The Nature of Schizophrenia

New Approaches to Research and Treatment

The Nature of Schizophrenia

New Approaches to Research and Treatment

Lyman C. Wynne

Professor, Department of Psychiatry
University of Rochester School of Medicine and Dentistry
Rochester, New York

Rue L. Cromwell

Professor, Department of Psychiatry
University of Rochester School of Medicine and Dentistry
Rochester, New York

Steven Matthysse

Associate Psychobiologist
Mailman Research Center
McLean Hospital
Belmont, Massachusetts

In Collaboration With:
Margaret L. Toohey
Bonnie J. Spring
Jonathan Sugarman

A Wiley Medical Publication
John Wiley & Sons
New York • Chichester • Brisbane • Toronto

Library of Congress Cataloging in Publication Data:

Wynne, Lyman C.
  The nature of schizophrenia.

  "A Wiley medical publication."
  1. Schizophrenia.   I. Cromwell, Rue L., joint
author.   II. Matthysse, Steven, joint author.
III. Title.

RC514.W96   616.8′982   77-28527
ISBN 0-471-02209-8

Printed in the United States of America

10 9 8 7 6 5 4 3 2 1

Principal Contributors

Lorraine G. Allan, Ph.D., Associate Professor, Department of Psychology, McMaster University, Hamilton, Ontario, Canada

E. James Anthony, M.D., Blanche F. Ittleson Professor of Child Psychiatry & Director, The Child Development Research Center, Washington University School of Medicine, St. Louis, Missouri

Robert F. Asarnow, Ph.D., Assistant Professor of Psychology, University of Waterloo, Waterloo, Ontario, Canada

Jack D. Barchas, M.D., Professor of Psychiatry & Behavioral Sciences, Stanford University School of Medicine, Stanford, California

Manfred E. Bleuler, M.D., Professor of Psychiatry, University of Zürich, Zürich, Switzerland

Monte S. Buchsbaum, M.D., Chief, Unit on Perceptual and Cognitive Studies, Biological Psychiatry Branch, National Institute of Mental Health, Bethesda, Maryland

Bertram D. Cohen, Ph.D., Professor, Department of Psychiatry, Rutgers Medical School of the College of Medicine & Dentistry of New Jersey, Piscataway, New Jersey

Patrick J. Collins, Ph.D., Department of Behavioral Sciences, New York Institute of Technology, Old Westbury, New York

Rue L. Cromwell, Ph.D., Professor of Psychiatry (Psychology), and Pediatrics, University of Rochester School of Medicine & Dentistry, Rochester, New York

John M. Davis, M.D., Professor of Psychiatry, University of Chicago; and Director of Research, Illinois State Psychiatric Institute, Chicago, Illinois

L. Erlenmeyer-Kimling, Ph.D., Associate Professor of Psychiatry and of Human Genetics and Development, Columbia University; Principal Research Scientist, Department of Medical Genetics, New York State Psychiatric Institute, New York, New York

Norman Garmezy, Ph.D., Professor of Psychology, University of Minnesota, Minneapolis, Minnesota; Clinical Professor of Psychiatry (Psychology), University of Rochester School of Medicine & Dentistry, Rochester, New York

Michael J. Goldstein, Ph.D., Professor of Psychology, University of California at Los Angeles, Los Angeles, California

Irving I. Gottesman, Ph.D., Professor of Psychology & Director, Behavioral Genetics Center, University of Minnesota, Minneapolis, Minnesota

Roy R. Grinker, Sr., M.D., Professor of Psychiatry Emeritus, University of Chicago; Director of the Schizophrenia Research Program, Michael Reese Hospital and Medical Center, Chicago, Illinois

John H. Gruzelier, Ph.D., Senior Lecturer in Psychology, Charing Cross Medical School, University of London, London, England

Barry Gurland, MRCP, MRCPsych, Associate Professor of Clinical Psychiatry, Columbia University College of Physicians & Surgeons; Chief, Department of Geriatrics Research, New York State Psychiatric Institute, New York, New York

Philip S. Holzman, Ph.D., Professor of Psychology, Department of Psychology and Social Relations, Harvard University, Cambridge, Massachusetts

Jerome Kagan, Ph.D., Professor of Human Development, Department of Psychology and Social Relations, Harvard University, Cambridge, Massachusetts

Martin M. Katz, Ph.D., Chief, Clinical Research Branch, Division of Extramural Research Programs, National Institute of Mental Health, Rockville, Maryland

Seymour S. Kety, M.D., Professor of Psychiatry, Harvard Medical School; Director, Mailman Research Center, McLean Hospital, Belmont, Massachusetts

Kenneth K. Kidd, Ph.D., Assistant Professor of Human Genetics, Yale University School of Medicine, New Haven, Connecticut

Dennis K. Kinney, Ph.D., Assistant Professor of Psychology, University of California at Los Angeles, Los Angeles, California

Conan Kornetsky, Ph.D., Professor of Psychiatry and Pharmacology, Department of Behavioral Pharmacology, Division of Psychiatry, Boston University Medical School, Boston, Massachusetts

Morton Kramer, Sc.D., Professor of Mental Hygiene, The Johns Hopkins University School of Hygiene and Public Health, Baltimore, Maryland

Einar Kringlen, Prof. Dr. Med., Professor of Psychiatry, University of Oslo Institute of Psychiatry, Oslo, Norway

Theodore Lidz, M.D., Sterling Professor of Psychiatry, Yale University School of Medicine, New Haven, Connecticut

Steven Matthysse, Ph.D., Assistant Professor of Psychobiology, Harvard Medical School; Associate Psychobiologist, Mailman Research Center, McLean Hospital, Belmont, Massachusetts

Thomas F. McNeil, Ph.D., Docent, Barnutvecklingsprojektet, Department of Psychiatry, University of Lund, Malmö, Sweden

Sarnoff A. Mednick, Ph.D., Dr. Med., Professor of Psychology, University of Southern California, Los Angeles, California; Director, Psykologisk Institute, Kommunehospitalet, Copenhagen, Denmark

Marek-Marsel Mesulam, M.D., Assistant Professor of Neurology, Harvard Neurological Unit, Beth Israel Hospital; Aphasia Research Center, Boston University School of Medicine, Boston, Massachusetts

Loren R. Mosher, M.D., Chief, Center for Studies of Schizophrenia, National Institute of Mental Health, Rockville, Maryland

H. B. M. Murphy, M.D., Ph.D., Professor of Psychiatry, McGill University, Montreal, Canada

Thomas F. Oltmanns, Ph.D., Assistant Professor, Department of Psychology, Indiana University, Bloomington, Indiana

S. R. Rochester, Ph.D., Assistant Professor, Department of Psychiatry, University of Toronto; Head, Research Psychology Section, Clarke Institute of Psychiatry, Toronto, Ontario, Canada

John Romano, M.D., Distinguished University Professor of Psychiatry, University of Rochester School of Medicine & Dentistry, Rochester, New York

Michael Rutter, M.D., FRCP, FRCPsych, DPM, Professor, Department of Child and Adolescent Psychiatry, Institute of Psychiatry, The Bethlem Royal Hospital and the Maudsley Hospital, University of London, London, England

Edward J. Sachar, M.D., Professor of Psychiatry and Chairman, Department of Psychiatry, Columbia University College of Physicians & Surgeons; Director, New York State Psychiatric Institute, New York, New York

Leonard F. Salzman, Ph.D., Professor of Psychiatry (Psychology), Psychology, and Medical Education & Communication, University of Rochester School of Medicine & Dentistry, Rochester, New York

Arnold J. Sameroff, Ph.D., Professor of Psychology, Pediatrics, and Psychiatry, University of Rochester, Rochester, New York

Norman Sartorius, M.D., Director, Division of Mental Health, World Health Organization, Geneva, Switzerland

David Shakow, Ph.D., Senior Research Psychologist, Mental Health Intramural Research Program, National Institute of Mental Health, Bethesda, Maryland

Margaret Thaler Singer, Ph.D., Clinical Professor of Psychiatry (Psychology), University of Rochester School of Medicine & Dentistry, Rochester, New York; Professor, Department of Psychiatry, University of California at San Francisco, San Francisco, California

Solomon H. Snyder, M.D., Professor of Psychiatry and Pharmacology, The Johns Hopkins University School of Medicine, Baltimore, Maryland

Robert L. Spitzer, M.D., Professor of Clinical Psychiatry, Columbia University College of Physicians & Surgeons; Chief of Psychiatric Research, Biometrics Research Department, New York State Psychiatric Institute, New York, New York

Herbert E. Spohn, Ph.D., Senior Research Psychologist, Department of Research, The Menninger Foundation, Topeka, Kansas

Bonnie J. Spring, Ph.D., Assistant Professor of Psychology and Social Relations, Department of Psychology and Social Relations, Harvard University, Cambridge, Massachusetts

Richard A. Steffy, Ph.D., Professor of Psychology, University of Waterloo, Waterloo, Ontario, Canada

Helm Stierlin, M.D., Ph.D., Professor and Director, Psychoanalytische Grundlagenforschung und Familientherapie, University of Heidelberg, Heidelberg, West Germany

John S. Strauss, M.D., Professor of Psychiatry and Director, Yale Psychiatric Institute, Yale University School of Medicine, New Haven, Connecticut

Erik Strömgren, M.D., Professor of Psychiatry, University of Aarhus; Medical Superintendent, Psychiatric Hospital, Risskov, Risskov, Denmark

Samuel Sutton, Ph.D., Professor of Psychiatry, Columbia University College of Physicians & Surgeons; Head, Department of Psychophysiology, New York State Psychiatric Institute, New York, New York

Ming T. Tsuang, M.D., Ph.D., Professor of Psychiatry, University of Iowa College of Medicine, Iowa City, Iowa

George E. Vaillant, M.D., Associate Professor of Psychiatry, Harvard Medical School, and The Cambridge Hospital, Cambridge, Massachusetts

Herbert G. Vaughan, Jr., M.D., Professor of Neuroscience & Neurology, Albert Einstein College of Medicine; Associate Director of the Rose F. Kennedy Center for Mental Retardation and Human Development, Bronx, New York

Peter H. Venables, Ph.D., Professor of Psychology, University of York, York, England

John K. Wing, M.D., Ph.D., Director, Medical Research Council, Social Psychiatry Unit; Professor of Social Psychiatry, Institute of Psychiatry, London, England

Julius Wishner, Ph.D., Professor of Psychology and in Psychiatry, University of Pennsylvania, Philadelphia, Pennsylvania

Richard Jed Wyatt, M.D., Chief, Laboratory of Clinical Psychopharmacology, National Institute of Mental Health, Saint Elizabeth's Hospital, Washington, District of Columbia

Lyman C. Wynne, M.D., Ph.D., Professor of Psychiatry, University of Rochester School of Medicine & Dentistry, Rochester, New York

Theodore P. Zahn, Ph.D., Research Psychologist, Laboratory of Psychology and Psychopathology, National Institute of Mental Health, Rockville, Maryland

Joseph Zubin, Ph.D., Distinguished Research Professor of Psychiatry, University of Pittsburgh School of Medicine; Staff Psychologist, V.A. Hospital, Pittsburgh, Pennsylvania; and Professor Emeritus of Psychology, Columbia University, New York, New York

Dedication

At the Second Rochester International Conference on Schizophrenia, on May 4, 1976, the University of Rochester proudly conferred Honorary Doctor of Science degrees on three of the world's leading contributors to understanding the nature of schizophrenia.

Manfred E. Bleuler   Erik Strömgren   Joseph Zubin

Manfred Eugen Bleuler

"I set myself the single task forty years ago of remaining in close touch with a large number of my patients for decades, regardless of whether they remained in the clinic or were returned to a free life." Manfred Bleuler's success in his undertaking is clearly demonstrated in his latest work, *Schizophrenic Mental Disorders in the Light of Long-Term Patient Observation,* now being translated into English. This is a unique work in psychiatry that reveals his intimate knowledge of his patients and their families in the hospital, their community, and their homes. In this work, he has specified clearly and thoroughly his criteria for the diagnosis of schizophrenia, assessed course and outcome, compared acute and chronic schizophrenia, and evaluated the impact of schizophrenic parents on their children at different ages.

Manfred Bleuler grew up in the renowned Burghölzli Hospital in Zurich in the setting of a truly pioneering center where the term schizophrenia was introduced by his father in 1911. After undergraduate medical education in Zurich, Kiel, and Geneva, he obtained postgraduate training in surgery, neurology, and adult and child psychiatry in Boston, New York, and Switzerland. In 1942 he was appointed Professor of Psychiatry at Zurich and Director of the University Psychiatric Clinic at the Burghölzli, and retained these posts until he returned in 1969. On the Burghölzli's 100th anniversary in 1970, he was especially honored by the Swiss government. He has received the Stanley R. Dean Award (United States) for his contributions to the understanding of schizophrenia, and has been elected to prestigious medical and scientific bodies in Switzerland, Germany, France, England, and the United States. Although he is renowned as a clinician, researcher, and teacher for his life work on schizophrenia, he also has contributed to the study of endocrinologic psychiatry, psychopathologic reactions to somatic diseases, alcoholism, and psychiatric disorders in the general population.

Erik Strömgren

Now recognized as the dean of Scandinavian psychiatry, Erik Strömgren was born and educated in Copenhagen. In 1945 he became Professor of Psychiatry at the University of Aarhus and Medical Superintendent of the Psychiatric Hospital at Risskov. From 1946–50, he also was in charge of the teaching of human genetics at the University. During his entire career, his attitude toward psychiatric research and therapy has been comprehensive. Over the years, he has created a teaching and research center in which the diverse subspecialties of psychiatry could be equally represented. He has taken an active part in the planning of psychiatric teaching, research, and clinical service facilities throughout Denmark and was a member of the Commission that planned the establishment of the new University of Odense.

For many years he was a member of the Danish National Committee of the UNESCO, a leader of the World Psychiatric Association, and a consultant to the World Health Organization. Since 1965 he has been a chief collaborating investigator in the WHO International Pilot Study of Schizophrenia. He has been the editor of *Acta Psychiatrica Scandinavica* since 1961. Awarded honorary membership in psychiatric scientific bodies in England, France, Germany, Switzerland, Sweden, and the United States, he has received several prizes for his research. In 1965 he gave the annual Kraepelin Lecture at the University of Munich, and in 1969 the Adolf Meyer Lecture of the American Psychiatric Association.

The works for which he is most famous are his studies of episodic and schizophreniform psychoses and extensive epidemiologic studies of the incidence and prevalence of mental illness, first on the island of Bornholm, and later on the island of Samsø and in Aarhus. At Samsø, the study led to the establishment of a comprehensive community mental health service. His interest in genetics is attested by numerous twin and family studies undertaken by him and members of his department. In psychiatric therapy, he introduced lithium in Denmark, followed by significant research conducted by Mogens Schou in his department. His numerous scientific papers written in Danish, German, French, and English, give evidence of the broad scope of his leadership.

Joseph Zubin

Joseph Zubin, born in Lithuania and educated at Baltimore City College, the Johns Hopkins University, and Columbia University, began his professional career over 45 years ago as volunteer resident intern in psychology at the New York State Psychiatric Institute. It was there, in 1956, that he founded the Biometrics Research Unit of the New York State Department of Mental Hygiene and, through his inspired leadership, made possible the participation of many scientific disciplines in its research into the problems of mental illness. Within his scientific work he has integrated areas of measurement, evaluation, anthropology, sociology, geriatrics, clinical psychiatry, experimental psychology, and learning and development.

As Professor of Psychology at Columbia since 1956, his zeal in teaching won for him the affection and respect of his students, not only for his interest in their futures, but particularly for his germinal capacity to entertain new ideas. He has served as a member and officer of many prestigious scientific bodies in the United States and has been associate editor and editor of journals of applied, experimental, and abnormal psychology. He has received many honors, including the Paul H. Hoch Memorial Lecture in 1968, the Distinguished Service Citation for Research of the New York State Department of Mental Hygiene in 1968, and a Certificate of Merit from the American Psychological Association in 1968. He received the degree, Honorary Doctor of Medicine, from the medical faculty of the University of Lund, Sweden, in 1972, the Stanley R. Dean Award for outstanding basic and clinical work in schizophrenia, in 1974, and was made an Honorary Life Member of the New York Academy of Sciences in 1974. ·

Citations to George A. Newbury and Richard A. Kern

Throughout history, active participation in philanthropy has been a particular characteristic of western societies. While the organization of philantropy in recent years has eliminated much of the spontaneity of giving, there are exceptions.

Most notable has been the generous and imaginative leadership of Scottish Rite Freemasonry, Northern Jurisdiction, in its pioneering support of basic and coordinated researches into the causes of schizophrenia. Yearly appropriations have increased steadily from the beginning allotment in 1934 of $15,000, to $500,000 in 1975. Since 1934, more than 200 separate investigations concerned with fields relevant to the study of the schizophrenic patient and his family have been financed at a cost of over $5,000,000.

In the Second Rochester International Conference on Schizophrenia, the University of Rochester honored two men: George A. Newbury, Sovereign Grand Commander, 1965–75, and Dr. Richard A. Kern, Honorary Sovereign Grand Commander. Building upon the firm foundation laid by Dr. Melvin M. Johnson, chief architect of the Schizophrenia Research Program, Justice George E. Bushnell, and the eminent scientists who have served on the advisory committees, Mr. Newbury and Dr. Kern have been primarily responsible for the growth of the Supreme Council Benevolent Foundation, which has enabled it to keep pace with the expanding financial requirements of the complex scientific investigations, and, most recently, has enabled it to establish the Dissertation Research Fellowship Program.

For their sustained devotion and support to the pursuit of new knowledge in an area of great public need, Robert L. Sproull, President, on behalf of the University of Rochester proudly presented its Presidential Citation to George Adelbert Newbury and to Richard Arminius Kern.

Preface

This volume arose out of a widely felt need for a major stocktaking of the state of knowledge on the schizophrenic disorders. Although in recent years various conferences and their proceedings have focused usefully on biologic and other aspects of schizophrenia, two conferences of 1967 provided a landmark assessment of this field by leading researchers. The proceedings of the First Rochester International Conference on Schizophrenia was published as *The Origins of Schizophrenia* (John Romano, editor). The Puerto Rico Conference, sponsored by the Foundations' Fund for Research in Psychiatry, was presented in written form as *The Transmission of Schizophrenia* (David Rosenthal and Seymour Kety, editors). Together, these 1967 conferences provided an historical reference point for the planning of two overlapping conferences held in Rochester, New York, on May 2–6, 1976: The Second Rochester International Conference on Schizophrenia and the Conference on Attention and Information Processing sponsored by the Scottish Rite Schizophrenia Research Program.

By bringing together reports of diverse investigators, the First Rochester Conference and the Puerto Rico Conference of 1967 helped consolidate points of view for the selection of studies that appeared to have borne fruit and were promising for the future. Especially influential were the preliminary reports of the adoption studies of schizophrenia "spectrum disorders" and the strategy of selecting research samples at "high risk" for future development of schizophrenic illness. Approaches to schizophrenia through psychophysiology and family interaction studies also were introduced.

By 1976 several trends, some new and some continuing, were evident and are represented in the present volume. While the contribution of one or more genetic factors to the predisposition to schizophrenic illness is now firmly accepted, the next steps of identifying genetic markers, clarifying genetic mechanisms, and understanding gene-environment interactions remain as elusive high priorities. In 1959, Kety set standards for biochemical studies of schizophrenia; subsequent progress has been steady, especially in the systematic use of drugs to elucidate neurotransmitter mechanisms.

Partly as a result of the presentations at the 1967 conferences by Mednick, a major change has been a burgeoning of longitudinal high-risk studies. Increasingly, these studies have been viewed in the context of developmental psychopathology. Some of these long-term programs have incorporated family interaction methods that will clarify the significance of family communication and related variables. Earlier research on family interaction had been difficult to interpret, especially because of the problem of "direction of effects," between family and individual.

Other risk research programs have emphasized the predictive value of psychophysiologic, neurophysiologic, and biochemical variables and are part of a dramatic new development in schizophrenia research during recent years: wide conviction that the concepts of attention and information processing are especially valuable because they bridge the gap between the biologic and psychologic realms. It is remarkable that attention can be studied over the entire range from schizophrenic language to single unit recording in the monkey brain. These elegant biologic techniques, building upon earlier psychophysiologic and neurophysiologic approaches, must be matched by precise formulations of the concepts of attention and information processing at the human level. Thus, the organizers of the Scottish Rite Conference believed this was an appropriate time to bring this biologic knowledge into closer relation with what is known about the psychology of schizophrenia.

No doubt stimulated by the pioneering long-term studies of Manfred Bleuler, a major development during the past decade has been a greater emphasis on comprehensive assessment of factors affecting the course of schizophrenic illness. This work, in turn, has been closely linked to a broad, fresh evaluation of diagnostic methods and criteria. In retrospect, perhaps this area involves the most striking shifts since 1967 when diagnostic criteria were mentioned only vaguely and standardized interview procedures were not used in any of the studies reported in Rochester and in Puerto Rico. Indeed, in a note to the editor, David Shakow expressed concern that there now was too much preoccupation with diagnostic measuring techniques: "This carried with it a lessening interest in the sophisticated clinical approach and an overdoing of measuring for measurement's sake. Perhaps the comments of Zubin, an (extreme) exponent of the measurement school, that this trend . . . had gone too far and it was necessary to look again at the phenomena substantively, was an outstanding aspect of the Second Rochester Conference."

At the same time, Kramer warned that diagnostic data have become woefully unavailable for epidemiologic studies. Only in Rochester, where the Monroe County Cumulative Psychiatric Case Register has been operational since 1960, are data available over time for comparison of epidemiologic trends in the United States. The data from that source, plus national census data on changes in population age groups, suggest that the next decade will produce an alarming increase in schizophrenics—at the very time when public funding for treatment facilities has been prematurely curtailed. More broadly, the need for research on basic familial, sociocultural and related epidemiologic factors influencing the onset, manifestations and chronicity of schizophrenia and other mental disorders (quite apart from the issue of their etiology) is urgently needed; the collaborative international studies by WHO and NIMH are a small and badly needed contribution to this relatively neglected area.

The editors believe that this volume includes information that will inform the practicing clinician as well as the active investigator. Treatment implications of research findings have been included throughout much of the volume; nevertheless, schizophrenic illness remains an enigma that challenges us to put into use not only all available scientific knowledge but also the full range of our therapeutic skills and human compassion.

LYMAN C. WYNNE
RUE L. CROMWELL
STEVEN MATTHYSSE

Acknowledgments

Second Rochester Conference on Schizophrenia: Building on the theme of "The Origin, Pathogenesis and Course of Schizophrenia and Related Disorders," the Second Rochester International Conference on Schizophrenia was planned and organized by a group of faculty at Rochester: Lyman C. Wynne and Rue L. Cromwell, Co-chairmen; Norman Garmezy, John Romano, Leonard F. Salzman, and John S. Strauss. This committee sought a program that explicitly would place schizophrenic disorders within a developmental framework, ranging from genetic and sociocultural precursors to those biologic, psychologic, interpersonal, and cultural factors that may influence vulnerability, onset, and course, or, alternatively, constitute assets that may help avert illness despite a predisposition. To assist in the difficult task of identifying both experienced and fresh contributors, those with an historical perspective and those with maps for major future exploration, a diverse Advisory Group was consulted about the program: Michael J. Goldstein, Martin Katz, Seymour S. Kety, Steven Matthysse, Loren R. Mosher, Norman Sartorius, David Shakow, and Erik Strömgren. We are grateful for their generosity in giving time and thought to this task. At the same time, the Advisory Group cannot be held responsible for what may be perceived as omissions or lack of representativeness in the roster of participants.

Among the sponsors of the Conference, we give special recognition and appreciation for fiscal and professional support from the Clinical Research Branch of the National Institute of Mental Health (Contract No. PLD-07401-76FS). Their assistance reflects a long-term interest in stimulating interchange among active investigators in schizophrenia and in obtaining reports which will assist in further planning for schizophrenia programs. Other contributors included: Hoffman-La Roche, Inc.; Merrell-National Laboratories; Sandoz Pharmaceuticals; Merck, Sharp, and Dohme Postgraduate Program; CIBA Pharmaceutical Company, and Abbott Laboratories.

Scottish Rite Conference on Attention and Information Processing: Simultaneously, the Schizophrenic Research Program of the Scottish Rite Freemasonry Benevolent Foundation planned a conference to consider recent advances in the rapidly growing field of attention and information processing that have become relevant, indeed pivotal, in much current research on schizophrenia. The Scottish Rite Schizophrenia Program is indebted to their organizing committee: Rue L. Cromwell, Norman Garmezy, Brendan Maher, David Shakow, Samuel Sutton, and Gerhard Werner.

Because of overlap in the advisory and planning groups for the two conferences, it quickly became apparent that there could be substantial duplication both in persons and topics. Hence we agreed to collaborate. The result was a plan to have both conferences in Rochester, with one afternoon jointly sponsored by the two groups (see chapters by Shakow, Holzman, Steffy, Gruzelier, Spohn, and Cromwell). This was followed by a day of shorter, more informal workshop papers in the conference sessions sponsored solely by the Scottish Rite Schizophrenia Research Program (see remainder of Sections III through VIII).

We especially thank Joyce Yutzy, Executive Assistant, for patient and painstaking attention to thousands of details that went into planning, conducting, and following up on these conferences. Additionally, we are grateful to Gladys Wilson for her invaluable administrative assistance for the Scottish Rite Conference. Finally, we express appreciation to the numerous alumni and current faculty and staff of the University of Rochester who contributed time, money, and interest to this meeting.

This Volume: The initial contributions to the volume proved to be substantially too lengthy for publication in a single book. Recognizing the importance of retaining in published form the comprehensive quality of the joint conference, we struggled to shorten all of the papers and to reserve some for publication in journal form only. These latter papers, presented in the Scottish Rite Conference, were of a technical and methodologic nature or dealt mainly with conceptual issues outside the field of schizophrenia. They will be of interest to many readers and will be published, along with the full versions of Scottish Rite Conference papers in this volume, in the *Journal of Psychiatric Research,* volume 15, 1978. John Wiley and Sons has kindly permitted the journal publication of these papers so that they are available in archival form. We are grateful to the many authors who cooperated with remarkably good grace and understanding in the necessary editorial decisions.

The editing and indexing requirements for a volume of this scope were truly enormous, both in converting the oral presentations to publishable form and in bringing about the needed shortening. As indicated on the title page, the editing of this volume was the collaborative effort of six persons. Margaret L. Toohey undertook the arduous task of editorial review of the manuscripts and references as a whole, together with preparation of the index. Bonnie Spring and Jonathan Sugarman made special editorial contributions to Sections III–VIII on attention and information processing.

LYMAN C. WYNNE
RUE L. CROMWELL
STEVEN MATTHYSSE

Contents

Section III. Central Nervous System and Psychophysiologic Approaches   159

Section IV. Information Processing and Schizophrenia   217

The Nature of Schizophrenia

New Approaches to Research and Treatment

The Central Core
of Madness

John Romano, M.D.

It happened over 40 years ago, when I was a house officer with Eugen Kahn at Yale. The patient was a recently admitted, very young man, who was frightened, perplexed, and hallucinating. Since he would not eat, he had to be tube-fed daily. On each occasion he had to be tube-fed twice, because after the first feeding, he would vomit. After the second feeding the food would stay down. When I asked, "Why do you vomit?" the patient answered, "Because I have no stomach." I replied, "Well, the second time I feed you the food stays down. Where does it go if you have no stomach?" Almost immediately the patient answered, "It goes to the upper peninsula." I tried as best I could to trace this idea to its source, to look for related ideas through a detailed review with the patient and his family of his past and present life history, through the use of projective tests, from his infrequent spontaneous remarks, and even by pondering over fragments of occasional dreams he recounted to me; but to no avail. It remained enigmatic, strange, nonunderstandable.

I learned later of the emphasis placed by Jaspers (1) on the significance of nonunderstandability as a criterion of schizophrenic symptomatology. Whether a given symptom can be understood or not, Jaspers believed, is determined by feeling oneself into the situation of the patient and assessing whether the symptom can be understood logically or emotionally as arising from the patient's affective state, his previous personality, or the current situation. But, as many have noted, this approach is somewhat vague and subjective. I have learned that it depends in great part on how much time you spend with a patient, how informed you are of his past and present life, and on the nature of the trust established between you and the patient. Whatever its significance, the nonunderstandability, together with the characteristic hallucinations, the thought disorders, the passivity experiences and their delusional interpretations—all occurring in a state of wakeful consciousness—have constituted a mosaic, a cluster of signs and symptoms that have demarcated this type of madness from others (2). Through the mists of antiquity the notion of paranoia emerged, and long before it acquired its modern, denotative, persecutory or projective meanings, it meant, more simply, beyond understanding and was used to describe the essence of madness.

Perceptive, seasoned clinicians, beginning with Thomas Willis in the seventeenth century, and others through the eighteenth and nineteenth centuries, differentiated what we call schizophrenia from melancholia, from mania due to fever and that due to wine, from the enfeeblement of the aged, and from brain damage. Although schizophrenia had

1

many names—stupidity, foolishness, vesania, idiocy, monomania, paranoia, and others—these earlier clinicians described the characteristics of family origin, endogenous cause, early onset, remitting or regressive course, bizarre ideas, dissociation of thought and emotion, and social withdrawal. All this occurred long before the more precise contributions of Morel, Hecker, Kahlbaum, Kraepelin, and Bleuler and the designations of dementia praecox and schizophrenia (3). Then, as now, other types of madness, like melancholia, mania, and the enfeeblement of the aged, seemed more open to empathic understanding and more consonant with human psychologic experience. Then, as now, this special type of madness, which we call schizophrenia, appeared to be the central core of madness or unreason.

Nine years ago, during the First Rochester International Conference on Schizophrenia, we drew attention to the magnitude of the prevalence of schizophrenia, the lack of agreement about its diagnosis and course, and the multiple conjectures about its origins—all attesting to the fact that it constitutes modern psychiatry's greatest challenge (4). It appeared then, as it does now, that the need for continuing studies was both urgent and imperative. One hoped that such studies would contribute not only to the understanding of schizophrenia in biologic as well as in psychologic terms, but also to our knowledge of perception, thought, memory, and emotion, to human growth and development, and to interaction within the family and other social groups. One of the objectives of the First Conference was to stimulate us, and we hoped others, to examine more critically what it is we know, or believe we know, and to seek new knowledge in all the areas relevant to our task.

We are encouraged to learn that in the past decade there appears to have been an increased world-wide interest in and support of the investigation of the schizophrenic patient and his family. This is attested to by the number of published scientific papers and monographs, the establishment of special journals, the international studies of diagnosis and course, the development of new methods of biologic research, and the frequent convening of interested groups in conferences such as the one in which we are now engaged.

Following our First Conference, and stimulated in great part by Norman Garmezy's seminar on vulnerability to psychopathology (1969), we initiated a pilot study, supported generously by the Scottish Rite Foundation and the Margo Cleveland Research Fund, in which Haroutun Babigian, Arthur Orgel, and Irving Weiner took major responsibilities and were joined later by Alfred and Clara Baldwin, then at Cornell, and now, happily for us, at Rochester. With the appointment of Lyman Wynne as department chairman (1971), we were able, under his leadership, to design and launch the University of Rochester Child and Family Study (NIMH grant MH-22836), whose objectives are:

1. to identify children who genetically are at high versus low risk for schizophrenia
2. to examine these groups through three classes of predictor variables
   a. diagnostic assessments of the biologic parents, with the implication of differing genetic loadings for the "high-risk" children of a schizophrenic parent versus the "low-risk" children of parents who have had other kinds of psychiatric disorders
   b. diverse patterns of psychosocial competence, adaptation, and biologic functioning of the children themselves
   c. constellations of factors in the family and school environments which may differentiate the high-risk from the low-risk children

3. to follow these families prospectively and to determine whether or not differences appear in later years or initial differences are maintained in developmental trends.

It has been my privilege in the past 5 years to return, after many intervening years, to active participation in clinical research as a part of the University of Rochester Child and Family Study. Together with my associate, Robert Geertsma, and our research technician, Sandra Squires Trieshmann, our assignment in the overall program has been to conduct investigations, supported by the Scottish Rite Foundation and the Margo Cleveland Research Fund, with the aim of identification of those characteristics of parents which are associated with vulnerability or invulnerability of children at high risk for schizophrenia. Identification here refers to:

1. the documentation of parental characteristics and the nature of the caretaking patterns of behavior from videotaped interviews
2. the characterization of parental object relations through adjective checklist studies
3. the analysis of clinical diagnosis, past and present, through current videotaped interviews of patient and spouse and through careful review of past hospital records

Briefly, I should like to present one diagnostic datum from our studies in progress and share with you several personal impressions of clinical research in this field. Of the first 97 families studied, 50 patients had been diagnosed as schizophrenic and 47 as nonschizophrenic during their inpatient period of study. Following our review of the hospital records and our current clinical diagnostic interviews with the former patient and spouse, we disagreed in over half the cases with the initial diagnosis of schizophrenia (26 of 50 patients); but we agreed in 95% of the cases initially diagnosed as nonschizophrenic. Then our clinical diagnoses were compared with those reached by John Strauss and his associates, who review past records and use standardized questionnaire interviews. Of the families studied thus far, there was 80% agreement between Strauss's and our group in the diagnosis of the patient while he was an inpatient.

Obviously, diagnosis remains an urgent and central problem of concern. Equally obvious is that most of us in the United States have tended to diagnose schizophrenia less rigorously than most of our European colleagues. However, I am heartened by evidence of a national movement in clinical practice for greater precision in diagnosis. From a practical point of view, it has now become necessary to discriminate carefully among schizophrenia, mania, the several types of depression, and other psychotic behavior to prescribe the appropriate medication. Both the United States-United Kingdom and the World Health Organization Studies attest to this greater interest and concern (5). (See the chapters by Sartorius and Gurland in this volume.)

One impression which we shall have to check later is that we are dealing with a particular type of schizophrenic, selected by design when the index patient is a parent. Rarely has illness in such patients begun in childhood or adolescence. Most frequently, particularly in women, it seems associated with the problems of young adulthood, including courtship, marriage, pregnancy and labor, parenthood, house-moving, employment, economic stress, relation to parents, and with mental illness in the families of origin. Most of our patients' illnesses have been short-term, a number with remitting course, with improvement assisted in many instances by medication and by family rally. While over one-half of our patients still receive some type of medication, either the major or minor tranquilizers, we found three-quarters of them to be currently asymptomatic. In the interests of homogeneity, the patients under study are exclusively white, predominantly middle-class, married, initially with an intact family and with male children aged 4, 7, or 10. While our population may be representative of a population of patients with these characteristics, it certainly is not representative of populations of schizophrenics frequently studied, namely, those of lower class patients with long-term illnesses, continuously hospitalized since early life, with little social competence, unmarried or divorced, and with limited or no experience in parenting. The need for those of us engaged in clinical studies to define clearly and fully the populations under study is evident. The possibility of biased conclusions from uneven selection of patients is obvious and a constant hazard.

Another impression is the recognition of the limits of usefulness, not to speak of validity or reliability, of research based on hospital records. Even in reasonably well-conducted clinical households, one often finds that the data one wishes are not available and that records, when legible, vary considerably in recording primary data of patient behavior. The fullest, most useful records are those prepared by our third-year medical students during their clinical assignment. Most observers prefer to record data in terms of inferred psychodynamics rather than at the phenotypic level of behavior. Terms such as "regression," "introjection," "homosexual panic," "cognitive slippage," and even more simply, "patient is depressed," or "hallucinated," or "paranoid," are used commonly without giving any material evidence of the specific behavior that led to the inference. I have also become disenchanted with reports from psychological tests which provide no primary data and invite one to hear the grass grow. Incidentally, the more recent the record, the more complete the charting of family genetic trees. Rarely does one find a report of the physical description of the person—dress, mannerisms, posture, gait, expression, height, weight, movement, and so forth. On another occasion I have noted, "In psychiatry we have been so fascinated by what we hear that we have neglected to look. We can well respond to the wisdom of that Dean of Malapropisms, Yogi Berra, when he said, 'You can observe a lot just by watching.'" (6)

Another impression is of the limited number of clinical psychiatrists engaged in these high-risk studies. In a quick review of the 20 ongoing research programs in the United States engaged in the search for the antecedents of schizophrenia, I found only 7 had psychiatrists as principal investigators, the rest being psychologists (7). This ratio may be representative of American psychiatrists engaged in clinical investigative work, and it is a personal disappointment that more psychiatrists are not involved in research of this type, particularly after the aspirations of those of us who initiated the USPHS Career Investigator Program many years ago. Furthermore, on my return to clinical investigative work, I am surprised to find that in many of these programs, including our own, few senior professional persons have direct contact with the research subject or patient, such contact being made principally by junior professionals or by technicians. The basic problem with this is again the crucial necessity to obtain an informed, sensitive, and precise appraisal of the subjects who will provide the primary data. Without such subject identification, the generalization of results and their comparison with results of other studies becomes indeterminate.

I have learned something about the hazards of research programs dealing with an almost infinite number of variables. There is, quite understandably, the compelling temptation to use methods familiar, available, and reliable to test what it is we wish to learn. How appropriate they may be to our task is another matter. John Dollard cautioned us years ago, "The first loyalty of a scientist is to his material; he must seek it where it can be found and grasp it as it permits. If he doesn't do this, he is likely to find himself an aimless imitator of others, of better methods not applicable to his field." (8)

I have also learned that we are apt to confuse two investigative purposes: that of hypothesis generation and that of hypothesis testing. One is concerned with discovery, the other with proof. I would predict that in large studies like ours, more will emerge as discovery, and less as proof.

Because computers can now handle thousands of variables, this has removed from the investigator's shoulders the need for him to select initially those variables that he wishes to use. One is reminded of Edith Wharton's remark about getting into the thick of thin things.

What has been most impressive to me is the old-fashioned altruism of the families who have participated in our studies, however one chooses to define altruism. In our study, even though a full explanation of the project was given at the time the subjects filled out appropriate consent forms, more than two-thirds appeared to retain little of what they had heard or read when I asked them about this in our interview, which usually takes place at the end of the study. Almost invariably, while they are not clear as to the purpose of the study, they appear to have enjoyed participating in it and have been impressed with the interest and kindness of those with whom they have met, even though at times they were somewhat puzzled as to why an endless number of silly questions was asked. Most often we hear: "We're really not sure what this is all about, but we and the children have enjoyed doing it. We wanted to take part in it to express our appreciation for having been helped in the past, and perhaps one day, while the information you are getting may not be useful to us, it may be to someone else." I wish sincerely that some of our militant philosophers, theologians, and ethicists, whose instant omniscience in matters of privacy and informed consent appears to be matched only by their overweaning arrogance, could hear some of these remarks and learn from them of the need of the patient to give something of himself, and recognize that among one's fundamental rights is the right to know and, one hopes, to know more, about the disturbance that affects his life. While we may not be able to reach the shores of the upper peninsula, perhaps we can be pointed in the right direction.

REFERENCES

1. Jaspers K: *General Psychopathology.* University of Chicago Press, 1963.

2. Fish FJ: *Schizophrenia.* Bristol, John Wright & Sons, Ltd, 1962.

3. Wender PH: Dementia praecox: the development of the concept. *Am J Psychiat* 119:1143–1151, 1963.

4. Romano J: *The Origins of Schizophrenia.* Excerpta Medica Foundation, Amsterdam, 1967, p 3.

5. Carpenter WT, Strauss JS, Bartko JJ: Flexible system for the diagnosis of schizophrenia. Report from the WHO international pilot study of schizophrenia. *Science* 182:1275–1278, 1973.

6. Romano J: On those from whom we learn. *California Medicine* 117:72–75, 1972.

7. Garmezy N: Children at risk: the search for the antecedents of schizophrenia. Part II: ongoing research programs, issues and interventions. *Schizophrenia Bull,* issue 9, pp 55–125, Summer 1974.

8. Dollard J: *Caste and Class in a Southern Town.* Second Ed., Harper & Bros., New York, 1949.

Section I

GENETIC TRANSMISSION

INTRODUCTION
Erik Strömgren, M.D.

Ten or fifteen years ago I would not have enjoyed being the chairman of a session on genetic transmission. Now, however, the situation is different. During the last years an encouraging development has taken place within psychiatric research. Bitter discussions on "nature versus nurture" in the etiology of schizophrenia have abated. There seems to be a general consensus that both play a part. There is still, however, ample room for discussion and many unclear areas: We do not know exactly *what* is inherited and certainly not *how* it is inherited. With regard to exogenous factors, very little is known except perhaps that they are very heterogeneous. Even if genetic and environmental factors are equally important in etiology, there still may be cases of schizophrenia that are primarily genetically determined and others that have a primary environmental causation. If this were so, it would be of great importance to distinguish such types clinically.

Until now, all concepts and determinations of schizophrenia have been clinical and, therefore, more or less arbitrary. No adequate agreement on diagnosis has been reached. Only certain severe, chronic types are regarded as definitely schizophenic by all schools of psychiatry. With regard to many of the other less severe types, opinions and labels vary widely: latent, pseudoneurotic, pseudopsychopathic, and acute schizophrenia; schizophreniform, reactive (or psychogenic), and schizoaffective psychosis, and so forth. The latter is regarded by some as a "true" schizophrenia and by others as an atypical form of manic-depressive disorder.

There are also many psychoses that have an organic basis but show schizophrenic symptomatology, e.g., certain epileptic psychosis and certain cases of Huntington's chorea. These are genetically determined but have no genetic relationship to schizophrenia. Finally, there are toxic psychoses caused by amphetamine which are often symptomatically indistinguishable from schizophrenia.

Therefore, it seems advisable in research on schizophrenia to include all kinds of schizophrenialike psychoses (with unknown etiology) and to work with the expectation that subdivisions will become evident and can be compared.

7

Chapter 1
Adult Offspring of Two Psychotic Parents, with Special Reference to Schizophrenia

Einar Kringlen, Prof. Dr. Med.

A study of offspring of two psychotic parents might throw light on the mode of genetic transmission, nosological problems, gene-environment interaction and antecedents of psychotic development, and factors that counteract deviant development.

The Mode of Genetic Transmission
The frequency of psychopathology in such children might support genetic recessivity, dominance, or polygenicity. If schizophrenia, for instance, is caused by a recessive gene, the schizophrenic parents would both have the pathologic gene in double dose (aa × aa), and all their children would be expected to develop the disease (all would be aa). If, on the other hand, schizophrenia is brought about by a dominant gene, both parents would normally harbor the gene in single dose, and three-fourths of the children would be expected to be schizophrenic. If multiple genes are involved in polygenic transmission, then the proportion of schizophrenic offspring is more uncertain and would depend on more complex genetic mechanisms. Thus, these empirically derived numbers of morbidity risk are of considerable importance for genetic theorizing with regard to schizophrenia.

Nosologic Problems
The degree of variability of psychopathology and normal personality functioning in these offspring should provide information about etiologic heterogeneity and specificity. Nosologic (classificatory) distinctions based on answers to etiologic questions would constitute an unusual scientific gain in psychiatry. For example, do schizophrenic parents beget manic-depressive children? Do manic-depressive parents breed schizophrenic offspring?

9

Gene-environment Interaction and Antecedents of Psychotic Development

Childen of two psychotic parents represent an extreme high-risk group that provides a sufficiently large set of psychotic offspring for comparative purposes. More specifically, such a study should offer an opportunity to assess the effects of various environmental factors. Many, but not all, children of such families have been exposed to extremely adverse parental influences and environmental conditions. Some have been reared by their psychotic parents; some have been separated from their parents and have grown up in foster homes or orphanages. Some have experienced their parents in acute psychosis; others have not been aware of their parents' psychotic behavior at all.

Factors That Counteract Deviant Behavior

Finally, a study of the life history of normal, well-adjusted individuals in such a group might throw light on factors that counteract deviant development. Instead of the traditional psychiatric question: "Why psychopathology?", the question should be reformulated to: "Why normality?"—perhaps a more interesting question with regard to persons under extreme genetic and environmental risk. It is obvious that such information would be useful for preventive psychiatry.

SAMPLE

Many family studies have started with psychotic offspring and then examined their parents. However, if one begins with psychotic children, one will obtain a sample of psychotic and nonpsychotic parents that most likely will not be representative of psychotic parents in general. Hence, we took as a starting point a sample of pairs of psychotic parents that were not preselected because of the characteristics of their offspring. All the married patients who had been hospitalized for a functional psychosis in two Norwegian mental hospitals (Valen and Neevengården) were selected. The names of their spouses were obtained and checked against the Norwegian central register of psychosis, with the assistance of local population registers. The original sample consisted of 22 parent pairs and their 70 offspring. (Seventeen pairs had been excluded because they were childless.) A preliminary report of this study has been given by Bastiansen and Kringlen (1).

Since this sample was too small to permit general conclusions, the material was enlarged by including other psychiatric hospitals in Norway (Dikemark, 1936–60, and Gaustad, Lier, and Universitetets psykiatriske klinikk, 1950–60). This produced 53 couples with 133 children. Five parent pairs had to be excluded later because the diagnosis of psychosis given by the hospitals could not be accepted. Finally, one child was excluded because he was under 20.

Accordingly, the final sample consisted of 48 couples where both parents had been hospitalized and discharged with a diagnosis of functional psychosis as classified in Scandinavia (schizophrenia, reactive psychosis, and manic-depressive illness), and these diagnoses were accepted by me and two of my research colleagues.[1] The offspring consisted of 58 males and 63 females, 121 subjects in all.

---

[1] Pål Abrahamsen, M.D. and Svenn Torgersen, cand. psychol.

METHODS

When the parents and their offspring had been identified, they were visited in their homes or institutions. However, many of the parents were old and some were dead. It was necessary to a large degree to rely on hospital records, which in the majority of cases provided sufficient information for a diagnostic evaluation.

Information about the offspring was obtained through semistructured interviews that covered life history, adult mental health status, and social functioning. Siblings were asked to describe each other, and in this way the data could be corrected and supplemented. Information also was obtained from general practitioners, psychiatrists, and psychiatric hospitals in case the person in question had been treated by these sources for mental problems. Supplementary information was sought from the central criminal register as well as the central psychosis register.

Diagnostic Classification

The subjects were classified according to conventional psychiatric diagnoses (13). The diagnosis of *schizophrenia* has been employed when the patient presented a typical clinical picture of so-called "process" schizophrenia. The primary symptoms, accompanied by clear consciousness, can be grouped as thinking disturbances, disintegration of emotions, autism, massive depersonalization and derealization, and marked feelings of influence and passivity.

Borderline schizophrenics usually have not displayed manifest psychotic symptoms. Clinically these patients might first appear as neurotics, but closer contact reveals a clinical picture more severe than typical neuroses and exhibiting diffuse and pervasive anxiety and/or disturbed ability for emotional closeness. In extended, less structured interviews, thinking disturbances often can be revealed.

Patients who showed marked neurotic personality traits such as sensitivity, dependency, and emotional restriction were classed as *neurotics*. Their main difficulties were in the area of interpersonal relationships with symptoms such as anxiety, obsessions, and somatic complaints of a psychologic origin.

The term *psychopathy* has been used when the personality was characterized by extreme impulsivity, egocentricity, emotional coldness, hostility, and absence of guilt feelings. Complications of crime and/or alcoholism were not unusual.

Normality means *clinical* normality, i.e., the individual might harbor psychologic conflicts and may have had periods when he has experienced tension, sleeping difficulties, sadness, or headache, but these troubles have been of a short duration and have never really interfered with ordinary functioning. In other words, the normal person in this study has not shown clear-cut psychotic, psychopathic, or neurotic traits or symptoms.

The subjects also were classified according to a global mental health rating scale, where 1 and 2 correspond to "normal"; 3 and 4, clear-cut neurotic or psychopathic disorder with moderate impairment; whereas 5 to 7 stand for gross impairment, chiefly of a psychotic nature. In practice, 5 signifies reactive psychosis, manic-depressive illness, or benign types of schizophrenia; 6, typical schizophrenia and 7, extremely severe schizophrenic disorder.

Before a final psychiatric diagnosis and a global mental health rating was attributed to parents and offspring, summaries of case histories were prepared. Two of my research colleagues and I then diagnosed the subjects independently without any knowledge of the relationship between them and their offspring. Complete agreement on psychiatric diagnosis was arrived at in 60% of the parents, and on mental health ratings, in 62%. For the offspring, complete agreement was 74% for diagnostic categories and 55% for mental health ratings. In the main, it is fair to conclude that the interrater reliability was high since the disagreement in all cases was of a minor nature. For instance, two raters, might diagnose a case manic-depressive (depression), and the third one, reactive psychosis (depressive type); or all three raters might agree on the diagnosis of normality, but two of them might attribute to the subject a mental health rating of 1, and the third rater, 2.

FINDINGS

Diagnoses of Parents

Table 1-1 shows the distribution of diagnoses in fathers and mothers. Reactive psychosis is the most common, followd by schizophrenia. This diagnostic distribution probably reflects the strict use in Norway of the diagnoses of schizophrenia and manic-depressive illness and the liberal use of the diagnosis of reactive psychosis. In the United States, for example, many patients with reactive psychosis would probably have been classified as schizophrenic or manic-depressive. There is no remarkable difference between fathers and mothers, except that mothers more often have an affective syndrome.

Table 1-2 shows the various combinations of psychotic parents. Schizophrenia × reactive psychosis is the most common combination followed by reactive psychosis × reactive psychosis. For one couple only, the diagnosis is manic-depressive illness in both parents.

Mortality of Offspring

In previous studies of the offspring of psychotic parents, the infant mortality has been extremely high. In the studies of Kahn (10) and Elsässer (3) of 99 births, 22 children died in early childhood, most in the first year of life, and perhaps some mortalities also were unknown to the authors. In the present series the infant mortality was not exceptionally high, even though I must admit that cases of mortality might have escaped our investigation. Of the total sample of 125 (126) offspring, 4 (5) were excluded because of death before the age of 15. (One boy died by accident at age 14.) The remaining deaths occurred at birth or shortly after. This perinatal death rate of about 4% does not deviate significantly from the rate in the general population. Essen-Möller (6) from Sweden and Reisby (16) from Denmark also failed to report any excessive mortality in offspring of schizophrenics.

Table 1-1. Diagnostic Distribution of Parents

Classification	Fathers	Mothers
Schizophrenia	19	23
Manic depressive illness	4	8
Reactive psychosis	25	17
Total	48	48

Table 1-2. Diagnostic Combinations in Parents

Schizophrenia × reactive psychosis	20
Reactive psychosis × reactive psychosis	9
Schizophrenia × schizophrenia	8
Schizophrenia × manic-depressive illness	6
Manic-depressive illness × reactive psychosis	4
Manic-depressive illness × manic depressive illness	1
Total	48

Diagnoses of Offspring

Tables 1-3 and 1-4 show the diagnoses in offspring. More than one-half are classified as normal, barely 30% neurotic, alcoholic, psychopathic, and mentally deficient, and 17% psychotic and borderline. In Table 1-4, the concept of psychosis is broadly applied and includes 10 cases of schizophrenia (8%), 3 cases of reactive psychosis, 1 case of manic-depressive illness, 1 suicide, and 5 borderline cases.

Age Distribution of Offspring

The mean age of the offspring is 38 years with a range of 22–65 years (see Table 1-5).

Genetic Aspects

As can be observed in Tables 1-6 and 1-7, the highest frequency of psychosis, and more specifically schizophrenia, is found in families of two schizophrenic parents, where seven (28%) of the children have been classified as psychotic or borderline, with five (20%) of these as schizophrenic.

Then follows the combination of schizophrenia × reactive psychosis, which produced 7 (17%) psychotic and borderline cases out of 42 offspring. Three (7%) of these are schizophrenic.

Table 1-3. Diagnosis of Offspring by Sex

Classification	Male	Female	Total
Schizophrenia	6	4	10
Reactive psychosis	1	2	3
Manic-depressive illness	1	—	1
Suicide	1	—	1
Borderline state	4	1	5
Alcoholism, psychopathy	5	—	5
Mental deficiency	1	1	2
Neurosis	8	24	32
Normality	31	31	62
Total	58	63	121

Table 1-4. Diagnostic Clusters of Offspring by Sex

Classification	Male		Female		Total	
	No.	%	No.	%	No.	%
Psychosis and borderline[a]	13	22.4	7	11.1	20	16.5
Alcoholism and psychopathy[b]	6	10.3	1	1.6	7	5.8
Neurosis	8	13.8	24	38.1	32	26.5
Normality	31	53.5	31	49.2	62	51.2
Total	58	100.0	63	100.0	121	100.0

[a] Four borderline and one suicide case included.
[b] Two cases of mental deficiency included.

The combination of a schizophrenic spouse with a manic-depressive partner is especially significant for genetic theory. Of the 12 offspring from such marriages, 2 (17%) were psychotic, both schizophrenic, and none were manic-depressive.

Adding together those combinations in which one parent was schizophrenic (married to a partner with either a reactive psychosis or a manic-depressive illness), only 9 (17%) of 54 offspring had any form of functional psychosis. However, 5 (9.3%) of these 9 psychotic offspring were typical schizophrenics. This figure is similar to reports summarized by Slater and Cowie (19) who conclude that the risk in offspring of one index schizophrenic parent (psychiatric status of spouse unspecified) is "in the neighborhood of 10%."

Fourteen combinations of parents with manic-depressive illness or reactive psychosis (m.d. × react., react. × react., m.d. × m.d.) produced only four "psychotic" offspring— one manic-depressive psychosis, one reactive psychosis, one suicide, and one borderline state (4/42, 9.5%)—but no schizophrenics.

A closer look at the offspring of two schizophrenic parents reveals that four of the seven offspring classified as psychotic are definitely schizophrenic; one is possibly schizophrenic, one has a diagnosis of reactive psychosis, and one is classified as borderline. In other words, 20% (5/25) of the offspring of two schizophrenic parents have developed schizophrenia or possible schizophrenia (see Table 1-7).

By age correction with Weinberg's short method, an expectancy figure of 29% (5/17) for schizophrenia is arrived at, a figure which must be considered a maximum figure

Table 1-5. Age-Distribution of Offspring by Sex[a]

Age	Male	Female	Total
22–29	17	12	29
30–39	20	24	44
40–49	14	15	29
50–59	6	9	15
60–65	1	2	3
Total	58	62	120

[a] A case of suicide (20-year-old male) excluded (case no. 9).

Table 1-6. Diagnostic Distribution in Offspring of Various Parent Combinations

Parents	No. of couples	Offspring				
		Psychosis[a]	Alcoholism/ psychopathy[b]	Neurosis	Normality	Total
Schiz. × schiz.	8	7 (28%)	1 (4%)	10 (40%)	7 (28%)	25
Schiz. × react.	20	7 (17%)	2 (5%)	7 (17%)	26 (62%)	42
Schiz. × m.d.	6	2 (17%)	2 (17%)	6 (50%)	2 (17%)	12
M.d. × react.	4	1 (11%)	2 (22%)	2 (22%)	4 (44%)	9
React. × react.	9	3 (11%)		5 (18%)	20 (71%)	28
M.d. × m.d.	1			2 (40%)	3 (60%)	5
Total	48	20	7	32	62	121

[a] Inclusion of borderline cases.
[b] Inclusion of two cases of mental deficiency.

since the mean age of the subjects who have not passed the risk period for schizophrenia is 36 years, at which age about 70% of potential schizophrenics have developed the disorder (14a,20).

> Morbidity risk figures are usually calculated by employing the abridged method of Weinberg, which assumes a period of risk in which each person in that age range is counted as half a case. Subjects who have not reached the risk period are excluded, whereas individuals who have passed the period of risk are counted as one full case. Weinberg's method is, however, problematic if new cases are not distributed evenly in the risk period. In schizophrenia the majority of new cases occur in the twenties and thirties. Accordingly, employment of the short method of Weinberg here, where the bulk of the nonschizophrenic offspring have lived through most of the risk period, leads to an overcorrection of age. Therefore, I have designated the calculated morbidity figure as a maximum figure.

Children of either sex should on simple genetic grounds be presumed to run an equal risk of developing schizophrenia. Previous investigations, however, have observed a higher rate of schizophrenia in female than in male offspring (17). In this series the tendency is in the opposite direction. The eight dual matings of schizophrenics had 25 offspring, 9 males and 16 females. Three (33%) of the 9 males and 2 (12.5%) of the 16

Table 1-7. Combinations of Psychotic Parents and Types of Psychosis in the Offspring

Parents	No. of couples	Offspring					
		Schiz.	React.	M.d.	Suicide	Bord.	Total
Schiz. × schiz.	8	5	1			1	25
Schiz. × react.	20	3	1			3	42
Schiz. × m.d.	6	2					12
M.d. × react.	4			1			9
React. × react.	9		1		1	1	28
M.d. × m.d.	1						5
Total	48	10	3	1	1	5	121

females have been classified as schizophrenics. The same tendency to schizophrenia and psychosis in general has been observed for the total group of offspring, where 9 of 58 males (16%) have a diagnosis of psychosis (including one suicide) compared with 6 of 63 females (10%). Inclusion of borderline cases gives a rate of 13/58 (22%) and 7/63 (11%) (see Table 1-3).

The average age of onset for the schizophrenic offspring was 22.6 years (range 18–27), with an average age of 25.8 years at first admission to hospital. Table 1-8 shows the mean ages for schizophrenic parents and their schizophrenic children with regard to onset of illness and first hospital admission. The difference in age of onset is 12.7 years later for the parents than for the offspring, and difference in age at first admission is 13.6 years. The main reason for later•onset and admission in the parents seems to be that persons who develop schizophrenia at a young age are less likely to marry, whereas persons who develop schizophenia later have had a chance of marrying before their illness.

Using the global mental health ratings, the parents and offspring appeared to have similar severity of illness. Seven of the fathers had ratings of 6 (typical schizophrenia) and the remaining one, 7. For the mothers, the ratings were 5 in one case, 6 in four, and 7 in three cases. The mean mental health rating for the offspring was 6.0 (6 in three cases, 5 in one case, and 7 in one case). There was no sex difference with regard to these ratings.

Nosologic Conclusions

Is there any relationship between type of functional psychosis in parents and children? The number of psychoses is small, but Table 1-6 seems to show a positive correlation. It is worth noting that all 10 schizophrenic offspring have at least one schizophrenic parent. In this sample of 121 offspring of dual-mated psychotic parents, no schizophrenic offspring are found who do not have at least one schizophrenic parent. The only manic-depressive offspring has a manic-depressive parent, but of the five offspring of a pair of manic-depressive parents, none have been manic-depressive or psychotic. All these offspring have passed the age of 50.

What about subtype of schizophrenia in parent and child? Table 1-9 contains limited information, but there evidently exists no strong relationship in this study. The table shows, for instance, that one couple consisting of a father with miscellaneous schizophrenic symptomatology and a paranoid schizophrenic mother have a nonparanoid schizophrenic offspring. The next dual mating of a nonparanoid schizophrenic father and a schizoaffective mother has bred a paranoid schizophrenic son.

Heston (9) and Karlsson (12) observed that many persons related to schizophrenics were artistically gifted, and they postulated a genetic connection between schizophrenia and creativity. These findings cannot be confirmed in this study. Six of the 121 offspring

Table 1-8. Mean Ages of Onset and First Hospitalization in Eight Schizophrenic Parent Pairs and Their Five Schizophrenic Offspring

	Fathers	*Mothers*	*Offspring*
Mean age of onset	33.9 yr (25–40)	36.6 yr (28–52)	22.6 yr (18–27)
Mean age at first admission	39.8 yr (30–55)	39.0 yr (31–55)	25.8 yr (20–29)

Table 1-9. Relation Between Subtype of Schizophrenia in Parents and Offspring

Parents		No. of Offspring	No. of Psychotic Offspring	Type of Psychosis of Offspring
(Fathers)	*(Mothers)*			
Schiz.-misc.[a]	× schiz.-par.	3	1	Schiz.-nonpar.
Schiz.-nonpar.	× schiz. aff.	2	1	Schiz.?-par.
Schiz.-misc.	× schiz.-misc.	3	2	Schiz.-par.; Schiz.-misc.
Schiz.-misc.	× schiz. aff.	5	1	Schiz.-misc.
Schiz.-par.	× schiz.-misc.	4	1	React. psych. (par.-depr. type)
Schiz. aff.	× schiz.-nonpar.	4		
Schiz.-misc.	× schiz.-par.	3		
Schiz.-misc.	× schiz.-misc.	1		
Total		25	6	

[a] Misc.—miscellaneous.

displayed particular artistic interests, although none had distinguished themselves in the field. Only 2 of the 28 children of schizophrenic parents could be said to be artistically gifted.

Nor can I confirm Heston's (9) findings of a relationship between schizophrenia and sociopathy and mental deficiency. Eleven offspring—one female—were listed in the Criminal Register, but the subjects' crimes were usually petty larceny committed as youths and often under the influence of alcohol. Two of these developed schizophrenia later on, and three, chronic alcoholism. Only six had been imprisoned, but most of them only for 3 or 4 weeks. It is true that some subjects were no shining lights, but only two offspring could be classified as mentally defective; both were patients in institutions for mentally deficient. However, neither had schizophrenic parents. I should add that one schizophrenic child, prior to her schizophrenic disorder, had displayed signs of low IQ.

Environmental Factors

It is obvious that children of schizophrenic parents in general must have experienced a wretched childhood and adolescence. Poor housing conditions, miserable economy, and a chaotic homelife with crazy rearing practices often have befallen these children. That such conditions must predispose to low self-esteem, sad memories, and conflicts—in short, a weak ego—goes without saying.

Does it matter which of the parents is schizophrenic in a couple where one is schizophrenic and the other psychotic, but not schizophrenic? One would expect that a schizophrenic mother would have a more detrimental effect on a child's development than a schizophrenic father.

The data support our hypothesis (Table 1-10). The frequency of severe psychopathology is higher in families where the mother is schizophrenic than in families where the father is schizophrenic (the other parent is psychotic, but not schizophrenic). The difference is not statistically significant, but the tendency is noteworthy and definitely worth testing on a larger sample. By exclusion of a case of reactive psychosis and two borderline cases, the difference is more marked—although still not statistically significant. Five of the 32 offspring (16%) born to schizophrenic mothers are schizophrenic,

Table 1-10. Psychopathology in the Offspring as a Function of Psychopathology in the Mothers and Fathers

Both Parents Psychotic	No. of Families	No. of Offspring	No. of Psychoses[a]	Percentage of Psychosis[a]
Mother schiz., father nonschiz.	15	32	7	21.8
Father schiz., mother nonschiz.	11	22	2	9.1

[a] Inclusion of borderline cases.

whereas only one of 22 children (5%) of schizophrenic fathers is schizophrenic. Age differences for the two groups cannot explain this finding. In fact, the mean age is higher in the offspring of schizophrenic fathers, namely, 37.5 years compared with 35.1 years for the offspring of schizophrenic mothers.

The Problem of Normality

One might at first find it unbelievable that so many subjects of schizophrenic parents have managed to develop into relatively normal human beings, considering the fact that these children experience both extreme genetic and environmental risks. What kind of skills and coping mechanisms did these people develop to have escaped serious mental disorder? I have no firm answer to this question, but I think that a summary picture of one family might throw some light on the question.

Family No. 14

This family consists of two psychotic parents, both schizophrenic, and their three children, two of whom are schizophrenics and the third quite normal.

The *mother* is by now 75 years old. She worked as a seamstress when she married at the age of 24. She has always been rather sensitive and suspicious, but at the same time extroverted. At the age of 27 she developed psychotic symptoms but was not hospitalized. Between ages of 31 and 32 she was hospitalized twice because of psychotic symptoms, confusion, hallucinations, and bizarre paranoid ideas. After this episode she seems always to have harbored vague paranoid ideas about spiritual connections between people.

The *father* died in 1966 at the age of 66. He was trained as a mechanic and in younger years had a good work record. He married at the age of 25. At the age of 31 he was admitted to a mental hospital in acute psychosis, excited, paranoid, maintaining that his wife was the Devil. He was hospitalized again at ages 33 and 42, hallucinated, anxious, and paranoid. In later years he worked regularly and received a disability pension.

The *first child* is a 49-year-old male schizophrenic. He remembers his childhood as a very depressive period, with conflicts in the home and quarrels between his parents. He was often beaten up by his father. He was not allowed to play with certain children and often felt lonely. His best time in childhood, he said, was when both his parents were hospitalized.

After school he started working as a mechanic. He was sensitive and suspicious, with a tendency to withdraw from hardships. He married at the age of 24. After a couple of years he began displaying deviant behavior, saying that he was not married and thinking that the police followed him. Gradually he developed serious schizophrenic symptoms and had to be admitted to a mental hospital. In recent years he has done some casual work. Now and then he still hallucinates, and he is always paranoid. He has received disability pension.

The *second child* is a normal, 48-year-old, married foreman who has never experienced nervous troubles. According to him, his parents and an uncle living in the same house tried to interfere in his play with other children, but he ignored their meddling and admonition. At an early age he realized that the situation at home was hopeless, and he spent much of his free time in a garage near his home. Here he experienced quite a different world as compared with his home milieu. He also felt that his father was the dominant figure at home, the mother being more compliant, but at the same time manipulating. At an early age he had decided to move from home as early as possible. After completing elementary school, he started to work and found a room for himself in the city at the age of 14. At 24 he married. All his life he has been active and clever at work and has moved up to be a foreman in a machine shop. His personality is rather relaxed and friendly, independent, and self-assertive. He has good relationships with friends and colleagues. Both husband and wife feel that their marriage is happy. That is also my impression from a home visit which was a comfortable experience indeed.

The *third child* is a 46-year-old female schizophrenic. The patient remembered her childhood as a dismal period in her life. She was a sensitive and sulky girl who often cried when scolded. She tells the same story as the older brother: her parents interfered in her activities and restricted her autonomy. She remembers her father as an extremely strict and furious man, and she often felt that his thoughts accompanied her. However, she was fond of her father, and it was painful for her that he frequently quarrelled with her mother. She felt that her mother never really understood her. Her parents' conflicting views on matters of upbringing distressed her. Frequently her mother permitted her something, for instance, going to a party, while her father, when he learned about it, refused to let her go.

She worked as a shop-assistant and later as a maid. After she had moved to Oslo to change jobs at the age of 23, she gradually developed symptoms of tiredness, somatic complaints, and finally restlessness and religious excitement. The following year she was admitted to a mental hospital, paranoid, with ideas that Jesus had transferred his thoughts to her. She has since been hospitalized eight times with schizophrenic symptoms—at first catatonic and paranoid; in later years, more autistic. At follow-up she was guarded, sensitive, troubled with auditory hallucinations, and unable to work.

In the case just presented, the family is not integrated in the society at large, partly because it is a working-class family living in an upper-class area and partly because the parents refused to accept the norms of the area by preventing the children from taking part in normal activities outside the family. All three children have been exposed to a noxious home milieu, a conflicting insecure atmosphere with an unpredictable father and a manipulating mother, an ambiguous communication pattern, an attempt to force the children into rigid role patterns by restricting their activities outside the family. And, finally, all the children have experienced separation from their parents in preschool years.

How do we explain the fact that two of the children developed a schizophrenic way of life and that the third one managed to grow up to be a normal human being? I cannot, of course, give a completely satisfactory explanation, but I can point to several significant differences in the childrens' development. The healthy offspring seemed to have been able at an early age to detach himself from the family. This was in fact his own explanation, when he was asked why he had managed to hold the pathologic situation in which he lived at bay. His parents and his father's family, particularly his paternal uncle, tried to interfere with his connections outside the home, but he closed his ears and went his own way. In a garage nearby he discovered quite another world compared with his home milieu. Here he was able to identify with normal male figures. Because he realized at an early age that his parents were sick, he escaped the danger of overidentification and overinvolvement with sick parents, and he could look at his crazy family-life with a sort of objective attitude. How he was able to break the vicious circle in which he too must have started, we do not know. Perhaps he got his chance when both parents were in the hospital when he was between 5 and 6 years old. An alternative interpretation would be that his genes predisposed him to a more independent and self-assertive life which made him able to break away from the pathologic family milieu.

DISCUSSION

Before I discuss my findings I should like to stress the limitations of my study. The sample is relatively small, and diagnosis in parents is a cause of uncertainty since evaluation has to be made in most cases almost entirely from records. The strength of the study is, however, that all the offspring have been identified and most of them personally investigated.

In the main, the findings indicate that the risk of psychotic development, and more specifically schizophrenia, increases when both parents are psychotic or schizophrenic. Whereas the risk of schizophrenia in the general population is considered to be around 1%, the risk to children of one schizophrenic parent is about 10%. Dual mating schizophrenics produce, according to the literature, about 35–45% schizophrenic offspring. Kallmann's (11) often-quoted figure of 68% in recent years has not been accepted. Based on the studies of Kahn (10), Schulz (18), and Elsässer (3), Rosenthal (17) estimated the morbidity expectancy rate to be about 35% (see Table 1-11). By inclusion of questionable schizophrenics, Erlenmeyer-Kimling (5) and Slater and Cowie (19) calculated the expectancy rate at about 46%.

My own figures show an uncorrected rate of 20% (5/25) for typical schizophrenia and 28% (7/25) when borderline cases are included. The rate for typical schizophrenia is 29% with age-corrections. This figure can be designated as a maximum figure since I have used the Weinberg short method. In this case the Weinberg method certainly overcorrects for age. In conclusion, I would maintain that it is reasonable to accept a rate of about 25% for my own sample. Based on the studies of Kahn (10), Schulz (18), Elsässer (3), and the present one, the rate is approximately 25–35%, the exact figure not being of great importance.

Table 1-11. Summary of Psychopathology in the Offspring of Schizophrenics Couples, Based on Six Studies

Investigator	Year	Country	No. of Couples	Offspring Schizo-phrenia	Schizo-phrenia?	Other Psy-chopathy	Normal	Total
Kahn	1923	Germany	8	7	2	5	3	17
Kallmann	1938	USA	12	13	3	16	3	35
Schulz	1940	Germany	30	13	5	22	20	60
Elsässer	1952	Germany	14	12	3	12	32	59
Lewis	1957	England	4	4		3	20	27
Kringlen	1976	Norway	8	4	1	13	7	25

Two general conclusions might be drawn from such a figure. First, the low morbid expectancy rate strongly supports the importance of environmental factors in schizophrenia. Second, such a low expectancy rate does not support a theory of simple recessive or dominant inheritance. With regard to polygenic inheritance the question is more complicated, but most would probably agree that with such a low expectancy rate heritability must be of a modest degree.

In prior studies more schizophrenics have been found among female than among male offspring. The female schizophrenics also seem to have been more severely ill in former samples. In fact, by combining the series of Kahn (10), Schulz (18), and Elsässer (3), it is observed that 20 of 68 females (29%) were schizophrenics as compared to 12 of 68 (18%) males. In the present study no such sex difference was observed. A slight tendency was actually observed in the opposite direction, both for the total sample and for the schizophrenic group. These findings are in line with observations made in twin research. In the older twin studies, concordance for schizophrenia was considerably higher in females than in males. In most recent studies, however, these differences seem to disappear. This is particularly true for my own study where I could find no difference between men and women when the data were based on intensive investigation with personal follow-ups (13).

Since children of either sex on simple genetic grounds should run an equal risk of developing schizophrenia, this difference must have an environmental explanation. Deficient sampling is unlikely since the investigators all started with parents, not psychotic children. The most reasonable interpretation of the data is that girls in former days were more strictly brought up and had less opportunity for social contacts than boys. With increasing female emancipation this sex-difference in upbringing and attitudes has diminished. These differential sex-rates in twin studies and studies of dual matings also could be related to the national culture. Young women in Scandinavia have, I think, enjoyed for many years greater intrafamilial and social freedom than females in Germany, for example. If these speculations are correct, they will also influence etiologic theory. Until now we have emphasized the importance of genetics and early environmental influences, such as etiologic factors in serious mental disorder. Could it be that we have underestimated the significance of the teenage-years for both healthy and deviant development?

What about the biological unity of schizophrenia? Do all the various types of schizophrenic disorder share a common genetic background? What about the specificity of the schizophrenic genotype? For example, are manic-depressive illness and reactive psychosis genetically related to schizophrenia? If the genes are important in schizophrenia, then these nosological questions are also relevant.

Our data showed no clear-cut connection between subtypes of schizophrenia in parents and children. The literature also presents a conflicting view. Family studies show in most cases that subtypes distribute themselves in the same family. Twin studies, however, show a rather strong association of subtypes in genetically identical twins (13,7). Identification processes in monozygotic twins might, however, be partly responsible for this strong correlation.

Although the numbers are small and even though the data suggest some overlapping between the various types of functional psychosis, it is worth noting that all the schizophrenic offspring were born to parents who were both schizophrenic or at least one was classifieed as schizophrenic. None of the reactive and manic-depressives produced schizophrenic offspring. Again these findings might be partly explained psychologically by postulating strong identification between child and parent. But, as Rosenthal (17) points out in the adoption studies of schizophrenia, where the child never had a parental model of psychosis with which to identify, no manic-depressive offspring has as yet been reported. More contradictory results have been published by Schulz (18) and Elsässer (3,4). It is a fact that offspring of manic-depressives sometimes develop schizophrenia. However, it is rare that children of schizophrenics become manic-depressive. A reasonable conclusion seems to be that if there is a genetic association between schizophrenia and manic-depressive psychosis, this connection is rather weak.

I am not going to discuss in any detail environmental factors, but it needs to be emphasized that many but not all children of two psychotic parents have experienced a disturbed childhood environment. The problem here, as so often in research on heredity and environment, is that there is usually a correlation between genes and milieu, and it is rarely possible to split genes from environment. Such is the case here too. For example, offspring from dual matings of reactive psychosis often have had a reasonable childhood and adolescence, whereas most of the offspring of schizophrenic couples have grown up under extremely unstable and often chaotic circumstances. On purely environmental grounds, higher frequencies of severe psychopathology are to be expected in the latter children.

It usually has been observed that when a parent of a schizophrenic is affected by the same disorder it is more often the mother than the father, a finding which apparently could support an interpretation of psychologic transmission of schizophrenia. However, this finding is easily explained by the fact that women marry earlier and secondly become schizophrenic later than men, thus having more fertile years. In this study the starting point was, however, the parents, and, accordingly, the finding that schizophrenic mothers produce more schizophrenic children than schizophrenic fathers is significant and in support of environmental factors. The literature on this point shows conflicting results. Neither Kallmann (11) nor Bleuler (2) observed any maternal effect. Reed et al (15), however, found in a large American chronic hospital population a risk of 20.1% psychosis in children of psychotic mothers, compared with 8.1% for children of psychotic fathers. Reanalysis of the schizophrenic parents by Hanson (8) showed that the spouses of the female schizophrenics were disproportionately more psychiatrically deviant than the spouses of the male schizophrenics. Thus, the higher frequency of psychosis in children of female than of male schizophrenics could be explained in part by differential spouse pathologic states in the two groups. This explanation, however, does not hold for my own sample, since the mean mental health rating was the same for spouses of male and female schizophrenics.

The frequency of severe mental disorder was of course high in the extreme-risk group reported here. However, the outlook for offspring of psychotic parents seems better than originally thought, considering Kallmann's (11) figure of 68%, Rosenthal's (17) estimate of 35% and, now, my own figure of 25%. Three-fourths of the offspring of schizophrenic couples in fact do not develop schizophrenia. This circumstance is from a scientific point of view intriguing, but from a practical psychiatric point of view, a relief.

What sort of psychologic mechanisms have the people developed who have escaped the destiny of serious mental disorder? I think that knowledge of their coping skills would aid us in developing preventive measures. As psychiatrists we naturally have focused attention on psychopathology and have not speculated too much on the question of normality, which is just as puzzling. Should we not more often ask, "Why normality?'' instead of "Why pathology?" Let us hope that this neglected area of schizophrenia research might be the new direction in psychiatric research in the coming years.

SUMMARY

A personal investigation of 121 offspring of 48 couples, of which both partners at some time in their adult life were hospitalized for functional psychosis, show that 17% (20/121) could be classified as psychotic or borderline. The highest frequency of psychoses and borderline states was found in the children of schizophrenic couples. Twenty-eight percent (7/25) of children of schizophrenics have been classified as psychotic or borderline and 20% (5/25) have developed clinical schizophrenia. Age correction provides us with a maximum expectancy-rate of 29% (5/17).

Our findings show that the risk of psychotic development increases when both parents are psychotic, and, in particular, schizophrenic. However, the risk seems not as high as has been previously maintained.

These findings suggest that environmental factors play a considerable role in schizophrenic development. The results give no support to any simple dominant or recessive transmission. If one accepts a polygenic transmission, one has to admit that based on these data the polygenic predisposition is of a rather modest degree. More than 70% of children of two schizophrenic parents do not develop schizophrenia despite a double risk genetically and environmentally.

The study revealed a positive correlation between type of functional psychosis in parent and child. However, no relationship between subtype of schizophrenia in parent and offspring was observed.

The frequency of severe psychopathology was higher in families of schizophrenic mothers than in families of schizophrenic fathers (the other parent is psychotic, but not schizophrenic).

The problem of normality is touched upon. More than one-half of the total sample of offspring is classified as clinically normal—51.2% (62/121). In the offspring of schizophrenic parents, 28% (7/25) were diagnosed as normal. Finally, a brief clinical description is given of a family which consists of two schizophrenic parents, one normal and two schizophrenic children.

REFERENCES

1. Bastiansen S, Kringlen E: Children of two psychotic parents, a preliminary report, in Rubinstein D (ed): *Psychotherapy of Schizophrenia*. Amsterdam, Excerpta Medica, 1972.

2. Bleuler M: *Die schizophrenen Geistesstorungen im Lichte langjähriger Kranken- und Familienges-chichten*. Stuttgart, Thieme, 1972.

3. Elsässer G: *Die Nachkommen geisteskranker Elternpaare*. Stuttgart, Thieme, 1952.

4. Elsässer G, Lehmann H, Pohlen M, Scheid T: Die Nachkommen geisteskranker Elternpaare: Nachuntersuchungen unter sozialpsychiatrischen, tiefenpsychologischen und genetischen Aspekten. *Fortschr Neurol Psychiat* 39:495–522, 1971.

5. Erlenmeyer-Kimling L: Studies on the offspring of two schizophrenic parents, in Rosenthal D, Kety SS (eds): *The Transmission of Schizophrenia*. Oxford, Pergamon, 1968.

6. Essen-Möller E: Untersuchungen über die Fruchtbarkeit gewisser Gruppen von Geisteskranken. *Acta Psychiat Scand* (suppl 8) (Diss. med. Lund), 1935.

7. Gottesman II, Shields J: *Schizophrenia and Genetics: A Twin Study Vantage Point.* New York, Academic Press, 1972.

8. Hanson DR: Cited by Gottesman II, Shields J: A critical review of recent adoption, twin and family studies of schizophrenia: Behavioral genetics perspectives. *Schiz Bull* 2:200, 1976.

9. Heston LL: Psychiatric disorders in foster home reared children of schizophrenic mothers. *Brit J Psychiat* 112:819–825, 1966.

10. Kahn E: Studien über Vererbung und Entstehung geistiger Störungen: IV, Schizoid und Schizophrenie im Erbung, *Monograph ges Neurol Psychiat* 36:1, 1923.

11. Kallmann FJ: *The Genetics of Schizophrenia.* New York, Augustin, 1938.

12. Karlsson JL: *The Biological Basis of Schizophrenia.* Springfield, Ill, Thomas, 1966.

13. Kringlen E: *Heredity and Environment in the Functional Psychoses.* vol. I–II, Oslo, Universitetsforlaget 1967; London, Heineman, 1968.

14. Lewis AJ: The offspring of parents both mentally ill. *Acta genet* 7:349–365, 1957.

14a. Ødegard, Ø: A statistical investigation of the incidence of mental disorder in Norway. *Psychiat Quart* 20:381–399, 1946.

15. Reed SC, Hartley C, Anderson VE, et al: *The Psychoses: Family Studies.* Philadelphia, Saunders, 1973.

16. Reisby N: Psychoses in children of schizophrenic mothers. *Acta Psychiat Scand* 43:8–19, 1967.

17. Rosenthal D: The offspring of schizophrenic couples. *J Psychiat Res* 4:169–188, 1966.

18. Schulz B: Zur Erbpathologie der Schizophrenie. *Z ges Neurol Psychiat.* 143:175–293, 1932.

19. Slater E, Cowie V: *The Genetics of Mental Disorders.* London, Oxford University Press, 1971.

20. Strömgren, E.: *Beitrage zur psychiatrischen Erblohre* Copenhagen, Munksgard, 1938.

Chapter 2

The Biologic and Adoptive Families of Adopted Individuals Who Became Schizophrenic: Prevalence of Mental Illness and Other Characteristics

Seymour S. Kety, M.D.
David Rosenthal, Ph.D.
Paul H. Wender, M.D.
Fini Schulsinger, M.D.
Bjørn Jacobsen, M.D.

In 1959 we reviewed the evidence supporting the operation of genetic factors in schizophrenia. This evidence consisted of a higher risk for schizophrenia in the blood relatives of schizophrenics than in the general population, a risk that was highly correlated with consanguinity, reaching its highest level in the offspring of two schizophrenic parents and in the monozygotic twins of schizophrenics. The possibility of selective and subjective bias had not been ruled out in most of the studies, and all suffered from an inability to control environmental variables adequately, some of which would be expected to vary with consanguinity. We concluded that an alternative approach would be the study of the prevalence of schizophrenia in the biologic and adoptive relatives of adopted individuals who became schizophrenic, and we suggested that only a national sample would provide a sufficient number of cases and the types of control necessary (1).

In 1962, three of us (Rosenthal, Wender, and Kety), who had independently devised different strategies that utilized adoption as a means of disentangling genetic and environmental variables, decided to pool our efforts. In 1963, with the invaluable

Research reviewed in this paper has been supported by the NIMH Intramural Program, Extramural grants MH15602 and MH25515, the Schizophrenia Research Program of the Scottish Rite, and the Foundations' Fund for Research in Psychiatry.

collaboration of Schulsinger, we began the compilation of a national sample of adopted individuals in Denmark. The sample consists of all individuals adopted, from the beginning of 1924 to the end of 1947, by persons other than their biologic relatives. The ages of the adoptees thus range, in 1976, from approximately 29 to 52 years. A total of 14,500 adoptees are included.

THE ORIGINAL STUDY, BASED ON INSTITUTIONAL RECORDS

The compilation was begun with the subsample of adoptions granted by the courts of the city and county of Copenhagen (the Greater Copenhagen Sample) and consisted of 5483 adoptees. From the central Psychiatric Register[1] and from the records of each of the psychiatric hospitals in Denmark, those adoptees who had ever been admitted to a mental hospital were identified and their records abstracted. Inclusion in the index (i.e., schizophrenic) group of adoptees required the unanimous agreement of four raters on a diagnosis of "definite schizophrenia," made after reading the abstracts but without knowledge of family history. We had previously agreed that for the purposes of this study, "schizophrenia" would include three subgroups: chronic or classical schizophrenia, latent or borderline schizophrenia, and acute schizophrenic reaction. In doing so we made no assumptions that these three syndromes were valid or necessarily related. The criteria used by each of us in making these diagnoses were presented in our first paper on mental illness in the biologic and adoptive relatives of schizophrenics (2) (Table 2-1). In the Greater Copenhagen Sample, 33 index cases were thus selected, and the total national sample of adoptees yielded 74. A control was chosen for each index case from adoptees who had no history of admission to a mental hospital, but who matched the index case in age, sex, length of time spent with the biologic mother, history before adoption, and socioeconomic status of the adoptive parents.

The biologic and adoptive relatives of the index and control probands were located through the adoption records which, with very few exceptions, identified the adoptive mother and father, the biologic mother and putative biologic father. There is, of course, the possibility of error in the last of these, but the requirements in Denmark that the putative father acknowledge paternity and contribute to the costs of maternity care and adoption would tend to minimize the error, and it is doubtful whether misidentification of a few biologic fathers could introduce a significant systematic bias into the results. In the case of one proband, three putative fathers were named in the adoption record, and all three were retained in the subsequent analysis. (Fortunately, schizophrenia was not found in any of them or their other offspring so the problem of appropriately weighting them did not arise.) The remarkable Folke and psychiatric population registers in Denmark permitted the identification of full siblings and half-siblings of the probands through the biologic and adoptive parents.

Ascertainment of mental illness and other forms of psychopathology in the relatives required a more exhaustive search than that which sufficed for the selection of index cases, where the purpose was simply to find those on whom a unanimous agreement on a diagnosis of definite schizophrenia could be reached. Because all the relatives had to be

[1] The authors wish to express their gratitude to Drs. Erik Strömgren and Annalise Dupont of the Institute of Psychiatric Demography in Aarhus for the use of the National Psychiatric Register.

Table 2-1. Diagnostic Criteria for Components of the Schizophrenia Spectrum[a]

A.		Definitely not schizophrenia (specify diagnosis).

B1.   Chronic schizophrenia ("chronic undifferentiated schizophrenia," "true schizophrenia," "process schizophrenia").

Characteristics: (1) Poor pre-psychotic adjustment; introverted; schizoid; shut-in; few peer contacts; few heterosexual contacts; usually unmarried; poor occupational adjustment. (2) Onset—gradual and without clear-cut psychologic precipitant. (3) Presenting picture—presence of primary Bleulerian characteristics; presence of clear rather than confused sensorium. (4) Posthospital course—failure to reach previous level of adjustment. (5) Tendency to chronicity.

B2.   Acute schizophrenic reaction (acute undifferentiated schizophrenic reaction, schizo-affective psychosis, possible schizophreniform psychosis, [acute] paranoid reaction, homosexual panic).

Characteristics: (1) Relatively good premorbid adjustment. (2) Relatively rapid onset of illness with clear-cut psychologic precipitant. (3) Presenting picture—presence of secondary symptoms and comparatively lesser evidence of primary ones; presence of affect (manic-depressive symptoms, feeling of guilt); cloudy rather than clear sensorium. (4) Post-hospital course—good. (5) Tendency to relatively brief episode(s) responding to drugs, EST, etc.

B3.   Borderline state (pseudoneurotic schizophrenia, borderline, ambulatory schizophrenia questionable simple schizophrenia, "psychotic character", severe schizoid individual).

Characteristics: (1) Thinking—strange or atypical mentation; thought shows tendency to ignore reality, logic and experience (to an excessive degree) resulting in poor adaptation to life experience (despite the presence of a normal IQ); fuzzy, murky, vague speech. (2) Experience—brief episodes of cognitive distortion (the patient can, and does, snap back but during the episode the idea has more the character of a delusion than an ego-alien obsessive thought); feelings of depersonalization, of strangeness or unfamiliarity with or toward the familiar; micropsychosis. (3) Affective—anhedonia—never experiences intense pleasure—never happy; no deep or intense involvement with anyone or anybody. (4) Interpersonal behavior—may appear poised, but lacking in depth ("as if" personality); sexual adjustment—chaotic fluctuation, mixture of hetero- and homosexuality. (5) Psychopathology—multiple neurotic manifestations which shift frequently (obsessive concerns, phobias, conversion, psychosomatic symptoms, etc.); severe wildespread anxiety.

C.   Inadequate personality.

Characteristics: A somewhat heterogeneous group consisting of individuals who would be classified as either inadequate or schizoid by the *APA Diagnostic Manual.* Persons so classified often had many of the characteristics of the B3 category, but to a considerably milder degree.

D1, 2, or 3.   Uncertain B1, 2, or 3 either because information is lacking or because even if enough information is available, the case does not fit clearly into an appropriate B category.

[a] From Kety SS et al (2).

Table 2-2. Schizophrenia Spectrum Diagnoses in the Biologic Families of Schizophrenic and Control Adoptees (Greater Copenhagen Sample)

	N	Definite Schizophrenia		Uncertain Schizophrenia		Schizoid or Inadequate Personality		Total Spectrum	
		N	(%)	N	(%)	N	(%)	N	(%)
Early study based on hospital records (Kety, Rosenthal, Wender, Schulsinger, 1968)									
Biologic relatives of schizophrenic adoptees	150	7	(4.7)	4	(2.7)	2	(1.3)	13	(8.7)
Biologic relatives of control adoptees	156	2	(1.3)	1	(0.6)	0	(0.0)	3	(1.9)
p^a =		0.077		n.s.		n.s.		0.007	
Most recent study, based on interviews (Kety, Rosenthal, Wender, Schulsinger, Jacobsen, 1975)									
Biologic relatives of schizophrenic adoptees	173	11	(6.4)	13	(7.5)	13	(7.5)	37	(21.4)
Biologic relatives of control adoptees	174	3	(1.7)	3	(1.7)	13	(7.5)	19	(10.9)
p =		0.026		0.009		n.s.		0.006	
Biologic half-sibs of schizophrenic adoptees	104	10	(9.6)	10	(9.6)	6	(5.8)	26	(25.0)
Biologic half-sibs of control adoptees	104	1	(1.0)	2	(1.9)	11	(10.6)	14	(13.5)
p =		0.005		0.017		n.s.		0.026	
Biologic paternal half-sibs of schizophrenic adoptees	63	8	(12.7)	6	(9.5)	4	(6.3)	18	(28.5)
Biologic paternal half-sibs of control adoptees	64	1	(1.6)	1	(1.6)	9	(14.1)	11	(17.2)
p =		0.015		0.055		n.s.		0.094	
Biologic families[b] of index adoptees	33	14	(42.4)	17	(51.5)			23	(69.6)
Biologic families of control adoptees	34	3	(8.8)	5	(14.7)			16	(47.0)
p =		0.002		0.001				n.s.	

[a] Fisher's one-tailed exact probability; n.s. (not significant) is listed for p values greater than 0.10.

[b] Tabulating number of probands whose biologic parents, sibs, or half-sibs include at least one diagnosis of definite, uncertain, or spectrum cumulatively.

given diagnoses and none could be rejected, it was necessary to recognize a category of "uncertain schizophrenia" where it was felt that schizophrenia was the most likely diagnosis but was necessarily questionable because the symptoms were too mild, too few, or too atypical. We were aware that in previous studies relatives and monozygotic twins of classical schizophrenics sometimes displayed such symptomatology or even milder syndromes best described as "schizoid" or "inadequate" personality. We developed a concept that we called the "schizophrenia spectrum" of disorders, which included schizoid or inadequate personality and uncertain schizophrenia as well as definite schizophrenia (chronic, latent, and acute). It was hoped that the results of the study would shed some light on the validity of these syndromes and their relationship to each other and to classical schizophrenia as Kraepelin had described it. In the case of the relatives, information relating to admission to mental hospitals was obtained as it was for the adoptees, but, in addition, searches were made through military records and court records, for information regarding psychiatric disorder in any of the relatives. The pertinent records were abstracted, translated into English, and edited to remove any clues that would permit a sophisticated reader to surmise the type of relationship (biologic or adoptive, index or control). As in the case of psychiatric diagnosis generally, we recognize that many of our diagnostic categories were vague and that our individual and consensus diagnoses were largely subjective. These diagnoses, however, were made without knowledge of the relationship of the relatives to the probands.

The major finding of the first study based on hospital and other records of the relatives in the Greater Copenhagen Sample was a highly significant concentration of diagnoses in the schizophrenic spectrum among biologic relatives of index cases compared with those of the controls; the adoptive relatives of index probands were not different from their controls in this respect, and neither group showed a higher prevalence of schizophrenic spectrum disorders than would have been expected in the general population (Table 2-2). The number of diagnoses representative of the various subgroups within the schizophrenia spectrum were too few in this sample to yield reliable differences. We, therefore, continued this approach through the total national sample of adoptees and simultaneously decided to conduct interviews with the relatives in the Copenhagen sample.

DIAGNOSES FROM PSYCHIATRIC INTERVIEWS OF RELATIVES IN THE GREATER COPENHAGEN STUDY

To obtain more information for the diagnosis of relatives in the Greater Copenhagen Sample, as well as to obtain more information regarding environmental variables, a second study was carried out on the same population of relatives, this time involving extensive interviews by a Danish psychiatrist Dr. Bjørn Jacobsen. More than 90% of the relatives alive and residing in Denmark, Norway, or Sweden were interviewed; the minority who refused were distributed evenly among the four types of relatives. The edited interviews were read by three American raters (Rosenthal, Wender, and Kety; Schulsinger was ruled out because of the possibility that as the Chief Psychiatrist of a large Copenhagen hospital he might have recognized some of the subjects). Independent, blind diagnoses were made by each, and a consensus diagnosis reached. A first report of the results (Tables 2-2 and 2-3) was presented in 1973 and eventually published (3). The various categories of mental illness outside the schizophrenia spectrum (organic, neurotic, affective, and personality disorders) were distributed randomly among the four populations of relatives, whereas schizophrenia spectrum disorders were significantly concentrated in the biologic relatives of the index probands, the only population related genetically to the schizophrenic adoptees. There were now enough diagnoses among the various subcategories to permit a statistical breakdown.

The categories of chronic schizophrenia, uncertain schizophrenia, and definite schizophrenia (including chronic, latent, and acute) each showed a significant concentration in the biologic index relatives compared with their controls, while the adoptive relatives who reared the schizophrenic adoptees showed no higher prevalence of any of these

Table 2-3. Schizophrenia Spectrum Diagnoses in the Adoptive Families of Schizophrenic and Control Adoptees (Greater Copenhagen Sample)

	N	Definite Schizophrenia		Uncertain Schizophrenia		Schizoid or Inadequate Personality		Total Spectrum	
		N	(%)	N	(%)	N	(%)	N	(%)
Early study based on hospital records (Kety, Rosenthal, Wender, Schulsinger, 1968)									
Adoptive relatives of schizophrenic adoptee	74	0	(0.0)	1	(1.4)	1	(1.4)	2	(2.7)
Adoptive relatives of control adoptees	83	2	(2.4)	1	(1.2)	0	(0.0)	3	(3.6)
p =		n.s.		n.s.		n.s.		n.s.	
Most recent study based on interviews (Kety, Rosenthal, Wender, Schulsinger, Jacobsen, 1975)									
Adoptive relatives of schizophrenic adoptees	74	1	(1.4)	1	(1.4)	2	(2.7)	4	(5.4)
Adoptive relatives of control adoptees	91	2	(2.2)	3	(3.3)	2	(2.2)	7	(7.7)
p =		n.s.		n.s.		n.s.		n.s.	
Adoptive families of index adoptees	33	1	(3.0)	3	(9.0)			5	(15.2)
Adoptive families of control adoptees	34	3	(8.8)	5	(14.7)			7	(20.6)
p =		n.s.		n.s.				n.s.	

Uncorrected prevalence of these diagnoses in the General population can be estimated using all adoptive relatives and biologic control relatives. The individual subsamples do not differ significantly from each other. For *definite* schizophrenia (from hospital records) the uncorrect prevalence is $\frac{4}{313}$ or 1.3%; for *definite* schizophrenia (from interview survey of the population), $\frac{6}{339}$ or 1.8%; for *uncertain* schizophrenia (from hospital records), $\frac{3}{313}$ or 1.0%; and for *uncertain* schizophrenia (from interview survey of the population), $\frac{7}{313}$ or 2.2%.

diagnoses than did their controls or what would be expected in the general population. On the other hand, the diagnoses of schizoid or inadequate personality were evenly distributed between the biologic index relatives and the biologic control relatives, so this study failed to adduce evidence of a relationship between these syndromes and schizophrenia. Some of our other studies support such a relationship (4), so the question is still unresolved. Perhaps further characterization of the personality characteristics that contribute to that diagnosis may make it possible to define those that are genetically related to schizophrenia.

Recognizing that a more conservative treatment of the data would be based on the 33 schizophrenic probands rather than on their relatives, we have carried out and reported such analyses. Seventeen (52%) of the 33 schizophrenic probands had one or more instances of definite or uncertain schizophrenia in their biologic relatives as compared with five (15%) in biologic families of 34 control adoptees (p = 0.001). Although this approach takes into account the fact that there are only 33 index cases in this sample, as well as controlling for some environmental variables if the family members live together, it also loses information because it disregards the amount of schizophrenia that exists in each family. Matthysse and Kidd have been developing a means of calculating the best estimate of genetic risk from the distribution of schizophrenia in families. Such an estimate would take this factor into consideration, and it is our plan to apply that type of analysis to our samples of probands and their families.

In an effort to rule out possible environmental factors such as *in utero* influences, birth trauma, and early mothering experience which adoptees may have received from their biologic mothers, we have examined the occurrence of schizophrenia in the biologic paternal half-siblings of the index and control probands since these relatives did not share the same uterus or neonatal mothering experience and thus have had no environmental influences in common with the adoptee. Although the number of these half-siblings was distributed evenly between index and control populations, there was a significantly high concentration of both definite and uncertain schizophrenia in the paternal half-siblings of the schizophrenic adoptees. Analyzing the results by the proband method, we find 10 index adoptees with definite or uncertain schizophrenia in biologic paternal half-siblings as compared with 2 control adoptees (p = 0.01). We regard this as the most compelling evidence we have that genetic factors operate significantly in the transmission of schizophrenia.

During the past 2 years we have been engaged in further analysis of the voluminous data derived in this study and in two other related studies, i.e., extension of the adoptive sample from Greater Copenhagen to all Denmark and a study of a matched sample of nonadopted individuals in Great Copenhagen.

DIAGNOSIS BASED ON MENTAL HOSPITAL RECORDS FOR THE TOTAL NATIONAL SAMPLE OF ADOPTEES AND THEIR RELATIVES

Proceeding as we had in the Greater Copenhagen study, we agreed on a diagnosis of "definite schizophrenia" in 41 additional index adoptees, now from the adoptee sample outside Greater Copenhagen. This has given us a total of 74 schizophrenic index adoptees from the total of 14,500 adoptees in all Denmark legally adopted by other than their biologic relatives from the beginning of 1924 to the end of 1947. Of the 74 index cases, 37 received a consensus diagnosis of chronic schizophrenia, 24 a diagnosis of latent schizophrenia, and 13 a diagnosis of acute schizophrenic reaction. Search of the adoption records and the Folkeregister identified a total of 1159 relatives of these probands and their matched controls, broken down as follows: biologic relations of index and controls, 405 and 387, respectively; adoptive relatives of index and controls, 173 and 194, respectively. The number of diagnoses in the schizophrenia spectrum and in its subgroups arrived at from abstracts of mental hospital records for each of these populations has now been ascertained. There is a highly significant concentration of spectrum disorders in the biologic relatives of the index cases (5.9%) as compared with the biologic relatives of the control case: (1.0%). No significant difference occurred between the two types of adoptive relatives, who with the control biologic relatives showed a prevalence of spectrum disorders (1.3%) in accord with the rate that would be expected in the general population. Because of the larger number of probands and relatives, the spectrum can be subdivided into its components with an indication that chronic schizophrenia, uncertain schizophrenia, and definite schizophrenia are concentrated in the biologic index relatives; there were very few diagnoses of acute schizophrenic reaction, schizoid, or inadequate personality, as was the case in the analysis based on hospital records for the Greater Copenhagen sample, and none of these diagnoses can be said to be concentrated in any of the populations.

The larger size of this sample also now makes possible a breakdown of the diagnoses in the biologic relatives of the index adoptees according to the type of schizophrenia found in these probands. The 37 index probands with a diagnosis of chronic schizophrenia had a total of 217 identified biologic relatives who yielded 6 diagnoses of chronic schizophrenia, 6 diagnoses of latent schizophrenia, one diagnosis of acute schizophrenia, 4 diagnoses of uncertain schizophrenia, and one schizoid personality. This appears to suggest that certain syndromes, milder than those described by Kraepelin, which we have diagnosed as latent and uncertain schizophrenia, may be genetically related to the classical syndrome, as others have suggested (5,6). The 24 probands with a diagnosis of latent schizophrenia had 128 identified biologic relatives who yielded one diagnosis of chronic schizophrenia, 3 of latent schizophrenia, and one each of uncertain schizophrenia and schizoid personality. These findings are also compatible with the inference above. The 13 probands diagnosed as acute schizophrenic reaction had 61 biologic relatives in none of whom was a diagnosis made within the schizophrenia spectrum. Although this fails to support the genetic relatedness of this syndrome to others in the spectrum, the further study based on exhaustive psychiatric interviews yielded four diagnoses of uncertain schizophrenia in the relatives of such probands. An analysis which is now underway of the specific symptomatic components that have gone into these diagnoses may help to resolve this issue.

SPECIFIC CHARACTERISTICS OF THE SYNDROMES WITHIN THE SCHIZOPHRENIA SPECTRUM

Up to the present time the diagnoses in the schizophrenia spectrum have been based on blind and global consensus diagnoses by several raters. The criteria used in the diagnoses of chronic, latent, and acute schizophrenia have been fairly explicit and were derived from the standard American source (DSM-II). The prevalence of these diagnoses' based on institutional records, in populations genetically related to schizophrenics and those not so related is comparable to those in the literature (see footnote, Table 2-3). These prevalences were elevated somewhat in both populations when based on an interview survey of 90% of the population, a more exhaustive form of ascertainment than is usually employed.

On the other hand, the criteria for our diagnosis of uncertain schizophrenia were considerably more vague, leaving each rater to perceive and evaluate symptoms which to him suggested schizophrenia as the most likely diagnosis. What we found, despite this lack of diagnostic specificity, was a consistent increase in the prevalence of the diagnosis of uncertain schizophrenia in individuals genetically related to schizophrenic probands as compared with those not so related. This diagnosis by the three raters in the interview study, independently and consensually, discriminated consistently the adoptive and biologic relatives at a high level of significance (p values of 0.003, 0.01, and 0.009, for each rater independently and 0.002 for their consensus). This appears to justify a more exhaustive search for those characteristics which permit that diagnosis. These biologic relatives are unique in having lived apart from and being largely unacquainted with the proband, which minimized the possibility of mimicry and other environmental influences in the development of these symptoms, and also of subjective bias in the diagnostic identification of these subjects. Hence, this approach permits a clearer evaluation of characteristics that are essentially genetic in origin.

ANALYSIS OF THE MATCHED NONADOPTED SAMPLE
IN GREATER COPENHAGEN

The roughly 50% discordance for schizophrenia found by numerous studies in monozygotic twins (5) constitutes clear evidence that nongenetic factors must operate in the development of schizophrenia. Our findings appear to permit the conclusion that these factors usually operate on a genetically transmitted vulnerability. If these nongenetic variables were intrafamilial, it would be expected that the process of adoption, by randomizing genetic and family-specific environmental variables, would reduce the prevalence of overt schizophrenia in the biologic relatives of schizophrenic adoptees. To examine that hypothesis, it was necessary to compare these prevalences, as found by us, with appropriate nonadoptive populations. It was clear to us that such a comparison could not be made with figures in the literature since the prevalence of diagnosed schizophrenia depends so heavily on means of ascertainment and diagnostic criteria. To keep these constant we decided to repeat the Greater Copenhagen study on a matched sample of nonadopted individuals.

That sample of adoptees was made up of 5483 adoptees, for each of whom a nonadopted control now was selected from census records of the city and county of Copenhagen, matching for age, sex, and socioeconomic class of the rearing family as approximated by the neighborhood of rearing. The matched control usually lived on the same street, often in the same apartment house as the adoptee.

Ascertainment of schizophrenia in the nonadopted sample followed exactly the same procedures as those used in the selection of the adoptee index cases. The possible bias of knowing that these were nonadopted individuals was avoided by carrying out the selection of index cases at the same time that the adoptee index cases were being selected for the remainder of Denmark, the two populations having been pooled and randomized. In this manner 31 index cases were identified in the nonadopted sample, compared with the 33 such probands who had been identified in the adopted sample. Thus, the incidence of definite schizophrenia in adopted individuals did not differ appreciably from the incidence in a matched sample of the general population. A comparable group of 31 matched controls were selected from the nonadopted sample with no history of admission to a mental hospital. The relatives of both groups of probands were identified and mental illness diagnosed using the same procedures applied to the biologic and adoptive relatives of the study outside Copenhagen. Again, all the relatives were randomized and the raters were blind regarding the relationship of a relative to a proband and whether the proband was index or control, adopted or nonadopted.

The prevalence of definite schizophrenia in the relatives of nonadopted schizophrenics was not significantly different from that in the biologic relatives of adopted schizophrenics, although the severity of the diagnoses appeared to be greater in the nonadopted group. Thus, whereas definite schizophrenia was comparable in prevalence (4.9% vs. 4.7% in the biologic relatives of nonadopted versus adopted schizophrenics), most of the schizophrenics in the biologic relatives of the nonadopted probands were diagnosed as chronic, while the majority of the affected biologic relatives of the adopted schizophrenics had been diagnosed as latent or uncertain in subtype. These tentative results are still based on global but blind diagnoses; if that distinction is also made by the use of the more explicit characteristics that are now being examined, it would suggest that the important role of intrafamilial environmental variables was to enhance the severity of the illness.

DIFFERENCE IN DEATH RATES BETWEEN BIOLOGICAL INDEX RELATIVES AND CONTROLS

In the analysis of the interview study on the Greater Copenhagen sample, we found and reported (3) a very interesting and highly significant ($p = 0.002$) higher death rate for the biologic relatives of index cases than for their controls. We have since searched the death records in Denmark as well as hospital records for the cause of death in each of these relatives. Analysis indicates that the preponderance of deaths can be accounted for by suicide (5 vs. 0 instances), possible suicide (3 vs. 0 instances), accidental death or homicide (5 vs. 0 instances), or sudden death with unknown cause (3 vs. 0 instances) for a total of 16 unnatural deaths in the biologic control relatives. Deaths from natural causes (19 vs. 15) are not significantly different between the two groups, indicating that the difference in death rate is probably not the result of a medical illness genetically associated with schizophrenia. Since suicide and violent death is considerably more common among schizophrenics than among the rest of the population, it is possible that some of these may have occurred in schizophrenics who had been unrecognized.

EXAMINATION OF THE POSSIBILITY OF SUBJECTIVE BIAS IN THE SELECTION OF INDEX AND CONTROL PROBANDS

In the first report of these studies in 1968, we pointed out and discussed a number of ascertainment, selective, or subjective biases that might have operated on the results despite our efforts to control them. A number of these would have operated to decrease the preponderance of schizophrenia in the biologic relatives of the index cases. The enlightened social system in Denmark makes it possible for a pregnant woman to obtain a legal abortion on the basis of a history of schizophrenia in herself or in the father. This, in addition to the relative infertility of overt schizophrenics, could have resulted in the removal from our sample of adoptees of a disproportionate fraction of those with schizophrenia in the biologic parents. In addition, we now know that the five suicides in biologic index relatives were in biologic parents. In a similar manner, the adoption process would be expected to screen out children born of parents with overt schizophrenia, thus further contributing to a reduction in the prevalence of overt schizophrenia in the biologic parents.

On the other hand, there are biases that could have operated to exaggerate the prevalence of diagnosed schizophrenia spectrum disorder in the biologic families of index cases. Possible knowledge of the relationship existing between an index case and a member of his biologic family, or knowledge of the existence of schizophrenia in the biologic family of an adoptee could have affected the tendency to notice, to record, to institutionalize, or to diagnose schizophrenia in one or the other individual on the part of professional or nonprofessional observers, or the selection of index cases and controls in such a way as to enhance the likelihood of finding schizophrenia in the biologic index relatives. It was our impression at the time that this leakage of information was small. Nevertheless, we accumulated all the available information pertinent to these questions and have recently analyzed it.

The original adoption documents and the records of the Mothers' Aid Agency in Denmark contain information that was known about mental illness in the biologic parents of the adoptees at the time of adoption, the health of the child, and reasons why the child was given up for adoption. Schulsinger, in abstracting and translating into English the hospital records of candidate index probands had included information relating to mental illness in the biologic family (which was deleted in the transcripts used in the selection process). Jacobsen has, in the past 2 years, prepared an independent and exhaustive review of the same hospital records.

We have reviewed their unedited transcripts as well as the information from the adoption and Mothers' Aid Agency and have reassured ourselves that there was very little information available that could have prejudiced our selection of probands. In no biologic parent was a diagnosis of schizophrenia recorded, but in 5 of the 33 index probands, a presumption of schizophrenia in a parent might conceivably have been made on the basis of suicide, "psychogenic depression of pregnancy," or schizophrenia in an avuncular relative. If these 5 probands and their biologic families are removed from our sample and the results recalculated, the significant differences we find for definite schizophrenia and for uncertain schizophrenia in biologic index relatives and families compared to their controls remain.

Another way in which the selection of probands might have been biased would be in the rejection of control adoptees because of information relating to schizophrenia in their biologic families. After the 33 index adoptees had been selected on the basis of a consensus diagnosis of definite schizophrenia, their histories between birth and adoption were obtained from the adoption documents and the records of the Mothers' Aid Agency. Then, for each index case, at least four candidate controls with no history of admission to a mental hospital were selected from adoptees appearing immediately before and after the index adoptee in our chronologically arranged adoption file. These candidates matched the index proband in sex and age. Information was then obtained on each candidate regarding preadoption history and socioeconomic status of the adoptive family. From that information one control was chosen for each index adoptee who matched best on socioeconomic status of adoptive family and on time spent with biologic mother or father, in a children's home, or with foster parents before transfer to the adopting family. That selection might conceivably have been influenced by information regarding mental illness in the biologic family.

We have reviewed the information we had at the time of that selection for each of the control adoptees chosen and for the 114 who were rejected. There was no information regarding schizophrenia in any of the biologic relatives. In only two was there any information regarding mental status—one biologic mother of the controls selected was feeble-minded, one biologic mother of the 114 rejected had committed suicide, and in both cases inclusion or rejection had been based only on the demographic criteria indicated earlier. We have found no basis for subjective bias in the selection of control or index probands.

Although the results we have reported are based on the original samples of index and control probands selected at the beginning of each study rather than on the basis of retrospective subdivisions, it has sometimes been useful to make such retrospective analyses on the basis of questions that have subsequently arisen. Because we did not know how many index cases would emerge from the samples, we did not restrict them only to adoptees who were separated from their biologic mothers very early. This was actually the case for approximately one-half of our probands, the others having been put out for adoption after several months or even a year. When the analyses have been restricted to the index cases and controls put out for adoption within the first month, in most instances simply because of illegitimacy, the prevalence of schizophrenic illness in the biologic relatives of index cases remains essentially the same, but it falls appreciably in the case of the controls (2). That is not unexpected, since putting children up for adoption an appreciable time after birth is usually for reasons other than illegitimacy, and often is done because of serious illness in one of the parents or because of marital disruption.

We have selected our controls from samples not known to have been hospitalized for mental illness, but that does not assure us of the absence of severe behavioral disturbances or even schizophrenia among them. In the case of the interview study, it was possible to interview and make psychiatric diagnoses blindly in a majority of these controls. When the control population of probands is restricted to those who are psychiatrically normal or with no suggestion of schizophrenia in their diagnoses, the prevalence of schizophrenia in the biologic relatives decreases substantially (3). These controls who have been screened by a psychiatric interview may be a useful comparison group in subsequent analyses that attempt to find symptoms or personality characteristics of the genetically vulnerable individual.

SUMMARY

Studies on adopted individuals and their families offer a means of dissociating genetic from environmental variables in the transmission of schizophrenia. The results of three studies that examined the prevalence of mental illness in the biologic and adoptive relatives of adoptees who eventually became schizophrenic are summarized.

The first study of the relatives of 33 schizophrenic adoptees and matched controls, identified among a total sample of 5483 adoptees in Greater Copenhagen, used blind consensus diagnoses based on abstracts of mental hospital records and found a highly significant concentration of schizophrenic spectrum disorders in the biologic relatives of the schizophrenic adoptees. A second study, based on psychiatric interviews with 90% of the living relatives, confirmed the results of the first but found, in addition, that diagnoses of chronic schizophrenia, definite schizophrenia, and uncertain schizophrenia were significantly higher in the biologic relatives of the schizophrenic adoptees while other mental disorders were randomly distributed. The biologic relatives of schizophrenic adoptees also showed a significantly higher death rate, accounted for by suicide, possible suicide, and accidental death.

A third study, which extended the first sample to all of Denmark, identified a total of 74 index adoptees whose biologic relatives, in confirmation of the first two studies, showed a significantly higher prevalence of definite and uncertain schizophrenia in comparison to the biologic relatives of their controls. In each of the three studies the prevalence of schizophrenia and schizophrenia spectrum disorders in the adoptive relatives of the schizophrenic adoptees was not significantly different from that in the control relatives.

Index adoptees who were diagnosed as typical chronic schizophrenics had significant numbers of biologic relatives diagnosed as latent or uncertain schizophrenia in addition to those with more typical schizophrenia, suggesting that these categories bear a genetic as well as a phenomenologic relationship to chronic schizophrenia. Adoptees with a diagnosis of acute schizophrenic reaction had relatively few schizophrenia-like disorders among their biologic relatives.

The prevalence of schizophrenia in an adopted population is not significantly different from that in a matched population of nonadopted individuals. The prevalence of schizophrenia in the biologic relatives of nonadopted and adopted schizophrenics is comparable, although the severity of the symptoms appears to be less in the biologic relatives of adopted schizophrenics.

REFERENCES

1. Kety SS: Biochemical theories of schizophrenia. A two-part critical review of current theories and of the evidence used to support them. *Science* 129:1528–1532, 1590–1596, 1959.
2. Kety SS, Rosenthal D, Wender PH, Schulsinger F: The types and prevalence of mental illness in the biological and adoptive families of adopted schizophrenics, in Rosenthal D, Kety SS (eds): *The Transmission of Schizophrenia*. Oxford, Pergamon 1968, pp 345–362.
3. Kety SS, Rosenthal D, Wender PH, Schulsinger F, Jacobsen B: Mental illness in the biological and adoptive families of adopted individuals who have become schizophrenic: A preliminary report based upon psychiatric interviews, in Fieve R, Rosenthal D, Brill H (eds): *Genetic Research In Psychiatry*. Baltimore and London, Johns Hopkins University Press, 1975, pp 147–165.
4. Rosenthal D: Discussion: The concept of subschizophrenic disorders. In: *Genetic Research in Psychiatry,* op. cit., pp 199–208.
5. Gottesman II, Shields J: *Schizophrenia and Genetics: A Twin Study Vantage Point.* New York, Academic Press, 1972.
6. Kallmann FJ: *The Genetics of Schizophrenia.* New York, Augustin, 1938.

Chapter 3
Environmental Factors in Schizophrenia: New Adoption Study Evidence

Dennis K. Kinney, Ph.D.
Bjørn Jacobsen, M.D.

Adoption studies have proven to be of great value in investigation of genetic factors in schizophrenia, as the previous chapter demonstrates. Adoption study data also have great potential for shedding light on the role of environmental factors in schizophrenia.

There is an abundance of empirical and theoretical reports that suggest a link between schizophrenia and various environmental factors, but as yet these reports have not provided definitive evidence of a causal relationship. Goldstein and Rodnick (1), for example, in a recent and scholarly review of research on the family environment and schizophrenia, conclude that current evidence—although promising and indicating the value of further investigation—"does not yet permit a clear-cut statement on the role of family factors in the development of schizophrenia." A similar conclusion appears to hold for evidence on other possible environmental factors in schizophrenia: we have some promising leads, but as yet no definitive proof.

In large part, the difficulty lies in not knowing whether environmental correlates of schizophrenia, particularly those that involve reactions of other people, are the cause or the effect of the schizophrenic's abnormal behavior. When all the subjects are schizophrenic, however, environmental factors *inversely* correlated with the degree of genetic risk are more likely to be causes rather than simply effects of the schizophrenic

Research reported in this paper was supported in part by USPHS Grant No. MH 25515 and by a grant from the Benevolent Foundation of Scottish Rite Freemasonry, Northern Jurisdiction, USA. Permission by Drs. Seymour Kety, David Rosenthal, Fini Schulsinger, and Paul Wender to use their Danish adoption study data is gratefully acknowledged, as is extensive advice and encouragement by Dr. Kety.

process. The reasoning behind our research strategy is that environmental factors contributing to schizophrenia should be more marked, on the average, in the life histories of schizophrenics for whom the hereditary predisposition is low or absent. Because our sample is adoptive, moreover, we are able to distinguish genetic and environmental factors that are confounded in nonadoptive samples. Finally, this method is potentially valuable because it makes inferences about causal factors in schizophrenia from the comparison of different subgroups of schizophrenics. Mednick points out in Chapter 41 that problems in drawing representative samples make differences *within* samples of schizophrenics more likely to be reliable and valid than differences *between* samples of schizophrenics and matched samples of nonschizophrenics.

METHODS AND RESULTS

As the first step in the analysis, the environments of 34 adopted schizophrenics from the Greater Copenhagen sample obtained by Kety et al (2) were reconstructed from their psychiatric case histories, adoption and birth records, and interviews with the adoptive parents and siblings of the schizophrenics. The data collected by Kety et al include psychiatric interviews conducted by Dr. Jacobsen with the biologic and adoptive relatives of the 34 adopted schizophrenics (the "index" probands) and of the 34 nonschizophrenic adoptees (the "control" probands) who had been matched on a number of criteria such as age, sex and socioeconomic status of the rearing family.[1] (Dr. Jacobsen was able to interview more than 90% of the relatives still alive and residing in Scandinavia; additional details concerning the method by which these adopted schizophrenics and their matched controls and relatives were obtained are described elsewhere, including the previous chapter, and will not be repeated here.)

Various aspects of each proband's life history (e.g., season and year of birth, likelihood of cerebral injuries after birth, chaotic family histories, parental personalities, and psychopathology) have been coded while remaining blind as to the subject's likely genetic risk for schizophrenia. (Genetic risk was estimated as high if the schizophrenic proband had a biologic parent, sibling, or half-sibling who was schizophrenic.)[2]

---

[1] In the Danish sample collected by Kety et al on which our study is based, there were 34 schizophrenic and 34 control adoptees who served as probands. Among the schizophrenic as well as the matched control probands, there was one pair of monozygotic twins. Kety et al decided for their genetic analyses (including those presented in this book) to treat each monozygotic twin pair as representing one rather than two probands, so they report *33* probands in their data. This decision makes good sense, since the twins are genetically identical and the focus of Kety et al was on genetic factors. In our own analyses, however, we were interested also in *environmental* factors, on which the monozygotic twins might differ significantly. It therefore seemed more reasonable to consider the twins as constituting two rather than only one proband; hence, in our data we list a total of 34 rather than 33 probands. In our analyses, therefore, each twin is counted separately; each relative of the twins, however, is counted only once.

[2] Ideally, one would like to have a more direct indication of genetic risk, such as a marker gene or biochemical trait. However, until we have such a marker, the presence of schizophrenia among close biologic relatives of adopted schizophrenics may be one of the best substitutes available to us for identifying individuals likely to be carrying a gene or genes for schizophrenia. At the same time, it should be possible to refine the estimates of genetic risk beyond the simple high- or low-risk dichotomy we have used in this study. This might be done, for example, by considering the number of biologic relatives for whom a definite diagnosis is available, the number of these diagnosed as schizophrenic, and their ages and degrees of genetic relatedness to the proband. Drs. Steven Matthysse and Kenneth Kidd are presently developing formulas that would provide quantitative estimates of degree of genetic risk using this kind of information, and we hope to use these in future analyses with these adopted schizophrenics.

Schizophrenics at high and low genetic risk were then compared for the presence or absence of these environmental factors.

Preliminary analyses of the data provide support for three general classes of environmental factors in schizophrenia: postnatal cerebral injury, season of birth (and possibly a related perinatal complication factor), and sociofamilial factors.

Postnatal Brain Damage

In the present sample of index schizophrenics, there were a number of cases where it seemed that the individual might have suffered organic brain injury after birth but prior to the onset of schizophrenic symptoms. These individuals seemed to be likely candidates for forms of schizophrenia that were primarily environmentally induced. If so, these postnatal "organic" schizophrenics should be concentrated among the group at low genetic risk for schizophrenia, and this is indeed what our data seem to indicate. For each index case, we estimated the likelihood of postnatally incurred brain damage on the basis of whether there appeared to be any physical signs of brain abnormalities (e.g., seizures or abnormal EEG recordings). We also looked for an indication of some postnatal cerebral injury (e.g., severe concussion with loss of consciousness, encephalitis, or drug toxicosis) that previous research had indicated as a potential cause of schizophrenia, and that had preceded the onset of schizophrenia in our subjects. Independent ratings of the likelihood of postnatally incurred brain injury by the first author and his research assistant showed good interrater reliability ($r = 0.94$, $p < 0.001$). Ratings of likely postnatal brain injury did tend to be more common in the adopted schizophrenics at *low* genetic risk, as predicted, and are significantly more common ($p = 0.03$, two-tailed test) in those who are at low genetic risk and also were born during the May–December period. (This period appears to have a lower risk for obstetric complications.) These preliminary results are encouraging, and we plan to conduct more detailed investigations in this area with Dr. Paul Wender.

Season of Birth

A second environmental factor we examined was season of birth. Recent studies in Denmark (3) and in England (4) confirm many previous reports of a statistically significant excess of schizophrenics born in the first three to four months of the year. [For reviews of this research, and possible explanatory variables, see Barry and Barry (5) and Dalen (6).] This excess of schizophrenic over normal births in the first few months of the year is relatively small (on the order of 5–15%), but Dalen (6) has shown that the proportion of January-to-April births is significantly greater among schizophrenics hospitalized for less than 3 years, whereas more chronic schizophrenics show a seasonal distribution of births more similar to normal individuals. Dalen suggests that the season-of-birth association may reflect a causal role for some pre- or perinatal complication factor. As Dalen notes, the more marked season-of-birth effect for less chronic schizophrenics suggests that schizophrenia may be etiologically heterogenous, and he points out that the seasonal distribution of certain obstetrical complications closely fits that for schizophrenia.

This suggested to us the hypothesis that schizophrenia caused by a seasonally related perinatal brain damage factor might represent a second set of cases in the index sample that were primarily phenocopies. If this were the case, we would expect to see January–

April births concentrated among schizophrenics at low genetic risk—and especially concentrated among schizophrenics at low "biologic" risk (i.e., those who had neither high genetic risk *nor* any sign of postnatally incurred brain injury). The results presented in Table 3-1 indicate that this is indeed the case. Among the 34 schizophrenic or "index" probands, there is a highly significant (p < 0.02) association between season of birth and genetic or postnatal risk. Thus 7 of 10 schizophrenics at low risk for genetic predisposition or postnatal brain injury were born during the January–April period, whereas this was true for only 5 of 24 schizophrenics at high risk. If we also include those nonproband schizophrenics (i.e., schizophrenics among the biologic or adoptive relatives of index or control probands) for whom we could make a good estimate of genetic risk, the difference is even more significant (p = 0.0002)—see Table 3-1.

It is also interesting to note in Table 3-1 that only 3 of 34 index probands have neither genetic risk, postnatal organic risk, nor January–April birth. Of these three, one was born on December 31 (one day away from the January–April period), while the biologic parents of the second case could not be interviewed because both had committed suicide. (As Kety et al and Tsuang et al note in this book, the death rate, especially for suicide, is higher among schizophrenics than in the normal population.) The data thus suggest the interesting possibility that some kind of organic impairment, be it genetic or environmental in origin, may be present in most cases of schizophrenia. The third case is remarkable in that it is the only schizophrenic proband who had an *adoptive* sibling diagnosed as a definite schizophrenic, and a chronic one at that. (Only one of the remaining 33 schizophrenic probands had an adoptive sibling suspected by Kety et al of being schizophrenic; this sibling was placed in the uncertain borderline category.)

To control for the possibility that the season of birth association might simply reflect a tendency for the biologic parents of schizophrenics to have more of their children during the cold months of the year, we compared the season of birth of high- and low-risk

Table 3-1. Proportion of January–April Births in Schizophrenics at High vs. Low Biological[a] Risk

	Schizophrenic Probands Only	Schizophrenic Probands and Nonprobands[b]
Low risk	7/10 (70.0%)	12/17 (70.6%)
High risk	5/24 (20.8%)	10/53 (18.9%)
p (low vs. high)[c]	0.019	0.0002

[a] "Biologic" risk is considered high if genetic risk and/or risk for postnatally incurred brain injury are present.

[b] Nonprobands include all biologic and adoptive relatives of both schizophrenic and control probands who could be categorized rather clearly as being at high or low biologic risk. Schizophrenics among the biologic relatives of the schizophrenic adoptive probands were considered as being at high risk. Other schizophrenics among the index and control relatives were regarded as low risk if none of their biologic relatives was schizophrenic. If schizophrenics were not biologically related to a schizophrenic proband, but had a nonproband biologic relative, they were excluded because genetic and social environmental factors were confounded, and biologic risk was therefore rather ambiguous.

[c] All tests are chi-square with appropriate correction; p-values two-tailed.

schizophrenics with that of their respective biologic relatives. Table 3-2 shows that low-risk schizophrenics differ on seasonal birth distribution from (a) their biologic relatives in the same way that they differ from (b) high-risk schizophrenics or from (c) all nonschizophrenics in the total sample (i.e., the group consisting of control probands as well as all nonschizophrenic biologic and adoptive relatives of index or control probands). Whether one looks at all biologic relatives or only biologic siblings and half-siblings, the result is the same. The case for a causal role of a season-of-birth factor is thus significantly strengthened.

Because the number of low-biologic-risk proband schizophrenics was rather small, we were interested in whether the tendency for low-risk schizophrenics to be born during the early months of the year might also hold for relatives other than these adopted schizophrenic probands. Therefore, we identified those schizophrenics other than the probands in the total sample who were most likely to be at low genetic risk (i.e., all low-genetic-risk schizophrenics among the biologic and adoptive relatives of either index or control probands). These were all nonproband schizophrenics who had no biologic relative with a diagnosis of schizophrenia. There were 7 of these, 5 of whom were born in January–April; by contrast only 2 of their 11 *non*schizophrenic relatives were born during this period (p < 0.03, Fisher's exact test, see Table 3-2).

Perhaps the most interesting season-of-birth finding is that the proportion of schizophrenics who were at high risk for genetic predisposition or postnatal brain damage and who were born in January–April is relatively low, as compared with all nonschizophrenics in the total study sample. Moreover, January–April births for these

Table 3-2. Proportion of January–April Births in Low-Biologic risk Schizophrenics Compared With Their Nonschizophrenic Biologic Relatives and All Nonschizophrenics in the Study Sample

Group	No. Born Jan.–April	No. Born May–Dec.	Percentage of Group Born Jan.–April
1. Probands (low-bio-risk schizophrenics)	7	3	70.0
2. Biol. sibs and halfsibs (of group 1)	6	15	28.6
3. Biol. parents, sibs and half-sibs (of group 1)	9	20	31.0
4. Nonprobands (low-bio-risk schizophrenics)	5	2	71.4
5. Nonschizophrenic biol relatives (of group 4)	2	13	13.3
6. All nonschizophrenics in study sample	119	207	36.5

Group 1 vs. 2 p = 0.073; Group 1 vs. 3 p = 0.073; Group 1 vs. 6 p = 0.068; Group 4 vs. 5 p = 0.028*; Group 4 vs. 6 p = 0.13.

* Two-tailed test, Fisher's exact. All other tests in table are chi-square, p-values two-tailed.

Note: Low-bio-risk schizophrenic probands are index probands with neither a biologic family history for schizophrenia nor any indication of postnatal brain injury. Low-bio-risk schizophrenic *non*probands are biologic or adoptive relatives of the index or control probands. Like the low-risk probands, they lack a biologic family history for schizophrenia.

Table 3-3. Proportion of January–April Births in Schizophrenics and Nonschizophrenics Among High-biologic-risk Index Probands and Their Biologic Relatives at High Risk

	High-biologic-risk Probands and All Biol. Relatives[a]	High-biologic-risk Probands and Biol. Sibs, Half-sibs
Schizophrenics	10/53 (18.9%)	10/45 (22.2%)
Nonschizophrenics	23/48 (47.9%)	21/40 (52.5%)
p[b]	0.004	0.008

Note: Biologic risk is considered high if genetic risk and/or risk for postnatally incurred brain injury are judged present.

[a] All biologic relatives includes parents, siblings, and half-siblings.

[b] Significance for schizophrenics vs. nonschizophrenics; all tests chi-square, p-values two-tailed.

high-biologic-risk schizophrenics were significantly lower than for their non-schizophrenic biological relatives (see Table 3-3).

This suggested to us that fetuses carrying a gene(s) for schizophrenia might be especially vulnerable to, and therefore more likely to suffer an early death from, an adverse factor associated with January–April births. We therefore checked to see whether schizophrenics at high risk for genetic factors alone would be significantly less likely than their biologic relatives to be born from January to April. Table 3-4 indicates that this is indeed the case; the significant difference (p < 0.02) as compared to nonschizophrenic biologic siblings and half-siblings is especially noteworthy.

Season-of-birth effects seem, in the present sample at least, to be limited to schizophrenics. For example, individuals at high- and low-genetic risk for schizophrenia do not differ from each other in the season of birth if they are diagnosed as normal or as having a psychiatric disorder other than schizophrenia. Nor do nonschizophrenic disorders show atypical birth-season trends in these data. Of particular interest is the fact that, if we do not control for genetic risk, the percentage of all January–April births is almost the same (31.4 vs. 36.5%; p, n.s., see Table 3-2) for all schizophrenics taken as a group as it is for nonschizophrenics.[3] Thus, if we had ignored genetic risk in looking for this environmental factor, we would have found no evidence at all for a season-of-birth effect. However, when we control for genetic risk in the total sample, we get a clear separation of schizophrenics and nonschizophrenics in season of birth. Moreover, if we look only at the index cases (where it was possible to exclude cases of likely postnatal brain damage from the low-risk group), the separation is especially marked:

[3] As we have noted, a slight excess of all schizophrenics born during January–April has been reported for Denmark as well as for its Northern European neighbors. However, it is not surprising that we do not find such an excess for all schizophrenics in our sample. For one thing, the excess of January–April births for all schizophrenics in other samples is usually on the order of 5–10%: an excess this small might fail to appear in our own relatively small sample as a result of sampling variation. Moreover, Videbech et al (3) have found that for Denmark there are yearly as well as the marked seasonal or monthly fluctuations in the ratios of schizophrenic to normal births. Inspection of the data of Videbech et al indicates that the large proportion of our cases were born during years in which the January-April birth excess for all schizophrenics was not particularly pronounced; this is interesting, and suggests that the season-of-birth effects we find when considering high-and low-risk schizophrenics might be even greater if birth year as well as season were taken into account.

Table 3-4. Proportion of January–April Births in Schizophrenics and Nonschizophrenics Among High-*Genetic*-risk Index Probands and Their Biologic Relatives

	High-genetic-risk Probands and Biol. Sibs, Half-sibs			High-genetic-risk Probands and Biol. Parents, Sibs, Half-sibs		
	No. Born Jan.–Apr.	No. Born May–Dec.	% Born Jan.–Apr.	No. Born Jan.–Apr.	No. Born May–Dec.	% Born Jan.–Apr.
Schizophrenics	9	29	23.7	9	37	19.6
Nonschizophrenics	21	19	52.5	23	25	47.9
Total	30	48	38.5	32	62	34.0
p[b]		0.017			0.007	

[a] Genetic risk is considered high if an individual is either (a) an adopted schizophrenic proband with at least one biologic relative who is schizophrenic or (b) a biologic relative of such a high-risk adopted schizophrenic.

[b] Significance for difference in proportion for schizophrenics vs. nonschizophrenics; all tests chi-square, p-values two-tailed.

21% of January–April births for the high-risk group versus 70% for the low-risk group (see Table 3-1). There would appear to be a more general methodological principle here: it may well be that many environmental factors in schizophrenia will not be evident unless we at the same time take genetic factors into account.

Conversely, our data also illustrate the possibility of clarifying genetic factors by taking environmental factors into account. For if we use the presence of postnatal brain injury risk and/or January–April season of birth to identify probable phenocopies among our 34 schizophrenic probands, we find that only 7 of 21 (33%) of the probable phenocopies are at high genetic risk. By contrast, 10 of the remaining 13 probands (77%) who are unlikely phenocopies are at high genetic risk ($p = 0.036$).

Sociofamilial Factors

So far, we have talked about perinatal and postnatal brain damage factors. However, the method of comparing high- and low-genetic-risk adopted schizophrenics may potentially be of even greater value in studying the causal role of the social environment in schizophrenia. There are at least three alternative hypotheses that can plausibly explain an association between an environmental factor and schizophrenia. The first of these hypothesis is that the environmental correlate in fact causes schizophrenia. However, it is just as plausible, on a priori grounds, that schizophrenia or some premorbid characteristic might have caused the environmental correlate. A third possibility is that both schizophrenia and the environmental correlate were caused by a third variable, and in nonadoptive samples this third variable may well be a genetic factor passed from the parent to the schizophrenic offspring. This is particularly likely if the environmental correlate is some parental behavior involving the schizophrenic child.

For example, suppose the parents of schizophrenics are found to treat their children differently than do the parents of nonschizophrenic controls. With a nonadoptive sample, it is difficult to be sure whether these different (and perhaps pathogenic) parental behaviors have causally contributed to their child's becoming schizophrenic. Instead, the parent's behavior might represent the indirect effects of a gene or genes which, when inherited by the child, have led to schizophrenia. Also, if the parents' behavior were not simply a manifestation of their genetic constitution, it might be more a response to, than a cause of, the child's schizophrenic behavior.

Certain studies, particularly those comparing identical twins who have been reared apart or those who were reared together but are discordant for schizophrenia, are at least potentially able to deal with the confounding of genotype and environment because they constitute natural experiments in which genetic factors are controlled while environmental factors are allowed to vary. However, even in discordant twin studies, it may be difficult to exclude the possibility that abnormal parental behavior may have been induced by the sick twin's schizophrenic or preschizophrenic behavior. Even prospective studies of children at high risk for schizophrenia cannot completely exclude this possibility. Even if it is found that some form of abnormal parental behavior (hypothesized to be schizophrenogenic) is found to *precede* the onset of schizophrenic symptoms, it is still possible that premorbid characteristics of the child may lead to both the parental behavior and the child's later schizophrenia or that the parental deviance is a reflection of genetic factors shared with their schizophrenic offspring. The advantage of comparing adoptive schizophrenics at high and low genetic risk is that this can separate genotype and postnatal environment and also help to exclude the induction hypothesis. That is, because all subjects being compared are schizophrenics, it is harder to argue that postnatal environmental differences between the groups differing in genetic risk are simply effects of the schizophrenia of the adoptive subjects.

Preliminary analyses of the present data provide some tentative support for possible parental personality factors influencing the postnatal environments of schizophrenics. For example, if we examine the psychiatric interview data on the adoptive parents of our schizophrenic probands, we find that, of those characteristics for which there is sufficient data to make valid comparisons, there are five that most clearly distinguish the adoptive parents of high- and low-genetic-risk index schizophrenics (p < 0.05, Fisher's exact test). On all five characteristics, the adoptive parents of the *low*-risk schizophrenic probands appear to rate less favorably. Four of these traits might reasonably be construed to represent features of a schizoid personality. These traits are: (a) subject's report of being shy and reserved as an adult, (b) subject's report of having been frequently teased as a child (c) interviewer's judgment of subject being restricted or lacking in spontaneity, and (d) subject's report of phobias in adulthood. All traits are more common in the adoptive parents of the *low*-genetic-risk schizophrenic probands. The fifth distinguishing trait is subject's report of academic performance in school, which is lower for the low-risk parents. The data thus suggest that some kind of social learning or family interaction variable may indeed be causally related to schizophrenia.

However, these results on the adoptive parents, although potentially of considerable interest, need to be interpreted with some caution because of possible biases in the data. First, interview data are available for only a minority of the adoptive parents. For most questionnaire items, including the items mentioned as differentiating adoptive parents of the high- versus low-genetic-risk schizophrenic probands, there are data from 25 adoptive parents, 13 parents of the high-risk probands and 12 of the low-risk (for various probands, interview data were present for one, two, or none of the adoptive parents; interview data were present for at least one adoptive parent of 21 index probands). Data are missing for various reasons, the most common being parental deaths. In other cases, adoptive parents refused to be interviewed, had left the country, or had simply disappeared. Although we have no evidence to suggest that such biases may have *differentially* affected the selection of the adoptive parents of high- and low-risk probands, this remains a possibility. Second, most of the adoptive parents are elderly, so their recollections of their own childhood (i.e., of their academic performance or of being teased in school) may span several decades. The mean ages of the adoptive parents of high- and low-risk probands are not significantly different, however, so age factors may not account for those differences found between the two groups of parents.

A third possible methodologic problem is that the personality differences between the low- and high-risk parents may reflect different attitudes in the two groups toward having reared a schizophrenic child; Dr. Jacobsen notes that in a few cases the adoptive parents of schizophrenics spontaneously reported to him that they had been able to discover that their child had a biologic family history of schizophrenia. It is Dr. Jacobsen's definite impression that this knowledge of a likely hereditary predisposition relieved a great deal of the guilt and anxiety these parents felt about having reared a schizophrenic. (It seems reasonable that this might be the case; Wender et al. (7), for example, similarly report that many adoptive parents of schizophrenics in their U.S. sample presented pictures of depression, social withdrawal, anxiety, and guilt as an apparent *reaction* to their child's schizophrenia.)

Adoptive parents who reared a schizophrenic *without* a biologic family history would not be able to relieve their possible guilt in this way. This difference might, therefore, account for some of the apparent personality differences we found between the two groups of adoptive parents. On the other hand, knowing that their adopted children had a biologic family history for schizophrenia might also have created a "self-fulfilling prophecy" in which the adoptive parents expect their child to become schizophrenic because of the biologic "taint." These parental expectancies might conceivably have contributed to their children becoming schizophrenic.

DISCUSSION

Postnatal Brain Damage and Season of Birth

It was our initial hypothesis that, while some forms of schizophrenia might be primarily hereditary, others could be regarded as phenocopies for which no specific genetic predisposition was required. These phenocopies might occur in a certain fraction of brain injuries in which the cerebral damage included circuits critical for the development of schizophrenic symptoms. However, such phenocopy schizophrenias would likely be more atypical, and perhaps less chronic and severe as well, in their course and symptomatology than the hereditary forms. These phenocopies might result from various forms of postnatal brain damage, as suggested by Davison and Bagley's review (8), or by prenatal or perinatal brain damage resulting from obstetric complications, as suggested by the research reviewed by McNeil and Kaij in this book. Our own adoption study data appear to provide support for this view, since signs of postnatal brain injury and January–April season of birth do seem to be more common among the schizophrenics at low genetic risk and among the acute and borderline as opposed to the chronic schizophrenics.

It is interesting to note that our results parallel those of other researchers who have found no excess of schizophrenia among the biologic relatives of individuals who develop schizophrenia following definite postnatal brain injury (see Chapter 5). There are also data that suggest a similar pattern in the affective disorders. Thus Hare, Price, and Slater (4) found a large excess of first-quarter-of-the-year births among English cases with mania, and Dalen (9) found evidence for perinatal complications and adult EEG abnormalities among manic patients lacking a family history of affective disorders. It would be interesting to analyze adoption study data on affective disorders in a manner similar to that done in the present paper for schizophrenia.

The fact that we find an excess of January–April births among low-biologic-risk schizophrenics and a deficit among those at high-biologic-risk is particularly interesting. Assuming we are able to replicate these findings in other samples, they could give us an important clue as to the environmental factors that are critical for the development of primarily hereditary forms of schizophrenia as well as for the phenocopies, and perhaps lead eventually to intervention that could prevent some forms of schizophrenia from occurring in the first place. One hypothesis suggested by these data is that similar perinatal environmental factors can cause brain injury leading to schizophrenia in individuals with or without a specific genetic vulnerability. This hypothesis would also posit that much less severe adverse perinatal factors would produce schizophrenia in a genetically vulnerable individual. Moreover, factors severe enough to produce schizophrenia-predisposing brain injury in a fetus or infant of low-genetic vulnerability would be more likely to cause death of the fetus that is genetically vulnerable.

It is also interesting to note in Table 3-4 that if we look at high-genetic-risk schizophrenic probands and their biologic siblings and half-siblings we can see that 29 of 48, or 60%, of those born in the May–December period are schizophrenic. However, among those born in the January–April period, only 9 of 30, or 30%, are schizophrenic, suggesting the possibility of a substantial pre- and perinatal mortality rate for fetuses and/or infants carrying the major gene.[4] This hypothesis is made more tenable by the fact that the January–April period has a high fetal and infant mortality rate in Scandinavia and that, of the various obstetric complications surveyed by Dalen (6), stillbirths show a season-of-birth-distribution that fits particularly well with that of schizophrenia.

While this hypothesis must be viewed with caution until it can be corroborated by other data, it has interesting implications for genetic as well as environmental theories. For example, attempts to account for deviations of actual family and general population incidence data for schizophrenia from those predicted by simple mendelian models of inheritance often have tended to invoke polygenic models and/or the notion of variable penetrance for the hypothesized gene, with the expression of the gene at the phenotypic level depending on some environmental factor(s). Our data, however, suggest the possibility that the admixture of major-gene schizophrenias with phenocopies, and a substantial early mortality rate among individuals carrying the schizophrenogenic gene, might be just as important in accounting for deviations from the predictions of simple mendelian models.

In any case, it seems quite likely that there is some factor associated with season of birth contributing to the development of schizophrenia. But just what might that factor be? Dalen (6) reports that, along with stillbirths, perinatal asphyxia is an obstetric problem whose seasonal distribution in Sweden has an especially good fit with that of schizophrenia. This fact, together with our data, seems to support the hypothesis of Mednick and Schulsinger and their colleagues (e.g., 10) that many cases of schizophrenia result from an asphyxia-producing obstetric complication acting on a generally vulnerable individual. However, as Dalen notes in his review, there are a number of other plausible agents, ranging from viruses and dietary factors to temperature extremes, that have marked seasonal variation as well as teratogenic precedents. To explore some of these possibilities (e.g., severe winter cold around the time of birth or hot summer temperatures during the first trimester), we plan to examine obstetric data and meteorological records relevant to our sample.

Finally, it is interesting to recall that our data suggested that nearly all schizophrenics in our sample might have some organic brain factor, either involving a hereditary predisposition or some kind of pre- or postnatal brain injury. As Goldstein and Rodnick (1) point out in their review, recent research on family factors has largely neglected the problem of why only certain children in a family develop schizophrenia; our data suggest that a major explanation may lie in the children's organic vulnerability.

---

[4] Note, however, that this suggestion that high-genetic-risk schizophrenics might be more likely to be born in May–December could be reconciled with other studies reporting a deficit of all schizophrenics born in May–December, only if phenocopies constituted a large enough proportion of all cases to produce a slight net excess of all schizophrenics born in January–April. In our data, this appears to be the case, with about one-half the schizophrenics in our total sample of probands and relatives being likely phenocopies, as judged from the absence of a biologic family history of schizophrenia.

Family and Social Environment

Even if it were the case that some type of organic brain dysfunction were involved in all cases of schizophrenia, however, this would not mean that social and environmental factors were unimportant. Fish (11), for example, in reviewing the most recent results of her long-term longitudinal study of infants at high risk for schizophrenia, notes that even in cases where infants clearly appeared to suffer from neurologic damage, the quality of the rearing environment provided by parental figures seems to have played a critical role in determining the clinical outcome of the child. Moreover, data on factors influencing intellectual development suggest that the quality of the family-social environment may be of particular importance for precisely those infants with congenital neurologic impairment. Evidence from several studies (12,13,14) suggests that there is a synergistic interaction between the quality of postnatal parental stimulation and the biologic integrity of the infant's nervous system. Thus the social class of the rearing parents is much more strongly associated with later IQ for children at high risk for neurologic damage—whether the children are at high risk because they are premature (12), exposed to severe delivery complications (13), or in the lowest quartiles of mental and motor development at 8 months (14). As Willerman (15) notes, the implications of such data are not only that poor postnatal environments are likely to be particularly devastating for the brain-damaged infant, but that, conversely, there is often cause for optimism with regard to the intellectual development of neurologically impaired infants, given a stimulating environment.

To us, these data argue strongly for greater consideration, by researchers of social and family environmental factors, of the interaction between these environmental factors an constitutional neurologic vulnerabilities. Consideration of such interactions betwee parental rearing practices and constitutional vulnerabilities becomes particularly critica if, as Fish (11) suggests, these interactions may be rather specific (e.g., if the parenta style that is beneficial for one infant is neutral or even harmful for another). Attemptir to control for such interactions could greatly help researchers of family and social facto in schizophrenia to better distinguish cause from effect, and to design intervention pr grams that are especially effective in meeting individual needs of high-risk children.

We suggest that the research strategy we have employed in the present paper (that comparing schizophrenics at high and low genetic risk) provides a relatively simple a direct method for beginning to identify environmental contributors to schizophrenia a their possible interactions with constitutional factors. Although we have applied t method to retrospective data, it also should be possible to use this research strate either in prospective studies involving large sets of children or in high-risk samp which are collected using risk criteria other than biologic family history schizophrenia. For examples of such alternative risk criteria see Fish (11) and Goldst and Rodnick (1).

Implications for Genetic Research

Finally, the approach and data we have described may be of use to researchers of gen factors in schizophrenia. At present, there is substantial evidence for some kin genetic factor in schizophrenia, but so far it has been difficult to demonstrate cor sively what that genetic factor or set of factors might be. For example, is the fact single gene, a major gene with minor gene modifiers, or a still more complex system? If there is a major gene, what is its mode of action and its penetrance in the homo- and heterozygous states? It may be difficult to establish which genetic model is correct so long as such genetic models are tested against etiologically heterogeneous samples of schizophrenics in which forms that are primarily environmentally induced are mixed together with forms that are primarily hereditary.

If, however, we were able to screen out the primarily environmental cases from our sample of schizophrenics, leaving only the primarily hereditary forms, the chances of our understanding the genetic mechanisms might be greater. The present data illustrate the possibility of this kind of screening. For as we noted earlier, if we use, for example, postnatal organic risk and January–April season of birth as indicators of our schizophrenic probands most likely to be phenocopies, we find that only 33% of these probable phenocopies among our index probands are at high genetic risk. By contrast, over 76% of the remaining index probands, who are unlikely phenocopies, are at high genetic risk. By using additional factors to remove phenocopies it may be possible to select samples of purely hereditary schizophrenia (or at least forms in which the genetic factor is more homogeneous) against which genetic models could be tested more adequately.

In conclusion, this study suggests the value of investigating the conjoint effects of genetic and environmental factors. On the one hand, controlling for genetic risk can help one in identifying environmental factors. Conversely, controlling for environmental factors may help in identifying the nature of genetic factors. Perhaps the moral of the research we have discussed is that we need better collaboration between researchers of genetic and environmental factors in schizophrenia.

REFERENCES

1. Goldstein MJ, Rodnick EH: The family's contribution to the etiology of schizophrenia: current status. *Schizophrenia Bulletin* 14:48, 1975.

2. Kety SS, Rosenthal D, Wender PH, Schulsinger F, Jacobsen B: Mental illness in the biological and adoptive families of adopted individuals who have become schizophrenic: a preliminary report based upon psychiatric interviews, in Fieve R, Brill H, Rosenthal D (eds): *Genetics and Psychopathology.* Baltimore, Johns Hopkins Press, 1975.

3. Videbech T, Weeks A, Dupont A: Endogenous psychoses and season of birth. *Acta Psychiat Scand* 50:202, 1975.

4. Hare EH, Price JS, Slater E: Mental disorder and season of birth: a national sample compared with the general population. *Brit J Psychiat* 124:81, 1974.

5. Barry H II, Barry H Jr: Season of birth in schizophrenics: its relationship to social class. *Arch Gen Psychiat* 11:385–391, 1964.

6. Dalen P: *Season of Birth: A Study of Schizophrenia and Other Mental Disorders.* Amsterdam, North-Holland Publishing Co, 1975.

7. Wender PH, Rosenthal D, Kety SS: A psychiatric assessment of the adoptive parents of schizophrenics, in Rosenthal D, Kety SS (eds): *The Transmission of Schizophrenia,* Proceedings of the Second Research Conference of the Foundations' Fund for Research in Psychiatry, Dorado, Puerto Rico, 1967.

8. Davison K, Bagley CR: Schizophrenia-like psychoses associated with organic disorders of the central nervous system: A review of the literature. *Brit J Psychiat,* Special Publication, No 4 p 113, 1969.

9. Dalen P: Family history, the electroencephalogram and perinatal factors in manic conditions. *Acta Psychiat Scand* 41:527, 1965.

10. Mednick SA, Mura E, Schulsinger F, et al: Prenatal conditions and infant development in children with schizophrenic parents. *Social Biology* 18:S103, 1971.

11. Fish B: Biologic antecedents of psychosis in children, in Freedman DX (ed): *Biology of the Major Psychoses.* New York, Raven Press, 1975, p 49.

12. Drillien C: *The Growth and Development of the Prematurely Born Infant.* Baltimore, Williams & Wilkins, 1964.

13. Werner EE, Bierman JM, French FE: *The Children of Kauai.* Honolulu, University of Hawaii Press, 1971.

14. Willerman L, Broman S, Fiedler M: Infant Development, preschool IQ and social class. *Child Development* 41:69, 1970.

15. Willerman L: Biosocial influences on human development. *Am J Orthopsychiatry* 42:452, 1972.

Chapter 4
Relatives of Schizophrenics, Manics, Depressives, and Controls: An Interview Study of 1331 First-Degree Relatives

Ming T. Tsuang, M.D., Ph.D.
Raymond R. Crowe, M.D.
George Winokur, M.D.
John Clancy, M.D.

In Iowa, we are currently conducting a combined follow-up and family study of cases of schizophrenia, mania, and depression, with a control group of surgical patients. We have approximately 500 index psychiatric cases, and, therefore, the study has been nicknamed "The Iowa 500." My topic here will be restricted to the family study and the rate of schizophrenia among the first-degree relatives because of the special interest for genetics. Before proceeding to the relatives, we would like to describe briefly the index cases who are the subjects of our follow-up study. All the psychiatric cases and controls in our study were admitted to University Hospitals, Iowa City, between 1934 and 1944. The psychiatric cases came from a review of records of 3800 consecutive admissions (1). Therefore, the length of follow-up is as much as 40 years for some patients.

Reliable diagnosis, especially of schizophrenia, remains the single most vexing problem in studies of mental disorders. We have tried to overcome this problem by utilizing

This study was supported by a grant from the United States Public Health Service No. MH 21489. Tom Bray, M.S., Robert Wiese, B.A., and Jerome Fleming, M.S. have participated in the collection and analysis of the data for this study.

a set of specified criteria which were considered appropriate to the purposes of this study because of their emphasis upon typical illness. A disadvantage of these criteria, however, is that their use results in the exclusion of many cases that otherwise undoubtedly would be diagnosed clinically as schizophrenia or affective disorder. But, because the criteria are relatively objective and specific, they minimize disagreement about choice of subjects for the research sample and their fixed nature maximizes ease of replication.

Two hundred schizophrenics were selected according to the criteria in Table 4-1. These criteria are somewhat abbreviated in the table. For example, the key element in the "verbal communication" criterion is that the person's verbal production is unintelligible. If the person were mute, for example, the diagnosis of schizophrenia could not be made because there would be no verbal production. We have stipulated that at least two of the five indented criteria would have to be present to make the diagnosis. "Alcoholism" or "drug abuse" must have been absent for at least one year prior to the onset of the psychosis.

A similar version of these criteria by Feighner et al (2) utilizes "Family History of Schizophrenia" (instead of "Blunted Affect") as one of the five optimal criteria. Since we were selecting a sample for a family study, this criterion was excluded from the selection criteria in order to avoid built-in bias in the schizophrenia group.

The requirement of a "six months' course" includes the stipulation that there was not a return to the premorbid level of psychosocial adjustment. The reference to "affective symptoms" in these criteria points up one of the perennial questions of psychiatry: Are schizophrenia and manic-depression two illnesses or one? (3) Another question is: How can you study or talk about schizophrenia without including mania and depression? One of the purposes of our study is to work on these questions; therefore, we are studying schizophrenia, mania, and depression simultaneously.

Table 4-2 gives criteria used to select 100 manics. "Hyperactivity" includes motor, social, and sexual activity. "Grandiosity" may be delusional. The two weeks' course includes the stipulation that there was no diagnosable preexisting psychiatric condition. There is likewise an exclusion criterion that is not indicated in the table, namely, that the affective symptoms *are not* accompanied by a massive or peculiar alteration of perception and thinking as a major manifestation of the illness. Once again, these criteria demonstrate an awareness of and a concern for "overlap" among the major functional psychoses.

Table 4-1. Research Criteria for Schizophrenia

Delusions/hallucinations in a clear sensorium, or
Lack of logical/understandable verbal communication
At least two of the following:

    Single
    Poor premorbid social/work history
    Absence of alcoholism/Drug abuse 1 year prior
    Onset before 40 years of age
    Blunted Affect

Absence of affective symptoms sufficient to qualify for
    a diagnosis of primary affective disorder
Six months' course

Table 4-2. Research Criteria for Mania

Euphoria/irritability
At least two of the following:

Hyperactivity
Push of Speech
Grandiosity
Flight of Ideas
Decreased Sleep
Distractibility

Two weeks' Course

Our 255 depressives were selected with the criteria in Table 4-3. The "weight loss" criterion is considered positive if it was 2 pounds a week or 10 or more pounds in a year when not dieting. The "sleep difficulty" includes both insomnia and hypersomnia. Decreased sex drive is included under "loss of interest in usual activities." The feelings of "self-reproach or guilt" may be delusional. These criteria would not be applied to an individual with life-threatening or incapacitating medical illness preceding and paralleling the depression. Also, as with the criteria for mania, there can be no preexisting diagnosable psychiatric illness or massive or peculiar alteration of perception and thinking.

Our study also includes a control population of hospitalized surgical patients matched on certain demographic variables and free of any psychiatric illness (see Table 4-4). The surgical control group represents a stratified, random sample of cases of appendectomy and herniorrhaphy from the University's Department of Surgery. Controls were drawn from the same admission time period as the psychiatric cases and had to be psychiatric symptom-free on chart review. A randomly selected case was discarded if the age at admission was less than 14 or greater than 61 (the range of ages for the psychiatric cases). There are 80 controls hospitalized for herniorrhaphy or appendectomy. We have, then, 685 surgical and psychiatric index cases who have been selected according to specified criteria.

Our interest then shifted to what kinds and rates of psychiatric disorder we might expect among the first-degree relatives. We are in the third year of this study. It took us

Table 4-3. Research Criteria for Depression

Dysphoric Mood (depressed, sad, blue)
At least four of the following:

Anorexia/weight loss
Sleep difficulty
Loss of energy
Agitation/retardation
Loss of interest in usual activities
Self-reproach/guilt
Diminished ability to think/concentrate
Recurrent thoughts of death/suicide

One months' course

Table 4-4. Method and Criteria for Selecting
the Control

---

80 appendectomy and 80 herniorrhaphy patients
Stratified random sample
Same admission time period: 1934–44
Same age range: 14–61 years old
Psychiatric symptom-free by history
Proportional matching for:
    Sex
    Socioeconomic status

---

one year to develop the interviewing instrument (4), and we have been in the field gathering data now for two years. As can be seen from Table 4-5, the 648 cases traced represent 95% of the index population. We have been able to interview personally 69% of the index cases who are still living. Preliminary analysis of outcome of these cases shows them to be well separated along diagnostic lines (5).

In our search for first-degree relatives, we have had access to extremely detailed family records from the hospital charts. Using information in the medical record, and current data from other family members, we have so far identified a total of 5315 first-degree relatives (see Table 4-6). For some relatives, we had only a name or such references as "three younger sibs." Despite such problems, we have traced to current address or death 4822 (91%) of the relatives. Although we have concentrated our family-study efforts on living relatives, personally interviewing 133 (59%) of them, we are also studying the deceased by interviewing their surviving relatives and, if available, their records at the state's four Mental Health Institutes.

Our primary data-gathering instrument is a structured interview form. This form is a hybrid of several familiar forms, but much shorter and much more appropriate to this largely nonhospitalized and psychiatrically normal population. The form, was designed to be used by specially trained interviewers and has been tested extensively for reliability. We are quite satisfied that it is adequate to meet the needs of the study.

Table 4-5. Current Follow-up Status of Index Cases

	Sc	*Mn*	*Dp*	*Cn*	*Tl*
N	200	100	225	160	685
Traced	192	91	216	149	648
% of N	*96*	*91*	*96*	*93*	*95*
Deceased	81	55	159	55	350
% of Traced	*42*	*60*	*74*	*37*	*54*
Living	111	36	57	94	298
% of Traced	*58*	*40*	*26*	*63*	*46*
Interviewed	86	23	35	63	207
% of Living	*77*	*64*	*61*	*67*	*69*

Sc: schizophrenia; Mn: Mania; Dp: depression; Cn: control; Tl: Total.

All interviews are conducted blind. The interviewers are given only the interviewee's name and address, with no information regarding diagnosis, family relationship, or whether the interviewee is an index case or a relative. The mean age of those interviewed is well beyond the risk period for schizophrenia.

The information on this interview form is being used in a blind diagnostic assessment of the study population. For a majority of the forms, we obtained a psychiatric assessment independently from two psychiatrists. Disagreements in this pair of diagnoses occasion a third, or even fourth, blind assessment from outside diagnosticians.

The results to date among the relatives for the frequency of schizophrenia and affective disorder, according to DSM-II, can be seen in Table 4-7. The highest rate of schizophrenia is found among the relatives of the schizophrenics; relatives of manics are next highest, then relatives of depressives; and, finally, the lowest rate of schizophrenia is found among the control relatives.

The trend here is in the expected direction in rank order of the rates for the relatives. There is a remarkable difference in the rates between the schizophrenia and the control relatives and between the schizophrenia and the depressive relatives. The difference between the relatives of the schizophrenics and the manics is not quite at a statistically significant level, but shows a trend (p = 0.07).

As far as the diagnosis of schizophrenia is concerned, the relatives of our index cases appear to have been separated out rather clearly. However, with regard to the actual rates of schizophrenia among the various relative groups, these figures appear low in comparison with other studies (6).

Table 4-6. Current Follow-up Status of First-Degree Relatives

	Sc	Mn	Dp	Cn	Tl
N	1211	807	1913	1384	5315
Traced	1091	736	1761	1234	4822
% of N	90	91	92	89	91
Deceased	568	411	1110	478	2567
% of Traced	52	56	63	39	53
Living	523	325	651	756	2255
% of Traced	48	44	37	61	47
Refused	113	60	127	112	412
% of Living	22	18	20	15	18
Located not interviewed	97	74	111	229	511
% of Living	18	23	17	30	23
Interviewed	314	195	408	414	1331
% of Living	60	60	63	55	59
Mean age of interviewed	60.3	56.6	58.0	50.6	56.2
	±13.0	±14.9	±14.9	±16.5	±15.3

Table 4-7. Frequency of Schizophrenia and
Affective Disorder in 1331 First-Degree Relatives

Index Diagnosis	N	Schizophrenia	Affective Disorder
Sc	314	16 (5.1%)	9 (2.9)
Mn	195	4 (2.1%)[a]	19 (9.7%)[c]
Dp	408	5 (1.2%)[b]	42 (10.3%)[c]
Cn	414	1 (0.2%)[c]	20 (4.8%)

p one-tailed (difference from Sc).
[a] p = 0.0689
[b] p < 0.01
[c] p < 0.001

There are several factors to consider when evaluating these results. First, it must be remembered that these are rates for only the living relatives who consented to be interviewed. Although we have not yet begun to analyze the reasons why some relatives refused interviews, it may be that we have interviewed the healthiest portion of the relatives. If this were the case, then these figures represent the minimum rates to be expected among these relatives.

Another plausible explanation has been suggested by our continuing analysis of the mortality experience of the index population. In comparison with the Iowa population, we are finding significant excess mortality among the psychiatric cases, particularly the schizophrenics. No such excess is being found among the controls. Very interestingly, the increased risk of death is most remarkable in the decade following admission. It may be that, among the deceased relatives, those who became psychiatrically ill were more likely to die and, therefore, be unavailable for interview. We do have some evidence that this indeed may be the case: from our review of those living and deceased relatives who have been admitted to psychiatric institutions, the ratio of the record reviewed for the living and the deceased is 1:2. It will be some time, however, before we are able to analyze this information on both the living and dead relatives, but we think it is realistic to expect that these rates will be increased significantly.

Another indication that the relatives of our index cases are being separated out rather effectively can be seen in the rates of affective disorder among this same group of relatives. The relatives of schizophrenics have the lowest rate, significantly lower than the rates among the relatives of manics and depressives.

We are in the process of analyzing the rates of other psychiatric diagnoses among the relatives. In summary, we have several data-gathering projects going on in an attempt to make our information about the families in this project as nearly complete as possible. Our presentation today has been a preliminary report of just one aspect of our family study. Our ultimate goal is to combine data from the current follow-up and family studies with the information obtained at the index admission. On the basis of this information, we hope to be able to revise the research diagnostic criteria and to select homogeneous subgroups of schizophrenics, manics, and depressives for future biological and psychosocial studies.

REFERENCES

1. Morrison J, Clancy J. Crowe RR, et al: The Iowa 500: Diagnostic validity in mania, depression, and schizophrenia. *Arch Gen Psychiat* 27:457–461, 1972.

2. Feighner JP, Robins E, Guze SB, et al: Diagnostic criteria for use in psychiatric research. *Arch Gen Psychiat* 26:57–63, 1972.

3. Tsuang MT: Schizophrenia and affective disorders: One illness or many? in Freedman DX (ed:) *Biology of the Major Psychoses.* New York, Raven Press, 1975, pp 27–47.

4. Tsuang MT, with the assistance of Bray T: *The Iowa Structured Psychiatric Interview—1974.* Iowa City, Department of Psychiatry, 1974.

5. Tsuang MT, Winokur G: The Iowa 500: Field work in a 35-year followup of depression, mania, and schizophrenia. *Can Psychiat Assoc J* 20:359–365.

6. Slater E, Cowie VS: *The Genetics of Mental Disorders.* London, Oxford University Press, 1971.

Chapter 5
Schizophrenia and Genetics: Where Are We? Are You Sure?

Irving I. Gottesman, Ph.D.

The fact that this is the Second Rochester International Conference on Schizophrenia is sufficient proof of the uncertainty that surrounds our knowledge about the etiology of the disorder that saps the lives of the afflicted and their families and our research energies. By the time of the Third Conference, in a decade or so, the contributions from genetic and biologic data and theorizing should bring us considerably closer to solving some of the etiologic issues than we are able to come today. The risk of being wrong that is inherent in such a prediction is one I am quite willing to take; I hope that the Third will be the next-to-last such Conference. This is not to say that no advances have been made since the Spring of 1967 when Rosenthal (1) and Kringlen (2) presented the only two papers directly concerned with genetic evidence at the First Rochester Conference, or the Summer of 1967 when Rosenthal and Kety convened the Dorado Beach meetings on *The Transmission of Schizophrenia* (3). There, other new twin studies were described; Slater (4) reviewed the earlier genetic evidence, and Shields (5) summarized the then current state of knowledge in a brilliant, far-ranging paper. It was at the latter meeting that the first details were revealed of the landmark series of Danish-American studies using adoption strategies, and in the intervening years we have been treated to a wealth of genetically oriented studies summarized in Slater and Cowie (6) and Gottesman and Shields (7,8). The papers in the section on genetic transmission of this volume continue the accumulation of relevant empirical information and elaborate on the themes of earlier research.

Since there is no infallible knowledge about the nature of the global explanatory constructs that bear the burden of our quest for understanding schizophrenia, it is hardly surprising that many different conclusions are drawn from the same empirical facts. The differing conclusions led to the various interchanges documented in the remainder of this volume. All or virtually all the participants in the Conference

I wish to acknowledge my long collaboration with James Shields, .
Institute of Psychiatry, London, from which much of this chapter
results. I also wish to thank The Benevolent Foundation of
Scottish Rite Freemasonry, Northern Jurisdiction, U.S.A. for their
support of my current research.

subscribed to some form of a diathesis-stressor framework (DSF) for explaining the appearance of schizophrenia. With the exception of Kringlen, the contributors to this section on genetic transmission emphasize a large and rather specific genetic "something" interacting with nonspecific, perhaps universal, environmental factors. It is the relative weight one places on the two classes of events that leads to one being clustered in the genetic camp or the environmental camp; we seem to agree that there is no valid dichotomy, but that these labels serve to identify preferred research strategies and data interpretations much like the labels Democrat-Republican or liberal-conservative do in other areas. Scientists may even "vote" in accordance with their intellectual parents-mentors and only change their allegiances after some kind of social-cognitive mobility.

There is no reluctance to calling galactosemia a genetic disease; all babies homozygous for this recessive disorder become affected when exposed to the universal agent in their diets, milk. When the genetic predisposition is relatively rare and the relevant environmental factor is common, it is clear that the disease is inherited. At the other end of this continuum of cause-specificity and weighting come the typical environmental diseases such as plague; everyone adequately exposed to the environmental vector becomes affected. When the genetic predisposition is relatively common and the relevant environmental factor is rare or infrequent, the disorder is called an environmental one. Favism, a hemolytic anemia that follows the eating of fava or broadbeans, provides a textbook example of genotype X (by) environment interaction. Only those persons with the X-linked G6PD variant enzyme deficiency develop favism, and then, only after eating the bean. Both the gene and the bean are necessary (neither by themselves is sufficient) for the disease to appear, and the disease is *both* a genetic and an environmental one. Schizophrenia falls between the two extremes of galactosemia and plague and has aspects analogous to the interaction in favism. It is the relative prevalence of the genetic predisposition to schizophrenia compared with the relative prevalence of alleged environmental causes that leads the genetic camp to prefer calling it a genetic disorder.

It is the consistency of the evidence in the literature (1,6,8) and in this section, together with the failure to confirm successive ad hoc environmentally oriented alternatives to the genetic kinds of arguments, rather than the results of any one or two studies or strategies, that is the strength of the (DSF) broad genetic hypothesis. The fact that the empirical data on the risks to various kinds of relatives of index cases or probands yields a pretty good fit to the predictions of one or more genetic models of transmission is a necessary but not sufficient condition for the credibility of genetic (DSF) hypotheses (cf. 9). For the sake of continuity with Rosenthal's review at the First Conference (1), and as a foundation for considerations about the newer data presented at the Second Conference, Table 5-1 presents a compilation (6,7,10) of the lifetime risks for developing schizophrenia among various kinds of relatives of schizophrenic probands, each to be evaluated against a lifetime risk in the general population of about 1%. Parents, siblings, and children are termed first-degree relatives, 50% gene overlap; half-sibs, uncles, nephews, and grandchildren are second-degree relatives, 25% gene overlap; and, first cousins are third degree relatives, 12.5% gene overlap. Identical twins (MZ), to be mentioned shortly, have 100% gene overlap, fraternal twins (DZ) have, like ordinary sibs, 50% gene overlap, while the offspring of two schizophrenics (dual matings) are awkward to describe in this fashion. (The child regression on the hypothetical midparent genotype for schizophrenia is 1.0, the same as the regression of one MZ twin on his/her co-twin.)

Table 5-1. Risks for Developing Schizophrenia in Relatives of Index Cases

| | | Schizophrenic | | | |
| | | Number | | % | |
Relationship	Total Relatives	(a)	(b)	(a)	(b)
Parents	7675	336	423	4.4	5.5
Sibs (all)	8505	724	865	8.5	10.2
Sibs (neither parent schizophrenic)	7535	621	731	8.2	9.7
Sibs (one parent schizophrenic)	675	93	116	13.8	17.2
Children	1227	151	170	12.3	13.9
Children of mating Schiz. × Schiz.	134	49	62	36.6	46.3
Half-sibs	311	10	11	3.2	3.5
Uncles and aunts	3376	68	123	2.0	3.6
Nephews and nieces	2315	52	61	2.2	2.6
Grandchildren	713	20	25	2.8	3.5
First cousins	2438	71	85	2.9	3.5

(a) Diagnostically certain cases only; (b) also including probable schizophrenics. Both columns of risk figures are age-corrected.

The foundation for thinking about the genetic aspects of schizophrenia would not be complete without an updated version of the results of the "modern" twin studies reported in 1967 by Kringlen (2), in addition to other studies that were unknown at that time. Table 5-2 (8) reports the pairwise and probandwise concordance rates for the studies conducted in Norway by Kringlen, in Denmark by Fischer, in the United Kingdom by Gottesman and Shields, in Finland by Tienari, and in the USA (World War II veterans) by Pollin et al. If you are a betting person, being the identical twin of a schizophrenic is still (cf. 11) the best single predictor of future schizophrenia; unfortunately that future is usually too short to be useful to high-risk methodology. The criterion for co-twin concordance adopted for Table 5-2 approximates the consensus diagnoses of a panel of six clinicians in the Gottesman and Shields study (7) and would correspond to a functional psychosis with schizophreniclike features, one not likely to be an affective psychosis. No age corrections have been applied to the concordance rates.

Kringlen's chapter in this section illustrates the use of another strategic population in psychiatric genetic studies, the offspring of dual mated schizophrenics and other diagnostic "crosses." Although the pooled data (4,12) from the older studies in Table 5-1 show a higher risk, 37% to 46%, than the risks reported in the Norwegian work, some of the individual studies that went into that average are quite close to Kringlen's report for the non-age-corrected findings. The discussion about the Norwegian data brought out the fact that the diagnoses of the offspring were not blind, i.e., the investigator knew the parental diagnoses at the time of interviewing or diagnosing the offspring; a similar procedure had been followed in the earlier studies, thereby leaving such work open to

Table 5-2. Schizophrenic Twin Studies (1963–1973): Concordance Rates for Schizophreniclike Psychoses[a]

	Kringlen	Fischer	Tienari	Gottesman/ Shields	Pollin
MZ pairs					
Pairwise range (investigator)	25–38	24–48	0–36	40–50	14–27
No. of pairs (used for "consensus")	55	21	17	22	95
Probandwise concordance (our "consensus")	45%	56%	35%	58%	43%
DZ pairs					
Pairwise range	4–10	10–19	5–14	9–10	4–5
No. of pairs	90	41	20	33	125
Probandwise concordance	15%	26%	13%	12%	9%

[a] From Gottesman II, Shields J (8).

the criticisms of "contaminated" diagnoses. Note, however, that the so-called contamination can work either to raise or to lower the risks, depending on the investigators' hypotheses.

The chapter by Tsuang et al in this section illustrates the modern application of the earliest strategy used in our field, the study of the risk to first degree relatives of schizophrenics. The diagnoses in the Iowa work were blind. Note that the risk of 5.1% to the interviewed first-degree relatives is not directly comparable to the risks reported in Table 5-1; the data are not age-corrected and, more importantly in this instance, the Iowa data must be compared with the population value of 0.2% they found in their own study when using the same standards applied to the relatives of schizophrenics. The data for first-degree relatives in Table 5-1 are to be compared with a lifetime risk of about 0.85%. The net effect of these considerations is to conclude that the Iowa group has confirmed the older European studies even with the added safeguards of blind diagnoses.

Another point brought out by the analyses of Tsuang et al is the failure of the diagnoses to "breed true to type"; that is, the relatives who become mentally disordered often suffer from conditions others than that of the proband, contrary to what we have been led to believe by the standard textbooks. Tsuang's earlier work (13) made this same point, and it can be illustrated with data from Ødegaard's (14) large-scale study using the Norwegian Psychosis Register. Table 5-3 illustrates some of Ødegaard's findings that focus on the overlap between the schizophrenias and the affective disorders; the data are *not* risk figures but are the proportion of already psychotic relatives who have the diagnoses in the table. The number of psychotic relatives ranged from 39 for atypical affective psychoses to 368 for schizophrenia with slight defect. If the Iowa data were to be examined in the same fashion, they would be quite compatible with the Norwegian data.

Table 5-3. Ødegaard's Diagnostic Distributions Within Families[a]

Proband Diagnosis	Percentage of Psychotic Relatives Diagnosed as		
	Schizophrenia	Reactive Psychosis	Affective Psychosis
Schizophrenia, severe defect	78.0%	7.3%	14.7%
Schizophrenia, slight defect	70.5%	15.7%	13.8%
Schizophrenia, no defect	45.8%	22.9%	31.3%
Atypical affective psychoses	35.9%	28.2%	35.9%
Manic-depressive psychoses	19.1%	10.6%	70.2%

[a] From Ødegaard Ø (14).

The chapter by Kety et al in this section illustrates another of the major strategies in psychiatric genetics, the examination of the biologic and adoptive relatives of adoptees who grew up to be schizophrenics. No other researchers have such data and they make an unique contribution to our knowledge. The chapter by Kinney and Jacobsen is mainly exploratory, but it has the merit of putting some meat on the bones of grouped data as well as illustrating the problems of genotype × environment interaction analyses in a concrete fashion. The complementary strategy of examining the adopted-away offspring of schizophrenics and their controls was used by Heston in the USA (15) and by Rosenthal et al (16,17) in Denmark. Wender et al (18) have further expanded these strategies to include the children of normals crossfostered into adoptive homes where a parental figure became schizophrenic. The latter study also was conducted in Denmark using the national adoption register and should not be confused with a Wender study reported in 1968 for an American sample of adoptive parents of schizophrenics that contribute to the chapter by Singer et al in this volume. Tables 5-4 and 5-5 present a summary of some of the findings in the three variations on the adoption theme so they might be considered at the same time as the data tabled earlier in this chapter that do not incorporate them. The symbols B and D represent definite and doubtful cases of schizophrenia, respectively, including acute, latent, and borderline, but excluding other so-called spectrum diagnoses by the Danish-American team.

Some of the problems and merits of these studies are discussed in (8). To state that adoption studies permit the disentangling of heredity from environment may be too pat and misleading.

Table 5-4. Danish Adoption Studies, 1975

Rosenthal Strategy	No.	B or D (%)
Children of schiz., not adopted (NA)	42	?
Children of schiz., adopted-away index (AI)	69	18.8
Children of normals, adopted-away control (AC)	79	10.1
Children ("purified") of normals, crossfostered to schiz. (CF)	21	4.8

Table 5-5. Danish Adoption Studies, 1975

Kety Strategy	No.	B or D (%)
Biol. parents of schiz. adoptees	66	12.1
Biol. parents of control adoptees	65	6.2
Adopt. parents of schiz. adoptees	63	1.6
Adopt. parents of control adoptees	68	4.4
Half-siblings of schiz. adoptees	104	19.2
Combined adopt., full, and half-siblings of control adoptees	143	6.3

Adoption studies wherein assumed similar genotypes are exposed to differential family rearing test specific environmental and interactional hypotheses. They cannot rule out genetic factors which would need to be studied with the same environmental factors but different genotypes. An adoption study of favism in which offspring of index cases placed in a nonbean community compared to controls reared by their own parents would find a zero incidence of favism in the adoptees. These findings could not rule out the necessity of a specific genotype that would only be discovered by means of family studies in a bean-ridden environment. Many are surprised by our claim (8) that the major accomplishment of the adoption studies was to rule out some environmental factors as either necessary or sufficient for the occurrence of schizophrenia. These factors had been proposed as ad hoc alternatives to the conclusions concerning genetic influences that had been drawn from family and twin studies. We see the role of adoption studies to be that of revealing specific triggering or protective environmental factors for children separated from their usual rearing environments. The positive results of the adoption work failed to refute the previous genetic plus environmental explanations/ conclusions, and thereby strengthened them. Adoption studies, better than any other, sort out family genes from that family's rearing environment. Of course, some adoptive homes will turn out to be poorly adapted to the child, but it is unreasonable to assume that even these as a group are as schizophrenogenic as a schizophrenic parent or as parents who, although not themselves schizophrenic, have managed to produce a child who developed schizophrenia. The trouble is that *schizophrenogenic* cannot be reliably defined. If it could be, we could define new high-risk samples based on a criterion other than being a close relative of a schizophrenic. It would be circular reasoning to say that the rearing of every schizophrenic must have been schizophrenogenic, and his/her genes must have been schizophrenogenic too, so it must have been the interaction of genes and environment. We could never refute by adoption studies the gene × family environment interaction hypothesis, and not even the canons of Popperian philosophy of science can help us here.

The emphasis so far in this chapter on the abnormalities seen in the relatives of schizophrenic probands as indicators of a genetic predisposition to schizophrenia does not at all do justice to the much larger proportion of relatives who are apparently symptom-free (19). Garmezy, Anthony, and Zubin later in this volume make the same point in connection with their emphasis on "invulnerability." It is informative to be able to illustrate such phenomena in the context of a genetic explanation for such invulnerability. Table 5-6 shows what Bleuler (20) found in the offspring of schizophrenics

Table 5-6. Status of Offspring Over Age 20 (N = 143)—Bleuler's Schizophrenics[a]

Mentally sound, noneccentric	73%
Eccentrics, personality deviations	18%
Retarded, epileptic	2%
Schizophrenic	7%
Age-corrected risk for schizophrenia	8.7%

[a] From Bleuler M (20).

whom he knew on an intimate basis compared to the brief contact of most investigators in this field. The 73% rate of mentally sound and noneccentric offspring can be explained most parsimoniously as the *absence* of the genetic predisposition, to be expected with the independent assortment of genes, although the presence of factors of invulnerability cannot be ruled out and, in fact, are expected within the diathesis-stressor framework (7,8,3).

It should be noted that most of the high-risk studies of schizophrenia are not formulated in an explicitly genetic framework, the latter being in the minority; investigators mainly make use of the higher empirical risks to the offspring of schizophrenics compared to the population base rate to conduct a prospective study of psychopathology efficiently. The study by Hanson, Gottesman, and Heston (21) illustrates the use of a genetic orientation to select a pattern of behaviors that individually did not distinguish the high-risk group from their pathologic or normal controls. The three "indicators" shown in Table 5-7 were selected a priori on the basis of earlier research on the offspring of schizophrenics. The results for a second group of normals (N = 27) not matched for SES, maternal age, and parity are omitted from the table. Of the total of 116 children examined when they reached age 7, only five hit on all three indicators; all five were the children of schizophrenics and would be our candidates for the subset of all high-risk children to become affected overtly later in life. To the extent that such a subset could in fact be picked out, the remainder of the group are not high risk and may

Table 5-7. Percentage of 7-year-old Children Positive for Indicators—Hanson, Gottesman, and Heston[a]

	Children of Parents who are		
Indicators	*Schizophrenic (N = 30)*	*Other Psychiatric Patients (N = 30)*	*Normals, Matched (N = 29)*
Poor motor skills	30%	10%	21%
Large within-person test score variance	53%	30%	28%
"Schizoid" behavior at 4 and 7 years	27%	3%	10%
Hits on only two indicators	10%	10%	17%
Hits on three indicators	17%	0%	0%

[a] From Hanson DR, Gottesman II, Heston LL (21).

even be thought of as less vulnerable than average. The idea behind this statement is that we are sampling from a finite set of genes without replacement and have thus "used up" the genetic contributors to later schizophrenia. The match between the hit rate of 17% (5/30) in the 7-year-olds and the risk for schizophrenia in the adult offspring of schizophrenics, 14% in Table 5-1, lends strength to our pessimistic inferences about these children.

Before concluding with a summarizing set of tenets about schizophrenia that must be reconciled with any comprehensive theory about its etiology, some comments are in order about genetic models of transmission to form a bridge to the remaining chapter in this section by Kidd. It might be thought that the two kinds of genetic theories, mono-genic and polygenic, would generate very different research strategies. The first should lead one to search for a specific biochemical abnormality, while the second should necessitate a multivariate, statistical approach. However, monogenic theories for schizophrenia now require many factors in addition to the posited necessary gene, and polygenic theories, far from excluding biochemical genetics, would be consistent with schizophrenia depending mainly on a multifactorially determined quantitative abnor-mality in a single biochemical system. The consequences of the two classes of theories are not as distinct as was supposed before the revolution in molecular biology that incor-porated gene regulation and before the advances in quantitative genetics that incor-porated the concept of individual genes with much larger effects than others in a system (22).

The concept of liability (9,23,24) is essential to understanding the strength and flexi-bility in the diathesis-stressor framework for attempts at understanding the etiology of schizophrenia. With the polygenic kinds of theories about schizophrenia, it can be shown that the proportion of the variance in the combined liability to developing schizophrenia is associated with genetic factors to the extent of about 80% (6,7,8). While environmental factors may contribute only about 20% to the variance of the combined liability to developing schizophrenia in the whole population, they will be critical in determining whether the individual with a high risk for genetic reasons breaks down or not. It is true that various lines of evidence reviewed so far converge to discredit shared family environment as important, but that still leaves as important for the individual those aspects of the environment not shared or those not experienced in the same way by others. Much of the work of social psychiatry (25), such as that of Birley, Brown, and Wing (see the chapter by Wing in this volume), speaks to the role of such presumptive idiosyncratic stressors and objective "life-events" of many kinds in precipitating onsets and relapses in some schizophrenics. Cases at the extreme tail of the distribution of genetic liability may infrequently have such objectively defined life-events prior to developing the disorder—perhaps any environment would be sufficiently stressful for them. However, for the larger number of individuals who are not so extremely predis-posed, these relatively gross events will presumably play a larger role (7,8).

CONCLUDING REMARKS

The following set of tenets, unencumbered by extensive documentation, may serve as a guide to organizing the diverse findings and interpretations offered at this Second Rochester International Conference on Schizophrenia so they might be used in the service of formulating etiologic theories. None of the tenets need be carved in stone, and some are put forward hesitantly since they depend on small sample sizes and so-far unreplicated findings. Consistency should be sought between the suggestions below and the suggestions in the remainder of this volume. The tenets are meant as both inclusion and exclusion criteria when used to test for consistency with other findings, but they are far from exhaustive of the examples that others in the field of psychiatric genetics might have chosen.

1. No environmental causes have been found that will invariably or even with moderate probability produce genuine schizophrenia in persons who are unrelated to a schizophrenic index case.

2. Schizophrenia occurs in both industrialized and undeveloped societies; in the former the lifetime risk (with conservative diagnostic standards) is usually about 1% by age 55.

3. Within large urban communities there is a marked social class gradient in the prevalence of schizophrenia, most of which can be attributed to premorbid downward social drift of predisposed persons (26).

4. The risk of schizophrenia to the relatives of index cases increases markedly with the degree of genetic relatedness (25%, 50%, 100%) even in the absence of shared, specific environments.

5. The identical twin concordance rates for schizophrenia are about three times those of fraternal twins and at least 30 times the general population rate.

6. More than one-half the MZ pairs in recent studies are discordant for schizophrenia despite sharing all their genes in common; MZ and DZ twins as such are not at a higher risk for schizophrenia than singletons.

7. Children of schizophrenics placed early for nonfamilial adoption still develop schizophrenia at rates considerably higher than the population rate, sometimes as high as those children reared by their affected parents.

8. Adoptive relatives of schizophrenic adoptees do not have elevated rates of schizophrenia, but the biologic relatives of the adoptees do have high rates.

9. Children of normal parents (N = 21) crossfostered into homes where a parental figure became schizophrenic do not show an increased rate of schizophrenia.

10. Identical twins reared apart from childhood (roughly 28 pairs) are concordant for schizophrenia to about the same extent as those reared together (7).

11. Gender/sex is not relevant in schizophrenia except for age at onset: paternal half-siblings of index schizophrenic adoptees are as often schizophrenic as the maternal half-siblings; offspring of male schizophrenics are as often schizophrenic as offspring of female schizophrenics; the sex ratio for schizophrenia is even by the end of the risk period; female twin pairs are not significantly more concordant than males (MZ) and opposite-sex fraternals are as concordant as same-sex fraternals in recent studies.

12. The risk to the relatives of schizophrenics varies with the severity of the proband's illness, the number of other relatives already affected, and, in the case of offspring, with the status of the other parent, e.g., from 1.8% (simple schiz. × normal) (27) to 46% (schiz. × schiz.).

13. The communication problems associated with early total deafness do little to increase the schizophrenia risks in the deaf sibs of deaf schizophrenic probands over the hearing sibs (28).

14. Probands whose schizophrenialike psychoses occur after head injuries have first degree relatives whose risks do not differ from the general population (29,30).

15. Since no corpus delicti has yet been identified that can be equated with a genotype for schizophrenia, the premorbid schizophrenic is currently not identifiable. Hence, ambiguity haunts the attempts to fit specific models of genetic transmission.

Wherever we look with an open mind in psychiatric genetics, we are confronted by uncertainty and challenges to conventional wisdom and traditions. The very useful and flexible concepts embodied in a diathesis-stressor framework that incorporates ontogeny and molecular biology reflects the kinds of uncertainty found in such an established science as physics with its Heisenberg Uncertainty principle. Surely human behavior is more undetermined than the behavior of atomic and subatomic particles. Look at diabetes, a disorder of man better understood and more objectively diagnosed than schizophrenia. We see considerable uncertainty about the degree of homogeneity of the condition with its early- and late-onset clinical forms. Expert analyses of the data have led to the conflicting conclusions that juvenile-onset cases are caused by viral infections; or, since they are early and the environment has had little time to exert its effects, they are even more genetic than the maturity-onset cases; or, two different independent genotypes are involved; or, the two clinical forms are merely ends of the same dimension representing variations in severity of one genetic condition; or, two genetic forms are involved, each with its own heritability, but with considerable genetic overlap between them (31). It is easy to see parallels between diabetes and schizophrenia and to see why *our* problem should be approached with "modest doubt."

REFERENCES

1. Rosenthal D: An historical and methodological review of genetic studies of schizophrenia, in Romano J (ed): *The Origins of Schizophrenia,* Proceedings of the First Rochester International Conference on Schizophrenia. Rochester, NY, 1967.

2. Kringlen E: Heredity and social factors in schizophrenic twins. An epidemiological clinical study, in Romano J (ed): *The Origins of Schizophrenia,* Proceedings of the First Rochester International Conference on Schizophrenia, Rochester, NY, 1967.

3. Rosenthal, D, Kety SS (eds): *The Transmission of Schizophrenia.* Oxford, Pergamon, 1968.

4. Slater E: A review of earlier evidence on genetic factors in schizophrenia, in Rosenthal D, Kety SS (eds): *The Transmission of Schizophrenia.* Oxford, Pergamon, 1968, p 15.

5. Shields J: Summary of the genetic evidence, in Rosenthal D, Kety. SS (eds): *The Transmission of Schizophrenia.* Oxford, Pergamon, 1968, p 95.

6. Slater E, Cowie V: *The Genetics of Mental Disorders.* London, Oxford Univ. Press, 1971.

7. Gottesman II, Shields J: *Schizophrenia and Genetics, A Twin Study Vantage Point.* New York, Academic Press, 1972.

8. Gottesman II, Shields J: A critical review of recent adoption, twin, and family studies of schizophrenia: behavioral genetics perspectives. *Schiz Bull* 2: 360, 1976.

9. Curnow RN, Smith C: Multifactorial models for familial diseases in man. *J Roy Stat Soc A* 138: 131, 1975.

10. Zerbin-Rüdin E: Endogene Psychosen, in Becker PE (ed): *Humangenetik,* vol V/2. Stuttgart, Thieme, 1967, p 446.

11. Meehl PE: Schizotaxia, schizotypy, schizophrenia. *Amer Psychol* 17:827, 1962.

12. Erlenmeyer-Kimling L: Studies on the offspring of two schizophrenic parents, in Rosenthal D, Kety SS (eds): *The Transmission of Schizophrenia*. Oxford, Pergamon, 1968, p. 65.

13. Tsuang MT: A study of pairs of sibs both hospitalized for mental disorder. *Brit J Psychiat* 113:283, 1967.

14. Ødegaard Ø: The multifactorial theory of inheritance in predisposition to schizophrenia, in Kaplan A (ed): *Genetic Factors in Schizophrenia,* Springfield, Ill, CC Thomas, 1972, p 256.

15. Heston LL: Psychiatric disorders in foster home reared children of schizophrenic mothers. *Brit J Psychiat* 112:819, 1966.

16. Rosenthal D, et al: Schizophrenics' offspring reared in adoptive homes, in Rosenthal D, Kety SS (eds): *The Transmission of Schizophrenia*. Oxford, Pergamon, 1968, p. 377.

17. Rosenthal D, Wender PH, Kety SS, et al: Parent-child relationships and psychopathological disorder in the child. *Arch Gen Psychiat* 32:466, 1975.

18. Wender PH, Rosenthal D, Kety SS, et al: Crossfostering: a research strategy for clarifying the role of genetic and experiential factors in the etiology of schizophrenia. *Arch Gen Psychiat* 30:121, 1974.

19. Shields J, Heston LL, Gottesman II: Schizophrenia and the schizoid: the problem for genetic analysis, in Fieve RR, Rosenthal D, Brill H (eds): *Genetic Research in Psychiatry*. Baltimore, Johns Hopkins Press, 1975, p 167.

20. Bleuler M: *Die schizophrenen Geistesstörungen im Lichte langjähriger Kranken- und Familienges-chichten*. Stuttgart, Thieme, 1972.

21. Hanson DR, Gottesman II, Heston LL: Some possible childhood indicators of adult schizophrenia inferred from the children of schizophrenics. *Brit J Psychiat* 129: 142, 1976.

22. Shields J, Gottesman II: Genetic studies of schizophrenia as signposts to biochemistry, in Iversen LL and Rose SPR: *Biochemistry and Mental Illness,* London, Biochemical Society, 1973, p 165.

23. Falconer DS: The inheritance of liability to certain diseases estimated from the incidence among relatives. *Ann Hum Genet* 29:51, 1965.

24. Reich T, James JW, Morris CA: The use of multiple thresholds in determining the mode of transmission of semi-continuous traits. *Ann Hum Genet* 36:163, 1972.

25. Brown GW, Birley JLT, Wing JK: Influence of family life on the course of schizophrenic disorders: a replication. *Brit J Psychiat* 121:241, 1972.

26. Kohn M: Social class and schizophrenia: a critical review and a reformulation. *Schiz Bull* 7:60, 1973.

27. Kallmann FJ: *The Genetics of Schizophrenia*. New York, Augustin, 1938.

28. Altshuler KZ, Sarlin B: Deafness and schizophrenia: interrelation of communication stress, maturation lag and schizophrenic risk, in Kallmann FJ (ed): *Expanding Goals of Genetics in Psychiatry*. New York, Grune and Stratton, 1962, p 52.

29. Zerbin-Rüdin E: "Schizophrenic" head injured persons and their families. Abst No 356. Report of 3rd Internat Cong Hum Genet, Chicago, 1966 (Complete report communicated personally by the author.)

30. Davison K, Bagley CR: Schizophrenia-like psychoses associated with organic disorders of the central nervous system: a review of the literature, in *Brit J Psychiat* Spec Publ No 4 (*Current Problems in Neuropsychiatry*) 1969, p 113.

31. Smith C: Statistical resolution of genetic heterogeneity in familial disease. *Ann Hum Genet* 39:281, 1976.

Chapter 6
A Genetic Perspective on Schizophrenia

Kenneth K. Kidd, Ph.D.

GENES AND ENVIRONMENT

Genetic studies of schizophrenia can be both challenging and frustrating to a geneticist: challenging because of the fascinating problems raised, but frustrating because there are no readily identifiable genes. Because of the ambiguities in the definition of schizophrenia and the absence of clear familial patterns, no definitive conclusions can be reached about the exact mode of the genetic transmission of schizophrenia (1,2). Nevertheless, there are two points that are quite clear to a geneticist.

The first is that genes must be involved in determining who becomes schizophrenic and who does not. The adoption studies of Kety et al (3) and Heston (4) provide the conclusive proof that some biologically transmitted genes increase the risk of an individual becoming schizophrenic. However, the adoption studies are not the only basis for reaching that conclusion. The data on familial clustering of schizophrenia have given impetus to genetic transmission hypotheses. In addition, the tremendous genetic variation among humans makes a genetic contribution to schizophrenia almost certain. We are now able to recognize polymorphic[1] variation at roughly 30% of the enzyme loci in every human population; any individual human is expected to be heterozygous at a minimum of 10% of all loci (5). This tremendous reservoir of genetic variation must influence almost all traits. Thus, it is inconceivable that genes could not to some degree be involved in determining who becomes schizophrenic and who does not.

The second point is that environmental factors must be involved in determining who develops schizophrenia. The monozygotic twin concordances are less than 100%; this is conclusive proof that identical genotypes do not always lead to identical phenotypes. Some aspect of development, the process that intervenes between the genes and the phenotype of the adult organism, is moderated by environment, i.e., by nongenetic factors. Variation in those factors is thus involved in determining who becomes schizophrenic and who does not. However, twin data are not the only basis for believing nongenetic factors are important. While the familial clustering suggests genetic contribu-

---

[1] Polymorphic: Two or more alleles at one locus, occurring with appreciable frequencies.

tions to schizophrenia, the absence of clear Mendelian patterns in those same families is suggestive of environmental factors being present as well. Moreover, just as the genetic variability of man makes a genetic contribution likely, a priori, so the behavioral nature of schizophrenia makes an environmental contribution seem almost certain, a priori.

However, those environmental factors need not be limited to psychosocial factors. The intrauterine environment, the nutritional status of the young child, and the number and severity of childhood diseases are all environmental factors that affect the growth and development of the individual and hence are theoretically relevant environmental factors in schizophrenia. In addition, for certain genetic models involving a major locus, the background genotype acts much as random noise and is confounded with nongenetic effects. For the sake of clarity it should be noted that the environmental factors being considered produce a lifetime liability or susceptibility to the disorder; they are not environmental factors that act to precipitate an episode of illness.

GENETIC MODELS

One must accept that both environmental *and* genetic factors operate in determining who becomes schizophrenic. Genetic analyses of family data must incorporate both factors; such analyses are possible. Many different models incorporating both genetic and environmental variation can be formulated. Most of the models fit the available data because the models have great flexibility and because the data are very general and tend to be complicated by diagnostic uncertainties. Where statistical tests are possible, few models can be excluded on the basis of available data. Thus, we are left with a surplus of models and the problem of finding ways to collect data that will allow testing of models with the possibility of excluding them.

The Multifactorial Model and the Single Major Locus Model

Two of the simplest models that have been applied to data on schizophrenia are the multifactorial (polygenic) threshold model (MF) and the single major locus threshold model (SML). These models are roughly illustrated graphically in Figure 6-1 A and B. Both models incorporate both genetic and environmental variation. Use of these models to study a syndrome like schizophrenia presents more problems than the study of simple genetic traits, but analyses are not impossible. These models and their applications to schizophrenia are discussed in more detail elsewhere (1,2,6). Here, it is sufficient to note that both models give equally valid representations of the available data on schizophrenia; neither model can exactly account for all available data, but both account almost equally for the most frequent and common types of family data.

SOME GENERAL "CONCLUSIONS"

Studying these models has made it clear that there can be no real argument over whether genes or environment are more important. Since both genes and environment must contribute to the development of every individual, it is impossible to say that any trait is due solely to genes or solely to environment. There probably are no purely genetic types or purely environmental types. Which is the more important in either an

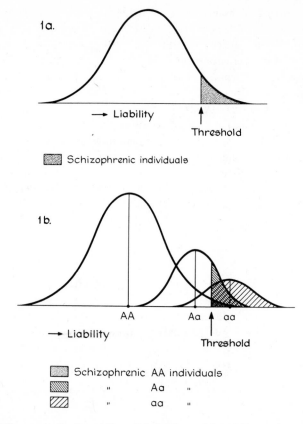

Figure 6-1. A. The generalized multifactorial (MF) model and **B.** single major locus (SML) model. In the MF model the liability is determined by additive genetic and environmental contributions; individuals exceeding the threshold are affected. In the SML model each genotype has a mean liability, but environmental contributions distribute individuals around that mean; individuals of any genotype can exceed the threshold and be affected. These models represent the extremes of a continuum; reality is probably intermediate. Reproduced from Kidd KK, Cavalli-Sforza LL (1).

individual or in the population seems to be a matter of opinion and is not answerable in a scientific sense.

The philosophical nature of the "argument" can be illustrated by considering a single major gene model which fits the available data reasonably well (2). A general incidence of 0.87% for schizophrenia and average incidences of 10.9% for schizophrenia among the offspring and sibs of schizophrenics can be explained by a two allele model with the pathogenic allele at a frequency anywhere between 0.3% and 2.2%. Figure 6-2 is a Venn diagram of the single locus solution using 1.36% as a representative allele frequency. Half of the homozygotes (small circle) for the pathogenic allele have schizophrenia; 25% of the heterozygotes (large circle) develop schizophrenia; and only .15% of the genetically less predisposing homozygotes (everything except those two circles) develop schizophrenia. Under these conditions the population of schizophrenics is composed of 78% of individuals who carry the gene, nearly all of whom are heterozygotes (crosshatched area) and 22% of individuals who do not carry the gene (lined part of middle circle). Thus, most schizophrenics have the gene, but (recalling that the penetrance for the heterozygotes is only 25%) most individuals with the gene do not become schizophrenic (lined area of large circle). There is no precise correspondence between genes and the disease phenotype because environment mediates the development of the individual from the blueprint in his genes. Depending on one's point of view, one can note the high frequency of schizophrenics having the pathogenic allele or one can note the high frequency of individuals with the pathogenic allele who do not become schizophrenic.

Another conclusion from the genetic analyses is that genetic heterogeneity almost certainly exists. Whatever the genetic model, some individuals with the disorder have a different genetic constitution than others. We have just discussed an example with a single locus model; a similar example could be cited for a multifactorial or polygenic model.

Genetic analyses cannot yet identify the precise nature of the genes involved in the transmission of schizophrenia because several different models give equally acceptable explanations. The fault lies in two areas: first, genetic analyses incorporating environmental effects are not sophisticated relative to other types of genetic analyses; and second, the common types of family data collected lack information that would enable one to discriminate among hypotheses. As more data become available, and as our methods of genetic analysis become more powerful, a much more definitive statement should become possible. However, these analyses are not useless at the current state. They do make useful quantitative predictions of heterogeneity in schizophrenia.

As Dr. Matthysse and I have recently suggested (2), these models may allow for ready interpretation of a significant correlation of a biochemical defect with schizophrenia. This is important since, as Figure 6-2 illustrates, any biochemical defect may occur in only a small fraction of all schizophrenics, especially if the detectable defect is limited to the homozygotes. That small fraction is still greatly increased over the fraction in controls. Such results from studying genetic models may also provide a useful framework

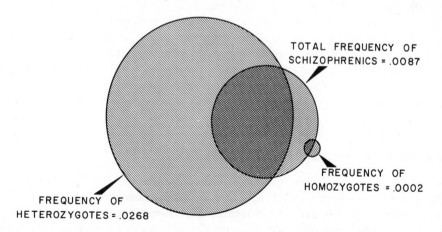

Figure 6-2. A Venn diagram of a specific numeric example of the possible SML solutions for schizophrenia. The three circles and their overlaps are drawn to scale and represent a small part of a total area that sums to 1; everything outside the circles represents unaffected genetically normal individuals. Based on data from Matthysse SW, Kidd KK (2).

for interpreting the existence of outlying individuals for an enzyme activity or biochemical substance. The models already have suggested a strategy for selecting individuals who have the highest probability of having a significant genetic loading, be it a high frequency of homozygosity on a single locus model or a particularly high genetic liability on the polygene model.

FAMILY AND POPULATION STUDIES

The most important broad area for study in schizophrenia is the interaction of genes and environment. Biochemical studies of the cells of affected patients will not elucidate the interaction of genes and environments. Family studies, studies of unaffected relatives as well as affected relatives, are necessary to elucidate the interactions that undoubtedly exist. The adoption studies being done by Kety et al (7) indicate that schizophrenia, per se, in the family is not an environmentally relevant factor for development of schizophrenia. While adoption studies do not completely clarify how genes and environment interact, Kinney and Jacobsen (8) are using that strategy to make an important advance. They appear to have identified some factors present in the life histories of schizophrenics whose biological families did not manifest the disorder. These cases may represent a subtype that is genetically unrelated to chronic schizophrenia. Those environmental factors may be primarily the ones associated with the lined part of the "schizophrenia" circle in Figure 6-2; they may not be relevant to the crosshatched part of that circle. It is possible that different environmental factors may be relevant to the different genotypic fractions.

Kringlen's study (9) and the "Iowa 500" study of Tsuang, Crowe, Winokur, and Clancy (10) are important complementary studies. A large body of family data, such as will result from the Iowa study, is necessary for any statistical analysis. Unfortunately, as already mentioned, the ordinary types of family data do not provide much power for discriminating among models. The incidence of affected offspring from two affected parents does provide some discriminating information. Simulation studies (1,11) indicate that, at least theoretically, the data will be very helpful. It is interesting to note that, according to the single major locus model, the incidence of affected offspring from two affected parents is identical, in the absence of a dominance variance, to the proband-wise concordance in monozygotic twins (2). Kringlen's estimate (9) of 25% to 35% is approximately in the range for monozygotic twin concordances (12).

GENETIC COUNSELING FOR SCHIZOPHRENIA

As a final comment I wish to urge clinicians to consider genetic counseling for schizophrenics and their families; it is now an appropriate procedure and should be utilized. It may not be necessary to mention this point to geneticists; indeed, genetic counseling for schizophrenia is already being done. However, I think psychiatrists have not sufficiently considered the familial concentration, and the need for genetic counseling, particularly for relatives of schizophrenics.

Genetic counseling is a multifaceted process of conveying information to individuals, helping them understand it, and helping them cope with the problem. Families need to be warned that schizophrenia might develop in other adult relatives and in children as they grow up. With early diagnosis and treatment much suffering may be avoided. At the same time families need to be reassured that the risk is relatively low (about 10% for children and siblings of a single schizophrenic) and that most relatives, including children, will not become schizophrenic. With the increasing emphasis on the rights of the patient to know and to be told all the relevant facts, it seems possible that in the near future a failure to mention the genetic or the familial concentration of schizophrenia, or the failure to refer the family of a schizophrenic for genetic counseling could be considered a serious failure on the part of the physician.

Although counseling cannot be based on a completely understood genetic and environmental model, excellent empirical data are available or are rapidly accumulating on the frequency with which schizophrenia of the various types occurs among the relatives of a schizophrenic proband. These data now provide sufficient information for genetic counseling. With the increase in family studies using defined criteria to investigate defined populations and with the rapidly increasing sophistication of our methods of genetic analysis and interpretation, much more precise and much better understood risk values should be available for specific family situations in the near future.

REFERENCES

1. Kidd KK, Cavalli-Sforza LL: An analysis of the genetics of schizophrenia. *Social Biology* 20:254, 1973.
2. Matthysse SW, Kidd KK: Estimating the genetic contribution to schizophrenia. *Am J Psychiatry* 133:185, 1976.
3. Kety SS, Rosenthal D, Wender PH, et al: Mental illness in the biological and adoptive families of adopted individuals who have become schizophrenic: a preliminary report based on psychiatric interviews, in Fieve RR, Rosenthal D, Brill H (eds): *Genetic Research in Psychiatry*. Baltimore, Johns Hopkins University Press, 1975, 147–165.
4. Heston LL: Psychiatric disorders in foster home reared children of schizophrenic mothers. *Brit J Psychiat* 112:819, 1966.
5. Harris H: *The Principles of Human Biochemical Genetics,* Oxford, North-Holland, 1975.
6. Elston RC, Campbell, MA: Schizophrenia: Evidence for the major gene hypothesis. *Behav Genet* 1:3, 1970.
7. Kety SS, Rosenthal D, Wender, PH, Schulsinger F, Jacobsen B: The biologic and adoptive families of adopted individuals who became schizophrenic: Prevalence of mental illness and other characteristics; in Wynne LC, Cromwell RL, Matthysse S (eds): *The Nature of Schizophrenia*. New York, John Wiley & Sons, 1978.
8. Kinney DK, Jacobsen B: Environmental factors in schizophrenia: New adoption study evidence, in Wynne LC, Cromwell RL, Matthysse S (eds): *The Nature of Schizophrenia*. New York, John Wiley & Sons, 1978.
9. Kringlen E: Adult offspring of two psychotic parents, with special reference to schizophrenia, in Wynne LC, Cromwell, RL, Matthysse S (eds): *The Nature of Schizophrenia*. New York, John Wiley & Sons, 1978.
10. Tsuang MT, Crowe RR, Winokur G, et al: Relatives of schizophrenics, manics, depressives, and controls: An interview study of 1331 first-degree relatives, in Wynne LC, Cromwell RL, Matthysse S (eds): *The Nature of Schizophrenia*. New York, John Wiley & Sons, 1978.
11. Kidd KK: unpublished.
12. Gottesman II, Shields J: Genetic theorizing and schizophrenia. *Brit J Psychiat* 122:15, 1973.

CONCLUDING COMMENTS
Rue L. Cromwell, Ph.D.

The discussion following the papers on genetic factors in schizophrenia covered topics that progressed from old and familiar questions to current issues to contemplations about the future. Asked in various ways, one old and familiar question was: Are the research data precise enough to justify a conclusion that some factors of schizophrenia are genetically transmitted? Assuming a positive answer, the question of a different role of genetics for the different categories of schizophrenia and schizophrenia-like psychoses was asked. Next, the genetic relation of schizophrenia to affective disorders considered different from schizophrenia was questioned. The relationship of schizophrenia to psychopathy, criminality in particular, and to death rate, suicide in particular, were discussed. Finally, comments concerning future research directions and applications were offered. More than in past conferences these discussions revealed that the interplay of genetic and strictly environmental factors has been accepted.

Does Genetic Transmission of Schizophrenia-related Factors Occur?

This Conference just might be the last one where the questions are seriously asked whether genetically transmitted factors play a role in schizophrenia. The story of schizophrenia genetics has been one of redoing and superseding older studies and data with better methodologies, yet finding evidence to some degree again that genetic factors exist. Still, the question of genetic factors is asked appropriately. Current methodologies have not answered all the questions.

The earlier studies of twins and other family relatives made the separation of genetic and environmental factors difficult. The major step in the last decade has been to apply the adoptee paradigm; where children, removed from their biologic parents at birth and adopted into other homes, were studied. In this paradigm a concordance of schizophrenia between biological parent and child who did not share the same psychosocial environment is compared with the concordance of adoptive parent and child, along with other appropriate comparisons. The greater concordance of schizophrenia between biologic parent and child is indeed evidence in support of some conclusion. The question is, what conclusion?

Norman Watt asked Seymour Kety if the biologic parents were not frequently lower class and the adoptive parents more frequently middle and upper class in socioeconomic status. If so, the results could potentially be explained by the greater incidence of schizophrenia in the lower classes. Kety conceded that class differences existed between the biologic and adoptive fathers but this was not what was tested. The comparison was between the biological relatives of the index (schizophrenic) adoptees and the biological relatives of the control (normal) adoptees. Here no difference in socioeconomic status existed.

What was not pointed out is that socioeconomic status need not be viewed independently of genetic variance. In the same sense that the study of genetics of behavior is justified, one can, if he chooses, study the genetics of a sociologic variable. And, indeed, biologically transmitted factors may contribute to social class similarities across generations within a family. In fact, one could potentially obtain positive concordance data across generations for the preference to own a particular make of automobile—using a co-twin, other co-relative, or adoptee paradigm. This extreme, perhaps absurd, example is useful, since it reminds us that in each of these paradigms we cannot make conclusions about what precisely is transmitted biologically. This is true whether the biologic factor mediates a set of behaviors, such as seen in schizophrenia, or a sociologic variable, such as that measured in socio-economic status.

While the presence of sociologic factors does not negate the possibility of genetic transmission, concern was nevertheless expressed about the defining boundaries of what is getting transmitted. Lidz, like others, was concerned about the concept of "schizophrenia spectrum." Lidz argued that classifications such as latent and uncertain latent schizophrenia broadened the concept beyond what is ordinarily considered schizophrenia. Here lies a crucial choice point in the endeavor to do behavioral genetic research in schizophrenia. Strictly speaking, if a researcher broadens the concept of schizophrenia in objective ways, as Kety's group did, the findings must be generalized to the more broadly defined group, not to what schizophrenia is ordinarily considered to be. If one looks only at data of traditional schizophrenias, Lidz argues, the evidence for biological transmission is not significant. But, there is another side to the argument. If one's intent is to investigate hypotheses concerning genetic transmission of schizophrenia, then the restriction of the investigation to only those who are or have been manifestly and severely ill with the disorder would be a naive one. Genetic determinants are present in a person from conception, and if any of these determinants contribute to schizophrenia they penetrate to phenotypic expression not from birth on but only later in life and even then not always in a full blown form. Thus, it would seem mandatory for the responsible investigator to make every attempt possible to include those in the index group who might be affected with the genetic traits. Granted, in reports one should distinguish those with the fully manifested form and those with lesser forms, as in the reporting of a "schizophrenia spectrum" by Kety and his group. The issue, then, is not whether "schizophrenia spectrum" cases should have been included in the study; the issue is whether the definitional criteria (based upon subtle clinical symptoms) represent the best way to do it. One now wonders whether the attention, information-processing, and psychophysiological "high-risk" indicators, discussed in other chapters, will not eventually provide better measures to identify those with genetic determinants of schizophrenia but in whom the disorder is not fully manifest.

Occasionally in the past the evidence for biological transmission of schizophrenia has been viewed as a discrediting of the possibility that family interaction and psychosocial factors may occur, and vice versa. This view has no logical merit. One credible view, presented elsewhere in this book and not yet substantiated, suggests that genetic determinants of schizophrenia concern only the vulnerability. How, when, and whether it becomes manifested may be determined completely by other factors, including the family and psychosocial ones. In the same sense that this conference *might* be the last one where questions are seriously asked about whether genetic determinants occur in schizophrenia, it *should* be the last one where data related to a genetic contribution is seen as a threat to or negation of data related to familial and other environmental contributions.

The major contribution of the adoptee method is its demonstration that factors other than postbirth ones can play a role in schizophrenia. Except for influences during the short period between birth and adoption, differences among adoptee groups attest to a prebirth or perinatal influence. Of the various influences that can potentially occur, a genetic influence is one.

Mindful of these limits of inference from adoptee paradigm data, the question of concordance among paternal half-siblings becomes important. It is here that the two relatives, having the same father, do not share the same uterine or birth canal environment. Thus, with paternal half-siblings concordant for schizophrenia the possible inference of genetic transmission is greater. Recognizing the importance of these data, a member of the audience asked the question whether half-siblings given up for adoption might come more often from families that are instable for environmental reasons as compared to comparable control half-siblings who are not given up for adoption. Another possibility is a familial tendency for some families to produce high numbers of half-siblings which are given up for adoption. Kety responded by saying that unwed mothers rather than families were usually the source of the adopted children. More important, he indicated that the number of half-siblings of the adoptees in his study remained unknown. While the Folkeregister in Denmark is comprehensive and precise, it does not list the illegitimate children of a father or the children of a mother whom she does not bring back to her home. Consequently, the total sample is now being investigated to find the other children of the biologic mothers or fathers who may have been adopted. Hopefully, as Kety indicated, the question raised here can be answered at a later time.

Other questions were raised regarding the precision of controls in studies that attest to genetic transmission. Gottesman asked Kringlen if the diagnoses of schizophrenic offspring in his study had been made blindly from knowledge of diagnosis of the parent. Kringlen indicated that he had knowledge of the parents' diagnoses when diagnosing the patients but that his two colleagues did not. Considerable effort had been given in each case to interclinician reliability of diagnostic judgment. Kringlen acknowledged that it is theoretically possible for a clinician to lean toward a diagnosis of schizophrenia if he knows that a parent has been diagnosed schizophrenic; however, much really depends on the strictness of criteria for separating the borderline patient from the one to be called schizophrenic. Attention was given to keeping these criteria explicit and constant. As for limitations of the study, Kringlen felt that the greater problem, instead of diagnostic bias and small sample, is that the people were mature in age upon follow-up. Consequently, older records must be relied upon for the diagnosis of their parents. On the positive side, all offspring had actually been identified in this particular study, and most had been personally interviewed. To illustrate the practical trade-off necessary in research control, Kringlen noted how attention to one factor can have a negative effect upon another. Families were approached carefully in order to insure a full size cooperative sample. Using clinicians who were unaware of parent diagnosis could have jeopardized this effort.

As the final comment to the dialogue of Kringlen and Gottesman, Strömgren indicated that knowledge of parents' diagnoses can operate in either direction. Besides the danger of including a case that should not be called schizophrenic, there is also the danger of leaning backwards to exclude a case that justifiably should be included in the schizophrenia group.

Boklage suggested that lateral dominance should be taken into consideration in genetic studies of schizophrenia. While monozygotic twins concordant for schizophrenia have handedness no different from normal monozygotic twins, the monozygotic twins discordant for schizophrenia, he reported, have a higher rate of cases that are not righthanded.

Another question concerning precision of control was directed by Gottesman to Tsuang. Gottesman noted that criteria used in the Iowa 500 study required schizophrenics to be single. This, Gottesman felt, exemplified an approach too restrictive and unusual to yield good conclusions. For example, in the U.K. 54% of female and 33% of male schizophrenics are married. Tsuang commented that single marital status was not a required criterion but only one of the optional criteria for the selection of his schizophrenic sample. He explained that the original purpose of the Iowa 500 study was not to study all cases of clinically diagnosed schizophrenia but to utilize and remain with stable criteria which might be a basis for revising the diagnostic system. He then noted that he felt that excluded cases should be studied also. Consequently, since he came to Iowa, he has identified 315 excluded cases with a clinical diagnosis of schizophrenia. Referring to these as Iowa non-500, he assured that they were under study.

Differences Among the Schizophrenialike Psychoses

Accepting the conclusion that some genetic factors operate in schizophrenia, Carpenter introduced the question of genetic contribution to acute schizophrenics in particular. This question has important implications for the delineation of schizophrenia-type psychoses in the future. Carpenter noted the separation by Kety and his group of the acute, borderline, and chronic patients and wondered about the present state of genetic research among subclassified schizophrenics.

Tsuang was the first to answer. He and his coworkers studied patients with acute onset of schizophrenic symptoms with evidence of precipitating circumstances. The family histories of these patients revealed that 1.3% of the first degree relatives were suffering from schizophrenic disorders but 7.6% of the relatives were diagnosed as affective disorders. This frequency of affective disorder, Tsuang indicated, is similar to the 8.3% found among the relatives of the affective disorders. While conclusive evidence from their study is not yet at hand, Tsuang's impression is that acute schizophrenics may be genetically closer to affective disorder than to chronic schizophrenia.

Strömgren responded next. Some years ago he and Joseph Welner studied families of patients with acute schizophrenialike psychoses who showed recovery. Evidence of schizophrenia in these families was no greater than in the general population; however, there was a greater risk of other types of psychosis, neurosis, and personality deviation.

Strömgren then asked McCabe to respond. McCabe had just completed reviewing a series of eight investigations from various countries where patients had what American psychiatrists would call acute schizophrenia. Various labels were used. Perris, in his monograph on cycloid psychosis, reported 28 different names that have been applied to the disorder. While the nosology is confusing, the genetic data are consistent. The rate of typical (chronic, process) schizophrenia among the first-degree relatives is so low that no genetic relationship between acute and typical chronic schizophrenia can be proposed. On the other hand, the first-degree relatives had an increased risk for similar (acute, atypical) psychoses and, to a lesser extent, manic depressive psychosis. Thus, the question is no longer one of the genetic relationship to chronic schizophrenia; the unresolved question is the relationship of acute schizophrenia to affective disorders and similar atypical psychoses.

McCabe did not go into the research problems engendered by the ambiguous use and different definitions for "acute schizophrenia," as used in American psychiatry. Nor did he point out that the disorder would not be referred to as schizophrenia, but instead as atypical or other psychosis, in certain other parts of the world. For an elaboration on ways in which "acute" and "chronic" are defined in different and confusing ways, the reader is referred to the "Concluding Comments" following the chapters on onset and course of schizophrenia.

Other Relationships to Affective Psychosis

In addition to the major evidence of independence between acute and chronic schizophrenia, other less familiar relationships were proposed and discussed. Tsuang commented on Morrison's paper published in *Archives of General Psychiatry,* January, 1973 on catatonic schizophrenia. Investigating excited versus retarded catatonic patients, he found that 28% of the excited qualified for a diagnosis of affective disorder, mostly bipolar, and 10% of the retarded qualified for the diagnosis of unipolar affective disorder. Dr. Azuela (Michigan) had observed a high prevalence of manic-depressive psychosis and suicide in Mexico, Puerto Rico, and Latin America, but by contrast, a relatively greater prevalence of schizophrenia among Spanish-speaking people in the United States. Tsuang felt that this difference was probably the result of differences in diagnostic criteria between countries rather than an epidemiologic difference.

Death and Suicide

The question of death rate in the genetic data was raised by Sheps (Harlem Hospital). He commented on concentration camp survivors and ex-prisoners of war returning from Japan and Korea, who had extremely high death rates from traffic accidents and other causes. The death rate seemed to be related to the intensity of stress in their war experience. Of 2000 prisoners of war returning from Korea, almost 50% were killed during the first year of their return. Among the remainder, traffic accident rate was 15 times higher than usual. In response, Tsuang reported that mortality in the Iowa data had been divided into four decades following first admission. During the first decade schizophrenics, manics, and depressives had unusually high mortality. After this, the death rate for manics and depressives dropped off to near normal, but the schizophrenic death rate remained high throughout the four decades. The causes of death and treatment received are now being studied in the attempt to explain this result.

The discussion turned to suicide when one conferee reported three outcomes for offspring of schizophrenics: schizophrenia, criminality, and death by suicide. In response, Tsuang noted that in the Iowa 500 sample after 40 years 10% of both the schizophrenics and the manic depressives who died committed suicide. These rates compare to less than 1% for suicide in the control sample.

Psychopathy and Criminality

The question of psychopathy and criminality was introduced by Mednick. In his Copenhagen studies these characteristics have been recorded in the mates of the schizophrenic patients. Using psychophysiological reactivity in the offspring as a dependent variable, he has found schizophrenics mated to psychopaths and criminals to have a reduced amplitude of response as compared to the elevation shown in children of schizophrenics with a different mating. Since the greater amplitude of response has been considered a schizophrenia-related characteristic, these results suggest that matings may produce genetic or genetic-environmental combinations that influence the incidence of schizophrenia in the offspring. Commenting on other relevant evidence, Mednick pointed out that Kallman reported in 1938 that schizophrenic women with a psychopathic mate had children whose schizophrenia rate was no different from those with a normal or other nonpsychopathic mate. On the other hand, in Kringlen's data on children where both parents are psychotic, Mednick opined that the rate of schizophrenia was lower than should be expected.

Gottesman emphasized the theoretical importance of Mednick's question. Is there a way of identifying antischizophrenic genes? Is there a way of identifying the contribution of the other parent? The genetics technique of diallele-cross, being used by Kringlen in Norway and by Fischer and Gottesman in Denmark, attempts to identify particular combinations that lead to reduced or increased risk in offspring. The use of biochemical as well as other variables in this genetic method, according to Gottesman, should not be overlooked.

A significantly higher percentage of pathology occurs in the spouses of schizophrenics, according to Tsuang, than in the spouses of manics and depressives. In the Iowa 500 data these pathologies in the mates included schizophrenia, alcoholism, and antisocial personality. Tsuang emphasized the importance of studying not only spouses but also the first degree relatives of spouses in order to confirm findings by Heston and others.

Kringlen reported that his study failed to confirm certain other findings concerning offspring of schizophrenics. Sociopathy, mental deficiency, and artistically gifted people were not more frequent than normal. Six of the 121 offspring displayed artistic interest, but none were distinguished. Eleven, including one female, were listed in the criminal register, but the crimes were early in life, petty in nature, often associated with alcoholic intoxication. Only six of the eleven had been in prison but mostly for less than four weeks. Two of the eleven later became schizophrenic. Only two had been institutionalized for mental deficiency. Another showed low IQ prior to her schizophrenic disorder. Kringlen felt that the high rate of sociopathy and psychopathy reported in some studies might be related to environmental factors. Crime rates in different countries should be taken into account. Mednick noted that differing results among Heston, Kringlen, himself, and others might result from the percentage of mating of schizophrenics with psychopaths. In his investigation the rate was 40%.

Kety noted that the possibility of selective mating should not be overlooked. One could argue that it would require a certain amount of psychopathy to impregnate an overtly schizophrenic woman, especially an unmarried one. When one removes that bias, many of the results may diminish or disappear. The combined incidence of psychopathy, drug addiction and suicide was significantly greater among biological relatives than controls. However, in the interview study where much more information was available, only suicide remained significant. Psychopathic and schizoid personalities had no greater prevalence among the relatives of schizophrenics than among control subjects. Since one cannot control or avoid natural mating preferences, noted Kety, the relationship of psychopathy to schizophrenia remains unclear.

Implications for the Future

The general question of whether genetic factors play a role in schizophrenia is an uninteresting one. If this proposition were not already true at the time of this

Conference, it should certainly be true in the future. To continue populational studies on the global concept of schizophrenia would probably have two consequences. As before, positive evidence of genetic transmission would be offered. As before, the practical limitations of any given paradigm would leave questions concerning certain confounding variables which could not be controlled. Does genetic transmission contribute to schizophrenia? As in other scientific pursuits, a critical analysis might always produce some measure of doubt.

The far greater question now is *how* the genetic influence occurs. Do different subgroups of schizophrenics have different genetic characteristics, as has been strongly suggested in the comparisons of acute and chronic schizophrenic data? Are these subgroups so genetically unrelated that the common term schizophrenia is inappropriate, or do different and independent genetic and environmental factors lead to a common path of chronic illness with common manifestations, treatment implications, and prognoses? What are the co-morbid features that accompany, facilitate, or inhibit schizophrenia? The questions concerning suicide, death rate, and psychopathy must be only a start.

As mentioned previously, the most currently used paradigms do not reveal *what* is being genetically transmitted. Is it a single or small number of schizophrenia-specific genes? Is it a widespread number, suggesting, as did Harry Stack Sullivan, that schizophrenia-specific genes may be so widely carried in the normal population that intervention on this level is futile?

Is it possible there are no schizophrenia-specific genes at all but instead genes which specifically affect stress vulnerability or some other factor which, under certain conditions in given individuals, precipitates a schizophrenic illness? Are these genes, whether schizophrenia-specific, stress-specific, or otherwise, the same or different from one family strain to another? If different, the collapsing of heterotypic data across families would mask out what we are trying to understand.

Finally, is it possible that the genetic factors now being identified have no specificity at all, even in the polygenic sense? That is, is the genetic contribution to schizophrenia merely an accumulation of diverse constitutional factors, different from one patient to the next, along with environmental factors, which leaves the individuals less able to cope in general? If so, what is being transmitted genetically could more usefully be viewed even within given families as a high versus low accumulation rather than as specific genes or groups of them. Unfortunately, the current popular paradigms cannot answer these questions or rule out these possibilities.

Genetic Linkage[1]

If certain genes are schizophrenia-specific or schizophrenia-predisposing, at least within given family pedigrees, on what chromosome are they? And, so long as we are asking the question, would our genetic data be more exact if we studied specific behavioral deficits present throughout premorbid, morbid, and remitted states rather than the variably expressed clinical syndrome of schizophrenia? Since the method of genetic linkage, which would answer these questions, has been infrequently used in schizophrenia research, further elaboration is appropriate.

In recent years gene mapping in man has become a productive field of research. This genetic method is aimed at pinpointing the location of particular genes on chromosomes.

[1] Based in part on discussions with Lowell R. Weitkamp.

Human somatic cells have 23 pairs of chromosomes. To date at least one genetic locus has been assigned to each chromosome, with a total of more than 150 human loci now assigned. An untold number are yet to be assigned.

For each of the 23 pairs of chromosomes one member of each pair is contributed by the mother and one by the father. However, when the individual forms a reproductive cell (sperm or egg) with 23 single chromosomes, it is not simply a matter of transmitting either the maternal or paternal member of each chromosomal pair. Instead, in the process of meiotic division each member of a pair may exchange segments of material with the other. That is, a number of corresponding segments of the two chromosomes trade places so that the resulting two chromosomes each contain maternal and paternal segments. After this crossover, the two chromosomes move apart and become part of the nuclei of separate reproductive cells, one containing the alternate maternal and paternal genetic material which the other one does not have.

The important outcome of this crossover for gene mapping is that the closer two genes are to each other on the same chromosomal chain the more likely they will be transmitted from generation to generation together. They will more likely be part of the same segment. Contrarily, if two genes are on different chromosomes, or if they are far apart (and go onto different segments) on the same chromosome, the probability that they will be transmitted together during meiosis is at chance (i.e., one-half).

As more and more marker genes become identified, the possibility of mapping still other genetic traits is increased. Along with other biologic and behavioral traits schizophrenia and its associated deficits have become an important focus of study. While linkage research will not indicate what the genetic determinants of schizophrenia are, it can tell us on what chromosome and where on it a genetic determinant exists. It will also contribute to knowledge regarding the singularity or plurality of genetic determinants of schizophrenia. Finally, the method will determine if different chromosomal locations are found in different families.

Turner (New York) gave an illustration of linkage research in which an attempt was made to demonstrate the existence of genetic determinants of schizophrenia on the same chromosome and in proximity to HL-A blood factors. Kidd pointed out the necessity of calculating probability values carefully when a number of genetic marker variables are being examined. All agreed that findings are yet too uncertain to draw any conclusions about the chromosomal location of schizophrenia determinants.

Genetic Counseling

Carpenter made the argument that genetic counseling has seldom been attended to in clinical work with schizophrenic patients. He related a recent experience in which patients were informed in advance about a genetic marker study. The patients revealed deep concerns about the genetic relevance of their illness. They asked appropriate questions. In their many years under the care of psychiatrists and other physicians no one had discussed these issues with them. The approach and methods for handling these concerns in patients is well part of the applied research task and the advancement of clinical training.

Section II

BIOCHEMICAL APPROACHES

INTRODUCTION
Seymour S. Kety, M.D.

Each Chairman has been asked to introduce his session with a discussion of the historical trends in that field in recent years, particularly in the period since the First Rochester Conference of 1967. There is little doubt that remarkable progress has been made in that short span in a number of biologic areas pertaining to schizophrenia. It is difficult to name another area of psychiatric research in which substantive progress in the accumulation of basic knowledge and in socially useful application has been as great. The chapter in the section on genetics and especially the comments of Drs. Gottesman, Kidd, and Strömgren, make it clear that there is no longer any basis for controversy regarding nature or nurture, since it is now obvious that both genetic and environmental variables operate in the transmission of schizophrenia.

If it is true that genetic factors are important in the etiology of schizophrenia, then biochemical factors must be important because the genes can express themselves only through biochemical processes. Although there is still a long way to go in elucidating the biologic pathways that genetic influences follow in their expression, the burgeoning of information in basic neurobiology has provided stimulating suggestions of what these processes may be and a body of knowledge that provides the foundations for further progress.

In the past two decades, a revolution has occurred in neurobiology in the form of the recognition that the synapse is a biochemical switch rather than an electrical junction. There is no doubt that the higher nervous activity which is especially characteristic of man and includes perception, cognition, motivation, mood, and other emotional and mental states, must be mediated through the multitudinous synapses of the brain. The recognition that these are chemical switches provides crucial loci at which metabolic processes, hormones, and drugs may affect these junctions and influence the psychologic processes they mediate. The metabolic processes in the biologic substrates of mental illness would be expected to affect particular synapses, and drugs that ameliorate these disorders should also act there.

It is now clear that all of the antidepressant drugs have important actions on monoaminergic synapses, enhancing, by one mechanism or another, the actions of norepinephrine, serotonin, dopamine, and quite possibly other less well-defined transmitters. Reserpine, the use of which in hypertension was accompanied in some individuals with a clinical depression very similar to the endogenous disorder, depletes synapses of these transmitters. More recently, compelling evidence has been adduced at clinical, electrophysiologic, and molecular levels that all the agents effective in relieving the psychosis of schizophrenia act on dopamine synapses to attenuate their activity.

Although it is fair to say that the mechanisms of action of the drugs effective in the treatment of mental disorder are becoming well defined, the metabolic and biochemical factors involved in schizophrenia and the affective disorders have not been elucidated. There are, however, for the first time, clear indications of where to search, plausible and heuristic hypotheses that can be formulated, powerful new techniques, and a cadre of psychiatrists well trained in the basic biologic sciences, highly motivated to explore these areas. The chapters in this section are written by a number of individuals who have contributed significantly to this remarkable progress.

Chapter 7
Dopamine and Schizophrenia

Solomon H. Snyder, M.D.

Why should anyone search for a specific chemical abnormality in schizophrenia? How do we know that such an abnormality exists at all? For many years these questions seemed quite valid and may have discouraged some investigators from pursuing biochemical problems of schizophrenia. The powerful genetic studies of recent years, especially those of Kety et al (1), have established rather unequivocally that at least a portion of schizophrenics suffer from a disease in which the vulnerability stems from genetic factors. It is almost a dogma of modern molecular biology that a genetic disturbance will be reflected in a biochemical abnormality. Hence, it is realistic to assume that one or more biochemical abnormalities exist in the bodies of schizophrenics, probably in the brain.

Searching for specific biochemical abnormalities by procedures such as fractionating urine or blood and attempting to discern some chemical present or absent uniquely in schizophrenics has not been a promising enterprise. There are literally millions of chemical candidates. Some researchers have sought particular types of chemicals because of what has been fashionable at the moment in brain chemistry or pharmacology. I have always been wary of such fashion-oriented research. The approach which I favor and which has been particularly useful in evaluating the role of dopamine in schizophrenia has been somewhat more systematic. I and other investigators have taken advantage of certain unique effects of drugs in schizophrenic patients, namely, that drugs such as amphetamine and related agents dramatically worsen the symptoms of schizophrenia while neuroleptic drugs alleviate the symptoms. These two groups of agents act selectively on brain dopamine but in opposite directions. Thus, one can titrate symptoms by manipulating brain dopamine. This tells us that dopamine "has something to do with schizophrenia." However, one cannot say whether its role is causal or only incidental. The manipulations of brain dopamine could well be several steps removed from the abnormal locus in the brains of schizophrenics. The only way to state definitively that dopamine plays a specific role in the pathophysiology of the disease is to demonstrate a specific abnormality of dopamine-related biochemistry in brains or body fluids of schizophrenics. This has never been done.

Regardless of the specific role of dopamine in schizophrenia, recent research has greatly clarified the mechanism of action of numerous important psychotropic drugs that act via dopamine. Moreover, such investigations have greatly advanced our understanding of neurotransmission in the brain. In this way, the clinical use of drugs in psychiatry, though initially derived from almost accidental discoveries, has provided the tools and stimulus for some of the most important discoveries in modern neurobiology. The remainder of this chapter will clarify the disposition of brain dopamine and interactions with various drugs.

DOPAMINE

Dopamine is one of the two principal catecholamines in the brain (Figure 7-1). "Catechol" refers to a benzene ring with two adjacent hydroxyl groups. In most areas of the brain, dopamine is merely the precursor of norepinephrine, to which it is transformed by the enzyme dopamine-beta-hydroxylase. However, some parts of the brain lack dopamine-beta-hydroxylase. There, dopamine is the only catecholamine constituent of specific neuronal pathways where it is the presumed neurotransmitter and where it can be visualized by histochemical fluorescent techniques (Figure 7-2).

The best known of these pathways has cell bodies in the substantia nigra of the brainstem with nerve terminals in the corpus striatum, the caudate nucleus, and putamen. This dopamine pathway is destroyed selectively in patients with idiopathic Parkinson's disease. The resultant dopamine depletion may be causally related to the symptoms of the disease. Replacing the missing dopamine by treatment with its amino acid precursor L-DOPA dramatically alleviates parkinsonian symptoms. It is reasonable to assume in Parkinson's disease that a "dopamine hypothesis" of causation has been translated into hard empirical evidence.

A dopamine pathway of importance to endocrinologists has cell bodies in the arcuate nucleus of the hypothalamus and nerve terminals synapsing on the portal vessels in the median eminence which convey releasing factors from the hypothalamus to the pituitary gland. Dopamine in these neurons regulates releasing factor activity and subsequent endocrine effects.

Other dopamine pathways may be more important to the symptoms of schizophrenia. Pathways with cell bodies close to the substantia nigra project to the nucleus accumbens and olfactory tubercle, both of which are components of the limbic system of the brain. The latter system regulates emotional behavior. Recently described dopamine pathways

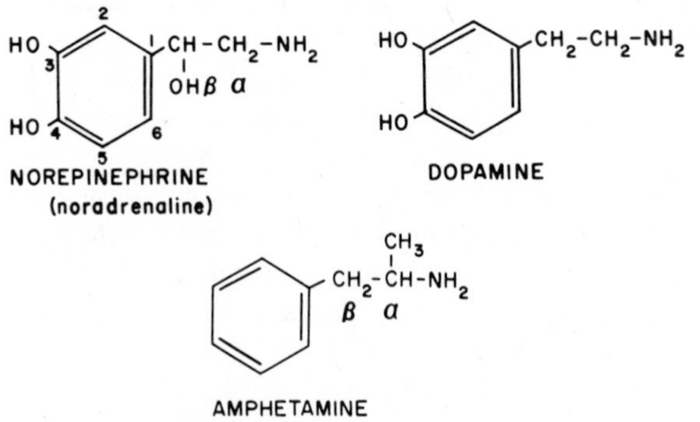

Figure 7-1. Structures of amphetamine, dopamine and norepinephrine.

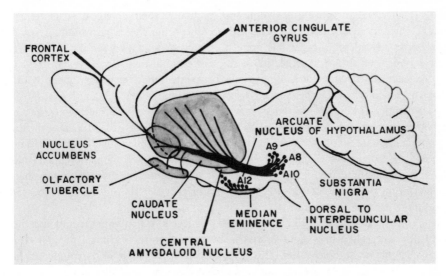

Figure 7-2. Dopamine and norepinephrine neuronal pathways in the brain.

with cell bodies in the same areas project to parts of the frontal, cingulate, and entorhinal cerebral cortex. These are phylogenetically older parts of the cerebral cortex linked in function to the limbic system.

NEUROLEPTIC ACTIONS

For many years, many psychiatrists seemingly have used neuroleptic drugs, such as the phenothiazines, as if they were sedatives, to help patients "behave" so they can be discharged into the community; or, if they are still too disturbed to be discharged, at least these drugs lessen the load on the ward staff. As a result of multihospital, collaborative NIMH and Veteran's Administration studies, it has become apparent that these drugs are doing something more and perhaps something unique. They activate some withdrawn schizophrenics as well as calm hyperactive patients. They do not merely relieve anxiety because benzodiazepines, which are more effective in treating nonschizophrenic, anxious patients than are phenothiazines, are no more effective than placebos in the treatment of schizophrenia. Other sedatives such as barbiturates are also no better than placebos. Moreover, neuroleptic drugs appear to act selectively on the "fundamental" symptoms of schizophrenia. Thus, although these drugs cannot be claimed to "cure" the disease, they do seem to possess an unique antischizophrenic action.

There are two major groups of neuroleptic drugs, the phenothiazines and butyrophenones. Although they are quite different in their chemical structures, these two groups of drugs have very similar pharmacologic properties. The major difference is that the butyrophenones are considerably more potent. Haloperidol (Haldol), the one commercially available butyrophenone in the United States, is about 50 times more potent than the parent phenothiazine, chlorpromazine (Thorazine). Among the phenothiazines there are wide discrepancies in potency, so fluphenazine (Prolixin, Permitil) is about as potent as haloperidol. These variations in potency are not attributable to differences in metabolism or penetration. Phenothiazines exist that are only partially effective or totally ineffective in treating schizophrenia, although their chemical structure is not greatly different from that of agents such as chlorpromazine. The availability of large numbers of neuroleptic agents has greatly assisted in searching for the mechanism of their action: One studies whether biochemical effects parallel clinical potency. That is, the biochemical effect to be sought would be exerted most strongly by the clinically potent agents and least by the ineffective or weak agents.

Neuroleptics are highly reactive chemicals and affect almost all biochemical processes that have been studied. For most of these biochemical effects, the clinically ineffective phenothiazines are similar to the clinically effective ones. When such is the case, one can rule out the particular biochemical effect as being associated with the clinical, therapeutic effects of the drugs. This has been done in a number of cases. The one pharmacologic action that correlates closely with clinical effects is the influence of neuroleptic drugs on dopamine disposition.

In 1962 Arvid Carlsson observed increases in levels of dopamine metabolites in the brain that were elicited by neuroleptics in proportion to their clinical potency (2). He postulated that these biochemical effects resulted from blockade of dopamine receptors. In the succeeding years, a large body of evidence has accumulated to indicate that he was indeed correct.

However, the first direct biochemical evidence is quite recent. In 1972 Paul Greengard and associates developed a means of detecting effects of dopamine related to its synaptic actions in a relatively simple biochemical system (3). They observed that an adenylate cyclase, an enzyme which forms cyclic AMP, responds selectively to dopamine and is localized in areas of the brain rich in dopamine nerve terminals. They reasoned that cyclic AMP, which is a universal second messenger for many hormones and neurotransmitters, might be the second messenger for dopamine neurotransmission. If so, the dopamine-sensitive adenylate cyclase would indirectly reflect dopamine postsynaptic receptor activity. Neuroleptic drugs block the stimulatory action of dopamine on the adenylate cyclase, and there is a rough correlation between the potencies of phenothiazine neuroleptics on the enzyme and their clinical actions. However, the correlation is by no means perfect, and there are some very serious discrepancies. For example, the butyrophenones, the most potent of all neuroleptics, are quite weak in inhibiting the dopamine-sensitive adenylate cyclase. Their relative potencies in this biochemical action do not parallel clinical effects. The discrepancies are sufficiently serious that numerous investigators concluded that butyrophenones, such as haloperidol, might act by some mechanism unrelated to dopamine. Alternatively, it was argued that no neuroleptics act by blocking dopamine receptors.

THE DOPAMINE RECEPTOR

This controversy was resolved when it became possible to identify by direct biochemical techniques the dopamine receptor, operationally defined as the recognition-binding site for dopamine. In our own laboratory (4–6) as well as in that of Phillip Seeman (7), we directly measured the binding of dopamine and haloperidol in radiolabeled forms to the dopamine receptor. In the past, such studies had not been feasible because the vast amount of binding of dopamine or any drugs to nonspecific ionic binding sites on membranes would obscure the small amount of specific binding to the dopamine receptors. By a variety of maneuvers, such as using low concentrations of highly radioactive agents and washing away the nonspecific binding vigorously but rapidly, it was possible to minimize the nonspecific binding and to detect interactions with the receptor. Proof that the binding involves the physiologic dopamine receptor derives from the close parallel between binding affinity and pharmacologic potency as well as the fact that binding sites are distributed throughout the brain in parallel with the distribution of dopamine innervation.

We found that while both dopamine and haloperidol bind to the dopamine receptor, they interact with different aspects of it. Dopamine and related agents, which stimulate the dopamine receptor and are called "agonists," are much more potent in inhibiting ^{3}H-dopamine than ^{3}H-haloperidol binding. By contrast, phenothiazine and butyrophenone neuroleptics, which are dopamine receptor antagonists, are much more potent in competing for ^{3}H-haloperidol than ^{3}H-dopamine binding sites. It appears that ^{3}H-dopamine and ^{3}H-haloperidol label distinct agonist and antagonist states of the dopamine receptor.

Presumably the two states of the dopamine receptor are interconvertible. The observations which provided a basis for inferring the existence of two states or conformations of the dopamine receptor resemble other observations in our laboratory which indicate that many, if not all, neurotransmitter receptors in the brain function in this fashion. Direct evidence for a two-state model has been obtained for receptors associated with the neurotransmitter actions of glycine, serotonin, the alpha-noradrenergic receptor, the beta-noradrenergic, muscarinic cholinergic, and opiate receptors (8). This model explains why certain drugs are agonists but others, as antagonists, block the actions of neurotransmitters. Agonist actions, and, hence, synaptic transmission, can take place only when an agent binds to the agonist state of the receptor. Antagonist drugs sequester antagonist states of the receptor, changing the equilibrium between the two receptor conformations so more unbound agonist receptors must convert into unbound antagonist receptors to maintain an appropriate equilibrium. Therefore, there will be fewer agonist conformations of the receptor available for the oncoming neurotransmitter.

The potencies of neuroleptics in competing for ^{3}H-dopamine binding are similar to their relative actions on the dopamine-sensitive adenylate cyclase and parallel clinical efficacy poorly. Appreciating that there are distinct agonist and antagonist states of the receptor, this finding is not altogether surprising; one would expect clinical potencies of antagonists to be predicted best by affinity for the antagonist state of the receptor. Indeed, we were gratified to observe a strikingly close correlation between clinical potencies of all neuroleptics, including phenothiazines and butyrophenones, with their ability to compete for 3H-haloperidol binding to the antagonist state of the dopamine receptor (Figure 7-3). This is especially impressive since clinical potencies are determined in part by absorption from the gastrointestinal tract, metabolism in the liver, urinary excretion, and differential ability to penetrate the brain. Fortunately, neuroleptics in general do not differ markedly in these parameters, so clinical potency in fact is a reasonably good reflection of affinity for receptor sites.

A similarly close correlation has been obtained between affinity for ^{3}H-haloperidol binding sites and the ability of neuroleptics to block stereotyped behavior induced by apomorphine or amphetamine. This stereotyped behavior in rats involves sniffing, licking, and gnawing in a compulsive, repetitive fashion. These drugs also elicit staring and

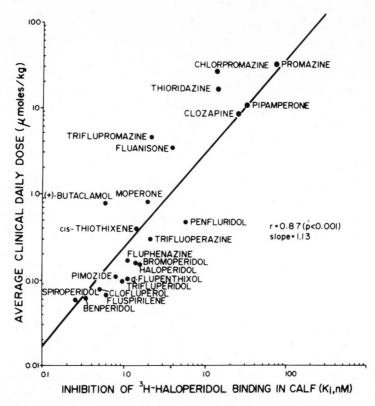

Figure 7-3. Neuroleptic antischizophrenic drugs: correlation between affinities for the binding of ^{3}H-haloperidol to dopamine receptors in corpus striatal membranes of calf brain and clinical potencies. Means of published daily dose ranges were converted to μmoles/kg assuming a human body weight of 70 kg. The correlation coefficient r = 0.87 is significant at the p < 0.001 level. Adapted from Snyder et al (13).

other stereotyped behavior in cats, dogs, and monkeys. Such behavior closely resembles that observed in human amphetamine addicts shortly prior to the onset of amphetamine psychosis. Amphetamine is known to act by directly releasing the catecholamines norepinephrine and dopamine which then act on their receptor sites. Apomorphine directly stimulates dopamine receptors itself. Pharmaceutical houses have known for years that the potencies of neuroleptics in blocking stereotypes behavior induced by apomorphine and amphetamine predicts quite well the antischizophrenic activity of these drugs.

In summary, direct biochemical identification of the dopamine receptor has made it possible to establish quite definitively that neuroleptics exert their clinical actions by a blockade of dopamine receptors. As a test of this concept, one might predict that decreasing available amounts of dopamine by inhibiting its synthesis should facilitate actions of neuroleptics. As predicted, treatment with alpha-methylparatyrosine, which blocks catecholamine synthesis, lowers the required dose of neuroleptics in chronic schizophrenic patients (9).

AMPHETAMINES

Two aspects of amphetamine actions are relevant to an understanding of schizophrenia. First, these drugs exacerbate selectively the symptoms of schizophrenia. John Davis and coworkers observed that small doses of methylphenidate (Ritalin) or amphetamine itself will floridly exacerbate the symptoms of schizophrenic patients (10). These low doses do not affect the symptoms of manic or depressed patients. They do not elicit an unique psychosis superimposed upon the schizophrenic symptoms. Instead, the patient's own symptoms are worsened. Hebephrenics become more hebephrenic, catatonics more catatonic, and so forth.

Amphetamines release norepinephrine as well as dopamine. Do more selective dopamine facilitating agents worsen schizophrenic symptoms? L-DOPA which is converted primarily to dopamine (although small amounts of norepinephrine are formed as well) is one of the most direct available means of increasing brain dopamine. Moderate doses of L-DOPA exacerbate schizophrenic symptoms much like the amphetamines (11). Thus, flooding dopamine receptors with more dopamine selectively worsens the symptoms of schizophrenia.

Amphetamine psychosis is an acute paranoid psychotic process that can be indistinguishable from acute paranoid schizophrenia. Most amphetamine addicts at one time or another experience such a psychosis. Controlled studies of this psychosis, first carried out by John Griffith in former amphetamine addict volunteers, demonstrated that the psychosis could not be due to precipitation of a latent schizophrenia because patients with any schizophrenic or schizoid tendencies were screened out of the study (12). Moreover amphetamine psychosis could not be a sleep deprivation psychosis because in some cases it appeared within 24 hours of the initiation of drug administration.

Some people have asked why one generally observes only paranoid psychotic processes in amphetamine psychoses of nonschizophrenics. If the catecholamine hypothesis of schizophrenia is valid, should not one observe an undifferentiated schizophreniform psychosis? It is asking quite a bit to expect acute administration of a drug to a nonschizophrenic-prone individual to mimic exactly all forms of acute schizophrenia, both nonparanoid and paranoid, as well as chronic schizophrenia. Also, drugs such as amphetamines produce multiple actions. For instance, through its actions on brain norepinephrine, amphetamine is thought to elicit its alerting effect. Perhaps amphetamine mimics schizophrenia through release of dopamine, while its effects on norepinephrine transform the syndrome into a paranoid process. Clinicians have long observed that acute paranoid schizophrenics are highly alert, as would be expected from the central stimulant alerting actions of amphetamine.

CONCLUSIONS

The effects of neuroleptics and amphetamines indicate that one can manipulate schizophrenic symptoms through the dopamine system. Which of the numerous dopamine pathways in the brain is involved? Presumably the nigrostriatal dopamine pathway is uniquely associated with the symptoms of Parkinson's disease and extrapyramidal side effects of neuroleptics. The best candidates for drug effects related to schizophrenia might be other dopamine pathways with terminals in the nucleus accumbens, olfactory tubercle, or cerebral cortex.

If there is a causal association between dopamine and schizophrenia, one should seek definitive evidence in postmortem studies of schizophrenic brain. Unfortunately, the absence of appropriate brain banks with well-preserved schizophrenic brains and matching controls has precluded much research in this area. With the availability of sensitive techniques for measuring biochemical parameters (including levels of neurotransmitters, enzymes involved in their synthesis and degradation, and in associated receptor sites), one should be able in the not too distant future to measure most features of the dopamine system in human postmortem samples.

Again, it bears repeating that although drug effects in schizophrenia involve brain dopamine, this by no means establishes that dopamine abnormalities are causally associated with schizophrenic symptoms. However, even if they are quite unrelated to the pathogenesis of the illness, the studies of brain dopamine have sparked research into numerous neurotransmitters and mechanisms of all information processing in the central nervous system.

REFERENCES

1. Kety SS, Rosenthal D, Wender PH, Schulsinger KF: The types and prevalence of mental illness in the biological and adoptive families of adopted schizophrenics. In Rosenthal D, Kety SS (eds): *The Transmission of Schizophrenia.* New York, Pergamon Press, 1968.

2. Carlsson A, Lindqvist M: Effect of chlorpromazine or haloperidol on the formation of 3-methoxytyramine and normetanephrine in mouse brain. *Acta Pharmacologica et Toxicologica* 20:140, 1963.

3. Greengard P: Possible role for cyclic nucleotides and phosphorylated membrane proteins in postsynaptic actions of neurotransmitters. *Nature* 260:101, 1976.

4. Burt DR, Enna SJ, Creese I, et al: Dopamine receptor binding in the corpus striatum of mammalian brain. *Proc Natl Acad Sci USA* 172:4655, 1975.

5. Creese I, Burt DR, Snyder SH: Dopamine receptor binding: differentiation of agonist and antagonist states with [^{3}H]-dopamine and [^{3}H]haloperidol. *Life Sciences* 17:993, 1975.

6. Creese I, Burt DR, Snyder SH: Dopamine receptor binding predicts clinical and pharmacological potencies of antischizophrenic drugs. *Science* 192:481, 1976.

7. Seeman P, Chau-Wong M, Tedesco J, et al: Brain receptor for antipsychotic drugs and dopamine: direct binding assays. *Proc Natl Acad Sci USA* 72:4376, 1975.

8. Snyder SH, Bennett JP Jr: Neurotransmitter receptors in the brain: biochemical identification. *Ann Rev Physiol* 38:153, 1976.

9. Walinder J, Skott A, Carlsson A, et al: Potentiation by metyrosine of thioridazine effects in chronic schizophrenics. *Arch Gen Psychiat* 33:501, 1976.

10. Janowsky DS, El-yousef MK, Davis JM, et al: Provocation of schizophrenic symptoms by intravenous methylphenidate. *Arch Gen Psychiat* 28:185, 1973.

11. Angrist B, Sathananthan G, Gershon S: Behavioral effects of L-DOPA in schizophrenic patients. *Psychopharmacologia* 31:1, 1973.

12. Griffith JD, Cavanaugh J, Held J, et al: Dextroamphetamine: evaluation of psychomimetic properties in man. *Arch Gen Psychiat* 26:97, 1972.

13. Snyder SH, Creese I, Burt DR: The brain's dopamine receptor: labeling with [^{3}H]dopamine and [^{3}H]haloperidol. *Psychopharmacology Communications* 1:663, 1975.

Chapter 8
Neuroendocrine Studies of Brain Dopamine Blockade in Humans

Edward J. Sachar, M.D.
Peter H. Gruen, M.D.
Norman Altman, M.D.
Gerhard Langer, M.D.
Frieda S. Halpern, M.A.

As several other chapters in this volume have emphasized, blockade of brain dopamine receptors is believed to be the essential property related to the antipsychotic action of neuroleptic drugs (1–3). In the study of this neuropharmacologic action, most of the work has been on the neostriatal dopamine system, either in intact animals or in vitro studies on neural tissue taken from this area (4). Other brain dopamine systems investigated include those of the incerto-hypothalamic, mesocortical, and mesolimbic tracts (5–10). This discussion focuses on yet another dopamine pathway, that of the tubero-infundibular tract, which plays a major role in regulating neuroendocrine function, including prolactin secretion. The fibers of this pathway have their origin in the arcuate nucleus and end in the median eminence, where released dopamine suppresses the secretion of prolactin from the anterior pituitary (possibly through the intermediate action of a prolactin inhibiting factor) (11). Thus, administration of dopamine agonists, such as L-DOPA, promptly suppresses plasma prolactin levels, while administration of dopamine antagonists, such as chlorpromazine, promptly stimulates prolactin secretion. This hormonal "read-out" of dopamine activity in the tuberoinfundibular system provides an unusual opportunity for the clinical psychopharmacologist, since it permits

*This work was supported in part by U.S.P.H.S. Grants MH-25133
and 5 MOL-RR-50; and a grant from Scottish Rite Freemasonry,
Northern Jurisdiction, United States.*
*We are also indebted to the Hormone Distribution Program of the
National Institute of Arthritis, Metabolism, and Digestive Diseases
for providing the human prolactin and antihuman prolactin serum
used in these studies.*

95

studies of brain dopamine activity in the intact human, both normal and schizophrenic. The other established methods for assessing brain dopamine activity are not as readily applicable to human subjects.

The first question we asked was whether there was any evidence for abnormal dopamine function in the tuberoinfundibular prolactin system in schizophrenics. Figure 8-1 shows that both unmedicated normal and schizophrenic subjects had similar baseline levels of plasma prolactin, and they responded similarly to a standard IM dose of 25 mg of chlorpromazine. Both groups also showed virtually identical prolactin suppression after receiving 500 mg of L-DOPA orally (Figure 8-2). Thus far, then, there is no evidence that the hypothesized brain dopamine disturbance in schizophrenia extends to the tuberoinfundibular prolactin system; and if it exists, it is probably a regional disturbance in another brain area.

The next question was whether the human prolactin response to neuroleptics, as an index of brain dopamine blockade, correlated well with the antipsychotic properties of the drugs. This would be another test, in man, of the dopamine blockade hypothesis of the therapeutic action of neuroleptics.

We tested, in humans, drugs in every class of neuroleptics, and we found an excellent correlation, indeed, as good as, or better than any other test of dopamine blockade in animals or in vitro. Thus, chlorpromazine, prochlorperazine, thioridazine, butaperazine, trifluoperazine, fluphenazine, haloperidol, pimozide, thiothixene, loxapine, and molindone all stimulated prolactin, consistent with their antipsychotic action (12). We also tested a phenothiazine as yet unevaluated for its antipsychotic properties, thiethylperazine, marketed as an antiemetic. We found it was a potent prolactin stimulator, and we predicted last year that it would have antipsychotic potency (13, Figure

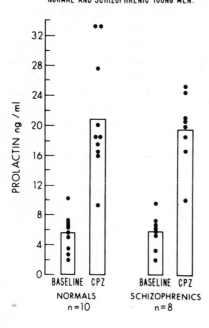

Figure 8-1. Highest plasma prolactin concentrations within two hours after 25 mg chlorpromazine IM in normal and schizophrenic young men.

PROLACTIN RESPONSE TO L−DOPA IN SCHIZOPHRENIC
AND NORMAL SUBJECTS (ALL MALES UNDER 35 y.o.)

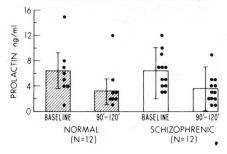

Figure 8-2. Mean plasma prolactin concentrations between 90 and 120 minutes after ingestion of 500 mg L-DOPA in normal and schizophrenic young men.

8-3). In an open trial of 10 patients conducted since then by Rotrosen, Angrist, Gershon, et al, this prediction has been borne out (14).

On the other hand, drugs with weak or absent antischizophrenic action, such as promazine, promethazine, diazepam, lithium, imipramine, desmethylimipramine, and amitriptyline, all failed to stimulate prolactin (12). The only exception to this highly consistent pattern was clozapine, an effective antischizophrenic drug that failed to stimulate prolactin in five subjects, although it has been found to stimulate prolactin in rats (15). On the whole, however, the prolactin test should be an excellent screening method for evaluating potentially antipsychotic drugs and should also be useful in monitoring outpatients for drug compliance. Our pilot studies indicate that criteria can be developed which should be about 90% accurate in determining whether a patient has been taking medication within the last 24 hours, namely, by measuring his plasma prolactin level (12).

Our next question was whether the prolactin response to neuroleptics was all-or-nothing, or whether the response was graded according to the dose and potency of the drug. The potency issue is of particular theoretical importance to the dopamine hypothesis because demonstration that the dopamine-blocking potency of the drug correlated well with its clinical potency has been a critical test of the theory.

First we conducted dose-prolactin response studies of chlorpromazine, haloperidol,

PLASMA PROLACTIN RESPONSE TO 10mg. THIETHYLPERAZINE I.M.

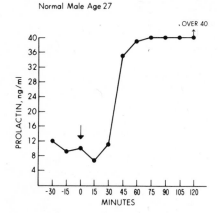

Figure 8-3. Plasma prolactin response to 10 mg thiethylperazine IM in a normal young man.

Table 8-1. Maximal Increases in Plasma Prolactin (ng/ml)
From Baseline After Varying Doses of Intramuscular
Haloperidol in the Same Group of Seven Normal Young Men

	Haloperidol Dose (mg)			
	0.25	0.5	1.0	1.5
◁prolactin	4.4	11.6	16.4	17.6
SD	3.2	3.5	5.2	4.2
	$p < 0.01$	$p < 0.025$	N.S.	

and butaperazine in normal subjects to determine the range of sensitivity of the response. Table 8-1 shows responses of four subjects to varying intramuscular doses of haloperidol. There is a clear and significant dose response curve from 0.25 mg to 0.5 mg to 1.0 mg. Note also, however, that 1.5 mg produced no larger changes in prolactin than 1 mg, suggesting that the system had become "saturated." We will return to this point shortly, but these data show both dose-response relations and an upper limit to the sensitivity of the system. The lower limits are indicated in Table 8-2 of prolactin responses of five subjects who received 12.5 mg and 25 mg of chlorpromazine IM. Once again the response to 25 mg was consistently greater than to 12.5 mg. However, only three of five subjects had a response to the smaller dose, thus indicating the lower limits of sensitivity. Figure 8-4 illustrates responses of four subjects to 2.5, 5, and 7.5 mg of butaperazine orally. Dose-response relations are apparent at 75, 90, and 105 minutes (with the differences between 2.5 and 7.5 mg statistically significant), but by 2 hours all subjects achieved a maximum response to all doses. Once again this indicated a "saturation" effect. By "saturation" we do not mean necessarily that the dopamine receptors have been fully saturated in this system, let alone in the other brain regions. Among many possibilities, the most likely, in our view, is that the higher doses have provided enough neuroleptic to block the action of the dopamine being tonically released from tuberoinfundibular neurones. Challenge by additional dopamine agonists should be capable of overriding the blockade by these doses of neuroleptics to suppress prolactin again.

Table 8-2. Change in Human Prolactin (ng/ml)
2 Hours After 12.5 mg and 25 mg of
Chlorpromazine IM

Subject	12.5 mg	25 mg
A	4.3	31.5
B	5.9	31.4
C	−1.1	13.1
D	−3.6	15.1
E	5.6	14.5
Mean	2.2	21.1
SD	4.3	9.4

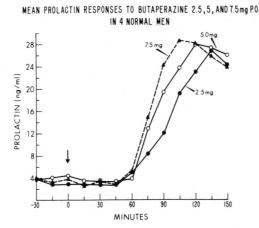

Figure 8-4. Plasma prolactin responses to 2.5, 5.0, and 7.5 mg butaperazine p.o. in four normal young men.

Two implications of these data should be emphasized, however. First, it is likely that a plateau of prolactin levels will be achieved rather soon after beginning a therapeutic dose regimen in schizophrenic patients, since these doses will, in general, be much greater than the doses required for a maximum prolactin response. A correlation between a large *therapeutic* dose and prolactin level, therefore, will be unlikely. It follows that a simple correlation between prolactin response and clinical response is equally unlikely if the patient is taking his medication and if it is in the therapeutic range. Second, in evaluating the relative potency of neuroleptic drugs in stimulating prolactin, care should be taken to administer doses within the range of sensitivity of the prolactin response.

With this latter consideration in mind, we have compared the prolactin responses to standard doses of chlorpromazine, thioridazine, butaperazine, trifluoperazine, and haloperidol in several normal subjects. Figure 8-5 presents an example of the prolactin responses of one subject to 50 mg of chlorpromazine, 50 mg of thioridazine, 5 mg of butaperazine, and 1 mg of haloperidol, all as oral concentrates. We then used a crude formula for evaluating relative prolactin stimulating potency per milligram of drug:

$$\frac{\text{prolactin ng/ml (peak-baseline concentration)}}{\text{mg drug given}}$$

The maximal increase of prolactin per milligram of drug was related to the similar figure for chlorpromazine, as the reference drug. The relative prolactin stimulating potency of thioridazine, butaperazine, and haloperidol are expressed as multiples of 1, the value for chlorpromazine (Table 8-3 and 8-4).

In two subjects, thioridazine was essentially equipotent with chlorpromazine, butaperazine 9 to 18 times more potent, and haloperidol 17 to 36 times more potent, quite consistent with the ratios of clinical potency reported for these drugs. In the next study, in three subjects, intramuscular doses of 25 mg chlorpromazine, 4 mg of trifluoperazine, and 1 mg of haloperidol were given. Haloperidol was 50 times more potent than chlorpromazine, while trifluoperazine was 12 times more potent than chlorpromazine in

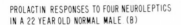

PROLACTIN RESPONSES TO FOUR NEUROLEPTICS
IN A 22 YEAR OLD NORMAL MALE (B)

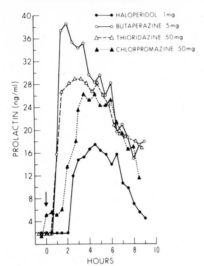

Figure 8-5. Plasma prolactin response to four neuroleptics in a normal young man.

stimulating prolactin (Table 8-3). These figures again accord strikingly well with average clinical potency of the drugs. It is also noteworthy that this prolactin test is unusual in that it is a single measure of dopamine blockade in which both thioridazine and haloperidol emerge with the right potency ratios. Thus, these data strongly support the dopamine blockade hypothesis of neuroleptics, and they also should provide an excellent tool for assessing probable clinical potency of new drugs.

Another clinical application of the prolactin response could be in the determination of the duration of action of neuroleptics. Meltzer and colleagues have shown that, after discontinuation of a course of typical oral neuroleptic medication, plasma prolactin concentration returns to normal within 48–72 hours (16). We have investigated prolactin responses to long-acting medication—depot fluphenazine enanthate. We find (Figure 8-6) that prolactin concentration remains elevated for about 2 weeks, consistent with reports of clinical duration of action of this drug.

We conclude by focusing on a more complex neuropharmacologic issue. The neostriatal dopamine system appears to differ in several ways from the hypothesized dopamine system where antipsychotic drugs exert their therapeutic effects, which we

Table 8-3. Human Prolactin-stimulating Potency of Oral Neuroleptics Relative to Chlorpromazine[a]

Subject	Chlorpromazine	Thioridazine	Butaperazine	Haloperidol
A	1	1.3	17.6	35.7
B	1	0.9	9.2	16.6

$$^a \frac{\Delta \text{ prolactin (ng/ml)}}{\text{mg drug}} \div \frac{\Delta \text{ prolactin (ng/ml)}}{\text{mg chlorpromazine}}$$

Table 8-4. Human Prolactin-stimulating Potency of Intramuscular Neuroleptics Relative to Chlorpromazine[a]

Subject	Chlorpromazine	Trifluoperazine	Haloperidol
A	1	6.6	18.2
B	1	10.1	30.9
C	1	19.1	104.0
Mean	1	11.9	51.0

[a] $\dfrac{\Delta \text{ prolactin (ng/ml)}}{\text{mg drug}} \div \dfrac{\Delta \text{ prolactin (ng/ml)}}{\text{mg chlorpromazine}}$

will call the "therapeutic" dopamine system. For example, tolerance rapidly develops to the extrapyramidal side effects induced by neuroleptics but not to their therapeutic effects (17). Again, antiparkinsonian-anticholinergic drugs rapidly and significantly reverse neuroleptic-induced extrapyramidal symptoms but without any major effect on the therapeutic potency. Conversely, cholinergic drugs like physostigmine worsen drug-induced parkinsonism in schizophrenics (18) but not their psychotic symptomatology (19). Again, thioridazine is weak in its effects on the intact neostriatum, although potent as an antipsychotic (20). Extrapyramidal symptoms, such as dystonias, often appear many hours after the peak blood level and penetration of drugs into the brain have been achieved (21). An explanation for some of these differences has been offered by several researchers who suggest a cholinergic antagonism of dopaminergic activity in the neostriatum but not in the "therapeutic" dopamine system (22).

In any case, we have studied some of these neuropharmacologic responses in the tuberoinfundibular prolactin system to see whether it behaves more like the neostriatal or more like the "therapeutic" dopamine system. With regard to thioridazine, we already have seen that it is equipotent with chlorpromazine in stimulating prolactin. [Regarding tolerance (Table 8-5), over a 4-week period of constant dose therapy with various neuroleptics, no decline in prolactin levels occurred in patients; that is, tolerance did *not* develop.] With regard to anticholinergic and cholinergic drugs (Figure 8-7), a variety of these agents (methscopolamine, neostigmine, scopolamine, diphenhydramine, and benztropine) administered singly and in combination did not affect prolactin secre-

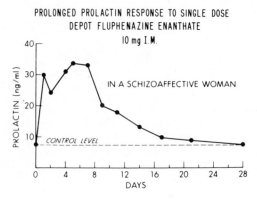

Figure 8-6. Prolonged plasma prolactin response to a single dose of fluphenazine enanthate IM in a schizo-affective woman.

Table 8-5. 8:30 A.M. Prolactin Levels (ng/ml) in Psychotics During Sustained Constant-Dose Neuroleptic Therapy

		Weeks			
Patient	1	2	3	4	mg Drug qd
A	14.0	9.3	15.2	14	Butaperazine 60
B	8.9	18.6	19.7	20	Thiothixene 20
C	14.1	14.0	12.7	16	Butaperazine 60
D	18.3	18.7	18.7	17	Butaperazine 80
E	31.3	30.9	30.1	31	Butaperazine 30
Mean	17.3	18.3	19.2	19.6	
SD	8.5	8.0	6.6	6.7	

tion in normal subjects. Similarly, the centrally-acting cholinergic drug physostigmine, when properly balanced by an adequate dose of the peripherally acting anticholinergic drug methscopolamine—which prevents side effects and physical distress—also had no effect on prolactin secretion (Figure 8-8). Thus, the tuberoinfundibular prolactin system appears to behave much more like the hypothesized "therapeutic" dopamine system than the neostriatum, which mediates extrapyramidal symptoms.

We have also noted in three subjects that after administration of neuroleptic drugs, dystonias occurred well after prolactin levels had fallen from their peak, but still prior to return to baseline. Given that prolactin is an index of brain dopamine blockade, the dystonias occurred while there was still evidence of residual blockade. These data are consistent with Davis's hypothesis that dystonias occur when the "built-in" anticholinergic-antiparkinsonian effects of the neuroleptic wear off, but while some dopamine blockade persists (21).

In summary then, the tuberoinfundibular prolactin system appears to us a highly useful model pathway for the neuropharmacologist and the clinical psychopharmacologist,

HUMAN PROLACTIN RESPONSES TO INTRAMUSCULAR
CENTRAL AND PERIPHERAL ANTICHOLINERGIC AND
CHOLINERGIC DRUGS

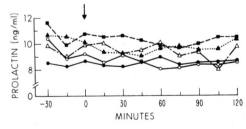

●——● METHSCOPOLAMINE - 0.25mg (N=5)
△---△ SCOPOLAMINE 0.4 + NEOSTIGMINE 0.125mg (N=5)
○——○ DIPHENHYDRAMINE - 50mg (N=5)
▲·······▲ NEOSTIGMINE - 0.25mg (N=4)
■---■ BENZTROPINE - 1mg (N=4)

Figure 8-7. Plasma prolactin response to intramuscular centrally and peripherally acting anticholinergic and cholinergic drugs in normal young men.

HUMAN PROLACTIN RESPONSES TO IM PHYSOSTIGMINE
(1mg) AND METHSCOPOLAMINE (0.25 AND 0.4mg)

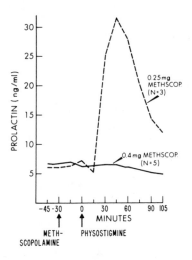

Figure 8-8. Plasma prolactin responses to 1 mg physostigmine IM combined with 0.25 mg and 0.4 mg methscopolamine in normal men.

both because of its neuropharmacologic similarities to the hypothesized "therapeutic" dopamine system and its ready applicability to the studies of humans, both normal and schizophrenic.

REFERENCES

1. Matthysse S: Antipsychotic drug actions: A clue to the neuropathology of schizophrenia. *Fed Proc* 32:200–205, 1973.

2. Snyder SH, Banerjee SP, Yamamuro HI, Greenberg D: Drugs, neurotransmitters, and schizophrenia. *Science* 184:1243–1253, 1974.

3. Snyder SH, Taylor KM, Coyle JT, et al: The role of brain dopamine in behavioral regulation and the actions of psychotropic drugs. *Amer J Psychiat* 127:119–207, 1970.

4. Klawans HL, Goetz C, Westheimer R: Pathophysiology of schizophrenia on the striatum. *Dis Nerv Syst* 33:711–719, 1972.

5. Björklund A, Lindvall O, Nobin A: Evidence of an incerto-hypothalamic dopamine neurone system in the rat. *Brain Res* 89:29–42, 1975.

6. Hökfelt T, Ljungdahl A, Fuxe K, et al: Dopamine nerve terminals in the rat limbic cortex: Aspects of the dopamine hypothesis of schizophrenia. *Science* 184:177–179, 1974.

7. Stevens JR: An anatomy of schizophrenia. *Arch Gen Psychiatry* 29:177–189, 1973.

8. Anden N-E: Dopamine turnover in the corpus striatum and the limbic system after treatment with neuroleptic and anti-acetylcholine drugs. *J Pharm Pharmacol* 24:905–906, 1972.

9. Anden N-E, Stock G: Effect of clozapine on the turnover of dopamine in the corpus striatum and in the limbic system. *J Pharm Pharmacol* 25:346–348, 1973.

10. Wiesel F-A, Sedvall G: Effect of antipsychotic drugs on homovanillic acid levels in striatum and olfactory tubercle of the rat. *Eur J Pharmacol* 30:364–367, 1975.

11. Wurtman RJ, Fernstrom JD: Neuroendocrine effects of psychotropic drugs, in Sachar EJ (ed): *Hormones, Behavior and Psychopathology*. New York, Raven Press, 1976, pp 144–151.

12. Gruen PH, Sachar EJ, Altman N, et al: Prolactin responses to neuroleptic Drugs, I: Relation to antidopaminergic and antipsychotic properties. *Arch Gen Psychiatry,* in press.

13. Sachar EJ, Gruen PH, Altman N, et al: The use of neuroendocrine techniques in psychopharmacological research, in Sachar EJ (ed): *Hormones, Behavior and Psychopathology.* New York, Raven Press, 1976, pp 161–176.

14. Rotrosen, J, Angrist B, Gershon S, et al: Neuroendocrine assessment of dopamine in schizophrenia, to be published.

15. Meltzer HY, Daniels S, Fang VS: Clozapine increases rat serum prolactin levels. *Life Sci* 17:339–342, 1975.

16. Meltzer HY, Fang VS: The effect of neuroleptics on serum prolactin in schizophrenic patients. *Arch Gen Psychiatry* 33:279–286, 1976.

17. Fann WE, Lake CR, Richman BW: Drug induced parkinsonism: a reevaluation. *Dis Nerv Syst* 36:91–93, 1975.

18. Abani LM, VanWoert MH, Bowers MB Jr: Physostigmine effects on phenothiazine induced extrapyramidal reactions. *Arch Neurol* 29:444–446, 1973.

19. Janowsky, DS, El-Yousef MK, Davis JM, et al: Antagonistic effects of physostigmine and methylphenidate in man. *Amer J Psychiat* 30:1370–1376, 1973.

20. Matthysse S: Dopamine and the pharmacology of schizophrenia: the state of the evidence. *J Psychiatr Res* 11:107–113, 1974.

21. Davis JM: Blood levels, drug interactions and dosage in psychiatric clinical pharmacology. Presented at Annual Meeting, Psychiatric Research Society, October 31–November 1, 1975, New York City.

22. Snyder S, Greenberg D, Yamamura HI: Antischizophrenic drugs and brain cholinergic receptors. *Arch Gen Psychiatry* 31:58–61, 1974.

Chapter 9
Dopamine Theory of Schizophrenia: A Two-Factor Theory

John M. Davis, M.D.

The previous chapters in this volume have reviewed various aspects of the current biochemical theories of schizophrenia. The dopamine theory underlies most but not all the recent research into the biology of schizophrenia. For this reason I will focus my discussion on the dopamine theory of schizophrenia. I will first try to summarize the theory and discuss the supportive evidence. For this purpose, I will emphasize work from our laboratory. Finally, I will provide a critique of the dopamine theory.

The dopamine theory essentially derives from the evidence for a common pharmacologic mechanism at work in drugs that benefit schizophrenic illness and in drugs that induce a schizophreniform illness. Historically, in terms of its basic paradigm, the dopamine theory of schizophrenia is comparable to the norepinephrine theory of depression. The norepinephrine theory of depression and mania essentially was derived from the fact that treatments known to benefit depression (ECT, tricyclic antidepressants, and monoamine oxidase inhibitors) increase norepinephrine, while drugs implicated in causing depression, such as reserpine and alpha-methyl dopa, decrease brain norepinephrine. Notwithstanding practical limitations, which demand that such theories be tested with special caution, the norepinephrine theory has generated a large body of empirical data, treatment strategies, and theoretical speculations. It is not surprising, therefore, that the same type of theorizing would be applied to schizophrenia, considering that the norepinephrine and the dopamine hypothesis are both derived from treatment in an heuristic manner.

The dopamine theory of schizophrenia follows from the early observations of Carlsson (1) that the possible mechanism of phenothiazine action was dopamine blockade. In this now classic paper, he provided the first evidence that phenothiazines are central dopamine blockers. This finding has been replicated using a variety of different pharmacologic techniques. It has also been verified by studies of several species' behavioral systems known to be under the control of a dopaminergic neural substrate. Subsequently, by extrapolating from the possible mechanism of therapeutic action of the antipsychotic drugs, Snyder (2) argued that abnormal dopamine levels may be involved in schizophrenia. In our laboratory, we have focused on empirical studies of man that may add new evidence to confirm or disconfirm this theory. I will not attempt a comprehensive review of this evidence but will restrict much of my empirical review to studies where I have had personal experience.

The dopamine theory of schizophrenia derives from the inference of a common denominator for drugs that help or cause psychoses. It has limitations in that the same logic on which the inference is based would also lead us to conclude that if pneumococcal pneumonia is helped by penicillin, it must surely be a penicillin deficiency disease. A drug can benefit a disease through an entirely different mechanism than that which causes the condition. Drugs can act through complicated chains of events, and the exact relationship between treatment and causes may be far more complicated than correcting a simple excess or deficiency. Penicillin kills the bacteria that are a causative factor in pneumonia. Hence the problem is to pin down the connection between treatment and etiology. To help do so, I conceptually differentiate three questions in dopamine theories: (a) Do antipsychotic drugs block dopamine receptors? (b) Do antipsychotic drugs produce their beneficial effect in schizophrenia through blockade of dopamine receptors? (c) Is dopamine involved in schizophrenia in some central causative way, or is its connection nonspecific?

With regard to the first of these questions, whether or not antipsychotics block dopamine receptors, there is overwhelming evidence that they do. Using a variety of pharmacologic techniques, this has been demonstrated in many different ways. For example, dopamine blockade leads to increased dopamine synthesis, and this has been shown with a variety of techniques. Blockade also has been found directly in single cell neurophysiologic recordings. It has been demonstrated on a molar level through studies of animal behaviors known to be mediated by dopamine. For example, antipsychotic drugs block stereotyped behavior (see Chapter 7). Since so many different methods are involved (neurophysiologic, pharmacologic, and behavioral), it is difficult to reach any conclusion other than that the antipsychotics block dopamine receptors. In this volume, Snyder describes further evidence for such blockade.

Unfortunately, there is an inductive leap from saying that antipsychotics block dopamine receptors and an answer to the second question: Do antipsychotic drugs benefit schizophrenia through their blockade of dopamine receptors? Drugs have many different pharmacologic effects, and it cannot be simply concluded because a drug has a given pharmacologic effect that the therapeutic response in a complex illness has been produced by that particular pharmacologic action. There is, however, substantial evidence that the mechanism by which antipsychotics benefit schizophrenia may in fact take place through blocking dopamine receptors. In the United States there are five marketed classes of antipsychotic drugs: the phenothiazine derivatives, the thioxanthenes, the butyrophenones, the indoles, and the dibenzoxepins. In addition, there are several experimental classes of antipsychotics, such as the acradines, that have definite antipsychotic properties. There is an abundance of evidence from a variety of different neurophysiologic, pharmacologic, and also animal-behavior systems to support the hypothesis that all these antipsychotic drugs block dopamine receptors. A great many phenothiazines have been studied in man, and only those phenothiazines that block dopamine receptors (i.e., those which share certain structural configurations such as the three-carbon chain) are effective antipsychotic agents. What is more important is that there are a number of structurally unrelated drugs that also share the property of producing dopamine blockade and also possess antipsychotic properties. Dr. Snyder, in Chapter 7, has elegantly extended the work on the dopamine blockade produced by the antipsychotics by directly measuring the affinity of antipsychotic drugs to the dopamine receptor and by showing a strikingly high correlation between the degree of dopamine blockade produced and the therapeutic potency of the antipsychotic agents.

It is also known that a variety of drugs produce pharmacologic effects in animals at doses well in excess of doses used in humans. Therefore, it is relevant to ask whether antipsychotic drugs produce dopamine blockade *in humans*. The best evidence that they do so at clinical doses is the fact that all the antipsychotic agents produce extrapyramidal side effects. This disturbance is similar to that of Parkinson's disease, a dopamine deficiency disease. Extrapyramidal side effects are consistent with the dopamine blockade theory of antipsychotic drug action. In addition, the beneficial effect of antipsychotic drugs in amphetamine psychosis or amphetamine overdose is consistent with the dopamine blockade hypothesis. Furthermore, antipsychotic drugs increase CSF levels of the dopamine metabolite homovanillic acid (HVA). This too is evidence of functional dopamine blockade. All these findings indicate that antipsychotic drugs produce dopamine blockade in doses typically used in man.

We would like to emphasize this point: the combined facts that a variety of apparently structurally dissimilar drugs all share the common pharmacologic property of producing dopamine blockade, and that all have beneficial effects in schizophrenia are evidence that the therapeutic effects occur through dopamine blockade. It would seem unlikely that so many different types of drugs could share more than one common pharmacologic property and that dopamine blockade was not involved in their antipsychotic actions. The fact that Snyder has found a quantitative relationship between blockade and potency greatly strengthens this conclusion. If a second, unknown pharmacologic property was a common denominator of all these drugs and dopamine blockade was merely a red herring, then the second, unrelated pharmacologic property would have to coincide in all these different drugs in a manner such that the quantitative degree of alteration of the unknown factor would correlate with the quantitative degree of dopamine blockade as well as with the quantitative degree of antipsychotic potency in man. In other words, the fact that dopamine blockade quantitatively correlates with potency makes it very unlikely that another unknown property could be this common denominator.

It is of interest to note that reserpine also has well-documented antipsychotic properties, although it is a less effective antipsychotic agent than the neuroleptic drugs. It lowers brain dopamine levels by interfering with dopamine storage in the storage vesicles. This is important evidence because reserpine produces an antipsychotic action that has a different type of antidopamine function, i.e., lowering dopamine levels rather than blocking dopamine receptors. Thus, schizophrenia is benefited by two pharmacologic classes of drugs, dopamine blockers and drugs that lower functional brain dopamine. Dopamine again is our common denominator. Reserpine also produces extrapyramidal side effects; this indicates that in doses used in man, dopamine blockade occurs.

Alpha-methyl-paratyrosine blocks dopamine synthesis and is without antipsychotic activity in man. It may be that, at the doses used, there was not enough inhibition of synthesis to lower brain dopamine levels to a pharmacologically significant extent. More will be said about the significance of this observation later. An additional crucial experiment was performed by Roos, Carlsson, and their coworkers in Sweden (3) demonstrating that if patients were simultaneously treated with alpha-methyl-paratyrosine, the dose of antipsychotic needed to produce a given degree of antipsychotic activity could be lowered markedly. Since alpha-methyl-paratyrosine is structurally quite dissimilar from the antipsychotic agents, there are most likely but few common parameters that these drugs share except for their effects on dopamine.

A methodologic point is in order here. The relationship between the dose of chlorpromazine and clinical response is such that most patients will have achieved the maximum possible clinical response when dosages of approximately 1000 mg per day are used, i.e., the dose response curve will reach its peak at that dose, and the incremental increase in response after that point would be only slight. It may be that whatever can be done to benefit schizophrenia through dopamine blockade is already accomplished by doses of that order of magnitude. That is, further antidopamine effects through any mechanism may not be that useful, since this dose of drug would cause the maximum effect that could be achieved in any dopaminergic action. If this is indeed the case, it would *not* be expected that one could augment therapy in this dose range by giving additional agents that affect dopamine through other mechanisms. However, if a very low dose of antipsychotic drug were used, this could indeed be potentiated by other antidopamine agents because full dopamine blockade is not initially achieved. I would conclude from this line of reasoning that the way to show potentiation of antipsychotic drugs by an agent which has antidopamine function through a different mechanism would be to use suboptimal doses of dopamine blocking antipsychotics and to see if the second agent can indeed potentiate the full antipsychotic response. This is precisely the strategy used by Walinder, Skott, Carlsson, and Roos (3).

Thus, to summarize the evidence, it is noted that otherwise markedly dissimilar drugs that share the property of lowering dopamine levels by blocking dopamine receptors all possess antipsychotic activities. It is unlikely that such diverse structures would share many common pharmacologic properties. Reserpine, acting through a different mechanism, lowers brain dopamine and helps schizophrenics. Alpha-methyl-paratyrosine, which blocks dopamine synthesis, potentiates the effects of the antipsychotic agents.

This discussion provides several lines of evidence that indicate, in my opinion, that the antipsychotic drugs act through dopamine blockade in benefiting schizophrenic patients. Whether this can be extended to say that schizophrenics have some functional overactivity in dopaminergic systems is another matter. However, the evidence that the antipsychotic drugs benefit schizophrenic patients through dopamine blockade is the first cornerstone of the dopamine theory of schizophrenia.

The second cornerstone of the dopamine theory of schizophrenia is that agents that release dopamine or otherwise raise dopamine levels in the synaptic cleft can worsen schizophrenia. Most importantly, a wide variety of drugs that act either through releasing dopamine or through potentiating dopamine by blocking its reuptake, or both, can cause a paranoid psychosis when given in high doses (4). These drugs include a wide variety of amphetamine-type psychomotor stimulants such as amphetamine or methylphenidate. Cocaine, which acts through a similar but not identical mechanism, also causes a paranoid psychosis. In our laboratory (5–8), we extended this line of evidence and showed that small intravenous doses of amphetamine or methylphenidate produce a florid exacerbation of schizophrenic psychosis in a patient who is actively schizophrenic. A similar dose of a psychomotor stimulant when given to normal subjects produced a very mild euphoria. This euphoria is measurable but not very pronounced. The subjects in these studies were given either a placebo infusion or a psychomotor stimulant infusion. The amount of methylphenidate used was sufficient for most subjects to realize they had received the methylphenidate as opposed to the placebo, but they were not absolutely certain. The same small dose markedly worsens, roughly doubles, the intensity of psychosis in a patient during an active schizophrenic episode. It seems, therefore, that schizophrenic patients are remarkably susceptible to small doses of dopamine releasing agents.

We distinguish these small dose effects *in schizophrenics* from amphetamine psychoses *in normal subjects* who take very high levels of amphetamine and who typically develop a *paranoid* psychosis. In contrast, for schizophrenic patients, very small intravenous doses of these psychomotor stimulants worsen the *preexisting* psychotic symptoms, i.e., if the patient is catatonic, the catatonic symptoms get worse; if the patient is hebephrenic, the hebephrenic symptoms get worse; in schizophrenics, the psychosis-worsening property of these psychomotor stimulants is not a uniform paranoid psychosis but, rather, a worsening of the preexisting symptoms. Since these agents act through releasing dopamine and then blocking the reuptake of the released dopamine, the activation of the psychosis is consistent with the dopamine theory of schizophrenia.

The exacerbation of schizophrenic symptoms produced by amphetamine was found to be attenuated if patients were also treated with pimozide (9). Pimozide is a fairly specific dopamine blocker. The fact that pimozide can reverse this amphetamine effect is evidence that amphetamine does indeed produce its effect via the release of dopamine rather than norepinephrine or serotonin.

The fact that L-amphetamine as well as D-amphetamine can produce a paranoid psychosis when given alone, or can worsen schizophrenia when given in small intravenous doses, is consistent with the interpretation that these effects were produced by dopamine release rather than by the dopamine "false transmitter type" metabolites (norephedrine or p-hydroxy-norephedrine). D-Amphetamine as opposed to L-amphetamine is metabolized to these false transmitters (5–8). In our laboratory we find that methylphenidate is much more potent than amphetamine in worsening schizophrenia (5–8). Methylphenidate releases dopamine from stored sites, while amphetamine releases newly synthesized dopamine. Reserpine, which affects storage, is an antipsychotic drug, whereas alpha-methyl-paratyrosine, which affects production of newly synthesized dopamine, is ineffective in schizophrenia. We would speculate that perhaps stored dopamine may be more involved in schizophrenia than newly synthesized dopamine. We also have observed a worsening of psychosis with amantadine, another drug that acts via a dopamine mechanism.

In our group, we performed a pilot trial to see if L-DOPA might have a beneficial effect on tardive dyskinesia. We discovered that this was not the case: these patients had their psychosis activated by L-DOPA. Since L-DOPA is converted to dopamine, this activation is consistent with the dopamine hypothesis of schizophrenia. In parkinsonian patients, L-DOPA occasionally produces a psychotic reaction, particularly in patients with preexisting mental disease. Also, L-DOPA activation of schizophrenia has sometimes been noted in experimental studies (10). It seems that schizophrenic patients are unusually susceptible either to drugs that release dopamine or to drugs that increase dopamine levels.

If schizophrenics are unusually susceptible to drugs that increase synthesis or release dopamine, it is reasonable to ask what mechanisms could be responsible for this. There are, of course, a variety of possible mechanisms. Schizophrenics could have an increase in dopamine synthesis, a decrease in reuptake, decreased degradation, and so forth. Some evidence is consistent with the hypothesis of decreased degradation. Wyatt, in Chapter 10 of this volume, has reported a variety of studies that show that schizophrenic patients have decreased monoamine oxidase (MAO) in their platelets. Platelets have been used as a model for central adrenergic neurons in a number of investigations since they share many common properties with neurons. Schizophrenia is a disease of young adulthood, and this is the time of the life cycle during which MAO levels are at their lowest. A decrease of MAO levels in schizophrenics is a finding that is consistent with a dopamine hypothesis and with the empirical evidence that schizophrenics are unusually susceptible to drugs that increase dopamine levels or increase the release of dopamine.

In collaboration with Zeller (11), our group has confirmed the initial work of Wyatt and Murphy (12). In a study using three different substrates (see Table 9-1), we found MAO levels decreased in all three substrates in schizophrenics. However, the degree of the decrease varies from substrate to substrate. We speculate that this may indicate that there is a qualitative difference in the MAO of schizophrenics as opposed to normal subjects. If it were just a decrease in activity without a qualitative change, an equal degree of decrease would be expected in all three substrates.

One important piece of negative information, which Barchas and his coworkers discussed in this symposium, was the observation that schizophrenic patients do not excrete elevated levels of the dopamine metabolite HVA in the cerebrospinal fluid. If schizophrenic patients did indeed synthesize abnormally large amounts of dopamine, their cerebrospinal fluid would be expected to show dopamine overactivity. The question then is this: If schizophrenia is not a disease of dopamine overproduction, could it be a disease involving supersensitive dopamine receptors, that is, a postsynaptic disease?

In the above discussion, we have considered the dopamine theory of schizophrenia: schizophrenic patients may have excess dopamine available in the synaptic cleft. A second possibility equally consistent with the evidence, however, would be that schizophrenic patients have supersensitive dopamine receptors. In this regard, it is of interest that pilot data in our laboratory (13) showed that schizophrenic patients have enhanced responses to growth hormone and to apomorphine. Apomorphine is, of course, a dopamine receptor stimulant. This result is very preliminary, but it does suggest that postsynaptic mechanisms should not be forgotten in hypotheses about dopamine mechanisms that may be involved in some way in schizophrenia.

Of course, both possibilities could be true. Speculations about possible abnormalities of biogenic amines that may play a causative role in schizophrenia involve an inductive leap from the empirical evidence. Since methods do not exist for the precise definition of biochemical mechanisms in the living human brain, the theories tend to be simple dynamic theories that focus on levels of a single amine. These usually identify an abnor-

Table 9-1. Platelet MAO Activities for Schizophrenic and Aged Matched Controls Expressed as Percentage of Control[a]

	p-Methoxybenzylamine	Tyramine	m-1-Osobenzylamine
Female Control	100%	100%	100%
Schizophrenic	38%*	32%*	65%*
Male Control	100%	100%	100%
Schizophrenic	43%*	39%*	69%*
	p < 0.002		

[a] From Zeller ET, et al (11).

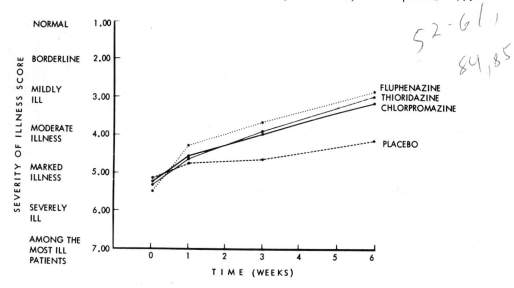

Figure 9-1. Time course of symptom relief with antipsychotic medication or placebo.

mality in the level of a single transmitter and, hence, are single-transmitter, single-disease theories. Those critical of these theories may refer to them as monomanias.

At this point, let me briefly provide a critique of the dopamine theory. This theory derives from drugs that cause or benefit schizophrenia. Generically, although some drugs do specifically antagonize some factor closely related to the cause of a given disease, other drugs benefit diseases through a manner that is distantly related to the actual cause or in a manner that is entirely nonspecific. Digitalis could benefit a patient with congenital heart disease, although obviously the congenital heart disease is a structural defect completely unrelated to the functional effect of digitalis. In addition to this philosophical point, there is evidence that is apparently inconsistent with the dopamine theory. Alpha-methyl-paratyrosine (AMPT) does reduce dopamine synthesis but is ineffective in treating schizophrenia. In nonschizophrenics, amphetamine does not produce schizophrenia in its diverse manifestations but, rather, only paranoid psychoses. Schizophrenics do not manifest excessive levels of HVA in the cerebrospinal fluid.

Some of these discrepancies may not be critical. The increased synthesis of dopamine, which is assumed to be responsible for schizophrenia, may be localized in the brain in such a place that cerebrospinal fluid HVA may not reflect the dopamine turnover in this particular location. Perhaps insufficient doses of AMPT were used in man. However, I wish to record here that anomalies and discrepancies between empirical data and these theories do exist. Although there may be plausible reasons why these do not constitute critical disconfirmation of the theory, a balanced presentation requires their mention.

The time course by which antipsychotic drugs relieve schizophrenia has been well studied (Figure 9-1). Schizophrenia gradually lessens over the course of 6 weeks or so of antipsychotic drug treatment. Dopamine receptors are blocked quite rapidly and, indeed, there is evidence that there may be some tolerance to dopamine blockade after several weeks, as measured by a reduction of extrapyramidal side effects and by lowered cerebrospinal HVA levels. In other words, the schizophrenic is benefiting from antipsychotic drugs at a time when tolerance is developing. If dopamine blockade were all there was to treating schizophrenia, it might be expected that schizophrenia would improve quite dramatically and remit within a few hours after an adequate dose of antipsychotics is given. Tolerance apparently does not develop to the antipsychotic effect of the neuroleptic drugs, yet it seems to develop for extrapyramidal side effects and also in terms of the biochemical reflection of dopamine blockade in cerebrospinal fluid HVA levels. Studies in our laboratories utilizing loading doses do not show that this hastens the recovery of schizophrenic patients (14).

A second related type of argument is as follows: In many physiologic systems, dopamine is opposed by acetylcholine in a mutually antagonistic relationship. Parkinson's disease and tardive dyskinesia are both good examples of this. The worsening of schizophrenia produced by methylphenidate can be antagonized by physostigmine, a drug that increases brain acetylcholine. Physostigmine alone does not benefit schizophrenia when given in a single injection. If one assumes that balances that apply to dopamine in parkinsonian movement disorders also apply to dopamine in schizophrenia, then it would be expected that physostigmine would have an antipsychotic effect. This does not seem to be the case in these acute experiments.

These considerations have led me to suggest a two-factor theory of schizophrenia. The nondopaminergic first factor may "turn on" a schizophrenic episode. The second factor, dopaminergic stimulation, may be involved in a neural system connected with the first factor but not identical to it. Excess dopamine may aggravate the first factor and "turn up the gain." Antipsychotics may turn down the gain by blocking dopaminergic stimulation. Once the gain is turned down, then normal reparation can take place. This would explain the slow time course of the antipsychotic action of the neuroleptics. The first factor would imply that schizophrenia is also mediated by some psychologic or physiologic factor other than dopamine levels.

Although controlled studies have focused on the antipsychotic effects of the neuroleptics in schizophrenia, there is a clinical opinion that these drugs also have an antipsychotic effect in some cases with organic brain damage and also in mentally defective patients who manifest psychoticlike symptoms. These drugs also are effective in mania. It would seem, therefore, that the label "antischizophrenic" is too specific. Antipsychotic implies that the drugs lessen many forms of psychosis or psychoticlike disorders. This implies that whatever their action is, it is not so specific as to apply only to schizophrenia. There is little doubt that the antipsychotic drugs produce substantial benefit in schizophrenia. To illustrate the quantitative amount of the drug-placebo difference, we have reanalyzed NIMH Collaborative Study 1 showing the relative percentage of patients who are much improved, and those who show no change or who deteriorate in a 6 weeks' trial (Figure 9-2). The drug-placebo difference is quite substantial. Apropos of the observations of many of the authors in other chapters of this volume that schizophrenia may be a heterogeneous disease, we note that about one-quarter of the patients improved substantially on placebo. This evidence from drug studies supports the concept of heterogeneity, that schizophrenia may not be a single diagnostic entity.

I would like to close this discussion by pointing out that the evidence that antipsychotics are dopamine blockers is overwhelming. When considering the hypothesis that the dopamine blockade properties of phenothiazines are the mechanisms by which they produce their antipsychotic effect, a reasonably strong case can be made from a variety

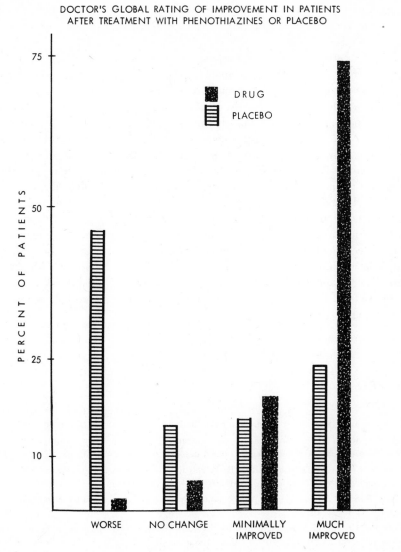

DOCTOR'S GLOBAL RATING OF IMPROVEMENT IN PATIENTS
AFTER TREATMENT WITH PHENOTHIAZINES OR PLACEBO

Figure 9-2. Doctor's global rating of improvement in patients after treatment with phenothiazines or placebo.

of evidence. Extending this line of thought to say that schizophrenia is caused by excess dopamine (presynaptically, postsynaptically, or both) involves a departure from a good deal of the experimental data. I have, therefore, suggested a second interpretation of the data, the two-factor theory of schizophrenia, which suggests that dopamine is not the "first" cause of schizophrenia but rather a modulator, and that the antipsychotic drugs turn down the gain, so to speak, and allow a normal repair process to take place. (This could not take place if the first factor was continually aggravated or irritated by the dopamine systems.) This two-factor theory implies some intimate relationship between my hypothesized first and second factors. The two-factor theory is obviously quite speculative. I am suggesting it not so much as a definitive explanation but, rather, as an illustration of the point that more than one interpretation of the data which has led to the dopamine theory is possible.

Actually, the dopamine theory of schizophrenia as such is somewhat removed from the data. I would like to make an analogy to psychoanalytic theory. That branch of psychoanalytic theory that is most speculative, and most removed from the observed data in actual psychoanalytic sessions, is metapsychologic psychoanalytic theory. In this sense, the dopamine theory of schizophrenia is a metapharmacologic-psychopharmacologic theory. As such, it is less a proven theory than a research strategy which may or may not ultimately be useful. The intent of my discussion has been to summarize, to parse conceptually those aspects of the dopamine theory that are quite well substantiated as opposed to the more speculative aspects. I would like to give the reader a general feel for the state of the art and to suggest an alternate theory. Since dopamine is affected by drugs that benefit or cause psychosis, it is, in my opinion, a lead which cannot be ignored. It is important to follow this evidence to see just how dopamine may be related to schizophrenia and just how dopamine blockade is beneficial to the schizophrenic patient. That dopamine crops up in a variety of situations connected with psychosis is undoubtedly true and, in this sense, dopamine is generating much smoke. But whether this is smoke from the fire at the core of schizophrenia or a mere smoke screen remains to be determined.

REFERENCES

1. Carlsson A, Lindqvist M: Effect of chlorpromazine and haloperidol on the formation of 3-methoxytyramine and normetanephrine in mouse brain. *Acta Pharmac (KBH)* 20:140, 1963.

2. Horn AS, Snyder SH: Chlorpromazine and dopamine: Conformational similarities that correlate with the antischizophrenic activity of phenothiazine drugs. *Proc Natl Acad Sci USA* 68:2325-2328, 1971.

3. Walinder J, Skott A, Carlsson A, Roos B: Potentiation by metyrosine of thioridazine effects in chronic schizophrenics, *Arch Gen Psychiat* 33:501-508, 1974.

4. Angrist B, Sathananthan G, et al: Amphetamine Psychosis: Behavioral and biochemical aspects. *J Psychiat Res* 11:13-23, 1974.

5. Davis JM: Critique of single amine theories: Evidence of a cholinergic influence in the major mental illnesses, in Freedman DX (ed): *Biology of the Major Psychoses.* New York, Raven Press, 1975, pp 333-342.

6. Davis JM: A two-factor theory of schizophrenia. *J Psychiat Res* 11:25-29, 1974.

7. Davis JM, Janowsky DS: Amphetamine and methylphenidate psychosis, in Usdin E, Snyder S (eds): *Frontiers in Catecholamine Research.* London, Pergamon, 1973, pp 977-987.

8. Janowsky DS, El-Yousef MK, Davis JM et al: Provocation of schizophrenic symptoms by intravenous administration of methylphenidate. *Arch Gen Psychiat* 28:185-190, 1973.

9. Docherty J, Van Kammen D, Jimerson D, et al: Amphetamine effects in schizophrenia versus depression. Paper presented at the Annual Meeting of the American Psychiatric Association, Miami, Florida, May 1976.

10. Angrist BM, Sathananthan K, et al: Behavioral and biochemical effects of L-Dopa in psychiatric patients, in Usdin E, Snyder S (eds): *Frontiers in Catecholamine Research.* London, Pergamon, 1973, pp 991-994.

11. Zeller ET, Boshes B, Davis JM, et al: Molecular aberration in platelet monoamine oxidase in schizophrenia. *Lancet* 1:1385, 1975.

12. Murphy DL, Wyatt RJ: Reduced monoamine oxidase activity in blood platelets from schizophrenic patients. *Nature* 238:225–226, 1972.

13. Pandey GN, Garver DL, Hengeveld C, et al: Postsynaptic supersensitivity in schizophrenia. *Sci Proc Am Psych Assn* 128:254, 1976.

14. Ericksen S, Haraszti J, Dekirmenjian H, et al: High vs standard dose of haloperidol in schizophrenia. *Sci Proc Am Psych Assn* 128:306, 1976.

Chapter 10
Is There an Endogenous Amphetamine? A Testable Hypothesis of Schizophrenia

Richard Jed Wyatt, M.D.

For a number of years it has been recognized that the psychosis produced by repeated administration of large doses of amphetamine is an excellent model for paranoid schizophrenia. The major deficit of the amphetamine psychosis-paranoid schizophrenia parallel is that many, but not all, observers have found that amphetamine-induced psychosis is not accompanied by a thought disorder, while a thought disorder is frequently used as a defining characteristic of schizophrenia. My own experience, and I suspect that of many clinicians, is that I frequently make the diagnosis of paranoid schizophrenia in the absence of a formal thought disorder.

As good as the amphetamine model may be, nobody has yet proposed that amphetamine is an endogenous compound or is capable of producing schizophrenia. Phenylethylamine (PEA) is an endogenous compound structurally identical to amphetamine except for the methyl group on the side chain alpha carbon (Figure 10-1). Because of this similarity, we and others have wondered whether PEA might act like an endogenous amphetamine and perhaps be responsible for some forms of schizophrenia, in particular, paranoid schizophrenia (1,2).

At the time a hypothesis is proposed, it is useful to describe by what criteria it can be judged. We have previously proposed nine criteria, some of which were originally suggested by Hollister (3), by which the PEA hypothesis might be evaluated. In this paper I shall describe and evaluate this hypothesis in the light of these criteria.

1. *The agent must be capable of mimicking clinical aspects of schizophrenia.* There are no direct data related to the question of whether or not PEA can produce psychotic behavior. However, phenylketonuric children who have very high PEA concentrations have been described as having autistic-like behavior and stereotypy similar to that which amphetamine produces (4). Perry et al (5) described two phenylketonuric adults with normal intelligence who were admitted to mental hospitals because of psychotic episodes and treated as schizophrenics. While we do not know if these behavioral disturbances

116

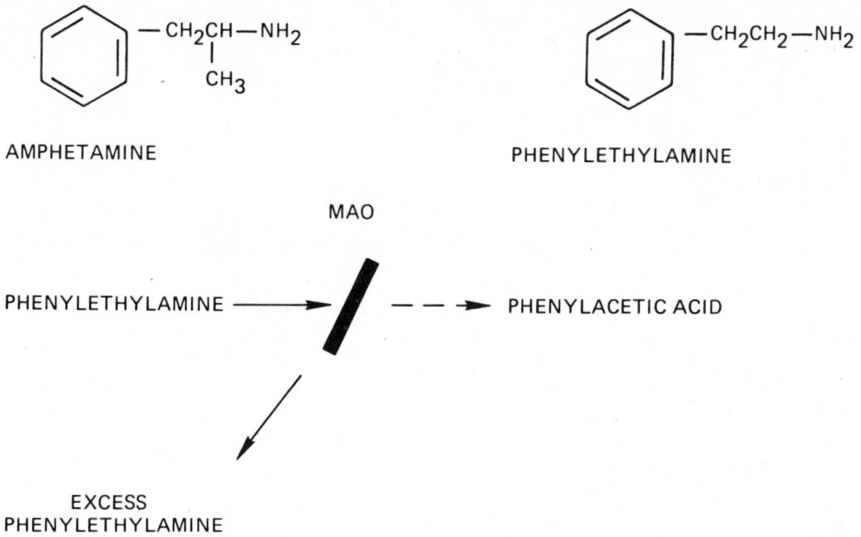

$$-CH_2CH-NH_2$$
$$\quad\quad | $$
$$\quad\quad CH_3$$

AMPHETAMINE

$$-CH_2CH_2-NH_2$$

PHENYLETHYLAMINE

MAO

PHENYLETHYLAMINE $\longrightarrow$ / $- - \rightarrow$ PHENYLACETIC ACID

EXCESS
PHENYLETHYLAMINE

Figure 10-1. Structural similarity between amphetamine and phenylethylamine. A block in the enzyme monoamine oxidase (MAO) would lead to an increase in phenylethylamine.

were due to PEA or what might happen if PEA were administered in prolonged high doses to man, its close relative, amphetamine, does produce a paranoid psychosis.

2. *The agent must be found in man.*   Jepson et al (6), Oates et al (7), Levine et al (8), Fischer et al (9), Boulton and Milward (10), Fischer and Heller (11), Fischer et al (12), Fischer et al (13), Schweitzer et al (14), and Inwang et al (15), using a variety of techniques, have found PEA in human urine. Good techniques for quantification of PEA in human tissues, however, are still in the developmental stage.

3. *The precursor of the agent should be found in man* (see criterion 4).   The amino acid phenylalanine, the precursor of PEA, is present in the diet and is found in man.

4. *The agent should be synthesized in man,* although the possibility remains that the agent could be of dietary origin.   The enzyme for converting phenylalanine to PEA is *l*-amino acid decarboxylase (16), which is known to be present in human brain (1). The affinity of PEA for the enzyme is very low (Km = 2×10^{-2} M), indicating conversion under normal circumstances would be slow. In spite of this, Levine et al (8) found that normal subjects given a phenylalanine load had increases in PEA excreted over a 24-hour period from 285 to 477 μg, while heterozygotes for phenylketonuria, metabolizing phenylalanine poorly, had increases from 387 to 1149 μg. Both normal subjects and phenylketonuric patients were pretreated with a monoamine oxidase inhibitor.

5. *The agent must be differently synthesized or metabolized in schizophrenics.* There are two studies that report PEA concentrations in the urine of schizophrenics. Fischer and Heller (11) reported markedly elevated PEA concentrations in four chronic schizophrenics while Schweitzer, Friedhoff, and Schwartz (14) found no differences between three acute schizophrenics and 18 controls.

There are a number of ways by which the concentration of PEA might be increased. Here we shall examine three (Figure 10-2). PEA is metabolized by the enzyme dopamine β-hydroxylase to form phenethanolamine. Wise, Baden, and Stein (17) reported that dopamine β-hydroxylase was markedly decreased in the autopsied brains of schizophrenics compared to that of controls. We (18) found only very small, nonsig-

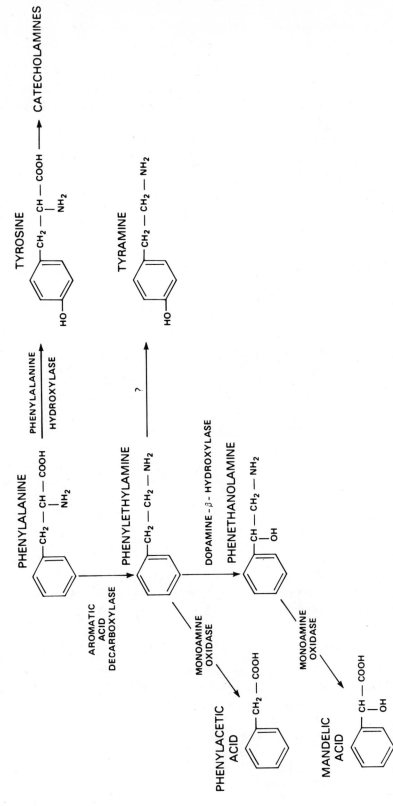

Figure 10-2. Metabolism of phenylethylamine from phenylalanine to phenylacetic acid and mandelic acid.

nificant decreases in the brains of schizophrenics and, contrary to the hypothesis proposed here, the patients with a paranoid diagnosis had, if anything, higher enzyme activities than those without (19). Furthermore, plasma concentrations of dopamine β-hydroxylase have been found repeatedly to be normal in schizophrenic patients (18).

Monoamine oxidase is perhaps the major route of PEA metabolism, and a reduction in this enzyme should increase PEA concentrations. Jepson et al (6) found that normal subjects excreted less than 20 μg PEA per 24 hours, while phenylketonurics excreted 10–20 μg. After treatment with a monoamine oxidase inhibitor, the values for the normal subjects increased to 60 μg, while those for the phenylketonurics increased to 3000 μg.

Tissue monoamine oxidase (MAO) is believed to exist in at least two forms conveniently referred to as type A and type B (20). PEA is the best endogenous substrate for the type B form which is found in the human platelet. We and other investigators (although not all) have found platelet monoamine oxidase to be decreased in some schizophrenic patients (Table 10-1, 22–36). Schildkraut, Herzog, Orsulak, et al (35) found that a subgroup of schizophrenic patients, identified on the basis of auditory hallucinations, had lower platelet MAO activity than patients without this symptom. Carpenter, Murphy, and Wyatt (28) found that the presence of paranoid and grandiose delusions helped discriminate (although not statistically significantly) a low MAO activity group of acute schizophrenic patients. Recently, using chart diagnoses (DSM II) of 36 chronic schizophrenic patients, we (21) found that all seven paranoid patients had platelet MAO activity below 9.16 units while only 18 of 29 nonparanoid schizophrenics were below this arbitrarily chosen break-off point (Fishers Exact Probability Test p <

Table 10-1. Platelet Monoamine Oxidase in Schizophrenic Patients as Percentage of Controls

Author	Patient Subtypes	Percentage of Controls
Murphy and Wyatt, 1972 (22)	Chronic and acute	41
Wyatt et al, 1973 (23)	Chronic and acute	61
Shaskan and Becker, 1974 (24)	Not stated	no difference
Friedman et al, 1974 (25)	Remitting	83
Nies et al, 1974 (26)	Less than 1 year of hospitalization	72–86[a]
Meltzer and Stahl, 1974 (27)	Chronic	32–52[a]
	Acute	45–69[a]
Carpenter et al, 1975 (28)	Acute	97
Zeller et al, 1975 (29)	Acute and chronic	39–43[a]
Bailey et al, 1975 (30)	Chronic	no difference
Cookson et al, 1975 (31)	Acute	low
Wyatt and Murphy, 1975 (32) Wyatt et al, 1975 (33) Murphy et al, 1976 (34)	Chronic	53 (females) and 71 (males)
Schildkraut et al, 1976 (35)	Nonparanoid Paranoid	~100 ~66
Domino and Khanna, 1976 (36)	Chronic	~46

[a] Used multiple substrates.

0.05). These three studies, all retrospective, indicate that paranoid schizophrenics may have lower platelet MAO activities than others, although confirmation of this by prospective studies would be most useful.

It is important that studies of brain MAO have not demonstrated differences between schizophrenics and controls. To date, no serious attempts to divide the schizophrenics into paranoid-nonparanoid subgroups for brain MAO have been made, and other peripheral tissues have not been studied.

If the deficit of type B MAO is more pervasive than just in the platelets, it might be expected that PEA might be elevated. It is recognized, however, that platelet MAO activity is low in some normals (37), patients with bipolar illness (38), and perhaps other psychiatric groups as well. Further, drugs that inhibit MAO do not generally produce psychosis. Thus, it is probably not sufficient to have low type B MAO to produce schizophrenia. Another simultaneous abnormality must be postulated, whether it be environmentally or genetically induced. Since schizophrenia is a disorder which itself has no obvious survival value in an evolutionary sense, it may be that having low MAO activity without a second abnormality is beneficial in some as yet undescribed manner. In fact, it has long been thought that unaffected relatives of schizophrenics might in some way be more creative than other normals.

A third postulated mechanism for increasing PEA is one we are presently considering. As mentioned previously, heterozygotes for phenylketonuria produce increased amounts of PEA. This is due to a partial deficit in the enzyme phenylalanine hydroxylase. Phenylalanine is therefore metabolized to PEA in greater than normal amounts.

What evidence is there that heterozygotes for phenylketonuria might be prone to schizophrenia? There are conflicting reports that family members of phenylketonurics have a high incidence of psychosis—seemingly a paranoid type. Folling (39) was the first to consider heterozygotes as unusually apt to suffer from psychiatric disorders when he found two relatives of a phenylketonuric patient to be schizophrenic. Penrose (40) also found the incidence of schizophrenia to be increased in a large pedigree of phenyl-ketonurics. Munro (41) found the incidence of psychosis to be twice the expected rate in siblings of phenylketonurics. It is of some interest that these psychotic patients were paranoid (42). Thompson (43) also found a high incidence of nonspecific mental disorders throughout life in families of phenylketonurics.

Blehova et al (44) found a high incidence of mental illness in family members of phenylketonurics. Kuznetsova (45) studied 300 parents of phenylketonurics and found four schizophrenics having a fairly benign course. When a correction for age was made, the frequency was 2.4% against 0.85% in the general population. However, since it was unlikely that severe chronic schizophrenics would have married and had children, a frequency index of a relatively benign form of illness was used for comparison (0.45%). Thus, heterozygotes were thought to have about five times the prevalence of schizophrenia as the general population.

Perry et al (46), Larson and Wyman (47), and Blumenthal (48), using large samples of relatives of phenylketonurics, could not confirm these findings. Blumenthal, however, only examined the parents of phenylketonurics having reasonably successful social adjustments and who might not be expected to be chronic schizophrenics.

Knox (49) at one time estimated that heterozygosity for phenylketonuria would account for 20% of mental illness. He apparently no longer holds this view (50).

There is also one report that schizophrenics might have abnormally high serum phenylalanine. Poisner (51) examined serum phenylalanine concentrations in 40 schizophrenic drug-free patients and 15 controls. The schizophrenics had a mean serum phenylalanine concentration of 2.65 mg% while the controls had one of 1.88 mg%, a statistically significant difference. There was no difference among schizophrenic subgroups.

Lippman (52), using a phenylalanine tolerance test, found 13 out of 50 schizophrenics were in a borderline range for being heterozygotes for phenylketonuria, and he suggested the possibility that the interaction of being heterozygotes for more than one entity might itself produce a disorder.

6. *Tolerance to the agent should not develop.* Unless a substance irreversibly damages the brain to produce schizophrenia, it would have to be continuously present or perhaps present in some cyclic fashion. Since schizophrenia is a disorder that lasts at least a few weeks and in most cases for years, the body would not become completely tolerant to a postulated biochemical substance producing it.

To test whether tolerance develops to PEA in the rat, PEA-induced stereotypy was examined. In rats given PEA (16 mg/kg, IP) in conjunction with the monoamine oxidase inhibitor pargyline (2 mg/kg, IV) three times a day, no tolerance developed in experiments lasting 3 and 7 days; however, longer periods of drug administration are necessary before a conclusion on the development of tolerance can be made.

7. *Neuroleptics must be capable of antagonizing the synthesis, increasing the metabolism, or antagonizing the effect of the agent.* Since neuroleptics are known to decrease, at least partially, schizophrenic symptoms, any proposed models of the disorder must take this into consideration. In rats, the neuroleptics pimozide, clozapine, haloperidol, and chlorpromazine decreased PEA-induced stereotypy. Diazepam, a psychoactive drug that does not alter schizophrenia, did not decrease the stereotypy.

The neuroleptics have been reported to be very efficacious in reversing the amphetamine-induced psychosis as well as blocking amphetamine- and PEA-induced behavioral changes in animals. If paranoid schizophrenia is in fact mimicked by amphetamine psychosis, it might be expected that the paranoid schizophrenic patient would have a good response to neuroleptics.

The question might be asked: How do paranoid compare to nonparanoid schizophrenics in their response to neuroleptics? Table 10-2 shows the results of seven studies using 11 neuroleptics in which the same neuroleptic was given to both paranoid and nonparanoid schizophrenic patients and the response compared between patient groups (53–59). The groupings were determined by either clinical diagnoses or factors distinguished by features of the subdiagnosis on the Brief Psychiatric Rating Scale (BPRS). The study by DeMaio (59) used a small number (10 paranoid and 12 nonparanoid) of patients and found no difference using clozapine. For the most part, the other comparisons showed differences in favor of paranoid patients who improved more than did nonparanoid ones, except in the case of haloperidol (53) which had a slightly greater effect on nonparanoid than paranoid schizophrenics.

These studies are far from conclusive, but they seem to favor the notion that paranoid schizophrenics and paranoid symptomatology respond better to neuroleptics than do nonparanoid patients or nonparanoid symptomatology.

8. *Diets deficient in the precursor should alter behavior of the patients.* We are currently testing this criterion by giving a diet low in phenylalanine to selected patients.

9. *A diet with a high amount of the substance or its precursor should make the illness worse.* Against this criterion is the study of Pollin et al (60). They gave 1-phenylalanine (20 gm/70 kg) with and without iproniazid (50 and 150 mg/70 kg) to chronic

Table 10-2. Preferential Sphere (Paranoid vs. Nonparanoid) of Drug Action by Diagnosis or by BPRS Factors[a]

Study	Drug	Paranoid Schizophrenics Improved More Than Nonparanoid
Hollister et al 1962 (53)	Thiopropazate	Yes
	Haloperidol	Worse
Hollister et al 1965 (54)	Triperidol	Yes
Bishop et al 1965 (55)	Trifluperidol	Yes
	Trifluoperazine	Yes
Hollister et al 1967 (56)	Acetophenazine	Yes
	Perphenazine	Yes
	Benzquinamide	Yes
Overall et al 1969 (57)	Thiothixene	Yes
Goldstein 1970 (58)	Thioridazine	Yes
DeMaio 1972 (59)	Clozapine	No difference

[a] There is no agreement when factors or diagnosis other than paranoid versus nonparanoid are used.

schizophrenic patients for 2 to 3 weeks. In none of these conditions was there a behavioral or mood change in the patients. Iproniazid, however, is a poor monoamine oxidase inhibitor of the "B" form of monoamine oxidase—the form that probably metabolizes PEA.

DISCUSSION

Phenylethylamine (PEA) may well be an endogenous analogue of amphetamine. To date, no serious data have been produced to argue against PEA's involvement in schizophrenia either in general or in patients specifically of a paranoid type. The crucial tests, however, have not been done, but compared to most hypotheses relating a cause to a major psychosis, testing the PEA hypothesis should be relatively easy. If the hypothesis is incorrect, it can be buried easily.

REFERENCES

1. Wyatt RJ, Cantor F, Gillin JC, et al: Ventricular fluid metabolites of phenolic amines and catecholamines, in Usdin E, Sandler M (eds): *Trace Amines in The Brain* Psychopharm Ser. Vol 1, Dekker, 1976.

2. Sandler M, Reynolds GP: Does phenylethylamine cause schizophrenia? *Lancet* 1(7950):70–71, 1976.

3. Hollister LE: *Chemical Psychosis-LSD and Related Drugs.* Springfield Ill, Charles C Thomas, 1968.

4. Hackney IM: Autistic behavior patterns in phenylketonuric children. *Can Psychiatr Assoc J* 12:333–334, 1967.

5. Perry TL, Hansen S, Tischler B, et al: Unrecognized adult phenylketonuria. *N Eng J Med* 289:395–398, 1973.

6. Jepson JB, Lovenberg W, Zaltzman P, et al: Amine metabolism, studied in normal and phenylketonuric humans by monoamine oxidase inhibition. *Proc Biochem Soc* 74:5, 1960.

7. Oates JA, Nirenberg PZ, Jepson JB, et al: Conversion of phenylalanine to phenethylamine in patients with phenylketonuria. *Proc Soc Exp Biol Med* 112:1078–1081, 1963.

8. Levine RJ, Nirenberg PZ, Udenfriend S, et al: Urinary excretion of phenethylamine and tyramine in normal subjects and heterozygous carriers of phenylketonuria. *Life Sci* 3:651–656, 1964.

9. Fischer E, Heller B, Miro AH: β-phenylethylamine in human urine. *Arzneim Forsch* 18:1486, 1968.

10. Boulton AA, Milward L: Separation detection and quantitative analysis of urinary β-phenylethylamine. *J Chromatogr* 57:287–296, 1971.

11. Fischer E, Heller B: Phenethylamine as a neurohumoral agent in brain. *Behav Neuropsychiatry* 4:8–11, 1972.

12. Fischer E, Spatz H, Saavedra JM, et al: Urinary elimination of phenylethylamine. *Biol Psychiatry* 5:139, 1972.

13. Fischer E, Spatz H, Fernandex Labriola RS, et al: Quantitative gas-chromatographic determination and infrared spectrographic identification of urinary phenethylamine. *Biol Psychiatry* 1:161–165, 1973.

14. Schweitzer JW, Friedhoff AJ, Schwartz R: Phenethylamine in normal urine. Failure to verify high values. *Biol Psychiatry* 10:227–286, 1975.

15. Inwang EE, Davis JM, Jones FD, et al: Amine modulation of abstinence syndrome in drug-dependence: Phenylethylamine and catecholamines. *Abstracts of Society of Biological Psychiatry Thirtieth Annual Convention* pp 54–55, 1975.

16. Lovenberg W, Weissbach H, Udenfriend S: Aromatic L-amino acid decarboxylase. *J Biol Chem* 237:89–93, 1962.

17. Wise CD, Baden MM, Stein L: Post-mortem measurements of enzymes in human brain: Evidence of a central noradrenergic deficit in schizophrenia. *J Psychiatr Res* 11:185–198, 1974.

18. Wyatt RJ, Schwartz MA, Erdelyi E, et al: Dopamine-beta-hydroxylase activity in the brains of chronic schizophrenic patients. *Science* 187:368–370, 1975.

19. Wise CD, Stein L: (No title) *Science* 187:370, 1975.

20. Yang HYT, Neff NH: β-phenylethylamine: A specific substrate for type B monoamine oxidase of brain. *J Pharmacol Exp Ther* 187:365–371, 1973.

21. Wyatt RJ, Potkin S, Walls P, et al: Clinical correlates of low platelet MAO in schizophrenic patients, in Kiskill J (ed): *Proceedings of Neuroscience International Symposium, Biological Procedures in Psychiatric Disorders,* to be published.

22. Murphy DL, Wyatt RJ: Reduced monoamine oxidase activity in blood platelets from schizophrenic patients. *Nature* 238:225–226, 1972.

23. Wyatt RJ, Murphy DL, Belmaker R, et al: Reduced monoamine oxidase in platelets: A possible genetic marker for vulnerability to schizophrenia. *Science* 179:916–918, 1973.

24. Shaskan EG, Becker RE: Platelet MAO in schizophrenics. Letter to the Editor. *Nature* 253(5493:659–660, 1974.

25. Friedman E, Shopsin B, Sathananthan G, et al: Blood platelet monoamine oxidase activity in psychiatric patients. *Am J Psychiatry* 131:1392–1394, 1974.

26. Nies A, Robinson DS, Harris LS, et al: Comparisons of monoamine oxidase substrate activity in twins, schizophrenics, depressives, and controls, in Usdin E (ed): *Neuropsychopharmacology of Monoamines and Their Regulatory Enzymes.* New York, Raven Press, 1974, pp 54–70.

27. Meltzer HY, Stahl SM: Platelet monoamine oxidase activity and substrate preferences in schizophrenic patients. *Res Commun Chem Pathol Pharmacol* 7:419–431, 1974.

28. Carpenter WT, Jr, Murphy DL, Wyatt RJ: Platelet monoamine oxidase activity in acute schizophrenia. *Am J Psychiatry* 132:438–441, 1975.

29. Zeller EA, Boshes B, Davis JM, et al: Molecular aberration in platelet monoamine oxidase in schizophrenia. *Lancet* 1:1385, 1975.

30. Bailey AR, Crow TJ, Johnstone EC, et al: Platelet monoamine oxidase activity in patients with chronic schizophrenic illness untreated by neuroleptic drugs. *Br J Pharmacol* 2:280, 1975.

31. Cookson IB, Owen F, Ridger PA: Platelet monoamine oxidase activity during the course of a schizophreniform psychosis. *Psychol Med* 5:314–317, 1975.

32. Wyatt RJ, Murphy DL: Neurotransmitter-related enzymes in the major psychiatric disorders: II MAO and DBH in schizophrenia, in Freedman DX (ed): *The Biology of the Major Psychoses: A Comparative Analysis.* New York, Raven Press, 1975, pp 289–296.

33. Wyatt RJ, Belmaker R, Murphy D: Low platelet monoamine oxidase and vulnerability to schizophrenia, in Mendlewicz J (ed): *Modern Problems of Pharmacopsychiatry: Genetics and Psychopharmacology.* Basel, Switzerland, Karger, 1975, pp 38–57.

34. Murphy D, Belmaker R, Wyatt RJ: Monoamine oxidase in schizophrenia and other behavioral disorders, in Matthysse S, Kety SS (eds): *Enzymes in the Neuropathology of Schizophrenia.* Oxford, Pergamon Press, 1976.

35. Schildkraut JJ, Herzog JM, Orsulak PJ, et al: Reduced platelet monoamine oxidase in a subgroup of schizophrenic patients. *Am J Psychiatry* 133:438–440, 1976.

36. Domino EF, Khanna SS: Decreased blood platelet MAO activity in unmedicated chronic schizophrenic patients. *Am J Psychiatry* 133:323–326, 1976.

37. Murphy DL, Donnelly CH, Miller L, et al: Platelet monoamine oxidase in chronic schizophrenia: Some enzyme characteristics relevant to reduced activity. *Arch Gen Psychiat* 33:1377–1381, 1976.

38. Murphy DL, Weiss R: Reduced monoamine oxidase activity in blood platelets from bipolar depressed patients. *Am J Psychiatry* 128:35–41, 1972.

39. Folling A: Uber ausscheideng von phenylBrenz trauBensaure in den Harn, als stoffwechsel anomalie in verbindung mit Imbezillitat. Hoppe Seyler Z. *Physiol Chem Physics* 227:169–176, 1934.

40. Penrose LS: Inheritance of phenylamentia (phenylketonuria). *Lancet* ii:192–194, 1935.

41. Munro TA: Phenylketonuria: Data on 47 British families. *Ann Eugen* 14:60–88, 1947.

42. Munro TA: Quoted in Pratt RT, Gardner D, Curzon G, et al: Phenylalanine tolerance in endogenous depression. *Br J Psychiatry* 109:624–628, 1957.

43. Thompson JH: Relatives of phenylketonuric patients. *J Ment Defic Res* I:67–78, 1957.

44. Blehova B, Hrubcova M, Bartonova M: Psychicke zateze vrodinach fenylketonuriku. *Cesk Pediatr* 18:701–706, 1963.

45. Kuznetsova LI: Frequency and phenotypic manifestations of schizophrenia in the parents of patients with phenylketonuria. *Sov Genet* 8:554–555, 1974.

46. Perry TL, Tischler B, Chapple JA: The incidence of mental illness in the relatives of individuals suffering from phenylketonuria or mongolism. *J Psychiatr Res* 4:51–57, 1966.

47. Larson CL, Wyman GE: Phenylketonuria: Mental illness in heterozygotes. *Psychiatr Clin* 1:367–374, 1968.

48. Blumenthal MD: Mental illness in parents of phenylketonuric children. *J Psychiatr Res* 5:59–74, 1967.

49. Knox WE: Phenylketonuria, in Stanbury JB, Wyngaarden JB, Fredrickson DS (eds): *The Metabolic Basis of Inherited Disease,* New York, McGraw-Hill, 1960, pp 321–382.

50. Knox WE: Phenylketonuria, in Stanbury JB, Wyngaarden JB, Fredrickson DS (eds): *The Metabolic Basis of Inherited Disease,* ed 3. New York, McGraw-Hill, 1972, pp 266–295.

51. Poisner AM: Serum phenylalanine in schizophrenia: Biochemical genetic aspects. *J Nerv Ment Dis* 131:74–76, 1960.

52. Lippman RW: The significance of heterozygosity for hereditary metabolic errors related to mental deficiency (oligomentia). *Am J Ment Defic* 63:320–324, 1958.

53. Hollister LE, Overall JE, Caffey E, et al: Controlled comparison of haloperidol with thiopropazate in newly admitted schizophrenics. *J Nerv Ment Dis* 135:544–549, 1962.

54. Hollister LE, Overall JE, Bennett JL, et al: Triperidol in newly admitted schizophrenics. *Am J Psychiatry* 122:96–98, 1965.

55. Bishop MP, Gallant DM: Trifluperidol in "paranoid" and "nonparanoid" schizophrenics. *Curr Ther Res* 7:96–101, 1965.

56. Hollister LE, Overall JE, Bennett JL, et al: Specific therapeutic actions of acetophenazine, perphenazine, and benzquinamide in newly admitted schizophrenic patients. *Clin Pharmacol Ther* 8:249–255, 1967.

57. Overall JE, Hollister LE, Shelton J, et al: Broad-spectrum screening of psychotherapeutic drugs: Thiothixene as an antipsychotic and depressant. *Clin Pharmacol Ther* 10:36–43, 1969.

58. Goldstein MJ: Premorbid adjustment, paranoid status, and patterns of response to phenothiazine in acute schizophrenia. *Schizophrenia Bulletin* 1:24–37, 1970.

59. DeMaio D: Clozapine, a novel major tranquilizer. *Arzneim Forsch* 22:919–923, 1972.

60. Pollin W, Cardon PV, Jr, Kety SS: Effects of amino acid feedings in schizophrenic patients treated with iproniazid. *Science* 133:104–105, 1961.

Chapter 11
Biogenic Amine Hypotheses of Schizophrenia

Jack D. Barchas, M.D.
Glen R. Elliott, Ph.D.
Philip A. Berger, M.D.

In recent years, the study of the biochemical and pharmacologic correlates of schizophrenia has yielded an impressive quantity of data. Despite this, the etiology and pathogenesis of schizophrenia are still unknown, and even the mechanisms by which some pharmacologic agents ameliorate schizophrenic symptoms remain obscure. Two major hypotheses have dominated investigations into the biologic substrate of schizophrenia: one suggests that the symptoms of schizophrenia result from the production of an endogenous psychotogen by abnormal methylation, while the other postulates that schizophrenia reflects a functional overactivity of one or more cerebral dopaminergic system.

THE TRANSMETHYLATION HYPOTHESIS OF SCHIZOPHRENIA

Observing that the hallucinogen mescaline is a methylated derivative of the catecholamines and that the synthesis of epinephrine involves an N-methylating enzyme, Osmond and Smythies (1) reasoned that this, or another enzyme, might methylate hydroxyl positions of catecholamines to yield a mescalinelike substance such as dimethoxyphenylethylamine (DMPEA) (Figure 11-1). This was the first suggestion that aberrant methylation of biogenic amines might be of etiologic significance in schizophrenia. Subsequently, the indoleamine 5-hydroxytryptamine (5-HT, serotonin) was also found in mammalian brains (2,3); and methylated indoleamines such as N,N-dimethyltryptamine (DMT), psilocin, psilocybin, and D-lysergic acid diethylamide (LSD-25) were shown to be powerful hallucinogens in man (Figure 11-1). [For a good compendium, see Usdin and Efron (4).] These findings led to an expansion of the original methylation hypothesis of Osmond and Smythies, which Kety (5) has called the "transmethylation" hypothesis of schizophrenia. This hypothesis postulates that schizophrenia arises from the abnormal accumulation of a psychotogenic N- or O-methylated biogenic amine derivative.

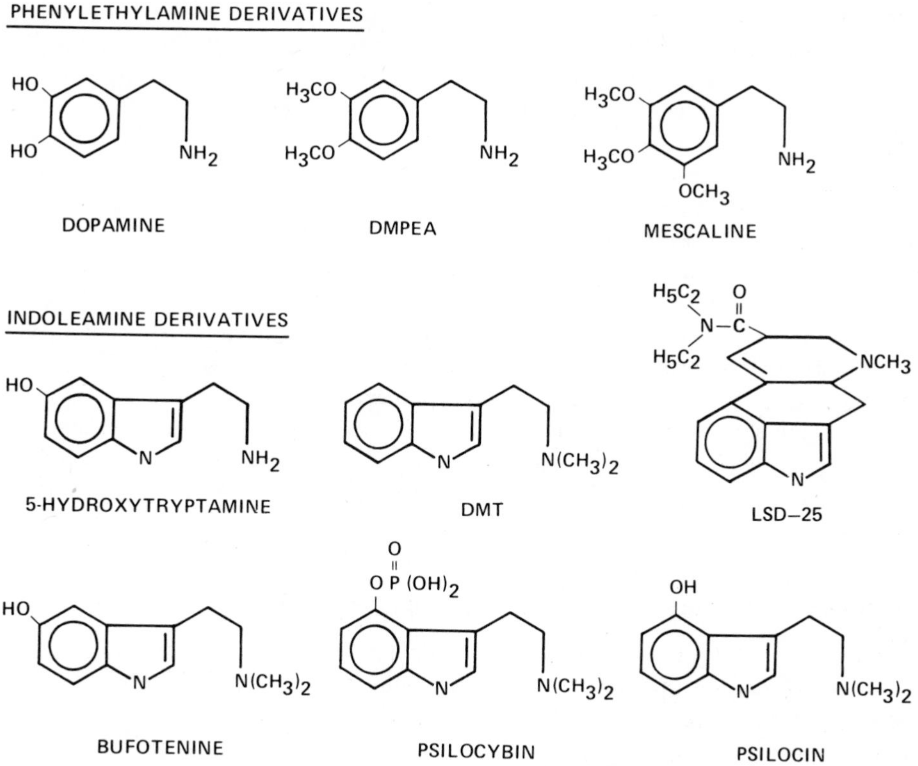

PHENYLETHYLAMINE DERIVATIVES

DOPAMINE   DMPEA   MESCALINE

INDOLEAMINE DERIVATIVES

5-HYDROXYTRYPTAMINE   DMT   LSD–25

BUFOTENINE   PSILOCYBIN   PSILOCIN

Figure 11-1. Compounds that are relevant to the transmethylation hypothesis.

It is convenient to divide the investigations of the transmethylation hypothesis into three types of studies: (a) attempts to identify methylated derivatives of biogenic amines in biological fluids, (b) attempts to alter the production of these methylated derivatives by pharmacological manipulations, and (c) efforts to identify and characterize enzymes that might form such compounds.

Excretion of Methylated Amines

Dimethoxyphenylethylamine (DMPEA)

As mentioned earlier, Osmond and Smythies (1) suggested that DMPEA might be a good candidate for their proposed endogenous psychotogen. In 1962, a compound identified as DMPEA was found in urine from 15 of 19 schizophrenics and none of 14 controls (6). This original report was followed by a large number of contradictory studies that have failed to establish not only whether DMPEA plays a role in schizophrenia but even whether its presence in urine is abnormal. [For a review, see Wyatt et al (7).]

Methylated Indoleamines

The search for methylated derivatives of indoleamines has also met with mixed results. Bufotenine (Figure 11-1) has been demonstrated in the urine of both schizophrenics and normal controls (7), as has DMT (8–10). However, no consistent differences between schizophrenics and controls have been found. Studies of plasma concentrations of methylated indoleamines have been equally inconclusive (7). Still, the recent report by Koslow (11), describing abnormally high concentrations of 5-methoxytryptamine in the CSF of schizophrenic and manic patients, suggests the need for further studies of methylated amines in the biologic fluids of normal subjects and schizophrenics.

It is important to emphasize that the failure of the above studies to identify a methylated amine that is uniquely associated with schizophrenia does not rule out the possibility of its existence. First, the number of possible candidates is enormous, and the list has in no way been studied exhaustively. Studies of many of them must await the development of sensitive and specific assays (10,12,13). Second, the selection of appropriate controls to eliminate unrelated effects of diet, drug treatment, hospitalization, and other factors is both crucial and extremely difficult. Third, it may be necessary to study schizophrenics longitudinally, since changes in excretion patterns might be more important than absolute concentrations (14,15). And finally, even without the above difficulties, it is conceivable that the important changes are occurring in specific cerebral nuclei, so monitoring at distant sites, such as plasma or even CSF, may simply fail to detect the important phenomena.

Attempts to Alter the Production of the Proposed Psychotogen

A second strategy used to evaluate the transmethylation hypothesis has been the attempt to alter schizophrenic symptoms by precursor loading with amino acids. This approach was stimulated by the report that patients receiving a monoamine oxidase (MAO) inhibitor showed an increase in psychotic symptoms when given large oral doses of methionine (16). It was suggested that methionine might be increasing psychotic symptoms by supplying methyl groups for transmethylation reactions. Since this first report, there have been at least 15 other studies on the effects of methionine loading in schizophrenia, summarized in a recent review (17). Despite a wide variety of study populations, drug regimens, and experimental designs, all studies report a deterioration in mental status during methionine loading. However, a controversy exists as to whether this deterioration represents a true increase in schizophrenic symptoms or an additional toxic psychosis. For example, in two reports, it was emphasized that methionine did not produce new symptoms but seemed to increase preexisting schizophrenic symptoms (18,19); yet, two other groups suggested that methionine loading probably induces a superimposed intoxication (20,21). Furthermore, even if schizophrenia is truly exacerbated by methionine loading, it is unclear that the effect is via an increase in methylation. It has been shown, however, that methionine loading increases the concentration of the methyl donor S-adenosylmethionine (SAM) in brain and liver (22). Thus, while the methionine loading studies have produced suggestive results, they neither confirm nor rule out the transmethylation hypothesis.

If, as suggested by the methionine-loading studies, schizophrenia is exacerbated by increasing methylations, then a decrease in methylation reactions might reasonably be expected to produce improvement in schizophrenics. The use of nicotinamide in schizophrenia was based, in part, on its ability to serve as an acceptor of methyl groups. Despite the continued use of this treatment by some physicians, careful studies have failed to find significant improvement in schizophrenic symptoms during nicotinamide administration (23,24). Using a somewhat different approach, another group found that low methionine diet also failed to cause significant improvement in schizophrenia (25).

Like the studies of methylated amines, efforts to alter psychotogen production have met with mixed results. Again, it is difficult to draw definitive conclusions from either the successes or the failures. Just as the excretion studies suffer from possible contamination by processes unrelated to the disease, so too are the loading studies unable to distinguish between specific effects on the systems of interest and general effects produced by large doses of the drugs. A further complication in these studies rests in the characterization of the schizophrenics themselves. As mentioned earlier, it is extremely difficult to differentiate between an increase in schizophrenic symptoms and the addition of symptoms of a toxic psychosis. Furthermore, nondrug variations from day-to-day changes in the behavior of schizophrenics may well be mistaken for the effects of the drug regimen.

Attempts to Identify N-Methylating Enzymes

The third approach to the investigation of the transmethylation hypothesis has entailed identification of enzymes which might methylate biogenic amines. In 1961, Axelrod (26) described an enzyme capable of transferring a methyl group from S-adenosylmethionine (SAM) to several indoleamine substrates (Figure 11-2A). This SAM enzyme, which Axelrod originally isolated from rabbit lung, also has been reported in chicken brain (27) and, recently, from human lung (28), blood (29), and brain (30). In an extensive study, Wyatt et al (29) investigated the activity of the SAM enzyme in red blood cells, plasma, and platelets. In a red-blood-cell preparation, there were no significant differences among normal subjects, chronic schizophrenics, and psychotic depressives. Nor were there differences in plasma activities between acute schizophrenics and age-matched controls. In contrast, platelet preparations from schizophrenics and psychotic depressives had higher activities than did those of normal controls, although this dif-

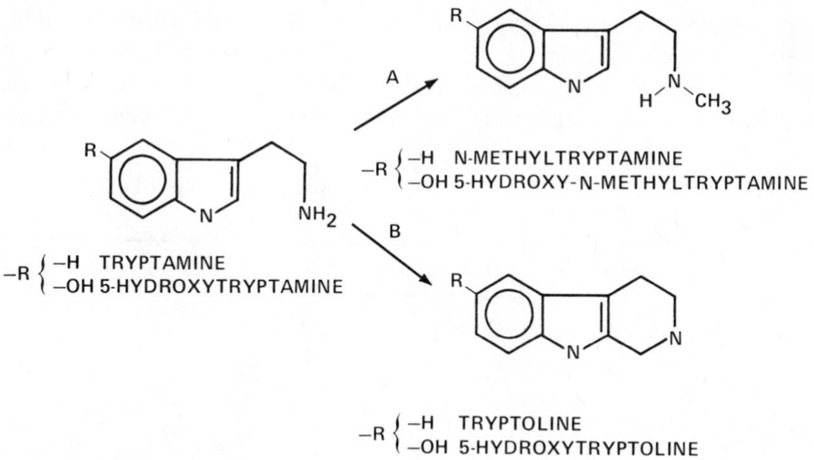

Figure 11-2. SAM- and 5-MTHF-dependent enzymatic reactions with tryptamines. *A.* As described in the text, N-methylation has been demonstrated unambiguously in some in vitro tissue preparations of the SAM-dependent enzymatic system. It has not been shown conclusively for a 5-MTHF-dependent enzymatic system. *B.* As described in the text, tryptoline formation appears to be the major, perhaps sole, reaction for in vitro preparations of the 5-MTHF-dependent enzymatic system. It may also be a significant competing reaction in some SAM-dependent enzymatic preparations.

ference was at least partially dependent on a dialyzable factor in the nonpsychotic group.

In a recent collaboration with Dr. Richard Jed Wyatt, at the National Institute of Mental Health, we undertook a study of SAM-dependent, N-methylating activity in autopsied brain parts of chronic schizophrenics and normal controls. The experimental details of this study are described elsewhere (31), but the general results are presented in Table 11-1. As shown, there were large differences among brain parts, as well as a tendency for schizophrenic values to be higher than normal values. However, there was a large overlap between the two groups. The results are further complicated by uncertainty about the product identification. Although the products of this SAM-dependent reaction have been absolutely identified as methylated tryptamines in some systems (28), there is also evidence suggesting that a competing reaction, illustrated in Figure 11-2B, also can occur (32). Although this latter reaction may well be merely an in vitro artifact in these preparations, the resulting compounds behave sufficiently like methylated tryptamines to interfere in many of the assays used to measure the "methylating" activity. Thus, changes in the actual level of methylating activity might possibly be masked by this competing reaction.

A new dimension was added to studies of N-methyltransferase enzymes by Laduron, who reported that an enzyme from rat brain used 5-methyltetrahydrofolic acid (5-MTHF) as a methyl donor and speculated that it might play a role in schizophrenia (33). This activity was soon confirmed by other investigators (34,35). Wyatt and Barchas were the first to demonstrate this activity in human brain (36) and platelets (37); however, they were unable to confirm that the products were N-methylated derivatives. Although the substrate specificities and the reaction kinetics of these preparations resembled those reported for other tissues, tryptamines yielded products which consistently displayed thin-layer chromatographic characteristics that were different from any of the possible N- or O-methylated derivatives. It was then determined by thin-layer chromatography, co-crystallization, and gas-liquid chromatography/mass spectrometry that methylation was not occurring in this system. Instead, the reaction involved the transfer of a one-carbon unit from 5-MTHF to the tryptamine substrate; this was followed by an intramolecular cyclization to yield a β-carboline which has been

Table 11-1. SAM-Dependent N-Methylating Activity in Autopsied Brain Parts of Controls and Chronic Schizophrenics[a]

	Controls	Schizophrenics
Cerebral cortex		
Orbital	1.06 ± 0.06 (9)	1.21 ± 0.05 (9) [114]
Temporal	1.45 ± 0.09 (7)	1.65 ± 0.14 (10) [114]
Occipital	5.77 ± 0.22 (8)	7.46 ± 0.77 (6) [129]
Amygdala	2.87 ± 0.13 (8)	2.76 ± 0.24 (6) [96]
Septal region	4.12 ± 0.31 (8)	4.42 ± 0.53 (8) [107]
Medial thalamus	1.56 ± 0.19 (9)	1.69 ± 0.19 (8) [108]

[a] Enzyme activities are presented as mean ± SEM and expressed as nmole/hr/g wet weight. Sample size is indicated in parentheses, while activity in schizophrenics as a percent of controls is shown in brackets. By analysis of variance, the differences between chronic schizophrenics and controls are not statistically significant for either enzyme. For additional experimental and analytical detail, see Erdelyi et al (31).

Table 11-2. Platelet Methylene Reductase Activity in Schizophrenic Patients and Control Subjects[a]

	N	Methylene Reductase Activity	
		Mean ± SEM	Range
Nonhospitalized controls	15	0.86 ± 0.12	0.15–1.36
Hospitalized controls	16	0.72 ± 0.13	0.01–1.84
Schizophrenics	18	1.17 ± 0.18	0.05–2.28
All subjects	49	0.93 ± 0.09	0.01–2.28

[a] Activities are expressed as nmole/hr/mg protein. There were no significant differences between schizophrenics and either hospitalized or nonhospitalized controls. For additional details, see Berger et al (52).

called a tryptoline (36,37) (Figure 11-2B). Similar results have been obtained with enzymatic preparations from other species and organs (38-40).

The physiologic significance of this 5-MTHF-dependent reaction is, as yet, unclear. Several investigators suggested that the enzymatic reaction might be limited to the production of free formaldehyde from the labile carbon unit on 5-MTHF, followed by a nonenzymatic reaction of formaldehyde with the tryptamines (36,41). This mechanism received considerable support with the demonstration by Taylor and Hanna (42) that the "tryptoline-forming" enzyme is indistinguishable from $N^{5,10}$-methylenetetrahydrafolate reductase (methylene reductase), the enzyme that converts 5,10-methylenetetrahydrofolic acid to 5-MTHF. Under in vitro conditions of high 5-MTHF concentrations, the reaction will proceed in the reverse direction, with subsequent release of free formaldehyde (43). Tryptoline formation also has been associated with methylene reductase activity in preparations from rat (44), pig (45), and man (46).

The studies just mentioned are consistent with the conclusion that the apparently enzymatic synthesis of tryptolines is strictly an in vitro artifact resulting from the formation of formaldehyde by the action of methylene reductase on excess 5-MTHF. Studies of partially purified preparations of the reductase enzyme suggest that, normally, enzyme kinetics and in vivo substrate concentrations would not favor this reverse reaction (47). Despite this, the system should not be lightly dismissed. Methylene reductase appears to function, in part, to prevent the build-up of 5,10-methylenetetrahydrofolate, which can be formed in several ways—among them, a reversible condensation of formaldehyde and tetrahydrofolic acid (48). Perhaps, therefore, subnormal methylene reductase activity could result in an elevation of tissue formaldehyde concentrations which might, in turn, induce nonenzymatic tryptoline formation (49).

In this regard, it is interesting to note that Mudd and Freeman (50,51) recently have described a patient with "schizophreniclike" symptoms. Not only was the methylene reductase activity in this patient far below normal, but the "schizophrenic" symptoms were markedly relieved by daily administration of folic acid.

Since methylene reductase activity had not been studied in schizophrenics, we decided to explore the possibility that this enzyme might be abnormal in such individuals. Table 11-2 presents data from a study of platelet methylene reductase activity in chronic schizophrenics and in hospitalized and nonhospitalized controls. All subjects were males, and the three groups were age-matched. As reported elsewhere (52), there were no signifi-

Table 11-3. Methylene Reductase Activity in Autopsied Brain Parts of Controls and Chronic Schizophrenics[a]

	Controls	Schizophrenics
Cerebral cortex		
Orbital	52.8 ± 6.06 (9)	37.6 ± 5.32 (9) [71]
Temporal	42.4 ± 7.73 (7)	27.2 ± 3.49 (10) [64]
Occipital	42.2 ± 4.68 (8)	24.6 ± 5.26 (6) [58]
Amygdala	52.5 ± 9.52 (8)	33.9 ± 5.17 (6) [65]
Septal region	41.4 ± 6.05 (8)	34.1 ± 5.24 (8) [82]
Medial thalamus	24.4 ± 3.87 (9)	15.4 ± 1.52 (8) [63]

[a] Enzyme activities are presented as mean ± SEM and expressed as nmole/hr/g wet weight. Number of samples are indicated in parentheses, while activity in schizophrenics as a percent of controls is shown in brackets. None of the schizophrenic activities was statistically different from control activities for any brain part. For additional experimental and analytical detail, see Barchas et al (53).

cant differences among the groups, although there was a small but significant correlation between age and methylene reductase activity (r = −0.31).

To rule out the possibility that changes in methylene reductase might be limited to the brain, we also examined the activity in autopsied brain parts, as part of the study mentioned earlier. These results are presented in Table 11-3 and will be published in full elsewhere (46,53). Again, we failed to find any significant differences between controls and schizophrenics. Schizophrenic activities averaged 58–82% of controls, depending on the brain region, but the standard errors for both groups were high. In addition, animal studies of the effects of delay between death and autopsy suggest that reductase activity drops fairly rapidly at room temperature. Schizophrenics had considerably longer delays to autopsy than did controls, offering a possible explanation for the depressed values (46,53).

Thus, this third approach to the investigation of the transmethylation hypothesis also has failed to provide any firm conclusions. Although the SAM-dependent enzyme is presently the only one known to N-methylate indoleamines, it is quite possible that other such enzymes exist. The recent discovery by Mandel (54) of a drug that can inhibit the SAM enzyme in vivo may provide an important means of examining what role, if any, this system has in schizophrenia. However, such investigations will depend on either the use of an appropriate animal model or the approval of the drug for human studies, both of which are presently problematic.

Current Status of the Transmethylation Hypothesis

More than 20 years after the transmethylation hypothesis was first expounded, no conclusions about its relevance to or involvement in schizophrenia can be drawn. Although a variety of methylated biogenic amines continue to be viable candidates for the endogenous psychotogen, none have been shown to occur only in schizophrenics or even to exist in relatively high concentration in schizophrenics alone. As Kety (5) observed a decade ago, however, the transmethylation hypothesis transcends studies of individual substances. This represents both a strength and a weakness. Although the theory remains viable, its utility as a focus for research is greatly limited by its inability to define more explicitly the substance or substances of potential interest.

THE DOPAMINE HYPOTHESIS OF SCHIZOPHRENIA

Dopaminergic systems have become a focus for much of the recent thinking about psychotic disorders, as has been carefully and thoughtfully presented by other authors in this section. While it is obvious that the dopamine hypothesis has generated a tremendous amount of exciting and important research, it continues to lack direct supporting evidence. The hypothesis rests primarily on the ability of known antipsychotic agents to inhibit dopamine (DA) activity. Marthe Vogt (55) has made an important analogy between current efforts to elucidate the biochemical basis of schizophrenia and earlier studies of Parkinson's disease. She noted that the earliest treatments of Parkinson's disease appeared to work by counteracting a hyperactive cholinergic system. Yet, subsequent studies have shown that this apparent excess of cholinergic activity arises from a severe dopaminergic deficiency. Might not a similar condition hold for DA in schizophrenia? For example, in this section, Drs. Snyder and Davis have noted that amphetamine exacerbates the symptoms of active schizophrenics but does not initiate a psychotic episode in a schizophrenic in remission. Is it possible that DA is involved in a potential compensatory system and thus works only in the presence of the underlying defect? Naturally, answers to these questions must await an extensive expansion of our knowledge about the functions of dopaminergic systems and about the overall changes that occur in cerebral function of schizophrenics.

Amphetamine Effects on Central Dopamine

The evidence implicating DA in amphetamine action is particularly varied. One important argument was introduced by Snyder in 1972 and relies on a pharmacologic difference between the D- and L-stereoisomers of amphetamine. In vitro studies on striatal synaptosomes indicated that they had nearly equal affinities for DA synaptosomes, but the D-form had a much greater affinity for norepinephrine (NE) synaptosomes (56). Clinical reports that D- and L-amphetamine were approximately equipotent in inducing psychosis (57) or worsening schizophrenic symptoms (58) led Snyder (56) to suggest that the amphetamines were acting through DA. Although elegant, this hypothesis has not been confirmed. It is not clear how the synaptosomal affinity of amphetamines correlates with their pharmacologic actions. Even if such a correlation were found, several investigators have been unable to confirm the reported asymmetry between the amphetamine stereoisomers (59-61). Still, DA remains a good candidate as a mediator of some of the actions of amphetamine. Certainly the recent demonstration that antipsychotics show a strong correlation between their inhibition of haloperidol binding and their effects on amphetamine- and apomorphine-induced behavioral syndromes suggests that this system may be involved (62). However, parallel effects on NE and on other neuronal transmitters and modulators remain to be examined.

Biochemical and Metabolic Studies of the Dopamine Hypothesis

Although the pharmacologic studies just described lend strong support to the conclusion that antipsychotics work through a central dopaminergic system, the evidence that schizophrenia results from a defect in that system is much weaker. As with the transmethylation hypothesis, investigators have employed a variety of approaches aimed at uncovering a defect in a DA system. Earlier in this section, Dr. Sachar discussed efforts to assess central DA activity indirectly through its effects on other systems such as

Table 11-4. Catecholamine Systems in Controls and Chronic Schizophrenics[a]

	Controls	Schizophrenics	
Tyrosine hydroxylase			
Head caudate	9.75 ± 3.39 (8)	5.88 ± 1.65 (10)	[60]
Putamen	7.48 ± 1.48 (8)	5.49 ± 1.69 (10)	[73]
Substantia nigra	5.32 ± 1.17 (9)	4.77 ± 1.24 (9)	[89]
Globus pallidus	3.44 ± 1.18 (9)	2.82 ± 1.14 (10)	[82]
DOPA decarboxylase			
Head caudate	9.50 ± 4.15 (8)	2.20 ± 0.84 (10)	[23]
Putamen	8.92 ± 2.62 (8)	5.72 ± 2.24 (10)	[64]
Substantia nigra	2.46 ± 0.99 (9)	2.17 ± 1.31 (9)	[88]
Globus pallidus	3.43 ± 1.44 (8)	1.61 ± 0.68 (9)	[47]
Dopamine-β-hydroxylase			
Hippocampus	41.2 ± 2.66 (9)	35.5 ± 2.31 (9)	[86]
Hypothalamus	140.8 ± 26.8 (9)	118.3 ± 23.5 (9)	[88]
Pons	77.3 ± 19.5 (9)	65.0 ± 14.3 (9)	[84]
Phenylethanolamine N-methyltransferase			
Hypothalamus	0.49 ± 0.10 (7)	0.37 ± 0.06 (10)	[76]
Catechol-O-methyltransferase			
Parietal cortex	9.61 ± 1.12 (9)	6.60 ± 1.73 (8)	[67]
Putamen	1.50 ± 0.43 (8)	1.17 ± 0.54 (10)	[78]
Pons	10.46 ± 2.76 (8)	7.96 ± 1.90 (10)	[76]
Dopamine-β-hydroxylase Inhibitor[b]			
Hippocampus	52.0 ± 7.2 (5)	45.0 ± 10.0 (5)	[86]
Hypothalamus	58.0 ± 3.9 (7)	61.0 ± 3.8 (10)	[105]

[a] Enzyme activities are expressed as mean ± SEM of substrate converted (nmole/hr/g wet weight). Sample size is indicated in parentheses, while activity in schizophrenics as a percent of control is shown in brackets. None of the activities in schizophrenics differed significantly from control activities for any parameter or brain region using two-tailed t-test. For additional experimental and analytical details, see Wyatt et al (88).

[b] Activity is expressed as percent inhibition of pure bovine adrenal medullary dopamine-β-hydroxylase.

prolactin. Two somewhat more direct attempts to monitor DA activity have involved measurement of the DA metabolite homovanillic acid (HVA) in CSF and our own investigations of activities of catecholamine enzymes obtained from autopsied brains of schizophrenics.

Measurement of HVA in CSF
To date, measurement of HVA in the spinal fluid of schizophrenics has failed to reveal differences from control values (63). It is possible that turnover, rather than absolute levels, is the important parameter. Probenecid has been used in some CSF studies to

prevent the migration of acid metabolites (64). In the only available study of HVA accumulation after probenecid, no differences between normals and unmedicated, acute schizophrenics could be detected (65). Further studies using the probenecid technique are indicated.

Since antipsychotic medications cause an acceleration of DA turnover in animals (66,67), they might be expected to increase HVA levels in human CSF. This could be an important indication that they are acting through DA systems. Sedvall has shown that, in some schizophrenic patients on antipsychotic medication, HVA is elevated in the CSF (68). This suggests that it will be interesting to determine the relationship between increases in HVA and clinical response to antipsychotic medication.

Measurement of Catecholamine Enzymes

An important aspect of our postmortem studies of schizophrenic brains, which have already been mentioned, entailed a careful examination of enzymes that are involved in the synthesis and degradation of the catecholamines. The results shown in Table 11-4 have been abstracted from the full report (69). As with methylene reductase, these enzymes generally appear to be somewhat less active in preparations from schizophrenic tissues than in those from controls. This may, again, reflect differences in ages, drug treatment, and autopsy status. To date, our data fail to reveal any consistent differences between schizophrenic and normal brains (53). In contrast to our own work, Stein and Wise have reported differences in dopamine-β-hydroxylase, which they relate to a possible defect in the noradrenergic reward system in schizophrenics (70). These discrepancies might arise from our selection of subjects, from differences in experimental detail, or from deterioration of active processes that cease at death. They might also result from a failure to monitor some critical aspect of the regulatory process, so any changes that are found are only coincidental. Alternatively, this system may not be central to the disease state, i.e., the observed variability may arise from compensatory changes induced by antipsychotic medications. Each of these possibilities will require considerably more study before its impact on the schizophrenic state can be assessed.

MONOAMINE OXIDASE IN SCHIZOPHRENIA

One enzyme for which possible involvement in schizophrenia has received particular attention has been monoamine oxidase (MAO). MAO has a major role in the metabolic degradation of synthetic and natural monoamines, including 5-HT, NE, and DA, and it may play a role in the regulation of the intracellular storage of amines (71). The importance of altered MAO activity to psychiatric disorders was first suggested by the antidepressant activity of the wide variety of medications that inhibit this enzyme (72).

The enzyme MAO is found in many human tissues. It is primarily a constituent of mitochondria, including the mitochondria isolated from synaptosomes (73). Recently, several groups of investigators, using different methods, have suggested that MAO may exist in multiple forms, with each form having different substrate and inhibitor specificities (74–76). The relative proportion of these multiple forms of MAO vary in different tissues. The exact role and relative importance of each of the multiple forms of MAO in psychiologic and pathologic states should be an exciting area for future research.

It has been suggested that human platelet MAO has characteristics in common with other MAOs, including those found in brain (77). In recent investigations by Murphy and Wyatt, a reduction in platelet MAO activities in some chronic schizophrenics has been found (78). These results have been confirmed by other groups of investigators (79–81). The decrease in platelet MAO activity does not seem to be a result either of chronic hospitalization or of antipsychotic medication. However, other studies have failed to find decreased platelet MAO activity in schizophrenic patients (82–84). Preliminary investigations have also failed to reveal any significant differences between the MAO activity in the postmortem brains of schizophrenics and controls (85,86).

These inconsistent results, like other inconsistencies in research findings with schizophrenics, might be explained by the presence of distinct subgroups of schizophrenic patients. Thus, patients with acute schizophrenia have been found to have normal platelet MAO activity (87). In addition, it recently has been reported that patients with auditory hallucinations have reduced platelet MAO activity, while schizophrenics without auditory hallucinations do not have reduced enzyme activity (80). Furthermore, studies on monozygotic twins discordant for schizophrenia suggest that reduced platelet MAO activity may correlate with a genetically determined vulnerability to schizophrenia, rather than to the actual presence of schizophrenic symptoms (87). The issue is further complicated by the finding that some patients with bipolar depression also have reduced platelet MAO activity (88). Clearly, further studies of platelet MAO activity in schizophrenic patients are necessary. In these studies, it will be important to control experimental conditions carefully. Diet, medications, and circulating hormones may all influence platelet MAO activity. Various substrates for MAO also must be used in the assessment of MAO activity, since it has been reported that platelet MAO activity is lower in some schizophrenics than in controls when tyramine and m-iodobenzylamine, but not tryptamine or octopamine, are used as substrates (79). It is possible that these differences reflect alterations in the active site of the enzyme (89).

Even if the finding of reduced platelet MAO activity in a subgroup of schizophrenic patients can be confirmed, its relationship to the pathogenesis of schizophrenia is unclear. For example, a reduction in MAO activity is consistent with nearly every hypothesis of schizophrenia which invokes a relative abundance of a biogenic amine. While it may produce a relative excess of dopamine, it might also contribute to an increase in methylated tryptamines. Furthermore, as Dr. Wyatt explained earlier in this section, low MAO activity should also contribute to the excessive production of phenylethylamine, another possible endogenous psychotogen. Thus, even if MAO activity is found to be altered in schizophrenia, it also will be necessary to establish what changes this defect actually induces in biogenic amine metabolism.

DIRECTIONS FOR FUTURE RESEARCH

In evaluating our understanding of the biologic substrates of schizophrenia, it is important not only to examine where we have been but also to ask where we are—or, perhaps, should be—going. Clearly, both the transmethylation and the dopamine hypotheses of schizophrenia have provided direction and purpose for important investigations into the biochemistry of schizophrenia. Just as clearly, they have not led to a complete understanding either of the etiologic factors that predispose toward schizophrenia or of the exact mechanisms that produce the psychotic state. Thus, although there is good reason to believe that dopaminergic systems are involved in some aspect of schizophrenia, there is, to date, no direct evidence for a defect in these systems in schizophrenics. Successful investigation of a complex disease process must entail a variety of independent but linked thrusts, ranging from basic biochemical to clinical. It seems useful, therefore, to review briefly some approaches that may be particularly essential for the elucidation of the etiology of schizophrenia.

Basic Biochemistry of Neuroregulators

In the last decade, we have made tremendous progress in unraveling the regulator mechanisms by which normal neuronal activity is controlled. Much of this work has concentrated on the regulation of neurotransmitter activity ranging from studies of the control of synthesizing rate through multicellular neuronal feedback loops. Furthermore, scientists have become increasingly aware of an expanding list of compounds that appear to act as neuromodulators, affecting the neuronal system indirectly by altering the synaptic state and, thus, changing its response pattern to incoming signals. In addition, evidence is accumulating that many of these parameters are strongly affected by genetic factors, in accord with the findings of many studies of a genetic component to schizophrenia. As our understanding of the normal role of the various neuroregulators improves, we can apply the information to a finer inspection of these systems in schizophrenics. We can look not only at enzyme activities but also at the activating mechanism for these enzymes. We can study as well the postsynaptic sites, such as receptors. Only a clear understanding of these other regulatory steps will allow us to formulate useful approaches to evaluating them in schizophrenics.

Interactions of Neuroregulatory Systems

One important concept that has arisen from our expanding awareness of the number and variety of neuroregulators involves the potential for parallel or balancing systems. Earlier, we mentioned that studies of patients with Parkinson's disease suggest a balance between dopaminergic and cholinergic systems. Earlier in this section, Dr. Davis has reviewed the evidence for an analogous balance hypothesis of schizophrenia. A balance hypothesis relating alteration of serotonergic systems with a relative increase of dopaminergic function is also possible. Complete evaluation of these hypotheses must await further clarification of the mechanisms controlling neuroregulator activity and will require an array of highly specific pharmacologic and physiologic tools with which to disrupt specific cerebral systems. The exciting work of the fluorescence histochemists and immunocytochemists is providing precise information about anatomic pathways of specific neuroregulator systems. As we begin to establish the physiologic significance of these pathways, it should be possible to determine what compensatory or parallel changes occur with their specific disruption.

Application of these techniques should greatly improve our understanding of the location and nature of the defects in schizophrenia. For example, the DA-ACh balance hypothesis suggests that changes in either of these systems should affect the psychotic state. Thus, Dr. Davis has already described experiments in which physostigmine, a cholinesterase inhibitor, reversed the amphetamine-induced exacerbation of psychotic symptoms. Delineation of the biochemical and physiologic systems responsible for this interesting phenomenon might provide valuable information about the disease process. Are changes in the dopaminergic systems of schizophrenics being masked by simultaneous changes in the cholinergic system? Would such changes be detected in investigations of acetylcholine (ACh) turnover or of the activities of enzymes involved in this system? What effects do the antipsychotics have on cholinergic activity, and do they act directly or through their effects on DA activity? These questions, along with analogous ones springing from other balance hypotheses, should provide a rich and fruitful area for future research efforts.

Interactions Between Neuroregulators and Behavior

Recently, there have been tremendous improvements in the technologies for obtaining samples from brain and for measuring small amounts of compounds which may be of interest. As an exciting outcome of these advances, investigators are now able to monitor cerebral function in conscious, behaving animals over long periods of time. Such experimental models may well prove to be a rich source of new information. For example, it is well known that schizophrenics handle stress badly and that, in animals, stress induces a number of changes in hormonal and neuroregulatory systems. Careful study of the time-course and sequence of these changes may yield important insight into ways in which stress produces its effects in schizophrenia.

It will also be important to apply these techniques to our studies of animal models of schizophrenia. To date, the inherently greater flexibility of monitoring cerebral function in animals is counterbalanced by uncertainty about the relevance of a particular animal model to schizophrenia, which appears to be a peculiarly human disorder. Thus, advances in this field depend on more than highly sophisticated biochemical measures: without a comparably sophisticated means of assessing the relevance of the model we are using, interpretation of the data becomes impossible. Thus, full realization of the potential utility of precise assessment of cerebral function must await parallel advances in the development of a good animal model of schizophrenia.

Clinical Aspects

Delineation of the biochemistry of schizophrenia also will depend on progress in investigations of its behavioral and psychological aspects. Clear examples of the importance of these dimensions of the problem are provided in other sections of this volume. Lacking a unique biochemical or behavioral marker for schizophrenia, we continue to rely on a variety of clinical manifestations to define the disorder. These manifestations have been classified in shifting arrays of subtypes which sometimes provide research leads, but at other times tend more to confuse than to clarify the study of biochemical correlates. Also, the biochemical inconsistencies associated with clinical changes over time remain to be examined. The careful work by Dr. Manfred Bleuler and others, following the clinical course of schizophrenics over long time periods, should greatly enhance our understanding of meaningful stages of the disease process.

Another area of great interest has been the attention to precise assessment of a variety of psychologic, sociologic, and physiologic parameters of schizophrenics and normal subjects. Such measures may enable us to focus more precisely on the essential features of schizophrenia so animal models and biochemical investigations may be designed accordingly. In addition, an understanding of characteristic deficits in schizophrenia may suggest additional therapeutic measures for those individuals who suffer from it.

CONCLUSION

It is encouraging that investigators have approached the Second Rochester International Conference on Schizophrenia, as reported in this volume, with such tremendous enthusiasm, not because we have the answers but, rather, because we have obtained enormous impetus toward obtaining them. Obviously, the common goal is to treat and, if possible, to prevent this extremely crippling disorder. Faced with an almost overwhelmingly complex disorder, we can only profit from opportunities such as these to evaluate carefully the current status of our own areas and to assess thoughtfully the potential impact of progress in others.

REFERENCES

1. Osmond H, Smythies J: Schizophrenia: a new approach. *J Ment Sci* 98:309–315, 1952.

2. Twarog BM, Page IH: Serotonin content of some mammalian tissues and urine and a method for its determination. *Am J Physiol* 175:157–161, 1953.

3. Amin HH, Crawford TBB, Gaddum JH: The distribution of substance P and 5-hydroxytryptamine in the central nervous system of the dog. *J Physiol (Lond)* 126:546–618, 1954.

4. Usdin E, Efron D (eds): *Psychotropic Drugs and Related Compounds,* ed 2. DHEW Publ No 72-9074. Washington, DC, US Government Printing Office, 1972.

5. Kety SS: Summary. The hypothetical relationships between amines and mental illness; a critical synthesis, Himwich HE, Kety SS, Smythies JR (eds): *Amines and Schizophrenia.* Oxford, Pergamon, 1967, pp 271–277.

6. Friedhoff AJ, Van Winkle E: The characteristics of an amine found in the urine of schizophrenic patients. *J Nerv Ment Dis* 135:550–555, 1962.

7. Wyatt RJ, Termini BA, Davis J: Biochemical and sleep studies of schizophrenia: a review of the literature—1960–1970. *Schizophrenia Bull* 4:10–66, 1971.

8. Narasimhachari N, Himwich HE: Gas chromatographic-mass spectrometric identification of N:N-dimethyltryptamine in urine samples from drug-free schizophrenic patients and its quantitation by the technique of single (selective) ion monitoring. *Biochem Biophys Res Comm* 55:1064–1071, 1973.

9. Mandel LR: Dimethyltryptamine: its biosynthesis and possible role in mental disease. *Psychopharmacol Bull* 10:55–56, 1974.

10. Wyatt RJ, Mandel LR, Ahn HS, et al: Gas chromatographic-mass spectrometric isotope dilution determination of N,N-dimethyltryptamine concentrations in normals and psychiatric patients. *Psychopharmacologia* 31:265–270, 1973.

11. Koslow S: N- and O-methylated tryptamines, in Usdin E, Hamburg DA, Barchas JD (eds): *Neuroregulators and Psychiatric Disorders.* Oxford, Oxford University Press, 1977, pp 210–219.

12. Creveling CR, Daly JW: Identification of 3,4-dimethoxyphenylethylamine from schizophrenia by mass spectrometry. *Nature* 216:190–191, 1967.

13. Barchas JD, Elliott GR, DoAmaral JR: Neurosciences applications of mass spectrometry. *Finnigan Spectra* 5:1–3, 1975.

14. Narasimhachari N, Plant J, Himwich HE: 3-4-Dimethoxyphenylethylamine, a normal or abnormal metabolite. *J Psychiatr Res* 9:325–328, 1972.

15. Braun G, Kalbhen DA, Müller J, et al: Nachweis und Bedeutung der intermittierenden Ausscheidung von 3,4-Dimethoxyphenyläthylamin (DMPEA) in Harn von Patienten mit akuter Schizophrenie. *Arch Psychiatr Nervenkr* 218:195–210, 1974.

16. Pollin W, Cardon PV, Kety SS: Effects of amino acid feeding in schizophrenic patients treated with iproniazid. *Science* 133:104–105, 1961.

17. Cohen SM, Nichols A, Wyatt R, et al: The administration of methionine to chronic schizophrenic patients: a review of ten studies. *Biol Psychiatr* 8:209–225, 1974.

18. Park LC, Baldessarini RJ, Kety SS: Methionine effects on chronic schizophrenics: patients treated with monoamine oxidase inhibitors. *Arch Gen Psychiatry* 12:346–351, 1965.

19. Berlet HH, Matsumoto K, Pscheidt GR, et al: Biochemical correlates of behavior in schizophrenic patients. *Arch Gen Psychiatry* 13:521–531, 1965.

20. Alexander F, Curtis GC III, Sprince H, et al: L-methionine and l-tryptophan feedings in nonpsychotic and schizophrenic patients with and without tranylcypromine. *J Nerv Ment Dis* 137:135–142, 1963.

21. Kakimoto Y, Sano I, Kanazawa A, et al: Metabolic effects of methionine loading in schizophrenic patients pretreated with a monoamine oxidase inhibitor. *Nature* 216:1110–1111, 1967.

22. Baldessarini RJ: Biological transmethylation involving S-adenosylmethionine: development of assay methods and implications for neuropsychiatry. *Int J Neurobiol* 18:41–67, 1975.

23. Meltzer H, Shader R, Grinspoon L: The behavioral effects of nicotinamide adenine dinucleotide in chronic schizophrenia. *Psychopharmacologia* 15:144–152, 1969.

24. Kline MS: Controlled evaluation of nicotinamide adenine dinucleotide in the treatment of chronic schizophrenic patients. *Brit J Psychiatr* 113:731–742, 1967.

25. Pscheidt GR, Berlet HH, Spaide J, et al: Variations of urinary creatinine and its correlation to secretion of indole metabolites in mental patients. *Clin Chim Acta* 13:229–334, 1961.

26. Axelrod J: Enzymatic formation of psychotomimetic metabolites from normally occurring metabolites. *Science* 124:343–344, 1961.

27. Morgan M, Mandell AJ: Indole(ethyl)amine N-methyltransferase in the brain. *Science* 165:492–493, 1969.

28. Mandel L, Ahn HS, VandenHeuval WJA, et al: Indoleamine-N-methyltransferase in human lung. *Biochem Pharmacol* 21:1197–1206, 1972.

29. Wyatt RJ, Saavedra JM, Axelrod, J: A dimethyltryptamine forming enzyme in human blood. *Amer J Psychiatr* 130:754–760, 1973.

30. Mandell AJ, Morgan M: Indole(ethyl)amine-N-methyltransferase in human brain. *Nature New Biol* 230:85–87, 1971.

31. Erdelyi E, Elliott GR, Wyatt RJ, et al: S-Adenosylmethionine-dependent N-methyltransferase activity in autopsied brain parts of chronic schizophrenics and controls, submitted.

32. Meller E, Rosengarten H, Friedhoff AJ: Conversion of C^{14}-S-adenosylmethionine to C^{14}-formaldehyde and condensation with indoleamines: a side reaction in N-methyl-transferase assay in blood. *Life Sci* 14:2167–2178, 1974.

33. Laduron P: N-methylation of dopamine to epinine in brain tissue using N-methyltetrahydrofolic acid as a methyl donor. *Nature New Biol* 238:212–213, 1972.

34. Hsu LL, Mandell AJ: Multiple N-methyltransferases for aromatic alkyl amines in brain. *Adv Biochem Psychopharmacol* 11:75–84, 1974.

35. Banerjee SP, Snyder SH: N-methyltetrahydrofolic acid: the physiological methyl donor in indoleamine N- and O-methylation. *Adv Biochem Psychopharmacol* 11:85–93, 1974.

36. Wyatt RJ, Erdelyi E, DoAmaral JR, et al: Tryptoline formation by a preparation from brain with 5-methyltetrahydrofolic acid and tryptamine. *Science* 187:853–855, 1975.

37. Barchas JD, Elliott GR, DoAmaral J, et al: Tryptolines: formation from tryptamine and 5-MTHF by human platelets. *Arch Gen Psychiatry* 31:862–867, 1974.

38. Mandel LR, Rosegay A, Walker RW, et al: 5-Methyltetrahydrofolic acid as a mediator in the formation of pyridoindoles. *Science* 186:741–743, 1974.

39. Hsu LL, Mandell AJ: Enzymatic formation of tetrahydro-β-carboline from tryptamine and 5-methyl-tetrahydrofolic acid in rat brain fractions: regional and subcellular distribution. *J Neurochem* 24:631–636, 1975.

40. Laduron P, Leysen J: Enzymatic formaldehyde production from 5-methyltetrahydrofolic acid: prior step to alkaloid formation. *Biochem Pharmacol* 24:929–952, 1975.

41. Meller E, Rosengarten H, Friedhoff AJ, et al: 5-Methyltetrahydrofolic acid is not a methyl donor for biogenic amines: enzymatic formation of formaldehyde. *Science* 187:171–173, 1975.

42. Taylor RT, Hanna ML: 5-Methyltetrahydrofolate aromatic alkylamine N-methyltransferase: an arte-fact of 5,10-methylenetetrahydrofolate reductase activity. *Life Sci* 17:111–112, 1975.

43. Donaldson KO, Keresztesy JC: Further evidence on the nature of prefolic A. *Biochem Biophys Res Comm* 5:289–292, 1961.

44. Ordonez LA, Caraballo J: Methylene reductase: responsible for the in vitro formation of formaldehyde from 5-methyltetrahydrofolic acid. *Psychopharmacol Comm* 1:253–260, 1975.

45. Pearson AGM, Turner AJ: Folate-dependent l-carbon transfer to biogenic amines mediated by methylenetetrahydrofolate reductase. *Nature* 258:173–174, 1975.

46. Sutherland K, Erdelyi E, Elliott, GR., et al: $N^{5,10}$-Methylenetetrahydro-reductase activity in autopsied brain parts of chronic schizophrenics and controls and in vitro tryptoline formation, submitted.

47. Kutzbach C, Stokstad ELR: Mammalian methylenetetrahydrofolate reductase. Partial purification, properties, and inhibition by S-adenosylmethionine. *Biochem Biophys Acta* 250:459–461, 1971.

48. Blakely RL: *The Biochemistry of Folic Acid and Related Pteridines.* Amsterdam, North Holland Publishing Company, 1969.

49. Elliott GR, Holman RB: Tryptolines as potential modulators of serotonergic function, in Usdin E, Hamburg DA, Barchas JD (eds) *Neuroregulators and Psychiatric Disorders.* Oxford, Oxford University Press, 1977, pp 220–228.

50. Mudd SH, Freeman JM: $N^{5,10}$-methylenetetrahydrofolate reductase deficiency and schizophrenia: a working hypothesis. *J Psychiatr Res* 11:259–262, 1974.

51. Freeman JM, Finkelstein JD, Mudd SH: Folate-responsive homocystinurea and "schizophrenia". A defect in methylation due to deficient 5,10-methylenetetrahydrofolate reductase activity. *N Engl J Med* 292:491–496, 1975.

52. Berger PA, Elliott GR, Erdelyi E, et al: Platelet methylene reductase activity in schizophrenia. *Arch. Gen. Psychiatry* 34:808–809, 1977.

53. Barchas JD, Berger PA, Elliott GR, et al: Studies of enzymes involved in biogenic amine metabolism in schizophrenia, in Usdin E Weiner N (eds) *Biochemistry and Function of Monoamine Enzymes.* New York, Marcel Dekker, in press.

54. Mandel LR: Inhibition of indoleamine-N-methyltransferase by 2,3,4,6,7,8-hexahydropyrrolo[1,2-a]-pyrimidine. *Biochem Pharmacol,* 25:2251–2256, 1976.

55. Vogt M: Behavioral effects of central catecholamines: concluding remarks, in Matthysse SW, Kety SS (eds), *Catecholamines and Schizophrenia.* Oxford, Pergamon Press, 1975, pp 183–184.

56. Snyder SH: Amphetamine psychosis: A "model" schizophrenia mediated by catecholamines. *Am J Psychiat* 130:67, 1973.

57. Angrist BM, Shopsin B, Gershon S: The comparative psychotomimetic effects of stereoisomers of amphetamine. *Nature* 234:152–153, 1971.

58. Davis JM, Janowski CA: Amphetamine and methylphenidate psychosis, in Usdin E and Snyder SH (eds) *Frontiers in Catecholamine Research.* New York, Pergamon Press, 1974, p 977–981.

59. Harris J, Baldessarini RJ: Effects of amphetamine analogs on the uptake of ^{3}H-catecholamines by homogenates of rat corpus striatum and cerebral cortex. *Neuropharmacol* 12:669–679, 1973.

60. Thornburg JE, Moore KE: Dopamine and norepinephrine uptake by rat brain synaptosomes: relative inhibitory potencies of l- and d-amphetamine and amantadine. *Res Comm Chem Pathol Pharmacol* 5:81–89, 1973.

61. Ferris RM, Tony FLM, Maxwell RAA: A comparison of the capacities of isomers of amphetamine deoxypipradol and methylphenidate to inhibit the uptake of tritiated catecholamines into rat cerebral cortex slices, synaptosomal preparations of rat cerebral cortex, hypothalamus and striatum and into adrenergic nerves of rabbit aorta. *J Pharmacol Exp Ther* 181:407–416, 1972.

62. Creese I, Burt DR, Snyder SH: Dopamine receptor binding predicts clinical and pharmacological potencies of antischizophrenic drugs. *Science* 192:481–483, 1976.

63. Rimon R, Roos B-E, Räkköläinen V, et al: The content of 5-hydroxyindoleacetic acid and homovanillic acid in the cerebrospinal fluid of patients with acute schizophrenia. *J Psychom Res* 15:375–378, 1971.

64. Neff NH, Tozer TN, Brodie BB: Application of steady-state kinetics to studies of the transfer of 5-hydroxyindoleacetic acid from brain to plasma. *J Pharmacol Exp Ther* 158:214–218, 1967.

65. Fink EB, Post RM, Carpenter WT, et al: CSF metabolites in acute schizophrenia. *New Research Abstracts,* APA Annual Meeting, May 1974, p 24.

66. Snyder SH: The dopamine hypothesis of schizophrenia: focus in the dopamine receptor. *Am J Psychiatry* 133:197–202, 1976.

67. Snyder SH, Creese I, Burt DR: The brain's dopamine receptor: labeling with (^{3}H)dopamine and (^{3}H)haloperidol. *Psychopharm Comm* 1:663–673, 1975.

68. Sedvall G, Fyrö B, Nyback H, et al: Mass fragmentometric determination of HVA in lumbar cerebrospinal fluid of schizophrenic patients during treatment with antipsychotic drugs. *J Psychiatr Res* 11:75–80, 1974.

69. Wyatt RJ, Erdelyi E, Schwartz M, et al: Catecholamine-related enzymes in the brains of schizophrenics and controls, submitted.

70. Wise CD, Baden MM, Stein L: Post-mortem measurements of enzymes in human brain: evidence of a central noradrenergic deficit in schizophrenia, in Matthysse SW, Kety SS (eds) *Catecholamines and Schizophrenia*. Oxford, Pergamon Press, 1974, pp 185–198.

71. Kopin IJ: Storage and metabolism of catecholamines: the role of monoamine oxidase. *Pharmacol Rev* 16:197–199, 1968.

72. Berger PA, Barchas JD: Monoamine oxidase inhibitors, in Usdin E, Forrest I (eds) *Psychotherapeutic Drugs*. New York, Marcel Dekker, 1977, pp. 1173–1216.

73. Aghajanian GK: Electron microscopic aspects of neural function, in Clark WG, del Giudice J (eds): *Principles of Psychopharmacology*. New York, Academic Press, 1970, pp 97–104.

74. Johnston JP: Some observations upon a new inhibitor of monoamine oxidase in brain tissues. *Biochem Pharmacol* 17:1285–1297, 1968.

75. Sandler M, Youdim BH: Multiple forms of monoamine oxidase: functional significance. *Pharmacol Rev* 24:331–348, 1972.

76. Neff NH, Yang HYT, Fuentes J: The use of selective monoamine oxidase inhibitor drugs to modify amine metabolism in brain, in Usdin E (ed) *Neuropsychopharmacology of Monoamines and Their Regulatory Enzymes*, New York, Raven Press, 1974, pp 49–57.

77. Murphy DL, Donnelly CH: Monoamine oxidase in man: enzyme characteristics in platelets, plasma and other human tissues, in Usdin E (ed) *Neuropsychopharmacology of Monoamines and Their Regulatory Enzymes,* New York, Raven Press, 1974, pp 71–85.

78. Murphy D, Wyatt RJ: Reduced monoamine oxidase activity in blood platelets from schizophrenic patients. *Nature* 238:225–226, 1972.

79. Meltzer HG, Stahl SM: Platelet monoamine oxidase activity and substrate preferences in schizophrenic patients. *Res Comm Chem Pathol Pharmacol* 7:419–431, 1974.

80. Schildkraut JJ, Herzog JM, Orsulak PJ, et al: Reduced platelet monoamine oxidase activity in a subgroup of schizophrenic patients. *Am J Psychiatr* 133:438–439, 1976.

81. Domino EF, Khanna SS: Decreased blood platelet MAO activity in unmedicated chronic schizophrenic patients. *Am J Psychiatr* 133:323–325, 1976.

82. Friedman E, Shopsin B, Sathananthan G, et al: Platelet monoamine oxidase activity in psychiatric patients. *Am J Psychiatr* 131:1392–1394, 1974.

83. Sashkan EG, Becker RE: Reduced platelet monoamine oxidase activity in schizophrenics. *Nature* 253:659, 1975.

84. Bailey AR, Crow TJ, Johnstone EC, et al: Platelet monoamine oxidase activity in patients with chronic schizophrenic illnesses untreated by neuroleptic drugs. *Br J Clin Pharmacol* 2:380P, 1975.

85. Domino EF, Krause RR, Bowers J: Various enzymes involved with putative neurotransmitters. *Arch Gen Psychiatr* 29:195–201, 1973.

86. Schwartz MA, Aikens AM, Wyatt RJ: Monoamine oxidase activity in brains from schizophrenic and mentally normal individuals. *Psychopharmacologia* 38:319–328, 1974.

87. Carpenter WT, Murphy DL, Wyatt RJ: Platelet monoamine oxidase activity in acute schizophrenia. *Am J Psychiatr* 132:438–440, 1975.

88. Murphy DL, Weiss R: Reduced monoamine oxidase activity in blood platelets from bipolar depressed patients. *Am J Psychiatr* 128:1351–1357, 1972.

89. Zeller EA, Boshes B, Davis JM, et al: Molecular aberration in platelet monoamine oxidase in schizophrenia. *Lancet* i:1385, 1975.

Chapter 12
A Survey of Other Biologic Research in Schizophrenia

Richard Jed Wyatt, M.D.
Llewellyn B. Bigelow, M.D.

It has been 9 years since the last Rochester Conference on Schizophrenia. During that time, researchers attempting to comprehend the ecology of the schizophrenic forest have cleared some new paths, abandoned others, and are more recently rediscovering some that had been trodden before, but later allowed to grow over. Although no compelling theories supported by irrefutable data have appeared, there has been some successful mapping of areas that can serve as staging points for future inquiry. In this chapter we will survey some of the salient points of biologically oriented research that have not been discussed elsewhere in this section.

INDOLEAMINE METABOLISM

Almost since its discovery in mammalian tissue, serotonin has been a candidate for a crucial role in the genesis of the schizophrenic syndrome. Early efforts directed at demonstrating abnormalities in serotonin metabolism in schizophrenics were unsuccessful. More recently some schizophrenics were found to have a less than normal REM sleep rebound after REM sleep deprivation. This observation rekindled interest in a possible serotonin deficiency since REM sleep is thought to be partially under the control of the serotonergic system (1).

Reasoning from the classic work done in the treatment of Parkinson's disease with L-DOPA, investigators embarked on a series of therapeutic trials giving the serotonin precursor, L-5-hydroxytryptophan, along with the peripheral decarboxylase inhibitor, α-methyldopa hydrazine (carbidopa), to chronic schizophrenics. The initial experiment produced modest improvement in about one-half of a sample of patients free of other drugs (2). Further trials have been carried out giving L-5-hydroxytryptophan to chronic schizophrenics in combination with standard neuroleptics (3). In this latter group the main result was an arousal of affect. Some patients appeared to improve mildly under these circumstances, but others appeared overwhelmed.

Gillin, Kaplan, and Wyatt found that 20 grams of tryptophan a day given to chronic schizophrenics had no effect (4). Domino and Krause (5) investigated the metabolic response of schizophrenics and controls to a tryptophan load. They found no major difference in concentrations or ratios of free versus bound tryptophan in schizophrenics. However, Bender and Bamji (6) found markedly decreased total tryptophan in a small group of chronic patients. Overall, these findings are in contrast to the reports of some success in the treatment of affective disorders with serotonin precursors (7), and they offer additional support to the biologic differentiation of schizophrenia and affective disorders.

Methylated indoleamines continue to arouse interest. The demonstration of an enzyme in human lung, platelets, and brain capable of forming the hallucinogenic substance dimethyltryptamine (DMT) has stimulated renewed efforts to demonstrate the presence of these substances in the blood and urine of schizophrenics. Reports in this area are conflicting; some found the presence of DMT, and others have not found it (8). In no case has the formation of DMT in man been demonstrated under physiologic conditions.

Another compound of interest, methylated serotonin or 5-methoxy-tryptamine, has been reported as elevated in the lumbar cerebrospinal fluid of schizophrenics as well as in other psychiatric patients (9). This is related to 5-methoxy-N,N-dimethyltryptamine which is a highly toxic substance in some species (10) and is said to be hallucinogenic (11).

ABNORMAL PROTEINS IN SCHIZOPHRENIA

Taraxein, the subject of much controversy in earlier years, has not continued to receive much attention, rather surprisingly, since one of the original findings associated with spiking in septal leads of schizophrenic patients has now been confirmed (12). Of further convergent interest is the recent intense investigation of nucleus accumbens. This anatomic way station in the septal area is known to be heavily innervated by dopaminergic neurons and is thought by some to be a principal gate between the limbic system and the rest of the brain (13).

Frohman, Harmison, Arthur, and Gottlieb (14) have continued their long-standing effort at clarifying the changes produced by schizophrenic sera on the aerobic metabolism of chicken erythrocytes. They have extended their observations to a new system—tryptophan uptake by chicken erythrocytes exposed to sera from schizophrenics and controls. Again they found differences in schizophrenic sera as compared to that of the controls and more recently have attributed this difference to the schizophrenic sera having an α-2-globulin predominantly in the alpha helical configuration. The tryptophan uptake data have been challenged by others (15). Frohman, Arthur, Yoon, and Gottlieb's finding of an abnormally configurated protein awaits confirmation, as does their very recent report of the existence of another intracellular protein responsible for shifting the structure of that globulin to a non-alpha configuration (16).

OTHER BIOLOGIC AREAS

As pointed out in a 1970 review of biochemical studies in schizophrenia (17), the best established difference between schizophrenics and matched controls was that schizophrenics as a group had diminished reponse to intradermal histamine challenge. However, the meaning of this awaits explanation.

"Megavitamin therapy," now called orthomolecular psychiatry, has continued to attract many serious workers in the field of schizophrenia. The initial positive results for niacin supplementation in schizophrenia were not borne out by later studies (18). The notion that large amounts of vitamins acting as co-factors might serve as therapy for some schizophrenics has remained tantalizing and has received further support from the case report of a patient with schizophreniform behavior and mental retardation who showed some improvement after being placed on supplementary folic acid (19). However, this appears to be an exception.

Clinicians often have commented on the presence of a peculiar odor associated with chronic schizophrenia. It has been all too easy to dismiss this smell as a product of poor hygiene. Smith, Thompson, and Koster (20) found evidence that this odor is due to trans-3-methyl-2-hexanoic acid, differentially secreted in the sweat of chronic schizophrenics; Perry, Melancon, Lesk, and Hansen were unable to confirm this (21).

The possibility that schizophrenic illness might be a behavioral consequence of a slow or latent viral infection has received at least hypothetical support from the discovery that Jacob-Creutzfeld disease may have such a pathogenesis. Certainly, patients with herpes encephalitis frequently have been initially diagnosed as suffering from schizophrenia (22). The leads that suggest a viral etiology for a subgroup of schizophrenics have been reviewed recently by Torrey and Peterson (23,24).

Meltzer's finding of elevated serum creatine phosphokinase (CPK) and aldolase in acute psychotic states has generated considerable research in the last decade [for review, see Meltzer (25)]. The elevated CPK appears to come from skeletal muscles. Concomitant with this enzyme rise there is microscopic evidence for aberrant neuronal growth in skeletal muscles in psychotic patients. The meaning of this finding is elusive at present, but it does present a biologic abnormality from which new hypotheses may be generated.

Interest in a regulatory role for peptides in the function of the central nervous system has burgeoned recently. Prange, Wilson, Lara, Alltop, and Breese's original work suggesting salutary clinical effects of a thyrotropin-releasing hormone factor in depression (26) and schizophrenia (27) has not been reproduced thus far (28,29). Modest benefits from injections of a crude extract of bovine pineal glands in conjunction with neuroleptics again have been reported in a selected population but do not occur in drug-free patients (30). Carroll has proposed that the failure of depressed patients' cortisol levels to be suppressed with dexamethasone may aid in differential diagnosis of schizophrenic versus depressive illness (31).

Gamma-aminobutyric acid (GABA) has long been suspected as an inhibitory modulator of neurotransmission in the spinal cord. Interest in GABA has been spurred with the recent demonstration that it is the transmitter for inhibitory neurons from the globus pallidus to the substantia nigra (32). This observation lent some weight to the report of Fredericksen that baclofen, presumed to be a GABA analog and agonist, might be of therapeutic benefit in schizophrenia (33). Subsequent clinical work has failed to support Frederiksen's report (34); in addition, baclofen has been reported to be more specifically an antagonist for substance P (35), although it will antagonize some behavioral effects of amphetamine (36). The lack of clinical effect for baclofen will be of theoretical interest when we understand the role of substance P.

Gluten has long been suggested as a pathogenic component of the diet of schizophrenic patients. A recent publication by Singh and Kay claimed support for this hypothesis (37). Varma, Varma, Allen, and Ward (38) have reported striking differences in excretion of mucopolysaccharides of schizophrenic patients as compared to controls. This finding awaits confirmation.

A new and potentially exciting finding is that of Issidorides, Stefanis, Varson, and Katsorchis (39) who have reported that the chromatin of polymorphonuclear leukocytes tends to undergo greater conformational changes in response to decondensing stimuli in schizophrenics than in normal subjects. If this finding can be confirmed, it will open an entirely new area of research in schizophrenia.

SUMMARY

There have been a number of expeditions into the schizophrenic forest. None have returned with "the fox," but many have offered reports that can help the future scientist plan the next exploration of that wilderness. It seems reasonable to hope that the next Rochester Conference will include reports of definitive reclassification of some patients currently sheltered under the diagnostic umbrella of schizophrenia into new groups of persons afflicted with one or more specific metabolic diseases.

REFERENCES

1. Wyatt RJ, Gillin JC: Biochemistry and human sleep. In Williams RL, Karacan I (eds): *Pharmacology of Sleep*. New York, John Wiley & Sons, 1976, pp 239–273.

2. Wyatt RH, Vaughan T, Galanter M, et al: Behavioral changes of chronic schizophrenic patients given L-5-hydroxytryptophan. *Science* 177:1124–1126, 1972.

3. Walls P, Bigelow L, Rauscher F, et al: Clinical effects of L-5-hydroxytryptophan plus haloperidol administration to chronic schizophrenics. *Abstracts of the American Psychiatric Association's 129th Annual Meeting*, 1976.

4. Gillin JC, Kaplan JA, Wyatt RJ: Clinical effects of tryptophan in chronic schizophrenic patients. *Biol Psychiatry* 11:635–639, 1976.

5. Domino EF, Krause RR: Plasma tryptophan tolerance curves in drug free normal controls, schizophrenic patients and prisoner volunteers. *J Psychiat Res* 10:247–261, 1974.

6. Bender DA, Bamji AN: Serum tryptophan binding in chlorpromazine-treated chronic schizophrenics. *J Neurochem* 22:805–809, 1974.

7. Asberg M, Thoren P, Traskman L, et al: Serotonin depression—A biochemical subgroup within the affective disorders? *Science* 191:478–480, 1976.

8. Gillin JC, Wyatt RJ: The psychedelic model of schizophrenia: the case of N,N-dimethyltryptamine (DMT). *Am J Psychiatry* 133:203–208, 1976.

9. Koslow SH, The biochemical and biobehavioral profile of 5-methoxy-tryptamine, in Usdin E, Sandler M (eds): *Trace Amines and the Brain*. New York, Marcel Dekker, 1976, pp 103–130.

10. Gillin JC, Tinklenberg J, Stoff DM, et al: 5-methoxy-N,N-dimethyltryptamine: behavioral and toxicological effects in animals. *Biol Psychiatry* 11:355–358, 1976.

11. Holmstedt BO, Windgren JE: Chemical constituents and pharmacology of South American snuffs, in Efron DH, Holmstedt B, Kline NS (eds): *Ethnopharmacologic Search for Psychoactive Drugs*. PHS Publication No. 1645, Superintendent of Documents, Washington, DC, pp 339–373, 1967.

12. Hanley J, Rickles WR, Crandall PH, et al: Automatic recognition of EEG correlates of behavior in a chronic schizophrenic patient. *Am J Psychiatry* 128:1524–1528, 1972.

13. Stevens JR: An anatomy of schizophrenia? *Arch Gen Psychiatry* 29:177-189, 1973.

14. Frohman CE, Harmison CR, Arthur RE, et al: Conformation of a unique plasma protein in schizophrenia. *Biol Psychiatry* 3:113-121, 1971.

15. Guchhait RB, Janson C, Price WH: Validity of plasma factor in schizophrenia as measured by tryptophan uptake. *Biol Psychiatry* 10:303-314, 1975.

16. Frohman CE, Arthur RE, Yooh HS, et al: Distribution and mechanism of the anti-S protein in human brain. *Biol Psychiatry* 7:53-61, 1973.

17. Wyatt RJ, Termini BA, Davis J: Biochemical and sleep studies of schizophrenia: a review of the literature 1960-1970, Part I: Biochemical studies. *Schizophrenia Bulletin* 4:10-44, 1971.

18. Wyatt RJ: A comment to Linus Pauling's megavitamin and orthomolecular therapy in psychiatry. *Am J Psychiatry* 131:1258-1262, 1974.

19. Freeman JM, Finkelstein JD, Mudd SH: Folate-responsive homocystinuria and schizophrenia. *N Eng J Med* 292:491-496, 1975.

20. Smith K, Thompson GF, Koster HD: Sweat in schizophrenic patients: identification of the odorous substance. *Science* 166:398-399, 1969.

21. Perry TL, Melancon SB, Lesk D, et al: Failure to detect trans-3-methyl-2-hexanoic acid in the sweat of schizophrenic patients. *Clin Chim Acta* 30:721-725, 1970.

22. Raskin DE, Frank SW: Herpes encephalitis with catatonic stupor. *Arch Gen Psychiatry* 31:544-546, 1974.

23. Torrey EF, Peterson MR: Slow and latent viruses in schizophrenia. *Lancet* II:22-24, 1973.

24. Torrey EF, Peterson MR: The viral hypothesis of schizophrenia. *Schizophrenia Bulletin* 2:136-146, 1976.

25. Meltzer HY: Neuromuscular dysfunction in schizophrenia. *Schizophrenia Bulletin* 2(1):106-146, 1976.

26. Prange AJ, Jr, Wilson IC, Lara PP, et al: Effects of thyrotropin-releasing hormone in depression. *Lancet* II:999-1002, 1972.

27. Wilson IC, Lara PP, Prange, AJ Jr: Thyrotropin-releasing hormone in schizophrenia. *Lancet* II:43-44, 1973.

28. Benkert O, Gordon A, Martschke D: The comparison of thyrotropin-releasing hormone, luteinising hormone-releasing hormone and placebo in depressive patients using a double-blind cross-over technique. *Psychopharmacologia* 40:191-198, 1974.

29. Bigelow LB, Gillin JC, Semal C, et al: Thyrotropin-releasing hormone in chronic schizophrenia. *Lancet* II:869-870, 1975.

30. Bigelow LB: Some effects of aqueous pineal extract administration on schizophrenia symptoms, in Altschule MD (ed): *Frontiers of Pineal Physiology*. Cambridge, Mass, The MIT Press, 1975, pp 225-263.

31. Carroll BJ: Limbic system-adrenal cortex regulation in depression and schizophrenia. *Psychosom Med* 38:106-121, 1976.

32. Kim JS, Bak IJ, Hassler R, et al: Role of γ-aminobutyric acid in extrapyramidal motor system. II: Some evidence for existence of a type of GABA-rich strionigral neurons. *Exp Brain Res* 14:95-104, 1971.

33. Frederiksen PK: Baclofen in the treatment of schizophrenia. *Lancet* I:702-703, 1975.

34. Simpson GM, Branchey MH, Shrivastava RK: Baclofen in schizophrenia. *Lancet* I:966-967, 1976.

35. Saito K, Konishi S, Masanori O: Antagonism between lioresal and substance P in rat spinal cord. *Brain Res* 97:177-180, 1975.

36. Ahlenius S, Carlsson A, Engel J: Antagonism by baclofen of the d-amphetamine-induced disruption of a successive discrimination in the rat. *J Neural Transm* 36:327-333, 1975.

37. Singh MM, Kay SR: Wheat gluten as a pathogenic factor in schizophrenia. *Science* 191:401-402, 1976.

38. Varma RS, Varma R, Allen WS, et al: Urinary excretion of acid mucopolysaccharides in schizophrenia. *Biochem Med* 11:358-369, 1974.

39. Issidorides MR, Stefanis CN, Varsou E, et al: Altered chromatin ultrastructure in neutrophils of schizophrenics. *Nature* 258:612-614, 1975.

Chapter 13
Missing Links

Steven Matthysse, Ph.D.

I have entitled my discussion "Missing Links" because I think there is an important missing link in the "dopamine theory." *Granted that neuroleptic drugs are dopamine blockers, why is dopamine blockade good for schizophrenia?*

The answer to this question might help us develop better screening tests for antischizophrenic drugs. The criterion used at present to develop screening tests—correlation of activity in the test system with potency of established antischizophrenic drugs—is really circular reasoning and is likely to lead to the development of future drugs very similar to the existing ones. It is now evident that the various dopaminergic test systems that are known in the brain do not respond identically to dopamine blocking drugs. Dopamine turnover in the striatum, and amphetamine-induced stereotypy, for example, are affected less by thioridazine than by chlorpromazine; dopamine-sensitive adenylate cyclase is weakly affected by haloperidol in comparison to its clinical potency (1). Exclusive use of stereotypy as a screening test is practically a guarantee that new antischizophrenic drugs will, like the old ones, have extrapyramidal side effects (2). By investigating what it is about dopamine blockade that confers antischizophrenic efficacy, we might be able to sharpen our test systems and to discover more specific and effective drugs.

Presumably in schizophrenia there is a trait that is affected primarily by dopamine blockade, while other traits improve secondarily. If we knew the primary trait, we would be able to classify patients with respect to it. Patients with high versus low values might be treated preferentially with different drugs. An underlying dopamine-sensitive psychologic process might be a risk factor with a more nearly mendelian pattern of inheritance and with a higher monozygotic twin concordance than the syndrome as a whole. The functional anatomy of the dopamine-sensitive trait could be studied in animals and would provide a rationale for morphologic and histochemical examination of brains from schizophrenic patients. While there are many dopamine-blocking drugs, their therapeutic effects are very similar (3). Important aspects of behavior—especially in the domains of motivation, affect, and interpersonal relations—remain impaired after drug treatment. By making precise what dopamine blockers do *not* do, we could begin to approach the biologic basis of residual symptoms.

Why, then, is dopamine blockade good for schizophrenia? The theory I would like to present arose by considering the two behavioral syndromes that can be most clearly related to excessive dopaminergic transmission: stereotyped behavior and Huntington's chorea. Stereotyped behavior consists of perseverative repetition of motor acts. If dopaminergic agonists were to produce similar mental effects, one would expect *inability to withdraw attention from the stimulus or idea on which it is focused.* In Huntington's chorea, there is excessive emergence of movement, as if subthreshold movements were not held under sufficient inhibition. While dopaminergic neurons are probably not involved in the primary pathology of Huntington's chorea, neuroleptics relieve the symptoms and L-DOPA makes them worse. If the same analogy were to hold in the mental sphere, one would expect *inability to deny attention to stimuli or ideas that are normally held below the theshold for awareness.*

The proposed hypothesis combines these two ideas: *the involuntary control of attention—its coupling to stimuli and internal states—is, at least in part, under the control of a dopaminergic system.* The evidence supporting the hypothesis comes from the effects of dopaminergic agonists, antagonists, and lesions in animals and man.

Agonists
Excessive fixation of attention is commonly observed in amphetamine overdose. Ellinwood (4) describes "engagement in tasks that primarily involve small bits or minutiae and a marked enhancement of perceptual acuity directed toward these minute objects." Very similar states ("stereotyped behavior") also can be provoked by amphetamine and apomorphine in animals. Monkeys, for example, will turn objects over and over in their hands for long periods of time. They may stare persistently at cagemates while following them around in the cage; they may groom one spot on their skin incessantly, even to the point of injury. Sacks (5) relates some striking instances in parkinsonian patients treated with L-DOPA:

> Miss D. would lift a tea-cup to her mouth, and find herself unable to put it down; she would reach for the sugar-bowl, and find her hand "stuck" to the bowl; when doing crosswords, she would find herself staring at a particular word, and be unable to shift either her gaze or her attention from it; and, most disquieting (not only for herself but for others), she would at times feel "compelled" to gaze into someone else's eyes . . .

Antagonists
Dopamine-blocking drugs, such as the neuroleptics, seem to counteract certain disturbances of involuntary attention. An action of chlorpromazine against attentional perseveration was one of the first clinical effects observed after the introduction of the drug (6):

> The obsession loses its imperative character—its dominant tonality—and tends to keep in the background; if it does not disappear, it loses its power of fixation; the patient indicates that, if the idea recurs, he can banish it easily from his mind and forget it. . . .

Spohn has reported (abstract in Chapter 26) that a decrease in "the readiness . . . to attend to experimenter and self-presented stimuli" (measured by changes in skin conductance and heart rate), as well as "reduction in excessive attention to the standard stimulus" (measured by visual fixation time in a size comparison test), occur early in chlorpromazine treatment of schizophrenic patients (7). Pimozide, which is a relatively more specific dopamine-blocker than the other antipsychotic drugs, is said to be effective in monosymptomatic hypochondriacal psychoses, where there is a fixed conviction of abnormal anatomy or physiology (8,9). One patient after treatment "could concentrate on matters other than the action of her cervical musculature . . . although her delusional belief was still elicited on direct questioning . . ."(10). Lesions of the nigrostriatal and mesolimbic dopamine tracts in rats cause "sensory neglect" of the opposite side of the body (absence of orienting response to tactile stimuli) (11).

The essential experimental question is: do disturbances in central dopaminergic systems, e.g., by amphetamine or apomorphine administration, disrupt the normal smooth coupling of attention to stimuli, motivational states, and cognitive processes? Such paradigms as crossmodal versus ipsimodal reaction time (12,13) and the detection of simultaneity .of events presented in two different channels (14) might be used to approach this question. The visual tracking ("pendulum") task used so successfully by Holzman (15) may also be a suitable test system, and I propose, in Chapter 30, a theory of visual tracking based on these principles.

REFERENCES

1. Matthysse S: In: *Neuroregulators and Psychiatric Disorders*. E. Usdin, D. A. Hamburg and J. D. Barchas, Eds. New York, Oxford University Press, 1977, pp 3–13.

2. Matthysse S: Theory of preclinical screening of antipsychotic drugs, in Clark WG, del Giudice J (eds): *Principles of Psychopharmacology*, ed 2, in press.

3. Hollister, LE: Clinical differences among phenothiazines in schizophrenics, in Forrest IS, Carr CJ, Usdin E (eds): *Phenothiazines and Structurally Related Drugs*. New York, Raven Press, 1974, pp 675–683.

4. Ellinwood EH, Sudilovsky A, Nelson LM: Evolving behavior in the clinical and experimental (model) psychosis. *Am J Psychiatry* 130:1088–1093, 1973.

5. Sacks O: *Awakenings*. Garden City, NY, Doubleday, 1974, p 38.

6. Sigwald J, Bouttier D: Le chlorhydrate de chloro-3(dimethylamino-3-propyl)-10-phenothiazine in pratique neuro-psychiatrique courante. *Ann Med* 54:150–184, 1953. Quoted in Swazey JP: *Chlorpromazine in Psychiatry: A Study of Therapeutic Innovation*. Cambridge, Mass, MIT Press, 1974.

7. Spohn HE, Lacoursiere R, Thompson K, et al: Phenothiazine effects on psychological and psychophysiological dysfunction in chronic schizophrenics. *Arch Gen Psychiat* 34:633–644, 1977.

8. Riding, J, Munro A: Pimozide in the treatment of monosymptomatic hypochondriacal psychosis. *Acta Psychiat Scand* 52:23–30, 1975.

9. Riding BEJ, Munro A: Pimozide in monosymptomatic psychosis. *Lancet* 1:400–401, 1975.

10. Reilly TM: Pimozide in monosymptomatic psychosis. *Lancet* 1:1385–1386, 1975.

11. Ungerstedt U, Pycock C: Functional correlates of dopamine neurotransmission. *Bull Schweiz Akad Med Wiss* 30:44–55, 1974.

12. Sutton S, Zubin J: Effect of sequence on reaction time in schizophrenia, in: Birren JE, Welford AT (eds): *Behavior, Aging and the Nervous System: Biological Determinants of Speed of Behavior and its Change with Age*. Springfield Ill, Charles C Thomas, 1965.

13. Waldbaum JK, Sutton S, Kerr J: Shift of sensory modality and reaction time in schizophrenia, in: Kietzman M, Sutton S, Zubin (eds): *Experimental Approaches to Psychopathology*. New York, Academic Press, 1975.

14. Kristofferson, A. B. Successiveness discrimination as a two-state quantal process. *Science* 158:1337–1339, 1967.

15. Holzman PS, Proctor LR, Levy DL, et al: Eye-tracking dysfunctions in schizophrenic patients and their relatives. *Arch Gen Psychiat* 31:143–151, 1974.

CONCLUDING COMMENTS
Rue L. Cromwell, Ph.D.

The floor discussion that followed the papers on biochemical approaches focused on both the general role of biochemistry in schizophrenia and certain specific strategies and hypotheses in biochemical research. Primarily, the discussion focused on the rationale for the prominence currently given to the dopamine hypothesis.

GENERAL ROLE OF BIOCHEMISTRY

Dr. Perez-Cruet (McGill University) asked whether research being presented was that of biochemistry antecedent or consequent to the schizophrenic disorder. After describing his recent experiments showing conditioning of dopamine metabolism using opiates as unconditioned stimuli (1) and quoting previous work where catalepsy induced by bulbocapnine was also conditionable (2), he proposed that it is still not clear whether the schizophrenic illness leads to changes in dopamine metabolism or whether alterations in dopamine metabolism antecede the schizophrenic illness. Later, Dr. Kety stated the issue in a different way: Is the neuroleptic drug acting on a biochemical process that has been induced by life experience or, instead, on a process that is primary to the schizophrenic disorder? Dr. Kety noted that many examples exist in which biochemical, physiologic, and other biologic changes in an organism result from life experience and can be modified and corrected by drugs. Dr. Snyder indicated that the problem in answering such a question is that no change in enzymes or neurotransmitters has been documented in the schizophrenic patient. Therefore, all we can say is that drugs that affect the schizophrenic in varying degrees involve the dopamine system in corresponding degrees. As many of the speakers had pointed out, one cannot therefore conclude or infer that something is aberrant in the dopamine system.

The best evidence that some biochemical factors are primary in schizophrenia, according to Dr. Kety, is the genetic evidence. If there are genetic determinants contributing to these illnesses, then there must be some primary biochemical disturbances in addition to those induced by environmental factors. Dr. Kety pointed out that the first stages of gene expression occur through biochemical processes.

In response to Dr. Kety's comment, Dr. Barchas emphasized that many biochemical factors are yet to be examined. For example, the enzyme tyrosine hydroxylase, rate-limiting in the formation of dopamine and norepinephrine, can be activated in response to acute stress on a very short-term basis. It is not known whether schizophrenics differ from normal subjects in their ability to activate this enzyme. Clearly, however, neurochemical processes in these systems can be altered in animals by life experience.

Dr. Bleuler felt that the discussed biochemical findings are of greatest value in the understanding of arousal and of the biologically based drives and impulses. Up to now, however, he implied, the biochemical findings have been less helpful in understanding schizophrenia in its human aspects. Dr. Matthysse indicated that he agreed in part but not completely. For example, Matthysse said, dopamine may have something to do with

151

attention, and a defect in attention may result in psychotic symptoms as a secondary feature (see Chapter 30).

Dr. Sachar continued with the same point. If the attentional defect is present to some extent before the flagrant psychosis, if the child at risk is struggling to focus attention, to form relationships as others do, then one would expect a secondary characterologic difficulty to develop. If the biochemical defect exists, it was argued, this is not the whole story. As with other organic defects, we will see the patient struggling, trying to compensate, trying to develop other ego skills, being puzzled and bewildered by the defects—the whole panoply of human efforts to cope and to adapt to some inner disturbance that he does not understand. Unfortunately, Dr. Sachar remarked, we who study and treat it do not yet fully understand it either.

Dr. Wyatt commented on the relevance that different possible subtypes of schizophrenia might have to the biochemical findings. He first acknowledged that three different types of disorders—affective, acute, chronic—can easily be conceived. However, regarding this issue, a number of questions are yet to be answered. First is the question of whether sufficient evidence exists for separate disorders or whether schizophrenia is a single disorder. Next is the question of whether neuroleptic drugs are uniformly efficacious in all the disorders. After this comes the question of whether the relationship between biochemical potency and clinical effectiveness, as reported by Dr. Snyder, is the same for all the disorders. Finally, with each disorder in turn, is the dopamine blockade effecting a primary or secondary deficit? It was agreed that much is yet to be done in understanding subclassifications of schizophrenia in biochemical terms.

Why the Emphasis upon Dopamine?

A major question in the discussion was why the dopamine hypothesis became emphasized more than other biochemical hypotheses. Essentially, the answer was that the major basis by which to propose a strategy to pursue biochemical factors was the correlation between activity in the biochemical system and the clinical effect on the mental disorder, as the drug dosage level is varied. Little question exists that neuroleptic drugs—phenothiazines, butyrophenones, and so forth—lead to some definite improvement in some schizophrenic patients. Unfortunately, for purposes of understanding the biochemistry of the schizophrenic disorder, these drugs have wide-ranging effects on different enzyme and neurotransmitter systems of the brain. When differences of therapeutic potency correspond closely to differences in the extent of a particular biochemical effect, then there is basis to suspect that the biochemical system may be more centrally involved with therapeutic action than a biochemical system where the correlation does not occur. Dopamine-blocking activity has been the biochemical variable most closely related to clinical effectiveness among drugs. Amphetamine-type drugs, such as methylphenidate (Ritalin), which makes schizophrenic symptoms worse, can also conceivably have their action through the dopamine pathway. While this strategy has pointed researchers in the direction of study of the brain dopamine systems, it does not necessarily imply that the biochemical disturbance in schizophrenia lies within that system.

Alpha-methyl-paratyrosine (AMPT)

Particular attention was paid to alpha-methyl-paratyrosine (AMPT) and the special role it plays in supporting the dopamine hypothesis in schizophrenia. While the clinically effective neuroleptic drugs block the activity of dopamine, AMPT blocks the synthesis of dopamine and other catecholamines. Therefore, if this compound were found to be clinically effective, it would contribute significantly to the notion that dopamine plays an important role in schizophrenic disorders. Dr. Snyder responded to the question of AMPT by first emphasizing that the data he presented indicated only that AMPT could synergize, i.e., increase the effectiveness of phenothiazines. The effectiveness of AMPT when used alone had not been demonstrated. He noted that it was a difficult drug to use and that complete blockade of dopamine synthesis may not be possible in dose levels which could be administered to man. Dr. Snyder doubted if the appropriate studies had been done to answer clearly and fully the role of AMPT. While AMPT may potentiate the antipsychotic effect of phenothiazines, Dr. Kety predicted that, when used alone, AMPT would actually worsen the apathy, anhedonia, and withdrawal symptoms of schizophrenia. These symptoms, he explained, appear to be related to the lessened activity of catecholamines.

In response to these comments, Dr. Wyatt called on Dr. Henry Nasrallah, who had recently completed a study of AMPT in Dr. Wyatt's laboratory. Dr. Nasrallah indicated that two studies using AMPT alone, reported in 1967, showed no improvement in schizophrenics. Three studies by Carlsson and his group, using the same research design, showed that with AMPT less thioridazine (Mellaril) was needed to treat schizophrenic patients. The study by Dr. Nasrallah showed that no improvement was observed by giving AMPT to symptomatic schizophrenic patients already on phenothiazines. A significant rise in plasma prolactin levels with AMPT was evidence of strong dopamine blocking, despite the lack of clinical improvement. Dr. Wyatt added that the results indicated a lack of differential symptom change with AMPT.

The Amphetamines and Methylphenidate

The other side of the coin, i.e., the role of methylphenidate (Ritalin) in making psychotic symptoms worse, received considerable attention. Dr. MacCrimmon (McMaster University, Ontario) quizzed Dr. Davis about the experimental controls for neuroleptic medication during the Ritalin injection experiment. That is, withdrawing and readministering the neuroleptic drugs could, instead of Ritalin, potentially account for the period of increased psychosis. In response, Dr. Davis explained that the patients were off neuroleptic medication before and during Ritalin injections. Afterward, most of them were on neuroleptics, but some of them were not. Some patients recovered spontaneously.

A major question, raised by Dr. Kornetsky, was why oral amphetamines had little effect on chronic schizophrenics in a study he had performed earlier. Dr. Snyder speculated that intravenous, rather than oral, administration may be crucial to the findings. Also, Ritalin, as opposed to amphetamines, is the more effective compound. The third explanation, of course, was that Ritalin worsens the symptoms in acute, but not in chronic, patients. In discussing these three alternatives, Dr. Davis agreed with Dr. Snyder that a large intravenous bolus of Ritalin was important to the effect. Dr. Kornetsky expressed surprise that with a 40-mg oral dose he could not get at least a minimal behavioral effect. As for type or stage of schizophrenia, Dr. Davis indicated that all his patients were acute or were in the acute phase of a recurrent episode. When patients were past their acute episode, the worsening of symptoms did not occur with Ritalin administration. Thus, it would appear that the data of Dr. Kornetsky and Dr.

Davis are in agreement regarding the lack of effect of these psychomotor stimulants in chronic schizophrenics.

While Ritalin worsens the symptoms of acute schizophrenics, it has proven efficacious in treating hyperkinetic children. Dr. Johnston (Indiana) asked how these two findings could be reconciled. Why do not the hyperkinetic children also become psychotic? Dr. Matthysse explained that, in relation to attention, chlorpromazine releases attention from sustained fixations in schizophrenics and Ritalin does the opposite. That is, Ritalin permits the individual to sustain attention on one stimulus or task for a longer time. Dr. Matthysse's comment was compatible with past research which has indicated that more sustained attention is needed in hyperkinetic children. Distractibility, not motor output, is the crucial feature of the disorder. Children are labeled hyperactive because of frequent shifting of attention from one activity or stimulus to another. The attentional deficit in schizophrenia, Dr. Matthysse explained, is at the other extreme, i.e., the inability to disattend, to withdraw, or to shift from a sustained attention.

Finally, an observation was made concerning the cognitive experience of schizophrenic patients who experience the controlled-blind sequence of injections of Ritalin and placebo, respectively. Dr. Davis noted that once the patients learned what specific drug had aroused their psychosis, they tended to view the psychosis as ego-alien, i.e., the result of this exogenous agent. Some patients recovered, were no longer schizophrenic, were discharged from the hospital free of drugs. Once free of psychosis, the Ritalin did not exacerbate or return the symptoms. He cautioned, however, that he would not advocate Ritalin as a therapeutic agent.

Prolactin

The major questions regarding prolactin were whether its elevation in phenothiazine-treated patients correlated with clinical therapeutic changes in the patient or with the magnitude of any in vivo chemical activity. These questions appeared consistent with the previously described research strategy that has placed emphasis upon the dopamine system. Dr. Cleghorn (McMaster University, Ontario) asked if Dr. Sachar had examined different doses of L-DOPA on the prolactin system. Dr. Sachar indicated that nothing had been done empirically on establishing a dose response curve with L-DOPA. However, a standard dose of 500 mg L-DOPA causes essentially the same suppression in all subjects. Schizophrenics and normals do not differ in stimulation of growth hormone with that amount of L-DOPA.

Conversely, with haloperidol, dose response studies indicate that prolactin level increases practically to the saturation point with 0.5 or 1.0 mg., which certainly is not a therapeutic dose. No prolactin response at all to anti-psychotic drugs would be grounds to suspect the patient was not taking his medication, or more rarely, was not absorbing it.

Dr. Sachar also noted that a clinical response does not occur with increasing prolactin levels because the prolactin response is immediate and apparently results from a saturation of the system that releases prolactin. The system that produces a therapeutic response takes about 6 weeks to operate and needs more of the neuroleptic to produce a clinically therapeutic response. The prolactin elevation is greater in some cases than in others. After 6 weeks, patients show varying degrees of improvement from the neuroleptic. However, these two variables, according to Dr. Sachar, are uncorrelated. What does account for the individual differences in prolactin elevation is not known.

Just how important, Dr. Kornetsky asked, is it if no difference occurs between schizophrenics and normal subjects in prolactin response to chlorpromazine within 120 minutes? Would differences occur if one waits longer? A number of years ago, he pointed out, he had found no difference in orthostatic hypertension among schizophrenic and normal "phenothiazine virgins," but he had observed marked differences 12 hours later. Dr. Sachar acknowledged the importance of this time dimension. Regarding prolactin, a number of stimulation and depession tests are yet to be done.

Dr. Sachar explained that a finding of no difference between schizophrenics and normal subjects in prolactin response would not be a disaster to the dopamine theory. No one, he feels, believes that schizophrenia resides in the neuroendocrine system. Regardless of prolactin, a disturbance in brain dopamine, brain dopamine receptors, or functional dopamine brain activity would still be suspected. Most people believe that the functional disturbance, if it exists, is occurring in a discrete area of the brain rather than diffusely through neuroendocrine hormones. The areas suggested by Dr. Snyder, i.e., the pathway to the frontal cortex and areas A8-A10 of the mesolimbic system, are worthy of further investigation.

As in the case of amphetamine response, the question was raised by Dr. Ettigi (Clark Institute of Psychiatry, Toronto) whether a prolactin response would occur in chronic schizophrenics. Research was described in which a group in Montreal studied chronic schizophrenics withdrawn from neuroleptics for 4 weeks after having been on them for over a year. They did not find a difference in prolactin response in some schizophrenics on long-term neuroleptic medication. Also, no difference was observed between schizophrenics and normal controls after withdrawal from neuroleptic medication. Dr. Sachar said he was unable to explain this finding and that it differed from the finding of Trackington who found prolactin was maintained at a high level in treated chronic schizophrenics. Asked if it were possible that residual neuroleptics in the system could account for the lack of change, Dr. Sachar cited the work of Meltzer. Meltzer found that patients withdrawn after several months from neuroleptics maintained their elevated prolactin levels a few days before they dropped back to normal. However, some other factor must be involved in studies where subjects do not serve as their own control.

The possible relationship of prolactin to diminished libido and testosterone levels was raised by Dr. Azuela (Michigan). He has had several patients on heavy doses of Mellaril who have complained of diminished libido. When their testosterone was tested, it was found to be low. Dr. Sachar stated that the relationship of testosterone and LH levels in the blood to libido in adult human subjects has never really been determined. Neuroleptics tend to inhibit the release of LH and LH-regulated hormones. Whether this is the source of the clinical concern regarding libido, Dr. Sachar concluded, is doubtful. Instead he felt that deficit symptoms, such as the lowered libido, would be expected as part of the untreated or untreatable aspect of the schizophrenic illness. That is, after the flagrant psychotic symptoms had been removed with neuroleptics, the patient is left without spark, without libido, without much human interest. Thus, the observation of diminished libido may be related to the process of schizophrenia—the part for which we have no way to intervene—rather than to the drugs.

Overview

A conclusion may be drawn from the discussion on biochemical approaches by first citing the following analogy. A well-known sociologic fact is that a downpour of rain greatly decreases the probability of street riots. One would hesitate to conclude that rain plays an important role in the etiology of street riots. To a lesser extent, but nevertheless with comfortable certainty, dopamine-blocking drugs decrease the probability of manifest schizophrenic symptoms in some patients. One likewise would hesitate to conclude that these drugs and the dopamine system play a primary role in the etiology of schizophrenia. Nor can one conclude the opposite. Thus, the question should be answered within the coming few years as to whether the "dopamine hypothesis" researchers are "sitting on top of" the major variables in the etiology of schizophrenia or, contrarily, whether dopamine is relatively remote from the key variables. As Dr. Kety has pointed out, the new generation of psychiatrists working on biochemical theories of schizophrenia no longer needs admonitions about etiological conclusions versus artifacts or secondary features. Nevertheless, the analogy cited here is useful for others of us outside the biological research field.

Also of note is the fact that the reduction of overt schizophrenic symptoms which occur with dopamine-blocking drugs happens not immediately but weeks later. This means that either a long time is required for the drugs to reach the site of action or, as suggested here, that the drug action merely clears the way for a second reparative action to take place. Elsewhere in this volume, the distinction has been made between the vulnerability and the waxing and waning of symptoms. How the proposed two-factor interpretation involving biochemistry relates to the "vulnerability versus manifest symptom" issue is a matter of considerable importance.

It may also be concluded safely that prolactin is useful in indicating when an antipsychotic drug is present in the body of a schizophrenic—at least, an acute schizophrenic. However, the hormonal level does not indicate the pathway of action for either the antipsychotic or the "worsening" effect in schizophrenic symptoms. Meanwhile, the strategy for biochemical hypotheses through correlating chemical effects with clinical benefit or worsening is a reasonable one.

REFERENCES

1. Perez-Cruet J: Conditioning of striatal dopamine metabolism with methadone, morphine, or bulbocapnine as an unconditioned stimulus. *Pavlovian Journal of Biological Sciences,* 1976.
2. Perez-Cruet J: Cardio-respiratory components of conditional catalepsy to bulbocapnine, in Brill H (ed): *Neuropharmacology,* Proceedings of the Collegium Internationale Neuropsychopharmacologicum. Congress Series #129, Excerpta Medica International, 1967, pp 912–917.

Seymour S. Kety, M.D.

It is now clear that several chemically different types of drugs attenuate the manifest schizophrenic symptoms in many patients, and that a blockade of dopamine synapses is their common pharmacologic action. One would hesitate to conclude that the dopamine system therefore plays a primary role in the etiology of schizophrenia. Since the dopamine system interacts with many other transmitter systems, including serotonin,

GABA, norepinephrine and certain polypeptides, any of these or others still undiscovered could be the site of the biochemical alteration, the existence of which is implied by the genetic evidence. It was known for some time that anticholinergic drugs helped to alleviate the symptoms of Parkinson's disease but we would have been in error had we concluded that cholinergic synapses were primarily involved. We now know that the disturbance in Parkinson's disease lies in dopamine pathways that are normally in balance with the cholinergic system.

Also of note is the fact that the reduction of overt schizophrenic symptoms which occurs with dopamine-blocking drugs happens not immediately but weeks later. This means that either a long time is required for the drugs to reach the site of action, or that the drug action clears the way for a second reparative action to take place. This second action could be biochemical, involving the induction of enzymes or receptors; it could lie in the anatomic, physiologic, or psychological domains or in the complex relationships among them.

It is obvious, however, that the common action of these drugs, which have been of remarkable benefit in the treatment of schizophrenia, on a particular neurotransmitter system is one of the most important leads we have had to the biologic mechanisms that may underlie schizophrenia. Further study of that system and of its interrelations with other neurotransmitters is clearly indicated.

Section III

CENTRAL NERVOUS SYSTEM AND PSYCHOPHYSIOLOGIC APPROACHES

Chapter 14
On the Possible Role of Neocortex and Its Limbic Connections in Attention and Schizophrenia

Marek-Marsel Mesulam, M.D.
Norman Geschwind, M.D.

ATTENTIONAL DEFICITS CAUSED BY STROKE IN HUMANS

Derangements in the complex process of selective attention are among the most common abnormalities of mental status encountered by the clinical neurologist. These patients are said to have "acute confusional states," "metabolic encephalopathies," or "delirium." Although a derangement of attention is the fundamental aspect of these conditions (1,2), many clinicians neglect this and stress such secondary manifestations as agitation or hallucinations. Most of these patients suffer from toxic or metabolic encephalopathies so the anatomic site of the responsible cerebral insult cannot be specified with certainty. However, in a small but significant number of cases, the derangement of attention emerges as a major manifestation of focal cerebral infarction. Since these infarcts are delimited, such cases offer a unique opportunity for investigating the anatomy of attention in man.

The derangements of attention that result from stroke may be divided into two syndromes. First, the cerebral infarct may result in a *global* deficit of attention that permeates the entire extrapersonal space and that impairs, pari passu, the coherence of perception, affect, thought, and indeed most aspects of behavior. On the other hand, other patients may show the dramatic neglect of only *one-half* of the extrapersonal space. In either condition, the derangement of "selective attention" is primary in the sense that it cannot be attributed to more elementary deficits in the spheres of arousal, sensation, language, or motor function.

Global derangements of attention have been described with strokes involving the

Supported by NIH grants NS 09211, 06209, 07011, and S01-RRO-5479-13.

occipito-temporal (3), parietal (4), or frontal (4) areas of the brain. As a consequence of the cerebral lesion, these patients develop a dramatic impairment of selective attention: the ability to direct and maintain vigilance is impaired; distractibility by irrelevant stimuli is augmented; and the ability to maintain a coherent stream of thought or to perform a sequence of goal-directed behavior is severely compromised. In addition, these patients also show severe abnormalities of affect which may range from senseless agitation (3) to apathy and sluggish indifference (4).

We have recently described three such patients who developed the acute onset of global inattention as a consequence of stroke (4). With the help of neuroradiologic procedures, it was suggested that the cerebral lesion was confined to the posterior parietal cortex in two of these cases and to prefrontal cortex in the third. Phylogenetic and myelogenetic considerations would suggest that these areas of the human brain constitute very advanced portions of association neocortex (5). Furthermore, in each of these cases the cerebral infarct was situated in the right cerebral hemisphere.

The data from these three cases lead to several implications of considerable interest. First, the observation that a circumscribed cerebral lesion confined to one hemisphere may cause severe and somewhat selective impairment in the ability to direct and maintain vigilance is rather surprising. In fact, it is likely that a significant number of patients like these end up in state hospitals with the erroneous diagnosis of functional psychosis, especially as a consequence of the associated abnormality in emotional behavior. Second, it is remarkable that the lesion in all three cases was in the *right* hemisphere: in fact, damage to the corresponding regions of the left hemisphere is known to result in language disorders without additional impairment of attention (5). Third, it is of interest that the responsible lesions are located predominantly in neocortex despite the somewhat prevalent tendency to associate "attention" with the functions of the brain stem reticular formation. However, since the efficient exercise of vigilance is a highly complex function that presupposes both recognition of what is irrelevant as well as elaborate processing of relevant information, it is likely that this process is highly dependent on neocortical mechanisms. In fact such a conclusion is implied by the dichotic listening experiments of Broadbent (6) and of Moray (7), as well as by investigations of the contingent negative variation (8) and sensory evoked responses (9).

The second syndrome which interferes with the process of selective attention results in a striking neglect of the sensory hemispace opposite to the involved cerebral hemisphere. In extreme cases, these patients may act as if one-half of the universe did not exist at all. One patient may shave only one-half of his face; another may only dress one-half of his body; still another may read only half of each sentence on a page. Indeed, we have seen an alcoholic patient who suffered such a stroke and was admitted to the hospital with florid withdrawal hallucinations in addition to severe unilateral neglect: the striking feature of this case was that all the hallucinations were located in one-half of the sensory space and no hallucinations were reported in the neglected sensory space!

As in the case of global inattention described earlier, this syndrome of unilateral neglect has been described with cerebral lesions in the parietal (10) or frontal (11) lobes. Although it has been suggested that the cerebral areas that are involved in the syndrome of unilateral neglect are also convergence zones for association neocortex, it is not yet known how their neuronal circuitries differ from those areas where strokes result in the *global* type of inattention. It is possible that the regions subserving global attention have different neural connections, or, alternatively, unilateral neglect may constitute either a milder form or a stage in the recovery of the lesion responsible for global inattention.

The clinicopathologic data to distinguish between these and other possibilities are not yet available.

Furthermore, as in the case of global inattention, instances of prolonged and severe unilateral neglect are most often seen with lesions in the *right* hemisphere (12). Although different interpretations have been advanced to account for this hemispheric asymmetry, one may postulate that the *right* hemisphere has a pivotal role in the process of selective attention (4), just as the left hemisphere is specialized for language. Indeed, the observation that the late component of visually evoked responses recorded over the right parietal region is of higher amplitude than that from the left is consistent with this conclusion.

Moreover, patients with unilateral inattention and right hemisphere lesions also show affective disturbances. These patients may act as if they ignored the "biologic stimulus value" (10) of events occurring in one side of the world. In addition, there may be more generalized abnormalities consisting of a global lack of concern for diseases or disability. Such affective disturbances are far less frequent with lesions in the left hemisphere. Thus, in either syndrome where a lesion in the right hemisphere leads to an impairment of attention, affect is also impaired. This parallelism in the integrity of "attention" and "emotion" is also noted in a number of other psychiatric and neurologic conditions, and schizophrenia is certainly no exception to this clinical correlation. Since several independent lines of investigation converge on the conclusion that the right cerebral hemisphere of man is also specialized for emotions (13,14), the anatomic basis of this clinical association may depend, at least in part, on the fact that the same cerebral hemisphere has a predominant role in regulating both attention and emotion.

PARIETAL INATTENTION IN THE RHESUS MONKEY AND ITS ANATOMIC CORRELATES

Unilateral inattention may be obtained in the rhesus monkey by means of ablations that include the inferior parietal lobule. Despite the apparent absence of significant sensory deficits, these animals fail to attend appropriately to contralateral visual, auditory, or somesthetic stimuli: for instance, in the absence of either weakness or visual field defect, the animal may fail to retrieve an apple located contralateral to the side of the lesion (15). Although analogies between the behavior of man and animals are often unwarranted, this behavior in the rhesus monkey is probably a reasonable model for the syndrome of unilateral inattention in man. More recently the activity of single neurons within this parietal region has been determined in the awake and behaving rhesus monkey (16). In the course of these elegant studies, the remarkable observation has been made that some neurons fire most rapidly when the animal fixates or follows with its eyes only those objects which are "desirable," such as food when hungry or liquid when thirsty.[1]

Anatomic data indicate that the inferior parietal lobule receives neural input from association neocortex, paralimbic cortex, the limbic system, and the brain stem (17). Although none of these connections may be unique to the inferior parietal lobule, this particular *constellation* may determine its role in the process of attention. Thus, a neocortical area which appears to be involved in the function of attention receives *direct*

---

[1] For further detail, see discussion by T. Yin in the *Journal of Psychiatric Research* version of the Proceedings, in press.

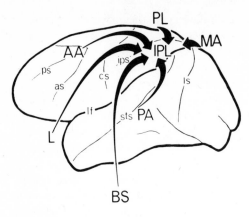

Figure 14-1. A schematic representation of the neural input converging within the inferior parietal lobule of the rhesus monkey. Abbreviations: AA: anterior association cortex: as: arcuate suleus; BS: brain stem; cs: central sulcus; IPL: inferior parietal lobule; ips: intraparietal sulcus; L: limbic areas; lf: lateral fissure; ls: lunate sulcus; MA: medial association cortex; PA: posterior association cortex; PL: paralimbic cortex; ps: principal sulcus; sts: superior temporal sulcus.

limbic and paralimbic input as well as input from "high order" association areas. This limbic and paralimbic input may be responsible for directing vigilance towards motivationally relevant events. Moreover, as a consequence of this input, the same cortical area also may be involved in the experience of emotion. Similar limbic-cortical connections also may be present in man and may explain the clinical association between derangements of attention and of affect.

LIMBIC-CORTICAL CONNECTIONS AND THEIR POSSIBLE RELEVANCE TO SCHIZOPHRENICS

Neuronal pathways interconnect parietal cortex with limbic structures which are known to constitute an anatomical substrate for affective behavior. One of these, the nucleus accumbens septi, receives input from two major limbic centers: the hippocampus and the amygdala. The dopaminergic projection from the limbic midbrain also reaches this

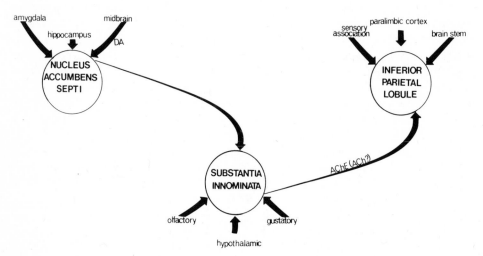

Figure 14-2. A diagram of neural pathways which connect limbic structures with parietal neocortex. Abbreviations: ACh: acetylcholine; AChE: acetylcholinesterase; DA: dopamine.

nucleus. It is on the basis of these limbic and dopaminergic connections that the nucleus accumbens septi has been implicated in the pathogenesis of schizophrenia (18). The distribution of the neural output from the nucleus accumbens septi is not known in great detail: however, there are indications that a major output is directed to the substantia innominata. In turn, the substantia innominata may be regarded as a convergence center for visceral information. For instance, in addition to the input from the nucleus accumbens septi, this region receives gustatory, olfactory and hypothalamic connections. Finally, the acetylcholinesterase-rich neurons of the substantia innominata send axons into parietal neocortex, thus completing a limbic-cortical neural connection within which dopaminergic and "cholinergic" synapses are both involved (17).

These anatomic connections indicate that the nucleus accumbens septi which has been implicated in the process of schizophrenia may be an important component in a pathway that connects limbic structures with neocortex by way of the substantia innominata. Accordingly, a structural or biochemical lesion at the level of the nucleus accumbens septi may significantly interfere with the access of neocortex to limbic information so a deficit of attention may emerge as one of the consequences. Alternatively, a lesion in the inferior parietal lobule may result in similar disconnection of cortex from the limbic system, a disconnection that may be partially responsible for the unilateral inattention seen in the rhesus monkey. Thus, anatomic considerations pertaining to schizophrenia, on one hand, and attentional disorders, on the other, may converge within this neural pathway. With respect to schizophrenia, this anatomic pathway enjoys two advantages. First, it becomes consistent with pharmacologic arguments that have implicated an additional dysfunction of cholinergic mechanisms in schizophrenia. Second, it provides direct anatomic pathways for the participation of *neocortex* in the complex phenomena that characterize schizophrenia.

Indeed, we would like to propose that the anatomic basis of many derangements of attention and affect may be found in dysfunctions that disrupt neural connections between neocortex and the limbic system. Such a disruption may interfere both with the reception of sensory information by limbic structures as well as with the ability of neocortex to initiate, to coordinate, or to inhibit complex behavior in response to the proper limbic cues. Consequently, significant and maladaptive discrepancies between stimulus and response may appear in the spheres of affective and attentive behavior. In fact, the phenomenology of many disorders of attention and emotion, and perhaps also of schizophrenia, may be conceptualized in terms of such discrepancies among drive, stimulus, and response which may result from a disruption of neural connections between limbic structures and neocortex.

REFERENCES

1. Chedru F, Geschwind N: Disorders of higher cortical functions in acute confusional states. *Cortex* 8:395, 1972.

2. Mesulam M-M, Geschwind N: Disordered mental states in the post-operative period. *Urologic Clin of N Amer* 3:199, 1976.

3. Horenstein S, Chamberlain W, Conomy J: Infarction of the fusiform and calcarine regions: Agitated delirium and hemianopia. *Trans Amer Neurol Assoc* 92:85, 1967.

4. Mesulam M-M, Waxman SG, Geschwind N, et al: Acute confusional states with right middle cerebral artery infarctions. *J Neurol Neurosurg Psychiat* 39:84, 1976.

5. Geschwind N: Disconnexion syndrome in animals and man. *Brain* 88:237, 585, 1965.

6. Broadbent DE: *Perception and Communication.* Oxford, Pergamon Press, 1958.

7. Moray N: Attention in dichotic listening: Affective cues and the influence of instructions. *Quart J Exp Psychol* 11:56, 1957.

8. Cohen J: The contingent negative variation in visual attention. *Electroenceph Clin Neurophysiol* 31:287, 1971.

9. Haider M, Spong P, Lindsley DB: Attention, vigilance, and cortical evoked potentials in humans. *Sci* 145:180, 1964.

10. Denny-Brown D, Meyer JS, Horenstein S: The significance of perceptual rivalry resulting from parietal lobe lesion. *Brain* 75:434, 1952.

11. Heilman KM, Valenstein E: Frontal lobe neglect in man. *Neurol* 22:660, 1972.

12. Joynt RJ, Goldstein MW: The minor cerebral hemisphere, in Friedlander WJ (ed): *Advances in Neurology 7.* New York, Raven Press, 1975, p 147.

13. Schwartz GE, Davidson RJ, Maer F: Right hemisphere lateralization for emotion in the human brain. *Sci* 190:286, 1975.

14. Gainotti G: Emotional behavior and hemispheric side of the lesion. *Cortex* 8:41, 1972.

15. Heilman KM, Pandya DN, Geschwind N: Trimodal inattention following parietal lobe ablations. *Trans Amer Neurol Assoc* 95:295, 1970.

16. Mountcastle VB, Lynch JC, Georgopoulos A, et al: Posterior parietal association cortex of the monkey: Command functions for operations within extrapersonal space. *J Neurophysiol* 38:871, 1975.

17. Mesulam MM, Van Hoesen GM, Pandya DN, et al: Limbic and sensory connections of the inferior parietal lobule (area PG) in the rhesus monkey: a study with a new method for horseradish peroxidase histochemistry. *Brain Res,* in press.

18. Matthysse S: Schizophrenia: Relationship to dopamine transmission motor control and feature extraction, in Schmitt FO, Worden FG (eds): *The Neurosciences. Third Study Program.* Cambridge, Mass, MIT Press, 1974, p 733.

Chapter 15
Bimodal States of Arousal and Lateralized Dysfunction in Schizophrenia: Effects of Chlorpromazine

John H. Gruzelier, Ph.D.

SCHIZOPHRENIA AND THE TEMPORAL-LIMBIC SYSTEM

Neuropsychopharmacology may provide unique insights about the etiology of schizophrenia. Delineation of the brain pathways that neuroleptic drugs act on and of those pathways that appear instrumental in producing or modulating schizophrenic behavior, will lead to an understanding of the central nervous system locus of schizophrenic symptoms.

Already this approach has yielded several observations to guide us—notably the action of psychotropic drugs on central neurotransmitter systems. Neuroleptic drugs that suppress the clinical signs of schizophrenia number among their effects action on catecholamine neurons including dopamine (1,2,3), noradrenaline (4,5,6), and possibly adrenaline (7). Psychotomimetic drugs that trigger schizophrenic-like hallucinations and delusions influence the cholinergic and serotonergic systems (8,9,10) and amphetamine, which induces a psychosis in many ways indistinguishable from paranoid schizophrenia, increases both dopamine and noradrenaline (11,12).

Caution should be observed in evaluating single systems in isolation, notably, the current preoccupation with dopamine. Neurotransmitter systems are seldom affected in isolation because selective blockade or stimulation of one transmitter system alters other systems as well. A more useful approach may be provided by neurotransmitter balance and interaction models (13,14). That multiple systems must be involved is also borne out by the consideration that chemotherapy varies from patient to patient. For example, one patient may respond in a similar fashion to any one of an array of drugs blocking dopamine or adrenergic activity, while another may require several days in combination. Some patients recoveries may be drug specific and other patients may be refractory to all drugs, singly or in combination. It is tempting to speculate whether the heterogeneity of schizophrenic symptoms may stem from a variety of patterns of neurotransmitter imbalance.

This evidence behooves us to consider the behavioral significance of transmitter systems and how these interact. Furthermore, the involvement of brain pathways—and not simply specific structures—suggests that in schizophrenia we have a disturbance of central neural systems with both specific and nonspecific effects. In support of this, the central actions of chlorpromazine [historically the drug of choice in the chemotherapy of schizophrenia (15)], are most clearly demonstrable with electrographic measures of cortical arousal and brainstem reticular activity, both of which have widespread nonspecific effects. Action upon more localized structures, such as those of the temporal-limbic system, are more obscure, at least within the range of standard clinical doses (16,17).

That the temporal-limbic systems may play an integral part in the target symptoms and psychological deficits or schizophrenia is suggested by a variety of evidence. Limbic structures such as the amygdala, hippocampus, and septum are instrumental in the integration of information-processing functions including perception, attention, and memory registration, as well as processes involved in learning, reinforcement, and emotion (18,19). A disruption of such functions may be central to the information-processing disabilities of schizophrenics. Parallels have been drawn between the behavior of chronic schizophrenics and the Kluver-Bucy syndrome in animals that results from temporal lobe ablation or amygdalectomy (20,21). Abnormal spiking from electrode placements in the septal area has been reported in schizophrenic patients during the course of psychotic episodes (22). Schizophrenic-like behavior has resulted from tumors or electrical stimulation of the hippocampus (23,24) and is reported in neurological patients with known damage to the temporal lobe. However, such behavioral sequelae are by no means restricted to lesions of these brain areas (25). The nonspecificity existing in relation to the latter issue may stem from the existence of a multitude of interconnecting neurochemical and anatomical pathways between limbic structures and others throughout the brain. Relevant to the findings to be reported here are those pathways acting on the cortical and brain-stem arousal systems, as well as those exerting modulatory influences upon the hypothalamus and endocrine systems (26,27).

Pharmacological evidence also points to the involvement of the limbic system in schizophrenia. Catecholamines are found in high concentrations in the limbic structures and pathways. Even though much current research has centered on the involvement of the striatal dopamine system, close evaluation of these studies shows that the mesolimbic dopamine pathways are at the very least a viable alternative for study. Much of the striatal dopamine theory hinges on evidence showing correlations between the clinical potency of neuroleptics and their efficacy in blocking stereotyped behavior. Dopamine is known to be a transmitter in the extrapyramidal system, and extrapyramidal symptoms are common side effects of many, though not all, neuroleptic drugs. This correlational evidence is far from exact. It is contradicted by the examples of a drug, such as thioridazine, that has marginal stereotypy blocking effects, yet whose antipsychotic effects are on a par with those of chlorpromazine (12, 28). The relevance of the striatal system is also called into question by the consideration that the extrapyramidal side effects can be prevented without affecting the therapeutic efficacy of the drugs. The theory is qualified further by findings on cerebrospinal homovanillic acid.

The alteration in this substance that accompanies the administration of chlorpromazine follows a different time course from the drug's effects upon psychotic symptoms. Homovanillic acid is an index of the turnover of striatal dopamine (29).

The necessary involvement of mesolimbic dopamine pathways is highlighted by evidence that clozapine (a neuroleptic without extrapyramidal effects) increases dopamine preferentially in the mesolimbic pathways rather than in the nigrostriatal tract or the tuberoinfundibular dopamine system. This drug also increases the turnover of noradrenaline and influences serotonergic transmission (7,30). Thus, there is suggestive evidence that in order to elucidate the gamut of schizophrenic symptomatology it is necessary to consider the involvement of temporal-limbic structures and pathways.

Investigations of hypothesized temporal-limbic disturbance in schizophrenia were initiated by using the autonomic component of the orienting response. The orienting response, or, as Pavlov termed it, the "what is it?" reflex (31), was studied in response to repeated stimuli without attentional significance. As Sokolov (32) defines it, this response is nonspecific with respect to stimulus quality and intensity and habituates as the stimulus is repeated. Habituation of the response is selective according to whether the stimulus is of attentional relevance. Sokolov accounts for the evaluative process by invoking the concept of a neuronal model of the stimulus, that is, a trace of the stimulus in memory. An orienting response results if there is a mismatch between the stimulus and its neuronal model. A discordance between the stimulus and memory trace may arise through a difference in temporal and contextual, as well as physical, properties of the stimulus array. At the same time, the habituation process relates to the organism's generalized arousal state and reflects an individual's degree of attentional responsiveness when in an idling state. It also reflects his readiness for interaction with the environment (32–35). A change in arousal may disrupt habituation and reintroduce the orienting response. It must be noted, however, that the precise behavioral significance of the autonomic components of this response is unclear. Theories that suggest that it reflects a registration of stimulus input in awareness (18,36) would appear out of keeping with the relatively slow time course of the response, which has a latency of one or two seconds.
the relatively slow time course of the response, which has a latency of one or two seconds.

The neuroanatomical basis of the orienting response to nonsignal stimuli is relatively well-defined (36–42). Systems centered on the amygdala determine, through their connections with hypothalamic and brainstem triggering mechanisms, whether or not the response occurs. Systems associated with the hippocampus control the rate of habituation of the response when it does occur. The amygdala has predominantly an ergotrophic function (43), and in its absence there tends to be an absence of autonomic orienting responses, though hyperresponding is occasionally found.

The hippocampus, in addition to exerting control over the rate of habituation, appears to influence temporal features of the response. The number of responses preceding an habituation criterion is correlated with the time taken for the response to return halfway to prestimulus levels in the direction of the habituation deficit accompanying short recovery time (82). Hippocampectomized monkeys show both habituation deficits and shorter half response recovery times (36,40). Central control of the response recovery time appears to stem from frontal-hippocampal influences, in view of the evidence of slow recovery times in monkeys with frontal ablations (38) and in schizophrenic patients with frontal leucotomies (author's works in progress). Whether the amygdala is similarly influenced by frontal pathways is less clearly defined.

Autonomic hyperresponding or hyporesponding to repeated, identical, simple stimuli is common among neurologic patients. However, there appears to be a distinction between temporal and parietal lobe as compared to frontal lobe patients. The former are hyperresponsive or hyporesponsive to nonsignal stimuli, but respond normally in certain attentional situations; the latter exhibit abnormal responses to both signal and nonsignal stimuli (45,46).

BIMODAL STATES OF AROUSAL IN SCHIZOPHRENIA

The orienting responses of schizophrenic patients were found to be bimodally distributed (20,46–56). In two samples totaling 127 patients, about half exhibited no responses to the 15 orienting stimuli, and the remainder showed a high incidence of responses that were slow to habituate. Healthy normal control patients exhibited responses that showed fast or moderate rates of habituation. Nonpsychotic psychiatric control patients showed approximately equal incidence of nonresponding, fast or moderate habituation and slow habituation. These results are summarized in Figure 15-1. The schizophrenic patients were heterogeneous as to diagnostic subtype within the bounds of British diagnostic criteria. They had active symptoms and were lightly medicated with phenothiazines. Electrodermal responding differences did not correspond to differences in diagnosis or medication.

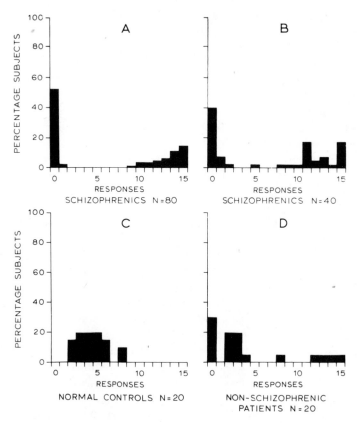

Figure 15-1. The incidence of skin conductance orienting responses to nonsignal tones in the two schizophrenic samples (A and B), in normal controls (C), and in nonschizophrenic patients (D).

Nine independent investigations in Europe and North America (a total of 17 experiments) have subsequently replicated a high incidence of nonresponding among schizophrenics (57–64). One series of largely retrospective studies has not found the same high incidence of nonresponders (66). However, methodologic issues may account for this discrepancy (67). Care is required in insuring that the orienting stimuli are not of attentional relevance. This is necessary because it was found that when schizophrenic patients attend to stimuli—especially when they prepared to make an overt response—both responders and nonresponders exhibited electrodermal responses (46). In view of the evidence above (45) of differential response of temporal and frontal lobe patients to signal and nonsignal stimuli, nonresponding in schizophrenia could represent a disorder of attentional processes located in temporal-limbic systems. This would include the amygdala and hippocampus rather than the frontal-limbic systems.

Nevertheless, the responder/nonresponder distinction does not simply reflect states of voluntary attention in responders and involuntary attention in nonresponders. All schizophrenic patients exhibit at least one form of attentional response to the orienting stimuli (53). This is a cardiac orienting response occurring within milliseconds of stimulus onset, a latency closer to the behavioral and electrocortical orienting response. In contrast, the orienting response in the autonomic nervous system has a latency of 1 or 2 seconds. It is the second component of the heart rate orienting response, which has a 1 or 2 second latency, that distinguishes electrodermal responders and nonresponders. This second component is an accelerative or decelerative response in responders and no response in nonresponders (53,68). Furthermore, in an experiment in which attention was required to distinguish between randomly presented signal and nonsignal tones, nonresponders exhibited a response to the signal tone only (46). This evidence and much of that which follows shows that the responder/nonresponder distinction, rather than simply reflecting a difference in attentional set, is indicative of two substantially different physiologic states in schizophrenia.

Under ordinary circumstances there is little correspondence between levels of physiologic activity across autonomic, cardiovascular, and somatic systems (69). However, in extreme states of emergency the organism can approach a unitary state of arousal in which the highly differentiated activities of the hypothalamus are harnassed to behavioral contingencies through the coordinating functions of the limbic forebrain. In schizophrenia it is hypothesized that this hypothalamic differentiation is undermined due to an imbalance of limbic-forebrain systems, so that even in a resting state there is a tendency towards a global state of arousal.

Evidence is now reviewed showing the existence of two states of arousal in schizophrenia. The presence or absence of electrodermal orienting responses in a nonsignal context provides indices of the two states. Schizophrenic patients subclassified with this index have been found to differ in their levels of physiologic activity, behavioral activity, pituitary-adrenal functioning and information-processing capacities, while chlorpromazine has been found to affect the two states differentially. Together this suggests a state of *high* arousal in patients with orienting responses and *low* arousal in patients without orienting responses.

The first source of evidence was the consistently higher levels of physiological activity in states of responding compared with states of nonresponding. This is shown in Table 15-1. Conversely, whether a schizophrenic patient has orienting responses may be predicted from levels of autonomic activity (67). This is illustrated by the distribution of scores obtained from discriminant function analyses of psychophysiologic measures (see

Table 15-1. Differences in Psychophysiologic Activity Between Electrodermal Responders (R) and Nonresponders (NR)

N		Variable	Statistical Significance
R	NR		
23	27	(noninstitutionalized) skin conductance level	p < 0.001
23	27	(noninstitutionalized) spontaneous fluctuations	p < 0.001
14	16	(institutionalized) skin conductance level	p < 0.05 one-tailed
14	16	(institutionalized) spontaneous fluctuations	p < 0.001
20	20	skin conductance level	p < 0.003
20	20	spontaneous fluctuations	p < 0.001
15	15	two-flash threshold	p < 0.001
12	12	two-flash threshold	p < 0.04
12	12	tonic skin conductance level	p < 0.001
30	30	heart rate	p < 0.001
15	15	(institutionalized) skin temperature	p < 0.001
10	10	(institutionalized) skin temperature	p < 0.02
10	10	(noninstitutionalized) skin temperature	NS
20	20	systolic blood pressure	p < 0.001
20	20	diastolic blood pressure	NS
10	10	heart rate variance	p < 0.002
10	10	heart rate variance	p < 0.001

Figure 15-2). In the first sample heart rate, skin conductance and spontaneous fluctuations in skin conductance differentiated the groups (p < 0.001) and correctly classified 85% of the patients. In the second sample the groups were selected so that heart rate levels were approximately the same (on this variable the groups had overlapped most in the first sample). The skin conductance variables together with systolic and diastolic blood pressure and finger skin temperature distinguished the groups (p < 0.001) and correctly classified 95% of the responders and nonresponders.

Ratings of behavioral arousal also showed group differences. Nurses who were blind to the patient's autonomic status rated responders higher than nonresponders on the Wittenborn Psychiatric Rating Scales of psychotic belligerence, manic state, anxiety, aggression, and attention-demanding behavior (47,56). When the behavioral ratings were added to the physiologic variables in the discriminant function analysis carried out on the first sample, all but one patient was correctly classified. Patients in long-stay wards were rated with Wittenborn scales relating to schizophrenic behavior. Scales of hebephrenic symptoms and delusions of grandeur when combined with spontaneous fluctuations led to the correct classification of all patients (p < 0.001). Excluding the physiologic variables, a discriminant function analysis with scales of hebephrenia, delusions of grandeur, motoric excitement, and compulsive-obsessive behavior gave rise to 86.7% correct classification (p < 0.005). On all of these scales responders were rated higher than nonresponders.

These findings are compatible with the hypothesized limbic basis of the responding and nonresponding arousal states. Electrical stimulation of the amygdala produces increased behavioral arousal and aggressive behavior, whereas lesions often produce the converse effects (22,70–74). Further compatible support was found in moderate positive correlations between the amplitude of the skin conductance orienting responses of responders and scales of assaultive behavior ($r = 0.65$, $p < 0.005$) and anxiety, psychotic belligerence, and compulsive-obsessive behavior (all $r = 0.45$, $p < 0.05$). The amygdala and hippocampus also have reciprocal influences on levels of physiologic activity (75–77).

Patients were all lightly medicated with phenothiazines. Reports of the effects of phenothiazines on both electrodermal activity and limbic mechanisms suggest that the bimodal states of arousal are unlikely to be drug effects; on the contrary, phenothiazines should militate against unitary states of arousal. This was tested in an experiment with up to 19 chronic schizophrenics who, having been stabilized on chlorpromazine for between 3 and 27 weeks, were examined intensively for 4 weeks on drug, for 4 weeks on placebo after withdrawal of drug, and for 4 weeks after drug was reinstated. Chlorpromazine was administered in standard clinical doses ranging between 100 and 800 mgs daily.

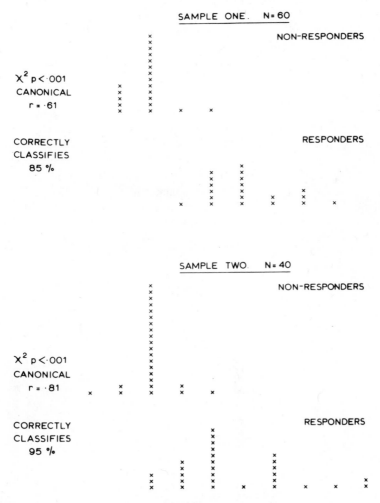

Figure 15-2. Discriminant function scores obtained from the levels of physiologic activity of electrodermal orienting responders and nonresponders.

A detailed report of the drug's effect upon psychophysiologic activity is reported elsewhere (65,116). While the drug withdrawal period—the length of which was determined by ethical considerations—was not long enough to free the patients of all long-term drug influences, the patients' clinical condition, rated by psychiatrists and nurses, showed evidence of deterioration in most cases. Therefore, the study did permit measurement of changes in the laboratory that accompany the development of primary symptoms. There was no systematic effect on skin conductance orienting responses (116). That nonresponding is not a drug effect is supported by more recent testing of patients admitted to the hospital drug-free, or withdrawn from short-acting drugs (and having no recent history of phenothiazine administration). Here the ratio of nonresponders to responders has been found to be about 2 to 1. Others have found evidence of nonresponding in chronic schizophrenics who never have had phenothiazines or any other neuroleptics (78).

The absence of a systematic drug effect on electrodermal responses to nonsignal stimuli contrasts with the clear-cut effect of chlorpromazine on electrodermal responses to stimuli with attentional significance. Chlorpromazine reduced the number ($p < 0.001$) and amplitude ($p < 0.003$) of responses to an unconditional stimulus in an autonomic conditioning paradigm (65).

Concerning levels of physiologic activity, the drug was found to have bidirectional effects (see Figure 15-3). It lowered levels of skin conductance ($p < 0.001$) and spontaneous fluctuations in skin conductance ($p < 0.001$) but increased heart rate ($p < 0.001$) and finger skin temperature ($p < 0.04$). The earlier finding of high arousal states in schizophrenic responders and low arousal states in nonresponders was replicated only when patients were withdrawn from the drug. A discriminant function analysis on heart rate and skin conductance levels and spontaneous fluctuations in skin conductance was significant and classified all but one responder and two nonresponders. When first on chlorpromazine, the discriminant function was not significant and classified only one of the five responders. When the drug was reinstated, the two patients (then responders) were correctly classified.

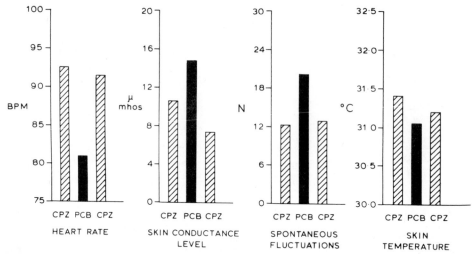

Figure 15-3. The effect of drug withdrawal on levels of autonomic activity.

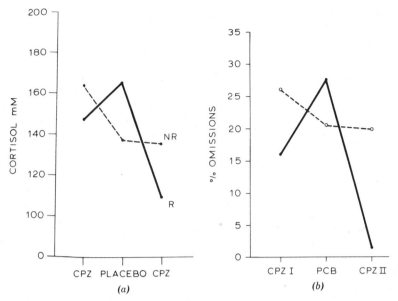

Figure 15-4. Cortisol levels (*a*) and percentages of omissions in the auditory discrimination task (*b*) for electrodermal responders and nonresponders.

The drug's effects on levels of physiologic activity are consistent with its central influences in reducing the activity of the sympathetic nervous system as well as its action on the peripheral nervous system, in particular its cholinergic blocking activity, important in view of the cholinergic mediation of electrodermal activity in the periphery.

With moderate doses of chlorpromazine the patients' electrodermal responding status no longer could be predicted from knowledge of levels of physiologic activity as accurately as when they were on placebo. Chlorpromazine appeared to fractionate the unitary nature of their state of arousal. In view of the fact that the drug influenced levels of physiologic activity, but not orienting responses to nonsignal stimuli, it may be inferred that the drug acts on nonspecific central arousal systems and peripheral autonomic functions rather than on specific temporal-limbic processes.

Limbic activity centered on the amygdala and hippocampus also controls the behavioral response to stress of the pituitary-adrenal axis. The effects are complex (79–82), but essentially the amygdala has an excitatory effect and the hippocampus an inhibitory one (83,84). In the chlorpromazine study, plasma cortisol levels were also measured and were examined as an index of pituitary-adrenal function (65). There are a multitude of potentially stressful influences that the schizophrenic patient may be exposed to by withdrawal of a drug acting to supress psychosis. Considering, too, how subjective and varied are patients' reactions to their hallucinations and delusions, group differences in cortisol with a classification based on autonomic responses to meaningless tones may seem difficult to demonstrate. Nevertheless, the results supported the neuropsychologic predictions. Responders were found to have higher levels of plasma cortisol than nonresponders ($p < 0.05$). The drug also had a tendency to shift the levels of the two groups in opposite directions (see Figure 15-4a).

The presence or absence or orienting responses in schizophrenic patients also coincides with differences in the processing of sensory information. In one experiment patients discriminated between single flashes and paired flashes having variable inter-flash intervals (50,52). On one occasion this was accompanied by white noise of moderate intensity. At first, without noise, nonresponders showed poorer two-flash resolution than responders. In the presence of noise, the sensitivity or precision of the discrimination (as measured by the slope of the psychophysical ogive) in some nonparanoid nonresponders improved markedly, beyond the level of the normal control group. These effects were independent of tendencies to make false positive errors, that is, a report of a double flash when only a single flash was present, a phenomenon that characterized the schizophrenic patients as a whole.

In another experiment patients were required to detect a slightly longer tone in a series of shorter tones (85). The eight patients who were nonresponders, irrespective of whether on drugs or off, were better able to distinguish longer from shorter sounds than those patients who had orienting responses on at least one occasion. The performance of responders, unlike nonresponders, also deteriorated when the rate of stimulus presentation was increased from 1 to 2 per second. The responders' higher omission scores coincided with higher false positive scores than found in nonresponders ($p < 0.05$). There also tended to be differential drug influences on the auditory discriminations of electrodermal responders and nonresponders (65). On drug, responders had fewer omissions, fewer false positives, and performance deteriorated less with faster presentation rate than on placebo. Nonresponders tended to show the opposite effects. These effects are shown in Figure 15-4b.

It is noteworthy that chlorpromazine had similar influences on cortisol levels and perceptual processing. This relation provides support for the extensive studies of Henkin (86) and colleagues who have shown systematic changes in perceptual discrimination across all sensory modalities in patients treated for disorders of the pituitary-adrenal system. Impaired perceptual discrimination was found to accompany high levels of circulating ACTH, an index of which is a raised level of cortisol. The finding that both cortisol level and perceptual discrimination vary with electrodermal responding and nonresponding supports evidence of an association between raised levels of ACTH and habituation deficits (87,88). Both phenomena may be ascribed to an imbalance in limbic processes in the direction of a loss of hippocampal inhibitory activity. Reciprocal influences between the amygdala and hippocampus also have been described with respect to levels of ACTH (84). The association of both cortisol and habituation deficits with omission scores in the auditory detection task implies that perceptual discrimination also may be modulated by limbic systems centered on the amygdala and hippocampus in support of animal studies (89-91).

These associations also are congruent with the inverted-U relation between performance, as reflected in omission scores, and arousal, here denoted by electrodermal responding and cortisol levels (92-97). The direction of change in these indices under chlorpromazine medication suggests that nonresponders are in a low state of arousal when on placebo and that the drug acts to increase limbic modulated arousal levels. Responders, on the other hand, are in a high state of arousal when on placebo, and the drug acts to lower limbic-modulated arousal levels. This is consistent with the manipulation of arousal by increasing stimulus presentation rate that led to deleterious performance in electrodermal responders as distinct from nonresponders. Conversely, the visual processing of some nonresponders was improved when arousal was increased with continuous noise. These results provide a test of two alternative views that either nonresponders are in a state of over-arousal and are located on the descending limb of the inverted-U relation between arousal and performance (58) or that nonresponders are in a state of under-arousal and are located on the ascending limb of the inverted-U curve (20,51). Support is found for the latter parsimonious view; it is the responders that are prone to over-arousal*.

LEFT HEMISPHERE DISTURBANCE IN SCHIZOPHRENIA

In the year the orienting response studies began, a report appeared of a survey of psychotic symptoms in 50 cases of temporal lobe epilepsy where foci were left-sided, right-sided, or bilateral in origin (111). Of those with schizophrenic psychoses without affective features, 43% had left-sided foci and 47.5% bilateral foci. Right-sided foci were in the minority (9/50 cases), but of those patients 6 had affective features. In a control group of 50 epileptic patients without psychotic features, unilateral foci of both hemispheres were represented in equal numbers. Thus, there was a tendency for schizophrenic psychosis in the absence of affective symptoms to involve the left hemisphere, and for affective psychosis, whether or not schizophrenic symptoms were present, to involve the right hemisphere.

On the basis of this evidence with epileptic patients, the author and colleagues have examined schizophrenic patients for evidence of impairment to the left hemisphere. After initial results that supported the hypothesis (48,49) this issue was examined in the chlorpromazine experiment in view of the possibility that the drug's action on left hemisphere activity might underlie its therapeutic efficacy in schizophrenia. At first glance the proposition that a drug acts differentially on the two brain hemispheres may appear fanciful, yet on two occasions, Serafetinides (112,113) discovered increases in EEG energy on dominant hemisphere as opposed to nondominant hemisphere recordings in some schizophrenic patients when they were administered chlorpromazine.

In 3 investigations the skin conductance orienting responses to nonsignal stimuli were monitored bilaterally. Some patients had gross response asymmetries in the direction of nonresponding on the left hand and responding, with slow habituation, on the right hand (48,49,116). In the majority of schizophrenic responders, responses were bilateral but with more bilateral asymmetries both in the number and amplitude of responses than occur in healthy controls. The direction of the asymmetry was a reduction in responding on the left hand compared with the right hand. Depressive patients showed the opposite asymmetry (49).

In view of evidence showing ipsilateral mediation of amygdaloid efferent influences (20,48), including the electrodermal orienting response (114,115), nonresponding on the

---

* There are other aspects of the orienting response that have psychopathological implications. Unlike normals, who show high reliability from one occasion to the next (98–100), schizophrenics, manic depressives, and some other patients with affective disorders switch from one extreme of responding to the other at different stages of the disorders (101–103). In responders, the more severe the clinical symptoms the greater tends to be the deficit in habituation (78,104). The number of responses also increases with tone intensity (20,58). There is a suggestion that patients whose symptoms remit with chemotherapy tend toward faster habituation (105). All of these features do not distinguish responders from nonresponders, indicating that they are not two extremes of a response continuum. The shape of the response is also important. The time taken for the response to return halfway to prestimulus level may be predictive of breakdown later in life in children with a process schizophrenic mother (106) and has been found to be shorter in many (20,46–49,107) but not all (108) schizophrenic patients. Electrodermal recovery time may be related to temporal features of information processing (20,36,44,47,109,160).

left hand may indicate a reduction of left-sided amygdaloid influences. There is suggestive evidence (20) that the efferent inhibitory influences of the hippocampus are
contralaterally projected and therefore the habituation deficits of the right hand also
may be of left-sided temporal-limbic origin. As all of the 140 schizophrenic patients
tested were dextral, with the exception of 2 who were ambidextrous, the lateralized deficits refer to the left hemisphere.

Chlorpromazine's action on orienting responses to nonsignal stimuli could be
evaluated only with the two patients who exhibited responses both on drugs and off.
Nevertheless, both patients showed a consistent effect (116). On drug and after drug
withdrawal, asymmetries in response amplitude were undirectional, whereas after drug
reinstatement the direction of asymmetry was variable. Here the drug's action on
response asymmetries appeared to interact with state of arousal. By the time of drug
reinstatement, patients were fully adapted to the laboratory proceedings. This was
reflected in their cortisol and electrodermal levels, which were then at their lowest. As
levels of physiologic activation were closer to a basal state, the drug's action may have
been more powerful.

The phenomenon that signal value induced responses in nonresponders made possible
examination of bilateral, asymmetries in nonresponders. Nonresponders also showed
lower left- than right-hand response amplitudes, but in this context the responses of
responders were bilaterally symmetrical (46). This may in part reflect the task demands,
in particular the need for an overt response which, while not triggering the response
involving the activity of both hemispheres, may have shifted the balance between them
in the more labile responders. This is discussed further (116) in reply to Uheriks' (117)
partial replication of electrodermal asymmetries in schizophrenia.

Electrodermal response asymmetries to signal stimuli were more clearly demonstrated
to an unconditional stimulus in an autonomic conditioning paradigm (67). The stimulus
was a 12 second, 75dB noise presented ten seconds after a conditional stimulus on half
the trials. Schizophrenic patients were examined on chlorpromazine as well as on
placebo. Patients responded to the unconditional stimulus with lower left- than right-
hand responses (p < 0.03) (see Figure 15-5). Nonpatient controls showed the opposite

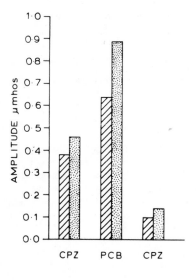

Figure 15-5. Bilateral skin conductance response
amplitudes to unconditional stimuli.

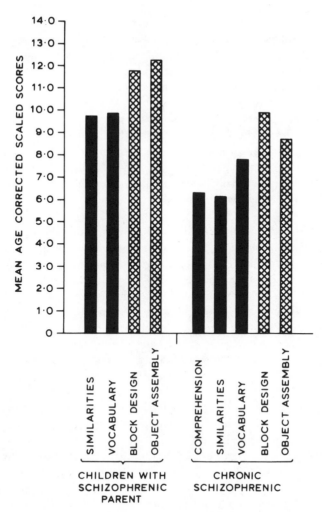

Figure 15-6. Wechsler subtests with left hemisphere and right hemisphere loadings (cross hatching) for children with a schizophrenic parent and chronic schizophrenic patients.

asymmetry (p < 0.008). The response asymmetry with patients was higher on placebo than on drug (p < 0.03), as was the overall magnitude of responses (p < 0.003). A Laterality Index (I) was computed by dividing the left-right difference × 100 by the sum of the left and right response amplitudes. This scaled the bilateral differences in response amplitudes in terms of their absolute size. An analysis with 'I' scores no longer showed a significant drug effect, indicating that the response amplitude asymmetry on placebo was due to the increase in amplitudes on both hands after drug withdrawal. Thus, with respect to signal responses the absence of bilateral asymmetries on drug was secondary to the drug's action in reducing response amplitudes on both hands.

Patterns of cognitive abilities also provided evidence suggestive of a left hemisphere deficit (see Figure 15-6). Subtests of the Wechsler Intelligence Scale for Children (WISC) were obtained from seventy-two 11-to-13-year-old children with a schizophrenic parent from a study of Mednick and Schulsinger. A comparison of verbal subtests that had dominant hemisphere factor loadings (for example, Similarities and Vocabulary) with subtests with nondominant hemisphere factor loadings (for example, Block Design and Object Assembly), showed a significant reduction in dominant relative to nondominant hemisphere abilities (118). Scores on the two verbal tests also were lower in children with a schizophrenic parent than in children whose parents were without known pathology (p < 0.05 and p < 0.01, respectively). Children whose parents had nonschizophrenic pathology including criminality showed a similar trend in subtest scores, but not to the same extent as the children with a schizophrenic parent. The latter represents a partial control for the possibility that the verbal subtest deficit represents an adverse home environment. As only a small percentage of the children with a schizophrenic parent will become schizophrenic themselves, reduced dominant hemisphere functioning may reflect a genetic liability factor related to schizophrenic vulnerability (119).

An essentially similar pattern of abilities has been found with the adult Wechsler subtests of chronic schizophrenics (118). A comparison of the mean scores of the subtests with high dominant hemisphere loadings (Comprehension, Similarities, and Vocabulary) with the subtests with high nondominant hemisphere loadings (Block Design and Object Assembly) showed a highly significant reduction in dominant hemisphere abilities (p < 0.001). While these results have been reported by others with chronic schizophrenics (120,121), they are by no means well established in the clinical literature. Wechsler's (122) report that anxiety and clinical disturbance will differentially impair performance subtests results may have a bearing on this issue. We insured that patients presented an optimal clinical picture before the WAIS was administered.

Evidence of bilateral differences in auditory perception has been found in the audiograms of schizophrenic patients. A threshold shift in the absolute sensitivity of the right ear while the sensitivity of the left ear remained stable occurred during the course of the 12-week chlorpromazine experiment (p < 0.009). Auditory thresholds were unaffected by drug withdrawal. A similar threshold shift has been found to occur from early morning to late afternoon (118,123). The shift occurred in the region of middle and high frequencies, that is, between 1000 and 8000 Hz. There is some evidence (124) that discriminations in the middle and high frequency range as distinct from lower frequencies may be affected by temporal lobe lesions. In line with the temporal-limbic hypothesis, the audiograms of schizophrenics showed on the average a 5dB hearing loss compared with those of healthy normals. What was not anticipated was a finding of superior sensitivity of schizophrenics at lower frequencies.

As the right-ear acuity of the schizophrenics was initially more sensitive than their left-ear acuity (p < 0.02), the dynamics of the right-ear threshold changes may have an affinity with the Russian dimension of strength of the nervous system (118,123). Initially keen sensory sensitivity that cannot be sustained with prolonged stimulation is characteristic of a nervous system susceptible to inhibitory factors such as adaptation and fatigue (125–127). In schizophrenia the left hemisphere appears especially susceptible.

Perceptual discrimination between tones of different durations also showed evidence of lateralized asymmetries in the same patients (85,118). On placebo there was a trend towards poorer right ear performance (p < 0.1). However, the lateralized deficit was reversed by chlorpromazine. With increasing time on drug, right-ear performance improved relative to left-ear performance (p < 0.05). That the reversal in the lateralized deficit was drug induced is further suggested by correlational evidence with the dose

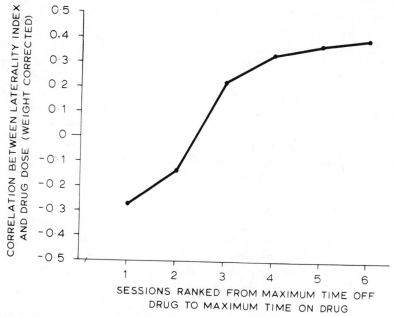

Figure 15-7. The relation of auditory discriminations to chlorpromazine dose level showing better left ear performance with maximum time off drug and better right ear performance with maximum time on drug.

level. 'I' scores, in this case obtained with omission scores, were correlated with the chlorpromazine dose levels (corrected for body weight when on drug). These are shown in Figure 15-7 where omission scores are plotted as a function of sessions ranked from maximum time off drug to maximum time on drug. Correlations were positive when the patients were on drug, indicating that the higher the dose the better the right-ear performance. Correlations were negative when patients were on placebo, indicating worse right ear performance the higher the dose level. In view of the predominantly contralateral projection of auditory pathways, improvement of right ear performance with chlorpromazine is consistent with its hypothesized beneficial effects upon left hemisphere processing.

CONCLUSION

At a strictly empirical level the psychophysiologic, endocrine, behavioral, and information-processing findings indicate that schizophrenic patients tend towards a state of unitary arousal. This may be a state of low arousal or a state of high arousal. Evidence of a similar incidence of the bimodal states at most stages of hospitalization should dispel the popular notion that the schizophrenic patient's arousal is always high. When the patients were subclassified according to arousal level, chlorpromazine was found to reestablish an equilibrium in central arousal processes, as distinct from reducing arousal, whether in a monotonic or nonmonotonic (inverted-U) direction. Central arousal was evaluated through information-processing abilities and levels of cortisol. Levels of autonomic arousal were altered in both directions by the peripheral and central actions of the drug. Such bidirectional effects also would have the effect of disrupting or fractionating a global arousal state.

The experiments were also directed at testing a neurophysiologic model of the locus of schizophrenic pathology that proposes that the disorder is primarily of left-sided, temporal-limbic origin. Support was found from orienting response abnormalities that occurred to nonsignal as distinct from signal stimuli, implying that temporal-limbic rather than frontal-limbic processes are involved. Differences between patients with and without orienting responses were consistent with an imbalance in the modulation of the hypothalamus, pituitary-adrenal axis and the brainstem reticular formation by systems centered on the amygdala and hippocampus. Chlorpromazine, while affecting central arousal measures differentially in patients with and without orienting reactions, did not influence the orienting response index itself, either by correcting deficits of habituation or by restoring responses in nonresponders. This suggests that the drug does not act directly on temporal-limbic processes. As chlorpromazine does not represent a panacea for schizophrenia, it would be of interest to compare its behavioral and therapeutic effects with drugs that do act specifically on temporal-limbic structures and pathways.

Evidence of left-sided deficits in schizophrenic patients was found at diverse levels of function. The bilateral asymmetries in orienting reactions were compatible with a reduction in left-sided amygdaloid influences. Auditory sensitivity at an absolute threshold showed a right ear threshold shift in conditions that may indicate that the left more than the right hemisphere manifests the dynamics of what Russian researchers term the 'inhibitory' nervous system. This dimension of central nervous activity has been associated with a loss of hippocampal inhibitory influences over the ascending reticular formation. It has been used as an explanatory device for earlier findings relating to the perceptual and autonomic functions of schizophrenic patients, but without reference to hemisphere differences. In view of the hemisphere imbalance in arousal, the contralateral hippocampal pathways may be of special relevance. A loss of left-sided hippocampal inhibitory influences may lead to excessive right hemisphere interference on left hemisphere processing via the hippocampal commissures.

A left-sided vulnerability to inhibition and fatigue may underlie verbal cognitive deficits of schizophrenic patients and of children with a genetic liability for schizophrenia. This may represent a trait which predisposes to breakdown. On chlorpromazine, some left-sided deficits in auditory processing were reversed, implying that some laterality effects are transient and are related to clinical state. The equalizing or reversal of bilateral asymmetries on chlorpromazine may reflect the reestablishing of an equilibrium in arousal processes between the brain hemispheres. This suggests a new interpretation of the neurophysiologic dynamics underlying the therapeutic efficacy of change beneficial to schizophrenia.

REFERENCES

1. Carlsson A, Lindqvist TM: Effect of chlorpromazine and haloperidol on formation of 3-methoxy-tyramine and normetanephrine in mouse brain. *Acta Pharmacol* 20:140, 1963.
2. Anden NE, Roos BE, Werdinius B: Effects of chlorpromazine haloperidol and reserpine on the levels of phenolic acids in the rabbit corpus striatum. *Life Sciences* 3:149, 1964.
3. Bobon DP, Janssen PAJ, Bobon J (eds): *The Neuroleptics.* Basel, Kager 1970.

4. Stein L, Wise CD: Possible etiology of schizophrenia: Progressive damage to the noradrenergic reward system by 6-hydroxydopamine. *Science* 171:1032, 1971.

5. Atsmon A, Blum I, Steiner M et al: Further studies with propranolol in psychotic patients. *Psychopharmacologia* (Berl.) 27:249, 1972.

6. Yorkston NJ, Zaki SA, Malik MKU et al: Propranolol in the control of schizophrenic symptoms: *Brit Med J* 765:633, 1974.

7. Fuxe K, Nystrom M, Tovi M et al: Central catecholamine neurons, behaviour and neuroleptic drugs: an analysis to understanding the involvement of catecholamines in schizophrenia. *J Psychiat Res* 11:151, 1974.

8. Axelrod J: Enzymatic formation of psychotomimetic metabolites from normally occurring compounds. *Science* 134:343, 1961.

9. Morgan M, Mandell AJ: An indole (ethyl) amine. N-methyl-transferase in the brain of the chick. *Science* 165:492, 1969.

10. Warburton DM: *Brain, Behaviour and Drugs.* London, John Wiley & Sons, 1975.

11. Snyder SH: Catecholamines in the brain as mediators of amphetamine psychosis. *Archs Gen Psychiat* 27:169, 1972.

12. Matthysse S: Dopamine and the pharmacology of schizophrenia: The state of the evidence. *J Psychiat Res* 11:197, 1974.

13. Friedhoff AJ, Alpert M: A dopaminergic-cholinergic mechanism in production of psychotic symptoms. *Biol Psychiat* 6:165, 1973.

14. Davis JM: A two factor theory of schizophrenia. *J Psychiat Res* 11:25, 1974.

15. Swazey JP: *Chlorpromazine in Psychiatry: A Study of Therapeutic Innovation.* Massachusetts, M.I.T. Press, 1974.

16. Grossman SP: Behavioral and electrophysiological effects of intracranial microinjections of phenothiazines. *Comm Beh Biol* 1:9, 1968.

17. Cytawa J, Kutulas G: Influence of chlorpromazine on emotional hyperreactivity resulting from septal forebrain injury. *Psychopharmacologia* 27:389, 1972.

18. Douglas RJ: The hippocampus and behavior. *Psychol Bull* 67:416, 1967.

19. Isaacson RL, Pribram KH (eds): *The Hippocampus.* Vol 2. New York, Plenum Press, 1975.

20. Gruzelier JH: The investigation of possible limbic dysfunction in schizophrenia by psychophysiological methods. PhD thesis, London University, 1973.

21. Torrey ES, Peterson MR: Schizophrenia and the limbic system. *Lancet* 942, 1974.

22. Heath RG, Monroe RR, Mickle WR: Stimulation of the amygdaloid nucleus in a schizophrenic patient *Amer J Psychiat* 111:862, 1955.

23. Malamud N: Psychiatric disorders with intracranial tumors of the limbic system. *Arch Neurol* 17:113, 1967.

24. Horowitz MJ, Adams JE: Hallucinations on brain stimulation: Evidence for revision of the Penfield hypotheses, in Keup W (ed): *Origins and Mechanisms of Hallucinations.* New York, Plenum Press, 1970, p 13.

25. Davison K, Bagley CR: Schizophrenia-like psychoses associated with organic disorders of the central nervous system, in Herrington RN (ed): *Current Problems in Neuropsychiatry.* London, Royal Medico-Psychological Association, 1969.

26. Jarrard LE: The hippocampus and motivation. *Psychol Bull* 79:1, 1973.

27. Isaacson RL, Pribram KH (eds): *The Hippocampus* Vol. 1 New York, Plenum Press, 1975.

28. Matthysse S: Antipsychotic drug actions: a clue to the neuropathology of schizophrenia? *Federation Proc* 32:200, 1973.

29. Post RM, Goodwin FK: Time-dependent effects of phenothiazines on dopamine turnover in psychiatric patients. *Science* 190:488, 1975.

30. Burki HR, Eichenberger E, Sayers AC et al: Clozapine and the dopamine hypothesis of schizophrenia, a critical appraisal. *Pharmakopsychiat* 8:115, 1975.

31. Pavlov IP: *Conditioned Reflexes and Psychiatry.* Translated Gantt WH. New York, Int Univ Press, 1941.

32. Sokolov EM: *Perception and the Conditioned Reflex.* New York, Macmillan, 1963.

33. Germana J: Central efferent processes and autonomic behavioural integration. *Psychophysiol* 6:78, 1969.

34. Bernstein AS: To what does the orienting response respond. *Psychophysiol* 6:338, 1969.

35. Venables PH: Input regulation and psychopathology, in Hammer M, Salzinger K, Sutton S (eds): *Psychopathology.* New York, John Wiley & Sons, 1973, p 261.

36. Pribram KH, McGuinness D: Arousal, activation and effort in the control of attention. *Psych Rev* 82:116, 1975.

37. Bagshaw MH, Kimble DP, Pribram KH: The GSR of monkeys during orienting and habituation and after ablation of the amygdala, hippocampus and inferotemporal cortex. *Neuropsychologica* 3:111, 1965.

38. Grueninger WE, Kimble DP, Grueninger J: GSR and corticosteroid response in monkeys with frontal ablations. *Neuropsychol* 3:205, 1965.

39. Kimble DP, Bagshaw MH, Pribram KH: The GSR of monkeys during orienting and habituation after selective partial ablations of the cingulate and frontal cortex. *Neuropsychol* 3:121, 1965.

40. Bagshaw MH, Benzies S: Multiple measures of the orienting reaction and their dissociation after amygdalectomy in monkeys. *Exp. Neurol* 20:175, 1968.

41. Holdstock TL: Autonomic reactivity following septal and amygdaloid lesions in white rats. *Physiol Behav* 4:603, 1969.

42. Holdstock TL: Plasticity of autonomic functions in rats with septal lesions. *Neuropsychologia* 8:147, 1970.

43. Isaacson RL: *The Limbic System.* New York, Plenum Press, 1975.

44. Edelberg R: The information content of the recovery limb of the electrodermal response. *Psychophsiol* 6:527, 1970.

45. Luria A, Homskaya ED: Frontal lobe and the regulation of arousal processes, in Mostofsky D. (ed): *Attention: Contemporary Theory and Research.* New York, Appleton 303:330, 1970.

46. Gruzelier JH, Venables PH: Skin conductance responses to tones with and without attentional significance in schizophrenic and non-schizophrenic patients. *Neuropsychologia* 11:221, 1973.

47. Gruzelier JH, Venables PH: Skin conductance orienting activity in a heterogeneous sample of schizophrenics: Possible evidence of limbic dysfunction. *J Nerv Ment Dis* 155:277, 1972.

48. Gruzelier JH: Bilateral asymmetry of skin conductance orienting activity and levels in schizophrenia. *J Biol Psychol* 1:21, 1973.

49. Gruzelier JH, Venables PH: Bimodality and lateral asymmetry of skin conductance orienting activity in schizophrenics: Replication and evidence of lateral asymmetry in patients with depression and disorders of personality. *Biol Psychiat* 8:55, 1974.

50. Gruzelier JH, Venables PH: Two-flash threshold, sensitivity and β in normal subjects and schizophrenics. *Quart J Exp Psychol* 26:594, 1974.

51. Gruzelier JH, Venables PH: Evidence of high and low arousal in schizophrenics. *Psychophsiol* 12:66, 1975.

52. Gruzelier JH, Venables PH: Relations between two-flash discrimination and electrodermal activity re-examined in schizophrenics and normals. *J Psych Res* 12:73, 1975.

53. Gruzelier JH: The cardiac responses of schizophrenics to orienting, signal and non-signal tones. *Biol Psychol* 3:143, 1975.

54. Venables PH: Progress in psychophysiology: Some applications in a field of abnormal psychology, in Venables PH, Christie MJ (eds): *Research in Psychophysiology.* London, John Wiley & Sons, 1975, p 418.

55. Venables PH: A Psychophysiological approach to research in schizophrenia, in Fowles DC (ed): *Clinical Applications of Psychophysiology.* New York, Columbia University Press, 1975.

56. Gruzelier JH: Clinical attributes of schizophrenic skin conductance responders and non-responders. *Psychol Med* 6:245, 1976.

57. Patterson T: Skin conductance responding/nonresponding and pupillimetrics in chronic schizophrenia: a confirmation of Gruzelier and Venables. *J Nerv Ment Dis* 163:200, 1976.

58. Lobstein TJ, Venables PH: Heart rate and skin conductance activity in schizophrenia. In preparation, 1976.

59. Rubens RL, Lapidus LB: Arousal patterns and stimulus barrier functioning in schizophrenia. *J Abn Psychol* (in press).

60. Rippon G: Personal communication 1976.

61. Mirkin T: Personal communication 1976.

62. Fedora O: Personal communication 1976.

63. Venables PH, Patterson T: (This volume, Chapter 16).

64. Straube E: Personal communication 1976.

65. Gruzelier JH, Hammond NV: The effect of chlorpromazine upon the psychophysiology of schizophrenics. *J Psychiat Res* (in press).

66. Zahn TP: On the bimodality of the distribution of the electrodermal orienting responses in schizophrenic patients. *J Nerv Ment Dis* 162:195, 1976.

67. Gruzelier JH: On the bimodality of the distribution of the electrodermal orienting responses in schizophrenia. Replications, refinements and behavioural relevance. In preparation.

68. Gruzelier JH, Hammond NV: Chlorpromazine and the heart rate activity of schizophrenic patients. (In preparation).

69. Lacey JI: Somatic response patterning and stress: Some revisions of activation theory, in Appley MH, Trumbull E (eds): *Psychological Stress.* New York, Appleton-Century-Crofts, 1967, p. 14.

70. Gloor P: Amygdala, in Field J (ed): *Handbook of Physiology,* Section I Neurophysiology Vol 2. Washington, American Physiological Society, 1960.

71. Goddard GV: Functions of the amygdala. *Psychol Bull* 62:8, 1964.

72. Delgado JMR: Free behaviour and brain stimulation. *International Review of Neurobiology* 6:349, 1964.

73. Pagano RR, Gault FP: Amygdala activity: a central measure of arousal *EEG Clin Neurophysiol* 17:255, 1964.

74. Fonberg E: The effect of hypothalamic and amygdalar lesions on alimentary behaviour and thermoregulation. *J de Physiologia* 63:249, 1971.

75. Yokata T, Sato A, Fujimori B: Inhibition of sympathetic activity by stimulation of limbic systems. *Jap J Physiol* 13:138, 1963.

76. Lang H, Tuovinen T, Valsala P: Amygdaloid after discharge and galvanic skin response. *EEG Clin Neurophysiol* 16:366, 1964.

77. Yokata T, Fujimori B: Effects of brain-stem stimulation upon hippocampal electrical activity, somatomotor reflexes and autonomic functions. *EEG Clin Neurophysiol* 16:375, 1964.

78. Frith CD, Baker HF, Deakin JFW, et al: Brain noradrenaline metabolism and psychophysiological variables in chronic schizophrenia. 1st. annual conference of the Brain Research Association, Bath, 1976.

79. Eleftheriou BF (ed): *The Neurobiology of the Amygdala.* New York, Plenum Press, 1972.

80. Bohus B: The Hippocampus and the Pituitary-Adrenal System Hormones, in Isaacson RL, Pribram KH (eds): *The Hippocampus.* New York, Plenum Press, 1975, p 323.

81. McGowan-Sass BK, Timiras PS: The Hippocampus and Homonal Cyclicity, in Isaacson RL, Pribram KH (eds): *The Hippocampus.* New York, Plenum Press, 1975, p 355.

82. Van Hartesveldt C: The Hippocampus and Regulation of the Hypothalamic-Hypophyseal-Adrenal Cortical Axis, in Isaacson RL, Pribram KH (eds): *The Hippocampus.* New York, Plenum Press, 1975, p. 375.

83. Mason JW: A review of psychoendocrine research on the pituitary-adrenal cortical system. *Psychosom Med* 30:576, 1968.

84. Knigge KM: Adrenocortical response to stress in rats with lesions in hippocampus and amygdala. *Proc Soc Exp Biol Med* 108:18, 1961.

85. Hammond NV, Gruzelier JH: Laterality, attention and rate effects in the auditory discrimination of chronic schizophrenics. The effect of treatment with chlorpromazine. *Quart J Exp Psychol* (in press).

86. Henkin R: The neuroendocrine control of perception, in Hamburg DA, Pribram KH, Stunkard AT (eds): *Perception and Its Disorders.* Baltimore, Williams and Wilkins, 1970.

87. Endroczi E: *Limbic System, Learning and Pituitary-Adrenal Function.* Budapest, Akademiae Kiado, 1972.

88. Levine S: Stress and behaviour, *Sci Amer* 224:26, 1971.

89. Fuster JM, Uyeda AA: Reactivity of Limbic neurons of the monkey to appetitive and aversive signals. *EEG and Clin Neurophysiol* 30:281, 1971.

90. Cain DP, Bindra D: Responses of amygdala single units to odors in the rat. *Exp Neurology* 35:98, 1972.

91. Conrad CD, Stumpf WE: Direct visual imput to the limbic system: Crossed retinal projections to the nucleus onterodoesalis thalami in the tree shrew. *Exp Brain Res* 23:141, 1975.

92. Yerkes RM, Dodson JD: The relation of strength of stimulus to rapidity of habit-formation. *J Comp Neurol Psychol* 18:459, 1908.

93. Duffy E: *Activation and Behavior.* New York, John Wiley & Sons Inc, 1962.

94. Freeman GL: The relationship between performance level and bodily activity level. *J Exp Psychol* 26:602, 1940.

95. Hebb DO: Drives and the c.n.s. (conceptual nervous system). *Psychol Rev* 62:243, 1955.

96. Malmo RB: Activation: a neuropsychological dimension. *Psychol Rev* 66:367, 1959.

97. Gruzelier JH, Lykken DT, Venables PH: Schizophrenia and arousal revisited: Two flash threshold and electrodermal activity in activated and non-activated conditions. *Arch Gen Psych* 26:427, 1972.

98. Siddle DAT, Heron PA: Reliability of electrodermal habituation measures under two conditions of stimulus intensity. *J Res Personality* (in press).

99. Bull RHC, Gale MA: The reliability and interrelationships between various measures of electrodermal activity. *J Exp Res Personality* 6:300, 1973.

100. O'Gorman JG: A comment on Koriat, Averill and Malmstrom's "Individual differences in habituation." *J Res Personality* 8:192, 1974.

101. Gruzelier JH: Switch process in schizophrenia? Paper presented at the meeting of the British Psychological Society, London, December, 1970.

102. Lader M: The psychophysiology of affective disorders. Psychophysiology Group, British Psychological Society, London, December, 1975.

103. Mawson C: Personal communication 1975.

104. Meares R, Horvath T: A physiological difference between hallucinosis and schizophrenia. *Brit J Psychiat* 122:687, 1973.

105. Stern JA, Surphlis W, Koff E: Electrodermal responsiveness as related to psychiatric diagnosis and prognosis. *Psychophysiol* 2:51, 1965.

106. Mednick SA, Schulsinger F: Some premorbid characteristics related to breakdown in children with schizophrenic mothers, in Rosenthal D, Kety SS (eds): *The Transmission of Schizophrenia.* London, Pergamon Press, 1968.

107. Ax AF, Bamford JL: The GSR recovery limb in chronic schizophrenia. *Psychophysiol* 7:145, 1971.

108. Maricq HR, Edelberg R: Electrodermal recovery rate in a schizophrenic population. *Psychophysiol* 12:630, 1975.

109. Edelberg R: Electrodermal recovery rate, goal orientation and aversion. *Psychophysiol* 9:512, 1972.

110. Venables PH: The recovery limb of the skin conductance response in "high-risk" research, in Mednick SA, Schulsinger F, Higgins J, et al (eds): *Genetics, Environment and Psychopathology.* Amsterdam, North Holland Publishing Co., 1974, p 117.

111. Flor-Henry P: Psychoses and temporal lobe epilepsy: a controlled investigation. *Epilepsia* 10:363, 1969.

112. Serafetinides EA: Laterality and voltage in the EEG of psychiatric patients. *Diseases of the Nervous System* 33:622, 1972.

113. Serafetinides EA: Voltage laterality in the EEG of psychiatric patients. *Diseases of the Nervous System* 34:190, 1973.

114. Luria AR, Homskaya ED: Le trouble du role regulateur du language au course des lesions au lobe frontal. *Neuropsychol* 1:9, 1963.

115. Sourek K: *The Nervous Control of Skin Potential in Man.* Praha: Nakladetelstvi Ceskoslovenska Akademic Ved, 1965.

116. Gruzelier JH, Hammond NV: The effect of chlorpromazine upon bilateral asymmetries of bioelectrical skin reactivity in schizophrenics. *Studia Psychologica* 19:40, 1977.

117. Uherik A: Interpretation of bilateral asymmetry of bioelectrical skin reactivity on schizophrenics. *Studia Psychologica* 17:51, 1975.

118. Gruzelier JH, Hammond NV: Schizophrenia: A dominant hemisphere temporal-limbic disorder? *Res Commun Psychol Psychiat Behav* 1:33, 1976.

119. Spring B, Zubin J: (This volume, Chapter 36).

120. Klonoff H, Fibiger CH, Hutton GH: Neuropsychological patterns in chronic schizophrenia. *J Nerv Ment Dis* 150:291, 1970.

121. Flor-Henry P, Yeudall LT, Stefanyk W et al: The neuropsychological correlates of the functional psychoses. *Psychiat Clin Psychol* 3:34, 1975.

122. Wechsler D: *The Measurement and Appraisal of Adult Intelligence,* ed. 4. Baltimore, Williams and Wilkins, 1958.

123. Gruzelier JH, Hammond NV: Gains, losses and lateral differences in the hearing of schziophrenic patients. In preparation.

124. Massopust LC, Wolin, LR, Frost V: Increases in auditory middle frequency discrimination thresholds after cortical ablations. *Exp Neurol* 28:299, 1970.

125. Nebylitsyn VD: Investigation of the connection between sensitivity and strength of the nervous system, in Gray JA (ed): *Pavlov's Typology.* Pergamon Press, Oxford, 1964.

126. Nebylitsyn VD, Gray, JA: *Biological Bases of Individual Behaviour.* New York and London, Academic Press, 1972.

127. Nebylitsyn VD: *Fundamental Properties of the Human Nervous System.* New York, Plenum Press, 1972.

Chapter 16
Speech Perception and Decision Processes in Relation to Skin Conductance and Pupillographic Measures in Schizophrenia

Peter H. Venables, Ph.D.
Terry Patterson, Ph.D.

SKIN CONDUCTANCE AND PUPILLOGRAPHY

In recent years two important findings have emerged from skin conductance research in schizophrenia. The long-term studies of Mednick and Schulsinger (18) in Denmark have implicated the recovery limb of the skin conductance orienting response (S.C.O.R.) as a significant factor in the prediction of schizophrenia. In these studies it has been demonstrated that the recovery of the S.C.O.R. is significantly faster in those children who will display schizophrenic symptomatology in later life. However, the mechanism of this aspect of the orienting response is not well understood despite the work of Edelberg and others (6,7).

It is not as yet certain whether the same mechanism underlies all components of the S.C.O.R. or whether it is possible to postulate a different mechanism to underlie some, or all, of the "time parameters" of skin conductance (latency, rise time, and recovery) as distinct from the "amplitude parameters" (basal level and amplitude of response) (31).

The second finding that has emerged with some clarity is that within a schizophrenic population the S.C.O.R. is absent in about 50% of these patients. This finding has been most distinctly stated by Gruzelier and Venables (8,9,11,32) but has been confirmed by Bernstein (personal communication) and Patterson (20). The responding/nonresponding dimension of the S.C.O.R. has been used by Gruzelier and Venables (10–12) to predict other variables such as heart rate, blood pressure and two-flash threshold [a suggested index of cortical "arousal" level (33)].

Thus two parameters have appeared from skin conductance recording (responding/ nonresponding and response recovery time) that have apparent usefulness in work with schizophrenics—in the first instance as a factor dividing adult schizophrenics into separate groups, and in the second as a diagnostic predictor while the patient is still in the premorbid state. Clearly it is of considerable importance to extend the work with both these findings, not only for its own sake but also because greater elucidation of the underlying mechanisms could be forthcoming.

Over a considerable number of years Rubin (22–27) has made the statement that pupillographic parameters show clear abnormalities in psychotic patients. Little attention however, has been paid to this work following the report of Hakerem, Sutton, and Zubin (13) that the "normal" population reported by Rubin has a much smaller variance than any that they had been able to find. Thus the abnormality of Rubin's psychotics was judged by deviation from a control population with excessively small variance. Unfortunately, no research has addressed itself to the possible connection of pupillary "light/dark" reflex behavior and other physiologic and behavioral measures in psychotics and normal subjects. Rubin proposes a model of adrenergic/cholinergic imbalance in the functional psychoses and although this may be speculative, the suggestion that pupil dilation is an adrenergic function and pupil constriction a cholinergic function (16) would appear to be reasonably well established. Thus, it would appear that pupil dilation parameters could be some index of noradrenergic peripheral nervous system activity, and pupil constriction parameters similarly could be related to peripheral cholinergic activity. It is always extremely difficult to extrapolate from peripheral to central measures in electrophysiology because of the problems of interpretation of function in relation to the "blood/brain barrier," and it, therefore, would not be wise to use pupillography as a measure of CNS activity until it has been checked out against some measures with known or strongly hypothesized central effects. However, if a relationship should exist between pupillography and skin conductance parameters, such information would be extremely interesting, even if, strictly, it only applied to a relationship between two peripheral physiologic measures.

It was with this background in mind that Patterson (19) conducted an experiment to examine the relation between skin conductance and pupillographic parameters in a group of 31 chronic schizophrenics. The measurement of the electrodermal variable was by a standard constant voltage technique (17) and the pupillographic measurement was based on the work of Rubin (25). One eye of the subject was photographed at a rate of two frames per second by a 16 mm cine camera. The subject was light adapted for 15 minutes to a standard 750-ft candle source in the pupillograph, and a few frames were taken before extinguishing the light and allowing the pupil to dilate for 60 seconds while being photographed in infra-red light. After 60 seconds, the white light was turned on again, and the constriction of the pupil was photographed for an additional 5 seconds. Measures of the pupil area were calculated for each of the 0.5-second frames exposed.

Using these techniques it was found that there was a relationship between the mean time taken for the S.C.O.R. (a series of 75 db 1000 Hz 1-second stimuli) to recover to 50% of its prestimulus value (rec t/2) and the light/dark reflex of the pupil. This relationship is shown schematically in Figure 16-1, where the total schizophrenic group is dichotomized on the basis of their SC responsivity into fast and slow recovery subgroups.

The most significant pupillographic parameter distinguishing the fast and slow recovery SC groups is the time to maximum pupil constriction from the dark-adapted

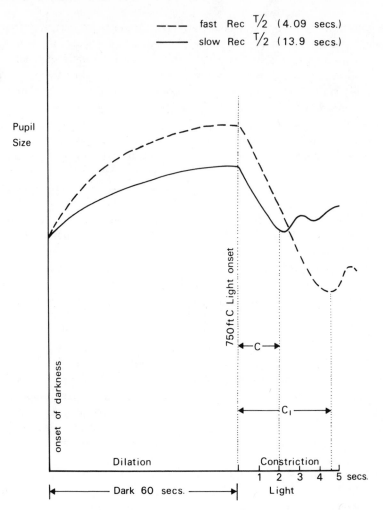

Figure 16-1. Pupil size as a function of time in schizophrenics with fast versus slow skin conductance recovery.

state, the difference between C and C′ in Figure 16-1. In addition, the rate and extent of pupillary dilation is greater in the fast recovery than the slow recovery group.

In a second set of experiments that looked at SC responsivity in another group of chronic schizophrenics and a group of normal subjects, a relationship was found between responding/nonresponding and pupillographic parameters. In brief, the pupillographic records of the patient responders were similar to the fast rec t/2 group previously reported (Figure 16-1), whereas the patient nonresponders performed (pupillographically) in a way akin to the slow rec t/2 group in Figure 16-1. The nonresponders showed very small dilation and constriction parameters in relation to the responders. Some degree of parsimony in these separate sets of findings comes from the observation (in both sets of data) that the S.C.O.R. of some schizophrenics habituates within one or two trials and no further responses are displayed to a series of 15 stimuli. These subjects have been named "Fast Habituators" (FH) by Patterson (20) and "trial-one responders" by Gruzelier (personal communication). The suggestion from this current work is that these subjects may represent an "intermediate" group between SC responders and nonresponders. This view is strengthened by the following observations: (a) The FH group show long latency and extremely long rec t/2. (b) The FH group also show a very low SC basal level, often indistinguishable on this parameter from the nonresponders (11). These observations, together with the pupillometric data, might suggest that whatever the mechanism that underlies rec t/2, an abnormality in this mechanism could possibly underly SC nonresponding in patients. When normal SC responders are compared to patient responders, there is no evidence for differences in their pupillometric light/dark reflex records. However, when the same normal subjects are compared to patient nonresponders, the latter show the same hyporeactivity of the pupil as do the slow rec t/2 group in Figure 16-1. It should be noted that all schizophrenics were receiving similar medication and, at least at the level of tonic heart rate, they apparently all showed equal chlorpromazine-induced tachycardia. These data are in need of replication, but they could well be of interest in future research.

CONCEPTUAL INTEGRATION OF WORK ON AUTONOMIC INDICES AND ITS POSSIBLE RELATION TO ATTENTIONAL PROCESSES

In an attempt to summarize the position, it is suggested that there is a range of skin conductance orienting activity to mild (75 db, slow rise time, 1000 Hz, 1 second) non-signal stimuli from those subjects who respond to a large number of stimuli and who show fast recovery of the S.C.O.R. to those who show no responding whatsoever, with an intermediate group (the fast habituators) who show perhaps one or two responses with slow recovery parameters. Schizophrenics tend to occupy both extreme positions on this range, while normal subjects are found in a more central distribution. This continuum of SC responding is parallel to a continuum of pupillary responding such that the subject showing fast S.C.O.R. recovery tends to exhibit slow time to maximum pupillary constriction, while the subject having a long S.C.O.R. recovery time, or showing no SC responding at all tends to show fast time to maximum pupillary constriction.

Venables (31) has reviewed possible central factors related to speeds of S.C.O.R. recovery, particularly in the light of data from Bagshaw and Kimble (1) where fast S.C.O.R. recovery time and lack of SC habituation is seen in monkeys with hippocampal lesions, while animals with amygdaloid lesions show no SC responsivity. With this in mind, it is suggested that the range of SC activity just outlined is related to a range of limbic activity from functional lack of hippocampal activity (amygdala dominance) to functional lack of amygdala activity (hippocampal dominance).

After reviewing a large amount of animal work with limbic lesions and the use of drugs affecting cholinergic activity, Douglas (5) came to the conclusion that the effects obtained with hippocampal lesions are paralleled by the effects obtained with anticholinergic drugs (i.e., cholinergic depletion). The suggestion is therefore that there is an operational relation between hippocampal inactivity, cholinergic depletion, and fast S.C.O.R. recovery.

Cholinergic depletion, it is suggested, is related to slow pupil constriction in that a small amount of cholinergic antagonism to adrenergically mediated pupil dilation would allow large pupil dilation, and that constriction would be limited in extent or take longer to achieve. The data from the experiments cited earlier show a relationship between fast S.C.O.R. recovery, slow time to constriction, and large pupillary dilation. On the other hand, it could be suggested that the slow rec t/2 group have excessive functional cholinergic activity. This would predict excessive antagonism to pupil dilation, thereby reducing it, and perhaps it also would predict faster pupil constriction. If these suggestions are applied to Figure 16-1 it can be seen that they fit quite well.

Douglas (4) suggests, "The amygdaloid system makes stimuli more figural while the hippocampal system converts figure into ground." Thus, where other than extremely restricted stimulus input is considered, it is possible that under amygdala dominance all the stimuli to which the subject is exposed become "figural." If this is so, then there is a destruction of the hierarchy of stimulus input, and the signal/noise ratio is worsened by the increase in "noise." Carlton (3) formulating a similar position from a response oriented theoretical position states, "Thus responses that were normally inhibited because of their correlation with non-reinforcement were emitted under conditions of attenuated cholinergic function." He is saying that there is a destruction of response hierarchy under cholinergic depletion, or, in terms of the linking suggestions made earlier, under hippocampal inactivity.

At the other extreme, hippocampal dominance would lead to the suggestion of destruction of hierarchy of stimulus input by the reduction of all stimuli to "ground"; in this case the signal/noise ratio is worsened by decrease in "signal." Thus, both hippocampal or amygdaloid dominance or cholinergic depletion or overactivity would predict lack of selectivity of attention and consequently poor performance by schizophrenics exhibiting autonomic features indicative of either end of the continuum outlined previously on tasks requiring selection of input signals from a complex or "noisy" background.

As an aside, it is perhaps important to note that, following the work of Hockey (14,15), it is possible to predict that when there is no differential range of probabilities in a set of stimuli forming an ensemble, changes in states of "arousal" have no effect on changing responses to these equiprobable stimuli. Thus, it might be suggested that however a schizophrenic's level of "arousal" might change as a reaction to the circumstances in which he finds himself, his range of attention still will remain broad. The suggestion would be that the characteristics of attentive function exhibited by schizophrenics occupying either extreme position would be relatively stable.

EXPERIMENTS ON ATTENTION AND SPEECH PERCEPTION

To examine some of these relationships Patterson (21) tested both schizophrenics and normal subjects on an auditory signal detection task. This consisted of the presentation of noise bursts every 3 seconds; 50% of the time at random, a signal (a 1000-Hz tone) was presented 2–3 db above the subject's threshold for this signal in noise, and a response to the signal stimuli was requested. Signal detection theory (SDT) d′ and beta were calculated in the usual way and the d′ results were plotted against "time to maximum pupil constriction."[1] In both patients and normal subjects, it was found that after 20–30 minutes of performance on the task, an inverted U function best fitted the data. Within the normal group, the "mid" constrictor group (those with a time to maximum constriction of 2–4 seconds) showed better sustained attention ability than

---

[1] d′ is classically defined as a measure of the observer's sensory capabilities or of the effective signal strength; β, on the other hand, is a measure of the degree of caution with which the observer works.

those subjects with constriction times either faster or slower. These differences in the normal group only appear after 20 minutes of performance on the SDT task, and the "mid" constrictors thereafter consistently show higher d' values. Within the schizophrenic group, the inverted U function of d' against "time to maximum pupil constriction" appeared much earlier in the task (5–10 minutes), but it had a shape similar to the normal subject's curve, i.e., the "mid" constrictors show better SDT d' over time than either the slow or fast constrictors.

Thus, the results are reasonably consonant with the theoretical position outlined previously where poor performance of extreme groups on the continuum of cholinergic activity or amygdaloid/hippocampal dominance is postulated. However, the results are not directly in line with the theorizing of Warburton (28) and Warburton and Brown (30). In the latter study the authors have demonstrated that with increasing doses of scopolamine (a cholinergic blocker) given to experimental animals, a dose-related decrement in signal detection d' (stimulus sensitivity) is observed. On the basis of this experiment, poor performance would be expected in the group hypothesized to have cholinergic depletion, i.e., those with fast S.C.O.R. recovery and slow time to pupillary constriction. While the inverted U-shaped curve relating d' to constriction time was found throughout the task with the schizophrenics and after 20 minutes in the normal groups, a linear relation between d' and constriction time was found during the first 15 minutes of the task. This relationship was in the direction of poor attentional performance with slow time to constriction and, thus, over this time period is in line with the Warburton and Brown (30) animal studies.

This linear relationship is paralleled by results on a speech perception task carried out by the same subjects. The subjects had to perceive and report normally reproduced and low pass filtered speech (all frequencies above 500 Hz filtered off at 18 db/octave). This paradigm closely follows that of Bull and Venables (2). The subjects with fast pupillary constriction (mean—1.5 seconds constriction time from the dark-adapted state) showed improved detection of low pass filtered speech in comparison to both the "mid" and "slow" constrictors, who were not distinguished on this task. Within the schizophrenic group, this effect was reduced but still tended in the same direction, with better low pass filtered speech performance being seen in the "fast" pupil constrictors. The better performance of normal subjects on both the signal detection and the speech perception task in those having pupillary activity showing fast constriction suggests that if fast constriction is paralleled by a degree of cholinergic overactivity, or amygdala dominance, the "figural accentuation" offered by these mechanisms is effective because it is not extreme or is adequately balanced by adrenergic activity. Clearly the conditions under which linear or curvilinear relationships between attentional performance and underlying physiologic function are shown requires more than this preliminary study before anything definitive can be suggested.

CONCLUSIONS

It is not novel to suggest cholinergic involvement in schizophrenia, and as a result of this hypothesis some of the most direct experimental/treatment-oriented manipulation of the schizophrenic CNS was done by Sherwood and coworkers in the 1950s (29). These researchers directly injected acetylcholinesterase into the cerebral ventricles of some schizophrenics. In some cases the results were immediate and dramatic reversal of extremely severe and long-standing schizophrenic symptoms. No effect was noted in other patients, and in some there was an exacerbation of symptoms. This is one of the very few examples of direct intervention in the schizophrenic CNS and its conclusions are directly in keeping with the view expressed here. It should also be noted that some of the effects noted during direct acetylcholinesterase infusion were pupillary changes and sweating. This perhaps gives slightly more credence to the notion that the pupillometric and skin conductance parameters reported here are some indication of central states.

In conclusion, the authors do not wish to put forward the notions discussed above as more than very tentative. Instead, it is our intention that the data and discussion given here be used to stimulate research. The results presented are still in process of experimentation, and it is therefore in the spirit of conjecture that this paper is presented with the hope that others will feel it worthwhile to extend the parameters that, in our hands, have promised exciting results.

REFERENCES

1. Bagshaw MH, Kimble D: Bimodal EDR orienting response characteristics of limbic lesioned monkeys correlates with schizophrenic patients. Paper read to Society for Psychophysiological Research, Boston, Mass, 1972.

2. Bull HC, Venables, PH: Speech perception in schizophrenia. *Brit J Psychiat* 125:350–354, 1974.

3. Carlton PL: Cholinergic mechanisms in the control of behavior by the brain. *Psych Res* 70:19–39, 1963.

4. Douglas JJ: The hippocampus and behaviour. *Psychol Bull* 67(6):416–442, 1967.

5. Douglas JJ: Pavlovian conditioning and the brain, in Boakes RA, Halliday MS (eds): *Inhibition and Learning*. London, Academic Press, 1972.

6. Edelberg R: The information content of the recovery limb of the electrodermal response. *Psychophysiology* 6(5):527–539, 1970.

7. Edelberg R: Electrical activity of the skin, in Greenfield NS, Sternbach RA (eds): *Handbook of Psychophysiology*. New York, Holt, Rinehart & Winston, 1972.

8. Gruzelier JH, Venables PH: Skin conductance orienting activity in a heterogeneous sample of schizophrenics. *J Nerv and Ment Dis* 155(4):277–287, 1972.

9. Gruzelier JH, Venables PH: Skin conductance responses to tones with and without attentional significance in schizophrenic and non-schizophrenic psychotic patients. *Neuropsychologia* 11:221–230, 1973.

10. Gruzelier JH, Venables PH: Two-flash threshold, sensitivity and β in normal subjects and schizophrenics. *Q J Exp Psychol* 26:594–604, 1974.

11. Gruzelier JH, Venables PH: Evidence of high and low levels of physiological arousal in schizophrenia. *Psychophysiology* 12(1):66–73, 1975.

12. Gruzelier JH, Venables PH: Relations between two-flash threshold discrimination and electrodermal activity, re-examined in schizophrenics and normals. *J Psychiat Res* 12:73–85, 1975.

13. Hakerem G, Sutton S, Zubin J: Pupillary reactions to light in schizophrenic patients and normals. *Ann NY Acad Sci* 105:820–831, 1964.

14. Hockey GRJ: The effect of loud noise on attentional selectivity. *Q J Exp Psychol* 22:28–36, 1970.

15. Hockey GRJ: Signal location and spatial location as possible bases for increased selectivity in noise. *Q J Exp Psychol* 22:37–42, 1970.

16. Loewenfeld IE: Mechanism of reflex dilation of the pupil: Historical review and experimental analysis. *Documenta Opthalmologica* 12:185–448, 1958.

17. Lykken DT, Venables PH: Direct measurement of skin conductance: A proposal for standardization. *Psychophysiology* 8:656–672, 1971.

18. Mednick SA, Schulsinger F: Some premorbid characteristics related to breakdown in children with schizophrenic mothers, in Rosenthal D, Kety SS (eds): *Transmission of Schizophrenia*. London, Pergamon, 1968.

19. Patterson T: Skin conductance recovery and pupillometrics in chronic schizophrenia. *Psychophysiology* 13:189–195, 1976.

20. Patterson T: Skin conductance responding/nonresponding and pupillometrics in chronic schizophrenia: a confirmation of Gruzelier and Venables. *J Nerv and Ment Dis* 1976, accepted for publication.

21. Patterson T: The relationship between skin conductance and pupillography in chronic schizophrenia. Unpublished PhD thesis, University of Reading, England, 1976.

22. Rubin LS: Pupillary reactivity as a measure of autonomic balance in the study of psychotic behaviour. *Trans NY Acad Sci* 22:509, 1960.

23. Rubin LS: Pupillary reactivity as a measure of adrenergic-cholinergic mechanisms in the study of psychotic behaviour. *J Nerv and Ment Dis* 130:386, 1960.

24. Rubin LS: Patterns of pupillary dilation and constriction in psychotic adults and autistic children. *J Nerv and Ment Dis* 133(2):130–142, 1961.

25. Rubin LS: Patterns of adrenergic-cholinergic imbalance in the functional psychoses. *Psych Rev* 69:501–519, 1962.

26. Rubin LS, Barry TJ: Autonomic Fatigue in Psychoses. *J Nerv and Ment Dis* 147:211, 1968.

27. Rubin LS, Barry TJ: The effects of conjunctional instillation of Eserine and homatrophine on pupillary reactivity in schizophrenics. *Biol Psychiat* 5(3):257–269, 1972.

28. Warburton DM: The cholinergic control of internal inhibition, in Boakes RA, Halliday MS (eds): *Inhibition and Learning*. London, Academic Press, 1972.

29. Warburton DM: Schizophrenics and experimental psychoses, in *Brain, Drugs and Behaviour*. London, John Wiley and Sons, 1975.

30. Warburton DM, Brown K: Attenuation of stimulus sensitivity induced by scopolamine. *Nature,* 230:126–127, 1971.

31. Venables PH: The recovery limb of the skin conductance response in "high-risk" research, in Mednick SA, Schulsinger F, Higgins J, et al (eds): *Genetics, Environment and Psychopathology*. Amsterdam, North Holland/American Elsevier, 1975, p 117.

32. Venables PH: A psychophysiological approach to research in schizophrenia, in Fowles DC (ed): *Clinical Applications of Psychophysiology*. New York, Columbia University Press, 1975.

33. Venables PH, Warwick-Evans LA: Cortical arousal and two-flash threshold. *Psychonom Sci* 8:231–232, 1967.

Chapter 17
Physiologic and Behavioral Correlates of Attention Dysfunction in Schizophrenic Patients

Conan Kornetsky, Ph.D.
Maressa Hecht Orzack, Ph.D.

Schizophrenic patients usually perform poorer than normal subjects on most behavioral tasks. It is our contention that many of the behavioral deficits seen in the schizophrenic can be accounted for by a primary attentional disorder and/or a general lack of interest by the patient in playing the psychologic games of the investigator. Much of the discordance in experiments with schizophrenic patients is probably due not only to the failure to obtain full participation of the patient but also to the failure to define adequately the study sample. Furthermore, experimental designs often suffer from the assumption that the disease state itself is a unitary function. Many investigators have attempted to subdivide their subject sample by subtype, i.e., paranoid versus nonparanoid, process versus reactive, good premorbid versus poor premorbid, and so forth; however, even this type of subdivision often has not given consistent results across a variety of experiments. In all these studies the dividing of the schizophrenic sample into subtypes has been on the basis of some clinical characteristic of the patient and the dependent variable has been some performance measure. In this report we will discuss a series of experiments in which we have used the opposite approach. The independent variable is the performance of the patients on a simple test of attention and the dependent variables are other performance tasks, various clinical subdivisions, and EEG recordings.

THE INDEPENDENT VARIABLE

In previous work, we have found that the performance of approximately 40% of chronic schizophrenics that we have tested on the Continuous Performance Test (CPT) is

Supported in part by NIMH grant MH12568. Dr. Kornetsky is an NIMH Research Scientist Awardee, MH1759.

poorer than that of all normal subjects we have tested (1). We have interpreted this impairment as resulting from an attentional deficit. This attentional deficit has been found in schizophrenic patients who were in good remission and not on medication (2). Patients receiving antipsychotic medication are less likely to show an attentional deficit than patients not receiving such medication (1,3). This chapter, for the most part, will review those experiments in which we have compared schizophrenic patients who perform well on the CPT to those patients who do poorly on the CPT. The CPT consists of the presentation of stimuli, usually but not necessarily letters, in a random sequence at a constant rate and for a brief exposure time. A critical stimulus "X" appears, on the average, every fifth stimulus presentation until a total of 50 critical stimuli are presented. The task for the subject is quite simple. He is asked to press a key each time and only when a critical stimulus is presented.

The exposure time for critical stimuli that we have used in most of our experiments has been 0.1 second with an interstimulus time of 1.0 second. Figure 17-1 shows a schematic representation of the time sequence and the types of correct or incorrect responses that can be made by the subject. With very young children, pictures have been substituted for letter stimuli. Auditory forms of the test also have been used, and the task can be made more difficult by having the subject respond to the "X" only when it follows an "A" in the sequence. It is our belief that the major critical component in the task is that it is an experimenter-paced task, and that the exposure time of stimuli is relatively brief (4). The use of the test with schizophrenic patients and the effects of drugs on test results in both animals and man are described by Kornetsky (5) and Kornetsky and Markowitz (6).

We have found that normal subjects rarely make more than two omission errors in 50 presentations of the critical stimulus. Schizophrenics who make two or less errors we have arbitrarily defined as the "goods" and those who make three or more errors as the "poors." Using this dichotomy, we proceeded to make a number of predictions based on the hypothesis that poor performance on the CPT by schizophrenic patients was a manifestation of an attentional deficit, and that this deficit in attention is due to a central state of hyperarousal. This central state of arousal may or may not be related to autonomic or behavioral arousal.

With these simple assumptions in mind, a number of predictions of differences between "goods" and "poors" were made in a series of experiments involving schizophrenic patients.

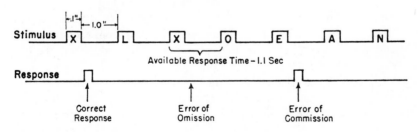

Figure 17-1. Schematic representation of the time sequence and types of errors on the CPT.

1. Poor performance on the CPT would be related to slow reaction time and disturbance in segmental set
2. Poor performance on the CPT would be associated with a higher incidence of fast activity in the EEG
3. Poor performance on the CPT would be associated with a lack of slow wave sleep.
4. Poor performance on the CPT would be associated with a greater amount of mental illness in the family

CPT AND REACTION TIME

Among the most consistent findings of a difference between schizophrenic and normal subjects are those associated with reaction time. More specifically, the schizophrenic patient is unable to maintain a readiness to respond at longer preparatory intervals (7). Zahn et al (8) demonstrated that the reaction time of schizophrenic patients is influenced not only by the preparatory interval for the specific trial but also by the length of the interval of the preceding trial.

Procedure

The subjects consisted of 19 chronic schizophrenic patients who had been hospitalized 2 or more years and 10 normal volunteer control subjects. None of the patients had received any pharmacotherapeutic drugs for at least 4 weeks at the time of the study.

All the subjects were tested on the CPT and also were administered the Digit Symbol Substitution Test (DSST). On the basis of performance on the CPT, the patients were divided into two groups. Nine of the patients were classified as poor performers on the CPT, and 10 as good performers. The latter group had three or more errors on the CPT. In the measurement of reaction time, the procedure used by Zahn et al (8) was replicated except that visual rather than auditory reaction time was measured. Five different preparatory intervals were used: 1, 2, 4, 7, and 15 seconds. They were presented in a quasirandom order so each interval preceded all other intervals an equal number of times, making a total of 52 trials.

Results

The reaction time as a function of the preparatory interval (PI) and the previous preparatory interval (PPI) is shown in Figure 17-2. The PPI is the preparatory interval preceding the target reaction time trial independent of the PI of the target interval. As can be seen, overall reaction time was slowest in the "poors" and fastest in the normal subjects. Each group was statistically significantly different from each of the other two groups. The figure also indicates that the "poors" were affected by both the PI and the PPI more than the "goods" or the normal subjects.

To determine more exactly the role of the PPI in reaction time, the reaction time for each target PI was averaged separately for those trials in which the PPI was shorter than the target interval and for those trials in which the PPI was longer than the target interval. This analysis is shown in Figure 17-3. For each group of subjects the difference in reaction time between the longer and shorter PPIs was statistically significant. The

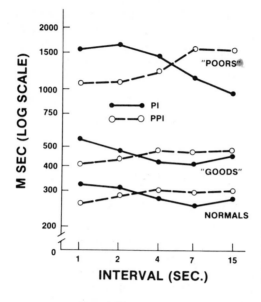

Figure 17-2. Reaction time as a function of the preparatory interval (PI) or the previous preparatory interval (PPI) for the good and poor performers on the CPT and for the normal subjects.

comparison between the groups is of interest for in the "poors" the PPI had no effect when the target interval was 4 seconds but had marked effects at the longer preparatory intervals.

Two results are apparent from this study. The reaction time of the "poors" is significantly slower than that of the "goods" who are significantly slower than the normal subjects. And, the reaction time of the "poors" is influenced more by the PPI than that of either the "goods" or the normal subjects. The major problem in interpreting these results is that in this study we found a significant difference in DSST performance

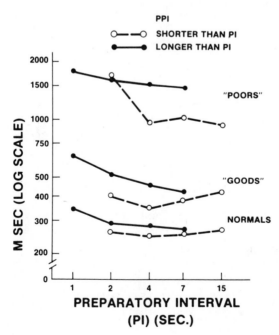

Figure 17-3. The reaction time for the three groups of subjects at each of the preparatory intervals (PI) as a function of whether or not the previous preparatory interval (PPI) was longer or shorter than the PI of the target reaction time trial.

between the "goods" and the "poors." The mean DSST scores were 42.8 and 23.5 for the "goods" and "poors" respectively. The mean score on the DSST for the normal subjects was 69.9. In previous studies in which we have controlled for years of education between groups, we have found no significant difference between patients and normal subjects on the DSST. Also, the "goods" and "poors" did not differ on the DSST in the previous studies.

CPT AND EEG

Previous investigations have consistently reported that the EEG of the chronic schizophrenic patient is characterized by a greater amount of fast and choppy activity than that of the nonschizophrenic (9,10). Also, patients receiving antipsychotic medication have more synchronous and slower activity on the EEG than do patients not receiving antipsychotic medication. We have found that patients receiving pharmacotherapy show a lesser attentional deficit than those not receiving medication (1,3).

The specific hypothesis in the present experiment was that the poor performers on the CPT would have more fast activity in their EEG records than would good performers. In addition to a comparison of the "goods" and the "poors," we also tested a group of normal volunteers with the prediction that they would have less fast activity in their EEG records than either of the schizophrenic groups.

Procedure

The subjects consisted of 25 chronic schizophrenic patients, hospitalized for 2 or more years. Eight of the patients were hospitalized, and 17 were living in the community under hospital supervision. All the patients were maintained on phenothiazine medication. Eight normal volunteers were used as a control group. Although the normal subjects were considerably younger than the patients (mean age—25; mean age of patients—48), the age of the "goods" was not significantly different than that of the "poors" in the sample of schizophrenic subjects.

All subjects were administered the CPT and, in addition, all patients were tested on the DSST. None of the normal controls made any errors on the CPT. The patients' mean error score on the CPT was 4.2. The 25 patients were divided into two groups on the basis of their CPT performance, 8 poor and 17 good performers. The two groups did not differ significantly either in their DSST performance or on the amount of medication they were receiving.

The EEG was continuously recorded while the subject was tested on the CPT. EEG frequencies were characterized into one of the following frequency bands: 1–3 Hz (delta), 4–7 Hz (theta), 8–13 Hz (alpha), 14–26 Hz (beta 1), and 27–40 Hz (beta 2).

The "poors" had more beta 2 activity than the "goods," although this difference did not reach statistical significance ($0.05 < p < 0.10$). The failure to find a statistically significant difference between the "goods" and "poors" in the amount of beta 2 is understandable in that all the schizophrenics were receiving phenothiazine medication and, as reported by Itil (10), the phenothiazines reduce the amount of EEG fast activity. Thus, if we were able to test these patients while they were not receiving medication, it is our belief that the difference in the amount of beta 2 would have been greater.

CPT PERFORMANCE AND SLOW-WAVE SLEEP

Previously published papers have reported that schizophrenic patients have little or no slow-wave sleep as compared to normal subjects (11,12). This absence of slow-wave sleep in some patients fits the arousal model of schizophrenia. Since we have postulated that poor performance on the CPT in schizophrenic patients is associated with central arousal, our model would predict that the absence of slow-wave sleep would be associated with poor performance on the CPT.[1]

Methods

Ten chronic schizophrenics who were not receiving antipsychotic medication were divided into two groups on the basis of their CPT performance. Five subjects were classified as "poors" and 5 subjects were classified as "goods." The EEG sleep patterns of the patients were monitored for eight consecutive nights. Only the data for the last six nights were used in the analysis. EEG scoring was done according to the Rechtschaffen and Kales method by trained laboratory personnel who were "blind" with regard to the CPT scores.

Results

Poor attenders had a smaller proportion of Stage IV (slow-wave) sleep than good attenders had. None of the other comparisons of the stages of sleep, including REM sleep, showed a statistically significant difference between the "goods" and the "poors." Most of the absence of slow-wave sleep could be accounted for by a higher percentage of stage II sleep in the "poors" than in the "goods," although this difference did not reach an acceptable probability level. The DSST performance of these two groups of patients did not differ nor did they differ in terms of age, years of hospitalization, or age of onset of the disease.

CPT AND ENVIRONMENTAL AND FAMILIAL PREDICTORS

The results of this study have been previously published (1), so we will only briefly summarize the findings. As in the previous experiments, a group of chronic schizophrenic patients was divided into two groups based on CPT performance. In this case we tested every diagnosed chronic schizophrenic who had been hospitalized for 2 or more years at Medfield State Hospital (Medfield, Massachusetts) and who was willing and could perform on a simple psychologic test. Only patients who obtained a score of 30 or more on the DSST were included. For further details of the selection of patients see Orzack and Kornetsky (1). The usable sample consisted of 69 patients; 27 were free of medication and 42 were receiving phenothiazines or phenothiazines and antiparkinsonism drugs. Of those patients not maintained on medications, 13 were classified as "poors" and 14 as "goods" based on the previously described CPT criterion. Despite a variety of variables looked at, including length of hospitalization and diagnostic subtype, the only

---

[1] This study was done with the collaboration of Ernest Hartmann. Details of the study will be published elsewhere.

Table 17-1. Incidence Of Mental Illness In Patients' Families As A Function Of CPT Performance and Medication[a]

No Medication

	Attention Behavior	
	"Poors"	*"Goods"*
Familial mental illness	8	3
No familial mental illness	5	11
Fisher's Exact Probability Test p = 0.05		
Mentally ill siblings	7	2
No mentally ill siblings	6	12
Fisher's Exact Probability Test p = 0.04		

Medication Status

	On	Off
Familial mental illness	32	11
No familial mental illness	10	16
Chi Square p < 0.01		

[a] From Orzack MH, and Kornetsky C (1).

variable that clearly separated the "goods" from the "poors" was a history of mental illness in the family. This is shown in Table 17-1. A positive score for mental illness was assigned if there was a history of illness in the immediate family or in aunts, uncles, and grandparents. Of the total sample of 69, 47 cases were given positive scores for mental illness, and in only 7 of the 47 was the mental illness not in the immediate family. Acceptable categories for mental illness were schizophrenia, alcoholism, depression, paranoia, manic-depression, and suicide. Of interest is the finding that the medicated patients had significantly more mental illness in the family than the nonmedication group (see Table 17-1). Since the determination of therapy was in the hands of the treating psychiatrist, this relationship would suggest that those with a history of mental illness tended to be patients who could not be maintained drug-free. In addition to these findings, the results supported previous findings that patients receiving pharmacotherapy perform significantly better on the CPT than do patients not on medication, with scores of 1.9 and 5.1 errors respectively.

DISCUSSION

It is our contention that despite the simplicity of the CPT, in some schizophrenics it is tapping a core performance deficit. It is a deficit that is reduced by antipsychotic medication, and that is present in some children at risk (13) as well as in some patients in remission. It is a deficit that correlates with a history of mental disturbance in the family. The deficit predicts the absence of slow-wave sleep and may be related to the amount of beta 2 activity in the EEG. And finally, poor performance on the CPT predicts a segmental set alteration in schizophrenic patients.

We have not found the deficit in CPT performance to be related to cognitive functioning, diagnostic subtype, duration of hospitalization, duration of illness, age, sex, race, ethnic background, marital status, education, or birth order.

The results reported are not without their shortcomings. The reaction time experiment was contaminated by the significant difference in DSST scores between the two groups of schizophrenic patients. The EEG experiment was contaminated by the fact that all patients were receiving phenothiazine medication. The dividing of schizophrenic patients into two groups simply on the basis of their performance on a test as simple as the CPT is by its nature a gross oversimplification of the disease process. Also, since the cooperation of the patient is needed in these studies, we are testing only a small biased sample of the chronic schizophrenic population. Thus, conclusions and inferences from the results must be guarded.

Further, there is the question concerning what the CPT actually measures. Are errors on the test a function of an attentional deficit as we have postulated, or do they reflect some failure in the response system of the subject? Further, and what is most surprising, how could a test in which a criterion of three or more errors in a testing session presenting approximately 250 stimuli predict such things as a history of mental illness in the family or the absence of slow-wave sleep? Although, with all these things in mind, it would be easy to dismiss any one of these findings, we are always amazed at the robust nature of the procedure.

The question that these data confront us with is what do they tell us about the schizophrenic? Are we tapping some core deficit or are we merely finding a correlation with factors that are correlated with the condition but not directly related to some core dysfunction in the central nervous system of the patient?

The studies we have reported here as well as others in our laboratory, both in animals as well as schizophrenics, lead us to believe that the deficit is real, and that it is not a matter of cooperation or motivation of the subject. We have postulated that the intervening variable accounting for the deficit is a level of central arousal that allows for competing stimuli, both internal and external, to interfere with the complete registration of the critical stimuli (14).

Although experimental results have not always supported the arousal hypothesis of schizophrenia, Zahn (15), in his review of the literature, states that most of the evidence from autonomic and electrophysiologic experiments indicates that the schizophrenic has a higher level of resting or "basal" level of arousal than the normal subject has. Most of the disagreement with the arousal model involves experiments in which autonomic nervous system measures of arousal were measured during test situations. In these experiments relative hypoarousal is associated with poor performance. Also, the use of contingent noxious stimuli to increase arousal does not result in impairment in performance of the schizophrenic patient as would be predicted by the arousal hypothesis (15).

Although it is beyond the scope of this paper to detail why there is apparent autonomic hypoarousal in schizophrenic patients during the test situations, there are factors that may confound these results. These are: in many of the experiments the schizophrenic subjects were receiving medication and there were differences in basal autonomic levels between the schizophrenic and the normal subjects.

In the experiments in which contingent noxious stimuli were used to increase arousal, the improved performance of the schizophrenic may allow for the focusing of attention on the task which was impaired because of a variety of competing stimuli.

As Zahn has suggested, schizophrenics may have both nonspecific arousal and relatively specific hypoarousal in test situations as compared to normal subjects. The nonspecific arousal is supported by the findings of Wohlberg and Kornetsky (2) and those of Stammeyer (16) in which the CPT performance of patients in remission or patients with an active process were tested under conditions of sensory overload. The other possibility is that central arousal does not necessarily correlate with autonomic arousal. The reports of increased fast activity in the EEG of schizophrenic patients as well as the experiment in which the EEG was recorded while the subject was taking the CPT suggest that poor performance on the CPT is related to fast activity in the CNS even when the EEG and performance scores are contaminated by drug therapy.

We have suggested that these findings fit the inverted U model with arousal level on the abscissa and performance on the ordinate. This model remains alive and well only if the postulated state of arousal is central nervous system activation and not autonomic activation.

REFERENCES

1. Orzack MH, Kornetsky C: Environmental and familial predictors of attention behavior in chronic schizophrenics. *J Psychiat Res* 9:21, 1971.

2. Wohlberg G, Kornetsky C: Sustained attention in remitted schizophrenics. *Arch Gen Psychiat* 28:533, 1973.

3. Orzack MH, Kornetsky C, Freeman H: The effects of daily administration of carphenazine on attention in schizophrenic patients. *Psychopharmacologia* Vol. 11, p. 31, 1967.

4. Kornetsky C, Orzack MH: A research note on some of the critical factors on the dissimilar effects of chlorpromazine and secobarbital on the digit symbol substitution and continuous performance tests. *Psychopharmacologia* 6:79, 1964.

5. Kornetsky C: The use of a simple test of attention as a measure of drug effects in schizophrenic patients. *Psychopharmacologia* 24:99, 1972.

6. Kornetsky C, Markowitz R: Animal models and schizophrenia, in Ingle D, Shein H (eds): *Model Systems in Biological Psychiatry.* Cambridge, Mass, MIT Press, 1975, p 26.

7. Shakow D: Segmental set; a theory of the formal psychological deficit in schizophrenia. *Arch Gen Psychiat* 6:1, 1962.

8. Zahn TP, Rosenthal D, Shakow D: Effects or irregular preparatory intervals on RT in schizophrenia. *J Abnorm Soc Psychol* 67:44, 1963.

9. Davis PA, Davis H: The electroencephalograms of psychotic patients. *Am J Psychiat* 95:1007, 1939.

10. Itil TM, Saletu, B, Davis S: EEG findings in chronic schizophrenics based on digital computer period analysis and analogue power spectra. *Biol Psychiat* 5:1, 1972.

11. Caldwell DF, Domino E: Differential levels of stage IV sleep in a group of clinically similar chronic schizophrenic patients. *Biol Psych* 1:131, 1969.

12. Traub AC: Sleep stage dificits in chronic schizophrenics. *Psych Reports* 31:815, 1972.

13. Grunebaum H, Weiss JL, and Gallant D: Attention in young children of psychotic mothers. *Am J Psychiat* 131:887, 1974.

14. Kornetsky C, Mirsky A: On certain psychopharmacological and physiological differences between schizophrenics and normal persons. *Psychopharmacologia* 8:309, 1966.

15. Zahn TP: Psychophysiological concomitants of task performance in schizophrenia, in Kietzman ML, Sutton S, Zubin J (eds): *Experimental Approaches to Psychopathology.* New York, Academic Press, 1975, p 109.

16. Stammeyer EC: The effects of distraction on performance in schizophrenic, psychoneurotic, and normal individuals. A Dissertation. Catholic University of America Press, Washington, DC, 1961.

Chapter 18
Toward a Neurophysiology of Schizophrenia

Herbert G. Vaughan, Jr., M.D.

Since Berger's pioneering studies of the human EEG (1), continuing efforts have been made to define electrophysiologic patterns characteristic of schizophrenic illness. In the absence of a satisfactory animal model of schizophrenia, neurophysiologic analyses of this disorder must necessarily be limited to data obtained from the scalp EEG, supplemented by rare opportunities to obtain intracranial recordings in psychiatric patients.

Although various alterations in the spontaneous EEG and in stimulus-evoked potentials have been described in schizophrenic patients, no electrophysiologic sign has been identified that is specific to schizophrenia or reliably discriminates schizophrenics from other individuals. See reviews by Mirsky (2) and Shagass (3–5).

This state of affairs is not entirely surprising inasmuch as schizophrenic illnesses encompass a wide range of behavioral and experiential symptomatology that would be associated with concurrent variations in underlying neurophysiologic processes. This heterogeneity of psychopathology is further compounded by neurophysiologically significant variables such as age, sex, and drug treatment. These circumstances constitute a substantial impediment to the discovery of pathognomonic electrophysiologic indices of schizophrenic illness, even if one accepts the notion that schizophrenia entails a specific "core" neurophysiologic dysfunction.

Although not entirely beyond the realm of possibility, the notion of a simple electrophysiologic "marker," specific to schizophrenia, appears implausible. A reliable marker would necessarily be insensitive to individual differences in symptomatology as well as to fluctuations in clinical course within each patient. Such an index would presumably reflect some stable, genetically determined biochemical or structural change. Since it is highly unlikely that a schizophrenogenic genome is expressed, even at the molecular level, as an invariant phenotype, neurophysiologic manifestations would be expected to reflect the phenotypic variations. Any latent genetic defect most likely would be manifested as a pathognomonic biochemical deviation rather than an electrophysiologic one. Neuroelectric activity within the central nervous system represents a resultant of highly complex neural processes involving the activity of systems that contain neurons with different neurotransmitters and varied patterns of excitatory and inhibitory synaptic architecture. There are few if any neuroelectric processes that can be observed in the intact behaving organism that uniquely reflect the action of specific neurochemical processes. For this reason alone, the detection and interpretation of deviant central neural processes almost certainly will require an analytic experimental approach that seeks electrophysiologic indices of characteristic *psychologic* patterns of evidence, rather than electrophysiologic signs of an underlying biochemical and/or structural defect.

Recent electrophysiologic studies have focused on the more reasonable goal of identifying neuroelectric indices of hypothesized dysfunction in neural systems that modulate arousal and attention. These efforts have been handicapped by the slippery nature of these psychophysiologic constructs and often present circular interpretations of the data. Electrophysiologic studies in schizophrenia also suffer from the same problems in subject selection and classification that have plagued behavioral experimentation, and there are few findings in this area whose reliability has been established by replication. Furthermore, no measurement, no matter how carefully made, is of value unless one knows what is being measured. In human electrophysiology it has seemed sufficient that some aspect of brain activity was being quantified. Ad hoc interpretations of arbitrarily selected measures often characterize electrophysiologic approaches to psychopathology (6). It is necessary to insist on more rigorous approaches to human psychoneurophysiologic investigations that utilize appropriate behavioral paradigms and to exploit fully the information contained in the available neuroelectric data.

THE ANALYSIS OF EVENT-RELATED CEREBRAL POTENTIALS

The electrical signals recorded from the scalp represent a biased sample of a vast number of individually complex cellular processes within the brain. It is a formidable challenge to extract information from these composite phenomena that can be related validly to psychologic data on the one hand and to cellular electrophysiology on the other. Many problems remain unsolved, and some are essentially insoluble due to inherent limitation in the information contained in the scalp-recorded EEG. Nevertheless, available analytic methods permit the extraction of significant information on timing, location, and magnitude of cerebral neuroelectric phenomena that can be directly related to concurrent psychologic processes. These methods utilize signal averaging techniques to extract from the EEG the brain potentials that are temporally related to specific events, such as stimuli or discrete motor acts, in combination with a topographic analysis that permits inferences to be drawn on the intracranial sources of these event-related potentials (ERP) (7). The principles of ERP analyses are discussed by Vaughan (8) and should be consulted for more detailed methodological information.

Inasmuch as the averaging technique involves the summation of neuroelectric activity synchronized with a discrete time reference, the physiologic data can be directly related to behavioral analyses, employing the information processing paradigm forwarded by Sternberg (9,10). The information processing approach is heuristically schematized in terms of psychological processes in Figure 18-1. The relationship between physiologic data and behavioral analyses is indicated below:

$$O(t) \xrightarrow[\substack{\uparrow ERP \downarrow \\ S \qquad R}]{\text{experience}}$$

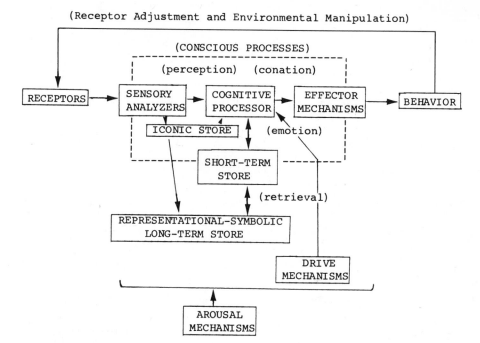

Figure 18-1. Heuristic flow diagram of central processing mechanisms. Input to arousal and drive mechanisms is not indicated nor are reciprocal interactions among processing components completely depicted.

In this diagram, the observable variables—stimuli (S), event-related brain potentials (ERP), and motor responses (R)—are depicted below the line that represents the sequence of internal neural processes. Concurrent experiential phenomena are represented above the line. It should be pointed out that while subjective experience cannot be observed directly, it is likely that a substantial portion of the central neural apparatus is involved in the generation of experiential phenomena. We can anticipate, therefore, that some of the electrical manifestations of central processes that reach the conscious level (see Figure 18-1) can be recorded from the scalp. Thus, we can contemplate the development of an objective neurophysiology of mental processes utilizing approaches derived from psychophysical methodology.

The information-processing scheme just depicted may be modified by eliminating the motor response, i.e., the classic averaged evoked potential (EP) paradigm, or by deleting the specific cueing stimuli for motor acts so as to record the motor potentials (MP) associated with self-initiated movements (11). The information-processing paradigm also can be elaborated to observe a temporally circumscribed sequence of neural activity associated with perceptual, cognitive, and motor activities at any desired level of complexity.

Of the various ERP, the EPs have been most intensively studied and illustrate the problems encountered in the interpretation of these data. The relevant variables in EP experiments are stimulus parameters, state of the organism at the time of the stimulation, EP waveform, and indices of the elicited sensory experience. EP studies generally have been formulated either as a means of analyzing sensory mechanisms or as an indication of organismic state.

EP AS MEASURES OF SENSORY INFORMATION PROCESSING

In the former context, the EPs are considered to reflect some aspect of sensory information processing and to depict, in part, the neural activity underlying sensory experience. These studies can be viewed as physiologic extensions of psychophysical investigations in which measures of sensory magnitude and of temporal properties are emphasized. It is important to recognize that EPs are not "simple" correlates of sensation. The measurable parameters of the EP waveform are determined by a multiplicity of variables and thus only partially reflect a given psychophysical dimension. For example, the amplitude of EPs is influenced by interstimulus interval (ISI) as well as by stimulus intensity, yet there is no relationship between subjective magnitude and ISI over the range within which large effects on EP amplitude are observed. For this reason alone, a direct correspondence between EP amplitude and perceived intensity cannot be assumed but must be established empirically. As yet, there are few direct demonstrations of quantitative relationships between measures and EP magnitude and sensory experience. We have examined this relationship in several studies (12,13).

It is assumed in these studies that EP amplitude reflects the magnitude of neural processes related to subjective intensity. There are no data in the literature that directly test this critical assumption. We have studied the relationships among stimulus intensity, subjective magnitude, and reaction time to electrocutaneous stimuli varied from just above threshold to the limit of tolerance in three normal subjects. Constant current pulses 0.5 msec in duration were delivered to the tip of the right index finger over the intensity range of 1.75 to 6 milliamperes at random intervals ranging from 2.5 to 5 sec. Runs of 100 stimuli were delivered and motor responses were made as rapidly as possible to each stimulus. At the end of each run of a given intensity, the subject assigned a numerical estimate of the "average" perceived intensity. The experiment was carried out in five sessions, with two runs at each of the five intensity levels presented randomly on each day. The magnitude estimates for each intensity were averaged across days to obtain a mean magnitude estimate. The magnitude estimation functions for each subject were very similar, whereas the EP amplitude gradients appeared to differ substantially when plotted linearly. Only when the data were corrected for threshold and plotted in log-log coordinates were the slopes of the EP amplitude gradient found to be similar. This relationship was found *only* for the late somatosensory component N140-P200 and not for any earlier component, again suggesting that this late activity is temporally related to the stimulus elicited sensory experience.

Thus, under appropriate conditions of recording and analysis, a systematic relationship between EP amplitude gradient and subjective magnitude has been shown. It cannot be concluded, however, that such a relationship might hold for other sensory modalities, without empirical confirmation; nor can it be presumed that EP measurements that are found to provide good psychophysiologic correlations under one set of experimental conditions will be valid under other conditions.

EP CORRELATES OF STATE

The assessment of organismic state, employing the EP as a physiologic probe, is complementary to the analysis of sensory processes. This approach has gained widespread use in studies of psychopathology. Two important facts must be recognized concerning the conceptual framework within which these studies are performed. First, any stimulus-elicited neural process is embedded within an enormous complex of ongoing nervous activity, much of which is unrelated to the stimulus-generated activity. Second, the activity generated by a stimulus is itself conditioned by the state of the nervous system at the time of stimulation. Thus, those aspects of organismic state that neither affect nor are affected by the stimulus, the "background" neural activity, can be distinguished from those portions of the ongoing neural processes that either alter or are altered by the stimulus.

In many investigations, the neural states at the time of stimulation are viewed as independent variables. These include such disparate organismic conditions as maturation, brain lesions, intelligence, and psychopathology, as well as more labile states induced by drugs and fluctuations in arousal and/or attention. In these studies, the usual procedure is to compare EPs obtained in two states or conditions (these may represent different subject groups differentiated according to some criterion). This strategy often has been seen as a method for defining "objective" indices of a hypothetical psychologic or physiologic state or entity. This demands that the validity of the postulated differentiation be established empirically, and it requires an operational definition of the state parameters that constitute the independent variable. In some circumstances this is not difficult, as in adult sleep stages or in maturational studies. By contrast, reliable and unambiguous definition of psychopathology and differences in waking arousal level present great challenges. The problem of inadequate operational definition has seriously confounded much of the experimental work in these areas, since the *conceptualization* of the entity may not necessarily correspond to an objectively definable condition of the organism. It would often be well to abandon cherished but ill-defined hypothetical constructs such as "arousal level," "attention," and perhaps even "schizophrenia" in favor of explicit operational definitions. When this is done, one is no longer dealing with somewhat mythical "states" but with variables that can be formulated within an information-processing paradigm.

It also must be noted that there is no certainty that the EP measures employed in an experimental assessment of "state" necessarily reflect changes in the parameter of interest. There is no a priori method for predicting the extent to which any arbitrarily selected EP measure might reflect some aspect of a complex psychologic construct. It appears highly unlikely that an arbitrarily selected EP measure would, by chance, be found to reflect in a meaningful way some unknown property of the nervous system specifically related to the construct under consideration.

In view of the complex physiologic organization of psychologic entities that fall under the rubric of organismic state, two value comparisons should be avoided whenever possible, since these tend to shed little light on the physiologic organization of the entity under consideration and are all too susceptible to ad hoc interpretation. As suggested in the following section, one should always attempt to formulate correlations between brain potentials and psychologic constructs that permit an independent behavioral definition of the psychologic processes that are concurrent with the electrophysiologic phenomena being recorded.

In summary, it is contended that constructs of state, while useful as concise representations of complex organismic conditions at some point in time, should not be employed as independent variables unless they are operationally defined and their putative measures have been independently validated.

ELECTROPHYSIOLOGIC CORRELATES OF PROCESSING STAGES

By employing a combination of the methods outlined below, it is possible to establish the timing and gross intracerebral sources of cerebral potentials associated with specific aspects of information processing associated with sensorimotor sequences. Although it is not necessary in all instances to employ a reaction time paradigm (e.g., a delayed discriminative response might be required), the RT task represents a powerful method for determining the temporal covariation of psychologic and neurophysiologic processes. The basic analytic approach comprises the following main features:

1. *Stage synchronization.* It is axiomatic that the neural processes necessary for generation of a specific behavioral response are temporally circumscribed by stimulus and response in RT tasks. Thus, selective averaging of brain potentials associated with the same response latency in a given RT task permits the resolution of a sequence of neural activity synchronized with both stimulus and response. This sequence of potentials is a representation of neural activity associated with the processes necessary for performance of the specific task. Since RT varies across trials, a series of average ERP representing different response latency ranges can be constructed. In Figure 18-2 such a set of ERP associated with a simple visual RT task is depicted.

2. *Subtractive identification of stages.* In this example, averaged visual EPs obtained without a mõtor response have been subtracted from the averaged ERP obtained in each of four response latency bands for the simple RT task. The subtracted records represent the *difference* in mean electrical activity associated with performance of the RT task. These difference potentials can, in principle, contain contributions from three sources of altered neural activity: (a) effects of general changes related to arousal, motivation, and so forth, (b) effects of specific attentional factors on the EP, and (c) activity specifically related to the additional task requirement, in this case, performance of a motor response. Although there is some unavoidable confounding of processes in the complication-subtraction method, the differential timing and spatial distribution of various components of the difference waveform often permits inferences to be drawn on the factors that contribute to the identified components.

3. *Topographic analysis of processing stages.* Definitive neurophysiologic study of specific processing mechanisms requires the identification of brain regions that participate in a specific process. Although a substantial amount of information on local specialization of brain mechanisms has been derived from analyses of the effects of focal lesions and stimulation, the actual spatiotemporal sequence of brain activity during specific psychologic processes can be disclosed only by direct observation of concurrent neural activity.

Scalp recordings provide only limited possibilities for localizing specific central processes, since the EEG and the ERP are degraded by the passive impedance of tissues that lie between the recording sites and the intracranial sources. Also, due to the composite nature of these volume conducted signals, information is lost on the potentials produced by individual neural generators.

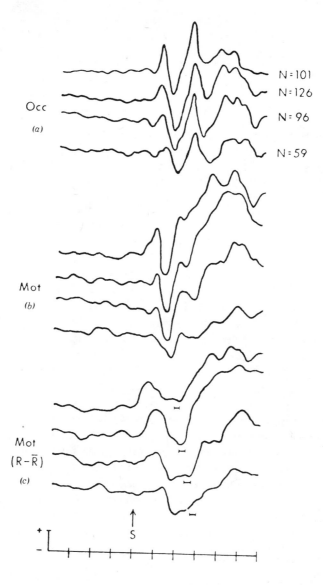

Figure 18-2. Averaged ERP obtained in a simple visual RT task: (a) recorded from midoccipital electrode referred to linked ears: (b,c) taken from an electrode placed overlying the estimated position of the contralateral hand area also referred to linked ears. ERP data has been segregated into four sets according to RT: 180–210 msec; 210–240 msec; 240–270 msec; 270–300 msec. The number of individual trials in each average is indicated to the right of the upper traces. Sets (a) and (b) depict ERP recorded during performance of the RT task. The data in set (c) are obtained by subtracting a comparable number of trials on which no response was made to the visual stimulus. By this method the cerebral potentials (MP) related to the motor response are uncovered and approximately synchronized (+ 15 msec). Note that the EP recorded from occipital and motor leads show primarily a decrease in amplitude with increasing RT with only minor shirts in latency, whereas the timing of the motor potentials follows the RT more closely. Calibration: 2.5 uV, 100 msec/division.

Potential shifts recorded from the scalp reflect extracellular currents generated by changes in cell membrane conductance. Definition of the electrical field at the scalp surface requires a knowledge of the strength and geometry of the current sources as well as of the specific impedances of the intervening tissues. Given these data, the scalp potential distribution can in theory be computed. It is not possible, however, to specify the sources of potentials within a volume conductor from a description of the surface potential field, since a given distribution could be generated by an infinite variety of source configurations. Despite this circumstance, which is often cited to point up the futility of attempting to utilize scalp potentials as a means of gaining access to information on intracranial neural processes, the prospects are not nearly as limited as might be supposed from a superficial consideration of the biophysical problem of scalp potential analysis. Fortunately, the task is not to define one of an infinite variety of source configurations but to select from a rather small number of alternatives that are determined by anatomic considerations.

A method for inferring the gross position and extent of the intracranial generators of ERP components has been developed and implemented (8). This technique involves comparison of the empirically defined scalp topography of ERP components with theoretical potential distributions computed from models of specific intracranial source configurations situated within a spherical conductive medium. The best source approximation can be selected by testing the empirical distributions against those produced by various anatomically and physiologically plausible source geometries. In combination with the methods for temporal definition of ERP components, the topographic data permit the identification of the timing and localization of processes related to specific, empirically determined processing requirements.

Over the past decade, we have carried out a series of detailed topographic analyses of ERP in normal subjects under a wide variety of stimulus and task conditions (7,14–18). These data provide normative information on the timing and topography of several types of ERP that can be considered to reflect neural mechanisms of information processing. Our human studies have been complemented in many cases by intracranial mapping studies in chronically implanted monkeys (19,20), which strongly support the validity both of our method for inferring intracranial sources and for the specific source attributions derived therefrom.

APPLICATION OF ERP TECHNIQUES IN SCHIZOPHRENIA

Normative studies are of crucial importance to define the psychologic processes that are temporally concurrent with specific ERP components. Once this has been accomplished, additional studies will be required to evaluate the impact of general organismic variables such as motivation, arousal level, and attentional factors on each of the ERP indices of processing stages. These studies should represent the highest priority for human electrophysiologic studies. There are, however, a number of relatively straightforward ERP investigations that could now be profitably pursued in schizophrenic patients.

The most obvious and potentially fruitful studies would explore the central source of the delayed simple RT responses that are so characteristic of schizophrenic patients. As yet, no studies have been performed utilizing stage synchronization and subtraction techniques. In general, EP studies in schizophrenics have found reduced amplitude and increased variability of most EP components [see Shagass (5) for review]. Although Shagass and colleagues (21) have made a preliminary examination of combined EP and

RT recording in normal subjects and psychiatric patients, they did not evaluate their data utilizing methods suitable for resolving processing stages, and they found intrasubject variability to be a serious impediment to their search for intergroup differences. The latter problem is to be expected, since substantial RT variability is characteristic of both normal and pathologic groups, with large variance being a particular hallmark of schizophrenic performance. The methods described previously use the temporal *distribution* of response latencies as a means for assessing the way in which specific processing stages contribute to this variability. The data presented by Shagass (3), as well as many other EP studies in schizophrenia, give little support to the notion that delayed motor response can be attributed to prolongation of sensory processing as reflected in EP latency changes. Thus, the processing deficiency responsible for prolonged RT in schizophrenics remains to be identified. Clearly, evidence on the timing of response-synchronized potentials is needed to clarify this issue.

After a detailed analysis of the electrophysiologic correlates of simple RT has been accomplished, examination of go/no-go and choice RT tasks would appear to be the next step. More complex paradigms employing performance tasks that tap attentional capacities (e.g., 22) also will provide data relevant to current theoretical issues in schizophrenic research. Experiments also can be designed to evaluate other possible processing impairments involving retrieval from short-term memory and various aspects of linguistic and symbolic processing.

An especially useful approach to the study of perceptual and cognitive processing of schizophrenic patients may be provided by topographic analyses of the cortical potentials associated with saccadic eye movements, either voluntarily initiated or occurring during the spontaneous scanning of visual scenes or during reading (16). The analysis of spontaneous scanning and the associated cortical potentials may be of particular value in schizophrenic patients since it is a largely involuntary activity that can provide data on the processing time for visual information without the voluntary motor response required in RT tasks.

Saccade-synchronized eye movement potentials (EMP) comprise both antecedent components, emanating from parietal and frontal eye fields that are thought to reflect processes that initiate the saccades, and later components, principally generated in occipital, parietal, and posterior temporal cortex, that reflect input and processing of visual information (16,23,24). The EMP potentials when recorded together with the distribution of intersaccade intervals during specific visual scanning tasks, provide direct information on the timing and localization of cortical activity associated with the processing of visual information. Since stimulus materials and task requirements can be varied to tap many aspects of visual processing, future study of EMP in schizophrenics should provide important insights into their scanning behavior and the cortical processes underlying it. These data could provide empirical substance to hypothesized defects in perceptual scanning mechanisms in schizophrenia.

RELEVANCE OF ERP STUDIES TO A NEUROPHYSIOLOGY OF SCHIZOPHRENIA

The data that ultimately may be obtained from ERP studies in schizophrenic patients will provide information on the timing and localization of cortical neural activity during the performance of specific sensorimotor and cognitive tasks. A picture should begin to emerge of spatiotemporal patterns of cortical activation that either differ from or fall within the normal range for various processing conditions. To the extent that the schizophrenic illness may disrupt specific processing mechanisms in which cortex plays a part, distinctive spatiotemporal ERP deviations may be observed that will point to pathophysiology within particular neural subsystems.

In view of the variety and variability of the clinical manifestations in schizophrenia, it is anticipated that ERP deviations will be similarly diverse and changeable. Conventionally, the large variance in behavioral and physiologic data from schizophrenic patients has been treated as error rather than as reflecting a characteristic feature of the illness which itself requires detailed analysis. Attention to the sources and nature of variability is necessary in ERP studies due to the inherently statistical character of the electrophysiologic data. Thus, as already emphasized, these data must be closely related to concurrent behavioral observations of response latency distributions and of errors. Indeed, it may well be that the analysis of the ERP associated with errors or temporally deviant responses will pinpoint the transient fluctuations in neurophysiologic organization that are characteristic of much schizophrenic symptomatology.

There is presently no reason to believe that psychoneurophysiologic dysfunction in schizophrenia is associated with cellular pathophysiology at the cortical level. Indeed, if current neuropharmacologic theories of schizophrenia are sustained, disordered neurotransmitter functions may be limited to the nigro-striatal and mesolimbic systems that are the principal central loci of dopaminergic action. Thus, the relationships of these systems to the cortical regions that generate scalp recorded ERP are likely to be critical to the interpretation of ERP deviations. Present information on neurophysiologic interactions among cortex, striatum, and limbic structures in behaving animals is minimal, yet the known anatomic and functional relationships that link these systems are strong and are likely to be central to the pathophysiology of perceptual and cognitive disturbances in schizophrenia (25,26). The systematic topographic projection of cerebral cortex onto the neostriatum (27) is of great significance for the interpretation of any localized abnormalities in cortical physiology that may be observed in schizophrenic patients.

Unfortunately, the cortical relations of the mesolimbic dopaminergic systems are indirect and as yet not fully defined, but there are important projections to nucleus accumbens septi from amygdala, pyriform cortex, and hippocampus. The possibility that electrical activity within the latter structures, under suitable recording and task conditions, could be identified in human scalp ERP data is a possibility well worth intensive investigation. These structures are directly related to the mesolimbic dopaminergic termination in nucleus accumbens and, due to their important role in affective and motivational processes, should be key structures in the mediation of those aspects of schizophrenic symptomatology. At this time, direct information on the electrical activity generated within limbic structures is seemingly inaccessible to scalp recording. Nevertheless, information on the circumstances under which ERP are recorded from these structures and on the volume conduction characteristics of these potentials can be readily obtained from intracranial recordings in primates, using the mapping techniques we have developed (e.g., 20), so the possibility of obtaining data on limbic system activity in man from scalp electrodes cannot be dismissed.

It will be necessary to relate human ERP data to intracranial recordings in primates to obtain a definitive identification and interpretation of the neurophysiologic substrates of the scalp recorded waveforms. As this endeavor progresses, opportunities for more detailed analysis of antipsychotic-psychotominetic drug effects on specific ERP in human and subhuman primates can be of value in evaluating their mechanism of action in relation to specific neurophysiologic systems. Since we seem to be a long way from ideal pharmacologic therapies for schizophrenic illness, more detailed information on the actions of therapeutic agents on the neurophysiologic systems that subserve specific psychologic processes appears to be necessary for a better understanding of psychopharmacologic actions in individual patients. The suitable application of ERP techniques during the course of drug therapy should prove valuable in this endeavor. It should be emphasized that the study of ERP promises a far greater yield of information than do studies that merely utilize the EEG and ERP as "indices" of simple or undefined central neural states. It is only when psychologic variables are linked to neurophysiologic observations in the analysis of ongoing information processing mechanisms that we will achieve a true neurophysiology of schizophrenia.

REFERENCES

1. Berger H: Uver das elektrenkephalogramm des menschen. I-XV. *Arch Psychiat Nervenkr.* (English translation by P. Gloor: Hans Berger on the electroencephalogram of man. *Electroenceph Clin Neurophysiol* (suppl 28, 1969).

2. Mirsky AF: Neuropsychological bases of schizophrenia. *Ann Rev Psychol* 20:321, 1969.

3. Shagass C: *Evoked Brain Potentials in Psychiatry.* New York, Plenum Press, 1972.

4. Shagass C: EEG and evoked potentials in the psychoses, in Freedman DX (ed): *Biology of Major Psychoses: A Comparative Analysis.* New York: Raven Press, 1975, p. 101.

5. Shagass C: An electrophysiological view of schizophrenia. *Biol Psychiat* 11:3, 1976.

6. Vaughan, HG Jr: Physiological approaches to psychopathology, in Kietzman ML, Sutton S, Zubin J (eds): *Experimental Approaches to Psychopathology.* New York, Academic Press, 1975, p 351.

7. Vaughan HG Jr: The relationship of brain activity to scalp recordings of event-related potentials, in Donchin E, Lindsley DB (eds): *Averaged Evoked Potentials: Methods, Results, Evaluations.* Washington, DC, National Aeronautics and Space Administration (NASA #SP-191), 1969, p 45.

8. Vaughan HG Jr: The analysis of scalp-recorded brain potentials, in Thompson RF, Patterson MM (eds): *Bioelectric Recording Techniques, Part B: Electroencephalography and Human Brain Potentials.* New York, Academic Press, 1974, p 157.

9. Sternberg S: Memory scanning: Mental processes revealed by reaction-time experiments. *Amer Sci* 57:421, 1969.

10. Sternberg S: The discovery of processing stages: Extensions of Donders' method, in Koster WG (ed): *Attention and Performance II.* Amsterdam, North-Holland Publishing Co, 1969, p 276 (reprinted from *Acta Psychologica* 30, 1969).

11. Gilden L, Vaughan HG Jr, Costa LD: Summated human EEG potentials with voluntary movement. *Electroenceph Clin Neurophysiol* 20:433, 1966.

12. Vaughan HG Jr: The perceptual and physiologic significance of visual evoked responses recorded from the scalp in man. *Clin Electroret,* suppl to *Vision Res* 203, 1966.

13. Vaughan HG Jr, Silverstein L: Metacontrast and evoked potentials: A reappraisal. *Sci* 160:207, 1968.

14. Vaughan HG Jr, Costa LD, Ritter W: Topography of the human motor potential. *Electroenceph Clin Neurophysiol* 25:1, 1968.

15. Vaughan HG Jr, Ritter W: The sources of auditory evoked responses recorded from the human scalp. *Electroenceph Clin Neurophysiol* 28:360, 1970.

16. Kurtzberg D, Vaughan HG Jr: Electrophysiological observations on the visuomotor system and visual neurosensorium, in Desmedt JE (ed): *Visual Evoked Potentials in Man: New Developments.* Oxford, Clarendon Press, 1976.

17. Simson R, Vaughan HG Jr, Ritter W: The scalp topography of potentials associated with missing visual or auditory stimuli. *Electroenceph Clin Neurophysiol* 40:33, 1976.

18. Simson R, Vaughan HG Jr, Ritter W: The scalp topography of potentials in auditory and visual discrimination tasks. *Electroenceph Clin Neurophysiol* 42:528, 1977.

19. Arezzo J, Vaughan HG Jr: Cortical potentials associated with voluntary movements in the monkey. *Brain Res* 88:99, 1975.

20. Arezzo J, Pickoff A, Vaughan HG Jr: The sources and intracerebral distribution of auditory evoked potentials in the alert rhesus monkey. *Brain Res* 90:57, 1975.

21. Shagass C, Straumanis JJ Jr, Overton DA: Electrophysiological recordings in the reaction time experiment: Exploratory studies for possible psychiatric research application. *Biol Psychiat* 5:271, 1973.

22. Friedman D, Vaughan HG Jr, Erlenmeyer-Kimling L: Task-related cortical potentials in children in two kinds of vigilance tasks, in Otto D (ed): *Proceedings of 4th International Conference on Event-Related Potentials of the Brain,* in press.

23. Vaughan HG Jr: A note on the visual neurosensorium, in Nicholson JP (ed): *Advances in Behavioral Biology,* vol 5. London, Plenum Press, 1972, p 167.

24. Kurtzberg D, Vaughan HG Jr: Electrocortical potentials associated with eye movement, in Zikmund V (ed): *The Oculomotor System and Brain Functions.* (Proc Intl Colloquium, Smolenice, Oct. 1970). London, Butterworths; Bratislava, Publishing House of the Slovak Academy of Sciences, 1973, p 137.

25. Stevens JR: An anatomy of schizophrenia? *Arch Gen Psychiat* 29:177, 1973.

26. Krauthamer GM: Catecholamines in behavior and sensorimotor integration: The neostriatal system, in Friedhoff AJ (ed): *Catecholamines and Behavior,* vol 1: *Basic Neurobiology.* New York, Plenum Press, 1975, p 59.

27. Kemp JM, Powell TPS: The connexions of the striatum and globus pallidus: Synthesis and speculation. *Phil Trans Royal Soc London Ser B* 262:441, 1971.

Section IV

INFORMATION PROCESSING AND SCHIZOPHRENIA

INTRODUCTION
David Shakow, Ph.D.

> The discovery of a reliable measure of . . . attention would appear to be one of the most important problems that await solution by the experimental psychology of the future.

Thus said Külpe, one of the major figures of psychology, in the *Outlines of Psychology,* in 1895. Moray, in his comment at the very end of his book on *Attention,* published some seven decades later, says of this quotation:

> Attention is back again, respectable both in theory and in practice. But despite the considerable recent progress it is perhaps salutary to end with an ancient but still valid call to better things. . . . (1969, p 194).

The field of attention is both complex and perplexing. However, progress is indeed being made. For one, there are the advances coming from information theory, and, for another, neural areas are being discovered which seem to have crucial relationships to the function of attention. Until recently, the latter have been relatively neglected areas that still remain somewhat enigmatic for psychology and to some extent enigmatic for neurophysiology as well. Among the different parts of the nervous system, the phylogenetically old and the neocortex, interrelationships to a degree heretofore not appreciated have been found. There are important internal control mechanisms, largely inhibitory throughout the system, even to the extent of controlling sensory input.

At the same time, however, we must be aware of the older notions of the attention mechanism, like those of James, who postulated two kinds of attention, an involuntary, effortless or passive attention, and an active or voluntary attention; Freud, who emphasized the concept of *Reizschutz;* and Sullivan, with his own concept of *selective inattention.* I might add a few more words about James, for his chapter on attention in the *Principles* is very insightful. For him, "the intimate nature of the attentive process"

217

involved: "1. The accommodation or adjustment of the sensory organs; and 2. The anticipatory preparation from within of the ideational centres concerned with the object to which the attention is paid" (1890, I, p 434). To this he adds, some pages later: "The only third process I can think of as always present is the *inhibition* of irrelevant movements and ideas" (italics mine, p 445). For James, then, the important aspects of the attentive process were adjustment of sensory organs, preperception, and inhibition of the irrelevant. James remarks further by paraphrasing Helmholtz' law of *inattention:*

> We leave all impressions *unnoticed* which are valueless to us as signs by which to discriminate things. . . . And all this is due to an inveterate habit we have contracted, of passing from them immediately to their import and letting their substantive nature alone. (p 456; italics mine)

This law of inattention is most important when dealing with schizophrenics, because it seems that for the schizophrenic all such impressions are *noticed* rather than "unnoticed," as Helmholtz would have it. This is the point emphasized particularly by Sullivan in his concept of "selective inattention" (1953, p 319).

REFERENCES

James, W: *Principles of Psychology.* New York, Holt, 1890.

Moray, N: *Attention: Selective Processes in Vision and Hearing.* London, Hutchinson, 1969.

Sullivan, H. S: *The Interpersonal Theory of Psychiatry.* New York, Norton, 1953.

Chapter 19
Attention and Information Processing: A Foundation for Understanding Schizophrenia?

Rue L. Cromwell, Ph.D.

The idea that schizophrenics are deficient in attention and information processing is not a new one. While the term "information processing" has been used only recently, it long has been acknowledged that schizophrenics do not process continuously and accurately their ongoing experience. Psychoanalytic writings have described schizophrenia in terms of a defense mechanism of withdrawal from reality. Loss of reality contract has been an oft-used clinical description. The present *Diagnostic and Statistical Manual* (DSM-II) defines schizophrenia in terms of a disturbance in reality relationships. Harry Stack Sullivan's concept of prototaxic level of functioning implied that the schizophrenic is global and undifferentiated in processing the continuity of experience.

TRADITIONAL UNDEREMPHASIS

In spite of these allusions, attention and information-processing measures have not captured the central interest of those studying schizophrenia. Elsewhere in this volume, Katz (1) suggests that pathology is judged as it deviates from the norm of a given community or ethnic group. In other words, the reported manifestations of schizophrenia vary from one group to another as a function of different concerns attached to these different manifestations. Extending this principle, I also would suggest that psychopathology is described and defined primarily in terms of how it deviates from the norms and expectancies of society in general. Certain manifestations of schizophrenia deviate enough to be viewed as bizarre, intolerable, or threatening. Other manifestations do not and they often are overlooked. This distinction is apparently so important that we

219

have different terms to refer to the tolerable and the intolerable manifestations. The tolerable manifestations are usually referred to as behavioral deficits. The intolerable ones are referred to as clinical symptoms. The intolerables, i.e., the clinical symptoms, have been the central focus by which to understand schizophrenia, not because they are more important in etiological, prognostic, or treatment considerations but because they are indeed intolerable to the patient and/or the community.

Perhaps the reason why attention and information processing have not been viewed as a dramatic or exciting feature of schizophrenia is that they are tolerable. No one has ever been arrested for a reaction time cross-over deficit. No one has been committed to an institution for velocity arrests in his eye-tracking. No one has been taken into psychiatric treatment because of overestimating the size of visual stimuli.

For eight decades now, disturbing and intolerable symptoms have been intensively studied in the attempt to explain schizophrenia. Little has been accomplished in genuine prevention or amelioration. These clinical symptoms have been elusive and fluctuating. Attempts to group them in diagnostic subcategories have led to severe problems in reliability. Clinical symptoms have been disappointing in their prognostic significance [e.g., Strauss and Carpenter (2)]. The papers in this Section reflect not so much a breakthrough as the need to back up and ask: "Are the behavior deficits, including attention and information processing, a possible key to the better understanding of schizophrenia?" Historically, of course, David Shakow and Joseph Zubin were the pioneers who first raised this question.

Many times when I have given research presentations, the question has been asked, "All of this you tell us about reaction time and size estimation is very interesting, but what does it have to do with schizophrenia?" A long-postponed, yet tentative, answer is expressed in the chapters of this volume, for example, in the diverse papers by Holzman, Steffy, Gruzelier, Asarnow, Spohn, Spring, and Cohen. To explain schizophrenia, perhaps these more subtle, more tolerable but probably more stable, manifestations are more important than the variably expressed incursive symptoms that jar the tolerance of most people on earth.

The Various Applications

How can these subtle and inoffensive variables contribute to the study of schizophrenia? Five ways are illustrated here. First, there has been a search for the common denominator in schizophrenic illnesses. Neither delusions, hallucinations, distorted thought and language, nor inappropriate, flat, or agitated affect characterize all schizophrenics. The identification of a common denominator at least would give an Aristotelian certitude to the schizophrenia classification. Reaction time, together with associative disturbances, perhaps has come the closest to serving as this common denominator. Even here, however, a simple mean reaction time deficit dwindles as the mental health status of the patient improves. Also, other pathologic states show slow mean reaction time. Thus, attention has turned to other more subtle and complex measures of reaction time, such as the cross-over effect and Steffy's resurgence effect, to pinpoint an unwavering characteristic. With such measures the prevalence of deficit among schizophrenics is high. One then is left to wonder if the exceptional cases result from lack of universality of the deficit within schizophrenia or from the poor reliability in diagnosing cases as schizophrenic.

Second, attention and information-processing measures have been used in the search for subgroupings of schizophrenia. Mindful of the long-held observation that undifferentiated schizophrenic groups have high intersubject, as well as intrasubject, variability on most measures, one strategy has been to identify subgroups within schizophrenia. If successful, variability would be less within subgroups and greater from one subgroup to another. These attempts often have led to subgroupings which look like only gradations in severity. When this happens, it suggests one common underlying disorder: schizophrenia. Simple reaction time (e.g., 3), correlated with mental health status in schizophrenia, is an example. A theoretically more provocative finding occurs when one defined subgroup of schizophrenia differs significantly in one direction while another subgroup differs significantly in the opposite direction from the normal control group. This has been demonstrated in measures such as size estimation (4) and incidental recall (5). When these subgroup differences are found, one is then left to determine whether the index for grouping is identifying different disorders or different cognitive styles with which the single pathologic state has been afflicted. Only the evidence of different treatment, prognosis and etiology factors in the subgroups could answer this.

Third, more recently, measures of attention and information processing have been used in the search for phenotypes that would be common to schizophrenics and those normal relatives who would share with them a genetic vulnerability for the disorder. Most popular among such approaches are the studies of high-risk children. In families with one schizophrenic parent, 10% to 15% of the offspring become schizophrenic as adults. The name of the game in high-risk studies is to identify what measures among the normally functioning, yet vulnerable, children will predict later psychotic breakdown. Asarnow's (6) span of apprehension measures show promise here. In the more traditional genetic study of discordant identical twins, the eye-tracking measures of Holzman et al (7) show promise.

Fourth, looking across the lifespan of the single individual rather than across the disturbed individual and his relatives, another search is beginning to take place for the indices of vulnerability. These indices would occur prior to, during, and after becoming schizophrenic. In this work the identified variable may or may not be a genetic phenotype. Again, this work is illustrated by Asarnow et al (6) who found span of apprehension deficit to be similar among high-risk children and remitted schizophrenics. It is also reflected in the recent ideas and work by Zubin and his coworkers (8).

Fifth, attentional and processing variables have been used to track the course of change in response to treatment. The work of Spohn et al (9) and Gruzelier (10) illustrate this well. In the final analysis, diagnostic constructs are defined in terms of (a) historical and/or (b) current observations which provide a basis for predicting (c) what treatment, if any, leads to (d) what level of outcome (e.g., see 11). If attentional and processing variables are useful in this endeavor, they may not necessarily have a role in the etiology of schizophrenia.

PROCESSING VERSUS AROUSAL

In studies of attention and information processing, reported here and elsewhere, one cannot avoid the fact that arousal is often mentioned. Venables (12) and Kornetsky (13) have been leaders in pointing to arousal disorder in schizophrenia and to its association with attentional and information-processing characteristics. Both Gruzelier (10) and Spohn (9) have dealt directly with this issue in this volume. Their results are provocative since they present different interpretations. While Spohn's results support the interpretation of hyperarousal in schizophrenics, Gruzelier interprets his data to indicate both hyperarousal and hypoarousal deviancies. Both investigators agree that schizophrenics do not conform to Lacey's interpretation (14) of independence among arousal systems. Among normal subjects Lacey has observed that high arousal expressed in one system, such as heart rate, is relatively independent of whether high arousal is expressed in another. The resolution of these diverging interpretations will be an important focus of future research. Much depends on what data can designate the schizophrenic "nonresponder," as described by Gruzelier and Venables, as hypoaroused. An alternative view has regarded such responses as defensive, stimulus-reducing, or inhibitory reactions in a hyperaroused individual.

Another question concerns the relationship of arousal to attentional deficit. Is the disorder of arousal, whether overresponding or underresponding, a necessary antecedent to the disorders of attention and information processing? Or, are the attentional and information processing disorders the more primary features? Does the schizophrenic experiencing information-processing difficulties become aroused, or does the arousal disorder create the difficulty in processing? As other alternatives, neither or both cause-effect relationships may exist.

To construct a picture of how arousal deviance might be primary to attentional/information-processing deviance in schizophrenia, one need only extrapolate the inverted U-shaped curve of performance as a function of arousal. At arousal levels below that shown on the U-shaped curve are the various stages of sleep. The first (upward) limb of the U-shaped curve associates low arousal with sluggish, unmotivated performance. As arousal increases, performance reaches optimum level. Then, on the second (downward) limb, performance, although remaining rational, deteriorates with increasing arousal. Suppose one can extrapolate to yet higher levels of arousal beyond breakdown of performance. At such high levels the organism might shift his resources away from the assigned performance goals simply to restore a more normal state of arousal. While we expect normal individuals to attend continuously, retain, organize, and use information in a rational way, the schizophrenic instead may be putting first things first. His attempts to get rid of punishingly high arousal may override the innate systems for dealing with information in the usual way. The model of amphetamine psychosis and the evidence of lack of stage IV sleep in cases of thought disorder (e.g., 15) would appear to be compatible with this interpretation of primacy of arousal over the processing deficit. With this interpretation one might expect a DSM-IV not to describe subgroups of schizophrenia; instead, the various manifestations of schizophrenia, previously grouped, merely would be viewed as levels of different cognitive and emotional response while coping with a disordered state of arousal.

The alternative view is also possible. The schizophrenic may be battling with a basic blockage in attending and assembling information. Because of frustration from the number of events that he cannot process adequately, the arousal may either overbound or become inhibited and reduced. That such a disquieted or quieted response occurs when an individual fails to function adequately is not new to either clinical or research literature. The question is whether it is antecedent to clinically manifested schizophrenia.

Depending on how the matter is clarified by future research, schizophrenia may be treated as an arousal disorder, an attention/information-processing disorder, or neither.

With the former two possibilities we may no longer think of a genetics of schizophrenia. Instead, we may think of a genetics of arousal or, on the other hand, attentional dysfunction. Instead of a biochemistry of schizophrenia, the biochemical pursuits may be aimed more directly to these specific deficits. Most important, these potential views of schizophrenia would tell us with more confidence where to intervene. Thus, the implications of the arousal versus processing issue are considerable.

While some of the issues just discussed are still on the horizon, other issues are becoming resolved. For decades past, the behavioral research in schizophrenia had been plagued with the overshadowing possibility that schizophrenics act the way they do—in reaction time, deviant word association, and other cognitive activity—because they do not care. That is, lack of motivation to perform well, as others do, in the psychologic laboratory may have been the parsimonious and sufficient explanation of the behavioral deficits. Much evidence has now accrued to make this explanation untenable. Holzman (7) carefully separates the eye-tracking deficit from those eye movements that are indeed heavily influenced by motivation. Gruzelier's findings (10) of laterality differences in electrodermal response demand an explanation other than motivation. Most exciting among the recent reaction time results has been the resurgence finding by Steffy (16). To expose the patient to a novel stimulus, wait 9 seconds, and then find a reaction time deficit that was not present 2 or 4 seconds earlier is an exciting revelation about the temporal characteristics of attention/information-processing. The precise and repeatedly demonstrated time relationships defy a motivational explanation. One may note also the findings of Cohen (17) of patients' language disturbance when designating one of two color patches so close in hue that no familiar labels are readily available. Is this finding related to subject motivation, to the resurgence deficit, 9 seconds after a novel stimulus, or to something else?

The story of schizophrenia research often has been one of traveling down blind alleys. We have yet to know if attention and information-processing deficits will prove to be an avenue.

REFERENCES

1. Katz MM, Sanborn KO, Lowery HA, et al: Ethnic studies in Hawaii: On psychopathology and social deviance, in Wynne LC, Cromwell RL, Matthysse S (eds): *The Nature of Schizophrenia*. [Ch. 51] New York, John Wiley & Sons, 1978.

2. Strauss JS, Carpenter WT Jr: Prediction of outcome in schizophrenia. *Archives of General Psychiatry* 27:739–746, 1972.

3. Rosenthal D, Lawlor WG, Zahn TP, et al: The relationship of some aspects of mental set to degree of schizophrenic disorganization. *Journal of Personality* 28:26–38, 1960.

4. Neale JM, Cromwell RL: Size estimation of schizophrenics as a function of stimulus presentation time. *Journal of Abnormal Psychology* 73:44–48, 1968.

5. Kar BC: Muller-Lyer illusion in schizophrenics as a function of field distraction and exposure time. Master's thesis, George Peabody College for Teachers, Nashville, Tenn, 1967.

6. Asarnow RF, Steffy RA, MacCrimmon DJ, et al: An attentional assessment of foster children at risk for schizophrenia, in Wynne LC, Cromwell RL, Matthysse S (eds): *The Nature of Schizophrenia*. [Ch. 34] New York, John Wiley & Sons, 1978.

7. Holzman PS, Levy DL, Proctor LR: The several qualities of attention in schizophrenia, in Wynne LC, Cromwell RL, Matthysse, S (eds): *The Nature of Schizophrenia*. [Ch. 29] New York, John Wiley & Sons, 1978.

8. Spring BJ, Zubin J: Attention and information processing as indicators of vulnerability to schizophrenic episodes, in Wynne LC, Cromwell RL, Matthysse S (eds): *The Nature of Schizophrenia.* [Ch. 36] New York, John Wiley & Sons, 1978.

9. Spohn HE, Lacoursiere RB, Thompson K, et al: The effects of antipsychotic drug treatment on attention and information processing in chronic schizophrenics, in Wynne LC, Cromwell RL, Matthysse S (eds): *The Nature of Schizophrenia.* [Ch. 26] New York, John Wiley & Sons, 1978.

10. Gruzelier JH: Bimodal States of Arousal and Lateralized Dysfunction in Schizophrenia, in Wynne LC, Cromwell RL, Matthysse S (eds): *The Nature of Schizophrenia.* [Ch. 15] New York, John Wiley & Sons, 1978.

11. Cromwell RL, Strauss JS, Blashfield RK: Criteria for classification systems, in Hobbs N (ed): *Issues in the Classification of Children: A Handbook of Categories, Labels, and Their Consequences.* Los Angeles, Jossey Bass, 1975.

12. Venables PH: Input dysfunction in schizophrenia, in Maher BA (ed): *Progress in Experimental Personality Research,* Vol 1. New York, Academic Press, 1964, pp 1–42.

13. Orzack MH, Kornetsky C, Freeman H: The effects of daily administration of carphenazine on attention in the schizophrenic patient. *Psychopharmacologia* 11:31, 1967.

14. Lacey JI: Somatic response patterning and stress: Some revisions of activation theory, in Appley MH, Trumbull, R (ed): *Psychological Stress.* New York, Appleton-Century-Crofts, 1967.

15. Caldwell DF, Domino EF: Patterns of sleep, in Tourney G, Gottlieb JS (eds): *Lafayette Clinic Studies on Schizophrenia.* Detroit, Wayne State University Press, 1971.

16. Steffy RA: An early cue sometimes impairs process schizophrenic performance, in Wynne LC, Cromwell RL, Matthysse S (eds): *The Nature of Schizophrenia.* [Ch. 20] New York, John Wiley & Sons, 1978.

17. Cohen BD: Self-editing deficits in schizophrenia, in Wynne LC, Cromwell RL, Matthysse S (eds): *The Nature of Schizophrenia.* [Ch. 31] New York, John Wiley & Sons, 1978.

Chapter 20
An Early Cue Sometimes Impairs Process Schizophrenic Performance

Richard A. Steffy, Ph.D.

This chapter reports recent work on the "time-linked impairment" pattern reported by Steffy and Galbraith (1) to characterize the effect of an early cue on the reaction time performance of process schizophrenics. In this account, manipulations of task parameters that produce the effect have been conducted with patients diagnosed as schizophrenic and judged to be in the process range of the process-reactive dimension, as determined by the modified Elgin Prognostic Rating Scale (2).

BACKGROUND

The Simple Reaction Time Task

The simple reaction time task is well known for its sensitivity to schizophrenic pathology. The precision of the procedure, replicability of results, and salience for theorizing about the nature of attentional deficits in schizophrenia have made it a virtual "north star" of schizophrenia research (3).

In its basic form the task has three primary stimulus features comprised of two signals with a delay interval between. The first signal is an alerting or "ready" signal designed to announce the beginning of each trial. Following that signal there is a delay or preparatory interval during which the subject is asked to wait vigilantly for the second stimulus which serves as a signal-to-respond (generally a finger lift or a retraction from a telegraph key). These task features have been studied to learn how procedural variation interacts with schizophrenic pathology. The latency of response, recorded in milliseconds, is generally used to assess experimental and subject variation.

This work was supported by Grant 408 from the Ontario Mental Health Foundation.

Maximum attention has been given in the literature to the study of two of these features. The signal-to-respond or imperative signal has been investigated in terms of the intensity (4), modality (5), and modality relationship among trials (6). The delay, or preparatory, interval has been investigated in relation to the length of the delay and the predictability of the various delays used across trials (7). Studies of these two features have provided support for various theoretical constructions of schizophrenic pathology, for example, Shakow (7) and Zubin (8).

Our work over the past several years has attempted to retrace some of the steps of Shakow and his colleagues (7) in exploring the time factor. Recently this exploration of the temporal factor has led us to be impressed with the salience of the earliest component, the ready signal, and other stimulus events given before or early in the trial.

Detrimental Effects of an Early Signal on Reaction Time Performance

There is some evidence that indicates that early, presumably helpful and informative, signals may have a detrimental influence on the reaction time performance of process schizophrenics, even though such signals have been provided to alert the subject and to assist performance. We came to this point of view from research in which a series of four consecutive trials having identical delay intervals—3 seconds or longer—was included in a random series of trial durations. This condition reliably produced a detrimental influence on the fourth trial of such a series in samples of process schizophrenics. In contrast, other subject groups reliably profitted from the presence of four identical or regular trials in a random series. A statistically reliable decrement has been observed in a series of experiments; 77% of 190 process schizophrenic subjects have shown this effect when their records were examined individually (9–12). This finding has suggested that the detection of the regularity of presentation in the four-trial series, although helpful to all other subject groups in producing a general improvement on the fourth trial relative to the first, has an impairing effect on most subjects in process schizophrenic groups. Although studied with different trial arrangement procedures, the classical studies by Rodnick and Shakow (13), Tizard and Venables (14), and other studies reviewed by Sutton and Zubin (6) permit similar conclusions about the effect of longer duration regular trials impairing schizophrenic performance relative to trials presented in random order.

These findings indicate that performance of process schizophrenics is impaired by the detection of redundancy in the series. The effects of a series of three redundant continuous trials in a random context on a fourth similar trial constitute a signal of some sort and is the first evidence that an early informative signal may have a detrimental influence on process schizophrenic subjects.

The Effect of an Early Signal Varies Over Time

Inspired by a finding of Mo (15) that verbal instruction had detrimental effects on the reaction time performance of schizophrenics at certain delay intervals and not at others, we sought to chart the time course of an early signal over a short time spectrum. In a recently reported study (1), we used preparatory intervals that ranged from 1 to 9 seconds to assess the impact and the temporal course of a signal given at the beginning of selected probe trials.

The following procedure was employed. Multiple standard reaction time trials (blocks of 25 trials) were used to establish a baseline of performance. The standard trials featured three signals, namely, a visual "ready" signal, a visual "get set" signal continuously present during the preparatory interval, and a visual "lift your finger" signal in addition to an auditory (tone) signal-to-respond. A special, infrequently presented (three trials out of each block of 25 regular trials) probe signal was used to assess the effect of early signals. Probe stimulation featured a 10 microsecond bright flash (approximately 25,000 foot candles) in the periphery of the visual field presented at the beginning of the trial along with a small alteration in the background of the "get set" signal field. The alteration was comprised of a frame of x's surrounding the words "get set" [see (1) for details]. Although confounded in the initial investigation, the two probe stimulus features—the flash and the background field alteration—are the basis for current parametric investigations of intensity, message, and other stimulus factors. For the time being, the informative signal was chosen to maximize the impact of the early signal on the trials. Figure 20-1 shows the outcome of a series of standard trials averaged together and the three probe trials averaged together for each block of five trial durations studied for normal and process schizophrenics. The standard trials show a typical performance function for regular trials in both groups. On the probe trial normal subjects showed only a small disadvantage if the signal-to-respond was delivered one second later, whereas the process schizophrenics were slower overall on the probe trials and showed a complex relationship to the standard trials with considerable variation over the temporal delays. In the publication of these findings (1), a difference score was created by subtracting the average standard trial from the average probe trial for each preparatory interval and plotted as a function of preparatory interval. As a difference score the data represented in Figure 20-1 for the normal control subjects showed a posi-

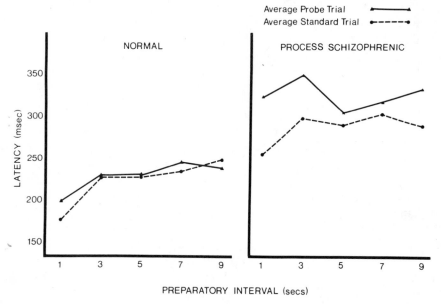

Figure 20-1. Latencies of standard regular trials and probe trials as a function of preparatory interval and pathology group. Data taken from Steffy RA, Galbraith K (1).

tive deviation from one second followed by no difference at the other delay intervals. Reactive schizophrenics sampled in that study (1) showed a pattern identical to the normal controls except that the probe stimulation produced a greater decrement (relative to their standard performance) on the one second trials. Nonschizophrenic patient controls showed no significant difference from standard trials as a function of probe stimulation at any of the five time periods sampled. The difference scores for the process schizophrenic patients showed a U-shaped trend in which the large deviation at 1, 3, and 9 seconds and the similarity of probe and standard at 5 and 7 seconds, depicted in Figure 20-1, yielded a nearly significant ($p < 0.10$) quadratic trend for that group. Two of the three control groups, the reactive schizophrenics and the normal subjects, showed only linear trends across trial duration without any evidence of the U-shaped effect.[1]

To interpret this data, the impairment at 1 and 3 seconds was considered to be an indication of the process schizophrenic's difficulty in recovering from the probe stimulation—especially, we thought, the bright flash. In the data presented, it is clear that the process group was impaired for as long as 3 seconds after the probe stimulus, whereas the other groups had shown complete recovery by 3 seconds.

The latter component of the function, namely, the decrement of performance at 9 seconds, was not easy to interpret. It was of some help to note that the relationship between the Elgin Prognostic Rating Scale scores, which were used to categorize the subjects as process or reactive, yielded a strong, highly significant, positive correlation with the reaction time difference (average probe minus average standard trial) score for the 9 second trial ($r = +0.70$), and that the relationship between the Elgin score and the performance at the 7 second point was -0.19. Taken together, the impression was conveyed that the more severely ill patients were showing the least deficit at 7 seconds and then sliding back at 9 seconds (1). This finding gave some encouragement that this decrement at 9 seconds was a meaningul event.

INVESTIGATION OF FEATURES OF THE EARLY SIGNAL

In the original report of the time-linked impairment effect, the influence of intensity in accounting for the U-shaped pattern had been tested in a second experiment (1). In that study the flash was removed from the probe stimulus, leaving only the frame of x's around the "get set" signal in a test of a new sample of process schizophrenics. Those findings (1) showed that the effect remained intact. A significant U-shaped function was obtained again. Analyses of the process schizophrenics in the original study and in the study omitting the flash from the probe stimulus showed that the presence of the flash yielded reliably larger difference scores (slower performance), but the presence of the flash did not interact with the delay interval (1). Consequently, the U-shaped temporal pattern may not be considered a result of the short-term flash imposed at trial onset.

Having ruled out the effect of one of the two features of the probe stimulation, we next turned to a study of the other feature, the background field alteration, comprised of the border surrounding the "get set" field on the probe trials. As reflected in Figure 20-2, removal of this apparently trivial modification of the visual field, using only the

---

[1] This data analysis in the Steffy and Galbraith report (1) included the two trials immediately following each of the three individual probes to appraise the extendent effect of probe stimulation.

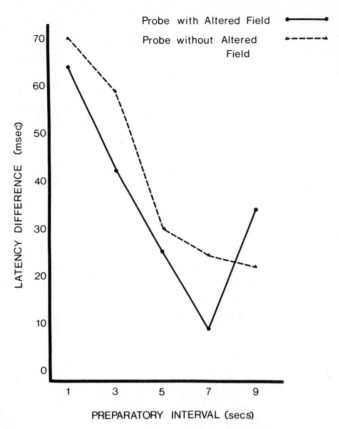

Figure 20-2. Latency difference scores obtained by process schizophrenics with and without the "get set" field alteration.

instantaneous flash procedure (low and high intensities were sampled), eliminated the U-shaped function.

Having eliminated the effect by removing the background stimulation, and having found the effect to be independent of intensity level of the flash, the subtle change in background stimulation presented during the delay is held to account for this distinctive pattern of impairment. A series of parametric studies has just begun to tease out the particular character of this feature of the early signal which is delivering the payload of the early signal effect.

Although presently unable to specify the mechanism of the time-linked impairment pattern, we speculate that this phenomenon reflects the special difficulty faced by the process schizophrenic patient when required to cope with an unexpected event. He appears slow to recover from the probe stimulation and his recovery process is unstable and short-lived. We have wondered if the recovery process, used to regain control by 5 seconds, may be itself an impairing influence that results in slow performance at 9 seconds (1). In this regard Epstein and Coleman (16) have argued that the schizophrenic is characterized by a poorly modulated inhibitory response to stimulation. The "all-or-none" inhibitory response they describe may be exacting a toll on the efficiency of performance at 9 seconds.

THE GENERALITY OF THE EFFECT

Awaiting further evidence on the nature of the effect, we have considered the generality of this pattern. If so subtle a stimulus as an alteration in background reliably produces a complex pattern of performance over time in process schizophrenics, one might wonder if there are other places where such impairment may have been manifested. Although only a handful of studies (15), in addition to this current series from our lab, have used discrete signals delivered by the experimeter, other types of early signal events have been examined in the reaction time literature, and they provide a basis for studying the effect of various early signals on performance as a function of time. For one, the strong and reliable proactive influences among trials in an irregular series may be considered as signal factors and examined for temporal effects. For example, it has been noticed (8, 17) that whenever a pair of identical preparatory interval trials are included in a random series, the second member of that pair provides the best overall performance for that duration. Consistent with the "immediacy hypothesis" of Salzinger (18) and the concept of "segmental set" advanced by Shakow (7), the particular features of any given trial serves to dispose the schizophrenic subject to respond efficiently to that same duration again. Consequently, the detection of any preparatory interval duration can be seen as an informative signal extending its effect to the subsequent trial. Consistent with the concern of this chapter, we sought to examine the influence of the first member of the equal duration pair on the second as a function of the trial duration.

Data examining the reaction time performance of schizophrenics as a function of both the preparatory interval (PI) of the current trial and the previous trial (the previous preparatory interval or PPI) were available in a classical report of Zahn, Rosenthal, and Shakow (19). In Figure 20-3 the trials in which the PPI equaled the PI are plotted for comparison with all the other trials averaged for each PI duration; one can see in Figure 20-3 that the paired trials are reliably faster than all the others except for the longest interval studied (15 seconds).[2] This finding gives support to the expectation that in longer duration trials the early signal does not facilitate and may impair, performance.

Similarly in work from our own laboratory, a set of four experiments conducted by Bellissimo (9,10) allow plots of the trials where a given trial was preceded immediately by another trial of similar duration. In Figure 20-4 separate experiments studying PI durations of 1, 3, and 7 seconds are averaged and presented along with the averages of experiments testing 5-, 7-, and 11-second durations. In these studies, comparisons between trials drawn from a random series and trials preceded by an equal delay interval again yield a decrement for the longer intervals.

CONCLUSION

In conclusion, this chapter has provided some evidence, that an early signal can be an impairing influence on reaction time performance of process schizophrenics, and that the extent of that impairment seems to be linked to a temporal course of information processing which has a particularly impairing impact at the longer intervals studied. Furthermore, these effects can be witnessed in a variety of reaction time situations in which the effect of an early signal can be traced over the period of time extending

[2] Data presented in Table 3, p 48 of that article (19).

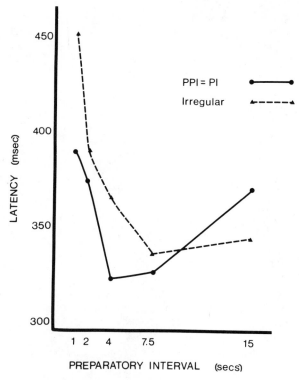

Figure 20-3. Reaction times on trials preceded by an equal duration trial (PPI = PI) and contrasted with irregular trials. Data taken from Zahn TP, Rosenthal D, Shakow D (19).

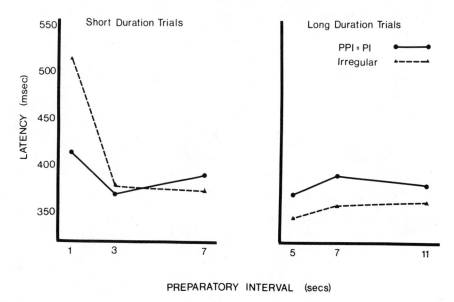

Figure 20-4. Reaction time for PPI = PI and irregular trial conditions as a function of two sets of preparatory interval durations. Data taken from studies by Bellissimo A, Steffy RA (9,10).

231

between the signal and the requirement to respond. This work raises questions about temporal factors in the processing of information and about the particular features of early signals (e.g., content, orienting, and distracting properties) that may lead to these time-linked impairments in process schizophrenics.

REFERENCES

1. Steffy RA, Galbraith K: The time course of a disruptive signal in the reaction time performance of process schizophrenic patients. *J Abnorm Psychol* 84:315, 1975.

2. Becker WC: The process-reactive distinction—A key to the problem of schizophrenia? *J Nerv Ment Dis* 129:442, 1959.

3. Cancro R, Sutton S, Kerr J, et al: Reaction time and prognosis in acute schizophrenia. *J Nerv Ment Dis* 153:351, 1971.

4. Grisell JL, Rosenbaum G: Effects of auditory intensity on simple reaction time of schizophrenics. *Percept Mot Skills* 18, 1964.

5. Venables PH, O'Connor N: Reaction times to auditory and visual stimulation in schizophrenic and normal subjects. *Quart J Exp Psychol* 11:1975, 1969.

6. Sutton S, Zubin J: Effect of sequence on reaction time in schizophrenia, in Welford A, Birren J (eds): *Behavior Aging and the Nervous System*. Springfield, Ill, Charles C Thomas, 1965.

7. Shakow D: Segmental set. *Arch Gen Psychiat* 6:1, 1962.

8. Zubin J: Problem of attention in schizophrenia, in Kietzman M, Sutton S, Zubin J (eds): *Experimental Approaches to Psychopathology*. New York, Academic Press, 1975.

9. Bellissimo A, Steffy RA: Redundancy-associated deficit in schizophrenic reaction time performance. *J Abnorm Psychol* 80:229, 1972.

10. Bellissimo A, Steffy RA: Reaction time performance in schizophrenia: Three studies of trial contextual influences on the crossover phenomenon. *J Abnorm Psychol* 84:210, 1975.

11. Steffy RA, Galbraith K: A comparison of segmental set and inhibitory deficit explanations of the crossover pattern in process schizophrenic reaction time. *J Abnorm Psychol* 83:227, 1974.

12. Kaplan RD: The crossover phenomenon: Three studies of the effect of training and information on process schizophrenics reaction time. Unpublished doctoral dissertation, University of Waterloo, Ontario, 1974.

13. Rodnick EH, Shakow D: Set in the schizophrenic as measured by a composite reaction time index. *Am J Psychiat* 97:214, 1940.

14. Tizard J, Venables PH: Reaction time responses by schizophrenics, mental defectives, and normal adults. *Am J Psychiat* 112:803, 1956.

15. Mo SS: Schizophrenic reaction time to sudden change of a fixed foreperiod. Unpublished doctoral dissertation, University of Pennsylvania, 1968.

16. Epstein S, Coleman M: Drive theories of schizophrenia. *Psychosom Med* 32:113, 1970.

17. Nideffer RM, Neale JM, Kopfstein JH, et al: The effect of previous preparatory intervals upon anticipatory responses in reaction time of schizophrenic and non-schizophrenic patients. *J Nerv Ment Dis* 153:360, 1971.

18. Salzinger K: The immediacy hypothesis and schizophrenia, in Yaker HM, Osmond H, Cheek F (eds): *Man's Place in Time*. New York, Doubleday-Doran, 1971.

19. Zahn TP, Rosenthal D, Shakow D: Effects of irregular preparatory intervals in reaction time in schizophrenia. *J Abnorm Soc Psychol* 67:14, 1963.

Chapter 21
Stages of Information Processing in Schizophrenia: Sternberg's Paradigm

Julius Wishner, Ph.D.
Marsha K. Stein, Ph.D.
August L. Peastrel, Ph.D.

The purpose of this chapter is to report initial results from a study that is part of a research program designed to identify loci of dysfunction in the information-processing systems of schizophrenics. A number of models of normal human information processing have been developed in cognitive psychology. For our purposes, we have chosen one constructed by Sternberg because of its conceptual clarity and extensive experimental support, and we report on its application to the study of schizophrenia.

GENERAL BACKGROUND

From Kraepelin on, and perhaps before, investigators have been intrigued by the slowness of schizophrenics as one reflection of their disorder. The modern history of this problem starts with the work of Shakow and Huston and the Worcester group (1–3) and extends to the current scene (4,5). Ignoring minor exceptions, it is a universal finding that schizophrenics are slower than controls, with the smallest differences appearing in simple reaction time (RT) at very short preparatory intervals. The details of the relevant experiments have been reviewed extensively (6–8).

Most germane to our current concerns are the hypotheses offered to account for the results. In general, they concentrate on input dysfunctions. Thus, Shakow (9) proposed that retardation of RT resulted from the inability of the schizophrenic to maintain the major set required by the situation, with the concomitant arousal of erratic minor sets. Wishner (10) has argued that the "segmental set" theory is a special case of inefficiency

This study was supported by grants from the Scottish Rite Schizophrenia Research Program to the first author and from the Society of Sigma Xi to the second author.

in schizophrenic behavior, which is generally diffuse in relation to task requirements. McGhie (11) emphasized attentional dysfunction localized at the filtering mechanism postulated by Broadbent (12,13). At the physiologic level, Venables (14,15) adduced evidence to support a theory of extreme levels of arousal as accounting for the variability of schizophrenic performance.

None of these theories is sufficiently precise to generate critical experiments. It is not surprising, therefore, that the overall results of the research undertaken to test them are inconclusive (7).

The most detailed attempt to deal with attentional dysfunction in schizophrenia has been that of Yates (16). He proposed that there are four "levels" at which dysfunction can occur in schizophrenic information processing: receptor, data processing, cognitive, and motor. These look very similar to the stages proposed by Sternberg. Indeed, there is reason to view Yates's idea as a first approximation to the more refined and operationally precise paradigm of Sternberg. Yates's theory has been criticized precisely for failing to prescribe experiments that could lead to clear-cut conclusions (17), for whatever dysfunctions are found at any of his "levels" could originate at any other level. No paradigm is provided for identifying loci of dysfunction. Sternberg's paradigm, as will be seen below, is not subject to such criticism.

STERNBERG'S PARADIGM

As a result of a series of experiments [for original experiments, see Sternberg (18,19); for summaries and theoretical development, see Sternberg (20-23)], Sternberg postulated four stages in information processing, as shown in Figure 21-1. Further, he has specified a set of experimental operations that affect each of the stages exclusively (top line of Figure 21-1), so appropriate experimentation can yield information concerning specific loci of effect on RT.

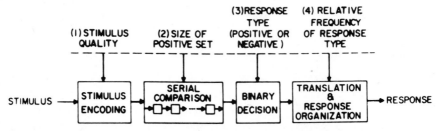

Figure 21-1. Processing stages in binary classification. Above the broken line are shown the four factors examined. Below the line is shown the analysis of RT inferred from additive relations between factor pairs 1&2, 1&3, 2&3, 2&4, and 3&4, the linear effect of factor 2, and other considerations described in the text. The quality of the test stimulus influences the duration of an encoding stage in which a stimulus representation is formed. This representation is then used in a serial-comparison stage, whose duration depends linearly on size of positive set; in each of its substages the representation is compared to a memory representation of one member of the set. In the third stage a binary decision is made that depends on whether a match has occurred during the serial-comparison stage that precedes it; its mean duration is greater for negative than for positive decisions. The selection of a response based on the decision is accomplished in the final stage whose duration depends on the relative frequency with which a response of that type is required. Copied from Sternberg S, Figure 6 (21).

A paradigmatic experiment is as follows: (a) the subject memorizes a set of digits; (b) a test digit is then presented; (c) if this digit is a member of the memory set, the subject responds in one way; if it is not, he responds in another. The measure is RT, measured from time of onset of the test stimulus to time of response.

Sternberg has shown the operational effects of the independent variables at the top of Figure 21-1 on each of his postulated stages. Thus, manipulating stimulus quality, e.g., intact versus degraded stimuli, affects RT via retardation of encoding with degraded stimuli but affects no other stage. Varying the size of the memory set affects speed of comparison of the stimulus serially with the items in the memory set. The presence or absence of the stimulus in the memory set affects decision time, absence resulting in longer RT, but again, without interaction with either stimulus quality or memory set size. Finally, the relative frequency of presentation of members of the positive set affects a translation and response organization stage, the greater the frequency the shorter the RT.

Sternberg's additive-factor model provides for a test of whether a variable affects only one stage of the RT process or more than one stage, by testing for interaction between factors. It is precisely this power of the model and paradigm that is the focus of this research program.

Application of Sternberg's Paradigm to Schizophrenia

Suppose we introduce the variable, schizophrenia versus control, into the experimental paradigm outlined above. The questions are:

1. Does schizophrenia simply add a processing stage (perhaps negativistic or withdrawn attitudinal stage prior to encoding) as might be inferred from simple delay of RT, without interaction with any other factor?

2. Does schizophrenia affect one or more of the other stages, with one or more interactions?

3. Are both additive (main effects) and interaction effects present?

The only previous attempt to apply Sternberg's paradigm to study schizophrenia is that of Checkosky.[1] He studied chronic schizophrenics, acute schizophrenics, and alcoholic controls using letters, digits, geometric figures, and colors. He varied intactness (implicating the encoding stage), memory-set size (implicating the serial comparison stage), and presence versus absence (implicating the decision stage). In all cases there were significant main effects, i.e., differences in intercept between the three groups but no difference in slope. In brief, for acute and chronic schizophrenics, Checkosky found no evidence of qualitatively different functioning from controls in the first three stages of Sternberg's model. For example, with respect to memory-set size, the extrapolated intercept at zero set size for chronic schizophrenics was 705 msec with a slope of 35 msec/item; for acute schizophrenics, the respective figures were 598 and 35; and for alcoholics, 488 and 34. The equivalent figures for Sternberg's subjects were 367 and 39.

One apparent exception to this conclusion has been reported by Yates and Korboot (24), who studied inspection time as a function of "complexity" of stimuli (akin to set size in the current proposal), using three types of materials (lines, words, symbols) in four groups of schizophrenics and two groups of neurotics. Unfortunately, they reported

[1] Unpublished data kindly made available to us by Dr. Stephen Checkosky.

only log transformations of their real time data. As Sternberg (21) has pointed out, additivity in general is destroyed by nonlinear transformations. He therefore specified the use of real time as the datum for all calculations. It is extremely difficult to interpret the Yates and Korboot data in the current context. Although an interaction between type of schizophrenia and set size appears to be implied, it must be remembered that their experiment does not fit in the memory-search paradigm. Their analysis of variance (on transformed data only) also indicates an interaction of diagnosis by type of stimulus material. Although type of material has been shown to be implicated in schizophrenic performance in various types of experiments (25–26), it is by no means certain that it will constitute either an interactive or additive factor in the Sternberg paradigm. It may simply affect one of the stages in the model; the serial comparison stage is a likely candidate. However, Checkosky's data do not support even this notion, in that he found no interactions regardless of type of material. Thus, the use of log transformations by Yates and Korboot may be responsible for statistical interactions even when none may exist in untransformed data.

Checkosky's data show no interactions between diagnosis and any of the factors implicating the first three stages. The fourth stage, translation and organization of the response, was not tested. Analysis of the experimental literature on output dysfunction in schizophrenia indicates that the omitted stage may be important in differentiating schizophrenics from normal subjects.

For example, Holzman et al (27,28) have described two experiments in which the subject is required to look at a moving pendulum while his eye movements are recorded. Fifty-two percent of their "recent" schizophrenics and 86% of their chronic schizophrenics showed deviant eye-tracking, compared to 22% of the manic-depressives, 21% of nonpsychotic patients, and 8% of a normal control group. Moreover, 44% of the relatives of schizophrenics but only 10% of the relatives of nonschizophrenics showed this phenomenon. The authors concluded that it was quite unlikely that the results were attributable to motivational and set variables. (See Holzman's chapters in this volume for a possible reinterpretation.)

At a directly physiologic level, Meltzer and his associates (29–31) have examined enzymatic and structural changes in the musculature of acutely psychotic patients and conclude that both myopathic and neuropathic components are involved.

At the level of organization of memory, Bauman and Kolisnyk (32,33) concluded that output interference had a more profound effect on the recall of schizophrenics than input interference. In one of their experiments (33), subjects learned 35 different seven-digit lists one at a time. Different serial positions were probed randomly after each list. When the interference was of the input variety, resulting from the interpolation of *items* between presentation and recall of the probed item, the results were the same for both groups. But when the interference was of the output, resulting from the interpolation of *responses* between presentation and recall, the schizophrenics were significantly poorer than controls. They concluded that "output interference is the major causative factor in the schizophrenic recall deficit."

In a similar vein, Wishner and Wahl (34), in a dichotic listening task, showed that at very slow rates of presentation, schizophrenics and controls did not differ significantly in accuracy of shadowing. At the same time, in later recall and recognition tests, schizophrenics showed marked inaccuracy in differentiating between the shadowed and distractor words. Thus, it was inferred that the dysfunction noted had to be beyond the input stage.

Thus, Checkosky may have omitted a critical variable in his survey of Sternberg's paradigm as it applies to schizophrenia. In the present study, a variable was included with the intention of testing for differences in psychomotor functioning.

In addition, it was decided to sample paranoid and nonparanoid schizophrenics, in view of the usual findings that paranoids function at a level between nonparanoids and normal subjects. In terms of the Sternberg paradigm, we were interested in whether this represents quantitative differences in intercepts or whether we will find differential slopes, indicating different loci of dysfunction.

SPECIFIC AIMS OF THE FIRST EXPERIMENT

The present study was designed to examine the information processing of paranoid and nonparanoid schizophrenics over the last three Sternberg stages: serial comparison, binary decision, and translation and organization of the response. The factors varied were the size of the positive set (two, three, or four digits), response type (positive or negative), and the number of hands used in responding (one versus two). The task was memory search and the fixed set procedure was used. As a test of the translation and response organization stage, one versus two hands was chosen over relative frequency, the usual factor varied for this stage. The manipulation of the latter variables has been shown in one study to influence the encoding stage as well as the translation and response organization stage (35). Based on pilot data, one versus two hands appeared to be a clearer measure of at least one aspect of the final stage. This, along with other stages, are always subject to further analysis and breakdown into several stages, as Sternberg has recognized.

PROCEDURES

The subjects were 10 nonparanoid schizophrenics, 10 paranoid schizophrenics, and 12 alcoholic control subjects.[2] They were drawn from populations at Norristown State Hospital, Norristown, Pennsylvania. Alcoholics were chosen to control partially for the effects of institutionalization and for effects not specific to the schizophrenic process that might occur generally in any psychopathologic group (36). Criteria for selection of subjects were: (a) male, (b) right-handed, (c) age: 18–55 years, (d) race: white, (e) education: minimum of 8 years, (f) no electroconvulsive shock treatments within 3 months of testing, (g) no brain damage or mental retardation, (h) paranoid schizophrenics must display an organized delusional system. The mean ages for the groups were: paranoids 33, nonparanoids 34, and alcoholics 39.

Almost all schizophrenics in the hospital are on antipsychotic medication, primarily phenothiazines. However, two studies (37,38) concerned with the effects of phenothiazine medication on performance of psychomotor tests showed little difference before and after drugs. The study which included a reaction time task (37) found a decrease in variability, but no change in mean speed. In any case, there is no a priori reason to expect these drugs to affect slopes differentially.

---

[2] These are the partial results available at the time of this report. See "Addendum as of March 1977" at the end of this chapter for outcome of completed experiment.

The test stimuli were digits mounted on 35 mm slides. The digits, when projected onto a screen, were 2.5 cm high. A trial consisted of the following events: (a) an intertrial interval of 4 seconds, (b) warning signal (illumination of lights) for 1.25 seconds, and (c) display of the test stimulus for 3 seconds whether or not the subject responded.

SET SELECTION

The positive memory sets were composed of two, three, or four digits. Each group of six subjects received a different group of memory sets. Obvious patterns, for example, all even or odd, were excluded.

It was intended to test each subject twice a day for six sessions over a period of 3 successive days. This was not possible in the case of six subjects, whose sessions were extended over one or more extra days when their schedules interfered. Each session lasted 35 minutes to 1 hour, and the sessions were separated by at least 2 hours.

At the beginning of each session, the subject was given an index card with the members of the positive set. After stating that he had memorized the numbers, the subject was presented with a set of cards, one digit per card, which he was instructed to sort into two piles, one containing the positive and the other, the negative numbers. If the subject made a mistake, he was asked to sort the cards again. This was repeated until the subject sorted the cards perfectly.

Each session was composed of 24 practice trials and 144 test trials. The subject was informed of his errors during the practice trials to further insure that he had correctly memorized the numbers. The subject was stopped during the test trials if he had made a number of errors. If this occurred, the subject was asked to repeat the numbers he had memorized and then to indicate the appropriate key response.

One digit was presented on each trial of the experiment. The subject decided whether or not the digit was a member of the positive set. He then pressed one of two keys. In the one-hand condition, half of the subjects responded to the positive set with their right hand and half with their left hand. Within the one-hand condition, half of the subjects responded "yes" with their index finger and "no" with their middle finger. This was reversed for the other half of the subjects. In the two-hand condition, half of the subjects responded to the positive set with the index finger of their right hand and to the negative set with the index finger of their left hand. Again, this was reversed for the other half of the subjects.

RESULTS AND INTERPRETATIONS

Mean error rates were 0.77% for alcoholics, 3.04% for paranoids, and 1.84% for nonparanoids, indicating the possibilities for valid RT results from these groups, since the error rates are within the limits generally accepted and justify confidence in the RTs as measures of information processing time.

A summary of the results of the analysis of variance of RT is given in Table 21-1.

The results of central interest are those involving interactions of diagnosis by the other independent variables. These are illustrated in Figure 21-2. There were no signifi-

Table 21-1. Summary of Results of Anova of RT

Variable	Schizophrenic Group Separately			Schizophrenic Group Combined		
	df	F	p	df	F	p
Diagnosis (D)	2,29	3.81	0.03	1,30	7.32	0.01
Set Size (S)	2,58	23.25	0.0001	2,60	23.09	0.0001
Positive-negative (P-N)	1,29	30.73	0.0001	1,30	31.72	0.0001
Hand (H)	1,29	1.28	0.27	1,30	1.33	0.26
D × S	4,58	1.47	0.22	2,60	1.72	0.18
D × P-N	2,29	1.50	0.24	1,30	3.03	0.09
D × H	2,29	0.24	0.79	1,30	0.48	0.50
S × P-N	2,58	0.17	0.84	2,60	0.18	0.83
S × H	2,58	0.53	0.60	2,60	0.55	0.59
P-N × H	1,29	5.04	0.03	1,30	5.19	0.03
D × S × P-N	4,58	0.10	0.98	2,60	0.10	0.90
D × S × H	4,58	0.73	0.58	2,60	1.37	0.26
D × P-N × H	2,29	0.54	0.59	1,30	1.02	0.32
S × P-N × H	2,58	2.75	0.07	2,60	2.76	0.07
D × S × P-N × H	4,58	0.76	0.55	2,60	0.62	0.55

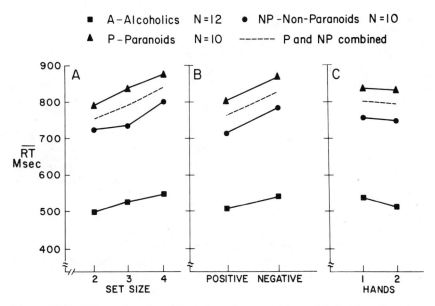

Figure 21-2. RT as a function of the independent variables and their interactions.

cant interactions involving diagnosis, i.e., the slopes for the schizophrenics were not signficantly different from the slopes for the alcoholics.

Since the paranoid and nonparanoid schizophrenics were not significantly different from each other, their data were combined, and these results are shown in the right half of Table 21-1 and by the dotted lines in Figure 21-2. Again, there were no significant interactions involving diagnosis.

There were significant main effects for the groups, i.e., intercepts of the schizophrenics were significantly different from those of the alcoholics. Thus, as is usually the case, schizophrenics were slower than controls.

The significant interaction of hands by positive (P)-negative(N) results from a mean difference of 37 msec between P and N with one hand responding, as compared to a mean difference of 63 msec with two hands responding. Such an interaction indicates that the hand factor may be affecting the third stage (Figure 21-1) in Sternberg's model, but in view of our failure to find this with college students in our pilot work, further speculation appears hazardous.

The tendency of paranoids to be slower than nonparanoids seen in Figure 21-2, although not significant, may reflect our diagnostic procedure. It will be recalled that overt evidence of a delusion was required to justify classification as paranoid. It may be that this requirement (in the face of medication) selected for a greater intensity of disorder.

From the standpoint of our central interest in differential slopes between groups, the results are negative. In the stages thus far surveyed by Checkosky and us, there is no evidence of a different mode of functioning for schizophrenics in the type of information processing tested by these methods.

DISCUSSION

Within the limits of the methods and materials used to this point, the results indicate that there is no special dysfunction of schizophrenics in the serial comparison and binary decision stages, the second and third stages in Sternberg's model. In these respects, this is a replication of Checkosky's results. Checkosky also has shown that there is no special dysfunction in the first stage, encoding. Our attempt to test the fourth stage, translation and organization of the response, must be considered unsuccessful. It might be useful to attempt to experiment with Sternberg's factor for the fourth stage, relative frequency, as well as with a stronger psychomotor variable, which would implicate gross movements.

The intercept differences remain unexplained in ways other than the theories outlined in the introduction to this report. It may well be that we are dealing with an overall disorganization factor in schizophrenia that is not specific to any stage of information processing in short-term memory experiments, thus, the greatly raised intercepts.

Before accepting such a conclusion, however, it would seem wise to eliminate decisively the possibilities of more precise analyses offered by modern cognitive psychology. There are the suggestions offered above, as well as other potentially fruitful approaches. For example, there is every reason to attempt to study the effects of distraction on information processing using visual stimuli, analogously to what has been done in the aural mode (34). In our laboratory, we are proceeding in this direction via visual stimuli with built-in distractors. In view of the focus of this conference, such manipulations seem natural to try.

In any case, systematic, step-by-step attempts to analyze the schizophrenic retardation in RT, utilizing the techniques made available to us by cognitive psychology, as well as others yet to be invented, would appear to be the surest road to a psychologic understanding of this phenomenon. Scattered attempts thus far, while laying some foundation, seem destined to leave us in puzzlement, if continued in unsystematic fashion.

ADDENDUM AS OF MARCH 1977

The experiment has now been completed. Analysis of the data according to the scheme detailed above yielded results identical in significance levels to those reported. However, additional analysis revealed one positive result and one trend of interest.

The trend is for more schizophrenics (13 of 24) than controls (3 of 12) to be slower with two hands than with one. Although not significant statistically, we are inclined to place some weight on this trend because in a subsequent study with female schizophrenics, the proportion of patients and controls exhibiting slower RT's with two hands was almost precisely the same: 50% and 25%, respectively. The modal difference among these patients was about 100 msec.; for the controls it was about 10 msec.

The positive result arose from dividing the schizophrenics and controls into fast and slow RT groups at their respective medians for mean RT over all conditions. Mathematically, mean RT is independent of the slope for any condition. A significant interaction ($p < 0.01$) was found between overall speed and set size for schizophrenics only. The slope for set size of the slow schizophrenics (about 74 msec/item) was more than three times as steep as the slope of the fast schizophrenics (22 msec/item). The last value was about the same as that of the slow controls (30 msec/item). Reanalysis of Checkosky's data in these terms also produced a significantly steeper slope for set size in slow schizophrenics.

Further, of the 12 slow schizophrenics in this study, 6 were in the two-hands slower group and 6 were in the two-hands faster groups. Thus, the underlying dimensions represented by the set size and hand factors, respectively, appear to be orthogonal. Tentatively, we identify these dimensions as rate of memory search and degree of motor coordination. Schizophrenics, then, may be characterized by: slow memory search and motor coordination; slow search and motor discoordination, fast search and motor discoordination, or defects on neither of these dimensions. Presumably, there are other characteristic dysfunctions at this level of analysis yet to be identified. Research directed to these ends is in progress.

REFERENCES

1. Shakow D: Psychological deficit in schizophrenia. *Behav Sci* 8:275–305, 1963.
2. Shakow D: Some observations on the psychology (and some fewer, on the biology) of schizophrenia. *J Nerv Ment Dis* 153:300–316, 1971.
3. Shakow D, and Huston PE: Studies of motor function in schizophrenia: I. Speed of tapping. *J Gen Psych* 15:63–106, 1936.
4. Bellissimo A, Steffy RA: Redundancy-associated deficit in schizophrenic reaction time performance. *J Ab Psych* 80:299–307, 1972.
5. Steffy RA, Galbraith K: A comparison of segmental set and inhibitory deficit explanations of the crossover pattern in process schizophrenic reaction time. *J Ab Psych* 83:227–233, 1974.

6. McGhie A: Attention and perception in schizophrenia, in Maher BA (ed): *Progress in Experimental Personality Research,* vol 5. New York, Academic Press, 1970.

7. Neale JM, Cromwell RL: Attention and schizophrenia, in Maher BA (ed): *Progress in Experimental Personality Research,* vol 5. New York, Academic Press, 1970.

8. Salzinger K: *Schizophrenia: Behavioral Aspects.* New York, John Wiley & Sons, 1973.

9. Shakow D: Segmental set: a theory of the formal psychological deficit in schizophrenia. *Arch Gen Psychiat* 6:1–17, 1962.

10. Wishner J: Response to the discussions. Symposium on clinical psychology and experimental psychopathology. *Bull l'Assoc Int Psych Appl* 14:74, 1965.

11. McGhie A: *Pathology of Attention.* Baltimore, Penguin, 1969.

12. Broadbent DE: *Perception and Communication.* Elmsford, NY, Pergamon, 1958.

13. Broadbent DE: *Decision and Stress.* New York, Academic Press, 1971.

14. Venables PH: Input dysfunction in schizophrenia, in Maher BA (ed): *Progress in Experimental Personality Research,* vol 1. New York, Academic Press, 1964.

15. Venables PH: Input regulation and psychopathology, in Hammer M, Salzinger K, Sutton S (eds): *Psychopathology: Contributions from the Social, Behavioral, and Biological Sciences.* New York, John Wiley & Sons, 1973.

16. Yates AJ: *Behavior Therapy.* New York, John Wiley & Sons, 1970, ch 14.

17. Wishner J: Convergent trends in psychopathology. *Proceedings of XVIIth International Congress of Applied Psychology,* vol I. Bruxelles, Editest, 1972.

18. Sternberg S: High-speed scanning in human memory. *Sci* 153:652–654, 1966.

19. Sternberg S: Two operations in character-recognition: some evidence from reaction-time measurements. *Percept Psychophys* 2:45–53, 1967.

20. Sternberg S: Memory-scanning: mental processes revealed by reaction-time experiments. *Amer Scient* 57, 421–457, 1969.

21. Sternberg S: The discovery of processing stages: extensions of Donders' method, in Koster WG (ed): Attention and performance II. Acta Psychologia 30:276–315, 1969.

22. Sternberg S: Decomposing mental processes with reaction-time data. Invited address, Midwestern Psychological Association Meeting, Detroit, 1971.

23. Sternberg S: Memory scanning: new findings and current controversies. *Quart J Exp Psych* 27:1–32, 1975.

24. Yates AJ, Korboot P: Speed of perceptual functioning in chronic nonparanoid schizophrenics. *J Ab Psych* 76, 453–461, 1970.

25. McGhie A, Chapman J, Lawson JS: The effect of distraction on schizophrenic performance: 2. Perception and immediate memory. *Brit J Psychiat* 111:383–390, 1965.

26. Lawson JS, McGhie A, Chapman J: Distractibility in schizophrenic and organic cerebral disease. *Brit J Psychiat* 113:527–535, 1967.

27. Holzman PS, Proctor LR, Hughes DW: Eye-tracking patterns in schizophrenia. *Sci* 181:179–181, 1973.

28. Holzman PS, Proctor LR, Levy DL, et al: Eye-tracking dysfunctions in schizophrenic patients and their relatives. *Arch Gen Psychiat* 31:143–151, 1974.

29. Meltzer HY: Muscle enzyme release in the acute psychoses. *Arch Gen Psychiat* 21:102–112, 1969.

30. Meltzer HY: Central core fibers in an acutely psychotic patient. Evidence for a neurogenic basis for the muscle abnormalities in the acute psychoses. *Arch Gen Psychiat* 27:125–132, 1972.

31. Meltzer HY, Crayton JW: Subterminal motor nerve abnormalities in psychotic patients. *Nature* 249:373–375, 1974.

32. Bauman E: Schizophrenic short-term memory: the role of organization at input. *J Consult Clin Psych* 36:14–19, 1971.

33. Bauman E, Kolisnyk E: Input and output interference in schizophrenic short-term memory. *Proceeding, 81st Annual Convention, American Psychological Association,* 1973.

34. Wishner J, Wahl O: Dichotic listening in schizophrenia. *J Consult Clin Psych* 42:538–546, 1974.

35. Miller JO, Pachella RC: Locus of the stimulus probability effect. *J Exp Psych* 101:227–231, 1973.

36. Wahl O, Wishner J: Schizophrenic thinking as measured by developmental tests. *J Nerv Ment Dis* 155:232–244, 1972.

37. Heilizer J: The effects of chlorpromazine upon psychomotor and psychiatric behavior of chronic schizophrenic patients. *J Nerv Ment Dis* 128:358–364, 1959.

38. Pearl D: Phenothiazine effects in chronic schizophrenia. *J Clin Psych* 18:86–89, 1962.

Chapter 22
Visual Temporal Integration in Psychiatric Patients

Patrick J. Collins, Ph.D.
Mitchell L. Kietzman, Ph.D.
Samuel Sutton, Ph.D.
Eleanor Shapiro, M.A.

Although clinical reports indicate that some schizophrenic patients display definite and profound differences from normal controls in the quality of their sensory and perceptual experiences (1–3), recent reviewers of this topic (4–5) have concluded that the existence of such differences remains an open and scientifically unanswered question, requiring more research with refined techniques. Several suggestions have been made to explain the discrepancy between the apparent sensory and perceptual impairment of patients (as indicated from anecdotal and clinical reports) and the fact that there has been no sustained or systematic experimental evidence of such sensory differences: (a) The poor performance of schizophrenic patients found in previous sensory studies (e.g., performance that is less accurate, slower, and more variable than that of normal subjects) may simply be due to the fact that they differ from normal controls in cognitive and motivational factors (6). For example, patients may differ from normal subjects in their degree of attention, their level of effort, or their attitudinal response biases, such as the degree of cautiousness (7). (b) If sensory differences do exist between psychiatric patients and normal subjects, they may be very small, in which case the relatively larger variability among patients would tend to obscure such differences. (c) Inaccurate or inappropriate grouping of psychiatric subjects on the basis of subjective clinical judgments may tend to obscure genuine differences in the experimental measures under consideration. (d) Traditional research designs and procedures used with cooperative volunteer normal

We thank R. Laupheimer and R. Simon for their assistance in instrumentation, J. Fleiss and I. Berenhaus for their assistance in data analysis, J. Endicott for her assistance in patient classification, and M. Wallach, Director, Kingsboro Psychiatric Center, for providing space and facilities. This research was supported by NIMH Grants MH-11688 and MH-18191 and by a N.Y. State Department of Mental Hygiene project grant.

subjects may not be appropriate with psychiatric patients who may be less cooperative and more difficult to test. (e) The more general problem in this type of research is that patient and nonpatient differences may not be attributable directly to the subject variable under consideration (psychiatric classification) but actually may be due to confounding by other uncontrolled subject variables (8).

When taken together, these problems require special research strategies that optimize the possibility of locating patient-normal sensory differences, if they exist. One such strategy is to design sensory experiments in which the performance of the patient is not necessarily inferior to that of the normal subject, but instead the performance reflects a sensory processing ability on the part of the patient that is different from that of the normal subject (e.g., a patient can do something the normal subject does not or cannot do). This would lend greater credence to a positive finding since the better performance on the part of the patient group could not then be dismissed as a by-product of generalized poor performance by patients in the testing situation. Additionally, it is important to use techniques and procedures that have been well investigated so potential difficulties and problems can be anticipated and the obtained results can be interpreted with maximum clarity. Finally, it is advantageous to employ an objective method for classifying patients such as is made possible by the use of a structured interview technique (9).

In the present study, schizophrenic patients, nonschizophrenic psychiatric patients, and normal controls were compared on the sensory measure of temporal integration. The theoretical basis for this work is derived from Bloch's law of stimulus intensity-time reciprocity (temporal integration) in visual psychophysics (10) and visual physiology. Recent studies have used simple reaction time as a psychophysical measure of the characteristics of temporal integration. These reaction time studies, using a number of experimental paradigms and a variety of experimental conditions, have shown that critical duration, i.e., the longest stimulus duration displaying complete temporal integration (intensity-time reciprocity) for simple reaction time, is very brief—briefer than estimates obtained for verbal discrimination and detection tasks under similar stimulus conditions. It may be as short as 10 milliseconds. Simple reaction time was chosen as the response measure in the present study because it is more easily performed by psychiatric patients than psychophysical tasks, and it has been thoroughly investigated both for patients and normal subjects. In our adaptation, reaction time has the virtue of measuring temporal integration without requiring any overt or "conscious" discrimination on the part of the subject (11a).

The basic strategy of our experiments involves the presentation of brief visual stimuli of the same luminance, but different durations. Two of the stimuli are equal-energy pulses of light—a 4-msec pulse and a double-pulse stimulus made up of two, 2-msec pulses with a varying dark interval separating the two pulses. The use of such double-pulse stimuli is an established procedure that is completely consistent with the logic of measuring complete intensity-time reciprocity, i.e., for stimulus durations shorter than critical duration, only total energy, not its distribution in time, determines the response. Simple reaction time responses to all stimuli are measured. The expectation is that very brief stimuli of the same energy (the 4-msec and the double-pulse stimuli) would produce the same reaction times if they are fully integrated, i.e., if their stimulus durations are below critical duration. Several studies (11,12,13) have shown that as the dark interval between the two pulses of the double-pulse stimulus is increased, a duration is reached at which reaction time increases and this increase is evidence that critical duration has been reached. Reaction time increases because part (or all) of the energy of the second pulse is not fully integrated for the reaction time response.

A 2-msec light pulse of the same luminance and therefore half the energy of the other stimuli was also included in this study to measure the reaction time difference between the 2- and 4-msec single pulses, which because of their brevity are presumed to be fully integrated. This difference, which indicates the effect of doubling luminous energy on the reaction times, is called the *energy effect* and serves as one indicator of the subject's cooperation in performing the task. For example, failure to obtain faster reaction times to the 4-msec stimulus than to the 2-msec stimulus would lead one to question if the subject was following instructions or if he understood the task.

The purpose of this study was to determine if there are differences in critical duration as measured by simple reaction time among psychiatric and nonpsychiatric subjects. The methodology and procedures employed were chosen to maximize the opportunity of finding such differences.

METHOD

Subjects

The subjects in the main study consisted of 19 psychiatric patients and 10 normal controls (all males). Alcoholics, drug addicts, organics, and uncooperative subjects were eliminated. The psychiatric patients were subdivided into a nonschizophrenic group (N = 9) and a schizophrenic group (N = 10), on the basis of a Current and Past Psychopathology Scales structured interview (CAPPS) (9). There were no statistically significant differences between the three groups with respect to age, ethnicity, education, and socioeconomic level.

All patients were undergoing phenothiazine therapy. Since the complete testing period was from 4 to 6 weeks for each patient, the phenothiazine medication and dosage varied during the testing period because the course of chemotherapy was regulated according to each individual's tolerance, side effects, and clinical response. The patients were selected with an attempt to equate the mean daily amount of phenothiazine taken during the testing period. For more specific details of the exact drugs and dosage levels, see Collins (14).

Apparatus

Chin and forehead rests were employed to obtain a stable position for the subject. The stimulus was a white-appearing circular target, viewed binocularly and foveally fixated. The reaction time response consisted of lifting the right index finger from a telegraph key.

Stimulus Conditions

The stimulus conditions are shown in the top portion of Figure 22-1. The three stimuli used in the experiment were all of the same luminance (0.2 mL) and of the following durations: (a) a 2-msec light pulse; (b) a 4-msec light pulse; and (c) a 6-msec stimulus consisting of two, 2-msec pulses separated by a 2-msec dark interval. Therefore, the 2-msec stimulus was half the energy of each of the other two stimuli, which themselves

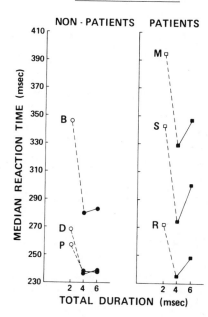

STIMULUS CONDITIONS

2 - MSEC SINGLE PULSE   4 - MSEC SINGLE PULSE

6 - MSEC DOUBLE PULSE

PRELIMINARY DATA

NON - PATIENTS   PATIENTS

MEDIAN REACTION TIME (msec)

TOTAL DURATION (msec)

Figure 22-1. The stimulus conditions are shown in the top panel. The bottom panel shows the preliminary reaction time data for three nonpatients (left side) and three psychiatric patients (right side). The total number of trials for a subject for each stimulus condition ranged from 22 to 128.

were equal in energy. The energy level of the 2-msec stimulus was approximately one-half a log unit above the detection threshold of one normal subject.

Procedure

The subject was seated in a light-tight booth and dark adapted for 5 minutes. On a signal from the experimenter that a block of trials was about to begin, the subject positioned his head in the chin rest, placed his right arm on a table with his index finger on the reaction time key, and fixated on the four red fixation lights. Each trial was initiated by the experimenter saying "ready" followed in approximately one second by a click. The click warning signal was followed, after a random variable foreperiod of 1–2 seconds, by one of the three stimuli. The subject was instructed to lift his finger as quickly as possible upon seeing the light. Reaction times were measured from stimulus onset. In each block of 30 trials, all three stimulus conditions were presented quasirandomly such that there were twice as many presentations of the 2-msec stimulus as either of the other two stimuli. The total number of trials for each subject was approximately 400, i.e., 2-msec pulse, N = 200; 4-msec pulse, N = 100; 6-msec double pulse, N = 100. There was a 9- to 11-second interval between trials. Short rest periods were given in the booth in the middle of a block and between blocks of trials. Sessions lasted approximately 40 minutes.

Prior to the running of the main study, preliminary data were collected from psychiatric patients and from nonpatients, using essentially the same apparatus, stimulus conditions, and procedures.

RESULTS

The bottom of Figure 22-1 shows the preliminary data for three nonpatients (subjects B, D, and P) and three psychiatric patients (subjects M, S, and R). These serve to illustrate the general direction of the findings. The unfilled symbols signify the half-energy, 2-msec stimulus, while the filled symbols show data from the two stimuli that are equal in energy (the 4-msec single pulse and the 6-msec double pulse). Median reaction time is shown as a function of total duration of the stimulus (the duration from the onset of the first pulse to the offset of the second pulse for the double-pulse stimulus or the duration of the stimulus itself for the single-pulse stimulus). All subjects showed a reaction time difference between the half-energy and full-energy stimuli (the 2- and 4-msec stimuli), suggesting they were doing the task properly. For the three nonpatients, the differences in reaction time to the 4-msec and 6-msec stimulus were small and varied around zero difference, a result entirely consistent with other results obtained from testing dozens of nonpatients under identical conditions. However, for the three psychiatric patients the reaction times to the 6-msec stimulus were markedly slower than the reaction times to the 4-msec stimulus, a result that would be obtained if critical duration were shorter than 6 msec for the patients.

For the main study, correlations were obtained between the mean and the standard deviation of the individual reaction time distributions for each condition within each group, before and after a logarithmic transformation of the data. None of the correlations for the transformed data was significant. Therefore, the subsequent analyses were performed using the transformed reaction times for each subject for the three stimulus conditions. Table 22-1 shows the group means and standard deviations for each condition. These group values are based upon the antilogs (in msec) of the means of the transformed reaction times, i.e., upon the geometric means, of the individual subjects. As expected, the patients exhibited slower and more variable reaction times than did the normal controls. The higher energy single-pulse stimulus (the 4-msec stimulus) produced faster reaction

Table 22-1. The Mean ($\bar{X}$) and Standard Deviation (SD) in Milliseconds of the Geometric Means for Three Stimulus Conditions for Each Group of Subjects

Diagnostic Groups	2 msec		4 msec		6 msec	
	$\bar{X}$	SD	$\bar{X}$	SD	$\bar{X}$	SD
Nonpatients (N = 10)	335	42.0	276	29.7	275	28.4
Nonschizophrenic patients (N = 9)	436	100.6	391	98.4	378	92.4
Schizophrenic patients (N = 10)	423	60.7	361	42.4	386	59.5

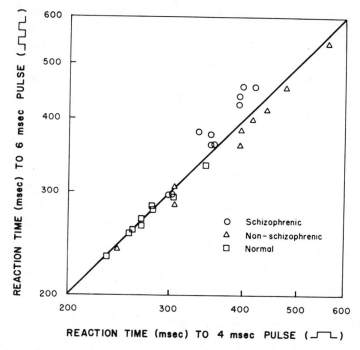

Figure 22-2. Scatter diagram of the geometric mean of reaction times to the 4- and 6-msec equal-energy pulses for all subjects of each of the three groups.

times than the lower energy single-pulse stimulus (the 2-msec stimulus). The fact that all patients showed a faster reaction time to the higher energy stimulus suggests that they were executing the task properly.

An analysis of variance was done (a 3 × 2 groups by conditions with repeated measures) to compare differences between the reaction times to the 4-msec single-pulse stimulus and the equal-energy 6-msec double-pulse stimulus across the three groups of subjects. The results showed a significant F for: (a) overall level of reaction time between groups (F = 9.97, d.f. = 2/26, p < 0.01), i.e., the groups differed in overall speed of response, as in the prior comparable F test for the 2- and 4-msec stimuli; (b) effects of stimulus conditions across groups (F = 30.52, d.f. = 1/26, p < 0.01); and (c) the groups by conditions interaction effects (F = 18.35, d.f. = 2/26, p < 0.01). The chief interest of this analysis was the significant interaction effect which is equivalent to a comparison between groups of the temporal integration effect, i.e., the reaction time differences to the 4- and 6-msec stimuli. Post hoc comparisons (Bonferroni t-test) of these reaction time differences for the group pairs only showed significant differences (slower reaction times to the 6-msec stimulus than to the 4-msec stimulus) for the schizophrenic group compared with the nonschizophrenic group (t = 5.62, p < 0.01) and compared with the normal group (t = 4.09, p < 0.01).

Figure 22-2 is a plot of the reaction time of each subject in the three groups for the two equal-energy stimuli, the 4-msec pulse (abscissa) and the 6-msec double-pulse (ordinate). The diagonal line shows the theoretical expectation of equal reaction times for the two equal-energy stimuli. The normal subjects (the squares) are distributed at this theoretical line. The nonschizophrenic patients (triangles) also fall near the line of equality although their range of reaction times is similar to that of the schizophrenic patients. Most of the schizophrenic patients (the circles) are distributed above the line of equal reaction times, indicating slower reaction times to the 6-msec double-pulse stimulus than to the 4-msec single-pulse stimulus of equal energy. Since the two stimuli tested were of equal energy, a significantly slower reaction time to the longer duration double-pulse stimulus for the schizophrenic subjects indicates failure of complete intensity-time reciprocity, i.e., only some portion of the energy of the second pulse is being integrated.

Several analyses were performed to evaluate possible effects of variations in the dosage of phenothiazine medication in our patient population on the differential integration results of this study. Correlations were calculated to test the relationship between the difference scores (the difference between the reaction times to the 4-msec and 6-msec equal-energy stimuli) and the daily drug dosage level. The nonschizophrenic group showed an unexplained significant negative relationship between the two measures ($r = -0.67$ $p < 0.05$), while the correlation within the schizophrenic group did not reach significance ($r = 0.34$).

The effects of long-term medication were analyzed by assigning each patient to one of three categories based on the length of time the patient was taking some form of phenothiazine medication. The categories were: (a) less than 6 months; (b) 6 months to 2 years; and (c) longer than 2 years. Pearson correlations computed between the categories (a, b, and c) and the reaction time difference scores indicated no relationship across the entire patient sample ($r = 0.18$) nor within the separate groups ($r = -0.29$ for the schizophrenic group and $r = 0.23$ for the nonschizophrenic group).

The six subjects who displayed the greatest reaction time difference between the two equal-energy stimuli (see Figure 22-2), i.e., were furthest from the equal reaction time line, shared a common symptom—evidence of speech disorganization on the CAPPS (this speech disorganization scale seems to be closely related to a formal thought disorder). Only one of the four remaining schizophrenic patients and none of the nonschizophrenic patients had a positive rating on speech disorganization.

DISCUSSION

The results of this investigation suggest that for the nonpatients and nonschizophrenic patients, critical duration is greater than 6-msec, while for the schizophrenic patients it is less than 6-msec. These data are interpreted to indicate a sensory difference between schizophrenic patients and other psychiatric patients and normal controls which, for several reasons, is believed not to be confounded by motivational and/or response bias differences. First, the differences in reaction time between the 4-msec pulse and the equal-energy, 6-msec double-pulse represent a psychomotor "discrimination" which the schizophenic subject is making and which the nonschizophrenic and normal subject cannot make. Subjects cannot differentiate these stimuli as evidenced by several psychophysical studies using verbal reports, which have shown that even under the most optimal conditions a dark interval of at least 15 to 20 msec is necessary for such a discrimination (15–17). Note that poor motivation and attention on the part of the schizophrenic patients, the bane of psychophysical experiments in psychopathology, cannot account for the ability of the schizophrenic patient to make a reaction time "discrimination" other subjects cannot make. On the contrary, poor motivation and attention would tend to mask such a difference.

Second, differences in response criterion and therefore response bias across stimulus conditions were not possible since all three stimuli were presented randomly by trial. Thus, there is no way that subjects could exercise a differential response bias prior to each presentation that would produce the obtained differences between the equal-energy stimuli.

The possibility still remains that different groups of subjects may have had, for the tasks as a whole, different response biases that conceivably could account for the group differences. For example, the psychiatric patients may have been "stricter" in responding, thus accounting for their slower reaction times. There are several reasons why we do not believe such a difference would explain our result, i.e., the relatively longer reaction time for the 6-msec pulse on the part of the schizophrenic patients. We have conducted a number of control experiments in normal subjects in which motivation and response criterion were manipulated. Although these factors affected the speed and variability of reaction time, they did not seem to alter systematically, or in a clear-cut way, the value of critical duration. Second, if the number of missed responses and/or the speed of responses are used as rough indicators of response bias, then the three groups of subjects could be compared for any criterion differences. On the average, the three groups of subjects did not differ in their frequency of missed responses, which suggests that they might not have differed in criterion. In terms of speed of reaction time, the two patient groups were not significantly different, yet only the schizophrenic patients showed the effect. These results, taken together, suggest that although the groups of subjects (especially the patient groups) did not differ in criterion, the schizophrenic group did differ in critical duration.

A recent development in sensory and perceptual research has been the adoption of an information-processing approach for studying behavior (18) and its physiologic correlates (19). However, some investigators (20,21) have expressed concern that visual information-processing research must give more attention to the importance of the stimulus (the pertinent stimulus dimensions and ways of measuring them) and to various sensory differences such as the limits of temporal resolution, differences in retinal sensitivity, or differences in visual acuity. We suggest that a first step in studying information processing would be to investigate sensory-processing phenomena, such as temporal integration. There are several advantages of using measures of temporal integration to test for differences in psychiatric patients. Temporal integration is a clearly defined and thoroughly investigated sensory process that can be tested using extremely simple stimuli of specified durations, intensities, and energies. Furthermore, the numerous physiologic and psychophysical studies of temporal integration help us to design investigations that avoid confounding by other sensory factors such as sensitivity and acuity.

The topic of information processing has been extended to the area of psychopathology (22–26) where it has been used as an explanatory model. Several theorists have posited either a sensory or an information processing dysfunction as basic to the schizophrenic disorder (3,22,23,25,26).

One of the most explicit discussions of schizophrenia as a deficit in information processing is offered by Yates (26). He suggests that the chain of behavior between stimulus and response can be divided into four stages. While failures of performance may occur at any or all these stages, Yates considers the second, or perceptual-processing, stage to be the one most likely to be impaired in the case of schizophrenic patients, and he suggests that the specific deficit in schizophrenics is an abnormally slow primary rate of information processing. This slow rate of processing for patients means that only a fragmentary part of the stimulation is successfully processed, and therefore over long periods of time, thought disorder or other symptomatology may appear. It is possible that Yates's "slower processing" may be related in part to what we refer to here as shorter critical durations with a reduction in integrated energy. Furthermore, Broen (22) discusses and refines Yates's processing model of psychopathology by speculating on how impairment in the speed of information processing, over a number of years, could come to influence the total functioning of an individual and thus may be related to the development of a chronic schizophrenic illness.

REFERENCES

1. Chapman J, McGhie A: A comparative study of disordered attention in schizophrenia. *J Ment Sci* 108:487, 1962.
2. Gross G, Huber G: Sensorische Storungen bei Schizophrenien. *Arch Psychiatr Nervenkr* 216:119, 1972.
3. Silverman J: Perceptual and neurophysiological analogues of "experience" in schizophrenic and LSD reactions, in Sankar DVS (ed): *Schizophrenia, Current Concepts and Research*. New York, PJD Publications, 1969, p 182.
4. Jenness D, Kietzman ML, Zubin J: Contributions of psychological science to psychiatry: Perception and cognition, in Freedman AM, Kaplan HI, Sadock BJ (eds): *Comprehensive Textbook of Psychiatry*, ed 2. Baltimore, Williams & Wilkins, 1975.
5. Zubin J, Salzinger K, Fleiss JL, et al: Biometric approach to psychopathology. *Ann Rev Psychol* 26:621, 1975.
6. Sutton S: Fact and artifact in the psychology of schizophrenia, in Hammer M, Salzinger K, Sutton S (eds): *Psychopathology: Contributions from the Social, Behavioral, and Biological Sciences*. New York, John Wiley & Sons, 1973.
7. Clark WC, Brown JC, Rutschmann J: Flicker sensitivity and response bias in psychiatric patients and normal subjects. *J Abnorm Psychol* 72:35, 1967.
8. Underwood BJ: *Psychological Research*. New York, Appleton-Century-Crofts, 1957.
9. Spitzer RL, Endicott J: DIAGNO II: Further developments in a computer program for psychiatric diagnosis. *Amer J Psychiatr* 125:12, 1969.
10. Bartlett NR: Thresholds as dependent on some energy relations and characteristics of the subject, in Graham CH (ed): *Vision and Visual Perception*. New York, John Wiley & Sons, 1965.
11. Kietzman ML, Gillam BJ: Visual temporal integration and simple reaction time. *Perception and Psychophysics* 11:333, 1972.
11a. Kietzman ML, Sutton S: Reaction time as a psychophysical method in psychiatric research. *Schizophrenic Bulletin*, in press.
12. Grossberg M: Frequencies and latencies in detecting two-flash stimuli. *Perception and Psychophysics* 7:377, 1970.
13. Pease VP: Effect of luminance and duration of interstimulus interval upon human reaction time. *J Opt Soc Amer* 62:1505, 1972.
14. Collins PJ: Reaction time measures of visual temporal integration in schizophrenic patients, other psychiatric patients, and normal subjects. Unpublished doctoral dissertation, Columbia University, 1972.
15. Kietzman ML: Two-pulse measures of temporal resolution as a function of stimulus energy. *J Opt Soc Amer* 57:809, 1967.

16. Lewis MF: Two-flash thresholds as a function of flash luminance and area. *Perception and Psychophysics* 4:241, 1968.

17. Mertens HW, Lewis MF: Temporal discrimination of two-pulse stimuli as a function of psychophysical method and luminance. *J Opt Soc Amer* 62:823, 1972.

18. Haber RN: *Information-processing Approaches to Visual Perception.* New York, Holt, Rinehart & Winston, 1969.

19. Fields WS, Abbott W (eds): *Information Storage and Neural Control.* Springfield, Ill, Charles C Thomas, 1963.

20. Eriksen CW, Spencer T: Rate of information processing in visual perception: Some results and methodological considerations. *J Exp Psychol Monogr* 79(2), Part 2, 1969, p 1.

21. Garner WR: The stimulus in information processing. *Amer Psychologist* 25:350, 1970.

22. Broen WE Jr: *Schizophrenia: Research and Theory.* New York, Academic Press, 1968.

23. Frith CD: Abnormalities of perception, in Eysenck HJ (ed): *Handbook of Abnormal Psychology,* ed 2. San Diego, Cal, Robert R Knapp, 1973.

24. Miller JG: Adjusting to overloads of information. *Dis Commun* 42:87, 1964.

25. Venables PH: Input dysfunction in schizophrenia, in Maher BA (ed): *Progress in Experimental Personality Research,* vol I. New York, Academic Press, 1964.

26. Yates AJ: Psychological deficit. *Ann Rev Psychol* 17:111, 1966.

Chapter 23
The Attention Switching Model: Implications for Research in Schizophrenia

Lorraine G. Allan, Ph.D.

The concept of attention has had an extremely uneven importance in the history of experimental psychology. In the late 1800s and early 1900s, attention was regarded as one of the core problems for experimental psychology. Then, with the rise of Behaviorism and Gestalt Psychology, the concept of attention fell into disrepute. It was not until 1958, with the publication of Broadbent's book, *Perception and Communication,* (7) that the seal of respectability again was put on experimental investigations of human attention. Since the 1950s, experimental research on attention has been abundant, fruitful, and exciting. However, it has become increasingly clear that many different kinds of behavior are included under the concept of attention. Some of these behaviors appear to bear little relation to one another except for being similarly classified as involving attention. In fact, one is struck by the disparities among attentional tasks rather than by any feature that the tasks have in common.

The hypothesis of an attentional deficit in schizophrenia has generated much research in recent years. However, as Neale and Cromwell (20) have pointed out:

> It is difficult to evaluate research and theory in attention in schizophrenia unless one has a good working definition of attention. Unfortunately, no such definition is available. (p 42)

Recently, the development of a *psychophysics of attention* has provided experimental psychology with a new means of investigating attention. This approach makes use of the methodology from modern quantitative psychophysics and is characterized by experiments that use extremely simple stimuli, and by theorizing which is specific and quantitative. The major purpose of this chapter is to acquaint the clinical investigator with psychophysical studies of attention. While experimental psychology has not provided a definition of attention, the methodology, the results, and the theorizing of psychophysical studies of attention may be of use to him.

254

Many of the experiments that I will be discussing were generated by a quantitative model, the attention-switching model, proposed by Kristofferson (10,11) and elaborated by Allan and Kristofferson (4) and by Allan (2). The model is concerned with the role of attention in the temporal processing of bimodal signals. There have been a number of suggestions in the clinical literature that schizophrenics have difficulty switching attention from a signal in one sensory modality to a signal in another modality (e.g., 8,14,17,24,25). The attention-switching model may be of value in generating experiments to test this hypothesis and in providing a theoretical framework for analyzing the data from such experiments. In fact, the few reports in the literature which have explored the attention-switching problem in schizophrenia have provided informative data and suggest that such an approach is promising.

The studies I will be discussing are of two kinds. They are concerned with the judgment of the temporal order of the occurrence of two bimodal signals or with the increment added to reaction time by uncertainty regarding the signal to be responded to in a bimodal discrimination task.

The determination of the source of errors made in judgments of temporal order and simultaneity is one of the oldest problems in experimental psychology. It is well known that the order of the *same* two temporally successive events can be judged correctly, in the reverse order, or even as simultaneous. This variability in the judgment of two temporal events was a major problem for the nineteenth century astronomer whose task was to determine when a star crossed a hairline in a telescope in relation to a series of clicks of a clock. This task required a precise judgment about the order of occurrence of a visual event and an auditory event. It was repeatedly found that these judgments varied among individual astronomers, and that "personal equations" had to be determined for each.

The cause of these individual differences was taken up by the new science of psychology, and it was explored by means of the "complication experiment." The subject was required to judge the temporal relation between the position of a rotating pointer and a click. He was to indicate whether the pointer reached a particular position before or after he heard the click. [The reader is referred to Boring (6) for a detailed description of the complication experiment.] The results of the complication experiments formed the foundation for Titchener's Law of Prior Entry:

> The stimulus for which we are predisposed requires less time than a like stimulus, for which we are unprepared, to produce its full conscious effect. (1908, p 251).

According to Titchener, the stimulus being attended is perceived more quickly than similar stimuli which are not being attended. The observed variability in judgments of order results from biased selective attention.

Convincing experimental support for Titchener's law was lacking until a recent report by Sternberg, Knoll, and Gates (22). To control the direction of the subject's attention, Sternberg et al combined judgments of order with a reaction time task. There were two types of trials, judgment trials and catch trials, presented randomly and with equal probability, during each block. On judgment trials two signals, S_A and S_B, were presented; their onsets were asynchronous by t msec, their offsets simultaneous. Prior to each session the subject was instructed to respond as quickly as possible to the onset of one of the signals (for example, S_A), and then to indicate the order of occurrence of the two onsets. On catch trials only the signal *not* to be responded to (in this case, S_B) was presented, and the subject was supposed to withhold his response. In essence the task allowed attention to be biased toward one signal by requiring a rapid and selective detection response to that signal.

In one experiment S_A was an auditory signal and S_B a cutaneous one; in another S_A was auditory and S_B was visual. The independent variables were the value of t (the asynchrony between the signal onsets) and the signal to be responded to (S_A or S_B). The values of t were varied randomly within a session, and the signal to be responded to was constant within a session and varied between sessions.

In both experiments, a large prior entry effect was demonstrated. The point of subjective simultaneity (PSS) was defined as the value of t at which the probability of responding that S_A occurred prior to S_B was equal to 0.50. The prior entry effect was defined as the difference between the value of PSS estimated when attention was biased toward S_B and the value of PSS estimated when attention was biased toward S_A. For the three well-practiced subjects in the auditory/cutaneous order judgment task, the size of the prior entry effect ranged from 69 msec to 79 msec. When attention was biased toward the auditory signal (S_A), the auditory onset *followed* the cutaneous onset by 40 msec; when attention was biased toward the cutaneous signal (S_B), the auditory onset *preceded* the cutaneous onset by 30 msec. The Sternberg et al (22) study convincingly demonstrates that the perceived order of two events can be strongly influenced by an attentional bias and suggests that selective attention is a plausible source of errors in order judgments.

The attention-switching model (2,4,10,11) explains order judgments in terms of an attentional mechanism. There are three basic postulates in the model.

1. There is an internal timing mechanism that generates a succession of equally spaced points in time. These points occur at the rate of one every q msec, and their occurrence is independent of the presentation of an external stimulus.

2. There are independent input or sensory channels and attention can be directed at only one such channel at a time. That is, information from independent channels are gated one at a time into a central processor.

3. Attention can be (but need not be) switched from one channel to another channel only at a time point. Therefore, the minimum waiting time to switch attention has a uniform distribution over a range of q msec.

In terms of the model, errors in judgments of temporal order are due to the waiting time to switch attention. For the temporal order of two successive signals in independent input channels to be correctly judged, it is necessary to observe the occurrence of the first signal, to switch attention to the channel of the second signal, and then to observe its occurrence. If the second signal already has occurred by the time the switching operation is completed, then the two signals cannot be distinguished from simultaneous signals, and there is no order information. To be specific, suppose a light and a tone come on simultaneously. The light is terminated, and then t msec later the tone is terminated. The subject is required to indicate which stimulus was terminated first. If the subject is attending to the light channel at light offset, he will perceive its offset. At the next time point he switches to the tone channel. If the tone is still on, he can make a correct judgment (the light offset occurred first). However, if the tone is no longer present, he has no information on which to base his temporal judgment. The tone could have offset before the light, simultaneously with the light, or after the light. The best he can do is guess.

The longer the duration of t, the greater the probability of a time point and therefore a correct response.

It should be emphasized that the attention-switching model is applicable only to signals in independent channels. In its present form, the model makes no predictions about the judgment of the order of two signals when both occur in the same channel. It is for this reason, that in all our evaluations of the model we have used bimodal signals.

As a psychophysical model the attention-switching model is a simple three-state model. It provides a mechanism for generating three states: a simultaneous state and two successive states, S_A followed by S_B and S_B followed by S_A. It specifies that these are in fact states, and that there are not degrees of simultaneity. When attention switches to another channel, and if the signal in that channel already has occurred, it does not matter how long ago that happened. The trace of the signal conveys no useful *temporal* information. Allan and Kristofferson (4,12) provide data that support this prediction of the model. Two light-tone pairs were presented sequentially on each trial. In each pair the onsets of the light and the tone were simultaneous, while their offsets were asynchronous. In one pair, the variable stimulus, the light offset always preceded the tone offset by t_v msec (t_v varied between 10 msec and 100 msec in 10 msec steps). In the other pair, the standard stimulus, the light offset followed the tone offset by t_s msec ($t_s = $ 0, 10, or 25 msec). On half of the trials the standard was presented first; on the remaining trials the variable was presented first.

To bias the subject's attention to the light signal, he was instructed that in each pair the light offset either preceded the tone offset or was simultaneous with the tone offset. That is, he was told that in the variable pair the light offset preceded the tone offset and in the standard pair the two offsets were simultaneous. His task was to indicate the pair in which the light offset preceded the tone offset, that is, to indicate whether the variable occurred first or second.

According to the attention-switching model, if the subject is attending to the light signal when it is terminated, the probability of a correct response, $P(C)$, will increase as a linear function of t_v, and will be independent of t_s. That is, performance should be invariant over changes in t_s. The data reported by Allan and Kristofferson (4) indicate that when attention was directed at the light signal, performance did indeed remain constant as the temporal relationship between the offsets in the standard pair was varied.

Another prediction of the model is that the perception of successiveness is both a necessary and sufficient condition for the perception of order. If the subject perceives two sequentially presented signals as successive, then he also will perceive correctly their order. Allan (1,2) presented data that are in accord with this prediction of the model.

We have found that the attention-switching model provides an excellent description of bimodal temporal order data, and in all the studies, the value of q has been estimated to be approximately 50 msec. It should be noted that the attention-switching model is not equivalent, either conceptually or in terms of certain predictions, to a discrete psychologic moment model. The defining characteristic of a discrete moment model is that internal or psychologic time is divided into discrete, nonoverlapping units or moments (e.g., 5,23). If two signals that are separated by t msec fall in the same moment, all order information is lost. The two temporally separated signals will be indistinguishable from the simultaneous presentation of the two signals, as far as order of occurrence is concerned. If the two signals fall in two different moments, their order always will be correctly perceived. In comparing the attention-switching model with a moment model, the important distinction is that in a moment model the probability of obtaining order information depends upon the value of t and the size of the moment. In the attention-switching model, the probability of obtaining order information *also* depends on the channel the subject is attending to. Allan (1) has demonstrated that under some conditions the two models yield very different predictions, and that while the experimental data are in accord with the attention-switching model, they are clearly inconsistent with a moment model.

The attention-switching model also has implications for measures of reaction time (RT) under certainty and uncertainty conditions (10). Two bimodal signals, a light and a tone, are presented, and the subject is required to respond to one of the signals. Under the certainty condition, the subject is told in advance which signal he is to respond to; under the uncertainty condition, he does not know to which of the two signals he will be required to respond. Since the proportion of trials on which the subject fails to pay attention to the relevant channel at the critical moment will be larger for the uncertainty condition, it is possible to make inferences about the waiting time to switch attention by comparing certainty RT with uncertainty RT. Kristofferson (10) found that the value of q estimated from certainty/uncertainty RT data was also approximately 50 msec. Furthermore, he has reported that there is a substantial correlation between values of q estimated from order judgments and the values estimated from RT data.

Kristofferson (13) compared latencies obtained from 12 normal and 12 chronic schizophrenic subjects under certainty and uncertainty conditions. A light and a tone were presented simultaneously. Then one of the signals was terminated, while the other continued to be present. The subject's task was to respond, by releasing a key, when the first of the two signals terminated. Under the certainty condition the subject was given exact knowledge as to which signal would terminate first. Under the uncertainty condition, either the light or the tone could terminate first. For each subject the increment, Δ, added to certainty RT by signal uncertainty was defined as

$$\Delta = T_L + T_S - t_L - t_S$$

where T_L and T_S denote the mean RT to the light and tone respectively under uncertainty, and t_L and t_S the mean RT to the light and tone under certainty. In essence, Kristofferson found that an increment was added to simple RT by signal uncertainty in both groups of subjects. However, the schizophrenic group had significantly greater values of Δ than did the normal subjects, and they showed greater variability in the estimates of Δ.

Two important features of Kristofferson's experiment should be emphasized. First, each subject acted as his own control. This eliminates differences between normal subjects and schizophrenics that might be attributed to level of motivation or cooperation. Second, the fact that the RTs of schizophrenics are longer than the RTs of normal subjects does not influence the estimate of Δ since this estimate is obtained from comparisons in which base RT is eliminated.

In terms of the attention-switching model there are two plausible interpretations of the larger Δ values shown by the schizophrenics. Either schizophrenics have a larger value of q than normal subjects do, or they are less likely to switch attention from one channel to the other at the earliest opportunity (the next time point). Kristofferson's data do not allow one to discriminate between these two alternatives.

Broen (8) presents data from two doctoral dissertations which investigated certainty/uncertainty RT in schizophrenics. Feeney (9) compared normal subjects, acute schizophrenics, and chronic schizophrenics. She replicated Kristofferson's findings in showing larger Δ values for chronic schizophrenics than for normal subjects. She also found that acute schizophrenics did not differ from normal subjects.

Meiselman (16) explored the possibility of reducing the difference in Δ between chronics and normals through an explicit training procedure. During pretraining, Δ values were determined for 23 chronic schizophrenics. The 20 with the largest Δ values (mean $\Delta = 184$ msec) were divided into two matched groups, experimental and control. During training, the experimental group was told that it was possible to improve performance, and was given praise or criticism contingent on speed of responding at the end of each block of trials. As well, trial-by-trial reinforcement contingent on fast responding was introduced. For example, if the subject's RT on a training trial was at least 10 msec faster than his mean on that type of trial during pretraining, he won 5 cents; otherwise he lost 5 cents. The training sessions for the control group were essentially identical to the pretraining session. That is, no statement about expected improvement was made, specific feedback on performance was not given, and contingent reinforcement was not used.

The major result was that the RT of the experimental group decreased during training, while that of the control group did not. The greatest improvement was in the RT performance of the experimental group under uncertainty. For the controls, Δ did not change from pretraining to training; for the experimentals, Δ decreased from approximately 200 msec to less than 50 msec.

Kristofferson (11) has shown that with normal subjects, trial-by-trial feedback results in improved successiveness discrimination performance. He suggested that this improvement could reflect a tendency on the part of the subject to increase the likelihood of switching attention at the next available opportunity. Broen did not discuss Meiselman's training results in terms of the attention-switching model. The decrease in Δ observed in chronic schizophrenics is reminiscent of Kristofferson's findings of improved successiveness performance in normals with feedback. Meiselman's training procedures may be inducing schizophrenics to switch attention at the next available opportunity.

Unfortunately, Meiselman (16) does not report any Δ values for normal subjects in her certainty/uncertainty task. The Δ values reported by Kristofferson for normals (mean $\Delta = 71$ msec) are similar to the Meiselman values for chronic schizophrenics who underwent training. Meiselman's data suggest that with appropriate training procedures, chronic schizophrenics may not differ from normals in terms of the increment added to RT due to channel uncertainty. Clearly, further data are needed before a more definitive conclusion can be reached.

CONCLUSION

I have presented a quantitative model that attributes both errors in the judgment of the order of occurrence of bimodal signals, and the increase in RT due to channel uncertainty, to the same source, namely, the waiting time to switch attention between sensory channels. The model has considerable empirical support. It has been argued in the literature that chronic schizophrenics have difficulty switching attention between modalities. Order judgments and uncertainty RT may be useful tools in investigating this hypothesis. Furthermore, since the attention-switching model is concerned specifically with switching attention between modalities, it could be useful in generating testable, precise predictions about schizophrenic performance. The few studies examining certainty/uncertainty RT in schizophrenics have proven informative.

I have concentrated on my own work, and on data directly related to the attention-switching model. There are many psychophysical investigations of attention that I have not discussed (e.g., 15,18,19,21), which may be of interest to clinical investigators. It would be extremely gratifying if psychophysical studies in attention did provide a methodology and a theoretical foundation that would be of use in clinical investigations of schizophrenia.

REFERENCES

1. Allan LG: Second guesses and the attention-switching model for successiveness. *Perception and Psychophysics* 17:65–68, 1975.

2. Allan LG: The relationship between judgments of successiveness and judgments of order. *Perception and Psychophysics* 18:29–36, 1975.

3. Allan LG: Temporal order psychometric functions based on confidence-rating data. *Perception and Psychophysics* 18:369–372, 1975.

4. Allan LG, Kristofferson AB: Successiveness discrimination: two models. *Perception and Psychophysics* 15:37–46, 1974.

5. Allport DA: Phenomenal simultaneity and the perceptual moment hypothesis. *British Journal of Psychology* 59:395–406, 1968.

6. Boring EG: *A History of Experimental Psychology*. New York, Appleton-Century-Crofts, 1950.

7. Broadbent DE: *Perception and Communication*. New York, Pergamon Press, 1958.

8. Broen WE Jr: Limiting the flood of stimulation: a protective deficit in chronic schizophrenia, in Solso RL (ed): *Contemporary Issues in Cognitive Psychology*. New York, Halsted Press, 1973. pp 191–211.

9. Feeney S: Breadth of cue utilization and ability to attend selectively in schizophrenics and normals. Unpublished doctoral dissertation, University of California, Los Angeles, 1971.

10. Kristofferson AB: Attention and psychophysical time. *Acta Psychologica* 27:93–100, 1967.

11. Kristofferson AB: Successiveness discrimination as a two-state quantal process. *Science* 158:1337–1339, 1967.

12. Kristofferson AB, Allan LG: Successiveness and duration discrimination, in Kornblum S (ed): *Attention and Performance IV*. New York, Academic Press, 1973, pp 737–749.

13. Kristofferson MW: Shifting attention between modalities: a comparison of schizophrenics and normals. *Journal of Abnormal Psychology* 72:388–394, 1967.

14. Lang PD, Buss AH: Psychological deficit in schizophrenia: II. Interference and activation. *Journal of Abnormal Psychology* 70:77–106, 1965.

15. Lindsay PH, Taylor MM, Forbes SM: Attention and multidimensional discrimination. *Perception and Psychophysics* 4:113–117, 1968.

16. Meiselman KC: Broadening dual modality cue utilization in chronic nonparanoid schizophrenics. *J Consult Clin Psychol* 41:447–453, 1973.

17. Mettler FA: Perceptual capacity, functions of the corpus striatum, and schizophrenia. *Psychiatric Quarterly* 29:89–111, 1955.

18. Moray N: Time sharing in auditory perception: effect of stimulus duration. *Journal of the Acousical Society of America* 47:660–661, 1970.

19. Moray N: Introductory experiments in auditory timesharing: detection of intensity and frequency increments. *Journal of the Acousical Society of America* 47:1071–1073, 1970.

20. Neale JM, Cromwell RL: Attention and schizophrenia. *Progress in Experimental Personality Research* 5:37–66, 1970.

21. Shiffrin RM, Grantham DW: Can attention be allocated to sensory modalities. *Perception and Psychophysics* 15:460–474, 1974.

22. Sternberg S, Knoll RL, Gates BA: Prior entry re-examined: effect of attentional bias on order perception. Unpublished manuscript. (Presented at the Annual meeting of the Psychonomic Society, November 1971, St. Louis, Mo).

23. Stroud JM: The fine structure of psychological time, in Quastler H (ed) *Information Theory and Psychology*. New York, Free Press, 1955.

24. Sutton S, Hakerem G, Zubin J, et al: The effect of shift of sensory modality on serial reaction-time: a comparison of schizophrenics and normals. *American Journal of Psychology* 74:224–232, 1961.

25. Sutton S, Zubin J: Effect of sequence on reaction time in schizophrenia, in Welford AT, Birren JE (eds): *Behavior, Aging, and the Nervous System*. Springfield, Ill, Charles C Thomas, 1964, pp 1–37.

26. Tichener EB: *Lectures on the Elementary Psychology of Feeling and Attention*. New York, Macmillan, 1908.

Chapter 24
Modality Shift
at the Crossroads

Samuel Sutton, Ph.D.
Bonnie J. Spring, Ph.D.
Patricia Tueting, Ph.D.

One can take two points of view toward the problem of attention and its measurement in schizophrenia. The weaker and less interesting hypothesis, substantiated by general observation of the phenomenology of the disorder, is that patients attend differently than normal subjects do. Presumably, this can be "explained" by the emotionally disturbed state of the patient, the fact that the patient is preoccupied with hallucinations and so on. As a by-product, or as simply another illustration of difference in attention, the patient performs less well at whatever experimental tasks we present. Such a set of assumptions does not necessarily make experimental tasks valueless. As King and others have shown, experimental tasks, e.g., reaction time, are such sensitive reflectors of patient behavior that they can be used to monitor the progress of therapy (1).

Stronger hypotheses are based on the possibility that specific experimental tasks represent an analysis of the difference in attention, a kind of attempt to specify or dissect the ill-defined concept of attention into its structural components. This is the kind of effort that Shakow and his collaborators (2) attempted in their formulation of the concept of segmental set. In a somewhat different vein, Salzinger (3) formulated the immediacy hypothesis, namely, that the patient is disproportionately influenced by stimuli that are relatively close in time and space.

Our own interest at the Psychophysiology Section of the Biometrics Research Unit began with a suggestion by Mettler (4) that some of the perceptual findings in schizophrenia might be interpreted as arising from a greater difficulty of shifting attention from one sensory modality to another. In our original experimental paradigm, devised by Hakerem, the subject responded by pressing the appropriate one of four keys as rapidly as possible in response to each of four stimuli: a high tone, a low tone, a red light flash, or a green light flash. Stimuli were presented in random order, without

We are indebted to Drs. Joseph Zubin and Muriel Hammer for a critical reading of the manuscript and to Ms. Marion Hartung for editorial assistance and drafting of figures. Supported in part by grant MH-27342 from the National Institute of Mental Health, United States Public Health Service.

warning and with random intervals (within some range, e.g., 3–5 seconds) between stimuli. In later experiments, we substituted a simple finger lift for all stimuli. In other words, no matter what stimulus was presented, the subject was to lift his finger as rapidly as possible. The findings for all variations of this paradigm were always the same and are essentially those shown in Figure 24-1.

Whether we studied acute or chronic schizophrenics, we found that as compared with normal subjects, the patients' reaction times were disproportionately retarded when the stimulus sequences involved a shift of sensory modality (III in Figure 24-1). Sequences involving different stimuli in the same modality (II in Figure 24-1) were used as baselines for this comparison. Patients also appear to show a disproportionate lengthening of reaction times to sequences involving different stimuli in the same sensory modality as compared with sequences involving identical stimuli (I in Figure 24-1), but this effect was not statistically significant.

This last question of the possibility of a disproportionate retardation in reaction time for schizophrenic patients as a result of difference *within* a modality never has been studied systematically. It is possible that had we made the two stimuli within a modality more different from each other, e.g., more different in frequency, we might have obtained a difference between patients and normal subjects in *intramodal* shift. If that were to turn out to be true, it would cast the *crossmodal* differences between patients and normal subjects in a different light. It would imply that the crossmodality effect that distinguishes between groups has nothing to do with sensory modality per se, but rather that, for the specific stimuli we happened to use, the magnitude of difference between the stimuli across modalities was greater than the magnitude of difference between the stimuli within modalities.

In the majority of our experiments, the significant modality shift differences between schizophrenic patients and normal subjects were found for reactions to sound stimuli (5). Reactions to light stimuli have been less consistent. Our suspicion is that this is an artifact of the relative intensity of the stimuli in the two modalities. In a more recent

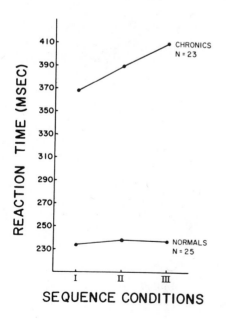

SEQUENCE CONDITIONS

Figure 24-1. Mean simple reaction time as a function of type of stimulus sequence for chronic schizophrenic patients and normal controls. I—identical sequences, II—nonidentical (ipsimodal) sequences, III—crossmodal sequences. Reproduced from Sutton S, Zubin J (5).

experiment (6) we set the sound and light stimuli at the same number of log units above absolute threshold. In this study, findings were consistent for both modalities.

Our original experiment provided no direct insight into the source of the modality shift retardation in schizophrenic patients. At least two interpretations were plausible: (a) a more enduring trace in the patients' nervous system which somehow interfered with speedy response to a subsequent different input [see (7) for a discussion of this alternative] or (b) patients' expectations differed from normal subjects in some manner. Although the stimuli occurred equally often, perhaps the patients for some reason usually expected that the modality of the stimulus would be repeated on the next trial. This would leave them more unprepared for a shift in modality and would result in a disproportionate lengthening of reaction time.

One factor that made us lean toward an expectancy hypothesis was that as we went from experiment to experiment, we were able to shift the intertrial interval with impunity, making it quite long in some cases. It seemed to us that this was inconsistent with a trace hypothesis. A trace should decrease in proportion to the intertrial interval, and patient-normal differences should wash out with long intervals.

Although there is no direct way to determine what the subject expects, we decided as a first approximation to use a guessing paradigm. In this experiment (6), we used only one light (a 10-millisecond light flash), and one sound (a 10-millisecond white noise burst). On each trial the subject guessed whether the next stimulus would be a sound or a light by pressing and holding down one of two keys clearly labeled "sound" or "light." When either the sound or the light was presented, the subject was to lift his finger as rapidly as possible.

The first evidence with respect to the expectancy hypothesis comes from the guessing data. We compared the patients and the normal subjects on the relative proportion of ipsimodal expectations to crossmodal expectations. Ipsimodal expectations were guesses that corresponded to the sensory modality of the stimulus of the previous trial; crossmodal expectations were guesses that did not correspond to the sensory modality of the stimulus of the previous trial. There were no statistically significant differences between the schizophrenic patients and the normal subjects in these proportions. Thus there is no support for the notion that the modality shift reaction time differences, which were statistically significant, are due to the fact that patients more often expect the stimulus in the next trial to be the same as the stimulus in the last trial (ipsimodal expectation). Even the direction of the imbalance is opposite to one that would account for the patient-normal differences on the basis of differences between groups in expectancy: 61% ipsimodal versus 39% crossmodal for normal subjects as compared with 55% versus 45% for schizophrenic patients.

Second, any argument that might be based on the notion that the modality shift difference between patients and normal subjects is due to the difference between groups in number of unfulfilled (wrong) expectations is in conflict with a detailed analysis of the reaction time data. The modality shift differences are only statistically significant for reaction times associated with correct guesses. Thus group differences in crossmodal retardation hardly can be based on different tendencies for the two groups with respect to incorrect predictions.

Perhaps the most devastating blow to an expectancy hypothesis comes from another portion of the Waldbaum et al experiment (6). In alternate blocks of trials, the experimenter told the subject prior to each trial whether the stimulus would be a sound or a light. The subject clearly demonstrated understanding of the instructions by depressing the correct button. In this condition then, there is no possibility of forming differential expectations. The subject knows the modality of each stimulus in advance. *Schizophrenic patients still show a disproportionate retardation after shift of sensory modality.* This appears to deal conclusively with the expectancy hypothesis and presumably leaves us with some kind of a trace hypothesis or some as yet unformulated interpretation.

Having effectively disposed of the expectancy hypothesis as the explanation for the crossmodal findings, we were brought up short by other crossmodal data that are best explained by the expectancy hypothesis. In a recent study, Levit (8,9) followed the Waldbaum paradigm quite closely. However, he recorded average evoked potentials from scalp. He did not use a reaction time response since, except in highly trained subjects, the movement and muscle tension involved are very likely to contaminate the scalp records. Instead he simply had subjects guess whether the next stimulus would be a sound or a light. He recorded the evoked responses from vertex to the sound and light stimuli which informed the subjects that their guesses were right or wrong. Levit's sample included psychotic depressive patients as well as schizophrenic and normal groups.

With respect to the guessing data, Levit confirmed the finding of Waldbaum et al that it is the normals who are biased toward ipsimodal expectations (60% vs 40%) rather than the schizophrenic patients (50% vs 50%). The bias of the psychotic depressive patients (58% vs 42%) was closer to that of the normal subjects.

To describe the evoked potential data, some information has to be presented on the properties of a component of the vertex potential known as $P\overline{300}$. In a series of studies over the last decade (10–13), we have shown that this component is larger the greater the amount of uncertainty which is reduced by the stimulus. This generalization has been conclusively demonstrated for objective uncertainty, e.g., as manipulated via the relative probabilities of different stimulus events. In general, the rarer the class of events, the greater the amplitude of $P\overline{300}$ to the presentation of stimuli belonging to that class. With objective uncertainty fixed, the generalization also holds for the amount of uncertainty perceived by the subject. In the experiment by Leifer et al (14), the relative probabilities of the stimuli were fixed, but $P\overline{300}$ differences between low- and high-probability events increased as the subjects learned the operative probabilities. In Levit's situation, the objective probability of ipsimodal and crossmodal sequences was 50:50. The guessing behavior of the schizophrenic patients indicated that this is what they accepted or perceived. In effect then, the relative level of uncertainty reduced by the occurrence of an ipsimodal or a crossmodal sequence was the same. However, the normal subjects and to a slightly lesser degree depressive patients guessed that ipsimodal sequences were more frequent (60%) than crossmodal sequences (40%). In other words they subjectively treated crossmodal sequences as if they were rarer events than ipsimodal sequences. Thus the occurrence of a crossmodal stimulus should yield a larger $P\overline{300}$ than an ipsimodal stimulus for normal subjects and for depressive patients, but there should be little or no difference between crossmodal and ipsimodal stimuli for the schizophrenic patients (Figure 24-2). This is essentially what was found. An example of the difference in crossmodal and ipsimodal waveforms for one subject is shown in Figure 24-3.

In summary then, the reaction time findings in the certain condition lend little or no support to a cognitive or expectancy formulation of the *reaction time* modality shift differences between schizophrenic patients and normals. The guessing behavior data are

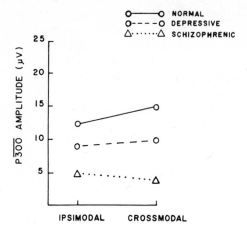

Figure 24-2. Amplitude of $\overline{P300}$ in the uncertain condition as a function of stimulus sequence. Values for light and sound stimuli are averaged together. From Levit (8).

also in conflict with an expectancy interpretation of the *reaction time* modality shift findings. But, paradoxically, the guessing behavior data are completely consistent with the *evoked potential* modality shift findings, and these in turn are best explained on the basis of an expectancy formulation.

One would think that some clarification might be achieved by testing the same subjects on guessing, reaction time, and evoked potentials—perhaps guessing and reaction

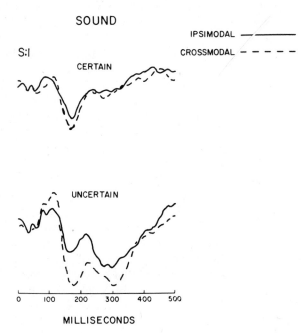

Figure 24-3. Average evoked responses to sound stimuli for one subject as a function of stimulus sequence in both the certain and uncertain condition. Adapted from Zubin J, Sutton S: Assessment of physiological, sensory, perceptual, psychomotor, and conceptual functioning in schizophrenic patients. *Acta Psychiatrica Scandinavica* 46 (suppl 219): 247–263, 1970.

time on one day and guessing and evoked potential on another day to avoid contaminating the evoked potentials with motor artifact. Our pilot work along these lines simply confirms the findings already reported and does not appear to shed any new light on the matter.

It should be noted that no paradox would obtain if in fact there were two crossmodal effects, one at the trace level and a different one at a cognitive or expectancy level. If this were true, then different experiments have yielded their effects by the fact that we have unwittingly combined the two sources of crossmodal effects in various mixes. Perhaps in the reaction time experiment, when subjects knew in advance what the next stimulus would be, our findings were primarily due to differences between groups in trace duration (7). On the other hand, in the evoked potential procedure which involved guessing and no reaction time, our findings may have been due primarily to differences between groups in the cognitive or expectancy domain. While such a formulation is not as parsimonious as one would like, it cannot be ignored in considering the design of new experiments.

At the beginning of this chapter we suggested that it might be possible to explain all the data by taking refuge in the hypothesis of a generalized attentional deficit in schizophrenia. Such an explanation certainly corresponds with the experimenter's subjective experience when dealing with schizophrenic patients. The patient appears to be less "with it" for all of our tasks. Such an approach might explain why the schizophrenic patient is guessing closer to 50:50. Perhaps because he is not attending to, or involved enough in the task, the patient does not form any elaborated strategies or expectations. His moment-to-moment expectations are governed by chance alone, and in this case chance happens to match the objective probability of stimulus occurrence. The fact that we do not obtain larger crossmodal $P\overline{300}$s in the evoked potential data of the schizophrenic patient would follow from the same reasoning. By not forming a systematic strategy, the schizophrenic patient may be treating each trial in isolation. He then would be less likely to assume, as the normal subject appears to, that crossmodal sequences are less frequent than ipsimodal sequences. As a result, the crossmodal $P\overline{300}$ would not be larger than the ipsimodal $P\overline{300}$, as is the case with normal controls.

While such an explanation cannot be dismissed, it encounters a number of difficulties. With respect to the reaction time task, there is nothing in the nature of the task that cues the subject that we will be interested in comparing reaction times to stimuli as a function of sequence of modality from trial to trial. Of course, different groups of subjects may form different expectancies with respect to sequence as was shown when guessing was used as an indicator of expectancy. What is more to the point is that, as designed, there is nothing in the nature of the task that would seem to require more attention for crossmodal sequences than for ipsimodal sequences. The subject's task is always the same, to lift his finger as rapidly as possible whether a light or a sound is presented. A generalized attention explanation must then somehow, on a post hoc basis, assume that a crossmodal sequence under these conditions requires more attention than an ipsimodal sequence, and that the proposed generalized impairment in schizophrenic attention results in disproportionately greater retardation for crossmodal sequences.

In one experiment, ipsimodal sequences as long as four in a row were presented before shifting to the other modality. One would assume that with a generalized attention impairment, schizophrenic patients would not gain as much from the repetition, i.e., their reaction time would not decrease as much, as did the reaction times of normals. In fact, for red light stimuli, reaction time does decrease as much for male and female schizophrenic patients as it does for male and female controls (Figure 24-4). For high tone stimuli, the same holds true for the comparison of females. For male subjects, the reaction times of the schizophrenic patients decrease *more* than that of the normal controls, i.e., they are gaining more from repetition than are the normal subjects. These data then provide no support, and in fact they may be considered in conflict with the hypothesis of a generalized attentional deficit in schizophrenic patients.

In the most recent crossmodal reaction time study, Spring (15) tested schizophrenic and depressed patients as well as healthy controls and siblings of the schizophrenic probands. All trials were administered in the certain condition, in which subjects are informed, prior to each trial, about the modality of the forthcoming stimulus. On half of the trials, constituting an experimenter-told condition, the tester orally told subjects which stimulus to expect. On the remaining trials, constituting a machine-told condition, an actual sound or light stimulus was presented to forewarn the subject. Findings indicated that both schizophrenic and depressed patients showed significantly greater than normal crossmodal retardation to sound stimuli. For reactions to light stimuli, the schizophrenic patients showed more crossmodal retardation than any other group. Siblings of schizophrenic patients did not differ significantly from controls on crossmodal retardation to either sound or light stimuli. Finally, the machine-told condition did not reduce the degree of schizophrenic patients' crossmodal retardation. This failure to find a difference between experimenter-told and machine-told conditions indicates that schizophrenic

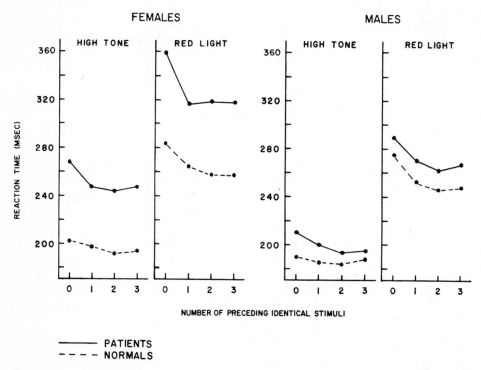

Figure 24-4. Mean simple reaction time as a function of the number of sequential red light and high tone stimuli for male and female normal controls and acute schizophrenic patients. Adapted from Sutton S, Zubin J (5).

crossmodal retardation in the certain condition cannot be attributed to patients' difficulty in utilizing verbal symbolic expectancy information.

Where does all of this leave us with respect to the nature of attentional organization in schizophrenic patients? Unfortunately, at this stage, not very far. The virtue, or, perhaps from another point of view, the fault, of tight experimental paradigms is that it is not easy to talk one's way around results that do not fit some formulation. Hopefully, these inconsistencies eventually will yield to ingenious experimentation.

REFERENCES

1. King HE: *Psychomotor Aspects of Mental Disease.* Cambridge Mass, Harvard University Press, 1954.

2. Shakow D: Psychological deficit in schizophrenia. *Behavioral Science* 8:275–305, 1963.

3. Salzinger K: An hypothesis about schizophrenic behavior. *American Journal of Psychotherapy* 25:601–614, 1971.

4. Mettler ·FA: Perceptual capacity, functions of the corpus striatum and schizophrenia. *Psychiatric Quarterly* 29:89–109, 1955.

5. Sutton S, Zubin J: Effect of sequence on reaction time in schizophrenia, in Welford AT, Birren JE (eds): *Behavior, Aging and the Nervous System.* Springfield Ill, Charles C Thomas, 1965, pp 562–597.

6. Waldbaum JK, Sutton S, Kerr J: Shift of sensory modality and reaction time in schizophrenia, in Kietzman ML, Sutton S, Zubin J (eds): *Experimental Approaches to Psychopathology.* New York, Academic Press, 1975, pp 167–176.

7. Zubin J: Problem of attention in schizophrenia, in Kietzman ML, Sutton S, Zubin J (eds): *Experimental Approaches to Psychopathology.* New York, Academic Press, 1975, pp 139–166.

8. Levit RA: Averaged evoked potential correlates of information processing in schizophrenics, psychotic depressives and normals. Doctoral dissertation, Columbia University, 1972. University Microfilms No. 72-20,051.

9. Levit RA, Sutton S, Zubin J: Evoked potential correlates of information processing in psychiatric patients. *Psychological Medicine* 3:487–494, 1973.

10. Sutton S, Braren M, Zubin J, et al: Evoked-potential correlates of stimulus uncertainty. *Science* 150:1187–1188, 1965.

11. Sutton S, Tueting P, Zubin J, et al: Information delivery and the sensory evoked potential. *Science* 155:1436–1439, 1967.

12. Tueting P, Sutton S, Zubin J: Quantitative evoked potential correlates of the probability of events. *Psychophysiology* 7:385–394, 1970.

13. Ruchkin DS, Sutton S: Equivocation and $\overline{P300}$ amplitude, in Otto D (ed): *Multidisciplinary Perspectives in Event-related Brain Potential Research.* Washington DC, US Government Printing Office, in press.

14. Leifer LJ, Otto DA, Hart SG, et al: Slow potential correlates of predictive behaviour during a complex learning task, in McCallum WC, Knott JR (eds): *The Responsive Brain.* Bristol England, John Wright and Sons, 1976, pp 65–70.

15. Spring BJ: Attention dysfunction in schizophrenic patients and their healthy siblings. Doctoral dissertation, Harvard University, 1977.

Section V

ATTENTION, PSYCHOPHARMACOLOGY, AND SCHIZOPHRENIA

Chapter 25

Short-term Outcome, Clinical Improvement, and Reaction Time Performance in Acute Schizophrenia

Theodore P. Zahn, Ph.D.
William T. Carpenter, Jr., M.D.
Thomas H. McGlashan, M.D.

Perhaps the earliest and most widely studied technique to measure attentional deficits in schizophrenia is the method of reaction time (RT) developed by Shakow and his collaborators (1,2). In this technique simple RT is measured as a function of the preparatory interval (PI)—the interval between a warning stimulus and the imperative stimulus—under both a "regular" condition (PI constant for a series of trials) and an "irregular," or variable PI, condition. Using this method it has been shown that the preparatory sets of schizophrenics are quite fragile. In addition to an overall slowness of RT apparent under even optimal conditions, schizophrenics are unable to take advantage of the regularity of the PI in the regular condition for more than a few seconds and are disproportionately impaired on trials with the shorter PIs in the irregular series, particularly when they have been preceded by a trial having a longer PI (3,4).

These features have been found in the performance of acute schizophrenic patients as well as in the performance of chronic schizophrenics on whom the original studies were made (5). Subjects with brain injuries, while having slow RT, do not show the same pattern of deficits with variations in the PI as do schizophrenics (6,7). Other psychiatric disorders, with the possible exception of depression, do not produce deficits to the same extent as does schizophrenia (5,8), but elderly subjects seem to show some of the PI-related features found in schizophrenia (9). Thus, the pattern of impairment described seems fairly, but perhaps not completely, specific to schizophrenia.

Dr Carpenter is presently at Maryland Psychiatric Research Center, Baltimore, Maryland; Dr. McGlashan is presently at Chestnut Lodge, Rockville, Maryland.

Rodnick and Shakow (2), taking advantage of the specific features of the curves relating RT to the length of the PI under regular and irregular conditions, developed an overall index of performance—the "Set Index"—which discriminated chronic schizophrenics from normal subjects without overlap. In our study comparing acute schizophrenics in the armed services with nonschizophrenic psychiatric inpatients, Rosenthal and I (Zahn) (5) found that while there was overlap between the two groups, the original Set Index discriminated the two groups better than various other indices that we thought might be more appropriate to our data. Further, the Set Index discriminates among chronic schizophrenics with varying degrees of psychopathology, a correlation of 0.89 having been found between this RT measure and ratings of global psychopathology (10). In an unpublished attempt to replicate this finding on 17 chronic schizophrenics, I found a correlation of 0.70 between the two measures. The lower correlation may have been due to including both male and female patients in the sample in the second study (only males were tested in the first one), a less adequate index, or a restricted range, of psychopathology in the second group.

The Set Index method, then, seems to be reflecting something fundamentally related to the schizophrenic process. In the present study, this test was given to drug-free acute schizophrenic patients on a research ward on two occasions: shortly after admission to the unit and 3–4 months later, shortly before they were to be discharged. The study was designed to answer two questions. First, does performance on this task have any short-term prognostic significance? Second, do changes in clinical condition produce comparable changes in performance on this task? That is, do within-subject differences in psychopathology relate to task performance in the same way that between-subject differences do.

METHOD AND RESULTS

The subjects were 46 acute schizophrenics who were inpatients on a research unit at the NIH Clinical Center, having been recruited from local community hospitals usually within a week after admission there. Diagnosis was made according to DSM-II criteria based on a 3-week evaluation. Use was made of a computerized diagnostic system (CATEGO) using Present State Examination interview data and by a system of increasingly stringent criteria derived from the International Pilot Study of Schizophrenia (11). The patients were tested 3 weeks after admission (admission test week) and had been given no medication during that time.

Improvement category was determined from ratings of global psychopathology made by the patients' therapist and by nurses during the admission test week and a similar test week following another 3-week drug-free period soon before discharge, after about 4 months of hospitalization. By comparison of admission and discharge ratings it was determined that 18 of the patients definitely had improved and 17 had not improved. The two groups were comparable in age, social class, and education, but there were 8 males and 10 females in the improved group and 4 males and 13 females in the not improved groups.

The RT procedure used was the same as in previous studies from this laboratory (5). The subjects were given 10 trials at each of 5 constant PIs: 1, 2, 4, 7, and 15 seconds, in that order. This regular procedure was followed by two 26-trial irregular series in which each PI occurred 5 times in a quasi-random order and was preceded by each PI including itself.

The patients who were subsequently to improve (TI) did not differ at the time of the admission test on any of the ratings of global psychopathology from those who were not to improve (NTI), but the two groups did, of course, differ at time of discharge. Statistical tests of the RT data are based on 2 × 2 (groups × sex) analyses of variance.

Curves relating mean RT to the length of the PI for regular and irregular series on the admission testing for the TI and NTI groups, are shown in Figure 25-1. Although the TI group appears markedly superior in performance to the NTI group, statistical analyses are not as impressive as the graph might suggest due to high variability. There are significant differences in mean RT level for most of the individual PIs under each procedure and for overall mean RT (p < 0.05). However, none of the features of the curves that have been found to be associated with schizophrenia in previous studies, such as their slopes and the effects of the preceding PI in the irregular series, are significantly different. The overall measure of performance—the Set Index—showed only a trend to be lower in the TI group (p < 0.20).

Comparisons were also made on the discharge tests of subjects with relatively low

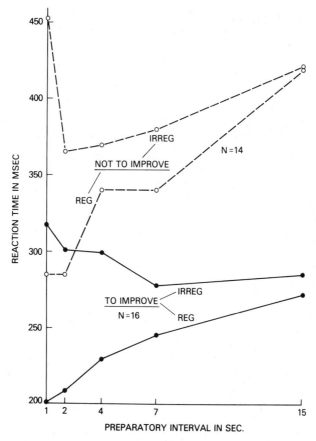

Figure 25-1. Reaction time as a function of length of preparatory interval: Admission test.

psychopathology ratings ("well") versus those who remained in an acute psychotic state ("sick"). Mean RT for the various PIs in each series are plotted in Figure 25-2. Although the mean differences between the groups are, in general, slightly smaller than for the admission testing, the significance of the differences is greater due to reduced variability and greater regularity of the data on this test. In addition to having faster RT ($p < 0.02$), the well group tended to have a smaller positive slope on the regular series ($p < 0.10$) and a less negative slope on the irregular series ($p < 0.10$); the difference between slopes was greater for the sick group ($p < 0.02$). In the irregular series, RT was slower for the sick group when the preceding PI was either shorter ($p < 0.01$) or longer ($p < 0.005$) than the PI, but the difference tended to be greater under the PPI longer condition ($p < 0.10$). These differences all have been found to characterize schizophrenic patients when compared with normal subjects. Finally, the Set Index discriminated these two groups ($p < 0.02$).

To evaluate the other major question addressed by this study, namely, whether changes in clinical state are accompanied by parallel changes in performance of this attentional task, the difference between admission and discharge tests was compared for those subjects who were rated and tested at both times according to whether they had improved clinically or not. These analyses show that the performance of most subjects, surprisingly, did not change appreciably. For example, the Set Indexes of most subjects in each group changed less than 100 msec, the proportion of these stable scores being

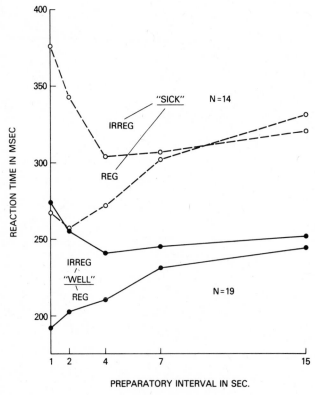

Figure 25-2. Reaction time as a function of length of prepatory interval: Discharge test.

slightly greater for the improved subjects (69% to 58%). Statistical tests of the admission-discharge difference scores on various parameters of the RT data showed that none of these differences reached significance at $p < 0.05$ for the improved group. Although there was somewhat more performance improvement in those clinically improved subjects with either large initial scores or large change scores (or both) than was true of the clinically unimproved patients, performance changes seem to be independent of clinical changes for most patients.

DISCUSSION

With respect to the question of short-term prognosis, the results show there is a moderately significant tendency for acute schizophrenic patients who will improve over the course of a short hospitalization to have faster RT about the time of admission than those patients who will not improve. This result is independent of global psychosis ratings at the time of testing. These findings confirm the findings of Cancro et al (12) who found that simple RT was correlated with a 3-year outcome measure also independently of clinical state. The results of these two studies are similar in another respect as well: in both studies it was the RT level that had the prognostic significance and not those aspects of the data that are thought to have a particular relationship to schizophrenia. In the Cancro study, using the variable stimulus modality technique of Sutton and Zubin (13), the crossmodal RT did not add significantly to the results obtained with simple RT. Similarly, in the present study, manipulations of the length and variability of the PI did not affect the two groups differentially.

It might be noted that this RT difference may be accompanied by physiologic changes that also differentiate the two prognosis groups. In two sessions previous to the one reported here, skin conductance and heart rate were recorded during rest, a series of simple tones, and a short RT procedure. The TI group showed evidence of higher baseline autonomic arousal and faster habituation of the skin conductance orienting response as compared to the NTI group and was more physiologically responsive than the NTI group to the RT task as manifested by a greater number and shorter latency of phasic electrodermal responses to the stimuli and greater cardiac deceleration during the foreperiod (14). The TI group was not significantly different from normal controls on these variables. Thus, patients with a good short-term prognosis appear to be characterized by a greater responsivity to the demands of the task situation manifested both psychophysiologically and behaviorally.

The significant superiority of the "well" patients over the still psychotic ones on the discharge test confirms the previous findings of a relationship of psychiatric condition to the Set Index obtained on a much more chronic group (10). It will be recalled that in addition to differing in simple RT as did the TI and NTI groups, these groups differed in several aspects of the data such as slopes, PPI effects, and the Set Index which have been associated with some specificity to schizophrenia. One possible explanation of these data is that there is in fact a "real" (i.e., replicable) effect of prognosis on the effects of the PI and PPI, but this is not apparent statistically, in this small sample, because of the high variability. Another hypothesis is that these "schizophrenic" aspects of the task are affected by differences in psychiatric condition while only simple RT is affected by prognosis.

This interpretation cannot be applied, however, to changes over time in the same individuals. The only systematic effect of an improvement in psychiatric condition seems to be that the group variance is reduced. Clinical improvement tends to be accompanied by RT performance improvement only for those subjects with very high initial levels. The general lack of change, which also was mirrored in the psychophysiologic variables mentioned earlier, suggests that most patients who will recover from an acute schizophrenic episode relatively quickly, despite manifesting equally severe symptomatology as those patients whose recovery is less rapid, retain a capacity to respond to environmental stimuli in a more normal fashion. It may be speculated that this environmental responsivity is in fact a critical attribute of the recovery process possibly by potentiating the effects of whatever healing experiences the patients might be exposed to.

It should be pointed out that the Phillips Scale of premorbid adjustment (15), which is widely used as a prognostic indicator, did not relate to either the psychophysiologic variables or the RT performance. Analyses comparing good and poor premorbid patients on these variables produced somewhat fewer statistically significant results than would be expected by chance alone, and there appears to be no systematic pattern in the results. Although the scale showed a trend to be related to the actual short-term outcome, this was not statistically significant. Thus, while premorbid social competence may be related to longer-term outcome, the speed of in-hospital recovery from an acute schizophrenic episode, especially under conditions of intensive treatment involving milieu-, pharmaco-, and psychotherapy, as was the case with the patients in this study, may be predictable at the time of hospital admission more by those physiologic and behavioral characteristics of the patients that reflect responsivity to the environment.

Since the initial testing occurred over 3 weeks after admission to the NIMH unit which, in turn, was preceded by another short hospitalization, there was already some opportunity for partial recovery from the psychotic episode. It would be important to know whether "normalization" of environmental responsivity already had occurred by the time of testing or whether such a capacity is relatively unaffected by a psychosis in some types of patients. The answer to this question might have etiologic importance and can be answered only by more frequent experimental and clinical observations.

REFERENCES

1. Huston PE, Shakow D, Riggs LA: Studies of motor function in schizophrenia: II. Reaction time. *J Gen Psychol* 16:39, 1937.

2. Rodnick EH, Shakow D: Set in the schizophrenic as measured by a composite reaction time index. *Am J Psychiat* 97:214, 1940.

3. Zahn TP, Rosenthal D, Shakow D: Reaction time in schizophrenic and normal subjects in relation to the sequence of series of regular preparatory intervals. *J Abnorm Soc Psychol* 63:161, 1961.

4. Zahn TP, Rosenthal D, Shakow D: Effects of irregular preparatory intervals on reaction time in schizophrenia, *J Abnorm Soc Psychol* 67:44, 1963.

5. Zahn TP, Rosenthal D: Preparatory set in acute schizophrenia. *J Nerv Ment Dis* 141:352, 1965.

6. Costa LD: Visual reaction time of patients with cerebral disease as a function of length and constancy of preparatory interval. *Percep Mot Skills* 14:391, 1962.

7. Olbrick R: Reaction time in brain-damaged and normal subjects to variable preparatory intervals. *J Nerv Ment Dis* 155:356, 1972.

8. Huston PE, Senf R: Psychopathology in schizophrenia and depression. I. Effect of amytal and amphetamine sulphate on level and maintenance of attention. *Amer J Psychiat* 109:131, 1952.

9. Botwinick J: Theories of antecedent conditions of speed of response, in Welford AT, Birren JE (eds): *Behavior, Aging and the Nervous System.* Springfield, Ill, Thomas, 1965, p 1.

10. Rosenthal D, Lawlor WG, Zahn TP, et al: The relationship of some aspects of mental set to degree of schizophrenic disorganization. *J Pers* 28:26, 1960.

11. World Health Organization: *The International Pilot Study of Schizophrenia, Vol 1.* Geneva, WHO, 1973.

12. Cancro R, Sutton S, Kerr J, et al: Reaction time and prognosis in actute schizophrenia. *J Nerv Ment Dis* 153:351, 1971.

13. Sutton S, Hakerem G, Zubin J, et al: The effect of shift of sensory modality on serial reaction-time: A comparison of schizophrenics and normals. *Amer J Psychol* 74:224, 1961.

14. Zahn TP, Carpenter WT, McGlashan TH: Autonomic variables related to short-term outcome in acute schizophrenic patients. Presented at annual meeting of The Society for Psychophysiological Research, Toronto, Ontario, 1975.

15. Phillips L: Case history data and prognosis in schizophrenics. *J Nerv Ment Dis* 117:515, 1953.

Chapter 26
The Effects of Antipsychotic Drug Treatment on Attention and Information Processing in Chronic Schizophrenics

Herbert E. Spohn, Ph.D.
Roy B. Lacoursiere, M.D.
Karen Thompson, R.N.
Lolafaye Coyne, Ph.D.

After more than 20 years of drug evaluation research, much is known about the power of the neuroleptic drugs to reduce or remove the symptoms of schizophrenia and to improve the hospital and community adjustment of schizophrenic patients (1–3). Much less is known about the effects of antipsychotic drug treatment on psychologic and psychophysiologic dysfunction, particularly on impairment of attention and information processing and on arousal states (4–7).

The principal objectives of the investigation reported here in synoptic form were to determine whether antipsychotic drug treatment in chronic schizophrenics modified attention-information processing and arousal-activation states and whether such modifications related to symptom reduction and therapeutic response.[1] These questions motivated and guided the design and methodology of a placebo-controlled investigation in which the performance of chronic schizophrenics on laboratory tests of attention-perception and cognitive dysfunction, as well as autonomic arousal and reactivity, were

---

[1] A full report of this investigation under the title: "Phenothiazine effects on psychological and psychophysiological dysfunction in chronic schizophrenics" appears in *Archives of General Psychiatry* 34:633, 1977.

followed over an 8-week period of chlorpromazine treatment and in which the clinical symptomatic course was assessed by symptom and global rating scales. Level of premorbid social adjustment, rated by the Phillips Scale (8), served as a dichotomous classification factor. After 40 schizophrenics were withdrawn from all antipsychotic medication for 6 weeks, 20 patients were randomly assigned to chlorpromazine treatment, and 20 patients to placebo. They were tested on four occasions during an 8-week treatment period by means of performance measures of attention-perception and cognitive dysfunction. Heart rate and skin conductance were monitored during testing, and clinical evaluation was performed by means of the Inpatient Multidimensional Psychiatric Rating Scale (9).

Results indicated that the antipsychotic drug treatment was associated with clinical improvement in the drug treatment group and deterioration in the placebo group. Therapeutic response was not demonstrably related to premorbid social-sexual adjustment. No significant differences between drug and placebo groups were demonstrable with the tests of cognitive dysfunction, including a proverbs test, a measure of overinclusive thinking, and the WAIS Digit Symbol Substitution Test.

However, measures of attentional-perceptual dysfunction revealed a normalizing effect of drug treatment. Reaction time and Continuous Performance Test results showed an improved ability to sustain "set" to task-relevant stimuli. A Span of Apprehension test indicated that the rate, or efficiency, of precognitive information processing increased with drug treatment.

Although basal skin conductance levels showed no time trends, the highest skin conductance level reached during the tests was significantly reduced in the drug group and increased in the placebo group. Amplitude of heart rate deceleration and amplitude of skin conductance response (corrected for initial level) were also significantly decreased over time in the drug group and increased in the placebo group.

The finding of reduced autonomic reactivity, or of autonomic deactivation, in the context of improvement on performance measures of attention affords some support for Kornetsky's chlorpromazine action model (10) which postulates that in schizophrenics performance improvement is contingent on reduction of hyperarousal to more optimal levels. Correlations of drug effects on set, selective attention, and precognitive information processing with degree of rated therapeutic response suggest that impaired attention-information processing may be a significant component in the psychopathology of chronic schizophrenics which phenothiazines are effective in reducing or removing.

REFERENCES

1. NIMH Psychopharmacology Service Center Collaborative Study Group. Phenothiazine treatment in acute schizophrenia. *Arch Gen Psychiat* 10:246, 1964.

2. Casey JF, Lasky JJ, Klett CJ, et al: Treatment of schizophrenic reactions with phenothiazine derivatives: A comparative study of chlorpromazine, triflupromazine, mepazine, prochlorperazine, perphenazine, and phenobarbital. *Am J Psychiat* 117:97, 1960.

3. Goldberg SC, Klerman GL, Cole JO: Changes in schizophrenic psychopathology and ward behaviour as a function of phenothiazine treatment. *Br J Psychiat* 111:120, 1965.

4. Neale JM, Cromwell RL: Attention and schizophrenia, in Maher BA (ed): *Progress in Experimental Personality Research, vol 8*. New York, Academic Press, 1976.

5. Callaway E III: Schizophrenia and interference—An analogy with a malfunctioning computer. *Arch Gen Psychiat* 22:139, 1970.

6. Venables PH: Input dysfunction in schizophrenia, in Maher BA (ed): *Progress in Experimental Personality Research,* vol 1. New York, Academic Press, 1964.

7. Lang PJ, Buss AH: Psychological deficit in schizophrenia: II. Interference and activation. *J Abnorm Psychol* 70:77, 1965.

8. Phillips L: Case history data and prognosis in schizophrenia. *J Nerv Ment Dis* 117:515, 1953.

9. Lorr M, Klett CJ: Inpatient multidimensional psychiatric scale (IMPS). Unpublished test manual. Washington, DC, Veterans Administration Hospital, 1966.

10. Kornetsky C, Mirsky AF: On certain psychopharmacological and physiological differences between schizophrenic and normal persons. *Psychopharmacologia* 8:309, 1966.

Chapter 27
The Effect of Antipsychotic Medication and Diagnostic Criteria on Distractibility in Schizophrenia

Thomas F. Oltmanns, Ph.D.
Jacques Ohayon, B.A.
John M. Neale, Ph.D.

The relative inability of some schizophrenic patients to attend selectively to sensory stimuli was noted in the earliest clinical observations of the disorder. Taking clinical reports into the laboratory, many investigators have sought to demonstrate that the presence of irrelevant stimuli interferes more with the perceptual and cognitive processes of schizophrenics than with the performance of various control samples. The typical design has required schizophrenics and control subjects to perform a simple perceptual or recall task in both the presence and absence of distracting stimuli. The usual result has been that schizophrenics' performance resembles that of control subjects more closely in the neutral, or no distractor, condition than in the distractor condition. Unfortunately, in most studies, the deficit of the schizophrenics with distracting stimuli may have reflected the psychometric properties of the measures employed rather than different levels of susceptibility to distraction.

Oltmanns and Neale (1) pursued this problem by constructing two pairs of short- and long- digit-span tests which were carefully matched for psychometric properties. The

This research was supported, in part, by Grant MH21145 from the National Institute of Mental Health. Dr. Oltmanns is now at the Department of Psychology, Indiana University, Bloomington, Indiana; Mr. Ohayon is now at the Department of Psychology, Univeristy of Pittsburgh, Pittsburgh Pennsylvania; Dr. Neale is at the State University of New York at Stony Brook.

short pair consisted of neutral items containing six digits and distractor items containing five relevant digits; the long pair was comprised of six-digit distractor items and neutral items containing seven and eight digits. Using these tests, we found that chronic, medicated schizophrenics performed less adequately on all four tests than did demographically matched normal subjects. However, for the shorter pair of tests, the discrepancy between schizophrenics' and normal subjects' scores was no greater in the distractor condition than in the neutral condition. A different picture emerged with the longer neutral and distractor tests: here the schizophrenics' performance on the distractor test was more greatly impaired.

EFFECT OF NEUROLEPTICS ON DISTRACTIBILITY

In these earlier studies of distractibility, the patients had been receiving antipsychotic medication for a number of years. If antipsychotic drugs improve the ability of schizophrenics to screen out irrelevant stimuli (2,3), the distractibility of schizophrenics after drug withdrawal should deteriorate significantly. In a study of this hypothesis, the neutral and distractor digit-span tests were administered to 14 chronic schizophrenics both before and two weeks after the withdrawal of antipsychotic medication. Fourteen other chronic schizophrenics were tested at 2-week intervals while on medication. All items were recorded on an audio tape and presented binaurally to the patient through stereo headphones. In the neutral tests, the patient heard a series of digits presented by a female voice at the approximate rate of one digit every two seconds. In the distractor tests, four irrelevant digits were read by a male voice in each of the intervals between relevant digits. Subjects were instructed to ignore the male voice. The task was to recall as many correctly ordered digits as possible. A group of 24 normal subjects also was tested: 10 male prison inmates and 14 hospital attendants. The three groups did not differ in educational history, and the two schizophrenic groups did not differ significantly in length of hospitalization. The normal subjects were younger than both groups of schizophrenics.

Overall, the performance of the schizophrenics while on medication was substantially inferior to that of the normal subjects. But, since our interest was in the degree of change caused by the presence of distraction, we were primarily concerned with two difference scores which were computed for each subject by subtracting his score on each distraction test from the matched neutral test. These "distraction indices" were near zero for each group at initial testing. The scores of the control schizophrenics staying on medication did not change at retesting for either the short or the long pairs of items, and the scores of the drug-withdrawal group did not change on the neutral items. However, the accuracy of the chronic schizophrenics at retesting when off neuroleptics was considerably impaired on both the short and long distraction tests, compared to their initial performance when on drugs. As evaluated using a Wilcoxon Signed-Ranks test for matched groups, this difference was significant for the longer distraction test ($t = 6.5$, $N_{s-r} = 13$, $p < 0.01$) but fell short of significance for the shorter distraction items.

Thus, these findings do not support the notion that chronic schizophrenic patients are abnormally distractible while on medication. While they are less accurate than normal subjects, their performance while on neuroleptics is not *differentially* impaired by distracting stimuli. The many previous reports of heightened distractibility in medicated, chronic patients may reflect the psychometric properties of the tasks rather than the abilities of the subjects.

The changes in performance by the group withdrawn from medication are striking. Since these patients' accuracy on the neutral tests remained unchanged, we may conclude that the altered cognitive abilities of these patients reflect a specific deficit beyond simple changes in cooperativeness, motivation, or general intelligence. Rather, the drugs appear to have a particular effect in assisting schizophrenics to screen out distracting stimuli. In their absence, a genuine deficit in selective attentive abilities becomes apparent.

DISTRACTIBILITY IN SCHIZOPHRENICS WITH BROAD VERSUS NARROW DIAGNOSES

The characteristics of the sample of patients employed in this study limited the interpretation of the findings. First, these schizophrenics had been hospitalized continuously for a mean of more than 10 years. Second, in the absence of a control group of nonschizophrenic psychiatric patients, we could not clearly attribute the observed deficit specifically to schizophrenia. Third, the diagnoses of the schizophrenics had been based on the rather broad DSM-II criteria and might not hold with more conservative criteria.

Therefore, in a second study we administered the same neutral and distractor tests to 47 less chronic schizophrenic patients, all receiving antipsychotic medication at the time of testing. They were separated into schizophrenic and nonschizophrenic groups first on the basis of their hospital diagnoses, yielding a group of 31 schizophrenics, with a mean of 3.7 previous hospitalizations and a mean of 7.7 months of hospitalization between the most recent admission and the time of testing. The 16 nonschizophrenics had been hospitalized, on the average, 2.0 times in the past and for a mean of 12.9 days since their most recent admission. The nonschizophrenic group carried hospital diagnoses of manic-depressive psychosis, depressive neurosis, reactive depression, psychotic depression, adjustment reaction to adult life, and personality disorder.

The schizophrenics' performance was significantly less accurate than that of both the normal and nonschizophrenic patient groups in each test condition. None of the differences between normal subjects and nonschizophrenic psychiatric patients were significant. Our principal interest, however, was not in overall accuracy but rather in the effect of distraction. Therefore, distraction indices were computed for each subject by subtracting each distraction test score from the corresponding neutral test score. Using hospital DSM-II diagnoses as the basis for diagnosing these relatively nonchronic schizophrenics, this schizophrenic group (on neuroleptics) was not more distractible than either of the other groups.

The psychiatric patients were reclassified as being either schizophrenic or nonschizophrenic on the basis of the more stringent Research Diagnostic Criteria (RDC) (4), which exclude patients with significant affective symptoms from a schizophrenic diagnosis. A subgroup of 21 RDC schizophrenics was compared with 20 RDC nonschizophrenic patients using one-way ANOVAs on the "distraction indices." A significant group effect $[F (2,62) = 3.25, p < 0.05]$ emerged on the distraction index derived from the shorter neutral and distractor tests. This data analysis revealed that the medicated RDC schizophrenics, unlike the DSM-II schizophrenics, were significantly more impaired by the distracting stimuli than were either the normals or the other psychiatric patients. The comparison of difference scores between the longer neutral and distractor tests was not significant.

Finally, the distraction indices of these 21 RDC schizophrenics were correlated with eight demographic characteristics (age, education, marital status, sex, number of admissions, total time in hospital, age at first admission, and number of ECT treatments) and 12 symptom ratings. There was a significant negative correlation between the number of admissions the patient had experienced and the degree of distractibility ($r = -0.52$, $p < 0.05$). The only current symptom rating that correlated significantly with distractibility was formal thought disorder ($r = 0.55$, $p < 0.01$) as defined by Spitzer, Endicott, and Robins (4).

In summary, these two studies substantiated clinical observations that many schizophrenic patients have difficulty in screening out distracting stimuli. Although chronic schizophrenics were less accurate on digit-span tests than normal subjects, they were not abnormally distractible while on antipsychotic medication but become so after 2 weeks of drug withdrawal.

Broadly diagnosed schizophrenics, including schizoaffectives, were not more distractible while on neuroleptics than were a diagnostically mixed group of other hospitalized psychiatric patients. However, when schizoaffective schizophrenics were excluded from the schizophrenic group, using Research Diagnostic Criteria, then the more narrowly diagnosed, medicated schizophrenics do reveal more distractibility on the digit-span tests than do the nonschizophrenic patients.

REFERENCES

1. Oltmanns TF, Neale JM: Schizophrenic performance when distractors are present: Attentional deficit or differential task difficulty? *J Abnorm Psychol* 84:205, 1975.

2. Chapman LJ, Knowles RR: The effects of phenothiazine on disordered thought in schizophrenia. *J Consult Psychol* 28:165, 1964.

3. Kornetsky C: The use of a simple test of attention as a measure of drug effects in schizophrenic patients. *Psychopharm* 24:99, 1972.

4. Spitzer RL, Endicott J, Robins E: *Research Diagnostic Criteria (RDC) for a Selected Group of Functional Disorders*. New York, Biometrics Research, New York State Psychiatric Institute, 1975.

Section VI

VISUAL TRACKING AND SCHIZOPHRENIA

Chapter 28
Pendulum Eye-Tracking in Remitted Psychiatric Patients

Leonard F. Salzman, Ph.D.
Robert H. Klein, Ph.D.
John S. Strauss, M.D.

Interest in a possible relationship between pendulum-tracking behavior and psychopathology can be traced back as early as 1908 when Diefendorf and Dodge (1) reported on pendulum eye-tracking disruption in a variety of patients, particularly in schizophrenics. More recent investigations of this phenomenon began with the report of Holzman, Proctor, and Hughes (2) describing a study of pendulum-tracking behavior in psychotic and nonpsychotic patients and in normal controls. Holzman et al (2) found that a heterogeneous group of schizophrenics showed markedly abnormal pendulum-tracking patterns while normal subjects showed little evidence of such abnormal tracking responses. Nonschizophrenic psychiatric controls tended to produce more abnormal tracking patterns than normal subjects, but significantly fewer than schizophrenics. Holzman interpreted his findings as providing possible evidence of difficulty in fine regulation of neuromuscular activity, but he did not discount the possibility that a core attentional deficit might be involved. In a subsequent paper Holzman, Proctor, Levy, Yasillo, Meltzer, and Hurt (3) reported further data supporting the initial findings of a relationship between impairment of smooth pursuit eye movement and schizophrenic pathologic state. As an important elaboration of this relationship, they reported the presence of impaired tracking in the first-degree relatives of schizophrenics.

Shagass, Amadeo, and Overton (4) replicated Holzman's work and confirmed the strong relationship between deviant pendulum-tracking and schizophrenic pathologic

This research was supported by NIMH Program Project Grant MH22836. The investigators in this study are Lyman Wynne (Principal Investigator), Alfred Baldwin, Clara Baldwin, Michael Chandler, Robert Cole, Elaine Faunce, Lawrence Fisher, Norman Garmezy, Robert Geertsma, David Harder, Howard Iker, Fredric Jones, Robert Klein, Ronald Kokes, Steven Munson, Barry Ritzler, John Romano, Leonard Salzman, Margaret Singer, Lawrence Space, and John Strauss. Investigators previously participating are Rue Cromwell, James Heriot, Gerald Rubenstein.

289

state. However, they also found the dysfunction to be present in patients with other psychoses, and they questioned whether this impairment is specific to schizophrenia. Klein, Salzman, Jones, and Ritzler (5) reported finding significant differences in pendulum-tracking between patients and normal subjects, but they found no differences between schizophrenic and nonschizophrenic patient groups.

Focusing on the possible relationship between pendulum-tracking and attention, Shagass, Roemer, and Amadeo (6) utilized an attention-enhancing procedure in a further investigation of the tracking dysfunction in psychiatric groups. Such a procedure greatly improved pendulum-tracking performance among both patients and nonpatients. Improvement was greatest among those with the worst baseline scores, but the differences between groups remained.

As part of a larger research project studying children at risk for the development of schizophrenia and their families (7,8), the present study examined pendulum-tracking performance among a group of women previously hospitalized for schizophrenia or for a severe, but nonschizophrenic, psychiatric illness. In this investigation it was possible to examine the relationship between psychopathologic state and pendulum-tracking performance among a group of subjects who had undergone a psychiatric hospitalization in the past, but who were at the time of testing, living in the community and, in many cases, were asymptomatic.

METHOD

The subects for this study are a subsample of a large group of families investigated in the University of Rochester Child and Family Study. Families participating in this project met the following criteria: at least one parent had been hospitalized at some time for functional psychiatric disorder (excluding alcoholism, drug abuse, and organic brain syndrome), there is a male child age 4, 7, or 10 years old, and the family is living together. Families in this study participate in an extensive program of investigations which includes studies of the children, the parents, and the family as a group. As part of those studies, an elaborate series of diagnostic procedures are performed on the identified (index) patient member of each family.

The subjects included in the study were 35 of the mothers in these families with a history of psychiatric hospitalization. Fourteen of these women had received a consensus diagnosis of schizophrenia by the research diagnostic teams, while 21 had been hospitalized for serious, but nonschizophrenic, psychiatric disorders. The diagnostic dichotomy, schizophrenia/nonschizophrenia, was reached by three investigators in the project (Drs. Castaneda, Romano, and Strauss) arriving at diagnostic agreement after reviewing all available information. The consensus diagnosis of schizophrenia was relatively narrow, including only about one-half of the patients receiving a hospital diagnosis of schizophrenia, but slightly more than would have been diagnosed schizophrenic using K. Schneider's first rank symptoms as a diagnostic criterion. (The relationship between psychophysiologic findings and diagnostic criteria other than consensus diagnosis will be reported when data collection on the total sample has been completed.)

The mean age of the subjects was 38.7. All families were in social class II–IV (9). The most recent hospitalization of the subjects was an average of 5 years before the time of their entry into the study. The women were all functioning in the community, and they were in at least partial remission from the severe symptoms that had necessitated hospitalization.

At the time of entry into the study, subjects were interviewed with a standardized sign and symptom inventory and psychiatric history forms of demonstrated reliability (8) as well as with less structured clinical interviews (10). In addition, all hospital records were subjected to intensive review to obtain symptom and psychiatric history data. From this review, ratings of symptomatology and social function were made using the Case Record Rating Scale (CRRS) (11). Data from all these sources were combined to make a rating of global mental health (12), and symptom data from all sources were combined to yield scores on several syndrome dimensions including a dimension of degree of psychosis. This dimension was a combination of ratings on individual symptoms including delusions, hallucinations, thinking disorder, incongruous affect, incomprehensibility, and bizarre behavior (13).

Patient diagnoses were arrived at clinically as well as by the two diagnostic teams in the project, each reaching a diagnosis independently and then meeting to reach a final consensus diagnosis.

The pendulum-tracking procedure was administered using the method described by Holzman et al (3).

RESULTS

The correlation between subjects' pendulum-tracking scores, diagnosis (schizophrenic vs. nonschizophrenic), measures of global adjustment, and ratings of level of psychotic symptomatology are presented in Table 28-1. Diagnosis was not related to pendulum-tracking performance nor were tracking scores related to the global measure of the patient's current functioning. The only measure significantly related to pendulum-tracking performance was that of the ratings of degree of psychosis at the time of the patient's prior hospitalization. As Table 28-1 also reveals, there is no relationship between time since hospitalization and pendulum-tracking scores.

Table 28-1. Correlations of Diagnostic and Symptom Variables with Pendulum-tracking scores

	Type Rating (N = 30)	Velocity Arrests (Sum) (N = 30)
Psychosis rating (hospitalization)	0.53[a]	0.61[a]
Psychosis rating (current)	0.07	0.02
Health-sickness (hospitalization)	−0.20	−0.04
Health-sickness (current)	−0.10	−0.11
Diagnosis (schiz., nonschiz.)	0.21	0.26
Time since hospitalization	−0.06	−0.11

[a] $p < 0.01$.

Table 28-2. Pendulum-tracking as a Function of Ratings of Psychotic Symptomatology at Time of Hospitalization

		Psychosis Rating			
		Minimal	Moderate	Severe	
Tracking type rating	X̄	2.00	2.00	2.82	$F(2, 27) = 4.03^a$
	SD	0.82	0.74	0.75	$p < 0.05$
	n	7	12	11	
Pendulum tracking					
Tracking velocity errors sum	X̄	46.57	44.08	68.45	$F(2, 27) = 3.61^a$
	SD	10.01	19.40	31.14	$p < 0.05$
	n	7	12	11	

[a] Newman-Keuls tests of differences between cell means reveal significant differences ($p < 0.05$) between the severe psychosis group and each of the other two groups.

Analyses of variance were performed on the pendulum-tracking data as a function of the ratings of severity of psychotic symptomatology at hospitalization. Those ratings were divided into a low-, a middle-, and a high-severity group based on the distribution of scores from a somewhat larger group of 67 female subjects for whom such data were available. As Table 28-2 reveals, the data for both measures of pendulum tracking indicate a significant difference in scores between those categorized as having severe psychotic symptomatology compared with those having either moderate or mild symptomatology at the time of hospitalization, while no differences are indicated between the mild and moderate groups. Newman-Keuls tests of the differences between individual cell means confirms that impression. Analyses of variance also were performed on the tracking scores in relation to the other measures of pathologic condition, including diagnosis. However, no significant differences were obtained.

DISCUSSION

Previous studies of the pendulum-tracking function have utilized both ratings of the degree of distortion in the tracking record and objective counts of velocity arrests as revealed by a derivative of the original analog record. Our data suggest that these two measures of the tracking performance are highly related and probably could be utilized interchangeably. In the future it may well be advisable to focus on velocity arrests as a more objective and replicable measure of tracking performance. Inspection of the direct analog record may continue to be of value, however, in identifying unusual or anomalous records that otherwise might go undetected. Our data further indicate that there is little information to be obtained from division of the velocity arrest scores into pre- and postalerting measures. Again, these scores are highly correlated and separate analyses (not reported here) produced no additional information about tracking performance that was not already evident from the velocity-arrest sum scores.

Klein et al (5) in a preliminary report noted a failure to distinguish schizophrenics from nonschizophrenic patient controls on a pendulum-tracking task, although patients as a group differed significantly from nonpatient controls. In the present study, data from an augmented sample point to the limited relationship between diagnosis and pendulum-tracking performance. This conclusion, however, must be tempered by the consideration that a majority of our schizophrenic patients were diagnosed as schizoaffective. As previous studies (3,4) have indicated, schizoaffectives' performance on the task tends to be intermediate between nonschizophrenic psychiatric controls and other schizophrenic subtypes.

Shagass (6) has provided strong evidence for the interpretation of pendulum-tracking difficulty as an attentional dysfunction. He demonstrated that a procedure that required subjects to focus carefully on the pendulum resulted in markedly improved tracking. Taken in conjuction with those data, our results suggest that attentional dysfunction is more related to degree of psychotic symptoms including hallucinations, delusions, disturbances in thinking, bizarre behavior, incomprehensibility, and incongruous affect, than to a specific diagnosis, or, for that matter, to general level of social and emotional functioning. These data are consistent with results reported by Holzman et al (3) regarding the association of significant levels of disturbance in thinking as measured by the Rorschach Delta Index to pendulum-tracking dysfunction.

An important aspect of the present study is that the subjects were functioning in a state of relative remission from previously severe clinical symptomatology. Substantial differences in past versus current levels of functioning were readily apparent, both in terms of the patients' overall level of social and emotional functioning and in terms of their degree of psychoticism. What is of particular interest, therefore, is the fact that although these subjects are currently in a state of remission, they show a relationship between their *past* levels of psychotic functioning and their *current* pendulum-tracking performance. This relationship exists in spite of the absence of a relationship between current level of social functioning or ratings of current psychotic symptoms and pendulum-tracking performance. One explanatory hypothesis which suggests itself is that pendulum-tracking performance which reflects attentional dysfunction can be thought of as a trait characteristic. Thus, the attentional disturbance implicated by disrupted pendulum-tracking performance may reflect an enduring index of vulnerability to specific symptom occurrence which is present independent of variations in a patient's current clinical state. In other words, individuals with attentional impairment, if they develop psychiatric disorders, may be more likely to manifest psychotic symptoms characterized by cognitive and perceptual distortion.

SUMMARY

Pendulum eye-tracking measurements were obtained from 35 women previously hospitalized for a serious psychiatric disorder. Although these subjects were largely in symptomatic remission, their pendulum-tracking records were significantly correlated with ratings of degree of psychosis present at the time of their hospitalization. Pendulum tracking was not related to diagnosis or to overall ratings of mental health. The results suggest the possibility of attention dysfunction as a trait characteristic, predictive of psychotic symptomatology when decompensation occurs.

REFERENCES

1. Diefendorf AR, Dodge R: An experimental study of the ocular reactions of the insane from photographic records. *Brain* 31:451, 1908.

2. Holzman PS, Proctor LR, Hughes DW: Eye-tracking patterns in schizophrenia. *Science* 181:197, 1973.

3. Holzman PS, Proctor LR, Levy DL, et al: Eye-tracking dysfunctions in schizophrenic patients and their relatives. *Arch Gen Psychiat* 31:143, 1974.

4. Shagass C, Amadeo M, Overton DA: Eye-tracking performance in psychiatric patients. *Biol Psychiat* 9:245, 1974.

5. Klein RH, Salzman LF, Jones F, et al: Eye-tracking in psychiatric patients and their offspring. *Psychophysiology* 13:186, 1976, abstract.

6. Shagass C, Roemer RA, Amadeo M: Eye-tracking performance and engagement of attention. *Arch Gen Psychiat* 33:121, 1976.

7. Garmezy N: Children at risk: The search for the antecedents of schizophrenia. Part 2: Ongoing research programs, issues and interventions. *Schizophrenia Bull* 9:55, 1974.

8. Strauss JS, Wynne LC, Cole R: Understanding the origins of psychopathology: Unique perspective of a multi-team vulnerability study. Presented at the Albert Einstein Medical School Department of Psychiatry, April 30, 1976.

9. Hollingshead A, Redlich, F: *Social Class and Mental Illness.* New York, Wiley, 1958.

10. World Health Organization: *The International Pilot Study of Schizophrenia. Vol. 1.* Geneva, WHO Press, 1973.

11. Strauss JS, Harder DW: The case rating scale: A method for rating symptoms and social function data from case records. *Comp Psychiat,* in press.

12. Spitzer RL, Gibbon M, Endicott J: *Global Assessment Scale.* Biometrics Research, New York State Department of Mental Hygiene, New York, 1974.

13. Harder DW, Strauss JS, Chandler M: Egocentrism in children of parents with a history of psychiatric disorder. Presented at the Annual Meeting of the American Psychological Association, 1976.

Chapter 29
The Several Qualities of Attention in Schizophrenia

Philip S. Holzman, Ph.D.
Deborah L. Levy, Ph.D.
Leonard R. Proctor, M.D.

Ever since systematic observation of madness began—and history records ancient descriptions of syndromes quite similar to those we know today—disturbances in the ability to attend have been given a prominent place either in explanations or descriptions of the abnormalities. In this chapter we present evidence for an impairment of a nonvoluntary form of attending in schizophrenia, the study of which has important implications for exploring the psychologic and neurophysiologic aspects of schizophrenia.

In the modern era, specific involvement of attention in schizophrenic psychoses received extended discussion in several of Kraepelin's texts. For example, he wrote (1):

> Attention: This behavior [dementia praecox] is without doubt [closely] related to the disorder of attention which we frequently find conspiciously developed in our patients. It is quite common for them to lose both inclination and ability on their own initiative to keep their attention fixed for any length of time. It is often difficult enough to make them attend at all. . . . But the patients do not take any notice of what they may perceive quite well, nor do they try to understand it; they do not follow what happens in their surroundings, even though it may happen to be of great importance to them. They do not pay attention to what is said to them, they do not trouble themselves about the meaning of what they read. . . In psychological experiments the patients cannot stick to the appointed exercise; they feel no need to collect their thoughts in the appointed manner or to reach a satisfactory solution. (pp 5–6)

Kraepelin distinguished between *Auffassung,* meaning registration of information and *Aufmerksamkeit,* meaning active attention. He wrote that in dementia praecox the former is rarely disturbed except for a narrowing of attention span in certain acute and

The work reported here was supported by grant number MH-19477, USPHS, and a grant from the Benevolent Foundation of the Scottish Rite, Northern Masonic Jurisdiction. Dr. Holzman is a recipient of Public Health Service Research Scientist Award (MH-70900).

terminal phases of the illness. Active attention, however, in the sense of sustained, directed, and concentrated effort, is almost always deficient in the disorder. Kraepelin also cited fluctuations in distractibility that range from hyperdistractibility to compulsive attentiveness to all incidental sensory stimulation.

Most modern reviews of empirical studies focus on the central role of impaired attention in schizophrenic dysfunctions, although many of these works fail to specify more precisely the nature of the impairment. For the term attention refers to several different processes and English, unlike German, has only the one term to denote the several qualities of attention. From the use of the term attention alone it is not possible to infer which of several possible meanings is invoked, for instance, processes of searching and selecting, sustaining a vigil, activating a set of functions, alerting, concentrating, or anticipating. "Not paying attention" also has been used to describe states of motivated inattention, distraction, and disregard, in the sense that Kraepelin has been quoted. It is in this sense of "not paying attention" that many investigators of psychopathology have employed the term "defect of attention" to explain schizophrenic impairment.

To refer aspects of schizophrenic behavior to a presumed failure of attention is not a sufficient explanation of these functional defects. Our understanding would deepen only if we could decide what specific processes of attention are functioning poorly. We could then search the network of complex functioning to locate the breakdown in the specific form of attention and then trace linkages to interferences with integrated behavior.

Serious examination of the various qualities of attention requires both phenomenologic description and efforts to press through to the psychologic and even the physiologic processes that are involved. In his discussion of attention, William James also distinguished involuntary, effortless, or passive attention from the active and voluntary form (2). It is the voluntary form that raises the issue of the kind and degree of interest that a person has in a thing or event. It seems to us that to assert that many schizophrenics display motivated inattention or voluntary distractibility does not advance us very far in understanding the mysteries of schizophrenia, for many conditions, transitory and quasi-permanent, from fatigue to chronic debilitating physical illness, can affect one's will or ability to attend. To say that a schizophrenic patient shows a disturbance of voluntary attention says little more than that the patient's interests are elsewhere. Freud, too, noted this characteristic of schizophrenics and referred to it as the withdrawal of cathexis (or interest) from the external world. And it is a further error to assume either that one understands the behavioral processes of disturbances of attention simply by naming them as such or that the demonstration of an impairment of attention in behavior dysfunctions such as psychosis precludes concomitant complex neurophysiologic dysfunctions.

The nonvoluntary aspect of attending in schizophrenia has received scant study, and the investigation of its role may yield more information about this mysterious form of madness than studies of voluntary attending. James wrote that the reflexive, involuntary form of attention has physiologic counterparts. These consist of the excitement of an appropriate cortical center and the adaptation by the sense organ and its muscular apparatus to make perception of the object as clear as possible. James was certain, within the limits of knowledge then available, that involuntary selective attention implies a neurophysiologic process. It is this infrastructure that we shall focus on in this chapter, arguing from empirical evidence that voluntary inattention in the sense that Kraepelin used it, while characteristic of most schizophrenics, is not specific to schizophrenia but that a particular quality of nonvoluntary attending that has a neurophysiologic underpinning shows significant impairment.

A chance observation concerning disordered smooth pursuit eye movements in schizophrenic patients confronted us with the problem of the several qualities of attention in schizophrenia. Our studies have shown that between 65% and 80% of schizophrenic patients, in contrast to about 6% of normal subjects, showed disordered smooth pursuit eye movements (3,4). The impairments were not due to the effects of neuroleptic drugs. Further, we found that about 45% of first-degree relatives of these patients, although never clinically ill, also had impaired pursuit movements. These results were essentially replicated by several other investigators, although Shagass (12) reported that most of his psychotic patients, manic-depressive patients included, showed this impairment.

Smooth pursuit is the name for the eye movement used in following or tracking as one watches a moving target. When evoked, these movements are controlled automatically in the presence of a moving object. The velocity of the target determines almost exactly the velocity of the eye. The adaptive function of the pursuit system is to maintain the image of the target on the fovea. Another kind of eye movement, the saccadic or rapid movement, acts to bring the image of the object onto the fovea. Saccadic movements are very rapid, at times attaining speeds up to 600 degrees a second in comparison with an upper limit of 36 degrees a second for pursuit movements. Several investigators have shown that the neural groups associated with slow and fast eye movements are at least partially independent (5,6). More recent studies indicate that the same oculomotor neurones participate in both types of eye movements (7,8). Horizontal saccades are probably represented cortically in the frontal lobes and pursuit movements originate cortically in the occipital-parietal (peristrate) visual association areas (9). Both types of eye movements are regulated in the cerebellum and in the pontine paramedian reticular formation just ventral to the medial longitudinal fasciculi (10).

Our experimental task calls for the subject to follow a pendulum that swings within 20 degrees of visual arc with a frequency of 0.4 Hz. In normal eye tracking the sinusoidal wave of the pendulum should be matched by a congruent sinusoidal movement of the eyes and an electronystagmograph can record those movements. Figure 29-1A shows normal eye tracking. Figure 29-1B, C, and D show types of impaired eye tracking. The derivative of these tracings, also shown in the figures, indicates the velocity of the eyes at each point, and from the velocity channel we can approximate the number of times the eyes stop moving when indeed they should be moving, a phenomenon we called "velocity arrests." Our earlier studies showed that schizophrenic patients and many of their first-degree relatives had tracings that resembled those in Figure 1B, C, and D and also had a greater number of velocity arrests than did nonschizophrenics.

This task requires that all subjects pay attention to the swinging pendulum and thus willing participation in the experiment is critical. But once the subject looks at the swinging pendulum, the pursuit system is triggered and the eyes follow the target. Instructions to re-alert the subjects significantly reduced the number of times the patients' eye speed exceeded that of the target, but this re-alerting instruction had no significant effect on the number of eye arrests. That is, the velocity arrest score was unaffected by voluntary activities, whereas errors of "velocity overshooting" were so affected. We believe that we demonstrated that voluntary behavior, motivated behavior, or "paying attention" in common parlance and in the sense implicated by Kraepelin in

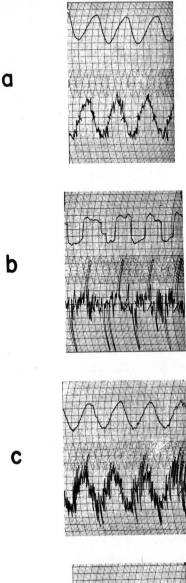

Figure 29-1. Four examples of pursuit eye movements. The stimulus is a pendulum. Top of each example shows the direct eye signal; the bottom shows the derivative of that signal, displaying eye velocity. *A.* Normal sinusoidal smooth pursuit pattern with 5.6 velocity arrests per cycle. *B.* Smooth tracking is replaced by saccadic shifts with 14.9 velocity arrests per cycle. *C.* Cogwheeling pursuit with 14.5 velocity arrests per cycle. *D.* Spikey pattern with 13.2 velocity arrests per cycle.

Aufmerksamkeit, is not the principal issue in the eye-tracking dysfunctions we described.

In a recent paper, Shagass et al (11) reported an interesting improvement of the pursuit task, one we have since routinely incorporated into our procedures. He placed arabic numbers on the pendulum. As the pendulum oscillates it also slowly rotates, thus displaying different numbers. The subject's task is to read the numbers silently as he tracks the pendulum. Shagass et al reported striking reductions in the number of eye arrests and a tendency for tracking to become smoother as a result of this procedure, although the differences between patients and normal subjects remained. None of the subjects in either Shagass's experiment or in our repetition of that work realized that their tracking was deviant, or that their tracking had improved when they were asked to read the numbers. It is this number-reading task that can help us to penetrate more deeply into the problem of attention in schizophrenia.

We have tested our subjects four times, twice in the usual way with a plain, unnumbered pendulum, then with numbers placed on the pendulum with the instruction to read the numbers silently while tracking it, and finally with the plain pendulum again. Figure 29-2 shows that schizophrenic patients improved significantly when they were asked to read the numbers silently; they reverted to their previous poor performance when tracking the plain pendulum. Normal subjects were again superior in all conditions.

When normal subjects are given Seconal, alcohol, or chloral hydrate, smooth pursuit markedly deteriorates from predrug levels. In the number-reading task even those drug-impaired performances improve, but the improvement lasts only as long as the numbers are present on the pendulum. Figure 29-3 shows this effect on the velocity arrest score in normal subjects after ingestion of chloral hydrate.

The number-reading task, however, is able to normalize only certain kinds of eye-tracking impairments. We have noted that there are two principal kinds of eye-tracking dysfunctions in our subjects. In type I, the pursuit movements are almost totally replaced by saccades. In type II, small amplitude rapid movements intrude upon the smooth tracking, leaving its general form intact but giving the tracings either a spikey or a "cogwheeled" appearance. We are not yet prepared to state which kind of dysfunction predominates in schizophrenic patients and in their relatives, although our impression is that type II, the "spikey" type, is the more common. Reading the numbers silently

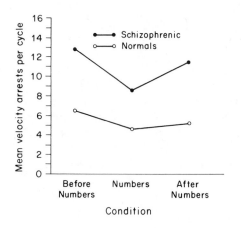

Figure 29-2. Effects of reading numbers silently while tracking pendulum. Velocity arrests decrease significantly for schizophrenics, and return to the previous high level after removal of numbers. Differences between schizophrenics and normal subjects remain significant for all conditions.

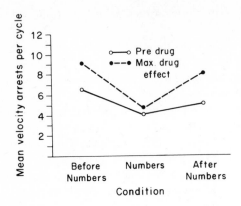

Figure 29-3. Effects of reading numbers silently while tracking pendulum for a group of normal subjects before and after the maximum effect of 1500 mg of chloral hydrate. Velocity arrests are minimized by the number-reading task and then return to previous high level after numbers are removed.

while tracking significantly improves type I—that in which saccadic shifts replace smooth pursuit. Figure 29-4 shows this effect. The number-reading task normalizes many of those records at least for several swings of the pendulum. When, however, the numbers are removed, most of the subjects showing this type of dysfunction revert to gross saccadic shifting.

Subjects with the type II dysfunction do not generally improve with the number-reading task, although we can observe a small reduction in the number of eye arrests. The tendency to normalize some of the spikey records is not very great, and the extent of these changes never results in unimpaired smooth-pursuit movements. Figures 29-5 and 29-6 show this effect. It is as if in type I tracking dysfunction, the pursuit system does not switch on, and in type II, other interferences do not switch off.

Type I tracking, in which smooth pursuit is almost completely replaced by saccades, could reflect an incapacity or a sluggishness to begin a pursuit movement—akinesia or bradykinesia. The number-reading task, which provides a more commanding stimulus than does the pendulum alone, may override this initial sluggishness and thus normalize the pursuit. Type I tracking dysfunction is also easily normalized (or very close to normalized) by re-alerting the subjects after 30 seconds. Subjects showing otherwise normal tracking may have episodes of type I dysfunction during a session.[1]

Type I tracking dysfunction represents a failure to activate the pursuit system which actually functions properly once in motion. In this first type of dysfunction, a simple cognitive task superimposed on the tracking task seems to recruit another system involving a different quality of attention and serves to augment the effectiveness of the pursuit system. In type II pattern, the superimposed and commanding cognitive task could be thought of as lending only a minor degree of help to reestablish some degree of suppression of the ataxic saccadic activity by invoking another functional system. When, however, the visual inhibitory controls are again suspended when number-reading ceases, the prior level of disinhibition of the saccadic system returns.

Perhaps an analogy may help us to understand the phenomenon of tracking improvement with the number-reading task. Many organic defects can be overcome or circumvented by introducing prostheses, or by invoking different but intact functions that may override or circumvent the dysfunction. For example, a person with a broken leg can

---

[1] Occasionally a normal subject who has a previously undetected oculomotor disturbance such as a gaze nystagmus will show yet another type of smooth pursuit disturbance.

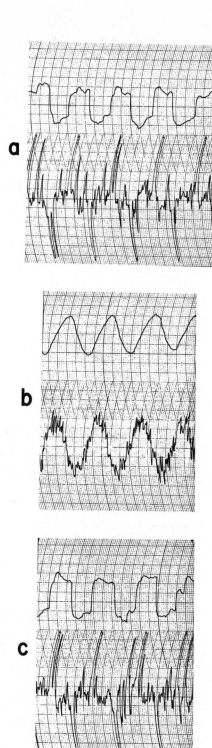

Figure 29-4. Effects of silent number-reading on eye-tracking pattern in which saccadic shifts replace smooth pursuit. *A.* Poor tracking. Velocity arrests: 10 per cycle. *B.* Normal pursuit pattern occurs during silent number-reading. Velocity arrests: 3 per cycle. *C.* Pursuit movement returns to saccadic shifts after removal of numbers from pendulum. Velocity arrests: 11 per cycle.

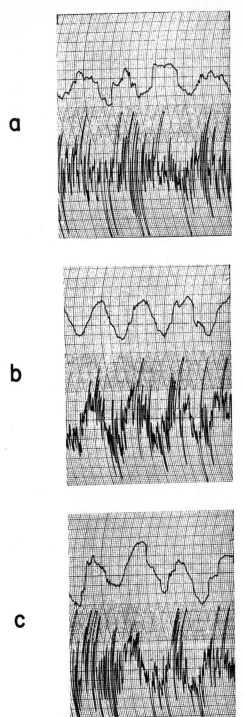

Figure 29-5. Spikey eye-tracking patterns. *A.* Before number-reading task. Velocity arrests: 16.8 per cycle. *B.* During number-reading task. Velocity arrests: 10.8 per cycle. *C.* After removal of numbers from pendulum. Velocity arrests: 18.4 per cycle.

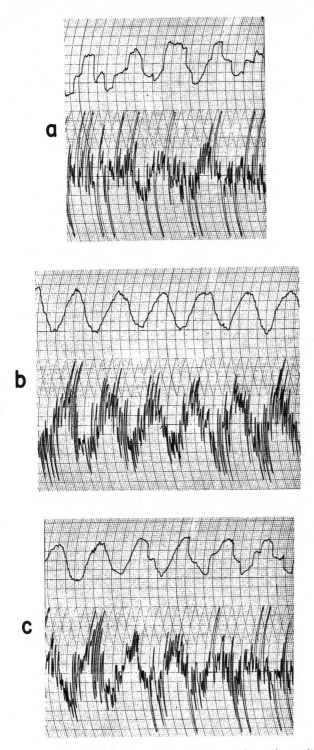

Figure 29-6. An eye-tracking pattern that includes both saccades and cogwheeling. *A.* Before number-reading task both cogwheeling and saccadic movements are present. Velocity arrests: 18. *B.* During number-reading task saccades disappear but cogwheeling remains. Velocity arrests: 11.6. *C.* After removal of numbers, a tendency for some saccadic shifts to return, and cogwheeling remains. Velocity arrests: 13.6.

walk if the leg is supported by a cast or the person walks with crutches. A parkinsonian patient with an at-rest tremor stops his tremor during a purposeful act, such as reaching for a wanted object. A stutterer can speak with fluency by markedly slowing his rate of speaking or by singing. The cast, the crutch, the intention, and the singing temporarily normalize the impaired functions. But one cannot reason from this effect that the original cause of the dysfunction is the absence of a cast or of an auxiliary intention. Likewise, one cannot parsimoniously attribute the eye-tracking dysfunctions to failures in the deployment of voluntary attention—to *Aufmerksamkeit*—simply because they are to some extent correctable by the voluntary attention mobilized by a dominating cognitive task. Since our subjects were already paying attention and were cooperating in the task, we conclude that motivational variables like inattentiveness are not involved in producing the eye-tracking dysfunctions. What is involved, however, is a failure to maintain a visual-attentive focus that is continually locked on to the oscillating pendulum, a failure of *cognitive centering,* in spite of the intention to do the task. Thus, the eye-tracking experiment supports the assumption that although schizophrenic patients may be inattentive, schizophrenia also involves a dysfunction in nonvoluntary attention. In the following paragraphs we shall try to develop the thesis that this quality of nonvoluntary attention has an identifiable neurophysiologic substrate.

At this juncture let us inventory our data to see the directions they point to.

1. We have shown that a large proportion of schizophrenic patients and their first-degree relatives manifest a dysfunction of smooth-pursuit eye movements.

2. There are two major kinds of eye-tracking dysfunctions. In type I, the pursuit movement either fails to start or is sluggish in starting and is replaced by grossly inaccurate, large amplitude saccadic movements. In type II, pursuit movement is interrupted by very brief and frequent eye arrests.

3. Type I can be improved or even completely normalized by either the number-reading task or simple re-alerting. Type II can at best be only modestly improved by the number-reading task.

4. The subjects are not aware either that they are tracking poorly or that they improve with the addition of the number-reading task.

5. There is no way to produce such eye movements unless the person is first paying attention to the swinging pendulum.

From these data we concluded that a disorder of nonvoluntary attention accounts for the eye-tracking dysfunction and is thus involved in schizophrenia. The number-reading task temporarily and differentially improves the deviant eye-tracking by mobilizing another cognitive system that relies on a different quality of attention from that called for in simple eye pursuit movements. As an aside, this finding is of special interest for the psychology of attention since the superimposition of one task on another usually interferes with performances of the first task. In this instance, however, the co-occurrence of a task requiring nonvoluntary attention with that requiring voluntary attention is synergistic and, as a mnemonic device helps one to to memorize, this second task improves performance.

6. The eye-tracking dysfunction is not specific for schizophrenia, and this nonspecificity may help us understand the meaning of the dysfunction in schizophrenia. Type II tracings have been described in persons who have multiple sclerosis, Parkinson's disease, brain-stem and hemispheric lesions, and some drug intoxications like those referable to alcohol and barbiturates. Type I deviations have been described in some cases of peripheral ocular disorders, multiple sclerosis, and in a few normal persons, Shagass et

al (12) reported impaired eye tracking in psychotic patients other than schizophrenics, although the types of tracking dysfunctions observed were not described. Eye tracking tends to show impairments with aging, and in our study of 74 normal persons who ranged from 15 to 59 years, we found a significant correlation of 0.36 between the number of eye arrests and age. The older a person is, the greater the number of arrests. These facts suggest that some kinds of central nervous system damages reflected in certain lesions, some toxicities, and in aging, show themselves in degrees of impaired eye tracking. It would thus seem likely that impaired eye tracking in schizophrenics and in their relatives also reflects a central nervous system dysfunction.

Examination of the quality of velocity arrest records in subjects with type II tracking impairments shows not one but two kinds of activity that occur during pursuit movements. One reflects the rapid saccadic shifts of the ocular globe. But from analysis of the power spectrum of the signals emitted there is also evidence of activity occurring at speeds far greater than the 600 degrees per second that the eyes are maximally capable of moving. These velocities are too rapid to have been produced by eye movements. Rather, they suggest that random, asynchronous neural firing is occurring in addition to the ocular saccades.

In another connection, Gregory (13), who proposed a signal detection theory of aging, suggested that as the organism ages, spontaneous and random discharge or "neural noise" increases. Since the signal-to-noise ratio is one determinant of the capacity to detect a signal, a low signal-to-noise ratio, as in the aging nervous system, would require a stronger or more commanding stimulus to be detected or discriminated than would be necessary in a nervous system with a higher signal-to-noise ratio. A major task of the central nervous system is to suppress or inhibit some other central nervous system activities. One may ask, then, whether the high number of eye arrests seen in schizophrenic patients and in many of their relatives represents increased and random neural firing or a failure of neural suppression. Since type II eye-tracking dysfunctions occur in degenerating conditions, including aging, it would be likely that the high speed asynchronous firing reflects not an increased acivity of some parts of the nervous system, but a failure of some inhibiting, modulating, or integrating control centers. It therefore would not be unreasonable to assume that a failure of such central nervous system inhibitory activities also accompanies schizophrenic conditions. Where in the central nervous system could such a presumed failure of inhibition occur? A promising place to look would be in the cerebellum and the pontine paramedian reticular formation where all types of oculomotor activity are regulated.

Whether we are dealing with a peripheral or a more general, pervasive phenomenon of the entire central nervous system remains to be investigated. We think it is plausible, however, that the eye-tracking dysfunctions inform us not simply of a disorder of the oculomotor system, but of a more general central nervous system disorder. The oculomotor system is probably a particularly felicitous one for studying some neural transmission processes since in the extraocular system the ratio of nerve to muscle is the lowest of any anatomic set, except perhaps for that of the larynx. Simple and manageable procedures for establishing the generality of these events beyond the oculomotor, however, are not yet developed.

In summary, we have presented evidence that nonvoluntary attending is disordered in schizophrenic conditions and, despite previous assumptions, that inattention, "heedless negligence," or failure to cooperate are not the specific attentional qualities that are disordered in schizophrenia. The data from our studies of smooth pursuit eye movements implicate a neurophysiological substrate of impaired nonvoluntary attention in schizophrenia. The neural dysfunction can be described as a failure of inhibitory, synchronizing or integrating systems which may be located in the brain stem. This failure shows itself in increased nonspecific high frequency neural noise during efferent activity.

REFERENCES

1. Kraepelin E: *Dementia Praecox and Paraphrenia.* Edinburgh, Livingston, 1919.
2. James W: *Principles of Psychology.* New York, Dover, 1950.
3. Holzman PS, Proctor LR, Hughes DW: Eye tracking patterns in schizophrenia. *Science* 181:179–181, 1973.
4. Holzman PS, Proctor LR, Levy DL, et al: Eye tracking dysfunctions in schizophrenic patients and their relatives. *Arch Gen Psychiat* 31:143–151, 1974.
5. Rashbass C: The relationship between saccadic and smooth tracking eye movements. *J Physiol* 159:326–378, 1961.
6. Wertheimer G: Eye movement responses to a horizontally moving visual stimulus. *Arch Ophthal* 52:932–941, 1954.
7. Fuchs AF, Luschei ES: Firing patterns of abducers neurons of alert monkeys in relationship to horizontal eye movement. *J Neurophysiol* 33:382–392, 1970.
8. Keller EL, Robinson DA: Abducens unit behavior in the monkey during vergence movements. *Vis Res* 12:369–382, 1972.
9. Robinson DA, Fuchs AF: Eye movements evoked by stimulation of the frontal eye fields. *J Neurophysiol* 32:637–649, 1969.
10. Cohen B, Komatsuzaki A, Bender MB: Electrooculographic syndrome in monkeys after pontine reticular formation lesions. *Arch Neurol* Chicago 18:78–92, 1968.
11. Shagass C, Roemer RA, Amadeo M: Eye tracking performance and engagement of attention. *Arch Gen Psychiat* 33:121–125, 1976.
12. Shagass C, Amadeo M, Overton DA: Eye tracking performance in psychiatric patients. *Biol Psychiatry* 9:245–260, 1974.
13. Gregory RL: Increase in "neurological noise" as a factor in aging. *Proceedings of the Fourth International Congress on Gerontology* 1:314–324, 1959.

Chapter 30
A Theory of the Relation Between Dopamine and Attention

Steven Matthysse, Ph.D.

The distinction between voluntary and involuntary shifts in the focus of attention has a long history in psychology. Bleuler (1) and Jaspers (2) made use of it in their psychiatric phenomenologies. Jaspers' definition of involuntary attention is simple and useful for our purposes: "being drawn towards something or being fascinated by it." Titchener constructed what was perhaps the most elaborate catalogue of determinants of attention, including fairly obvious stimulus features such as intensity and movement, but also some that were to prove interesting in future research, such as novelty and stimulus cessation (3). Titchener also indicated that certain stimulus qualities might be especially compelling for no apparent reason—"the taste of bitter, the smell of musk, the sight of yellow . . . the least trace of them fascinates me"—and internal perceptions as well—"pains that we 'cannot get away from,'" and "intimate, worrying, wicked things." The existence of these involuntary determinants by no means indicates any defect in the organism's relationship to its environment; for efficient functioning a smooth coupling of attention to stimuli, motivational states and cognitive processes is necessary, just as compensatory visual shifts must be made as the organism changes direction.

The hypothesis I would like to propose is that *shifts in the focus of attention—its coupling to stimuli and internal states—are, at least in part, under the control of a dopaminergic system.* At this stage of our knowledge, it is best to be cautious in assigning an anatomic locus for this system; it might be limbic, striatal, or cortical. The effect of dopaminergic agonists seems to be overinvestment of attention in stimuli, both external and internal. The normal function of the dopaminergic system may be efficient coordination of shifts in the focus of attention, rather than regulation of its intensity, just as motor neurons are concerned with the detailed pattern of muscle activity, although cholinergic agonists and antagonists affect muscle tone. The evidence supporting the theory comes

This research was supported by Alcohol, Drug Abuse, and Mental Health Administration Grant MH-25515 from the National Institute of Mental Health.

from the effects of dopaminergic agonists, antagonists, and lesions in animals and man (see chapter 13 for review).

It may be possible to arrive at an objective criterion for distinguishing "voluntary" from "involuntary" shifts in the focus of attention by considering a specific attentional system, the control of eye movement. Spontaneous eye movements are always saccadic, whereas the eye movements in tracking a moving stimulus are smooth. I would like to suggest that this characteristic of eye movements holds for all shifts in the focus of attention: *voluntary shifts in the focus of attention are always saccadic, whereas involuntary shifts can be smooth.* Furthermore, I would suggest that *saccadic shifts cannot occur in the midst of continuous changes, but only at moments when internal and external determinants of attention have reached a state of balance.*

These principles can be directly applied to the pendulum phenomenon, which Holzman has discussed in the previous chapter. "Positive velocity errors" may be caused by voluntary, hence saccadic, shifts of attention (4). The prominence of "velocity arrests" in the records may be a consequence of the fact that zero-crossings of velocity are unlike other level-crossings; at such moments the involuntary determinants of attention may have reached a state of balance, when voluntary attentional saccades are facilitated. Shifts of attention at these points might be manifested by positive velocity errors, or by prolongation of the velocity zero as attention is voluntarily diverted elsewhere, so it is not merely an instantaneous zero-crossing but an actual arrest, occupying a finite duration. Three predictions can be tested: (a) saccadic eye movements and velocity arrests in the tracking record should tend to have velocity zeros as points of origin (not always—since the saccade is facilitated by the stationarity of the internal state of attention, which may not be faithfully indicated by the absence of eye movement); (b) the acceleration of the eye may sometimes be discontinuous at velocity zeros, so an actual arrest occurs rather than merely an instantaneous zero-crossing; (c) saccadic disturbances should be more frequent at the extremes of the pendulum's motion than in the center, since at these points the pendulum is stationary and attentional determinants are likely to be in balance.

The same principles can be applied to Maher's analysis of schizophrenic language (5). Ends of clauses are moments of attentional balance, when the determination exercised by the linguistic unit is weakest; and these are the points at which attentional saccades (associative intrusions) are most likely. Commas, in other words, are analogous to the end-points of the pendulum's swing.

A quantitative analysis of pendulum tracking errors can be developed according to these principles. Let the pendulum displacement be $x_0(t) = -a \cos (2\pi t/\tau_0)$, where a is the amplitude of the pendulum's swing and τ_0 is its period. Suppose the eye to be correctly aligned with the pendulum, with respect to both position and velocity, at some time t_0. From t_0 until the time of the first zero-crossing of velocity ($x'(t) = 0$, where x(t) is the displacement of the eye), the tracking movements of the eye are expected to be under involuntary control. At the time of the first zero-crossing, the results are unpredictable. There may be a saccade, a prolongation of the zero (arrest), or a zero-crossing without incident. Indeed, it is an open question whether zero-crossings are followed by discontinuous events more frequently in schizophrenics than in normals. But since saccadic interference is unlikely (according to our theory) until the first zero-crossing of velocity, we can attempt to predict the probability distribution of the location of the first-zero-crossing.

We assume that x(t), the displacement of the eye, satisfies the differential equation

$$\frac{d^2x}{dt^2} = \frac{d^2x_0}{dt^2} - K(x - x_0) + I(t)$$

The restoring acceleration is assumed to be proportional to the tracking error (proportionality constant K). The eye is subjected to a perturbing acceleration I(t), which is a random process. We will make the natural assumption that I(t) is an Ornstein-Uhlenbeck process, i.e., $I(t_1)$ and $I(t_2)$ are normally distributed with zero means and covariance $\alpha e^{-\rho|t_1-t_2|}$. This process was originally introduced in the theory of Brownian motion (6). $1/\rho$ is a measure of the persistence of the fluctuations in time; if α is proportional to ρ and $\rho \rightarrow \infty$, I(t) becomes white noise (fluctuations with no persistence in time). One may think of I(t) as representing excitations from attention-controlling systems competing with the tracking task; α is an estimate of their magnitude, and ρ of their rate of decay. Thus the tracking is governed by three parameters: K, α, and ρ. All three may vary independently as a result of drug treatment or psychopathology. Conceivably K is elevated in an individual who is stimulus-bound and is depressed in one whose awareness of the environment is obtunded. α would presumably measure the pressure for emergence of task-irrelevant determining tendencies, i.e., preconscious ideas and impulses. ρ might be high (low persistence of perturbations) in hebephrenics, low in catatonics. Determination of K, α, and ρ may be more revealing than counting the number of tracking errors. In principle, it is possible to determine them from the angular distribution of saccades, as will be shown below.

The solution of the stochastic differential equation is somewhat complicated, and details have been omitted. If $K \gg \rho^2$ (perturbations persist substantially in time, unlike white noise), the probability density of a zero-crossing of velocity at time t is

$$\lambda(t) = (\sqrt{K}/\pi)e^{-V_m^2 K \sin^2 (2\pi t/\tau_0)/\alpha(2\rho\tau + 1)}$$

In this formula K, α, and ρ are the parameters defined above; V_m is the maximum velocity of the pendulum; τ is the time elapsed since initialization (correct alignment of the position and velocity of the eye with respect to the pendulum); τ_0 is the pendulum's period. The formula can be interpreted more graphically by constructing a "form factor" g, which contains, essentially, the dependence of error rate on pendulum phase. Assume initialization occurs as the pendulum begins its swing. τ/τ_0 is thus 0 at the extreme left, ¼ at the lowest point, ½ at the extreme right, ¾ at the return to the lowest point, etc. The form factor,

$$g(\tau/\tau_0) = e^{-\sin^2 (2\pi \tau/\tau_0)/[2\rho\tau_0(\tau/\tau_0) + 1]}$$

depends only on the persistence parameter ρ and the period τ_0.

$$\lambda(\tau/\tau_0) = (\sqrt{K}/\pi)g(\tau/\tau_0)^{V_m^2 K/\alpha}$$

is the probability density of zero-crossings of velocity. The probability density is highly dependent on pendulum phase, as is shown in Figure 30-1 in which the form factor $g(\tau/\tau_0)$ is plotted for $\rho\tau_0 = 1$. The effect of the form factor can be large, because the exponent $V_m^2 K/\alpha$ will normally be $\gg 1$. At the extreme right end, $\tau/\tau_0 = \frac{1}{2}$ and $g(\tau/\tau_0) = 1$, so $\lambda(\frac{1}{2}) = \sqrt{K}/\pi$, from which K can be determined independently of α and ρ. The formula does not apply after the first zero-crossing of velocity after initialization,

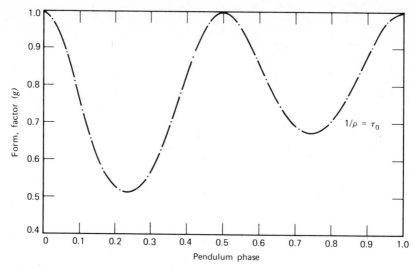

Figure 30-1. Theoretical dependence of velocity arrests on pendulum phase.

because at that point voluntary processes are facilitated: saccades or velocity arrests for a finite interval, to which the Ornstein-Uhlenbeck process does not apply.

A drug might decrease both K and α, with little or no net effect on the average density of tracking errors. Conceivably chlorpromazine does this (i.e., decreases responsiveness to the external stimulus but also decreases intensity of distracting tendencies), and the conflicting actions might explain why this drug, although a dopamine blocker, does not substantially affect tracking errors. (7). Since amphetamine and apomorphine cause animals (and humans) to become stimulus-bound, they should increase K, but their overall effect on tracking performance may depend on what they do to α and ρ. Analysis of the angular distribution of tracking errors may be useful both in subtyping schizophrenic patients and in exploring the relationship between dopamine and attention.

REFERENCES

1. Bleuler E: *Textbook of Psychiatry*. New York, Macmillan, 1924, p 40.

2. Jaspers K: *General Psychopathology*. Chicago, University of Chicago Press, 1963, pp 138–9.

3. Titchener EB: *Lectures on the Elementary Psychology of Feeling and Attention*. New York, Macmillan, 1908, pp 180 ff.

4. Holzman PS, Proctor LR, Levy DL, et al: Eye-tracking dysfunctions in schizophrenic patients and their relatives. *Arch Gen Psychiat* 31:143–151, 1974.

5. Maher B: The language of schizophrenia: a review and interpretation. *Brit J Psychiat* 120:3–17, 1972.

6. Ornstein LS, Uhlenbeck GE: On the theory of the Brownian motion. *Phys Rev* 36:823–841, 1930.

7. Holzman PS, Levy DL, Uhlenhuth EH, et al: Smooth-pursuit eye movements, and Diazepam, CPZ, and Secobarbital. *Psychopharmacologia* (Berl) 44:111–115, 1975.

Section VII
ATTENTION AND COMMUNICATION

Chapter 31
Self-Editing Deficits in Schizophrenia

Bertram D. Cohen, Ph.D.

When manifest, disturbances in language usage are among the most convincing symptoms of a schizophrenic psychosis. These symptoms, however, are not impairments in language per se but are impairments of interpersonal communication. Thus, measures of *communicability* are much more effective discriminators of schizophrenic from normal (or neurotic) speech than are measures of linguistic structure, style, or content (10,14).

In the studies to be considered in this paper, the communicability of an utterance is defined in terms of the accuracy with which listeners use the utterance as a basis for identifying a speaker's referent. The basic paradigm involves the presentation of an explicit set (display) of stimulus objects to a subject (speaker) who is instructed to provide a verbal response to one of them (the referent) such that a listener, given the response, will be able to pick the referent out of the display. This essential paradigm has been adapted to the study of referent-communication in normal children and normal adults, as well as in adults suffering from schizophrenia (6,9,11,16,17).

The purpose of the experiments to be considered here has not been simply to demonstrate that a schizophrenic speaker's utterances are lower in communicability (communication accuracy) than those of normal subjects but rather to specify what goes wrong, compared to the process through which normal speakers select appropriate responses. I will consider first the source of the schizophrenic speaker deficit; second, theory and data concerning the nature of dysfunctional self-editing in schizophrenia; and third, changes in the schizophrenic speaker's communication process from early to late-term in the course of the disorder.

THE SOURCE OF THE SPEAKER DEFICIT: DEVIANT REPERTOIRES OR FAULTY SELF-EDITING?

It is possible that a schizophrenic speaker's associations, meanings, or descriptions of a referent object are idiosyncratic, and that communication failures, therefore, are due to

The research summarized in this paper has been supported in part by NSF Grant GS-40265.

313

differences between speaker and listener in their referent-response repertoires. Alternatively, the schizophrenic speaker's referent-response repertoires may be nondeviant, but he fails to edit out responses inappropriate to the momentary context before they intrude into overt speech.

In an initial study, Cohen and Camhi (3) assigned schizophrenic and normal subjects to speaker or listener roles. Schizophrenics were poorer than normal subjects in communication accuracy as speakers but not as listeners. These results held regardless of whether the patients were listening (or speaking) to other patients or to normal subjects. Since the patients, as listeners, were able to identify speakers' referents on the basis of mutually shared referent-response associations, it was concluded that the schizophrenic *speaker* deficit was not due to deviant associative repertoires. Smith (15) confirmed the Cohen and Camhi findings of poor communication accuracy for schizophrenic speakers. In addition, he demonstrated that schizophrenic speakers are prone to respond on the basis of culturally common referent-response associations, even in situations in which unusual associations would be more appropriate. The evidence from both of these studies indicates that schizophrenic speaker deficits are due to impaired self-editing.

Cohen and Camhi interpreted their findings as evidence of faulty integration of the editing with the associative stages of a two-stage model of the normal speaker process proposed earlier by Rosenberg and Cohen (12,13). In brief, this interpretation asserts that schizophrenic speakers draw ("sample") potential referent-responses from the same underlying repertoires as do normal subjects, but when inappropriate responses are sampled, they are less likely to be edited out ("rejected") prior to their intrusion into speech.

THE SELF-EDITING MALFUNCTION: FAILURE TO EDIT, OR INABILITY TO IGNORE THE EDITED-OUT RESPONSE?

If the schizophrenic speaker deficit in communication accuracy is due to faulty self-editing, what is the nature of this malfunction? It is possible, for example, that the speaker fails to self-edit altogether, thus emitting responses that are of little use to listeners. A second possibility is that he is unable to ignore rejected referent-responses once they occur to him, despite his awareness of their inappropriateness.

The first of these hypotheses, termed the Impulsive Speaker Model, implies a failure to consider the nonreferents from which referents need to be distinguished and, in effect, a failure to consider the cognitive situation of the listener. In contrast, the second hypothesis, termed the Perseverative Speaker Model, implies an unsuccessful struggle by the schizophrenic speaker to replace inappropriate with more appropriate responses despite the speaker's active consideration of such contextual factors as the nonreferents from which referents will need to be distinguished by his listener.

To examine these alternative interpretations of the self-editing deficit, Cohen, Nachmani, and Rosenberg (4) used a color description task in which early, acute schizophrenic and normal control speakers were asked to describe referent colors (Munsell discs). The self-editing requirements of the displays were manipulated by systematically varying the similarity in hue between the referent and nonreferent colors in the displays.

According to the Rosenberg-Cohen model, a normal speaker's color description is the outcome of a repetitive two-stage process. In the first, "sampling," stage the speaker is thought to sample, but not necessarily emit, a response from his repertoire of potential descriptions of the referent color. The probability that any given description will be sampled is proportional to the strength of its association with the referent color, alone. Thus, the response most likely to be sampled is the common color name of the referent, regardless of what other (nonreferent) colors might be included in the display. Self-editing is believed to occur in the second, "comparison," stage in which the speaker compares the referent, and nonreferent colors in the display: the stronger the association to the referent—relative to the nonreferent(s)—the more probable it is that the response will be emitted as an acceptable communication, and the process terminated. If the association with a nonreferent is equal to or stronger than the association with the referent, the response more probably will be rejected, in which case the process is assumed to recycle: the speaker again samples a description, compares, and either emits or rejects, and so forth. Ultimately, a response is sampled, "passes" the self-editing stage test, and is emitted, thus terminating the process.

Since colors similar in hue tend to evoke overlapping descriptions (1), the more similar the colors in a display, the more rigorous its self-editing requirements. In a low-similarity display little or no self-editing is required since the response most likely to be sampled is the common color name.

Normal speakers typically show increased response latencies (the time to initiate a description) as display similarity increases. Normal speakers will usually increase the lengths of their descriptions (number of words) as display similarity increases (8) because a common color name will not distinguish the referent color under high levels of display similarity and will tend to be replaced by longer and more complex descriptions, insofar as the speaker intends to communicate accurately to his listeners. Thus, response time and utterance length can be used as indices of the amount of self-editing activity engaged in by speakers.

If the Impulsive Speaker Model (failure to self-edit) is an accurate description of the schizophrenic speaker, little or no change in the latency or length of speakers' referent-responses will result from increases in display similarity since, according to this model, the speaker is not influenced by the nonreferents in the display. The findings of the Cohen et al experiment (4), show that the schizophrenic speakers were actually *more* responsive than the normal subjects to increasing display similarity (Figures 31-1 and 31-2).

Since these schizophrenic speakers' communication accuracy scores were lower than those of the normal subjects, it is also clear that their increased self-editing did not result in better quality referent-responses. The patients may have been trying harder to edit out poor responses but were succeeding less.

The alternative hypothesis, the Perseverative Speaker Model, posits that the speaker is actively editing out inappropriate referent-responses. However, each time a response is rejected, it is perseveratively resampled and the speaker is denied access to other potential responses in his repertoire of responses. Ultimately, after multiple recyclings of the sampling → comparison → rejection → (re)sampling → and so forth, sequence, the perseverative response passes the self-editing stage and is emitted.

According to the Perseverative Speaker Model, the response ultimately emitted should be the same as the one initially sampled; hence, although response time should increase with increasing display similarity (see Figure 31-1), utterance length should remain constant. Since, in fact, the schizophrenic speakers' utterance lengths actually showed abnormally large increments with increasing similarity, something beyond perseveration must be considered (see Figure 31-2).

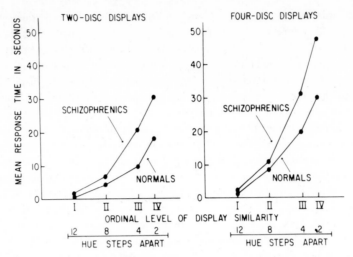

Figure 31-1. Increases in response latency with increases in display similarity in the Cohen et al experiment. From Cohen BD, Nachmani G, Rosenberg S (4).

Examination of the schizophrenic speaker protocols indicated that their excess verbal content often occurred in the form of loosely connected chains of responses rather than coherent descriptions. That is, following the initial latent period, the speaker's overt utterances consisted of elements that appeared to be sampled from their repertoires of associations to prior segments of the utterance rather than from the objective referent (the color disc). Such a chaining tendency, combined with an initial covert perseverative period, accounts for the schizophrenic increments both in utterance length and in latent time under conditions of increasing display similarity. Cohen (2) includes an extensive sample of the verbatim speaker-protocols on which this hypothesis is based.

This third hypothesis, termed the Perseverative-Chaining Model, implies that schizophrenic speakers struggle to communicate accurately to listeners but, as with the

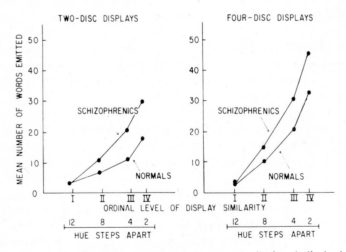

Figure 31-2. Increases in description lengths with increases in display similarity in the Cohen et al experiment. From Cohen BD, Nachmani G, Rosenberg S (4).

Perseverative Speaker Model, their active self-editing decisions to reject inappropriate responses are rendered ineffectual by the perseverative tendency. This covert perseverative cycle is interrupted only when the speaker stops trying to sample a new response from his repertoire of names or descriptions of the referent color and instead samples from his repertoire of *associations* to the perseverative response. (For example, a patient, having implicitly perseverated "orange," which is inadequate to communicate the color in the given display, finally breaks from it by talking about vitamin C.) Since the newly sampled response is also likely to be inadequate to communicate the referent, the speaker, now expressing sampled-but-rejected responses overtly, continues to seek further possible descriptions by sampling from his associations to each prior response in what has become a "chain." Since each new element in this chain is also likely to be rejected, the speaker continues talking until he either finds an apt response (fortuitously) or "passes" a poor one.

DOES SELF-EDITING BEHAVIOR VARY WITH CHRONICITY OF SCHIZOPHRENIA?

The findings on which the Perseverative-Chaining hypothesis was based involved acute, first-admission patients seen early in their hospital stay. It seems reasonable that early-term patients struggle to edit out inappropriate responses in spite of the perseverative handicap. Although this persistence may continue throughout the course of the illness, alternatively, long-term patients, continually frustrated by the perseverative tendency, may give up, as futile, attempts to edit out sampled but inappropriate responses. Their performance then is a truncated one-stage, sampling-only process conforming to the Impulsive Speaker Model.

To test this hypothesis, Kantorowitz and Cohen (7) administered a color-description task to chronic process (Phillips Scale) and equally chronic reactive schizophrenic inpatients of a Veterans Administration Hospital and to a group of normal controls. The patients' cumulative duration of hospitalization ranged from 6 to 10 years.

Similar to the results of prior studies, the schizophrenic speakers, process or reactive, were poorer than the normal subjects in communication accuracy, as measured by the referent choices of a (normal) listener panel. But, instead of showing signs of more self-editing activity than the controls, the long-term patients showed *less*; that is, they showed little or no increases in response latency or length, either absolutely or in comparison with the normal control speakers. Compared with the process schizophrenics, the reactive patients were somewhat more responsive to display similarity, but not significantly so. These results suggest strongly that for long-term schizophrenics, the Impulsive Speaker Model holds as a description of their referent-communication processes.

There were two further observations that support the Impulsive Speaker Model as a description of these long-term patients' speaker processes. First, their response times were significantly *faster* than those of the control subjects. Second, their referent descriptions rarely went beyond common color names even for high-similarity displays. Both these features of their responses indicate that long-term patients are prone to sample and edit without putting their responses through a self-editing stage.

An additional aspect of the Kantorowitz and Cohen data was disclosed when the patients were divided into two equal groups on the basis of clinical ratings of the prevalence of paranoid symptoms in their current clinical pictures. No differences were found between the paranoid and nonparanoid groupings, either in communication accuracy or in the indices of self-editing activity. However, a clear difference was found in the overall average utterance lengths of their responses. The mean number of words per description was tabulated for each patient and the median of this distribution was used to establish a boundary between "terse" and "verbose" speakers. The 2 × 2 table, shown here, indicates that the paranoids' utterance lengths were significantly shorter than the nonparanoids; $\chi^2 = 8.57, p\ .01$.

		Mean number of Words per Description	
		Terse	Verbose
Diagnosis	Paranoid	11	4
	Nonparanoid	3	12

A similar 2 × 2 analysis comparing the process and reactive patient groups suggested that the process patients were more terse. However, the resulting chi square value (3.34) was not significant at the 0.05 level.

Apparently, long-term patients with paranoid features supplement the Impulsive Speaker adjustment by keeping their communications short. Possibly, long-term process schizophrenics (paranoid or nonparanoid) do the same. (There was no correlation between the process-reactive and paranoid-nonparanoid ratings in this long-term patient sample.) Finally, neither terseness nor verbosity conveyed any special communication accuracy advantage to the speakers in any of the schizophrenic subgroups.

Although the long-term patient data do not, in themselves, provide evidence of a perseverative tendency, I am nevertheless strongly inclined to favor the hypothesis that the same basic perseverative tendency—the inability to reject a sampled response effectively—underlies the speaker deficits in both early- and long-term schizophrenia. The difference between the two is that whereas early, acute patients attempt to compensate for the perseverative handicap via the chaining mechanism, long-term patients do not bother to try and, instead, are more prone to emit what they sample and let it go at that.

Looked at this way, chronic schizophrenia is a condition in which patients yield to the "pull" of referent stimuli, becoming progressively less responsive to contextual cues as determinants of thought, speech, and possibly perception. Perhaps, too, as a mean of adjusting on the basis of this limited mode of interpersonal communication, such patients seek or drift into simplified life settings (for example, many custodial institutions). These are settings in which the dominant response is appropriate for most of the referents that speakers might need to communicate and, hence, little or no self-editing is required. Such settings would seem to be well-suited to the cognitive skills of patients such as those Cromwell (5) has termed "high redundancy" schizophrenics. For a fuller discussion of this and other implications of the perseverative hypothesis for the psychopathology of referent-communication in early- and long-term schizophrenia, see Cohen (2).

REFERENCES

1. Brown R, Lenneberg EH: A study of language and cognition. *J Abn Social Psychol* 49:454–462, 1954.
2. Cohen BD: Referent communication disturbances in schizophrenia, in Schwartz S (ed): *Language and Cognition in Schizophrenia*. Philadelphia, Ehrlbaum Associates, in press.
3. Cohen BD, Camhi J: Schizophrenic performance in word-communication task. *J Abn Psychol* 72:240–246, 1967.
4. Cohen BD, Nachmani G, Rosenberg S: Referent communication disturbances in acute schizophrenia. *J Abn Psychol* 83:1–13, 1974.
5. Cromwell R: Strategies for studying schizophrenic behavior. *Psychopharmacologia* 24:121–146, 1972.
6. Glucksberg S, Krauss RM, Weisberg R: Referential communication in nursery school children: Method and some preliminary findings. *J Experimental Child Psychol* 3:333–342, 1966.
7. Kantorowitz D, Cohen BD: Referent communication in chronic schizophrenia, *J Abn Social Psychol* 86:1–9, 1977.
8. Krauss RM, Weinheimer S: The effect of referent array and communication mode on verbal encoding. *J Verbal Learning and Verbal Behav* 6:359–363, 1967.
9. Lantz De L, Stefflre V: Language and cognition revisited. *J Abn Social Psychol* 69:472–481, 1964.
10. Lorenz M: Problems posed by schizophrenic language. *Arch Gen Psychiat* 4:603–610, 1961.
11. Rosenberg S: The development of referential skills in children, in Schiefelbusch RL (ed): *Language of the Mentally Retarded*. Baltimore, University Park Press, 1972.
12. Rosenberg S, Cohen BD: Speakers' and listeners' processes in a word-communication task. *Science* 145:1201–1203, 1964.
13. Rosenberg S, Cohen BD: Referential processes of speakers and listeners. *Psychol Review* 73:208–231, 1966.
14. Salzinger K: *Schizophrenia: Behavioral Aspects,* New York, John Wiley & Sons, 1973.
15. Smith E: Associative and editing processes in schizophrenic communication. *J Abn Psychol* 75:182–186, 1970.
16. Triandis HC: Cognitive similarity and communication in a dyad. *Human Relations* 13:175–183, 1960.
17. Werner H, Kaplan B: *Symbol formation*. New York, John Wiley & Sons, 1963.

Chapter 32
Are Language Disorders in Acute Schizophrenia Actually Information-processing Problems?

S. R. Rochester, Ph.D.

In the past 7 years, my colleagues and I have studied the use of language by acute schizophrenic speakers and listeners. In this chapter, that work is summarized in a set of hypotheses about the nature of language disorder in acute schizophrenia.

PSYCHOLINGUISTIC HYPOTHESES

The psycholinguistic hypotheses may be characterized briefly as follows:

1. The acute schizophrenic speaker/listener is for the most part an adequate user of language.[1]
   a. As a listener, the schizophrenic subject uses syntax as a basis for information processing, just as normal listeners do.
   b. As a speaker, the schizophrenic subject forms syntactically adequate clauses and uses a lexicon that is generally familiar to native speakers of English.
2. When the schizophrenic speaker fails to communicate verbally, it is because she/he fails to account for the listener's immediate needs.
   a. The schizophrenic speaker sometimes fails to provide the listener with accurate information about which parts of the message are "new" and which parts have already been "given."

[1] These descriptions do not necessarily apply to chronic patients or other persons who have been removed from ordinary language use for long periods (e.g., persons who have lived as isolates or those who have been long-term patients in institutions).

I gratefully acknowledge the continued support of the Benevolent Foundation of Scottish Rite Freemasonry, Northern Jurisdiction, USA, and the Clarke Institute Associates' Research Fund.

    b. The schizophrenic speaker fails to provide as many cohesive links between clauses as normal speakers.

3. The schizophrenic speaker who shows clinical signs of thought-process disorder accommodates to the listener's immediate needs less than schizophrenic speakers who show no clear thought disorder.

These three hypotheses summarize the bulk of our findings with psycholinguistic variables. They form the basis for our more general hypotheses about language use by schizophrenic speakers and listeners. To understand the more general hypotheses, however, it is necessary to view the psycholinguistic data in more detail.

PSYCHOLINGUISTIC DATA

Hypothesis 1

Hypothesis 1 states that the acute schizophrenic speaker/listener tends to use language adequately for the most part.

Before the last decade, this statement would probably have been considered absurd. Virtually all the literature describing the schizophrenias and especially that focusing on language portrayed the schizophrenic speaker as essentially incompetent. Virtually all studies argued that schizophrenic subjects could not produce or perceive normal speech. However, with the efforts of Gerver (1) and Truscott (2), this trend began to reverse.

Gerver presented chronic schizophrenic listeners and controls with normal sentences (e.g.: Trains carry passengers across the country.), with sentences which were syntactically adequate but semantically anomalous (e.g.: Trains steal elephants around the highways.), and with random strings (e.g., on trains hive elephants simplify). Subjects listened to the sentences and repeated them aloud. Gerver found that although schizophrenic subjects recalled fewer words than control subjects did, both groups recalled normal sentences most accurately, and they recalled grammatical sentences better than random strings. Moreover, the rate of increase in recall for schizophrenic subjects across the three sentence types was at least as large as the control subjects' rate.

Truscott's (2) investigation, our own work (3), and Carpenter's (4) recent study support and extend Gerver's findings. It now seems clear that, although schizophrenic listeners tend to be less accurate than normal subjects in recalling sentences, the inferior performance is not due to an inability to use "the organization inherent in language" (5).

In addition to this relatively recent evidence about the linguistic abilities of listeners, there are some similar data for the schizophrenic speaker. Two sorts of studies are relevant here and both are rare. One is based on the argument that whatever language aberrations are seen in schizophrenia, are also seen in normal discourse (6). The other posits that the essential events of normal discourse also occur in the speech of schizophrenic subjects. This is difficult to demonstrate. If one finds no differences between schizophrenic and normal speakers on a linguistic variable, one cannot conclude that the groups are the same on that variable. As a result, failures to find differences are dismissed and investigators tend to report only those variables that discriminate schizophrenic from normal speakers. This trend is unfortunate because it is deceptive. It means that, in the literature at least, one has a picture of a schizophrenic speaker who is essentially different from a normal speaker. Our psycholinguistic analyses of schizophrenic and normal speakers suggest that the opposite is true.

Our studies suggest that schizophrenic speakers use the same procedures as normal speakers. While it is difficult to present this as a convincing argument in terms of speaker differences, it is possible to show these similarities in terms of effects on normal judges. In a recent study (7), we recorded unstructured interviews with 40 acute schizophrenic subjects and 20 normal controls. Three-minute samples from the interviews were transcribed and the transcriptions given to 10 lay judges. The judges were asked to act as editors, and to mark any clauses that seemed to disrupt the flow of the discourse. The fact that schizophrenic subjects were generally adequate speakers was shown in two ways. First, half the schizophrenic speakers were almost indistinguishable from the normal controls. These were schizophrenic subjects who showed no clear signs of thought disorder to our clinical judges. Second, even those schizophrenic subjects who were thought-disordered were understood by our lay judges: most (80%) thought-disordered speakers had less than 16% of the clauses in their discourse disrupted, and none had more than 30% disrupted.

These findings on schizophrenic speakers and the data on schizophrenic listeners support the hypothesis that the schizophrenic speaker/listener is able to produce and perceive normal language, for the most part. To the extent that this hypothesis is supported, it permits us to recognize the linguistic competence of the schizophrenic subject and to search beyond linguistic boundaries for the source of communication difficulties in schizophrenia.

Hypotheses 2 and 3

Hypotheses 2 and 3 state that the acute schizophrenic speaker fails to account for the listener's immediate needs. Hypothesis 2 suggests that this is true of schizophrenic as opposed to normal speakers, and Hypothesis 3 suggests that this is true of thought-disordered schizophrenic speakers as opposed to those who show no clinical signs of thought-disorder.

One way the speaker can fail the listener is to provide misleading cues about the location of referents. For example, if the speaker mentions *that old hat,* the listener expects to find more information about *that hat* elsewhere in the utterance context. The information may be in the immediate situation or in the listener's recent memory of the verbal context. If the referent is in fact recoverable, the speaker's guidance to the listener has been helpful. If the referent is nowhere to be found, the guidance has been misleading.

Helpful guidance would seem to be an art usually practiced by native speakers of English. However, acute schizophrenic speakers, especially those who are thought-disordered, seem to lack the art. Consider the following sample taken from the connected discourse of a thought-disordered speaker:

a. but what's to say there's nothing up in that ice age
b. the ice age that is yet to come supposedly this summer and this winter coming up
c. you could see quite a recession of them
d. and then they come on pretty strong

Each segment is rather well-formed in itself, but the text of the four segments is not fully coherent. The problem seems to be that segments (c) and (d) contain noun phrases

Table 32-1. Retrieval Categories for Definite Noun Phrases

Category	Location of Referent	Example[a]
Explicit referents		
Verbal	Explicit verbal context	A **donkey** was loaded with salt and *he* went to cross a river.
Situational	Explicit situational context	I am reading *this* now.
Implicit referents		
Bridging	Implicit verbal context	There's a **house** with two people standing in *the door*.
Unclear referents		
Addition	Not clear	A donkey was crossing *the other river*.
Ambiguous	Not clear	**A commuter** and **a skier** are on a ski lift and *he* looks completely unconcerned.

[a] The item in bold type is the *definite noun phrase;* items that are italicized are the referents.

(*them* and *they*) which require supplementary information to be understood. The noun phrases presuppose some referent, but, when we search for the referent, we can find no candidate that is obviously correct.

From 60–80% of all noun phrases used by normal speakers require referents to be understood. We examined all such noun phrases (which we termed "definite noun phrases") in speech samples from several contexts for normal and acute schizophrenic subjects (8). For each definite noun phrase, we had coders decide where the referent for that noun phrase was located. Table 32-1 shows the various categories of locations and gives examples of each category.

One finding is of particular interest here. First, unclear referents (seen in the example given previously) were virtually never used by normal speakers, but they were used by thought-disordered speakers quite often. For instance, in narratives, 2% of the normal speakers' noun phrases had unclear referents, whereas 19% of those from thought-disordered had unclear referents. This is a highly reliable finding. In addition, nonthought-disordered schizophrenic speakers used fewer unclear referents (12%) than did thought-disordered subjects. In other contexts, while there was no difference according to thought disorder, schizophrenic speakers again used more unclear referents than did normal speakers.

This result suggests an obvious failure on the part of schizophrenic—and especially thought-disordered—speakers. They fail to provide clear referents for noun phases that require referents and therefore pose a profound problem for the listener. They send the listener to search for information that does not exist.

AN INTERIM HYPOTHESIS AND ITS PROBLEMS

Results of the sort described in the previous sections led us to the following picture of the acute schizophrenic speaker/listener. This person uses language adequately for the most part. Occasionally, however, he fails to communicate, largely because the speaker fails to account for the listener's immediate needs. For example, the speaker may fail to provide referents when a referent has been promised or to facilitate transitions from clause to clause (9).

These results and others pointing to a neglect of the listener suggested an interpersonal failure. We hypothesized that the schizophrenic speaker must be ignoring or avoiding the listener, and that this interpersonal process was responsible for the communication problems we observed.

This explanation has been troublesome for several reasons. (a) It does not fit with the fact that the schizophrenic speaker engages in some interpersonal processes with little difficulty. For example, our subjects were able to pose questions, issue demands, answer queries, and carry out other social-role aspects of language in a fairly appropriate manner. (b) In our paralinguistic analyses (10), we found that schizophrenic speakers (and especially thought-disordered speakers) pause longer at clause boundaries than within clauses. This suggests problems with information-control processes, since clause boundaries seem to be critical points of integration for information flow. (c) Finally, in our earlier research on listeners (11), we found that nonsyntactic information processing severely limits the schizophrenic listener's ability to decode sentences. These findings led us to suspect that information-processing problems rather than interpersonal failure lay at the root of the schizophrenic's communication difficulties.

Recently, we have reevaluated our linguistic data in light of a model developed by Robin Fawcett (12,13). It depicts the actions and processes of a language user in terms of six functional subsystems. What is remarkable about these subsystems is that there is only one that is tailored to the immediate needs of the listener. The "Informational System," as Fawcett terms it, is the only component in which the speaker assesses the listener's state of ignorance (or knowledge) on a moment-to-moment basis. All other subsystems presume a more general audience in which the listener either is an ideal member of some language community or a particular person frozen in time.

The speaker using the informational network must determine the balance of information needed by the particular listener being addressed. To do this correctly, the speaker must estimate how much of the content of the sentence is already familiar to the listener. The speaker must discover whether a referent item or event (a) is already in the immediate physical context, (b) is in the prior verbal context of the discourse, or (c) is so well-known to the listener that it need not be described fully.

These decisions are precisely the ones that seem difficult for the schizophrenic speakers we have studied. And this is reasonable since the set of procedures involved is unusually demanding. These procedures not only require many decisions about a particular (and often newly-encountered) listener but, more importantly, demand continual accessing of short-term memory to evaluate the listener's needs. What the listener knows after clause n is different from what he/she knows after clause $n + 1$, so the speaker's presumptive model of the listener must be updated after every clause. This means that speakers must constantly check their short-term memory store to determine what they just said and what is presumably now known by their listeners.

Following Fawcett's model, therefore, we hypothesize:

4. The language subsystem used to account for a listener's immediate needs, the Informational System, demands unusually complex information processing from the speaker. The

complexity derives from the speaker's need to continually update and retrieve information from a short-term memory store.

and from our own investigations, we hypothesize:

5. The schizophrenic speaker, and especially the thought-disordered speaker, has difficulty with short-term encoding and/or retrieval operations, and consequently she/he has difficulty using the Informational System of the language.

We are hypothesizing that the schizophrenic speaker, and especially the thought-disordered speaker, fails to account for a listener's immediate needs because of short-term memory limitations. (Note again that this hypothesis is restricted to schizophrenic patients who have not been deprived of opportunities for ordinary discourse.)

AN ARGUMENT FOR SHORT-TERM MEMORY LIMITATIONS IN SCHIZOPHRENIC DISCOURSE

At a general level, we can offer an account of how short-term memory limitations might be responsible for the breakdown of discourse seen in the early stages of acute schizophrenia. The complexities of producing discourse require the coding and recoding of linguistic information. The selective distribution of attention is more or less critical for the operation of these processes, some processes requiring more attention than others. It is likely that some processes go on simultaneously with others under normal circumstances. For example, the use of syntax to determine the general form of an idea and the rapid accessing of previously processed information to connect with new information may represent processes that normally occur at about the same time. These processes depend not only on a knowledge of sentence syntax and word meanings but also on the "shifting of attention among various components, only some of which can occupy a limited capacity working memory at a given time" (14).

From our work to date, it appears that the most vulnerable of these several processing skills are those which require the rapid shifting of attention between prior clause (or the immediate situation) and the clause being produced. These are the skills that Maher (15) proposed as problematic in the schizophrenic speaker. And these are the skills involved in Fawcett's Informational Component, in which the speaker must determine the redundancy balance that is optimal to meet the listener's immediate needs. Skills that do not require this shifting, on the other hand, are probably less vulnerable to early disruption. For example, the syntactic structure of a clause and most lexical choices do not seem to require a rapid shifting of attention. Therefore, clausal syntax and most of the lexicon should remain intact in discourse until after the Informational Component begins to deteriorate. It should not be possible to find major syntactic disruptions or frequent inappropriate word choices without finding failures in referential cues and inappropriate cohesion.

We are not postulating that the *capacity* of the schizophrenic speaker's short-term memory is limited. Evidence for this is scanty and, taken overall, unconvincing (4,16,17). Rather, we find it more persuasive to argue that discourse failures of acute schizophrenics involve the manner in which their limited capacity memory system is used (14,18). The control functions that permit access to working memory are at issue here, rather than the capacity of short-term memory to hold lists of words or digits or random dot patterns.

SOME PREDICTIONS

To summarize this argument, it is tenable that limitations in the use of short-term memory are a major factor in the schizophrenic speaker's failure to account for the immediate needs of the listener. This hypothesis predicts some further disruptions of discourse that have not yet been studied systematically. One prediction concerns the distance between an item and its referent. Normally, we would expect that speakers maintain some constant lag between an item and its referent in the verbal context. The lag may be on the order of 2–3 independent clauses, and it may vary with situations and with the interpersonal relationship between speaker and listener. However, in a brief conversation, the lag should be small and approximately constant. For the schizophrenic, and especially the thought-disordered speaker, however, we would expect the lag to be broad and highly variable. If the speaker does not recall clearly how and when an item was referenced, he/she should confuse the listener by the use of widely divergent referencing distances.

A more general and more interesting prediction concerns the course of language breakdown that should occur in acute schizophrenia.[2] If it is true that discourse breakdown is not essentially linguistic but instead reflects more general information processing problems, then systems of language should break down in order of the complexity of the processing demands. What we are proposing is not a particular order of breakdown so much as the view that those functional aspects of language which demand the greatest attentional shifting will be the earliest to break down.

REFERENCES

1. Gerver D: Linguistic rules and the perception and recall of speech by schizophrenic patients. *British J Social Clin Psychol* 6:204–211, 1967.
2. Truscott IP: Contextual restraint and schizophrenic language. *J Consult Clinical Psychol* 35:189–194, 1970.
3. Rochester SR, Harris J, Seeman MV: Sentence processing in schizophrenic listeners. *J Abn Psychol* 82:350–356, 1973.
4. Carpenter MD: Sensitivity to syntactic structure: Good versus poor pre-morbid schizophrenics. *J Abn Psychol* 85,41–50, 1976.
5. Lawson JS, MacGhie A, Chapman J: Perception of speech in schizophrenia. *Brit J Psychiat* 110:375–380, 1964.
6. Fromkin VA: A linguist looks at "schizophrenic language." *Brain and Language* 2(4):498–503, 1975.
7. Rochester SR, Martin J, Thurston S: Thought process disorder in schizophrenia: The listener's task. *Brain and Language* 4:95–114, 1977.

[2] It may be accurate to discuss language breakdown in acute psychosis. Since there is evidence of "thought disorder" in serious depressive illness (19), severe mania (20), and in many organic syndromes, and since our results are most dramatic for thought-disordered speakers, it is possible that our findings are not unique to schizophrenia. To determine the specificity of our predictions, we will need to test a greater variety of patient groups.

8. Rochester SR, Martin J: The art of referring: The speaker's use of noun phrases to instruct the listener, in Freedle R (ed): *Discourse Comprehension and Production*, Vol 1. Norwood, NJ, Ablex Publishing Corp, 1977, pp 245–269.

9. Martin J, Rochester SR: Cohesion and reference in schizophrenic speech, in Makkai A, Makkai VB (eds): *The First LACUS Forum 1974*. Columbia, SC, Hornbeam Press, 1975, pp 302–311.

10. Rochester SR, Thurston S, Rupp J: Hesitations as clues to failures in coherence: Studies of the thought-disordered speaker, in Rosenberg S (ed): *Sentence Production: Developments in Research Theory*. Hillsdale, NJ, Erlbaum Associates, 1977, pp 65–88.

11. Rochester SR: The role of information processing in the sentence decoding of schizophrenic listeners. *J Nerv Ment Dis* 157(2):217, 1973.

12. Fawcett R: Generating sentence in systematic functional grammar. Paper presented at the meeting of the Linguistics Association of Great Britain, Sheffield, November 1972.

13. Fawcett R: Systematic functional grammar in a cognitive model of language. Paper presented at the meeting of the Linguistics Association of Great Britain, Sheffield, November, 1972.

14. Perfetti CA, Goldman SR: Discourse memory and reading comprehension skill. *J Verbal Learning and Verbal Behav* 14:33–42, 1976.

15. Maher B: The language of schizophrenia: A review and interpretation. *Brit J Psychiat* 120:3–17, 1972.

16. Koh SD, Kayton L, Schwarz C: The structure of word storage in the permanent memory on nonpsychotic schizophrenics. *J Consult Clin Psychol* 42(6):879–887, 1974.

17. Koh SD, Peterson RA: Perceptual memory for numerousness in "nonpsychotic schizophrenics." *J Abn Psychol* 83:215–226, 1974.

18. Perfetti CA, Hoagboam T: The relationship between single word decoding and reading comprehension skill. *J Educ Psychol* 67:461–469, 1975.

19. Ianzito BM, Cadoret RJ, Pugh DP: Thought disorder in depression. *Amer J Psychiat* 131(6):703–707, 1974.

20. Carlson GA, Goodwin FK: The stages of mania. *Arch Gen Psychiat* 28:221–228, 1973.

CONCLUDING COMMENTS: B. COHEN AND S. R. ROCHESTER

Bertram Cohen: Readers may find it useful to compare Rochester's hypotheses (and methods) with that presented in my paper in which a perseverative process is posited as basic to referent-communication disturbances in schizophrenia. Rochester's hypothesis makes contact with mine insofar as the inability to shift attention is related to perseveration. I share Rochester's preference for a model in which the schizophenic speaker's "interpersonal failure" is derived from a more basic information-processing deficit. However, it is possible that interpersonal variables act to magnify the dysfunctional effects on self-editing of the basic deficit; for example, anxiety induced by anticipation of a listener's hostility might further acutely impair the speaker's ability to shift attention flexibly enough to maintain adequate interpersonal communication.

Rochester's data were obtained from unstructured interviews, rather than from laboratory procedures in which the speaker's need to access working memory might be experimentally heightened. This may bear on the low frequency of disturbed speech in her data. Speakers who suffer from the hypothesized inability to shift attention fast enough to take full advantage of working memory may learn to control their own output in unstructured interviews or casual conversations. Perhaps, thought-disordered patients are those who have (as yet) been less successful in acquiring this form of defensive adaptation.

S. R. Rochester: Cohen's studies are among the few careful experimental studies of the schizophrenic speaker. My own investigations of speakers are not truly experimental, but rather phenomenologic. My colleagues and I attempt to describe the language characteristics of schizophrenic speech while Cohen and his co-investigators manipulate variables that may be critical to the schizophrenic speaker's decisions. These two approaches, the experimental and the phenomenologic, seem excellent complements to each other: the experimental work offers strong tests of particular questions, while the phenomenologic approach presents a broad perspective from which to view the range of language production problems in schizophrenia.

However, it seems important to challenge Cohen's formulations on the ground that they are not rich enough to account for all the data. He argues that the performance of an acute, short-term schizophrenic speaker is due to the operation of a perseverative process. In this process, the speaker repeatedly cycles back to inappropriate responses, or at best, she/he associates to inappropriate responses. This formulation, and its variants, is put forward to account for the schizophrenic speaker's problems in communicating. Specifically, Cohen attempts to account for the speaker's lack of "accuracy" in identifying referents for the listener. We observed that thought-disordered speakers use more noun phrases with referents that are unclear or ambiguous than do other schizophrenic speakers or normal subjects. It is difficult to see how a perseveration hypothesis could predict this difference.

Thought-disordered speakers paused longer than other schizophrenic speakers and normals at clause boundaries, but this increase in pause time did not result in more coherent discourse. Cohen infers that his data support a perseverative model: the schizophrenic subjects are actively editing their inappropriate responses, he argues, but with each edit, the response is resampled, and the speaker is unable to produce other responses.

This formulation seems to imply that long latencies should be followed by repetitions of a response, or, with the Perseverative-Chaining Model, by loosely connected chains of responses. We did not find this. Nor did we find any one-to-one relationship between clauses preceded by long pauses and incoherent clauses. It is plausible that an information control process was disturbed, so that access to the previous propositional content was delayed.

Although Cohen's formulations do not account for our data, our model is also very limited. After all, with our extensive linguistic analyses, we could only account for 38% of lay judges' discriminations of thought disorder. And, although we have proposed a model to predict the course of language breakdown in acute psychosis, we have not yet spelled out which systems will break down first and which later, nor have we tested these predictions. I think it is very important to keep our failures in mind, lest we forget that we are trying to build a model of the actual language user. From our failures, we may learn enough to build a psychologically viable model of the schizophrenic speaker, and this offers the truly exciting promise of a framework for integrating language data with information-processing theories and other models of the schizophrenic process.

Chapter 33
Attentional Processes in Verbal Behavior

Margaret Thaler Singer, Ph.D.

Although the literature on schizophrenia is filled with diverse and discrepant findings, two formulations about schizophrenics are widely accepted, namely, that schizophrenics tend to have communication disorders, and that they appear to have attentional problems. It is to the interface of these two domains of behavior that Dr. Lyman Wynne and I have directed much of our research over the years with families. We have explored how parents and their offspring share or fail to share foci of attention and meaning in conversations (2–31). To do so, we have developed a series of strategies for studying communication in various settings and in a series of communication tasks. Because of our long-standing interest in the attentional and communication problems of schizophrenics, we have studied in particular those features of the family context that we have hypothesized might be relevant to these issues.

ATTENTION AND COMMUNICATION

One of our assumptions has been that certain properties of verbal behavior are manifestations of attentional processes. When one person is conversing with another, his remarks reveal aspects of how his attentional processes are functioning. To select and arrange his words, he must properly deploy and guide his attention. He must attend to his inner thoughts, keep his listener in mind, handle outer stimuli, and plan ahead to his next remarks. That is, he must deploy his attention to search, select, formulate, and state his ideas. He must turn inwardly so he can recall, select, and reason about mental contents and past memories and adapt them to the situational demands as he sees them. However, he must not allow the irrelevant inner or outer stimuli to capture his attention. Thus, we assume that his verbal remarks constantly are derived from ongoing attentional processes.

His verbal statements are the products of his attending to both external stimulus requirements and to his inner associative processes and contents, typically in the setting of a transaction with another human being oriented to achieving shared foci of attention and meaning. In other words, the form (style) of his verbalizations reveal, albeit indirectly, certain properties of his attentional processes.

In turn, his verbal behavior has an impact on the attention and information processing within his listener. A speaker's remarks can make easy, if clearly presented, the
attending by his listener and facilitate the sharing of foci of attention and the sharing of
meaning between them (7–9,12–16,22–31). Elsewhere, we have addressed ourselves to
the issues of the impact of a speaker's deviances of communication and attention on a
listener (7–9,12–16). We conceptualize conversations as series of shared foci of attention
during which meanings are exchanged by the participants.

If the impact a speaker makes on a listener causes the listener to think that the
speaker is grossly violating a number of conversational rules, the speaker is judged
harshly by the listener. In fact, down through the ages the imputing of madness has
rested heavily on a listener concluding that a speaker's remarks were outside the bounds
of reason and the relevant rules of conversation. Many of these rules of conversation
carry the expectation that the listener should be able to attend in regular and predictable
ways to what is being said. When a speaker phrases his thoughts in ways that affront
such attentional expectancies, his remarks are experienced negatively and a listener,
even when he does not comment, is usually bothered or distressed.

Although there are many verbal and attentional behaviors that have been attributed
to various subgroups of schizophrenic persons, here it is possible only to select and to
comment on two major kinds of attentional difficulties frequently noted in the verbal
productions of schizophrenics. We are directing certain research efforts to the study of
these attentional problems as they affect conversations in which schizophrenic persons
participate.

There are two broad types of attentional problems, which we label attentional repetitions and attentional breaks, that can be detected in the verbal behavior of most
schizophrenics. While these features will be described separately to define and to
illustrate them, in any actual spoken passage most schizophrenic persons display both
kinds intermingled. However, certain other subgroups of schizophrenic persons appear
to exhibit more of one or the other kind. For ease of exposition, the two major kinds will
be discussed separately as attentional repetitions and attentional breaks.

ATTENTIONAL REPETITIONS

Attentional repetitions are those indications that a person seemingly is unable to move
on in his thinking for one of two reasons—his attention is blank and he is finding no
ideas, or he cannot drop an idea that has come into mind. In the first form of repetitions, the speaker's silence and behavior may suggest that his attentional search for ideas
has become hung-up, caught, somehow stuck; for the time being his mind is blank—
ideas are not possible. A stoppage has occurred. He attempts to attend to his associative
processes and yet indicates to his listener that his attention is "stuck on a blank period."
For example, the speaker may say, "I uh, I uh, I can't think of anything. Nothing
comes to mind. I just can't think of anything." His words reveal that he momentarily
feels that no ideas are possible for him. He cannot pursue an associative search. His
attention is stuck; a thought deprivation may have occurred.

The second form of the attentional repetition is one with content. The speaker cannot
drop an idea, a word, a phrase, a theme, and he repeatedly re-uses it in quick succession. The word, phrase, or idea will not fade. It captures or penetrates into attention,
and perseveratively is repeated. Either it captures and holds the person's attention, and

he blatantly restates a word or idea, or the notion seems to be simply penetrating or intruding into attention and is reappearing within a passage beyond the number of times that we normally expect to hear it.

A man viewing Rorschach Card IV said: "That looks like a boot. Well you *put your foot*, in here. *Your foot*, it fits in there, and it's ah through right that part. *Put your foot* through the top of the boot. You know, what I mean? Just like these boots I got on. *Put your foot* through the top of the boot, slide it in." Here we see the phrase and idea of "put your foot" continuing to intrude into the passage.

Such mental processes catch up the speaker's attention, and he is seemingly unable to let go of an idea. The notion hovers too long, reappears, or fails to fade away, and the passage thus takes on a reiterative quality. To some degree new thoughts may be possible and his attention moves on. However, there is a continual interspersing and reiteration of the old ideas, which should have faded or dropped away into the new ideas.

This theme-lag, or failure of an idea to fade, is involved in what Cromwell and Dokecki (1) termed the disattention phenomenon they noted in schizophrenics:

> It is proposed that an important dysfunction in schizophrenia is the inability to disattend from stimuli. Disattention is the adaptive ability of an organism to withdraw his attention from a stimulus after having attended to it. Much of the disorganization in schizophrenic behavior follows from attempts to deal with this disattention deficit. It is further proposed that this deficit has far-reaching effects on many of the symptoms that are manifested in schizophrenia. (p 249).

Thus, our formulation and that of Cromwell and Dokecki, both of which were independently derived from studying schizophrenic behavior from different data, have reached the same conclusions.

To summarize, I have noted two forms of attentional repetition: (a) attention that is arrested and the speaker has difficulty finding an idea, and (b) repetition when content is achieved but repeated, either blatantly or as a theme, and interspersed into subsequent thoughts and remarks. In the latter attentional problem, ideas fail to fade or drop out once they have gained a focus and centrality in attention.

ATTENTIONAL BREAKS IN VERBAL REMARKS

The second group of verbal episodes, breaks or jumps in content and context, occur when the speaker's words suggest to the listener that the speaker has jumped to another thought without connecting the old idea to what he is now saying. Sometimes it seems as if material has intruded into the speaker's awareness and captivates his attention momentarily; he says it aloud—material most persons learn not to express because it is distracting to listeners. This is one of the conversational rules most persons follow, keeping continuity for the listener paramount and not saying aloud irrelevant or distracting idiosyncratic associations. For whatever reasons, the speaker thus fails to label what has happened, to notify the listener about what he is doing and where his attention has gone. His remarks seem fragmented (21,22). The schizophrenic speaker may or may not return to the dropped idea. If he does, the return to the original topic may be as abrupt as was the departure from it. The impact upon the listener is to engender a sense of bewilderment because he has not been supplied with the connections for these remarks.

FAMILY COMMUNICATION AND ATTENTION

In one area of our research, Dr. Lyman Wynne and I are attempting to make inferences about attentional features that may be inferred from verbal transactions of schizophrenic persons engaging in conversational interchanges with a standardized starting point. We are developing a scoring system for attentional difficulties underlying schizophrenic communication and examining how these verbal measures correlate with laboratory measures of attention.

Further, these current efforts are an extension of our early formulations about what we have posited as the main transactional difficulties that we find in the families of schizophrenics:

> We find that communication in the families of schizophrenics is especially disturbed at the attentional level, whereas in the families of borderline, neurotic, and normal individuals, communication disorders are more prominent *later on after* an attentional focus has been shared by two or more persons. (12, p 147)

As one step in our present effort to trace the problems of schizophrenics in maintaining a shared focus of attention, we have been studying and comparing verbatim transcripts of the verbal productions of all the members of a series of families, those containing young adult schizophrenic offspring and those containing nonpsychotic offspring, comparing these families on the same procedures gathered in standardized fashion. We have been working to develop a manual that aids raters in detecting and classifying various attentional problems in these transcripts of verbatim conversations. We have begun to inspect these transcripts for the types of attentional problems that are seen in the blockings, the repetitions and the jumps in verbal remarks described earlier. We are asking where, when, and under what conditions in conversations do each of a variety of subgroups of attentional problems occur in any given schizophrenic.

Much of my research with Dr. Wynne has assessed various stylistic (formal) features of family communication, especially the comparison of families containing young adult schizophrenics. Also, in research on a series of monozygotic twins, some concordant and some discordant for schizophrenia, and some nonschizophrenic controls, we became interested in studying the attentional aspects of verbal behavior in these twins and their parents. We noted that certain of the psychologic tests given these persons were replete with instances in which a speaker's words suggested a transient inability to disattend, to move on in communication. On further inspection, this characteristic was evident across a number of verbal tasks (TAT, Rorschach, research interviews, and so forth). Further inspection of the verbatim typescripts of tape-recorded verbal transactions from all members of these families revealed that certain families contained several individuals who seemed to share certain attentional qualities. Various groups of families could be put together based on classifications used in our earlier work. Some of the patterns noted seemed related to our earlier concepts of amorphous and fragmented thinking (6,7,8,21,22). In that work we had described the attention of the amorphous schizophrenic as being poorly focused, the continuity of his communication as being impaired by blocking, gaps, laconic indefiniteness, and vagueness, all of which give the overall picture of "underinclusive" thought disorder. In contrast we noted that the fragmented schizophrenic was able to focus attention fairly clearly for brief moments, but that his communication was disrupted by inner and outer distractions, by bits and pieces of intermingled memories and current stimuli with the overall effect being that of the "overinclusive" thought disorder (6).

The attentional repetitions, or attentional perseveration, referred to earlier in this presentation can be illustrated in the following passage. The example shows how a schizophrenic's attention becomes "caught" so that "moving on" in a conversation is impeded. The verbatim speech sample occurred while viewing Card IV of the Rorschach. The italicized words indicate the "hanging on," perseveration, or the failure of an idea to fade.

Well, this looks like a couple of boots that are leaning up against a fireplace or something. Uh they've got little tassels *hanging down*. These things *hanging* down here. And very possibly it could be a Christmas stocking too, I guess, *hanging down, hanging* off of a, there's maybe the stockings *hanging down* waiting to be, looks like they're full of Christmas toys or candy or something. Let's see what else it could be. Well, uh, I don't know. I dunno, didn't see anything.

Later, the patient expressed the notion that he had "run out of ideas" *after* being caught up with the one idea.

His twin brother on Card X displayed a comparable attention defect:

Well, *this* appears to be *another, another head* here, *this* is *one head, this* is *another head, this* is *one, this's another head.*

On Card I of the Rorschach the mother of the twins said:

Could be grass or something growing *up*—growing *up* on a mountain side, straight *up*, or maybe *scrub, shrubbery*, you know, little *shrubs, shrubbery.*

On Card VIII she said:

Well, again, I see animals. It could be either ah uh, you know, reaching *up*, and also they could be squirrels or something which have been eating *up* the tree, *up* in a tree, some food they found *up* there.

Although the father in this family did not display the inability to let go of an idea, he did have what may be a related problem, namely, an extreme impoverishment of thought, as if he were unable to focus attention at all. Whereas his two sons and wife became stuck on one idea, he became stuck with no idea:

Card I: (After failing to get an idea of his own, said to the tester;) You're not ready to make any suggestion to me.

Card III: Well, that kind of sticks me there. I just don't seem to be able to tie that one at all. Sorry, that's about all on that one.

Card IV: Well, let's see. Afraid that's about all I can find there. (Said after not findihg any response for the blot.)

Card V: I couldn't make much sense of anything in particular.

Card VII: I dunno. It could be part of a fishing pole, but all the rest of it, I'm lost on.

Card VIII: Be astounded at the true answers of what they are, wouldn't we, hunh?

Card X: I'll have to pass this one, 'cause there ain't nothin' in there that I can see.

The following excerpt from a young female schizophrenic's Rorschach illustrates how her attention fragments and how a listener is left to find or to sort out connections between her ideas.

Card VI: And this looks like a part of the southeastern United States coast from side and side, with this being Florida and vaguely this, and the saying that goes: life in neither black nor white but different shades of grey—which are my sorority colors, excuse me, you know what I'd like to do sometime? Is take take all the charts and records and mail them off to a ghost author and get nine-tenths of the property. No I'll write myself. I want a book that might interest him.

Her nonschizophrenic twin sister shared this same kind of fitful attention, but despite breaks in communication, she does manage to persist with a theme:

Card X: That's ah, that's someone ridin' a horse. This is his feet hangin' down, I mean, I mean, this is the horse's tail hangin' down. This is the end of the horse. And that's one of the horse's legs. In other words, that ah more, more like, I mean uh from here on up's the horse's leg, but this is the—uh looks like, where it might be the end of the—whoever it is ah, well by whatchacall a-a stirrup or where you put your feet. And uh only I didn't see the rest of the horse's figger. And it could be hid from the trees. But this little part where it looks like that's up on the horse's back. And this is the end of the horse's body. And uh that's—be his leg down—but the other part of the horse is hid among the trees.

These brief illustrations from members of the same families are presented to indicate how we approach verbal behavior features in a series of families of schizophrenic young adults. It is not to be implied that simplistic counting of attentional blockings, perseverations, and breaks in communication are sufficient for the exploration or definition of the parameters of schizophrenia. Rather, we reason that since attentional problems are one of the central features in schizophrenics' behavior, we believe that their study in transactional communication deserves special consideration.

The foregoing examples, first, from the family members whose attention appeared to become caught and fixed, and last, from two sisters whose attention seemed replete with breaks, are samples of the verbal behaviors that we are attempting to classify and to study as part of our continuing exploration of attentional problems in schizophrenics. Our work is family-oriented, and we therefore study how all members of a family go about sharing or failing to share a focus of attention at the start of verbal interchanges with another person. If a shared focus of attention is achieved, we then attempt to study any problems between the participants that emerge in the maintenance of this shared focus.

In summary, the concepts of features which we have labeled as attentional blocking, repetition and perseveration, and as breaks and fragments, have much in common with the concepts of failure to disattend and the problems of segmental set which others, using different methods, have described. Work with families of schizophrenics permits the study and comparison of individual attentional and language styles within and across families. We have developed scoring criteria for classifying attentional qualities inferrable from verbal remarks made during research procedures given to family members as individuals, as couples, and as whole families. We continue to evaluate items that categorize forms of perseveration, reiteration of words, ideas, themes, and sets toward tasks. A companion set of items to classify attentional repetitions and breaks is being refined to see how reliably this can be applied to verbatim typescripts of communication across different research tasks. Thus, the interrelationships between attention and communication within an individual and within his family remain one of our central research interests.

REFERENCES

1. Cromwell RL, Dokecki PR: Schizophrenic language: A disattention interpretation, in Rosenberg S, Koplin JH (eds): *Developments in Applied Psycholinguistic Research.* New York, Macmillan, 1968, pp 209–261.

2. Loveland NT, Wynne LC, Singer MT: The family Rorschach: A method for studying family interaction. *Family Process* 2:187–215, 1963.

3. Morris GO, Wynne LC: Schizophrenic offspring and parental styles of communication: A predictive study using family therapy excerpts. *Psychiat* 28:19–44, 1965.

4. Singer MT, Wynne LC: Differentiating characteristics of the parents of childhood schizophrenics, childhood neurotics, and young adult schizophrenics. *Amer J Psychiat* 120:234–243, 1963.

5. Singer MT: A Rorschach view of the family, in Rosenthal D: *The Genain Quadruplets: A Case Study and Theoretical Analysis of Heredity and Environment in Schizophrenia.* New York, Basic Books, 1963.

6. Singer MT: *Stylistic variables in family research.* Paper presented at a symposium sponsored by Marquette University and Milwaukee Psychiatric Hospital, October 1964.

7. Singer MT, Wynne LC: Thought disorder and family relations of schizophrenics: III. Methodology using projective techniques. *Arch Gen Psychiat,* 12:187–200, 1965.

8. Singer MT, Wynne LC: Thought disorder and family relations of schizophrenics: IV. Results and implications. *Arch Gen Psychiat* 12:201–212, 1965.

9. Singer MT, Wynne LC: Principles for scoring communication defects and deviances in parents of schizophrenics: Rorschach and TAT scoring manuals. *Psychiatry* 29:260–288, 1966.

10. Singer MT, Wynne LC: Communication styles in parents of normals, neurotics and schizophrenics: some findings using a new Rorschach scoring manual. *American Psychiatric Association Research Report* 20:25–38, 1966.

11. Singer MT: The consensus Rorschach and family transactions. *J Proj Tech and Pers Assess* 32:348–351, 1968.

12. Singer MT: Family transactions and schizophrenia: I. recent research findings, in Romano J (ed): *The Origins of Schizophrenia,* Amsterdam, Excerpta Medica International Congress Series, No 151, 1967, pp 147–164.

13. Singer MT: *Scoring Manual for Communication Deviances Seen in Individually Administered Rorschachs.* Revision, 1973 (mimeographed, 100 pp).

14. Singer MT: The borderline diagnosis and psychological tests: review and research, in Hartocollis, P (ed): *Borderline Personality Disorders.* New York, International Universities Press, 1977.

15. Singer MT: The Rorschach as a transaction, in Rickers-Ovsiankina MA (ed): *Rorschach Psychology.* Huntington, New York, Krieger, 1977, pp 455–485.

16. Singer MT: Impact versus diagnosis: a new approach to assessment techniques in family research and therapy. *Family Process,* in press.

17. Wynne LC, Singer MT, Toohey ML: Communication of the adoptive parents of schizophrenics, in Jørstad J, Ugelstad E (eds): *Schizophrenia 75.* Oslo, Universitetsforlaget, 1975, pp 413–451.

18. Wild C, Singer MT, Rosman B, et al: Measuring disordered styles of thinking: Using the Object Sorting test on parents of schizophrenic patients. *Arch Gen Psychiat* 13:471–476, 1965.

19. Wynne LC, Ryckoff I, Day J, et al: Pseudomutuality in the family relations of schizophrenics. *Psychiat* 21:205, 1958.

20. Wynne LC: The study of intrafamilial alignments and splits in exploratory family therapy, in Ackerman N, Beatman FL, Sherman SN (eds): *Exploring the Base for Family Therapy.* New York, Family Service Association of America, 1961, pp 95–115.

21. Wynne LC, Singer MT: Thought disorder and family relations of schizophrenics: I. A research strategy. *Arch Gen Psychiat* 9:191–198, 1963.

22. Wynne LC, Singer MT: Thought disorder and family relations of schizophrenics: II. A classification of forms of thinking. *Arch Gen Psychiat* 9:199–206, 1963.

23. Wynne LC, Singer MT: The transcultural study of schizophrenics and their families. Proceedings of Joint Meeting of the American Psychiatric Association and the Japanese Society of Psychiatry and Neurology. *Folia Psychiatrica et Neurologica Japonica,* suppl 7, (May) 1963, pp 28–29.

24. Wynne LC, Singer MT: *Thinking disorders and family transactions.* Presented to Joint Meeting of the American Psychiatric Association and American Psychoanalytic Association, Los Angeles, California, May 4, 1964.

25. Wynne LC, Singer MT: *Schizophrenic impairment in sharing foci of attention: A conceptual basis for viewing schizophrenics and their families in research and therapy.* Presented as the Bertram H. Roberts' Memorial Lecture, Yale University, New Haven, Conn, 1966.

26. Wynne LC: Family transactions and schizophrenia: II. Conceptual considerations for a research strategy, in Romano J (ed): *The Origins of Schizophrenia.* Amsterdam, Excerpta Medica, 1967, pp 165–178.

27. Wynne LC: Methodologic and conceptual issues in the study of schizophrenics and their families. *J Psychiat Res 6* (suppl 1):185, 1968.

28. Wynne LC: Family research on the pathogenesis of schizophrenia: Intermediate variables in the study of families at high risk, in Doucet P, Laurin C (eds): *Problems of Psychosis.* Amsterdam, Excerpta Medica, 1971, pp 401–423.

29. Wynne LC: Communication disorders and the quest for relatedness in families of schizophrenics. *Am J Psychoanal* 30:100, 1971.

30. Wynne LC, Caudill M, Kasahara Y, et al: Translation problems in the cross-cultural study of psychopathology: a comparison of Japanese and American disorders of thinking and communication, unpublished.

31. Wynne LC, Singer MT, Bartko J, et al: Schizophrenics and their families: Research on parental communication, in Tanner JM (ed): *Developments in Psychiatric Research.* London, Hodden & Stoughton, 1977, pp 254–286.

Section VIII

ATTENTIONAL PROCESSES IN VULNERABILITY TO SCHIZOPHRENIA

Chapter 34
An Attentional Assessment of Foster Children at Risk for Schizophrenia

R. F. Asarnow, Ph.D.
R. A. Steffy, Ph.D.
D. J. MacCrimmon, M.D.
J. M. Cleghorn, M.D.

Attentional dysfunction has long been considered a prominent characteristic of schizophrenia. Kraepelin (17) maintained that "impaired attention" is a major symptom of schizophrenia. Bleuler (3) described two types of attentional disturbances found in schizophrenics. Some schizophrenics were described as pathologically over-emphasizing their sense impressions, while others were described as ignoring the outside world completely.

More recently the construct of attentional deficit has been used in an attempt to integrate findings of impaired performance obtained from the assessment of schizophrenic patients on a wide variety of laboratory tasks. Lang and Buss (19), Venables (37), and Silverman (34) have attempted to integrate diverse findings of impaired schizophrenic performance by characterizing these impairments as instances of attentional deficit. There are problems with the construct of attentional deficit, for example, the term attention itself is a label covering a broad variety of functions (25,26). Nonetheless, it seems to be the case that tasks with attentional demands seem to be particularly sensitive to schizophrenic pathologic states.

Grant support for this project was provided by an Ontario Mental Health Foundation grant (No. 387) to Cleghorn and MacCrimmon, an Ontario Mental Health Foundation grant (No. 512-74B) to Asarnow and MacCrimmon, a University of Waterloo research grant to Asarnow, and an Ontario Mental Health Foundation grant (No. 408-72D) to Steffy.
The authors acknowledge the assistance of Marnie Griffin in the collection of data and of Linda Siegel in the design of the Concept Attainment Task employed in this study.

While work with adult schizophrenics has suggested the importance of attentional dysfunction in terms of both clinical symptoms and impaired performance, very little is known about attentional functioning in the prodromal or premorbid state. Some indirect evidence is available, however, to suggest premorbid attentional problems. For example, using data from child guidance clinic files, Ricks and Berry (32) report that a substantial number of adult schizophrenics show a poor attention span during adolescence.

The experimental literature on attentional functioning in children at risk for schizophrenia [see Garmezy (10,11) for a review of background and current status of high-risk research] also provides some evidence to suggest the presence of attentional dysfunction in a risk population even though only a small portion (10–15%) are expected to acquire a diagnosis of schizophrenia in adulthood. Grunebaum, Weiss, Gallant, and Cohler (13) have reported that children of psychotic mothers, particularly those of schizophrenic mothers, made significantly more errors of commission on the Continuous Performance Test, an attention demanding task, than did children of control mothers. Marcus (21) has found that the offspring of schizophrenic women have slow reaction times. Pursuing these leads, which suggest that children of schizophrenic mothers are handicapped in their performance on attention demanding tasks, the present study surveyed the performances of offspring of schizophrenic mothers, as compared with a foster and a community control group, on a battery of eight attention-demanding tasks. The tasks were chosen to sample a variety of the processes subsumed under the rubric of attention [see discussion by Zubin (41) regarding different attentional processes assessed in the schizophrenia literature]. Special emphasis was given to choosing tasks known to be sensitive discriminators of adult schizophrenic pathologic states. In effect, we were attempting to determine whether processes observed in adult schizophrenic patients can be detected in children at risk for schizophrenia.

Our interest in determining if children at risk for schizophrenia show the same kind of attentional impairment as adult schizophrenics was inspired by the possibility that the impaired performance of hospitalized schizophrenics might reflect the social and medical consequences of the disorder (the effects of institutionalization, medication, stigmatization, the sick role, and so forth) rather than the direct behavioral manifestations of the disorder. For example, Mednick and McNeil (23) have argued that certain perceptual anomalies observed in hospitalized schizophrenics may be caused by institutionalization per se rather than by schizophrenia. The remedy they proposed for this confounding of the social and medical consequences of schizophrenia with the direct behavioral manifestations of the disorder is to study individuals prior to the onset of clinical symptoms who are at heightened risk to become schizophrenic. Presumably measures that differentiate high-risk from control groups would not be influenced by the aforementioned nuisance variables. Thus in the present study, if measures known to be sensitive to adult schizophrenic pathologic states were to prove successful in detecting individuals at risk for schizophrenia, this would suggest that those measures are tapping processes central to schizophrenia and not epiphenomena.

Tasks selected for inclusion in the battery generally met the following criteria: (a) Cross-sectional research with frankly schizophrenic adult subjects had demonstrated the sensitivity of the task to schizophrenic pathology. (b) The task was suitable for work with adolescents between the ages of 15 and 18. (c) The task could be administered in a standardized fashion, provided objective observation, and had generally good psychometric properties.

Two specific questions guided the design and analyses in the present study: Can children at risk for schizophrenia be differentiated from other children on the basis of deficient attentional functioning? Within the high-risk group, is there a subset of children who are characterized by a similar performance pattern on the attention-demanding tasks?

To answer the first question, the attentional functioning of a group of foster children whose biologic mothers were schizophrenic (the high-risk group) were compared with a group of foster children without a family history of psychopathology (the foster control group) and a group of children living with their biologic parents, none of whom have a history of psychiatric disorder (the community control group). A high-risk foster population was chosen to test children who were not currently suffering from the unstabilizing influences of severe psychopathologic states in their homes. Although these children had lived for considerable periods of time (approximately 7 years) with their biologic parents, on the average, they had spent the last 8 years of their lives in foster homes. Since the fostering experience might be expected to have had a detrimental influence on the psychologic well-being of these children, a matched foster control group was included. A community control group was used to assess the effects of foster placements and to provide normative data.

The second question arose because a risk marker of maternal history of schizophrenia leads one to expect only about 10–15% of the children in the study to become schizophrenic as adults (33). In effect, when comparing the high-risk group with the control groups, it is this small subset of children within the high-risk group who are expected to move the group means in such a way as to differentiate the high-risk group from the control groups. This is a problematic enterprise given (a) the relatively small number of these children and (b) the fact that variations in the attentional functioning of these children may be relatively subtle. In the present study, multivariate statistical procedures were used that allowed the classification of children on the basis of commonalities in their attentional functioning. If 10–15% of children at high-risk are expected to acquire a diagnosis of schizophrenia later in life, and if attentional dysfunction is present in the premorbid state, one might hope to detect a subset of the high-risk children who are especially vulnerable on the basis of poor performance across a number of attentional demanding tasks. Obviously, for an attentionally defined subset to be definitively considered as showing a special vulnerability, follow-up data will be required.

METHODOLOGY

Subject Selection

Foster child placement agencies in southern Ontario were contacted and their cooperation solicited to compose a list of foster children between the ages of 12 and 18 and to identify the biologic mothers of these foster children. A list of 892 mothers was generated. This list was cross-checked with a central psychiatric registry which yielded a list of 161 mothers with a history of psychiatric hospitalization. Next, the list of 161 biologic mothers was cross-checked with the case files of psychiatric hospitals in southern Ontario. It was determined that 65 of these women had a hospital discharge diagnosis of schizophrenia. A maternal history of schizophrenia was used as the risk marker rather than paternal history because previous experience suggested that maternity could be more reliably established than could paternity (22). The case histories of these 65 mothers were then reviewed independently by two psychiatrists to confirm the adequacy of the mother's discharge diagnosis. The criteria used to assess the adequacy of diagnosis were (a) continuity of illness—continuous hospitalization for at least 1 year or at least three separate admissions, and (b) evidence of formal thought disorder, flattened affect, lack of volition, and psychomotor disorder. Presence of only delusions and/or hallucinations was not accepted as sufficient evidence of schizophrenia. Only cases in which the two raters reached independent agreement were accepted for inclusion in the study. A total of 28 women with 33 children received a project diagnosis of schizophrenia. The foster parents of the children were then contacted and their cooperation was sought in making their foster child available for testing. This yielded a total of 10 subjects. Of the 25 subjects who were not tested, 4 refused to cooperate, 14 could not be tracked down, 2 were institutionalized in mental retardation units, 2 were institutionalized in psychiatric facilities, and 3 were reported by the foster agencies to be showing evidence of behavior problems.

The 10 children in the foster control group were identified by selecting cases from foster agency files and yoking them to the index subjects on the following criteria: sex, age (plus or minus 6 months), race, religion, and age at placement. The names of the biologic parents of these control cases were submitted to a central psychiatric registry, where search of the records for all Ontario hospitals was made. Report of hospitalization for either biologic parent led to rejection of the control case. One foster control case was selected as a yoked control for each index case. The second group of control subjects, the community control group, was constituted to control for the effects of foster placement. School authorities were contacted and asked to identify a list of students between the ages of 12 and 16 who were doing average work in school and who were regarded by teachers as well adjusted. Subjects were then selected from this school setting in such a way as to make the community control group comparable to the high-risk and foster control groups in terms of age, sex, and year in school. Ten adolescents were included in this group.

No children with a history of perinatal difficulties or a central nervous system disorder were included in the study.

Subject Characteristics

Table 34-1 shows the means and standard deviations for the high-risk, foster, and community control groups for age, sex, school grade, age at placement, and the number of foster placements. Group means were analyzed using simple analysis of variance. The results of that analysis revealed that the groups were comparable in age, sex, and school grade. The high-risk and foster control groups were comparable in the age of separation from biologic parents and in number of foster placements.

The Tasks

As indicated, the purpose of this study was to identify patterns of attentional functioning characteristic of children at risk for schizophrenia. To accomplish this, a battery of attention demanding tasks was composed. The measures selected met the criteria discussed in the preceding section. The individual tests are listed and described below.

Table 34-1. Characteristics of High-risk and Foster and Community Control Groups

Variables	High-risk	Foster Control	Community Control	Chi Square or F Values[a]
Age at testing				
Mean	16.11	16.10	15.40	
SD	1.61	1.66	1.26	0.69
Sex				
Mean	1.55	1.60	1.60	
SD	0.52	0.51	0.51	0.02
School grade				
Mean	8.77	10.00	9.70	
SD	1.20	1.94	1.56	1.50
Age at placement				
Mean	8.88	8.20		
SD	2.93	4.91		0.42
Number of placements				
Mean	2.44	2.10		
SD	1.23	1.37		0.48

[a] Chi square for Sex differences, F for the other variables.

Competing Voices

This is a dichotic listening task developed by Rappaport (30) in which a target message of random digits is presented sterophonically while distractor messages of random digits are coincidentally presented monaurally. The subject's task was to hear and to write the stereo message while ignoring the distracting messages. The extent of distraction was systematically manipulated by increasing the number of irrelevant messages (0, 4, 6, or 12). The subject's score was the total number of errors under the four conditions of information load studied. Rappaport (30) has reported this task to be sensitive to the pathologic state of attention found in schizophrenic subjects, and he has regarded deficits on the competing voices task to result from dysfunction of the selective attention system.

Concept Attainment Task

The concept attainment task used in this study is a modification of the Walker and Bourne (39) procedure. The subjects were instructed to sort cards into one of two categories based on criteria known, initially, only to the experimenter. Subjects were informed when they sorted incorrectly. The number of irrelevant stimulus dimensions present in the cards to be sorted was manipulated requiring subjects to focus on the relevant dimensions and disregard the irrelevant dimensions. The subject's score consisted of the number of incorrect sorts for each of four sets of cards. Adinolfi and Barocas (1) and Payne (29) have found schizophrenics to perform in an impaired manner relative to normal control subjects on this type of task, and they have attributed the deficient concept attainment performance of some schizophrenics to a failure of selective attention, particularly the ability to ignore irrelevant stimulus dimensions.

Continuous Performance Test (CPT)

This test requires subjects to monitor a visual display in which digits are presented tachistoscopically for 80 milliseconds with 1100-millisecond interstimulus intervals. Subjects were instructed to press a telegraph key each time a critical stimulus (the digit 7) appeared and only when the critical stimulus appeared. The critical stimulus appeared randomly on 20% of the trials. Two scores were computed for each subject on this task: the number of errors of omission (the number of times the subject fails to press when the critical stimulus was present) and the number of errors of commission (the number of times the subject pressed when the critical stimulus was not present). Kornetsky and his group (15,16, 28) have used this task in conjunction with the DSST to study attentional dysfunction in schizophrenic adults.

Digit Symbol Substitution Test (DSST)

This test is one of the subtests of the WAIS intelligence test. The DSST is a time-limited task that requires subjects to match geometric forms to digits. The number of items completed in 90 seconds is the score for this task. Mednick (22) and Landau et al (18) have found the DSST useful in identifying groups of children at risk for schizophrenia.

Simple Reaction Time

This procedure requires subjects to respond (typically finger retraction from a button) "as fast as possible" to a signal. A preliminary "ready" signal indicates the individual trial onset. In our study the subject was required to respond to an auditory imperative signal that was presented 1 to 10 seconds after the start of each trial. Trials varied in predictability of the intersignal delay, the so-called preparatory interval. Latency scores were averaged to represent performance differences resulting from variations in these temporal parameters. An extensive literature over four decades has found that variations in the length and certainty of the time interval between the two signals have produced variations in performance in schizophrenic samples quite distinctive from control groups (2,5,35).

Span of Apprehension

This task requires subjects to report the presence of a tachistoscopically presented target stimulus (the letters T or F). The complexity of the stimulus array in which the target stimuli is embedded was manipulated by systematically increasing the number of nonrelevant stimuli (0, 2, 4, or 9 extra letters). Subjects receive four scores in this paradigm, consisting of the number of correct detections of the target stimuli under each of the four conditions of array complexity studied. Neale and his coworkers (27) have demonstrated the span of apprehension to be sensitive to schizophrenic pathologic state.

Spokes Test

This is a modification of one of the subtests of the Halstead-Reitan battery, the Trailmaking Test (31). Subjects were required to connect either numbers or letters and numbers from a point or origin in sequence. The total time required to connect the numbers in alternation or letters and numbers in alternation, provided the scores for this task. Each time the subject made an error, he was instructed by the experimenter to start again.

Stroop Color-Word Test

This test requires subjects selectively to attend and to report the names of color words that are encumbered by colored ink that is incongruent with the meaning of the word, for example, the word "red" printed in blue ink. Subjects were trained to report colors and names in preliminary phases of the test and then were required to handle the competing situation by attending to only the relevant stimulus dimension. The time required to read without error the colors or names of colors provided the score for each subject. Wagner and Krus (38) have reported this task was effective in discriminating schizophrenics from normal subjects.

Testing Procedure

The children were tested in the offices of the foster agency which had jurisdiction over them. This was done because the children had experience going to these offices and would not likely be unduly alarmed by being asked to appear at these offices. The interviewing and testing took a complete day including time for lunch. Children in the community control group were tested at their high school.

On arrival at the testing site, the child was met by a research assistant who would be that child's tester for the day. After the purpose of the study was explained to the child, and his consent to participate in the study obtained, a fact sheet of biographic information was completed. The research assistant then introduced the child to a psychiatrist, who was blind to which children were in the high-risk group, and who conducted a standardized psychiatric interview using the format developed by Spitzer, Endicott, Fleiss and Cohen (36), the Psychiatric Status Schedule. The research assistant then instructed the child how to complete the MMPI. Preliminary review of the Psychiatric Status Schedule data indicated that none of the children were showing the classical symptoms of schizophrenia. A more extensive report of the results of the clinical findings will be presented in another paper. After a rest period, testing on the McMaster-Waterloo attentional test battery commenced. After three tests, subjects were taken to lunch. The balance of testing was completed after lunch. Three orders of administration of the tests were employed. Preliminary analysis of the data revealed no effect of order of administration.

RESULTS

The first question to which this study addressed itself was whether the high-risk group could be differentiated from the control groups on the basis of deficient attentional performance. To answer this question, the performance of the three groups of children on the eight attention-demanding tasks was compared using a simple analysis of variance. Table 34-2 presents the means, standard deviations, and F values for the high-risk, foster, and community control groups on the 25 subscores yielded by the eight attention-demanding tasks in the test battery. The second column ("score") of Table 34-2 indicates the nature of the dependent variable used in a particular task. In the third column ("variable"), the various conditions within a task are reported. Examination of Table 34-2 reveals a general tendency across tasks for the high-risk group to perform less adequately than did the foster control group who, in turn, performed less adequately than did the community control group. There was also a tendency for increased variability to occur within the high-risk group on the tasks that best discriminated the high-risk group from the two control groups. As seen in Table 34-2, the measures that best differentiated the high-risk group from the two control groups were (a) the Spokes Test, particularly the more complex version of that task, Spokes B; (b) the complex stimulus array condition, (seven elements) of the Span of Apprehension; and (c) the

Table 34-2. Attentional Performance of High-risk and Foster and Community Control Groups

Task	Score	Variable		High-risk		Foster Control		Community Control		F Value
				Mean	SD	Mean	SD	Mean	SD	
Competing Voices	Number of errors	Number of voices:	1	0.25	0.50	0.68	1.59	0.08	0.24	0.98
			3	8.56	11.37	3.90	1.81	3.50	2.51	1.71
			7	12.39	9.97	8.45	2.61	6.60	1.37	2.43[a]
			13	8.28	7.83	7.05	3.61	5.20	2.75	0.88
Concept Attainment	Errors to criterion	Number of stimulus dimensions:	3	3.44	1.33	2.40	1.43	1.70	0.68	5.26[c]
			4	3.00	0.87	2.40	1.08	1.70	0.68	5.18[c]
			5	6.89	2.93	3.80	2.49	5.20	1.40	4.22[b]
			6	9.11	3.89	8.10	3.00	6.50	1.43	1.97
Continuous Performance Test	Number of errors of commission and omission	Errors of commission		1.33	3.64	2.40	4.88	1.50	1.90	0.24
		Errors of omission		2.22	3.53	1.70	1.83	1.10	1.10	0.56
Digit Symbol Substitution Test	Number completed	DSST		47.00	9.18	49.50	12.83	56.30	8.29	2.09
Simple Reaction Time	Latency difference (in msec.) between	Preparatory interval:	1	945.22	56.77	936.32	38.77	957.59	26.38	0.65
			4	994.62	65.09	979.26	12.46	986.62	40.33	0.29

Measure									
irregular and regular trials at preparatory interval of 1, 4, and 7 secs. (−1000 added to difference)		7	1014.03	38.53	1003.89	39.32	991.65	46.05	0.69
Latency (msec.)			316.11	107.13	287.53	64.01	280.84	39.56	0.60
Span of Apprehension	Number of correct detections	Series of 15 irregular trials							
		Number of elements in array: 1	39.00	2.00	39.70	0.48	40.00	0.00	1.88
		3	38.78	1.20	39.20	1.03	39.20	0.92	0.50
		5	35.44	2.83	37.10	2.28	37.90	2.03	2.58[a]
		10	30.00	4.00	32.70	3.13	34.80	2.62	5.28[c]
Spokes Test	Total Time (secs.)	Spokes A	40.13	12.83	35.10	8.69	29.56	7.92	2.70[a]
		Spokes B	91.53	32.60	58.32	21.81	49.71	9.05	9.05[c]
Stroop Test	Total time (secs.)	Read color words	6.59	1.38	7.14	2.47	6.48	1.57	0.32
		Name colors	8.77	2.00	8.91	1.79	7.66	1.14	1.60
		Read color words (interference condition)	7.61	2.38	8.03	11.30	7.62	1.43	0.15
		Name colors (interference condition—4 trials)	68.01	11.37	63.43	14.36	59.85	10.38	1.10

[a] = $p < 0.10$.
[b] = $p < 0.05$.
[c] = $p < 0.01$.

Concept Attainment task, particularly the three least difficult conditions. Considering each of these differences in greater detail with post hoc comparisons of pairs of scores obtained from the Neuman-Keuls Test, the following pattern of results was observed.

On the Span of Apprehension, the high-risk group was comparable to the foster control and community control groups on the simple stimulus arrays. However, the high-risk group showed a much more rapid decrement in their accuracy of detection of the critical stimulus as the number of elements in which the critical stimulus was embedded was increased. On the most complex stimulus array (Span 10), the high-risk group made significantly fewer detections than did the foster control ($p < 0.05$) and the community control ($p < 0.05$) groups.

On all but the most complex version of the Concept Attainment task, the high-risk group made significantly more errors to criteria than the community control (CA 3 $p < 0.05$, CA 4 $p < 0.10$, CA 5 $p < 0.05$) group did. The high-risk group made significantly more errors than the foster control group on the second most simple condition of the Concept Attainment Task (CA 4 $p < 0.05$).

On the Spokes Test, the high-risk group took significantly longer to complete the maze on the complex version of the Spokes than did the foster control ($p < 0.01$) and community control ($p < 0.01$) groups. The differences were only marginally significant on the simple version of the Spokes Test.

The Competing Voices task yielded marginally significant differences. On the condition in which 7 voices were presented, the high-risk group tended to make more errors than the foster control ($p < 0.10$) and community control ($p < 0.10$) groups did. There were no differences among the three groups on the trials when 1, 3, and 13 voices were presented. It may be noted that the 1- and 13-voice conditions ordinarily yield fewer errors (20) and are thereby the simpler levels on this test.

The high-risk group was comparable to the other two groups of subjects on the Continuous Performance Test and the Stroop Test. On the DSST the high-risk group did not significantly differ from the foster control group but tended to complete fewer items than did the community control group.

On the crossover indices derived from the Simple Reaction time task, there was a tendency for the high-risk group to show redundancy-associated impairment (a slower reaction time on regular trials relative to irregular trials with the same preparatory interval at the longest preparatory interval of 7 seconds (2). On a series of 15 random preliminary trials, the high-risk group tended to have a slower average latency than did the foster and community control groups. The inflated variance in the high-risk group for this index ($SD = 107.13$) was due to a few markedly deviant subjects who had very slow latencies on this task.

To summarize the findings, the high-risk group took longer to complete the complex version of the Spokes Test and made more errors on the simple conditions of the Concept Attainment task. On the Span of Apprehension task the high-risk group showed a greater decrement in the accuracy with which they could detect a critical stimulus as the complexity of the stimulus array in which the target stimulus was embedded was increased. Their ability to detect the target voice in the Competing Voices task also tended to be differentially impaired by the addition of irrelevant voices.

These findings leave open the question as to whether a particular subgroup of poorly performing high-risk subjects were causing the differences or whether different combinations of subjects within the high-risk group accounted for the group differences depending on the particular measures. It was considered important to determine if a subset of subjects in the high-risk group produced differences across the tasks that differentiated the high-risk from foster and community control groups, or whether different subjects within the high-risk group performed in an extreme, deficient manner on different tasks. If the latter was true (i.e., different subjects performed poorly on different tests), all that could be concluded was that on some attention-demanding tasks the high-risk group was impaired when compared with the foster and community control groups, and that different subjects showed impairment on different tasks. It would then follow that any characterization of the performance "profile" of the high-risk group generated by merely summarizing the tasks on which the high-risk group performed in a deficient manner as compared with the control groups would probably not be representative of the profiles of the individual subjects in the high-risk group. On the other hand, if a subset of subjects produced most of the differences across the tasks that differentiated the high-risk group from the other groups, the identification and characterization of that subset of subjects is of interest rather than the overall group profile.

Consequently the second formal question asked of this data set was whether a subset of children within the high-risk group were impaired on the most discriminating tasks or were different children within the high-risk group impaired on different tasks? One way to answer this question was to examine the intercorrelations between the measures. Because of the small number of subjects, correlations were not computed separately for each group of subjects. High intercorrelations between the measures would indicate that subjects were consistent in their performance across tasks. A high correlation was observed between subjects' scores on the Spokes B and most complex condition of the Span of Apprehension ($r = -0.61$). However, the correlation between the subject's scores on the most discriminating condition of the Concept Attainment task and their scores on the Spokes B test ($r = +0.27$) and the correlations between the subject's scores on the most discriminating condition of the Concept Attainment task and their scores on the most complex condition of the Span of Apprehension ($r = -0.14$) were substantially lower. It thus seems to be the case that subjects' scores were relatively comparable across the complex version of the Span of Apprehension task and the complex version of the Spokes Test, but that different subjects were contributing to impaired performance on the Concept Attainment task.

Another way to view the question as to whether or not the same children are contributing to differences across tasks is by identifying the subjects who scored in the bottom third on the three most discriminating tasks. On the complex versions of the Span of Apprehension and Spokes Test, seven high-risk children had scores in the bottom third (10 worst scores) on *both* tasks. Five of these seven high-risk children scored in the bottom third on the Concept Attainment task. Thus it appears there is a subset of high-risk children who are performing in a deviant fashion across the tasks that differentiate the high-risk from the foster and the community control groups.

To corroborate these impressions, a cluster analysis was used to detect whether there were subsets of children within the high-risk group who were identifiable on the basis of common patterns of performance *across* all tasks in the attentional battery. To use a cluster analysis, the ratio of variables to subjects had to be reduced. This was accomplished by factor analyzing the 25 scores generated by the eight attention-demanding tasks using the PA-1 factor analysis program in the SPSS package. Again because of the small number of subjects, the factor analyses were not computed separately for each subject group. A varimax rotation of the axes was performed. It was found that five factors accounted for 79% of the variance within the matrix. Factor scores on these five factors were computed for each subject. The five factor scores for each subject were then sub-jected to a hierarchical cluster analysis technique developed by Howard and Harris (14). Cluster analysis is a multivariate procedure that classifies subjects on the basis of com-monalities along specified dimensions. The Howard-Harris cluster program forms groups of subjects using an object by variables matrix as the data set. The program requires a minimum within group variance at each level of clustering (12). In the present case, clusters of subjects generated by the Howard-Harris program at each level of clustering would show minimal within cluster variance and maximal between cluster variance. The subject clusters so generated are in effect empirically derived typologies of subjects classified on the basis of commonalities in attentional functioning. Hierarchical cluster analysis as opposed to other forms of cluster analysis classifies *all* subjects at each level of resolution. Table 34-3 shows the distribution of subjects classified into a four-cluster resolution on the basis of commonalities in their attentional performance, inde-pendent of group classification, case record, personality or psychiatric assessment, and other information. Inspection of Table 34-3 reveals that one cluster, III, consists of but one subject, a member of the original high-risk group. Cluster IV consists of four high-risk children and one foster control child. Cluster I consists of one high risk child, three foster control children and nine community control children. Cluster II consists of three high-risk children, five foster control children, and one community control child. A chi-square conducted on the frequency distribution in Table 34-3 confirms the impression that different patterns of attentional performance are associated with the three groups (χ^2 = 17.03, df = 3, p < 0.009). In summary, patterns of attentional performance (represented by clusters III and IV) were observed that occur predominantly in the high-risk group and account for five of those nine children.

Table 34-4 presents the means, standard deviations, and F values for the attentional performance on the eight attention-demanding tasks for the four clusters of attentionally defined subjects. Since cluster III consisted of only one child, the simple analyses of variance were conducted on comparisons between clusters I, II, and IV. As before, com-parisons between pairs of groups were made with the Neuman-Keuls Test. Across all tasks which differentiated clusters I, II, and III, subjects in cluster I performed in a superior fashion. By contrast, the cluster of one high-risk child, cluster III, showed impaired performance across all tasks.

The most interesting subgroup was cluster IV, comprised of four high-risk and one foster control child. This subgroup showed significantly impaired performance relative to clusters I (Span 5 p < 0.05, Span 10 p < 0.01) and II (Span 5 p < 0.05, Span 10 p < 0.05) on the complex versions of the Span of Apprehension task and complex version of the Spokes Test (p < 0.01 for both comparisons). In addition, they were significantly

Table 34-3. Distribution of Four Attentional Clusters Across the High-risk and Foster and Community Control Groups

	Cluster			
Group	I	II	III	IV
High-risk	1	3	1	4
Foster control	4	5	0	1
Community control	9	1	0	0

impaired relative to cluster I (p < 0.05) on the condition in the Competing Voices task in which seven voices were presented. Subjects in this cluster performed quite well on the Continuous Performance Test, the average reaction time to a random series of trials, and the simple versions of the Span of Apprehension task. Across a number of tasks, subjects in cluster IV tended to show differential impairment as a function of increase in the amount of information that had to be processed. We have termed this pattern an "overload" pattern of performance. This pattern is defined on the Span of Apprehension task and the Competing Voice task by the tendency of these subjects to show greater decrements relative to other subjects in their accuracy of detection of target stimuli as the ratio of noise to signal is increased. On the Spokes Test, as the complexity of the task was increased, they again were differentially impaired. In addition, subjects in this group relative to subjects in cluster I showed impaired performance on the Digit Symbol Substitution Test (p < 0.05) but did not differ from subjects in cluster II. It is interesting to note that on the Stroop Test and on the Concept Attainment task where difficulty level was also manipulated, subjects in cluster IV were *not* differentially affected by increase in complexity.

Subjects in cluster II, with one exception, were intermediate in their performance between subjects in cluster I and cluster IV. The one exception was the Stroop Test where subjects in this cluster took significantly (p < 0.05 for all comparisons) longer to read color words and name colors than did subjects in clusters I and IV.

The five high-risk children in clusters III and IV are the same subset of high-risk children who performed in the bottom third of subjects across the Span of Apprehension task, the Spokes Test, and the Concept Attainment task. Thus, using three different methods of identifying subsets of subjects, we converge on five high-risk subjects who performed in a deficient manner across a number of tasks. One of these children showed impairment across all tasks. The other four high-risk children, in addition to one foster control child in cluster IV, showed impairment primarily on perceptual motor tasks when the complexity of the task was increased, usually by increasing the ratio of noise to signal.

DISCUSSION

The results of this study indicate the presence of attentional dysfunction in children at risk for future schizophrenia. More specifically, the high-risk group showed significantly lower levels of performance on some attention-demanding tasks, notably the complex versions of the Span of Apprehension task and Spokes Test and the simple conditions of the Concept Attainment task. A tendency to inaccuracy also was observed on the complex condition of the Competing Voices task. Examination of low-scoring subjects and intercorrelations between tasks revealed that within the high-risk group there was a subset of subjects who were showing impairment across these tasks to produce the overall low group means. When subjects were classified on the basis of commonalities of attentional performance across tasks using cluster analysis, two clusters of subjects were identified; one included five of the nine high-risk children, and the other included only children from a control group.

One cluster contained only one high-risk child. His performance was characterized by poor levels of performance across seven of the eight tasks. Indeed, this child was the lowest scorer in the entire study on these measures. His reaction time latencies were of

Table 34-4. Attentional Performance of Four Attentional Clusters

Task	Score	Variable		I		II		III		IV		F Value
				Mean	SD	Mean	SD	Mean	SD	Mean	SD	
Competing voices	Number of errors	Number of voices:	1	0.07	0.21	0.19	0.50	2.00		1.10	2.19	2.31
			3	3.03	1.94	4.50	2.02	29.50		7.70	11.12	1.75
			7	6.32	1.76	9.22	2.37	29.00		12.30	9.97	3.69[b]
			13	4.64	2.79	7.55	3.49	27.50		7.30	3.21	3.15[b]
Concept Attainment	Errors to criterion	Number of stimulus dimensions:	3	2.14	1.23	2.67	1.12	5.00		2.60	1.82	0.51
			4	2.14	0.95	2.55	1.13	3.00		2.40	1.14	0.45
			5	4.28	1.98	5.44	2.19	10.00		6.60	3.65	1.90
			6	6.78	2.52	8.00	3.08	12.00		9.80	3.27	2.15
Continuous Performance Test	Number of errors of commission and omission	Errors of commission		2.35	4.29	0.80	0.83	11.00		0.00	0.0	1.32
		Errors of omission		1.07	1.14	2.49	1.51	11.00		0.00	0.0	7.45[b]
Digit Symbol Substitution Test	Number completed	DSST		57.30	10.48	45.60	6.84	30.00		47.80	5.12	5.58[b]
Simple Reaction Time	Latency difference (in msec.) between	Preparatory interval:	1	961.70	29.46	919.60	35.76	1015.40		937.90	53.59	0.90
			4	985.30	32.82	988.20	41.92	850.70		1014.40	14.17	1.39

352

	irregular and regular trials at preparatory interval of 1, 4, and 7 secs. (−1000 added to difference)	7	991.70	40.44	1011.30	37.27	1093.60	1000.40	32.86	0.71
	Latency (msec.)	Series of 15 irregular trials	285.50	37.88	307.10	108.41	459.00	261.80	20.50	0.75
Span of Apprehension	Number of correct detections	Number of elements in array: 1	39.90	0.27	39.70	0.44	34.00	39.40	0.89	2.25
		3	39.20	1.05	39.20	0.83	37.00	38.80	1.10	0.35
		5	37.80	2.08	37.40	1.67	32.00	34.20	2.49	5.99[b]
		10	34.50	2.53	32.80	3.49	26.00	28.20	1.92	9.30[b]
Spokes Test	Total Time (secs.)	Spokes A	30.40	8.09	37.80	9.11	59.90	36.60	12.02	2.05
		Spokes B	49.80	9.97	62.90	20.92	145.10	99.20	24.02	15.80[c]
Stroop Test	Total time (secs.)	Read color words	5.75	0.94	8.54	2.05	7.50	6.14	0.57	11.28[a]
		Name colors	7.32	1.02	9.91	1.24	12.00	8.06	1.06	13.81[b]
		Read color words (interference condition)	7.12	1.59	9.26	1.44	8.40	6.80	0.91	6.73[b]
		Name colors (interference condition—4 trials)	55.82	8.17	71.14	12.55	84.80	67.68	4.64	7.56[b]

[a] = $p < 0.10$.
[b] = $p < 0.05$.
[c] = $p < 0.01$.

an order of magnitude found in chronic adult schizophrenics. His performance on the Spokes Test was comparable to that of brain-damaged patients. The number of impulsive errors and errors of commission made by this child on the Continuous Performance Test was comparable to that made by adult schizophrenic patients. This child's performance was consistent with a picture of diffuse neuropathology which manifests itself in impaired performance on a variety of perceptual motor tasks. In many ways this child resembled Fish's (8,9) description of Peter, a child who showed perceptual motor anomalies early in life and later acquired a diagnosis of schizophrenia.

The other cluster of particular interest was comprised of four high-risk and one foster control subject. These subjects were characterized by adequate performance on simple tasks, for example the Continuous Performance Test, Reaction Time, and the simple conditions of the Span of Apprehension and Competing Voices tasks, but showed differential impairment as a result of an increase in task complexity. An increase in task complexity was produced by increasing the amount of information on tasks in which the subject was required to detect target stimuli while holding constant the stimulus exposure time. On both the Span of Apprehension and the Competing Voices tasks, this group of subjects was comparable to subjects in clusters in I and II on the simple levels of these tasks. However, they showed a more rapid decrement in the accuracy with which they could detect target stimuli, voices or letters, as the number of irrelevant stimuli in which the target stimulus was imbedded was increased. We have termed this pattern of performance an "overload" pattern.

Chapman and Chapman (4) recently have pointed out some difficulties in making inferences from findings of differential deficit. In particular, they have noted that what may seem to be differential impairment in subjects may merely reflect the differential reliability or difficulty levels of tasks. In the context of the present study, the question arises: Are subjects who show the overload pattern merely showing an effect of task difficulty in general, or are they sharing an effect due to the specific way difficulty was increased in the study, i.e., increase in the amount of information to be processed while holding constant the time available to process the information? The fact that subjects in cluster IV were *not* differentially affected by increases in difficulty level on the Concept Attainment task and Stroop Test in which difficulty level was also manipulated suggests that there may be something special about the way difficulty level was produced in the Competing Voices and Span of Apprehension task and in the Spokes Tests that results in a differential effect of difficulty level on those tests rather than a general psychometric effect of difficulty level per se.

An adequate explanation for the overload pattern would have to take into account the parameters of stimulus exposure time and amount of information to be processed. The notion of limited channel capacity advanced by Yates (40) could well prove to be a valuable construct in helping us to understand the processes which underlie the overload pattern.

The finding in our study of attentional dysfunction in children at risk for schizophrenia is consistent with the recent findings of Grunebaum, et al (13) and Erlenmeyer-Kimling (7). Using a modification of the CPT in which distractor stimuli were presented, both Grunebaum et al and Erlenmeyer-Kimling found that high-risk children made significantly more errors under the distraction condition than did control children. It should be noted that the modification of the CPT employed by Grunebaum et al and Erlenmeyer-Kimling was different from the one used in our study. Indeed, the distractor condition of the CPT, which permitted identification of high-risk children in their studies, is more similar to the Span of Apprehension and Competing Voices tasks we used than it is to our version of the CPT. Erlenmeyer-Kimling concludes "that when distractors are present high-risk children seem to have difficulty in maintaining sustained attention." The results of our study are consistent with her conclusions.

It is intriguing to note that the mean score of 47 on the Digit Symbol Substitution Test obtained by the high-risk group in the present study is quite similar to the score obtained by the high-risk subjects in Mednick's (22) study (a mean score of 48) on the coding task from the WISC, which is analagous to the Digit Symbol Substitution Test on the WAIS. The somewhat slower reaction times on a series of irregular trials of the high-risk group, while not attaining statistical significance, are consistent with Marcus's (21) finding of slow reaction time in the adolescent offspring of schizophrenic women.

The detection of attentional dysfunction in a group of children at risk for schizophrenia free from major clinical symptoms raises the possibility that attentional dysfunction is part of the schizophrenic diathesis, not merely a reflection of a general psychiatric disorder. The fact that the high-risk children in our study were foster children permits us to rule out the currently disruptive effect of living with a psychotic parent. Their impaired performance is due either to the mother's genes or *early* training or both, but not the current disruptive effects of the mother. That the high-risk group can be differentiated from the foster control group means that the reduced efficiency of attentional functioning observed in our study is not due merely to the hard knocks that accrue to foster children.

Other clinical groups of children also show attentional dysfunction, for example, Dykman et al (6) have suggested that an attentional deficit underlies a wide range of impairments observed among learning disabled children. Further research is needed to determine whether the attentional dysfunction observed in high-risk children is qualitatively different from the attentional impairment observed in hyperactive children.

The small number of subjects used in this investigation requires cautious interpretation of the findings. Clearly, replication is needed before one can determine whether attentional dysfunction does indeed occur in a significant subset of children at risk for schizophrenia. Moreover, the predictive validity of the attentional clusters identified in our study can only be established by the results of follow-up investigations, the results of which will not be available for another 15 years. However, the results of this study clearly suggest the utility of conducting an attentional assessment using multiple attention-demanding measures in attempting to identify children at risk for schizophrenia. In addition, given the importance of the identification of subsets within the high-risk group, the utility of cluster analysis as a tool in the identification of subgroups of subjects seems to be most promising.

POSTSCRIPT

An interesting perspective to view the results of the present investigation is provided by a recent study (42) in which two of us (Asarnow and MacCrimmon) used the identical Span of Apprehension task described in this chapter with three additional groups of subjects: schizophrenic patients in clinical remission living in the community; hospitalized, acutely disturbed schizophrenics; and normal control subjects. Figure 34-1, which combines the Span of Apprehension data from the new study by Asarnow and MacCrimmon (42) and from the study reported in this chapter, presents the number of correct detections of the

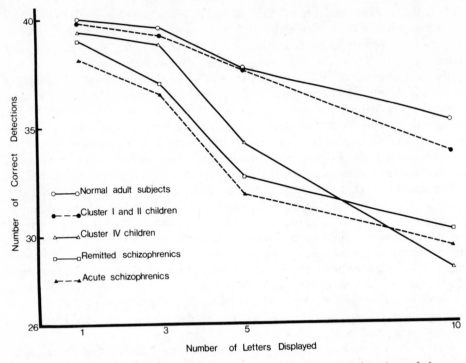

Figure 34-1. *Span of Apprehension Data:* Mean number of correct detections of the target stimulus as a function of complexity of stimulus array for: normal adult controls, acute hospitalized schizophrenics, remitted schizophrenics, cluster IV children, and clusters I and II children combined.

target stimulus as a function of the complexity of stimulus array for five groups: (a) acute schizophrenics, (b) remitted schizophrenics, (c) normal adult controls, (d) cluster IV children, and (e) clusters I and II children combined. The data were analyzed by five groups (between) by four complexity levels of stimulus array (within) a mixed model analysis of variance that yielded significant main effects of groups, $F(4,83) = 13.69$, p < 0.001, and of complexity of stimulus array, $F(3,249) = 200.78$, p < 0.001. The significant interaction of group by complexity levels, $F(12,249) = 5.54$, p < 0.001, was analyzed using the Neuman-Keuls test for differences between pairs of groups. The results of this analysis revealed that the five groups did not differ in their performance when only 1 and 3 elements were in the array; however, on the arrays of 5 and 10 elements, the hospitalized acute schizophrenics, the remitted schizophrenics, and the children in cluster IV made significantly fewer correct detections of the target stimulus than did the normal adult controls and the lower-risk children of clusters I and II (p < 0.01 for all comparisons). Also, the acute and the remitted schizophrenics and the children in cluster IV showed a significantly greater decrement in their accuracy of detection of the target stimulus as the complexity of the stimulus array was increased. The children in cluster IV *did not* significantly differ from the adult acute and remitted schizophrenics.

Although the number of subjects is small and these results need to be replicated, we find it fascinating to see patients in clinical remission who previously manifested schizophrenic symptoms, patients who at time of testing were actively schizophrenic and a subgroup of children from the high-risk study—four of whom fell in the high-risk group—all showing the same pattern and level of performance. These findings suggest that the span of apprehension is not reflecting merely the onset of acute psychiatric impairment or the social and medical consequence of acquiring a diagnosis of schizophrenia, but rather is sensitive to schizophrenic processes that are independent of clinical state. The results of the present study, in conjunction with the findings of Asarnow and MacCrimmon (42), raise the intriguing possibility that the span of apprehension may be tapping an underlying vulnerability to schizophrenia, a "schizotypic" condition (43).

REFERENCES

1. Adinolfi AA, Barocas P: Conceptual performance in schizophrenics. *J Clin Psychol* 26:167–171, 1970.

2. Bellissimo A, Steffy RA: Redundancy-associated deficit in schizophrenic reaction time performance. *J Abnorm Psychol* 80:229–307, 1972.

3. Bleuler E: *Dementia Praecox or the Group of Schizophrenics.* New York, International Universities Press, 1950.

4. Chapman LJ, Chapman JP: Problems in the measurement of cognitive deficit. *Psychological Bulletin* 79:380–385, 1973.

5. Cromwell RL, Rosenthal D, Shakow D, et al: Reaction time, locus of control, choice behavior, and descriptions of parental behavior in schizophrenic and normal subjects. *Journal of Personality* 29:363–379, 1961.

6. Dykman R, Ackerman R, Clements S, et al: Specific learning disabilities: An attentional deficit syndrome, in Mykleburst H (ed): *Progress in Learning Disabilities,* vol 2. New York, Grune and Stratton, 1971.

7. Erlenmeyer-Kimling L: A prospective study of children at risk for schizophrenia: Methodological considerations and some preliminary findings, in Wirt R, Winokur G, Roff M (eds): *Life History Research in Psychopathology* vol 4. Minneapolis, University of Minnesota Press, 1975, p. 23.

8. Fish B, Shapiro T, Halpern F, et al: The prediction of schizophrenia in infancy: II A ten year follow-up of predictions made at one month of age, in Hoch P, Zubin J (eds): *Psychopathology of Schizophrenia.* New York, Grune and Stratton, 1966.

9. Fish B, Hagin R: Visual-motor disorder in infants at risk for schizophrenia. *Arch Gen Psychiat* 27:594–596, 1972.

10. Garmezy N, Streitman S: Children at risk: The search for the antecedents of schizophrenia. Part I: Conceptual models and research methods. *Schizophrenia Bulletin* 8:14–90, 1974.

11. Garmezy N: Children at risk: The search for the antecedents of schizophrenia. Part II: Ongoing research programs, issues and intervention. *Schizophrenia Bulletin* 9:55–125, 1974.

12. Green PE, Rao VR: *Applied multi-dimensional scaling.* New York, Holt, Rinehart and Winston, 1972.

13. Grunebaum M, Weiss J, Gallant D, et al: Attention in young children of psychotic mothers. *Amer J Psychiat* 131:887–891, 1974.

14. Howard N, Harris B: A hierarchical grouping routine, IBM 360/65 Fortran program. *University of Pennsylvania Computer Center,* 1966.

15. Kornetsky C, Orzack M: A research note on some of the critical factors on the dissimilar effects of chlorpromazine and secobarbital on the digit symbol substitution and continuous performance tests. *Psychopharmacologia* 6:79–86, 1964.

16. Kornetsky C: The use of a simple test of attention as a measure of drug effects in schizophrenic patients. *Psychopharmacologia* 24:99–106, 1972.

17. Kraepelin E: *Dementia Praecox and Paraphrenia.* Chicago, Medical Books, 1919.

18. Landau R, Harth P, Othnam N, et al: The influence of psychotic parents on their children's development. *Amer J Psychiat* 129:38–43, 1972.

19. Lang PH, Buss AH: Psychological deficit in schizophrenia: Interference and activation. *J Abnorm Psychol* 70:77–106, 1965.

20. MacCrimmon DJ, Sigal JJ, Streiner DL: Differential diagnosis of schizophrenic and nonschizophrenic adolescents by tests based on interference theory. *Canadian Psychiatric Association Journal* 19:279–285, 1974.

21. Marcus LM: Studies of attention in children vulnerable to psychopathology. Unpublished Ph.D. dissertation. Minneapolis, University of Minnesota, 1972.

22. Mednick SA: The children of schizophrenics: Serious difficulties in current research methodologies which suggest the use of the "High-Risk Group" method, in Romano J (ed): *The Origins of Schizophrenia.* Amsterdam, Excerpta Medica Foundation, 1967.

23. Mednick SA, McNeil TF: Current methodology in research on the etiology of schizophrenia: Serious difficulties which suggest the use of the high-risk group method. *Psychological Bulletin* 70:(6)681–693, 1968.

24. Mednick S, Schulsinger F: Some premorbid characteristics related to breakdown in children with schizophrenic mothers, in Kety S, Rosenthal D (eds): *Transmission of Schizophrenia.* Oxford, Pergamon Press, 1968, p 267.

25. Moray N: *Attention.* New York, Academic Press, 1970.

26. Neale J, Cromwell R: Attention and schizophrenia, in Cancro R (ed): *Annual Review of the Schizophrenic Syndrome,* vol 2. New York, Brunner/Mazel, 1972.

27. Neale JM, McIntyre CW, Fox R, et al: Span of apprehension in acute schizophrenics. *J Abnorm Psychol* 74:593–596, 1969.

28. Orzack MH, Kornetsky C: Attention dysfunction in chronic schizophrenia. *Arch Gen Psychiat* 14:323–326, 1966.

29. Payne RW: The measurement and significance of overinclusive thinking and retardation in schizophrenic patients, in Hoch PH, Zubin J (eds): *Psychopathology of Schizophrenia.* New York, Grune and Stratton, 1966.

30. Rappaport M: Attention to competing voice messages by nonacute schizophrenic patients. Effects of message load, drugs, dosage levels and patient background. *J Nerv Ment Dis* 146:404–411, 1968.

31. Reitan FM: The comparative effects of placebo, Ultran, and meprobromate on psychologic test performances. *Antibiotic Medicine and Clinical Therapy* 4:158–163, 1957.

32. Ricks DF, Berry JC: Family and symptom patterns that precede schizophrenia, in Roff M, Ricks DF (eds): *Life History Research in Psychopathology.* Minneapolis, University of Minnesota Press, 1972.

33. Rosenthal D: *Genetic Theory and Abnormal Behavior.* New York, McGraw-Hill, 1970.

34. Silverman J: The problem of attention in research and theory in schizophrenia. *Psychol Rev* 71:352–379, 1964.

35. Shakow D: Segmental set. *Arch Gen Psychiat* 6:17–32, 1962.

36. Spitzer RL, Endicott J, Fleiss JL, et al: The psychiatric status schedule: A technique for evaluating psychopathology and impairment in role functioning. *Arch Gen Psychiat* 23:41–55, 1970.

37. Venables PH: Input dysfunction in schizophrenia, in Maher BA (ed): *Progress in Experimental Personality Research.* New York, Academic Press, 1964, pp 1–47.

38. Wagner S, Krus DM: Effects of lysergic acid diethylamide, and differences between normals and schizophrenics on the Stroop color-word test. *Journal of Neuropsychiatry* 2:76–81, 1960.

39. Walker CM, Bourne IC: The identification of concepts as a function of amounts of relevant and irrelevant information. *Amer J Psychol* 16:410–417, 1961.

40. Yates A: Psychological deficit. *Annual Review of Psychology* 17:111–144, 1966.

41. Zubin J: Problem of attention in schizophrenia, in Kietzman M, Sutton S, Zubin J (eds): *Experimental Approaches to Psychopathology.* New York, Academic Press, 1975.

42. Asarnow RF, MacCrimmon DJ: Residual attentional deficit in clinically remitted schizophrenics: In search of a marker of vulnerability. Manuscript submitted for publication, 1977.

43. Meehl PE: Schizotaxia, schizotypy, schizophrenia. *Amer Psychol* 17:827–838, 1962.

Chapter 35
Attentional Measures in a Study of Children at High-Risk for Schizophrenia

L. Erlenmeyer-Kimling, Ph.D.
Barbara Cornblatt, Ph.D.

This is a report of two measures of attention and distractibility that were included in the original test battery of a prospective study of children of schizophrenic parents (1,2). The experimental procedures from which these measures were adapted had been reported to show attentional dysfunctions in schizophrenic patients and were of interest for theories concerned with faulty filtering of stimulus input. Our expectation was that some of our high-risk subjects might exhibit similar, although possibly not so profound, impairments if disturbances in attention are part of the process that leads to schizophrenia rather than being the symptoms of the illness. Our purpose here is to describe very briefly the measures and the results of preliminary analyses in our sample of high-risk and low-risk children.[1]

THE MEASURES

The two attentional measures were part of a day-long testing session which included psychophysiologic and psychologic tests, a neurologic examination, and a videotaped interview (3). The battery was administered to 205 children who were between the ages of 7 and 12 years at the time of first testing (1971–73); most of the subjects have now been retested 2 or 3 years following the first examination. The sample was composed of 44 children with schizophrenic mothers, 23 with schizophrenic fathers, 13 with two schizophrenic parents; 25 with a parent who had a psychiatric disorder other than schizophrenia; and 100 children with "normal" parents (i.e., parents who had no psy-

---

[1] The data reported here are part of B. Cornblatt's doctoral dissertation.

This research was supported in part by a USPHS Grant MH19560 from the National Institute of Mental Health and by the Department of Mental Hygiene of New York State.

chiatric treatment). Only children with one schizophrenic parent and normal controls are considered here. Children of patients, schizophrenic or otherwise, were located by screening consecutive admissions to psychiatric facilities in the greater New York metropolitan area; children of normal parents were located through contacts with public school systems. Details of the ascertainment and diagnostic procedures appear elsewhere (3).

Continuous Performance Test

One of our two measures of attention and distractibility was based on a task that Rosvold and colleagues (4) designed to detect lapses of attention as a function of brain damage and that Kornetsky, Mirsky, and their colleagues (5,6,7) have used extensively in the study of schizophrenic patients. At least some subgroups of schizophrenic patients have been found to do more poorly, as measured by number of response errors, on this continuous performance test (CPT) than either the normal controls or the non-schizophrenic patients. The CPT in the foregoing studies required the subject to respond to a target stimulus whenever it appeared in a series of stimuli or only when it was immediately preceded by another specified stimulus. An adaptation of the CPT, using pictures rather than letters of the alphabet, was employed by Anderson and colleagues (8) in a study of phenylketonuric children.

In a pilot phase of our study, both the Anderson et al (8) pictorial version and the original letter version of the CPT were tried on a group of normal 7–12-year-old children. Both versions were found to be too easy and, therefore, incapable of detecting individual differences.[2] Furthermore, because we wished to test the hypothesis that high-risk subjects might show greater impairment of performance as a function of the introduction of external distractors, it was necessary to add a distraction condition to our continuous performance test. The considerably modified version of the CPT which we adopted also provided an opportunity to obtain reaction time measures on an attentional task under distraction (D) and no distraction ($\overline{D}$) conditions.

More detailed descriptions of our CPT appear elsewhere (9,10). Slides of playing cards were used as stimuli. Subjects were told to respond as rapidly as possible by pressing a response key when a slide appeared that was identical in both number and suit to the preceding slide, and they were instructed to ignore the voice that would occasionally be heard through the earphones. Distraction consisted of a tape recorded woman's voice reciting digits at rates of presentation varying from fast to slow. (Three earlier versions of "distraction" were discarded in piloting the measures because they appeared to have no effect on the performance of pilot children. The recitation of digits, however, did impair performance in this group and was perceived to be moderately irritating.)

Four blocks of $\overline{D}$ trials and four blocks of D trials were counterbalanced over the administration of the CPT. A total of 320 trials (slides) was presented in each condition, of which 40 (per condition) immediately followed an identical slide and therefore required a response. Another 40 pairs of slides per condition were identical in playing card number

---

[2] In a discussion earlier in this Conference, Dr. Kornetsky observed that Grunebaum and his colleagues have recently employed a version of the CPT that discriminates between four-year-old children of schizophrenic mothers and control children but fails to discriminate at age seven because by that age the task is too easy to detect individual differences.

but not in suit. These were treated as "false alarms" in the signal detection analyses that were applied to the data, and the remaining trials were simply called "others."[3]

The CPT in our laboratory thus yielded the following performance indices: (a) number of errors of omission (target trials missed); (b) number of errors of commission, divisible into "false alarms" and "others," or the sum of both; (c) reaction time on target trials. Signal detection analyses yielding d' and β values also were calculated (9). The effects of distraction could be evaluated by comparing the various performance indices in the $\overline{D}$ and D conditions.

Attention Span

An auditory attention span task was modified from a procedure reported by Lawson, McGhie, and Chapman (11) in a study of schizophrenic patients and, in particular, from the procedure used by Hawks and Robinson (12) in an attempt to compare Yates's (13) hypothesis that schizophrenics process information at an abnormally slow rate with the hypothesis advanced by McGhie (14) and others suggesting that schizophrenics are extremely susceptible to irrelevant stimulation owing to the breakdown of a filtering mechanism.

In our adaptation of the attention span task, sequences of either three or five letters were recited by a female voice at either a fast or a slow rate of presentation (one letter/ second or one letter/1.5 seconds) in a tape recording played into the subject's earphones. The subject was required to recall each sequence immediately following its presentation. Twenty-four trials counterbalanced for rate of presentation and length of the sequence, were presented without distraction, and 24 trials, similarly counterbalanced, were presented with distraction. Distraction consisted of a male voice reciting letters in the intervals between the target letters that were given in the female voice. Subjects were told to ignore the male voice.

Each recalled sequence was scored as totally correct if all letters were repeated in correct order without omissions or intrusions, and otherwise it was scored as incorrect.

HYPOTHESES

Several hypotheses were advanced concerning the respective performance of the high-risk and control subjects.

Specifically, among the hypotheses for the CPT (9) were: (a) that high-risk subjects would make more errors of both omission and commission than would the control subjects in $\overline{D}$; (b) that reaction time would be longer in high-risk subjects in $\overline{D}$; and (c) that the between-group discrepancy on all performance indices would increase in the D condition.[4]

---

[3] The CPT with slight modifications, including recording of visual evoked responses, was administered in a second round of testing approximately two years after the first testing. Preliminary analyses comparing the two rounds show highly significant intrasubject correlations for the various performance indices, indicating that test performance is reasonably stable over time.

[4] It was further hypothesized that in the signal detection analyses the discriminability index, d', would be lower in high-risk subjects than in controls. This expectation was confirmed (9), suggesting that, compared to the controls, the high-risk subjects are less able to discriminate between stimuli. No predictions were made regarding the likelihood ratio criterion, β, and no significant differences were found (9); thus, "response bias" does not appear to be more optimal in controls than in high-risk subjects.

For the attention span task, it was expected: (a) that high-risk subjects would produce more incorrectly recalled sequences than would the controls; and (b) that these differences would be magnified in the distraction condition, D. It was also considered possible that the performance of the high-risk subjects would deteriorate with the faster rate of presentation and with longer sequences (i.e., five letters versus three letters), although the Hawks and Robinson (12) study of schizophrenic patients showed no effects of rate of presentation within the range used and yielded unclear results with respect to sequence length.

RESULTS

As Table 35-1 illustrates, some but not all of our hypotheses regarding performance on the CPT were supported. The high-risk subjects made more errors of omission to target trials than did controls in both the $\bar{D}$ and D conditions as expected. They did not respond more frequently to "false alarms" but did respond significantly more often to "other" irrelevant trials. The total number of errors of commission—summed over "false alarms" and "others"—was also significantly greater in the high-risk group. There were, however, no significant differences between the groups with respect to reaction time in either $\bar{D}$ or D.

The role of distraction was as had been hypothesized, with both groups doing more poorly in the D condition than in $\bar{D}$ on all performance indices, although these within group differences did not all reach the 0.05 level of significance. The high-risk group performed more poorly under distraction than did the controls on all indices, although in the case of "false alarms," total errors of commission, and reaction time, the difference between groups was not significant. The third row for each index in Table 35-1 indicates whether there was a significant difference between the high-risk and control groups in the degree to which performance on the given index was affected by distraction. The high-risk group showed a significantly greater decline in performance as a result of distraction for errors of omission and "others." Between-group differences were in this same direction for the remaining indices but were not significant.

A more complete report on the data from the CPT, including results of the signal detection analyses, appears elsewhere (9).

As Table 35-1 shows, the attention span task was generally less effective than the CPT in differentiating between high-risk and control subjects. There was no difference between the groups on the three-letter sequence or the slow rate of presentation in either $\bar{D}$ or D. On the five-letter sequence and the fast rate of presentation, the high-risk group performed significantly more poorly than did the controls but only in the no distraction condition. Distraction produced a very large decrement in performance in both groups, without discriminating between them.

Because group comparisons are only a first step in high-risk research,[5] a further set of analyses of the two attentional measures is important. These analyses employed eight performance indices—namely, on the CPT errors of omission, "false alarms," "other"

[5] Because not all children with a schizophrenic parent are genetically at risk for schizophrenia (only 50% if dominant transmission is involved, fewer if polygenic) and only about 12% are expected actually to manifest a schizophrenic psychosis, the true strategy of high-risk research involves the search, within the high-risk sample, for a subgroup of individuals whose deviance on several selected indices suggests that they are *the* vulnerable members of the sample. The analyses described here are a preliminary step in this direction.

Table 35-1. Summary of Main Findings in Comparisons of the High-risk and Normal Control Groups on the CPT and Attention Span Task

Continuous Performance Test			Attention Span Task		
Performance index[a]	Test Condition[b]	Result of HR vs. NC[c]	Performance Index[a]	Test Condition[b]	Result of HR vs. NC[c]
Error of ommission: target trials	$\bar{D}$	HR > NC (p = 0.058)	Trials missed: 3 letter sequence, summed over presentation rates	$\bar{D}$	(n.s.)
	D	HR > NC (p = 0.012)		D	(n.s.)
	Diff. ($\bar{D}$ – D)	(n.s.)		Diff. ($\bar{D}$ – D)	(n.s.)
Error of commission: "false alarms"	$\bar{D}$	(n.s.)	Trials missed: 5 letter sequence, summed over presentation rates	$\bar{D}$	HR > NC (p = 0.028)
	D	(n.s.)		D	(n.s.)
	Diff. ($\bar{D}$ – D)	(n.s.)		Diff. ($\bar{D}$ – D)	(n.s.)
Error of commission: "others"	$\bar{D}$	HR > NC (p < 0.001)	Trials missed: slow presentation rate, summed over sequence lengths	$\bar{D}$	(n.s.)
	D	HR > NC (p < 0.001)		D	(n.s.)
	Diff. ($\bar{D}$ – D)	HR > NC (p = 0.043)		Diff. ($\bar{D}$ – D)	(n.s.)
Error of commission: Total ("false alarms + others")	$\bar{D}$	HR > NC (p = 0.024)	Trials missed: fast presentation rate, summed over sequence lengths	$\bar{D}$	HR > NC (p = 0.022)
	D	HR > NC (p = 0.050)		D	(n.s.)
	Diff. ($\bar{D}$ – D)	(n.s.)		Diff. ($\bar{D}$ – D)	(n.s.)
Reaction time: target trials	$\bar{D}$	(n.s.)			
	D	(n.s.)			
	Diff. ($\bar{D}$ – D)	(n.s.)			

[a] See text for description.
[b] Distraction D and no distraction $\bar{D}$.
[c] HR—high-risk group, NC—normal control group.

Table 35-2. Comparison of High-risk and Normal Control Groups with Respect to the Number of Performance Indices on Which Individual Subjects Scored in the Worst 5% (or Beyond) of the Standardized Distribution

Number of Performance Indices	High-Risk Group Number of Subjects[a]	% of Total	Normal Control Group Number of Subjects[a]	% of Total
0	23	39.7	66	71.7
1	14	24.1	17	18.5
2	10	17.2	5	5.4
3	7	12.2	4	4.4
4	3	5.2	0	
5	1	1.7	0	
Total	58[a]	100.0	92[a]	100.0

[a] Number of subjects for whom complete data were available on both the CPT and the attention span task.

errors all in $\overline{D}$, as well as the same three indices in D, and on the attention span task, trials missed on five-letter sequences in $\overline{D}$ and in D. For each performance index, standardized scores were obtained for the normal control group, and the worst (i.e., poorest performance on that particular index) 5% of the group was identified. Subjects in the high-risk group whose standard scores were at least as extreme (in the same direction) were then located. As Table 35-2 shows, 71.7% of the control subjects did not fall into the extreme 5% of the distribution for their group on *any* performance index, while this was true for only 39.7% of the high-risk subjects. Moreover, as can be seen, none of the controls scored in the extreme 5% on more than three performance indices, while 6.9% of the high-risk subjects did so. If the cut-off point is set at three indices with extreme scores, 19.1% of the high-risk subjects and 4.4% of the controls were below the cut-off point with extreme scores on three or more indices. Finally, each of the 11 high-risk subjects thus identified was found to have a standard score on two or more indices that was considerably more deviant than the most extreme score obtained by a control subject on that particular index.[6]

CONCLUSION

Our experience with adaptations of the continuous performance test and an attention span task reported in the literature (12) serves to illustrate some of the special difficulties of high-risk research in attempting to apply measures that differentiate schizophrenic and normal adults to the assessment of children. The attention span task is on the whole, although not entirely, a poor discriminator of our two groups of subjects; the distraction condition at least is evidently too difficult for subjects in the 7- to 12-year age range. The CPT is a moderately efficient discriminator in this age range but may not be so in the longitudinal follow-up as our subjects move into adolescence.

[6] We wish to thank Dr. Yvonne Stellingwerf for her contribution to the above analyses.

Nevertheless, the measures together flag for further observation a subgroup of high-risk subjects whose performance on attentional tasks appears to be excessively disturbed. Whether this same subgroup respresents the truly vulnerable members of the high-risk sample, and whether the same subgroup will be identified by other components of our test battery, remains to be seen. Further analyses of the CPT and attention span task and their relation to clinical assessments of our subjects are now being carried out.

REFERENCES

1. Erlenmeyer-Kimling L: Prospective study of children of schizophrenic parents. USPHS Grant number MH 19560, 1970.

2. Erlenmeyer-Kimling L: Prospective study of children of schizophrenic parents. USPHS Grant number MH 19560, 1974.

3. Erlenmeyer-Kimling L: A prospective study of children at risk for schizophrenia: Methodological considerations and some preliminary findings, in Wirt RD, Winokur G, Roff M (eds): *Life History Research on Psychopathology,* vol 4. Minneapolis, University of Minnesota Press, 1975, p 23.

4. Rosvold HE, Mirsky AF, Sarason J, et al: A continuous performance test of brain damage. *J Consulting Psychol* 20:343, 1956.

5. Mirsky AF, Kornetsky C: On the dissimilar effects of drugs on the Digit Symbol Substitution and Continuous Performance Tests. *Psychopharmacologia* 5:161, 1964.

6. Orzack MH, Kornetsky C: Attention dysfunction in chronic schizophrenia. *Arch Gen Psychiat* 14:323, 1966.

7. Kornetsky C, Mirsky AF: On certain psychopharmacological and physiological differences between schizophrenic and normal persons. *Psychopharmacologia* 8:309, 1966.

8. Anderson VE, Siegel FS, Fisch RO, et al: Responses of phenylketonuric children on a continuous performance test. *J Abnorm Psychol* 74:358, 1969.

9. Rutschmann J, Cornblatt B, Erlenmeyer-Kimling L: Sustained attention in children at risk for schizophrenia. *Arch Gen Psychiat* 34:571, 1977.

10. Cornblatt B, Rutschmann J, Erlenmeyer-Kimling L: Comparison of children at risk for schizophrenia and normal controls on a continuous performance test. Paper presented at the 83rd annual meeting of the American Psychological Association, Chicago, August 30–September 3, 1975.

11. Lawson JS, McGhie A, Chapman J: Distractibility in schizophrenia and organic cerebral disease. *Brit J Psychiat* 113:527, 1967.

12. Hawks DV, Robinson KN: Information processing in schizophrenia: The effect of varying rate of presentation and introducing interference. *Brit J Soc Clin Psychol* 10:30, 1971.

13. Yates AJ: Data processing levels in thought disorder in schizophrenia. *Aust J Psychol* 18:103, 1966.

14. McGhie A, Chapman J, Lawson JS: The effect of distraction on schizophrenic performance. I. Perception and immediate memory. *Brit J Psychiat* 111:383, 1965.

Chapter 36
Attention and Information Processing as Indicators of Vulnerability to Schizophrenic Episodes

Bonnie J. Spring, Ph.D.
Joseph Zubin, Ph.D.

As a descriptive model, we find it useful to distinguish between *vulnerability* to schizophrenia which is a relatively permanent, enduring trait and *episodes* of schizophrenic disorder that are waxing and waning states. According to this model, episodes of schizophrenia ensue when endogenous and exogenous challengers surpass a threshold set by the individual's dispositional level of vulnerability. When such challenging events subside, the patient shows at least some degree of recovery, and sometimes even reattains his premorbid level of functioning. However, even when a schizophrenic's state has normalized, his vulnerability persists and leaves him at risk for future episodes of schizophrenia.

The various etiologic models of schizophrenia have been presented elsewhere (1). Here it will suffice to suggest that vulnerability to schizophrenia may originate in many ways. Biologic models emphasize etiologic forces arising from an individual's internal make-up: his genes, biochemistry, and neurophysiology. Field theory models stress the role of exogenous forces impinging on the maturation, learning, and immediate behavior of the individual.

The different etiologic models often agree in predicting that a particular group of individuals will be vulnerable to schizophrenia, although these predictions are based on different rationales. Most models predict that siblings of schizophrenics represent a

Supported in part by National Institute of Mental Health Grant
MH303-1117A.

group at some risk for schizophrenia, since they share numerous possible sources of vulnerability with the schizophrenic probands. These include a shared gene pool, similar intra-uterine environments, common family and community interaction experiences, exposure to the same diseases, diets, physical environments, and so forth.

Because of the evidence that disturbed sensation, perception, and attention may be central characteristics of the schizophrenic syndrome (2–4), our selection of potential vulnerability indicators has been influenced by the neurophysiologic model of schizophrenia. This model seeks the causes of schizophrenic symptoms in disorders of central nervous system functioning and the capacity to take in and process information. Disturbances of information processing have a prima-facie link with the schizophrenic psychopathologic state because patients' subjective complaints so often include altered perceptual experience, distractibility, and flooding or loss of the ability to differentiate figure from ground (2–3). Even if these disturbances do not produce or cause schizophrenia, they may serve as "culture-free" markers of that disorder or of vulnerability to it.

We are investigating a variety of information-processing indicators to distinguish between two types: those that mark the trait of vulnerability to schizophrenia and those that mark episodes of schizophrenia. The sample consists of recently hospitalized schizophrenic patients, their close-in-age siblings who have never manifested severe psychiatric disturbance, nonschizophrenic psychiatric control subjects, and healthy controls without a family history of psychiatric disturbance. Schizophrenic patients are also retested after their symptoms have subsided. We will designate as potential markers of vulnerability to schizophrenia performance anomalies that display two characteristics: (a) The characteristic is not present in nonschizophrenic psychiatric patients or healthy control individuals but does appear in both the nonaffected sibling and the schizophrenic proband, (b) The anomaly persists in "recovered" schizophrenics. Anomalies found in both groups "at risk" for schizophrenia (unaffected siblings and "recovered" patients) but bearing no relationship to the manifest psychopathologic state, would appear to be associated with the underlying vulnerability to schizophrenia. In contrast, promising candidates to mark the beginnings and ends of episodes of schizophrenia would be those characteristics that deviate only in highly symptomatic schizophrenic patients and normalize in retested "recovered" cases.

MEASUREMENT TECHNIQUES

The battery of assessment techniques consists of procedures previously found to reveal differences in the information-processing characteristics of healthy subjects, schizophrenic patients, and depressed individuals. Some techniques can be considered primarily sensory in nature; others assess physiologic, psychophysic, attentional, and language processes. All the techniques are listed below. More detailed descriptions will be given for procedures illustrating some general "methodologic maxims" that have been followed at the Biometrics Research Unit. Many of these maxims have recently been articulated by Sutton (5) as useful guidelines in designing test procedures for psychiatric research. The relevant techniques are:

1. Dichotic listening as a measure of the ability to maintain selective attention.
2. Simple reaction time to ipsimodal and crossmodal stimulus sequences, measuring the ability to shift attention.

3. Pupillary dilation to ipsimodal and crossmodal stimulus sequences.
4. Evoked potential to ipsimodal and crossmodal stimulus sequences.
5. Pupillary constriction to simple light stimuli.
6. Pursuit eye movements.
7. Visual threshold and visual temporal integration.
8. Auditory threshold and auditory reaction time facilitation by the addition of a masking stimulus.
9. Comprehensibility of verbal utterances as measured by the cloze procedure.

METHODOLOGIC MAXIMS

The maxims advanced are designed to contend with a fundamental pitfall in schizophrenia research. The pitfall is that confirmation can be obtained for almost any theory of schizophrenia as long as the theory predicts that schizophrenics will perform more poorly than normal subjects on a given experimental task. Therefore, certain precautions are needed to obtain meaningful patient data and to shed light on the factors responsible for schizophrenic behavior.

1. *Test procedures should be as simple as possible.* Two forms of simplicity are desirable. (a) *The response required of the subject should be as simple as possible,* so as not to place excessive demands on the subject's willingness to cooperate or to follow complex instructions. This demand is perhaps most readily met when simple physiologic recordings are taken, as two of our procedures illustrate.

In one test, visual and auditory evoked potentials are recorded from the scalp when subjects are either told in advance (certain condition) or asked to guess (uncertain condition) whether the stimulus on the next trial will be a light or a sound. Figure 36-1 shows evoked potential waveforms recorded from 10 normal controls, 10 depressed patients, and 10 schizophrenic patients. The solid tracing represents a waveform generated in the certain condition; the dotted line shows a wave recorded under conditions of uncertainty. Both groups of psychiatric patients were tested while receiving phenothiazine medication. This sample of tracings illustrates the finding of Levit et al (6,6A) that the effect of uncertainty in enhancing a late positive component of the evoked potential (P$\overline{300}$) is greatest in the normal group and least in the schizophrenic group. Levit also presented subjects who were naive with respect to evoked potentials with the 10 sets of three waveforms recorded in the uncertain condition. When instructed to select the "most different" waveform in each triad, subjects overwhelmingly identified the schizophrenic trace as the maverick.

In another procedure, subjects are simply asked to fixate while the extent of pupillary contraction to a single light pulse is assessed. Figure 36-2 illustrates the findings of Lidsky et al (7) comparing the pupillary reactions of recently admitted, drug-free psychiatric patients with those of normal controls. All but 7 of the 51 patients were diagnosed as schizophrenic by hospital psychiatrists. The data are presented in the form of a cumulative distribution, whereby a value on the ordinate shows the percentage of subjects whose contraction exceeds any given value on the abscissa. Results indicate that patients show reduced contraction of the pupil to light. Moreover, the reaction to light differentiates patients and normal subjects quite strikingly, such that the response distributions show only 20% overlap.

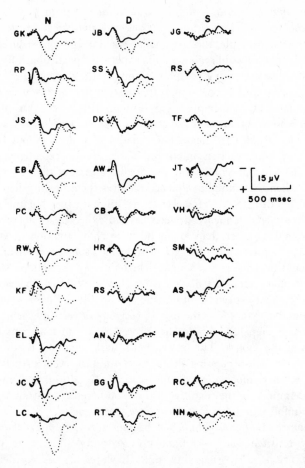

Figure 36-1. Evoked potential waveforms recorded from 10 normal subjects (N), 10 depressed patients (D), and 10 schizophrenic patients (S). Solid tracings represent waveforms generated in the certain condition. Dotted lines show waveforms recorded under conditions of uncertainty. From Levit RA (6a).

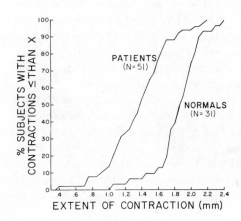

Figure 36-2. Cumulative distributions of patients and normal subjects as a function of the extent of contraction to a single light pulse. From Lidsky A, Hakerem G, Sutton S (7).

(b) *Task requirements should be simple in the respect that the procedure engages few systems of psychologic function aside from the one in which the deviant process is thought to reside.* For example, the crossmodal reaction time procedure was devised to test the hypothesis that schizophrenic patients experience particular difficulty in shifting attention. Rather than presenting complex cognitive stimuli that might evoke dysfunctions in high-level conceptual functioning, the procedure requires attentional switching between different modalities of simple energy stimuli. Very brief preparatory intervals of between 1.5 and 3.5 seconds are used, so as not to confound attentional switching ability with the capacity to sustain attention or to estimate the duration of long time intervals.

When simple finger-lift reaction time is tested for serially presented sequences of light and sound stimuli, schizophrenics show the predicted greater than normal lengthening of reaction time when the stimulus sequence requires them to shift their attention from one modality to another (8–9). However, it is still possible that the schizophrenic's impairment in crossmodal sequences reflects deviant expectancies about the modality of the upcoming stimulus rather than an inability to shift attention. To control for the variable of cognitive expectations, Kriegel (9) informed subjects of whether the stimulus on each trial would be a light or a sound. Schizophrenics continue to show the greater than normal crossmodal retardation even when they are told in advance what stimulus to expect. In our current experimentation, subjects are always informed of the nature of the upcoming stimulus. Moreover, the usual procedure of verbally conveying expectancy information is being compared with another procedure in which an actual light or sound stimulus forewarns the subject. The latter, more "task-syntonic" condition, is expected to reduce the information-processing demands of the task even further by making the form of the expectancy information distinct and in the appropriate modality for each stimulus and by eliminating the cognitive translation necessary to transform verbal symbolic expectancy information into an appropriate sensory set.

2. *The phenomenon of interest should be monitored in more than one response system, and, if possible, with simultaneous recording.* To study the physiologic response of the brain to crossmodality shift, Levit et al (6) recorded scalp evoked potentials to stimulus sequences involving light and sound. Simultaneous physiologic and psychomotor recording were not desirable in this case because of the danger of contaminating the evoked potential with movement artifact or with cortical activity reflecting motor processes. Findings showed that, whereas depressive and normal subjects tend to have larger N_1-P_3 amplitudes in the crossmodal condition, schizophrenics tend to display larger amplitudes in the ipsimodal condition. In the current study, subjects tested on the crossmodal reaction time procedure are subsequently tested by simultaneous monitoring of the vertex evoked potential and pupillary dilation response to certain and uncertain crossmodal and ipsimodal stimulus sequences. By obtaining all three responses for the same subject, it will be possible to determine whether pupillary dilation and P_3 amplitude preserve their previously discovered parallelism (10) and conform to the crossmodality psychomotor response pattern of any given subject.

3. *If nonschizophrenic psychiatric patients constitute a control group, the test battery should include at least one procedure on which this group's performance markedly differs either qualitatively or quantitatively from that of schizophrenics and normal controls.* The general rationale for including a nonschizophrenic psychiatric control group in a research design is to demonstrate that a relevant performance characteristic pertains specifically to schizophrenia rather than to psychosis or to psychiatric disorder in general. If it is to be argued that different diagnostic groups suffer from discrete

disorders rather than from the same disorder with more or less severity, then test results should bear out this theory. The usual finding that normal subjects perform adequately, psychiatric controls somewhat worse, and schizophrenics very poorly conforms as well if not better to the theory of differing severity as it does to the theory of discrete functional psychiatric disorders.

A test of auditory reaction time facilitation demonstrates the desired discontinuity in performances by schizophrenics and psychotically depressed patients. Bruder et al (11) examined the extent to which reaction time to a high intensity click is reduced when the standard click is paired with a second click. Clicks were presented in a forward masking paradigm in which the more intense click preceded the less intense. Testing was done at each of three different intervals (2, 7, and 15 mseconds) separating clicks in a pair. Affectively psychotic subjects showed a significantly greater reduction in reaction time to the click pair relative to the single click than did schizophrenics and nonpatients. In fact, schizophrenic patients displayed slightly less facilitation than did healthy controls. Moreover, when the interval separating clicks in a pair was increased to 15 mseconds, affectively ill patients showed a marked decrease in reaction time not observed in either of the other groups.

4. *Test procedures should be sought for which patient performance is in some sense better than normal.* The auditory reaction time facilitation procedure is illustrative in that affective psychotic patients show more improvement or better facilitation than do the controls. The great advantage of such findings is that it is difficult to attribute them to extraneous factors such as the patient's poor motivation, failure to comprehend or follow instructions, or more general problems.

The dichotic listening procedure is another technique that can yield better-than-normal patient performance. This task also will be used to illustrate three final methodologic maxims. Dichotic listening is a classic test of the ability to maintain selective attention while filtering out distracting material. The test should therefore index any tendency for schizophrenics to be excessively distractible. In this procedure, subjects wear stereo earphones and are simultaneously presented with two different verbal messages, one to each ear. The instructions are to ignore the message presented to one ear, while attending to the other message and "shadowing" or repeating it word-by-word.

When messages are presented at a fairly rapid rate, schizophrenics make more shadowing errors than controls (12–13). However, if schizophrenics are in fact excessively distractible, they should do *better* than controls on another aspect of the dichotic test. They should surpass healthy controls in the extent to which they process information on the irrelevant, distracting channel. Processing of the competing channel is typically assessed by asking subjects to recall or recognize words previously presented to the unattended ear. Two problems with this procedure are noteworthy. First, the subject is effectively placed in a double bind, having first been asked to ignore and then subsequently been asked to report on the competing message. Second, one must devise a way of distinguishing between two aspects of memory performance: the subject's sensitivity, or the extent to which he has processed information on the irrelevant channel, and the subject's criterion, or the extent to which he is willing to *report* having processed distracting material. Previous work on schizophrenic memory for distractors (12–13) suggests that the two variables may be difficult to disentangle, since patients and normal controls differ in their tendencies to make "false alarms," or to claim to remember words that have not in fact been heard.

5. *Whenever appropriate, research on psychiatric patients should either control the criterion variable or obtain separate estimates of sensitivity and criterion.* One strategy to avoid the confounding of sensitivity and criterion is to have subjects *show* by their performance rather than *tell* whether distractors have been processed. This objective can be attained by presenting novel pairs of words on the unshadowed channel and by subsequently testing to see how readily subjects learn to remember these paired-associates. To the extent that a schizophrenic subject has been biased toward attending to the distracting pairs, and has begun to learn to associate them during the shadowing task, he should find it relatively easy to learn these particular word pairs in a paired-associate memory task. But should his paired-associate memory for distractors exceed that of normal subjects in an absolute sense? Almost certainly not, because the schizophrenic's generally low level of memory ability will prevent him from being able to demonstrate an advantage in a simple group comparison. Rather than "covary out" the confounding variable of memory ability, an alternative strategy is to use an "own control" design.

6. *The own-control design can be used to control for differences between patients and normals on a confounding variable.* Two measurements can be taken in such a way that the confounding variable enters equally into both measures, and the variable of interest enters only into one. In the dichotic listening example, the group's ability to learn to remember pairs of words presented as distractors is compared with its baseline ability to learn new pairs of words not previously presented. The relationship between the group means on the two variables is plotted for all groups, so each group serves as its own control on the variable of baseline memory ability. Regression analyses can then be used to discern the general trend or "law" relating the two variables for the majority of groups, and it can be seen whether the experimental group deviates from the general trend (16).

7. *To establish the factors responsible for a performance anomaly, it should be demonstrated that the performance pattern fluctuates as a consequence of manipulations affecting the psychologic system that is hypothesized to be responsible for the anomaly.* If schizophrenics' deviant performance on the dichotic listening test is due to dysfunctional attention, the deviance should be normalized by manipulations that effectively engage attention. Kahneman (17) has reviewed evidence suggesting that voluntary control over attention is limited. The degree of attention invested in a task is primarily determined by intrinsic task demands rather than by volition. Spare processing capacity cannot be engaged by an easy task as readily as by a hard one.

It can be expected that the schizophrenic's tendency toward distractibility will be most evident when the shadowing task exerts few intrinsic constraints on attention. Attention will be most free to wander when the main message is easy to predict or highly redundant. On the other hand, manipulations that engage attention by making the shadowed message difficult and unpredictable should minimize and possibly even normalize deviant attentional performance.

In a pilot experiment conducted by Spring (18), the dichotic test was administered to nonpatient controls and to hospitalized psychiatric patients diagnosed according to research criteria (19). All subjects shadowed four familiar proverbs and four matched unpredictable sentences. Proverbs and unpredictable sentences were presented in semi-randomized order and equally often to the right and left ears. Sentences were presented at such a slow rate (slightly less than one syllable per second) that very few patients or nonpatients made any shadowing errors. A set of three pairs of words (proverb pairs) was presented as the competing message for each proverb; and a matched set of word pairs (unpredictable pairs) co-occurred with each unpredictable sentence. Sentences were matched on the syntax and Thorndike-Lorge frequency of each component word. Proverbs were rehearsed in advance to ensure familiarity. Word pairs consisted of one-syllable, high frequency words coupled to be difficult for paired-associate learning by pairing stimulus words low in imagery value with response words low in association value. When shadowing was completed, subjects were asked to memorize a list of paired words that included all proverb pairs and all unpredictable pairs in addition to nine new (neutral) pairs of words. On each memory trial, subjects studied and were tested on all 15 pairs, until the entire list was learned to a criterion of one perfect trial or until eight trials had been completed.

Distractibility was measured by a savings, or better performance, on learning to associate word pairs previously presented on the secondary tape channel, relative to baseline performance on new pairs of words. The savings on proverb pairs relative to baseline indexed distractibility when the shadowing task was predictable and the demand on attention was minimal. Savings on unpredictable pairs would indicate distractibility during a difficult, attention-engaging main channel task.

At this point it might be noted that there were many discrepancies between patients' hospital diagnoses and the diagnoses assigned according to research diagnostic criteria. The great majority of patients in the sample received hospital diagnoses of schizophrenia. Research diagnoses made with a knowledge of hospital diagnoses but blind as to test performance assigned patients almost equally across a broader range of diagnostic categories. One consequence of these discrepancies is an inadvertent drug control procedure. Among the patients receiving phenothiazine therapy were 5 of the 7 schizophrenics, 3 of the 7 depressed patients, 4 of the 7 schizoaffective depressed patients, 3 of the 5 schizoaffective manic patients, and all the 5 manic patients. There was no systematic relationship between medication and test performance across all diagnostic groups.

For all groups except schizophrenics and depressed patients, the number correct is about equal for proverb pairs and neutral pairs. The schizophrenic group deviates significantly from this trend ($t_{2\ d.f.} = 13.25$, $p < 0.01$) and shows a savings or better performance on learning pairs presented as distractors during an easy, predictable message. This finding suggests that schizophrenic patients profited from their distractibility during the shadowing task and began learning to associate the word pairs presented simultaneously with predictable sentences. Most groups appear not to have learned these associations during tape presentation—they learn the proverb pairs only as easily as the new pairs. Depressed patients also differ significantly from the main trend ($t_{2\ d.f.} = -21.21$, $p < 0.01$) but in an entirely different direction. They do not learn the proverb pairs as easily as new pairs. Instead they seem to have acquired an active inhibition that makes pairs previously presented as distractors more difficult to learn.

Figure 36-3 shows the consistency of these effects for all individuals in a group. For subjects in all groups except the schizophrenic and depressed, chance seems to govern whether there is a savings or a decrement on learning proverb pairs relative to baseline learning on new pairs. However, every single individual in the schizophrenic and depressed groups scores consistently with the trend for the mean group performance.

When the main channel message is unpredictable and, hence, should engage attention very effectively, *all* groups show a deficit relative to baseline in learning the associated

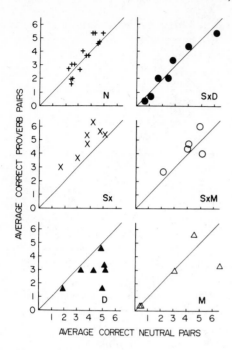

Figure 36-3. Average number correct on proverb pairs relative to average number correct on neutral (new) pairs for every subject in each group. From Spring B (18).

pairs. This "inhibition" effect is significantly more marked for the depressed ($t_{2\ d.f.}$ = -10.07, $p < 0.01$) and the schizoaffective depressed ($t_{2\ d.f.}$ = -13.93, $p < 0.01$) groups. The schizophrenics do not depart from the trend for the other groups. Thus their performance is normalized by the attention-engaging manipulation.

REFERENCES

1. Zubin J: Scientific models for psychopathology in the '70s. *Seminars in Psychiatry* 4:283, 1972.

2. Freedman BJ: The subjective experience of perceptual and cognitive disturbances in schizophrenia. *Arch Gen Psychiat* 30:333, 1974.

3. McGhie A, Chapman JS: Disorders of attention and perception in early schizophrenia. *Brit J Med Psychol* 34:103, 1961.

4. Venables P: Input dysfunction in schizophrenia, in Maher B (ed): *Progress in Experimental Personality Research*, vol 1. New York, Academic Press, 1964.

5. Sutton S: Fact and artifact in the psychology of schizophrenia. In Hammer M, Salzinger K, Sutton S (eds): *Psychopathology: Contributions from the Social, Behavioral, and Biological Sciences.* New York, John Wiley & Sons, 1972.

6. Levit RA, Sutton S, Zubin J: Evoked potential correlates of information processing in psychiatric patients. *Psych Medicine* 3:487, 1973.

6a. Levit RA: Averaged evoked potential correlates of information processing in schizophrenics, psychotic depressives and normals. (Doctoral dissertation, Columbia University, 1972). University Microfilms No. 72-20, 051.

7. Lidsky A, Hakerem G, Sutton S: Pupillary reactions to single light pulses in psychiatric patients and normals. *J Nerv Ment Dis* 153:286, 1971.

8. Sutton S, Zubin J: Effect of sequence on reaction time in schizophrenia. In Birren JE, Welford AT (eds): *Behavior, Aging and the Nervous System: Biological Determinants of Speed of Behavior and its Change with Age.* Springfield, Ill, Charles C Thomas, 1965.

9. Kriegel J: Reaction time in schizophrenics and normals as a function of stimulus uncertainty, guessing, and modality shift. Doctoral dissertation, Columbia University, 1967.

10. Friedman D, Hakerem G, Sutton S, et al: Effect of stimulus uncertainty on the pupillary dilation response and the vertex evoked potential. *Elect and Clin Neur* 34:475, 1973.

11. Bruder GE, Sutton S, Babkoff H, et al: Auditory signal detectability and facilitation of simple reaction time in psychiatric patients and nonpatients. *Psych Med* 5:260, 1975.

12. Payne RW, Hochberg AC, Hawks DV: Dichotic stimulation as a method of assessing disorder of attention in overinclusive schizophrenic patients. *J Ab Psych* 76:185, 1970.

13. Wishner J, Wahl O: Dichotic listening in schizophrenia. *J Cons Clin Psych* 42:538, 1974.

14. Russell PN, Bannatyne PA, Smith JF: Associative strength as a mode of organization in recall and recognition: a comparison of schizophrenics and normals. *J Ab Psych* 84:122, 1975.

15. Traupmann K: Effects of categorization and imagery on recognition and recall by process and reactive schizophrenics. *J Ab Psych* 84:307, 1975.

16. Fleiss JL, Tanur JM: The analysis of covariance in psychopathology. In Hammer M, Salzinger K, Sutton S (eds): *Psychopathology: Contributions from the Social, Behavioral, and Biological Sciences.* New York, John Wiley & Sons, 1972.

17. Kahneman D: *Attention and Effort.* Englewood Cliffs, NJ: Prentice-Hall, 1973.

18. Spring B: Dichotic listening in psychiatric patients. Unpublished manuscript, Harvard University, 1975.

19. Spitzer RL, Endicott J, Robins E: Research diagnostic criteria for a selected group of functional disorders. Biometrics Research, New York State Department of Mental Hygiene, 1975.

Chapter 37
Smooth Pursuit Eye Movements in Twins Discordant for Schizophrenia

Philip S. Holzman, Ph.D.
Einar Kringlen, Prof. Dr. Med.
Deborah L. Levy, Ph.D.
Leonard R. Proctor, M.D.
Shelby Haberman, Ph.D.

In a series of studies we reported that between 65% and 80% of schizophrenic patients have disordered pursuit eye movements, compared with about 15% in other psychiatric populations and 6% in the normal population. Of equal interest was the finding that about 45–50% of first-degree relatives of the schizophrenics also showed the same kind of eye-tracking impairments, compared with a prevalence in the families of other psychotic patients that was no greater than that found in the normal population (1,2). This association of disordered pursuit eye movements with schizophrenia and with members of the families of schizophrenics suggested that deviant pursuit eye movements may represent a genetic indicator of schizophrenia. This hypothesis would be confirmed if monozygotic (MZ) and dizygotic (DZ) twins who are discordant for schizophrenia were concordant for deviant eye tracking. This chapter describes such a study.

Smooth pursuit eye movements are those attendant upon following a moving target, and the speed of the target determines almost exactly the speed of the eyes. Rapid or saccadic movements are those that occur when fixation shifts, as when a person looks about a room from one object to another. In saccadic shifts, the eye can move at very rapid

The work reported here was supported by grant number MH-19477, USPHS, and a grant from the Benevolent Foundation of the Scottish Rite, Northern Masonic Jurisdiction. Dr. Holzman is a recipient of public Health Service Research Scientist Award (MH-70900). We wish to thank Nicholas J. Yasillo, Drs. Pål Abrahamsen, and Haldis Lie for important contributions to this study.

376

speeds, at times up to 600 degrees a second. In contrast, following movements break down into saccadic shifts if the target moves faster than about 40 degrees a second.

A simple test of pursuit eye movements requires a subject to follow a pendulum. The pendulum, of course, oscillates at a continuously varying velocity, at first accelerating to a maximum and then decelerating to zero velocity. Electronystagmographic recording permits the investigator to obtain a permanent record of eye movements during the pursuit task (1,2). In good pursuit eye movements the eyes should reproduce the sinusoidal wave form of the pendulum. Figure 37-1 shows four examples of pursuit movements. Normal eye tracking is represented in Figures 37-1a and 37-1b. Deviations in eye tracking, such as those illustrated in Figures 37-1c and 37-1d are found in persons with some hemispheric and brain-stem lesions, multiple sclerosis, Parkinson's disease, and some drug intoxications, particularly barbiturate and alcohol (3).

In our studies we found that deviant eye-tracking patterns in young schizophrenic patients occurred without the presence of organic disease, and in a large number of their first-degree relatives the poor tracking occurred without either the presence of clinical schizophrenia or of an organic pathologic condition. Indeed, none of the relatives examined had visited a psychiatric facility for treatment for themselves, and all were functioning quite adequately in the social and occupational areas. Table 37-1 shows the association of poor eye tracking with schizophrenia as diagnosed clinically by a team of psychiatrists.

We have used a second, more quantitative score to describe the pursuit eye movement deviations. This score tabulates the number of times the eyes stop moving when they should actually be moving if they were to track accurately. This score is obtained from the first derivative of the direct eye movement recording, using a differentiator coupler in the ENG. Figure 37-2 shows the direct tracing and the differentiator tracing, with the velocity of the eyes in the right and left directions. Points labeled "a" refer to the zero velocity of the eyes when the target was momentarily stationary. Points labeled "c", however, refer to an eye arrest when the eyes should actually be moving. We called these *velocity arrests*. We scored as velocity arrests all eye movements that returned to at least within 2 mm of the zero velocity line, which corresponds to 4 degrees per second. The biserial correlation between velocity arrests and good and bad tracking is 0.85 in our subjects. The velocity arrest scores also discriminated among our patient groups as Table 37-1 shows.

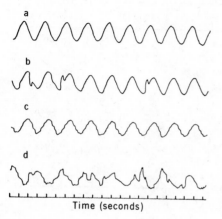

Figure 37-1. Four eye-tracking patterns in response to moving pendulum. Tracings a and b are considered normal; tracings c and d are considered abnormal. From Benitez JT (10).

Table 37-1. Frequency of Normal and Deviant Eye Tracking of Pendulum and Number of Velocity Arrests per Cycle in Each Group of Subjects Using Hospital Diagnoses[a]

Group	Tracking Type			Velocity Arrests/ Cycle
	Number	Normal	Deviant	
Schizophrenia	75	26	49	9.89
Manic-depressive	9	7	2	8.66
Nonpsychotic	19	15	4	7.69
Relatives of schizophrenics	34	19	15	10.48
Relatives of non-schizophrenics	19	17	2	6.70
Normal controls	72	66	6	6.76
Total	228	150	78	

[a] From Holzman PS et al (2).

We used a second method of diagnosis, one based on blind assessments of psychologic test protocols. This diagnosis relied not on symptoms as did the hospital psychiatrists' diagnosis but also on the special forms of thought organization and reality contact detected by the psychologist in the verbatim psychologic test records. When this method of diagnosis is employed, the relationship of poor eye tracking to schizophrenia improves as shown in Table 37-2.

We found no differences in eye tracking on the basis of either a paranoid-nonparanoid dimension or the Phillips Scale. The reader is referred to our previous papers (1,2) for more complete details of method and scoring.

The high prevalence of poor eye tracking in the first-degree relatives of the schizophrenic patients suggested that poor eye tracking may be under genetic control.

Table 37-2. Frequency of Normal and Deviant Eye Tracking of Pendulum and Number of Velocity Arrests per Cycle in Each Group of Subjects Using Psychologic Test Diagnoses[a]

Test Diagnosis	Tracking Type			Velocity Arrest/ Cycle
	Number	Normal	Deviant	
Schizophrenic	58	14	44	10.90
Other psychotics	18	15	3	5.77
Nonpsychotic	18	17	1	6.45
Relatives of schizophrenics	32	16	16	11.00
Relatives of non-schizophrenics	21	20	1	6.27
Normal controls	72	66	6	6.76
Total	219			

[a] From Holzman PS et al (2).

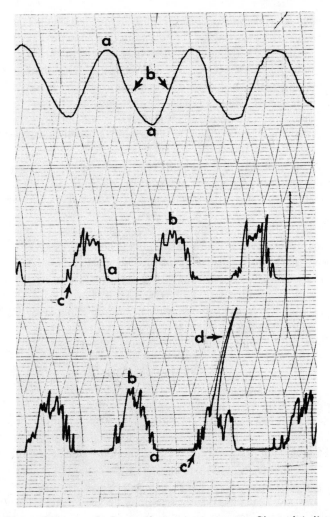

Figure 37-2. Eye-tracking record of normal pursuit movements. Channel 1 displays direct eye movement. Channels 2 and 3 display velocity of the eyes in right and left directions, respectively. Points a indicate eyes are stopped at times pendulum is stopped. Points c indicate velocity arrests, when eyes stop although they should be moving for accurate pursuit. Point d indicates velocity overshoot.

Since the early part of the twentieth century, investigators had noticed that madness tended to appear in some families more than in others. On the basis of such pedigree investigations, analysts have attempted to formulate genetic hypotheses about the mode of transmission but without much consensus. Twin studies have established a concordance rate for schizophrenia between 30–40% for MZ twins and between 8–10% for DZ twins (4,5,6), and crossfostering studies (7) have found that the number of schizophrenic offspring of biologic parents who are schizophrenic is approximately the same whether or not those children have been reared in adoptive or biologic homes. The rates of psychopathology in biologic relatives of schizophrenics have been reported to be higher than in the adoptive relatives (8), but the small numbers of subjects in these crossfostering studies have made more definite statements difficult to formulate. These studies have established a genetic component in the propensity to become schizophrenic but have left unanswered questions about the mode of transmission, what is transmitted, and the moderating or inhibiting effects of environment or constitution. A significant handicap in attempting to map the genetic transmission of schizophrenic predisposition is the absence of an objective indicator of schizophrenia, one that can be reliably and unequivocally reproduced and does not require clinical assessment of schizophrenic behavior itself. The eye-tracking dysfunction may qualify as such a genetic indicator of the predisposition for schizophrenia.

To test the viability of disordered pursuit eye movements as a genetic indicator, we examined the concordance of poor eye tracking in MZ and DZ twins who were discordant for schizophrenia. Kringlen had previously studied such a group and in 1967 published his findings (4). His sampling and analysis made use of sophisticated methods, and his conclusions were stated modestly. In that study, concordance figures for schizophrenia ranged from 25–38% in MZ twins and 4–10% in DZ twins, depending on whether a narrow or broad concept of schizophrenia was employed. The difference in concordance rates for MZ and DZ twins with respect to schizophrenia was statistically significant and thus supported a genetic factor in the etiology of schizophrenia. However, the concordance rates were much smaller than had previously been reported. Such a sample in which the discordant MZ twins represented between 62% and 75% of the sample seemed ideally suited for exploring the concordance of disordered eye tracking.

A complete description of the sample can be found in Kringlen's monograph (4), where the method of ascertainment, diagnostic criteria, concordance computations, and other relevant data are set forth in detail. For the present study, we selected from among that sample those twin pairs who were available for testing during a 2-month period in 1975. To insure that eye-tracking records would be evaluated blindly, without knowledge of the twinship relationship and the kind of eye tracking in the pairs, a list of four-digit random numbers was drawn up, and each subject was assigned a random number as the subject was tested. The identities of the subjects were retained by Kringlen, who kept the other three authors uninformed as to the twinships, diagnoses, and relationships among the people we had tested. Eye movements were recorded with a differential preamplifier driving an FM reel-to-reel magnetic recorder. Thus, since no visual record was displayed, no tracings could be examined. Most subjects were tested in their own homes, which were located throughout the southern half of Norway. A few subjects came to the University Psychiatric Clinic in Oslo and a few schizophrenic probands who were still hospitalized were tested in the hospitals. We were able to arrange for the transportation to Oslo of four persons from the far north of Norway. Only two sets of twins were tested in the same session.

We used the same procedure for testing smooth pursuit movements as that outlined in previous publications (1,2) with the modification that subjects were tested four times in a single session. Trials 1 and 2 followed the procedure previously used: subjects were asked to follow the pendulum as it traversed 20 degrees of visual arc. Then, after a brief test for spontaneous and gaze nystagmus, there was a third test of smooth pursuit movements, this time using the procedures suggested by Shagass et al (9). In these procedures arabic numerals were placed on the pendulum. The fourth trial was the same as trials one and two.

Following the test of smooth pursuit movements we drew from the subject 10 cc of venous blood which was sent to the Forensic Medical Institute, University of Oslo, for zygosity determinations using the following systems: ABO, MNS, Rhesus, Lewis, P., Duffy, Kell, Gm, and Gc. Complete similarity on all systems determined monozygosity. Most of these subjects had previously been tested for zygosity a decade ago, but in some the Institute performed retyping and typed a few not previously tested.

After all the data had been gathered, the tapes were sent to the United States where the signals were displayed on paper for visual analysis and scoring. Three of us independently scored each record. We determined whether the tracking was *good* or *bad* for each of the four trials and counted the number of velocity arrests per cycle for each of the four trials. There was very high agreement among the scores (over 95%), and, after consensus was reached on the few disagreements of qualitative scoring, a single consensus score was reached. The quantitative score—the number of velocity arrests— was the average of all four trials, and the qualitative score—whether A or B—was also the average of the four trials. On a prearranged date these scores were sent to Kringlen in Norway who, on the same date, set to Chicago the names, relationships of the subjects, and zygosity determinations. The data could be evaluated and processed only after this mutual exchange of codes and scores had taken place.

Ten sets of MZ and 15 sets of DZ twins were tested in Norway. Of the MZ pairs two sets were concordant for schizophrenia, two sets were partially concordant (that is, the co-twin, although never hospitalized and not psychotic, manfested some behavioral peculiarities) and six sets were discordant. One set of the MZ twins discordant for schizophrenia and tested in the United States was added to the group, making 11 MZ pairs. One pair of DZ twins was partially concordant and 14 were discordant.

RESULTS

Table 37-3 contains the data for these twin sets.

Association of B Tracking with Schizophrenia

Table 37-3 shows that there were 26 twin probands whose conditions had been diagnosed as schizophrenic. In addition, two MZ co-twins had at one time been hospitalized for a schizophrenic condition. Thus, 28 subjects in this sample had conditions diagnosed as schizophrenia for which hospitalization had been indicated, either at present or in the past. Seven of the MZ probands and 11 of the DZ probands had poor eye tracking. Of the two concordant MZ co-twins one had poor eye tracking. Thus, 19 of 28 schizophrenic persons (68%) in this sample had eye-tracking dysfunctions. This prevalence is within the range of our previous findings of 65–80% for schizophrenic patients and thus confirms the association of disordered pursuit eye movements with schizophrenia in this sample.

Within the 24 discordant co-twins—those without a diagnosis of schizophrenia—13 or 54% had B tracking. Table 37-3 shows that there were 4 of 9 (44%) nonschizophrenic MZ twins and 9 of 15 (60%) nonschizophrenic DZ co-twins who showed B tracking. This prevalence of 54% is similar to our previous findings of about 45% of the first-degree relatives of schizophrenics who showed B tracking.

Table 37-3. Sex, Age, and Eye-tracking Performance of 11 MZ and 15 DZ Twins[a]

Twin Pairs		Sex	Age	Mean Log Vel. Arr./5 Cycles Over 4 Trials[b]	Eye-tracking Type
MZ	1a	M	62	1.9096	B
	1b[c]			1.9782	B
MZ	2a	F	47	1.5748	B
	2b[c]			1.4620	A
MZ	3a	M	55	1.5908	A
	3b[d]			1.3748	A
MZ	4a	M	61	1.7160	B
	4b[d]			1.5739	A
MZ	5a	M	55	1.3007	A
	5b			1.2374	A
MZ	6a	M	73	1.5674	B
	6b			1.7383	B
MZ	7a	F	56	1.7657	B
	7b		–	1.7403	B

Twin Pairs		Sex	Age	Mean Log Vel. Arr./5 Cycles Over 4 Trials	Eye-Tracking Type
DZ	2a	M	54	1.4204	A
	2b			1.4073	A
DZ	3a	F	63	1.9174	B
	3b			1.7156	B
DZ	4a	F	59	1.6365	B
	4b			1.5144	A
DZ	5a	M	46	1.7989	B
	5b			1.6918	B
DZ	6a	M	56	1.7662	B
	6b			1.8001	B
DZ	7a	M	55	1.8968	B
	7b			1.7550	B
DZ	8a	M	55	2.1042	B
	8b			1.4851	A

Zygosity	Pair	Sex	Velocity arrest	Mean log score	Type		Zygosity	Pair	Sex	Velocity arrest	Mean log score	Type
MZ	8a	F	35	1.4294	A		DZ	9a	M	58	1.4356	A
	8b			1.4725	A			9b			1.7631	B
MZ	9a	F	59	2.0109	B		DZ	10a	F	62	1.8115	B
	9b			1.6984	B			10b			1.8354	B
MZ	10a	F	56	1.5205	A		DZ	11a	M	52	1.3567	A
	10b			1.6037	A			11b			1.5529	A
MZ	11a	M	21	1.7959	B		DZ	12a	F	73	1.8707	B
	11b			1.7294	B			12b			1.9867	B
DZ	1a	M	47	1.8654	B		DZ	13a	M	58	1.7703	B
	1b[d]			1.8415	B			13b			1.5091	A
							DZ	14a	F	45	1.6170	A
								14b			1.6292	B
							DZ	15a	F	53	1.9463	B
								15b			2.0329	A

[a] Velocity arrest scores are expressed as the mean log of four tracking trials, five cycles per trial. The eye-tracking type, whether good (A) or bad (B), is the average judgment of the four trials. In each pair, the proband is labeled a and the co-twin b.

[b] Log transformation was used to normalize the distribution of scores.

[c] Concordant for schizophrenia.

[d] Partially concordant for schizophrenia.

Concordance for Eye Tracking

A Pearson product-moment correlation was computed between MZ and DZ pairs with respect to the quantitative index of tracking movements, the velocity arrest scores. The correlation is 0.77 for MZ twins (p = 0.005) and 0.40 (p = 0.15) between DZ pairs. These values remain the same when corrected for age and attenuation. They are reasonably close to the theoretical values for genetic association which would be 1 and 0.50. These values, however, are not significantly different from each other, a reflection of the small sample size and the attendant large variances.

With respect to the concordance on the qualitative typing of eye tracking, whether A or B, (Table 37-4 shows that 5 of 7 (71%) of the MZ sets and 7 of 13 (54%) of the DZ sets were concordant for poor eye tracking, using pair-wise concordance. The concordance rates for clinical schizophrenia in these samples is 18–36% for MZ and 0–13% for DZ twins, depending on the broadness of the diagnostic criteria. The data thus show a considerably higher concordance for poor eye tracking than for clinical schizophrenia. Of the two sets of MZ twins who were concordant for schizophrenia, one pair was concordant for poor eye tracking and one discordant.

Within the MZ sets there is a significant tendency for tracking performance to be congruent; that is, probands with A or B tracking tend to have co-twins with the same kind of tracking (Fisher's Exact Test, p = 0.045, one-tail). But within the DZ sets that tendency is no greater than chance. The significance levels are restrained by the small sample size. It is worth noting, moreover, that there were two DZ probands who had A tracking but whose nonschizophrenic co-twins had B tracking.

It is of some interest to inspect the tracking patterns of some of the twin sets. These patterns show that concordance statistics can only allude to the high degree of similarity. The illustrations (Figures 37-3, 37-4, and 37-5) show that where there is concordance, the kinds of tracking errors made by the twins are strikingly similar.

These data are consistent with an interpretation of a nonrandom association of deviant eye tracking in this twin sample. The correlations of velocity arrest scores within the MZ and DZ pairs are close to the predicted genetic values. The pair-wise concord-

Table 37-4. Prevalence of Good and Bad Pendulum Eye Tracking in Probands of Four Different Groups Together With Eye Tracking Type in First-Degree Family Members

Diagnosis	Proband Eye Tracking Type	No.	Mother A	Mother B	Father A	Father B	Sibs A	Sibs B
Schizophrenic	A	10	7	0	5	2	2	4
	B	15	5	7	2	7	6	7
Nonschizophrenic psychotic	A	7	2	1	2	0	8	2
	B	0	0	0	0	0	0	0
Nonpsychotic	A	7	3	0	4	0	4	1
	B	0	0	0	0	0	0	0
Normal	A	11	8	3	8	1	10	0
	B	0	0	0	0	0	0	0

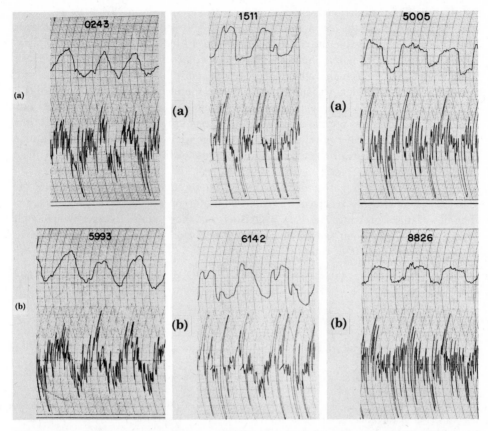

Figure 37-3, 37-4, 37-5. Pendulum eye-tracking records of three sets of twins. The first record of each pair is that of the proband. The figures illustrate concordance in smooth pursuit eye movement patterns within twin pairs.

ance rates for the qualitative classification of poor eye tracking are in the correct direction for genetic effects, but the small numbers of twin pairs limit the extent to which it is prudent to draw firm conclusions. The MZ-DZ ratio in this study, for example, would be consistent not only with a genetic influence on deviant eye tracking, but also with environmental influences. The latter would include viral or toxic etiologies.

Nevertheless, it is worthwhile to examine the family data we have collected thus far in Chicago to buttress conclusions about familial association. Table 37-4 shows the type of eye tracking for probands in three diagnostic classifications and for normals and for the first-degree relatives of these subjects.

It is striking that poor eye tracking is quite widespread in the schizophrenics and in their families. When the schizophrenic member has A tracking, the prevalence of B tracking in the families is lower than in the schizophrenics but still higher than in other groups.

These data strengthen the probability that the association of deviant eye pursuit movements with schizophrenia is at least partly under genetic regulation. This conclusion must be qualified by two cautions.

First, the small number of subjects seriously limits the statistical significance that can be gleaned. The correlation coefficient of velocity arrests within MZ pairs of 0.77 is highly significant, but the correlation coefficient of 0.40 within the DZ group falls short of 0.441 which is the value the correlation must exceed for significance at the 0.05 level with 13 degrees of freedom. The estimate of pair-wise concordance, likewise, would be more reliable if twice as many subjects had been included.

Second, the mean age of the subjects in the twin sample is 55. There is evidence that eye tracking accuracy declines with age and the number of velocity arrests increases with age (9). In our previous normal sample of 72 subjects in which the age range was from 15 to 59 years, the number of velocity arrests and age were correlated 0.36. A replication of this study should therefore include a young cohort of discordant twins, preferably those in the third decade of life.

We are continuing to gather data to answer the question of whether deviant smooth pursuit eye movements represent a genetic indicator of schizophrenic predisposition. The observations presented here are promising, but they require a larger twin sample from a younger age group and a wider family study before conclusions about the genetic status can be assumed to be robust.

REFERENCES

1. Holzman PS, Proctor LR, Hughes DW: Eye tracking patterns in schizophrenia. *Science* 181:179–181, 1973.

2. Holzman PS, Proctor LR, Levy DL, et al: Eye tracking dysfunctions in schizophrenic patients and their relatives. *Arch Gen Psychiat* 31:143–151, 1974.

3. Hagt WF, Frisen L: Supranuclear ocular motor control. Some clinical considerations-1974, in Lennerstrand G, Bach-y-Rita P (eds): *Basic Mechanisms of Ocular Activity and Their Clinical Implications.* Oxford and New York, Pergamon Press, 1975.

4. Kringlen E: *Heredity and Environment in the Functional Psychoses.* Oslo, Universitetetsforlaget, 1967.

5. Gottesman II, Shields J: *Schizophrenia and Genetics.* New York, Academic Press, 1972.

6. Tienari P: Schizophrenia in Finnish male twins, in Lader MH (ed): *Studies of Schizophrenia. Brit J Psychiat* Spec Publ No 10, 1975.

7. Wender PH, Rosenthal D, Kety SS, et al: Crossfostering. *Arch Gen Psychiat* 30:121–128, 1974.

8. Kety SS, Rosenthal D, Wender PH, et al: Mental illness in the biological and adoptive families of adopted individuals who have become schizophrenic, in Fieve R, Rosenthal D, Brill H (eds): *Genetic Research in Psychiatry.* Baltimore, Johns Hopkins Press, 1975.

9. Shagass C, Amadeo M, Overton DA: Eye tracking performance in psychiatric patients. *Biol Psychiatry* 9:245–260, 1974.

10. Benitez JT: Eye tracking and optokinetic tests: Diagnostic significance in peripheral and central vestibular disorders. *Laryngoscope* 80:834–848, 1970.

Chapter 38
Platelet Monoamine Oxidase, Plasma Dopamine-beta-hydroxylase and Attention in a "Biochemical High-Risk" Sample

M. S. Buchsbaum, M.D.
D. L. Murphy, M.D.
R. D. Coursey, Ph.D.
C. R. Lake, M.D.
M. G. Zeigler, M.D.

Low levels of both monoamine oxidase (MAO) and dopamine-beta-hydroxylase (DBH) have been postulated as being associated with schizophrenic symptomatology. Of the two enzymes, more supporting data by far have been found for MAO as measured in platelets.

Low MAO activity has been reported in a number of studies to be lower in patients with chronic schizophrenia (1), co-twins of schizophrenics (2) as well as in patients with bipolar (manic-depressive) disorders (3). Since MAO is an important enzyme in the degradation of both catecholamines and indoleamines, the finding of low MAO levels in schizophrenics would be consistent with two of the leading conceptualizations of biochemical abnormalities in the major psychoses—the transmethylation and dopamine

The authors wish to thank S. Potter, G. Palmer, S. Hookanson, A. Nichols, and T. Cridlin for technical assistance with the DBH and MAO assays and C. King for assistance with the neurophysiological and behavioral data.

hypotheses. Further, platelet MAO activity is under genetic control as shown by studies of twins (4,5).

Despite this positive evidence, it remains a possibility that the low platelet MAO activity observed might be due to some artifact of hospitalization or treatment factors. While Wyatt et al (2) had demonstrated low MAO levels in co-twins of schizophrenics discordant for schizophrenia, reanalysis of the data (6) suggested the possibility that at least some lowering of the MAO might be a concomitant of being schizophrenic. To avoid these confounding factors, we integrated the usual biochemical paradigm of measuring biologic factors in psychiatric patients with the "high-risk" approach of studying individuals at risk for developing an illness and produced a new "biochemically-at-risk" strategy. Here, the hypothesized "vulnerable" proband was selected from a normal population by a biologic measure alone, low platelet MAO activity, rather than by the usual familial relationship to a patient.

A population of individuals potentially at risk for psychiatric disorders was identified by screening 375 college student volunteers for low platelet MAO activity levels. The lower and upper 10% of the population in MAO activity were interviewed and tested psychophysiologically. Family history data were obtained.

To summarize briefly our results reported elsewhere (7), low-MAO probands reported more frequent psychiatric or psychologic counseling. Families of male low-MAO probands had an eightfold increase in the incidence of suicide or attempted suicide over those of high-MAO probands. On psychologic test measures, low-MAO probands also showed stimulus seeking, high scores on the Barron ego strength scale, more active leisure time activities (6), and significantly more time socializing each day. While such a pattern is consistent with the association of low MAO and bipolar affective disorders, it neither resembles that reported in familial schizophrenia high-risk studies nor in retrospective studies of the premorbid behavior of schizophrenics (8). One explanation of the discrepancies between these MAO findings and the many reports linking low MAO and chronic schizophrenia may be that low MAO is one of several contributing biologic factors increasing the risk for psychopathology in the major psychoses.

DBH seemed to us to be a second possible biologic factor that might operate in conjunction with low MAO to produce schizophrenic rather than affective symptoms. Low DBH levels, like low MAO levels, would be consistent with a dopamine overload concept of schizophrenia. Like MAO, DBH is under genetic control (9), and individual differences have correlated with behavioral measures (10,11). However, studies of patients with schizophrenia (12,13,14) or identical twins discordant for schizophrenia (9), did not provide positive evidence for a reduction in plasma DBH activity. One postmortem study indicated reduced DBH activity in brains of schizophrenic patients (15), but this was not supported in a second study (16). Nevertheless, earlier data associating psychotic symptoms with the administration of the DBH inhibitor disulfiram (17) paralleled similar observations with MAO inhibitors and suggested that further studies could be valuable. Although depressives were not reported to have low DBH activities (18), recently Meltzer et al (19) reported low DBH in a subgroup of psychotically depressed unipolar patients. Since both low MAO and low DBH levels might lead to central increases in dopamine, subjects with both low MAO and low DBH levels might be particularly vulnerable to psychotic symptoms. Wyatt (20) has suggested that individuals low in MAO activity might be unable to metabolize adequately phenylethylamine (a naturally occurring amphetaminelike compound derived from phenylalanine), especially if they had high levels of phenylalanine as in individuals heterozygous for phenylketonuria. Since DBH might also catabolize phenylethylamine, the low DBH-low MAO combination might again be associated with a special vulnerability.

Since our subjects were not psychiatric patients, psychologic and psychophysiologic measures associated with schizophrenia seemed most appropriate to assess any biologic vulnerability. From studies of reaction time reviewed elsewhere (e.g., 21) and presented at this Conference, it has been clearly demonstrated that schizophrenic patients have difficulty in sustaining attention to stimuli. Even drug-free remitted schizophrenics have difficulty in sustaining attention to stimuli in a continuous performance task (CPT) (22). The cortical average evoked response (AER) is diminished in amplitude if subjects disregard the stimulus and increased if subjects attend (e.g., 23). Smaller amplitude AERs have been generally reported in schizophrenics (24a) especially under conditions of attentional demands such as stimuli being uncertain (25) or infrequent (26). Thus both CPT and AER seemed appropriate measures for study of our biochemically-at-risk population.

METHODS

A total of 375 college students and university employees (203 men and 172 women, ages 18–38) were recruited from local sources and were paid $5.00 each for giving an initial blood sample.

Blood samples were analyzed for platelet counts and for platelet MAO activities using ^{14}C benzylamine as the substrate (5) and are reported in units of nanomoles/108 platelets/hr. The top and bottom 10% of the sample were then contacted for further study; complete data, as described below, were obtained from 87%. The final groups of high- and low-MAO individuals were selected on the basis of their mean platelet MAO activity from both the initial screening and repeat visit values; the high and low groups were separated by four MAO units. Since males had lower mean values than females (10.1 vs. 13.2, $t = 7.36$, $p < 0.001$), the limits for the low and high groups were chosen separately (7). Eighty-four percent of the low males but only 17% of the females fell below the mean of a group of chronic schizophrenics studied previously.

On the repeat visit, plasma was obtained for measurement of DBH by a radioenzymatic assay described elsewhere (27). All subjects had been asked to discontinue any medications at the time of the second blood sample. Neither MAO inhibitors nor DBH inhibitors had been used by any of the sample, and none of the drugs that had been previousiy used by the individuals (e.g., marijuana) is known to be MAO or DBH inhibitors in concentrations used in man.

Subjects participated in a structured interview on personal and family history (7) and were studied using perceptual and cognitive tasks and AER measures. The interviewers, test givers, and subjects were not aware of the laboratory results, and all the information was kept separate until the final data analysis.

AER Attention Procedure

Each subject received the same sequence of stimuli in two runs. Two sets of instructions were used, in random order. Four intensities of light and four intensities of 500-Hz tones were presented in a constrained random sequence. Each stimulus was 500 msec followed by a 500-msec interstimulus interval. Each intensity of light and tone was presented 64 times. Stimuli were generated and responses averaged by an on-line computer system (24). The light flashes were displayed on a translucent screen, rear-illuminated by fluorescent tubes, and the auditory stimuli were presented through a high fidelity speaker in front of the subject. EEG was recorded from vertex (Cz-right ear) and the temporoparietal area (Wernicke's area, 28), and responses to each of the four intensities were averaged on-line (see 29 for further details). AERs were divided into three time bands centered on P100 (76–112 msec), N140 (116–152 msec), and P200 (168–248 msec). These time bands generally coincide with the positive (P1), negative (N1) and positive (P2) triphasic sequence usually identified in the visual evoked response. The area in each time band was then calculated for use as an amplitude measure, as described earlier (29), following techniques used elsewhere (30,31).

During the "light attention" instructional condition the subject was instructed to count the number of times consecutive light flashes were of the same intensity, disregarding any intervening tones. During the "tone attention" instruction the same task was reassigned for the tone stimuli, with the intervening lights being ignored. Thus, visual AERs were computed under conditions of selective attention and inattention. The negative component at 140 msec (N140 or N1) is especially affected by selective attention (32), and this effect is most clear at low stimulus intensities for both visual (33) and auditory (34) modalities. A lack of increase in N140 amplitude for low-intensity stimuli under the selective attention condition would be a fairly specific indicator of a selective attention deficit.

Sustained Attention Measure

Rosvold's (35) Continuous Performance Test was modified to allow a greater performance range in normal subjects. A sequence of single numerals was presented to the subject on an LED display. The subject is requested to push a button if a "6" appears if and only if it is preceded by a "4." The failure to do so is an omission error; pressing the button for a number outside the critical sequence is a commission error. Since normals normally make less than 5% errors, we increased the error rate by reducing the interstimulus interval by 5% following each correct identification and increased the interval by 5% following each error. Subjects were instructed to work to maximize the stimulus presentation rate. A total of 600 digits were presented which contained 60 "4-6" combinations, 420 nontarget numerals, and 60 "4s" not followed by a "6." Median interstimulus interval for the last 200 stimuli formed a third summary score.

RESULTS

Subjects showed a wide range of plasma DBH values (23 to 2448) with a mean of 1094 units in males and 1197 units in females ($p < 0.10$ by t-test). Consistent with earlier reports (36), no significant relationship between MAO and DBH levels could be demonstrated by correlational analysis. For certain analyses, subjects were divided into high- and low-DBH groups on the basis of the median DBH in the total sample (1134). The mean of the high group (1670 $\pm$ SD 380) was roughly similar to a group of patients with a clinical and genetic pattern compatible with the autosomal dominant for torsion dystonia observed by Wooten et al (37).

DBH and AER Attention Effects

Overall, higher levels of DBH were associated with greater amplitude increases for the visual AER in the attending condition (counting light pairs) over the amplitude in the nonattending condition (counting tone pairs). The correlation between plasma DBH level and the difference between the N140 visual AER amplitude when counting stimulus pairs and when counting tones was 0.28 for the vertex lead (n = 68, p < 0.05) and 0.31 for left temporoparietal area (p < 0.05). This effect was far greater for low-intensity stimuli than for high-intensity stimuli. For example, at the lowest stimulus intensity the high-DBH group showed a significant mean amplitude increase of 30% (0.9 microvolts) in the visual AER when subjects attended (counting light stimulus pairs), but at the highest intensity the amplitude decreased by 1%. The low-DBH group also showed the same intensity effect but, in contrast to the high-DBH group, their amplitudes decreased both at the lowest intensity (1%) and the highest (12%).

MAO and AER Attention Effects

No significant correlations were found between MAO levels and AER attentional effects, nor did low-intensity attention effects distinguish the groups.

Combined DBH and MAO Attention Effects

The relationship between DBH levels and AER attentional effects was far stronger in the low MAO group, as shown in Figure 38-1. As was previously found for DBH alone, the differences are most marked for low intensities. Table 38-1 shows the mean differences in microvolts between N140 visual AER amplitude in the attending condition and the nonattending condition. Low-MAO/high-DBH subjects showed a mean increase of 37% in AER amplitude at the lowest intensity, vertex lead, whereas high-MAO/high-DBH subjects showed only a 25% increase. For the temperoparietal area, the comparison was 52% and 7%. The interaction among MAO, DBH, and magnitude

Table 38-1. Attention Effects on AER N140 Component for Mean of Two Lowest Intensities

	Low DBH	High DBH
Low MAO		
vertex	−0.32	1.23[a]
temporoparietal	−0.02	0.95[b]
High MAO		
vertex	−0.01	0.55
temporoparietal	0.28	−0.04

[a] Low DBH different from high DBH, t-test, p < 0.01.

[b] Low MAO different from high MAO, t-test, P < 0.05.

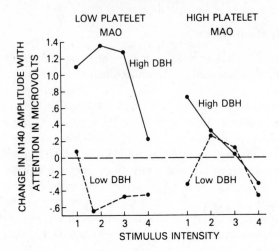

AER ATTENTION EFFECTS AND NEUROTRANSMITTER
RELATED ENZYMES

Figure 38-1. Differences in visual AER amplitude for the negative component at 140 msec between two attentional conditions, counting visual stimulus pairs and counting randomly interspersed auditory stimuli. Note that the AER amplitude enhancement was greatest in high DBH/low MAO subjects, and that the effect was maximal at low intensities.

of the attentional effect was statistically confirmed with a three-way analysis of variance (MAO level × DBH level × stimulus intensity, $F = 5.13$, d.f. 1, 65; $p < 0.05$ for the three-way interaction). It also should be noted that as a group, high-DBH subjects showed a statistically significant difference between the two attentional conditions for the visual AER N140 component, whereas the low-DBH group did not. The P100 and P200 components tended to show these trends, although the results did not reach statistical significance.

Continuous Performance Test

Subjects with low MAO and high DBH made significantly fewer errors of commission (by t-test, $p < 0.05$) than subjects with low MAO and low DBH—the type of error previously associated with performance in remitted schizophrenics (Table 38-2). The cor-

Table 38-2. Continuous Performance Task

	Minimum ISI in msec	Errors of Commission	Errors of Omission
Low MAO			
Low DBH	339	12.9[a]	13.6
High DBH	331	10.6	14.1
High MAO			
Low DBH	345	12.4	14.2
High DBH	347	13.6	13.4

[a] Low DBH different from high-DBH/low-MAO group (t-test, $p < 0.05$).

relation between DBH and errors of commission in low-MAO subjects was −0.403. As observed with the AER measure, the best attentional performance was seen in the low-MAO/high-DBH group with no significant DBH effect in the high-MAO group. No significant effect was observed for the interstimulus interval measure.

DISCUSSION

In this study we observed an association between high levels of plasma DBH and both enhanced selective attention, as inferred from AER measures, and vigilance performance, as measured by a continuous performance task. While this DBH/attention relationship was present in our entire sample, it was primarily in a group of individuals with low levels of platelet MAO activity that DBH was a correlate of attentional performance. This combination of findings brings together two somewhat disparate approaches to the biology of schizophrenia.

From the many systematic studies of reaction time (see 21) and concurrent autonomic psychophysiology (38), it appears that schizophrenic patients have difficulty in sustaining attention to stimuli. AER measures of attention are relatively newer and have been used in fewer studies of schizophrenics than reaction time or vigilance performance. Nevertheless, smaller amplitude increases over baseline when stimuli are uncertain (25) or infrequent (26) have been reported. Diminished contingent negative variation, an indicator of expectancy, has been reported in schizophrenics (39,40). The observed high variability in schizophrenic AERs has been interpreted as reflecting fluctuating attention and a decreased capacity to disregard redundant events (41).

AERs also have been reported to be influenced by brain monoamines in ways consistent with our data and with Wyatt's (20) speculations about phenylethylamine or other endogenous hallucinogens. Sabelli et al (42) report that, while injection of phenylethylamine alone failed to influence visual AERs in the rabbit, the slow negative component was abolished in animals pretreated with MAO inhibitors; the duration of this effect was prolonged by DBH inhibitors. Shaffer and McKean (43) report that lowering dietary phenylalanine in phenylketonuric humans resulted in discriminative visual AERs to patterned stimuli. Dimethyltryptamine has also been reported to diminish AER amplitude in humans (44).

For these reasons, the association of individual differences in attentional performance with levels of two neurochemical enzymes important to the metabolism of dopamine and/or false neurotransmitters is significant for the study of the psychotic disorders. It should be noted that neither the biochemical findings nor the psychologic ones are entirely unique to schizophrenia. Low MAO levels have been found in patients with bipolar affective illness and chronic but not acute schizophrenia (1), and low DBH levels have been found in a psychotic subgroup of unipolar depressives (19) but not in other psychotic groups. Similarly, diminished CNVs were found to be characteristic of depressives (39) as well as schizophrenics. Our finding linking poorer attentional performance and low-MAO/low-DBH levels in nonhospitalized nonpatients suggests that abnormalities in these biologic indicators previously observed in psychiatric inpatients are not merely artifacts of hospitalization or illness but are related to psychologic variables of possible relevance to the clinical psychiatric syndromes. While there is some evidence supporting a relationship between platelet and brain MAO activity (5), it is not yet clear how plasma DBH activities relate to tissue DBH activity. Thus, for the present, these findings cannot be considered as direct evidence supporting the hypothesis of alteration in brain enzyme activities in patients with schizophrenia or affective disorders.

SUMMARY

A group of subjects potentially at risk for psychiatric disorders was identified by screening 375 college students for low platelet monoamine oxidase (MAO) levels. The lower and upper 10% in MAO activity were studied with the continuous performance task measure of attentional vigilance and average evoked response (AER) measures of selective attention. Plasma dopamine-beta-hydroxylase also was measured. Among individuals low in both platelet MAO and plasma DBH, attentional performance on both measures was poor in comparison to individuals with high MAO or high DBH levels. The biochemical-high-risk strategy used here reduces the biologic heterogeneity of the sample and eliminates hospitalization and treatment factors that may confound many biochemical studies. While the relationships between peripheral enzyme levels and central monoamine metabolism are poorly understood, these results are nevertheless consistent with leading conceptualizations of biochemical abnormalities in the major psychoses—the dopamine, transmethylation and false neurotransmitter hypotheses.

REFERENCES

1. Wyatt RJ, Murphy DL: Low platelet monoamine oxidase activity and schizophrenia. *Schizophrenia Bull* 2:77, 1976.
2. Wyatt RJ, Murphy DL, Belmaker R, et al: Reduced monoamine oxidase activity in platelets: A possible genetic marker for vulnerability to schizophrenia. *Science* 173:916, 1973.
3. Murphy DL, Weiss R: Reduced monoamine oxidase activity in blood platelets from bipolar depressed patients. *Amer J Psychiat* 128:1351, 1972.
4. Nies A, Robinson DS, Lamborn KR, et al: Genetic control of platelet and plasma monoamine oxidase activity. *Arch Gen Psychiat* 28:834, 1973.
5. Murphy DL, Belmaker R, Wyatt RJ: Monoamine oxidase in schizophrenia and other behavioral disorders. *J Psychiat Res* 11:221, 1974.
6. Schooler C, Zahn, TP, Murphy DL, et al: Psychological correlates of MAO activity in normals. *J Nerv Ment Dis,* in press.
7. Buchsbaum MS, Coursey RD, Murphy DL: The biochemical-high-risk paradigm: Behavioral and familial correlates of low platelet monoamine oxidase activity. *Science,* 194:339, 1976.
8. Garmezy N: Children at risk: The search for the antecedents of schizophrenia. *Schizophrenia Bull* No. 8:14, 1974.
9. Lamprecht F, Wyatt RJ, Belmaker R, et al: Plasma dopamine-beta-hydroxylase in identical twins discordant for schizophrenia, In Usdin E, Snyder SH (eds): *Frontiers in Catecholamine Research.* New York, Pergamon Press, 1973, p 1123.
10. Ewing JA, Rouse BA, Mueller RA: Alcohol susceptibility and plasma dopamine-beta-hydroxylase activity. *Res Comm in Chemical Pathology and Pharmacology* 8:551, 1974.
11. Ewing JA, Rouse BA, Mills KC, et al: Dopamine-beta-hydroxylase activity as a predictor of response to alcohol. *Japan J Stud Alcohol* 10:61, 1975.
12. Dunner DL, Cohen CK, Weinshilboum RM et al: The activity of dopamine-beta-hydroxylase and methionine activating enzyme in the blood of schizophrenic patients. *Biol Psychiat* 6:215, 1973.

13. Shopsin B, Freedman LS, Goldstein M, et al: Serum DBH activity and affective states. *Psychopharmacologia* 27:11, 1972.

14. Wetterberg L, Aberg H, Ross SB, et al: Plasma DBH activity in hypertension and various neuropsychiatric disorders. *Scand J Clin Lab Invest* 30:283, 1972.

15. Wise CD, Stein L: Dopamine-beta-hydroxylase deficits in the brains of schizophrenic patients. *Science* 181:344, 1973.

16. Wyatt RJ, Schwartz MA, Erdelyi E, et al: Dopamine-beta-hydroxylase activity in brains of chronic schizophrenic patients. *Science* 187:368, 1975.

17. Angst VJ: Zur frange der psychosen bei behandlung mit disulfiram. *Schweiz Med Wschr* 86:1304, 1956.

18. Levitt M, Dunner DL, Mendlewicz J, et al: Plasma dopamine-beta-hydroxylase activity in affective disorders. *Psychopharmacologia* 46:205, 1976.

19. Meltzer HY, Cho HW, Carroll BJ, et al: Serum dopamine-beta-hydroxylase activity in the affective psychoses and schizophrenia. *Arch Gen Psychiat* 33:585, 1976.

20. Wyatt RJ, Gillin JC, Stoff DM, et al: Beta-phenylethylamine (PEA) and the neuropsychiatric disturbances. In Usdin E, Barchas J, Hamburg D (eds): *Neuroregulators and Psychiatric Disorders*. New York, Oxford University Press, 1977, p 31.

21. Zubin J: Problem of attention in schizophrenia. In Kietzman ML, Sutton S, Zubin J (eds): *Experimental Approaches to Psychopathology*. New York, Academic Press, 1975, p. 139.

22. Wohlberg GW, Kornetsky C: Sustained attention in remitted schizophrenics. *Arch Gen Psychiat* 28:533, 1973.

23. Hillyard SA, Hink RF, Schwent VL, et al: Electrical signs of selective attention in the human brain. *Science* 182:177, 1973.

24. Maugh TH: Medium sized computers: Bringing computers into the lab. *Science* 182:270, 1973.

24a. Landau SG, Buchsbaum MS, Carpenter W, et al: Schizophrenia and stimulus intensity control. *Arch Gen Psychiat* 32:1239, 1975.

25. Levit RA, Sutton S, Zubin J: Evoked potential correlates of information processing in psychiatric patients. *Psychological Medicine* 3:487, 1973.

26. Roth WT, Cannon EH: Some features of the auditory evoked response in schizophrenics. *Arch Gen Psychiat* 27:466, 1972.

27. Molinoff PB, Weinshilboum R, Axelrod J: A sensitive enzymatic assay for dopamine-beta-hydroxylase. *J Pharmacol Exp Ther* 178:425, 1971.

28. Matsumiya Y, Tagliasco V, Lombroso CT, et al: Auditory evoked response: Meaningfulness of stimuli and interhemispheric asymmetry. *Science* 175:790, 1972.

29. Coursey RD, Buchsbaum MS, Frankel BL: Personality measures and evoked responses in chronic insomniacs. *J Abnorm Psychol* 84:239, 1975.

30. Shagass C: *Evoked Brain Potentials in Psychiatry*. New York, Plenum Press, 1972, pp 169–173.

31. Soskis DA, Shagass C: Evoked potential tests of augmenting-reducing, *Psychophysiology* 11:175, 1974.

32. Schwent VL, Hillyard SA, Galambos R: Selective attention and the auditory vertex potential. I. Effects of stimulus delivery rate. *Electroencephalogr Clin Neurophysiol* 40:604, 1976.

33. Schechter G, Buchsbaum MS: The effects of attention, stimulus intensity and individual differences on the average evoked response. *Psychophysiology* 10:392, 1973.

34. Schwent VL, Hillyard SA, Galambos R: Selective attention and the auditory vertex potential. II. Effects of signal intensity and masking noise. *Electroencephalogr Clin Neurophysiol* 40:615, 1976.

35. Rosvold HE, Mirsky AF, Sarason L, et al: A continuous performance test of brain damage. *J Cons Psychol* 20:343, 1956.

36. Belmaker R, Beckman H, Goodwin F, et al: Relationships between platelet and plasma MAO, plasma DBH and urinary 3-methoxy-4-hydroxy phenylglycol. *Life Sciences* 16:273, 1975.

37. Wooten GF, Eldridge R, Axelrod J, et al: Elevated plasma dopamine-beta-hydroxylase activity in autosomal dominant torsion dystonia. *New Engl J Med* 288:284, 1973.

38. Zahn TP: Psychophysiological concomitants of task performance in schizophrenia. In Kietzman ML, Sutton S, Zubin J (eds): *Experimental Approaches to Psychopathology*. New York, Academic Press, 1975, p 109.

39. Small JG, Small IF: Contingent negative variation (CNV) correlations with psychiatric diagnosis. *Arch Gen Psychiat* 25:550, 1971.

40. Timsit-Berthier M, Delaunoy J, Koninckx N, et al: Slow potential changes in psychiatry. I. Contingent negative variation. *Electroencephalogr Clin Neurophysiol* 35:355, 1973.

41. Jones RT, Callaway E: Auditory evoked responses in schizophrenia—a reassessment. *Biol Psychiat* 2:291, 1970.

42. Sabelli HC, Vazquez AJ, Flavin D: Behavioral and electrophysiological effects of phenylethanolamine and 2-phenylethylamine. *Psychopharmacologia* 42:117, 1975.

43. Schafer EWP, McKean CM: Evidence that monoamines influence human evoked potentials. *Brain Research* 99:49, 1975.

44. Arnold OH: N,N-Dimethyltryptamin: Einige erste verleichsergebnisse. *Arzneim-Forsch* 25:972, 1975.

Section IX

HIGH RISK AND PREMORBID DEVELOPMENT

INTRODUCTION
E. James Anthony, M.D.

In this section the majority of the authors are engaged in prospective studies of infant, child, and adolescent subjects at high risk for schizophrenia. They address themselves to the examination of various hypotheses related to what has been termed schizophrenia-in-the-making. As the studies have progressed, questions have presented themselves in increasing numbers while answers, as in any longitudinal investigation, have lagged behind. Karl Popper remarked that the growth of knowledge in any branch of science results from a process closely resembling what Darwin termed "natural selection" (1). At any given moment in the evolution of a scientific area, what one knows derives from those hypotheses that have demonstrated their comparative fitness by surviving in the struggle for existence, a competitive contention that gradually eliminates the unfit hypotheses. With regard to high-risk research, as will be evident from the contributions that follow, the field is still far from being able to ascertain fitness or unfitness with any degree of confidence, so a host of hypotheses continue to haunt the current scene without being adequately disconfirmed and discarded. Furthermore, the proponents of some of the most fragile and almost moribund hypotheses tend to conserve them with a peculiar and passionate attachment, even when they fail the test of satisfying the calculus of probabilities. There is always the hope that these conjectures (for that is frequently all that they are) represent bold anticipations of things to come, with their validation lying in the future.

In spite of the still embryonic nature of the work, there is no doubt that the concept of risk has opened up a new world of research that permits the early study of the later established disorder. It has furnished us at least three possible ways of observing the genesis of schizophrenia by identifying subject populations with expectancies for morbid

397

development very much higher than those in the general population. Criteria for selection have been based mainly on tainted parentage, premorbid clinical characteristics, or neurologic dysfunctions presumably stemming from birth complications. Such criteria have provided samples of susceptibles with a 10–15% liability to future schizophrenia but a 40–60% liability to a wide range of current or future psychopathologic states, far more extensive than the entities included in the so-called schizophrenia spectrum disorders (2).

Risk research also has generated a new metalanguage that is fast obtaining an appreciable vocabulary. Although the epigenetic aspect has come increasingly to the forefront with a more balanced understanding of the continuous interactions between inherent and acquired susceptibilities (vulnerability), inherent and acquired risks to which the individual is exposed, and inherent and acquired capacities for mastering them (competence) in relation to the eventual outcome of health or disorder, clinicians, in general, appear to favor a deficit research strategy. Too, they appear to pay more attention to factors conducing to vulnerability, while nonclinicians have focused their attention on the elements of resilience and competence. The two approaches have understandably utilized the particular strengths belonging to the two types of researchers who have entered this special field and, taken together, they have enhanced the development in the field. The two concepts of vulnerability and competence likewise convey the important realization that not every child at high risk is liable to become disturbed or psychotic, and that the proper study of risk entails an understanding not only of the individuals who succumb but also of those who remain remarkably immune.

One can look at resilience and vulnerability in several different ways. For example, one can envisage the resilient subject as someone who has so far been fortunate in evading a precipitating stressfulness; or as one with such "super" combinations of competence, confidence, and adeptness in solving both cognitive and emotional problems as to make him "superphrenic," with perhaps an Achilles heel that eventually brings him down; and, finally, one can see him, more clinically, as a heavily defended person who "pays" in emotional terms for his invulnerability, which is reminiscent of Hinkle's (3) finding of the development of a kind of "emotional insulation" in people who had lived through demanding life situations in a state of well-being. Such individuals appeared to have only shallow attachments to people, goals, or groups, and they readily shifted to other relationships when established relationships were disrupted. "There was an almost 'sociopathic' flavor to some of them." "They behaved as if their own well-being were one of their primary concerns. They avoided situations that would make demands on them if they felt they could not, or did not want to meet these demands." For these reasons, they were apt to refuse promotions because they did not want the increased responsibility, overtime work because it was too tiring, transfers because they were "too much trouble," and they divorced themselves from relatives in trouble and refused to worry about them because there was nothing they could do about it. In St. Louis, we have observed such psychologic characteristics and attitudes in our group of "invulnerable" children, suggesting that this might play a role in the apparent immunity to the psychotic influence (4).

There also seemed to be three types of vulnerable children: (a) those who did quite well as long as they remained relatively encapsulated within a sheltered home setting and no drastic changes were made in their life situation; (b) those who, from birth onward, were of such poor physical and mental fiber that they responded to any and every stressor nonspecifically with transient decompensations and an efflorescence of symptoms, and who gave the general impression, in terms of Spenserian evolutionary theory, that they were poorly differentiated, poorly integrated, and totally dependent on a continuing tolerance and acceptance from the environment; and (c) there were those whose vulnerability seemed closely linked to the specific stressors associated with schizophrenia, such as thought disorder, communication deviance, and affective incongruence.

Being vulnerable can create a feeling tone of vulnerability, a generalized sense of insecurity and lack of safety that develops over time (5). These children seem aware of their incompetence in dealing with problematical situations and have little or no confidence in their capacities for mastering them. They behave like victims of a fate that is inevitable and of a course of events that cannot be altered. Clinically, they stand out in the family circle as being most closely identifiable with the sick parents, most involved in the elements of that sickness, and most responsive to any shifts in the mental status of the parents, and tending to interpret these in terms of their own experiences. To know how a child feels about the parents' illness, one must approach him directly. Psychotic illness, as a specific stressor for the child, is not quite the same illness as the one perceived and diagnosed by the clinician. The child's view is related not to the clinical diagnosis but to the behavior of the parent as it impinges on the child, and this behavior often may have particular components for a particular child in the family. Thus, it depends on the degree to which the child has been drawn into the maelstrom of the illusional and hallucinatory systems of the parent (6). Another factor also contributes to the stressful nature of parental psychosis for the child: it would seem that what taxes his adaptive capacity and coping skills is not simply the degree of severity of the disorder as rated by the psychiatrist but the range of transformation undergone by the parent from his best to his worst behavior (as measured, for example, by ratings on the Global Assessment Scale).

The child, living in the milieu of psychosis, can develop disturbances that can be regarded as identificatory, antecedent, or reactive. Miniature decompensations seem to punctuate the course of development of the vulnerable child and these "micropsychoses" tend to increase in frequency and intensity as the child enters adolescence and adult life. Now that many of the longitudinal risk investigations are entering the peak-age period for the development of schizophrenia, more opportunity will be available to study such "breakdowns" in greater detail, as is possible with the prospective mode of observation (7).

The clinical view has been emphasized in this introduction to provide some measure of balance in relation to the more laboratory types of investigation to be described by other contributors.

REFERENCES

1. Popper K: Evolution and the tree of knowledge, in: *Objective Knowledge: An Evolutionary Approach.* Oxford, Clarendon Press, 1972, p 261.
2. Kety S, Rosenthal D, Wender P, et al: The types and prevalence of mental illness in the biological and adoptive families of adoptive schizophrenics, in Rosenthal D, Kety S (eds): *The Transmission of Schizophrenia.* New York, Pergamon Press, 1968.
3. Hinkle L: The effect of exposure to culture change, social change, and changes in interpersonal rela-

tionships on health, in Dohrenwend BS, Dohrenwend BP: *Stressful Life Events*. New York, John Wiley & Sons, 1974, p 41.

4. Anthony EJ: The syndrome of the psychologically invulnerable child, in Anthony EJ and Koupernik C (eds): *The Child in His Family: Children at Psychiatric Risk*. New York, John Wiley & Sons, 1974, pp 529–544.

5. Anthony EJ: The syndrome of the psychologically vulnerable child, in Anthony EJ and Koupernik C (eds): *The Child in His Family: Children at Psychiatric Risk*. New York, John Wiley & Sons, 1974, pp 3–10.

6. Anthony EJ: A clinical evaluation of children with psychotic parents. *Am J Psychiat* 126:177, 1969.

7. Anthony EJ: The developmental precursors of adult schizophrenia. *J Psychiat Res* 6 (suppl 1):293, 1968.

Chapter 39

Obstetric Factors in the Development of Schizophrenia: Complications in the Births of Preschizophrenics and in Reproduction by Schizophrenic Parents

Thomas F. McNeil, Ph.D.
Lennart Kaij, M.D.

Obstetric complications (OCs) have been extensively studied as somatic, environmental *antecedents to* a broad range of psychiatric disorders, including schizophrenia, in the offspring. A majority of the studies of OCs antecedent to schizophrenia have focused on childhood schizophrenics rather than on adult schizophrenics. On the other hand, the distinction between childhood and adult schizophrenia typically has been overlooked when formulating the etiologic factors in adult schizophrenia. What is now needed is a review of the OC evidence regarding adult schizophrenics.

In recent years there has been a proliferation of studies of OCs in reproduction by schizophrenic parents, this interest having been stimulated by genetic high-risk studies of the offspring of schizophrenics (1,2). The theoretical relationship between OCs antecedent to schizophrenia and OCs in reproduction by schizophrenics often has been misinterpreted, with the rate of OCs in parents who at any time have been diagnosed as

*Preparation of this literature review has been partially supported
by PHS Research Grant No. 18857 from NIMH and by Grant No.
3793 from the Swedish Medical Research Council.*

schizophrenic being considered as prima facie evidence for or against the etiologic role of OCs in the later development of schizophrenia.

In the current presentation, we first shall outline a number of alternative hypotheses regarding the etiologic role of OCs in the development of schizophrenia. Next, we shall delineate the types of studies and research strategies used to investigate the relationship between OCs and schizophrenia, review the existing empirical data regarding these hypotheses, and discuss methodologic issues and the fit between hypotheses and data. Finally, we shall present new data from our ongoing study of OCs in the histories of adult schizophrenics.

The terminology we use in the present review is the following: By obstetric complications (OCs) we mean the general class of *somatic* deviations from an expected, "normal" course of events during pregnancy, labor and delivery, and the early neonatal period studied prior to discharge from the puerperal ward. Spontaneous abortions, fetal and neonatal deaths, and congenital malformations are thus included within OCs. The limits of an expected, "normal" course of events are selected quite arbitrarily and fluctuate among studies; most researchers have recorded those OCs which the obstetric personnel regard as complications. Some studies also include a mother's obstetric history, psychologic status, and even demographic characteristics (e.g., unmarried status) as OCs.

Within OCs, pregnancy complications or "PCs" cover the period from conception to the onset of labor; birth complications or "BCs" include the period during labor and delivery; and neonatal complications or "NCs" cover the period from the birth of the child through 2–4 weeks postpartum (or until discharge from the puerperal ward). Prematurity and other prenatal developmental deviations (like "small-for-date" status) have variously been considered PCs, BCs, or NCs in different studies. "Total OCs" refer to the sum of PCs, BCs, and NCs studied in a given project.

WORKING HYPOTHESES OF OCs' ETIOLOGIC ROLE IN SCHIZOPHRENIA

The following hypotheses (not necessarily mutually exclusive) are presented as guidelines for evaluating the theoretical relevance of the empirical data presented below, and we shall focus on some of the more common, basic interpretations of these data.

Hypotheses I–V concern the role of OCs, types of OCs, and types of schizophrenia; Hypotheses VI–IX, the relationship between OCs and other etiologic factors; and Hypotheses X–XII, the origin of OCs associated with schizophrenia.

Hypothesis I. The "no relationship" hypothesis: OCs are entirely unrelated to schizophrenia.

Hypothesis II. The "inverse relationship" hypothesis: OCs decrease risk for schizophrenia.

Hypothesis III. The "continuum of casualty" hypothesis: A broad range of OCs increases risk for all types of schizophrenia (among other disorders).

Hypothesis IV. The "specific OC" hypothesis: A particular type of OC or different OCs with similar effects increase risk for all types of schizophrenia.

Hypothesis V. The "schizophrenia subtype" hypothesis: OCs increase risk for one subtype of schizophrenia (e.g., regarding symptomatology, prognosis, illness course, degree of organicity) but not for schizophrenia in general.

Hypothesis VI. The "OC phenocopy" hypothesis: Given the already well-established genetic component in schizophrenia (3), OCs are an etiologic factor alternative to genetic influence, OCs being related to "organic phenocopies" of "real", genetic-based schizophrenia. Co-occurrence of a genetic influence and OCs in schizophrenics would be no greater than that expected by chance.

Hypothesis VII. The "OC-plus-gene additive" hypothesis:[1] While both OCs and genetic influence *each* increase risk for schizophrenia, the combination of OCs and genetic influence has no unique or multiplicative effect, but rather it has a higher potency (approximately equal to the sum of the two factors) for schizophrenia than does either factor by itself.

Hypothesis VIII. The "OC-gene interaction" hypothesis:[1] OCs and genetic factors combine in a more than additive manner to increase risk for schizophrenia. Other formulations of this hypothesis are that OCs increase risk for schizophrenia only in genetically predisposed persons or that OCs "trigger" the genetic potential for schizophrenia.

Hypothesis IX. The "OC and other environmental factors" hypothesis: OCs either interact with or add to other environmental factors, increasing risk for schizophrenia. This hypothesis covers the situation in which OCs would establish a set of conditions that would then increase risk for schizophrenia, as suggested by Pollin and Stabenau (4).

Hypothesis X. The "OC stress" hypothesis: The occurrence of OCs is independent of other factors associated with schizophrenia (e.g., genetic influence), and OCs have an independent, "stressful" effect on the offspring, thus increasing risk for schizophrenia.

Hypothesis XI. The "non-etiological epiphenomenon" hypothesis: OCs are a direct consequence of other factors associated with schizophrenia (e.g., genetic influence, parental characteristics) and have no independent, "stressful" effects that increase risk for schizophrenia in the offspring.

Hypothesis XII. The "secondary-consequence" hypothesis: OCs are a secondary consequence of other factors associated with schizophrenia (e.g., maternal medication, environmental conditions), but the OCs have etiologic effects that increase risk for schizophrenia in the offspring.

OCs ANTECEDENT TO ADULT SCHIZOPHRENIA

The OC histories of adult schizophrenics have received little empirical attention, in comparison with OC histories of childhood schizophrenics. While some genetic data (5) suggest biologic unity between adult and childhood schizophrenia, the relationship between the two disorders remains unclear (3). Schizophrenia in childhood is, in any case, not representative of adult schizophrenia (3,6), and etiologic factors, especially of an environmental nature, like OCs, need not necessarily be the same for childhood and adult schizophrenia.

Samples and Methodology

As shown in Table 39-1, the six articles we could find regarding OCs for adult schizophrenic groups (excluding twin and high-risk samples) consisted of one study of birthweight by Lane and Albee (7) and a series of studies of birthweight and OCs by

---

[1] Rosenthal (3) cites a number of models for stress-diathesis "interaction," and these overlap with Hypotheses VII and VIII to a certain extent.

Table 39-1. Empirical Studies of OCs in the Births of Adult Schizophrenic Samples

Study	Index Subjects (Age) [Diagnosis]	Control Subjects	Source OC data	Comparison: Schiz. > Controls in OC frequency	Other Results
Lane and Albee (7)	52 adult schiz. (age unstated) [apparently hospital diagnosis]	115 sibs	birth certificates, some birth records	$p < 0.01$ lower birth-weight (mean diff. = 6 oz) n.s. schiz. two times more often prema-ture	results not dependent on sex or birth order
Woerner et al (12)	46 schiz. (15–35 yrs.) [criteria referenced] 67 personality disorders	54 sibs (37 normal, 17 abnormal)	retrospective maternal interview (100%): PCs, birth certificate (91%): BCs, birth records (48%): NCs (blind coding)	schiz. vs. normals: $p = 0.03$ PCs, $p < 0.02$ BCs, $p < 0.02$ total OCs schiz. vs. abnormals: n.s.: PCs, BCs, or total OCs. zero NCs among 48 schiz. + sib records	n.s. OCs for male vs. female subjects n.s. OCs for schiz. vs. personality disorders
Pollack et al (10)	33 schiz. (25 chronic, 5 paranoid, 2 schizo-affective, 1 acute) (15–32 yrs.) [hospital diagnosis]	33 normal sibs (13–35 yrs.)	retrospective maternal questionnaire and interview (blind coding)	n.s. trend more frequent and severe OCs for schiz. n.s. birthweight	

Study	Subjects	Controls	Data source	OC findings	Results
Woerner et al (11)	34 schiz. (15–35 yrs.) [criteria referenced]	42 sibs (13–37 yrs.)	hospital records or birth certificates	n.s. (p < 0.10) birth-weight (mean difference = 5.8 oz) n.s. length at birth no prematurity among subjects	
Pollack and Greenberg (8)	51 schiz. (mostly chronic undifferentiated) (15–34 yrs.) [hospital diagnosis; excluded subjects with neurologic disease]	none	maternal reports	45% with moderate or severe OCs	OCs related to lower age at first hospitalization (p < 0.01), at first treatment (p < 0.01), and lower I.Q. (p < 0.01 moderate vs. no OC) n.s. trends OCs related to abnormal EEG, childhood deviation, and psychologic test evidence of CNS dysfunction
Pollack et al (9)	74 schiz. (15–57 years) [rediagnosis by researcher]	none	psychiatric records (?)	47.3% suspected early MBD, rated from birth and childhood history	MBD subjects had poorer outcome at 3-yr posthospital follow-up (p < 0.01)

Pollack and colleagues (8–12). The schizophrenics were chosen from hospital populations, which, in the Pollack series, represented white, primarily middle-class, voluntary patients. Diagnostic categories were clearly defined in more recent studies (13). Schizophrenics with known neurological disease were excluded from one study (8). All control samples consisted of siblings, including a subgroup of abnormal siblings in the most recent article (12).

Studies of OCs other than birthweight and infant length relied, at least in part, upon retrospective maternal reports, with Woerner et al (12) supplementing these with birth certificates for 91% and birth records for 48% of the sample. The birth records, which were used primarily to obtain information about NCs, failed to identify a single NC for 48 schizophrenics and siblings—an unexpected result considering the frequency of NCs found in some retrospective studies (14). These studies of OCs employed blind rating and coding of the OCs for index versus control subjects.

Results

Two separate studies found schizophrenics to weigh an average of about 6 oz (170 g) less than their siblings at birth, this difference reaching statistical significance for Lane and Albee (7) but not ($p < 0.10$) for Woerner et al (11). Prematurity was twice as frequent among schizophrenics as among siblings but statistically nonsignificant in the Lane and Albee sample; however, not a single premature subject was found among the total of 76 schizophrenics and siblings studied by Woerner et al (11).

Pollack et al (10) used retrospective maternal reports to study OCs and found a nonsignificant trend toward more frequent and more severe OCs for schizophrenics than for normal siblings. A more recent study by the same researchers (12), using additional data from birth certificates and records, found significantly more PCs, BCs, and Total OCs for schizophrenics as contrasted with normal siblings; no OC measure was significantly different for schizophrenics versus psychiatrically abnormal siblings.

Interestingly, schizophrenia subgroup analyses by Pollack and Greenberg (8) showed OCs ("degree of paranatal abnormality") to be significantly related to lower I.Q., and to lower age at first psychiatric treatment and at first psychiatric hospitalization. OCs also showed a nonsignificant trend toward being related to childhood deviancy (poor social adjustment and learning difficulties), abnormal EEG, and psychologic test evidence of CNS dysfunction—which is notable since schizophrenics with "evidence of neurologic disease" had been excluded during sample selection. In another study (9), schizophrenics rated as having suspected early minimal brain damage, based on birth and childhood history, showed a significantly poorer outcome at 3-year posthospital follow-up.

In summary, the few available studies seem to indicate that OCs, but not necessarily lower birthweight, are differentially characteristic of the births of adult schizophrenics, and that histories of OCs in the schizophrenic samples relate to relatively early adult onset, lower I.Q., and poorer outcome.

OCs AS DISCRIMINATORS WITHIN TWIN AND HIGH-RISK SAMPLES

Twins

Studies of monozygotic (MZ) twins discordant for schizophrenia or for severity of schizophrenia provide a valuable means of studying the effect of environmental factors such as OCs while holding genetic factors constant. Two limitations cited for OC studies using the discordant-twin technique are that (a) twins are a birth complication, thus potentially yielding many OCs and possibly inflating the apparent relevance of OCs to the etiology of schizophrenia, and (b) even consistent findings of within-pair differences may be small and, thus, possibly irrelevant to the development of schizophrenia in nontwins.

While a definitive and exhaustive review of sampling and diagnostic procedures for all the separate studies including discordant MZ twins is beyond the scope of this chapter, excellent reviews are to be found in Gottesman and Shields (15) and Fischer (16). Rather than reporting the OC results for the single studies, often with very small discordant samples, we have chosen to make use of previous summaries by Pollin and Stabenau (4) and Gottesman and Shields (15), showing OC characteristics of discordant MZ twins from a number of studies.

Intrapair Birthweights and Schizophrenia

Pollin and Stabenau's (4) compilation of data (found in the literature) for 100 pairs of MZ twins discordant for schizophrenia or severity of schizophrenia[2] provided evidence for a relationship between the development of schizophrenia and lower birthweight within the pair. While Pollin and Stabenau found lighter birthweight to be twice as frequent among the schizophrenics as compared with their co-twins, a more recent compilation of 82 discordant pairs by Gottesman and Shields (15), using data from five studies which they considered to have representative samples (15,17–20), showed lighter birthweight to be equally distributed among the schizophrenics and their co-twins. The differences in results stem from the fact that the two summaries share only 31 pairs (19,20) among their respective 100 and 82 pairs. Fischer's (16) twin study, which is not included in the above summaries, had largely missing data regarding birthweights. Rosenthal's (21) interesting study of the Genain quadruplets is relevant within the framework of multiple birth studies. He found that, while the entire reproduction involving the quadruplets was filled with complications, the two quads with the highest birthweights had the lowest severity. In summary, the existing data regarding the relationship between schizophrenia and discordant MZ twin birthweights appear to be inconclusive at the present time.

BCs and Schizophrenia

Pollin and Stabenau's summary (4) for the 100 discordant MZ pairs showed that "any BC" (N = 30 intrapair differences) and "asphyxia at birth" (N = 15 intrapair differences) were each four times more frequent for the schizophrenics within the discordant pairs. Since the choice of studies for compilation by Gottesman and Shields produced considerable change in the results regarding birthweight, the question may be raised as to whether the above BCs results would hold up in their choice of "representative" studies. Since Gottesman and Shields presented no summary data regarding BCs, we have performed our own compilation of BCs within discordant MZ twin pairs in the "representative" studies (15,17–20) used by Gottesman and Shields.

As shown in Table 39-2, the five studies showed a total of 39 discordant MZ pairs with an intrapair difference in BCs. In total, 71.8% of these pairs showed more BCs for

---

[2] Both major summaries (4,15) contain some pairs concordant for schizophrenia but discordant for severity (15, p 46). For simplicity of presentation, we use the term "schizophrenic" to denote even those twins who were the more severely schizophrenic within pairs concordant for diagnosis.

Table 39-2. Birth Complications for MZ Twin Pairs Discordant for (Severity of) Schizophrenia, from "Representative Samples" Chosen by Gottesman and Shields (15)

Study	Intrapair Differences in Birth Complications	
	More BCs for the (More Severely) Schizophrenic Twin	More BCs for the Normal or the Less Severely Schizophrenic Co-twin
Gottesman & Shields (15)[a] [Case histories: "BCs"]	4	1
Tienari (20) [Table p 112: "more difficult birth"]	5	2
Kringlen (18) [Table 48, p 119: "difficult birth"]	4	3
Inouye (17)[a] [Table 8, p 529: "asphyxia neonatorum"]	8	2
Slater (19)[a] [Table 14, p 50: "more difficult birth"]	7	3
Total	28[b] (71.8%)	11[b] (28.2%)
Pollin and Stabenau (4) ["any BC"]	24 (80.0%)	6 (20.0%)

[a] Included pairs discordant for severity of schizophrenia.

[b] Binomial: p = 0.01, two-tailed.

the schizophrenic twin. BCs were thus found 2.55 times more often for the schizophrenic twin than for the co-twin, a highly significant difference (p = 0.01, two-tailed). The limited information regarding the specific nature of the BCs prevents a closer evaluation of the type of BCs involved in these differences. Fischer's study (16), which is not included in the above summaries, showed very few recorded OCs, which probably reflects the fact that the birth records were from 1878–1912 for the discordant pairs. In summary, both the older studies and the newer ones show an association between BCs and schizophrenia in discordant MZ twin pairs.

Methodologic Considerations about OCs in Twin Studies

To our knowledge, all reviewed studies of discordant MZ twins, with the exception of Fischer's (16), obtained OC information retrospectively from relatives or from the twins themselves. Our impression from reading the case histories from more recent studies (15,16,20) is that the OC data are very sparse and generally of poor quality. There are obvious difficulties in requiring mothers (or twins!) to recall and report BCs for each of the same-sexed, identical twins at least 2 decades after the birth and after one twin has become schizophrenic. Despite these methodologic difficulties, the twin data regarding BCs are of considerable interest. Questions of the representativeness of twin OC results seem less critical when taken within the context of this review, since the twin BC data fit well with the results from single-born schizophrenics, and the data thus complement one another.

High-risk Samples

The offspring of schizophrenic parents provide a genetic high-risk (HR) group within which to study the interplay of genetic risk and environmental factors such as OCs (2). The only published study yet to relate OCs in the births of the offspring to their adult psychiatric status is that of Mednick and Schulsinger (22) who, in 1962, began a longitudinal study of 207 HR offspring of severely schizophrenic women and 104 offspring of control women. A 5-year follow-up showed 20 of the HR offspring to have become "severely abnormal" (not necessarily schizophrenic), and these "sick" subjects were then matched for demographic variables and 1962-mental status with 20 HR "well" offspring whose mental status had remained the same or improved, and with 20 low-risk (LR), normal "control" offspring.

Data regarding OCs in the births of these groups were obtained from forms completed by midwives attending the subjects' births (1942–1952). These forms have been described by Mednick as an "adequate but not ideal" source of OC information (23). Hospital birth records for the offspring have not been collected to date.

The first analysis of the frequency of *single OCs* among sick-well-control groups showed no significant differences (22), but subsequent reanalysis (24) in terms of total OCs showed *at least one OC* for "70% of the members of the sick group", 15% of the well group, and 36% of the control group.

However, Mizrahi's (25) unpublished report of these data, subsequent to Mednick's publication of them in 1970 (24), showed that the midwife records were missing for one sick, six well, and five control subjects. While the data available for the sick and well subjects still showed a higher proportion of sick subjects with at least one OC, the differences were less impressive than the 70% versus 15% originally reported by Mednick, and the chi-square analysis of "sick" versus "well" data done by Mizrahi (26, p 70) was on the boundary between significance-nonsignificance, depending on whether the Yates correction was used.

To our knowledge, Mednick has never presented the specific complications and frequencies representing "at least one OC," but these data for 19 sick, 14 well, and 15 control subjects are presented in the unpublished manuscript by Mizrahi (25). The OCs considered to represent "a history of severe perinatal distress" (27, p 103) for the 19 sick subjects are the following: 1 abnormal presentation, 3 premature ruptures of membranes[3], 6 prolonged labors, 2 forceps deliveries (unspecified position), *1 asphyxia,* 4 prematures, 1 multiple birth, 1 placental abnormality, and 1 umbilical cord complication. Further variables for the sick subjects are 16 cases with anesthetics (79–93% for the well and control subjects), 5 labor stimulants (much higher for the control subjects), 2 episiotomies (indication unstated), and 1 abnormal maternal reproductive history. The OCs most differentially characteristic, but nonsignificantly so, of the sick subjects were prolonged labor (31.6%, 0%, and 13.3% for the sick, well, and control groups) and prematurity (21.1%, 7.1%, and 6.7%, respectively).

Mednick (24) further found that OCs in the HR group were related to GSR rapid onset, rapid recovery, and poor habituation of response, plus poor extinction of conditioned response; the OCs, being of different frequencies in the sick versus well groups, *thus* accounted for the GSR differences between the sick and well subjects. Other

---

[3] The term, "dry birth," as consistently used by Mednick and Mizrahi, refers to rupture of amnionic membranes prior to active labor and not to "oligohydramniosis," called dry-birth in older literature (29,30), which is a rare and serious condition.

analyses (23) evaluated the possible mode of interplay between OCs and genetic risk regarding GSR patterns; these analyses showed additive effects for amplitude (large) and recovery (fast), while true interactive effects were found for latency (fast). Since OCs were not strongly related to GSR patterns among the LR subjects, Mednick concluded that OCs "trigger some characteristic which may be genetically predisposed" (24, p 56).

These results led Mednick (24) to formulate the theory that OCs result in anoxia that selectively damages the hippocampus, and this subsequently leads to schizophrenia in the genetically predisposed person. This theory has been criticized on neurophysiologic grounds by Kessler and Neale (28). An evaluation of the theory from an obstetric viewpoint is also indicated: In Mednick's own sample, only 1 of 19 sick subjects showed clinical evidence of anoxia (as judged from the midwife reports), namely the 1 asphyctic child.[4] In addition, a number of the other OCs found more often among the sick subjects than among the well subjects could increase the *risk* for but not necessarily lead to anoxia. All the OCs noted were birth complications, and any signs of asphyxia would thus have been available for observation by the midwives. Mednick's OC data might permit an *inferred* hypothesis concerning *risk* for anoxia, but provide little substantial evidence for the hypothesis since the hypothesized condition was not reported to have occurred.

The OC results from the Mednick-Schulsinger project, while suffering from an incompleteness regarding OC data and sketchy reporting, appear to be interesting findings, especially in relationship to the GSR parameters. These findings need to be replicated both in independent studies and with the "real" schizophrenics among the HR group. Mednick (32) recently has indicated that 15 of the HR subjects have become "severely schizophrenic" and that "perinatal difficulties mark the schizophrenics." We look forward to a presentation of these results.

In an as-yet unpublished study, Mirdal, Rosenthal, Wender, and Schulsinger investigated the relationship between "schizophrenicity" in adulthood (in the offspring) and OCs in the births of offspring of schizophrenic and control parents. The presence (vs. absence) of "any OC" is reported to be unrelated to the degree of "schizophrenicity" of offspring of schizophrenic parents. In contrast, the presence of OCs was related to *lower* "schizophrenicity" for control offspring. While further interpretation of these data must await their publication, the data do not support the hypothesis that OCs raise the risk for schizophrenia in genetically predisposed individuals.

While the high-risk area is still relatively young in terms of results, it promises potentially valuable contributions regarding knowledge of the etiologic role of OCs in the development of schizophrenia.

OCs IN REPRODUCTION BY SCHIZOPHRENIC PARENTS

Theoretical Relevance of the Studies

As stated previously, only one high-risk study (24) to date has published results regarding the relationship of OCs to adult mental status in the offspring. When the ongoing

---

[4] While the terms, anoxia and asphyxia, are often used interchangeably in clinical praxis (most likely in Danish midwife reports from 1942–1952), a clarification of these terms might be theoretically helpful: *Anoxia* is the "absence or deficiency of oxygen, as reduction of oxygen in body tissues below physiologic levels" (31) and, as such, is not observable through clinical methods. *Asphyxia* is the "apparent or actual cessation of life due to interruption of effective gaseous exchange in the lungs" (31) and is thus clinically observable.

high-risk studies (1) begin to find schizophrenia in the offspring, it will be possible to use high-risk study data to evaluate OCs in the births of these subjects as possible *antecedents* to schizophrenia. Until then, we are left with comparing rates of OCs for schizophrenic parents with those for control subjects and seeking relationships between OCs and other variables within the high- and low-risk groups. Data from such studies will fit well with other existing data regarding OCs in reproduction by mentally ill women.

The comparison of OCs in reproduction by schizophrenic and control parents may potentially yield information about (a) psychosomatic theories of psychologic stress and OCs, (b) epiphenomenal consequences of being schizophrenic, (c) general offspring risk as a consequence of OCs, (d) theories of interaction between OCs and genetic factors, and (e) even the "true nature" of schizophrenia [given some serendipitous finding like that of Shearer et al (33)].

While these topics are of considerable interest, it must be stressed that *the rates of OCs in reproduction by schizophrenic parents cannot,* given the available data, *show that OCs do or do not contribute to the development of schizophrenia in the offspring.* For example, if maximum differences in OC rates between schizophrenic and control parents were observed, and if every reproduction by a schizophrenic parent were attended by, e.g., severe asphyxia in the fetus, then asphyxia could not selectively relate to the development of schizophrenia in only that part of the high-risk group that will become schizophrenic; in such a case, asphyxia would seem to be a consequence or correlate of schizophrenia in the parent. On the other hand, if the reproduction by schizophrenic parents and by control parents produced exactly the same number and type of OCs, the OCs that occur nevertheless could be related differentially to the development of schizophrenia in the high-risk offspring.

Empirical Studies of OCs

Samples and Methodology

Table 39-3 presents information regarding samples, source of OC data, and results of 20 studies of reproduction by schizophrenic parents. While all studies included reproduction by schizophrenic mothers, a number of studies (27,34–38) also included reproduction by schizophrenic fathers. These comparisons of reproduction by schizophrenic mothers and by schizophrenic fathers are of value in evaluating possible OC consequences of schizophrenia. Samples of schizophrenic mothers included reproduction before, during, and after the onset of schizophrenia, and some samples (39,40) studied only women delivering offspring in psychiatric hospitals. In all studies, except Schachter's (41,42), the parents studied had been hospitalized psychiatric patients at some time; Schachter's studies included patients from prenatal clinics, and 39% of the women judged to be schizophrenic had had no previous psychiatric contact (42).

Hospital diagnoses of schizophrenia were used in sample selection in a number of studies (39,43,44), but some recent studies have used more standardized procedures of rediagnosis using psychiatric records, patient interviews, or testing with CAPPS (45). The types of schizophrenia included for study typically have been "spectrum" varieties, including process-chronic, acute, borderline, schizophreniform, schizoaffective, and so forth. These different subtypes typically have been collapsed into one "schizophrenic" group; only two studies analyzed OC data separately for "continuous" vs. acute types (37) and for process vs. schizophreniclike samples (46).

Table 39-3. Empirical Studies of Obstetric Complications in Reproductions by Schizophrenic Parents

Study	Schizophrenic Sample [Diagnostic Criteria]	Control Sample	OC Data Source	Results: Schiz. > controls in OC frequency	Other Results
McNeil and Kaij (46)	32 reprod. by 20 process schiz. mothers 38 reprod. by 22 schiz.-like mothers (SLP) [criteria given; organics excluded]	32 + 38 matched from delivery series	pregnancy and birth records (100%) (blind scoring)	schiz. vs. control: n.s. PCs, BCs, NCs, placental Cs, total OCs, or all specific OCs SLP vs. control: n.s. as above	schiz. vs. SLP: n.s. OCs Both index group n.s. OCs male vs. female offspring birth before vs. after first hospitalization: *schiz*—n.s. PCs, BCs, Plac. Cs, NCs; p = 0.04 more developmental deviation *before* first hospitalization; *SLP*—p < 0.05 more BCs and NCs *after* first hospitalization
McNeil et al (55)	99 reprod. by endogenous psychotic mothers (including 70 schiz. or SLP)	none for this analysis	(severity rated from psychiatric records)		n.s.: total OCs for subjects actively disturbed vs. not disturbed during pregnancy trend: fewer OCs for Ss seriously disturbed postpartum (p < 0.01 for first births)
Mednick et al (27)	83 reprod. by 57 schiz. mothers and 26 schiz. fathers [schiz. spectrum included acute and borderline]	83 reprod. by matched normal subjects 83 reprod. by "character disorder" parents	birth records (100%) (blind scoring)	schiz. vs. other: n.s. PCs or BCs. n.s. lower birthweight[a] Schiz. and CD vs. normal: more NCs (signif.?)	schiz. only: more PCs for female than male offspring; more PCs in births before than after illness onset; PCs and BCs correlated with NCs; <3000 g birthweight correlated with 1-yr retarded development
Mura, Mednick, et al (50)	same as (27)	83 new controls	same as (27)	p < 0.01 lower birthweight	
Mizrahi, Mednick, et al (51) and Mednick and Schulsinger (22)	166 reprod. by 112 process schiz. mothers (Mednick-Schulsinger project subjects)	90 reprod. by 84 control mothers	midwife birth records (100%) (not blind scoring)	n.s.: weighted OCs, severity of OCs, total OCs, each separate OC, or birthweight	schiz. before vs. after breakdown: n.s. total OCs, weighted OCs, or severity of OCs schiz.: n.s. OCs for male vs. female offspring

Study	Subjects	Data source	Findings	Comments
Hanson, Gottesman, and Heston (35), and Hanson (34)	33 reprod. by 14 schiz. mothers and 15 schiz. fathers [20 chronic, 3 acute, 1 schizophreniform, 5 borderline]; 36 nonschiz. psychiatric patients; 33 matched normals; 33 unmatched normals	birth records (100%)	schiz. vs. other: n.s. total OCs, specific OCs, or birthweight.	lower offspring I.Q. (7 yrs) related to edema and vaginal bleeding only in continuous schiz. group; I.Q.-OC relationship unaffected by male vs. female offspring or mother vs. father. No relation: birthweight-I.Q.
Rieder, Broman, and Rosenthal (37)	45 reprod. by 28 mothers and 17 fathers with "continuous schiz." (chronic, borderline, schizoaffective); 15 reprod. by 15 parents with "acute schiz." [criteria given]; 45 + 15 matched control subjects; 6580 population controls	pregnancy and birth records (100%) (blind scoring)	both schiz. types vs. matched controls: n.s. edema, vaginal bleeding, hypertension, 5-min. Apgar score, or use of conduction anesthetic. continuous schiz. vs. pop: schiz. p < 0.05 more vaginal bleeding; all other OCs n.s.	
Rieder et al (36)	93 reprod. by 46 schiz. mothers and 33 schiz. fathers; 60 reprod. by 24 mothers and 22 fathers with "possible schiz."; 57 reprod. by 16 mothers and 21 fathers with nonschiz. disturbance [criteria given]; 2 matched controls for each index	NINDS data; hospital records for deaths	schiz. vs. controls: p = 0.053 fetal or neonatal deaths, p < 0.01 more fetal deaths of "unknown cause", p < 0.05 more perinatal deaths of "unknown cause"; other index vs. controls: n.s. deaths; each index vs. controls: n.s. birthweight	
Schachter, Lachin, Spruill et al. (42)	79 reprod. by 79 schiz. mothers (39% no previous psychiatric contact) [criteria given, included CAPPS (45)]; 62 reprod. by 62 healthy mothers; 343 reprod. by 343 mothers with nonschiz. disorders	birth records (100%)	schiz. vs. all controls: n.s. specific OCs[b], PCs, BCs, total OCs, birthweight, or prematurity.	all subjects: no relation OCs and maternal anxiety or depression during pregnancy
Schachter et al (41)	23 reprod. by 22 schiz. mothers; 25 reprod. by 25 "low-certainty" schiz. mothers; 64 reprod. by nonschiz. women	birth records (100%)	schiz. vs. other: p < 0.01 more BCs and short gestation	
	16 reprod. by 16 schiz. mothers; 23 reprod. by 23 low-certainty schiz. mothers; 18 reprod. by 18 nonschiz. mothers	birth	n.s. birthweight or Apgar score among 3 groups: n.s. PCs, BCs, Apgar score, or gestational age	schiz. only: high delivery medication related to lower offspring heart rate acceleration

413

Table 39-3. (continued)

Study	Schizophrenic Sample [Diagnostic Criteria]	Control Sample	OC Data Source	Results: Schiz. > controls in OC frequency	Other Results
Sameroff and Zax (43)	12 reprod. by 12 schiz. mothers [hospital diagnosis]	12 reprod. by 12 neurotic-depressed mothers / 12 reprod. by 12 normal mothers	birth records (100%)	Among 3 groups: n.s. BCs	Significantly more BCs and abnormal EEG (combined) for schiz. & neurotic-depressed more major OCs for more severe 50% of schiz. and neurotic-depressed.
	13 reprod. by 13 schiz. mothers [criteria given, incl. CAPPS]	13 reprod. by 13 neurotic-depressed mothers / 13 reprod. by 13 normal mothers	birth records (100%)	Among 3 groups and schiz. vs. neurotic-depressed: n.s. BCs	BCs related to severe disturbance among both disturbed groups
Sobel (39)	222 reprod. by 218 schiz. mothers (pregnant and delivered in mental hospital) [hospital diagnosis]	population rates	psychiatric records	8.1% stillborn and neonatal deaths for schiz. vs. 3.6% for general population malformations: 3.2% schiz. vs. 0.8–1.3% gen. population	
Paffenbarger et al (53)	126 reprod. by 126 postpartum psychotics (57 schiz., 27 m.d., 42 undifferentiated) [all first psychotic episode; hospital diagnosis?]	252 reprod. from same delivery sequence	birth records	n.s. OC differences among 3 index diagnostic types	all patients vs. control: $p < 0.05$ total OCs. $p < 0.05$ PCs. $p < 0.01$ short gestation. $p = 0.02$ more perinatal mortality. significantly lower (live) birthweight
Soichet (40)	767 reprod. by schiz. women delivered in psychiatric hospitals [hospital diagnosis]	none	questionnaire to psychiatric hospitals	2 among 767 with preeclampsia; none with eclampsia	
Wiedorn (54)	127 reprod. by 57 black women and 28 reproduction by 15 white women with "acute schiz. psychotic episodes" [criteria unstated; hospital diagnosis rechecked by author]	150 reprod. by 54 black control women	birth records	$p = 0.001$ more toxemia (blacks only; n.s. white schiz. vs. black controls)	$p = 0.02$ more toxemia before (vs. after) first psychotic episode. most toxemia in first pregnancy and in pregnancy right before first episode

Study	Sample	Controls	Data source	Results	Additional results
DeHorn and Strauss (44)	130 reprod. by 23 white male schiz. and 35 white female schiz. (twin reprod. excluded) [hospital diagnosis]	150 reprod. by 75 nonschiz. psychiatric patients	state birthweight norms; birth certificates	offspring birthweight: n.s. both fathers and mothers vs. state norms; n.s. schiz. mothers vs. other patient mothers; $p < 0.05$ heavier for schiz. fathers vs. other patient fathers; gestational age: n.s. schiz. parents vs. other patient parents	n.s. schiz. vs. other patients near or after first breakdown. $p < 0.05$ schiz. *heavier* than other patients before breakdown
Yarden and Suranyi (52)	44 reprod. by mothers schiz. during pregnancy; 21 reprod. by mothers with post-partum schiz. reactions (excluded twins, birth injured, and malformed offspring) [hospital diagnosis]	35 reprod. by mothers somatically ill during pregnancy	birth records	offspring birthweight: n.s. schiz. vs. somatic; n.s. schiz-postpartum vs. somatic; n.s. schiz. vs. schiz-postpartum	female offspring heavier in *all 3 groups*
Lane and Albee (38)	162 reprod. by 66 schiz. mothers and 119 reprod. by 45 schiz. fathers [hospital diagnosis]	national birthweight norms	birth certificates and birth records	n.s. birthweight	no difference in birthweight for mothers vs. fathers

[a] The chi-square value cited in the article is incorrect, and this birthweight variable is not significant (50).

[b] Two specific OCs showed statistical significance but represented only one case each of "abnormal presentation" and "cord prolapse" for schizophrenics versus zero frequency for controls.

The obstetric data and samples in the schizophrenic parent studies are typically of a considerably better scientific quality than those reported previously for the "antecedent" studies. Most of the current samples studied births from the 1950s to the 1970s. No study used maternal recall to measure OCs; most studies obtained birth records or birth certificates (for birthweight) for all subjects. A number of samples are associated with prospective high-risk studies (22,27,43), and two of the studies (35–37) made use of existing OC data in the Collaborative Perinatal Study of the NINDS (47). While some of the studies investigated only one type of OC, e.g., toxemia or low birthweight, many studies investigated summary variables for PCs, BCs, and so forth, plus a considerable number of evaluations of rates of specific OCs. Scoring of OCs was done blindly with respect to index versus control status in at least three studies (27,37,46).

Results

1. *Offspring birthweight:* The finding of significantly lower birthweights for offspring of schizophrenics as compared with those of controls by Mednick et al (27) received considerable attention and has led to discussions of the stress versus diathesis nature of lowered birthweight in high-risk subjects (48,49). The reported results were, in fact, not statistically significant, but a more recent study (50) rematched the control group and reported birthweight differences reaching statistical significance. However, as can be seen in Table 39-3, this finding of lower birthweight for the offspring of schizophrenics generally has not been corroborated by other studies. In summary, nine different studies (27,35,36,38,41,42,46,51,52) found no significant differences in birthweights for offspring of schizophrenics versus those of controls, two studies (50,53) found significantly lower birthweights for schizophrenics'/postpartum psychotics' offspring, and one study (44) found significantly higher birthweights for the offspring of schizophrenic fathers. Even among the studies showing nonsignificant differences, the direction of the birthweight differences was inconsistent.

2. *OCs:* Seven different studies (27,35,37,42,43,46,51) showed nonsignificant differences among PCs, BCs, total OCs, and single OCs in the reproduction by schizophrenic parents as compared with those of control parents.[5] Only Paffenbarger et al (53), studying postpartum psychotics (including 45% schizophrenic type), found significantly more OCs for patients than for controls. Schachter et al (41) found significantly more BCs for one schizophrenic mother sample but did not confirm this in another sample presented in the same article, nor in their earlier, unpublished study with a larger sample (42). Regarding toxemia, Wiedorn's (54) study, which showed significantly more toxemia for black schizophrenic mothers than for black controls, has not been confirmed in other studies (35,40,42,46,51), and Wiedorn's results can be viewed as unrepresentative—toxemia not being differentially characteristic of schizophrenic mothers. In summary, reproduction by schizophrenics, as contrasted with reproduction by controls, with few exceptions, has not been found to be characterized by increased rates of PCs, BCs, NCs, or total OCs.

3. *Fetal and neonatal deaths and malformations:* Sobel (39) studied psychiatric records of schizophrenic women delivering in mental hospitals and found higher rates of offspring malformations, stillbirths, and neonatal deaths for schizophrenics as compared

---

[5] Sameroff and Zax (43) found significantly more deviations for schizophrenic mothers by combining BCs *and* abnormal offspring EEGs into a single variable, but BCs by themselves were not significantly different between the groups.

with the general population. Paffenbarger et al (53) found increased rates of perinatal death for offspring of women with postpartum psychoses. A more recent study by Rieder et al (36), using OC data from the Boston sample of the Collaborative Project, investigated rates of fetal and neonatal deaths in reproduction by schizophrenic, "possibly schizophrenic," nonschizophrenic index, and control mothers and fathers. Only the schizophrenics differed from the controls in having more fetal and neonatal deaths, this difference being statistically significant for cases with "unknown" cause (N = 7 deaths). The schizophrenic-control difference was not significant when spontaneous abortions before the twentieth week of pregnancy were excluded. The cause of the deaths generally could not be traced to maternal medication, and some data argued against a genetic causality.

The other sample from the Collaborative Project (34) evidenced one fetal death and one neonatal death (both of unknown cause) among 33 births from schizophrenic parents, compared with no deaths for 66 controls. Two fetal deaths also were noted among 36 offspring of nonschizophrenic psychiatric patients, which, together with the results of Paffenbarger et al (53), suggests that the elevated rate of deaths is not associated only with schizophrenia.

4. *Birthweight of offspring of schizophrenic fathers versus schizophrenic mothers:* Mednick's (27) original, nonsignificant finding of lowered birthweight seemed to be more characteristic of offspring of schizophrenic fathers than of schizophrenic mothers. Studies by Lane and Albee (38) and Hanson et al (34,35) showed very little difference in birthweights for offspring of schizophrenic mothers as compared with those of schizophrenic fathers. DeHorn and Strauss (44) found schizophrenic fathers' offspring to weigh 202 g *more* than schizophrenic mothers' offspring and 240 g *more* than control fathers' offspring, both latter groups showing normal birthweights. Thus, no consistent trends have been found regarding the birthweights of the offspring of schizophrenic fathers versus schizophrenic mothers.

5. *OCs in reproduction by schizophrenic fathers versus mothers:* No consistency is found in results among the few studies that published results in a form that allows direct comparison of OCs in reproduction by schizophrenic fathers as compared with those by schizophrenic mothers. Mednick stated (27) that PCs were especially characteristic of daughters of schizophrenic fathers. Rieder et al (37) found the relationship between OCs and lowered offspring I.Q. to be at least as strong when the father was a "continuous" schizophrenic as when the mother was a "continuous" schizophrenic. Rieder et al (36) found that, in all cases except one, perinatal deaths occurred when the mother (or both mother and father) was schizophrenic. Hanson et al (35) found somewhat lower 1-minute Apgar scores in offspring of mothers, and no difference in gestational age for births from schizophrenic mothers versus fathers having at least one OC was significantly more characteristic of reproduction by schizophrenic fathers than of those of schizophrenic mothers (χ^2 = 4.25, 1 d.f., p < 0.05, our calculation). These diverse results might at least suggest that reproduction by schizophrenic mothers is not attended by more OCs than is reproduction by schizophrenic fathers.

6. *OCs in reproductions before versus after onset of schizophrenia:* Wiedorn (54) found almost unparallelled rates of toxemia for schizophrenics before, as contrasted with after, the first psychotic episode. Mednick et al (27) found more PCs in reproductions before breakdown for schizophrenia. However, Mizrahi et al's (51) study of the original Mednick-Schulsinger sample (22) showed no significant difference in total OCs or severity of OCs before as compared with after onset. McNeil and Kaij (46) found no dif-

ferences in PCs, BCs, NCs or placental deviations for process schizophrenics before versus after first hospitalization; in contrast, schizophreniclike psychotics (corresponding somewhat to American acute schizophrenics) showed more PCs, BCs, and NCs *after* first hospitalization. Prenatal developmental deviations were more frequent for both diagnostic groups in reproduction before first hospitalization. Mednick et al (27) found lower offspring birthweight for schizophrenic mothers breaking down during pregnancy or within one year postpartum, reminiscent of Paffenbarger et al's (53) finding of lower birthweight for offspring of postpartum psychotics. However, DeHorn and Strauss (44) found schizophrenics' offspring born before first psychiatric contact to weigh more than control offspring. In summary, the data regarding OC rates in reproduction before versus after onset of schizophrenia seem inconsistent.

7. *Severity of maternal schizophrenia and OCs:* Sameroff and Zax (43) found more BCs for the more severely ill halves of samples of both schizophrenic and neurotically depressed mothers, with severity defined in terms of extent of previous psychiatric care. McNeil et al (55) found no relationship between degree of active maternal mental disturbance during pregnancy and total OC rates for endogenous psychotics (including 70% schizophrenics or schizophreniclike psychotics); serious mental disturbance postpartum was significantly negatively related to OCs in first births. Schachter et al (42) found that mentally disturbed obstetric patients, including schizophrenics, showed significantly higher rates of anxiety and depression during pregnancy than did control patients, but neither anxiety nor depression was significantly related to presence of OCs. In another study by Schachter (41), two samples of schizophrenic mothers, as contrasted with controls, both evidenced significantly more anxiety and depression during pregnancy; while one of these samples showed more OCs than did controls, the other sample did not. The data regarding severity of maternal schizophrenia and OC rates thus appear to be inconsistent at this time.

8. *Sex of offspring and maternal disturbance* (not included in Table 39-3): Lane (56) found an unexpectedly high rate of female offspring born to schizophrenic women, suggesting a teratogenic effect on male fetuses. This proportion has not been upheld in other studies. In the seven samples reviewed here (27,34,41,44,46,51,52), 45% of the 495 offspring of schizophrenic mothers were female. A more specific relationship between the sex of offspring and the timing of development of schizophrenia in mothers was posited by Shearer et al (33) and by Taylor (57), who found evidence that schizophrenics who developed psychoses within one month of conception gave live birth only to female offspring. Schorer (58) found no corroboration of this result. McNeil et al (59), while using not entirely comparable methods, found the offspring sex ratio to be very similar for schizophrenic and schizophreniclike mothers who were disturbed during pregnancy when compared with those who were not disturbed.

Further studies by Taylor (60,61) suggested a causal relationship between onset of schizophrenic symptomatology within one month postpartum and the birth of male offspring. Two independent studies by Melges (62) and Schorer (58) both showed no predominance of male offspring born to women with onset of schizophrenia in the first month postpartum. In our own study (59), schizophrenics who became (more severely) disturbed postpartum showed a nonsignificant tendency to give birth to more female than male offspring. In summary, the available studies do not show a consistent relationship between maternal schizophrenic disturbance and sex of offspring.

9. *Sex of offspring and OCs:* Mednick et al (27) found more PCs for female than for male offspring of schizophrenics, contrary to the expected increase of OCs for males. In contrast, Mednick's original sample (51) showed no significant differences in OCs for

male versus female offspring (but sex did show an interaction with parity in which first-born males of schizophrenics had the highest rates of OCs, while later-born males of schizophrenics had OC rates lower than those of the controls). Yarden and Suranyi (52) found female offspring of schizophrenics to weigh more than males at birth, but this reversal of expected proportions was true and of the same magnitude for control offspring. In contrast, DeHorn and Strauss (44) found male offspring to be heavier than females both for schizophrenic and control parents. Our study (46) showed no significant differences in PCs, BCs, placental Cs, or NCs for male versus female offspring of schizophrenics. In summary, the significant findings may well be chance results among a large number of analyses.

10. *Relationships between OCs and other variables:* A question of considerable interest in terms of possible interactions between genetic and OC factors is whether OCs have special effects within these genetic high-risk groups. Mednick's (24) finding of a relationship between OCs and GSR patterns already has been discussed within the context of the adult psychiatric status of the offspring. A number of other recent studies also have shown relevant results.

Gallant (63), studying very small samples, found BCs to be especially related to Bayley Scale scores among offspring of psychotic mothers (versus controls) tested at 8 months of age. BCs were related to twice as much "scatter" (within-test variation) for the offspring of psychotic mothers as for control offspring, and the author concluded that "having both a psychotic mother and perinatal complications results in unevenness in development, and, inferentially, greater vulnerability to developmental maladaption" (63, p 216). However, the three offspring of psychotic mothers *with BCs* had a total developmental quotient of 107, which was comparable to that of the control offspring (D.Q. = 107.2). Retarded development (D.Q. = 95) was found for the three offspring of psychotic mothers *without BCs*. Both developmental unevenness *and* retardation have been viewed as relevant to schizophrenia, and, as Fish commented elsewhere, "delayed motor landmarks could . . . be extremely important" (49, p 118).

Mednick et al (27) have also related OCs to developmental rates in offspring of schizophrenic and nonschizophrenic index and normal controls. Only in the offspring of schizophrenic parents was birthweight below 3000 g related to retarded motor development during the first year of life. Both Fish (49) and Heston (48) interpreted the lower birthweight and poor development as most likely reflecting a schizophrenic genotype rather than an external precipitating event. Mednick further found an unexpected relationship in which PC scale scores were associated with "physical condition, illness, and accidents" for offspring of schizophrenic offspring of mothers, neurologic symptoms in nonschizophrenic psychiatric patients, and developmental retardation in normals' offspring at the one-year examination.

Two studies found a relationship between delivery anesthetic and other variables: Schachter et al (41) found a unique pattern among schizophrenics' offspring in which the level of maternal delivery medication was negatively related to neonatal heart rate (acceleration) response 2 days postpartum. Rieder et al (37) found that only for the "continuous" schizophrenic group was "conduction anesthetic," but not gaseous anesthetic, related to lower offspring I.Q. at 7 years of age. Furthermore, face-hand edema, vaginal bleeding, and low Apgar score were each related to lower I.Q., but again, only among the offspring of "continuous" schizophrenics. Lower birthweight divided at Mednick's boundary (above/below 3000 g) failed to show any relationship to lower I.Q. at 7 years of age.

These results, while interesting, need to be replicated with other samples, especially since the data often are based on small samples. Like many other types of schizophrenia studies, these findings are somewhat difficult to integrate into a comprehensive pattern, since, for example, lower I.Q. has not generally been found to be related to risk for schizophrenia (15,35).

Summary
The present status of this rich and complex literature regarding OCs in reproduction by schizophrenic parents might be summarized in the following manner: The majority of studies show (a) no differences in birthweights for offspring of schizophrenics versus controls, and (b) no differences in rates of PCs, BCs, NCs, total OCs, or specific OCs in reproduction by schizophrenics versus controls. (c) Four studies show some apparent increase in fetal and neonatal deaths and malformations in reproduction by schizophrenic parents (especially mothers), but this may not be characteristic only of schizophrenics.

The results of the other comparisons are more variable, but suggest (d) no consistent differences in birthweights of offspring of schizophrenic mothers versus fathers, (e) no consistent increase in OCs in reproduction by schizophrenic mothers, as contrasted with fathers, (f) no consistent differences in OC rates in reproduction before versus after onset of schizophrenia in mothers, (g) no consistent relationship between OC rates and severity of maternal schizophrenia, (h) no consistent relationship between maternal schizophrenic disturbance and sex of the offspring, and (i) no consistent relationship between OC rates and sex of the offspring. (j) Some recent data suggest that OCs may have special effects on other characteristics of the offspring (I.Q., GSR patterns, developmental rate) within the high-risk groups.

In any case, the reproduction by schizophrenics does not appear to be very different from that of controls in terms of OC rates. Many of the first, positive results have not been corroborated in numerous other studies, but, *in the apparent drive to make theoretical "progress," this lack of corroboration has largely been ignored, and the original findings are still being cited.* However, we believe that these negative findings may be of theoretical relevance to the etiology of schizophrenia.

DISCUSSION

Methodologic and OC Scoring Issues

Retrospective Maternal Recall of OCs
A majority of the studies of OCs antecedent to both adult and childhood schizophrenia used retrospective maternal reports as at least one major source of OC information. While some studies (64–67) suggest unreliability of parental information regarding OC histories (other than birthweight), Pollack and Woerner (68) suggested that inaccuracy in reporting by parents most likely concerns errors of omission. However, Rutt and Offord (69) and Taft and Goldfarb (70) have raised the possibility of selective memory and reporting and/or unconscious falsification of OC histories by parents whose offspring are schizophrenic. Taft and Goldfarb have observed that mothers of psychotic children give more detailed histories for the psychotics than for the nonpsychotic siblings, and these mothers also give more detailed histories than do mothers of control children.

Two different arguments have been used against such criticism: (a) Pollack and Greenberg (8), using maternal reports of OCs, found high rates of OCs for subjects with personality trait disorders but not for subjects with affective disorders; they concluded that it is unlikely that mothers would differentially or falsely report OC histories for children with different types of disturbance. (b) Significant differences in OC histories of schizophrenics versus controls have been found using all OC information sources *and* using only birth records in two different studies (70,71). Thus, while the significant results based on hospital birth records might suggest that the other significant results were not entirely a function of inaccurate maternal reporting, the question still remains as to the degree of veracity of OC data based on retrospective maternal recall. Such data are, in any case, unlikely to provide a basis for sophisticated or detailed analysis of obstetric variables.

Number of Analyses and Statistical Significance

Many of the studies reviewed here have used a large number of statistical analyses, and few studies have discussed the number of analyses that might be expected to yield statistical significance by chance alone. Some studies even fail to indicate the specific number of variables studied. This lack of clarity in reporting is even more problematic in inter-correlations among a large number of variables, since the reader has no way of knowing the number of possible combinations underlying the few significant and "highly interesting" relationships that are presented. In the absence of clear information concerning variables and analyses, the reader may be left wondering about the real significance of the statistically significant results presented in each study; thus, we have attempted to compare results across different, independent studies, and seek consistent trends unlikely to be the result of random variations.

Scoring of OCs

Scoring and combining OCs for analysis is one of the most problematic areas of the study of OCs as antecedent to schizophrenia. The crux of the scoring issue is that composite, summary OC scores (as currently used) are empirically useful but not theoretically satisfactory[6] in terms of determining which OCs and how OCs increase risk for schizophrenia in the offspring.

Two arguments support the use of summary scores: (a) From an empirical point of view, the frequency of each OC is usually so low that statistical significance is seldom reached for specific OCs (12,24,72) *even when* summary OC scores show highly significant differences between schizophrenics and controls. These significant differences, which suggest that something deviant or a lot of deviancy has occurred in these births, are facts to be taken seriously when found in so many different studies. Further analysis of OC type is nevertheless needed. (b) From a theoretical viewpoint, different, selected specific OCs have communality in terms of inferred effects on the fetus, and these communalities should form a sophisticated basis for further analysis as a complement to the more standardly used summary variables.

---

[6] Our usual OC summary scores may be as unsatisfactory as the hypothetical obstetrician who creates an "MC Score" (mental complications) which is the sum of any and all psychologic symptoms and signs, such as suicide, nervousness before examinations, hallucinations, promiscuity, and so forth, plus risk-associated conditions like inner-city residence and lower socioeconomic status.

What is an OC?

This rhetorical-sounding question has practical relevance to the current area because studies often have included such extremely broad types of variables within the OC-framework. If the reproducing mother is being studied as a phenomenon (e.g., reproduction by schizophrenic parents), especially in terms of psycho-obstetrics, then inclusion of a broad range of OCs and obstetric parameters may be of interest. However, if the intention is to study the effect of the OCs on the offspring, it would be best to study OCs that have a presumed effect on the fetus and not to include conditions that only increase risk for OCs, which can themselves be noted if they occur. A good case in point is a mother's (bad) obstetric history, which many studies have included as an OC in the *current* reproduction; obstetric history is studied by obstetric services because of increased risk for OCs in the current reproduction, but we feel that this should not be counted as an OC per se since any resulting OCs can themselves be noted.

Diagnosis of Schizophrenia

Much in the same way as OCs are bunched together into summary scores, many studies are characterized by a lack of clinical analysis of the mental disturbances subsumed within the category "schizophrenia," a fact that does not enhance the possibility of a sophisticated analysis of the role of OCs in interaction with genetic factors, as noted in Rieder et al (37).

Fit Between Hypotheses and Data

We have presented a number of hypotheses regarding the relationship of OCs to schizophrenia as a framework for interpreting the literature presented. The primary purpose of most of the studies reviewed here apparently has been to evaluate evidence concerning whether preschizophrenics have more OCs than do controls, or whether schizophrenic parents have more OCs than do controls; more refined, additional study required to obtain evidence for or against the different hypotheses has not been a general characteristic of the studies. Nevertheless, some evaluation of the hypotheses in terms of the available data is possible. Data from 17 empirical studies of OCs in the births of childhood schizophrenics and autistics (73), excluded from review here because of space limitations, are relevant for testing the hypotheses, and these childhood studies are included below where relevant.

The extensive number of significant, positive relationships between OCs and schizophrenia allows us to reject Hypothesis I that OCs have no relationship to schizophrenia, and Hypothesis II that OCs decrease risk for schizophrenia. All other hypotheses, stated in a positive form, seem to be supported by at least one among hundreds of different results, and we therefore concentrate on the weight of available evidence.

Hypothesis III (continuum of casualty),[7] that a broad range of OCs increases risk for schizophrenia in general, seems, at face value, to be well supported by the antecedent studies. This, being the most inclusive hypothesis, may have received differential support through lack of further subgroup or sub-OC analysis necessary for testing the other hypotheses.

---

[7] This hypothesis was taken from the more general hypothesis of a "continuum of reproductive casualty extending from death through varying degrees of neuropsychiatric disability," posited by Pasamanick (74, p. 91).

Hypothesis IV (specific OC), that a specific type of OC increases risk for schizophrenia, has not received very much support from the studies. Most comparisons for single OCs have not reached statistical significance, and our suggested technique using OC-communalities has not been employed. Our attempts (73) to identify specific OCs making up the summary variables which produce significant results in studies of childhood psychotics yielded the tentative conclusion that the specific OCs most characteristic of the histories of childhood psychotics *across six different studies* (69,71,72,75–77) were toxemia, bleeding during pregnancy/threatened spontaneous abortion, and asphyxia. These observations must be viewed with considerable caution, both because the exact frequency of the specific OCs for the samples is largely unobtainable from the published reports and because the different OCs were not consistently included for study.

Hypothesis V (schizophrenia subtype), that OCs increase risk for one type of schizophrenia but not for schizophrenia in general, has not been supported in any consistent manner. For childhood schizophrenics, OCs were not related to degree of organicity (73), to abnormal EEGs (69), nor to outcome at 6-year follow-up (78). OCs' relationship to I.Q. was inconsistent across two studies (69,78), but OCs did relate to the retarded motor and speech development (75). Pollack and Greenberg's study (8) of adult schizophrenics showed OCs to be related to lower I.Q., lower age at first treatment, and poor outcome, but not significantly to CNS disturbance. (New data to be presented below bear upon this hypothesis.)

Thus, as the data presently stand regarding the first group of hypotheses (Hypotheses I–V), the results seem to favor the "continuum of casualty" hypothesis, but this may very well be because of the lack of further evidence necessary for supporting the other hypotheses rather than because of direct evidence against them.

Hypothesis VI (OC phenocopy), that OCs produce organic phenocopies alternative to genetic-based schizophrenia, has not received much support. A strong relationship between OC history and degree of organicity has not been found in these studies, as noted previously for Hypothesis V. Other possible evidence for Hypothesis VI would be found if family mental illness were not observed for schizophrenics with OCs, but high rates of family mental illness were observed for schizophrenics without OCs. The little data available do not support this either: Rutt and Offord (69) found OCs in childhood schizophrenics to be unrelated to mental illness in their families. Gittelman and Birch (78), who found high rates of OCs for their schizophrenic sample, found CNS pathologic conditions in the sample to be unrelated to family psychopathologic state. The little direct evidence available does not appear to support the OC-phenocopy hypothesis.

Hypotheses VII and VIII, concerning additive and interactive relationships between OCs and genetic factors, can be evaluated with both qualitative and quantitative associations. From a qualitative viewpoint, that OCs relate to other characteristics *only* within genetically high-risk groups suggests an interaction rather than an additive relationship, and data from Mednick (24), Rieder et al (37), and Schachter et al (41) show relationships between OCs or delivery anesthetics and other variables (I.Q., autonomic responsivity) only within the high-risk samples. From a quantitative viewpoint, Mednick's (23) data suggested additive effects of OCs and genetic risk on GSR amplitude and recovery but interactive effects on GSR latency. Gallant's (63) data might suggest different interplay modes on developmental quotient versus scatter. In general, the little existing data support both interactive and additive hypotheses, and OCs and genetic factors may quite possibly have different modes of interplay for different characteristics related to schizophrenia.

Hypothesis IX, that OCs interact with other environmental factors, has received primary support from Pollin and Stabenau's (4) own study of MZ twins discordant for schizophrenia, in which lower birthweight or other early somatic trauma produced a relative physiologic incompetence that, in turn, led to parental attitudes and family relationship patterns which produced dependency and identity problems, all setting the stage for personality development conducive to the development of schizophrenia. Other studies of nonschizophrenics have provided evidence that perinatal complications render children more vulnerable to stressful familial factors, resulting in retarded development (79) and increased levels of disturbance during childhood (80).

Hypotheses X–XII concern the origin of OCs associated with schizophrenia, and we consider these hypotheses as a group. The hypotheses are difficult to prove or to disprove directly, but we offer the following arguments: (a) That reproduction by schizophrenic mothers does not appear to produce more OCs than does reproduction by schizophrenic fathers might suggest that the OCs which occur are not a result of schizophrenia or mental illness-correlates within the mother carrying and delivering the offspring. (b) That reproduction by schizophrenic parents does not have more OCs than those of controls suggests that OCs are not epiphenomenal consequences of schizophrenia or mental illness. (c) The elevated OC rates associated with preschizophrenics might alternatively be considered to be results of "schizophrenic" genes in the preschizophrenic person or stressful factors independent of genetic influence. (d) That the types of OCs that precede schizophrenia do not (given present evidence) appear to differ substantially from those associated with Pasamanick's continuum of casualty (74) makes it unlikely that the OCs antecedent to schizophrenia are the result of "schizophrenic" genes while the same types of OCs antecedent to other neuropsychiatric disorders are the result of other factors.

In summary, the weight of evidence at the present time might support the hypotheses that OCs in general increase risk for all types of schizophrenia (perhaps by lack of further evidence), that OCs seem to interact with genetic influence toward schizophrenia, and that OCs occurring prior to schizophrenia in the offspring are independent, stressful factors and not a manifestation of "schizophrenic" genes. Many of the critical studies and analyses necessary to obtain support for alternative hypotheses have not yet been done, and new evidence forthcoming in the future could very well prove this tentative summary to be partially or wholly incorrect.

NEW STUDY OF OCs ANTECEDENT TO ADULT SCHIZOPHRENIA

The literature review just discussed suggested the need for additional OC data for (a) a carefully-diagnosed, (b) representative sample of adult schizophrenics, and (c) a well-matched control group, with (d) OC data obtained from hospital birth records, (e) evaluated and coded blindly with respect to index and control status. We are currently conducting such a retrospective study, and present this first report on the subsample of subjects studied to date.

Samples and Methods

Adult schizophrenics are being sampled from among all male and female patients born after 1944, hospitalized in the comprehensive, adult inpatient psychiatric facilities in southwest Sweden, and having a hospital diagnosis of a psychosis that is not apparently of manic-depressive or organic nature. Standardized rediagnosis of the patients by means of psychiatric records is being done by the second author (LK), in accordance with diagnostic practices used in our ongoing high-risk project.

In the current retrospective study, each patient is placed in one of three diagnostic categories: (a) Process schizophrenia (excluding patients with predominantly affective symptoms, clouding of consciousness, subnormal intelligence before onset, or clear signs of organic disturbance including epilepsy), (b) Schizophreniclike psychosis or SLP (including atypical endogenous, schizoaffective, schizophreniform, confusional, and reactive psychoses, and postpartum psychoses with schizophrenic symptomatology), and (c) Neither a nor b.

Thus far, we have studied the obstetric records for the first 100 schizophrenic cases, i.e., 54 process schizophrenics and 46 SLPs, who were born in Malmö. The potential residential mobility of the patients between the two fixed time points—birth and psychiatric hospitalization in the sampling region—is about 100 miles, and the subjects may also have moved about prior to and after hospitalization.

The hospital birth records were obtained for all 100 subjects from the archives of Malmö General Hospital, the comprehensive delivery facility for the city of Malmö. One control case was individually matched for each index case, matching for (a) same delivery sequence (alternating before and after the index), (b) maternal parity, age, social class, and marital status at delivery, (c) offspring's sex, and (d) control offspring alive at discharge from the hospital.

The birth records were scored and coded by the first author (TM), who was blind with respect to index and control status and index diagnostic status of the subjects. All scoring systems for OCs, including summary variables, were determined before breaking the index-control codes.

A total of 57 single OCs were studied, and weighted summary scores were compiled for PCs, BCs, NCs, and total OCs. An attempt was made to include only OCs of a potentially serious nature in the summary scores and, further, to count each complication pattern only once in each summary score.[8] A special communality score for oxygen deprivation was also calculated, in which the highest points were given for repeated evidence of oxygen deprivation, the next highest points were given for a single occasion of oxygen deprivation, and the lowest points were given for several delivery conditions that considerably increase risk for oxygen deprivation.

The data analyses performed thus far compared process schizophrenics with their controls and SLPs with their controls. Based on the literature reviewed, the hypothesis tested was that schizophrenics have significantly more OCs than do their controls.

Results

The SLPs did not significantly differ from their controls on total OCs, any other summary variable, or any single complication, except jaundice which was more frequent for controls.[9] In contrast, the process schizophrenics had significantly more total OCs than did controls [$p = 0.038$, Wilcoxon matched-pairs signed ranks test (81)]. Breaking this

---

[8] The variables studied and the scoring systems used will be described in detail when the results for the full samples are presented; this information is currently available from the authors on request.

[9] Seventeen single OCs had sufficient frequency to yield potential significance, and about 1 of the 17 might be expected to be significant at the 0.05 level by chance.

total difference down to other summary scores, the process schizophrenics had significantly more NCs than did controls ($p = 0.02$), including primarily preterm and small-for-date status, asphyxia and respiratory distress, and jaundice. The next most discriminating summary score was the oxygen-deprivation score which showed more complications for process schizophrenics at the 0.11 probability level; the single complications contributing most to these differences were asphyxia, long labor, and inertia of labor. Similarly, the summary score BCs showed more complications for the process schizophrenics at the 0.15 probability level. The summary score PCs showed no difference between process schizophrenics and controls.

With the current sample sizes, 22 single OCs had sufficient frequency potentially to reach statistical significance by Fisher's exact probability test; one of these would be expected to be significant at the 0.05 level by chance. Preeclampsia and inertia of labor were each significantly more frequent for process schizophrenics than for controls (each at $p = 0.03$), and the physician's diagnosis of the baby as "preterm, immature, or dysmature" was differentially characteristic of the process schizophrenics (versus controls) at the 0.056 level.

Thus, the first 100 index cases showed that schizophreniclike psychotic adults did not evidence a significant increase in OCs in their own births, as contrasted with their matched controls, but process schizophrenic adults had significantly more total OCs, significantly more NCs, including prematurity and small-for-date status, and a tendency toward more oxygen deprivation and more birth complications, as contrasted with controls. Further intragroup analyses and the study of relationships between OCs and additional psychiatric parameters await the collection of several hundred index cases.

CONCLUSION

While the extensive literature on etiologic factors in schizophrenia, presented in this and other volumes, suggests that obstetric complications are definitely not the sole answer to the etiology of schizophrenia, the extensive literature reviewed in this section and the new results presented also suggest that obstetric complications are a risk-increasing factor to be taken seriously in the etiology of schizophrenia. The most important tasks remaining would seem to be to investigate in what ways such complications affect the developing individual, in what way they relate to other premorbid characteristics of schizophrenics, and in what way they interact with or complement other etiologic factors in the development of schizophrenia.

REFERENCES

1. Garmezy N: Children at risk: The search for the antecedents of schizophrenia. Part II. Ongoing research programs, issues, and intervention. *Schizophrenia Bull* 9:55, 1974.
2. Mednick SA, McNeil TF: Current methodology in research on the etiology of schizophrenia: Serious difficulties which suggest the use of the high-risk-group method. *Psychol Bull* 70:681, 1968.
3. Rosenthal D: *Genetic Theory and Abnormal Behavior*. New York, McGraw-Hill, 1970.
4. Pollin W, Stabenau JR: Biological, psychological and historical differences in a series of monozygotic twins discordant for schizophrenia, in Rosenthal D, Kety SS (eds): *The Transmission of Schizophrenia*. London, Pergamon Press, 1968.

5. Kallmann FJ, Roth B: Genetic aspects of preadolescent schizophrenia. *Am J Psychiatry* 112:599, 1956.

6. Kanner L: *Child Psychiatry*. Springfield, Ill, Thomas, 1957.

7. Lane EA, Albee GW: Comparative birth weights of schizophrenics and their siblings. *J Psychol* 64:227, 1966.

8. Pollack M, Greenberg IM: Paranatal complications in hospitalized schizophrenic and nonschizophrenic patients. *J Hillside Hosp* 15:191, 1966.

9. Pollack M, Levenstein S, Klein DF: A three-year posthospital follow-up of adolescent and adult schizophrenics. *Am J Orthopsychiatry* 38:94, 1968.

10. Pollack M, Woerner MG, Goodman W, et al: Childhood development patterns of hospitalized adult schizophrenic and non-schizophrenic patients and their siblings. *Am J Orthopsychiatry* 36:510, 1966.

11. Woerner MG, Pollack M, Klein DF: Birth weight and length in schizophrenics, personality disorders and their siblings. *Br J Psychiatry* 118:461, 1971.

12. Woerner MG, Pollack M, Klein DF: Pregnancy and birth complications in psychiatric patients: A comparison of schizophrenic and personality disorder patients with their siblings. *Acta Psychiatr Scand* 49:712, 1973.

13. Klein DF: Importance of psychiatric diagnosis in prediction of clinical drug effects. *Arch Gen Psychiatry* 16:118, 1967.

14. McNeil TF, Kaij L: Reproduction among female mental patients: Obstetric complications and physical size of offspring. *Acta Psychiatr Scand* 50:3, 1974.

15. Gottesman II, Shields J: *Schizophrenia and Genetics*. New York, Academic Press, 1972.

16. Fischer M: Genetic and environmental factors in schizophrenia: A study of schizophrenic twins and their families. *Acta Psychiatr Scand*, suppl 238, 1973.

17. Inouye E: Similarity and dissimilarity of schizophrenia in twins. *Proc Third World Congr Psychiatry* 1:524, 1961.

18. Kringlen E: *Heredity and Environment in the Functional Psychoses*. Oslo, Universitetsforlaget, 1967.

19. Slater E: *Psychotic and Neurotic Illnesses in Twins*. London, Her Majesty's Stationery Office, 1953.

20. Tienari P: Psychiatric illness in identical twins. *Acta Psychiatr Scand*, Suppl 171, 1963.

21. Rosenthal D: *The Genain Quadruplets*. New York, Basic Books, 1963.

22. Mednick SA, Schulsinger F: Some premorbid characteristics related to breakdown in children with schizophrenic mothers. *J Psychiatr Res* 6:354, 1968.

23. Mednick SA, Schulsinger F: Studies of children at high risk for schizophrenia, in Mednick S, Schulsinger F, Higgins J, et al (eds): *Genetics, Environment and Psychopathology*. Amsterdam, North-Holland, 1974.

24. Mednick SA: Breakdown in individuals at high risk for schizophrenia: possible predispositional perinatal factors. *Ment Hyg* 54:50, 1970.

25. Mizrahi GK: Perinatal complications in children of schizophrenic mothers. Unpublished manuscript, 1971.

26. Mizrahi GK: *Perinatal Complications*. Unpublished dissertation, Copenhagen University, 1969.

27. Mednick SA, Mura E, Schulsinger F, et al: Perinatal conditions and infant development in children with schizophrenic parents. *Soc Biol* 18(suppl):103, 1971.

28. Kessler P, Neale JM: Hippocampal damage and schizophrenia: A critique of Mednick's theory. *J Abnorm Psychol* 83:91, 1974.

29. Brody S: *Obstetrik och Gynekologi*. Stockholm, Almqvist & Wiksell, 1970.

30. Greenhill JP: *Obstetrics*, ed 13. Philadelphia, Saunders, 1965.

31. *Dorland's Pocket Medical Dictionary*, ed 21. Philadelphia, Saunders, 1968.

32. Mednick SA: personal communication, 1975.

33. Shearer ML, Davidson RT, Finch SM: The sex ratio of offspring born to state hospitalized schizophrenic women. *J Psychiatr Res* 5:349, 1967.

34. Hanson DR: Children of schizophrenic mothers or fathers compared to children of other psychiatric controls: Their first eight years. Unpublished manuscript, 1974.

35. Hanson DR, Gottesman II, Heston LL: Some possible childhood indicators of adult schizophrenia inferred from children of schizophrenics. *Br J Psychiatry*, 129:142, 1976.

36. Rieder RO, Rosenthal D, Wender P, et al: The offspring of schizophrenics. Fetal and neonatal deaths. *Arch Gen Psychiatry* 32:200, 1975.

37. Rieder RO, Broman SH, Rosenthal D: The offspring of schizophrenics. II: Perinatal factors and intelligence. Unpublished manuscript, 1976.

38. Lane EA, Albee GW: The birth weight of children born to schizophrenic women. *J Psychol* 74:157, 1970.

39. Sobel DE: Infant mortality and malformations in children of schizophrenic women. Preliminary data and suggested research. *Psychiatr Q* 35:60, 1961.

40. Soichet S: Emotional factors in toxemia of pregnancy. *Am J Obstet Gynecol* 77:1065, 1959.

41. Schachter J, Kerr J, Lachin JM, et al: Newborn offspring of a schizophrenic parent: Cardiac reactivity to auditory stimuli. *Psychophysiology* 12:483, 1975.

42. Schachter J, Lachin J, Spruill L, et al: Maternal psychopathology and complications of pregnancy and delivery. Unpublished manuscript.

43. Sameroff AJ, Zax M: Perinatal characteristics of the offspring of schizophrenic women. *J Nerv Ment Dis* 157:191, 1973.

44. DeHorn AB, Strauss ME: Offspring birthweights of male and female schizophrenics. Unpublished manuscript, 1976.

45. Spitzer RL, Endicott J: Diagno II: Further developments in a computer program for psychiatric diagnosis. *Am J Psychiatry* 125:12, 1969.

46. McNeil TF, Kaij L: Obstetric complications and physical size of offspring of schizophrenic, schizophrenic-like, and control mothers. *Br J Psychiatry* 123:341, 1973.

47. National Institute of Neurological Diseases and Stroke: *The Women and Their Pregnancies.* Washington, DC, US Government Printing Office, 1972.

48. Heston LL: Discussion: Schizophrenia—onset in infancy? *Soc Biol* 18:114, 1971.

49. Fish B: Discussion: Genetic or traumatic developmental deviation? *Soc Biol* 18:117, 1971.

50. Mura E, Mednick SA, Schulsinger F, et al: Erratum and further analysis. Perinatal conditions and infant development in children with schizophrenic parents. *Soc Biol* 20:111, 1973.

51. Mizrahi Mirdal GK, Mednick SA, Schulsinger F, et al: Perinatal complications in children of schizophrenic mothers. *Acta Psychiatr Scand* 50:553, 1974.

52. Yarden PE, Suranyi I: The early development of institutionalized children of schizophrenic mothers. *Dis Nerv Syst* 29:380, 1968.

53. Paffenbarger RS, Steinmetz CH, Pooler BG, et al: The picture puzzle of the postpartum psychoses. *J Chronic Dis* 13:161, 1961.

54. Wiedorn WS: Toxemia of pregnancy and schizophrenia. *J Nerv Ment Dis* 120:1, 1954.

55. McNeil TF, Persson-Blennow I, Kaij L: Reproduction in female psychiatric patients: Severity of mental disturbance near reproduction and rates of obstetric complications. *Acta Psychiatr Scand* 50:23, 1974.

56. Lane EA: The sex ratio of children born to schizophrenics and a theory of stress. *Psychol Rec* 19:579, 1969.

57. Taylor MA: Sex ratios of newborns: Associated with prepartum and postpartum schizophrenia. *Science* 164:723, 1969.

58. Schorer CE: Gestational schizophrenia. *Can Psychiatr Assoc J* 17(suppl):259, 1972.

59. McNeil TF, Kaij L, Persson-Blennow I: Offspring sex and degree of active maternal mental disturbance near reproduction among female mental patients. *Compr Psychiatry* 16:69, 1975.

60. Taylor MA, Levine R: Puerperal schizophrenia: A physiological interaction between mother and fetus. *Biol Psychiatry* 1:97, 1969.

61. Taylor MA: Sex ratios of newborns and schizophrenia. *Science* 168:151, 1970.

62. Melges FT: Postpartum psychiatric reactions: Time of onset and sex ratio of newborns. *Science* 166:1026, 1970.

63. Gallant DH: Children of mentally ill mothers, in Grunebaum H, Weiss J, Cohler B, et al (eds): *Mentally Ill Mothers and Their Children.* Chicago, University of Chicago Press, 1975.

64. Wenar C: The reliability of developmental histories. *Psychosom Med* 25:505, 1963.

65. Robbins LC: The accuracy of parental recall of aspects of child development and of child rearing practices. *J Abnorm Soc Psychol* 66:261, 1963.

66. Drake ME, Ober G: Parental medical histories of mental retardates as compared and evaluated against newborn and hospitalization records. *Am J Ment Defic* 67:688, 1963.

67. Pyles MK, Stolz HR, MacFarlane JW: The accuracy of mothers' reports on birth and developmental data. *Child Dev* 6:165, 1935.

68. Pollack M, Woerner MG: Pre- and perinatal complications and "childhood schizophrenia": A comparison of 5 controlled studies. *J Child Psychol Psychiatry* 7:235, 1966.

69. Rutt CN, Offord DR: Prenatal and perinatal complications in childhood schizophrenics and their siblings. *J Nerv Ment Dis* 152:324, 1971.

70. Taft LT, Goldfarb W: Prenatal and perinatal factors in childhood schizophrenia. *Dev Med Child Neurol* 6:32, 1964.

71. Vorster D: An investigation into the part played by organic factors in childhood schizophrenia. *J Ment Sci* 106:494, 1960.

72. Mura EL: Perinatal differences: A comparison of child psychiatric patients and their siblings. *Psychiatr Q* 48:239, 1974.

73. McNeil TF, Kaij L: Obstetric complications in the histories of childhood schizophrenics and infantile autistics, in preparation.

74. Pasamanick B, Knobloch H: Epidemiologic studies on the complications of pregnancy and the birth process, in Caplan G (ed): *Prevention of Mental Disorders in Children*. New York, Basic Books, 1961.

75. Whittam H, Simon GB, Mittler PJ: The early development of psychotic children and their sibs. *Dev Med Child Neurol* 8:552, 1966.

76. Knobloch H, Pasamanick B: Some etiologic and prognostic factors in early infantile autism and psychosis, in Knobloch H, Pasamanick B (eds): *Developmental Diagnosis*. Hagerstown, Md., Harper & Row, 1974.

77. Hinton GG: Childhood psychosis or mental retardation: A diagnostic dilemma. II. Pediatric and neurological aspects. *Can Med Assoc J* 89:1020, 1963.

78. Gittelman M, Birch HG: Childhood schizophrenia: Intellect, neurologic status, perinatal risk, prognosis, and family pathology. *Arch Gen Psychiatry* 17:16, 1967.

79. Werner E, Simonian K, Bierman JM, et al: Cumulative effect of perinatal complications and deprived environment on physical, intellectual, and social development of preschool children. *Pediatrics* 39:490, 1967.

80. Drillien, CM: *The Growth and Development of the Prematurely Born Infant*. Edinburgh, Livingstone, 1964.

81. Siegel S: *Nonparametric Statistics*. NY, McGraw-Hill, 1956.

Chapter 40
In Search of Schizophrenia: Young Offspring of Schizophrenic Women

Arnold J. Sameroff, Ph.D.
Melvin Zax, Ph.D.

The Rochester Conference is designed to produce a definitive statement of our current understanding of schizophrenia. Such conferences are essential to provide a perspective of the field as a whole to those studying different aspects of the disorder. It is a major tribute to those participating here that we all appreciate that schizophrenia is a complex phenomenon and, further, that work on no single aspect is going to allow us to capture the full flavor of the entity itself. For lack of time I must forego the issue of whether schizophrenia is really an entity, a series of entities, or no entity at all, as some in our field have been led to claim. These views are explored quite well in other sections of this volume.

Those of us in the area of risk research have taken for granted that an abnormally high percentage of individuals with psychiatric problems emerge from certain populations. The goal of "risk" research is to identify the premorbid characteristics that would allow the prediction and hopefully the prevention of such deviant developmental outcomes.

The study of schizophrenia is especially amenable to risk research because a relatively large proportion of relatives of schizophrenics share the diagnosis. This familial characteristic of the disorder clearly implicates a hereditary mechanism in its etiology. Although as late as 10 years ago the genetic and environmental bases for schizophrenia found equal support, in the last decade the preponderance of evidence, especially that emerging from the Danish adoption studies, has led toward an almost unanimous psy-

Research reported here has been supported by Grants from the National Institute of Mental Health and the Grant Foundation.

chiatric concordance that biologic genetic factors are fundamental to the etiology of schizophrenia.

This genetic position in regard to schizophrenia fits well with the current return to nativism to explain other kinds of deviant development. Attributing low IQs to racial differences, and hyperactivity in school children to constitutional factors, also fits the etiologic model that is used to explain schizophrenia's emergence. All that remains in any of these disorders is to trace the connections between the genetic or constitutional factors and the actual resultant dysfunction.

It is at this point that our problems really begin. As Jackson (1) so neatly pointed out in his critique of genetic hypotheses:

> Until the ill-defined concept of "personality" can be broken down into enduring traits that are shown to have a genetic basis, it is surely fruitless to look for a genetic mechanism behind the symptomatic disorder of schizophrenia.

Jackson identifies two central problems in his statement. The first is to define schizophrenia in terms of some set of enduring personality traits, and the second is to trace the connections between these traits and some constitutional variable.

The uniqueness of the project we are about to describe lies in the fact that it is committed to neither a constitutional nor an environmental theory of schizophrenia. What we have attempted to do is to assess from birth both sets of influences to determine their relative contribution to any future aberrance found in our sample of children.

We have proposed five possible models for understanding the development of a schizophrenic disorder, two with specific constitutional factors, two with specific environmental factors, and the last with neither specific constitutional nor specific environmental factors.

The single-factor views posit a condition that produces schizophrenia (or some variant of it, e.g., spectrum disorders) in all individuals having that condition. In the constitutional form (Model 1), one view would be that a gene (3) produces schizophrenia. In the environmental form (Model 2), certain schizophrenogenic social situations, for example, living with specific types of impossible conflicts, would produce schizophrenia in any child.

There is insufficient evidence today to prompt many to accept these one-sided single-factor views and most have moved to some multifactor position. In two of the multifactor positions we identify (Models 3 and 4), schizophrenia can still be clearly specified as resulting from some specific constitutional or environmental cause, but a cause that is

Table 40-1. Etiologic Models of Schizophrenia

	Component Causes	
	Constitution	Environment
Single-Factor Views		
Model 1. Constitutional:	Schizophrenia	Irrelevant
Model 2. Environmental:	Irrelevant	Schizophrenogenic
Multi-Factor Views		
Model 3. Constitutional:	Specific predisposition	Nonspecific stress
Model 4. Environmental:	Nonspecific vulnerability	Specific disposition
Model 5. Transactional:	Nonspecific vulnerability	Nonspecific stress

more predisposing than disposing. In other words, either defects in a child's nature or nurture may produce schizophrenia, but either requires fertile soil for its development.

On the constitutional side (Model 3), the defects may reside in a genetic diathesis (4) or in a specific area of brain damage (5). The individual with these defects need not become schizophrenic if he or she grows up in an environment with low stress levels. It is only when his or her resistance drops below a certain threshold that he or she "catches" schizophrenia. On the environmental side (Model 4), the interactional position would argue that the "germ" resides in the caretaking environment, either in the form of deviant communication patterns (6) or family interactions (7). Not every child subject to these environments would become schizophrenic. A heightened susceptibility through some constitutional vulnerability would be required. Such general vulnerabilities might consist of physical deviancies resulting from delivery complications (8), temperamental variations in attentional distributions, or perceptual hypersensitivities.

The difference between the first four models and the transactional view (Model 5) is that each of the former posits a specific cause for a schizophrenic outcome. The transactional view does not argue for any *specific* developmental precursor, either constitutional or environmental. Rather, schizophrenia is treated as one of a full range of potential "normal" outcomes of development (9). The use of the word normal here may seem out of place, but from a developmental point of view normality resides in the ability of the organism to adapt to its environment. To the extent that a schizophrenic outcome is the result of the transactions between a specific child coping with his own specific environment, then an outcome that permits functional survival within that environment can be considered both adaptive and normal. This view can be seen in the cross-cultural writings of Erikson (10) and intracultural speculations of Laing (11). It also has been elaborated elsewhere in a more general form (12).

The five models reduce to two foci for research investigation. Whether one conceives of a constitutional factor as producing some form of schizophrenia in every carrier or merely predisposing the carrier toward schizophrenia, one must be able to identify some unique difference between such individuals and their peers. Similarly, whether one considers an environmental factor as producing schizophrenia in any individual raised in that environment or merely acting as a predisposing agent, one must be able to identify some unique characteristic of that environment.

Given these two foci, we must then identify our criteria for disorder. Since it would not be useful in a study of children during the first 4 years of life to use a diagnosis of schizophrenia as a criterion, we have turned to an intermediary stage as found, for example, in Meehl's (2) notion of schizotaxia. Schizotaxia can be dimensionalized into those characteristics usually present in schizophrenic personalities. These would include the three central characteristics—thought disorder, affective disorder, and social alienation—as well as a fourth characteristic more recently described involving neurologic or biochemical impairment affecting attention and information processing.

ROCHESTER DEVELOPMENTAL PSYCHOPATHOLOGY STUDY

In 1968, we (8) initiated a study emulating the work of Mednick and Schulsinger (13). Our study differed in two essential characteristics from the Copenhagen study. Mednick's and Schulsinger's subjects were the adolescent offspring of schizophrenic women.

This enabled them to follow these children through early adulthood, making an actual diagnosis of schizophrenia a realizable outcome measure during the investigators' lifetimes. In contrast, we felt that the ideal point in time to search for constitutional differences would be at birth when the infant had not yet been subject to the social consequences of life with a schizophrenic mother. Accordingly, we began our study with pregnant schizophrenic women and planned to follow their offspring through the first 4 years of life.

In addition, we felt that it was necessary to use additional control groups. As Mednick and McNeil (14) pointed out in their original justification of the high-risk strategy for studying schizophrenia, many of the characteristics that have been attributed to schizophrenia have really been the *consequences* of the diagnosis rather than of the disorder itself. These consequences include the effects of labeling and institutionalization. Similarly, we felt that a schizophrenic mother might influence her offspring in many ways that might be a consequence of the chronicity or severity of her mental illness per se, rather than something specifically related to her diagnosis. In short, our strategy was to include control populations that would allow us to assess the effects of separate aspects of psychiatric diagnosis, chronicity of disturbance, severity of disturbance, and social competency, as well as the general characteristics of social class, race, educational level, and family constellation.

Sample

Three hundred thirty-seven pregnant women were recruited for study over a 4-year period. Before delivery the women underwent a clinical interview based on the Current and Past Psychopathology Scale developed by Spitzer and Endicott (15). From the interview and case records each woman was given a diagnosis, a chronicity rating, a severity of illness rating, and a social competency score.

The chronicity of psychologic disturbance was defined by the frequency of psychiatric contact plus the need for and length of institutionalization. The least chronic category involved subjects who had had no previous psychiatric contact and were diagnosed as having no mental illness on the basis of the interview. The most chronic category included subjects who had had in excess of four psychiatric contacts or more than one year of institutionalization.

The severity of the mental illness score was based on an evaluation of emotional state, current functioning at home and at work, and the general level of social adjustment. Our social competence score, developed by Barbara Fox (16), was based on six measures similar to those used in the Zigler and Phillips scale (17).

For our analysis of the effects of a schizophrenic mother on the development of her child, four groups based on the psychiatric diagnosis were formed from the total sample: (a) a schizophrenic group, with 29 mothers, (b) a neurotic-depressive group, with 57 mothers, (c) a personality-disordered group, with 41 mothers, and (d) a no-mental-illness group, with 80 mothers. The no-mental-illness control group was matched to the other groups on the basis of age, race, socioeconomic status, number of children, education, and sex of child.

When the four groups were compared on mental health criteria other than diagnosis, it was found that the schizophrenic women as a group were more chronically ill, more severely ill in current symptomatology, and more socially incompetent.

As a control for chronicity, all the women in our sample were divided into four groups based on their psychiatric histories. Similarly, three groups were formed based on the severity of psychopathology rating.

Any differences between the schizophrenic and other diagnostic groups then could be evaluated in terms of either chronicity or severity of mental illness independent of diagnosis to determine which factor was making the greatest contribution to the outcome measures.

Outcome Measures

Our longitudinal study included six assessment ages, at least 16 investigators, and ultimately will probably produce 6000 variables. The assessments were made during pregnancy, at birth, and then at 4, 12, 30, and 48 months of age, both in the home and in the laboratory. The investigators included Haroutun Babigian, Fredric Jones, Ralph Barocas, and a host of graduate students and research technicians. We have nearly completed the assessment of the entire sample through 30 months of age, and about one-quarter of the sample at 4 years. At each age we have subdivided our assessment variables into four sets, each focused on what we believe to be domains of behavior related to potential mental illness outcomes. These four are (a) perceptual-motor functioning, (b) cognitive functioning, (c) affective functioning, and (d) social functioning.

Perceptual-motor Functioning

Perceptual-motor functioning was tested at birth with the Brazelton Assessment Scales (18). The newborns were also monitored for autonomic responsivity in a sensory stimulation task. At 4, 12, and 30 months of age they were tested with the Bayley Infant Development Scales which included scores for psychomotor performance. Physical health was assessed from birth records and also from a medical history form filled out by the mothers when the children were 30 and 48 months of age.

Cognitive Functioning

Cognitive performance at birth was measured by tests of alertness and habituation on the Brazelton scales. At 4, 12, and 30 months the mental development index of the Bayley scales was used, while at 48 months we shifted to the Wechsler Preschool and Primary Scale of Intelligence (WPPSI). The Peabody Picture Vocabulary Test (PPVT) was also given at both 30 and 48 months of age.

Affective Functioning

The child's emotional responsivity was assessed at birth from irritability and associated scores on the Brazelton scale. At 4 months, mood, threshold to stimulation, and intensity of response were scored from a maternal questionnaire. Emotionality was recorded during observations of mother-infant interactions in the home at 4 and 12 months of age. During the psychometric testing in the laboratory, the examiner scored measures of emotional responsivity during the 4, 12, 30, and 48 month laboratory sessions. At 30 and 48 months of age additional information was obtained from the Rochester Adaptive Behavior Interview (RABI), a detailed maternal interview designed by Fredric Jones (19).

Social Functioning

The social behavior of a newborn is hard to define, but we judged alertness and consolability to be its primary constituents. At 4 and 12 months, the mother-infant social interactions were observed and recorded in the home setting. At 4, 12, 30, and 48 months, ratings of the child's social responsiveness were made by the examiner during the psychometric evaluation. At 4 months the child was placed in a laboratory situation where differential looking and smiling at a mother versus a stranger could be measured. At the later testings, the child's reactions to separation from his or her mother were scored. A social history and the results of the RABI provided us with additional sources of information on the child's social behavior.

RESULTS

The ultimate goal of our study is to identify children at 4 years of age who are making inadequate developmental adjustments. For the purpose of this brief presentation we will limit the discussion to those deviant outcomes that can be specifically attributed to being the child of a mother with a diagnosis of schizophrenia.

I am sorry to report that when all other factors are controlled we have been unable to identify *any* characteristics in 30-month-old offspring of schizophrenic women that differentiate them from the offspring of women without a diagnosis of schizophrenia. We have a long way to go before our mass of data will have yielded their last bit of information. It is possible that among the complex interactions to be investigated in our home observations and laboratory assessments we will yet find subtle differences. However, in the current analyses we have not found such differences.

Cognitive Functioning

Let us illustrate with some of our findings from two assessment domains, cognitive functioning and social-emotional adaptation. Figure 40-1 contains the data from the psychometric testing at 4, 12, 30, and 48 months of age. The IQ scores at each age have been converted to Z-scores (mean of 0 and standard deviation of 1) to improve visual comparability across age. At 4 and 12 months the scores are from the Bayley Mental Development Indices, while at 30 and 48 months they are from the Peabody Picture Vocabulary Test. In the first graph it can be seen that at early ages schizophrenic's offspring seem to do more poorly. When separate analyses are made for severity and chronicity, this early retardation appears to be a function of the severity of their mother's mental illness, as can be seen in the graph. Moreover, by 30 months of age this effect dissipates, and no differences can be found among groups based on any of the psychiatric considerations. However, when the same data are viewed from the perspective of socioeconomic status, as in the last group, completely opposite results appear. There are no differences during the early sensory-motor period, but during the third year when language becomes relevant to IQ performance, the effects of social class differences are enormous.

Social-Emotional Adaptation

At 30 months of age a global rating was obtained for each child from the RABI. The ratings were on a scale ranging from a low score of 1 reflecting a happy child with superior relationships to a score of 5 reflecting a child with extreme or bizarre behavior and intense adjustment problems. Only one infant in our sample received a score of 5. He was placed in the fourth category to simplify Figure 40-2.

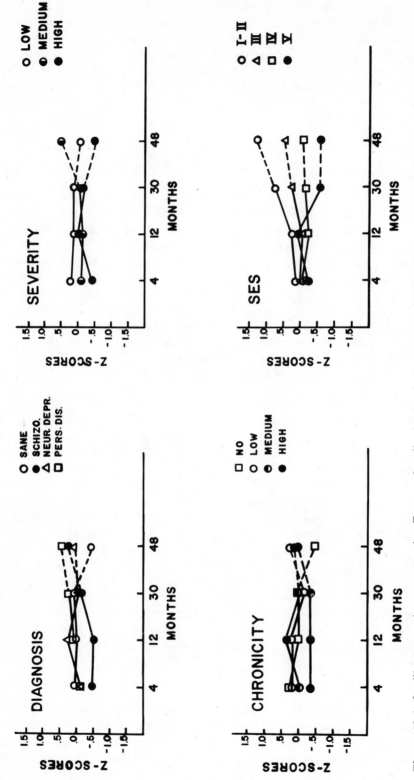

Figure 40-1. Intelligence quotients, expressed as Z-scores, for offspring in relation to maternal diagnosis, chronicity, severity and social class. The scores at 4 and 12 months are based on the Bayley Mental Development Index, and at 30 and 48 months on the Peabody Picture Vocabulary Test.

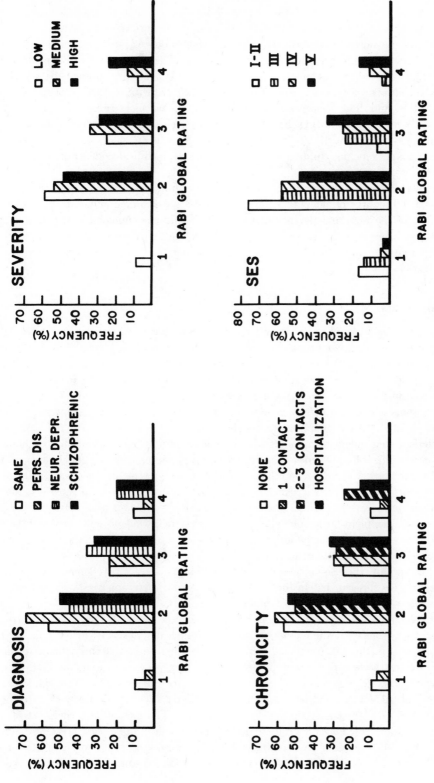

Figure 40-2. The distribution of adaptive behavior (RABI) global rating scores for 30-month-old infants, in relation to maternal diagnosis, chronicity, severity, and social class.

437

In this figure one can see the distribution of 30-month global ratings based on either mother's diagnosis, the severity of her mental illness, or her socioeconomic status.

In the diagnostic group analysis only the offspring of neurotic-depressive mothers had scores significantly different from those of the controls. The schizophrenic's offspring had higher than average scores but not significantly so. When we examined the severity groups, the effects were much clearer. The more symptomatic the mother's illness, the less adaptive the child. The socioeconomic status graph is even more revealing. A powerful linear effect is evident, showing that children of lower-class mothers scored as being significantly less competent than higher SES groups. What is especially interesting here is that our SES data include children whose mothers show no clinical evidence of any mental illness.

What we can conclude from the analysis of both cognitive and social-emotional adaptiveness at 30 months of age is that the effects of the social milieu appear to overpower the effects of the maternal psychopathologic state. The epidemiologic model that one should bear in mind is that most schizophrenics are not the offspring of schizophrenics. Our research also must be directed at understanding the sources of deviancy in this preponderant group.

Schizophrenia

But what then of schizophrenia? We began by arguing that schizophrenia is transmitted to the offspring of schizophrenic women, yet we can find no evidence of such transmission during the first 30 months of life. Let us divide this question into two parts. The first will be directed toward existing evidence for such transmission early in life, and the second will deal with our own views of how such transmission might occur.

The strongest evidence for the genetic transmission of schizophrenia comes from the adoption studies. In the adoption studies the assumption is made that the only unique characteristic that the offspring of a schizophrenic woman brings into the adoptive home is his or her schizophrenic genes. If mental disorder is an outcome for that child, then it must be attributed to those genetic factors. In our study, 6 of the 29 offspring in the schizophrenic group were placed in either adoptive or foster homes. Of those six, four spent their newborn period in an intensive care nursery—three for prematurity and one for a cardiac problem. It would appear, then, that many offspring of schizophrenic women who are given up for adoption may carry more uniqueness with them than their schizophrenic genetic endowment.

Let us amplify this point through a reexamination of our psychometric data. In Figure 40-1 we showed that in the schizophrenic group there appeared to be an early retardation which disappeared by 30 months of age.

We suggested that retardation was more the consequence of such factors as the severity and chronicity of the mother's illness than of her diagnosis of schizophrenia. Let us go one step further. By removing from the schizophrenic sample three infants being raised in foster homes, these early differences disappear. Two of the infants had been sufficiently premature as to be placed in a special care nursery. The third, while not from the special nursery, did have a birthweight of only 2800 grams, fairly close to the 2500-gram, low-birthweight criterion for prematurity. The lack of differences between the now-purified schizophrenic group and the control group can be seen in Figure 40-3. These data, although based on a small sample, raise important questions about the conclusions derived from adoption studies where the initial condition of the newborn was

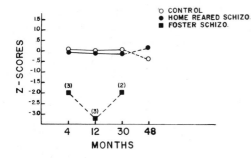

Figure 40-3. Intelligence quotients, expressed as Z-scores, for offspring of normal control mothers, and of schizophrenic mothers. The infants of the schizophrenic mothers who were home reared and reared in foster homes are displayed separately.

not taken into consideration. The rearing of a nonoptimal infant in a nonoptimal environment contributes major risk factors which must be added to genetic factors in any prognostication of outcome.

As for pregnancy and delivery complications themselves, our findings are in accord with the work of McNeil and Kaij (20) and others who have reported no differences between diagnostic groups in this respect. There has been a recent flurry of interest in reports of fetal deaths associated with the pregnancy of schizophrenic women: Reider and his associates (21) have reported a higher number of unexplained fetal deaths in schizophrenic women—7 of 93 schizophrenics as compared with 7 out of 423 controls. By contrast, in our sample we found no perinatal deaths in our schizophrenic group, but we did find 4 deaths among the 56 subjects in our neurotic-depressive group. We do not wish to draw major conclusions from these contradictory findings based on a small number of deaths, but we would be cautious of over-generalizations from such small samples.

Another hypothesis about the offspring of schizophrenic women is that their developmental scores may not differ on the average from those of other infants but that there is a greater variability between age periods. We have not found this to be true in our sample. On the contrary, research in development has shown that change and transformation are the rule rather than the exception for the developmental scores of *normal* infants during the first 2 years of life (22). In comparison with the appropriate control groups we have not found a greater variability in the development of our schizophrenic offspring. Furthermore, where major shifts in developmental status have occurred we have been able to identify familial factors which intruded at the point of shift. These factors were found for infants both in the schizophrenic group and in other groups.

How then does the schizophrenic mother transmit schizophrenia to her offspring? At the outset we argued for five possible models for the etiology of schizophrenia. Of these, two required the identification of some unique constitutional variable that differentiated offspring of schizophrenic women from their peers. Our inability to make such an identification within the first 30 months has shifted our focus to the characteristics of the environment in which the infant is raised. Our current belief is that schizophrenia is a socially transmitted disorder that requires a receiver capable of interpreting the message. The intellectual incompetence of the young infant makes it highly unlikely that he can learn the schizophrenic facts of life. As he grows in cognitive and linguistic skill, he becomes increasingly competent at identifying and adapting to the craziness in his social environment. Current theory in developmental psychology argues that the child does not internalize the logical structure of his world until the close of the preoperational period, somewhere between 4 and 7 years of age (23). It is during this period when we would expect to strike paydirt, that is, when we would expect to find children at risk for schizophrenia beginning to differentiate from those destined for more general forms of mental incompetency or competency.

SUMMARY

Let us reiterate our findings. Our results are *not* that offspring of schizophrenic women are a healthy, happy, intelligent, adaptive lot. Our measures have shown that they have high levels of illness, fearfulness, sadness, retardation, and social maladaptiveness. However, this does not make them uniquely different from the offspring of women with other severe or chronic mental disorders, or even children of psychiatrically normal women from the lower socioeconomic strata of our society. Without the appropriate control groups built into our study, we might have been led into the error of attributing these differences to the effects of a schizophrenic heritage.

We hope that our results, while not yet contributing to a greater understanding of the specific etiology of schizophrenia, have at least added to an understanding of the methodologies by which schizophrenia may be approached.

To conclude, we would like to make an important analogy between the study of schizophrenia and that of cancer. The initial research on cancer saw it as a singular biologic entity with a singular cause. The results of that research have come to recognize cancer as a deviation in the developmental pattern of the organism which has both inspired and required research into the basic mechanisms of biologic development. Similarly, the research failures resulting from the study of schizophrenia as a single identifiable disorder with a single identifiable cause now require us also to change our views. We believe that schizophrenia should be seen as a deviation in the developmental adaptation of the child. This view would require research into the basic mechanisms of psychologic and social development. The study of developmental psychopathology has opened new perspectives not only on the sources of incompetency but also, as has been noted by Norman Garmezy (24), the correlative study of the sources of competency. It is only within the enriched and enriching study of the matrix of human development that one can see this range of developmental outcomes in their appropriate perspective.

REFERENCES

1. Jackson DD: Schizophrenia. *Scien Amer,* August, 1962.
2. Meehl PE: Schizotaxia, schizotypy, schizophrenia. *Am Psychol* 17:827, 1962.
3. Heston LL: The genetics of schizophrenic and schizoid disease. *Science* 249: 1970.
4. Rosenthal D: *Genetic Theory and Abnormal Behavior,* New York, McGraw-Hill, 1970.
5. Mednick SA: Breakdown in individuals at high risk for schizophrenia: Possible predispositional perinatal factors. *Ment Hyg* 54:50, 1970.
6. Singer MT, Wynne LC: Differentiating characteristics of parents of childhood schizophrenics, childhood neurotics, and young adult schizophrenics. *Am J Psy* 120:234, 1963.
7. Lidz T: The nature and origins of schizophrenic disorders. *An Int Med* 77:639, 1972.

8. Sameroff AJ, Zax M: Neonatal characteristics of offspring of schizophrenic and neurotically-depressed mothers. *J Ner Men Dis,* 157:191, 1973a.

9. Werner H: The concept of development from a comparative and organismic point of view, in Harris DB (ed): *The Concept of Development.* Minneapolis, University of Minnesota Press, 1957.

10. Erikson EH: *Childhood and Society,* ed 2. New York, Norton, 1963.

11. Laing RD, Esterson A: *Sanity, Madness, and the Family,* New York, Basic Books, 1964.

12. Sameroff AJ: Early influences on development: Fact or fancy? *Mer Pal Quart* 1975.

13. Mednick SA, Schulsinger F: Factors related to breakdown in children at high risk for schizophrenia, in Roff, M, Ricks, DF (eds): *Life History Research in Psychopathology,* Vol 1. Minneapolis, University of Minnesota Press, 1970, p 51.

14. Mednick SA, McNeil TF: Current methodology in research on the etiology of schizophrenia. *Psych Bull* 70:681, 1968.

15. Spitzer R, Endicott J: Diagno II. Further developments in a computer program for psychiatric diagnosis. *Am J Psy* 125:12, 1969.

16. Fox BA: *Socioeconomic Status, Psychopathology, and Socialization.* Unpublished master's dissertation, University of Rochester, 1975.

17. Zigler E, Phillips L: Social competence and the process-reactive-distraction on psychopathology. *J Ab Soc Psy* 65:215, 1962.

18. Brazelton TB: *Neonatal Behavioral Assessment Scale.* London, Heinemann, 1973.

19. Jones FH: The Rochester adaptive behavior inventory: A parallel series of instruments for assessing social competence during early and middle childhood and adolescence, in Strauss, J, Babigian, H, Roff, M (eds): *The Origins and Course of Psychopathology: Methods of Longitudinal Research.* New York, Plenum, 1977, p 249.

20. McNeil TF, Kaij L: Obstetric complications and physical size of offspring of schizophrenic, schizophrenic-like, and control mothers. *Brit J Psy* 123:341, 1973.

21. Reider RO, Rosenthal D, Wender P, Blumental H: The offspring of schizophrenics: Fetal and neonatal deaths. *Arch. Gen Psy* 32:200, 1975.

22. McCall RB, Hogarty PS, Hurlbut N: Transitions in infant sensorimotor development and the predictions of childhood IQ. *Am Psy* 27:728, 1972.

23. Piaget J: *Psychology of Intelligence.* New York, Harcourt, Brace & World, 1950.

24. Garmezy N: The study of competence in children at risk for severe psychopathology, in Anthony EJ, Koupernik C (eds), *The Child in His Family: Children at Psychiatric Risk.* New York, Wiley, 1974.

Chapter 41
Berkson's Fallacy and High-Risk Research

Sarnoff A. Mednick, Ph.D., Dr. Med.

In Copenhagen we are now in the 14th year of our 1962 high-risk (HR) study that began with a group of 207 HR offspring of severely schizophrenic mothers and a matched group of 104 LR children without known mental illness in the parents or grandparents. Initially, the children were between 10 and 20 years of age (mean, 15 years). In 1967, the first wave of breakdowns in the offspring were studied, and in 1972–74 we brought in our subjects for an intensive diagnostic assessment (1,2). Of the HR subjects, the diagnostician, Hanne Schulsinger, identified 34 (Schizophrenia Group) as being (a) schizophrenic, borderline schizophrenic, or schizoid, (b) *and* having received psychiatric treatment, *and* (c) receiving a global rating of high severity of psychiatric illness, that is, a rating of 4 or above in the Current and Past Psychopathology Scales (3).

In 1970, we entered a second longitudinal study, part of a larger perinatal research project at the University Hospital in Copenhagen (4). By reference to central registers in Denmark, we culled those parents who had had a diagnosis of schizophrenia and matched them with a psychiatric control group of parents with "character disorders" and with a normal control group. We were then able to go back to the obstetrical and pediatric data on the pregnancies, births, and 1-year examinations of the children.

In the course of the data analyses on the 1962 HR project and the 1970 perinatal HR project we have made certain methodological observations which will be the focus of my remarks. From the beginning, it seemed perfectly clear that the HR method was a second choice for prospective research. It would have been more satisfactory to have assembled a large birth cohort (of perhaps 10,000 children), examined them intensively, and followed them to see who would become schizophrenic. The disadvantage with this plan was that the proportion of eventual schizophrenics would be rather small. Instead, I decided to examine HR subjects (5).

One of the advantages of the HR method is the higher rate of schizophrenia among children of schizophrenics. Some of the disadvantages revolve around the fact that the design involves biased selection of cases. Some attempt to overcome this bias takes the form of control groups matched for relevant factors. But do we really know what factors are relevant? We must begin to face the fact that almost any control group selected will

This research is supported by USPHS Grant MH25325.

be biased in some respects. For example, for valid generalizations of findings, the number of controls should be proportionate to the number in the population to which you wish to generalize. Otherwise the generalization is likely to be highly fallacious. This fallacy in design is well known in epidemiology; it has a name, Berkson's Fallacy.

> "If the subpopulation . . . of a group X and its control not-X, is not representative in the ratio of the marginal totals of X and not-X . . . in the general population, then association will appear even if *none* exists in the general population from which the study population is drawn" (6).

I might add that assocations that *do* exist in the general population may also be *masked* by control groups not representative of the not-X population. This means that another investigator drawing a small control sample from the same population, in the same manner, may select a sample unrepresentative in some other way. This problem is very likely at the root of most failures to replicate in the behavioral sciences. The situation may become even more unfortunate if you begin to apply specific selection criteria. These criteria may introduce a host of unknown biasing factors which might distort your results in unexpected ways.

SOME EXAMPLES

Severity of Parent's Illness

A child's risk for schizophrenia in almost all cases has been defined by a parent's diagnosis. But there is more than one type or grade of schizophrenia. In 1962, Schulsinger and I simply scoured the mental hospitals of Zealand for the most chronic, process schizophrenic women with children between the ages of 10–20 years. In the 1970, perinatal HR study, on the other hand, we examined the children of *all* parents with any schizophrenia diagnosis in a cohort of 9,006 consecutive deliveries. The perinatal sample parents have a wider range of grades of schizophrenia. What effect does this have on the characteristics of their children?

Figure 41-1 shows the results of a neurological examination of the HR children and the control group at one year of age. Figure 41-2 reveals the status of their motor development at one year of age. In both cases the subdiagnosis of the parents of the HR group is related significantly to their children's level of functioning.

If one HR investigator in Scandinavia uses a narrow definition of schizophrenia while another in the U.S. uses a broader definition, and they both study the neurological status of their HR children, then their failure to replicate one another's results may simply be a function of the proportion of borderline schizophrenia in their HR parents.

Puberty

If skin conductance in *children* is being examined and the results compared with another study on skin conductance in *adolescents,* before one generalizes about the results, it may be useful to know that, for a number of measures, boys after puberty evidence an increase in skin conductance lability and girls become relatively less labile. (These results are from our 1970 perinatal HR project.) Before comparisons of absolute or relative levels of lability are possible, ages, sex ratios, and measures should be taken into account.

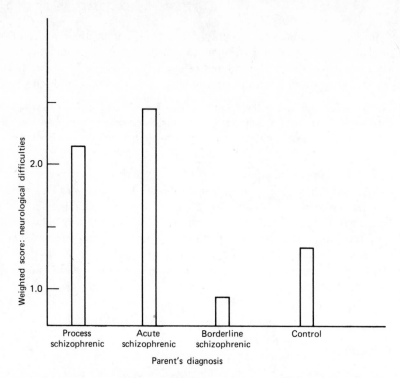

Figure 41-1. Parent's schizophrenia subtype and child's 1-year neurologic examination, from 1970 Perinatal High-Risk Project (F (5/207) = 2.89, p < 0.05).

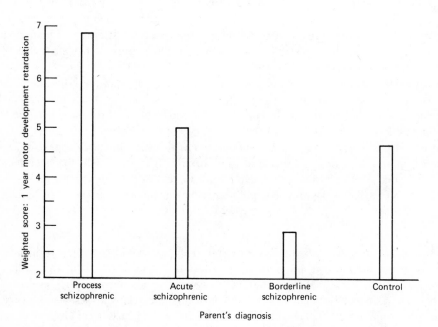

Figure 41-2. Parent's schizophrenia subtype and child's 1-year motor development retardation, from 1970 Perinatal High-Risk Project (F (5/191) = 2.85, p < 0.05).

Symptom Pattern

Not only severity of illness, but also specific symptom pattern may relate differentially to certain variables. When we re-examined the 1962 skin conductance recovery of the 34 HR individuals in the Schizophrenia Group, we found their electrodermal recovery to be very fast.

Our pleasure in these results was considerably tempered by the fact that variability of electrodermal recovery scores was rather high within the Schizophrenia Group. In order to better understand this high variance we did a canonical correlation to see which of a set of symptoms would correlate with which of a set of skin conductance variables in the HR subjects. Hallucinations and delusions correlated rather well with electrodermal recovery ($r = .49, p < 0.0005$). Individuals in the Schizophrenia Group without hallucinations and delusions do not tend to have fast skin conductance recovery. Hence, the large variance. This means that comparability of results relating to recovery may in part depend on the salience of hallucinatory and delusional symptoms in the study populations.[1]

Psychopathy and Criminality

Almost 40 years ago Franz Kallmann (7) called our attention to the fact that there was an unusually large amount of criminality in children of schizophrenics. One of three interpretations he offered was that schizophrenic patients assortatively mate with psychopaths and criminals. Kirkegaard-Sørensen and Mednick (8) have recently reported results supporting this interpretation. Of the fathers of the 1962 HR children, 49.6% were known to the police; 39.6% had been convicted at least once. These rates of criminality are far above the average for Danish men of their age and social status.

It is probably safe to conjecture that in most cases when one selects mothers who are schizophrenic, they will have very frequently mated with criminal and psychopathic men. If the asocial behavior of the mates is not registered by the investigator, and not considered in evaluating the behavior of the children, some unaccounted-for variance will likely be influencing HR-LR differences. Probably this factor has influenced most HR studies. From our own work and research in the literature, we are convinced that a child's psychophysiology is one variable which is strongly influenced by the criminality of his father.

Lykken (9) first reported the skin conductance hyporesponsiveness of the sociopathic individual. This finding has been replicated by Hare (10), Schalling and Levander (11), and Schmauk (12), (see review by Siddle (13)). I have reported on the remarkably slow electrodermal recovery of the criminal and psychopath (14,15). I came across this finding first when I studied the psychophysiology of those individuals from the 1962 HR study who became criminal. My findings on recovery have since been replicated by other studies of prison inmates: Siddle et al (13) and Hinton (18) in England, Bader-Bartfai and Schalling (16) in Sweden, by Hare (17) on maximum security prisoners in Canada. As a consequence of this research and despite the fact that we have not personally examined fathers of HR subjects, we can guess that they would be hyporesponsive and evidence very slow recovery.

While we have not examined the HR fathers, we have examined children of HR fathers. In Figure 4 we present the skin conductance responsiveness of children with and

---

[1] Subsequent to this analysis, two of the 34 Schizophrenia Group subjects were dropped from this Group. One was found to not have received psychiatric treatment; additional information changed a diagnosis to personality disorder. There was not sufficient time to redo the data analysis, but inspection revealed that the results for these two subjects tended to work against the results presented in Figure 3.

without criminal fathers from the 1970 perinatal study. As can be seen, the children of the criminal fathers evidence electrodermal behavior which resembles that which we would anticipate from their fathers. Note especially the effect on the recovery function of the skin conductance response. We have evidence from a twin study that the recovery function is, in some part, genetically influenced (19).

We must assume then, that HR fathers will tend to be more sociopathic than will LR fathers. Table 41-1 gives us an inkling as to what effect this might have on comparisons of the psychophysiology of the HR and LR children. If we expect *hyper*responsiveness from HR children, then the *hypo*responsiveness stemming from their having criminal fathers would tend to reduce HR-LR psychophysiological differences. Van Dyke analysed psychophysiological differences between HR and LR individuals using data from a study by Rosenthal done at the Psykologisk Institut. These investigators permitted me to examine criminality information on the parents of their subjects. As expected, the HR fathers are more severely criminal. They have been in jail an average of 4.73 months. The LR fathers had been in jail an average of 1.84 months. (I should mention that these are biological fathers of adoptees; they tend to be very highly criminal, Hutchings and Mednick (20)). It should also be mentioned that the HR sons have spent over twice the number of months in jail as the LR sons (1.3 months compared to .6 months). These criminality differences will tend to push electrodermal responsiveness in one direction while the schizophrenia risk differences will push in the opposite direction. Van Dyke (21) reports that in his data, this produced a draw, with the HR group, however, evidencing greater frequency and amplitude of response and slower habituation. (Van Dyke's "HR" subjects were actually surprisingly healthy adults, not significantly different in rating of mental health from their controls). Kirkegaard-Sørensen and Mednick (8) mention the possibility that, for a HR child, inheriting some of the autonomic *hypo*responsiveness of a criminal father could tend to be protective against schizophrenia.

Results from our 1962 HR study also point in this same direction. When we compare *our* 34 who were schizophrenic spectrum diagnoses with the remaining HR and LR groups on mean electrodermal recovery rate over all trials, we find that the schizophrenics have a rather rapid rate of recovery; the differences are highly significant (see Figure 41-3). When we consider just the 34 schizophrenia spectrum individuals and divide these into those with criminality in the family (mother, father or subject) and those without registered criminality, we find (in Table 41-2) that the criminality has a considerable effect on recovery rate.

Because of the apparent mutual attraction of female schizophrenics and male psycho-

Table 41-1. Skin conductance characteristics of children with criminal and non-criminal fathers

	Mean				
	Non-criminal	Criminal	F	DF	P
Number of Responses	2.79	1.55	8.51	1,187	<.01
Latency	2.05	2.38	5.32	1,95	<.05
½ Recovery time (X)	3.75	5.43	4.26	1,90	<.05
½ Recovery time (minimal)	2.26	4.33	8.80	1,90	<.01

Note: During orienting response testing, the child was presented 14 times with a tone of 1000 cps.

Table 41-2. Electrodermal recovery rate and familial criminality for 34 schizophrenia spectrum children. ($\chi^2 (1) = 9.70, p < 0.005$)

	Recovery rate all trials		
	Number slower than median	*Number faster than median*	
Criminality in family	12	3	15
No criminality	4	15	19
	16	18	34

paths and criminals, the influence of criminality on HR research will be with us as long as we define risk in terms of the mother's schizophrenia. In our own 1962 HR study we managed to match for criminality of the HR and LR fathers. This occurred as an indirect consequence of the fact that we matched for rearing in children's homes. For the HR subjects, their children's home experience was brought about by the schizophrenia in their family. For the LR subjects (who were screened for mental illness) their children's home experience was brought about by their father's criminality. As a consequence, the two groups of fathers were very well matched for level of criminality (8).

Intactness of Family

Erlenmeyer-Kimling and associates are conducting a HR study in New York City. Partly to be able to study both parents properly, she selected 7–12 year old children only from *intact* HR families and *intact* control families. Garmezy has reported that Erlenmeyer-Kimling did not find important psychophysiological differences between her

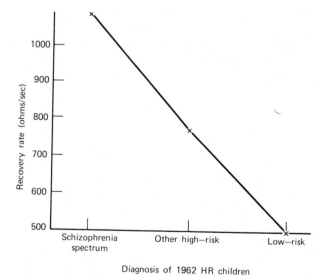

Diagnosis of 1962 HR children

Figure 41-3. Premorbid recovery rates for schizophrenics and other high-risk and low-risk subjects (F (2/296) = 5.33, p < 0.01).

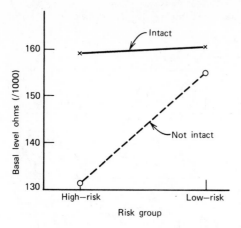

Figure 41-4. Mean basal level ohms resistance (over all trials) of high-risk and low-risk groups by intactness of family (1962 H R Project) (F (3/307) = 3.14, p < 0.025).

HR and LR groups. This finding has been contrasted with our Copenhagen finding of distinctive psychophysiological differences.

Our HR subjects in 1962 were selected because they had severely process, schizophrenic, hospitalized mothers living on the island of Zealand. There were no other restrictions in their selection. As a consequence, only about a quarter of the 1962 HR children would have been selected by Erlenmeyer-Kimling for her study; three-quarters of our group would have been rejected because the families were not intact at the proper age level. Of the 34 Schizophrenia Group subjects, only 14% would have been selected using the criterion of intactness of family. We have found that intactness of family also biases other aspects of our data.

I can illustrate this, showing the psychophysiological behavior of HR and LR subjects who come from intact families or do not come from intact families. As a consequence of our coding, the intactness is measured between the ages of 6–10 instead of 7–12 years. It is assumed that this difference did not produce critical effects on the psychophysiology.

Figures 41-4 through 41-8 describe the psychophysiology of the groups. As can be seen, our results for intact families are similar to those Garmezy reports for Erlenmeyer-Kimling, that is, no important HR-LR differences for offspring of intact families. The HR-LR psychophysiologic differences occur only in offspring of the families which are not intact.

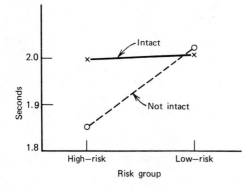

Figure 41-5. Mean electrodermal response latency (over all trials) of high-risk and low-risk groups by intactness of family (F (3/304) = 4.50, p < 0.005).

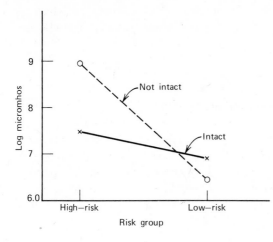

Figure 41-6. Mean by conductance amplitude (over all trials) of high-risk and low-risk groups by intactness of family (F (3/307) = 7.17, p < 0.0001).

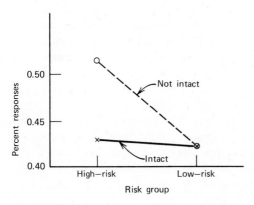

Figure 41-7. Percentage of scorable electrodermal responses (over all trials) of high-risk and low-risk groups by intactness of family (F (3/307) = 5.22, p < 0.002).

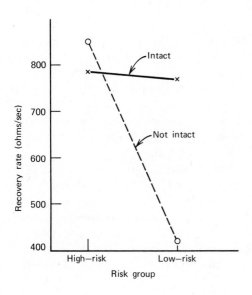

Figure 41-8. Mean recovery rate (over all trials) of high-risk and low-risk groups by intactness of family (F (3/302) = 2.58, p < 0.052).

449

The selection criterion "intactness of family" apparently contains elements which differentially affect the psychophysiological behavior of our subject groups. The HR subjects coming from not-intact families seem to be more psychophysiologically labile than the LR subjects coming from not-intact families. We suspect that the variable of intactness reflects something concerning the seriousness of illness of the schizophrenic mother. This may be partly responsible for the findings that we observe.

We should caution that by simply having redefined our groups in accordance with the criterion of intactness of family between the ages of 6–10, we do not automatically make our data perfectly comparable to that of Erlenmeyer-Kimling's. Intactness of family with a schizophrenic mother in Denmark in 1962 may not mean the same as intactness of family in New York City in 1972. There have been changing patterns of psychiatric treatment over the ten years; there is a cultural difference as well as a difference in criteria for diagnoses of schizophrenia.

SUMMARY

These considerations underline the need for a prospective birth cohort study of a population of perhaps 10,000 consecutive deliveries in a well-defined area and time. Granted, the study will take 35–40 years to complete. Granted, there will be problems concerning informed consent, etc. But with Berkson's Fallacy peering over our shoulders, it is clearly the only satisfactory approach to HR-LR comparisons.

Barring this approach, what other possibilities are there? We must be suspicious of the suitability of our LR controls because we sample so few of them in any one study. The situation is better when we consider our HR subjects. We must be aware of the correlates and effects of specific selection criteria such as family intactness, or adoptive status or a parent's subdiagnosis. Aside from these special circumstances, for the HR group we can better achieve representative sampling. This would mean that findings from analyses *within* the HR group will very likely be more readily generalized. Here we refer to analyses such as those made by Janes and Stern (22) who examined electrodermal factors as a function of psychopathology in HR children. Their results were in agreement with reports on the Sick, Well and Control Groups of the 1962 HR project (23).

An example of an analysis within the HR group, is illustrated by the comparison shown in Figure 3 of electrodermal recovery rates between the 34 individuals now schizophrenic and the other HR subjects. In this type of analysis we fulfill Berkson's conditions for generalization of findings. The ratio of the marginal totals for HR schizophrenics and HR not-schizophrenics will tend to correspond to the ratio in the general HR population. Whether these findings can then be generalized to non-HR populations can be best ascertained by the birth cohort study. While waiting for that project, we can make do by comparing our HR research findings with results of studies of schizophrenics. For example, the Janes and Stern finding, the findings on the Sick, Well and Control Groups of the 1962 HR study and the findings on the newly diagnosed schizophrenics reported in this paper (Figure 3) all tend to suggest that fast autonomic recovery is predispositional or at least a premorbid characteristic of poor adjustment, mental illness and schizophrenia. When we examine the literature on autonomic recovery in schizophrenics, there is one study reporting no differences (24), but Ax and Bamford (25), Gruzelier and Venables (26) Gruzelier (27), and Novelly,

Graham and Ax (28) all report considerably faster recovery for schizophrenics than for other deviant and non-deviant controls. We should not be blind to the dangers of Berkson's Fallacy in these latter studies.

REFERENCES

1. Mednick SA, Schulsinger F, Schulsinger H: Schizophrenia in children of schizophrenic mothers, in Davids A (ed): *Childhood Personality and Psychopathology: Current Topics,* Volume 2. New York, John Wiley, 1975, 221–252.

2. Schulsinger H: A ten-year follow-up of children of schizophrenic mothers: The clinical assessment. *Acta Psychiatrica Scandinavica* 53:371–386, 1976.

3. Endicott J, Spitzer R: Current and past psychopathology scales (CAPPS). *Archives of General Psychiatry,* 27:678–687, 1972.

4. Mednick SA, Mura E, Schulsinger F, et al: Perinatal conditions and infant development in children with schizophrenic parents. *Social Biology* 18:103–113, 1971.

5. Mednick SA: The early and advanced schizophrenic, in Mednick SA and Higgins J (eds): *Current Research in Schizophrenia.* Ann Arbor, Edwards, 1960.

6. Berkson J: The statistical study of association between smoking and lung cancer. Proceedings of Staff Meetings Mayo Clinic. 1955, 319–348.

7. Kallmann FJ: *The Genetics of Schizophrenia.* New York, J.J. Augustin, 1938.

8. Kirkegaard-Sørensen L, Mednick SA: Registered criminality in families with children at high risk for schizophrenia. *Journal of Abnormal Psychology,* 84:197–204, 1975.

9. Lykken DTA: A study of anxiety in the sociopathic personality. *Journal of Abnormal and Social Psychology,* 55:6–10, 1957.

10. Hare RD: *Psychopathy: Theory and Research.* New York, John Wiley, 1970.

11. Schalling D, Levander S: Spontaneous fluctuations in skin conductance during anticipation of pain in two delinquent groups, differing in anxiety-proneness. Psychological Institute, Stockholm, 1967.

12. Schmauk FJ: Punishment, arousal, and avoidance learning in sociopaths. *Journal of Abnormal Psychology,* 76:325–335, 1970.

13. Siddle DAT: Electrodermal acitivity and psychopathy, in Christiansen KO and Mednick SA (eds): *Biosocial Bases of Criminal Behavior.* New York, Gardner Press, Inc., 1977.

14. Mednick SA: Electrodermal recovery and psychopathology, in Mednick SA, Schulsinger F, Higgens J, et al (eds): *Genetics, Environment and Psychopathology.* Amsterdam, North Holland/Elsevier, 1974.

15. Loeb J, Mednick SA: A prospective study of predictors of criminality: Electrodermal response patterns, in Christiansen KO and Mednick SA (eds): *Biosocial Bases of Criminal Behavior.* New York, Gardner Press, Inc., 1977.

16. Bader-Bartfai A, Schalling D: Recovery times of skin conductance responses as related to some personality and physiological variables. Psychological Institute, Stockholm, 1974.

17. Hare RD: Paper presented at Les Arcs, France, September, 1975.

18. Hinton J: Personal communication.

19. Bell B, Mednick SA, Gottesman II et al: Electrodermal parameters in male twins, in Christiansen KO and Mednick SA (eds): *Biosocial Bases of Criminal Behavior.* New York, Gardner Press, Inc., 1977.

20. Hutchings B, Mednick SA: Registered criminality in the adopted and biological parents of registered male criminal adoptees, in Mednick SA, Schulsinger F, Higgins J, et al (eds): *Genetics, Environment and Psychopathology.* Amsterdam, North Holland/Elsevier, 1974, 215–230.

21. Van Dyke JL, Rosenthal D, Rasmussen PV: Electrodermal functioning in adopted-away offspring of schizophrenics. *Journal of Psychiatric Research,* 10:199–215, 1974.

22. Janes CL, Stern JA: Electrodermal response configuration as a function of rated psychopathology in children, in press.

23. Mednick SA, Schulsinger F: Some premorbid characteristics related to breakdown in children with schizophrenic mothers. *Journal of Psychiatric Research,* 6:267–291, 1968.

24. Maricq HR, Edelberg R: Electrodermal recovery rate in a schizophrenic population. *Psychophysiology,* 12:630–633, 1975.

25. Ax AF, Bamford JL: The GSR recovery limb in chronic schizophrenia. *Psychophysiology,* 7:145–147, 1970.

26. Gruzelier JH, Venables PH: Skin conductance orienting activity in a heterogeneous sample of schizophrenics. Possible evidence of limbic dysfunction. *Journal of Nervous and Mental Disease,* 155:277–287, 1972.

27. Gruzelier JH: Bilateral asymmetry of skin conductance orienting activity and levels in schizophrenics. *Biological Psychology,* 1:21–42, 1973.

28. Novelly RA, Graham JJ, Ax AF: Psychophysiological correlates of temporal lobe epilepsy. Paper presented at Psychophysiological Society Meeting, Salt Lake City, 1974.

Chapter 42
Cognition and Affect in the Human Infant

Jerome Kagan, Ph.D.

The primary purpose of this chapter is to suggest that during the last third of the first year the human infant enters a new stage of cognitive functioning that is characterized by an enhanced capacity to retrieve representations of past events that are not in the immediate psychologic field and to compare those representations, or schemata, with present experience. Since restriction of variety in environmental experience or impaired functioning of the central nervous system can alter the time of appearance of the behaviors that characterize this stage, investigators seeking predictive indexes of future psychopathologic states might consider studying this developmental period.

THE GROWTH OF RETRIEVAL AND COMPARATIVE COMPETENCES

During the last third of the first year a variety of new behaviors emerge. Although they appear on the surface to be very different from one another, we believe that they share at least one common mechanism. This mechanism is the capacity to retrieve schemata of past events in the absence of supporting stimuli and to compare those schemata with present experience in the service of assimilation. Let us first list some of these changes.

Increased Attentiveness

Toward the end of the first year the infant often displays more prolonged attention to a variety of discrepant events than he did when he was 6 or 7 months old. If an interesting event is shown to infants from 4 through 30 months of age in either a cross-section or longitudinal design, there is often, but not always, a U-shaped relationship between age and fixation, with a trough around 7 to 9 months. For example, if masks or drawings of human faces are shown to children, attention is prolonged from ages 4 to 6 months, markedly lower for the next few months, and then increases through the second and third years (6). This growth function for attention also occurs to nonsocial episodes. We

This research was supported by grants from the Grant Foundation, Carnegie Corporation of New York, and Office of Child Development.

recently administered to American and rural Guatemalan children a dynamic sequence in which a hand moved an orange rod across a traverse of 180 degrees to contact a bank of three lightbulbs which were then lit. After a series of familiarization trials, the child saw five repetitions of a discrepant transformation of the original event. The movement of the rod was omitted, the hand touched the orange rod, but the rod did not move and 3 seconds later the light appeared. After the transformation trials, the child again saw three trials of the original standard. Attention to the transformation and return trials showed a U-shaped relationship with a trough at 7½ months for both American and Guatemalan children living in subsistence rural villages.

The American children also were exposed to an episode in which they were familiarized with a 4-second tape recording of a meaningful sentence spoken by a female voice. After familiarization trials, they heard a discrepant phrase spoken by the same voice. One of the salient behaviors that occurs to auditory episodes is a searching movement in which the infant becomes alert and motorically immobile while his eyes move in regular saccadic search movements. The growth function for searching is U-shaped with a trough at 7½ months to standard, transformation, and return trials.

Object Permanence

The child's ability to retrieve an object that he watched being covered or hidden also appears at about 8 or 9 months. It is probably not a coincidence that the likelihood of the child's reaching for an audible object in total darkness also begins to increase at this time. Moreover, the increased disposition to reach for an audible object after 7 months of age also appears in blind infants (1,3).

Inhibition to a Discrepant Event

Prior to 8 months, the infant reaches almost at once to a novel object that is presented after repeated presentation of a familiarized standard, while a 12 month old shows an obvious delay before reaching for the novel object (8). A capacity for motor inhibition to an unexpected event is not new, for newborns will inhibit both limb movement and sucking to a sudden onset of stimulation but not to a change in psychologic information.

Wariness of Discrepancies

There is a dramatic increase in the likelihood of wariness and crying to an event whose major characteristic is that it is a discrepant transformation of earlier or immediately past experience. Scarr and Salapatek (10) exposed infants 2 to 23 months of age to six different discrepant events—a stranger approaching the child, the visual cliff, a jack-in-the-box, a mechanical dog that moved, facial masks, and a loud noise. Infants younger than 7 months rarely showed any behavioral signs of wariness toward any of these events. The peak display of wariness usually occurred between 11 and 18 months for most of these episodes.

The effect of the appearance of a stranger on the child has been investigated many times in the last 20 years, and the consensus from these studies is in accord with the data summarized by Scarr and Salapatek. Inhibition, facial wariness, or overt distress is rare prior to 7 months and grows dramatically between that time and the end of the first year (2,7,11–14).

To preview our interpretation, we suggest that the appearance of the wariness is the result of the emergence of the ability to retrieve from memory a schema related to the child's present experience and to compare the retrieved structures with the present in an attempt to resolve the inconsistency. The occurrence of wariness to unfamiliar events, which is not a typical reaction, is a result of the child's failure to resolve the inconsistency between the ongoing discrepant event and his knowledge, despite an attempt to do so. We also believe that this interpretation is relevant to the phenomenon of separation anxiety.

Separation Distress

A phenomenon that emerges toward the end of the first year has acquired the name separation anxiety because the child becomes upset when he is separated from his primary caretaker. That label is misleading since the child is far less likely to cry when he leaves his mother or is taken from her than when she leaves him. Moreover, if a 1 year old crawls or walks from his mother into an empty room so he has no visual access to her, he will show minimal signs of distress (9). But if his mother should leave him, the probability that he will fret is much greater. Moreover, if the father or another familiar adult remains with the child when the mother leaves, he is unlikely to become upset. It is only when a parent leaves the infant with a stranger or alone in an unfamiliar setting that he is likely to show apprehension. Thus if the mother's departure occurs in a familiar context, like the living room of the home, the child is less likely to become distressed than if the separation occurs in an unfamiliar setting. If the mother leaves the child by an unfamiliar exit in the home (a closet), he will show more apprehension than if she leaves by a familiar one, like the front door. These data imply that a primary incentive for the distress is the discrepant quality of the event.

There are two quite different aspects of this phenomenon. The first is the growth function for separation distress; the second concerns individual differences in intensity of distress during the period of its display. We are primarily concerned with the former. Controlled investigations of separation distress reveal that the probability of signs of protest to maternal departure, like crying or inhibition of play, are low prior to 9 months of age, rise rapidly from 9 to 18 months, and then begin to decline. This finding has been found several times in American samples. We recently have studied the developmental course of separation protest in children from four settings outside the United States—lower class Ladino families living in the city of Antigua, Guatemala, Indian families residing in the isolated agricultural village of San Pedro on Lake Atitlan in northwest Guatemala, Israeli kibutzim where infants spend most of the day in an infant house, and Bushmen families living on the Kalahari Desert. In all four samples the occurrence of crying following maternal departure when left with a stranger was minimal prior to 9 months, increased to a peak value between 12 and 15 months, and then declined (5).

Additionally, we recently completed a study in which children attended a research day care center 5 days a week from 3½ to 29 months of age. Each child in the day care group was paired with a control child of the same sex, social class, and ethnic group who was being raised at home. The child's reactions to his mother's leaving him alone in a strange room were observed regularly from 3½ to 29 months of age. The growth function was identical for both the day care and home reared children for both probability of crying and the delay between departure and distress, and, as in the earlier study, separation fear did not occur reliably until 9 to 12 months of age, peaking during the second year. Moreover, separation protest is only a few months delayed in blind children, emerging between 10 and 19 months with a median age of 11 months, close to the median age for sighted infants. This is remarkable considering the fact that the child cannot see that the parent has departed. The incentive event for the blind child's distress is the sudden absence of the mother's voice or the absence of the sounds that accompany her bodily movements (3).

The Suggestion of an Invariant Sequence

We have recently administered a series of tasks to American and Mayan Indian children. The American sample consisted of eight children who were followed longitudinally from 5 to 11 months of age. The Indian sample was cross-sectional and consisted of 34 children, 7 to 20 months old. The procedures involved:

Vacillation to Familiar and Novel Objects
The child was offered a toy and allowed to play with it for 15 seconds. After that period the toy was removed gently and a few second later the child was presented with two toys, the one he had just manipulated and a new one. The coder noted which toy the child looked at and also visual vacillation between the two toys. The child received five trials with five different toys.

Object Permanence
The child was administered a simple object permanence problem in which the examiner hid a toy under a cloth and coded whether or not the child reached for the toy. All children were also given the classic "A not B paradigm." Two cloths were placed in front of the child. The examiner hid a toy under one cloth and allowed the child to reach for it on three separate trials at that location. On the fourth trial, the toy was hidden under the other cloth while the child watched. The delay between hiding the toy and allowing the child to reach was less than 3 seconds.

Separation Protest
The child was allowed to play with a set of toys. When the child was happy and content, the mother left the child alone with an unfamiliar woman. Time playing and occurrence of crying were coded.

Play
The child was allowed to play with a set of toys for 15 minutes. A major variable of interest was a category called symbolic play in which the child treated an object as having some referential meaning or as representing a real object in his environment (using a toy comb to comb one's hair or feeding imaginary food to a doll).

Although the American children were a few months ahead of the Indians, the sequence was the same for both groups. Vacillation was the first response in most children. This was followed closely by object permanence, then separation protest, and finally the appearance of symbolism in play (see Table 42-1).

Table 42-1. Age at Which 50% of an Age Cohort Displayed Each of the Behavioral Variables

Variable	American Children	Indian Children
Vacillation on half the trials	6.5 months	10 months
Correct performance on object permanence problems	7 months	11 months
Cry to separation	10 months	13 months
Appearance of symbolism in play	11 months	14 months

AN INTERPRETATION

We suggest that one element common to these behavioral changes is a qualitative increase in the ability to retrieve schemata of prior events, a growth in what contemporary psychologists would call memory capacity. The most persuasive support for that idea comes from a study showing that an 8-month-old child will make an error in the "A not B" procedure if the delay between hiding of the object and the child's reaching for it is long (say 7 seconds) but not if it is 3 seconds or less. The child of 10 or 11 months will not make this error under any reasonable delay.

We suggest that the child shows increased attention to the transformation and return trials of an original familiarized standard because he is able to retrieve the schema for the original event and compare it with his present experience. He reaches for a hidden audible sound because he actively generates a schema for objects that in the past have made sounds. He pauses to vacillate because he actively retrieves the past experience and compares it with the present. He shows object permanence because he actively generates the idea of the absent object. He displays symbolic play because he can actively retrieve the action he witnessed with a toy. Now let us try to apply this idea to separation anxiety.

Following maternal departure, the child generates from memory the schema of her presence and compares it with the present, attempting to resolve the inconsistency. This process is necessary but not sufficient to bear the burden of explanation because the child does not display fear in other situations where he generates a schema of a past event, as when no object is found under a cloth after the child watched an adult place one there. Moreover, a 1 year old compares past with present all through the day in many contexts and does not usually show fear. Thus the new memory competence is necessary but not sufficient. An additional factor must be posited, and we believe it is the ability to generate anticipations of the future. Anticipating the mother's presence as she rises to leave is not the same competence as retrieving a past event and comparing it with the present. If the 1 year old anticipates an unpleasant event, like pain or danger, he is likely to cry. We do not believe this is an acquired conditioned anxiety reaction because it strains the imagination to assume that all over the world infants between 9 and 13 months of age, even those who are with their mothers most of the day, suddenly expect an unpleasant event when their mother leaves them, independent of the frequency of past distress when the mother was absent. We believe that the 1 year old has a capacity to try to anticipate the future. He attempts to predict what might happen following departure. Inability to generate a substantive prediciton, combined with the inability to resolve the inconsistency between the schema of her earlier presence and her absence, produces uncertainty and, in some children, inhibition of play and crying. Moreover, it is likely that if the child does not have a behavior to deal with the uncertainty, distress is most likely to occur. If he has such a response, his distress will be buffered.

In summary, the distress that follows separation is a product of several new competences: the new ability to retrieve a past schema and to compare it with the present in order to resolve the inconsistency and the ability to attempt to predict possibilities. Failure to resolve the inconsistency or to make the prediction produces uncertainty. And if the child has no response to the state of uncertainty, crying may occur.

DISCUSSION

The data are persuasive of the notion that in normal infants there is a fundamental change in cognitive functioning between 8 and 12 months of age. It seems likely that these new competences are mediated by maturing processes in the central nervous system, perhaps related to frontal lobe functions. Serious deviation from this timetable implies unusual rearing experiences or anomalous central nervous system development. Investigators who believe that schizophrenia has a biologic basis that can be revealed by psychologic observations of infants might focus their empirical probes on this period. If infants at risk for schizophrenia do not show unusual behavior on these variables, at least we will have eliminated another possibility. And that is progress.

REFERENCES

1. Bower TGR: *Development in Infancy*. San Francisco, Calif, WH Freeman & Co, 1974.
2. Bronson GW: Infants' reactions to unfamiliar persons and novel objects. *Monographs of the Society for Research in Child Development*. 37:3, 1972.
3. Fraiberg S: Parallel and divergent patterns in blind and sighted infants. *Psychoanalytic Study of the Child* 23:264, 1968.
4. Fraiberg S: The development of human attachments in infants blind from birth. *Merrill Palmer Quarterly* 21:315, 1975.
5. Kagan J: Emergent themes in human development. *American Scientist*, 64:186, 1976.
6. Kagan J: Do infants think? *Scientific American* 226:74, 1972.
7. Morgan GA, Ricciuti HN: Infants' responses to strangers during the first year, in Foss BM (ed): *Determinants of Infant Behavior*, vol 4. London, Methuen & Co, 1969.
8. Parry MH: Infant wariness and stimulus discrepancy. *Journal of Experimental Child Psychology* 16:377, 1973.
9. Rheingold HL, Eckerman CO: The infant separates himself from his mother. *Science* 168:78, 1970.
10. Scarr S, Salapatek P: Patterns of fear development during infancy. *Merrill Palmer Quarterly* 16:53, 1970.
11. Schaffer HR: The onset of fear of strangers and the incongruity hypothesis. *Journal of Child Psychology and Psychiatry* 7:95, 1966.

12. Spitz RA: Anxiety in infancy: A study of its manifestation in the first year of life. *International Journal of Psychoanalysis* 31:138, 1950.

13. Stevens AG: Attachment behavior, separation anxiety and stranger anxiety in polymatrically reared infants, in Schaffer HR (ed): *The Origins of Human Social Relations.* New York, Academic Press, 1971.

14. Tennes KH, Lampl EE: Stranger and separation anxiety in infancy. *Journal of Nervous and Mental Diseases* 139:247, 1969.

Chapter 43
Observations on High-Risk Research and Premorbid Development in Schizophrenia

Norman Garmezy, Ph.D.

When *The Origins of Schizophrenia* (1), the proceedings of the First Rochester International Conference on Schizophrenia, was published a decade ago, risk research was represented solely by a paper by Sarnoff Mednick (2) and my commentary that this study would be "oft-cited" (a new high for conservatism in predicting research trends), and that the future for developmental research in schizophrenia lay with the longitudinal study (3). Others appear to have shared that view, including those whose papers now appear in this volume and others whose research programs are presented in abbreviated form at the conclusion of this section of the volume.

It would, however, be a mistake to conclude that risk investigations represent an entirely new development in research on the psychopathology of schizophrenia. The classical clinical contributions of Bender, Fish, M. Bleuler, and others have been cited in a recent review (4,5). Their descendants now are responsible for the numerous ongoing programs of research on the developmental study of children at risk that are underway in Canada, Denmark, Israel, Mauritius, Sweden, and the United States.

One can trace back to Kraepelin evidence of a fleeting concern for such children. In his scholarly treatise on *Dementia Praecox and Paraphrenia*, Kraepelin (6) provided a masterly 250-page description of the phenomenology of schizophrenia. In a final chapter, only four and a half pages in length, titled "How to Combat It," Kraepelin used 199 words to comment on children at risk:

> In children of such characteristics as we so very frequently find in the previous history of
> dementia praecox one might think of an attempt at prophylaxis especially if the malady had

*The preparation of this paper has been supported by an NIMH
Research Career Award and a grant from the Supreme Council
33° A.: A.: Scottish Rite, Northern Masonic Jurisdiction
(Schizophrenia Research Program).*

been already observed in the parents or brothers or sisters. Whether it is possible in such circumstances to ward off the outbreak of the threatening disease, we do not know. But in any case it will be advisable to promote to the utmost of one's power general bodily development and to avoid one-sided training in brain work, as it may well be assumed that a vigorous body grown up under natural conditions will be in a better position to overcome the danger than a child exposed to the influences of effeminacy, of poverty, and of exact routine, and especially of city education. Childhood spent in the country with plenty of open air, bodily exercise, escalation beginning late without ambitious aims, simple food, would be the principal points to keep in view. Meyer, who regards dementia praecox essentially as the effect of unfavorable influences of life and education on personalities with abnormal dispositions, hopes by all these measures to be able to prevent the development of the malady. (p 253)

Embedded within those 199 words are a surprisingly large number of conjectures that can be viewed as forerunners of aspects of current research on children vulnerable to schizophrenia. Consider three of them:

1. *The passage defines the criterion for what is currently the dominant mode for identifying risk, namely the genetic base for the disorder.* The pregnant phrase that identifies this bias is Kraepelin's allusion to concern for a specific type of child—those in whom "the malady had already been observed in the parents or brothers or sisters."

2. *To the genetic diathesis, Kraepelin joins a set of specific environmental stressors.* Diathesis-stress theory, despite its imprecision in defining both predisposition and potentiator, has retained a powerful hold on both the genetically minded and environmentally minded proponents of etiology in schizophrenia. To his implicit genetic position, Kraepelin's admonition "to promote to the utmost" bodily development, to abjure an overemphasis on brain work, and to avoid the dangers of effeminacy, poverty, exact routine, and city education, provides a link to concern with gender identity, social isolation, overideational reflectiveness, compulsive routine, and the debilitating patterns that accompany lower social class status, all of which are viewed as stressors in the 1970s.

3. *Kraepelin provides a brief glimpse into the possibility of intervention with risk children, but he remains sufficiently unconvinced of the efficacy of the suggested procedures so he attributes them to the hopes of Adolf Meyer.* Provide the resources for exercise, temper overweaning aspirations, make available a less stressful environment marked by good nutrition, play, fresh air, and nonurbanization, and the course of psychopathology may be stayed. It is interesting to note that stress reduction and a training atmosphere for children characterized by warmth, support, and the reinforcement of more adaptive behaviors are reflected in the pioneering intervention efforts now underway in some risk research groups as widely scattered as Mauritius (Mednick, Schulsinger, and Venables), St. Louis, Missouri (Anthony and colleagues), and Burlington, Vermont (Rolf and colleagues).

Kraepelin's word picture was drawn in the first decades of the twentieth century. In the 60-year span that separates Kraepelin's writings from those of contemporary investigators, marked changes have occurred in our views of schizophrenia. Old arguments of gene versus environment have been abandoned by all except a small band of biophobes or psychophobes; today the dispute is more likely to center on theoretical formulations of the nature of those genetic and environmental contributions and the weights to be assigned such factors on the basis of empirical studies. The issue of single versus multiple genes finds a similar representation in the decision whether to study a single overriding aspect of the child's environment (e.g., family relations) rather than to focus on multiple environmental and personality determinants.

The most marked change of all, however, over the past half century has been recognition of the temporal nature of the disorder. If you scratch a psychopathologist in the mid-1970s, a developmentalist bleeds, and it does not matter whether that psychopathologist pledges primary allegiance to genetics, biology, dynamic or descriptive psychiatry, or to psychology.

Schizophrenia is the quintessential developmental disorder. As such, it is of primary importance to trace the early years of a patient-in-the-making prospectively, rather than retrospectively, if we are to provide an accurate scientific account of that disorder.

I make this point as prologue to an irreverent question. Imagine that the year is 2006 and we are again assembled for what is now the Fifth Rochester International Conference on Schizophrenia. Retirement and rocking chairs have either claimed or shortly will claim the likes of Mednick, Schulsinger, Anthony, Sameroff, McNeil, Kaij, and company. As the new century dawns, a youthful, callow invitee, intent on publishing rather than perishing, is asked to review the early studies on risk-for-schizophrenia research for the Intergalactic Institute of Mental Health. He sets out to trace early longitudinal investigations, surveys the now definitive follow-up data, assigns the children now grown to middle age into disordered and adaptive groups, and comes to the inescapable conclusion that efficiency of predictions, based on the independent variables that were used to categorize the children and the dependent variables that were introduced to measure their biologic and psychologic statuses, is depressingly low.

What then might be the judgment rendered about the contributions of risk research in the 1970s? I believe the answer to that question should be framed by two questions rather than a single one. (a) Did we do a good job in tracking the development of children born to schizophrenic parentage (or selected, perhaps, on other reasonably wise, theoretical bases) through infancy, childhood, adolescence, and early maturity? (b) Were we able to predict from our *clinical* and *experimental* data who would become schizophrenic?

If we have been able to construct studies capable of mapping the first question, then, even in the event of a negative answer to the second question, ours will have been a significant contribution. For what we will have provided for psychiatry and developmental psychology would be the first steps toward the growth of knowledge essential for understanding the relationship between the range of predisposition and the diversity of outcomes unbiased by information about such outcomes. Here would be the beginnings of a developmental psychopathology of schizophrenia and its related disorders.

Piaget (7) captured this viewpoint in his foreword to a recent volume, *Explorations in Child Psychiatry*. In referring to a goal that he sees as "very necessary yet difficult to attain," Piaget writes:

> This goal is the synthesis of developmental psychology with all the other aspects of child psychology into *a science of ontogenetic development* from birth to maturity encompassing three points of view—the biological, the behavioral, and the internalization of the behavioral into mental life. This synthesis is indeed necessary since it is not possible to understand a disorder or a developmental arrest without having a sufficient knowledge of the ensemble of elements that has brought it about. . . . However, since there are those who remain normal in situations where others become variously disturbed, the meaning of the disorder to be remedied can be extremely diverse, and in order to grasp it, it is necessary to immerse oneself in the ensemble at the different developmental stages, the order of which is by no means fortuitous but resembles the orderly sequence of stages observed in embryogenesis. (vii)

Piaget then concludes:

> To put it briefly, developmental psychologists . . . are looking forward with great expectation to the emergence of *developmental psychopathology* as a new discipline still struggling to organize its own relevant field of knowledge. They are hoping especially that in spite of all the obstacles in the way and the huge amount of creative effort required for the purpose that this science will constitute itself on an interdisciplinary basis as wide as possible and on a common language that helps to unify what is precise and generalizable. (ix)

As for the second question that inquires into the efficiency of our predictions, were we able to answer it affirmatively, history would, of course, judge our efforts more favorably. What I find rather disconcerting, however, is that we seem to be more oriented to the second question than to the first. The first question demands a longitudinal context; the second need not. To develop information about the prepotency of variables that may have etiologic significance does not necessarily require that we begin with a longitudinal design. Cross-sectional studies of different age groups joined by comparisons with other target and normal groups of children, as well as with active and remitted adult schizophrenics, may prove to be a wiser course in the early search for potential precursors to schizophrenia. I call your attention to the fact that this research strategy characterizes the efforts reported by Asarnow et al (see Chapter 34), and by Hanson, Gottesman, and Heston (8) in a recent publication.

In elaborating on this viewpoint, let me consider the problem of the selection of variables by which to examine children at risk. The opening-up of any research area poses a decision as to what warrants study. The answer to such a question is likely to be primitive (witness Kraepelin's commentary) when contrasted with the standards of later research that will be performed. "What goes with what?" is scarcely a hallmark of sophisticated scientific inquiry, but we need not be ashamed of admitting to an early overinclusiveness in choosing variables designed to answer an admittedly nonspecific question. What should be obvious, however, is that early stages of research should not require a premature declaration that we are on an etiologic quest. What seems to be far more necessary initially is to establish better criteria for selecting variables to examine during this formative stage of research.

At a recent World Health Organization conference (9) on risk research, I described one such set of criteria as a platform for debate by risk investigators. Briefly, I suggested: (a) the importance of studying those attributes that are clearly evident in varying degrees of intensity at different stages of the schizophrenic process; (b) that the proportion of subjects manifesting these attributes at least roughly approximate anticipated incidences for the disorder. (I now have come to view this criterion as suspect unless we have adequate knowledge of the factors that influence such rates, such as differential threshold values, genetic and experiential contributions of parents and spouse, and chronicity or acuteness of disorder. Compare Mednick, Chapter 41.) (c) The variable should be one likely to serve as a basic substrate for the expression of adequacy in thought, perception, and skill acquisition in the areas of economic and social exchange. (d) The variable should be a stable one, resistant to causal shifts in motivational level, practice, fatigue, and so forth.

Given this or any other set of criteria, where does one begin in the selection of variables? This question serves to introduce my discussion of the chapters that have been presented on high-risk research and premorbid development.

McNEIL-KAIJ

I would observe that the McNeil-Kaij chapter on obstetric factors in the development of schizophrenia (Chapter 39) seems to me to be the very exemplar of a review that should be a prerequisite in evaluating a variable that is to be considered for inclusion in a study of risk. Their critique incorporates a systematic account of the range of hypotheses that can be generated regarding the *etiologic role* of obstetric complications (OCs) in schizophrenia. Great insightfulness is evident in the exposition of 12 possible hypotheses related both to diathesis and to stress. The authors then proceed to a careful examination of the available empirical data on OCs when viewed against their presence in the histories of children at risk as defined by schizophrenia in their parents and also the self-same evidence in adult schizophrenics of early and late onset, and as discriminators in monozygotic twins discordant for schizophrenia. The subsequent careful mapping of the available data in terms of their relevance to the hypotheses initially set forth in their paper, the effort to define and to evaluate the presence of OCs in a broad spectrum of samples potentially related to schizophrenia, and the careful delineation of potentially confounding factors present not only in measuring OCs, but also in the various samples of subjects that have been studied, commends this paper as one that is a tribute to the scholarship of the authors. It is in every detail a major contribution to high-risk research in schizophrenia.

One comes away from this review convinced that despite disparate results across different studies, "obstetric complications are a risk-increasing factor to be taken seriously in the etiology of schizophrenia." It is for future investigations, including the one currently underway by the authors in Malmo, Sweden, to provide the answers to questions such as the interaction of OCs with other etiologic factors, their consequences for later adaptation, and their possible influence on the patterning of disorder if and when it eventuates.

The McNeil-Kaij chapter sets a standard for risk researchers. Were each risk research group either collaboratively or independently to prepare in similar fashion as definitive an appraisal and critique of the research literature of those variables to which these research teams are committed, their contributions both to the predisposition to and the psychopathology of schizophrenia would be of great value.

SAMEROFF-ZAX

Let me now move beyond pregnancy and birth to infancy and the preschool years as viewed by Sameroff and Zax in Chapter 40 on young offspring of schizophrenic women. With regard to the five models they have presented, I see these primarily as expository. It would be very difficult to find a responsible or knowledgeable investigator who would consider either Model 1 (constitutional) or Model 2 (environmental) as tenable in these times. Even for the multifactor views, the issue of specificity or nonspecificity more often is based on gaps in knowledge than on ideologic or theoretical perspectives. One chooses the path of nonspecificity in the absence of knowing just where specificity with regard to environmental or constitutional determinants is to be found. Sameroff's and Zax's transactional model is just that—a model for the description of nonspecificity to diathesis and stress that will undoubtedly have to undergo modification as more and more data are accumulated in the course of risk investigations. Models, after all, are only tentative theoretical structures erected to integrate subsets of existent data and for predicting new relationships within a given subject domain. Sameroff and Zax have chosen a transactional model on the basis of their existent data; the elements for predicting interrelationships are still undefined and essentially unexplored.

Models are suggestive in positing what the phenomena that interest us can be like rather than what they truly are. Their virtue lies in the efficacy with which they generate testable hypotheses. Inevitably, a good model that serves that primary function must meet its demise, for a model is never the exposition of a true faith, but is constructed to be relinquished. This means that in the search for new domains of knowledge, models can and should coexist. As Abraham Kaplan (10) has written: "The dangers are not in working with models but in working with too few, and those too much alike, and above all, in belittling any effort to work with anything else" (p 293).

A premature fixity of view poses danger to the scientific enterprise. In Kaplan's words, "The danger is that the model limits our awareness of unexplored possibilities of conceptualization. We tinker with the model when we might be better occupied with the subject-matter itself."

Clearly, Sameroff and Zax have not ignored their subject matter. Tracing the history of their project, it is evident that they have been empiricists first, model builders second. But it is necessary to recognize that the transactional model is one cast, at best, in Kaplan's delineation of the *eristic* style—i.e., one that emphasizes experimentation, data collection, and deduction. This style is a considerable distance removed from the goal of more tightly constructed models in which rigorous and logical conceptualizations are joined to explicit rules for deriving propositions and for testing them by equally rigorous mathematical proofs. One cannot fault Sameroff and Zax for the insubstantial nature of their model. In risk research, alternative models would be equally imprecise. I merely wish to make the point that it is important to recognize that there may be less than meets the eye when data are matched to model.

What I find more invigorating in the Sameroff-Zax paper are the data they present in the context of a short-term longitudinal design. The tracing of the earliest years of the offspring of schizophrenic women and others born to mothers who either have had neurotic depressive or personality disorders, or freedom from mental disorder, provides a focus on that period in a child's life that is critical for the development of attachment, socialization, and cognitive competence. (As we see, Kagan's chapter also emphasizes the significance of the latter part of the first year of life for the evocation of cognitive competence.)

By studying children up to four years of age, Sameroff and Zax have enlarged their focus to allow them to study the development of abilities and attributes that later may come to be associated with the evolution of competence in work, at play, and in love, and even perhaps to expectations of success as opposed to failure in achievement strivings (Whitehorn's criteria for defining the mentally healthy individual). The fact that the study extends only to the child's fourth year of life is unfortunate and tantalizing, for it places the child on the threshold of school entry and the early school years during which competence can best be evaluated. One would hope for continued follow-up of the children, at least for several years beyond the projected termination date of the study, to insure the study of adaptation in the school setting with its demands for economic (work), cognitive, and social competence.

A particular strength of the Sameroff-Zax study is to be found in their wise selection of two psychopathologic control groups. These have enabled them to make comparisons on variables that, given a less adequate design, could have led to the specification of schizophrenia-related attributions. Instead they have demonstrated effects that tend to be correlated with a wider band of more generalized disturbing maternal environments. It is the presence of control group data that has generated the feedback that has led the investigators to attribute nonspecificity to constitution and environment in the context of their transactional model.

Their results appear to implicate poverty (low SES) as a profoundly powerful determiner of competence in offspring, even of those born to normal control mothers. Thus, they conclude that "the effects of the social milieu appear to overpower the effects of maternal psychopathology." But it is also suggested that *some* of the offspring of schizophrenic mothers may bear certain unique characteristics at birth that parallel those described by McNeil and Kaij. Thus, of six offspring placed for adoption, three were maintained in an intensive care nursery because of prematurity. Whether this too may reflect a component of genetic endowment has been argued by Heston (11) and Fish (12). What is intriguing, however, is the affirmation in Sameroff's and Zax's paper of the central theme evident in McNeil's and Kaij's review. One can only look forward eagerly to the future outpouring of data from this program of research on neonatal and early childhood factors in serious maternal mental disorder.

MEDNICK

The research strategy designed by Sameroff and Zax in its broadest outline is one borrowed from the pioneering studies on risk conducted by Mednick and Schulsinger in Denmark. It is a tribute to the staying power of that research program that now 10 years after his initial presentation at the First Rochester International Conference on Schizophrenia, Mednick returns to provide us with some provocative new findings from Denmark.

It is 15 years since the initiation of that project and Mednick, using data drawn from his group's longitudinal study, has focused in Chapter 41 on the dangers of a too early assertion of failure by new investigative teams to replicate either their findings or those that may be obtained in another laboratory. He argues, rightfully, that consideration must be given to a variety of factors that may well influence behavioral and biologic observations that are seemingly in dispute. He illustrates his group's position by referring to the correlates of such factors as severity of parental illness (a factor McNeil and Kaij find to be critical in report of OCs in offspring), intactness of the family, age of the cohort, specific presence of delusions and hallucinations in the parent's symptom picture, and antisociality in the nonschizophrenic spouse. In the course of his analytic review of reported differences, Mednick effects some reconciliations using examples drawn from both true and hypothetical, nonreplicative samples. His group's attention to the role of criminality in fathers and the possible consequences of such a factor on psychophysiologic functioning is particularly interesting in the light of the data he reports of the high proportions of instances of assortative matings of schizophrenic mothers with criminal fathers. The data appear to suggest that the presence of criminality in fathers affects electrodermal recovery rate in those risk offspring who have been diagnosed as suffering from a "schizophrenic spectrum disorder."

The distribution of known outcomes has recently been reported by H. Schulsinger (13). Of the original 207 high-risk children, 173 have now received a reevaluation of their current psychiatric status. Results of several methods of affirming diagnosis (PSE, CAPPS, clinical interview) reveal a diagnosis of schizophrenia for all three diagnostic systems of 8 subjects (4.6%). Only one low-risk subject out of 91 was schizophrenic and was later found, after the "low-risk" classification had been made, to have a mother who had had psychotic episodes. The use of less stringent criteria (consensus with two diagnostic systems out of three) provides for larger Ns, with an increase in the number of schizophrenics to 15 (8.7%) plus 55 patients (31.8%) with borderline states, including schizoid and paranoid personality disorders.

Given more determinate outcomes such as these, it is now possible to examine various biologic and behavioral data against this more determinate criterion of psychiatric diagnosis. Assessment of commonalities or noncommonalities between risk studies against such an outcome criterion would constitute a more adequate test of the reliability of findings. Such outcomes, however, are not as yet available to researchers of risk programs, other than the Denmark study. It is, however, possible to evaluate at this point cohort and task differences in an effort to account for nonreplications. Before I proceed to a commentary on some aspects of Mednick's reanalyses of his data, I would like to make an observation about the resolution of discrepancies in findings across research groups. Science suffers under an adversary orientation. When discrepancies occur in a field as immature as psychopathology, the first line of analysis must always be a search for cohort variation. The second line involves task variation. The resolution of discrepancies based on these two factors is far more likely to lead to scientific advances than are the orations of adversaries.

Mednick has reported on his effort to reconcile disparities in the psychophysiologic findings obtained by his group in Copenhagen and Erlenmeyer-Kimling's research team at the New York Psychiatric Institute. This effort has implicated differences in the selection criterion of family intactness for admission to the two research programs. One can only commend the reasonableness of the effort at reinterpretation and review of the disparate findings. It may be of some interest, as a measure of my agreement with this task set, to quote from a comment I had made earlier at the Sixth Conference of the Society for Life History Research in Psychopathology (14) following the presentation by Dr. Erlenmeyer-Kimling (15) of some of her preliminary findings. The transcript indicates the following query:

> . . . are you sure the subjects that you're getting are comparable? For example, what does a comparison of demographic attributes reveal? If you select intact families, it narrows the generalizations to be drawn. Thus, your second criterion (married at time of admission) heightens the likelihood that you are testing a more fertile sample of costs. To the extent that specific variables suggest a lessened genetic weighting and to the extent that these relate to a more favorable prognosis, it may well be that some of the differences that are being obtained are differences that are a function of variations in the competence attributes of parents. The problem of replication becomes one not only of replication of procedures but also of needed replications using comparable selection criteria. When you look at the various risk projects, they vary greatly in terms of such comparability. I believe that Mednick and Schulsinger did not require the constraint of an intact family. A minimum of 16 percent of their risk sample had been in children's homes for a minimum of at least five years. That obviously means that a very substantial number of index cases did not come from intact families. (p 40)

Clearly there is no disagreement here with Mednick's search for the source of the disparity. Intactness or nonintactness of the family may be a highly relevant control variable. I believe, however, that it is now necessary that we go further in examining the "intact family" variable. What does "intactness" mean in each study? In the case of the Copenhagen study, does it include all families in which the children had not been placed in the "children's homes" to which I alluded? In the New York project, does intactness at the time of admission imply intactness over the entire time span prior to the family's participation in the project? What of the placement history of the child in the New York study? If children have been placed out for fostering although the mother and father are still living together, does that situation also denote family intactness? What of intactness as a function of the age of the child (Copenhagen average age is 15.1; New York, 9.6)?

Finally, what exactly does family intactness imply? Intactness as a variable poses the same problem as does social class—interesting but far too global and undifferentiated a concept. Our Minnesota research in inner city schools makes clear to us that a large number of single-parent families do exist, and that in many instances single parents do provide more warmth and support than would an intact family torn by dissension. To understand the components of intactness, we must "psychologize" the intact-family variable if we are to provide more meaningful tests of comparability across risk samples. "Psychologizing" family intactness in psychopathology, particularly schizophrenia, would appear to imply a more positive prognosis, heightened interpersonal competence, and lessened severity of the disorder. Of these, the more readily rated is severity. Indeed, the most recent analysis of the Copenhagen project provides ratings of severity of psychopathology, across all diagnostic types, for both the high-risk and low-risk subjects (13, p 379).

One can now ask whether severity of the disorder within the Copenhagen and New York samples provides a better matching variable than diagnosis against which to compare the offsprings' psychophysiologic states in the two studies. I present this suggestion to illustrate how efforts to reconcile disparities can perhaps be treated by a more determinate review of the meaning attached to cohort attributes to ascertain whether failures to replicate may be definitive or artifactual. Similar meticulous analyses would be required of potential variations in tasks, instructions, and the settings in which tests or observations are carried out. What this means, given the small Ns that inevitably characterize risk research efforts, is summed up in an assertion that my colleague Irving Gottesman has made. The risk researcher must retain his clinical acumen, let alone his experimental sophistication, to provide the astute analysis of persons, situations, and events that good clinicians are capable of doing. The parity of this clinical component with one's research skills poses the unique challenge of risk research.

ASARNOW ET AL

I turn now to a more specific problem, namely the in-depth study of a variable once the decision has been made that here is a factor worthy of *pilot* investigation. This approach is exemplified in Chapter 34 by Dr. Robert Asarnow and his colleagues who constitute the talented and newly formed University of Waterloo-McMaster University risk research team. Their interest lies in attentional processes in children at risk, an interest shared by research teams operating in Minneapolis, New York City, Stony Brook, Rochester, Boston, and so forth. Clearly, attentional function and dysfunction appears to be a fertile area for study in the investigation of risk potential in children (16). But there are some unique aspects to the research generated by this new and welcome addition to the ranks of risk researchers.

These investigators have set for themselves the difficult task of attempting to compare (a) a group of children at risk who have been placed away from their schizophrenic mothers, with (b) a foster control group similarly placed, but in the absence of mental disorder in the biologic parents, and (c) a sample of normal children in the community who are living with their own parents.

We can immediately recognize two realities: there is a massive task of subject identification involved and the resultant Ns can only be very small. The central focus of the study is on the use of multiple attentional measures with these small samples. Their use of a hierarchical cluster analysis of factors associated with these multiple measures to provide subsets of more homogeneous subjects in terms of their performance qualities is distinctly advantageous to a large-scale multivariate study in which very different types of abilities and attributes are assayed through brief, single-shot, nonrepeated tasks on very small numbers of children.

Even then, we limp noticeably in our efforts to assess children at risk, not merely because of our limited numbers of subjects, but because we also lack basic normative developmental data on numerous tasks that are relevant to our assessment strategies. Similarly, the unavailability of equivalent types of data on other types of risk samples, such as anti-social, hyperactive, and internalizing children, or offspring of depressed and personality disordered mothers (cf. Sameroff and Zax), restricts our efforts to relate specific performance deficits on specific tasks to specific forms of vulnerability. The Asarnow et al chapter points up the problem of small Ns, for they have elected to institute an environmental control, control-foster placement of the child at risk (although I suspect that the control is negated by the late age at which foster home placements of the children at risk were made). Nevertheless, the strength of this pilot investigation appears to reside in the multiple methods used to assess attentional dysfunction in the limited number of cases available to the investigators. One can appreciate the problem of methods posed for the Waterloo-McMaster team by reference to a bit of psychology's history.

The attentional construct has always been an elusive, catch-all term, far too inclusive and too little integrative in its definitional breadth. In one of his last papers, written shortly before his death in 1968, Professor E. G. Boring (17) prepared to review the history of the experimental study of the psychology of attention. Unfortunately, he did not live to complete the review which, given Boring's erudition, would have helped to clarify the reasons for the murkiness of the concept. We do know, however, that Boring too found himself segmented by the effort, for in his outline of the projected paper he cited "ten overlapping little histories" from which the concept of attention had been derived. These were the histories associated with a diverse set of tasks, among which were included reaction time, span of apprehension, the duration and the focus of attention, the "complication experiment" which involves the use of synchronous stimuli from cross-sensory modalities, all of which have come down to the present in the form of attentional measures.

It should surprise no one that some of these procedures appear to be more effective than others, or that deficit performance on one does not insure deficit performance on another. Even among chronic schizophrenics, the intercorrelations between different measures of attention tend to be rather low (18). Anticipating the subtle effects, if any, that are likely to be manifested in functional and cooperative children at risk, one can only envision even more restricted correlations and greater difficulty in selecting out a subset of consistently deficient subjects.

Examination of the Asarnow et al results, however, reveals index and control group differences with a reasonably high degree of consistency, albeit restricted magnitude. (There are also some discrepant findings suggesting the operation of chance factors, but these are relatively inconsequential.) It is this search for consistency that led the investigators to their hierarchical cluster analysis.

This strategy is not unlike the method used by Hanson et al (8) in a study Gottesman has described in Chapter 5. In their investigation, they used a sample of 116 children who had participated in the Collaborative Study of Cerebral Palsy, Mental Retardation, and other Neurological and Sensory Disorders of Infancy and Childhood, conducted under the auspices of the Perinatal Branch of the National Institute of Neurological Disease and Stroke. Drawing upon those cases that had been included in a Minnesota sample that contained a parent who had had a psychiatric hospitalization, the investigators generated consensus diagnoses based on case record and MMPI data. Three groups of children were then studied: 33 children with a schizophrenic parent; 36 others in which a psychiatrically hospitalized but nonschizophrenic parent was in evidence, and a group of children of normal parents matched for maternal age, social class, and parity.

The investigators then selected three a priori "indicators" suggestive of a predispositional pattern for future schizophrenia: "(1) poor motor skills; (2) large intraindividual inconsistencies in performance on cognitive tasks; and (3) observations of 'schizoid'-like behaviors, including apathy, withdrawal and emotional flatness mixed, somewhat paradoxically, with emotional instability, irritability, and negativism" (pp 146–147). The investigators then proceeded to use a method for maximizing chi-square differences between the high-risk sample and the comparison groups. Children who showed the three components at ages 4 and 7 numbered five, a finding above chance, and all proved to be the offspring of schizophrenic parents.

Asarnow's et al hierarchical clustering method and the maximizing chi-square method utilized by Hanson et al share a common achievement and a common problem. Both groups have selected on a rational basis variables that would appear to accompany risk potential. Both use statistical techniques to succeed in maximizing differences on these variables between their index and control samples. The shortcoming lies in the fragility engendered by such maximizing methods, for inevitably replication across subsequent samples is difficult to attain. Obviously, the larger the Ns in such groups, the more likely will be the possibility of subsequent replications, but small risk samples make the likelihood of such replications more remote.

Until these results can be replicated, however, they must remain interesting efforts to bootstrap one's way toward the selection of powerful and reliable indicators of risk. For the Waterloo-McMaster group, a partial replication might be attempted excluding the fostering variable. This would ease the logistical problem for the investigators without sacrificing markedly the power of Cluster IV (the overload pattern). Hanson, Gottesman, and Heston have a different road that can be travelled. The Collaborative Study embraced 12 participating University hospitals; the presence of 11 other institutions provides the wherewithal for additional replications. It is my understanding that one such effort using a Boston sample is currently underway in the Laboratory of Psychology of the National Institute of Mental Health under the direction of Reider and Rosenthal. Replication here would mean a careful notation by risk researchers that there exists a triad of factors worthy of inclusion in a longitudinal study.

The second aspect of the Asarnow et al study that I find admirable is their effort to compare the attentional performance of the children at risk with adult schizophrenics, both hospitalized and remitted, and normal adult controls. Note the parallels in this program of laboratory research both to McNeil's and Kaij's library research and to the criteria for variable selection that had been suggested earlier. It is the systematic interplay of studies of children and adult schizophrenics (with their attendant psychopathologic and normal controls) that can provide tentative affirmations that there may exist precursor variables capable of differentiating those children who are at risk from those who seemingly are not. In this context, the use of remitted schizophrenic patients seems to provide a particularly powerful bootstrap with which to evaluate variables that may have predictive import in risk studies. It is this systematic study of cohort variations that provides the analytic base for reconciling disparities and recognizing consistencies across risk investigations.

KAGAN

Finally, a comment about Kagan's chapter. I think it noteworthy that Kagan, a developmental psychologist, was invited to present a paper on high risk and premorbid development. Kagan's scientific interests have always been broadly reflective of developmental psychology. For a viable developmental psychopathology to emerge, it will be necessary for it to reflect the union of developmental psychology and developmental biology. Thus, the representation in this section of papers of one parent of that union is most welcome.

Kagan's message to risk researchers is to study maturational lags in cognitive competencies that generally occur in the last third of the first year in the life of the human infant. I am intrigued by the qualities of attention, anticipation, and attachment suggested in his paper. He views lags in these areas as implying either unusual rearing circumstances or maldevelopment of central nervous system functioning. Thus we again confront risk potential derived out of biologic or environmental anomalies.

I draw a more general conclusion for risk investigators from Kagan's chapter. In the earliest years of a child's life, our best predictors of subsequent maladaptation may well be found in those variables that reflect maturational lags or inconsistencies. In the later years of childhood, variables that reflect incompetencies in the spheres of cognition, emotionality, and socialization are more likely bets for risk investigations. Reviews of the literature of risk research suggest that this is a reasonably tenable hypothesis.

In closing, I would like to comment briefly on an observation that Sir Aubrey Lewis (19) made upon presenting a paper at the First International Congress of Human Genetics held in Copenhagen in August, 1956. Professor Lewis' paper was titled "The Offspring of Parents Both Mentally Ill." In his opening sentence, he suggested a posture that could well be emulated by all engaged in risk investigations: "I present this brief paper diffidently because of the lapse of time—over 20 years—since the material was obtained. . . ."

Professors Lewis's "diffidence" was a function of the many factors that he had encountered in the course of generating his risk research project. Those ills beset all risk investigators—the long journey to disorder, the restricted samples, the difficulty of ascertainment of offspring, the uncertainty of parental diagnoses, the absence or elusive presence of signs of disorder in the offspring, the difficulty of data analysis, the absence of psychiatric registries, and the limitations of case record data.

These are limitations that are a way of the research lives of those of us who study risk for schizophrenia. Diffidence is not in and of itself a virtue, but I believe that it can keep us from leaping to too rapid a conclusion that the resolution of the enormously complex problem of the etiology of schizophrenia is just around the risk researcher's corner; it may also keep us from an excess of pessimism engendered by our failure to resolve etiologic controversies implicating gene and environment in schizophrenia. Risk research is simply a part of the fabric of research that is necessary for achieving, ultimately, an understanding of the origins and nature of schizophrenia. In that sense, we share a common mission with our colleagues who at this Conference have provided a broad view of the diverse investigative efforts that are required before we can effect a resolution of the enigma of schizophrenia.

REFERENCES

1. Romano J (ed): *The Origins of Schizophrenia.* Amsterdam, Excerpta Medica Foundation, 1967.

2. Mednick SA: The children of schizophrenics: Serious difficulties in current research methodologies which suggest the use of the "high-risk group" method, in Romano J (ed): *The Origins of Schizophrenia.* Amsterdam, Excerpta Medica Foundation, 1967.

3. Garmezy N: Contributions of experimental psychology to understanding the origins of schizophrenia, in Romano J (ed): *The Origins of Schizophrenia.* Amsterdam, Excerpta Medica Foundation, 1967.

4. Garmezy N (with Streitman S): Children at risk: The search for the antecedents of schizophrenia. Part I: Conceptual models and research methods. *Schiz Bull* No. 8:14, 1974.

5. Garmezy N: Children at risk: The search for the antecedents of schizophrenia. Part II: Ongoing research programs, issues and intervention. *Schiz Bull* No. 9:55, 1974.

6. Kraepelin E: *Dementia Praecox and Paraphrenia.* Edinburgh, E. S. Livingston, 1919.

7. Piaget J: Foreword, in Anthony EJ (ed): *Explorations in Child Psychiatry.* New York, Plenum Press, 1975.

8. Hanson DR, Gottesman II, Heston LL: Some possible childhood indicators of adult schizophrenia inferred from children of schizophrenics. *Br J Psychiat* 129:142, 1976.

9. Garmezy N: Review of current knowledge of early detection: Characteristics of high risk subjects in *Conference on Primary Prevention of Schizophrenia in High Risk Groups,* W.H.O. Technical Report, Geneva, in press.

10. Kaplan A: *The Conduct of Inquiry.* San Francisco, Chandler Publishing Co, 1964.

11. Heston LL: Discussion: Schizophrenia—onset in infancy. *Soc Biol* 18:114, 1971.

12. Fish B: Discussion: Genetic or traumatic developmental deviation? *Soc Biol* 18:117, 1971.

13. Schulsinger H: A ten-year follow-up of children of schizophrenic mothers: Clinical assessment. *Acta Psychiat Scand* 53:371, 1976.

14. Wirt RD, Winokur G, Roff M (eds): *Life History Research in Psychopathology,* vol IV. Minneapolis, University of Minnesota Press, 1975.

15. Erlenmeyer-Kimling L: A prospective study of children at risk for schizophrenia: Methodological considerations and some preliminary findings, in Wirt RD, Winokur G, Roff M (eds): *Life History Research in Psychopathology,* vol IV. Minneapolis, University of Minnesota Press, 1975.

16. Garmezy N: Attention processes in adult schizophrenia and in children at risk. *J Psychiat, Res,* in press.

17. Boring EG: Attention: Research and beliefs concerning the conception of scientific psychology before 1930, in Mostofsky DI (ed): *Attention: Contemporary Theory and Analysis.* New York, Appleton-Century-Crofts, 1970.

18. Kopfstein JH, Neale JM: A multivariate study of attention dysfunction in schizophrenia. *J Abn Psychol* 80:294, 1972.

19. Lewis A: The offspring of parents both mentally ill. *Acta Genet et Statistica Medica* 7:349, 1957.

Chapter 44
Current Status of a Sample of Other High-Risk Research Programs

Norman Garmezy, Ph.D.

The papers presented at the Conference reflect only a cross-sectional slice of current research in the study of children vulnerable to psychopathology. Dr. Anthony, who chaired the scientific session on High Risk and Premorbid Development, and the authors of Chapters 34–41 and 43–46, are all active investigators in research on risk-for-schizophrenia. There are many other research groups engaged in related efforts within this area. A tabular description, accompanied by relevant citations, of 19 ongoing research programs, has appeared in two recent publications (1,2). Here I present brief additional descriptions of current programs of risk research to provide the interested reader with a broadened perspective on this field and the investigative efforts of its adherents.

UNIVERSITY OF ROCHESTER, ROCHESTER NY (L. C. WYNNE and J. S. STRAUSS)

The University of Rochester Child and Family Study (NIMH grant MH22836) is a project investigating developmental patterns in children of families in which a parent has been hospitalized for psychiatric disorder, schizophrenic, or otherwise. It is a longitudinal study designed to discover relationships among parent characteristics, patterns of family interaction and communication, and both competence and maladaption in the children.

In assessing these relationships, this project retains diagnosis of parental schizophrenia (using both broad and narrow criteria) as a variable of presumed genetic risk and also evaluates the dimensions of chronicity and severity of parental psychopathology, social and work functioning of the parents, family communication disorders, and psychophysiologic and behavioral precursors of psychiatric disorder in the child.

Eleven research teams participate in a project that thus incorporates study of diverse sets of variables: (a) *children's* birth and developmental history, psychophysiologic characteristics (autonomic, cortical evoked responses, eye tracking), censure-praise responses, intelligence and projective personality tests, Piagetian developmental

473

measures, peer and teacher assessments of school behavior, and the assessment of the child's general adaption and clinical symptomatology; (b) *family* and marital relationships as evaluated in interviews oriented to parenting and caretaking patterns, genetic history, and intrafamilial communication patterns as revealed in family Consensus Rorschach procedures and in a free play situation; (c) individual *parents,* both the index who has been a psychiatric patient and the spouse, assessed on the basis of past psychiatric case records, current standardized psychiatric interviews and an extensive psychologic test battery. These serve to evaluate symptoms, social relations, work function and diagnosis, and a variety of cognitive, perceptual, and attentional processes.

The project employs a longitudinal convergent design in which families that have a target male child of the ages 4, 7, or 10 are selected for study. A follow-up evaluation 3 years later provides for the convergence aspect of the design, enabling the research team to test the feasibility of utilizing a 3-year follow-up period to cover a critical 9-year age span in evaluating developmental patterns of children and the factors that may affect them.

As of June, 1976, more than 100 families had been fully evaluated. A sample of statistically significant preliminary findings include: (a) compared with normative samples, these children of a parent with a history of psychiatric hospitalization already showed, at ages 4, 7, and 10, substantial levels of dysfunction in home, school, and clinic; (b) the parents' diagnoses (schizophrenic/nonschizophrenic) relate significantly to several measures of psychophysiologic functioning, such as measures of autonomic reactivity and conditioning, in their children; (c) the most significant relationship between severity of parent psychosis and their own abnormal eye-tracking pattern is not with the parents' *current* severity of psychosis, at the time of research study, but with the severity at the time of "key" hospitalization, an average of 5 years prior to study (see Chapter 28 for details); (d) in a "free play" situation in which the interaction of both parents with the target child is observed, the index parent is significantly less active and the spouse more active, with these tendencies of *both* parents related to independent ratings of the severity of psychiatric difficulties of the index parent at the time of study, but *not* to the severity of parental illness at the time of key hospitalization; (e) deviance in family communication patterns measured in individual parent Rorschach tests and in Consensus Family Rorschach procedures relates significantly to independent measures of the children's competence functioning in school, while several parental diagnostic measures all fail to relate to the same child-school measures, (f) egocentric perception in the child, using Piagetian measures, is significantly related to severity of parental psychosis but inversely related to severity of parental depression at the time of hospitalization. Other aspects of this research program are reported by one of the senior investigators, Dr. John Romano, in the introductory chapter of this volume.

Currently, the first wave of the 3-year follow-ups is underway, with acceptance of continued participation exceeding 80% of the original subject groups.

EDISON CHILD DEVELOPMENT RESEARCH CENTER, ST. LOUIS MO (E. J. ANTHONY)

This risk research program is aimed at evaluating adolescents and adults at genetic risk for psychosis. Its object is to monitor the development of 193 children with a psychotic parent (either schizophrenic or manic-depressive) through a period of 3 years, and to compare their development with 98 children of physically ill (tuberculous) parents and

138 children of parents who have experienced no significant mental or physical illness. Thus the subject group comprises a total of 420 children who currently range in age from 7 to 26 years. These offspring and all members of their intact nuclear family group have been intensively studied along a number of different parameters (demographic, physical, psychophysiologic, anthropologic, psychiatric, psychologic, experimental, and social). Based on these data, predictions of risk potential and prognosis have all been made, with about 25% of the children in the experimental group having been categorized as being at highest risk and vulnerability. During the next four years, 186 of the oldest children (14–26 years) are expected to pass through a crucial period for the genesis of certain types of psychosis. In his introductory comments to this section, Dr. Anthony has given a clinical overview of the variety of patterns of competence and vulnerability in these children.

Follow-up investigations have focused on the emerging life patterns of the subjects, their achieved level of competence, and their inner life experiences as reported in interviews and through projective personality measures. The follow-up instruments, designed to test children at 3-year intervals, are quite extensive and range from a self-administered General Information Questionnaire to assessments of home atmosphere and the family environment, school assessments, cognitive measures, and so forth.

An initial testing phase extended over a 5-year period. 1967–1971. During this period, 105 families were tested, including 27 characterized by one parent who was schizophrenic, 19 who were manic-depressive, 20 who were physically ill, and 39 in which both parents were psychiatrically normal.

First reports of decompensation requiring hospitalization in adolescent subjects at genetic high risk for psychosis suggest tentative hypotheses for further study. These initial adolescent breakdowns have been associated with: (a) age of the offspring at the time of the parental psychosis (within the first 7 years); (b) a coinciding acute deterioration and rehospitalization of the parent; (c) life stresses that have increased prior to onset; (d) significant changes in affective levels and frustration tolerance; (e) signals of incipient "breakdown" that preclude the onset by at least 3 months, and a prevailing sense of social incompetence that also heralds the attack.

UNIVERSITY OF MINNESOTA, MINNEAPOLIS, MINN (N. GARMEZY AND V. DEVINE)

The long-term goal of the Minnesota project ("Project Competence") is to study the development of competence skills in various groups of children varying in their predisposition to psychopathologic conditions in later life. For the target children in this program, heightened predisposition typically is ascertained in one of two ways: the psychiatric status of parents and the adaptive or maladaptive patterns of behavior exhibited by the children. Since large numbers of control children are also studied, the research program embraces the investigation of children "at risk" as well as their nonrisk counterparts.

On the assumption that fundamental to the acquisition of competence skills is the ability to focus and maintain attention effectively in a variety of situations, emphasis in the research program has been on three elements:

1. Observations conducted during laboratory studies of selective and sustained attention
2. Observations made in the naturalistic setting of the classroom

3. Efforts to provide reliable and valid measures of children's social and economic (work) competence

The Minnesota project differs from other programs of research in a number of particulars. The first is the broadened definition given to risk. Instead of using a single target population, four target groups have been studied: (a) children of schizophrenic mothers; (b) children of nonpsychotic depressive and personality-disordered mothers; (c) children seen at a community child guidance for acting-out behaviors ("externalizers"); and (d) clinic children presenting symptoms of fears, phobias, withdrawal, social isolation, and so forth ("internalizers"). Recent studies have also included a group of hyperactive clinic children free of antisocial behavior. Control groups have typically included matched and randomly selected children from the target child's classroom.

Second, two major elements in the studies have been the measurement of competence and maturity attributes in these children, together with indices of attentional functioning.

Third, the studies have been cross-sectional, rather than longitudinal in design, with short-term follow-up studies conducted in an effort to trace competence qualities over a 3-to-5-year span.

Fourth, ages of the children tested have been in the range of 10–12 years (grades 4–6) and 13–14 years (grades 7–8). In each study substantial numbers of children located in large numbers of widely distributed classrooms have been evaluated (e.g., 113 classrooms involving 362 children; 80 classrooms and 240 children). An ongoing study of sustained attention will, upon completion, approximate 300 participating children.

Findings

Some of the results of previous studies conducted under Project Competence include the following:

1. As indexed by teachers' judgments, peer preference, and academic achievement, reduced competence generally characterizes the behavioral patterns of groups of antisocial children and the children of schizophrenic mothers. Children of depressive and personality-disordered mothers also give evidence of lowered levels of competence but not to so great an extent as do the first two groups. Among the target groups, the overinhibited clinic children appear to be rated the most competent of all by their classmates.

2. The quality of attentional functioning tends to follow the order set out in number 1, but there is overlap among the groups.

3. Normal control children both matched and random are basically equivalent in competence and attentional ratings and are superior to the target groups, across groups, and all targets on short-term follow-up reveal poorer school performance. To some extent such deficits appear to be related to poor attentional behavior in laboratory tasks.

4. Efforts to improve attentional behavior by the use of environmental supports, experimental cues, and information giving, indicates that all target groups can be brought up to the level of their normal control counterparts with the exception of children born to schizophrenic mothers.

Studies of attentional functioning now underway include vigilance tasks, reaction time studies using cross-sensory stimuli, and tests of incidental versus central learning.

Measures of social or core competence continue to serve as correlates of the attentional performance data.

NEW YORK STATE PSYCHIATRIC INSTITUTE, NEW YORK, NY (L. ERLENMEYER-KIMLING)

Dr. Erlenmeyer-Kimling has studied subgroups of children at different degrees of risk for schizophrenia (i.e., children of two schizophrenic parents, children of one schizophrenic parent, and children of normal parents or of parents with other psychiatric disorders) for the purpose of pinpointing early psychobiologic indicators of vulnerability and for evaluating the development of these children. Her original sample of children were tested when they were 7–12 years of age, between December 1971 and February 1973. Her findings with attentional measures obtained from this sample are reported in Chapter 35. Continual contact has been maintained with the families by telephone at 6-month intervals, and the children have been retested 2–3 years following their first examination. As of 1976, Dr. Erlenmeyer-Kimling noted the following follow-up clinical data on the 205 children:

> Two subjects with two schizophrenic parents and one subject with a schizophrenic mother have been admitted to a psychiatric hospital since their initial inclusion in the study. In addition, a substantial number of subjects are now receiving therapy, counseling, or other forms of treatment. Including the hospitalized offspring, percentages of subjects receiving treatment are:

Children of:	schizophrenic mother	16%
	schizophrenic father	26%
	two schizophrenic parents	54%
	other psychiatric parents	4%
	"normal" parents	4%

Dr. Erlenmeyer-Kimling rightfully cautions, however, that no conclusions can be drawn at this time "regarding need for treatment and eventual outcome."

Collection of a second sample is underway (1976–78). This sample too will consist of 7-to-12-year-old children, with N's projected as follows: 40 children of schizophrenic mothers; 40 children of schizophrenic fathers; 30 children of two schizophrenic parents; 40 children of parents with affective disorders; and 110 children of normal parents. The normal control group is to be matched one-to-one for age, sex, socioeconomic status, and ethnic background of the family to children in the three groups with schizophrenic parents.

Included in the evaluation methods are home visits, during which time a 2- to 3-hour structured interview is conducted with the parents and covers personal and family histories, pregnancy, birth, developmental, health, behavioral, and school histories on all children in the family. In addition, there is an effort to assess the effects of parental illness on the children. MMPIs are administered to the parents together with a variety of psychologic tests to their children.

Laboratory visits are subsequently initiated following the home visit to secure a wide-ranging set of data including tests of vigilance, attention span, motor performance, a neurologic evaluation, psychophysiologic (autonomic) recordings under conditioning, and generalization and extinction procedures. A second laboratory visit includes tests of auditory thresholds, EEG, auditory and visual evoked responses, and alpha attenuation. School evaluations have recently been added to the project and will be collected by Norman Watt and a group of risk researchers from the University of Massachusetts.

STATE UNIVERSITY OF NEW YORK, STONY BROOK, NY (J. M. NEALE, S. WEINTRAUB)

The Stony Brook Project also focuses on the academic and social competence of school-age children with either a schizophrenic or a depressed parent and children whose parents have no psychiatric history.

There are four major areas of assessment: (a) the mental status and social histories of both parents; (b) the general quality of the marriage and home environment; (c) descriptive information on the academic and social adjustment of the children as perceived by parents, teachers, peers, and selves; and (d) laboratory studies of cognitive processes, attention, emotional responsivity, and social interaction.

Families are recruited from local psychiatric facilities. New admissions are screened to determine if these patients have children in school. If so, the project is explained to the patient, consent is obtained, and assessment of the patient is then begun. The patient's spouse is also contacted and a visit is made to the home, at which time the spouse is evaluated. Later, after the patient has returned home, another visit to the family is made to gather information about the children as well as the quality of marital and family functioning.

A large portion of the project involves a longitudinal study of the children with a continuing 6-month contacts. Follow-up studies on both school and laboratory are conducted every 2 years using the same assessment procedures.

Diagnostic assessment procedures of the patient include (a) CAPPS, (b) MMPI, (c) a patient adjustment scale with the spouse as informant, and (d) an abstract of the patient's hospital record. Items a–c are also administered to the spouse with the patient as the informant for the spouse's adjustment scale. Marital adjustment tests are used to evaluate the marital relationship.

The assessment of the children has a wider range and includes measures of intelligence and academic performance, social adjustment, and interpersonal competence, teacher's ratings, and parental ratings of the child's behavior. Laboratory studies include measures of attentional dysfunction, information processing, distractibility, object sorting, referential communication, and emotional responsiveness.

In June 1976, the tested sample consisted of 91 families with a schizophrenic parent (60 mothers; 31 fathers; 200 children), 58 families with a depressed parent (36 mothers; 22 fathers; 120 children), and 60 control families (125 children). New families are still being collected to insure a larger representation of disordered fathers.

Preliminary findings indicate that the children of both schizophrenic and depressed mothers were rated by teachers as showing more "classroom disturbance, impatience, disrespect-defiance, and inattentiveness-withdrawal" than did the children of normal mothers. Children in the two groups with patient mothers also were rated lower on "comprehension, creative initiative, and relatedness to teacher."

Notably, however, teachers did *not* discriminate children of schizophrenic mothers from those of depressive mothers, even though the behavior pattern of the offspring of schizophrenic mothers was similar to that reported in studies that did not use a comparison group of children of depressive mothers. The Weintraub-Neale data suggest that lack of a psychiatrically disturbed, but nonschizophrenic, comparison group has led others to an erroneous impression that the children of schizophrenic mothers have *specific* characteristics.

MASSACHUSETTS MENTAL HEALTH CENTER, BOSTON, MASS (H. GRUNEBAUM)

Between 1968 and 1971, a sample of 50 children, from early infancy to 5 years of age, who had psychotic mothers, were acquired as a sample through state hospitals in the Boston area. The mothers had mixed, usually chronic psychiatric diagnoses— schizophrenia, psychotic depression, and manic-depressive illness. The families were demographically fairly homogeneous: white, all intact marriages at the beginning of the study, and working class or lower-middle class. A normal control sample was acquired, carefully matched by age, sex of youngest child, ethnicity, socioeconomic class, and peer position of children. The psychotic mothers were offered home nursing aftercare, half of them seen "intensively," on the average of once a week, and the other half seen "minimally," with infrequent visits and occasional telephone calls.

A variety of studies of the mother and the children comparing normal and patient samples and within-patient samples in terms of diagnoses have been conducted with the children and the mothers. The children have been followed-up subsequently at ages 1,3,5, and 6; currently a comprehensive follow-up study (3–4 years later) is being carried out with these mothers and children.

Results to date include the following:

1. Significant impairment was found in the development of cognition and attention in the 1-, 3-, and 5-year old children of psychotic mothers, but not in the 6 year olds. Diagnosis of the mother was related to the degree of developmental lag; the children of schizophrenic mothers were the most impaired, followed by the children of schizoaffective and affective mothers.

2. However, longer-term clinical follow-up data, partially analyzed, suggest that children of depressed mothers are *more* impaired than children of schizophrenic mothers. Most of the marriages stayed intact; the investigators have a preliminary impression that in the families in which the parents have separated the children are doing better when they have stayed with the nonpsychotic father.

3. Comparing treatment groups, children of intensively treated mothers were rated as more adaptive on a number of scales of affect expression and task competence, while exhibiting no difference in IQ and scales of social interaction.

4. At the end of treatment the intensive-treatment mothers, as compared with the minimal-treatment controls, reported significantly greater feelings of self-worth, increased confidence in their ability to work on their problems by themselves, and greater improvement in their ability to care for their children and to respond affectionately to their husbands.

It is clear from the diverse examples in this volume that the longitudinal-developmental study of children at risk represents a comparatively new orientation in the study of antecedents to the psychopathology of schizophrenia. For the most part, ongoing research programs are of recent origin, data are still being collected, statistical analysis, at best, is partial or not as yet undertaken. It is fair to say that only now are researchers growing aware of methodologic uncertainties and marked logistical difficulties that characterize studies of these vulnerable children.

We are still in an early era of research where adult schizophrenics' behaviors, intuition, and imitation tend to guide the selection of variables to be studied. Perhaps the most striking aspect of the findings to date is the growing realization that the search is not for attributes that merely statistically differentiate children-at-risk from their controls but, rather, for a subset of children who show more stable infirmities of deficit behaviors that are more likely to reflect the emergence of later incompetence rather than adaptation.

REFERENCES

1. Garmezy N: Children at risk: The search for the antecedents of schizophrenia. Part II. Ongoing research programs, issues and intervention. *Schiz Bull* No. 9:55, 1974.
2. Garmezy N: The experimental study of children vulnerable to psychopathology, in Davids A (ed): *Child Personality and Psychopathology: Current Topics, Vol 2*. New York, Wiley Inter-Science, 1975.

CONCLUDING COMMENTS ON TREATMENT IMPLICATIONS
E. James Anthony, M.D.

Given the undeniable fact that between 40–50% of children at high genetic risk for schizophrenia exhibit a variety of disturbances of variable intensity during the course of development as a result of identificatory, antecedent, or reactive mechanisms, the important question arises as to whether anything can be done to treat these conditions and thereby prevent them from becoming more serious and irreversible. In St. Louis, as an integral part of our prospective research in this area, we have established an ongoing research clinic to which about one-third of our total sample of high-risk children have been admitted. Since, on ethical grounds, we had no option open to us but to treat the children who needed it, we decided to carry out an investigation into the efficacy of various therapeutic measures (1). As in all work with children, the treatment carries the additional and possible implication of prevention of adult disorder, but it will be many years before a follow-up on our sample will disclose how effective the usual therapeutic measures, such as individual and group psychotherapy, catharsis, environmental support, and "ego therapy" aimed at helping the child to encounter the specific effects of parental psychosis, will have been.

Being born of psychosis and into psychosis undoubtedly carries with it a double developmental hazard stemming from both genetic and environmental sources. In about half the children, a wide spectrum of disturbances ensues, sometimes emerging episodically with every crisis of development, environmental change, or psychosis; but in other children, the impact leads to more sustained disorder as manifested in "shut-in" and eccentric characteristics. Some of these disturbances may subside with separation from the sick parent, but others persist, suggesting a more endogenous genesis. In clinical practice, it is difficult to disentangle genetic from environmental components although one or the other may seem to predominate.

When the child is examined directly and over a period of time, the amount of psychopathology uncovered exceeds that uncovered through secondhand reports by parents and teachers, even when the interviewer is kept "blind." Furthermore, the experience of living with psychosis is not easily communicated, especially in the case of the younger child, through paper and pencil methods or questionnaire responses. On the other hand, the sensitivities tapped in an interview may lead the clinician to an exaggerated notion of the traumata involved without allowance for the protective function of habituation and emotional insulation. The peculiar family milieu may enable the child to generate a system of defenses and masteries that enables it to survive psychologically. However, even allowing for such compensations, there is no doubt that a chaotic psychosis can strain the psychologic stamina and resources of some vulnerable children to a breaking point. The "headline" experiences—the attacks, the paranoid accusations, the incestuous approaches, the brutalities—seem easier for the child to endure than the constant confusions, mystifications, inconsistencies, and other seemingly minor problems of everyday living. It is not abnormality itself that proves so disturbing but the oscillations between normality and abnormality, and the wider these are, the more difficult it is for the child to sustain.

481

One must admit at this point that empathy is not a research tool that lends itself to very precise findings susceptible to replication. Yet, it would be self-limiting for the clinical investigator to shelve this well-developed capacity in himself and not make at least qualitative use of it in the service of furthering knowledge. This raises the pertinent question whether the sensitivity and experience of the clinician in clinical research adds to the total picture created by the more objective methods. With this in mind, one can put oneself into the shoes of children who form a captive audience to the disturbing spectacle of a disintegrating human psyche with whom they are very deeply involved. The children are participant observers in this engrossing situation from which the clinician is mostly excluded, and it is always surprising that more use is not made of the child informant in this respect. Our experience has been that they are able to furnish meticulous information on the incipient stages of psychosis, details that are often lost on the adult observer. We have often remarked that the child's observations are among the most valid that we possess and that the child is able, with his naive judgments, to perceive the "emperor's new clothes" for what they are.

When one examines these high-risk subjects, especially at the time when the parental psychosis is active, one is confronted with a catalog of reactions that run a wide gamut of negative feelings. First of all, the parent's psychosis is often experienced as a psychic loss and followed by a period of bereavement during which the grief is generally masked (2). We have seen several examples of a depressive reaction following the onset of the illness. Other disturbing affects include feelings of guilt (associated with the child's belief that his bad behavior has driven the parent crazy, or associated with experiencing relief at the parent's departure to a hospital), feelings of shame (when the parent's bizarre conduct becomes public knowledge, or when the parent misbehaves grossly in front of the child's peers), fear (at being attacked physically or sexually), anxiety (at becoming crazy oneself), and perplexity (at being subjected to contradictory and inconsistent demands). Overall, there is frequently a high degree of ambivalence toward the sick parent.

These are the basic concerns that harass the children. Although steeped in reality, they are also further elaborated with primitive fantasy. For instance, a 9-year-old boy brought his very psychotic mother in to see me and said desparately: "At night she sometimes tries to fuck me—please stop her!" He was right: she did try to do this, but over and above the actuality was a profound terror, that he was also able to verbalize, that she would injure his private parts and end up by destroying him. What can one do to help children in this sometimes extraordinary human predicament? It is not enough to study their attentionality, their incipient thought disorder, or their psychophysiologic responses, however much these add to our total understanding not only of the individual case but also of the group as a whole. At each step in this process where help is not available to the child, he is drawn further and further into a miasma of unwholesome experiences from which it is increasingly difficult for him to extricate himself.

Here I must speak for myself as someone who wears two hats—clinical and investigative—and is often not too sure which one he has on his head at any given time. The research hat allows me to put distance between myself and the subject, to objectify the encounter, and to quantify my judgment on a six-point scale. It is obvious that I cannot help when I am wearing this hat! One cannot, to quote the poet, botanize on one's mother's grave. To be therapeutic, I must put my measuring tape away and become involved, concerned, and less data-oriented. Having thus recaptured my humanity and therapeutic sense, I can take a number of steps toward relieving the high pressure of feeling within the child.

The classical therapeutic posture is not helpful in such situations since the child's distress frequently demands crisis measures. However, I can begin to listen to his own account of the contact with psychosis without interrogating him, that is, collecting data; I can begin to share his concerns with him and allow him to abreact his feelings as needed. I can help to de-mystify the arcane and esoteric features of psychosis and to make sense out of erstwhile nonsense. I can help to restore some degree of continuity to the incompatible images generated by the parent at different times. I can make myself available when the crisis of psychosis has arisen, and I can lend my own reality to counteract the unreality of the parent. At times, I can mediate between child and parent, explaining one to the other and also can act as a buffer when provocations from both sides become extreme. I can counsel parents who have a deficient knowledge and understanding of parenthood about the essentials of adequate child rearing, without creating in them a sense of harmfulness. It is important to take the psychotic parent seriously as a parent and help him or her to deal with the vicissitudes of everyday parenting without putting them too much on the defensive. This tactful monitoring of the parental function has an immediate ameliorative effect on the parent and, subsequently, on the child. We have found that when both parent and child become mutually disrupted by anxiety, offering them the same medication seems to help them both; or to put it another way, if it helps the parent, it also seems to help the child.

Our experience, therefore, with high-risk children has shown that a special clinic run in close conjunction with the research is an indispensable adjunct if one is to meet the responsibilities associated with risk research. The risks are everywhere. There is always a risk that the subjects will become disturbed, and a constant risk that a beautiful research design will be offset by contaminating interventions.

An important thing to remember when dealing with the high-risk subject and his family is that we should not carry our rationality and realism too blatantly as a badge of our professional sanity since this can add to the distance between investigator and subject and strain the therapeutic and research alliance. Some investigators are so defensively nonpsychotic that they are quite unable to empathize with the psychotic experience and thus lose an invaluable research tool. To maintain effective contact with this particular research population, one has to try to locate oneself on the same spectrum, even though our irrationalities and irrealities are comparatively trivial and short-lived.

In following these children prospectively, we have been struck by the insidious way in which the susceptible ones gradually develop patient characteristics and begin eventually to behave like potential or actual "mental patients." The main thrust of our intervention has been toward preventing or putting a stop to this transformation. Does what we do seem to help? A short-term appraisal would suggest that it does, but whether it has any long-term prophylactic value still remains to be seen. If we can abort the adolescent breakdown, there is a chance that the predicted psychotic outcome will be less inevitable. Unfortunately, as in all outcome studies, the results may confound rather than clarify these various issues.

REFERENCES

1. Anthony EJ: A risk-vulnerability intervention model for children of psychotic parents, in Anthony EJ and Koupernik C (eds): *Children at Psychiatric Risk.* New York, John Wiley & Sons, 1974, pp 99–121.
2. Anthony EJ: Mourning and psychic loss of the parent, in Anthony EJ and Koupernik, C (eds): *The Impact of Disease and Death.* New York, John Wiley & Sons, 1973, pp 255–264.

FAMILY RELATIONSHIPS AND COMMUNICATION

Chapter 45
Familial Precursors of Schizophrenia Spectrum Disorders

Michael J. Goldstein, Ph.D.
Eliot H. Rodnick, Ph.D.
James E. Jones, Ph.D.
Sigrid R. McPherson, Ph.D.
Kathryn L. West, Ph.D.

The belief that disordered family relationships may be a significant factor in the development of schizophrenia is not new. In a recent review of the empirical evidence on this issue, two of us [Goldstein and Rodnick (1)] conclude that the question reduces to three testable assumptions.

Assumption 1: Families of schizophrenics are discriminably different from those containing offspring with other types of disturbances, particularly in role relationships, affect, and communication style.

Assumption 2: These differences occur early enough and are sufficiently enduring in the life experience of the potential schizophrenic to have a significant impact on his development.

Assumption 3: Disordered family relationships are a necessary but not sufficient condition for the development of schizophrenia.

The research presented here was supported by grants from National Institute of Mental Health, 08744 and 13512 and the Grant Foundation. James E. Jones's participation in this project was supported in part by a Scottish Rite Predoctoral Fellowship in schizophrenia research. The authors would like to express their appreciation to Lewis J. Judd, Armand Alkire, Nancy Beakel and Fredric H. Jones for their significant contributions to this project. Special thanks are due Lin Ng who devised and implemented the computer programs necessary for the analysis of complex interactional data.

Paper presented at the Second Rochester International Conference on Schizophrenia, May 2-5, 1976, Rochester, New York.

Data regarding Assumption 1 has been reviewed previously (1), and the authors have concluded that there was a considerable degree of evidence for disordered communication in families of schizophrenics. Evidence for unique role relationships and affective tone appeared more variable across diverse studies. Assumption 3 recognizes that current evidence suggests the importance of other factors in the development of schizophrenia, including genetic and constitutional components.

This chapter will focus on Assumption 2 which questions whether distinctive patterns of intrafamilial relationships precede the emergence of schizophrenia and schizophrenia spectrum disorders in the offspring. Since previous research has emphasized patterns of distorted communication, these will receive special but not exclusive attention. The data reported in this chapter are derived from the UCLA Family Project, a longitudinal prospective study of intrafamilial relationships.

THE UCLA FAMILY PROJECT

The UCLA Family Project (2) was designed specifically to study intrafamilial relationships in a sample of individuals assumed to have acceptable variance in their degree of risk for subsequent schizophrenia and schizophrenialike conditions. The subjects selected for study were nonpsychotic but emotionally disturbed adolescents seen at an outpatient clinic and living at home with intact families. We assumed that the level of disturbance, being moderate in nature, was not as severe in its impact upon the family system as that caused by an offspring who is already psychotic. The basis for assuming that at least some of these adolescents were at risk for schizophrenia was derived from the general hypothesis that adolescence is a critical period in personality development, and that failures at this point would increase the probability of subsequent difficulties. The expectation that such a sample would be expected to contain a sufficient number of preschizophrenics is supported by the findings of Nameche, Waring, and Ricks (3) and Robins (4) who followed up comparable clinic populations. More specifically, the design involved the contrast of subgroups of disturbed adolescents, believed to be at greater than normal risk for schizophrenia-type disorders, with other subgroups of disturbed teenagers probably at risk for other adult problems, but not schizophrenia.

It was felt that the critical issue was whether families of preschizophrenics were distinctively different from families of other disturbed adolescent groups, and not whether they could be differentiated from normal family groups. While normal families are important for certain research questions, their motivation for participating in intensive studies of family relationships is likely to differ from the families of this study who were uniformly seeking treatment. By working within the psychopathologic spectrum, one can assume relatively equal motivation across groups of subjects in terms of anxiety over the adolescent, desire for help, and willingness to reveal intimate details of family life.

Definitions of Risk

Defining risk in this project has been an iterative process, beginning with the manifest disturbance of the adolescent and including other variables as they became available.

Problem Groups

The initial task involved an exclusion of psychotic adolescents and a definition of problem groups within the nonpsychotic disturbed adolescent range. These groups were defined empirically from the presenting problems of the disturbed but nonpsychotic adolescents in terms of the locus of the problem and the degree of passivity-activity of the behavioral difficulties.

Group I. Aggressive, Antisocial Adolescent: characterized by poorly controlled, impulsive, and acting-out behavior. Even when some degree of inner tension or subjective distress may be present, this is clearly subordinate to the aggressive patterns that appear in many areas, in school, in peer relationships, and with the law, but not predominantly in the home.

Group II. Adolescent in Active Family Conflict: characterized by a defiant, disrespectful stance toward parents, belligerence, and antagonism primarily in the family setting. Signs of inner distress or turmoil are often present, e.g., tension, anxiety, and somatic complaints. There are few manifestations of aggression or rebelliousness outside of the family.

Group III. Passive, Negative Adolescent: characterized by negativism, sullenness, and indirect forms of hostility or defiance toward authorities. In contrast to Group II, overt defiance and temper outbursts are infrequent, and there is a superficial compliance with the wishes of adults. School difficulties are frequent, typically described as underachievement, but with little evidence of disruptive behavior.

Group IV. Withdrawn, Socially Isolated Adolescent: characterized by marked isolation, general uncommunicativeness, few, if any, friends, and excessive dependence on one or both parents. Gross fears or signs of marked anxiety and tension are often present. Much of their unstructured time is spent in solitary pursuits.

The predominant locus of the problem for groups I and III is outside the home, and for groups II and IV, inside the home. Although groups I and II are more active, and groups III and IV more passive, the activity dimension has proved less valuable than the locus.

Subsequent to defining the four groups, an attempt was made to establish working hypotheses concerning risk level from the literature on adult schizophrenia (5). The poor premorbid patient demonstrates an adolescent history of extreme social withdrawal and low involvement with the opposite sex. The parallel between the description of the poor premorbid pattern and the withdrawn socially isolated teenager was close enough for the project to define this group IV as having greater than normal risk for schizophrenia.

Other literature (3,4,6), suggests another preschizophrenic pattern among adolescents characterized by stormy, acting-out behavior confined largely to the family group. These descriptions resembled adolescents in the active family conflict group, group II; therefore, this group was designated as a second high-risk group. Thus, groups II and IV, the adolescents in active family conflict and withdrawn, socially isolated adolescents were tentatively defined as at greater than normal risk, while the other two groups (I and III) were expected to have lower risk for schizophrenia.

Severity of Adolescent Psychopathology

A second predictor of psychopathology at 5-year follow-up in young adulthood was the overall severity of psychopathology already present at initial clinic visit. From descriptive statements about the adolescent's behavioral assets and liabilities made by the parents during intake, F. H. Jones (7) sorted subjects blindly into three groups representing the dimension of severity of maladaptive behavior. On a three-point scale, those who showed a mixed picture of such symptoms as sullenness, anxiety, feelings of inadequacy, and passive negativism, but also with sizable areas of adequate functioning, were given a rating of 1; those who showed multiple contacts with the police for problems of acting out, 2; and those who showed more extreme disturbances, with marked anxiety, sexual difficulties, and severe depression, including contemplation of suicide, 3.

Parental Communication Deviance

The definition of risk on the basis of the form and severity of the adolescent's presenting problem fulfilled a need for preliminary indicators of risk. However, to establish continuity with the family studies of schizophrenia, it was felt that a third criterion of risk derived from these studies would also be useful. The communication deviance concept of Singer and Wynne, which has proven useful in discriminating parents of schizophrenics from other groups of parents (8,9), appeared highly relevant for use with the UCLA project families. Application of the Singer and Wynne measures to our data permitted an estimate of risk for schizophrenia based on the degree to which parents manifested communication deviances of the type and frequency found by these investigators in parents whose offspring had already become schizophrenic. The project was designed to obtain projective test data, using the Thematic Apperception Test (TAT), from each member of the family. A scoring system for the TAT which assessed communication deviance using the same principles previously described by Singer and Wynne (11), was developed by one of the authors, J. E. Jones (10), with the help of Margaret Singer.

Factor score patterns of parental TAT communication deviances discriminated parents of schizophrenics in a separate sample of parents previously studied by Wynne and Singer at NIMH. J. E. Jones used these patterns to establish rules for assigning the UCLA adolescents to one of three categories of hypothesized risk for schizophrenia—high, intermediate, and low (10). For example, an adolescent whose parents both had a high frequency of TAT communication deviances, comparable to the parents of persons already diagnosed as schizophrenics, was placed in the category of hypothesized high risk for schizophrenia.

Thus, in this study, risk for schizophrenia (and spectrum disorders) in the offspring was not defined on the basis of the usual "genetic" criterion of diagnosed schizophrenia in one or both parents. Rather, a second indicator of risk for schizophrenia in the adolescent offspring was defined by the independent empirical classification of parental TAT scores of communication deviance, obtained prospectively at the time of initial assessment.

A key aspect of the UCLA project is to follow up, at 5- and 10-year intervals, the index cases into early adulthood and to trace their subsequent histories of positive and negative adaptation. In this chapter, we are presenting data on the psychiatric status at 5-year follow-up of 23 male index cases in relationship to (a) their behavior as teenagers (problem group and initial severity) and (b) the presence or absence of communication deviances in the parental TATs obtained 5 years previously at intake.

The 5-Year Follow-Up Assessment Procedure: All cases seen initially were contacted 5 years later, at ages 20–21, for a follow-up evaluation. This first follow-up consisted of (a) an interview with the parents which focused on the social adjustment of the offspring, (b) a separate interview with the young adult which covered many aspects of personality and social development as well as assessment of psychiatric symptoms, (c) psychologic testing of the young adult using the Minnesota Multiphasic Personality Inventory (MMPI), the Zulliger Test (a three-card Rorschach-type test), a Word Association Test, and two questionnaires, filled out by the young adult, which covered drug usage and sexual history. All interviews and testing were tape-recorded.

A tape of the interview with each young adult was given to one of two psychologists (Michael J. Goldstein and James E. Jones) who were blind as to the prior clinical and research records of the case and had never worked with the person or his family as researchers or clinicians. The psychologist reviewed the tape, abstracted the significant material in it, and attempted to summarize his findings using two diagnostic instruments, the Research Diagnostic Criteria (RDC), developed by Spitzer, Endicott, and Robins (12), and the Borderline Evaluation Schedule, developed by Gunderson (13). Each then reviewed an abstract of the parental interview and the psychologic test protocol to determine if additional data might modify the diagnostic impression. With those few cases for which the first listener was not confident of his diagnosis, the second psychologist independently listened to the entire tape and made his own diagnosis. For each of these cases, the second diagnosis was similar enough to the first for a consensus diagnosis to be easily reached by discussion.

These final diagnoses at follow-up then were used to assign subjects to a position on a seven-category scale originally used by Wender et al (14) in their adoption studies. Definite schizophrenia is assigned to category 7, probable schizophrenia and definite borderline to category 6, and probable borderlines and schizoid and paranoid characters to category 5. In keeping with previous analyses of Wender, the combined categories 5–7 are considered to cover the "schizophrenia spectrum."

The distinction between the spectrum and nonspectrum cases was verified from another data base, namely, scores obtained blindly from the Zulliger Test by another set of raters prior to the rating of the interviews. The DeVos index of unpleasant content (15) and two fabulized combination scores suggested by M. T. Singer (16) revealed a highly significant differentiation (p = 0.005) between spectrum and nonspectrum cases, thus supporting the clinical diagnostic differentiation.

RESULTS

The data presented in this chapter relate to two general issues. First, what relationship exists between (a) the form (problem group) and severity of adolescent psychopathology and (b) the later incidence of borderline and schizophrenic symptomatology in early adulthood? Second, are parental attributes of the type identified by Wynne et al (9), in their analysis of communication disorder in parents of schizophrenics, present *prior* to the onset of schizophrenic spectrum disorders and predictive of those disorders in the offspring?

Adolescent Psychopathology and Early Adult Diagnosis

Table 45-1 presents the relationship between the fourfold behavior problem manifested in adolescence and the placement on the seven-point diagnostic scale for early adulthood. Because of the small number of cases, these data are collapsed into diagnostic categories 1–4 and 5–7, with the latter considered as the extended schizophrenia spectrum. Here we see that Group III, the passive, negative group, stands out in its small number of cases in the 5–7 categories. This trend supports the hypothesis that Group III adolescents are at low risk for schizophrenia and borderline disorders in early adulthood. However, it is difficult to see marked differences among the other three diagnostic groups, although there is a suggestion that a high-risk group, Group IV, with-

Table 45-1. Adolescent Problem Group as a Predictor of Psychopathology at 5-Year Follow-up

Adolescent Problem Groups and Hypothesized Risk	Psychopathology at Follow-Up	
	Nonspectrum (Categories 1–4)	Schiz. Spectrum (Categories 5–7)
I Aggressive antisocial (low)	2	2
II Active family conflict (high)	3	4
III Passive, negative (low)	5	1
IV Withdrawn, socially isolated (high)	2	4

drawn, socially isolated adolescents, appear more frequently in the schizophrenia spectrum in early adulthood. With the size of sample analyzed at this time, these trends are not statistically significant. (Note: additional cases in Group I followed up later all fell in the nonspectrum category as hypothesized.)

The global ratings of adolescent psychopathology at the time of clinic intake were dichotomized, comparing serious (level 3) problems with a low or moderate degree of severity (levels 1 and 2). In Table 45-2, we see a significant relationship between the initial severity of problem behavior and the diagnostic assignments at 5-year follow-up ($p < 0.005$).

The five cases with initial level 3 ratings uniformly fall into the schizophrenia spectrum 5 years later. Although initial behavior ratings of levels 1 and 2 predominantly predict a follow-up diagnosis outside the schizophrenia spectrum, some initially low-rated cases do appear in the schizophrenia spectrum at follow-up. Thus, the presence of nonpsychotic but serious problems of coping in adolescence is a positive predictor, but

Table 45-2. Severity of Adolescent Behavior as a Predictor of Psychopathology at 5-Year Follow-up[a]

Initial Adolescent Severity of Psychopathology	Psychopathology at Follow-Up	
	Nonspectrum (Categories 1–4)	Schiz. Spectrum (Categories 5–7)
Initially serious but non-psychotic behavior (rating of 3)	0	5
No extreme initial behavior (ratings of 1 and 2)	12	5

[a] P = 0.01 (Fisher's exact test).

not the *only* precursor, of subsequent borderline and schizophrenia diagnoses. Further long-term study with larger samples and combinations of indicators seems indicated.

Parental Communication Deviance and Early Adult Psychopathology

Earlier in this chapter we indicated that risk of schizophrenia in an offspring can be estimated from parental attributes, especially those related to clarity of communication. Such assessment, when derived from TAT protocols, requires verbatim transcripts which were available in only 16 of the 23 cases in this report.

Table 45-3 presents the relationship between the risk for schizophrenia in the adolescents (high versus intermediate and low) based on initial parent communication deviance measures and the diagnosis of the offspring at follow-up in early adulthood. Parents with high communication deviance scores and hence designated as having adolescents at "high risk" for a later schizophrenia spectrum disorder do indeed have offspring who already have a significant frequency of schizophrenia spectrum diagnosis when they reach young adulthood (p = 0.025).

A Combined Index of Adolescent Problem Severity and Parental Communication Disorder

Since the severity of adolescent behavior disorder and parental communication at initial assessment *both* predict the later diagnosis of schizophrenia spectrum disorder in these offspring, the next step was to consider whether a combined index of these two factors would predict more effectively. In Table 45-4, the 16 cases with both parental and adolescent measures at intake have been delineated into three groups: (a) five cases with both high parental communication deviances and extreme adolescent behavior; (b) three cases with high parental communication deviance and minimal or mild severity of initial adolescent behavior problem; and (c) eight cases with low or mild initial measures for both the parents and the adolescent. Although none of the adolescents were initially psychotic or within the schizophrenia spectrum, seven of the 16 were so diagnosed by the time of the 5-year follow-up. Of those seven, six had parents with a high frequency of parental communication deviance at initial assessment. However, five of these seven spectrum cases had both precursors—serious behavior problems in adolescence and high

Table 45-3. Parental Communication as a Predictor of Psychopathology in Young Adult Offspring at 5-Year Follow-up[a]

Parental Communication Deviance as a Risk Estimate for Schizophrenia in Offspring	Offspring Psychopathology at Follow-Up	
	Nonspectrum (Categories 1–4)	Schiz. Spectrum (Categories 5–7)
High	2	6
Intermediate	6	1
Low	1	0

[a] P = 0.025 (one-tailed), Fisher's exact test, combining intermediate- and low-risk groups.

Table 45-4. Relationship Between Severity of Adolescent's Initial Symptoms, Initial Parental Communication Disorder, and 5-Year Follow-up in Early Adulthood

	Follow-Up Diagnoses of Offspring	
Combined Indices at Initial Assessment	Nonspectrum (Categories 1–4)	Schiz. Spectrum (Categories 5–7)
High frequency of parental communication deviance; serious coping problems of adolescent offspring	0	5
High frequency of parental communication deviance; low or moderate severity of adolescent problems	2	1
Low or moderate frequency of parental communication deviance; low or moderate severity of adolescent behavior	7	1

parental communication deviance; in contrast, seven of the nine nonspectrum cases at follow-up had neither the parental nor the adolescent high-risk indicators at initial assessment. (Note: two of the seven spectrum cases at this early stage of follow-up were "definite" schizophrenics—category 7 on the Wender scale.) Of the total sample of 23 cases (seven of which did not have parental TAT testing at intake), nine (39%) were diagnosed in the schizophrenia spectrum at follow-up.

Relationship between Parental Behavior in TATs and in Family Interaction

The presumption in using parental projective test data to estimate communication style is that individual test performance is a microcosm of what takes place among family members in their recurring direct interactions with one another. In an effort to learn how individual test behavior relates to interactional behavior with other family members, we analyzed the data derived from samples of video-taped family interaction. The data are based on a "confrontation" phase in the initial family assessment procedure (17) in which family members are left alone, first in parental dyads and then in a triadic grouping with the index offspring, to discuss emotionally relevant family problems.

First, we examined interaction behavior which we believe is comparable to certain communication deviances scored on the parental TATs. Failure to acknowledge the speech of another seemed a particularly significant way to disrupt focus of attention in family discussions. Therefore, we applied the Mishler-Waxler "acknowledgment" (18) scale [as modified by McPherson (19)] to the verbatim transcripts of the triadic discussion between father, mother, and index offspring. Figure 45-1 presents the frequencies of the four categories of the acknowledgment scale in the families with adolescents designated as at high, intermediate, and low risk for schizophrenia spectrum disorder on the basis of the parental TAT data. Other studies have shown that "partial" acknowledgment appears to be as adequate as "complete" acknowledgment in

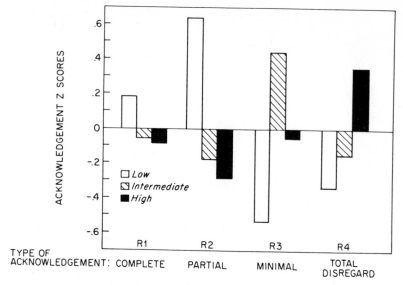

Figure 45-1. Mean of parents' summed scores for four types of acknowledgment (R1, R2, R3, and R4) in families hypothesized to be at low (L), intermediate (I), and high (H) risk for schizophrenia in an offspring, based on parental communication deviance scores.

"ordinary" family interaction. Significant differences were found between two acknowledgment categories, partial acknowledgment and total disregard for the previous speaker's remarks. The parents of the "low-risk" families, defined by the independent parental TAT measures, stand out from the other two risk groups by their marked frequency of acknowledging and extending the remarks of the previous speaker, with a low frequency of total disregard. In contrast, the "high-risk" parents show an inverse relationship on these two categories of the acknowledgment scale.

In an effort to determine factors other than communication deviance that might be operative in these individual parent-child relationships, McPherson has been analyzing the video tapes of dyadic interactions using two sets of codes, one that indexes the manifest intent of the verbal behavior and a second that classifies nonverbal behavior. Preliminarily, she has found that parents of high- and low-risk families differ in their use of positive suggestions (see Figure 45-2). In Figure 45-2, we see that "high-risk" parents,

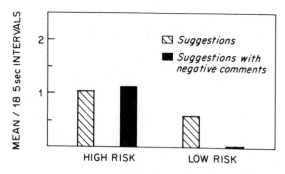

Figure 45-2. Mean number of positive parental suggestions and positive parental suggestions made together with negative comments in same 5-second intervals.

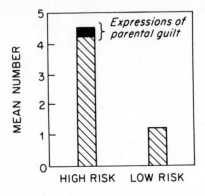

Figure 45-3. Mean number of combined self-defending statements and explicit expressions of guilt made during selected intervals by parents of adolescents hypothesized to be at high and low risk for schizophrenia.

so classified from prior TAT behavior, somewhat surprisingly offer more positive suggestions concerning what the offspring might do to solve his problem than do "low-risk" parents. However, the high-risk parents are markedly and statistically more prone than low-risk parents to offer negative comments (criticism, complaints, sarcasm, and so on) in the *same* 5-second interval in which the positive suggestions are offered—a contradictory communication, although not a true double-bind.

In another type of analysis, McPherson has coded parental verbal behavior in segments of the dyadic interaction in which the offspring was engaging in a certain type of nonverbal behavior, namely, looking away from the parent and staring at the floor. She reasoned that this nonverbal behavior could be construed as a signal and that subsequent parental response to this signal would be interesting to code. In Figure 45-3, we see two classes of parental verbal behavior, self-defending statements and expressions of guilt after their offspring looked away. Here we see that the "high-risk" parents (with frequent TAT communication deviances) are far more likely to react to this offspring's nonverbal cue with defensiveness or, less frequently, an explicit expression of guilt. These data suggest that the defensiveness of parents who also show frequent communication deviance may be another significant parameter of the intrafamilial climate, as well as difficulties in focal attention observed when both parents are present. One interesting hypothesis is that the "high-risk" parent utilizes self-defending statements in a fashion that leaves the offspring with a sense that it is *his* fault that he fails to understand what takes place in other family contexts.

DISCUSSION

The data presented in this chapter must be interpreted with caution since more cases in the sample remain to be studied and a much longer period of follow-up beyond the first years of adulthood is necessary before the risk period of 15–45 years for schizophrenia has passed. Despite these limitations, certain trends appears in the data. First, there is a modest relationship between the form of the problem of the adolescent and the later diagnosis in early adulthood of borderline and schizophrenia spectrum disorders. Most clearly, adolescent passive-negativism manifest *outside* the home predicts to a nonspectrum diagnosis at follow-up.

Second, the severity of psychopathology noted in mid-adolescence is a positive predictor of schizophrenia spectrum diagnosis at 5-year follow-up; for some subjects, there appears to be continuity in the severity of psychopathology from adolescence to early adulthood. However, the absence of extreme adolescent behavior does not exclude subsequent schizophrenia spectrum disorders. Thus, some patterns of severe early adult psychopathology appear discontinuous with adolescent adjustment.

Third, there is a strong relationship between parental communication deviance at initial assessment and the independent diagnosis of schizophrenia spectrum disorders at follow-up in the early adulthood of the offspring.

How may the severity of adolescent symptomatology and parents' communication style be integrated into the same etiologic model? When the two factors are considered together, there are a number of alternative hypotheses. First, parental communication disorder may be a necessary but not sufficient condition for the development of both serious coping problems in mid-adolescence and also of subsequent schizophrenia spectrum disorders in adulthood. Once behavioral problems have begun, deviant environment may be necessary to amplify the problems to psychotic propositions. The TAT measure of parental communication deviance is obviously a limited means of sampling relevant tendencies to communication disorder. However, of the seven offspring who were given a schizophrenic spectrum diagnosis as young adults, none, as adolescents, had had parents with low TAT communication deviance scores. Although a sample of this size cannot test the hypothesis, the finding suggests that further evaluation is warranted.

Second, extreme behavior of adolescents and parental communication disorder may be causally independent factors that interact, if at all, only *after* each has emerged on the basis of other factors. Given an adolescent with disturbance of indeterminate etiology, residence in a family with confused and blurred communication may inhibit movement toward problem solution and adaption to subsequent life stress. Very preliminary data from other segments of our program are congruent with the converse of this hypothesis: regardless of the initial severity of the adolescent problem, ratings of clear parental communication appear to predict symptomatic improvement during the 5-year follow-up period. Once again, a larger sample is needed.

Third, parental communication deviance may be completely reactive to characteristics of the child. However, at intake the parents of eight of 16 adolescents already showed marked communication disorder preceding, not following, psychosis or borderline symptoms in the offspring. Six of these eight did in fact become more disturbed, and were diagnosed in the schizophrenia spectrum, 5 years *after* the parental communication disorder had been identified. Nevertheless, we cannot reject the hypothesis that the deviant parental communication styles may have been reactive to the *non*psychotic adolescent psychopathology or to more subtle temperamental characteristics of the adolescent. From this viewpoint, parental communication deviance may be a useful reflection of important nonsymptomatic characteristics of the adolescent, but it may not be etiologically related to either adolescent or early adult psychopathology.

Fourth, extreme symptoms of the adolescent and parental communication deviance may form a mutually enhancing, positive feedback loop that would predict a steadily deteriorating course. In this model, each factor is seen as reactive to and amplifying the other. Extreme behavior would deteriorate in an environment of parental communication disorder. Conversely, parental communication deviance both would foster spectrum symptoms and itself would increase in reaction to extreme behavior of the offspring, at least above a certain threshold. Five of the eight adolescents with parents having high communication deviance scores also showed serious coping problems at initial assessment; hence, this overlap leaves open the likelihood that such developmental processes may be underway by mid-adolescence. Obviously, a quite complex design is required to test this model more fully. Data are needed from prospective studies which begin earlier in life to determine the temporal links between parental communication disorder and adolescent psychopathology before we can choose between these sets of etiologic hypotheses.

REFERENCES

1. Goldstein MJ, Rodnick EH: The family's contribution to the etiology of schizophrenia: Current status. *Schiz Bull* 14:48, 1975.

2. Rodnick EH, Goldstein MJ: A research strategy for studying risk for schizophrenia during adolescence and early adulthood, in Anthony EJ and Koupernik C (eds): *The Child in his Family: Children at Psychiatric Risk,* vol 3. New York, John Wiley & Sons, 1974, pp 507–526.

3. Nameche GF, Waring M, Ricks DF: Early indicators of outcome in schizophrenia. *J Nerv Ment Dis* 139:232, 1964.

4. Robins LN: *Deviant Children Grown Up.* Baltimore, Williams and Wilkins, 1966.

5. Rodnick EH, Garmezy N: An experimental approach to the study of motivation in schizophrenia, in Jones MR (ed): *Nebraska Symposium on Motivation.* Lincoln, University of Nebraska Press, 1957, p 109.

6. Arieti S: *Interpretation of Schizophrenia.* New York, Robert Bruner, 1955.

7. Jones FH: A four-year followup of vulnerable adolescents: The prediction of outcomes in early adulthood from measures of social competence, coping style and overall level of adjustment. *J Nerv Ment Dis* 159:20, 1974.

8. Singer MT, Wynne LC: Thought disorder and family relations of schizophrenics. IV. Results and implications. *Arch Gen Psychiat* 12:201, 1965.

9. Wynne LC, Singer MT, Bartko JJ, Toohey ML: Schizophrenics and their families: Recent research on parental communication. In Tanner JM (ed) *Developments in Psychiatric Research.* London, Hodden & Stoughton, Ltd., 1977, pp 254–286.

10. Jones JE: Transactional style deviance in the families of disturbed adolescents. Ph.D. dissertation, University of California, Los Angeles, 1974.

11. Singer MT, Wynne LC: Principles for scoring communication defects and deviances in parents of schizophrenics: Rorschach and TAT scoring manuals. *Psychiat* 29:260, 1966.

12. Spitzer RL, Endicott J, Robins E: *Research Diagnostic Criteria RDC for a Selected Group of Functional Disorders,* ed 2. New York, Biometrics Research, New York State Psychiatric Institute, 1975.

13. Gunderson JG: Characteristics of borderlines, in Hartocollis P (ed): *Borderline Personality Disorders:The Concepts, the Syndrome, the Patient.* New York, International Universities Press, 1977.

14. Wender PH, Rosenthal D, Kety SS: A psychiatric assessment of the adoptive parents of schizophrenics, in Rosenthal D, Kety SS (eds): *The Transmission of Schizophrenia.* Oxford, Pergamon Press, 1968, pp 235–250.

15. DeVos G: A quantitative approach to affective symbolism in Rorschach responses. *J Proj Tech* 16:133, 1952.

16. Singer MT: The borderline diagnosis and psychological tests: Review and research, in Hartocollis P (ed): *Borderline Personality Disorders: The Concept, the Syndrome, the Patient.* New York, International Universities Press, 1977.

17. Goldstein MJ, Judd LL, Rodnick EH, et al: A method for studying social influences and coping patterns within families of disturbed adolescents. *J Nerv Ment Dis* 159:20, 1974.

18. Mishler EG, Waxler NE: *Interaction in Families.* New York, John Wiley & Sons, 1968.

19. McPherson SR, Goldstein MJ, Rodnick EH: Who listens? Who communicates? How? *Arch Gen Psychiat* 28:393, 1973.

Chapter 46
Communication Disorders and the Families of Schizophrenics

Margaret T. Singer, Ph.D.
Lyman C. Wynne, M.D., Ph.D.
Margaret L. Toohey, B.A.

In our collaboration of the past 18 years, many colleagues, students and research assistants in Bethesda, Berkeley, and Rochester have contributed their support and dedicated efforts to family research which will be partially summarized here. The members of approximately 600 families have participated in our various research projects. By permitting us to study their family transactions, they have joined with us in seeking, a step at a time, to understand the context of those perplexing human states and conditions that are called the schizophrenias. In addition, colleagues in a variety of other settings, especially in Boston, Chicago, Houston, London, Los Angeles, New Haven, New York, and Palo Alto have examined various aspects of the hypotheses, methods, and conclusions which will be noted in this brief overview.

PARENTAL COMMUNICATION DEVIANCES

We have found that disordered styles of communication are a distinguishing feature of families with young adult schizophrenics. There are numerous ways in which the sharing of attention and meaning go astray in these families. We have described various aspects of family communication—attentional, cognitive, affective, and relational—and have developed reliable procedures for scoring many of these features in a variety of test situations. What we have concluded is that in the families of schizophrenics, communication processes appear already disturbed when the basic phase of focusing attention and sharing foci of attention begins. In the families of borderline, neurotic, and normal individuals, communication problems also occur but are more evident later on in communication sequences, *after* an attentional focus has been initially shared by two or more persons (1–3).

Although we and our colleagues have given many different tasks to families, we will emphasize here data from studies using the Rorschach inkblots. Over the years, we have not used the Rorschach procedure in its traditional way to make inferences about a person's intrapsychic life. Rather, we have used it as an analogue of those many daily occurrences in which two or more individuals attempt to establish a consensually shared view of ambiguous reality. In the communication of the Rorschach procedure, the subject proposes a focus of attention, labels what he "sees," and offers an interpretation of its meaning to the other. In turn, the listener asks for clarification or elaboration and may comment if and when a focus of attention on a percept and meaning has been understood and shared. The Rorschach inkblots provide standardized starting points for sampling the extent to which attentional foci and meanings are selected and become shared with a listener during a communication sequence. This procedure elicits two functions essential to effective parenting: *naming* (especially in the initial viewing portion of the individual Rorschach) and *explaining* (especially in the later inquiry portion). These are basic, repeated components of parent-child verbal exchanges of the formative years in which verbal and thinking styles of children become patterned (4).

In a manual of "communication deviance" categories found in verbatim Rorschach transactions, we score as disordered or deviant communication those features of the "naming and explaining" by the subject that distract and befuddle a listener who is attempting to share the meanings attributed to the inkblots by the speaker. These categories of communication deviances are described and exemplified in detail elsewhere (1,5) and are listed in Table 46-1. Instead of being able to follow and comprehend a line of thought and to visualize what the speaker is describing, a person listening to a type of communication which is defined as deviant in these categories finds himself puzzled about what he is hearing and what he should think. The listener is unable to construct a consistent visual image or a consistent construct from the speaker's words. Table 46-1 lists six factors of 32 categories of deviances (plus high word count) which we have examined in our empirical studies; each of these 32 categories separately differentiates (p < .01) the parents of schizophrenics from other parents. The Rorschach protocols were blindly

Table 46-1. Classification of Rorschach Communication Scoring Categories* Based upon Factor Analysis of Scores for 72 NIMH Parents of Schizophrenics

Category	Factor Loading
Factor 1: *Odd, hard-to-follow, ambiguous remarks* (11.1% of variance)	
1 Unintelligible remarks	.74
2 Ordinary words or phrases used oddly or out of context	.72
3 Uncorrected speech fragments	.66
4 Inconsistent and ambiguous references	.63
5 Odd, tangential, inappropriate remarks	.61
6 Partial disqualifications	.60
7 High total word count	.46
8 Odd sentence construction	.41
Factor 2: *Distracted and distracting failures to sustain task set* (7.4%)	
9 Forgetting responses	.65
10 Hopping around among responses	.56

Table 46-1. (Continued)

Category	Factor Loading
11 Concrete-set responses	.53
12 Interruptions of examiner's speeches	.52
13 Retractions and denials	.50
14 Responses in negative form	.50
Factor 3: *Unstable perceptions and thinking* (9.4%)	
15 Unstable percepts	.69
16 Incompatible alternatives	.65
17 Subjunctive "if" responses	.57
18 Failure to verify own responses	.53
7 High total word count	.47
8 Odd sentence construction	.45
19 Nonsequitur reasoning	.41
20 References to "they" and intent of others	.40
Factor 4: *Nihilistic and idiosyncratic task orientation* (8.1%)	
21 Nihilistic remarks	.74
22 Idiosyncratic, private terms	.59
13 Retractions and denials	.57
18 Failures to verify own responses	.51
23 Temporary card rejection followed by a response	.50
Factor 5: *Extraneous, illogical, contradictory comments* (8.5%)	
24 Illogical combinations of percepts and categories	.69
25 Contradictory information	.63
26 Extraneous questions and remarks	.58
27 Clanged associations, rhymed phrases, word play	.64
28 Derogatory, disparaging, critical remarks	.46
7 High total word count	.44
19 Nonsequitur reasoning	.40
Factor 6: *Abstract, indefinite, discursive vagueness* (6.1%)	
29 Abstract, global terms	.57
30 Gross indefiniteness	.54
14 Responses in negative form	.54
31 Nonverbal disruptions	.48
20 References to "they" and intent of others	.41
32 Repetition of words or phrases	−.42

* Of 41 categories listed in the original 1966 scoring manual (1), nine have been eliminated because they were statistically non-differentiating of parents of schizophrenics from other parents. Only one discriminating category, "Question" responses, failed to load > .40 on any of the six factors. High total word count was added as a deviance category in this factor analysis, in order to see with what categories it was associated; however, high word count is not a discriminating variable in its own right. See Table 46-2. All factor loadings ≥ .40 are listed; defining loadings are ≥ .50. Varimax rotation of six factors accounts for a total of 50.6% of variance.

scored from verbatim transcripts of tape-recordings; the late adolescent and young adult offspring were independently diagnosed without knowledge of the parental Rorschachs, and the Rorschach testers were not aware of the research diagnoses of the offspring.

Figure 46-1 presents data from one study using this manual. In this sample of 114 families assessed at the National Institute of Mental Health, Bethesda, Maryland, the parents of normal and neurotic subjects appear similar to each other but differ from the parents of both remitting and nonremitting schizophrenics, who are similar to one another on this quantitative measure. However, the parents of the borderline young adults have scores which overlap both those of the parents of the schizophrenics and nonschizophrenics (6).

Within each parental pair, the normal and neurotic offspring tend to have parents who both have low communication deviance scores. Young adult offspring with a borderline syndrome tend to have one parent with a high and one parent with a low com-

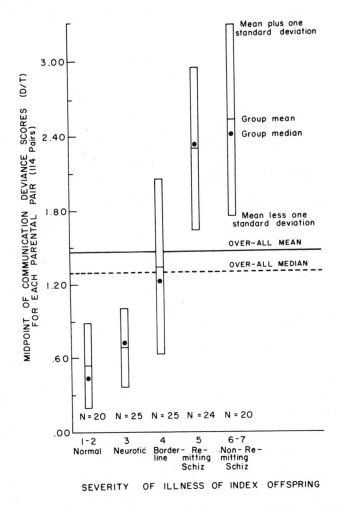

Figure 46-1. Parental Communication Deviances and Severity of Illness of Index Offspring. Reprinted with permission from Tanner JE (ed.): *Developments in Psychiatric Research*, London, Hodder and Stoughton, 1977, p 277.

Table 46-2. Discriminant Analysis of Variables Hypothetically Relevant to Severity of Psychiatric Disorder of Index Offspring[a]

Independent Variables	F	P
1. Communication deviance score, fathers	27.30	<0.0005
2. Communication deviance score, mothers	25.22	<0.0005
3. Severity of disorder, fathers	16.00	<0.0005
4. Severity of disorder, mothers	10.69	<0.0005
5. Age of Indexes	8.84	<0.0005
6. Communication deviance score, indexes	8.84	<0.0005
7. Age of fathers	5.59	<0.0005
8. Age of mothers	4.57	<0.01
9. Occupational level, fathers	4.55	<0.01
10. Years of education, indexes	3.75	<0.01
11. Years of education, fathers	3.47	≤0.01
12. Years of education, mothers	1.83	N.S.
13. Total word count, indexes	1.59	N.S.
14. Sex of indexes	1.31	N.S.
15. Total word count, mothers	1.22	N.S.
16. Total word count, fathers	0.66	N.S.

[a] Dependent variable: severity of clinical disorder of index offspring. In this table, all the independent variables entered into the analysis concurrently. The F values for each variable are equivalent to an analysis of variance for that variable, indicating its power, considered separately from the other variables, to discriminate among the index offspring at the seven levels of severity of disorder of the index offspring.

munication deviance score. With offspring who are young adult schizophrenics, both parents tend to have high deviance scores. Thus, there is a progressive increase, without apparent discontinuities, in the mean scores for parent groups in relation to the increasing severity of illness of their index offspring. It is important to note that if offspring with a borderline diagnosis had been selectively eliminated, as in a study by Hirsch and Leff (7), our data would have given a misleading impression of a dichotomy in parental communication scores and would have incorrectly suggested that high scores are specific for the parents of schizophrenics. Clearly, a continuum is apparent in these scores.

Table 46-2 shows the results of a discriminant function analysis in which 16 predictor variables were compared as to their differentiation of the severity of disorder in the index offspring in these families. Note that while a number of variables significantly predict the severity of disorder of an index offspring, it is the communication deviance scores of parents which rank highest as predictors (6).

Of special interest are the data on word count shown in Table 46-2. Hirsch and Leff (7) attempted a replication of our study with 40 pairs of parents, half with a schizophrenic offspring and half with a neurotic offspring. Despite serious methodologic shortcomings in their procedure for administering and scoring the Rorschachs, they found that the mean number of D/T scores (number of deviances divided by number of transactions or responses) for the parents of schizophrenics was 1.33, and for the parents of neurotics 0.88 (p < 0.05). However, noting a high correlation of word count and deviance scores, they suggested that number of deviances was primarily a function of word count. We have noted that excessive verbosity impairs comprehension and that certain categories of communication deviances, but not other categories, necessitate extra words. Excess verbosity probably impairs sharing of meaning and foci of attention and, as indicated in the factor analysis shown in Table 46-1, may be an index, when combined with certain other communication problems, of what we have conceptualized as "communication deviances". Thus, the Hirsch-Leff finding stands as a confirmation of our work, although the extent to which it constituted a replication is highly dubious, especially because their method of administration differed substantially from ours.

To re-assess the question of whether frequency of communication deviance is a function of word count, we examined the relationship between deviance scores and word count in the sample of 114 subjects, in a sample of 59 pairs of parents previously studied (2), and in 57 parental Rorschachs in an adoptive study (8). Using exactly the same statistical technique as that proposed by Hirsch and Leff, but also several other multivariate techniques, we consistently have found that when the effect of word count is statistically removed, the difference in deviance scores between parental groups actually heightens, not diminishes, as Hirsch and Leff expected. In Table 46-2, word count is shown to be a nondiscriminating variable. Especially noteworthy is the contrast between the lack of discrimination between parental groups when parental word count is the predictor variable compared to the highly significant discrimination with parental D/T scores.

Using analysis of covariance, as proposed by Hirsch and Leff, we found that the parental deviance scores, for the parents as a pair and for the fathers and mothers separately, continued to discriminate severity of disorder in index offspring, even when the effects of the parents' *own* severity of disorder, their Rorschach word count, and major demographic variables are each taken into account. As we had hypothesized, the discriminations are most striking for the parents as pairs, but also are highly significant for fathers and mothers separately ($p < 0.001$).

In this and other studies by us, and in cross-validating replications and a number of recent related studies by others (9-19), the type and severity of communication disorders in parents predict clinically assessed severity of psychiatric disorder in index late adolescent and young adult offspring of those families. Therefore, we have concluded that the study of a family's verbal transactions is a useful approach for both research on psychopathology and personality development and for planning therapeutic interventions (20).

THE CONCEPT OF COMMUNICATION DISORDER

Having found conceptual and clinical support for the hypothesis that specific links exist between the parents' style of communicating and the severity of diagnosis of their offspring, we evolved a broadened conceptualization of what is usually called thought disorder or language disorder—terms that take thinking and language out of their interpersonal context. We suggest that the term "communication disorder" is a more comprehensive and appropriate term. "Communication" takes into account the transaction in which thinking and language are embedded; it implies a verbal interchange, e.g., in patient-interviewer dyads and in family relationships (21). Schizophrenics have difficulties not only with thinking but also with *sharing* their experience, that is, in communicating.

However, schizophrenic communication disorders are obviously not of one class. By analyzing clusters of communication features, we have begun to characterize *sub*groups of schizophrenics and their families. We drew upon and extended the broadest and probably most widely accepted developmental principle in biology and psychology, as stated by Heinz Werner: "Wherever development occurs, it proceeds from a state of relative globality and lack of differentiation to a state of increasing differentiation, articulation, and hierarchic integration" (22). We found that the formal and stylistic aspects of the functioning of young adult schizophrenics, as well as the communication styles found within their families, could be characterized in terms of degrees and varieties of differentiation and integration. We coined the terms "amorphous" and "fragmented" to label the patterns we found in the communication and experience disorders shared in two major groups of schizophrenic young adults (23) (see Table 46-3). Generally, the amorphous schizophrenics show the laconic, impoverished indefiniteness and poorly differentiated focusing of so-called "process" schizophrenics. Patients with fragmented forms of schizophrenic communication disorder more consistently have relatively clear, differentiated styles of attending, perceiving, and communicating, but suffer preponderantly from a serious failure in articulation and integration of their ideas. Thus, the "fragmented" schizophrenic patients are highly vulnerable to emotional stress and show abrupt, often paranoid, maladaptive attention to task-irrelevant stimuli. We have found that by studying parental communication in sufficient detail, we can predictively describe forms of experience disorder and personality functioning that offspring will present (6,17,18,24,25). We also have found, in factor analyses of our communication deviance categories, other leads for future research on subtypes of schizophrenia.

Table 46-3. Two Major Forms of Schizophrenic Experiencing

Amorphous	Fragmented
Attention:	Attention:
poorly focused, drifts	fairly clearly focused for brief moments
Perception:	Perception:
uncertain and blurred	relatively well differentiated, but bits and pieces of memories and current stimuli become intermixed
Communication:	Communication:
loses continuity due to gaps, blocking, laconic indefiniteness, vagueness, often giving picture of "under-inclusive" thought disorder	disrupted by inner and outer distractions, giving picture of "overinclusive" poorly integrated thought disorder
Affect:	Affect:
flat, impoverished, hypohedonic	relatively alert and anxious, often with efforts to control the turmoil of powerfully intrusive thoughts, feelings and impulses
History:	History:
usually poor pre-morbid history with developmental failure rather than regression	usually relatively good pre-morbid history, often with successes and skills that have regressively been lost

Tentatively, we believe that there also are implications for differential treatment of the families of amorphous schizophrenics, in contrast to those containing fragmented young adult schizophrenics (20).

RECIPROCAL PROCESSES WITHIN FAMILIES

We have emphasized for many years that family living does not consist of one-way streets leading from parents to children. Rather, psychologic impact in families is reciprocal, within and across generations, in communication patterns which define the roles of family members and the boundaries of families as small social units or "systems." Each child brings to the family certain temperamental and personal attributes that presumably have both biologic and psychologic components, and that have an impact on parents and siblings, just as parental characteristics have an impact on each child.

The roles of all family members must differ for the family to function as a social unit, with role changes over time that optimally relate to the sex, age, biologic characteristics, and developmental needs of each family member; such roles are often rigid and stereotyped in the families of schizophrenics (26). These psychosocial considerations lead to the expectation of differences between family members, even when genetic similarities may be high, as with twins. In the past, some authors have naively suggested that the offspring of one, or especially two, schizophrenic parents are necessarily exposed to psychologic risk; such authors apparently failed to realize that "impact" is not a simple function of parental symptoms but must be assessed in a more complex framework that includes the concepts of social roles, family systems, and developmental psychology. Explicit data about each family member and about actual family communication are needed to assess hypotheses about diverse risk factors considered alternatively or in combination. Examples of such data are to be found in the "high-risk" research underway in Rochester and UCLA (see Chapters 44 and 45).

We have been interested in the differing roles of parents, especially whether one parent may modify the impact of the other on a child's perceptions and understanding. Such influences may be corrective of a deviant parent, passively collusive, or actively aggravating of the deviant impact. In our research, we first study each parent's communication with a stranger (tester). Then we study how the parents communicate directly with each other, for example, in our Spouse Consensus Rorschach in which the marital pair is asked to reach agreement on Rorschach percepts. Then, in the Family Consensus Rorschach, all family members meet together. We also have used other standardized tasks to sample family communication directly (16,17,21,25). These sessions are videotaped or recorded and verbatim typescripts are then made available for detailed scoring of communication deviances and other aspects of interaction.

Although the individual impact of each parent is important, it is our observation that children also seem to take into their own functioning complex derivatives of effects of the *overall* family interaction. In sociologic terms, the family as an internally differentiated social system has an impact on development. We find that each parent may, in roles outside the family, or with other kinds of emotional support, manifest many positive attributes and personal assets that are not evident in intrafamilial transactions. Hence, corrective potentialities shown under other, extrafamilial circumstances may not be operative and not available within the family for internalization by the children (19).

A related point concerns the communication styles of the siblings of schizophrenics. We have found that the communication deviance scores of the "well" siblings of schizophrenic young adults are greater than those in siblings of offspring from the other diagnostic groups (6). This suggests that these siblings measurably share *some* of the communication styles used in their families, even though their other behaviors are such that they do not usually carry psychiatric diagnoses.

However, the deviance scores for both the index offspring and their siblings are consistently *lower* across diagnostic groups than are the scores of the corresponding parental groups. In constructing the manual, we sought to identify features in Rorschach communication that we had found especially frequent in the Rorschach protocols of our initial samples of parents of schizophrenics. Because of the role differences between parents and their offspring, we would not expect parental communication features to be necessarily prominent in the symptomatically ill schizophrenic offspring. In contrast, test measures of "thought disorder" are intended to correspond to degrees of overt symptomatology and should show higher scores in the overtly symptomatic family members. Our hypothesis of psychosocial differences between parents and children leads to directly opposite expectations, namely, that the schizophrenic offspring should have *fewer* communication deviances than their nonschizophrenic parents. In Table 46-2, our hypothesis appears to be supported by the fact that the parental deviance scores predict the symptomatic disorder of the index offspring better than does the offspring's own deviance score. Also, the mean deviance scores, adjusted after an analysis of covariance, were lower for both remitting and nonremitting schizophrenics than for their parents (6).

PARENTAL CLINICAL DIAGNOSES AND COMMUNICATION DEVIANCES

Parental clinical diagnoses as one set of variables, and parental communication deviance scores as another set of independently measured variables, appear to be statistically separable, as shown in the discriminant analyses in Table 46-2. In that Table, we showed that the parental clinical diagnoses and their deviance scores on the Rorschach *each* predict to offspring diagnosis to a statistically significant degree.

A different kind of finding, summarized in Table 46-4, compares the severity of clinical illness of index offspring and the clinical diagnoses assigned to the parents (6). Note the diagnoses of the parents of the nonremitting ("process") schizophrenics: 75% of these patients had one or both parents who themselves were clinically diagnosed as borderline or worse, while only 21% of the remitting schizophrenics had parents with such diagnoses. This difference is statistically significant at the 0.001 level. Thus, although the overall *quantitative* scores of parental communication deviances do not differentiate parents of remitting versus nonremitting schizophrenics, the diagnosis of parental borderline syndrome appears to be of special value in differentiating nonremitting from remitting schizophrenics.

Gunderson and Singer (27) have described such persons who tentatively are diagnosed as having a "borderline syndrome." Foremost among their personality features is a tendency to reason loosely and to become difficult to follow when external structure is not provided. Such persons typically function well in structured occupational roles (and in structured psychologic tests and interviews) but, as parents, contribute very loose and confusing conversational exchanges in family relationships (and in open-ended "projective" tests) when they are responsible for establishing the goals, structure, and affective tone of family tasks and relationships.

Another study in which ratings of parental psychopathology and ratings of parental communication deviances were obtained separately was carried out in an Adoptive Parent Study in Bethesda with Wender, Rosenthal, and Kety (28,29). (This study should not be confused with the Danish adoptive studies.) Three small groups of parents were compared: (a) the biological parents of a group of schizophrenics, (b) the adoptive parents of schizophrenics, and (c) the adoptive parents of a group of normal young adults. Wender et al reported results obtained when diagnoses were compared in these parental groups. More recently, we have studied the communication deviance variable in these same parents. We made blind ratings of communication deviances in the verbatim transcripts of the tape-recorded parental Rorschach records (8). First, using global assessments similar to those of an earlier study (24), the communication patterns of the adoptive parents who had reared a schizophrenic were successfully differentiated from the adoptive parents of nonschizophrenic offspring. However, the adoptive schizophrenic parents were indistinguishable from the comparison group of biologic parents who have reared a schizophrenic offspring (see Table 46-5). Also, for those protocols that were suitable for scoring with the communication manual, the mean frequency of deviances were similar for the adoptive and biologic parents who had reared clinically matched schizophrenic offspring; but both had significantly higher deviance scores than the adoptive parents of nonschizophrenics (Table 46-6). In contrast, Wender et al (28,29) had found that the psychopathology ratings of the parents of the biologic schizophrenics were worse than those of parents of the adoptive schizophrenics. Thus, the psychopathology ratings and the communication deviance scores appeared to measure dif-

Table 46-4. Comparisons of Severity of Index Offspring's Illness and Clinical Parental Diagnoses

Severity of Illness of Index Offspring	Parental Diagnoses			
	Both Parents Normal or Neurotic (Severity 1–3)	One Parent Normal or Neurotic One Borderline or Psychotic	Both Parents Borderline or Psychotic (Severity 4–7)	N
Normal 1–2	19 (95%)	1 (5%)	0	20
Neurotic 3	23 (92%)	2 (8%)	0	25
Borderline 4	21 (84%)	4 (16%)	0	25
Remitting schiz. 5	19 (79.2%)	5 (21%)	0	24
Nonremitting schiz. 6–7	5 (25%)	7 (35%)	8 (40%)	20

Table 46-5. Global Assessment of Parental Rorschach Communication and offspring Diagnosis

Offspring Diagnosis and Adoptive Status	Schizophrenic Offspring Predicted from Parental Communication	Nonschizophrenic Offspring Predicted from Parental Communication
(BS) Schiz. Offspring Reared by Biologic Parents	7	0
(AS) Schiz. Offspring Reared by Adoptive Parents	9	0
(AN) Nonschiz. Offspring Reared by Adoptive Parents	0	10

ferent parental characteristics—a finding similar to that reported previously when these variables were statistically separated.

Wender et al (28) and Rosenthal (30) have proposed that parental psychopathology be regarded as an indicator of the genetic loading that may be transmitted to the biologic offspring; hence they have tentatively interpreted the psychopathology data in the Adoptive Parents Study as supporting a genetics hypothesis. The communication deviance variable was devised to measure psychosocial impact, not psychopathology in the traditional sense. If the communication variable is tentatively assumed to be more heavily weighted by psychosocial-experiential components than is psychopathology, then the

Table 46-6. Mean Frequency of Rorschach Communication Deviances in Parental Groups (CD/WC)[a]

Offspring Diagnosis and Adoptive Status	Parental Pairs Having Complete Rorschachs[b]
Schizophrenic offspring reared by biologic parents (BS)	0.122 (N = 6)
Schizophrenic offspring reared by adoptive parents (AS)	0.121 (N = 7)
Nonschizophrenic offspring reared by adoptive parents (AN)	0.049 (N = 8)

[a] The CD/WC index is deviance rate adjusted for number of words used: number of deviances divided by word count.

[b] The CD/WC ratio has been summed for each parental pair for whom both the initial viewing and inquiry portions of the Rorschach tests were scorable. The means of these sums for the parental pairs in each of the three groups are given. The Ns in each group are smaller than in Table 46-5 because some protocols were administered in a manner that permitted global assessment but not systematic scoring with the communication deviance manual.

communication deviance data from the same parents may support a psychosocial hypothesis. Because different measures—parental diagnoses and parental communication deviances—were used by Wender et al and by us, the results are complementary and are consistent with the hypothesis that *both* genetic and psychosocial (experiential) factors interact in their contributions to the emergence of overt schizophrenia.

FUTURE DIRECTIONS

In this brief overview of some of our research findings, we have chosen a few highlights that have direct implications for future research. In recent times, we have shifted our attention to studying families with younger offspring to see what can be learned about families which, by actuarial criteria, have offspring at risk for developing personality aberrations. With our new longitudinal samples, we are now testing prospectively a number of hypotheses that emerged from the earlier studies of families with offspring who had reached adulthood carrying diagnoses ranging from normality to nonremitting schizophrenia. We expect to continue to examine families from a systems point of view, to use an epigenetic concept of development building on features having diverse origins, to assess the multidirectional impact of family members on one another, and to test further our assumption that stylistic attributes of communication are both enduring and predictive of behavior that will emerge in later years.

REFERENCES

1. Singer MT, Wynne LC: Principles for scoring communication defects and deviances in parents of schizophrenics: Rorschach and TAT scoring manuals. *Psychiat 29:*260, 1966.

2. Singer MT: Family transactions and schizophrenia: I. Recent research findings, in Romano J (ed): *The Origins of Schizophrenia.* Amsterdam, Excerpta Medica, 1967, p 147.

3. Wynne LC: Family transactions and schizophrenia: II. Conceptual considerations for a research strategy, in Romano J (ed): *The Origins of Schizophrenia.* Amsterdam, Excerpta Medica, 1967, p 165.

4. Singer MT: The Rorschach as a transaction, in Rickers-Ovsiankina MA (ed): *Rorschach Psychology.* Huntington, NY, Robert E Krieger, 1977, p 455.

5. Singer MT: *Scoring Manual for Communication Deviances Seen in Individually Administered Rorschachs.* Revision, 1973 (mimeographed, 100 pp).

6. Wynne LC, Singer MT, Bartko J, et al: Schizophrenics and their families: Recent research on parental communication, in Tanner JM (ed): *Developments in Psychiatric Research.* London, Hodder and Stoughton, Ltd, 1977, pp 254–286.

7. Hirsch SR, Leff JP: *Abnormalities in Parents of Schizophrenics.* London, Oxford Univ Press, 1975.

8. Wynne LC, Singer MT, Toohey ML: Communication of the adoptive parents of schizophrenics, in Jørstad J, Ugelstad E (eds): *Schizophrenia 75.* Oslo, Universitetsforlaget, 1976, p 413.

9. Glaser, RB: Family, spouse and individual Rorschach responses of families with and without young adult schizophrenic offspring. Unpublished thesis, University of California, Berkeley, 1975.

10. Golden HK: Deviant thinking in parents of schizophrenics: an exploration of the concept of schizotaxia. Unpublished dissertation, New York University, 1973.

11. Hassan, SA: Transactional and contextual invalidation between the parents of disturbed families: A comparative study. *Fam Proc* 13:53, 1974.

12. Johnston H: Test features of schizophrenics and their families. Unpublished dissertation, University of Chicago, 1975.

13. Jones JE: Transactional style deviance in families of disturbed adolescents. Unpublished dissertation, University of California, Los Angeles, 1975.

14. Kuka RE: The relationship of parental communication to offspring psychopathology. Unpublished dissertation, University of California, Berkeley, 1973.

15. Lidz T, Fleck S, Cornelison AR: *Schizophrenia and the Family.* New York, International University Press, 1955.

16. Loveland NT, Singer MT, Wynne LC: The family Rorschach: A new method for studying family interaction. *Fam Proc* 2:187, 1963.

17. Morris GO, Wynne LC: Schizophrenic offspring and parental styles of communication: A predictive study using excerpts of family therapy recordings. *Psychiat* 28:19, 1965.

18. Singer MT, Wynne LC: Differentiating characteristics of the parents of childhood schizophrenics, childhood neurotics, and young adult schizophrenics. *Am J Psychiat* 120:234, 1963.

19. Singer MT: A Rorschach view of the family, in Rosenthal D (ed): *The Genain Quadruplets: A Case Study and Theoretical Analysis of Heredity and Environment in Schizophrenia.* New York, Basic Books, 1963.

20. Wynne LC: Some indications and contraindications for exploratory family therapy, in Boszormenyi-Nagy I, Framo JL (eds): *Intensive Family Therapy.* New York, Harper & Row, 1965, p 289.

21. Wynne LC: Communication disorders and the quest for relatedness in families of schizophrenics. *Am J Psychoanal* 30:100, 1971.

22. Werner H: *Comparative Psychology of Mental Development.* New York, Science Editions, Inc, 1961.

23. Wynne LC, Singer MT: Thought disorder and family relations of schizophrenics: II. A classification of forms of thinking. *Arch Gen Psychiat* 9:199, 1963.

24. Singer MT, Wynne LC: Thought disorder and family relations of schizophrenics: IV. Results and implications. *Arch Gen Psychiat* 12:201, 1965.

25. Wynne LC: Methodologic and conceptual issues in the study of schizophrenics and their families. *J Psychiat Res* 6 (suppl 1):185, 1968.

26. Ryckoff I, Day J, Wynne LC: Maintenance of stereotyped roles in the families of schizophrenics. *AMA Arch Psychiat* 1:93, 1959.

27. Gunderson JG, Singer MT: Defining borderline patients: An overview. *Am J Psychiat* 132:1, 1975.

28. Wender PH, Rosenthal D, Kety SF: A psychiatric assessment of adoptive parents of schizophrenics, in Rosenthal D, Kety SF (eds): *The Transmission of Schizophrenia.* New York, Pergamon Press, 1968, p 235.

29. Wender PH, Rosenthal D, Kety SF: The psychiatric adjustment of the adoptive parents of schizophrenics. *Amer J Psychiat* 127:1013, 1971.

30. Rosenthal D: A program of research on heredity in schizophrenia. *Behav. Sci* 16:3, 1971.

Chapter 47
Communication Deviance and Diagnostic Differences

Michael Rutter, M.D., F.R.C.P., F.R.C.Psych, D.P.M.

As well demonstrated by Hirsch's and Leff's (1) excellent review of the topic, there is now considerable literature on family influences in the causation of schizophrenia. The studies vary greatly in quality; some lack the most elementary precautions and some include extravagant claims which far outrun the empirical findings. Even so, it may be generally agreed on the basis of the better investigations that (a) more parents of schizophrenics are psychiatrically disturbed than are parents of normal children; (b) there is a link between "allusive thinking" in schizophrenics and their parents, but this is also true of normal people in whom it occurs less frequently; (c) the parents of schizophrenics show more conflict and disharmony than do the parents of other psychiatric patients; (d) mothers of schizophrenics show more concern and protectiveness than do mothers of normal offspring; (e) schizophrenics involved in intense relationships with their relatives or spouses are more likely to relapse than are those whose relationships are less intense; and (f) the evidence on parental communication deviance is contradictory (1). Let us focus on this last contradiction since the Wynne and Singer findings are used by Goldstein et al (2) as a crucial part of their argument. They warrant careful attention for two rather different reasons. First, the results suggest a particularly strong association between abnormal family communication patterns and schizophrenia. Second, the careful and systematic replication by Hirsch and Leff produced very different results. Why?

Before considering the possible reasons a brief word is necessary on the results of the studies. Wynne et al (3) found that communication deviance (as assessed from Rorschach responses) is so very much more common in the parents of schizophrenics than in those of neurotics or normal offspring that there is virtually no overlap between the schizophrenic and these two groups. Hirsch and Leff (1) on the other hand, found only a small difference in the same direction, and even that difference ceased to be statistically significant when the number of words used was taken into account. It should be noted that Hirsch and Leff went to unusual lengths to learn Wynne's and Singer's methods, and

512

Margaret Singer scored all their protocols—an admirable piece of cooperation between two research groups.

When two important studies come up with contradictory findings, it is always necessary to search very carefully for the correct explanation for the discrepancy. Often a failure to replicate may throw important light on the basic mechanisms involved (4), and a dismissal of one or other as just "wrong" is likely to throw away valuable information. What explanations may be put forward in this case? First, it could be simply chance variations. This suggestion lacks plausibility in view of the size of the samples and the degree of the difference between their results. Second, one of the two studies might be incompetent or dishonest. Again there is nothing to support that suggestion. Third, there could be a referral bias in one or other of the samples. This is most unlikely in the Hirsch and Leff study, but it could apply to the Wynne and Singer investigation. On the other hand, there are reasons for doubting that this is a sufficient explanation (1).

Fourth, the methodology might differ in some crucial respect. Two possibilities have been suggested. Hirsch and Leff (1) noted in their own findings that communication deviance was correlated with verbosity, and that when the word count was included in the analysis of covariance, the difference between groups became negligible. However, as this was not so in the Wynne et al (3) data, this cannot account for the discrepancy between the two studies. Wynne, on the other hand, has argued that Hirsch's and Leff's largely negative findings were due to their using a method of administering the Rorschach test that inhibited the expression of deviance. However, Margaret Singer had made this suggestion in 1968 during the Hirsch and Leff study, and as a result they altered their techniques for the second half of the investigation (1). As Singer correctly predicted, the change of technique did indeed increase the amount of communication deviance expressed. On the other hand, since it did so equally in both the neurotic and schizophrenic groups and since the new technique in no way affected the intergroup difference, clearly this cannot be the explanation for the disparity between the studies.

A fifth explanation is that the difference in results might be a consequence of variations in diagnostic practice. This could work in either of two ways. On the one hand, the difference might lie in the control groups. If the Hirsch and Leff neurotic sample included some borderline schizophrenics, this could explain why they had failed to find any marked difference between groups. This possibility can be discounted in that the difference between the two studies lay in the scores of the schizophrenic families and *not* in the scores of the neurotic families. That leaves the last possibility that the explanation lies in the way schizophrenia was diagnosed in the two studies. We know that there are marked differences between US and UK psychiatrists in their diagnosis of schizophrenia (5,6), and it is highly probable that similar differences existed between the Hirsch and Leff and the Wynne and Singer groups of schizophrenics.

This suggestion is supported by the available descriptions of the samples (1). The English sample consisted mainly of patients with acute florid psychoses, half of whom were experiencing their first admission and few of whom had psychotic parents. In contrast the American sample had more chronic disorders associated with a strong family history of schizophrenia but often without active delusions and hallucinations.

It is sometimes thought that the US-UK difference in the diagnosis of schizophrenia is a matter of severity: that English schizophrenics are more severely ill. However, this is a misleading oversimplification, and certainly so far as the Wynne and Singer sample is concerned, there is every indication they were dealing with chronic handicapping disorders, probably more so than with Hirsch's and Leff's acute psychoses. That is not the distinction. The difference lies in the American emphasis on severe and chronic personality disorganization as the main feature of schizophrenia (see 7), as distinct from the British emphasis on the presence of delusions, hallucinations, and a particular form of thought disorder as a necessary part of the acute psychotic manifestations.

At the moment we lack adequate data to test the hypothesis that the discrepancy between these two important studies is due to diagnostic differences, but it seems to be the one most likely to account for the observations. If it proves to be correct, what are the implications?

We need not waste time arguing whether the UK or US practice provides the "true" diagnosis of schizophrenia, as we do not yet know what is schizophrenia. Rather, the question should be—what are the differences between the schizophrenics diagnosed in the two countries? Obviously, to some extent, they differ in symptomatology, but do they also differ in etiology? The Hirsch and Leff findings suggest that they may do. It appears that abnormal family communication patterns may not be associated with acute florid psychoses with delusions and hallucinations and that they are more strongly associated with that variety of severe and serious personality disorganization termed schizophrenia in the US but given some other diagnosis in the UK. Such distinctions, certainly, at the very least, warrant systematic testing, and it is to be hoped that Hirsch and Leff and Wynne and Singer will continue their collaboration to test this hypothesis using methods of Rorschach administration most appropriate to the eliciting of communication deviance.

Let me now turn to the UCLA study undertaken by Goldstein and his colleagues (2). It has many strengths, it is prospective, it includes a variety of essential controls, it involves a wide range of measures, and it provides the possibility of comparing the Wynne and Singer projective test measures with observed family interactions. The observations of family interaction and communication seem to me particularly searching and well thought out. For all these reasons their findings require very careful scrutiny and consideration. Their results show a set of associations between adolescent symptomatology, parental communication deviance, and the development of so-called schizophrenia spectrum disorders.

What conclusions can be drawn? Goldstein infers that parental communication deviance probably predisposes to schizophrenia spectrum disorders. However, it should be noted that there were only two cases of definite schizophrenia (too few for conclusions on this group), and it remains uncertain how far the spectrum should extend. While the adoptee findings have been used as a justification of the spectrum concept, the evidence is weak in view of the extent to which schizophrenics mate with sociopaths.

However, let us accept that the UCLA findings do indeed show a most interesting relationship between parental communication deviance and particular pattern of psychiatric disorder. That is not in dispute and it should be recognized that the finding is an important one. The only serious doubt is how far the finding has to do with schizophrenia. What is the evidence? First, the link is assumed on the basis of previous findings that many schizophrenics showed psychiatric abnormalities before becoming overtly psychotic (9,10). That is well substantiated, but the same studies also showed that the prepsychotic abnormalities were very varied and nonspecific in type. The second piece of evidence concerns the projective test results. Goldstein relies here on the Wynne and Singer findings. But as I have already noted, the Hirsch and Leff data were rather different. Not only do some families of neurotics also show deviant communications, but it may well be that the most abnormal communication patterns are associated with those borderline cases termed schizophrenia in the US but not in the UK. Again there is the obvious need to relate Goldstein's family communication measures to specific diagnoses, using reliable and valid diagnostic tools.

Let us now suppose that the association is confirmed. What would it mean? Goldstein put forward various possibilities, all of which need to be considered. However, he did not include the possibility that the deviant communication reflects genetically determined attributes rather than any kind of environmental interaction. As Wynne and his colleagues (8,11) have appreciated, this possibility could be tested through the study of schizophrenic adoptees. If the communication deviance were to be evident in the adoptive parents of schizophrenics but not in their biological parents who did not rear them, this would rule out a genetic effect. Wynne et al found that communication deviance did apply to a small sample of adoptive parents of schizophrenics, but unfortunately it was not possible to examine the biologic parents. This still leaves the question unanswered in that although it makes a purely genetic explanation of deviant communication unlikely, it leaves open Goldstein's third possibility, namely, that the communication deviance is a reaction to the child's characteristics. The issue deserves further study.

Environmental influences also may be explored through study of course and prognosis. The investigations by George Brown and his colleagues (12,13) point the way. They found that intense negative feelings in the family predisposed to a higher relapse rate in schizophrenia. The results strongly suggest an etiologic relationship in which family emotions affect the course of schizophrenia. Does the same apply to parental communication patterns? Even more important, are improvements in family communication associated with changes for the better in the course of schizophrenia? Evidence of this kind is needed to test causal hypotheses.

One last point. In the past many investigators have tended to ask how much of the variation can be attributed to nature and how much to nurture? But less attention has been paid to interaction effects. Goldstein suggests some ways in which they may occur and often research suggests their possible importance. For example, the studies of both Crowe (14) and Hutchings and Mednick (15) suggest that the same environmental influences which have little or no effect in the absence of genetic susceptibility may have an important causal effect in the case of individuals who are vulnerable by virtue of heredity. In short, one of the ways in which genetic factors operate is to increase susceptibility to environmental hazards. Our own studies of chronic family stresses also emphasize the importance of interaction effects (16). I should add that all these studies refer to conduct or antisocial disorders and not to schizophrenia. However, the same may apply to schizophrenia. Certainly, the possibility of genetic-environmental interactions warrants serious study.

Let me conclude by stating that improved methods of studying family interactions and better research strategies are opening up important new avenues of investigation. It is clear that family difficulties and disorders of various kinds are associated with the broad group of schizophrenic disorders. Also, the evidence strongly suggests that family influences help shape the course of schizophrenics. However, the processes and mechanisms remain ill understood. Moreover, it is uncertain whether the family stresses are specific to schizophrenia or rather predispose to a wide range of psychiatric conditions. Finally, it has yet to be determined which variety of schizophrenia spectrum disorders is associated with communication deviance. The resolution of these questions gives us plenty to work on during the next decade, and the answers should provide a good basis for the next Rochester conference in 1986!

REFERENCES

1. Hirsch SR, Leff JP: *Abnormalities in Parents of Schizophrenics.* (Institute of Psychiatry: Maudsley Monograph no 22). London, Oxford University Press, 1975.

2. Goldstein MJ, Rodnick EH, Jones JE, et al: Family Precursors of schizophrenia spectrum disorders, chapter 45, this volume, 1978.

3. Wynne LC, Singer MT, Bartko JJ, et al: Schizophrenics and Their Families: Recent Research on Parental Communication, in Tanner JM (ed): *Developments in Psychiatric Research.* London, Hodder and Stoughton, 1977, pp 254–286.

4. Rutter M: Epidemiological Strategies and Psychiatric Concepts in Research on the Vulnerable Child, in Anthony EJ, Koupernik C (eds): *The Child in the Family, vol 3. Children at Psychiatric Risk.* London, Wiley, 1974.

5. Cooper JE, Kendell RE, Gurland BJ, et al: *Psychiatric Diagnosis in New York and London.* (Institute of Psychiatry: Maudsley Monograph no 22). London, Oxford University Press, 1972.

6. World Health Organization: *The International Pilot Study of Schizophrenia*, vol 1. Geneva, WHO, 1973.

7. Lidz T, Fleck S: Schizophrenia, Human Integration and the Role of the Family, in Jackson DD (ed): *The Etiology of Schizophrenia.* New York, Basic Books, 1960, p 323.

8. Singer MT, Wynne LC, Toohey ML: Communication Disorders and the Families of Schizophrenics, Wynne LC, Cromwell RL, Matthysse S (eds): *The Nature of Schizophrenia.* John Wiley & Sons, 1978.

9. Offord DR, Cross LA: Behavioral antecedents of adult schizophrenia. *Arch gen Psychiat* 21:267, 1969.

10. Rutter M: Childhood schizophrenia reconsidered. *J Autism Childhood Schiz* 2:315, 1972.

11. Wynne LC, Singer MT, Toohey MC: Communication of the adoptive parents of schizophrenics, in Jørstad J, Ugelstad E (eds): *Schizophrenia 75,* Oslo, Norway, Universitetsforlaget, 1976, pp 413–452.

12. Brown GW, Monck EM, Carstairs GM, et al: Influence of family life on the course of schizophrenic illness. *Brit J Prev Soc Med* 16:55, 1962.

13. Brown GW, Birley JLT, Wing JK: Influence of family life on the course of schizophrenic disorders: a replication. *Brit J Psychiat* 14:241, 1972.

14. Crowe RR: An adoption study of antisocial personality. *Arch Gen Psychiat* 31:785, 1974.

15. Hutchings B, Mednick SA: Registered Criminality in the Adoptive and Biological Parents of Registered Male Adoptees, in Mednick SA et al (eds): *Genetics, Environment and Psychopathology.* Amsterdam, North Holland, 1974, p. 215.

16. Rutter M: Early Sources of Security and Competence, in Bruner J, Garton A (eds): *Human Growth and Development.* London, Oxford University Press, in press.

Chapter 48
The Transmission of Irrationality Reconsidered

Helm Stierlin, M.D., Ph.D.

In a seminal paper published in 1958 on the transmission of irrationality, Lidz, Cornelison, Terry, and Fleck (1) pointed out that the detailed study of the families of schizophrenics unexpectedly reveals distorted and even bizarre reasoning in the parents, even in those who have never been hospitalized or would not be indexed as psychotic in broad epidemiologic surveys. These authors hypothesized that the schizophrenic patient has been "raised amidst irrationality and chronically exposed to intrafamilial communications that distort and deny what should be the obvious interpretation of the environment."

TWO PERSPECTIVES ON THE TRANSMISSION OF SCHIZOPHRENIA

Emphasizing that they were "describing what exists in the family rather than explaining how it came about," Lidz et al stressed that "both genetic and environmental factors may well be involved" (1). Today we still see the transmission of irrationality unfold within two perspectives—one biogenic, the other sociogenic. Within both there exist "givens" of transmission, such as structures, traits, dispositions, and sets. Modes of transmission correspond to those givens, and the modes and givens are believed to shape as well as to delimit phenomena, including forms of irrationality, which we associate with schizophrenia.

However, the two perspectives differ as to which givens and modes prevail. Within the first perspective, these fit into a biologic framework. The emphasis is on genetic, and perhaps phylogenetic, transmission. Man's genes, encoding and transmitting information, are seen as shaping biopsychologic structures and processes. Biogenetic transmission is even held to shape grammatical structures, as described by Chomsky (2), or the expression of emotions in men and animals, as suggested by Darwin (3). Such views could link with modern theories on the etiology of schizophrenia: Faulty grammar or inappropriately expressed emotions as well as man's cognitive styles, attentional processes, and psychophysiologic response dispositions may be biogenetic factors contributing to irrationality in schizophrenia.

Within the sociogenic perspective, however, such biogenetic givens and modes become less relevant, albeit not irrelevant. Here the key givens are norms, values, roles, attitudes, and verbal and nonverbal communicational tools which vary with time and society, yet provide intrasocietal cohesion, meaning, and sanction. To transmit these givens, a social mode of transmission is required. This mode accounts for the perpetuation of cultures, just as the phylogenetic mode accounts for the perpetuation of animal species. Although the social mode operates within confines set phylogenetically, in another sense it represents a radical widening of these confines. We may say the sociogenic mode transcends the biogenetic mode in the sense in which Hegel (3) used the term "aufheben," which means to conserve, to lift up (i.e., change qualitatively), as well as to cancel.

SCHIZOPHRENIA AS DERAILMENT OF SOCIALIZATION

Most theories of social transmission have built on the concept of "socialization"; schizophrenia, in light of these theories, can be considered a derailment of socialization. Socialization of man hinges on a special biopsychologic and relational configuration. At its basis is a child partially programmed by instincts (or innate behavior patterns), yet also significantly and enduringly dependent on socializing agents, particularly his parents and other family members. These agents, equipped with a "stronger reality" (5), transmit to the child the givens of his culture which he must learn and/or internalize. If he fails to do so in a consistent and socially adaptive fashion, we expect confusion, disturbances of identity and self-object differentiation, anomie, and possibly schizophrenia.

Within this broad framework, researchers distinguish among several groups of factors (or rearing variables), operating singly or conjointly, that may cause socialization to derail. All these have been implicated in schizophrenia.

First, the essential givens from the culture—e.g., categories of language, norms, and communicational tools, and so on—required for survival in any complex society may, for one reason or another, be unavailable for internalization.

Second, such givens of cultural nutriment may be available but are transmitted confusingly and in disregard for the child's age-appropriate needs and capacities. Consequently, the child or young adult is mystified, misdefined to himself, led astray in the symbolic jungle, trained in irrationality, and so forth, as described in an ever growing literature by such authors as Bateson et al (6), Lidz et al (7,8), Wynne and Singer (9–11), Laing (12), and many others.

Third, and interweaving with the first two factors, the interpersonal scenario required for socialization—the relationship between socializor and socializee—may be amiss. Optimally, this relationship should allow for trust and attachment and also for the development of mutual individuation and relative separation. At the same time, it should facilitate ever new levels of a mature interdependence. Yet there exist, as we know, many relationships that thwart such positive development. Here the child's dependency on mature caretakers, the basis of all socialization, is short-circuited or exploited, and his moves toward mutual individuation and mature interdependence become blocked or skewed. This, too, is held to contribute to schizophrenic developments. Many data and observations, as recently reviewed by Wynne (13), accord with such a view of contributions to schizophrenic etiology and pathogenesis. A somewhat different perspective which our group increasingly has come to adopt has derived mainly from further clinical work with families of schizophrenics. This perspective revolves around the concept of *delegation*.

DELEGATION WITHIN A MULTIGENERATIONAL PERSPECTIVE

The nature and dynamics of delegation have been elaborated elsewhere (14–17), and here a few summarizing remarks must suffice. Delegation derives from the Latin *"delegare"* which has two major meanings: "to send out" and "to entrust with a mission (or missions)." Delegation becomes possible when there exist strong, personalized bonds of loyalty, bonds forged chiefly during a child's early dependence on his parents and family. In the context of such intimate dependence, the child responds to signals, often given covertly, that reflect his delegator's wishes, expectations, fears, and fantasies. In responding to these signals, the child stakes out his life's major missions. He tries to execute these missions because of his need to be loved and to be loyal, and to find direction and meaning, a sense of mission and of personal importance in his life.

Delegation, thus understood, qualifies the meanings of concepts such as separation, autonomy, and individuation, for a delegate's separation and autonomy remain relative and conditional. While his missions may require him to separate and individuate, he is also kept on the leash of loyalty; while he is sent out, he is also held back; and whatever autonomy he exerts needs to comply with the loyalty he must prove and the missions he must execute.

Since I began to view delegation in this manner some 8 years ago, it has become the focus of a theoretical framework conceptualizing healthy as well as pathologic processes, and I have revised my notions on social transmission accordingly. Ideas of Boszormenyi-Nagy (18,19) in particular have entered into this framework. As a result, we are now inclined to say: Transmission via delegation transcends as well as conserves socialization, just as social transmission as such transcends and conserves phylogenetic transmission.

Foremost, it reveals a multigenerational perspective, familiar to the family therapist of schizophrenic patients, but less familiar to individual psychotherapists and nonclinical researchers. Within this perspective, one observes determinants of long-range behavior that are comparable to those other determinants—or intermediate variables—that schizophrenia researchers recently have come to stress, such as psychophysiologic response dispositions or communicational styles in families. However, the determinants revealed through the concept "delegation" also encompass forces that are not covered, or only insufficiently, by those better known constructs.

To help understand these processes, I note two additional meanings contained in the Latin *"delegare"*: *lex, legis* (law) and an early root, *lego* (collect or gather). *Ligare* (to bind) is disputedly a related early root. These root meanings of delegation, even more than those mentioned earlier ("to send out" and "to entrust with missions") broadly imply strong and lasting obligations and expectations that presumably operate as significant determinants of human behavior. These various aspects of delegation operate on individual-psychologic, transactional, intergenerational, and, possibly, existential levels.

On the first, individual-psychologic level, inner motivational sets, dispositions, and organizing principles of behavior with a dynamic "steering" function are involved in the delegating processes. These sets underlie and shape an individual's more specific attitudes and interactions and bear on his age-appropriate individuation and separation. In schizophrenia, we conceptualize these motivational sets as interfering with age-appropriate individuation-separation and social learning within the delegating process. Also, on the transactional level (and possibly the existential level), these forces reflect interpersonal and intergenerational scenarios or systems that may cause the delegating process to derail.

This derailment can happen in a number of ways. First, the missions may be such as to overtax cruelly a delegate, as when a child of medium talents must turn into the shining academic star his parents vainly tried to become. Second, there may be a conflict of missions, as when a child is commissioned to serve as a provider of excitement to his emotionally and sexually starved parents, and, at the same time, must be a stable and responsible adult on whom his parents can rely. Third, and interwoven with the above, there may be a conflict of loyalties, as when a delegate, while serving as one parent's delegate, necessarily betrays his loyalty to the other.

In short, as a consequence of such derailments there may result "missions impossible": any vulnerable individual, as a delegate of his parents or forebears, may become overburdened, possibly to the breaking point, and, therefore, fail in his age-appropriate individuation-separation and, eventually, in his socialization. Certain forms of such failure may then contribute to schizophrenia, typically during adolescence when the most strenuous tasks of individuation-separation occur.

"MISSIONS IMPOSSIBLE" AS FOUND IN SCHIZOPHRENIC DEVELOPMENT

I shall mention only a few of the "missions impossible" that we have found typically to devolve upon adolescents destined to become, and later diagnosed as, schizophrenic. First, there are missions that serve the parents' avoidance of shame or guilt (20). Such missions may destroy a delegate's self worth, integrity, and basic trust when he is made the container of the parents' disowned weakness, ineptness, messiness, or even madness (21). A special version of this kind of mission may occur when parents, haunted by the shameful spectre of mad ancestors, as described by Scott, Ashworth, and Montanez (22–24), may prophesy, search for, and induce "madness" in a given child. The ever-feared and ever-present madness is, in effect, then deposited in and behaviorally fulfilled by one or more receptive family members. There the madness remains available for the parents' constant scrutiny and worried agitation, yet safely disowned by them (21).

Second, certain missions may aim at sparing one's parents and/or other family members the painful work of mourning that is necessary for further individuation-separation within the family. We have found repeatedly in families with a schizophrenic offspring how this offspring has lived out the life of an unmourned family member, most often a sibling. Paul and Grosser (25) have well described "operant mourning" and the consequences when this bereavement process has been blocked and distorted.

Third, certain extreme types of missions may overburden a delegate while they also pull him (or her) in different directions and thus create an additional severe conflict of missions. Such a delegate, for example, a child of medium talents, may have to succeed as the famous pianist his mother failed to become, and thereby act as an extended arm for the maintenance of her self-esteem. This task requires him to move out and compete aggressively, yet at the same time he may have the conflicting and confusing mission of remaining her ever dependent, ever home-bound baby. By remaining babyish, he confirms her as a good and loving mother, yet he also helps her to cope with the deprivations she once suffered as a child in that he allows her now to give to him as she needed to be given to by her parents. Elsewhere I have written about such persons as "bound delegates" (15,17).

Fourth, certain missions imply extremely destructive conflicts of loyalties, as when a child, loyalty-bound to one parent, is commissioned to disparage or even destroy the other parent. Lidz et al (26) has described such destructive loyalty conflicts in the context of "marital schisms."

Unfortunately, space limitations do not allow me to trace in detail how derailments of delegation, resulting in overburdening, conflictual missions, may underlie, if not trigger, clinical schizophrenia (or schizophrenic spectrum disorders). An illustrative vignette, ·chosen from among numerous similar ones, must suffice. This vignette concerns 18-year-old Margot (pseudonym), and her family, whom we recently saw at our Heidelberg Institute.

Example of a Derailed Delegating Process

According to the account given initially by the family to the hospital psychiatrist, Margot had always been a studious, likeable, and essentially normal girl until she had changed about 18 months before admission, for reasons the family did not understand. She stopped going to school and roamed the woods at night, often half-naked, loitered in hippy hangouts, and was promiscuous in a strange, depersonalized way. The following 18 months after psychiatric hospitalization, she was more or less continuously incoherent, bizarre, silly, and unapproachable. She was usually disheveled, withdrawn, and seemingly absorbed in listening to voices. Her hospital diagnosis was schizophrenia, hebephrenic type.

She was then seen with her family by a therapist who was actively supportive of both the family and patient. In these meetings, she appeared strikingly less disturbed and fragmented than she was on the ward. Her behavior became understandable when seen in the context of conflictual missions in which she served as the family delegate. Most importantly, these missions seemed aimed at insuring her mother's tenuous psychologic survival. Not long before Margot's change in behavior began, her father had unexpectedly died of a heart attack and left her undereducated and home-bound mother overcome by fear, self-doubts, and loneliness. At night her mother began to hallucinate and made a suicide attempt. When Margot became ill, the mother's symptoms subsided. As long as she had Margot to worry about, the mother said, she could forget about killing herself. By thinking of Margot as her "helpless and needful child," she mustered the strength to survive. Thus, it devolved upon Margot to provide her mother with a meaning in life as well as with worries that both distressed and vitalized the mother.

Further, it was learned that the father's mother for a number of years had had an illness very much like that of Margot's. This woman had for some years embodied the family's frightening potential for madness. Later, Margot's bizarre behavior reenacted in minute detail the earlier behavior of her grandmother. Margot's illness can be conceptualized as involving a delegated mission to be the bearer of the family madness. It is noteworthy that this family context was not recognized at all when Margot was simply diagnosed and treated in a conventional manner as an individual hospitalized patient.

Clinical schizophrenia within this model thus reveals a drama of exploitation and counter-exploitation, of tragic binding and, at the same time, of mutual alienation, of complexly reverberating vicious circles. In this drama, exploitatively delegating parents often emerge as delegates of their own parents, unwittingly taking their children to account for what these parents did to them, and bindees turn out to be binders, and victims, victimizers.

DELEGATION AND DEVIANT PARENTAL COMMUNICATION

How then can we reconcile this model, emphasizing derailments of delegation, overburdening, and conflictual missions, with findings from current research as presented in this volume? Such findings, as here and elsewhere reported by Goldstein, Rodnick, Jones et al (27,28), as well as by Wynne, Singer Bartko, and Toohey (29), and Wynne, Singer, and Toohey (30) in their recent paper on adoptive parents of schizophrenics, confirm one group of variables as powerful predictors of schizophrenia: parental communication deviances. What then, we must ask, is the relation of these deviances to the delegating process?

In answering this question, we must keep in mind that not all deeply conflictual missions entail psychopathology and/or schizophrenia. Rather, they may also generate adaptive and even creative solutions. This compares to how we today assess the pathogenic versus creative potential inherent in so-called double-binds: Not all "double-binds," even intense, lasting and inescapable ones, eventuate in schizophrenia, as a growing literature attests. Rather, as Wynne (31) has pointed out, the *in*ability to escape double-binds, even though causing deepest anguish, may also spur one's creative passions and may, or may not, contribute to schizophrenic illness. The same, we believe, holds true for overburdening and seemingly irreconcilable missions, as here described.

We suggest that deviant communicational styles of parents do have an impact and affect deeply any delegate's chances to cope adaptively and creatively with difficult missions. In fact, such styles may well be a crucial element determining how delegations unfold, and/or derail, and/or eventuate in schizophrenia.

Here we must recall that Wynne and Singer's work on communication deviances has gone beyond familiar notions of the "double-bind" (5), the disqualification of meaning (32), mystification (12), and so forth, in that their work has generated complex, but nonetheless testable hypotheses and predictions, and afforded a much more detailed view of pathogenic family relationships than did the earlier clinical constructs.

At the same time, their work shows how the pathogenic and "corrective" influences of family members may interact and tip the balance toward relative health or schizophrenia. We may speak of a "differential exposure" to deviant communication. For example, one parent, according to Wynne and Singer's findings, may counteract the "schizophrenogenic" contributions of the other, as when a "straight-thinking," down-to-earth father may neutralize a scatter-brained and mystifying mother. The more forcefully such a father asserts his stronger reality, the more likely will he pull a vulnerable child away from the mother's "schizophrenogenic" orbit. By the same token, we assume that the more such a father allows meaning to emerge and stand, and positions within the family to be differentiated and articulated, the more will he also enable an exploitatively delegated child—and the other family members as well—to struggle creatively with any difficult and conflictual missions.

In the light of these considerations, we would like to emphasize the following as perhaps the most central factors bearing upon a child's development toward, or away from, schizophrenia (or schizophrenic spectrum disorders): (a) encumbrances by "missions impossible," reflecting relationships within the immediate family as well as an intergenerational legacy; (b) the differential exposure to parental transactional communication deviances that may negate a delegate's chances to cope with such missions adaptively and/or creatively; and, finally, (c) the transactional patterns that monitor such exposure, and may, or may not allow for escape routes and/or compensations.

PATTERNS OF BINDING AND EXPELLING

In earlier works (14–17), I described two extreme transactional patterns which may, albeit in opposite ways, interfere with an adaptive and successful delegation—the transactional modes of binding and expelling. We assume the impact of communication deviances will be different when combined with binding versus expelling. Where the binding mode dominates, centripetal forces prevail, and a child's age-appropriate separation is delayed, if not blocked. Psychologically, such a child remains locked into the family ghetto. According to our clinical experience, this may be so even in cases where outwardly we find mostly alienation and/or strife between parents and offspring, and where joint living at home has, in Scott's (22) words, become "untenable." The offspring may be bound by an ever-flowing regressive gratification, sapping his will to separate and individuate, or he may be bound by an excessive and enslaving loyalty, causing him to reel under unbearable guilt should he ever, in thought or action, try to separate from his parents. But, further, he may be bound also by the kind of unsettling and confusing communication which Wynne and Singer's communication deviance measure taps (29). This, then, we have reason to believe maximizes all other forms of binding and impairs from the outset the cognitive and perceptual tools an offspring would need to individuate intrapsychically and to separate interpersonally.

Here we have spoken of "cognitive" or "ego" binding, a binding that more than anything else appears to interfere with an individual's capacity to distinguish what is "Me" and "Not-Me," to differentiate his own motives, feelings, and ideas from those of others, and to focus attention flexibly in accordance with varying tasks and interpersonal settings. By the same token, such binding appears to interfere with one's ability to understand, define, evaluate, reject, and/or reconcile one's missions, as well as to bear the anguish and inner conflict should these become "impossible."

In the other extreme transactional mode, called the expelling mode, centrifugal forces dominate. Here an offspring, rather than being bound, suffers serious rejection and neglect. He develops a precocious autonomy but pays for it with, in the words of Wynne (33), massive attachment deficit and a diminished/absent sense of self-esteem. Such children will be damaged, and they too will respond to differential communication deviances, especially when exposed to them during their normative and vulnerable years. Yet they may, we believe, have better chances than "bound" ones to undo the effects of such exposure, and to communicate with, as well as learn from, peers and adults other than their parents.

In the light of these considerations, we can speculate that the four groups of troubled adolescents ("aggressive, antisocial," "active family conflict," "passive, negative," and "withdrawn, socially isolated") described by Goldstein et al (27,28), encompass different transactional scenarios with different exposures to communication deviances and different kinds and degrees of delegation. Thus, the first high-risk group ("active family conflict") may mainly refer to "bound delegates" stalemated in pseudohostile wrangles (34), and the second high-risk group ("withdrawn, socially isolated") may include "bound delegates" who have failed to make active efforts at individuation or have given up after an inconclusive struggle. By contrast, the two other groups might contain more expellees or expelled delegates, i.e., children less encumbered by difficult and conflictual missions and, therefore, in a better position to individuate-separate and learn from outside influences.

To build these hypotheses, finer distinctions and more data are needed. That, however, should not deter us from attempts to integrate findings and hypotheses from different areas—therapeutic, clinical, social, and biopsychological—that may throw light on this puzzling and tragic condition we call schizophrenia.

REFERENCES

1. Lidz T, Cornelison AR, Terry D, et al: Intrafamilial environment of the schizophrenic patient. VI. The transmission of irrationality. *AMA Arch Neurol & Psychiat* 79:305, 1958.

2. Chomsky N: *Language and Mind*. New York, Harcourt Brace & World, 1968.

3. Darwin C (1872): *The Expression of the Emotions in Man and Animals*. Chicago, University of Chicago Press, 1965.

4. Hegel G (1806): *The Phenomenology of the Spirit*, Baille JB (trans), 2 vols. London, Swann Sonnenschein, 1910.

5. Stierlin H: The adaptation to the "stronger" person's reality, *Psychiat* 22:143, 1959.

6. Bateson C, Jackson D, Haley J, et al: Toward a theory of schizophrenia, *Behav Sci* 1:251, 1956.

7. Lidz T, Fleck S, Cornelison AR: *Schizophrenia and the Family*. New York, International Universities Press, 1965.

8. Lidz T: *The Origin and Treatment of Schizophrenic Disorders*. New York, Basic Books, 1973.

9. Wynne LC, Singer MT: Thought disorder and family relations of schizophrenics: I. A research strategy. *Arch Gen Psychiat* 9:191, 1963.

10. Singer MT, Wynne LC: Thought disorder and family relations of schizophrenics: IV. Results and implications. *Arch Gen Psychiat* 12:201, 1965.

11. Wynne LC: The injection and the concealment of meaning in the family relations and psychotherapy of schizophrenics, in Rubinstein D, Alanen YO (eds): *Psychotherapy of Schizophrenia*. Amsterdam, Excerpta Medica, 1972, pp 180–193.

12. Laing RD: Mystification, confusion, and conflict, in Boszormenyi-Nagy I, Framo JL (eds): *Intensive Family Therapy*. New York, Harper & Row, 1965.

13. Wynne LC: Psychopathological aspects of psychoses: Nongenetic factors in the family setting, in *Research on Disorders of the Mind: Progress and Prospects*. Washington, US Dept Health, Educ & Welfare, 1977, pp 38–44.

14. Stierlin H: The adolescent as delegate of his parents, *Aust and NZ J Psychiat* 7:249, 1973.

15. Stierlin H: *Separating Parents and Adolescents. A Perspective on Running Away, Schizophrenia, and Waywardness*. New York, Quadrangle, 1974.

16. Stierlin H: Family dynamics and separation patterns of potential schizophrenics, in Rubinstein D, Alanen YO (eds): *Proceedings of the Fourth International Symposium on Psychotherapy of Schizophrenia*. Amsterdam, Excerpta Medica, 1972, pp 169–179.

17. Stierlin H: *Adolf Hitler—Familienperspektiven*. Frankfurt, Suhrkamp, 1975. English edition: *Adolf Hitler—A Family Perspective*. New York, The Psychohistory Press, 1976.

18. Boszormenyi-Nagy I: Loyalty implications of the transference model in psychotherapy. *Arch Gen Psychiat* 27:374, 1972.

19. Boszormenyi-Nagy I, Spark G: *Invisible Loyalties*. New York, Harper & Row, 1973.

20. Stierlin H: Shame and guilt in family relations: Theoretical and clinical aspects. *Arch Gen Psychiat* 30:38, 1974.

21. Stierlin H: The dynamics of owning and disowning: Psychoanalytic and family perspectives. *Fam Proc* 15:277, 1976.

22. Scott RD, Ashworth PL: The "axis value" and the transfer of psychosis. A scored analysis of the interaction in the families of schizophrenic patients. *Brit J Med Psychol* 38:97, 1965.

23. Scott RD, Ashworth PL: The shadow of the ancestor: A historical factor in the transmission of schizophrenia. *Brit J Med Psychol* 42:13, 1969.

24. Scott RD, Montanez A: The nature of tenable and untenable patient-parent relationships and their connection with hospital outcome, in Rubinstein D, Alanen YO (eds): *Psychotherapy of Schizophrenia*. Amsterdam, Excerpta Medica, 1972, pp 226–242.

25. Paul N, Grosser G: Operational mourning and its role in conjoint family therapy. *Comm Ment Health J* 1:339, 1965.

26. Lidz T, Cornelison AR, Fleck S, et al: The Intrafamilial environment of schizophrenic patients: II. Marital schism and marital skew. *Am J Psychiat* 114:241, 1957.

27. Goldstein MJ, Rodnick EH, Jones JE, et al: Familial precursors of schizophrenia spectrum disorders, Wynne LC, Cromwell RL, Matthysse S (eds): *The Nature of Schizophrenia*. John Wiley & Sons, 1978.

28. Goldstein MJ, Judd LL, Rodnick EH et al: A method for studying social influence and coping patterns within families of disturbed adolescents. *J Nerv Ment Dis* 147:233, 1968.

29. Wynne LC, Singer MT, Bartko J, et al: Schizophrenics and their families: Recent research on parental communication, in Tanner JM (ed): *Developments in Psychiatric Research*. London, Hodder & Stoughton, Ltd., 1976, pp 254–286.

30. Wynne LC, Singer MT, Toohey ML: Communication of the adoptive parents of schizophrenics, in Jørstad J, Ugelstad E (eds): *Schizophrenia 1975: Psychotherapy, Family Therapy, Research*. Oslo, Universitetsforlaget Scandinavian University Books, 1976, pp 413–451.

31. Wynne LC: Über Qual und schöpferische Leidenschaft im Banne des "double-bind"—eine Neuformulierung. *Familiendynamik* 1:24, 1976.

32. Haley J: The family of the schizophrenic. A model system. *J Nerv Ment Dis* 129:357, 1959.

33. Wynne LC: Overview, in Wynne LC, Cromwell RL, Matthysse (eds): *The Nature of Schizophrenia*. John Wiley & Sons, 1978.

34. Wynne LC: The study of intrafamilial alignments and splits in exploratory family therapy, in Ackerman N, Beatman FL, Sherman SN (eds): *Exploring the Base for Family Therapy*. New York: Family Service Assn of America, 1961, pp 95–115.

Chapter 49
Egocentric Cognitive Regression and the Family Setting of Schizophrenic Disorders

Theodore Lidz, M.D.

Concluding this Section on family studies, I wish to emphasize that there need not be any essential conflict between genetic-biological orientations and familial-sociocultural approaches to the study of schizophrenic disorders. Like all other animals, humans are endowed with a genetically transmitted makeup that enables them to live within a limited range of physical environments, but because they can communicate verbally, think reflectively, and plan toward a future, as well as use tools, they can modify environments to suit their limited physiological capacities. Because people can transmit what they learn across generations, learning becomes cumulative; children are born into a cultural heritage and thereby can assimilate from those who raise them the adaptive techniques needed to survive in the physical and social environment in which they live. The genetic makeup of human beings requires that they grow up in a social system and assimilate a culture in order to be able to survive and mature; they must learn the language of their culture in order to communicate with others upon whose collaboration their lives depend; and they must learn to use their inborn cognitive equipment to be able to guide themselves into the future. Unless we understand that infants are born with a dual endowment, a genetic inheritance and a cultural heritage, we can never correctly understand their development and how it can become disordered. The genes transmit the physical structure which in humans involves the unique capacity for symbolic functioning, but most of the specifically human adaptive techniques are not born into persons, but are acquired by assimilation from the social, cultural, and interpersonal environment.

The family is an essential derivative of the biological makeup of humans. Every society depends upon the family, or some planned substitute for it, to mediate between the child's cultural and biological endowments, and between the individual and society, as well as to inculcate the instrumental techniques of the culture, particularly the culture's language. The family is the primary agency of the society for nurturing children, for providing the structure necessary for integrating their personalities, and for socializing and enculturating them. Any attempt to understand personality development or maldevelopment independently of the family matrix in which it occurs is bound to err, because such simplifications eliminate essential factors in the process.

The distortions and disorganizations of language and thought that are characteristic of schizophrenic disorders, together with the profound regression of some patients that can lead to an almost vegetative existence, have led investigators to conclude that schizophrenic patients must suffer from a disorder of brain functioning. The strong familial incidence led to a commonly held conviction that the disorder is essentially genetically conveyed. It is reasonable to believe that some children are born with defective physical endowments that eventually lead to deterioration of the brain, to physiological dysfunction of the brain, or to faulty interaction with parental persons that leads more or less inevitably to a psychotic development. The search for anatomical lesions, toxic metabolic products, endocrine abnormalities, vitamin deficiencies, etc., has been pursued vigorously. The findings of an etiologic agent or abnormality have been numerous, but none has been substantiated. It is of interest that at this meeting, in contrast to some previous ones, the fascinating findings concerning how anti-psychotic drugs work have properly not been considered synonymous with uncovering the cause of schizophrenia. As it has become apparent that schizophrenic patients do not suffer a degradation of intellectual potential, that seriously delusional patients may, under proper circumstances, carry out highly complicated intellectual functions, that patients need not become deteriorated, and that many patients improve greatly over time with or without treatment, pathophysiological theories have been modified to hypothesize that something goes awry neurophysiologically when the patient is under stress—the reticular activating system no longer filters stimuli adequately because of the secretion of an abnormal metabolite, or because of the excessive secretion or diminished depletion of a neurotransmitter, etc. Such posited abnormalities may be genetic, may result from some acquired metabolic imbalance, or they may even be a consequence of severe emotional disturbance rather than a cause of it. However, the familial incidence, heightened by Kallmann's (2A) erroneous report of an 86 percent concordance rate in monozygotic twins, led to wide acceptance of the belief that whatever the nature of the physiological disorder that eventually would be uncovered, it would be a disorder that was transmitted genetically.

Starting in the 1940's, a few of us, noting that schizophrenic patients always seemed to emerge from seriously disturbed or distorted family settings, began to study the patients' families of origin. We soon developed hypotheses that could include, but did not require, a genetic factor or a biochemical dysfunction of the brain. Further, inconsistencies were found in the various genetic studies, particularly Kallmann's, that led to greatly improved sampling techniques and to studies that found concordance rates in monozygotic twins between 16 and 40 percent, making it credible that the concordance might be due to familial environmental factors or, at least, that the genetic factor was not of predominant importance. It became plausible that environmental factors, including detrimental intrafamilial influences now apparent to virtually all who studied such families, might have major significance.

These studies of familial environmental factors have now moved beyond hypothesis formation to the development of a coherent theory based on observable data that clarifies essential aspects of the origin and nature of schizophrenic disorders. In the theory I have developed, the introduction of Piagetian concepts of cognitive development to our under-standing of schizophrenic thought disorders has clarified many problems and opened the way for the solution of others; it also has permitted the development of a comprehensive theory based on the observable and ascertainable, rather than on conjecture about unknown genetic and biochemical abnormalities. A theory is not a statement of completed knowledge, but a formulation of underlying principles connecting and explaining observed phenomena; and I believe that sufficient connecting links between phenomena now have been established to enable us to move beyond the hypotheses to theory building.

I shall merely sketch some of the salient features of my theory here because a more complete version can be found in my book *The Origin and Treatment of Schizophrenic Disorders* (5). There are two interrelated aspects to the theory. The first has to do with how the parental personalities and the transactions within the family prevent a child from differentiating adequately from the mother, separating from the family, and gain-ing a sufficiently coherent integration to achieve an ego identity, a capacity for intimacy, and the ability to become reasonably self-sufficient by the end of adolescence. The second has to do with the development of the cognitive disorder that forms the critical attribute of the category of mental disorders we designate as schizophrenic.

The families in which schizophrenic patients grow up do not provide a proper developmental milieu for many reasons. My colleagues and I have considered schizophrenic disorders to be deficiency diseases, that is, a deficiency due to the family's inability to provide adequate nurturance, structuring, socialization, and enculturation for the developing child (7). However, I now believe that more specific distorting influences can be isolated. We have tended to divide these families into *schismatic* families in which the two parents are in abiding conflict, undercutting the worth of the other to the child, and the child is not only used to complete a parent's life and salvage the marriage but his psychic structure is torn apart by the internalization of two irrecon-cilable parents; and *skewed* families in which one parent, usually the mother, does not establish boundaries between herself and the child, uses the child to complete her life, and continues to be extremely intrusive into the child's life though impervious to the child's needs and feelings as a separate individual, behavior not countered by a passive spouse, etc.

Both types of families have certain characteristics in common: the use of the child to complete a parent's life or maintain the parents' marriage, which keeps the child from directing his energies and attention for his own development; the inability of one or both parents to appreciate that others, particularly family members, are separate individuals, interfering with the child's development of self-boundaries; the failure of the parent of the same sex as the child to provide an acceptable model for identification, together with the undercutting of that parent's worth by the spouse; the disruption of boundaries between the generations; the parents' confusions in their gender-linked roles; the feel-ings of emptiness or hopelessness about life conveyed by one or both parents; the distor-tion of perceptions, feelings, and meanings to preserve a parent's tenuous emotional equilibrium; and other disturbances in verbal and non-verbal communication that per-vade the family transactions.

It now appears firmly established that although an insufficient cause in itself, a child will rarely, if ever, become schizophrenic unless the intrafamilial communication is markedly disordered. My colleagues and I described how the child's perception of events and feelings is distorted or invalidated to fit the parents' distortions or feel rejected (6); Bateson, Jackson et al. (1) described the double-bind; Laing (3), the process of mystification; Searles (9), the efforts to drive the other crazy; Wynne and Singer (10), the amorphous and fragmented styles of communication.

The schizophrenic patient's thought disorder has been described and defined in a variety of ways. Eugen Bleuler described it as a derailment of associations. Various investigators have considered the same phenomena to be manifestations of deficiencies in forming or maintaining categories; and I have emphasized that category formation serves as a means of filtering out extraneous associations (4). The designation of schizophrenic thinking as "overinclusive" is a highly useful way of describing what happens with the breakdown in categorization. What has been overlooked is that the over-inclusiveness is primarily *egocentric* in Piaget's usage of the term "egocentric." The patient typically believes that what others do and say centers on him, as in delusions of reference or persecutory delusional systems; or he believes that his thoughts influence others and even the inanimate universe. Stated in such terms, we find ourselves in a familiar area for Piaget has pointed out that the preoperational child is egocentrically unable to realize that "experience contains fortuitous occurrences" and is likely to believe that anything which happens is done to affect him or results from his wishes or feelings. Category formation must remain limited and defective if the self intrudes into all categories.

Now, many of the characteristics that have commonly been observed in parents of schizophrenics can be considered as manifestations of profound egocentricity; the intrusiveness into the child's life but imperviousness to the child's feelings; the inability to differentiate their own needs and feelings from their child's, or to grasp that the child views the situation differently than they do; the use of the child as an adjunct to their own lives—in general, the inability to form boundaries between the self and the child. The egocentric parent, thus, cannot properly accommodate to the child's needs but requires the immature child to fit into the parent's needs and orientation. The egocentricities of the parent and child are reciprocal in many respects but the child is more sensitive to the needs of others as he has always had to accommodate to the parent's needs and ways of perceiving; and he gains direction not from his own impulses, desires, and plans, but from noting the feelings and moods of others. The patient comes to know that he can affect his parents profoundly by his own thoughts and feelings. In a sense the patient becomes more parent-centered then egocentric, but his feelings of being central to his parents' lives lead to feelings of being central and important to everyone but also of being controlled by others.

Now, when we translate various clinical observations of schizophrenic patients into a Piagetian frame of reference, many facets of the puzzle fall into place. A basic problem of schizophrenic patients is found in their poor self-boundaries; the failure to differentiate properly between the self and others, and between what arises within the self and what is outside the self. This failure is characteristic of the egocentricity of the sensori-motor period which infants overcome as they establish object constancy and differentiate from the mother. The schizophrenic patients, however, have not remained fixated at this primitive level of cognitive development though they may never have fully surmounted it.

We must comprehend the later types of cognition that Piaget has described to examine how the cognitive regressions typical of schizophrenic disorders occur. Egocentrism, for Piaget, means both the overevaluation of cognitive means of producing change and also the distortion of reality to satisfy the needs of the individual. Egocentrism increases each time the developmental process brings the child into a new and untried field of cognitive action and slowly subsides as the child masters the new field, only to reappear as the child again moves into a new stage of development. At first, preoperational children do not differentiate fantasy from reality or words from the objects they designate. They believe that inanimate objects have wills of their own, that parental figures control natural events, that their own thoughts affect nature. These are all ideas which we commonly encounter in schizophrenic patients. Children gradually overcome such notions and at this time move into the stage of concrete operations when new egocentric distortions arise. At first they do not grasp that persons in a different place from the self do not have the same view of an object as they do, and must still overcome the misunderstandings which arise because they cannot really grasp the fact that other persons have different points of view. As we study schizophrenic communications, we note the vagaries which arise because patients do not realize that they must orient others to what they are thinking and talking about. However, it is the egocentricity which arises early in adolescence that seems particularly pertinent to schizophrenic states.

Commonly, schizophrenic patients move into mid- or late adolescence before regressing cognitively as well as emotionally. They reach the developmental period when they are confronted by such psychosocial tasks as achieving independence from the parental family, a life plan, an ego identity, and a capacity for intimacy. These are tasks which trouble all adolescents but are particularly difficult for those who become schizophrenic because of the intrafamilial impediments to their development. Such obstacles include the limitations of extrafamilial socialization commonly found in schizophrenic persons brought about by the various peculiarities and fears of their parents.

Adolescents also undergo a major transformation which has been disregarded in psychodynamic developmental theories. They enter the stage of formal operations. They become capable of conceptualizing, of thinking reflectively, of thinking about thinking. Instead of simply proceeding from the real to the possible as they did previously, they can now plan from the possible to the real, and in so doing may never return from the mental realm of the possible. It is an expansive period of hopes and dreams which, at first, is untempered by the need to prove the feasibility of an ideal, or go through the tangible stages of convincing others and the laborious measures required to bring a plan to realization. It is, as Inhelder and Piaget (2) state, "a phase in which the adolescent attributes an unlimited power to his own thoughts so that the dream of a glorious future or of transforming the world through ideas . . . seems to be not only fantasy but also an effective action which in itself modifies the empirical world." Often it takes years to overcome this egocentricity and to recognize that thinking things out for oneself is very different from convincing others and from working them out in the real world. It is a characteristic of youth to formulate plans mentally and go on to construct imagined brilliant outcomes, but the ability to do so contains a trap into which the vulnerable may fall. The egocentric aspects of formal operations are overcome through increasing socialization, which brings the youth in contact with persons of different orientations and forces a reevaluation of his own concepts. They are also affected by undertaking a real job in which accomplishment counts more than imagined results, and by relating intimately to another person who has different habits, ideas, and beliefs.

Often the first indications that a youth may be in danger of becoming schizophrenic come when he cannot find a path into adulthood, goals fail to jell and instead become more diffuse and he remains in the realm of fantasied achievements. Of course, not all such ego diffusions of adolescence have a schizophrenic outcome, but for some the difficulties in socializing limit the necessary decentering, and confusions of sexual identity as well as other impediments to personality integration that result from growing up in a disturbed and confusing home now block the development of a coherent ego identity and the crucial emergence of an adult.

As part of his inability to move through adolescence, the youth who becomes schizophrenic fails to decenter cognitively. Feeling hopeless about the future and permeated by despair of ever becoming a person in his own right, or terrified at responsibilities he cannot assume, the youth develops more elaborate fantasy solutions and regresses cognitively as well as emotionally. Poorly grounded in reality testing and with tenuous boundaries between the self and others, he finds a way out of his real developmental dilemma by falling back to childhood forms of egocentric cognition. All egocentrism, whatever the specific type and from whatever stage of development, is bound together by the common characteristic of reliance on the "omnipotence of thought"—an unconscious belief in the efficacy of thought. Desperately seeking for meaning which seems hidden to him but obvious to others, and for direction which he cannot find, everything takes on heightened relevance and becomes personally meaningful. Unable to direct the self, he passively seeks direction from others or from supernatural powers through interpreting signs and references; and he comes to believe that his life is being directed or influenced by others. The patient finds himself affected by every fortuitous occurrence as he again believes himself central to all that happens. He can again give precedence to fantasy over reality, to belief in animism and in the efficacy of the magic of the wish.

To some degree, he will regress even more profoundly and, like the early preoedipal child, confuse the self and non-self, and what arises within him and what comes from outside of him. The results are far-reaching and devastating. Categorizations he had developed are now seriously impaired, and with the loss of the filtering function of categories, inappropriate associations intrude and derail his thought and communication. Thinking becomes syncretic and metonymic which in itself permits him to connect everything with everything and to justify further his egocentric distortions.

With this disruption of categorical thinking another source of schizophrenic thought breaks through. In order to understand the importance of category formation in thought and communication as well as the function of categories in filtering out the extraneous, we must understand that a person's experience unfolds in a ceaseless flow and in order to perceive, understand, and think about experiences they must be devided into categories. Experience, we may say, is continuous, whereas categories are discrete. There are innumerable ways of categorizing experiences and each culture does so differently; and to some degree all persons categorize slightly differently depending upon their education and experiences. To form categories, boundaries or hiatuses are established by repressing what lies between them. In particular, taboos are placed on material that would obliterate fundamental categories such as between the self and non-self upon which all further categorization rests, on such matters as fusion between child and mother, on fantasies of fusion in incest, and similarly of what might blur the basic categories of male and female—such as homosexuality and transvestite behavior. It is in such areas—the differentiation between self and non-self, parent and child, and maleness and femaleness, that parents of schizophrenic patients are particularly deficient. Further, proper categorization rests upon establishing and maintaining "object constancy." The relationship between object constancy and category formation is a complex matter that I shall not discuss here.

With this breakdown in category formation, schizophrenic persons because of the faulty repression in their early years may become preoccupied with material that lies between categories, and with fantasies of fusions of self and a mothering figure, with "polymorphous perverse" fantasies confusing genitals and other orifices, with cannibalistic impulses, with delusions of changing sex and other such matters that are usually eliminated from awareness very early in life and for which no clear categories even exist. It is in this *intercategorical realm*, preoccupied with such material, that some schizophrenics spend much of their time: fantasying and yet fearing their incestuous and devouring impulses, their desires to fuse with others, change sex, reenter the womb, etc. Still, no matter how profound the regression, the schizophrenic is not a child and much of what he has acquired remains available to him. The retained capacities explain the patchiness and shifting character of the thought disorder, and why such persons can continue to function well in some areas and under certain conditions.

I shall not here seek to account for the entire range of thought disorders. It is apparent that paranoid delusions and hallucinations are also concerned with boundary problems, the search for direction as well as control from others, and egocentric cognition. When the situation is no longer acute, the schizophrenic can often think competently except in areas that create emotional turmoil or at times of stress and decision. In chronic patients (8) the use of defensive cognitive styles such as evasive ambiguity or constrictive literality may overshadow all other cognitive disturbances.

In this brief sketch I have not entered upon all of the ramifications of the theory, or upon all that it can explain, but I believe sufficiently to indicate how it brings coherence to the basic phenomenology of schizophrenic disorders together with the findings of family studies about the patient's developmental settings. It permits us to understand the various gradations of severity and chronicity and the admixtures of manifestations with affective, hypochondriacal, sociopathic, and obsessive disorders. It becomes apparent that some individuals will become psychotic at an early age and become chronic because they have never achieved any semblance of integration as an independent person, whereas others regress after attaining some more mature personality capabilities and cognitive functioning and are not as seriously or, necessarily, as permanently impaired. Further, if we understand that many of the various disturbances of cognition commonly observed in schizophrenic patients are regressions of various types of egocentric cognition found in all children and adolescents, we need not believe that they are caused by some brain dysfunction and may even realize that, perhaps, they cannot be; but rather result from gross disturbances in personality development that derive from growing up in a particular type of disturbed family setting in which there are serious communicative disturbances.

REFERENCES

1. Bateson G, Jackson D, et al: Toward a theory of schizophrenia. *Behav Sci* 1:251–264, 1956.

2. Inhelder B, Piaget J: *The Growth of Logical Thinking from Childhood to Adolescence.* New York, Basic Books, 1958.

2A. Kallmann FJ: The genetic theory of schizophrenia: An analysis of 691 schizophrenic twin index families. *Amer J Psychiat* 103:309–322, 1946.

3. Laing R: *The Self and Others: Further Studies in Sanity and Madness.* London, Tavistock Publications, 1962.

4. Lidz T: The family, language, and the transmission of schizophrenia, in Rosenthal D, Kety S (eds): *The Transmission of Schizophrenia*. Oxford, Pergamon Press, 1968.

5. Lidz T: *The Origin and Treatment of Schizophrenic Disorders*. New York, Basic Books, 1973.

6. Lidz T, Cornelison A, Terry D, et al: The transmission of irrationality (1958) in Lidz T, Fleck S, Cornelison A: *Schizophrenia and the Family*. New York, International Universities Press, 1965.

7. Lidz T, Fleck S: Family studies and a theory of schizophrenia (1964), in Lidz T, Fleck S, Cornelison A: *Schizophrenia and the Family*. New York, International Universities Press, 1965.

8. Lorenz M: Criticism as approach to schizophrenic language. *Arch Gen Psychiat* 9:235–245, 1963.

9. Searles HF: The effort to drive the other person crazy: An element in the aetiology and psychotherapy of schizophrenia. *Brit J Med Psychol* 32:1–18, 1959.

10. Wynne LC, Singer MT: Thought disorder and family relations of schizophrenics: II. A classification of forms of thinking. *Arch Gen Psychiat* 9:191–206, 1963.

CONCLUDING COMMENTS
Lyman C. Wynne, M.D., Ph.D.

A developmental point of view usefully can be applied to delineate three major questions about the family relationships of schizophrenics: (a) What are the *current characteristics* of the family context of schizophrenics after a family member already has been diagnosed as having a disorder? (b) What are the *precursors* in family communication and family patterns and relationships of later schizophrenic illness of a family member? (c) What aspects of family communication patterns have *consequences* for later course and outcome of schizophrenic illness?

CURRENT FAMILY CHARACTERISTICS

Complementarity in Family Relationships
The papers in this Section on Family Relationships and Communication make a definite shift in perspective from the traditional orientation to schizophrenic symptoms and schizophrenic persons. Terms such as "thought disorder," "language disorder," "attentional disorder," "affect disorder," and "allusive thinking" (1) focus on intra-individual or intrapsychic aspects of the person, or on the hypothesized disorder or disease within the person. Actually—and this point often is ignored—these concepts are abstracted or extracted from behavior *in interaction* with an interviewer, tester, family member, or other person (minimally in a setting provided or observed by another person). As Harry Stack Sullivan pointed out, interpersonal, not intrapersonal, behavior is the explicit and empirical starting point for clinical interviews and diagnosis. Although the studies in the 1950s of the families of schizophrenics relied on retrospective and indirect attitudinal reports, the main emphasis on empirical family research for over a decade has been to study interpersonal behavior directly, through observation and usually taperecordings of samples.

In family studies, an additional concept of great importance is the complementarity that develops between persons who have repeated, patterned relationships with one another. Complementarity means that the communication patterns and other behavior of individual family members will mesh with one another in predictable forms, and that the behavioral manifestations of the individuals will predictably differ from one another. Taking this perspective, family researchers have asked: Can we learn about the current function of schizophrenic behavior, regardless of origins or causes, by examining the family context of such behavior in more detail? Given the presence of a family member with "schizophrenic" behavior, what communication patterns of other family members are complementary to that of the schizophrenic member?

Parental communication deviance (2, 3, and Chapters 45–46) is a concept that was developed through application of this formulation of complementarity within family systems. A synonym of communication deviance, "transactional style deviance" (4–6), as well as terms such as "emotional overinvolvement" and "expressed emotion" (7–9), "parental egocentricity" (10 and Chapter 49), and "delegation" and "binding" (11 and Chapter 48) all implicitly make use of the notion of complementarity. These terms all

534

describe not the schizophrenic but other family members who have interacted repeatedly with the identified patient. Although parents and offspring share participation in the same family system, such "sharing" does *not* imply that the individual family members have the same roles, behavior, or experiences. Rather, the roles and behavior of individual family members are hypothesized explicitly by family theorists to differ from one another because role complementarity and reciprocity within social systems are necessary for the integration of any enduring interpersonal relationship. Therefore, the methods and criteria for assessing the behaviors of *non*schizophrenic family members need to differ from the methods for assessing symptomatology of schizophrenics or potential schizophrenics. What is conceptually important about this point is the hypothesis, now partially confirmed, that these differences between family members are not random but are systematic and are predictable from psychosocial principles, but would not be deduced from hypotheses of genetic similarities.

Complementarity between family members has been studied with a measure of parental communication deviance, as reported in Chapter 46. Categories of these deviances were selected because of their hypothesized linkage to the "thought disorders" of diagnosed schizophrenic family members (3, 12, 13). To test this hypothesis, Wynne, Singer, and Toohey (2) predicted and confirmed that schizophrenic offspring should have *fewer* "communication deviances" than their nonschizophrenic parents, even though these offspring-patients clearly showed more evidence of traditional measures of schizophrenic thought disorder and characteristic delusions.

In the communication deviance categories (see Table 46-1), some of the categories have the impact of involving ("holding") the listener by offering an idea that is simultaneously but unclearly disqualified while other categories identify derogatory, disparaging, and critical remarks. Thus, the components of communication deviance appear to be conceptually similar to the "expressed emotion," "emotional overinvolvement" and "critical, hostile comments" by key relatives studied by Brown and his colleagues (7–9) with a different research method. Lidz also has emphasized the concepts of emotional overinvolvement and reciprocity between schizophrenics and their parents. This point is exemplified in his observation that the cognitive egocentricities of the parent and the schizophrenic offspring are reciprocal and differ in many respects. While parental egocentricity serves to protect his or her emotional balance, this leaves the patient vulnerable because he is oriented to the parent's needs rather than to investing his energies and attention in his own development (10). Stierlin's concept of "binding" (11) also has many of the qualities of emotional overinvolvement, but his concept of "delegation" from parent to offspring is a more complex psychological process that may continue despite physical separation.

Methodological Advances and Pitfalls

In this volume and in the literature at the present time, there still is an inadequate appreciation of the multiplicity of empirical techniques available for studying family interaction and communication. Riskin and Faunce (12) made a valuable and comprehensive review of these methods in 1972. Subsequently, other methods have proliferated (e.g., 13–15), especially in the high-risk research programs that emphasize family interaction methods at UCLA and Rochester (see Chapters 44–46). (Much of this work has been prepared for doctoral dissertations and is not yet available in general publications.)

Most importantly, evidence is accumulating for the validation of communication deviance as a broad construct with several major components (see Chapters 45–46). For example, acknowledgment, the interpersonal process that occurs when a person is responded to in a relevant manner, is conceptually a component of communication deviance. Lack of acknowledgment in family communication is most easily assessed by studying family interaction directly without an interviewer present, as in the consensus Family Rorschach (16). Other forms of communication deviances that first were studied in individual parental Rorschachs also are found in parental Thematic Apperception Tests (TAT) (5). Herman and Jones found that in families with lack of acknowledgment in the Family Rorschach, the parents showed a high frequency of communication deviances in their individual TATs (17).

Hopefully, such studies will soon correct a common misconception expressed by Hirsch and Leff (18), who had concluded that the individual Rorschach was the only "adequate" method available for studying communication deviance in parents (18, p 170). Actually, a variety of procedures for studying family communication, including interaction directly between family members in the absence of an interviewer, have been in use since 1963 (12,16,19).

In correspondence contributing to this discussion, Seymour Kety raised the question of whether parental communication sampled by individual Rorschach testing is characteristic of interaction in a "natural" setting. Inferences about this issue can be drawn from comparisons of family interaction obtained using different tasks, especially in the absence of an interviewer. The study by Herman and Jones (17) is one such comparison.

Additionally, external criteria, such as independent measures of child behavior in the school, can be used to validate whether the communication indices are meaningful, though what is "natural" is a more dubious and elusive notion. Using data from the Rochester high-risk sample of families, Doane (20) has found that parental communication deviance measured in the Consensus Rorschach with the whole family significantly predicts levels of social and cognitive competence in 7- and 10-year-old male offspring. Individual mother (not father) Rorschachs also predict significantly but less well to competence levels of offspring. In terms of family systems theory, the superiority of predictions derived from samples of the more "natural" direct communication of parents and children with one another, rather than with a tester, makes conceptual sense and underlines the point that the individual Rorschach is not the only or the optimal procedure for assessing communication deviance.

Partly as an accident of history, individual Rorschach protocols were readily accessible at the time of the early efforts to define the communication deviance concept operationally for empirical research and to facilitate progress from the provocative but untestable clinical formulations of the 1950s. The method had the advantage of eliciting communication beginning with standard stimuli *if* standard instructions and comments also are used by the testers. However, most Rorschach testers are not research-oriented and do not use a standardized, limited set of questions, nor do they use the transactional frame of reference, in which the tester explicitly is part of the interchange that is essential in the study of communication deviance (21). The most crucial portion of the individual Rorschach for the elicitation of communication deviances clearly is the Inquiry ("explaining") portion in which dialogue between tester and subject must occur; when properly administered, the Inquiry portion of the Rorschach elicits greater intergroup differences between parents than does the Initial Viewing ("naming") portion.

However, standardization in the method of administering the Inquiry for research purposes, and in scoring the protocols, is more complex and difficult to learn than Singer and Wynne originally realized. The difficulties became apparent in the study by Hirsch and

Leff that is discussed by Rutter in Chapter 47. As Singer and Wynne have found with other inexperienced testers using the Rorschach technique for this research purpose, Hirsch did not contribute to the Inquiry dialogue with an appropriate and standardized quality and amount of questioning. Subsequent experience and data analysis have shown that a far more rigorous training program in the technique of test administration is needed to achieve standardization.

After Hirsch obtained highly nonstandard protocols, especially in the Inquiry portion, for the first half of his sample, he was advised to change technique for the second half. Unfortunately, his second method was still nonstandard though now in a different way. Rutter (see Chapter 47) was persuaded to give credence to the Hirsch-Leff data because he noted that the second technique left unchanged a quantitative intergroup difference between the parents of the schizophrenics and the neurotics, even though the total quantitative levels had grossly changed. More importantly, the distribution of deviance categories in both groups changed radically from that obtained in the first half and also differed grossly from any of the numerous samples of parents tested and scored with this method before and since. Because these basic data from the Inquiry in Hirsch's protocols are not comparable with data from other studies, Wynne, in commenting on Rutter's paper, expressed the view that a sound scientific stance would be to refrain from drawing substantive conclusions from the Hirsch-Leff report and to use the study for identifying methodologic pitfalls that are avoided in current research at UCLA and Rochester.

Situational Anxiety and Communication Deviance

Kety raised another methodologic question—whether the parental communication deviances in the Rorschach study of adoptive parents of schizophrenics (see Chapter 46) may have been a situational consequence of "test anxiety" that may result from testing parents in a clinical setting where they might have believed their parenting of a disturbed offspring was being criticized. He cited a study by Schopler and Loftin (22) in which Object Sorting Test (OST) performance was compared for parents who had been interviewed about their normal child and parents who had been interviewed about their psychotic child (mean age, 7 years). Anxiety clearly does affect certain kinds of test performance.

However, the evidence is weak that parental communicative deviance is induced because of test anxiety. First, the Schopler-Loftin study did not assess communication deviance in the OST but, rather, concept formation, using Lovibond's scoring method (23). Wild et al (24), in 1965, showed that the Lovibond scoring criteria are much less adequate for differentiating parents of young adult schizophrenics from other parents than is the method of scoring communication deviances adapted from the Rorschach by Singer and Wild for use with verbatim OST records.

Second, applying a direct measure of anxiety developed by DeVos and Singer (25) to the Rorschach protocols obtained in the adoptive study (26) discussed by Kety, the parents of adoptive schizophrenics and biologic schizophrenics did not differ in anxiety levels. These same Rorschach protocols, when scored with the communication deviance measure, differentiated both the parents of the adoptive and biologic schizophrenics from the parents of the adoptive normals (see Chapter 46). Although a minority of parents in each group was anxious (but not differently for the adoptive and biologic schizophrenic groups), the anxiety levels were not correlated with the communication deviance scores of the same parents.

Third, parents of nonschizophrenic, seriously neurotic psychiatric patients have been studied with the Rorschach communication deviance measure (2). Compared with parents of matched normal offspring, these parents, who had every reason to be anxious about their hospitalized offspring, did not have increased frequencies of communication deviance scores compared to the parents of the normal control group (see Figure 46-1).

Fourth, preliminary data using the multiple family interaction techniques in the Rochester high-risk research program, in which a parent (not an offspring) in each family has had a hospitalized psychiatric illness, we have been impressed that most of these parents do *not* show a high frequency of communication deviances (and by that criterion have offspring at low risk, not high risk, for later schizophrenia). All of these parents could have been expected to show considerable "situational anxiety" as the result of the research study conducted in the hospital where they themselves had been inpatients. As documented elsewhere (2), communication deviance and symptomatic psychopathology can be separated out as variables in family research.

Diagnostic Differences

An issue relevant to future research was raised by Rutter concerning the possible effects of diagnostic differences in sampling patients in family studies. The problems here were similar to those raised later in Section XIII on Diagnostic and Conceptual Issues. Rutter suggested that Goldstein's family communication measures needed to be related to "specific diagnoses, using reliable and valid diagnostic tools," and that some patients diagnosed as schizophrenic by Wynne would be "given some other diagnoses in the UK." Both Goldstein and Wynne objected to these generalizations about their research diagnoses, made by Rutter on the basis of studies of US-UK clinical practices by others. For their research purposes, neither Goldstein nor Wynne had relied on hospital or clinic record diagnoses. Instead, they had used stringent research criteria and, in recent years, the same kind of standard diagnostic interview schedules that are used in London.

Contrary to Rutter's impression, Wynne pointed out that the schizophrenics in the NIMH sample did not include patients who lacked current or historical evidence of characteristic delusions or hallucinations and who merely had "severe and serious personality disorganization termed schizophrenia in the US" but not in the UK. Patients with serious schizoid and paranoid personality disorders, but not having a history of "characteristic" florid schizophrenic symptoms, were given nonschizophrenic research diagnoses at the severity level of 4 ("borderline") in the US study. The "nonremitting schizophrenics," severity level of 7, in the US sample were all chronic hebephrenic and paranoid schizophrenics, a diagnostic group that was not included in the UK sample. Rutter surmised that such patients would be most likely to have parents with high frequencies of communication deviances. However, the data reported by Wynne et al (2) and summarized by Singer in Chapter 46, showed no significant differences between the parents of remitting and nonremitting schizophrenics. The parents of the nonremitting schizophrenics did show significantly more severe *clinical* symptomatology, suggesting to Wynne and Singer that parental psychopathology and communication deviance may interact to produce offspring who appear to have so-called "process" features.

Quite apart from the problems of Rorschach methodology discussed above, Wynne agreed with Rutter that comparison of the US and UK samples is difficult because of differences in sampling and diagnostic assessments.

PRECURSORS OF SCHIZOPHRENIA IN FAMILY RELATIONSHIPS

Although methodologic studies of *current* family relationships are still needed, interest shifted, when the high-risk research approach became established, to the study of family relationships *prior* to the onset of schizophrenic disorder. The pioneering risk research by Mednick and Schulsinger (27) indicated that a significant factor contributing to later psychopathology in children at high risk for schizophrenia is the family relationship variable of separation. The first prospective study in which parental communication deviance was defined as a risk variable in the absence of parental schizophrenia is the important work of Goldstein and his colleagues (see Chapter 45).

In discussing the findings of high communication deviance in adoptive parents of schizophrenics (28), Kety stressed the hypothesis that the deviant parental communication patterns could be the result of having reared a schizophrenic offspring rather than being an etiologic factor in the development of schizophrenia. A choice between these alternative hypotheses cannot be made conclusively from data first obtained after the schizophrenic illness has developed, even in adoptive samples. Rather, evidence such as that from UCLA and from other prospective studies, such as those in Rochester and St. Louis, are needed to assess more fully the important question of direction of effects. However, this is not, strictly speaking, an etiologic issue in the sense of "ultimate," specific causal factors. Nevertheless, data about family relationships that could be of great importance for planning early treatment and prevention will come from the study of intermediate outcomes.

From this standpoint, Wynne has described family communication variables not as etiologic but as intermediate between genetic endowment and symptoms, and perhaps formative and contributory to acquired vulnerability (2, 29, and Chapter 61). Thus, a modest and practical goal for family studies at this time is to clarify the chain of sequential changes that occur developmentally and lead to schizophrenic outcomes.

Study of developmental precursors of *positive*, healthy outcomes that come about despite the presence of risk factors for schizophrenia too often are overlooked during the zealous search for antecedents of psychopathology. Statistically, about 90% of the offspring of a schizophrenic parent do not develop schizophrenia. What are the "protective" or "corrective" factors in their genes, in their family relationships, or in their broader cultural context? Wynne et al (2) have noted that if one parent with serious individual communication deviance problems has a spouse with positive, corrective features, the offspring may have minor psychiatric problems but rarely will develop typical schizophrenia. In Chapter 2, Kety reports data with similar implications, that intrafamilial environmental variables may modify the severity of illness, from "chronic" to "latent" or "uncertain" subtypes.

CONSEQUENCES OF FAMILY RELATIONSHIPS FOR OUTCOME

Most of the work on the consequences of family relationships for later course and outcome of schizophrenic episodes has been clinical. Some clinicians have acted on the assumption that the difficult relationships within the families cannot be altered and that keeping the patient apart from the family (at least physically) will be therapeutic. Many families, however, are emotionally embroiled and cannot readily disengage. In addition, nearly all families of schizophrenics before they become entrenched in positions of despair and recrimination, have valuable potentialities and often deep loyalties or wishes to aid one another, despite their difficulties in doing so.

Family therapy was introduced to assist and guide families in drawing upon their capacities to rally and to grow despite liabilities that may co-exist in individual family members and in the family as a social unit (30). Unfortunately, some families, and even some poorly trained or uninformed psychiatrists, sometimes have construed or allowed family therapy to become a setting for continuation of the blaming that often is associated with the onset of any poorly understood or frightening illness. In contrast, competent family therapists set as their first task the reduction of doubt and self-blame that many, if not most, families bring to the clinic or hospital. Guidance in restructuring family relationships and communication must be implemented through providing clear and feasible tasks for the family members to carry out with one another in a reciprocally supportive manner. Interpretations by the therapist of psychodynamic "insights" are apt to be more confusing than useful for these families. Social skill building and integration with other treatment programs, including medication, often is indicated.

Regretably, very little longitudinal research has been carried out thus far to provide underpinnings for these clinical observations in therapy with the families of schizophrenics. However, very promising results have been obtained in one series of studies in which George Brown et al (7,8) and Vaughn and Leff (9) have shown that the variables of "expressed emotion"—emotional overinvolvement, hostility, and critical comments—by key relatives about newly admitted schizophrenics predict to their status at the time of nine-month follow-up. Interestingly, not the psychotic symptoms, but other more enduring attributes of the patient seem to be the focus of the criticism that is associated with later relapse. Earlier in my discussion of current family characteristics, I suggested that "expressed emotion" descriptively is a component of communication deviance, which clearly includes both affective and cognitive factors (see Chapter 46). However, empirical research combining Brown's method with other measures in treatment-oriented research has not yet been carried out. Although the studies of expressed emotion have considerable importance for understanding the contributions of family relationships to the course of schizophrenic disorders, one should beware of transposing these findings to an etiologic or precursor model.

FUTURE DIRECTIONS

The need is obvious for continuation and expansion of research in which family interaction variables are incorporated into high-risk studies of the precursors and treatment studies of the consequences of schizophrenic illness. Reliance on single measures of such a complex area as family relationships seems foolhardy and apt to be misleading. Several major classes of methods and variables that hypothetically are directly relevant to family interaction should be included in future studies of the families of schizophrenics:

(a) Improved *genetic data* providing pedigrees of mental illness, preferably combined with genetic marker studies as soon as feasible, should be obtained from the same families that are studied with communication methods. When endophenotypic indicators of genetic vulnerability are combined with direct measures of family communication, then the beginnings of true gene-environment interaction effects at the family level will become a reality.

(b) *Standardized diagnostic procedures* with each family member need to be utilized in studies of family communication in order to extend the observations reported here about the degree to which psychopathology and communication deviance may or may not be linked to each other. More than traditional labels are required. Clarification of criteria and multiple axes are especially needed for the assessment of those nonhospitalized, often untreated, relatives of schizophrenics who infrequently are seen in ordinary practice, but who are seen in systematic family research, whether the research is oriented to genetics or to the family interactional context. Such family members, even in "blind" assessments, often end up with "spectrum" and "borderline" diagnoses that satisfy almost no one. For example, in the Conference discussion, the same point, that firm conclusions cannot be drawn when one makes "schizophrenic spectrum" diagnoses, was made by Rutter in questioning Goldstein's family interaction data, and by Lidz in challenging Kety's adoption data (31).

(c) Better measures of individual *premorbid adjustment* (32) need to be introduced in order to assess how these fit into the picture of the developmental unfolding of family patterns.

(d) Psychophysiologic and linguistic studies of *attentional* functions need to be linked to measures of communicational disorders. Even though, as this volume has documented, attention is a primary ingredient of communication, especially in schizophrenic communication, explicit studies linking the methods and concepts of attention and communication still are lacking.

(e) *Cultural and epidemiologic* studies of the family context are still infrequent. The next Section of this volume is concerned with these approaches. In the discussion, Kenneth Kidd stressed the importance, as in Murphy's work (see Chapter 52) of controlling for genetic variation by considering the same ethnic groups in different cultural situations. Social class variables probably have been underemphasized in these papers, both in their own right and as a context for family variables. The hypotheses on social class in relation to schizophrenia, proposed by Kohn (33), remain to be assessed.

REFERENCES

1. McConaghy N: The use of an Object Sorting Test in elucidating the hereditary factor in schizophrenia. *J Neurol Neurosurg Psychiat* 22, 243–246, 1959.

2. Wynne LC, Singer MT, Bartko JJ, et al: Schizophrenics and their families: Recent research on parental communication, in Tanner JM (ed): *Developments in Psychiatric Research.* London, Hodden & Stoughton, 1977, pp 254–286.

3. Singer MT, Wynne LC: Principles for scoring communication deviances in parents of schizophrenics: Rorschach and TAT scoring manuals. *Psychiat* 29, 260–288, 1966.

4. Jones JE, Rodnick E, Goldstein M, et al: Parental transactional style deviance in families of disturbed adolescents as an indicator of risk schizophrenia. *Arch Gen Psychiat* 34, 71–74, 1977.

5. Jones JE: Patterns of transactional style deviance in the TAT's of parents of schizophrenics. *Fam Proc* 16, 327–337, 1977.

6. Wild CM, Shapiro LN, Goldenberg L: Transactional communication disturbances in families of male schizophrenics. *Fam Proc* 14, 131–160, 1975.

7. Brown GW, Monck EM, Carstairs GM, et al: Influence of family life on the course of schizophrenic illness. *Brit J Prev Soc Med* 16, 55–68, 1962.

8. Brown GW, Birley JLT, Wing JK: Influence of family life on the course of schizophrenic disorders: A replication. *Brit J Psychiat* 121, 241–258, 1972.

9. Vaughn CE, Leff JP: The influence of family and social factors on the course of psychiatric illness: A comparison of schizophrenic and depressed neurotic patients. *Brit J Psychiat* 129, 125–137, 1976.

10. Lidz T: *The Origin and Treatment of Schizophrenic Disorders.* New York, Basic Books, Inc., Publishers, 1973.

11. Stierlin H: Psychoanalytic approaches to schizophrenia in the light of a family model. *Int Rev Psychoanal* 1, 169–178, 1974.

12. Riskin JM, Faunce EE: An evaluative review of family interaction research. *Fam Proc* 11, 365–455, 1972.

13. Wild CM, Shapiro LN, Abelin T: Communication patterns and role structure in families of male schizophrenics. *Arch Gen Psychiat* 34, 58–70, 1977.

14. Shapiro LN, Wild CM: The product of the consensus Rorschach in families of male schizophrenics. *Fam Proc* 15, 211–224, 1976.

15. Hassan SA: Transactional and contextual invalidation between the parents of disturbed families: A comparative study. *Fam Proc* 13, 53–76, 1974.

16. Loveland NT, Wynne LC, Singer MT: The family Rorschach: A new method for studying family interaction. *Fam Proc* 2, 187–215, 1963.

17. Herman BF, Jones JE: Lack of acknowledgment in the family Rorschachs of families with a child at risk for schizophrenia. *Fam Proc* 15, 289–302, 1976.

18. Hirsch SR, Leff JP: *Abnormalities in Parents of Schizophrenics.* London, Oxford University Press, 1975.

19. Mishler EG, Waxler NE: *Interaction in Families.* New York, John Wiley & Sons, 1968.

20. Doane JA: Parental communication deviance as a predictor of child competence in families with a schizophrenic and nonschizophrenic parent. Doctoral dissertation, Department of Psychology, University of Rochester, Rochester, New York, 1977.

21. Singer MT: The Rorschach as a transaction, in Rickers-Ovsiankina MA (eds): *Rorschach Psychology.* Huntington, New York, Robert E Krieger Publishing Co., 1977, pp 455–485.

22. Schopler E, Loftin J: Thought disorders in parents of psychotic children. *Arch Gen Psychiat* 20, 174–181, 1969.

23. Lovibond S: The Object Sorting Test and conceptual thinking in schizophrenia. *Aust J Psychiat* 5, 52–70, 1954.

24. Wild CM, Singer MT, Rosman B, et al: Measuring disordered styles of thinking: Using the Object Sorting Test on parents of schizophrenic patients. *Arch Gen Psychiat* 13, 471–476, 1965.

25. DeVos G: A quantitative approach to affective symbolism in Roschach responses. *J Proj Tech* 16, 133–150, 1952.

26. Wender PH, Rosenthal D, Kety SS: A psychiatric assessment of the adoptive parents of schizophrenics, in Rosenthal D, Kety SS (eds): *The Transmission of Schizophrenia.* New York, Pergamon Press, 1968, pp 235–250.

27. Mednick SA, Schulsinger H, Schulsinger F: Schizophrenia in children of schizophrenic mothers, in Davids A (ed): *Child Personality and Psychopathology: Current Topics,* vol 2. New York, John Wiley & Sons, 1975, pp 217–252.

28. Wynne LC, Singer MT, Toohey ML: Communication of the adoptive parents of schizophrenics, in Jørstad J, Ugelstad E (eds): *Schizophrenia 75.* Olso, Universitetsforlaget, 1976, pp 413–452.

29. Wynne LC: Family research in the pathogenesis of schizophrenia: Intermediate variables in the study of families at high risk, in Doucet P, Laurin C (eds): *Problems of Psychosis.* Amsterdam, Excerpta Medica, 1971, pp 401–423.

30. Wynne LC: Some guidelines for exploratory conjoint family therapy, in Haley J (ed): *Changing Families.* New York, Grune & Stratton, 1971, pp 96–115.

31. Lidz T: Commentary on "A critical review of recent adoption, twin, and family studies of schizophrenia: Behavioral genetics perspectives. *Schiz Bull* 2, 402–412, 1976.

32. Kokes RF, Strauss JS, Klorman R: Measuring premorbid adjustment: The instruments and their development. *Schiz Bull* 3, 182–213, 1977.

33. Kohn ML: Class, family and schizophrenia: A reformulation. *Social Forces* 50, 295–313, 1972.

EPIDEMIOLOGIC AND SOCIOCULTURAL APPROACHES

Chapter 50
Population Changes and Schizophrenia, 1970–1985

Morton Kramer, Sc.D.

Despite many advances in knowledge about schizophrenia during the past 25 years, bio-statisticians and epidemiologists still experience considerable difficulty in developing reliable and valid estimates of incidence and prevalence rates of this disorder specific for age, sex, race, and various demographic factors for the United States and different countries of the world (1,2). The basic problem that still impedes obtaining such data on schizophrenia is the absence of sensitive and specific case-finding techniques for this disorder that can be applied uniformly within and among countries. Frost (3) stated in his classic essay on epidemiology:

> ... since description of the distribution of any disease in a population obviously requires that the disease must be recognized when it occurs, the development of epidemiology must follow and be limited by that of clinical diagnosis and of the rather complex machinery required for the systematic collection of morbidity statistics and mortality statistics.

Considerable progress has been made in the development of demographic data and of the methods used in the collection, processing, and analysis of morbidity and mortality data. Of particular importance to the mental health field are the advances that have been made in collection, processing, and analysis of national, state, and local data on diagnostic and demographic characteristics of persons who use mental health facilities (4). Indeed, these advances have outdistanced by far progress that has been made in developing techniques for collecting the so-called numerator data required to establish incidence and prevalence rates for schizophrenia in noninstitutional populations, and, for that matter, for all the other mental disorders.

The psychiatric case register of Monroe County, NY, is an outstanding example of data collection at the local level that has considerable importance at the state, national, and even international levels. Work on the register was initiated by Drs. E. M. Gardner, H. C. Miles, and J. Romano. Dr. H. Babigian joined the staff in 1963, and, as a result of his dedicated efforts, has kept the register viable over the years. Dr.

Romano provided strong support for this activity and encouraged the use of register data for administrative and research purposes, and now Dr. Wynne is doing likewise. Financial support for this activity has come from various sources including the State Department of Mental Hygiene, the Monroe County Board of Mental Health, the University of Rochester, and the National Institute of Mental Health.[1]

This register is the only viable data collection operation of its kind and scope in the US which, at this time, provides systematic data on persons with mental disorders in a form that makes it possible to determine incidence and prevalence *like* rates for these disorders. A register makes it possible to obtain unduplicated counts of individuals in addition to the episodes of care experienced by each individual. The reason for adding the adjective *like* to incidence and prevalence rates is that the numerator data are derived from reports from all the facilities that provide psychiatric services to the residents of Monroe County, including private psychiatrists. Such data are still subject to the limitation that they are administrative-type epidemiologic data rather than so-called "true" epidemiologic data that describe how many new cases of a disorder occur in a specified population during a defined interval of time and how many cases of a disorder there are as of a given moment of time or during a given interval of time, whether or not the person with the disorder is under care of a facility that reports to the register (7). Another limitation of register data is that the diagnoses reported to it are dependent on the diagnostic practices and biases of the psychiatrists in the various facilities that report to the register.

On the positive side, the register collates reports on a single individual over time, thus making it possible to develop unduplicated counts of individuals and to relate the episodes of care experienced by an individual within defined periods of time to that individual. Also, the register is population based, i.e., it applies to a clearly defined population group. This makes it possible to determine an unduplicated count of residents of the catchment area who use at least one of the facilities that report to the register. By using this number as a numerator and the population of the catchment area as a denominator, one can then determine the proportion of persons in the catchment area who use a psychiatric facility specific for age, sex, race, socioeconomic status, marital status, and other demographic factors. As a result of this unique property, namely, provision of unduplicated counts of individuals who are members of a defined population base, the register is a source of basic data for answering a variety of questions that cannot be answered by data collected in national and state reporting programs. For the most part, these latter programs provide data on numbers of episodes of care experienced by individuals who use one or more of the facilities in the universe of facilities in the reporting program. Collection of data on the unduplicated number of persons who accounted for the episodes of care is an operation too complex to be carried out on a state-wide or national basis.

Central to the purposes of this paper is a table recently published by Dr. Babigian that provides treated incidence and prevalence rates of schizophrenia for Monroe County for the year 1970 specific for age, sex, and race (8). The numerator of the incidence rate consists of the total unduplicated number of residents of Monroe County (a) who had their first lifetime contact with any psychiatric facility during 1970 (excluding both those previously listed in this register and those who reported that they had had previous ambulatory or inpatient psychiatric contact anywhere else) and (b) who received a

---

[1] Readers interested in the history of the development of the register may consult references 5 and 6.

diagnosis of schizophrenia in the records of the Monroe County register during that year. The numerator of the prevalence rates contains all persons, residents of Monroe County, undergoing treatment during 1970 in the total network of mental health facilities in Monroe County, including hospitalized and nonhospitalized patients. Incidence rate is defined as the number of new cases of diagnosed schizophrenia occurring during that year per 1000 population, and prevalence rate is the number of cases of diagnosed schizophrenia known to have received care during 1970 per 1000 population. These rates will be referred to as treated incidence (T.I.) and treated prevalence (T.P.) to distinguish them from incidence and prevalence rates determined in epidemiologic surveys of the general population of an area (9,10). It is my intention to demonstrate that these T.I. and T.P. data have an importance that transcends the boundaries of this County. They will be viewed against population changes expected in the United States between 1970 and 1985 and will be used to speculate on the numbers of schizophrenics known to US psychiatric facilities in 1970 and on the possible order of magnitude of the number of such persons, by age and race, that might be expected in the US in 1985. These hypothetical estimates have important implications for the planning of services to meet the needs of persons suffering from schizophrenia and the manpower that will be required to do this. But, more than that, they will highlight several major problems that need to be investigated and solved. Hopefully, the results of such research will facilitate the development of the technology needed to collect the basic data required to establish reliable and valid comparative data on the incidence and prevalence of schizophrenia.

POPULATION, INCIDENCE, AND PREVALENCE DATA

The population data that were used as the denominator of the treated incidence and prevalence rates are given in Table 50-1. As of 1970, the population of Monroe County was 711,820. Of this number, 45% were white males; 48% white females; 3% nonwhite males; and 4% nonwhite females. The distribution of these persons by age is given in Table 50-1.

Table 50-1. Distribution of Population by Age, Sex, and Color, Monroe County, NY, 1970 Census[a]

Age (Years)	All Persons	White			Nonwhite		
		Total	Male	Female	Total	Male	Female
All ages	711,820	659,878	318,051	341,827	51,942	24,891	27,051
Under 15	205,588	183,899	94,211	89,688	21,689	10,867	10,822
15–24	121,208	111,694	53,347	58,347	9,514	4,184	5,330
25–34	91,966	83,915	41,404	42,511	8,051	3,692	4,359
35–44	79,884	74,222	36,452	37,770	5,662	2,747	2,915
45–54	82,262	78,670	37,499	41,171	3,592	1,785	1,807
55–64	62,038	60,052	28,339	31,713	1,986	956	1,030
65+	68,874	67,426	26,799	40,627	1,448	660	788

[a] Data in this table are derived from source documents provided by the University of Rochester, School of Medicine and Dentistry, Department of Psychiatry, Division of Community Mental Health and Preventive Psychiatry.

The treated incidence rates were based on 485 new cases of schizophrenia reported to the Monroe County Register in 1970, and the treated prevalence rates are based on 3319 cases under treatment during 1970. The distributions of the new cases and the corresponding T.I. rates by age and sex are given in Table 50-2. Corresponding data for cases under care are given in Table 50-3. The treated incidence and treated prevalence rates are shown in Figure 50-1.

For the white population, the age-adjusted incidence rate for males (0.74 per 1000) is 1.40 times that for females (0.53 per 1000). For the nonwhites, the age-adjusted male rate (1.60 per 1000) is 1.22 times that for females (1.31). The rate for nonwhite males is 2.16 times that for white males, while the rate for nonwhite females is 2.47 times that for white females.

The rates for nonwhites are considerably in excess of those for whites in every age group for both males and females. For each race-sex group the rates are low for persons under 15 years of age. They rise to a maximum in the age group 15–24 years for white males (2.57 per 1000) and for nonwhite males (3.58 per 1000). For females, the rates

Table 50-2. Number of New Cases of Schizophrenia Reported to Register and Treated Incidence Rates per 1000 Population Specific for Age, Sex, and Color, Monroe County 1970[a]

Age (Years)	Total	White			Nonwhite		
		Both Sexes	Male	Female	Both Sexes	Male	Female
Treated Incidence Rates per 1000 Population							
Total	0.72	0.62	0.72	0.54	1.41	1.45	1.37
Age Adj.[b]	0.72	0.63	0.74	0.53	1.44	1.60	1.31
<15	0.08	0.05	0.07	0.03	0.32	0.27	0.37
15–24	1.77	1.68	2.57	0.98	2.73	3.58	2.07
25–34	1.37	1.25	1.21	1.30	2.61	1.89	3.22
35–44	0.74	0.69	0.49	0.88	1.41	1.46	1.37
45–54	0.60	0.52	0.51	0.54	2.23	2.80	1.67
55–64	0.26	0.22	0.18	0.25	1.51	2.10	0.97
65+	0.06	0.06	—	0.09	—	—	—
Number of New Cases							
Total	485	412	230	182	73	36	37
<15	17	10	7	3	7	3	4
15–24	214	188	131	57	26	15	11
25–34	126	105	50	55	21	7	14
35–44	59	51	18	33	8	4	4
45–54	49	41	19	22	8	5	3
55–64	16	13	5	8	3	2	1
65+	4	4	—	4	—	—	—

[a] Recalculated from Babigian HM (8, Table II, p 862).

[b] Population of Monroe County, as enumerated by age, sex, and color in 1970 Census is used as standard.

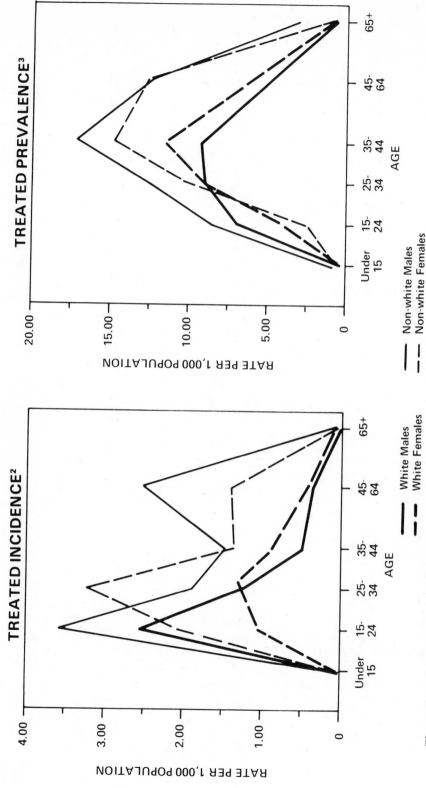

Figure 50-1. Age specific treated incidence and prevalence rates per 1000 population for schizophrenia for Monroe County, NY, by race and sex, 1970.

1. From Babigian HM: (8, pp 862, 863).
2. Treated Incidence = Number of new cases of schizophrenia (hospitalized and not hospitalized) reported to Monroe County Case Register during calendar year 1970, per 1000 population.
3. Treated Prevalence = Number of cases of schizophrenia (hospitalized and not hospitalized) known to have received care during 1970, per 1000 population.

549

Table 50-3. Number of Cases of Schizophrenia Under Care (Hospitalized and Not Hospitalized) and Treated Prevalence Rates per 1000 Population, Specific for Age, Sex, and Color, Monroe County 1970[a]

Age (Years)	Total	White Both Sexes	White Male	White Female	Nonwhite Both Sexes	Nonwhite Male	Nonwhite Female
			Treated Prevalence Rates per 1000 Population				
Total	4.78	4.55	4.49	4.61	6.08	6.91	5.32
Age Adj.[b]	4.78	4.53	4.46	4.59	6.94	7.89	6.15
<15	0.36	0.34	0.47	0.20	0.51	0.64	0.37
15–24	5.35	5.34	6.69	4.11	5.47	8.60	3.00
25–34	9.13	8.94	8.74	9.13	11.18	12.46	10.09
35–44	10.78	10.39	9.30	11.44	15.90	17.11	14.75
45–54	7.25	6.88	6.16	7.53	15.31	14.57	16.05
55–64	3.77	3.65	2.75	4.45	7.55	8.37	6.80
65+	0.96	0.93	0.63	1.13	2.07	3.03	1.27
			Number of Cases				
Total	3,319	3,003	1,428	1,575	316	172	144
<15	73	62	44	18	11	7	4
15–24	649	597	357	240	52	36	16
25–34	840	750	362	388	90	46	44
35–44	861	771	339	432	90	47	43
45–54	596	541	231	310	55	26	29
55–64	234	219	78	141	15	8	7
65+	66	63	17	46	3	2	1

[a] From Babigian HM (8, Table IV, p 863).

[b] Population of Monroe County as enumerated by age, sex, and color in 1970 Census is used as standard.

reach a maximum in the age group 25–34 years (1.30 per 1000 for white and 3.22 per 1000 for nonwhite females).

With respect to one-year prevalence, the age-adjusted rate for nonwhite males (7.89 per 1000) is 1.77 times that for white males (4.46 per 1000) and that for nonwhite females (6.15 per 1000) is 1.34 times that for white females (4.59 per 1000). The maximum rates for nonwhite and white males occur in the age group 35–44 years (17.11 per 1000 and 9.30 per 1000, respectively). For nonwhite females, the maximum rate occurs in the age group 45–54 years (16.05 per 1000) and for white females in the age group 35–44 years (9.30 per 1000). The rates for males in the age group 65 years and over are 0.63 per 1000 in the white population and 3.03 per 1000 in the nonwhite. The corresponding rates for females are 1.13 per 1000 and 1.27 per 1000, respectively. The higher treated incidence and prevalence rates for the nonwhite population as compared to the white have been noted by many other investigators (2,11,12,13,14,15).

PROBABILITY OF DEVELOPING SCHIZOPHRENIA

The consequences of treated incidence rates of the level reported for Monroe County may be further illustrated by using these rates to determine the probability of a person born in 1970 having at least one admission to a psychiatric facility at some time during his lifetime. This probability, which should not be confused with lifetime prevalence, is a function of the treated incidence rates and of the mortality rates of the life table used in the computation. Accordingly, the race-sex incidence rates, specific for age, were applied to several different life tables to illustrate the effect on this probability of different levels of mortality of the community in which the patient resides. Thus, the age specific T.I. rates by race and sex were applied to the following life tables: (a) the table specific for each race-sex group; (b) the table for white females to illustrate what the result would be if the rates operated in a population with a very low level of mortality; and (c) the table for non-white males to illustrate what the result would be if rates operated in a population with a very high level of mortality. These probabilities are shown in Table 50-4, calculated using the US Life Tables for 1970 (32).

When the age-sex-race specific incidence rates are applied to their respective life tables, the probabilities are for white males and females, 4.8% and 3.9%; for nonwhite males and females, 10.0% and 8.9%. Thus, the probability for nonwhite females is 2.3 times that for white females.

Table 50-4. Probability of a Person Born in 1970 Experiencing During His Lifetime at Least One Admission to a Psychiatric Facility With a Diagnosis of Schizophrenia[a]

Race-Sex Group	Life Table Used		
	That Specific to Each Race-Sex Group[b]	That with Lowest Death Rates[c]	That with Highest Death Rates[d]
	Probability (Percent)		
White			
Male	4.76	4.88	4.51
Female	3.94	3.94	3.49
Other than white			
Male	10.04	11.53	10.04
Female	8.94	9.38	8.37
All races and sexes	6.92	7.44	6.60

[a] Based on Monroe County age-specific treated incidence rates for 1970 and different levels of mortality in the community in which the treated incidence (T.I.) rate would operate.

[b] For this computation the age specific T.I. rates for each race-sex group were applied to the stationary population ($_nL_x$) for the corresponding race-sex groups, i.e., T.I. rates for white males were applied to 1970 life table for white males; T.I. rates for nonwhite males to the life table for nonwhite males, and so forth (32).

[c] For this computation the age specific T.I. rates for each race-sex group were applied to the life table for white females (a group with lowest mortality).

[d] For this computation the age specific T.I. rates for each age-race-sex group were applied to the life table for nonwhite males (the group with the highest mortality).

The hypothetical nature of these estimates must be emphasized. They describe the chances of an individual born in Monroe County in 1970 developing schizophrenia some time during his lifetime if he lived in a stable population subjected throughout his lifetime to the stated levels of mortality that existed in 1970 and the stated treated incidence rates of schizophrenia for that year.

The probabilities of developing schizophrenia, particularly for the nonwhite population, are among the highest of which this writer is aware. However, it is impossible to determine the extent to which these differences by race may be due to a tendency, on the part of psychiatrists in the facilities that report to the register, to diagnose blacks as schizophrenics more frequently than whites and to diagnose them less frequently as affectively ill.

Babigian et al (16) carried out a study that provides some indication of the consistency with which specified diagnostic terms are applied to all patients by psychiatrists in the multiple agencies that report to the psychiatric case register. The study population was derived from the 3491 patients reported to the register during 1961 by private psychiatrists, an inpatient observation unit, and the emergency unit of an outpatient department of a university hospital. Of these patients, 35% had one or more episodes of psychiatric services subsequent to their initial one. In 79% of these cases, the diagnosis on second and subsequent contacts remained the same as that on the first contact. Chronic brain syndrome was the diagnostic category for which diagnostic consistency was the highest, 92%. For schizophrenia the corresponding figure was 70%, and for affective psychosis, 40%. The time interval between consecutive contacts did not affect materially the diagnoses.

Differences in consistency of diagnosis by race were not reported. However, Simon et al (17) carried out a relevant study on 130 new admissions (86 white and 44 black) between the ages of 20–50 years, to one or more state hospitals in New York City. Techniques developed in the US-UK Diagnostic Study were used to determine differences between a hospital diagnosis and a diagnosis determined by a structured mental-state interview (18). Each patient received two diagnoses—one by the hospital staff and one by the project staff based on the structured interview and scales and categories of psychopathology derived from it. According to the hospital diagnosis, race and diagnosis were strongly associated: a diagnosis of schizophrenia rather than affective illness was given far more frequently to blacks than to whites. According to the project staff diagnosis, there was no significant association between race and the project's diagnosis. Studies of this type are needed to determine the extent to which schizophrenia may possibly be over-diagnosed in the nonwhite population and affective disorders underdiagnosed in the facilities reporting to the Monroe County Register.

IMPLICATIONS OF CHANGES IN SIZE AND COMPOSITION OF POPULATION OF THE UNITED STATES FOR THE NUMBER OF NEW CASES OF SCHIZOPHRENIA AND THE NUMBER UNDER CARE PER YEAR

Unfortunately, the age-race specific treated incidence and prevalence rates of the type described in Tables 50-2 and 50-3 are not available for the US. However, the rates for Monroe County provide a basis for speculating on what the situation in the US would have been in 1970 if the T.I. and T.P. rates of the order of magnitude reported for Monroe County existed in the US in 1970. Another computation was carried out to

Table 50-5. US Populations, Actual 1970[a] and Estimated 1985,[b] and Numerical and Percent Change in US Populations, 1970–1985, by Age and Color

Age (Years)	1970			1985		
	Total	White	Nonwhite	Total	White	Nonwhite
	Population (in Thousands)					
Total	203,212	177,749	25,463	234,069	200,548	33,521
Under 15	57,900	49,002	8,898	53,892	44,382	9,510
15–24	35,441	30,652	4,789	38,496	32,087	6,409
25–34	24,907	21,779	3,128	39,846	33,989	5,857
35–44	23,089	20,328	2,761	31,332	27,334	3,998
45–64	41,810	37,658	4,152	43,844	38,673	5,171
65+	20,065	18,330	1,735	26,659	24,083	2,576
	Change in Number of Persons (in Thousands) 1970–85			Percent Change in Number of Persons 1970–85		
Total	30,857	22,799	8,058	15.2	12.8	31.6
Under 15	−4,008	−4,620	612	−6.9	−9.4	6.9
15–24	3,055	1,435	1,620	8.6	4.7	33.8
25–34	14,939	12,210	2,729	60.0	56.1	87.2
35–44	8,243	7,006	1,237	35.7	34.5	44.8
45–64	2,034	1,015	1,019	4.9	2.7	24.5
65+	6,594	5,753	841	32.9	31.4	48.5

[a] From US Bureau of the Census (31, Table 52).

[b] From US Bureau of the Census (19, Table 8). Series II projection—projection is based on the estimated July 1, 1974 population and assumes a slight reduction in mortality, an annual net immigration of 400,000 per year and an ultimate cohort fertility level (average number of lifetime births per woman) at the replacement level figure of 2.1.

illustrate the effect of changes expected to occur in the size of the population of the US by 1985 on the number of treated schizophrenics, assuming the 1970 T.I. and T.P. rates for Monroe County can be applied to the population of the US in 1985.

Estimated Population Changes for the US, 1970–1985

The 1985 population estimate used in these computations is the so-called Series II projection published by the US Bureau of the Census in October 1975 (19). The Series II projection is a moderate one. It is based on the estimated July 1, 1974 population and assumes a slight reduction in mortality, an annual net immigration of 400,000 per year, and an ultimate cohort fertility level (average number of lifetime births per woman) at the replacement level figure of 2.1.[2] Such an estimate indicates that the population of the US would grow from 212 million in 1974 to 262 million in year 2000, an increase of 24%. The annual growth rate would increase to 1% during the early 1980s and then would decline to 0.6% by the end of the century.

Table 50-5 and Figure 50-2 show the expected changes in the composition of the

[2] Replacement level fertility is that level of fertility required for the population to replace itself with the projected mortality rates and in the absence of net immigration.

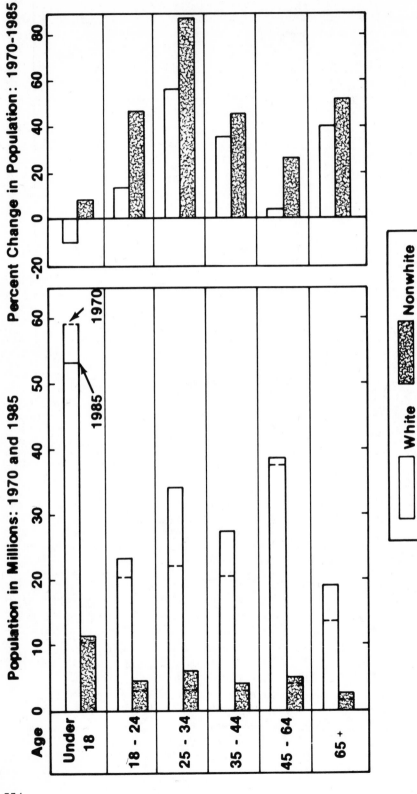

Figure 50-2. Population US 1970 and 1985 (estimated) and percent change 1970–1985 by age and color. From US Bureau of the Census (31, Table 52) and US Bureau of the Census (19, Table 8).

population of the US between 1970 and 1985 specific for age and race. By 1985, the population of the US will have increased to about 234.1 million persons, 15.2% greater than in 1970 (203,212 million). The increase will be 13% for whites (from 177.7 to 200.5 million), and 32% for nonwhites (from 25.5 to 33.5 million). Nonwhites are expected to constitute about 14% of the population in 1985 as compared to 13% in 1970. The relative increases expected in the size of each age group of the nonwhite population range from an 87% increase in the age group 25–34 years to 7% in the age group under 15 years. These increases are considerably in excess of those in the white population which range from 56% in the age group 25–34, to 3% in the age group 45–64 years. The number of white children in the age group under 15 years will *decrease* by 9%. Of particular importance is the fact that large relative increases will be occurring in numbers of persons in those age groups that are known to experience very high—usually the highest—incidence and prevalence rates for schizophrenia, namely, age groups 15–24, 25–34, and 35–44 years.

Estimated Number of New Cases, 1970 and 1985

Table 50-6 shows the estimated number of new cases that would have entered treatment in the US during 1970 for the first time, if Monroe County T.I. rates applied, and the number expected to do so in 1985, assuming no change in the T.I. rates. Thus, there would have been 147,139 new cases of schizophrenia in the US during 1970 (110,982 white and 36,157 nonwhite). The number of new cases that would occur during 1985 is 185,649, an increase of 38,510 (26.2%). The expected increase in number of new white cases in 1985 is 23,016 (20.7% increase) and nonwhite, 15,494 (42.9% increase).

The relative increases vary in each age group and, in these computations, would be the same as the relative increases in the population of the US in the specified age group (Figure 50-3). For example, in the age group 25–34, the number of new cases in the white population would have increased by 56% (from 27,224 to 42,486) and for the nonwhite population by 87% (from 8,164 to 15,287). Of particular interest is the change in the population under 15 years. There would be a *decrease* of 9% in white cases and a 7% *increase* in the nonwhite cases.

It is important to note that the overall percent increase in expected numbers of new cases of schizophrenia exceeds the overall percent increase for the general population. The reason is that the highest treated incidence rates for schizophrenia occur in those age groups where the expected relative increases in population are also the highest: 15–24 years, 25–34 years, and 35–44 years (see Table 50-5). Thus, although the expected relative increase in total population for whites is 13% and for nonwhites 32%, the corresponding increases in new cases of schizophrenia would be 21% and 43%, respectively.

The above estimates assumed no increase in age specific T.I. rates. However, if an increase in rates were to have been hypothesized on top of the population increase (e.g., 0.5%/year in each age-sex-race group), then the new cases would have increased by an additional 7.5%.

Indeed, it cannot be emphasized too strongly that the number of new cases of schizophrenia will continue to increase until research produces the knowledge needed to prevent their occurrence. As of this moment in time, it is impossible to predict the date by which sufficient knowledge about the etiology of this disorder and, equally important, the methods needed to apply this knowledge will have been developed. It is equally impossible to predict when it will be possible to begin achieving significant reductions in the rate at which new cases of this disorder are being added to our population. Even though a major research breakthrough would occur, the likelihood of achieving significant reductions in new cases quickly would seem to be quite small in view of the large increases expected in the size of the population groups in which the risk of acquiring this disorder is known to be high. Very effective and efficient methods of prevention would be required to counterbalance the increases in numbers of new cases that can be expected to occur as a result of population increases shown in Table 50-6.

The preceding discussion applied only to schizophrenia. However, similar computations can be made to illustrate the effect of population changes on brain syndromes, neuroses, personality disorders, and affective disorders.

Estimated Number of Cases Under Care 1970 and 1985

The preceding discussion considered factors related to the treated incidence of mental disorders, i.e., the annual rate at which *new* cases of these disorders are occurring. A

Table 50-6. Effect of Population Changes on Annual Number of *New* Cases of Schizophrenia Assuming Treated Incidence Rates of Monroe County for 1970 Applied to US Population in 1970 and 1985 (Estimated)[a]

Age (Years)	1970 (Estimate)[b]			1985 (Projected Estimate)[c]		
	Total	White	Nonwhite	Total	White	Nonwhite
	New Cases During Year					
All ages	147,139	110,982	36,157	185,649	133,998	51,651
Under 15	5,297	2,450	2,847	5,262	2,219	3,043
15–24	64,569	51,495	13,074	71,403	53,906	17,497
25–34	35,388	27,224	8,164	57,773	42,486	15,287
35–44	17,919	14,026	3,893	24,497	18,860	5,637
45–64	22,866	14,687	8,179	25,269	15,082	10,187
65+	1,100	1,100	—	1,445	1,445	—
	Change in Number of New Cases 1970–85			Percent Change in Number of New Cases 1970–85		
All ages	38,510	23,016	15,494	26.2	20.7	42.9
Under 15	−35	−231	196	−0.7	−9.4	6.9
15–24	6,834	2,411	4,423	10.6	4.7	33.8
25–34	22,385	15,262	7,123	63.3	56.1	87.2
35–44	6,578	4,834	1,744	36.7	34.5	44.8
45–64	2,403	395	2,008	10.5	2.7	24.6
65+	345	345	—	31.4	31.4	—

[a] Computations are based on the assumption that the 1970 age-color specific incidence rates for Monroe County, NY, applied to the actual population of the United States in 1970 and the projected population of the US in 1985 by age and race.

[b] The source of the US population figures for 1970 that were applied to the 1970 age-color specific rates for Monroe County, NY, was: US Bureau of the Census (31, Table 52).

[c] The source of the US population projections for 1985 that were applied to the 1970 age-color specific incidence rates for Monroe County, NY, was: US Bureau of the Census (19, Table 8—Series II projection).

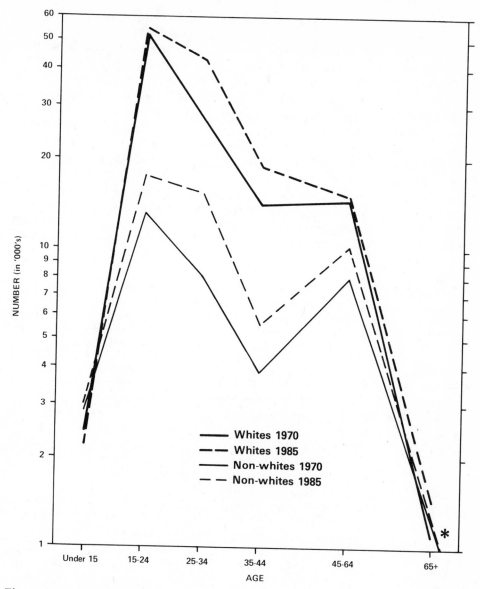

Figure 50-3. Estimated number of new cases[1] of schizophrenia occurring in the US during specified years 1970 and 1985 by age and color.
1. Numbers based on the assumption that the 1970 incidence rates for Monroe County, NY, applied to the population in the US in 1970 and 1985.

consideration of factors that affect the treated prevalence of mental disorders (i.e., the number of cases under care in the population as of a given moment in time) indicates that prevalence will also increase. Prevalence is dependent on not only the incidence but also the duration of these disorders, i.e., the interval between date of occurrence and date of their termination, variously defined as the date of remission, the date of "cure," date of death, depending on the question under study.

Table 50-7 illustrates the changes to be expected in treated prevalence merely as a result of shifts in the size and age distribution of the population of the US between 1970 and 1985. Again, let us draw on the age-race specific treated prevalence rates of Monroe County. Assume these rates applied to the corresponding age-race groups of the population of the US in 1985 as well as in 1970, then the treated prevalence of schizophrenia would increase by 272,834 cases (28.0%), with a 24.6% increase for whites and a 44.7% increase for nonwhites. Here, again, the relative increases in the various age groups would be the same as in the general population (Figure 50-4). In the age group 25–34 years, for example, the number of cases in the white population would increase from 194,704 in 1970 to 303,862 in 1985, or by 56%, and in the nonwhite from 34,971 to 65,481, or by 87%.

Note, again, that the relative increase in total number of cases of schizophrenia (28%) exceeds the corresponding increase in the general population of the US (15%). As with incidence, the highest prevalence rates occur in those age groups in which the relative increases in population are also the highest (e.g., 15–24, 25–34, and 35–44 years).

Table 50-7. Effect of Population Changes on Annual Number of Cases of Schizophrenia (Hospitalized and Nonhospitalized) Assuming Treated Prevalence Rates of Monroe County for 1970 Applied to US Population in 1970 and 1985 (Estimated)[a]

Age (Years)	1970 (Estimate)[b]			1985 (Projected Estimate)[c]		
	Total	White	Nonwhite	Total	White	Nonwhite
	Number of Cases Receiving Care During Year					
All ages	974,972	809,668	165,304	1,247,806	1,008,622	239,184
Under 15	21,199	16,661	4,538	19,940	15,090	4,850
15–24	189,878	163,682	26,196	206,402	171,345	35,057
25–34	229,675	194,704	34,971	369,343	303,862	65,481
35–44	255,108	211,208	43,900	347,568	284,000	63,568
45–64	258,474	206,366	52,108	276,824	211,928	64,896
65+	20,638	17,047	3,591	27,729	22,397	5,332
	Change in Number of Cases Receiving Care 1970–85			Percent Change in Number of Cases Receiving Care 1970–85		
All ages	272,834	198,954	73,880	28.0	24.6	44.7
Under 15	−1,259	−1,571	312	−5.9	−9.4	6.9
15–24	16,524	7,663	8,861	8.7	4.7	33.8
25–34	139,668	109,158	30,510	60.8	56.1	87.2
35–44	92,460	72,792	19,668	36.2	34.5	44.8
45–64	18,350	5,562	12,788	7.1	2.7	24.5
65+	7,091	5,350	1,741	34.4	31.4	48.5

[a] Computations based on the assumption that the 1970 age-color specific prevalence rates for Monroe County, NY, applied to the actual population of the United States in 1970 and the projected population of the United States in 1985 by age and race.

[b] Source of US population figures for 1970 that were applied to the 1970 age-color specific rates for Monroe County, NY, was US Bureau of the Census (31, Table 52).

[c] Source of US population projections for 1985 that were applied to the 1970 prevalence rates for Monroe County, NY, was US Bureau of the Census (19, Table 8—Series II projection).

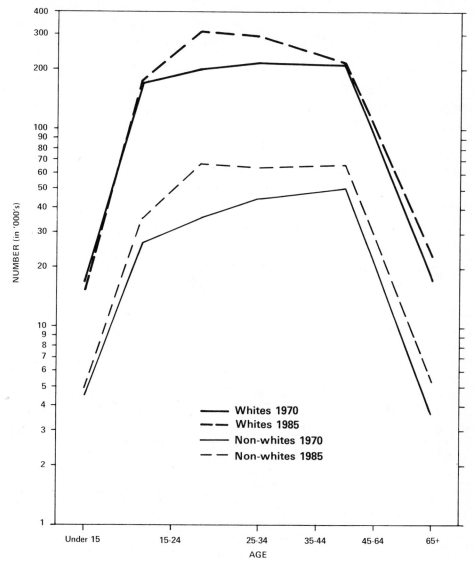

Figure 50-4. Estimated number of cases of schizophrenia (hospitalized and non-hospitalized) receiving care during year in the US, by age and color, 1970 and 1985.
1. Numbers based on the assumption that the 1970 prevalence rates for Monroe County, NY, applied to the population in the US in 1970 and 1985.

Similarly, a decrease would occur among white children under 15 years and an increase in the number of nonwhite children in this age group.

Mortality and Mental Disorders

In considering factors that determine the size of the population of persons with mental disorders in a country, it is essential to take into account those factors that can affect mortality rates not only of the persons who have a mental disorder but also of those who do not have such disorders. Indeed, factors that operate to increase the longevity of the mentally ill and the not mentally ill will tend to increase the prevalence of mental disorders.

Let us first consider the mortality of the mentally ill. A variety of studies have demonstrated that the age-specific mortality rates among the mentally ill—those hospitalized, as well as those under care of outpatient clinics, private psychiatrists, and psychiatric units of general hospitals—are considerably in excess of those in the corresponding age groups of the general population. Several studies have demonstrated the excess mortality of patients diagnosed as schizophrenic, both those in institutions and those under community care (2,20,21). For example, Babigian and Odoroff (21) showed that the age-adjusted death rate of males in the Monroe County Register diagnosed as schizophrenic was 1.6 times that of the male population of Monroe County and that for females, 1.9 times that of the corresponding female population.

The excess mortality of persons with mental disorders is the result of a variety of factors. These include (a) the high fatality rates for many of the conditions that cause or are associated with organic brain syndromes (e.g., infectious diseases, metabolic disorders, neoplasms, cerebrovascular diseases, skull fractures, intracranial injuries, poisonings); (b) patterns of behavior and attitudes of persons with mental disorders which, in turn, affect their life style, living arrangements, general health status, and the extent to which they seek and obtain psychiatric and medical care and related human services; (c) the extent to which psychiatrists are able to predict suicidal and violent behavior in patients and are successful in preventing such acts; (d) possible effects of somatic, pharmacologic, and other treatment procedures for mental disorders on essential life processes; (e) problems specific to the hospital, nursing home, or other facility in which the patient receives treatment (e.g., lack of adherence to sanitary, safety, and other standards for hospitals, clinics, and so forth; inadequate and substandard psychiatric care, medical care, and related health maintenance services; inadequate staff); (f) problems associated with long-term institutionalization that affect the physical and mental health and the social well being of patients; and (g) possibly unique factors associated with the etiology of a specific mental disorder which may, in some way as yet unknown, subject individuals with such a disorder to an increased risk of mortality.

Thus, activities that tend to reduce mortality rates of the mentally ill resulting from any of the factors just mentioned will tend to increase the number of mentally ill in our population. The application of advances in public health practice that resulted in better levels of environmental sanitation, control of tuberculosis, syphilis and other infectious diseases, improved diet, and improved general medical care, led to reductions in the mortality rates of the institutionalized mentally ill (2). Advances in clinical medicine have also prolonged the lives of the large population of aged persons who suffer from brain syndromes with cerebral arteriosclerosis and senile brain disease.

It is to be hoped that the new treatment methods for schizophrenia and affective disorders will also increase the longevity of persons with these disorders. It is also to be hoped that the large number of persons now under care of community based psychiatric programs will receive whatever psychiatric, medical, health, and social services they may need to improve their overall state of physical and mental health and social well being. Such services should tend to decrease the excess mortality of schizophrenics.

However, adequate provision of these services requires the strengthening of existing community mental health services. A recent study on the prevention of hospitalization in schizophrenia (22,23) indicates that the provision of adequate community services to formerly hospitalized schizophrenic patients will require the structuring of such services on an intensive and aggressive basis. Davis et al (22) state: " . . . the most important finding of the study was that chronic schizophrenics, in order to remain successfully in the community, must have continuous supervision and medication. They and their families must receive social services and psychological support to alleviate the all too familiar patterns of personal and family disorganization." For this to be achieved they further state: " . . . if clinics are to play a major role in providing community care for schizophrenic patients, the laissez-faire model and its assumptions will have to be replaced by an aggressive delivery system designed to deal with chronic, marginal patients, like the psychotics in this study and those who comprise the bulk of state hospital populations."

DISCUSSION

This chapter has illustrated types of data that have been generated from the Monroe County Register on the treated incidence and prevalence of schizophrenia by age, sex, and race, and on some of their uses. The unique appeal of these data is that they are an approximation—how good we don't know—of the "true" national differential incidence and prevalence rates specific for age, race, sex, and various demographic subgroups.

These data from the Monroe County Register can be used to answer certain questions and direct the attention of administrators and researchers to significant trends and issues. Indeed, if the diagnostic data on schizophrenia are correct, and the sex and racial differences between treated incidence and prevalence rates are real differences, they have important implications. Even if the data are not precisely correct, they still have importance for raising many questions that require further research. Such questions about the data from the register concern: reliability of diagnoses by psychiatrists reporting to the register; the relationship of *treated* incidence and prevalence rates to *true* rates of incidence and prevalence; the extent to which differences in rates of treated disorders are reflective of socioeconomic, racial and other factors that influence which facilities are used for treatment; the possibility that age variations believed to exist in the *true* incidence rates of schizophrenia in the so-called risk period of 15–44 years are biased by the inverted V-shaped curves that are based on *treated* incidences (low rates in childhood and old age, high in age groups from 20–34 years).

These questions can only be answered by research designed to eliminate the confusion that exists in the literature on epidemiology of schizophrenia and to develop improved case-finding instruments and diagnostic techniques for which I recommend a number of studies:

1. *Development of a glossary of morbidity indexes:* A profusion of terms in the literature on epidemiology of mental disorders include: true incidence, treated incidence, lifetime incidence, expectation of developing a disorder, morbid risk, and morbidity risk; true prevalence, point prevalence, interval prevalence, period prevalence, and lifetime prevalence. When each of these terms is dissected, it is apparent that it has been used with quite variable meanings. A manual to reduce confusion in the use of these basic terms is urgently needed.

2. *Research on case-finding techniques:* The development of more sensitive and specific case-finding techniques is a sine qua non if we are ever to answer questions concerning differential incidence and prevalence of schizophrenia and other mental

disorders within and among countries by age, race, sex, and other demographic and cultural factors.

3. *Research on diagnostic practice:* Much has been accomplished over the past 10–15 years in developing techniques for research on diagnostic comparability. The techniques developed in the US-UK Diagnostic Study (18) and those developed by the WHO in their program on standardization of psychiatric diagnosis and statistics (24) and the International Pilot Study of Schizophrenia (IPSS) (25) are excellent examples of what needs to be extended in the future.

4. *Follow-up studies of persons with mental disorders:* The IPSS (25) has developed schedules that can be used to assess clinical status and community adjustment at follow-up of patients in different countries. These can be adapted for use in similar studies in the US. Davis et al (23) published the instruments they used in their follow-up study of schizophrenics. Of particular importance are studies of differential outcome in white and nonwhite patients. Results of such studies may throw further light on the higher treated prevalence rates for nonwhites as compared with those for whites. One of the important variables to consider in these studies is the living arrangements of white and nonwhite persons, particularly of those in the high-risk age groups, 25–34 and 35–44. Tabulations of current population data on marital status and living arrangements of the US population in 1975 (26) emphasize the differences in the distribution of the white and nonwhite population in relation to composition of their households, the proportion of persons who live in families, the role each person occupies in a family, the proportion who live alone, and the proportion who live with nonrelated individuals (Table 50-8). These differences must be taken into account in studies of factors that influence use of psychiatric facilities and that affect course and outcome (27,28).

5. *Genetic studies:* Research on the genetics of schizophrenia has been carried out on predominantly white populations. The high rates of treated mental disorders for nonwhites have been reported not only for Monroe County, but for other areas of the US (11,13,29). These findings emphasize the need for a better understanding of the reasons for these differences, including the possible role of genetic factors in the etiology of schizophrenia in the members of different racial and cultural groups. Research on these issues is urgent in view of the increased interest in the mental health of blacks and other minority groups and, particularly, in view of the large increases expected in the size of the nonwhite population.

6. *Aging of schizophrenics:* The hypothetical projections of the number of schizophrenics that might be expected to be under care in the US in 1985 indicate their number in the age group 65 years and over will increase (Table 50-5). Indeed, such an increase is to be expected because of the effect of improved medical, psychiatric, and social services for the large number of schizophrenics who are now under care of outpatient clinics and community mental health centers, as well as for those who are in mental hospitals and nursing homes. Studies are needed that will provide information on the consequences of superimposed cerebral arteriosclerosis, senile brain disease, and other chronic illnesses on the course of schizophrenia and the needs of schizophrenics for medical care, psychiatric care, social services, and living arrangements. Such data are needed to fill present gaps in clinical knowledge about the course of schizophrenia in the aged and to plan programs and services for this increasingly large population of disabled individuals.

7. *Cross-cultural research:* Earlier in this chapter, the implications of expected increases in the population of the US between 1970 and 1985 for the expected numbers

of schizophrenics in 1985 were discussed. Of particular importance to those involved in cross-cultural research and in planning mental health services at the international level is the fact that even larger increases will occur in the population of certain world areas in those age groups in which the reported incidence of schizophrenia is high, namely, age groups 15–24, 25–34, and 35–44 years. According to estimates prepared by the Population Division of the United Nations (30), the population of the world will increase between 1970 and 1985 by 36% (Table 50-9). For the more developed regions, the number will increase by 17%, and for the less developed, by 44%. As of 1970, about 70% of the world's population was in the developing countries, and by 1985 this proportion will increase to 74%. In 1970 the percentage of the world's population that resided in the developing regions was only 45% in the age group 65 years and over, but was higher in younger age groups, reaching 78% in the age group under 15. By 1985, it is estimated that these percentages will have increased in each age group by substantial amounts, up to 81% of the population of the world under 15 years of age.

Expected percent increases for each age group are shown in Figures 50-5 and 50-6 for major regions of the world. These data emphasize that large absolute and relative increases in the numbers of persons in the high-risk age groups 15–24, 25–34, and 35–44 years will occur in most regions of the world. The increases in the countries of South Asia, Africa, and Latin America will be particularly large, while those in Europe and the USSR will be somewhat smaller because of the effect of lowered birth rates and population losses during and following World War II.

High prevalence rates for schizophrenia have been reported in many countries of the world (1,2). Although the majority of studies that reported these rates have been done in the US and Europe, some have been done in the Asiatic countries (Japan, Formosa, Korea, India, and Iran). The reported lifetime prevalence rates vary from 1.0 per 1000 to 10.0 per 1000. Although these data are not methodologically comparable, they underscore the fact that sizeable proportions of the populations studied have had an attack of a disorder which competent research workers in each country called schizophrenia. If we accept the premise that the age groups at high risk of developing this disorder are the same as those reported in the US and other countries of the world, then the increases in population expected in the various areas of the world emphasize that the *number* of schizophrenics throughout the world will increase simply because the populations are increasing in the age groups in which the incidence and prevalence rates of this disorder are high. Thus, it becomes increasingly important to acquire reliable information on factors that influence the development, course, and outcome of schizophrenia among persons living under diverse social, economic, political, and cultural conditions. Such knowledge is important not only for theoretical, clinical, and epidemiologic purposes but also for use by public health authorities throughout the world in their efforts to establish effective and efficient programs to control this serious disorder and to recruit and train the manpower that will be needed to accomplish this.

8. *Establishment of a limited number of additional registers in the US:* Lastly, it is important to have register data similar to that for Monroe County for other sections of the US. This would make it possible to obtain comparative data on and a broader perspective about patterns of use of psychiatric services and variations in treated incidence and prevalence, and to provide sampling frames for follow-up, evaluative and other types of studies of persons who have received psychiatric services. Unfortunately, issues revolving around confidentiality of data and privacy—issues that have been successfully handled thus far by the Monroe County Register—and the costs involved in

Table 50-8. Number and Percent Distribution of Persons 25–34 and 35–44 Years of Age by Family Status by Sex and Color, United States, March, 1975[a]

Family Status	25–34 Year Age Group						35–44 Year Age Group					
	Males			Females			Males			Females		
	Total	White	Nonwhite	Total	White	Nonwhite	Total	White	Nonwhite	Total	White	Nonwhite
	Number (in Thousands)											
Total	14,776	13,103	1,673	15,316	13,270	2,046	10,992	9,745	1,247	11,615	10,075	1,540
In families	12,782	11,436	1,346	14,234	12,355	1,879	10,046	8,968	1,078	11,171	9,720	1,451
Head of family	11,094	10,094	1,000	1,613	1,071	542	9,343	8,399	944	1,510	1,030	480
Wife of head	N.A.[b]	N.A.	N.A.	11,545	10,443	1,102	N.A.	N.A.	N.A.	9,207	8,343	864
Child of head	1,383	1,135	248	859	688	171	497	423	74	343	267	76
Other relative of head	304	207	97	217	153	64	206	145	61	112	79	33
Primary individual[c]	1,440	1,250	190	844	712	132	668	543	125	356	285	71
Secondary individuals[d]	554	417	137	236	203	33	278	234	44	88	70	18
In households	512	385	127	207	175	32	232	192	40	65	49	16
In group quarters	42	32	10	29	28	1	46	42	4	22	20	2

Percent Distribution

Total	100.0	100.0	100.0	100.0	100.0	100.0	100.0	100.0	100.0	100.0	100.0	100.0
In families	86.5	87.3	80.5	92.9	93.1	91.8	91.4	92.0	86.4	96.2	96.5	94.2
Head of family	75.1	77.0	59.8	10.5	8.1	26.5	85.0	86.2	75.7	13.0	10.2	31.1
Wife of head	N.A.	N.A.	N.A.	75.4	78.7	53.9	N.A.	N.A.	N.A.	79.3	82.8	56.1
Child of head	9.4	8.7	14.8	5.6	5.2	8.4	4.5	4.3	5.9	3.0	2.6	4.9
Other relative of head	2.0	1.5	5.8	1.4	1.1	3.1	1.9	1.5	4.9	0.9	0.8	2.2
Primary individual[c]	9.7	9.5	11.4	5.5	5.4	6.5	6.1	5.6	10.0	3.1	2.8	4.6
Secondary individuals[d]	3.7	3.2	8.2	1.5	1.5	1.6	2.5	2.4	3.5	0.8	0.7	1.2
In households	3.4	2.9	7.6	1.3	1.3	1.6	2.1	2.0	3.2	0.6	0.5	1.1
In group quarters	0.3	0.2	0.6	0.2	0.2	0.0[e]	0.4	0.4	0.3	0.2	0.2	0.1

[a] From US Bureau of the Census, (26, Table 2).

[b] N.A.—not applicable.

[c] Persons who are heads of household and either live alone or with other nonrelated persons.

[d] Either persons who live in households but who are unrelated to the head or other persons in that household, or persons who live in group quarters.

[e] Percent greater than 0, but less than 0.05.

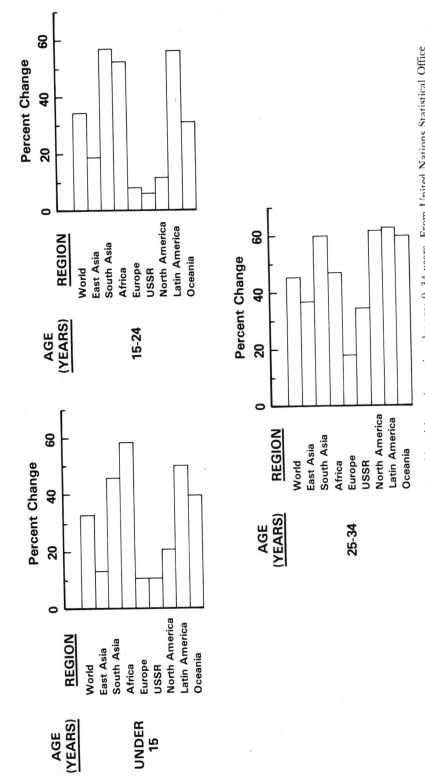

Figure 50-5. Percent change, 1970–85, in population of world and its major regions by age: 0–34 years. From United Nations Statistical Office (30, Table A-4).

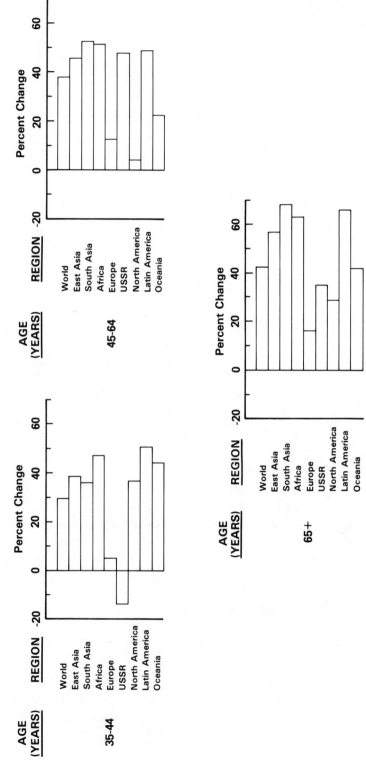

Figure 50-6. Percent change, 1970–85, in population of world and its major regions by age: 35 years and over. From United Nations Statistical Office (30, Table A-4).

Table 50-9. Estimated population of world (median variant) 1970 and 1985[a] and numerical and percent change in world population 1970–1985, for more and less developed regions of the world by age

Age (years)	1970			1985		
	Total	More Developed Regions	Less Developed Regions	Total	More Developed Regions	Less Developed Regions
	Population (in Thousands)					
Total[b]	3,631,798	1,090,297	2,541,501	4,933,463	1,274,995	3,658,468
Under 15	1,344,406	292,746	1,051,660	1,790,047	339,619	1,455,428
15–24	665,422	182,311	483,111	895,120	194,514	700,606
25–34	498,359	148,727	349,632	724,565	191,888	532,677
35–44	409,986	143,816	266,170	530,603	156,994	373,609
45–64	524,309	217,839	306,470	723,208	264,856	458,352
65+	189,318	104,859	84,459	269,919	132,123	137,796
	Change in Number of Persons (in Thousands) 1970–1985			Percent Change in Number of Persons 1970–1985		
Total	1,301,665	184,698	1,116,967	35.8	16.9	43.9
Under 15	445,641	41,873	403,768	33.1	14.3	38.4
15–24	229,698	12,203	217,495	34.5	6.7	45.0
25–34	226,206	43,161	183,045	48.4	29.0	52.4
35–44	120,617	13,178	107,439	29.4	9.2	40.4
45–64	198,899	47,017	151,882	37.9	21.6	49.6
65+	80,601	27,264	53,337	42.6	26.0	63.2

[a] Estimates prepared by United Nations Population Division; Median Variant: Table A-4 in United Nations Department of Economic and Social Affairs (1973): World Population Prospects as Assessed in 1968. UN: New York.

[b] Individual age groups will not necessarily add to total due to rounding.

developing and maintaining such data systems make it increasingly difficult to establish new ones. Nevertheless, efforts should be made to establish a limited number of new registers in carefully selected locations. In the meantime, it is increasingly important that the Monroe County Register continue to be maintained as a valuable resource for information on the treated incidence, duration, and prevalence of mental disorders and for research on other relevant issues.

SUMMARY

The psychiatric case register for Monroe County, NY, is a unique resource for systematic data on the patterns of use of psychiatric facilities by the residents of a defined catchment area and on variations in treated incidence and prevalence rates of psychiatric disorders by age, sex, race, and other demographic variables. This chapter uses recently published data on the treated incidence and prevalence rates of schizophrenia during 1970 among the residents of Monroe County to illustrate variations in these rates by age, sex and race. The treated incidence rate of schizophrenia is defined as the unduplicated number of residents of Monroe County who had their first lifetime contact with any psychiatric facility during 1970 and who received a diagnosis of schizophrenia in Monroe County during that year. The treated prevalence rate is defined as the number of residents of Monroe County with a diagnosis of schizophrenia undergoing treatment during 1970 in the total network of mental health facilities in Monroe County, including hospitalized and nonhospitalized patients, per 1000 population.

These rates were used as a basis for illustrating the implications that expected changes between 1970 and 1985 in the size and distribution of the population of the US by age and race have for the number of schizophrenics that might be expected in our country in 1985. To illustrate, the relative increases in the white population in high risk age groups would be as follows 15–24 years, 4.7%; 25–34 years, 56%; and 35–44 years, 35%. The corresponding increases for nonwhites would be 34%, 87%, and 45%, respectively. Under the assumption that the age-specific treated incidence rates in 1985 would be the same as those in 1970, these increases in general population would mean that the number of new cases of schizophrenia entering treatment would have increased by the same amounts. Similar considerations apply to treated prevalence. The 1970 Monroe County rates were used as a basis for speculating on the order of magnitude of the numbers that might be involved.

It is emphasized that the number of new cases of schizophrenia throughout the world will continue to increase until research produces the knowledge needed to prevent their occurrence. Even if a major research breakthrough were to occur, the likelihood of achieving significant reductions in new cases quickly would seem to be quite small in view of the large increases in the size of the population groups in which the risk of acquiring this disorder is known to be high. Very effective and efficient methods of prevention would be required to counterbalance increases in numbers of new cases that can be expected to occur solely as a result of anticipated population increases. The potential effects of improved medical, psychiatric, and social services for persons suffering from schizophrenia and other mental disorders were also considered. It is predicted that such services will increase the longevity of persons with mental disorders. The net effect of this will be to increase the number of persons in our population with mental disorders.

A review of population trends in the various regions of the world emphasizes that large absolute and relative increases in the numbers of persons in the high risk age groups 15–24, 25–34, and 35–44 years will occur in most regions of the world. The increases in the countries of South Asia, Africa, and Latin America will be particularly large, while those in Europe and the USSR will be somewhat smaller because of the effect of lowered birth rates and population losses during and following World War II. If the premise is accepted that age-specific incidence rates for schizophrenia are essentially the same universally, then the number of schizophrenics throughout the world can be expected to increase merely as a result of the expected increases in the population. This will happen unless significant decreases occur in the incidence rate of schizophrenia during the next decade.

The differences in the treated incidence and prevalence rates specific for age, race and sex, reported for Monroe County, raise questions that need to be answered with additional research in the following areas: case-finding techniques for use in epidemiologic surveys; diagnostic practice; follow-up studies of schizophrenia; genetics of schizophrenia; aging of schizophrenics. Particular emphasis should be given to studies that will determine if there are racial differences in incidence and course of schizophrenia among different subgroups of the population of the US and of other countries of the world.

Two other recommendations were made. One relates to the need for a glossary of technical terms currently found in the literature on the epidemiology of schizophrenia. The other relates to the importance of developing a limited number of additional case registers in carefully selected locations in the United States.

REFERENCES

1. Lin T, Standley CC: *The Scope of Epidemiology in Psychiatry,* WHO Public Health Paper No 16. Geneva, World Health Organization, 1962.

2. Yolles SF, Kramer M: Vital statistics, in Bellak L, Loeb L (eds): *The Schizophrenic Syndrome.* New York, Grune and Stratton, 1969.

3. Frost WH: Epidemiology, in Nelson Looseleaf System *Public Health and Preventive Medicine,* vol 2. New York, Thomas Nelson and Sons, 1927, p 163. (Reprinted in papers of Wade Hampton Frost. Maxcy KF (ed): *A Contribution to Epidemiologic Method.* New York, Commonwealth Fund, 1941.)

4. Kramer M: Some perspectives on the role of biostatistics and epidemiology in the prevention and control of mental disorders. *Health and Society, The Milbank Memorial Fund Quarterly,* Summer 1975.

5. Gardner EA, Miles HC, Bahn AK, et al: All psychiatric experience in a community. A cumulative survey: Report of first year's experience. *Arch Gen Psychiatry* 9:369, 1963.

6. Babigian HM: The role of psychiatric case registers in the longitudinal study of psychopathology, in Roff M, Robins L, Pollack M (eds): *Life History Research in Psychopathology,* vol. 2. Minneapolis, University of Minnesota Press, 1972, p 155.

7. World Health Organization Expert Committee on Mental Health: Epidemiology of mental disorders. *WHO Tech Rep Ser* 185, 1960.

8. Babigian HM: Schizophrenia: Epidemiology, in Freedman AM, Kaplan H, Sadock BJ (eds): *Comprehensive Textbook of Psychiatry II,* vol. 1, ed 2. Baltimore, Williams and Wilkins, 1975.

9. Kramer M: A discussion of the concepts of incidence and prevalence as related to epidemiologic studies of mental disorders. *Am J Public Health* 47:826, 1957.

10. Kramer M: Relationship of first admission rates to a mental hospital to "true" incidence rate, (Annex 2), in Kramer M: *Applications of Mental Health Statistics.* Geneva, World Health Organization, 1969, p 108.

11. Malzberg B: *Social and Biological Aspects of Mental Disease.* Utica, State Hospitals Press, 1940.

12. Pasamanick B: Myths regarding prevalence of mental diseases in the American Negro. *J Natl Med Assoc* 56:6, 1964.

13. Kramer M, Rosen BM, Willis EM: Definitions and distributions of mental disorders in a racist society, in Willie CV, Kramer BM, Brown BS (eds): *Racism and Mental Health: Essays.* Pittsburgh, University of Pittsburgh Press, 1973.

14. Pollack ES, Redick RW, Norman VB, et al: Socioeconomic and family characteristics of patients admitted to psychiatric services. *Am J Public Health* 54:506, 1964.

15. Kramer M, Pollack ES, Redick RW, et al: *Mental Disorders/Suicide,* Vital and Health Statistics Monographs, American Public Health Association. Cambridge, Mass, Harvard University Press, 1972, ch 6.

16. Babigian HM, Gardner EA, Miles HC, et al: Diagnostic consistency and change in a follow-up study of 1215 patients. *Amer J Psychiatry* 121:895, 1965.

17. Simon RJ, Fleiss JL, Gurland BJ, et al: Depression and schizophrenia in hospitalized black and white mental patients. *Arch Gen Psychiatry* 28:509, 1973.

18. Cooper JE, Kendell RE, Gurland BJ, et al: *Psychiatric Diagnosis in New York and London.* (Maudsley Monograph no 20). London, Oxford University Press, 1972.

19. US Bureau of the Census: *Current Population Reports, Population Estimates and Projections.* Series P-25, No. 601. Projections of the Population of the United States: 1975 to 2050. Washington, DC, US Government Printing Office, 1975.

20. Malzberg, B: *Mortality Among Patients with Mental Disease.* Utica, NY, State Hospitals Press, 1934.

21. Babigian HM, Odoroff CL: The mortality experience of a population with psychiatric illness. *Am J Psychiatry* 126:470, 1969.

22. Davis AE, Dinitz S, Pasamanick B: The prevention of hospitalization in schizophrenia: Five years after an experimental program. *Am J Orthopsychiatry* 42:375, 1972.

23. Davis AE, Dinitz S, Pasamanick B: *Schizophrenics in the New Custodial Community.* Columbus, Ohio State University Press, 1974.

24. Shepherd M, Brooke EM, Cooper JE, et al: An experimental approach to psychiatric diagnosis: An international study. *Acta Psychiatr Scand* 44 (suppl 201), 1968.

25. World Health Organization: *Report of the International Pilot Study of Schizophrenia.* Geneva, World Health Organization, 1973.

26. US Bureau of the Census: *Current Population Reports, Population Characteristics.* Series P-20, No. 287. Marital Status and Living Arrangements: March 1975. Washington, DC, US Government Printing Office, 1975.

27. Redick RW, Johnson C: Marital status, living arrangements and family characteristics of admissions to state and county mental hospitals and outpatient psychiatric clinics, United States 1970. *Statistical Note 100, February 1974.* Rockville, Maryland, Biometry Branch, National Institute of Mental Health, 1974.

28. Pollack ES: Mental health indices of family health. *WHO World Health Statistics Report* 28:278, 1975.

29. Taube CA: Admission rates to state and county mental hospitals by age, sex, and color, United States, 1969. *Statistical Note 41, February 1971.* Rockville, Maryland, Biometry Branch, National Institute of Mental Health, 1971.

30. United Nations Statistical Office: World Population Prospects As Assessed in 1968. *Population Studies,* No 53. New York, United Nations, 1973.

31. US Bureau of the Census: *US Census of Population, 1970, General Population Characteristics.* PC(1)-B-B1. Washington, DC, US Government Printing Office, 1970.

32. US Department of Health, Education and Welfare, National Center for Health Statistics: *Vital Statistics of the United States, 1970.* Vol II, Section 5, Life Tables. DHEW Publication No. (HRA)-1104, 1974.

33. Jablensky A, Sartorius N: Culture and schizophrenia. (Editorial) *Psychol Med* 5:113, 1975.

Chapter 51
Ethnic Studies in Hawaii: On Psychopathology and Social Deviance

Martin M. Katz, Ph.D.
Kenneth O. Sanborn, Ph.D.
H. Alice Lowery, M.S.
Judith Ching, M.A.

The role of culture in the etiology and expression of psychopathology remains obscure. Those of us who have worked for some time in this field are aware that there are very few sound experimental studies that permit definitive conclusions concerning the interaction of culture and psychosis.

In our own work (1,2,3) and in more recent reviews of the subjects (4,5), certain glaring limitations to our knowledge are quite evident. We know that culture influences the ways in which psychopathologic states are actually expressed, but we know very little about the process of how that comes about or what mechanisms underlie the similarities and variations in the overt characteristics of psychosis. In a recently prepared monograph on the Hawaii investigations (6), we discussed in detail the objectives of these studies since conceptual clarity is critical in attempting to deal with such complex notions as culture and psychopathologic states.

Thus, we state as the primary long-term objective, "to elaborate on the understanding of the nature of psychosis through investigating and contrasting its forms in different ethnocultural groups." Second, we wished to study how culture actually influences the

A summary of the Hawaii Research Program presented at the Second Rochester International Conference on Schizophrenia, Rochester, New York, May 2–5, 1976. The opinions expressed in this chapter are those of the authors and do not necessarily represent any official position of the National Institute of Mental Health.

572

ways in which psychosis is expressed, and third, we wanted to determine what can be learned about culture itself through the study of this interaction.

BACKGROUND

The development of the research program was strongly influenced by the results of two studies, one carried out at NIMH (7) and one, in Hawaii (8). We were aware from research conducted within the framework of the NIMH Collaborative Study of Drugs and Schizophrenia of the diversity of behavior and symptom patterns that comprise this major category of functional psychosis. The fact that schizophrenia can express itself in many forms is, of course, well accepted and is reflected in the descriptions of the classical subtypes in the standard nomenclature. Nevertheless, the heterogeneity of behavioral patterns as they occurred among the carefully diagnosed patients in that national study, e.g., the fact that several types of "paranoid schizophrenia" were identified, was still striking.

In a phenomenologic analysis of the social behavior and symptoms of some 400 of these patients prior to their entering the various hospitals, six distinctive patterns were identified (9). The types ranged from a "belligerent, manic" behavioral pattern marked by a paranoid quality, to a "withdrawn, periodically agitated, fearful" pattern. Convinced then, that this major form of psychosis, even when rigorously diagnosed, can express itself in a range of diverse forms, the question of central interest is whether the concept of "schizophrenia" represents several distinct disorders or variations on a single disorder of obscure etiology. The "types" in the latter case would be seen as merely reflecting expressive differences in psychosocial background and style (i.e., in personality).

Prior research on the influence of personality and of culture on the ways in which psychosis is expressed have not resolved this basic issue. Given the fact of diversity in form of expression, however, we can ask what such studies (of cultural differences in behavioral pattern) can tell us about the nature of psychosis, about its underlying mechanisms, or about the conflicts specific to the culture itself that brings about the condition.

That schizophrenia is expressed differently across cultures has, as noted, been reported consistently over the years (5). Enright and Jaeckle compared the patterns of manifest symptoms and social behavior of samples of paranoid schizophrenic patients of Japanese and Filipino extraction in Hawaii (8). The differences found in these two patient groups were again striking. The Japanese were more "seclusive, withdrawn," the Filipino, more manic-like, more belligerent in their behavior. In that setting, the evidence that cultural background influences the ways in which psychosis is expressed is, therefore, compelling. Furthermore, these ethnic types resemble closely two of the types identified in the sample from the NIMH study. Having found ways of characterizing their overt psychopathologic state, the questions that then guided the current work were: Do these variations in form have anything to tell us about the *nature* of psychosis and about the mechanisms of how the disorder or the conflicts it represents get translated into manifest "symptoms" or disturbed behavior? How does the characteristic symptom pattern for an ethnic group relate to conflicts central to the culture itself?

In the Hawaii investigation we, therefore, took as the first task the setting out in clear, descriptive form the nature of the behavior and the affect that comprise "psychopathology" in each of these diverse ethnic groups.

SETTING AND METHOD

We required a setting in which at least two ethnocultural situations were represented. Hawaii provided a very convenient laboratory for studying ways in which psychopathologic states are manifested in different cultural groups. For one thing, the Islands have representatives of such disparate cultural groups as the Western, the Oriental, the Malayan, and the Polynesian. Furthermore, in this particular setting, all the groups speak a common language. With severe functional mental disorder as our focus of interest, we noted the advantage of only one state hospital and only one general hospital to which most of the severely disturbed are referred.

In this research program, we viewed "psychosis" as both a *clinical* and a *sociologic* phenomenon. The work has, therefore, been guided by two very different disciplinary and research orientations. One is the more traditional "clinical model" for studies in cross-cultural psychopathology, an investigational approach relying on the professionals, the experts who are both observers and vehicles of measurement. The other model is "sociologic" in that it relies on the ethnic community itself for the definition of mental disorder and for the source of observation.

The results of more recent work in the field of cross-cultural psychopathology (10,11) reinforced the importance of adopting an investigational approach that brings to bear the power of several methodologies and several perspectives (or vantages) on the same behavior. We had learned in prior cross-national studies (of the perception of patient behavior and emotion) that the "perceptual thresholds" of representative viewers from different cultures, whether they be professional or lay people, are likely to vary widely as a function of the norms of the viewers' culture and the type of emotion or behavior they are observing (12).

Thus, we had to introduce a number of vantage points in the study of one ethnic group, in this case that of the "professional," the psychiatrist or psychologist, which fits our "clinical model," that of the ethnic community itself, and that of other ethnic communities with whom they live. Further, we varied the context in which the observations were made, the social background, i.e., the hospital and the community, within which psychopathology is expressed and defined. To assess the meaning of "disturbed" behavior, we found that we eventually would have to investigate what is "normal" for that ethnic community, professionals and experts aside.

The characterization of the typical patterns of social behavior and psychopathology of any one ethnic group requires the bringing together of observations from each of these vantage points to construct a multifaceted picture of that group. These configurations would consist of (a) "pathology", as seen by the clinical experts; (b) disturbed social behavior, as seen by the ethnic community; (c) normality, as perceived and defined by the ethnic community; and (d) deviance and normality, as seen by representatives of other ethnic communities, people who live and interact with this group.

In interpreting such patterns, we eventually will construct meaningful, relevant pictures of how ethnic groups are similar and how they differ. By contrasting such pictures, we expect also to uncover principles related to the mechanisms underlying the expression of psychosis. We began then, with an investigation of the nature of "psychosis," that which is common to the process of how one comes to be identified and diagnosed as "mentally disturbed" in his culture.

The character of this approach required the application of standard methods for interviewing and for describing the symptomatology of severely disturbed patients from several Hawaii ethnic groups. We tried to overcome the principal methodologic limitations of prior studies in this area through application of the following procedures: (a) use of a standardized clinical interview across all ethnic groups (Mental Status Schedule) (13); (b) use of a standard set of scales for rating psychiatric symptoms (Inpatient Multidimensional Psychiatric Scales) (14); and (c) investigation of psychopathology and social behavior in more than one setting, i.e., in the hospital and in the community by use of a standard method for measuring disturbed social behavior (Katz Adjustment Scales, KAS) (15). Further controls relevant to cross-cultural studies were also instituted, such as those for sex, social class, age, and marital status.

It became evident early in the course of the first investigation that to answer the critical questions about the influence of culture, "normal" baselines were essential. We later initiated a second major investigation aimed at deriving baselines of social behavior and symptoms for each of the ethnic groups. This phase involved the administration of one of the descriptive methods, the adjustment scales, to representative "normal" samples of each of the ethnic groups in the community (16). With this rather unique facet for a cross-cultural study, we also would be able through an empirical approach to investigate the sociologic problem of how the community itself defines mental disorder.

CLINICAL STUDY

Our inital patient sample consisted of all admissions to Hawaii State Hospital (from the ages of 20 to 50, from selected ethnic groups) for severe functional psychosis. Collection of the sample of 300 patients proceeded over a period of 2 years (1966–1968). Five ethnic groups were included: Hawaii-Japanese, Hawaii-Caucasian, Portuguese, Filipino[1], and Part-Hawaiians. All patients were interviewed and rated within 3 days of admission. Our "normal" sample was drawn later (1968) from a representative sample of 1200 households in Hawaii and provided subsamples for each of the ethnic groups included in the patient group.

The results of the clinical studies have been reported in detail elsewhere (1,6). Here we will summarize the findings that have emerged from that study.

1. Patients from the different ethnic groups did manifest psychosis differently when judged by a varied group of experienced clinicians in the hospital setting. The contrast was most marked between the Hawaii-Japanese and the Hawaii-Caucasian patients, but there were variations in emotional and behavioral patterns among all groups.
2. The differences were most pronounced in the expression of emotional states, i.e., hostility, anxiety, depression, and apathy (see Figure 51-1).

---

[1] Admissions of Filipino women during this period were very rare; only Filipino men were included in the sample. Both sexes were represented equally in the other ethnic groups. Portuguese are a distinct ethnic group in Hawaii.

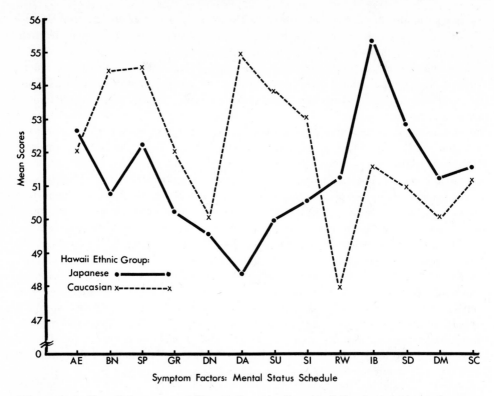

Figure 51-1. Hawaii-Japanese and Hawaii-Caucasian functional disorders: patterns of symptomatology in the hospital. *Note:* AE = agitation-excitement; BN = belligerence-negativisim; SP = suspicion-persecution-hallucinations; GR = grandiosity; DN = denial of illness; DA = depression-anxiety; SU = suicide-self mutilation; SI = social isolation; RW = retardation-emotional withdrawal; IB = inappropriate-bizarre; SD = speech disorganization; DM = disorientation-memory. From Katz, M.M., Sanborn, K.O. and Gudeman, H.: Characterizing differences in psychopathology among ethnic groups in Hawaii. In: *Social Psychiatry*, Redlich, F. (ed.), Baltimore: Williams and Wilkins, 1969.

3. The Hawaii-Caucasian psychotic was viewed by clinicians as significantly more "emotional" in quality—the Hawaii-Japanese, more schizoid, more withdrawn and apathetic.

4. On factors descriptive of the major indicators, the "core" characteristics of psychosis, i.e., in the cognitive, perceptual, and motoric spheres, there were few differences, if any, among the ethnic groups—all had similar levels of disturbance in *"paranoid projection, motor-disturbance, grandiosity, disorientation, conceptual disorganization"* (14).

The distinctions between the two ethnic groups were, however, very clear.[2] The Caucasians projected an image of heightened affect in all spheres, i.e., in level of hostility,

---

[2] The comparison of the Hawaii-Japanese and Hawaii-Caucasian is presented here because they are the most prominent of ethnic groups in Hawaii, accounting for some two-thirds of the population.

excited behavior, anxiety, and depression; the Japanese, of a more withdrawn-retarded, restrained picture of psychosis.

The more overriding question is whether these differences are reflecting real differences in the way ethnic background influences the expression of psychosis, the central issue in this study, or whether they are simply an artifact of the stage of psychosis at which various groups enter their members into a hospital. We presume, on the basis of experience in Hawaii, that the Japanese are more resistant to admitting family members to the mental hospital. There are, also, the issues of how Western training and Western "eyes" influence the observation of symptoms, the emotion expressed, and how valid the judgments are concerning the nature of these behaviors. The results are likely to be the outcome of the interaction of all these factors. What is true here is that, given samples of severely disturbed patients admitted from several diverse ethnic communities, trained clinical professionals see and report wide differences in the manner in which psychosis is expressed. These differences are somewhat consistent with what might have been expected from prior cross-national studies of psychopathology and from prior theory about the cultural characteristics of those groups.

In seeking to sort out further the bases for these differences, we turned to another source of information about the actual emotional and behavioral expression of these patients. That source was their own ethnic community. Their behavior would be described in another, more natural context, the community, and by someone more like themselves in ethnic background and social class.

COMMUNITY STUDY

In the community study the same set of problems was pursued, but from the standpoint of the ethnic group itself. If these patients were described at the time when they were most severely disturbed, i.e., just prior to admission to the hospital, how would they compare? What similarities and what differences among ethnic groups would result? How would the descriptions from the vantage of the community compare with those of the professionals?

This second major approach then focused on characterizing the kind of behavior and emotion manifested by people who were designated psychotic in a particular ethnic community. This behavior was described through the observations and judgments of members of the ethnic group itself to determine whether: (a) ethnic communities differ in their concepts and definitions of psychosis; (b) if so, how each ethnic community characterizes psychosis, or what we will later call severe "social deviance," and whether, (c) there are similarities in the ways psychosis is manifested in the various ethnic groups.

A third level of analysis would attempt to integrate the *pattern of pathology* and that of *social deviance* from the two standpoints, the "clinical" and the "sociologic," to better comprehend the nature of psychosis and its mechanisms, and to characterize more fully the various ethnic patterns of psychopathology.

The central method in this phase was the *relatives' ratings of symptoms and social behavior.*[3] The inventory was completed on each patient in the course of an interview

[3] The R forms of the KAS.

with a family member or someone who had been in close contact with the patient over the several weeks prior to hospital admission. A profile of scores, based on the factors described in Table 51-1, was generated for each of the 300 patients. These factors span social behavior, emotional expression, signs of distress, and qualities of normal and abnormal cognitive and perceptual activity. The mean factor scores for each ethnic group represent a pattern for that group.

Our first question, similar to that raised in the clinical study, was how comparable in expression and severity are the five groups; then, specifically, how comparable are the Japanese and the Caucasians.

The results of the comparison were striking in that very few differences were found among the five ethnic groups. There was one respect in which the Caucasian men turned out to be significantly different from men in other ethnic samples, namely, their relatives

Table 51-1. KAS[a] Form R1: Examples of Items Within Each Cluster

Belligerence (4)[b]	*Suspicious* (4)	*Nervousness* (4)
Angry and broke things	Thought people were talking about him	Got nervous easily
Got into fights	Acted as if suspicious	Jittery
Cursed at people	Said people were trying to make him do or think things	Worried or fretted
Verbal expansiveness (5)	*Anxiety* (6)	*Bizarreness* (5)
Spoke very loudly	Had strange fears	Had bad dreams
Talked too much	Afraid something terrible was going to happen	Acted as if he saw people or things
Bragged how good he is	Got suddenly frightened for no reason	Did strange things
Negativism (9)	*Withdrawal and retardation* (6)	*Hyperactivity* (3)
Not cooperative	Just sat	Was restless
Did the opposite	Quiet	Did same thing over and over
Deliberately upset routine	Moved about very slowly	
	Helplessness (4)	
	Cried easily	
	Acted helpless	
	Acted as if he could not concentrate on one thing	
	General psychopathology (24)	
	Laughed or cried at strange times	
	Got very excited for no reason	
	Talked without making sense	

[a] Katz Adjustment Scale.

[b] The number in parentheses indicates the total number of items within each cluster.

rated them as more "helpless." Other than this isolated finding, we found no significant differences among ethnic groups on any of the eleven social behavior and symptom variables measured by the KAS (6).

COMMENT

The differences that can be attributed to ethnicity in these five samples are, therefore, very minimal. The tendency for the Caucasian men to project a more "helpless," low performance picture is, however, consistent with their description from the clinical study of having significantly more depressive affect. The most outstanding aspect of these results was the failure to find any major differences among the groups. The various ethnic groups do *not* project distinctive patterns in the community. In view of the findings in the clinical study and the prevalent theory that differences in behavioral and emotional expression should be exaggerated in mental disorder, the results were unexpected.

In one sense, there must be more universality about the frequency with which certain kinds of behaviors and emotions associated with psychosis have to occur, i.e., the amount of obstreperous behavior, anxiety, suspiciousness, and withdrawal. All these appear to occur at similar levels for each ethnic group, although the patterns of expression across groups may differ slightly. It may be that there are certain standards of deviance within a community as a whole that have to be met before a person can qualify as being ill. Whatever the reasons, it is hard to distinguish the groups. The alternative hypotheses one must entertain are: (a) In the eyes of each community these patients exhibit similar amounts of these varieties of behavior, i.e., when people are disturbed they show similar signs—become more hostile, more anxious, entertain more bizarre ideas, become more helpless and suspicious—regardless of the cultural group to which they belong. There are, in other words, only so many ways in which people can manifest psychosis. (b) The method for measuring social behavior is not sufficiently sensitive to discriminate differences in these various categories of behavior,[4] e.g., there are insufficient items; the descriptors are not designed to bring out the ethnic specifics for that group.

Let us assume, however, that large differences are not evident in the ways the severely mentally disturbed of each of these communities appear to relate and behave. We are aware, on the basis of the evidence in the Hawaii second phase, that differences exist among the *"normal"* patterns of social behavior and emotional expression among these groups (16). How would the pattern of social behavior presented by psychotic patients look in relation to that which constitutes "normal" behavior in each ethnic community? Given normal baselines for each community, it was possible both to increase the sensitivity of the method, i.e., in experimental terms (by providing what could be viewed as a set of "before" scores on these variables), and to examine the meanings of the discrete behavioral categories *relative* to these community baselines. In these terms, a behavior is "psychopathologic" to the extent that it is found to deviate sharply from what is considered normal or typical in that ethnic group.

[4] In view of the KAS technique's capacity to distinguish among types of schizophrenics (17), social classes, the sexes (18), and changes in clinical state (19), this possible explanation is questionable.

We expected, in fact, that each community would place different weights on these behavioral factors, that each has its own concept of what constitutes deviant behavior, and that each will define psychopathology somewhat differently. To the extent, therefore, that we could apply "norms" as baselines for measuring these behaviors, the method would permit estimating the degree and the pattern of social deviance reflected by those identified as mentally disordered. It was this line of reasoning that contributed to the rationale for the second phase of the work, the development of the study of "normality" in the various ethnic groups of the Hawaii community.[5]

ETHNICITY AND "SOCIAL DEVIANCE"

In the following analysis, we attempted to define and to compare the patterns of social deviance for each of the ethnic groups and to compare the clinical and community descriptions for a particular ethnic group.

Operationally, the pattern of cluster scores derived for a representative "normal" ethnic group was used as a baseline from which the pattern of scores derived from the sample of hospitalized patients of that ethnic group was contrasted. The result was a profile of discrepancies, the peaks identifying those areas of behavior in the mentally disordered that are found to be most "*deviant*" from the "normal" for each ethnic group. The interpretation of this discrepancy pattern led to an empirical definition of psychosis for that community.[6] We asked first whether these empirically derived patterns of social deviance differ among ethnic groups. If so, we would then interpret the differences in the patterns, the ways in which they are distinguished, and specify the significant departures in social deviance for each group.

RESULTS AND COMMENTS

A new set of KAS scores for each patient in Study 1, based on the discrepancy between his profile of cluster scores and the norms for the ethnic groups was computed.[7] A two-way (groups by measures) profile analysis of variance which contrasts the four groups indicated that both the levels and the patterns of the groups differed significantly (6).[8] The significant interaction indicated that the relationship among the behavioral factors within a particular ethnic group differed from the relationships of these factors within

---

[5] The field study of social behavior in a representative sample of "normals" across ethnic groups involved administering the *relative's rating method* to a community sample of approximately 1200 subjects. The results depicting the varying patterns and the similarities are presented in Sanborn and Katz (16).

[6] The definition is viewed as "empirical" because it is based on the ratings of observed behavior of samples of normals and patients, rather than on generalized attitudes of the raters of that ethnic community.

[7] The norms are based on a sample of 300 raters (from the total of 1200 in the Hawaii Normal Study) (16) who used the 2-point (the same as that used in the patient study) rather than the 4-point scale of item intensity. The sample of 300 is representative, having been selected randomly from the entire sample of 1200. The norms are controlled for age and sex of the patient. In this analysis, as was done with the clinical data, a series of analyses evaluating the role and contribution of demographic variables was conducted. Those having direct relevance to the analysis of ethnic differences are reported in the text.

[8] The details of this ANOVA are presented in (6). Only those groups with both men and women were included.

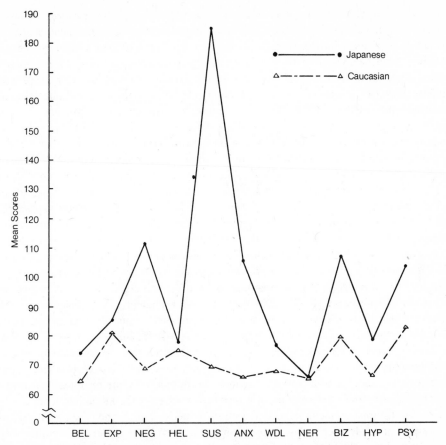

Figure 51-2. Ethnic group comparisons on relatives' ratings of social behavior. (KAS): Patterns of social deviance (profiles of difference scores between ratings of psychiatric patients and ratings of normals within each ethnic group).

the other groups. The patterns of "social deviance" among these groups, therefore, differed. Examples of these patterns, the Hawaii-Japanese and Hawaii-Caucasian, are displayed in Figure 51-2.

To summarize the results of this phase of the investigation:

1. Of all the Hawaii ethnic groups, the behavior of the *Japanese* was shown to be most deviant from that which constitutes normality in their own community. As shown in Figure 51-2, the profile of deviance scores for the Japanese patients was most marked in those areas that ordinarily signify a panic-like state or acute psychosis (severe anxiety and bizarre thinking), and in social behavior reflected by suspiciousness of others, extreme negativism, and hyperactivity.

2. Not shown in the data of Figure 51-2, the Caucasians were most deviant on the factor of the community's dissatisfaction with what they were doing with their free time; when only the lower social class groups were compared, more deviance was perceived in the "helplessness" of the Caucasian men, their inability to make decisions, and to perform.

What the social deviance pattern appears to be reflecting is that the concept of mental disorder which is internal to that community may be idiosyncratic to their view of the world and may not be observed easily by the outsider. Thus, on the basis of the descriptions of patient behavior that were provided by the community prior to the use of ethnic norms, it was difficult to discriminate among these groups. We may, therefore, expect that clinicians who see patients from ethnic groups other than their own, will have difficulty "reading" the behavior. Regardless of the underlying reasons, it is now clear that the ethnic communities were identifying distinct disorders that were seen in ways different from each other. If we now view these results from the standpoint of what they reflect in the attitudes and the concepts that the ethnic community has in regard to the meaning and nature of mental disorder, we see other implications.

The implications of these findings in regard to the meaning for the *Japanese* indicate, as reflected in Figure 51-2, their sensitivity to such factors as suspiciousness and anxiety, and that family members must be seen as manifesting a greater amount of psychopathology than is evident in all other groups before they will be referred to hospitals. The attribute of "suspiciousness" distinguished the Japanese patient—it stood out in the overall picture of that which constitutes deviance for the Japanese.

In seeking an interpretation of this finding, we are reminded of the preeminent role of "trust" in Japanese society.[9] The literal meaning of the factor of "suspiciousness" does, in fact, reflect a great deal of distrust of the environment and of other people by the mentally disturbed Japanese. The fact that distrust attains such an importance in the Japanese concept of social deviance—despite the fact that their overt behavior was not very different from that in other groups—implies that this types of behavior carried greater significance than do other behaviors. To pursue this line of thought, it implies that the Japanese have less tolerance for distrustful behavior than do other groups.

For the *Caucasian* men, it was a decline in performance and "helplessness," the inability to make decisions, that seemed most to disturb his community. Helplessness is often associated with the state of depression. We can ask in this case whether these factors are not related to the importance of independence and performance in Western Mainland society.[10]

These interpretations of the social deviance data thus point to those factors that are more salient in a group's concept of deviance, those that are viewed as more disruptive, more disturbing to the order of their social living.

SUMMARY

What findings were anticipated and which of them were different than might have been expected on the basis of prior notions and findings concerning ethnic psychopathology?

The hospitalized *Hawaii-Japanese* schizophrenic has been described (8) as likely to be contained, seclusive, emotionally shallow; he is said to be chronically schizoid in his general demeanor and is viewed as severely schizophrenic. The clinical picture we derived from the ratings by professional clinicians at Hawaii State Hospital was similar. Their

---

[9] Discussions with Dr. Takie Lebra, Department of Sociology, University of Hawaii, have been very helpful here.

[10] We cannot, in this brief chapter, do justice to the potential complexity of social and cultural explanations required to interpret these results fully.

descriptions of the Hawaii-Japanese, based on the standard interview and the IMPS, were of the chronic, withdrawn, type of schizophrenic with "blunted" affect.

The picture derived from the community, however, differed sharply from that of the clinicians. Although the behavior described by the informants would ordinarily indicate the presence of severe psychosis, the elements that distinguished this group are more consistent with an "acute" state, e.g., anxiety, bordering on panic. In emphasizing the anxiety, the community was also calling attention to the strong feelings of emotion evident in the patient, contrasting sharply with the shallow picture described by the clinician. The outstanding feature of the Japanese description of the patient's social behavior is the high level of "distrust," of suspicious, paranoid behavior, which appears to run directly counter to a central theme in Japanese values. It is this feature that appears to be central to the Japanese community's concept of deviance.

Disorder in the hospitalized *Hawaii-Caucasian* psychotic was in the clinical analysis more affective in quality than in the other groups, particularly as regards the emotions of depression and hostility, and less schizoid in general behavior. The analysis of community perception would tend, in emphasizing "helplessness" and decline in performance in the man, to support the picture derived from the clinical interview analysis. The clinical and community picture, therefore, do not conflict; they appear to be viewing the same behavior but with different emphases. The similarity in perceptions might be expected since the professional's ethnic background is not too unlike that of the patient's community.[11]

THEORETICAL IMPLICATIONS

There are a number of findings in the investigation that provoke reconsideration of certain assumptions concerning the relationship of normal to abnormal behavior in a culture. One derives from the anthropologic notion that the study of psychopathology in cultural groups provides an indirect but graphic approach to the understanding of what is "normal," and a path toward identifying the central basic values of that culture. In the language of psychopathology, it would be necessary to differentiate those formal aspects of psychosis, e.g., "disorders of thought," "failure of the capacity to distinguish reality from fantasy," from the stamp any particular ethnic or social group puts on the expression of that disturbance. Our investigation was not designed to answer whether the formal categories of psychosis, e.g., schizophrenia, are universal. It was directed more toward identifying those principles that underlie the nature of psychosis and those aspects of disorder that appear to be shaped primarily by the culture. In that respect, it is possible to view the primacy of "suspiciousness" in the Japanese psychosis, and "helplessness" in the Hawaii-Caucasian, as reflecting the dark side of central themes in these ethnic societies, i.e., the importance of trust and of control of outer emotions in the Japanese and of independence and productivity for the Caucasians.

As to differences in order of priority between clinicians and the community, the studies of the Portuguese and Filipino ethnic groups within the Hawaii community indicate that certain behaviors are already at a high level, are more like what is "normal" for that ethnic community, and thus may have to be interpreted differently in the

---

[11] Although most of the clinicians were from the U.S. Mainland, there were several with European and South American backgrounds. All were Western trained, i.e., U.S. and European Schools of Psychiatry.

analysis of the psychosis. "Hyperactivity," for example, has low diagnostic significance for the Portuguese, but belligerence suggests psychopathology for the Filipino community.

The professional, oriented as he is to the "disease" model, focuses on the form of psychosis, presumably those characteristics that identify psychosis in any setting. Thus, he may not always be in tune with what the central meaning of psychosis is to a particular ethnic group. The concept of psychosis must be expanded. For the individual, it appears to be shaped by forces that are primarily internal (on the assumption that some breakdown in organization has occurred); but in reflecting the dark negative side of a cultural value, it appears also to be a sign of moving against or breaking out of that cultural framework. Thus, the "disease" and "social deviance" model concepts come into conflict. Is psychosis simply a "breakdown in integrity of the organism" or is it a purposeful moving against the culture? It is, most probably we assume, both of these.

Professionals should be prepared in dealing with ethnic issues to move away from the disease model and to begin to integrate what the community is trying to tell them are the core features of psychosis for that culture. These concepts, then, must be integrated into professional understanding, not as another set of "symptoms," but as a way of understanding the *meanings* of the psychosis, perhaps its prime functions. The problem of which part of the psychosis is the outcome of biologic or psychologic breakdown, and which part is cultural acting out is still unresolved. The scientist must continue to work at the problem of analysis of the relative influence of these forces. It would be desirable for clinicians to move away from the strictly psychopathologic outlook and to concentrate on recreating the whole, i.e., the form *and* the social content.

In this respect, the community's picture of psychosis is central to this kind of understanding because it is less concerned with what may be the formal aspects of psychosis and is more focused on its social aspects, and its meaning as regards support or disruption of basic harmony in that community.

REFERENCES

1. Katz MM, Gudeman H, Sanborn KO: Characterizing differences in psychopathology among ethnic groups: a preliminary report on Hawaii-Japanese and Mainland-American schizophrenics, in Caudill W, Lin T (eds): *Mental Health Research in Asia and the Pacific*. Honolulu, East-West Center Press, 1969.

2. Katz MM, Sanborn KO, Gudeman H: Characterizing differences in psychopathology among ethnic groups in Hawaii, in Redlich F (ed): *Social Psychiatry*. Baltimore, Williams and Wilkins, 1969.

3. Katz MM, Sanborn KO: Multiethnic studies of psychopathology and normality in Hawaii, in Brown BS, Torrey EF (eds): *International Collaboration in Mental Health*. DHEW Publication No. (HSM) 73-9120. Washington, DC, US Government Printing Office, 1973.

4. Draguns J: Comparisons of psychopathology across cultures: Issues, findings, directions. *Journal of Cross-cultural Psychology* 4(1):9–47, 1973.

5. Sartorius N, Jablensky A: Culture and Schizophrenia. *Psychol Medicine* 5, (2) May 1975.

6. Katz MM, Sanborn KO, with Lowery HA, Ching J: Multiethnic studies in Hawaii: on psychopathology and social deviance, unpublished manuscript.

7. NIMH-PSC Collaborative Study Group: Effectiveness of phenothiazine treatment of acute schizophrenic psychoses. *Arch Gen Psychiatry* 10:246–261, 1964.

8. Enright J, Jaeckle W: Psychiatric symptoms and diagnoses in two sub-cultures. *International Journal of Social Psychiatry* 9:12–17, 1963.

9. Katz MM, Lowery HA, Cole JO: Behavior patterns of schizophrenics in the community, in Lorr M (ed): *Explorations in Typing Psychotics*. Oxford, Pergamon Press, 1965.

10. Cooper JE, Kendell RE, Gurland BJ, et al: *Psychiatric Diagnosis in New York and London*. (Maudsley Monograph Series no 20). London, Oxford University Press, 1972.

11. World Health Organization: *The International Pilot Study of Schizophrenia*, vol 1. Geneva, WHO, 1973.

12. Katz MM, Cole JO, Lowery HA: Studies of the diagnostic process: the influence of symptom perception, past experience and ethnic background on diagnostic decisions. *American Journal of Psychiatry* 125:7, 1969.

13. Spitzer RL, Fleiss JL, Endicott J, et al: The mental status schedule: properties of factor analytically devised scale, *Archives of General Psychiatry* 16:487–493, 1967.

14. Lorr M, Klett J, McNair DM, et al: *Inpatient Multi-dimensional Psychiatric Scale*. Palo Alto, California, Consulting Psychologists Press, pp 3–4, 1962.

15. Katz MM, Lyerly SB: Methods of measuring adjustment and social behavior in the community: I. Rationale, description, discriminative validity and scale development. *Psychological Reports* 13:503–535, 1963.

16. Sanborn KO, Katz MM: Multiethnic studies of normality in Hawaii, unpublished manuscript.

17. Katz MM: A phenomenological typology of schizophrenia, in Katz MM, Cole JO, Barton WE (eds): *The Role and Methodology of Classification in Psychiatry and Psychopathology*. Public Health Publication No. 1584. Washington, DC, US Government Printing Office, 1968.

18. Hogarty GE, Katz MM: Norms of adjustment and social behavior. *Archives of General Psychiatry* 25:470–480, 1971.

19. Schooler NR, Goldberg SC, Boothe H, et al: One year after discharge: community adjustment of schizophrenic patients. *American Journal of Psychiatry* 123:8, 1967.

Chapter 52
Cultural Influences on Incidence, Course, and Treatment Response

H. B. M. Murphy, M.D., Ph.D.

When schizophrenia in two or more populations differs markedly with respect to incidence, symptomatology, or course, one looks first to the processes of diagnosis and case-finding for explanation, then, to some form of genetic predisposition or selection, and finally, to environmental factors. The environmental factors can be either physical or sociocultural, and the sociocultural groups tend to be called social if the two groups derive from the same society but cultural if they derive from different societies.

Cultural explanations for disease are not popular, and when one is searching for causes, they tend to be looked at last and to receive the least serious examination. This is because accusing a culture of being disease producing is like casting doubt on someone's religion, and this today, as the British would say, is "not the done thing." Moreover, if one starts questioning someone else's religious or cultural beliefs, then one can end up by questioning the sanity of one's own. Yet the influence of culture on illness is still a valid field for scientific enquiry.

In Chapter 51 in this volume, Dr. Martin Katz has shown how culture can affect symptomatology; in this chapter I wish to touch briefly on the more fundamental question of its possible influence on incidence or risk and on chronicity. Because of space limitations, I will limit myself largely to new developments during the past 9 years, leaving the reader to look up my earlier review (1) of the subject for previous evidence.

INCIDENCE

In that previous review, attention was drawn to situations in Asia, West Africa, Europe, and North America where exceptionally high rates of schizophrenia in certain delimited populations appeared to have a cultural basis. Nothing new has come out of Asia; the main European example has been confirmed as to the excess of schizophrenia (2) but unconfirmed as to a cultural explanation; and only very indirect evidence has been

586

forthcoming regarding the African case. [Rwegellera (3) has shown that West African immigrants to Britain have much higher rates of psychosis than do other immigrant groups such as the West Indians who are equally disadvantaged as to migrational stresses, education, and occupation.] However, one of the North American examples cited was the overseas Irish; and it has now been abundantly shown, as Figure 52-1 illustrates, that in their homeland the schizophrenia rate is very much higher.

When one sees such a picture, as I noted earlier, one does not immediately jump to a cultural explanation. Rather, one thinks of a difference in diagnostic criteria and of case-referral patterns; then one thinks of genetic selection; then, of noncultural environmental factors and, only reluctantly, of cultural ones. However, it has been shown that the diagnostic criteria are not less strict in Ireland than in England (4), and that the mean duration of hospitalization (and hence presumably severity of illness) is not less than elsewhere (5), so the high morbidity level seems genuine.

Concerning genetics, the Irish church has always been very strict against consanguineous marriages. Geneticists claim that the Irish are a very mixed people, not deriving from any one stock, and that their reproductive pattern over the past 200 years should have hampered the transmission of a schizophrenic predisposition since the mean age at marriage is late, the great majority of known schizophrenics never marry, and illegitimate births are rare (6).

Social selection by emigration was an obvious factor to consider, but when the country is divided into districts there is no correlation between the schizophrenia rates and the emigration ones (7). The late and rapid industrialization of Southern Ireland might also be thought by some to be a possible factor, but it is in the countryside and not in the towns that the highest rates of schizophrenia are found (5). Finally, if one thinks of some physical agent in the food, air, or other aspect of the environment, one has to remember that Northern Ireland shares this physical environment but, as Figure 52-1

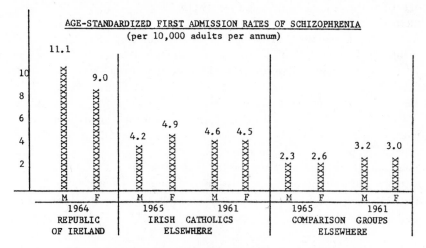

1965 -- Northern Ireland; Roman Catholics and remainder.
1961 — Canada; British-origin; Roman Catholics*& remainder.
    (* In Canada, the British-origin Roman Catholics are
        predominantly of Irish origin.)

Figure 52-1. Incidence of schizophrenia in Southern Ireland Catholics; Northern Ireland Catholics; British-Canadian Catholics, Irish origin; Northern Ireland non-Catholics; and Canadian non-Catholics. From the table in Murphy HBM (6).

shows, has a much lower rate of schizophrenia, particularly among the Protestants. Accordingly, none of the more obvious, noncultural explanations appear able to account for the whole of the marked difference that Figure 52-1 depicts. Almost certainly, some of these factors partly contribute, for we have learnt by now that schizophrenia is multifactorial. However, the way is clear for a consideration of whether some cultural factor could have been operating.

Before one can search for such a factor, one has preferably to have some sort of theory or hypothesis as to how culture might be affecting the risk of developing schizophrenia. I have offered such a theory under the title, "Schizophrenia-evoking Role of Complex Social Tasks" (8,9). Briefly, the theory assumes that genetic or other organic factors can produce a deficit in information processing, particularly with respect to the recognition of relevance or relatedness; but this deficit is of varying degree so that what we call schizophrenia often only arises when the information-processing function is persistently overburdened. In the laboratory this overburdening can easily be induced in schizophrenics, with a resultant, temporary increase in symptoms, by providing competing signals and demanding that the patient respond only to one. In real life the overburdening can occur when key figures in the schizophrenia-prone person's environment persistently demand that he decipher complex social messages or reconcile apparently contradictory ones, and prevent him from escaping from this task. The overburdening can occur within the family, as the work of Bateson (10), Wynne (11), and most recently Stierlin (Chapter 48) have attempted to demonstrate, but it can also occur outside the family. For instance, one can argue that the North American urban lower class [but not the lower class everywhere (12)] carries such a burden through being told that a normal man can achieve success by his own efforts while at the same time being confronted with a social structure that impedes upward mobility. Similarly, I have shown that the high rate of schizophrenia in French-Canadian rural women is probably linked to a conflict in teachings regarding the woman's role in that society (13).

In Southern Ireland one finds that a high complexity of social communication is not merely common but is expected and is an important source of entertainment. The country has been called the land of the "double think and double speak" (14); anthropologists have described how widespread ridicule is in some rural areas (15); and an Irish psychiatrist has written protesting against one form of ridicule in which "the victim is never sure whether the ridiculer is serious or not" (16). It is my opinion, therefore, that this cultural pattern among the Irish does evoke schizophrenia in persons with an information-processing defect, provided, as is true in the villages, such persons cannot escape the experience. Such an hypothesis would explain why the rate drops markedly (but not entirely) not merely when the Irish emigrate, but when they are living in the more culturally mixed Northern Ireland and in Dublin. However, the hypothesis needs testing (and is testable) so the next decade may see some clarification of this idea.

COURSE AND OUTCOME

The strongest reasons for suspecting a cultural factor in the course of schizophrenia are to be found in the 2-year and 5-year follow-up data from the International Pilot Study of Schizophrenia. (See Chapter 57.) Because the cultural dimension has not yet been fully discussed in that study, I prefer to refer to some earlier evidence.

In Figure 52-2, a comparison of follow-up data from Britain and from the Island of Mauritius shows that although the percentage of patients needing continuous hospitalization is virtually the same for the two islands, the percentages of patients running intermittent or semichronic courses are very different. Since the diagnostic criteria and incidence rates in the two locations have been shown to be very similar (17), the simplest explanation for this finding is to posit two types of schizophrenia, one chronic and resistant to sociocultural factors, the other less chronic and more susceptible. Such an explanation would harmonize with European ideas regarding the difference between "true" or "process" schizophrenia and the schizophreniform psychoses, and it would also enable one to argue that for the "true" variety there is no real difference between societies.

Unfortunately, further evidence does not support so simple a theory. Figures 52-3 and 52-4 present data from two other sources, the Caribbean and Canada, that suggest strongly that in people of the same genetic origin who live in different social settings, there can be considerable variation in the course of schizophrenia, with not just the "full recovery" but also the "fully chronic" categories being reduced when the frequency of intermediate courses increases. The people of St. Thomas in the Caribbean are largely of African origin, like the greater part of the Mauritius population, but when hospitalized schizophrenics were followed up in St. Thomas, they showed a very different pattern from that found in Mauritius (18). In Canada, the people of traditional ("old") and modern ("new") French-Canadian communities were of the same genetic origin and largely shared the same cultural values, but again the courses of illness showed marked differences. (The three "old" communities were scattered over a wide region, with no intermarriage, the same being true of the three "new" ones; and the scatter of rates within each three was narrow.) It seems more probable from these data, therefore, that there are not two schizophrenias, one chronic and the other variable, but either a single schizophrenia or many schizophrenias, with chronicity being affected by the social

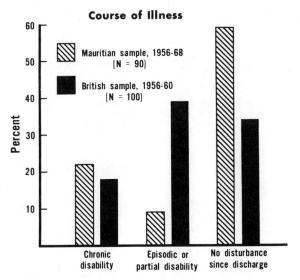

Figure 52-2. Comparison of Mauritian and British schizophrenics by course of illness as assessed twelve and five years after admission. Reproduced from Murphy HBM, Raman AC (17).

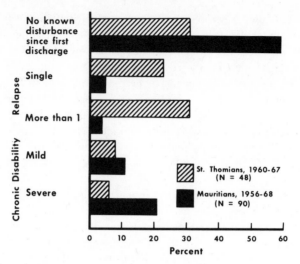

Figure 52-3. Course of illness in schizophrenic patients in the Caribbean (US Virgin Islands) and in Mauritius, over 5 and 12 years respectively. Reproduced from Murphy HBM (18).

setting. Wing (Chapter 53) has discussed familial and what might be called microsocial factors affecting course; I wish to discuss macrosocial ones.

When one contrasts Mauritius with Britain, there are marked differences in cultural orientation. When one contrasts Mauritius with St. Thomas, or the "old" French-Canadian communities with the "new" ones, the cultural orientations are relatively similar, although not identical. There are, however, considerable differences in social organization and the way in which the cultural values are supported. In both Mauritius and Britain the social support of the ex-mental hospital patient is quite good, but the expectations that the culture imposes on such a patient are very different. In the "old" and "new" French-Canadian communities, the cultural expectations directed at a

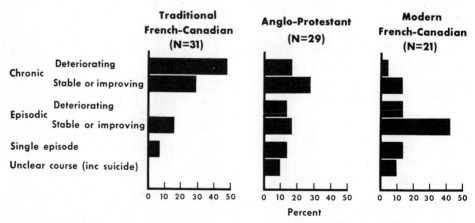

Figure 52-4. Courses of illness from three types of community in eastern Canada. (Chi square = 8.99; p = 0.02 for 2df, comparing chronic and nonchronic course.) Reproduced from Murphy HBM (18).

patient are relatively similar, but the community support of the patients is very different. It is this combination of expectations and support that, I think, accounts for most of the variation between the distribution of different courses of schizophrenia across societies.

The point I am attempting to make may be easier to grasp if we think not of whole societies but of those social microcosms, mental hospitals. We know that hospitals have varied greatly in the proportions of their schizophrenic patients that become long-stay. I suggest that the two main *intrinsic* factors affecting these proportions are the hospital's treatment philosophy or view of mental illness and its efficiency. Official views of mental illness have varied from the moral to the organic, from being a permanent handicap for which society has a duty to provide assistance, to being a conquerable disease which enough effort and skill should be able to cure. The proportion of long-stay patients is usually significantly higher when the "permanent handicap" view is held, no matter how well-intentioned and hard-working the staff may be, than when the "curable disease" view of insanity applies. However, the difference in the proportion of long-stay patients can be negligible in two hospitals with different philosophies if neither administration is efficient enough to insure that its philosophy is followed. If a belief in curability is coupled with a belief that illness is a personal responsibility, then patients may achieve only a brief recovery before relapsing, since both staff and patients tend to regard the latter as "poor devils" with insufficient character. On the other hand, if the curability belief is linked to a belief in an external causality, as by some infection or trauma, then relapses are likely to be less frequent, since both staff and patients tend to think of the external cause as having been destroyed.

Extrapolate from this model to whole societies, and one can see that the risk of chronicity is greatest where the cultural tradition is strong, as in the "old" French-Canadian communities, and where insanity has been and continues to be seen as a permanent disability. Conversely, this risk of chronicity will be least where the society views insanity as curable or, alternatively, as caused by some external agent that can depart as mysteriously as it came, something which is broadly true of the two main Mauritius peoples with their belief in witchcraft and malicious spirits. Where cultural traditions and social norms are less strongly held, as in the "new" French-Canadian communities and in some parts of the Caribbean, the course of schizophrenia is more idiosyncratic, with most patients neither completely recovering (since the social protection from stress is insufficient) nor becoming completely chronic (since the sick-role norms are not enforced). Similarly, where cultural traditions are strong and treatment-oriented, but where individuals are held accountable for their own behavior, as in Britain, then the task of attempting to account for his own behavior during the psychosis may be so difficult that, as argued earlier, the schizophrenia-prone individual is pushed back into his psychosis and relapses each time he feels well enough to attempt to confront his personal accountability. Moreover, these differences in accountability will occur almost regardless of what the official professional and governmental policy regarding mental disorder may be, since the expectations which the patient has internalized during childhood and the behavior of the public toward him are of key importance, more so than the expectations and behavior of the professionals that are assigned temporarily to deal with him.

It may be argued that the sociocultural factors that I have been proposing relate to the sick-role and not to schizophrenia, but I would suggest that the two cannot be kept separate so easily. If we follow Kraepelinian and Scandinavian concepts of schizophrenia as essentially a chronic disease, then we must ask how far this essential feature is culturally induced, not merely through the imposition of a prescribed sick-role but through the schizophrenia-reinvoking effect of trying to fight against that sick-role imposition.

RESPONSES TO DRUG THERAPY

The foregoing are the simpler ways in which one can see culture as possibly affecting the risk and course of schizophrenia, but there are hints that the matter may be much more complex. Neurologic studies on animals suggest that considerable modifications in the microstructure of the brain can be achieved through manipulation of the social environment, and some of the developmental studies of schizophrenia (see other chapters in this volume) suggest that the relevant neurophysiology may be affected by experience. Hence culture could have an effect on brain mechanisms and thence on the risk of schizophrenia at a much more basic level than I have been discussing.

The one type of evidence suggestive of this relates to ethnic differences in the responses of schizophrenics to psychotropic drugs. Most of the illustrations that we have of this—and there are many, although not often cited—compound so many factors that it is difficult to make a special case for a cultural explanation. Either the assessors have not been the same for all patients, or there has been a racial as well as a cultural difference, or the patients could have been chosen according to different criteria, or the social settings and therapies have not been held constant, and so on (19). However, when colleagues in Djakarta kindly provided me with drug trial data from samples of schizophrenic patients who had been selected and rated according to uniform criteria, had been treated by the same doctors in the same wards and with the same trial drugs, but had various cultural backgrounds, most of these complications were circumvented. It then became apparent that with the same drug in the same mean dosage per kilo of body weight, some symptoms disappeared significantly faster in patients of one culture than in patients of another, these cultures deriving from the same race but being respectively matrilineal and patrilineal in tradition (20). Only post hoc hypotheses can be offered as to why that difference appeared, but the finding suggests at least that cultural background should be routinely recorded and analyzed in large clinical drug trials. After that it might then be possible to judge whether this is a line of inquiry that deserves pursuing.

CONCLUSIONS

From the evidence presented here, there are two levels at which culture needs to be thought about by workers in the field of schizophrenia. First, but more difficult, one needs to ask whether one's own culture, or the culture in which one is working, is in some sense "schizophrenogenic." Second, one needs to ask whether cultural factors have been taken sufficiently into account in appraising the results of one's treatment or research. On the first point the question is not whether a culture is "causing" schizophrenia—the answer will always be no—but whether it is contributing to the difficulties of the schizophrenia-prone by imposing expectations or conditions that are not essential for the longer-term welfare of its people. On the second point, one needs to ask not merely whether culture is a concomitant variable that one should be studying, but whether it could be an antecedent variable that is affecting one's sample and contributing to the fact that one is getting results that differ from those of someone working elsewhere. Sanua (21) pointed this out many years ago with respect to the persons comprising the patient and control populations of various studies of the family dynamics of schizophrenia.

Psychiatrists and their fellow workers prove to know surprisingly little about culture, which in any event is quite a complex concept. For this reason, it is not going to be sufficient merely to record the cultural background of one's subjects or include various cultural groups in one's study (although this is better than nothing). To handle the variable adequately one must know what it means to be a Japanese, Scot, Papuan, and so forth, and what has contributed to such a cultural identity—something that usually means calling in a specialist, an anthropologist with specific knowledge of the groups under study. To handle the variable well, one must know what cultural elements have contributed to one's own identity.

REFERENCES

1. Murphy HBM: Cultural factors in the genesis of schizophrenia, in Rosenthal D, Kety SS (eds): *The Transmission of Schizophrenia.* London, Pergamon Press, 1968, p 137.

2. Crocetti GM et al: Selected aspects of the epidemiology of psychoses in Croatia, Yugoslavia; Part III. *Am J Epidem* 94:126, 1971.

3. Rwegellera GGC: Psychiatric morbidity among West Africans and West Indians living in London, unpublished manuscript.

4. Kelleher MJ, Copeland JRM: Psychiatric diagnosis in Cork and London; results of a cross-national pilot study. *J Irish Med Assn* 66:553, 1973.

5. Walsh D: *The 1963 Irish Psychiatric Hospital Census.* Dublin, Medico-social Research Board, N.D.

6. Murphy HBM: Alcoholism and schizophrenia in the Irish; an overview. *Transcult Psychiat Res Rev* 12:116, 1975.

7. Walsh D, Walsh B: Mental illness in the Republic of Ireland; first admissions. *J Irish Med Assn* 63:365, 1970.

8. Murphy HBM: The evocative role of complex social tasks, in Kaplan AR (ed): *Genetic Factors in "Schizophrenia."* Springfield, Ill, Charles C Thomas, 1972, p 407.

9. Murphy HBM: Sociocultural factors in schizophrenia: a compromise theory, in Zubin J, Freyhan FA (eds): *Social Psychiatry.* New York, Grune & Stratton, 1968, p 74.

10. Bateson G, Jackson D, Haley J et al: Toward a theory of schizophrenia. *Behav Sci* 1:251, 1956.

11. Wynne LC, Singer MT: Thought disorder and family relations in schizophrenia. *Arch Gen Psychiat* 9:191, 1963.

12. Murphy HBM: Culture and mental disorder in Singapore, in Opler MK (ed): *Culture and Mental Health.* New York, Macmillan, 1959, p 291.

13. Murphy HBM, Lemieux M: Quelques considérations sur le taux élevé de schizophrénie dans un type de communauté canadienne-française. *Canad Psychiat Assn J,* vol 12, Numéro Spécial S71, 1967.

14. Tracy H: *Mind You, I've Said Nothing!* London, Methuen, 1953.

15. Messenger JC: *Inis Beag.* New York, Holt Rinehart & Winston, 1969.

16. Dunne D: Psychiatric problems in County Mayo. *Corridor Echo,* 1970. Quoted by Greeley AM, in *That Most Distressful Nation: The Taming of the American Irish.* Chicago, Quadrangle Books, 1972.

17. Murphy HBM, Raman AC: The chronicity of schizophrenia in indigenous tropical peoples. *Brit J Psychiat* 118:489, 1971.

18. Murphy HBM: Chronicité. communauté et culture, in Chiland C, Béquart P (eds): *Traitements au Long Cours des Etats Psychotiques.* Toulouse, Privat, 1974.

19. Murphy HBM: Ethnic variations in drug response: Results of an international survey. *Transcult Psychiat Res Rev* 6:5, 1969.

20. Murphy HBM: Psychopharmacologie et variations ethno-culturelles. *Confrontations Psychiatriques* 9:163, 1972.

21. Sanua V: The sociocultural aspects of schizophrenia: a review of the literature, in Bellak L, Loeb L (eds): *The Schizophrenic Syndrome.* New York, Grune & Stratton, 1969.

Section XII

ONSET AND COURSE

INTRODUCTION
Joseph Zubin, Ph.D.

The literature on onset and course of schizophrenia is one of the most extensive in psychopathology, but it is poor on fact and rich in theory. The main thrust of this section of the volume is to winnow the fancy from the facts.

Onset: A widely held clinical impression has been that sudden onset leads to a poor outcome while gradual, insidious onset leads to a poor outcome. To test this impression, a survey of the world literature was conducted in 1961 by Zubin *et al* (1), and 177 studies were found that assessed type of onset clinically as either sudden or gradual. In each study, those with sudden onset had a superior outcome.

Indirect measures of type of onset based on premorbid personality assessment were obtained in 563 other studies in which the premorbid personality of the patients was assessed with regard to cyclothymic versus schizoid characteristics, psychosexual development, social and work history, interest in the environment, duration of illness prior to hospitalization, and presence of precipitating factors. The patients who had a good premorbid personality adjustment fared much better then those who had a poor premorbid adjustment in 531 out of the 563 studies. Only 21 studies showed a contrary trend, and 11 showed no decisive advantage in outcome for either the good or the poor premorbid patients.

The seeming advantage of sudden onset, predicting favorable outcome, has held true over the years despite the introduction of new therapies and changes in patient management. A recent study in the drug era by Gittelman-Klein and Klein (2) confirmed this finding for the premorbid schizoid (asocial) group, who fared poorly, but not for the nonschizoid (nonasocial) group whose outcome varied from very poor to very good. Why the good premorbid patients often improve while the poor premorbid patients do not, raises a fundamental question regarding the efficacy of therapy. By choosing good premorbid patients for any new therapy, its efficacy can be made to appear quite high. Many therapies may have achieved early prominence by such a selection. If it is also true that good premorbid patients more often experience spontaneous improvement, this too may produce the impression of a higher efficacy than the treatment warrants.

If we were to choose candidates for canonization into laws among the generalizations in psychopathology, the law that sudden onset leads to good outcome while gradual onset leads to poor outcome, and the law that good premorbid patients improve while poor premorbid patients do not, would rank high. However, determining the type of onset retrospectively is very difficult; identification of valid prospective clues appears to be even more elusive. It requires detailed knowledge of early school adjustment, family relationships, type and quality of adolescent friendship patterns, work history, including first jobs during vacation periods, and social and psychosexual adjustment. Sudden versus insidious changes in these variables ought to be apparent before the illness is diagnosed. One example of an attempt at finding indications of insidious onset was the study of friendship patterns in early adolescence (13–14 year olds) by Kreisman (3). She found, in a retrospective study, that there was little behavioral difference between the preschizophrenics and their normal controls in sociability as measured by overt participation in friendship relationships. However, they differed significantly in their feelings about friendship, e.g., feelings of loneliness and satisfaction with regard to friendship and intimacy. Apparently, before overt signs of schizophrenia appeared, some of the preschizophrenics evinced experiential precursors of the later clinical episode.

Outcome: One of the results of a survey of follow-up studies by Staudt and Zubin (4) concluded that up to the drug era, when mere release from the hospital was a significant outcome, the results indicated that about one-third of the patients seemed to improve, one-third remained unchanged, and one-third deteriorated. This generalization is another candidate for canonization as a law. The only change that has occurred since the drug era is that the middle third can now be released; it is this group that turned our formerly custodial institutions into "revolving-door hospitals."

We were puzzled by the ubiquity of the $\frac{1}{3}$-$\frac{1}{3}$-$\frac{1}{3}$ law and tried to find some explanation for it. One explanation leans on the possibility that the law does not reflect outcome as much as it reflects human judgment when faced with the uncertainty engendered by a classification task without specified objective criteria. Two extreme groups can always be selected, leaving a residual group in the middle. Windle (5) has pointed out that if the initial and final assessment of the patient has a reliability of 0.57, it follows, through statistical regression, that about one-third would shift from a lower to a higher level (improve). Following this reasoning, it may be possible to demonstrate that one-third would shift downward (deteriorate), and one-third would remain in the middle (unchanged).

The need for developing objective criteria for measuring improvement is paramount. The evaluation of outcome in the past has been made largely by the judgment of the clinician, by the patient, by the family, by important others, by society, especially with regard to employability and social acceptance, and by the after-care provided by the delivery system of health services. These judgments are not the most unbiased, do not always coincide, and may not be linearly related. The development of an integrated approach across these factors for assessing outcome is a dire necessity. Instead of appealing to multiple regression methods which depend upon such assumptions as linear relationships, we may find that it is more useful to apply typological analyses in which the patterning across these factors is sought.

These are some of the challenges we face, and at least some of these problems are clarified in this volume.

REFERENCES

1. Zubin J, Sutton S, Salzinger K et al: A Biometric approach to prognosis in schizophrenia, in Hoch PH, Zubin J (eds): *Epidemiology in the Mental Disorders*. New York, Grune & Stratton, 1961, p 143–203.

2. Gittelman-Klein R, Klein DF: Premorbid asocial adjustment and prognosis in schizophrenia. *J Psychiat Res* 7:35–53, 1969.

3. Kreisman D: Social interaction and intimacy in preschizophrenic adolescence, in Zubin J, Freedman AM (eds): *The Psychopathology of Adolescence*. New York, London, Grune & Stratton, 1970.

4. Staudt V, Zubin J: A biometric evaluation of the somatotherapies in schizophrenia. *Psychol Bull* 54:171–196, 1957.

5. Windle C: Prognosis of mental subnormals: A critical review of research. *Amer J Ment Defic,* Suppl 5:180, March 1962.

Chapter 53
Social Influences on the Course of Schizophrenia

John K. Wing, M.D., Ph.D.

THE COURSE OF SCHIZOPHRENIA

When discussing a condition that often runs a long and fluctuating course, it is important to define one's terms. The concept of *course* can be applied retrospectively to individual cases, such as those discussed by Kisker (1) and Minkowski (2), taking into account a large number of influences that might have been important and endeavoring to reach a judgment as to which actually did play a part in deciding the sequence of events and the outcome. The concept also can be applied more generally, as a sort of statistical abstraction, based upon the observation of what happens in a large number of cases over a given period of time.

Four main elements contributing to course need to be distinguished (3). First, there is the clinical condition itself, which may be acute, intermittent or chronic. The frequency and length of acute relapses or of the remissions between them provides one kind of index of the clinical course. Second, the severity of the chronic intrinsic impairments is another element. When the condition is untreated, and assuming a constant environment, a clearcut tendency towards a particular clinical course and outcome is known as the "natural" history.

Third, there are secondary handicaps which are not part of the disease process itself but which accumulate whenever a disease is characterized by frequent relapses or by chronic intrinsic impairments. These handicaps include altered self-attitudes and expectations, and the addition of new habits that make it increasingly difficult for the individual to follow an ordinary domestic and working life. These changes often mirror the attitudes toward the handicapped person of important people in the social environment. Institutionalism is an extreme example. At its heart lies an increasing acceptance by the patient of the standards and way of life of the institution and an inability, therefore, to live any other. (Thomas Mann, in *The Magic Mountain,* wrote an extraordinarily detailed and accurate account of the processes of institutionalism at work in a tuberculosis sanato-

This paper has been based largely on work carried out in the
MRC Social Psychiatry Unit during the past twenty years. Much
credit is due to Aubrey Lewis who founded the Unit and was its
first director.

599

rium.) There are, of course, many other types of secondary handicaps, such as a lack of confidence in one's ability to find and hold down a suitable job.

The fourth element contributing to the course consists of extrinsic disadvantages of various kinds that would be handicapping in their own right even without the supervention of an illness. A poor education, a lack of vocational skills, a low intelligence, an absence of social supports, are all disadvantageous in themselves.

Each of these four components can vary independently of the others. Each contributes to the degree of social disablement that is present at any given point in time (that is, to successive "outcomes"), and each contributes in a different way to the development of the social course. I have discussed their definition in some detail elsewhere (4). Most studies of the course of schizophrenia have not attempted to distinguish between them.

Kraepelin's follow-up data suggested that only about 17% of inpatients treated at the psychiatric clinic in Heidelberg were reasonably well "socially adjusted" many years later (5). Mayer-Gross followed up 260 patients out of a total of 294 admitted to the same clinic in 1912 and 1913, Sixteen years later, some 35% had made "social recoveries" and 5% were socially disabled but out of the hospital. There was, however, a high death rate (43%) among those who had remained in the hospital (6).

Most early descriptions of the course of schizophrenia were based on hospital records. Up to the 1930s, about 60% of all patients hospitalized for schizophrenia were likely to remain there indefinitely after their first admission; about 20% were severely impaired but could be discharged from the hospital, and about 20% made a reasonable recovery (7–9). It was usually assumed in these studies that patients who remained in the hospital or died there were clinically severely ill. This assumption must now be challenged. There is considerable evidence that length of stay is not solely an index of clinical morbidity. In three British mental hospitals only 66% of long-stay schizophrenic patients showed severe symptoms (14). Factors such as marital status (10), occupation (11), and even the extent to which patients were visited during the first month after admission (12) also determined length of stay. Institutionalism must have insured that many patients remained in the hospital, and wanted to do so, although they were not severely clinically impaired. These patients were, perhaps, the ones with extrinsic disadvantages, such as a lack of social ties, even before admission (13,14). In addition to these factors, there is evidence that the social environment of many hospitals actually had an influence on the intrinsic impairments of schizophrenia as well as on the secondary handicaps.

The symptomatic course therefore may have been somewhat better early in this century than appears from the studies quoted. Figures collected during the era of "moral treatment" over a century ago confirm this view (15,16). More recently, Harris and his colleagues studied 125 schizophrenic patients admitted to the Maudsley Hospital in London for deep insulin treatment between 1945 and 1950 (17). The death rate was very low, as in all recent studies. Forty-five percent of patients were regarded as "social recoveries" 5 years after admission and another 21% were socially disabled but out of the hospital. A study of 111 schizophrenic patients first admitted to three British mental hospitals in 1956 and followed up through 5 years of the "phenothiazine era," found that 56% were "social recoveries," 34% were socially disabled, and only 11% were still in the hospital (18). Thus the social course, as measured by the proportion of "socially adjusted" and "outside hospital" patients, appears to have improved throughout the century.

To compare the figures quoted so far, the assumption has to be made that the concept of schizophrenia used in the various studies was the same. Of course it was not. But if we wish to investigate either the clinical or the social course, and certainly if we wish to know how the clinical course is influenced by social events in order to try to construct a rational system of social treatment, it is important that an attempt should be made to arrive at a communicable system of clinical description and classification. A good deal has been written about this problem in recent years and considerable progress has been made (19–22).

I will briefly summarize the descriptive syndromes that seem of particular relevance. A disease concept is based on a network of interlocking theories put forward to explain the clinical syndromes. There is considerable evidence that genetic, biochemical, pharmacologic, neuropsychologic, and social theories are beginning at last to converge for the concept of schizophrenia. For present purposes, however, I shall be concerned mainly with the syndromes themselves and the way they appear to be influenced by social circumstances.

THE ACUTE AND CHRONIC SCHIZOPHRENIC SYNDROMES

Recent large-scale international studies have greatly clarified the way psychiatrists use clinical information to arrive at a diagnosis (19,20). Certain important aspects of clinical interviewing of acutely ill patients can now be made fairly precise and reliable so psychiatrists using a common technique can produce approximately comparable data no matter what part of the world they and the patient live in or what language they speak (22). Once a decision is reached about the symptoms and syndromes present, a categorization is made according to a hierarchy of priorities, with sensorial changes at the top of the list, followed by schizophrenic symptoms, and so on (20–23). This system cannot be applied to the more chronic impairments, however, and so it is necessary to consider acute and chronic syndromes separately.

The Acute Syndromes

So far as schizophrenia is concerned, there is a large central syndrome (containing Schneider's first-rank symptoms and a number of other symptoms, e.g., thought echo, thought insertion, delusions of control, and certain kinds of auditory hallucination) that is almost universally regarded by clinicians as characteristic. (For the moment, we can disregard those conditions that seem to be caused by cerebral pathology or by substances such as amphetamine or alcohol.) In the WHO study, the central syndrome was present in two-thirds of all disorders labeled schizophrenic. There were of course many other symptoms as well. In fact, the presence of first-rank symptoms seemed to guarantee that a whole range of other psychotic and neurotic phenomena also would be present. None, however, was as discriminating between clinical diagnoses of schizophrenia, mania, and depressive disorders as the first-rank symptoms. Although first-rank symptoms were present in 17% of patients clinically diagnosed as having manic psychoses (24), subsequent international studies have shown that this degree of discrimination can be improved (25,26).

There are of course many kinds of delusional syndromes other than the central one, and 17% of the cases diagnosed in the WHO study as schizophrenic were characterized by one or more of them in the absence of the central syndrome. Most psychiatrists called these conditions schizophrenic, although sometimes they were just called "paranoid psychoses." It would seem sensible to retain the option of keeping them separate since they can always be recombined with the more central conditions if necessary for statistical or conceptual purposes.

A small proportion (6%) of cases diagnosed as schizophrenic in the WHO survey had not shown the central or other delusional syndromes but were presumably classified on the basis of disturbances of behavior, affect, or speech, or on other characteristics such as change in personality. It may be that some of these cases might have been better described in other terms—Asperger's syndrome, for example, or the chronic sequelae of encephalitis. A further 10% were called schizophrenic in spite of the fact that some other classification, such as mania or psychotic depression, could be made on the basis of the clinical phenomena, and in spite of the absence of any of the syndromes described earlier. Again, it is possible that other criteria, such as personality change, were being taken into account. These results show that an agreed clinical classification of the acute condition can be reached in a substantial proportion of cases, even in a wide-ranging international study where considerable disagreement might be expected.

The characteristic central syndrome often has a fairly sharp onset. Both patient and clinician can tell quite easily whether symptoms of the first rank are present or absent. However, such symptoms are commonly preceded, accompanied, or followed by chronic syndromes that can be much more difficult to recognize.

The Chronic Syndromes

The set of behaviors associated with social withdrawal—slowness, underactivity, blunting of affect, poverty of speech, and so forth—can range from a severe stupor to a passive avoidance of social interaction that is only regarded as part of schizophrenia because it has persisted since the appearance of the acute condition. This syndrome of "clinical poverty" can be measured reliably when it is fairly severe and the observations are made in an institutional setting (27). A score on social withdrawal and associated behaviors is highly correlated with measures of social performance and with measures of physiologic arousal (28,29). It also predicts the individual's ability to communicate using verbal or nonverbal language. The most severely impaired person can convey little information through the use of language: the voice is monotonous, words are few and may convey little meaning, the facial expression is wooden, the bodily posture and gait is stiff, little use is made of gesture.

It is much more difficult to recognize the chronic syndrome reliably when it is mild and the observations are not made in a hospital setting, even when it is known that the individuals concerned have had schizophrenia in the past (30,31). A problem therefore arises as to the nature of mild conditions characterized by social withdrawal and associated behaviors found in people who have *never* had any of the more acute and florid manifestations of schizophrenia. It is by no means evident that they should be labeled "schizophrenic" and, in fact, there are many other possible labels.

A similar problem arises with respect to other aspects of personality, behavior, and modes of thinking that often accompany or follow the acute central syndrome and paranoid syndromes—for example, vagueness and incoherence of speech, unpredictability of thought and action, and an inability to concentrate thought on a central issue. If one or more such characteristics occur without the florid symptoms, should the person be regarded as "schizophrenic?" There are, after all, many other possibilities.

It is to meet this kind of question that special subgroups have been created: simple, pseudoneurotic, pseudopsychopathic, preclinical, borderline, sluggish, and so on. It has not been demonstrated that any of these categories can be precisely defined and reliably recognized in a hospital population, let alone among the public at large. There is evidence linked to much less clear-cut traits (even, for example, to creativity), but this does not in any way justify using these traits for making a diagnosis (32). The ethical problems involved are sometimes overlooked, and they have been heightened by the apparent ease with which some people have been admitted to the hospital and treated as if they had a full-blown picture of acute schizophrenia on evidence that is, to say the least, exiguous (33–35).

Unfortunately, very few scientific papers on the subject of schizophrenia include a clinical description that is sufficiently precise to allow even approximate replication. One can, of course, hope that any large series of acutely ill or chronically handicapped patients will include a fair proportion of comparable cases, but this cannot be taken for granted (36–38).

In the remainder of this chapter, I shall use the term "schizophrenic" to describe only people who have at some time shown the acute central syndrome or paranoid delusional syndromes. Much of the time, of course, such people are "in remission" so far as the acute symptoms are concerned, but they are often handicapped by chronic impairments associated with the clinical poverty syndrome or marked thought disorder. I shall *not* use the term "schizophrenia" to cover that wide and amorphous group of people who are withdrawn or odd but who have never shown evidence of the acute central or paranoid syndromes. Hence, I shall mainly be concerned with people who develop long-term impairments and a high vulnerability to relapse, but it is important to remember that this does not include at least one-third of those who are diagnosed as schizophrenic (18).

EMPIRICAL EVIDENCE FOR SOCIAL INFLUENCES ON THE COURSE OF SCHIZOPHRENIA

In reviewing work on social factors claimed to influence the course of schizophrenia, it is necessary to distinguish among three hypotheses. First, there is the possibility that social events or experiences occurring during infancy and early childhood contribute to a subsequent clinical onset of schizophrenia and perhaps also influence its severity and outcome. Second, there is the possibility that social events or experiences occurring during later childhood have a similar influence. Third, there is the rather different order of claim that first onset, risk of relapse, and subsequent course are influenced by proximate social events.

The first two of these claims are difficult to deal with under the heading of empirical evidence since very little is available, although current longitudinal studies might eventually produce it (39). Most of the scientific work relies on the demonstration of current abnormalities in the parents or relatives of people with identified "schizophrenia" compared with the relatives of control subjects. Even when the design and method are impeccable, the results can be interpreted in many different ways (36).

Hypotheses concerning the *immediate* effect of social factors on the course of schizophrenia are somewhat easier to test, and it is curious that relatively little attention has been paid to work in this field. My review of such work will be divided into two parts: one concerned with the social reactivity of the clinical poverty syndrome, the other with social factors that affect liability to relapse with an acute episode.

The Social Reactivity of the Clinical Poverty Syndrome

Many descriptive studies, notably by Belknap (40), Dunham and Weinberg (41) and Goffman (42), have been made of the ill effects of large and poverty-stricken institutions on their long-stay inmates. Most have not, however, attempted to separate cause and effect. It has been assumed that any association found between a deprived environment and a disadvantaged patient must be due to the former rather than to the latter. Only Robert Sommer (43) pointed out that chronically handicapped patients might, to some extent at least, create their own environment.

In the pre-phenothiazine days, many of the experiments designed to evaluate social therapies, such as "total push," had disappointing results. The experimental group did not improve and, if anything, the control group got worse (44–47). However, there was also evidence that the performance of chronic schizophrenic patients improved with practice, and that there were ways of motivating them to perform better (48–53).

A characteristic of the learning curve in studies of the output of chronic schizophrenic patients was a slow and linear improvement due to practice, which contrasted with the negatively accelerated form usually seen in normal people and the severely mentally retarded. This effect was clearly evident in an experiment by Wing and Freudenberg (54) in which severely impaired schizophrenic patients, not on medication, were given extra social activation in a workshop setting by well-known and trusted nurses. Superimposed on the slow and linear improvement due to practice was a clear-cut increment in output with onset of extra social stimulation, and a sharp decrement when stimulation was withdrawn. Members of the control group, who were well aware that they were missing something, deteriorated and then recovered in the same specific way. There was no transfer of effect from the workshop to other social settings; it seemed completely situation-specific.

It could be said that the nurses in this experiment were passively exercising for the patients functions that the latter were unable to exercise actively for themselves, in the hope that active function would eventually return. This is an excellent principle of rehabilitation, which has obvious implications for social treatment.

A larger study therefore was mounted, in which the hypothesis was tested that the social environment in which long-stay schizophrenic patients lived would have a measurable influence on the severity of the characteristics of the clinical poverty syndrome (14). A sample of long-stay schizophrenic women in three large psychiatric hospitals, each the main treatment agency for its area, was interviewed, and information was collected concerning the poverty or richness of the hospital social environment experienced by each patient. There were marked social differences between the hospitals in terms of numbers of personal possessions owned by patients, the attitudes of nurses toward them, the amount of contact with the outside world, the restrictiveness of ward regimes and the amount of time spent by the patient in various activities. Thus, the hypothesis could be tested that there should be equivalent clinical differences between the three series of patients and, indeed, even between the patients of one hospital if their social environments differed. The results were compatible with the hypothesis, particularly in terms of aspects of the patients' clinical condition such as social withdrawal, flatness of affect, poverty of speech, slowness, and underactivity. Of all the social indices used, the one that correlated most highly with clinical condition was length of time doing nothing.

Since the three groups were followed over an 8-year period, during which time social conditions improved a good deal and, in certain instances, deteriorated again, it was possible to make a number of quite rigorous tests of the hypothesis, but not to disprove it. An increase in social poverty was accompanied by an increase in clinical poverty, while social improvement was accompanied by clinical improvement. Drug treatment was not related to improvement. The hospital where the highest doses were used by no means had the best results.

We must remember that we are discussing "symptoms" that many people regard as fundamental to schizophrenia. It is true that negative symptoms very often did not disappear entirely, even when active rehabilitation was maintained and the patient was discharged (31,55), but the improvement was measurable and useful.

Several other studies since then have demonstrated the modifiability of negative impairments in schizophrenia and confirmed that many patients remain vulnerable to understimulating social conditions, whether these are found at home or in hostels, day centers, or agencies for the destitute (30,56). Simply discharging a patient from the hospital gives no guarantee that impairments will be minimized since, for reasons to be discussed later, he may return to or even actively seek out socially impoverished surroundings.

Social Factors Precipitating Relapse

In one of the experiments carried out to assess the value of social methods of treatment of long-stay schizophrenic patients, we noticed that six out of 45 moderately handicapped patients suffered from a recrudescence of florid delusions, that had not been in evidence for years, during the first week of a course at a rehabilitation unit outside the hospital. Most of the patients came from a hospital where very little preparation had been given before the course began (31). Stone and Eldred (57) described a similar phenomenon and, more recently, Goldberg and his colleagues have confirmed it under quite different conditions (58).

Thus it appears that the florid symptoms of schizophrenia may be profoundly influenced by environmental events. Two kinds of study have thrown further light on this observation. The first was carried out by Brown and Birley (59) who showed that there was a marked increase in the frequency of occurrence of certain life events during the few weeks immediately prior to an acute onset or relapse of schizophrenia. This was true even when events that might have been the result, rather than the cause, of an earlier unnoticed clinical deterioration, were excluded. Some of the events were positive rather than negative—a promotion at work, an engagement to be married, or moving into a new apartment. Others were more obviously threatening. It appeared that people in this series were more likely to relapse if exposed to many different kinds of change in their social environment, and that they found everyday life stressful at a lower threshold than most people.

A second group of studies dealt with the relationship between patient and key relative after discharge from hospital. In four separate studies, it has been shown that measurements of some aspects of these relationships are strongly associated with the likelihood of subsequent relapse with an acute schizophrenic breakdown (60–63). The simplest and most easily measured predictive factor was the number of critical comments made by the relative about the patient, but ratings of hostility and emotional overinvolvement were also found to be important. On the basis of these measures, families could be divided into two approximately equal groups, characterized by high or low degrees of expressed emotion. Two other important variables were the amount of face-to-face contact between patient and key relative during the previous week, divided approximately at the median, and whether or not the patient was taking medication during the follow-up period or at time of relapse.

Patients who spent much time in face-to-face contact with relatives expressing high emotion, and who were not taking medication, had a very high relapse rate (92%). If one or the other protective factor—medication or low face-to-face contact—was present, the relapse rate was markedly reduced (40–50%). If both protective factors were present, or if the patient returned to a low-emotion home, relapse was least likely (15%). In fact, in the low-emotion families, medication contributed nothing to prevention of relapse (63).

It should be noted that at least half of the key relatives provided an excellent environment for the patient. In the remainder, many of the relatives were undoubtedly reacting to prior disturbance in the patients, and this emotional response then formed part of a vicious circle leading to further breakdown.

Thus there seem to be at least two fundamental processes at work. On the one hand, an understimulating social environment tends to increase symptoms such as social withdrawal, apathy, inertia, and lack of initiative. This process is seen best in the old-fashioned type of mental hospital, but it can quite easily occur in the community as well. On the other hand, there is the tendency to break down, with an effusion of florid symptoms, under conditions of social overstimulation. This second process is most frequently seen outside the hospital, but it also can be seen within it. This outline of a theory depends on the assumption that negative symptoms are a protective reaction against the painful effects of social interaction when one has inadequate equipment for communication. When the patient is allowed to withdraw, he does so, and the process can easily go too far. When he is not allowed to withdraw but is faced with what appear to be impossible demands, the underlying thinking disorder becomes clinically manifest in florid symptoms (14).

The schizophrenic patient with a fairly severe degree of impairment and vulnerability is balanced, at the optimum, on a knife-edge. On one side is the tendency toward overdoing the protective social withdrawal. On the other side, particularly if the patient is forced into social interaction with no possibility of controlling the degree of stimulation, there is the danger of acute relapse. The latter danger is increased by overintrusive attempts at rehabilitation, by analogous efforts toward obtaining a social response by a relative who does not understand the nature of the impairment, and by more accidental environmental pressures that involve the necessity for making decisions that are so complex or difficult that the patient's ability to cope is exceeded.

The optimal social environment therefore is structured, with neutral (i.e., not highly emotionally involved) stimulation to perform up to achievable standards, with little necessity for complex decision making but with some degree of control over the amount of social stimulation left in the patient's own hands. It is in these circumstances that a relationship of trust and confidence is most likely to develop with professional staff or family members and the need for phenothiazine medication is likely to be minimal (3,64–66).

This clinical formulation has drawn on and can be supported by a long series of studies on the nature of the psychologic deficits in schizophrenia and their relationship to psychophysiologic factors such as psychomotor slowness, degree of overarousal, wide span of attention, information overload (67–72). Much of such work was carried out with long-hospitalized patients; it has been difficult to test nonhospitalized patients in remission as well as during acute attacks, when they are not receiving phenothiazine medication. Moreover, some of the concepts used, such as overarousal, are too simple to bear all the explanatory burdens that sometimes have been placed on them, as Claridge (73) pointed out. Above all, the heterogeneity of the disorders sometimes included under the heading of schizophrenia has not always been taken into account, so experiments have proved difficult to replicate with precision. A great deal more remains to be explained. In particular, the mechanism remains obscure for symptoms such as thought echo or thought insertion, which are direct descriptions of the patient's experience with very little elaboration.

CHANGING THE COURSE OF SCHIZOPHRENIA BY SOCIAL ACTION

The Clinical and the Social Course

Discussions of the course and outcome of schizophrenia rarely differentiate the four main elements discussed previously. Two elements—acute onset or relapse with florid delusional or hallucinatory symptoms and the development of chronic syndromes, such as the one associated with social withdrawal—are clinical in nature. Neither can be used to predict the other. The florid symptoms present during one acute attack of schizophrenia are good predictors of the florid symptoms that will be present during a subsequent acute attack (74). This meets one of Sydenham's criteria for a disease syndrome, and in this sense, it is permissible to speak of "the course of schizophrenia." The acute symptoms do not, however, predict the future severity of the clinical poverty syndrome. Only the severity of social withdrawal and associated behaviors (14,18), and the indices of social performance with which they are correlated (14,27–29), can do that. Like predicts like. The social circumstances that tend to precipitate or prevent relapse, or to increase or decrease the severity of chronic impairments, are an added hazard to prediction.

The other two elements contributing to social disablement—secondary handicaps and extrinsic disadvantages—are social in nature. The prediction of institutionalism (14,75) and other forms of secondary handicap, such as a lack of self-confidence in ability to get and hold down a suitable job (76,77), requires yet further variables to be taken into account. The course of "social disablement," i.e., the overall deficit in social performance resulting from the interaction of all four components over time, should not be equated with the course of "schizophrenia" or taken as a measure of it.

Since at least some of the factors that influence the development of social disablement in schizophrenia, as in many other conditions, are modifiable, it is clear that any idea of inevitable clinical deterioration, i.e. deficit remorselessly increasing over time, must be rejected. Manfred Bleuler (78,79) has extensively and elegantly documented this fact, and Foulds and Dixon (80) were able to demonstrate it by measurement. Sufficient environmental influences have been demonstrated to allow an attempt to bring together some of the ways in which the course of schizophrenia might be deliberately influenced.

Table 53-1 contains a schematic summary of possible preventable adverse influences. The prophylactic action that might be taken can be discussed under three headings:

Table 53-1. Social Factors Causing Extra Disadvantage to People with Schizophrenia

Component of Social Disablement	Adverse Factors
1. Acute syndromes	Precipitating events
	Social intrusiveness of important others, too much face-to-face contact
	Discontinuing medication
2. Chronic syndromes	Social understimulation
3. Secondary handicaps	Unfavorable attitudes and expectations of important others
	Lack of opportunity to practice social skills
	Isolation from everyday social life
	Enforced pauperism
4. Extrinsic disadvantages	Poverty, poor education, lack of vocational skills, other forms of deprivation

1. Specific—medication, achieving an optimal level of social stimulation, avoiding precipitating events, acquiring an understanding of the clinical impairments and their reactivity
2. Remedial—social skills and vocational training, counselling, advocacy, and support;
3. Provision of appropriate social and medical services—crisis intervention and relief, day and residential environments graded in degree of support and shelter, disability pensions at the level given to other disabled people.

The remedial aspects have been dealt with by Cumming and Cumming (81) who made the plausible suggestion that the acquisition of social skills would enable a handicapped person to deal more competently with everyday problems and thus to be able to anticipate and to deal with crises as they arise, and also better able to cope with emotional problems. Liberman and his colleagues (82) have worked out the principles of social skills training in detail.

The provision of adequate social and medical services cannot be dealt with here, but I have attempted elsewhere to consider how far their organization and administration can be based on rational principles of therapy and prevention (83–85).

The section that follows will be concerned mainly with specific aspects of secondary and tertiary prevention, seen through the eyes, first, of sufferers themselves and then through the eyes of relatives.

Perception of Afflicted People and Their Relatives

Over a period of time, an individual with schizophrenia can acquire considerable experience of his own vulnerabilities and impairments and the factors that make them better or worse. Table 53-2 lists the factors that can theoretically be brought under control. Medication is the most obvious, although the patient's attitude depends a good deal on how it is presented by doctor and relatives. The factors involved are no different in principle from those operating in the case of chronic diseases like diabetes or parkinsonism. Taking medication for a long time is an admission of deficiency, and acquiring the necessary insight is painful. Moreover, quite apart from the obvious extrapyramidal side effects, some patients complain of a feeling of being damped down, depressed, or unable to enjoy life while taking phenothiazines. Three comments from intelligent patients (86) were as follows:

> It is a feeling that somehow I am not functioning to my fullest capacity, which is very disagreeable, especially when I have no schizophrenic symptoms.
>
> I think I prefer to be a little bit mad than overdosed by major tranquilizers.
>
> My joy in living went . . . leaving only a death wish. I could no longer think clearly and quickly, which made my work impossibly difficult.

About one-third of those started on fluphenazine injections do not continue with them. Clearly, attention to dosage and prescribing antiparkinsonian drugs will help to avoid side effects, but there are always going to be patients who refuse medication, even when they are aware that florid symptoms will return. This does not mean that nothing more can be done.

There are some useful hints for professional people in a recent collection of essays written by highly intelligent and articulate patients who had come through the experience of schizophrenia and acquired a good deal of insight (86). One wrote that he knew he should not get too emotionally involved in arguments with other people, for example on topics such as politics or religion, because he might well begin to feel he was being persecuted.

Table 53-2. Factors Important to the Patient in Secondary and Tertiary Prevention of Schizophrenic Symptoms[a]   *Coping Skills*

1. *Controllable by patient if some insight attained*
   Self-understanding and self-education
   Recognition of difficulties of others, particularly relatives
   Recognition and avoidance of triggering situations
   Relaxation if stress is unavoidable
   Specific and restricted social withdrawal (e.g., from arguments, intrusive relatives, some love affairs, overcomplex work, etc.)
   Avoidance of general withdrawal (solitary living, wandering)
   Taking medication

2. *Partly controllable by patient (depends on others as well)*
   Helping others (e.g., relatives, friends) to adjust to patient's disabilities
   Finding activities within competence
   Finding suitable companions (not intrusive) and practicing controlled social interaction
   Finding work at suitable level (speed, complexity, social relationships)

3. *Not controllable by patient*
   Critical family attitudes, nagging about medication, social intrusiveness
   Availability and quality of day or residential services
   Attitudes of professional people
   Expectations of employers

[a] The more severely impaired the patient, the less likely he is to be in control and the more likely to be dependent on others for help.

There is a sensitivity in myself and I have to try to harden my emotions and cut myself off from potentially dangerous situations . . . When I get worked up, I often experience a slight recurrence of delusional thoughts. I begin to notice coincidences that otherwise I should not have noticed. I might see someone I hadn't expected to see. Then I might start testing some theory. Let me see whether that car turns the corner behind me. If so, is it still there several turnings later? Then it must be following me! I now feel that I have sufficient knowledge of myself to know that this kind of thinking is dangerous. I can control my mind sufficiently to prevent such thoughts getting out of control and destroying my inner self.

Another patient developed a relaxation technique, and whenever he felt delusional or hallucinatory experiences coming on he would "switch off." He found that in this way he could avoid them. From a theoretical point of view, this is quite a feasible suggestion, although it is very doubtful how many patients can acquire this degree of skill.

Social withdrawal is, of course, a technique that many people with schizophrenia consciously or unconsciously develop for avoiding too much social stimulation. Communication is often difficult and even painful. It is therefore simpler to avoid it. One patient solved the problem by sleeping during the day when his relatives were about and only getting up during the night when they had gone to bed. For the same reason, some patients welcome socially isolated surroundings and prefer anonymity to fellowship. Clearly, this tendency can go far beyond what is useful for self-protection and can lead eventually to a greatly increased negative impairment. But insight *can* lead to better self-management. One well-educated woman chose her male friends from among men who were less intelligent than herself because she became less emotionally involved and could control the relationship better.

Table 53-2 also lists some of the factors that are less easy or impossible for the patient to control. Many sufferers come to learn that they are unable to cope with work at the level or speed that they had previously attained. The difficulty may also be with workmates or supervisors. There also may be a tendency to make mistakes when complex decisions have to be made, particularly when under pressure (31,76). The ability to accept a handicap and take lower level work to adjust to it requires a degree of self-knowledge and realism that many of us do not possess, schizophrenic or not. Most patients, of course, are not highly intelligent and articulate; those who are, have to speak for their fellows. But the less capacity an individual has for recognizing his own intrinsic, secondary, and extrinsic disabilities, the more important become the attitudes of those with whom he or she lives.

Since relatives are almost as much in the front line as patients, as far as living with schizophrenia is concerned, it is surprising that there have been so few surveys of their views on the subject. In recent studies, it has been clear that many relatives are well aware of the behavioral problems described earlier (87–89). One of the major complaints was that when they asked for professional advice as to the best way to react, they received no answer at all, or the question was simply turned back to them. Table 53-3 summarizes the factors relatives can control.

Relatives do, of course, acquire considerable experience of coping with difficult behavior, but their methods are often by trial and error. Some learn not to argue with a deluded patient; others never learn. Some discover just how far they may go in trying to stimulate a rather slow and apathetic individual without arousing resentment. Others push too hard, find that they make matters worse and then retreat into inactivity themselves. Some never give up intruding until the patient is driven out of the home.

Table 53-3. Factors Important to Relatives in Secondary and Tertiary Prevention of Schizophrenic Symptoms[a]

1. *Controllable by relative if some insight attained*

   Creating a noncritical, accepting environment
   Attempting to reach optimal degree of social interaction (neither intrusive nor avoiding)
   Keeping aims realistic
   Learning how to cope with fluctuating insight by changes in own behavior
   Learning how to respond to delusions or bizarre behavior
   Calling medical or social help and learning what help can be given
   Discovering what welfare arrangements are available and how to use them

2. *Partly controllable by relative*

   Patient's attitude to self, to relatives, to medication, etc.
   Obtaining reward from patient's presence in family
   Divisions of opinion within family

3. *Not controllable by relative*

   Availability and quality of services
   Attitudes of professionals (sometimes carping and dismissive)
   Ability of professionals to give useful advice on management
   Expectations and reactions of employers, neighbors, etc.

[a] The more severely impaired the patient, the less likely is the relative to be able to modify the impairments and the more the emphasis shifts toward protection and shelter.

One of the most difficult problems is when the patient fluctuates in degree of insight. Table 53-3 shows some of the factors that are difficult for the relative to influence. At one moment, the patient may be completely out of control and need compulsory treatment; at another he may approach his own ordinary self but be apparently unaware of his previous behavior. The change needed in the attitude of a relative, from emotionally neutral nurse to emotionally involved parent or spouse, is quite unnatural and very difficult to achieve and maintain. Critical comments made by relatives, except those related to recent acute relapse, are almost always concerned with longstanding problems such as lack of affection, interest, and communication (89).

Other problems mentioned by relatives included the emotional strain they felt (often very understandable), their social isolation, the divisive effects of differences of opinion within the family, the agony of knowing what to say to children, the difficulty in getting help in times of emergency, the lack of sheltered environments (particularly hostels and sheltered workshops), and the various difficulties associated with obtaining help at home, welfare benefits, brief periods of freedom from responsibility, and so on.

The social problems of parents are, of course, very different from those of husbands or wives (62). If neighbors come to call, it is fairly socially acceptable for a mother to say that her son is handicapped, thus explaining the fact that he dashes to the safety of his room as soon as the doorbell rings and does not come down until the visitors have gone. Such behavior by a husband or wife is much more difficult for the other partner to explain, particularly if there are small children about.

One of the chief preoccupations, particularly among elderly widows living with a middle-aged handicapped son or daughter, was the future. Who would give such devoted care when the parent died? One father called it the W.I.A.G. (when I am gone) syndrome (18,88).

Tables 53-1, 53-2, and 53-3 contain the basis for rational intervention by the medical and social services. There is a good deal of argument as to who should provide what kind of help. Since we rightly tend to expect the patient and the relatives to help themselves, it is only fair to expect the doctor, nurse, or social worker to do their best to mobilize the appropriate services without too much contention as to whose job it is. It is also a duty that *all* those concerned should acquire at least a minimal degree of understanding of the nature of schizophrenia and the principal influences on its course.

Table 53-4 summarizes the points at which intervention can be made. The first requirement is to try to develop an appropriate relationship with the patient and to sustain the relatives in their equivalent attempts. It is only in the context of such relationships that it is possible to assess the aims and handicaps of the patient and the intricacies of the family or other social situation, and to devise a plan of treatment and advice that will need to be adjusted frequently over a period of years. It is not suggested that careful attention to these factors will altogether prevent the acute and chronic syndromes of schizophrenia, or the accumulation of secondary and extrinsic disadvantages, but this strategy is most likely to minimize the development of extra handicaps and to capitalize on natural healing processes. As Manfred Bleuler (78) has pointed out, schizophrenia remains a chronic condition. In that respect it is similar to many other disabling diseases, and the observation should mark the beginning of our attempts to help, not their end.

Cultural Factors Affecting the Course of Schizophrenia

Murphy and Raman (90) found, in a follow-up study in Mauritius, that the course of schizophrenia seemed more benign there than would have been expected from a study carried out in England (18). Data from the International Pilot Study of Schizophrenia (74) give some support for this view, although many other explanations are, of course, tenable. If further investigations lend support to this idea, it would be worthwhile looking at the factors we have been discussing to discover whether the social environment in which people with schizophrenia live in developing countries makes their impact less obtrusive. The family structure may make a concerned but neutral attitude easier for relatives to adopt. A lower expectation for occupational performance may result in less

Table 53-4. Help From Medical, Nursing, and Social Work Professionals in Secondary and Tertiary Prevention of Schizophrenic Symptoms

---

Develop relationship with patient and relatives (this will require sympathy, skill in taking history, and help with services)

Make correct diagnosis

Prescribe medication with awareness of side effects and social factors influencing dosage

Prescribe services: medical, residential, day, occupational (i.e., be aware of availability and quality)

Make sure available welfare benefits are understood

Counsel patient and counsel relatives on best way to live with schizophrenia

Social action and advocacy to improve quality and availability of services

---

anxiety. Afflicted people may be less often labeled as socially incompetent and, thus, better able to maintain an acceptable self-image.

However this might be, and there are several other quite plausible explanations for the facts, I think it indisputable that the next great clinical challenge is to see whether we can devise means of improving the prognosis, not simply in individual cases—most clinicians think they can do that—but overall, so we shall be able to demonstrate unequivocally the effect on relapse rates and levels of social performance.

REFERENCES

1. Kisker KP: *Der Erlebniswandel des Schizophrenen.* Berlin, Springer, 1960.

2. Minkowski E: *La Schizophrenie.* Paris, Desclée de Brouwer, 1953.

3. Wing JK: Impairments in schizophrenia: A rational basis for social treatment, in Wirt, RD, Winokur G, Roff M (eds): *Life History Research in Psychopathology,* vol 4. Minneapolis, University of Minnesota Press, 1975.

4. Wing JK: Principles of evaluation, in Wing JK, and Hailey AM (eds): *Evaluating a Community Psychiatric Service.* London, Oxford University Press, 1972.

5. Kraepelin E: *Psychiatrie,* ed 8. Leipzig, 1910.

6. Mayer-Gross W: Die schizophrenie, in Bumke O (ed): *Handbuch der Geisteskrankheiten, Band IX.* Berlin, Springer, 1932.

7. Brown GW: Length of hospital stay and schizophrenia. *Acta Psychiat Neurol Scand* 35:414, 1960.

8. Hastings DW: Follow-up results in psychiatric illness. *Amer J Psychiat* 114:12, 1958.

9. Malamud W, Render IN: Course and prognosis in schizophrenia. *Amer J Psychiat* 95:1039, 1939.

10. Ødegard Ø: Marriage and mental disease. *J Ment Sci* 92:35, 1946.

11. Cooper B: Social class and prognosis in schizophrenia. *Brit J Prev Soc Med* 15:17, 1961.

12. Brown GW: Social factors influencing length of hospital stay of schizophrenic patients. *Brit Med J* 2:1300, 1959.

13. Wing JK: Institutionalism in mental hospitals. *Brit J Soc Clin Psychol* 1:38, 1962.

14. Wing JK, Brown GW: *Institutionalism and Schizophrenia.* London, Cambridge University Press, 1970.

15. Bockoven JS: Moral treatment in American psychiatry. *J Nerv Ment Dis* 124:167 and 292, 1956.

16. Jones K: *A History of the Mental Health Services.* London, Routledge, 1972.

17. Harris A, Linker I, Norris V, et al: Schizophrenia: a social and prognostic study. *Brit J Prev Soc Med* 10:107, 1956.

18. Brown GW, Bone M, Dalison B, et al: *Schizophrenia and Social Care.* London, Oxford University Press, 1966.

19. Cooper JE, Kendell RE, Gurland BJ, et al: *Psychiatric Diagnosis in New York and London.* (Maudsley Monograph no 20). London, Oxford University Press, 1972.

20. World Health Organization: *The International Pilot Study of Schizophrenia.* Geneva, WHO, 1973.

21. World Health Organization: *Glossary of Mental Disorders and Guide to their Classification.* Geneva, WHO, 1974.

22. Wing JK, Cooper JE, Sartorius N: *The Description and Classification of Psychiatric Symptoms: An Instruction Manual for the PSE and CATEGO System.* London, Cambridge University Press, 1974.

23. Foulds GA, Bedford A: Hierarchy of classes of personal illness. *Psychol Med* 5:181, 1975.

24. Wing JK, Nixon JM: Discriminating symptoms in schizophrenia. *Arch Gen Psychiat* 32:853, 1975.

25. Scharfetter C, Moebt H, Wing JK: Diagnosis of functional psychoses: comparison of clinical and computerized classifications. *Arch Psychiat Neurol Sci* 222:61, 1976.

26. Wing JK, Nixon JM, von Cranach M, et al: Further developments of the PSE and CATEGO system. *Arch Psychiat Neurol Sci* 224:151, 1977.

27. Wing JK: A simple and reliable subclassification of chronic schizophrenia. *J Ment Sci* 107:862, 1961.

28. Venables PH, Wing JK: Level of arousal and the subclassification of schizophrenia. *Arch Gen Psychiat* 7:114, 1962.

29. Catterson A, Bennett DH, Freudenberg RK: A survey of long-stay schizophrenic patients. *Brit J Psychiat* 109:750, 1963.

30. Hewett S, Ryan P, Wing JK: Living without the mental hospitals. *J Soc Policy* 4:391, 1975.

31. Wing JK, Bennett DH, Denham J: *The Industrial Rehabilitation of Long-stay Schizophrenic Patients.* Medical Research Council memo no 42. London, HMSO, 1964.

32. Heston LL: Psychiatric disorders in foster home reared children of schizophrenic mothers. *Brit J Psychiat* 112:819, 1966.

33. Rosenhan DL: On being sane in insane places. *Science* 179:250, 1973.

34. Scheff TJ: The societal reaction to deviance. *Social Problems* 2:401, 1964.

35. Wing JK: Psychiatry in the Soviet Union. *Brit Med J* 1:433, 1974.

36. Hirsch SR, Leff JP: *Abnormality in Parents of Schizophrenics: A Review of the Literature and an Investigation of Communication Defects and Deviances.* London, Oxford University Press, 1975.

37. Wynne LC: Methodologic and conceptual issues in the study of schizophrenics and their families, in Rosenthal D, Kety SS (eds): *The Transmission of Schizophrenia.* London and New York, Pergamon, 1968.

38. Wynne LC: Family research on the pathogenesis of schizophrenia, in Doncet P, Laurin C (eds): *Problems of Psychosis.* Excerpta Medica International Congress Series, no 194, 1971.

39. Mednick SA, Schulsinger F, Higgins J, et al: *Genetics, Environment and Psychopathology.* New York, American Elsevier, 1974.

40. Belknap I: *Human Problems of a State Mental Hospital.* New York, McGraw-Hill, 1956.

41. Dunham HW, Weinberg SK: *Culture of the State Mental Hospital.* Detroit, Mich, Wayne State University Press, 1960.

42. Goffman E: On the characteristics of total institutions, in Cressey DR (ed): *The Prison.* New York, Holt, Rinehart and Winston, 1961.

43. Sommer R: Patients who grow old in a mental hospital. *Geriatrics* 14:581, 1959.

44. Bennett DH, Robertson JPS: The effects of habit training on chronic schizophrenic patients. *J Ment Sci* 101:664, 1955.

45. Galioni EF, Adams FH, Tallman FF: Intensive treatment of back-ward patients. A controlled pilot study. *Amer J Psychiat* 109:576, 1953.

46. Maas HS, Varon E, Rosenthal D: A technique for studying the social behavior of schizophrenics. *J Abnorm Soc Psychol* 46:119, 1951.

47. Powdermaker FB, Frank JD: *Group Psychotherapy.* Cambridge, Mass, Harvard University Press, 1953.

48. Carstairs GM, O'Connor N, Rawnsley K: The organization of a hospital workshop for chronic psychotic patients. *Brit J Prev Soc Med,* 10:136, 1956.

49. Garmezy N: Stimulus differentiation by schizophrenic and normal subjects under conditions of reward and punishment. *J Personality* 20:253, 1952.

50. Gatewood LC: An experimental study of dementia praecox. *Psychol Monog* 11:2, 1909.

51. Peters HN, Jenkins RL: Improvement of chronic schizophrenic patients with guided problem-solving motivated by hunger. *Psychiat Quart Sup* 28:84, 1954.

52. O'Connor N, Heron A, Carstairs GM: Work performance of chronic schizophrenics. *Occup Psychol* 30:1, 1956.

53. O'Connor N, Rawnsley K: Incentives with paranoid and non-paranoid schizophrenics in a workshop. *Brit J Med Psychol* 32:133, 1959.

54. Wing JK, Freudenberg RK: The response of severely ill chronic schizophrenic patients to social stimulation. *Amer J Psychiat* 118:311, 1961.

55. Wing JK: A pilot experiment on the rehabilitation of long-hospitalized male schizophrenic patients. *Brit J Prev Soc Med* 14:173, 1960.

56. Tidmarsh D, Wood S: Psychiatric aspects of destitution, in Wing JK, Hailey, AM (eds): *Evaluating a Community Psychiatric Service.* London, Oxford University Press, 1972.

57. Stone AA, Eldred SH: Delusion formation during the activation of chronic schizophrenic patients. *Arch Gen Psychiat* 1:177, 1959.

58. Goldberg SC, Schooler NR, Hogarty GE, et al: Prediction of relapse in schizophrenic outpatients treated by drug and sociotherapy. *Arch Gen Psychiat* 34:171, 1977.

59. Brown GW, Birley JLT: Social precipitants of severe psychiatric disorders, in Hare EH, Wing JK (eds): *Psychiatric Epidemiology.* London, Oxford University Press, 1970.

60. Brown GW: Experiences of discharged chronic schizophrenic patients in various types of living group. *Milbank Mem Fund Quart* 37:105, 1959.

61. Brown GW, Monck E, Carstairs GM, et al: Influence of family life on the course of schziophrenic illness. *Brit J Prev Soc Med* 16:55, 1962.

62. Brown GW, Birley JLT, Wing JK: Influence of family life on the course of schizophrenic disorders: a replication. *Brit J Psychiat* 121:241, 1972.

63. Vaughn C, Leff JP: The influence of family and social factors on the course of psychiatric illness. *Brit J Psychiat* 129:125, 1976.

64. Hirsch SR, Gaind R, Rohde PD, et al: Out-patient maintenance of chronic schizophrenic patients with long-acting fluphenazine: double blind placebo trial. *Brit Med J* 1:633, 1973.

65. Leff JP, Wing JK: Trial of maintenance therapy in schizophrenia. *Brit Med J* 3:599, 1971.

66. Wing JK, Leff JP, Hirsch SR: Preventive treatment of schizophrenia: some theoretical and methodological issues, in Cole JO, Freedman AM, Friedhoff AJ (eds): *Psychopathology and Psychopharmacology.* Baltimore, Johns Hopkins University Press, 1973.

67. McGhie A, Chapman J: Disorders of attention and perception in early schizophrenia. *Brit J Med Psychol* 34:103, 1961.

68. Mirsky AF, Kornetsky C: On the dissimilar effects of drugs on the digit symbol substitution and continuous performance tests. *Psychopharmacologia* 5:161, 1964.

69. Silverman J: The problem of attention in research and theory in schizophrenia. *Psychol Rev* 71:352, 1964.

70. Tizard J, Venables PH: The influence of extraneous stimulation on the reaction time of schizophrenics. *Brit J Psychol* 48:299, 1957.

71. Venables PH: The effect of auditory and visual stimuli on the skin potential response of schizophrenics. *Brain* 83:77, 1960.

72. Venables PH: The relation of two flash and two click thresholds to withdrawal in paranoid and non-paranoid schizophrenics. *Brit J Clin Soc Psychol* 6:60, 1967.

73. Claridge G: The schizophrenias as nervous types. *Brit J Psychiat* 121:1, 1972.

74. Sartorius N, Jablensky A, Strömgren E: Validity of diagnostic concepts across cultures, Wynne LC, Cromwell RL, Matthysse S (eds): *The Nature of Schizophrenia.* John Wiley & Sons, 1978.

75. Wing JK: Institutionalism in mental hospitals. *Brit J Clin Soc Psychol* 1:38, 1962.

76. Wing JK: A pilot experiment on the rehabilitation of long-hospitalised male schizophrenic patients. *Brit J Prev Soc Med* 14:173.

77. Wing JK: Social and psychological changes in a rehabilitation unit. *Soc Psychiat* 1:21, 1966.

78. Bleuler M: *Die Schizophrenen Geistesstorungen im Lichte Langjahriger Kranken und Familiengeschichte,* Stuttgart, Thieme, 1972.

79. Lewis AJ: Manfred Bleuler's *The Schizophrenic Mental Disorders:* an exposition and a review. *Psychol Med* 3:385, 1973.

80. Foulds GA, Dixon P: The nature of intellectual deficit in schizophrenia. *Brit J Clin Soc Psychol* 1:199, 1962.

81. Cumming JH, Cumming E: *Ego and Milieu.* New York, Atherton Press, 1962.

82. Liberman RP, King LW, DeRisi WJ, et al: *Personal Effectiveness.* Champaign, Ill, Research Press, 1975.

83. Wing JK: Institutional influences on mental disorders, in *Psychiatrie der Gegenwart, Band III, 2 Aufl.* Berlin, Springer Verlag, 1975.

84. Wing JK: Planning and evaluating services for chronically handicapped psychiatric patients in the UK, in Stein L and Test MA (eds): *Alternatives to Mental Hospital Treatment.* New York, Plenum, 1977.

85. Wing JK, Hailey AM: *Evaluating a Community Psychiatric Service. The Camberwell Register,* 1964–1971. London, Oxford University Press, 1972.

86. Wing JK (ed): *Schizophrenia from Within.* London, National Schizophrenia Fellowship, 1975.

87. Creer C: Living with schizophrenia. *Social Work Today* 6:2, 1975.

88. Creer C, Wing JK: *Schizophrenia at Home.* London, National Schizophrenia Fellowship, 1974.

89. Vaughn C, Leff J: Interaction characteristics in families of schizophrenic patients, in Katschnig H (ed): *Die andere Seite der Schizophrenie.* Vienna: Urban & Schwarzenberg, 1977.

90. Murphy HBM, Raman AC: The chronicity of schizophrenia in indigenous tropical peoples: results of a 12 year follow-up survey. *Brit J Psychiat* 118:489, 1971.

Chapter 54
The Course of Schizophrenia as a Developmental Process

John S. Strauss, M.D.
Ronald F. Kokes, Ph.D.
William T. Carpenter, Jr., M.D.
Barry A. Ritzler, Ph.D.

Since the definition of dementia praecox by Kraepelin and its re-definition by Bleuler as schizophrenia, clinicians and investigators have usually emphasized the uniqueness of this disorder, contrasting it to other types of psychopathology. Although the conceptualizing of schizophrenia was a major step in focusing treatment and research efforts, the emphasis on its uniqueness may have obscured important similarities this syndrome shares with other psychiatric disorders and with human function more generally.

One important aspect of viewing schizophrenia as unique has been the belief that the characteristics and predictors of its course are different from the characteristics and predictors of course in other disorders. This view has been supported by two kinds of information: data suggesting that the course of schizophrenia is rather stereotyped, marked by deterioration or, at best, by residual disability (1,2) and data suggesting that the variables of prognostic importance in schizophrenia are not predictors for the course in other kinds of psychopathology (3,4).

Theoretically, the concept of a unique course and its predictors implies a natural history view of schizophrenia, a view that its evolution is rather fixed and stereotyped, probably biologically determined and relatively immutable unless a specific—probably biological—intervention is made. The pervasiveness of this natural history approach is reflected in many statements made about schizophrenia. For example, the natural history view that the course of schizophrenia has unique predictors is reflected in the commonly held opinion (5) that poor social relationships prior to the onset of chronic

This research was supported in part by NIMH Grants No. MN00006-01 and MH25466-01.

schizophrenic symptoms are specific indicators that the disease has begun even before the symptoms appear.

An approach contrasting to the natural history view is provided by the developmental orientation. That view conceptualizes the evolution of disorder as part of an individual's longitudinal history following general rules of human development and learning. The developmental view implies that the course of schizophrenia and the prediction of its outcome are not unique and, in fact, share many similarities with the characteristics and predictors of the course in other kinds of psychopathology.

The choice of accepting the natural history rather than the developmental conceptualization has many practical implications. For example, belief in a unique, immutable course of schizophrenia is reflected in the tendency to use prolonged or deteriorating course of disorder as a diagnostic criterion for schizophrenia (6,7). This belief is further reflected in the tendencies (a) to utilize scarce resources for intensive psychosocial treatment primarily for nonschizophrenics because these patients are presumed to have a more modifiable future (8) and (b) to limit, for patient care review and related purposes, hospitalization coverage for schizophrenia to 2 or 3 weeks, durations that rarely serve to provide more than symptom reduction.

But is the course of disorder in schizophrenia really unique? Are not variables of prognostic importance predictors of outcome in other psychiatric disorders as well? Studies supporting the hypothesis that course and predictors are specific in schizophrenia have provided useful information, but they often have involved methodologic problems that limited their value for comparing schizophrenia with other disorders. These problems have included the tendencies to study mostly chronically hospitalized schizophrenic populations, to use length or frequency of hospitalization as the only outcome variable, to use unstandardized methods for evaluating patients, to investigate patients retrospectively, and to study schizophrenics without comparison diagnostic groups or, if studying comparison groups, failing to control for nondiagnostic variables. More adequate methodology for the study of course would require a prospective study using reliable assessment techniques, control groups of nonschizophrenics comparable to the schizophrenics in terms of nondiagnostic variables, and measures of several aspects of outcome function and their premorbid predictors.

This report describes such a study using these methods to explore three issues that are central for determining whether the course of schizophrenia and the predictors of this course are truly unique:

1. Is the course of schizophrenia relatively similar for most patients with the disorder, or is there wide variation in outcome, ranging from complete recovery to severe disability?
2. Is the course of schizophrenia unique to that disorder, or is a similar course also found with other kinds of psychopathology?
3. Are there specific predicators of the course and outcome of schizophrenia that are only important in that disorder, or are the same prognostic variables important for other diagnostic categories of severe psychopathology?

In this report, we will explore these issues by describing the combined findings of two prospective follow-up studies of schizophrenics and nonschizophrenics.

SUBJECTS

The subjects from which these data were drawn were first admissions for psychiatric disorder studied in two separate research projects. The first of these projects is the International Pilot Study of Schizophrenia (IPSS). The IPSS (9) is a transcultural psychiatric investigation of 1202 patients in nine countries—Colombia, Czechoslovakia, Denmark, India, Nigeria, Taiwan, the Union of Soviet Socialist Republics, the United Kingdom, and the United States of America. It was designed as a pilot study to lay scientific groundwork for future international epidemiologic research on schizophrenia and other psychiatric disorders. The second study providing data for this report is the First Admission Study (FAS), an investigation of all first admissions for functional psychiatric disorder over a one-year period from two catchment areas in Monroe County (Rochester), New York. The FAS is an investigation of the clinical, demographic, and diagnostic characteristics of this population on admission. It is also a prospective study with a follow-up phase to evaluate the characteristics that may determine outcome in these patients. At this time, about one-third of the follow-up phase of the FAS has been completed.

Both the IPSS and the FAS have involved the study of a diagnostically and demographically heterogeneous group of psychiatric admissions, excluding, however, patients who had definite evidence of organic brain disease, alcoholism, or drug abuse. The data presented in this report involve only the first admissions from the Washington subjects of the IPSS (28 diagnosed schizophrenics and 9 nonschizophrenics) and the first 47 subjects (35 nonschizophrenics and 12 diagnosed schizophrenics) from the FAS on whom follow-up has been completed. For the data analyses reported here, these two groups were pooled, yielding a group of 40 diagnosed schizophrenics and 44 diagnosed nonschizophrenics (34 neurotics, personality disorders, and situational reactions, 1 affective psychotic, 6 "other" psychotics [e.g., reactive psychosis, paranoid state], and 3 "other" [2 unspecified depression, 1 anorexia nervosa]). Diagnoses were made using the guidelines of DSM-II. All the 84 patients were first admissions. The distribution of the subjects for age, sex, race, and social class (Hollingshead Index) is presented in Table 54-1. The schizophrenics were somewhat younger and of lower social class.

PROCEDURES

Subjects from both cohorts were evaluated within 2 weeks of admission with standardized interviews of demonstrated reliability (9,10). These procedures included inter-

Table 54-1. Demographic Characteristics of the Subject Cohort

	Schizophrenics	Nonschizophrenics
Mean age[a]	24.9	29.6
Race (B/W)	5/35	7/37
Sex (M/F)	19/21	15/39
Mean social class[a]	3.6	2.9

[a] Significantly different (t-test) p < 0.025.

views for collecting information on the patients' symptoms and signs (Present State Examination and Psychiatric Assessment Interview), a standard Psychiatric History Interview to collect information about previous psychiatric problems and social relationships, and a Social Data Interview to obtain information on work functioning and demographic characteristics. Data were collected by interviewing the patient, reviewing the case records, and interviewing a family member whenever possible. From the information collected with these schedules, a set of items to predict outcome was rated on a prognostic scale of demonstrated reliability (11).

Two years after admission, the patients and available family members were again interviewed using standardized forms designed to obtain follow-up information. From these data, items were rated on the Strauss-Carpenter Level of Function Scale measuring duration of hospitalization, level of social functioning, and level of work functioning in the year prior to follow-up, and severity of symptoms in the month prior to follow-up. The reliability of this scale has been demonstrated (12).

RESULTS

The first task was to determine whether outcome results from schizophrenics fell within a narrow range. To accomplish this, the 2-year outcome scores for each item (symptoms, hospitalization, social relations, and work functioning) and for total outcome were plotted. These plots showed a wide range of outcomes with many subjects in the no disability category. An example of this distribution is demonstrated by the curve for the total outcome scores presented in Figure 54-1, showing 15% of schizophrenics with no impairment and 40% in the best three categories of a 17-point scale-rating disability at outcome.

The second task was to compare the outcome findings of the schizophrenic and the nonschizophrenic groups. This comparison (Table 54-2) showed that although there was a trend toward the schizophrenics being worse on all outcome measures, there were no significant differences between the two groups on measures of social relationships,

Table 54-2. Comparison of Mean Outcome Scores[a] Between Schizophrenics and Nonschizophrenics

	Mean Outcome Scores		
	Schizophrenics	Nonschizophrenics	Significance of Difference[b]
Duration of hospitalization	3.5	3.9	0.02
Social relations	3.1	3.2	N.S.
Employment	3.0	3.3	N.S.
Symptom severity	2.7	3.1	N.S.
Total outcome	12.2	13.5	0.05

[a] Range: 0 (worst)–4 (best) except for total outcome: 0 (worst)–16 (best).

[b] t-test.

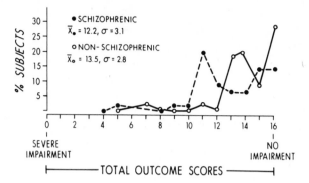

Figure 54-1. Two-year outcome of first admission schizophrenics and nonschizophrenics.

work functioning, and symptom severity at follow-up. The schizophrenics were significantly worse in duration of hospitalization during the year prior to follow-up and in total outcome scores. Although these two differences were statistically significant for total outcome, the actual magnitude of difference between the *means* was very small in clinical terms (a 1.3 difference in a total outcome score that ranges from 0 to 16). Comparison of the total outcome score *profiles* of these two groups revealed that they were significantly different (p = 0.01, Kolmogorov-Smirnov two-sample test). There was considerable overlap between the groups (Figure 54-1), but the nonschizophrenics had a somewhat higher percentage in the no-deficit category than the schizophrenics, a finding similar to that reported elsewhere with data from all patients, including readmissions, from the Washington Center IPSS cohort (13).

The third task was to determine whether similar predictors of outcome were found in both the schizophrenic and nonschizophrenic patients. For the schizophrenics, the pattern of product-moment correlations between predictors and outcome variables previously reported (11,14) was again found (Table 54-3). The two best predictors of outcome were level of social relations and level of work functioning (employment) in the year prior to admission. Each of these was the best predictor of its corresponding outcome variable. The two, when added, gave the best prediction of all outcome variables. The third predictor used in the earlier studies, duration of previous hospitalization, was not applicable for this group of first admission patients.

Table 54-3. Correlations[a] (Product-Moment) Between Predictors and Outcome Variables for Schizophrenics/Nonschizophrenics[b]

| Predictors at First Admission | Two-Year Outcome Measure | | | | |
	Duration of Hospitalization	Employment	Social Relations	Symptom Severity	Total
1. Employment	/.37	37/41	39/	46/34	52/34
2. Social Relations			75/49		41/37
3. Sum of 1 and 2	/.35	27/37	67/37	46/28	55/47

[a] Significant at p < 0.05.

[b] Schizophrenics N = 40, nonschizophrenics N = 44.

The product-moment correlation between predictors and outcome variables was also calculated for the nonschizophrenics to determine whether predictor-outcome relationships similar to those in the schizophrenics were found in this group. The results were practically identical to those for the diagnosed schizophrenics (Table 54-3). The same variables were found to have predictive value, and the same correspondence between predictors and outcome measures was demonstrated.

Finally, to obtain an estimate of the relative prognostic value of diagnostic and nondiagnostic variables, scores on a composite predictor (sum of social relations and work) were dichotomized, and the outcome scores of patients in these two prognostic groups were compared with those of the schizophrenic-nonschizophrenic dichotomy. Results showed that diagnosis was the only significant predictor of hospitalization, and that the dichotomized prognostic function items were the only significant predictors of symptom severity and social relations. Both diagnosis and the composite predictor were significantly related to total outcome.

Having demonstrated several similarities between the schizophrenics and nonschizophrenics in outcome levels (with the exception of hospitalization and the marginal difference in total outcome, which will be discussed subsequently), and having demonstrated the similarity of predictor-outcome relationships in both groups, the next step was to analyze these findings in more detail. First, two statistical issues that had been raised with earlier studies were investigated[1]. One question was whether unusual distribution patterns may be present in such data that might produce misleading results when statistical techniques assuming equal intervals between data points are used. The second question was whether there is greater predictive power at one or the other end of the prognostic score continuum, for example, whether good prognostic ratings predict good outcome but poor prognostic scores predict nothing.

To determine whether unjustified assumptions of interval characteristics in the data accounted for the correlations identified, Kendall's Tau was calculated for the predictor-outcome relationships. This technique assumes ordinal but not interval data. The same important predictors and the same significant relationships between the corresponding predictor and outcome variables were found as had been noted with product-moment correlation techniques (Table 54-4).

To determine whether predictors at one end of the scale were more powerful than at the other end, scatter plots of predictor-outcome relationships were reviewed. Although the majority of the subjects had both good prognostic scores and good outcome, the relationships between these scores at the favorable end of the continuum did not appear any stronger than between predictors and outcome at the unfavorable end. For example, by dividing total outcome into two categories and the sum of the two prognostic variables into three categories, the categories having been selected to provide at least minimum Ns in all cells (Table 54-5), four-fifths of all patients in the best prognostic group fell into the better outcome category and four-fifths of all patients in the worst prognostic group fell into the worse outcome category. To determine statistically if one end of the prognostic range was accounting for most of the predictive power, the prognostic continuum was dichotomized on two separate analyses using different splitting points for each analysis. Each set of dichotomous groups was then correlated (product-moment correlation) with outcome scores. Results of these analyses showed that no matter which

The authors wish to express their gratitude to Drs. Donald Klein and Samuel Guze for their helpful suggestions.

Table 54-4. Correlations[a] (Kendall's Tau) Between Predictors and Outcome Variables for Schizophrenics/Nonschizophrenics[b]

Predictors at First Admission	Two-Year Outcome Measure				
	Duration of Hospitalization	Employment	Social Relations	Symptom Severity	Total
1. Employment	/.32	33/34	'30/	39/36	38/29
2. Social relations			60/49		24/
3. Sum of 1 and 2		24/	47/35	35/	38/21

[a] Significant at p < 0.05.

[b] Schizophrenics N = 40, nonschizophrenics N = 44.

extreme of the prognostic continuum had its impact reduced by being combined with the mid-range values, the correlation of dichotomized prognosis with outcome was practically identical[2].

To evaluate the exceptions to the predictor-outcome relationships, the scatter plots were reviewed to identify patients from the study who were located in the extreme off-diagonal cells of a 3 × 3 matrix, i.e., those patients for whom predictor-outcome relationships did not hold. There were three subjects, all nonschizophrenics. Review of their data files showed that two of these subjects were from the FAS. They had been disorganized enough at the time of the initial interviews to have been considered poor informants, and data from other sources were not obtainable. The third patient (from the IPSS) had good prognostic scores and poor 2-year outcome. She was someone on whom 5-year outcome data collected as part of the IPSS were also available. This woman had experienced a long period of disability following hospitalization. However, at 5-year follow-up she exhibited practically no impairment (total outcome score of 15) and appeared by that time to have returned to her earlier level of functioning.

Of course, such a post hoc review of findings that do not fit a predictive analysis must be accepted with reservations. To provide further, although still not definitive, information on these issues, a review was made of subjects from the IPSS group of previously admitted patients who did not fit the predictor-outcome correlations (prognostic scores at one extreme were associated with outcome scores at the opposite extreme); the findings were similar. In one of the two instances of poor outcome in a patient with high prognostic scores and poor outcome, the interviewer had clearly underestimated the patient's pathology in his ratings, accepting too readily (as demonstrated by later review of the case record) her story of having minimal problems prior to admission. In the other instance with poor outcome and good prognostic ratings, the woman had previously experienced severe difficulties in all prognostic areas, but in the year prior to admission for which the prognostic items were rated, she had a temporary improvement in her functioning. For one of the two patients who had received poor prognostic ratings and had good outcome, the previous function had been underestimated. The patient had been in a confused state at initial evaluation and only information of poor quality was available at the time. For the other patient with low prognostic scores but good 2-year outcome, 5-year follow-up data were also available. Unlike the 5-year results for most

[2] The authors wish to express their appreciation for the statistical advice of Dr. Howard Iker.

Table 54-5. Predictor and Outcome Relationships With Categorized Variables

		Total Outcome Scores		
		0–11 (worse)	12–16 (better)	Total
Sum of Social Relations and Work Prognostic Variables	0–3 (worst)	8	2	10
	4–6	7	22	29
	7 and 8 (best)	9	36	45
	Total	24	60	84

other patients, this patient was considerably worse than at the 2-year follow-up. For this person, it appeared, in retrospect, that the 2-year follow-up occurred during a rather temporary period of remission in a woman who had otherwise fared poorly over the 5-year period after the initial evaluation.

COMMENT

These results must be viewed as building on findings from other studies. One finding from those studies suggested that outcome in schizophrenia may be quite heterogeneous (13,15,16), a finding also noted here. Earlier studies further showed that the various symptom-based methods for arriving at a diagnosis of schizophrenia are not differentially effective for predicting outcome (13,17), so there is little reason to suspect that the findings in this report are attributable primarily to the particular symptom-diagnostic criteria used. Earlier studies also have shown that 2-year outcome findings are good approximations of longer-term outcome (14), so the outcome results reported here can be viewed as reflecting the probable course of the disorder beyond 2 years. The relative stability of outcome following the first 6–12 months after admission has also been reported elsewhere (18–20).

The present results, although preliminary since they do not include all the data that will be available from the FAS, suggest that levels of outcome functioning in schizophrenia overlap considerably with outcome in other severe psychiatric disorders. The results also show that when important prognostic factors such as number of previous admissions are controlled, the diagnosis of schizophrenia *per se* has limited value as a predictor of outcome. Its major prognostic value is limited to being a predictor of hospitalization. On the other hand, levels of previous work functioning and social relationships, even when dichotomized, are significant predictors of several aspects of outcome functioning in both schizophrenic and nonschizophrenic disorders. It is possible, of course, that other more specific measures of outcome functioning could be developed (e.g., measures of certain qualities, rather than levels, of social relationships) that would specifically distinguish schizophrenics from nonschizophrenics. Although several research groups, including our own, are attempting to develop such measures, little success has yet been attained because of major problems in establishing norms and reliability.

The results showing that social relationship and work functioning are the best predictors of their corresponding outcome functionings support earlier findings (14,21). These relationships suggest that each of these variables should be viewed as representing a semi-independent, psychologic, longitudinal process. The relationships defining these processes are sufficiently robust that they do not disappear if nonparametric analyses are used, and exceptions have appeared to be attributable to measurement error.

The significance of these longitudinal processes and their lack of specificity for schizophrenia are shown by their importance as predictors of outcome in nonschizophrenics as well as in schizophrenics. Although this finding may appear to contradict results reported by other investigators, review of the outcome criteria used in those studies reveals that no such conflict exists. Studies by Rosen et al (4) and Bromet et al (3), failing to find prognostic importance of social relationships in disorders other than schizophrenia, used only duration of hospitalization or occurrence of rehospitalization as outcome criteria. Such hospitalization measures, while important approximations of outcome, have significant limitations. For example, lack of rehospitalization, rather than indicating recovery, may reflect prolonged, severe disability involving custodial care outside of a hospital setting (12,22,23). The present results agree with the findings of Rosen et al (4) and Bromet et al (3) in not demonstrating a significant correlation between preadmission social relationships and later hospitalization in nonschizophrenics. However, when other outcome measures are also evaluated, the results show important predictor-outcome relationships, thus disconfirming the specificity of these relationships for schizophrenia hypothesized by the earlier studies.

The work of Brown et al (24) and its replication (25) also have been interpreted as suggesting that social relations functioning has a unique role in determining outcome in schizophrenia. The authors viewed their findings as showing that patients diagnosed as schizophrenics are different from other people in that close personal relationships have adverse effects on the course of schizophrenic disorder. Careful scrutiny of those findings, however, suggests that living in a hostile environment, not closeness itself, was the crucial determinant hindering the schizophrenic's return to full human functioning. Perhaps this finding is not so different from what would be learned by studying patients with other severe psychiatric disorders.

One result of particular interest in our data was that the schizophrenia-nonschizophrenia dichotomy was significant prognostically for only one outcome variable, duration of hospitalization in the year prior to a 2-year follow-up. It seems possible that when schizophrenic symptoms recur, their quality may be particularly frightening and may lead to more pressure for rehospitalization than would be true for patients who present with a recurrence of less anxiety-arousing symptoms.

To speculate further, perhaps deterioration may have been promoted in these patients by past treatment systems which emphasized long-term institutional care with concomitant patient isolation. On the one hand, the association of schizophrenic symptoms and the chronicity promoted partly by the society's response to those symptoms may have contributed to the inaccurate conclusion that schizophrenia necessarily has a chronic and deteriorating course. On the other hand, our data do not show, nor do we imply, that schizophrenia necessarily has a good prognosis; in fact, our results, along with other findings (17), suggest that the average outcome in schizophrenia is somewhat worse than that for other disorders. The present findings do indicate, however, that this course is far from stereotyped.

How do these results relate to the traditional conception of schizophrenia? The view that the course of disorder in schizophrenia was stereotyped has been related to the natural history theory of disease that has long used in the interpretation of medical problems. In the eighteenth century Sydenham showed that the course of certain illnesses followed a characteristic evolution, had rather specific predictors, and was more or less similar for all cases unless altered by some extraordinary event or definitive treatment. Using this concept, and noting symptoms and signs as well, Sydenham discovered that scarlet fever, measles, and other disorders were separate diseases.

This natural history concept was used in the nineteenth century by Kraepelin to help define dementia praecox. He viewed the natural history of this disorder as following a deteriorating course that terminated in one of several specific end states. For many, Kraepelin's natural history concept has continued to be a major part of the view of schizophrenia. This particular natural history concept, besides having been used to imply poor outcome, often has been associated with the view that the course of this disorder is primarily biologically determined (26,27). Those who hold the natural history view also tend to believe that currently available biologic and psychosocial treatments should be used primarily for promoting symptomatic and "social" recovery, but that considerable residual disability is to be expected. The implication appears to be that the ultimate treatment for schizophrenia will have to be biologic, and that intensive psychosocial treatment of such patients is not warranted. These beliefs are frequently translated into practice.

Genetic and biochemical findings are occasionally used to support this cluster of views, although it is generally recognized that the evidence from these areas—good as it is—is not specific enough to provide the definitive explanation regarding determinants of the course in schizophrenia. The natural history concept often has proved valuable for understanding many disorders, but its application as the sole or primary explanation for the course of schizophrenia may have been premature.

By demonstrating the heterogeneity of outcome in schizophrenia, its overlap with outcome in other severe psychopathologic states, and the existence of predictors of outcome that are important both in schizophrenia and other psychiatric disorders, the results reported here emphasize the key role of factors affecting course of disorder that transcend a specific disease process. The main prognostic variables in schizophrenia are not characteristics exclusive to that disorder but are common human behaviors with important developmental roots that reach back into earliest childhood (28). For that reason, a theory of the course of schizophrenia is needed which incorporates a longitudinal perspective that is also relevant to the general emerging patterns of human behavior.

A developmental model meets this need. Such a model emphasizes the general rules that affect consistency and change in human behavior. It recognizes that many variables, including genetic and biochemical factors, social relationships, the expectations of others, life events, and the individual's personality structure, influence the unfolding of behavior. To understand more fully the developmental components in the course of schizophrenia, it will be particularly important to study them in the context of the developmental processes of childhood, adolescence, and adulthood more generally (29–31). To clarify further the way in which the longitudinal processes, social relations functioning, and work functioning affect the course of schizophrenia and other psychiatric disorders, it will also be important to determine whether these functions primarily determine vulnerability to disorders and limited capacity for recovery (32), or whether they are actually intrinsic parts of the disorders (33).

The developmental model has major implications for understanding determinants of the course in schizophrenia. Since social relations and work are behavior-molded through developmental processes, the findings suggest that variables known to influence functioning and change in these areas should be considered as potential major factors affecting the course of schizophrenia. These factors include variables ranging from bio-logic processes that may involve particular perceptual and response tendencies (35), to labeling and other social processes (36,37) that may affect competence and motivation. Between these extremes, other determinants of behavior and development include such variables as family characteristics, work history, and social class, all of which have been shown to have important relationships to schizophrenia.

A major focus on developmental processes also has ramifications for treatment choice and treatment goals. One implication is that the developmental processes probably can be influenced significantly by psychosocial therapies such as individual psychotherapy (38–40), family psychotherapy (41), milieu treatment (23,42), and behavior modifica-tion techniques (43). Unfortunately, evaluation of the effectiveness of these techniques in schizophrenia has been hampered by methodologic complexity and inadequate assess-ment of outcome. However, it is probably erroneous, and certainly premature, to con-clude that psychosocial approaches are of only limited value for dealing with the behavioral determinants that influence the course of schizophrenia.

In research, the developmental approach to understanding the course of schizophrenia implies that findings from many sources must be integrated. These sources include the findings of societal reaction theorists who emphasize the dangers of labeling and freezing a person into a role of permanent disability, of psychodynamic theorists who view intrapsychic and interpersonal conflicts as impediments to growth and inducements to abnormal functioning, and of biological investigators who emphasize genetic and biochemical factors in human maladaptive behavior. Investigations in the field of psy-chosomatic illness (44–47) have much to teach about how integration of such diverse sources of information can be accomplished.

Although the findings presented here support the developmental model, they do not demonstrate that a modified natural history model is invalid. In fact, it may be most useful to combine these views in a mixed model of the course of disease. There are, after all, even physical illnesses, in which natural histories have been demonstrated, in which developmental factors appear to play a major role in determining outcome. An important prognostic factor in tuberculosis, for example, is the patient's social competence (34).

Perhaps the only view that does not fit easily with a full recognition of the role of developmental factors in the course of schizophrenia is a fatalistic one. In one form, this view suggests that so-called "social" recovery, implying a return to some functioning but never with the fullness of life experienced by other humans, is all that ever can be hoped for. In another form, this view suggests that supportive treatment or rehabilitation is all that is indicated for schizophrenics and that permanent disability is to be expected.

Rather than such fatalistic conclusions, our findings suggest that the optimal blend of psychotherapeutic, rehabilitative, and psychopharmacologic treatment for schizophrenia remains to be determined, and new methods in all these areas are required. It would be a mistake to fall back on the concept of inexorable deterioration or necessarily permanent disability, or to be satisfied with "social" recovery and merely supportive treatment. It also would seem erroneous to use a purely natural history model as a justification for inadequate interest and resources for carrying out intensive treatment and research in these areas (8). If schizophrenia, and perhaps other severe psychiatric disorders, are complex processes involving a major contribution from developmental factors, we need to focus our treatment and research more vigorously on these factors.

ACKNOWLEDGMENT

This chapter is based partly on the data and experience obtained during the participation of the authors in the International Pilot Study of Schizophrenia, a project sponsored by the World Health Organization, and funded by the World Health Organization, the National Institute of Mental Health (United States), and the participating field research centers. The collaborating investigators on this study have been:

> At Headquarters in WHO, Geneva, Dr. N. Sartorius (principal investigator), Dr. T. Y. Lin (former principal investigator), Miss E. M. Brooke, Dr. F. Engelsmann, Dr. G. Ginsburg, Mr. M. Kimura, Dr. A. Richman and Dr. R. Shapiro. In the field research centers in: Aarhus, Dr. E. Strömgren (chief collaborating investigator), Dr. A. Bertelsen, Dr. N. Engkilde, Dr. M. Fischer, Dr. C. Flach, and Dr. N. Juel-Nielsen; Agra, Dr. K. C. Dube (chief collaborating investigator) and Dr. B. S. Yadav; Cali, Dr. C. Leon (chief collaborating investigator), Dr. G. Calderon, and Dr. E. Zambrano; Ibadan, Dr. T. A. Lambo (chief collaborating investigator) and Dr. T. Asuni; London, Dr. J. K. Wing (chief collaborating investigator), Dr. J. Birley and Dr. J. P. Leff; Moscow, Dr. R. A. Nadzharov (chief collaborating investigator) and Dr. N. M. Zharikov; Prague, Dr. L. Hanzlicek (chief collaborating investigator) and Dr. C. Skoda; Taipei, Dr. C. C. Chen (chief collaborating investigator) and Dr. M. T. Tsuang; Washington, Dr. J. Strauss and Dr. L. Wynne (chief collaborating investigators), Dr. J. Bartko and Dr. W. Carpenter.

A list of other staff contributing to the IPSS can be found in volume 1 of the Report of the IPSS, WHO, Geneva, 1973.

Findings and views in this chapter that represent the results from data collected in the Washington Center of the IPSS do not necessarily reflect the views of the collaborating investigators from other centers or WHO. The authors gratefully acknowledge the cooperation of Morris Cafritz Memorial Hospital, Washington, D.C.; Prince Georges General Hospital, Cheverly, Maryland; and Spring Grove State Hospital, Catonsville, Maryland.

REFERENCES

1. Bleuler E: *Dementia Praecox or the Group of Schizophrenias,* Zinkin J (transl). New York, International Universities Press, 1950.
2. Wing JK: Impairments in schizophrenia: A rational basis for social treatment, in Wirt RD, Winokur G, Roff M (eds): *Life History Research in Psychopathology,* vol 4. Minneapolis, University of Minnesota Press, 1975.

3. Bromet E, Harrow M, Kasl S: Premorbid functioning and outcome in schizophrenics and nonschizophrenics. *Arch Gen Psychiat* 30:203–207, 1974.

4. Rosen B, Klein DF, Levenstein S, et al: Social competence and posthospital outcome among schizophrenic and nonschizophrenic psychiatric patients. *J Abn Psychol* 74(3):401–404, 1969.

5. Zubin J: Chairman's remarks. Second Rochester International Conference on Schizophrenia. Rochester, NY, May 2–5, 1976.

6. Leonhard K: The question of prognosis in schizophrenia. *Int J Psychiat* 2:630–635, 1966.

7. Feighner JP, et al: Diagnostic criteria for use in psychiatric research. *Arch Gen Psychiat* 26:57–63, 1972.

8. Strauss JS, Frader MA: Justifying intensive psychotherapy for schizophrenia in a community treatment center. In Jørstad J, Ugelstad E: (eds): *Schizophrenia 75: Psychotherapy, Family Studies, Research.* Oslo, University of Oslo Press, 1976, pp 145–158.

9. World Health Organization: *The International Pilot Study of Schizophrenia,* vol 1. Geneva, WHO, 1973.

10. Strauss JS, Kokes RF, Ritzler BA, et al: Crucial patterns of psychiatric disorder. Presented in the New Research Section of the 129th Annual Meeting of the American Psychiatric Association, Miami Beach, May 10–14, 1976.

11. Strauss JS, Carpenter WT Jr: Prediction of outcome in schizophrenia. II. Relationships between predictor and outcome variables. *Arch Gen Psychiat* 15(3):205–212, 1974.

12. Strauss JS, Carpenter WT Jr: Prediction of outcome in schizophrenia. I. Characteristics of outcome. *Arch Gen Psychiat* 27:739–746, 1972.

13. Strauss JS, Carpenter WT Jr: Characteristic symptoms and outcome in schizophrenia. *Arch Gen Psychiat* 30:429–434, 1974.

14. Strauss JS, Carpenter WT Jr: Prediction of outcome in schizophrenia. III. Five-year outcome and its predictors. A report from the International Pilot Study of Schizophrenia. *Arch Gen Psychiat* 34:159–163, 1977.

15. Bleuler M: A 23-year longitudinal study of 208 schizophrenics and impressions in regard to the nature of schizophrenia, in Rosenthal D, Kety SS (eds): *The Transmission of Schizophrenia.* Oxford, Pergamon Press, 1968, pp 3–12.

16. Brown GW, Bone M, Dalison B, et al: *Schizophrenia and Social Care.* London, Oxford University Press, 1966.

17. Hawk AB, Carpenter WT Jr, Strauss JS: Diagnostic criteria and 5-year outcome in schizophrenia: A report from the International Pilot Study of Schizophrenia. *Arch Gen Psychiat* 32:343–347, 1975.

18. Bleuler M: The long term course of the schizophrenic psychoses. *Psychol Med* 4:244–254, 1974.

19. Achte KA: *On Prognosis and Rehabilitation in Schizophrenia and Paranoid Psychoses.* Copenhagen, E Munksgaard, 1967.

20. Astrup C, Noreik K: *Functional Psychoses: Diagnostic and Prognostic Models.* Springfield, Ill, Charles C Thomas, 1966.

21. Strauss JS, Carpenter WT Jr, Bartko JJ: Speculations on the processes that underlie schizophrenic symptoms. *Schizophrenia Bulletin* 11:61–70, 1974.

22. Lamb RH, Goertzel V: Discharged mental patients: Are they really in the community? *Arch Gen Psychiat* 24:29–34, 1971.

23. Carpenter WT Jr, McGlashan TH, Strauss JS: The treatment of acute schizophrenia without drugs: An investigation of some current assumptions. *Amer J Psychiat,* 134:14–20, 1977.

24. Brown GW, Carstairs GM, Topping GG: The post-hospital adjustment of chronic mental patients. *Lancet* ii:685, 1958.

25. Brown GW, Birley JLT, Wing JK: Influence of family life on the course of schizophrenic disorders: A replication. *Brit J Psychiat* 121(562):241–258, 1972.

26. Soskis DA: Aetiological models of schizophrenia: Relationships to diagnosis and treatment. *Brit J Psychiat* 120(557):367–373, 1972.

27. Frias CA: A transcultural survey of psychiatric opinion on schizophrenia. *Comprehen Psychiat* 15(3):225–231, 1974.

28. Jones FH: A 4-year follow-up of vulnerable adolescents: The prediction of outcomes in early adulthood from measures of social competence, coping style, and overall level of psychopathology. *J Nerv Ment Dis* 159(1):20–39, 1974.

29. Erickson E: *Childhood and Society.* New York, W. W. Norton, 1950.

30. Levinson D, McKee B: The psychosocial development of men in early adulthood and the mid-life transition, in Ricks DF, Thomas A, Roff M (eds): *Life History Research in Psychopathology.* Minneapolis, University of Minnesota Press, 1974, pp 243–248.

31. Vaillant GE: The evolution of adaptive and defensive behaviors during the adult life cycle, abstracted. *J Am Psychoanal Assoc* 19:110–115, 1971.

32. Spring B, Zubin J: Vulnerability to schizophrenic episodes and their prevention in adults. Delivered before the First Vermont Conference on the Primary Prevention of Psychopathology. University of Vermont, Burlington, June 25–28, 1975.

33. Phillips L: *Human Adaptation and its Failures.* New York, Academic Press, 1968.

34. Cassel J: Social science theory as a source of hypotheses in epidemiological research. *Amer J Pub Health* 9(54):1482–1488, 1964.

35. Silverman J: The problem of attention in research and theory in schizophrenia. *Psychol Rev* 71(5):352–379, 1964.

36. Scheff TJ: The labelling theory of mental illness. *Amer Sociol Rev* 39:444–452, 1974.

37. Rosenhan DL: On being sane in insane places. *Science* 179:250–257, 1973.

38. Sullivan HS: *The Interpersonal Theory of Psychiatry.* New York, Norton, 1953.

39. Fromm-Reichman F: *Principles of Intensive Psychotherapy.* Chicago, University of Chicago Press, 1950.

40. Searles H: *Collected Papers on Schizophrenia and Related Subjects.* New York, International Universities Press, 1965.

41. Beels CC: Family and social management of schizophrenia. *Schizophrenia Bulletin* 13:97–118, 1975.

42. Jones M: *The Therapeutic Community.* New York, Basic Books, 1953.

43. Hagen RL: Behavioral therapies and the treatment of schizophrenics. *Schizophrenia Bulletin* 13:70–96, 1975.

44. Ader R: The influences of psychological factors on disease susceptibility in animals, in Conalty ML (ed): *Husbandry of Laboratory Animals.* London, Academic Press, 1967, pp 219–238.

45. Engel GL: A psychological setting of somatic disease: The "giving up-given up" complex. *Proceedings of the Royal Society of Medicine* 60:553–555, 1967.

46. Reiser MF: Changing theoretical concepts in psychosomatic medicine. *American Handbook of Psychiatry,* vol 4. New York, Basic Books, 1975.

47. Weiner H: Presidential address: Some comments on the transduction of experience by the brain: Implications for our understanding of the relationship of mind to body. *Psychosom Med* 34(4):355–380, 1972.

Chapter 55
The Long-Term Course of Schizophrenic Psychoses

Manfred E. Bleuler, M.D.

Research on the long-term course of schizophrenia started 80 years ago. It will never come to an end, but we may venture to state: It has reached its first and most important aim; namely, we have just reached the point where we are able to draw reliable conclusions from representative and diverse experience. It definitely clarifies the main trends of the life history of schizophrenics, at least of schizophrenics in this century, in countries of Western civilization, and under average conditions of treatment. Such a reliable knowledge of the long-term course of schizophrenic psychoses is certainly an important contribution to the understanding of the nature of schizophrenia and to the future progress in prophylaxis of the disease and the care and treatment of schizophrenic patients.

First I shall point out how tremendous have been the difficulties to be overcome before we could gain our present knowledge. I shall then briefly mention the main clinical studies on which this knowledge is based. And it is my principal purpose to formulate basic ideas about the essentials of the life histories of patients after the onset of their psychoses.

Research on the course of schizophrenia was futile as long as it was not made clear what we understood by the designation "schizophrenia." Different psychiatric schools even now define schizophrenia in different ways. The large majority of psychiatrists, however, will clearly know what disturbances are meant when I only mention a few criteria for the diagnosis. They are acknowledged by all the students of the long-term course to whose studies I refer. First, we consider schizophrenia as a real psychosis in the social and psychologic sense–the designation psychosis or its synonyms has had for centuries. All patients included in the statistics I will summarize have gone through a severe psychotic phase at least once in their life. All of them were diagnosed by several psychiatrists as schizophrenics, and they would be considered as schizophrenic by nearly all psychiatrists all over the world. Borderline cases that could just as well be described as psychopaths, schizoid personalities, neurotics, or pseudoneurotics, are excluded from the diagnosis, even though some psychiatrists would label them as schizophrenics.

The second important point in describing the diagnostic procedure would seem evident: In studying the course of a disease, we must not consider this course as a diagnostic criterion! Obvious as this statement seems, it often has been forgotten by older clinicians. They hesitated to accept the diagnosis of schizophrenia if the prognosis were favorable. In the studies I consider in this chapter, the diagnosis of schizophrenia has been made independently of prognosis and course.

Third, we do not call a psychosis schizophrenic if it develops in evident connection with physical disease, if we can consider it a symptomatic schizophrenia, if it has amnesic and other psychoorganic features, even when the psychopathologic condition temporarily resembles true schizophrenia, as for instance in certain cases of brain tumor or certain intoxications.

I trust that on the grounds of these remarks you have a clear idea of what I mean when I use the term "schizophrenia." It is not necessary to describe further to you as psychiatrists the principal diagnostic criteria. You are familiar with the psychopathologic state labeled "schizophrenic."

Another difficulty which has not been overcome by older investigators concerns the selection of the patients to be studied. We are interested in knowing the average fate of all schizophrenics of certain cultural surroundings and are not eager to know how things look only with regard to a selected group of patients of a particular hospital with its particular admission policy. The main procedure in preventing errors of selection consists in comparing the course of the disease in many different groups of patients in different hospitals, in different countries, in different decades of the century. The statistics I am going to summarize do indeed concern the most varied groups of patients. In these statistics are included even schizophrenics who have never been hospitalized. Therefore, I think that the statements I am going to make hold good for the average course of schizophrenia in our time and in our culture.

I have no time to mention how the statistical errors of older investigations have been avoided. Everything possible has been done to avoid them in the statistics I am going to summarize, and the conventional sources of error have been carefully considered.

My own studies (1–7) of the course of schizophrenic psychoses started in Boston and White Plains, New York, in 1929, and were continued without interruption for more than 40 years. Within the last 3 years, I have had to stop working with my patients, but I have compared my results with the excellent studies of Christian Müller and Luc Ciompi (8) in Lausanne, Gert Huber, Gisela Gross, and Robert Schüttler (9,10) in southern Germany, and H. Hinterhuber (11) in Austria. These researches were performed independently of each other and, hence, the fact that these results correspond to each other heightens their validity.

My main study deals with 208 schizophrenics of the Burghölzli Clinic admitted after I became its head in 1942. I have treated all of them personally and have personally followed their destiny until death, or for at least 22 years, together with the destiny of their parents, siblings, marital partners, and children. I have also collected observations of many other groups of schizophrenics hospitalized in an alpine valley, in Basel, and in New York, cases of schizophrenia with good and bad outcomes, schizophrenics treated with different methods, and so forth. All these groups together comprise 1158 schizophrenic patients whose course I have studied over long periods. Altogether, the three other teams of investigators mentioned studied the course of 950 schizophrenics. The observations I am going to summarize are, therefore, considerable in number.

On an average, after 5 years' duration the psychosis does not progress any further. It tends, rather, to improve. Twenty, 25, 30, and more years after onset of the psychosis, the proportion of recovered to improved and to nonimproved patients remains about the same 5 years after onset. This statement is just as valid if we use other criteria such as hospitalization, earning capacity, or the general psychiatric condition. The same patients are not always in a good or bad condition, hospitalized or not hospitalized. What remains unchanged are the *proportions* of recovered to nonrecovered and of hospitalized to nonhospitalized patients.

The *tendency to improvement* is not evident if we only consider these rough statistics (recovered or not, hospitalized or not) but becomes very evident if we consider the condition of the individual patients carefully and in detail. The closer we live together with patients, even the most chronic ones, the more astonished we are at fluctuations in their condition. The great majority of the alterations in the course of many years after onset of the psychosis are clearly in the direction of improvement. The improvements are manifold in nature. Some of the patients who have hardly ever uttered coherent sentences start to speak or behave as if they were healthy on certain occasions, for instance, when on leave, at hospital festivities, or on the occasion of a catastrophe such as exploding bombs in wartime. I have seen improvements after 40 years' duration of a severe chronic psychosis. And, what is even more amazing, a schizophrenic may recover after having been psychotic and hospitalized for decades. Such a late, complete recovery is rare, but it occurs.

The circumstances under which late improvements or late recoveries take place are of the most varied kind. The death of a member of the family toward whom the patient was very ambivalent is such an occasion. A change of hospital environment or a physical disease or weakness of old age is another. Frequently, the improvement follows a reactivation of therapy, but successful active therapy may be of the most varied nature: psychotherapeutic, psychopharmacologic, or psychosocial approaches of any kind. This would seem of importance when we discuss the "right" therapeutic policy.

While late improvements are very frequent in patients who have had acute psychotic episodes in the past, they are very rare in those whose psychosis has steadily and chronically progressed to deterioration. This observation should stimulate our therapeutic interest even in these steadily progressing psychoses. Of great relevance seems to me to be the clinical observation that even in these chronic patients who have never improved with respect to hospital status, skillful examination reveals hidden behind the psychosis an intact inner life. In the time of Kraepelin, it was already known that memory and perception remain intact. Later it was observed that discernment—the ability to reason and to think logically—is never lost, but continues along with the illogical and chaotic inner life. And even more, I found it fascinating to discover and to evoke very normal, very fine emotions, signs of an intact and warm emotional life in chronic schizophrenics.

On the other hand, it is true that many improved schizophrenics who have recoverd from active psychotic symptoms remain underactive, lack personal initiative, and have somewhat apathetic, colorless personalities. With regard to the nature of this deterioration in spontaneous activity, Gert Huber and his team disagree with our opinion in Zürich. Gert Huber is inclined to compare the impoverished personality after a schizophrenic psychosis with the condition after psychosurgery or localized cerebral diseases. I should prefer to compare it with the impoverished personality after long-standing frustration in a concentration camp or after an uneventful, unsatisfactory life during which the person's talents and abilities had no occasion to develop.

Having described the general tendencies of the long-term course of schizophrenic development, I now shall cite a few figures characterizing the long-term course from another point of view.

At least 25% of all schizophrenics recover entirely and remain recovered for good. The qualifications of full recovery include a lack of psychotic signs, a normal social integration, and the ability to work. It is, however, not a reasonable criterion for full recovery that the former schizophrenic should view all that has gone on during the psychosis in the same way as the objective observer does. It is quite natural that the recovered schizophrenic patient looks back to his psychotic life in a subjective manner, that a resentment may remain where there has been a delusional idea of persecution, or that he occasionally may disagree with the psychiatrist about the cause and consequence of his abnormal behavior. For example, the former patient may still regard his past behavior as a natural reaction to unjustifiable attitudes of others, whereas the psychiatrist may believe that these attitudes of others were more a reaction to the abnormal behavior of the patient.

Naturally, the rate of favorable and long-standing recoveries fluctuate somewhat between the different groups of patients who have been studied. The extremes are 20% and 40%, but these extremes are due to unrepresentative selection and small numbers with considerable standard errors. If we take together the average and the largest and most representative groups, the statement of at least 25% full, long-standing recoveries holds good, and it can be considered very reliable because other investigators—Huber, Müller, and Hinterhuber—as well as myself, have found a long-standing recovery rate of 26%.

On the other hand, about 10% of schizophrenics remain permanently hospitalized as severe psychotics. This is a frightening number. However, it is a low number when viewed against the old opinion that schizophrenia by its very nature is a progressive disease that as a rule causes severe, life-long invalidism.

Intermediately, at least half of the patients (but less than three-quarters) alternate for decades between acute psychotic phases and phases of improvement or recovery. Only at a very advanced age do the acute relapses become rarer.

I have mentioned that at least 25% of the patients arrive at a lasting recovery. However, the number of recovered patients at a given moment after the onset of the disease is much higher and reaches almost 50%. Some of these patients, however, will have acute relapses. If one does not consider the overall condition but only the capacity to do useful work, the percentage of working patients at a given moment later than 5 years after the onset of the disease is even higher than 50%.

I might add some statistics on hospitalization alone: after the fifth year of the duration of the psychosis, about 25% of all schizophrenics are hospitalized at a given moment and 75% are not. On the average, a schizophrenic once hospitalized in the middle of this century had to expect that he would spend one-third of his future life in a hospital and two-thirds outside. This statistic is less shocking if we know that the number of hospital years includes hospitalizations on account of old age, not merely on account of schizophrenia.

All these figures are chosen from among many others collected to characterize the average course of schizophrenia. Although it is unnecessary to cite additional figures, one more statement is important: of the 25% of the patients who had reached a long-lasting favorable condition, not one was under long-term neuroleptic or other pharmacologic treatment, nor were most of the recovered patients cared for by welfare agencies. This should not be forgotten in judging the value of lasting prophylaxis with drugs or of regular after-care of discharged schizophrenic patients.

At this time, I must point out that statistics not only confirm the general impression that the average course of schizophrenic psychoses has changed during this century but also give some interesting details that were not recognized before. Every clinician knows that the most severe psychotic conditions are milder now than before. The so-called catastrophic schizophrenia, which is characterized by a very acute onset of a severe psychosis early in life followed without any interruption by a lifelong, very severe, chronic psychosis, has practically disappeared within the last decade. Also chronicity of schizophrenic psychoses (and in particular, chronic hospitalization of schizophrenics) has become less frequent, while phasic course (and hospital discharges and readmissions) has become more frequent. The changes, however, are not so great as to influence more rough figures of groups studied in the earlier and later decades of this century.

If the prognosis of schizophrenia has improved during this century, such improvement certainly does not hold good for every aspect of schizophrenia. It is somewhat discouraging that the number of total recoveries of long-standing duration has not increased, as far as statistics demonstrate. And it is also discouraging that the number of chronic forms that progress to severe deterioration have hardly diminished. These observations should stimulate therapeutic research with the aim of hastening hospital discharge, of finding ways to long-standing recovery, and of influencing even the course of chronic progressive schizophrenic patients.

A careful analysis of these patients who were mainly admitted before 1950, some before 1930, shows that the factor that contributed most to their improvement was the improvement of hospital therapy. For these patients, there had been great progress in social and environmental therapy compared with the conditions before World War I. On the other hand, they had not yet been treated as outpatients in modern after-care programs.

Now, however, the question is: What therapeutic method has been mainly responsible for success—pharmacotherapy, psychotherapy, or environmental therapy? An analysis of my statistics from the middle of this century shows that success is not due mainly to one treatment method but to an overall improvement and activation of therapy and care for the patients. Any therapeutic technique can be replaced by another good one, provided the technique includes one of the following: an active therapeutic community, sudden confrontation with stress,[1] or general tranquilization. Prominent clinicians like Aubrey Lewis expressed this opinion 20 years ago. Further research shows that they were right.

The statistics reveal many other interesting facts with regard to influences on the long-term course of schizophrenia. I shall select one of them: a disturbed relationship with relatives and well-loved persons and, in particular, a broken parental home are much more frequent in the life history of schizophrenic women than of schizophrenic

---

Acute stress was the main therapeutic factor in ancient techniques—for example, that of inoculating schizophrenics with malarial parasites—for treating schizophrenia; and it is one of the therapeutic factors in the more modern shock therapies. A better form of stress can be introduced by giving the patient unexpected responsibilities, by suddenly changing the hospital environment, by sudden discharge from the hospital, or by sudden appropriate interpretation of the patient's behavior.

men. Broken parental home in the anamneses of schizophrenic women is also significantly more frequent than in the average population, which is hardly the case in the history of schizophrenic men. There is no proof as yet, but it is probable that trouble in competition with other men and with authority are more frequent in the anamneses of male schizophrenics. In accordance with these data from anamneses, the morbid ideas of schizophrenic women frequently are centered on family members and well-loved persons, while those of schizophrenic males are on competition with other men and homosexual problems. This and many other observations demonstrate that the course of schizophrenia is influenced by psychodynamic events that are active in any person.

Another observation is interesting: in the anamneses of schizophrenics there exists a highly significant correlation between prepsychotic schizoid personality and broken homes or miserable childhood conditions of any kind. The development of schizoid personality traits has, therefore, much to do with adverse living conditions in childhood. Since a schizoid personality is in itself a disposition to schizophrenia and to an unfavorable course of schizophrenia, we must assume that living conditions in childhood are a factor in later schizophrenia.

These are only a few examples selected from many others to demonstrate how much the results of research on the life history of schizophrenics contribute to the theory of schizophrenia. They demonstrate, for instance, that the course of schizophrenic psychoses is not compatible with the assumption that schizophrenia is the result of any progressive brain disease, caused, for example, by a metabolic intoxication. On the other hand, they demonstrate that manifold psychologic influences act together to help form the course and the outcome of schizophrenic psychoses. It is a fascinating research task to study them. Even more important, the fact that course and outcome can be influenced must encourage our therapeutic activity. The discovery that so much of the inner life of the schizophrenic remains human, natural, and healthy, is a futher reason to appreciate the high significance of the therapy for schizophrenic patients.

REFERENCES

1. Bleuler M: *Krankheitsverlauf, Persönlichkeit und Verwandtschaft Schizophrener & ihre gegenseitigen Beziehungen.* Leipzig, Thieme, 1941.
2. Bleuler M: Das Wesen der Schizophrenieremission nach Schockbehandlung. *Zeitschrift gesamte Neurologie und Psychiatrie* 173:553, 1941.
3. Bleuler M: Die spätschizophrenen Krankheitsbilder. *Fortschr Neurol* 15:259, 1943.
4. Bleuler M: *Endokrinologische Psychiatrie.* Stuttgart, Thieme, 1954.
5. Bleuler M: A 23-year longitudinal study of 208 schizophrenics, in Rosenthal D (ed): *Transmission of Schizophrenia.* Oxford, Pergammon Press, 1968, p 3.
6. Bleuler M: *Die schizophrenen Geistesstorungen: im Lichte langjahriger Kranken—und Familien—Geschichten.* Stuttgart, Thieme, 1972.
7. Bleuler M: The long-term course of the schizophrenic psychoses. *Psychological Medicine*, 4:244, 1974.
8. Ciompi L, Müller C: *Lebensweg & Alter der Schizophrenen.* Berlin, Springer, 1976.
9. Gross G, Huber G, Schuettler R: Verlaufs- & sozialpsychiatrische Erhebungen bei Schizophrenen. *Nervenarzt* 42:292, 1971.
10. Huber G: Schizophrene Verläufe. *Dtsch Med Wschr* 89:212, 1964.
11. Hinterhuber H: Zur Katamnese der Schizophrenien. *Fortschr Neurol* 41:528, 1973.

Chapter 56

The Distinction Between Prognosis and Diagnosis in Schizophrenia: A Discussion of Manfred Bleuler's Paper

George E. Vaillant, M.D.

Fifty years ago, Adolph Meyer suggested that we need "less discussions of generalities and more records of well-observed cases—especially records of lifetimes, not merely snatches of picturesque symptoms" (1). Manfred Bleuler's work over the last 30 years has provided us with those records. He reports that his review of the life histories of almost 2000 schizophrenics reveals that at any given point in time 25% achieve full remission, an additional 50% make at least a partial social remission, and 25% remain social invalids or hospitalized. He supports his findings by citing data from Lausanne, southern Germany, and Austria. In a scholarly work, Joseph Stephens reviewed the world literature on long-term follow-up in schizophrenia and has amply corroborated Bleuler's findings (2).

More important, Bleuler reports that after the first 5 years of their disease, schizophrenics do not continue to get worse—at least statistically. That is to say that for every patient who becomes more socially debilitated, another patient will improve. Thus, if we can spare our patients the indignity of chronic institutionalization and if we can provide some supportive after-care, the purported progressive deterioration of schizophrenics, originally reported by Kraepelin and still widely believed by many psychiatrists, does not, in fact, characterize the group of schizophrenias. Bleuler also cautions that, contrary to popular belief, schizophrenics who achieve full remission do not require phenothiazines to maintain this remission. My findings from a smaller sample support this observation (3).

Bleuler emphasizes the fact that prognosis is different from diagnosis, but he does not discuss the prognostic factors that differentiate the schizophrenics destined to make complete remission from those who will suffer a chronic course. The evidence from long-term follow-up studies certainly supports Bleuler and militates against those who argue for a sharp dichotomy between reactive and process schizophrenias (4,5,15). If they are followed for long periods, Bleuler reports that some individuals with a diagnosis of process schizophrenia will pass to full remission; other investigators agree that on long-term follow-up 30–50% of the so-called reactive psychoses, schizophreniform psychoses, and benign stupors with a good prognosis nevertheless evolve into a chronic schizophrenic picture (6–9).

Thus, on the one hand, if combined with a hospital stay of at least a few weeks, any accepted means of diagnosing schizophrenia will identify individuals more prone to develop lifelong defects in working and loving than patients with other diagnoses. (Despite Strauss's hopeful chapter in this volume, long-term follow-up studies reveal that only one-third of the individuals reliably diagnosed as schizophrenic will ever marry and that 50% will spend much of their lives unemployed and another 25% underemployed.) On the other hand, the more the patient's schizophrenic state resembles an affective, a reactive, or a toxic psychosis, the more likely he or she is to enjoy remission.

Let me review that generalization in greater detail. First, schizophrenics who recover are more likely to manifest confusion, stressful precipitants, and an acute onset. This is consistent with toxic psychosis and is one reason that the terms Gjessing's syndrome, oneirophrenia, infection-exhaustion psychosis, and postpartum psychosis have been used to relabel such remitting patients.

Second, well-diagnosed schizophrenics who recover are far more likely to manifest emotional precipitants, acute onset, and a good premorbid adjustment. They are more likely to be married at the time of hospital admission. Thus, it is not surprising that terms like benign stupor, schizophreniform, and psychogenic or reactive psychosis have been applied to such patients.

Third, schizophrenics who recover are more likely to manifest affective symptoms and a heredity positive for affective psychosis but negative for schizophrenic psychosis. This finding explains why terms like schizomania, schizoaffective, cycloid, and "misdiagnosed manic-depressive" have been common.

Finally, prognostic indicators of chronicity in schizophrenia predict chronicity in all psychoses. Thus, several studies reveal that manic-depressives with insidious onset, clear sensoria, schizoid premorbid adjustment, and heredities positive for symptoms suggestive of schizophrenia are likely to suffer a chronic course (10–12).

In our efforts to relabel the remitting schizophrenics, we must remember that it is the sheer number of favorable prognostic symptoms—outlined in reviews by Langfeldt, Stephens, and Zubin et al—that provides the most powerful means of predicting remission (2,13,14). Accurate diagnosis finishes a poor second. For example, I have recently followed up a cohort of 55 remitting schizophrenics. These patients represented that fraction (20–25%) of all schizophrenics admitted to the Massachusetts Mental Health Center (Boston Psychopathic Hospital) between 1959 and 1962 who were known to have achieved full remission (1–2 years after index admission). In some respects, most of these patients resembled toxic *and* reactive *and* affective psychosis (15). However—and it is a big however—10 to 15 years later 40% of these patients manifested a course that could be described as "process." The patients in this *subgroup* of remitting schizophrenics have spent an average of 25% of their time in a hospital and continued to show psychotic symptoms and/or severe social deficits when in the community. Nevertheless, on first admission these 22 remitting patients were just as likely to have shown affective symptoms and an heredity positive for affective psychosis as those remitting schizophrenics who remained well.

In a similar vein, before this cohort of schizophrenics was assembled, the diagnosis of several patients was changed from schizophrenic to some other label. However, this relabeled group of nonschizophrenics enjoyed a good prognosis only to the degree that they manifested favorable prognostic symptoms. I suspect that even when we know the etiologic agents of both the schizophrenias and the affective psychoses, and unequivocal diagnosis is possible, there will continue to be schizophrenics who recover and affective psychotics who go on to chronic courses. Prognosis and diagnosis are different dimensions.

The most intriguing and perhaps most important finding reported by Manfred Bleuler is that after 20–30 years some so-called process schizophrenics seem to "mature" out of their illness. In personal communications, Joseph Zubin, John Clausen, Nils Retterstöl, and Eric Strömgren have reported the same observations. contradiction to the Kraepelinian notion of a deteriorating course, the defects of some schizophrenics may, like some character disorders, yield to the maturation of personality that goes on during the adult life cycle. The reason that this important finding has hitherto not been appreciated may be due to the fact that the average clinician loses contact with schizophrenics who do well and that chronic hospitalization makes schizophrenics worse. Clearly, this is an area of research demanding high priority in the future.

REFERENCES

1. Meyer A: Quoted by Lewis, N: Research in dementia praecox. The National Committee for Mental Hygiene, 1936.
2. Stephens JH: Long-term course and prognosis in schizophrenia. *Seminars in Psychiatry* 2:464–485, 1970.
3. Vaillant GE, Ewalt JR, Semrad, EV: Current Therapeutic Results in Schizophrenia. *N Engl J Med* 271:280–283, 1964.
4. Taylor MA, Abrams R: Manic-depressive illness and good prognosis schizophrenia. *Amer J Psychiat* 132:741–742, 1975.
5. Robins E, Guze SB: Establishment of diagnostic validity in psychiatric illness: Its application to schizophrenia. *Amer J Psychiat* 126:983–987, 1970.
6. Rachlin HL: A Follow-up study of Hoch's benign stupor cases. *Amer J Psychiat* 92:531–558, 1935.
7. Faergeman PM: *Psychogenic Psychoses*. London, Butterworth, 1963.
8. Noreik K, Astrup C, Dalgard OS, et al: A prolonged follow-up of acute schizophrenic and schizophreniform psychoses. *Acta Psychiatrica Scandinavia* 43:432–443, 1967.
9. Eitinger L, Laane C, Langfeldt G: Prognostic value of clinical picture and therapeutic value of physical treatment in schizophrenia and schizophreniform states. *Acta Psychiat Scand* 33:33–53, 1958.
10. Astrup C, Holmboe R: A follow-up study of 270 patients with acute affective psychoses. *Acta Psychiat Scand* 34:7–65, 1959.
11. Hunt, RC, Appel KE: Prognosis in the psychoses lying midway between schizophrenia and manic-depressive psychoses. *Am J Psychiat* 93:313–339, 1936.

12. Lewis N, Hubbard LD: The mechanisms and prognostic aspects of the manic-depressive-schizophrenic combinations in manic-depressive psychosis, in *Annual Review of Nervous and Mental Diseases*, vol 2. Baltimore, Williams & Wilkins, 1931, pp 539–608.

13. Langfeldt G: *Schizophreniform States*. Copenhagen, E. Munksgaard 1939.

14. Zubin J, Sutton S, Salizinger K, et al: A biometric approach to prognosis in schizophrenia, in Hoch P, Zubin J (eds): *Comparative Epidemiology of the Mental Disorders*. New York, Grune & Stratton, 1961.

15. Vaillant GE: Prospective prediction of schizophrenic remission. *Arch Gen Psychiat* 11:509–518, 1964.

A. CONCLUDING COMMENTS

Joseph Zubin, Ph.D.

Despite vast differences in the geographical origin of our panelists, ranging from London to Zurich, Boston to Rochester and New York, the degree of disagreement is rather meager and the degree of consensus rather remarkable. We all agree on the following:

1. First, schizophrenia today is much less disabling than in the first half of this century.
2. The course of the disorder, even when little or no therapeutic or custodial intervention takes place, is rather varied.
3. The assumption that psychosocial therapeutic approaches are of limited value is no longer tenable.
4. Close relationships with family or important others in itself is not disabling to the schizophrenic, but close involvement with hostile environments is.
5. Social impoverishment leads to clinical impoverishment, whereas social enrichment leads to clinical improvement.
6. The vulnerability concept is regarded as useful by all participants.

There is no consensus on the following: 1) acceptance of the concept of a "natural history" of schizophrenia; 2) the expected proportions of recovered, improved, and chronically ill; 3) the degree of heterogeneity-homogeneity in outcome; and 4) the role of triggering events in onset of an episode.

How did the panel deal with role of type of onset (sudden or insidious) and type of outcome in relation to good versus poor premorbid patients? Is it possible to find some integrating principle that could contain the various consensual agreements that were reached? Without wishing to foist another paper onto the session, I would like to suggest that the concept of *vulnerability* is a good candidate for integrating the agreements and disagreements. If we assume that the permanent characteristic of the schizophrenic is not the disorder but the vulnerability to the disorder, and that the episodes of the disorder are time limited, we can provide the desired integration. Vulnerability is the proneness to develop an episode when sufficient stress-producing life events (external as well as internal) occur that exceed the stress-tolerance of the person. When the stress level again falls below the threshold, the person returns more or less to his premorbid level and resumes his place in society. If he had a good premorbid level of adaptation, he will be regarded as recovered or improved. If his premorbid adaptation level was poor, he may be mistakenly regarded as continuing in his episode even though the episode is ended and he has returned to his premorbid, albeit poor, level. In the past, many patients failed to recapture their premorbid level because of iatrogenic effects such as hospitalism or other impediments imposed by the sick role. Today, I believe that the role of iatrogenically produced deficits has been reduced though not eliminated.

Consequently, a more optimistic view of schizophrenia has resulted. This optimism has been further aided and abetted by follow-up studies of entire cohorts of patients such as those conducted by Professor Manfred Bleuler. He points out that his father's rather

641

pessimistic attitude towards outcome of schizophrenia was based on limited follow-ups of rehospitalized patients, since he never saw again those who were so well-recovered that they never returned to the clinic.

It should be understood, however, that not all the patients returning to or remaining in the hospital are still in their original episode. For some, the episode is over and yet they may continue to be treated as if they were still sick, sometimes maintained continuously on drugs until tardive dyskinesia sets in. This is one of the reasons that monitoring of the beginning and end of episodes is so essential. Part of the variability in outcome probably reflects variability in the degree of premorbid adjustment to which the patients return at the end of the episode, as well as the variability in degree of vulnerability. Hence, variable outcome should not be taken as evidence of the non-applicability of the concept of a natural history of the disorder.

Another important source of variability in onset and in outcome is the fact that, unlike somatic disorders, behavioral disorders are judged on the basis of observed behavior. But this observed behavior includes not only manifestations of the focal disorder but also the premorbid personality and premorbid ecological niche on which the focal disorder is imposed. This, in part, is what Professor Wing refers to as the extrinsic disadvantages, unconnected with the disorder. For this reason it is well to try to separate, if possible, the "illness," which combines the focal disorder and its impact on the premorbid personality, from the focal disorder itself. That is, the observed illness is unique to each individual, depending upon his distinctive premorbid personality, even though theoretically the focal disorder may be conceptualized as independent of the premorbid personality. This may explain why clinical schizophrenia appears so variable. If we had knowledge of the focal disorder of schizophrenia itself, it might prove to be no more variable than somatic disorders. For this reason also, we need not deny the existence of a natural history for schizophrenia.

The relation between prognosis and vulnerability remains unclear. Prognostic indicators tell us what may happen after an individual develops an episode, but they do not predict who will have an episode nor who is more prone to have one. This is why measures of vulnerability must be developed independent of prognosis of outcome so that preventive methods can be utilized for the prevention of episodes in the first place.

The relationships among premorbid personality, onset, and outcome of schizophrenia are very complicated. Elsewhere (1), I have pointed out that premorbid personality may be related to the occurrence of an episode of schizophrenia in one of three ways: 1) the future schizophrenic has a premorbid personality which eventually blooms into the psychosis (a hypothesis probably congenial to psychoanalysis); 2) the premorbid personality is independent of the occurrence of the disorder (a disease model probably congenial to Kraepelin); and 3) the premorbid personality interacts with the disorder (probably a view congenial to Adolf Meyer). The available data do not lend any overwhelming weight to any one of these possibilities. The studies of Essen-Möller (2) and Hagnell (3) utilizing Sjöbring's (4) method of personality assessment, however, lend support to the second hypothesis—that is, independence, and it may be valuable in future work to adopt this null hypothesis in order to test if it is tenable.

Perhaps the most rapid advance made in the fields of onset and outcome during the last decade has been the provision of systematic structured interviews and rating scales for assessing these factors. There has been a virtual explosion of diagnostic techniques which have capitalized on the accumulated observations of 34 centuries of sagacious clinicians, and have systematized them. However, the inundation of new techniques one after another, reminiscent of the sorcerer's apprentice dilemma, must now somehow be stopped and a return made to detailed, firsthand observations of patients. Otherwise, our clinical understanding will not deepen.

In summary, this panel has provided a new view of schizophrenia, freeing it from the previous pessimistic view regarding its persistence and deteriorating outcome. The views expressed, expecially by Bleuler and Wing, offer a veritable Emancipation Proclamation for schizophrenics. It is possible that if we regard only the vulnerability to schizophrenia as being more or less permanent, but the episode(s) of the disorder as being time-limited and recoverable, much of the apparent confusion and variability can be explained.

Regarding the existence of a natural history for schizophrenia, even the natural course of a river, from which the analogy probably arose, is not preordained for all rivers, since the course depends on the rainfall, nature of terrain, etc. Nevertheless, there are certain generalizations which can be made about the course of rivers based upon geological considerations. In the case of schizophrenia, if we could separate the focal disorder from the broader illness, we may, at least conceptually, find it possible to accept the natural history approach.

Thus, adapting a Newtonian view in which we postulate both that a body once set in motion will continue forever and that friction with surfaces will gradually halt the body, we can by analogy hypothesize that there is an expected course for schizophrenia even though this course can be modified by degree of vulnerability and the ecological niche which the person occupies in life.

REFERENCES

1. Zubin J: Psychopathology and the social sciences, in Klineberg O, Christie R (eds): *Perspectives in Social Psychology.* New York, Holt, Rinehart & Winston, 1965, p. 189–207.
2. Essen-Möller E: *Individual Traits and Morbidity in a Swedish Rural Population.* Copenhagen, Ejnar Munksgaard, 1956.
3. Hagnell O: *A Prospective Study of the Incidence of Mental Disorder.* Stockholm, Svenska Bokförlaget, 1966.
4. Sjöbring H: Personality structure and development—a model and its application. (Translated by Essen-Möller E). *Acta Psychiat Scand,* Suppl 244, 1973.

B. DISCUSSION: INTEGRATION AND EDITORIAL COMMENT

Rue L. Cromwell, Ph.D.

The floor discussion that followed the papers on Onset and Course was directed toward three specific themes. While a number of issues in the onset and course of schizophrenia were not mentioned, those that were discussed seemed to reflect the current status of thinking in this field.

I. OPTIMISM REGARDING OUTCOME

The first theme was a new optimism about outcome of schizophrenic psychoses. This optimistic view, spearheaded by the data of Bleuler, but also reflected in the other papers, seems to have at least four different sources. First, a greater sophistication in philosophy of science has encouraged diagnosticians not to use incurability as part of the definition of a disorder. Instead, diagnostic concepts, including schizophrenia, should be defined in terms of currently available data and, as a separate matter, judged for their usefulness in predicting matters such as curability. Second, past studies have failed to put adequate emphasis upon the outcome of schizophrenic patients who did not return to or remain in psychiatric care. These individuals who eventually become lost to the view of clinicians are likely to have more favorable courses. Third, recent experiences with deinstitutionalization and community psychiatry have allowed some separation in the study of effects of institutionalization and of the schizophrenic disorder itself. Previously, the debilitating effects of long term institutionalization had often been attributed to the psychosis. Fourth, and still unresolved as to importance, the more optimistic outlook may in part be the result of how the psychotic cohort under study is defined. How many days must a patient be ill before he is included in the study group? Clearly, those with short illnesses (e.g., less than a month) have a better prognosis. This definitional artifact would not account for those cases of positive recovery after a long illness.

While the note of optimism and the rejection of past negative views about the course of schizophrenia were validly made, a counterpoint of caution was also presented. Vaillant, in his paper, noted that a high proportion of patients he had earlier reported as recovered later suffered a relapse. Spitzer, acknowledging the valid and useful data presented by Strauss, expressed concern that Strauss' findings on prognostic nonspecificity among mental disorders might be misinterpreted. While Strauss pointed to the lack of specificity or uniqueness in course and outcome of schizophrenia as compared to other hospitalized mental patients, Spitzer noted that the length of illness and the readmission record remains greater for schizophrenics than for nonschizophrenic psychiatric patients.

As these discussions proceeded, the ambiguity in the terms *acute* and *chronic* in current psychiatry was very apparent. Sometimes referring to floridity of symptoms, sometimes referring to length of illness or hospitalization, sometimes referring to sudden vs. slow onset of psychosis, and sometimes referring to a loose combination of these defining criteria, the terms *acute* and *chronic* still remain a liability in communication among psychiatrists.

II. WHY SYMPTOMS ARE A POOR BASIS TO PREDICT OUTCOME

A second theme, and indeed a complex one, concerned the growing recognition that symptoms are highly variable. They are expressed differently from individual to individual as well as from time to time within the same individual. They come and go. Their measurement usually lacks high reliability. Their value for differential treatment decisions and differential prognostic statements is far less than we would like to believe. The work of Strauss and Carpenter (1), and other groups as well, attest to the fact that a patient's functioning during the years following a diagnosis of schizophrenia is best understood not from the symptoms he displayed but from his functioning prior to the diagnosis of schizophrenia. Paradoxically, the very basis for diagnosing an individual schizophrenic, i.e., his clinical symptoms, is at the same time elusive in providing a systematic basis for understanding etiology, treatment, or prognosis. The discussion reflected several approaches toward resolving this dilemma.

Dr. V. G. Levit (Rockland Research Institute) suggested an approach to case identification based upon the concept of pathokynesis or nosodromia, i.e., a succession of symptom complexes as the patient continues the course of schizophrenia. Fleeting symptoms, he feels, could better serve as a basis for diagnosis if we focused on their temporal relationship to other fleeting symptoms. The relationship between external clinical manifestations and underlying process could thereby be better understood. In responding to this point, Strauss noted that this succession of events is not being overlooked in current research, that the concepts of course and prognosis themselves directly imply the sequencing of clinical manifestations. The remaining question, of course, is where the line is drawn definitionally to indicate what earlier segment of the sequential chain of symptoms is sufficient to diagnose the individual but is still useful in implementing treatment and in predicting later segments of the chain.

There was a discussion of a second and partially related approach to diagnosis, namely, viewing symptoms in clusters which reflect an underlying syndrome or process. This approach does not necessarily organize symptoms in terms of sequence of display but concerns concordance of display. The discussion revives to this author the distinction between monothetic and polythetic approaches to classification. As defined by Sneath and Sokal (2), a monothetic approach requires that certain cardinal features be present in all members of the class, e.g., in all schizophrenics. A polythetic approach to classification requires only that a sufficient number of representative features be present to define membership in the class. With the latter classification system, two individuals might be diagnosed as schizophrenic who have no overlap with each other in symptomatology so long as each had the required number of schizophrenia-type symptoms. Thus, with this approach, stability would be sought in the assumption of a common underlying process or syndrome rather than in the specific symptoms themselves.

A third view, offered by Dr. Marcus Sheffer was that more work is needed to sort out different schizophrenia-like syndromes. These are exemplified by oneirophrenia, a state of confusion and clouded consciousness described by Meduna (3); Gjessing's syndrome, the periodic psychosis resulting from problems in nitrogen metabolism; the Scandinavian concept of schizophreniform psychoses, and so on. Inherent to this approach is the underlying assumption that in the field of schizophrenia we are dealing with a number of underlying disease entities which should be considered separately, and, once so considered, this would allow some resolution to the current problem of symptom variability. In response to Sheffer, Vaillant cautioned against the development of terminology and definitions which are not uniformly defined and used by the world community.

A fourth and relatively more recent view, elaborated by Zubin in his concluding comments as chairman, is that the stable and unchanging aspect of schizophrenia is the underlying vulnerability of the individual to endogenous and exogenous life stresses.

Outcome of schizophrenia vs. outcome of man: an observation. Our anthropologic and archeologic data on the nature and evolution of man indicate his survival and ascent to superiority on earth has been closely linked to a finite number of distinctive features. First, his pattern of mating is intimate not only in biological sexual aspects but also in social caretaking. Second, there is an acceptance of community which has led to increasingly specialized work, to social affiliations, and to protective support. Third is the ability to form new functional concepts, especially those which free him increasingly from the drudgeries of biological survival in favor of more time to understand and enjoy his environment and himself as a person.

One cannot escape the observation that these features, so basic to the civil evolution of man, are also the ones, far more than the psychotic symptoms, which predict how well a given patient will do, before, during, and after his schizophrenic illness. One cannot escape the fact that these same basic features predict outcome in other life stresses, such as tuberculosis, response to hemodialysis, loss of physical ability to perform a given vocation, loss of employment through economic crisis, and so on. One can only conclude that schizophrenia is not an all-encompassing illness which sets the patient apart from his fellow man. Instead, the schizophrenic patient's destiny is determined much the same as the destinies of all people are determined. Much of the work on the course and outcome of schizophrenia tells us more about the course and outcome of man than it tells us about schizophrenia.

III. WHAT IS TREATED WHEN TREATING SCHIZOPHRENIA

A third theme of the discussion, sparked by the paper by Wing, concerned the question of what is being treated by the treatment agents for schizophrenia. Recognizing that over-emotionality in family relatives can be detrimental to the schizophrenic patient, a questioner in the audience asked Dr. Wing if it would not be wise to evaluate the family as a basis for prescribing drugs to the schizophrenic patient. Dr. Wing agreed but extended the point. Some relatives are over-emotional but more than half, in two recent studies, provided a neutral environment which seemed to be therapeutic. On the other hand, some therapists are over-emotional, and they then also have detrimental results. One of the objects of social treatment, he asserted, is to protect against intruding stimuli. Phenothiazines seem more effective when the patient is living in an over-stimulating social environment. Altering this environment may allow more patients to manage without maintenance medication. Some patients have been able to educate those they are living with in order to keep themselves stimulus-protected.

From Dr. Wing's view, the withdrawing of a patient from stimulus input, and the indication to his relatives that he must withdraw, does not necessarily indicate a worsening of his condition. Instead, it may be viewed as effective self-treatment. Patients, he indicated, have much to teach doctors and nurses, as well as their relatives, about how to modify the social environment. Because we do not know the long-term side effects of drugs, Dr. Wing suggested that other alternatives for protection against intruding stimuli, if effective, may be preferable. However, because schizophrenics are also vulnerable to under-stimulation and its consequent negative impairments, it is necessary to try to maintain a balance.

The comments by Wing, which advocated treatment without drugs when possible, led directly to a discussion of whether phenothiazines retard normal development. As one issue, questions were raised, but not answered, about how the fetus is affected when phenothiazines are administered to a pregnant woman. As another issue, Dr. D. P. vanKammen (National Institute of Mental Health) indicated that approximately one-third of their research patients taken off drugs tended to improve and lose their more severe psychotic symptoms within two to four weeks. Interestingly, these appeared to be good premorbid schizophrenics, with low platelet MAO and low spinal fluid 5HIAA (serotonin turnover). When some of these patients relapsed later, it seemed very hard to treat them with neuroleptics. This description was reminiscent of the report by the research group of Goldstein (4) that good premorbid nonparanoid schizophrenics are least responsive and sometimes impaired by phenothiazine medication.

Another important concern of Dr. vanKammen's was the long-term prognosis of chronic schizophrenics. In his program, chronic patients have emerged psychosis-free with drug treatment but appeared arrested at their premorbid level of social functioning. They frequently displayed immature behavior like thirteen- or fourteen-year-old children. What is the long-term outcome of these patients who are in early adulthood but who missed out on the developmental stages of adolescence and peer group experiences? Will they respond to psychotherapy and social-skill training, or do they stay at this impaired nonpsychotic stage for the rest of their lives? This may explain why some may not want to take anti-psychotic agents and prefer the horror of their familiar psychotic experience.

Dr. Strauss took the position that we simply do not know whether phenothiazine drugs cause a retardation in social development. Zubin, as he elaborated in his concluding comments, was concerned about the possibility of statistical artifacts when evaluating change. Zubin did concede, however, that the good premorbid patients tend to get better anyway. Because of this, a benign neglect (in line with Wing's suggestion of protection against intrusive stimulation) should perhaps be their preferred treatment. The great emphasis of research, Zubin felt, should be on factors governing change in the poor premorbid schizophrenics.

Dr. H. B. M. Murphy then tied together the previous lines of discussion concerning stimulus intrusion and social development. He noted that a shelter against stimulation in lives of schizophrenic patients may produce a drop in symptoms but that social reintegration does not occur. Lack of social reintegration of patients in quiet foster homes was given as an example (5). Consequently, Dr. Murphy asked Dr. Wing if there is some way to assess how much stimulation would be good for a patient? While one patient may profit from stimulus shelter, another might profit from a stimulus push which would result in better social integration. Dr. Wing, noting that he was unaware of any such assessment procedure, indicated that one must monitor each patient and his individual history in order to make such a judgment. The question raised by Dr. Murphy, however, is suggestive of stimulus deprivation research (6) with long-term hospitalized schizophrenics. After two hours in a stimulus-deprivation chamber, poor premorbid schizophrenics improve in performance and verbalize a preference for the deprivation, while good premorbid schizophrenics did the opposite.

REFERENCES

1. Strauss JS, Carpenter WT Jr: Prediction of outcome in schizophrenia. *Archives of General Psychiatry*, 27:739–746, 1972.

2. Sneath PHA, Sokal RR: *Numerical Taxonomy; The Principles & Practice of Numerical Classification.* San Francisco, W. H. Freedman, 1973.

3. Meduna LJ: *Oneirophrenia*. Urbana, University of Illinois Press, 1950.

4. Goldstein MJ: Premorbid adjustment, paranoid status, and patterns of response to phenothiazine in acute schizophrenia. *Schizophrenia Bulletin* No. 3:24–37, 1970.

5. Murphy HBM, Engelsmann F, Tcheng-Laroche: The influence of foster-home cure on psychiatric patients. *Archives of General Psychiatry*, 33:179–183, 1976.

6. Mehl M, Cromwell RL: The effect of brief sensory deprivation and sensory stimulation on the cognitive functions of chronic schizophrenia. *Journal of Nervous and Mental Disease*, 148:586–596, 1969.

C. EDITORIAL COMMENT: THE PROBLEM OF ONSET
Lyman C. Wynne, M.D., Ph.D.

Our intent when planning the Second Rochester International Conference of Schizophrenia was to assess the status of studies of the onset of schizophrenic disorders, as well as course and outcome. However, the reader will note that except for comments by Wing and Zubin, introducing this Section, little actually is said about the type of onset and the conditions surrounding onset. Dr. Zubin referred to his 1961 survey of the world literature in which direct clinical evaluation of onset as "sudden" versus "gradual" had been noted in 177 studies, and 563 other studies had general data about premorbid conditions which inferentially could be used to assess "sudden" versus "gradual" onset. He went on to assert that a candidate for canonization as a law of psychopathology is the generalization that "sudden onset leads to good outcome while gradual onset leads to poor outcome" (1).

Unfortunately, very little systematic research has focused on onset as a topic in its own right. On the one hand, many case reports of small samples of patients describe in rich detail the subjective and experiential side of the attentional, perceptual, cognitive, and interpersonal disturbances that occur during "acute" schizophrenic episodes. In a fine review of this literature, Barbara Freedman (2) concludes that "the multiform possible alterations in perception and cognition do lead rather reliably to the progressive loss of a sense of self and to the depersonalizing feeling of loss of control over one's thoughts, feelings, and behaviors that characterize the onset of an acute schizophrenic psychosis." However, she goes on to acknowledge the difficulties of generalizing from these accounts to onset for the "average," less articulate schizophrenic.

On the other hand, when statistically significant samples are assembled, only the variable of rate of onset usually has been studied, and that assessment typically has come from routine case records; how the primary clinical data have been collected, by whom, and how reliably, rarely has been explained.

Onset is a variable that has been incorporated into a number of instruments developed for other purposes. For example, prognostic measures, such as the Elgin Prognostic Scale (3), include subscales on rate of onset and precipitating events. Usually the data from these subscales are not separately analyzed. Factor analyses of the items have suggested that other features, such as schizoid withdrawal and reality distortion, are more prognostically significant than type of onset (4,5). The prognostic scales by Vaillant (6) and by Astrup and Noreik (7) have defined as "acute" those disorders which reach "full-blown psychosis" in six months or less. Onset variables were included as part of a multi-dimensional approach to prognosis and outcome. Useful as these studies have been for this intended purpose, they have not clarified how diverse kinds of onset fit into the concept of schizophrenia.

Another body of research has been concerned with good versus poor premorbid adjustment using measures that again do not directly assess the rate or conditions of onset. Recently, an excellent, comprehensive review and critique of premorbid adjustment in schizophrenia has been prepared by Strauss, Kokes, Klorman, and Sacksteder (8). As Zubin et al (1) noted, premorbid measures commonly have been assumed to be indirect indices of type of onset. Again, these approaches have left the issue of onset itself poorly studied and conceptualized. However, because of the strategic relevance of increased knowledge of onset for improved early treatment, this area deserves significantly more attention.

Defining onset of schizophrenia is far more difficult than might be assumed from the seemingly clear terms "sudden" or "insidious" and leads directly into fundamental problems lying at the heart of the concept of schizophrenia. In the last 15 years, several studies have attempted to assess precipitating factors of sudden or acute onset (9–13). However, in these studies the cases with gradual onset already have been excluded, so that a comprehensive picture of onset cannot be evaluated. Indeed, if one takes the view which has been proposed for the new DSM-III of the American Psychiatric Association, then acute onset cases no longer would be classified as schizophrenic (see Chapter 58). The working assumption in DSM-III is that psychoses of sudden onset in which there are no obvious brain lesions or toxic factors cannot be diagnosed reliably; the course over the first six months may clarify whether a term such as "brief reactive psychosis" will be appropriate or whether this is a beginning of an affective disorder, a schizoaffective psychosis, or a typical schizophrenic psychosis. I believe that most clinicians would agree that cases do occur in which the onset is sudden, with no noteworthy evidence of premorbid difficulties and with subsequent symptoms and course that nevertheless fit other criteria for "typical" schizophrenia. However, soon after a psychotic onset, reliability of diagnosis is especially low and a conservative position would be to suspend diagnostic judgment.

If one takes the view that a diagnostic criterion for schizophrenia is gradual or "insidious" onset, then studies of onset obviously are still more complicated. Eugen Bleuler clearly recognized these difficulties in 1911:

> The onset of schizophrenia is usually an insidious one, though the relatives of the patients generally insist that it first started acutely. . . . However, whenever we have a thorough case history, it is an exception if we are not able to detect the previous, earlier signs of disease whether it be nervous symptoms, character changes, or even direct overt schizophrenic manifestations. It is certainly difficult to evaluate personality changes when they do not point directly to the disease, or when the later manifest illness did not evolve from this character . . . . Yet, it is impossible to say whether the personality changes had already belonged to the disease picture itself or not . . .
>
> Frequently, the differentiation of schizophrenic characteristics from what might be called "original" peculiarities makes for unsurmountable difficulties. Yet there are early character anomalies which can be demonstrated by careful case histories in more than half the individuals who later become schizophrenic: the tendency to seclusion, withdrawal, together with moderate or severe degrees of irritability. . . . It is certain that many a schizophrenia can be traced back into the early years of the patient's life, and many manifest illnesses are

simply intensifications of an already existing character. It seems probable to me that these autistic character anomalies constitute the first symptoms of the disease. . . . Often, however, not even the most searching examination by an expert succeeds in demonstrating the presence of any specific symptoms in those early years. As a rule, the relatives do not see or do not want to see the first and early signs of mental illness; and they often prevent us from making a correct diagnosis during a consultation.

Thus when we speak of the initial symptoms of schizophrenia, we must limit ourselves to the first symptoms which come to notice. All too often we do not know the first real manifestations. (14, pp 251–252)

Thus, for Eugen Bleuler and all who have followed, the question of onset and the nature of schizophrenia as a concept are intimately interwoven. The key issue is whether schizophrenic disorders are defined by characteristic florid symptomatology, with "onset" marked quite explicitly by the appearance of these symptoms, or whether schizophrenia is defined in terms of underlying pathologic process, the onset of which has few manifest indicators.

When the nature or timing of the onset is obscured by the kind of difficulties described by Eugen Bleuler, the study of vulnerability, of enduring, predisposing traits, will be given more emphasis. As is evident in this volume, the predominant thrust of schizophrenia research has involved an orientation to vulnerability and premorbid adjustment (8) with comparatively few studies of acute onset and precipitating factors.

The study of precipitating factors can take place only when one is working with a concept that implies the relatively sudden onset of florid, psychotic symptoms. A useful distinction has been made by Brown et al (11) between the triggering and formative effects of life events in relation to onset. Comparing discernible events preceding depressive versus schizophrenic disorders, Brown concludes that life events have a formative effect in depressive disorders but a triggering effect in schizophrenic disorders. That is, he concludes that the schizophrenic disorders would have occurred before long for other reasons in the absence of the precipitating event. However, schizophrenics were accepted in his study only if onset could be identified as occurring within the 13 weeks before hospital admission. This meant that only 40% of all admitted schizophrenic patients were included. Additionally, events were excluded if there was any suggestion that they were produced by the disorder itself. Also, these investigators went through an extensive list of events that on commonsense grounds are likely to be emotionally important for many people. However, as they note, this meant that events with personal and idiosyncratic meanings inevitably would be excluded. A study by Beck and Worthen (10) that compared precipitating stressors for schizophrenic and depressive illness with a different method found that they could identify successfully a clear precipitant, of any degree of hazard, for only half of the schizophrenics, but they also concluded that this may have occurred because of "the private nature of the symbolic process of many schizophrenics."

REFERENCES

1. Zubin J, Sutton S, Salzinger K, et al: A biometric approach to prognosis in schizophrenia, in Hoch PH and Zubin J: *Comparative Epidemiology of the Mental Disorders.* New York, Grune & Stratton, 1961, pp 143–203.

2. Freedman BJ: The subjective experience of perceptual and cognitive disturbances in schizophrenia. *Arch Gen Psychiat* 30:333–340, 1974.

3. Wittman P: Scale for measuring prognosis in schizophrenic patients. *Elgin State Hospital Papers* 4:20–33, 1941.

4. Lorr M, Wittman P, Schanberger W: An analysis of the Elgin Prognostic Scale, *J Clin Psychol* 7:260–263, 1951.

5. Longabaugh R, Eldred SH: Pre-morbid adjustments, schizoid personality and onset of illness as predictors of post-hospitalization function. *J Psychiat Res* 10:19–29, 1973.

6. Vaillant GE: The prediction of recovery in schizophrenia. *J Nerv Ment Dis* 135:534–543, 1962.

7. Astrup C, Noreik K: *Functional Psychoses, Diagnostic and Prognostic Models.* Springfield, Ill., Charles C Thomas, Publisher, 1966.

8. Strauss JS, Kokes RF, Klorman R, et al: Premorbid adjustment in schizophrenia: concepts, measures, and implications. Part I. The concept of premorbid adjustment. *Schiz Bull* 3:182–185, 1977.

9. Birley JLT, Brown GW: Crises and life changes preceding the onset or relapse of acute schizophrenia: Clinical aspects. *Brit J Psychiat* 116:327–333, 1970.

10. Beck JC, Worthen K: Precipitating stress, crisis theory, and hospitalization in schizophrenia and depression. *Arch Gen Psychiat* 26:123–129, 1972.

11. Brown GW, Harris TO, Peto J: Life events and psychiatric disorders. Part 2: nature of causal link. *Psychol Med* 3:159–176, 1973.

12. Donlon PT, Blacker KH: Stages of schizophrenic decompensation and reintegration. *J Nerv Ment Dis* 157:200–209, 1973.

13. Jacobs S, Meyers J: Recent life events and acute schizophrenic psychosis: A controlled study. *J Nerv Ment Dis* 62:75–87, 1976.

14. Bleuler E: *Dementia Praecox or the Group Schizophrenias.* New York, International Universities Press, 1950.

Section XIII

DIAGNOSTIC AND CONCEPTUAL ISSUES

INTRODUCTION
Roy R. Grinker, Sr., M.D.

In my opinion, diagnosis is one of the most important issues confronting modern psychiatry—despite the publicity given to the speeches and writings of a fringe group of mythologists within and without our discipline. Diagnoses and classifications are the first scientific steps to answer the question, "What is schizophrenia?" Without better answers to this question, we cannot possibly approach or resolve the "how" and "why" questions that bear on causes, course, and adaptations.

However, the results of earlier attempts at delineation of types of mental illness and the present long list of various classifications are no longer adequate. This means that we must keep trying. Let me indicate a few continuing issues about the diagnosis of schizophrenia. First, many schizophrenics seem to have elevated, excited moods resembling mania. Others are depressed and suicidal, although this mood should be discriminated from anhedonia. We hedge on the label for these patients, diagnosing them neither clearly schizophrenic nor clearly manic-depressive but schizoaffective. There is no evidence from the clinical data that schizophrenic and manic-depressive thought disorder is identical. About 20% of manic-depressives do have some form of thought disorder, but, in my opinion, this is quite different from that of the schizophrenic.

The thought disorders characteristic of schizophrenias are still not well defined. Many psychologists have confused adolescent turmoil with schizophrenia on the Rorschach test. We still need to determine the presence or absence and the quality and quantity of thought disorders in schizophrenics in remission from an acute psychotic breakdown.

A second difficulty arises with the attempt to designate acute schizophrenia with one or several psychotic breakdowns as a disease different from the slowly progressive

653

chronic schizophrenia. This distinction has led to the diagnosis of a psychiatric mishmash called the schizophrenic spectrum in the families of index schizophrenics. The "spectrum" may not be found in the families of acute schizophrenics.

Unfortunately, Holzman and I have been misquoted recently as describing spectrum types as examples of the protean characteristics of schizophrenia. A schizophrenic spectrum is an important issue in current research. However, we do not wish to use the spectrum concept for neurotic or psychopathologic traits in families or siblings of index schizophrenics; such names are loosely used and may apply to everyone. Diagnosis and classification would need to take many steps backward if spectrum concepts have any validity as genetic indicators of schizophrenia. The supposed absence of spectrum diagnoses in relatives of acute schizophrenic index cases is not an indication that acute schizophrenics are genetically unrelated to the other types. Clinicians know that one or several acute breakdowns may precede the development of a chronic and often irreversible course. An attack of acute bronchitis may be the first sign of carcinoma of the lung. The fate of acute schizophrenics can only be determined by a long-term follow-up past age 40.

A third issue is the changing manifestations of psychiatric disorders: instead of florid conversion hysteria, mania, catatonia, and hebephrenia, we now see more restricted and constricted characters.

Fourth, diagnosis is also affected by the variability in the life histories of schizophrenics from time to time. The subtypes may shift from one to another; the acute may eventually become chronic, and the chronic may, even after decades, show at least some degree of reversibility. In this connection we should avoid identifying schizophrenia with psychosis; psychoses may be toxic, infectious, traumatic, drug, senile, and so forth. In my view, most schizophrenics never have a psychotic break. Moreover, recovery from a psychotic break is no indication that the process was not schizophrenia.

Finally, there is a voluminous literature on schizophrenia that no one can completely encompass except by a regiment of abstractors. What seems clear is that schizophrenia is a system diagnosable by the presence of biopsychosocial components inefficiently controlled or regulated by an organizational principle. Specific predisposition, derived from biogenetic factors, is sensitive to a wide variety of precipitating stimuli. Prior to the overt onset, prediction is almost impossible from the premorbid state. Even after a psychotic break or the recognition of thought disorder in a quiescent schizophrenic, the prediction of future attacks is very difficult. There are no single causes, and linear relationships between causes and effects have not been established.

What we can state is that when the schizophrenic organization weakens or breaks, we may observe two classes of symptoms as originally formulated by Hughlings Jackson. One is the loss of functional control determined by the absence of "high level" organization of thinking and feeling. The other is the presence of old functions, always alive but repressed or controlled until revived by the absence or weakness of higher level regulation.

A related diagnostic problem concerns the adaptive or so-called restitutive functions attempting to compensate for the lost functions or to cover up the revived functions of the schizophrenic process. Adaptation is often successful and no further difficulties ensue. However, a short-term outcome is not definitive.

How do we make a prediction? Is early life anhedonia a predictor of chronicity? Which acute cases become chronic? Do paranoid trends presage a later schizophrenia?

Do specific family patterns encouraging overprotection and prolongation of symbiotic relationships have a role in prediction? The following observations have developed from our own research. In 45% of our sample a grandparent has died 2 years before or after the subject's birth, apparently altering the mother's parenting role. On special T.A.T. cards the mother is more dependent on the child than the reverse, and one-third of our subjects were brought up by single parents.

Where can we turn for help? Certainly, use of computer techniques can deal with the necessary large quantities of research data and the large numbers of subjects. But here again the computer is dependent on input from the clinician whose training experience, expertise, and biases are important variables.

The use of old hospital records such as the Iowa 500 records of 1933–44 is inefficient because of the variability of those who have prepared them and the changing character of mental disorders. Follow-back is a precarious technique dependent on defensive memories and inadequate data. Study of families with high-risk children is possible only when we have defined what we call "high risk."

The procedure most likely to be of value is the follow-up. This is fraught with difficulties that can, however, be overcome. There is a high attrition rate of patients in the schizophrenic samples: moving to unknown areas, suicide, death from other causes, reluctance to discuss a painful area, and so forth. It requires the use of an outpatient clinic, beds for rehospitalization, and re-interviews and ratings by the same psychiatrists who first performed these functions. One person should be employed to do all telephone interviews and help subjects to fill out questionnaires.

In my view, outcome data with comparison groups composed of nonschizophrenic hospitalized patients and healthy subjects over a period of 15 to 20 years, or until the subjects reach age 40, should give us the best results, providing the intervening life situations and conditions are sufficiently taken into consideration. It is only then that we will be able to answer the "what" question of schizophrenia and its subtypes.

Chapter 57
Validity of Diagnostic Concepts Across Cultures: A Preliminary Report from the International Pilot Study of Schizophrenia

Norman Sartorius, M.D.
Assen Jablensky, M.D.
Erik Strömgren, M.D.
Robert Shapiro, M.D.

More than 70 years ago, Kraepelin made a strong case for "comparative psychiatry" which he defined as "the observation of mental disorders in different groups of people." He also argued that comparative studies should advance our knowledge in two basic ways: by throwing "light on the causes of mental disorders" and by providing "means of determining the influence which the patient's personality exerts on the particular form his illness assumes." Kraepelin's expectations were met only in a limited way by subsequent psychiatric research, for reasons that he himself pointed out in 1904: "Reliable comparison is, of course, only possible if we are able to draw clear distinctions between identifiable illnesses, as well as between clinical states; moreover, our clinical concepts vary so widely that for the foreseeable future such comparison is possible only if the observations are made by one and the same observer" (1).

The research strategy that Kraepelin saw as the only possible one was applied in many studies on the distribution, clinical picture, course, and outcome of schizophrenia. It became increasingly evident, however, that it was difficult to compare the results or to draw clear conclusions from individual studies about the nature of schizophrenia even when they were done by one observer because of the use of different diagnostic criteria, the imprecision and variation in the definition of outcome criteria, the lack of standardized and reliable methods of psychiatric assessment, and variations in the methods of follow-up. The difficulties became incomparably larger when different investigators were involved.

Against this background, the International Pilot Study of Schizophrenia (IPSS) set out to lay methodologic groundwork for future epidemiologic and other research in schizophrenia and the other functional psychoses, by attempting to answer certain basic methodologic questions and to provide information about the nature of schizophrenia. The study began in 1966 as a large-scale, cross-cultural collaborative project carried out simultaneously in nine countries differing considerably in their sociocultural characteristics: China, Colombia, Czechoslovakia, Denmark, India, Nigeria, the Union of Soviet Socialist Republics, the United Kingdom, and the United States of America (2). The study was sponsored by WHO and funded jointly by the World Health Organization (WHO), the National Institute of Mental Health (NIMH), and the nine field research centers.

With regard to methodology, the IPSS aimed:

1. to investigate the feasibility of large-scale international studies requiring the collaboration of psychiatrists and other mental health workers from different cultural and theoretical backgrounds
2. to develop standardized instruments and procedures for psychiatric assessment that could be applied reliably in a variety of cultural settings
3. to train teams of research workers to use such instruments and procedures so that comparable observations could be made in developed and developing countries.

With regard to information on the nature of schizophrenia, the study set out to explore in what sense it could be said that schizophrenic disorders exist in different parts of the world, that is, to identify similarities and dissimilarities between groups of patients who are diagnosed as suffering from schizophrenia in different cultures as well as between groups of patients with diagnosis of schizophrenia and with the diagnosis of other functional psychoses; to determine the extent to which dissimilarities between schizophrenic patients in different settings are the result of variations in diagnostic practice and to what extent a reflection of genuine culture-related differences in the manifestations of the disorder; and to investigate whether the course and outcome of schizophrenia differ from country to country.

Before discussing results obtained so far and, in particular, those pertaining to the reliability and validity of the diagnosis of schizophrenia, the methodology of the study will be described briefly.

METHODS OF THE INTERNATIONAL PILOT STUDY OF SCHIZOPHRENIA

The IPSS was carried out in three phases: a preliminary phase, an initial evaluation phase, and a follow-up phase. During the preliminary phase, administrative, operational, and organizational procedures were established and tested. In the initial evaluation phase, a total of 1202 patients were selected for study in the nine field research centers, and given a detailed standardized clinical examination. Of these 1202 patients,

811 had received a clinical diagnosis of schizophrenia, 164 a diagnosis of affective psychosis, and 277 of other psychoses and of nonpsychotic conditions. In the follow-up phase, the original patients were traced and reexamined twice, 2 years and 5 years after the initial evaluation. For the 2-year follow-up, 97.1% of all patients were traced, and in all centers except one an average of 82.1% were seen and reexamined. In the 5-year follow-up study, an average of 75.0% of the original patients were re-investigated (in four of the centers the percentage was above 90).

By design, the IPSS was not an epidemiologic study, and no attempt was made to compose samples representative of patient populations in the centers. Instead, a number of operationally defined selection criteria were used to insure inclusion in the project of patients within the age range 15–44, who had nonorganic, psychotic illnesses of a relatively recent onset and who would be likely to be available for follow-up. Patients with signs of an organic cerebral condition, of severe mental retardation, or of a physical illness that could explain the psychosis were excluded.

Eight instruments were used to assess patients in the initial evaluation phase of the study, among which the three basic instruments were the Present State Examination (PSE), a Psychiatric History Schedule, and a Social Description Schedule.

The PSE is a guide to structuring the clinical psychiatric interview to obtain systematic coverage of all areas of psychopathology usually explored in the course of a comprehensive clinical examination. The instrument includes 360 items arranged in sections that are used for probing or cross-examining. Ratings of psychopathology—reported and observed—are made on ordinal scales of intensity or duration of symptoms, according to specified rules, and in agreement with guidelines and standard definitions given in an accompanying glossary. The PSE procedure can be adjusted flexibly to the clinician's individual style. One of the main characteristics of the method is that ratings of the patient's symptoms depend not only on the patient's responses to questions but also on the examining clinician's overall judgment about the presence or absence of psychopathologic phenomena.

For the purposes of the study, the PSE was translated into seven languages and inter-language equivalence was achieved through the reiterative back-translation method and "target-checks" of meaning.

The psychiatrists from the collaborating centers received intensive training in the use of the instrument prior to the data collection phase, and the reliability of their assessments was controlled through series of simultaneous interviews repeated at regular intervals in the course of the study. Such exercises took place both between investigators within individual centers and between investigators from different centers. On the level of individual PSE items, the intraclass correlation coefficient between raters within centers was, on the average, 0.77. When items were combined into "units of analysis" corresponding to symptoms, or into larger groupings reflecting broad areas of psychopathology, such as delusions, hallucinations, and so forth, reliability was even higher, of the order of 0.81–0.84. Intercenter reliability was somewhat lower—median intraclass correlation coefficient values being 0.45 for units of analysis and 0.57 for groups of units, but sufficiently high to allow intercenter comparisons of psychopathology.

The two other principal instruments—the Psychiatric History and the Social Description schedules—covered systematically the past history of the patient and provided data on his social environment, socioeconomic status, occupational and educational record. The investigators using these schedules received considerable prior training. In view of the difficulties in assessing the reliability of such instruments across cultures, the rigorous procedure used in the case of the PSE was replaced by simpler methods with particular emphasis on joint training and development of agreed definitions.

During the 2-year and 5-year reevaluations, the patients were reexamined with the PSE and with follow-up history and social description instruments. In addition to pre-coded ratings, narrative histories of the patients' progress during the follow-up phase were supplied by the centers. These narrative histories were rated on a number of course and outcome variables (e.g., length of the episode of inclusion, proportion of the follow-up period during which the patient was in psychotic episodes, pattern of course, clinical type of subsequent episodes, level of social functioning, overall outcome), and this information was used to supplement ratings made in the schedules, and to evaluate course and outcome.

DIAGNOSTIC AND CLASSIFICATORY PROCEDURES

Since one of the important aims of the study was to investigate how the diagnostic concept of schizophrenia was applied in different settings, and whether a diagnosis of a schizophrenic disorder made at one point in time predicted characteristics of subsequent course and outcome of the patients in different cultures, several different methods were developed and applied to the diagnostic classification of patients: clinical diagnosis, computer-simulated reference diagnosis, a mathematical clustering technique, and a combination of these methods.

Clinical diagnosis of schizophrenic and other disorders included in the study was recorded in terms of ICD categories. The intracenter reliability of clinical diagnosis, measured as agreement rates obtained in series of paired simultaneous interviews, proved to be very high: the agreement on a diagnosis of schizophrenia was on the average 91.3%.

To standardize the diagnostic procedure and provide a reference classification of the study patients, the CATEGO computer program (3), which incorporated diagnostic principles generally accepted in European psychiatry, was developed. The program involves a stepwise decision process in which symptoms and syndromes receive a priori fixed diagnostic weights. The program relies considerably, but not exclusively, on some key symptoms which include, for example, Schneider's "first-rank" symptoms of schizophrenia. A patient, however, could be allocated to the diagnostic class corresponding to schizophrenia even in the absence of such key symptoms, if a sufficient number of other, less clear-cut manifestations of schizophrenia were present. The computer classification of patients turned out to be in agreement with the clinical diagnosis in a very high proportion (87%) of the patients. In patients who had positive ratings on "first-rank" symptoms, the agreement between a clinical and a computer diagnosis of schizophrenia reached 95%.

McKeon's hierarchical clustering method (4) provided a third classification of the patients by grouping all 1202 patients into 10 statistical clusters on the basis of maximum number of common characteristics.

Finally, the patients on whom the clinical and the computer diagnosis of schizophrenia agreed, and who were classified into the three statistical clusters that turned out to contain more schizophrenic patients than could be expected on a random basis, were designated as a "concordant" group of schizophrenics. These patients were analyzed further as distinct from those who had received a diagnosis of schizophrenia but were not classified as schizophrenic by the computer program, nor included in the statistical clusters containing an excess number of schizophrenics. The "concordant" group was of particular interest since it included patients for whom the diagnosis of schizophrenia was least influenced by the individual predilections of the diagnosticians, and, therefore, could be expected to provide clues to possible transcultural features of the disorder. Patients belonging to the "concordant" group were identified in all the nine centers of the study.

ASSESSMENTS OF THE CONTENT VALIDITY OF THE DIAGNOSIS OF SCHIZOPHRENIA

If content validity is defined as the degree to which the symptoms of patients classified into a diagnostic category are similar, and, at the same time, are different from the symptoms of patients allocated to other diagnostic groups, the results of IPSS provide strong support for the content validity of the concept of schizophrenia in each of the different cultural settings in which the study took place. When interpreting this finding, one must bear in mind that the study was not based on a population sample, and that the possibility exists for some conditions that could have been diagnosed as "probably schizophrenic" to have escaped inclusion in the study because of the application of inclusion/exclusion criteria.

With this proviso, it is possible to state that in all cultures involved, there were patients diagnosed as schizophrenic who had very similar psychopathologic characteristics. Evidence for this were the comparisons by means of analysis of variance, of the symptom profiles obtained within the different centers by condensing the scores of 129 symptoms (units of analysis) into scores on 27 groups of units of analysis (Table 57-1). In all centers, the patients with a clinical diagnosis of schizophrenia had high scores on lack of insight, predelusional signs (such as delusional mood, ideas of reference, and perplexity), flatness of affect, auditory hallucinations (except in Washington), and experiences of control. Scores were also high on delusions, derealization, and disturbances of mood, but they were low on psychomotor disorder, pseudohallucinations, and affective changes other than incongruous affect. Of the 36 possible comparisons of symptom profiles of schizophrenics among centers, high degrees of similarity ($P <$ 0.001) were obtained in 32.

That this similarity of the symptom profiles of schizophrenic patients was not due to an excessive preponderance of a few diagnostically nonspecific, general manifestations of psychotic disorder (such as lack of insight or poor rapport), was demonstrated by a series of discriminant function analyses the aim of which was to differentiate in terms of overall symptomatology and to give a statistical measure of the distance between the groups of schizophrenic patients and the patients in other diagnostic groups of the functional psychoses. When ratings on all the 129 symptoms were considered in such analyses, the schizophrenic patients were separated very clearly from all other diagnostic groups. Figure 57-1 shows the degree of separation that could be achieved with pooled data from all the centers between groups of 507 schizophrenic and 71 psychotic depressive patients on initial and on follow-up evaluation in terms of 129 symptoms. The distributions are plotted against the values of the discriminant function representing a weighted linear compound of the ratings on all the 129 symptoms, and the mean

Table 57-1. Composition of Groups of Units of Analysis[a]

Groups	Units of Analysis (Symptoms)	Groups	Units of Analysis (Symptoms)
1. Quantitative psychomotor disorder	1. Overactivity 2. Retardation 3. Stupor 14. Repetitive movements		51. Fantastic 52. Sexual 53. Impending doom
		9. Neurasthenic complaints	54. Obsessive thoughts 55. Worries 56. Lack of concentration 57. Memory difficulties 58. Hypochondriacal 59. Undecided 119. Decreased interest
2. Qualitative psychomotor disorder	4. Negativism 5. Compliance 7. Stereotypies 9. Grimacing 10. Posturing 11. Mannerisms 12. Hallucinatory behaviour 13. Waxy flexibility		
		10. Lack of insight	60. Lack of insight
3. Quantitative disorder of form of thinking (and speech)	15. Flight of ideas 16. Pressure of speech 18. Mutism 19. Restricted speech 124. Distractibility	11. Distortion of self-perception	61. Changed appearance 63. Looking at self 64. Break of self-identity
4. Qualitative disorder of form of thinking (and speech)	20. Neologisms 21. Klang association 22. Speech dissociation 23. Irrelevance 25. Blocking 26. Stereotypy of speech 27. Echolalia	12. Derealization	62. Derealization 65. Distortion of time perception
		13. Auditory hallucinations	66. Presence of verbal hallucinations 67. Voices speak to patient 69. Nonverbal auditory hallucinations 70. Presence of auditory hallucinations
5. Affect-laden thoughts	28. Gloomy thoughts 29. Elated thoughts 30. Hopelessness 31. Suicidal thoughts	14. "Characteristic" hallucinations	68. Voices speak full sentences 72. Voices discussing patient 73. Hallucinations from body 74. Voices comment on patient's thoughts 75. Voices speak thoughts
6. Predelusional signs	33. Delusional mood 34. Ideas of reference 35. Questioning reasons for being 37. Perplexity		
7. Experiences of control	38. Thought alienation 39. Thoughts spoken aloud 40. Delusions of control	15. Other hallucinations	76. Visual 77. Tactile 78. Olfactory 79. Sexual 80. Somatic 81. Gustatory
8. Delusions	41. Persecution 42. Guilt 43. Self-depreciation 44. Nihilistic 45. Grandeur 46. Reference 47. Presence of delusional system 48. Hypochondriacal 49. Special mission 50. Religious	16. Pseudo-hallucinations	82. Auditory 83. Visual
		17. Depressed—elated	32. Special depression 84. Depressed mood 85. Observed elated mood

662

Table 57-1. (Continued)

Groups	Units of Analysis (Symptoms)	Groups	Units of Analysis (Symptoms)
18. Anxiety, tension, irritability	86. Morose mood 88. Irritability 89. Tension 90. Situation anxiety 91. Anxiety	24. Other behavioural change	6. Talking to self 17. Disorder of pitch 96. Giggling to self 100. Demonstrative
19. Flatness	92. Flatness 93. Apathy	25. Psycho-physical	111. Early waking 112. Worse in morning 113. Worse in evening 114. Diminished appetite
20. Incongruity	95. Incongruity of affect		115. Sleep problems 116. Increased appetite 117. Increased libido
21. Other affective change	94. Ecstatic mood 97. Haughtiness 98. Ambivalence 101. Lability of affect 102. Ambitendence		118. Decreased energy 120. Decreased libido 121. Constipation
22. Indication of personality change	8. Odd appearance and behaviour 103. Change of interest 104. Change of sex behaviour 105. Autism 106. Abnormal tidiness 110. Social withdrawal	26. Cooperation difficulties, circumstances-related	125. Biological treatment 128. Environmental circumstances 129. Speech impediments
		27. Cooperation difficulties, patient-related	36. Suspiciousness 122. Suggestibility 123. Poor rapport 126. Unwilling to cooperate [a]
23. Disregard for social norms	108. Disregard for norms 109. Self-neglect		127. Inadequate description

[a] Five units of analysis ("perseveration," "frequent auditory hallucinations," "groaning," "loss of emotions," and "increased interest") were excluded because they did not fit well into any of the groups and it was considered inappropriate to create five new groups to accommodate them.

distance between the two groups is given as Mahalanobis's distance coefficient (D) indicating the level of discrimination between the two distributions (5). A higher discrimination was obtained when only patients classified as schizophrenic by the CATEGO computer program were compared with the other diagnostic groups.

Considering that a cross-cultural study is a very stringent test for the validity of a diagnostic classification, these results suggest that the diagnostic concept and classification of schizophrenia can be applied in different cultural settings and appear to be based on consistent symptom patterns which can be identified and described in a standardized and reliable way.

PRELIMINARY ASSESSMENTS OF THE PREDICTIVE VALIDITY OF THE DIAGNOSIS OF SCHIZOPHRENIA

Predictive validity of diagnosis was defined for the purposes of the analysis performed on IPSS material as the degree to which the classification of patients into a particular diag-

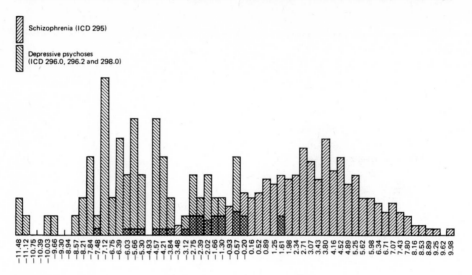

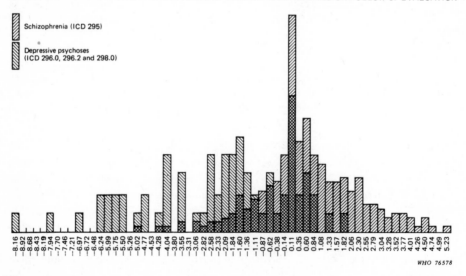

WHO 76578

Figure 57-1. Pooled data from all centers: Symptom profiles of schizophrenic and depressive psychotic patients.

nostic category predicted subsequent symptoms, course, and outcome of the patients. Thus, it was hypothesized that the diagnosis had predictive validity if patients allocated to one category had similar subsequent evolution of their disorders, and this evolution was distinguishable from that experienced by patients classified into other diagnostic categories.

Preliminary conclusions on the predictive validity of the diagnosis of schizophrenia in the IPSS can now be made with regard to the 2-year follow-up (which corresponds to what E. Bleuler termed "*Streckenprognose*" or interim prognosis of the disorder) (6).

The results indicate that the diagnostic classification of patients on initial evaluation did predict qualitatively the subsequent symptom patterns of those patients who remained ill, or had psychotic relapses, in the course of the follow-up period. For example, 72% of the schizophrenic patients who were psychotic on follow-up, were categorized into the same CATEGO classes as on initial evaluation by the computer program using follow-up mental-state data. Although there was a marked tendency for the symptom picture of the schizophrenic and other functional psychotic patients to "flatten out" with time in the sense that there were fewer florid or "productive" symptoms and more "negative" or deficit symptoms, the diagnostic groups remained symptomatically distinct at the cross-section of the 2-year follow-up evaluation. For example, as shown by Figure 57-1, the coefficient (Mahalanobis's D) based on discriminant function analysis, which measured the weighted symptomatic distance between the group of patients with clinical diagnosis of schizophrenia and the patients with clinical diagnosis of depressive psychosis, decreased from 2.83 to 1.70. Such decrease, or loss of discrimination, occurred to a much lesser degree, or not at all, between the group of depressives and the groups defined as schizophrenic by the CATEGO program, and the "concordant" group. This suggests that the criteria that defined these two groups tended to be more stable and consistent over time than the varying constellations of symptoms used by the clinicians in making a diagnosis.

Symptomatic criteria and diagnostic categories, however, turned out to be far less effective predictors of 2-year course and outcome defined by dimensions such as length of initial illness episode, proportion of the follow-up during which the patient was in psychotic episodes, pattern of course (e.g., remitting, with or without relapses, recurrent, or continuous), degree of social impairment, or a combination of several of these measures. Two aspects of the results deserve special mention.

First, patients diagnosed as schizophrenic on initial evaluation showed a high variability of course and outcome. When the range of possible outcomes was divided into five overall outcome categories, 26% of the schizophrenics fell into the best outcome group, 18% fell into the worst outcome group, and the remaining 56% were distributed over the three intermediate categories (Figure 57-2). Of all study patients with a diagnosis of schizophrenia, 27% had a single, relatively short psychotic episode followed by full recovery without relapses and social impairment. On the other hand, 26% never had a remission during the 2-year period.

Second, when course and outcome of the schizophrenic patients were analyzed by centers and by groups of centers, consistent and highly significant differences emerged between patients in the developing countries and patients in the developed countries. On virtually all course and outcome measures, the group of schizophrenic patients from Agra, Cali, and Ibadan, on the average, had better course and outcome than the group of patients from Aarhus, London, Moscow, Prague, and Washington (Figure 57-3). These differences in course and outcome were not removed when the groups were con-

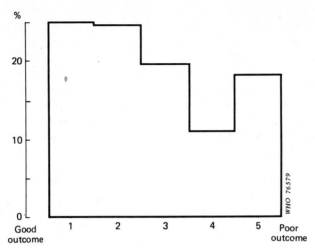

Figure 57-2. Distribution of 543 followed-up schizophrenic patients over five categories of 2-year overall outcome.

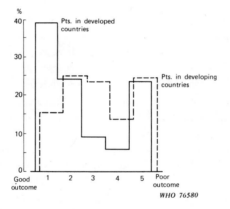

Figure 57-3. Distribution of the followed-up schizophrenic patients in developing and developed countries over 5 categories of 2-year overall outcome.
Categories of outcome: 1 = *very favorable*—includes: psychotic for less than 15% of the follow-up period, then full remission; no severe social impairment; 2 = *favorable*—includes any of the following: (a) psychotic for less than·15% of the follow-up period, then remission with some residual symptoms but no severe social impairment; (b) psychotic for 16–45% of the follow-up period, then full remission and no severe social impairment; 3 = *intermediate*—includes any of the following: (a) psychotic for less than 15% of the follow-up period, then remission with or without residual symptoms, but with social impairment; (b) psychotic for 16–45% of the follow-up period, then either remission with residual symptoms but no severe social impairment or full remission with severe social impairment; (c) psychotic for 46–75% of the follow-up period, then remission (full or with residual symptoms) but no severe social impairment; 4 = *unfavorable*—includes any of the following: (a) psychotic for 46–75% of the follow-up period, then full remission but severe social impairment; (b) psychotic for over 76% of the follow-up period, then remission (full or with residual symptoms) but no severe social impairment; 5 = *very unfavorable*—includes any of the following: (a) psychotic for 46–75% of the follow-up period, then remission with residual symptoms and severe social impairment; (b) psychotic for over 76% of the follow-up period, then remission (full or with residual symptoms) and severe social impairment.

666

trolled for such variables as length of previous illness (before inclusion into the study), presenting symptoms, and so forth. Thus, the results so far suggest the possibility of existence of culture-related differences in the course of schizophrenia.

Statistical techniques, such as the stepwise multiple regression analysis, were used to identify specific predictors of course and outcome within the diagnostic entity of schizophrenia. It was possible to show that no single variable, and no combination of "key" variables among those assessed on initial evaluation, could fully predict ratings on course and outcome measures. Using larger sets of 15 predictor variables, it was possible to explain up to one-third of the variance of some of the measures of course and outcome. Such sets of "best" predictors turned out to contain fewer than expected mental state-related variables but included many social, premorbid personality and past illness history characteristics. The degree of social isolation at the time of initial evaluation for example was highly correlated with an outcome of continuous illness without remissions (Table 57-2).

CONCLUSION

The IPSS has been the first large-scale effort to cope with the problem identified by Kraepelin in 1904 as a lack of common concepts and language among psychiatrists. This lack precluded the conduct of comparative studies of the mental disorders by researchers in different settings and of different background. The results obtained so far in the IPSS suggest that considerable progress has been achieved in the field of psychiatric research methodology since the time of Kraepelin's judgment. The findings reported here, in the fiftieth anniversary year of Kraepelin's death, demonstrate the existence of identifiable and comparable schizophrenic disorders in different cultures and parts of the world.

Furthermore, evidence has been obtained that culture-related factors may influence profoundly the course and outcome of schizophrenia, as anticipated by Kraepelin. However, the deeper nature of the entity that he delineated remains elusive and complex. Therefore, the multifactorial approach in studies concerning the nature of schizophrenia and its development appears as the most promising strategy to achieve further progress of knowledge.

ACKNOWLEDGMENT

This report is based on data and experience obtained during the participation of the authors in the International Pilot Study of Schizophrenia (IPSS), a project sponsored by the World Health Organization and funded by the World Health Organization, the United States National Institute of Mental Health, and the participating field research centers.

The collaborating investigators in this study have been Dr. N. Sartorius, principal investigator, Dr. T.-Y. Lin, former principal investigator, and Ms. E. M. Brooke, Dr. F. Engelsmann, Dr. G. Ginsburg, Mr. W. Gulbinat, Dr. A. Jablensky, Mr. M. Kimura, Dr. A. Richman, and Dr. R. Shapiro at the Headquarters of the World Health Organization in Geneva, Switzerland; Dr. E. Strömgren, chief collaborating investigator, and Dr. A. Bertelsen, Dr. M. Fischer, Dr. C. Flack and Dr. N. Juel-Nielsen at the field research center in Aarhus, Denmark; Dr. K. C. Dube, chief collaborating investi-

Table 57-2. Predictors of Several Measures of Course and Outcome in Schizophrenic Patients (All Centers)

Course and Outcome Variable and Number of Patients in the Analysis	Best Predictors	% Variance Explained by Five Best Predictors
Length of the episode of inclusion (565 patients)	Length of episode prior to initial assessment Social isolation Score on derealization Psychiatric treatment in the past History of behavior disturbance	15
Proportion of the follow-up period in which the patient was in psychotic episodes (559 patients)	Social isolation Length of episode prior to initial assessment Psychiatric treatment in the past Sex Type of onset	12
Full remission without relapses after the initial episode (154 patients)	Sudden onset No psychiatric treatment in the past No personality change Married Short duration of episode prior to initial assessment	14
Remittent course with relapses (172 patients)	Female sex Depression or elation Higher occupational level Neurotic complaints Absence of precipitating stress	7
Continuous illness, no remissions (150 patients)	Long duration episode prior to initial assessment Social isolation Divorced, separated, or widowed Absence of derealization History of behavior disturbance	14
Level of Social impairment on follow-up (585 patients)	Social isolation Long duration of episode prior to initial assessment Psychiatric treatment in the past Marital status other than currently married No physical illness or disability in the past	20

gator, and Dr. B. S. Yadav at the field research center in Agra, India; Dr. C. Leon, chief collaborating investigator, and Dr. G. Calderon and Dr. E. Zambrano at the field research center in Cali, Colombia; Dr. T. A. Lambo, chief collaborating investigator, and Dr. T. Asuni and Dr. M. O. Olatawura at the field research center in Ibadan, Nigeria; Dr. J. K. Wing, chief collaborating investigator, and Dr. J. Birley and Dr. J. P. Leff at the field research center in London, England; Dr. R. A. Nadzharov, chief collaborating investigator, and Dr. N. M. Zharikov at the field research center in Moscow, USSR; Dr. L. Hanzlicek, chief collaborating investigator, and Dr. C. Skoda at the field research center in Prague, Czechoslovakia; Dr. C. C. Chen and Dr. M. T. Tsuang, at the field research center in Taipei, China; and Dr. L. Wynne and Dr. J. Strauss, chief collaborating investigators, and Dr. J. Bartko and Dr. W. Carpenter at the field research center in Washington, DC.

A list of other staff contributing to the IPSS can be found in volume 1 of the *Report of the International Pilot Study of Schizophrenia*.

REFERENCES

1. Kraepelin E: *Vergleichende Psychiatrie*, 1904. English translation in Hirsch SH, Shepherd M (eds): *Themes and Variations in European Psychiatry*. Bristol, England, John Wright & Sons, 1974.

2. World Health Organization: *Report of the International Pilot Study of Schizophrenia*. vol 1. Geneva, WHO, 1973.

3. Wing JK, Cooper JE, Sartorius N: *The Measurement and Classification of Psychiatric Symptoms*. London, Cambridge University Press, 1973.

4. McKeon JJ: *Hierarchical Cluster Analysis*. Washington, DC, George Washington University Biometric Laboratory, 1967.

5. Overall JE, Klett CJ: *Applied Multivariate Analysis*. New York, McGraw-Hill, 1972.

6. Bleuler E: Quoted after Jaspers, K. *General Psychopathology*. Manchester, England, Manchester University Press, and Chicago, University of Chicago Press, 1963.

Chapter 58
Proposed Classification of Schizophrenia in DSM-III

Robert L. Spitzer, M.D.
Nancy Andreasen, M.D., Ph.D.
Jean Endicott, Ph.D.
Robert A. Woodruff, Jr., M.D.

The greatest obstacle to research in the schizophrenic disorders is the lack of a clear and widely agreed upon definition of the concept. The publication in 1979 of the ninth revision of the *International Classification of Diseases* (ICD-9) and the third edition of the American Psychiatric Association's *Diagnostic and Statistical Manual* (DSM-III) provides an opportunity to define these conditions with greater clarity than previously has been achieved. The Task Force on Nomenclature and Statistics of the American Psychiatric Association, which has the responsibility of developing DSM-III, is in the fortunate position of being able to review the completed definition of schizophrenia which will appear in the ICD-9 glossary.

Unlike the mandate to the Task Force that developed DSM-II in 1968 to make it equivalent to ICD-8, the mandate to the current Task Force is to develop the most useful classification possible given the current state of knowledge and only secondarily to insure some degree of correspondence with ICD-9. Although we have retained for the most part the diagnostic subtypes listed in ICD-9, we have attempted to improve their reliability and validity by: (a) describing systematically and with greater detail and specificity various aspects of these conditions, namely, as "essential" and "associated" features, onset, course, complications, predisposing factors, prevalence and sex ratio, familial pattern, and differential diagnosis; (b) adding a fifth and sixth digit to the four-digit ICD-9 codes to permit further subtyping where appropriate; and (c) providing operational criteria to assist clinicians in applying uniform standards for evaluating individual psychopathology. Previous work has shown that such operational criteria

All authors are members of the American Psychiatric Association Task Force on Nomenclature and Statistics.

greatly improve the interjudge reliability of psychiatric diagnosis as compared with the use of existing standard diagnostic glossaries (1).

Our first problem was to delimit the boundaries of the concept. The concept of schizophrenia presented in DSM-III will be restricted to illnesses in which at some time there have been characteristic delusions or hallucinations or marked formal thought disorder. (These symptoms will all be defined in a glossary section of DSM-III.) Borderline or latent subtypes which were included in DSM-II as Latent Schizophrenia (a category which also appears in ICD-9 without definition) have been eliminated. Patients who were given this diagnosis in DSM-II will probably be given a personality diagnosis noted at a severe level in DSM-III. The category of Simple Schizophrenia has also been eliminated because of the difficulty in differentiating it from severe personality disorders and the lack of evidence that such patients share important features with the other subtypes of schizophrenia. Patients who have not been frankly psychotic and who were formerly diagnosed under the categories of Latent Schizophrenia or Simple Schizophrenia can be diagnosed under the new category of Schizotypal Personality Disorder.

Although the concept of schizophrenia has been narrowed by requiring the presence of specific psychotic symptoms, it does not require that there be a chronic or deteriorating course. On the other hand, many observers have noted that brief psychotic episodes, often associated with stress, or which develop in individuals without pre-existing psychopathology, have been unsatisfactorily diagnosed as schizophrenic in DSM-I and II because there were no alternative categories. Therefore, the DSM-III definition of a Schizophrenic Disorder will require at least six months of illness, including a prodromal or residual phase, before the diagnosis can be made. For psychoses of shorter duration, two additional categories can be considered—Brief Reactive Psychosis and Atypical Psychosis. Other alternative categories for classifying psychotic reactions as either Affective or Paranoid Disorders are also operationally defined. We believe that this will greatly affect future American diagnostic practice.

Although DSM-II acknowledged that delusions and hallucinations do occur in the Affective Disorders, it was common American practice to make a diagnosis of schizophrenia unless the delusions and hallucinations obviously were related to the disorder of affect. DSM-III permits the diagnosis of an Affective Disorder even if there are delusions or hallucinations that cannot be readily attributed to the disorder of affect, unless they are one of a small group of Schneiderian first-rank symptoms, which have been shown to be indicative of schizophrenia in cross-national studies (2,3). In a similar fashion, DSM-III explicitly recognizes that formal thought disorder occurs in mania and is only diagnostic of schizophrenia in the absence of the manic syndrome. This will further reduce the American tendency to underdiagnose mania and overdiagnose schizophrenia (4).

A major change in classifying the subtypes of schizophrenic disorders in DSM-III is the provision for classifying both the course of the illness for all subtypes and the phenomenology of the current episode. The use of both course and phenomenology is in line with a vast research literature that suggests the potential power of a multi-axial approach as contrasted with the traditional approach which included course in the definition of only some of the phenomenologic subtypes. Thus, in DSM-II, it was only possible to indicate the course by the two undifferentiated subtypes, acute and chronic.

By and large, the classification of the clinical subtypes based on phenomenology is similar to that of DSM-II and ICD-8. However, some names or definitions have been changed to clarify the concepts. Hebephrenia, which in the United States has largely been restricted to patients with silly and regressive behavior, has been given the primary name of Disorganized to emphasize the essential feature of marked disorganization of thought. This corresponds to the general use of this category by our European colleagues. The Residual category has been defined so it now more closely corresponds to the European use of this term, in that psychotic symptoms may persist but are not prominent. Many patients diagnosed under the category Chronic, Undifferentiated according to DSM-I and II will now be classified as Residual. The American category of Undifferentiated has thus been split into either Residual, for those patients whose clinical picture has become less floridly psychotic, and a Mixed type, for those few patients who cannot be classified into any of the other specific subtypes.

The inclusion of the depressive and manic Schizoaffective subtypes within schizophrenia in DSM-III is done with the recognition that controversy exists as to whether or not Schizoaffective Disorder should be considered an atypical form of Affective Disorder, a subtype of schizophrenia, or a separate group (5–7). We also recognize the lack of consensus on how to define this group. Some restrict the category to acute onset with good premorbid features, while others use it for patients who at any time in their lives have shown evidence of both a disorder of affect and of schizophrenia, even if there was no temporal overlap. DSM-III defines this subgroup phenomenologically, requiring some temporal overlap of both the active phase of schizophrenia and the full depressive or manic syndrome. We have not yet resolved the problem of how to classify a patient with a Residual subtype of schizophrenia who subsequently develops a depressive or manic syndrome, without reactivation of the florid schizophrenic symptoms.

The lifelong course of the illness up to the present time will be coded in the sixth digit as either Acute, Subacute, Subchronic, Chronic, or in Remission. In DSM-I and II, an acute schizophrenic episode was sometimes used to signify a new or first episode and sometimes an acute exacerbation of a patient with chronic schizophrenia. In DSM-III, the term acute will be limited to individuals who have episodes of illness that are sudden in onset, of short duration, and, if there has been a previous episode, it was followed by recovery at least to the premorbid state, without characteristic residual symptoms. The term chronic will mean that there have been significant signs of schizophrenia more or less continuously present for at least the last two years. The Subacute and Subchronic categories will be for intermediate courses.

What follows is an initial draft of the DSM-III classification and definition of the schizophrenic disorders. Although the entire text of DSM-III as of January 1977, is included here for completeness, modifications are planned based on the careful review and suggestions made at the Rochester Conference. A recent major modification has been the deletion of a subtype—Confusional. This is included in ICD-9 as an equivalent to an acute schizophrenic episode. Criticisms have indicated that patients who have a sudden onset of confusion and emotional turmoil should probably be classified elsewhere, and the Confusional type eliminated. Many will recover quickly, and these should be classified elsewhere, for example, as Brief Reactive Psychosis. Others will have an associated mood disturbance and should be classified as Schizoaffective, manic or depressed. A few will have no predominant pattern of symptoms and should be classified as Mixed subtype.

Several other aspects of the text and criteria that follow are being considered for modification. The issue of subtyping is still under discussion since some colleagues reviewing the present classification have thought the deletion of the Simple type of schizophrenia to be premature. The criterion of a minimum two-week duration of symptoms has aroused considerable controversy. Discussion has centered on whether any duration should be specified at all and on what the duration should be if one is to be specified. This issue has not as yet finally been resolved.

We expect that the text that follows will be revised on the basis of critical review, field trial use, and further suggestions for improvement. Our hope is that the eventual definition will achieve the following goals:

1. to facilitate research by providing investigators with a definition that is more precise than the definitions offered in previous diagnostic manuals

2. to improve training by providing a fuller description of various aspects of the disorder

3. to bring the American concept of the disorder, which previously has been more broadly defined, closer to that used by our European colleagues

4. to develop a classification that is consistent with the research data which have been collected over the years

5. to assist clinical practice by providing information of value in differential diagnosis.

REFERENCES

1. Spitzer RL, Endicott J, Robins E: Clinical criteria for psychiatric diagnosis and DSM-III. *Am J Psychiatry* 132:11, 1975.

2. World Health Organization: *International Pilot Study of Schizophrenia.* vol 1. Geneva, World Health Organization Press, 1973.

3. Wing JK, Cooper JE, Sartorius N: *Measurement and Classification of Psychiatric Symptoms; An Instruction for the PSE and CATEGO Program.* London, Cambridge University Press, 1974.

4. Cooper JE, Kendall RE, Gurland BJ, et al: *Psychiatric Diagnosis in New York and London: A Comparative Study of Mental Hospital Admissions.* (Maudsley Monograph no 20). London, Oxford University Press, 1972.

5. Clayton PH, Rodin L, Winokur G: Family history studies: III. Schizoaffective disorder, clinical and genetic factors including a one to two year follow-up. *Compr Psychiatry* 9:31-39, 1968.

6. Slater E, Tsuang MT: Abnormality on paternal and maternal sides: Observations in schizophrenia and manic-depression. *J Med Genet* 5:197-199, 1968.

7. Spitzer RL, Endicott J, Robins E: *Research Diagnostic Criteria (RDC) for a Selected Group of Functional Disorders,* ed 2. New York, New York State Psychiatric Institute, 1975.

SCHIZOPHRENIC DISORDERS: PROPOSED DSM-III DESCRIPTION AS OF APRIL, 1977.

Essential Features

A group of disorders characterized by a disorganization of a previous level of functioning involving multiple aspects of psychologic functioning and not explainable by any of the specific conditions listed under the Organic Mental Disorders.

As defined here, at some time during the illness a Schizophrenic Disorder always involves at least one of the following: delusions, hallucinations, or formal thought disorder. No single clinical feature is generally agreed to be unique to this condition and evident in every case or at every phase of the illness. However, usually there are several characteristic disturbances in the form and content of thinking, perception, affect, the sense of self, volition, relationship to the external world, and motor behavior.

The limits of the concept of Schizophrenia are still unclear. Some approaches to defining the concept have emphasized the tendency toward a deteriorating course (Krae-pelinian), the presence of specific underlying disturbances in psychologic processes (Bleulerian), or pathognomonic symptoms or symptom complexes (Schneiderian). The approach taken here does not limit the concept to illnesses with a chronic and deteriorating course. Neither does it include borderline or latent forms which may appear to share common disturbances in underlying psychological processes attributed to the severe forms of the disorder. This manual utilizes clinical criteria which include both a minimal duration and a characteristic symptom picture in an effort to identify a group of conditions that have validity in terms of response to somatic therapy, presence of a familial pattern, a tendency toward onset in early adult life, recurrence, chronicity, and severe functional impairment.

Form of Thought

A disturbance in form of thought, as distinguished from content of thought, is often present. In most clinical situations, the disorder in thought processes is inferred from the way the patient speaks, and it is assumed that language is representative of thought.

Formal thought disorder may manifest itself in a variety of ways. In loosening of associations, the form of thought is determined not by logical and relevant associations, but by incidental ones, such as sound, alliteration, or other unrelated details, so the association between one idea and the next is not obvious. This is manifested in speech in which the patient repeatedly says things in juxtaposition which lack a readily understandable relationship or when he shifts idiosyncratically from one frame of reference to another. When poverty of content of speech is present, the speech is adequate in amount but conveys little information because of vagueness, talking past the point, empty repetitions or use of stereotyped or obscure phrases. Thinking may be illogical (other than as evidenced by delusions, hallucinations, or other abnormalities of content) in that facts are obscured, distorted or excluded. When the form of thought is severely impaired, it results in incoherence. Other common types of formal thought disorder include neologisms, perseveration, and blocking. (See glossary for definitions.)

Content of Thought

The major disturbance in the content of thought involves delusions that often are multiple, fragmented, and bizarre. However, simple persecutory delusions involving the belief that others are spying or surveilling, spreading false rumors, or planning harm are common. Delusions of reference, in which unrelated events are given personal significance, are also common. For example, a newspaper article or television program may be interpreted as giving a special personal message, usually of a negative or pejorative nature. Certain delusions appear to be very characteristic of this disorder. These include, for instance, the belief or experience that a patient's thoughts, as they occur, are broadcast from his head into the external world so that others can hear them (thought broadcasting); that thoughts, which are not his own are inserted into his mind (thought insertion); that thoughts have been removed from his head (thought withdrawal); or that his feelings, impulses, thoughts or actions are not his own and are imposed upon him by some external force (delusions of being controlled or delusions of passivity).

Perception

The major disturbances in perception are various forms of hallucinations. Although they may occur in all modalities, by far the most common are auditory hallucinations, frequently involving voices heard from outside of the head. The voices may be familiar, may be responded to, and commonly make insulting statements. The voices may be solitary or multiple. Voices speaking directly to the patient or commenting on his ongoing behavior without apparent relationship to depression or elation are particularly characteristic. Occasionally the auditory hallucinations are of sounds rather than voices. Bodily hallucinations (haptic) may be present and typically involve electrical, tingling, or burning sensations. Frequently these are localized in the sexual organs. Visual, gustatory, and olfactory hallucinations also occur, but with less frequency, and should always raise the question of the possible presence of an Organic Mental Disorder.

Affect

The disturbance in affective expression often involves either flattening of affect or inappropriateness of affect. In flattening of affect there is a lack of emotional responsiveness, which gives the patient a detached, alien, and remote quality. For example, when told of the death of a parent or sibling, there may be no emotional response. Inappropriateness of affect refers to an incongruity between the content of speech or the current situation and the emotional expression that accompanies it. For example, while discussing how he is being tortured by electrical shocks administered by his persecutors, a patient with Paranoid Schizophrenia may laugh or smile. The patient may complain that he no longer responds emotionally with his normal intensity or, in extreme cases, that he no longer has any feelings at all.

Unfortunately, despite the importance of affective disturbance in Schizophrenia, its usefulness in making the diagnosis is limited because the judgment of it is often unreliable except when it is present in extreme form. Furthermore, the antipsychotic drugs can produce a state which is nearly identical to the affective flattening seen in Schizophrenia.

Sense of Self

The sense of self which gives the normal person his feeling of individuality, uniqueness, and self-direction is frequently disturbed. This is sometimes referred to as a loss of ego boundaries and may manifest itself in some of the specific delusions or hallucinations described above, particularly those involving control by some outside forces.

Volition

Almost always there is some disturbance in self-initiated goal-directed activity. It may take the form of inadequate interest or drive, or inability to successfully complete a course of action. More rarely, pronounced ambivalence regarding two opposite courses of action may lead to near cessation of goal-directed activity.

Relationship to the External World

Frequently there is a tendency to withdraw from involvement with the external world and to become preoccupied with ideas and fantasies which are egocentric and illogical, and in which objective facts then tend to be obscured, distorted,or excluded. Severe forms of this are referred to as autism.

Motor Behavior

Various disturbances in motor behavior may be seen, particularly in the severe and chronic or more acutely florid forms. There may be a marked decrease in reactivity to the environment with a reduction of spontaneous movements and activity, and the patient may appear to be unaware of the nature of his surroundings (as in catatonic stupor). The patient may maintain a rigid posture against any efforts to move him (as in catatonic rigidity). There may be apparently purposeless and stereotyped excited motor activity not influenced by external stimuli (as in catatonic excitement). The patient may voluntarily assume inappropriate or bizarre posture (as in catatonic posturing). In addition, there may be mannerisms, grimacing, or waxy flexibility.

Associated Features

Almost any psychiatric symptom may occur as an associated feature. The patient may appear perplexed, disheveled, or eccentrically groomed or dressed. Abnormalities of psychomotor activity are common with either pacing, rocking, or apathetic immobility. Ritualistic or stereotyped behavior which may be associated with magical thinking may occur. Dysphoric mood is common, especially in the acute subtype and during exacerbations of the chronic subtypes; it may take the form of depression, anxiety, anger, or a mixture of these. Depersonalization, derealization, simple ideas of reference and illusions are commonly present, as are hypochondriacal concerns that may or may not be delusional. Typically there is no disturbance in consciousness, although during a period of florid symptoms the patient may be confused, perplexed and even disoriented or show impairment in memory.

Onset

The age at onset is frequently during adolescence or early adult life, although it may be late adult life or more rarely during childhood. Frequently, prior to the development of the full-blown syndrome there are difficulties which may include social withdrawal, diminished effectiveness at school or work, and the development of various specific symptoms, such as depression or anxiety. A change in personality may be noted by friends or relatives. The length of this prodromal period is extremely variable. In those cases where the prodromal period is characterized by an insidious downhill course over many years, the likelihood is that once the psychotic symptoms emerge, the disorder is already chronic.

Course

Although the course is extremely variable, as defined here, the duration of the illness must be at least 2 weeks measured from the time when there was the first noticeable change in the patient's usual condition. Usually this earliest change does not involve the psychotic symptoms but rather such prodromal symptoms as social withdrawal, irritability, and lack of drive.

Following the initial episode, a *complete* return to premorbid functioning is unusual. In fact, some clinicians would question the diagnosis under such circumstances. However, the concept of Schizophrenia used herein does not exclude the possibility of complete recovery, and the frequency of this course is unknown. There is a strong tendency for exacerbations requiring therapeutic intervention, usually with increasing residual impairment between episodes. Numerous studies have indicated a group of factors which are associated with a good prognosis: a family history of Affective Disorder, good premorbid personality with adequate social functioning, abrupt onset, the presence of precipitating events, onset late in life, and a clinical picture that involves confusion, perplexity, depression, or elation.

Because a knowledge of course is of such importance for planning treatment, and because differences in course may reflect fundamental differences in subgroups of the Schizophrenic Disorders, course is used here as one axis of classification in addition to the cross-sectional clinical phenomenology. The course has been operationally divided into four categories: acute, subacute, subchronic, and chronic. The acute form by and large corresponds to the concept of "good prognosis schizophrenia," whereas the more severe forms of what is here called chronic correspond to the concept of "process" or "bad prognosis schizophrenia."

Impairment and Complications

The degree of social impairment is almost invariably severe at some point during the illness, frequently requiring extensive supervision to insure that the patient's basic biologic needs are met and that he is protected from the consequences of his poor judgment, cognitive impairment, or acting on the basis of his delusional beliefs. Following the initial episode, and between subsequent episodes, the degree of disability can vary widely. Some patients have essentially none, whereas others are severely impaired and require prolonged institutional care.

The illness is so pervasive that it is difficult to separate the complications from the manifestations of the impairment. These include failure of educational achievement, work performance below that appropriate to education, social isolation, and inability to develop or maintain close interpersonal relationships. Although violent acts performed by individuals with this disorder may achieve notoriety, it is not known whether the incidence of violent acts is higher than in the nonschizophrenic population. The life expectancy is shorter than that of the general population due to an increased suicide rate and death from a variety of other causes, some of which have, at least previously, been associated with institutional care. Others are probably associated with the economically deprived environments in which many individuals with these disorders live.

Premorbid Personality and Predisposing Factors

There are a number of factors which are associated with the later development of the overt illness. The degree to which they are early signs of the illness, or merely predispose to the development of the illness, is unclear.

The personality of individuals who later develop the overt illness is often described as schizoid or shy and withdrawn. Often they have few, if any, close friends. Some show antisocial behavior, usually as isolates or marginal group members. Academic difficulties of various kinds are common. In contrast, some individuals who later develop the illness apparently function in a highly effective way and in no way show signs of psychopathology.

Often children who later develop the illness are described as sickly and in fact are more likely to have had a low birth weight, some signs of central nervous system dysfunction ("soft neurologic signs"), or a lower IQ than their siblings. There is some evidence that there is an increased likelihood of Schizophrenia among patients with convulsive disorder, particularly temporal lobe seizures.

The diagnosis is made more commonly among the lower socioeconomic groups. The reasons for this are still under investigation.

Various specific patterns of family interaction have been posited as being of etiologic significance in the development of the illness. None of the various hypotheses have as yet been confirmed.

Prevalence and Sex Ratio

Despite the difficulties in defining the disorder, most epidemiologic studies indicate a lifetime prevalence of the disorder in almost all societies that have been studied of approximately 1%. The sex ratio is approximately equal.

Familial Pattern

All investigators have found a higher incidence of the disorder among biologically related family members. This includes studies in which the adopted offspring of individuals with Schizophrenia have been raised by normal parents. Twin studies consistently show a higher concordance rate for monozygotic twins than dizygotic twins, while dizygotic twins have the same concordance rate as nontwin siblings. However, being a monozygotic twin does not of itself predispose one to the development of a Schizophrenic Disorder. Although genetic factors have been proven to be involved in the development of the illness, the relatively low concordance rate even in monozygotic twins indicates the importance of nongenetic factors.

Differential Diagnosis

The differential diagnosis of Schizophrenia involves distinguishing it from a variety of conditions. Organic Mental Disorders often present with symptoms which suggest Schizophrenia. The Drug Induced and Senile Organic Mental Disorders often present with a syndrome which resembles Schizophrenia because of the presence of hallucinations or delusions. Examples are Alcoholic Hallucinosis or intoxication due to amphetamine or an hallucinogen. Formal thought disorder and blunt or inappropriate affect are also commonly seen in Organic Mental Disorders, such as the senile dementias and frontal lobe tumors, or after cerebral trauma. Even though some forms of acute schizophrenia are associated with confusion, the presence of disorientation or memory impairment strongly suggests an Organic Mental Disorder. The diagnosis of Schizophrenia should not be made until the evidence indicates that the episode of illness is not due to any of the Organic Mental Disorders. This does not mean that Organic Mental Disorders and Schizophrenia as two separate disorders may not coexist in the same individual.

The Paranoid Disorders are distinguished from Schizophrenia by the absence of prominent hallucinations, formal thought disorder, or those forms of delusions which in this manual are regarded as indicating Schizophrenia.

The differential diagnosis with psychotic forms of the Affective Disorders, particularly with mania, is of special importance because of the different treatment implications.

By definition, Schizophrenia cannot be diagnosed unless the illness has lasted more than 2 weeks, whereas Brief Reactive Psychosis cannot be diagnosed if the illness lasts more than 2 weeks. Schizophrenia differs from Factitious Psychiatric Disorder in that in the latter the symptoms are present only when the patient thinks he is being observed.

Psychotic patients who do not have the characteristic symptoms that are listed in the operational criteria for Schizophrenia should not be given the diagnosis of

Schizophrenia merely because they do not meet the criteria for any of the other specific disorders which may be of psychotic proportion. Such patients should be categorized as Other or Unspecified Psychosis. Likewise, patients who manifest the characteristic symptoms, but in whom the illness, including the prodromal period, is of less than 2 weeks' duration, should not be given a diagnosis of Schizophrenia. Both types of patients should be categorized as Other or Unspecified Psychosis until either the clinical features include the characteristic features of Schizophrenia or the duration exceeds 2 weeks.

Patients with severe personality disorders may manifest transient psychotic symptoms. However, the quick return to the usual level of functioning distinguishes this exacerbation from Schizophrenia. Patients with Schizotypal Personality Disorder (Latent Schizophrenia) may show oddities of communication and behavior and social isolation which are suggestive of mild forms of Schizophrenia. In fact, this is the basis for including the latent and simple categories of Schizophrenia in some classification systems. However, the stability of these conditions and the absence of a florid symptom picture at some phase during the illness has led to their inclusion among the Personality Disorders rather than the subtypes of Schizophrenia.

The low level of social functioning, the oddities of behavior, the impoverished affect and cognition all associated with mental retardation may suggest a chronic form of Schizophrenia. Both diagnoses in the same individual should only be made when there is certainty that the symptoms suggesting Schizophrenia, such as delusions or hallucinations, are definitely present and not the result of difficulties in communication.

The patient with a severe Obsessive Compulsive Disorder occasionally develops explanatory ideas to account for symptoms which are difficult to distinguish from delusions. At the same time, obsessive or compulsive symptoms can be seen in Schizophrenia. Usually, the patient with Obsessive Compulsive Disorder recognizes that his symptoms and thinking are irrational even when dominated by them.

Individuals who are members of religious or other subcultural groups may have beliefs or experiences which are difficult to distinguish from pathologic delusions or hallucinations. When such experiences are explainable by identification with such subcultural groups or values, they should not be considered evidence of Schizophrenia. Useful clues that such experiences should not be considered pathologic include the occurrence of the experience during religious ceremonies or other religious contexts, and the acceptance by the subgroup and the individual himself of the behavior as normal or desirable.

Operational Criteria for a Schizophrenic Disorder

A. At least one symptom from any of the following during an active phase of the illness:

   Characteristic delusions

   1. Delusions of being controlled (or influenced), thought broadcasting, insertion, or withdrawal.

   2. Multiple or bizarre delusions (do not include if seen concurrent with depressive or manic syndrome).

   3. Somatic, grandiose, religious, nihilistic, or other delusions without persecutory or jealous content.

   4. Delusions of any type if accompanied by hallucinations of any type.

Characteristic hallucinations

5. Auditory hallucinations in which either a voice keeps up a running commentary on the patient's behaviors or thoughts as they occur, or two or more voices converse with each other.

6. Auditory hallucinations with content having no apparent relation to depression or elation, spoken to the subject on several occasions, and not limited to one or two words.

7. Hallucinations of any type throughout the day for several days or intermittently for at least 1 month unless all the content is clearly related to depression or elation.

Formal thought disorder

8. Marked formal thought disorder if accompanied by either blunted or inappropriate affect, delusions or hallucinations of any type, or grossly disorganized behavior (do not include if seen concurrent with a manic syndrome).

B. Signs of the illness have lasted at least six months from the onset of a noticeable change in the patient's usual condition (current signs of the illness may be residual symptoms only, such as extreme social withdrawal, blunted, or inappropriate affect, mild formal thought disorder, or unusual thoughts or perceptual experiences).

C. The illness is not apparently due to any of the Organic Mental Disorders previously listed.

Subclassification

Methods for subclassifying Schizophrenia have changed with time. In this manual, Schizophrenia is classified on two axes: the course of the illness which is indicated in the fifth digit, and the phenomenology of the current episode, which is indicated in the fourth digit.

The course of illness was chosen as one axis because of the importance for prognosis. The two ends, acute and chronic, roughly correspond to the concepts of "good prognosis" or "reactive," and "poor prognosis" or "process" Schizophrenia.

The phenomenologic subtypes are subcategorized to reflect the major cross-sectional clinical syndromes despite the knowledge that some are less stable over time than others and that their prognostic and treatment implications are variable. Changes in the phenomenologic subtypes should not be made unless the shift in the predominant clinical picture persists for more than several weeks. Because the simple and latent types imply nonpsychotic forms of the disorder, the use of these terms is not recommended.

Phenomenologic Subtypes

295.1x Disorganized [Hebephrenic]

The essential feature is marked disorganization of thought, and affect that is flat, incongruous, or silly. Fragmentary delusions or hallucinations with the content not organized into a coherent theme are common associated features.

Other associated features include grimaces, mannerisms, hypochondriacal complaints, extreme social withdrawal, and other oddities of behavior.

This clinical picture is usually associated with poor premorbid personality, an early and insidious onset, and a chronic course without significant remissions. Social impairment is usually extreme.

Operational Criteria for Disorganized Subtype

A. Meets the criteria for Schizophrenia.

B. Marked formal thought disorder (as defined in this manual).

C. Affect which is flat, incongruous, or silly.

295.2x Catatonic

The essential feature is a marked psychomotor disturbance which may involve particular forms of stupor, rigidity, excitement, or posturing. Sometimes there is a rapid alternation between the extremes of excitement and stupor. Associated features include negativism, stereotypes, mannerisms, and waxy flexibility. Mutism is particularly common.

This subtype tends to be associated with two different courses: one with an abrupt onset that frequently is followed by periodic remissions and recurrences (sometimes called periodic catatonia), and the other with a chronic course without remission.

During catatonic stupor or excitement the patient needs careful supervision and his illness may constitute a medical emergency because of the risks of starvation, exhaustion, or inflicting injury on himself or others.

This subtype formerly was among the most common. It is now rare in Europe and North America.

Operational Criteria for Catatonic Subtype

A. Meets the criteria for Schizophrenia

B. Throughout the active period of the current episode of illness the clinical picture is dominated by any of the following catatonic symptoms:

1. Catatonic stupor or mutism (marked decrease in reactivity to environment and/or reduction of spontaneous movements and activity).

2. Catatonic rigidity (maintains a rigid posture against efforts to move him).

3. Catatonic excitement (apparently purposeless and stereotyped excited motor activity not influenced by external stimuli).

4. Catatonic posturing (voluntary assumption of inappropriate or bizarre posture).

295.3x Paranoid

The essential feature is a clinical picture dominated by the relative persistence of, or preoccupation with, persecutory or grandiose delusions, or hallucinations with a persecutory or grandiose content. In addition, there may be delusions of jealousy.

Associated features include anger which may lead to violence, argumentativeness, fearfulness, delusions of reference, and concerns about sexual identity, object choice, functioning, and autonomy. Formal thought disorder may be absent or mild. The impairment in functioning may be minimal if the delusional material is not acted upon, since gross disorganization of behavior is relatively rare. Likewise, affective responsiveness may be preserved. Often there is either a stilted formal quality or an extreme intenseness to interpersonal interactions.

The onset tends to be later in life than the other subtypes. As a subtype, it is more stable over time than the other subtypes. There is also some evidence that the relatives of patients with Paranoid Schizophrenia are more likely to have the same subtype of Schizophrenia among ill relatives.

Operational Criteria for Paranoid Subtype

A. Meets the criteria for Schizophrenia.

B. Throughout the active period of the current episode of illness the clinical picture is dominated by the relative persistence of, or preoccupation with, one or more of the following:

1. Persecutory delusions.

2. Grandiose delusions.

3. Delusions of jealousy.

4. Hallucinations with a persecutory or grandiose content.

295.7x Schizoaffective, Depressed

The essential feature is the presence of a prominent and persistent depressive syndrome overlapping temporally to some degree with an active period of symptoms of Schizophrenia, i.e., delusions, hallucinations, or formal thought disorder. Sometimes the illness may begin with the schizophrenic symptoms and the depressive syndrome concurrently. In other cases, either the depressive syndrome or the schizophrenic symptoms may persist for a considerable period of time before or after the appearance of the other.

The clinical picture consists of varying admixtures of mood and psychotic schizophrenic symptoms. The complication of suicide is more common than with the other subtypes.

The course is frequently acute. It may occur only once, be recurrent, or become chronic.

There is some evidence, based on family history, course, and response to treatment, that suggests that the acute form of this subtype may be an atypical form of Affective Disorder.

This category should not be used when a patient has had a full recovery from Schizophrenia and then develops a depressive syndrome. Such a patient should receive a diagnosis of one of the Episodic Affective Disorders.

If a patient with an active form of one of the other subtypes develops the depressive syndrome, the subtype diagnosis should not be changed to Schizoaffective, Depressed, unless the depressive syndrome persists for more than several weeks and overlaps temporally with psychotic schizophrenic symptoms.

Schizoaffective, Depressed, should not be diagnosed when a patient with Schizophrenia, Residual Subtype becomes depressed without any activation of the psychotic schizophrenic symptoms. In such an instance, the first question is whether the depression is so severe, persistent, and distinct as to warrant an additional diagnosis. If it is, it should be diagnosed as Adjustment Disorder with Depressed Mood if it appears to be reactive to an identifiable psychosocial stressor and if the full depressive syndrome is not present. If the full depressive syndrome is present, it should be diagnosed as Atypical Depressive Disorder, whether or not it is reactive.

Operational Criteria for Schizoaffective, Depressed Subtype

A. Meets the criteria for Schizophrenia.

B. Dysphoric mood characterized by symptoms such as the following: depressed, sad, blue, hopeless, low, down in the dumps, "don't care anymore," irritable, worried. The mood disturbance must be prominent and relatively persistent but not necessarily the most dominant symptom. It does not include momentary shifts from one dysphoric mood to another dysphoric mood, e.g., anxiety to depression to anger, such as are seen in states of acute psychotic turmoil.

C. At least four of the following symptoms:

1. Poor appetite or weight loss or increased appetite or weight gain (change of a pound a week over several weeks or 10 pounds a year when not dieting).

2. Sleep difficulty or sleeping too much.

3. Loss of energy, fatigability, or tiredness.

4. Psychomotor agitation or retardation (but not mere subjective feeling of restlessness or being slowed down).

5. Loss of interest or pleasure in usual activities or decrease in sexual drive (do not include if limited to a period when delusional or hallucinating).

6. Feelings of self-reproach or excessive or inappropriate guilt (either may be delusional).

7. Complaints or evidence of diminished ability to think or concentrate such as slowed thinking or indecisiveness (do not include if associated with obvious formal thought disorder).

8. Recurrent thoughts of death or suicide, including thoughts of wishing to be dead.

D. The affective symptoms overlap temporally to some degree with the psychotic schizophrenic symptoms (delusions, hallucinations, marked formal thought disorder).

295.8x Schizoaffective, Manic

The essential feature is the presence of a prominent and persistent manic syndrome overlapping temporally to some degree with an active period of symptoms of Schizophrenia, i.e., delusions, hallucinations, or formal thought disorder. Sometimes the illness may begin with the schizophrenic symptoms and the manic syndrome concurrently. In other cases, either the manic syndrome or the schizophrenic symptoms may persist for a considerable period of time before or after the appearance of the other.

The clinical picture consists of varying admixtures of mood and schizophrenic symptoms. Transient depressive symptoms are common and may include suicidal behavior.

The course is usually acute and may be recurrent.

There is some evidence, based on family history, course, and response to threatment, that suggests that the acute form of this subtype may be an atypical form of Affective Disorder.

This category should not be used when a patient has had a full recovery from Schizophrenia and then develops a manic syndrome. Such a patient should receive a diagnosis of one of the Episodic Affective Disorders.

If a patient with an active form of one of the other subtypes develops the manic syndrome, the subtype diagnosis should not be changed to Schizoaffective, Manic, unless the manic syndrome persists for more than several weeks.

Operational Criteria for Schizoaffective, Manic Subtype

A. Meets the criteria for Schizophrenia.

B. One or more distinct periods with a predominantly elevated, expansive, or irritable mood. The elevated, expansive, or irritable mood must be a prominent part of the illness and relatively persistent although it may alternate with depressed mood. Do not include if mood change is apparently due to alcohol or drug intoxication.

C. If mood is elevated or expansive, at least three of the following symptom categories must be definitely present to a significant degree (four if mood is only irritable).

1. More active than usual—either socially, at work, sexually, or physically restless.
2. More talkative than usual or feels a pressure to keep talking.
3. Flight of ideas or subjective experience that thoughts are racing.
4. Inflated self-esteem (grandiosity, which may be delusional).
5. Decreased need for sleep.
6. Distractibility, i.e., attention is too easily drawn to unimportant or irrelevant external stimuli.
7. Excessive involvement in activities without recognizing the high potential for painful consequences, e.g., buying sprees, sexual indiscretions, foolish business investments, reckless driving.

D. The affective symptoms overlap temporally to some degree with the psychotic schizophrenic symptoms (delusions, hallucinations, marked formal thought disorder).

295.9x Mixed Undifferentiated

This category should be used when the episode of illness is characterized by prominent psychotic symptoms which cannot be classified in any single category previously listed.

Operational Criteria for Mixed Subtype

A. Meets the criteria for Schizophrenia.

B. Psychotic symptoms are prominent (delusions, hallucinations, formal thought disorder, or grossly bizarre behavior).

C. Does not meet the criteria for any of the previously listed specific active subtypes or meets the criteria for more than one.

295.6x Residual

This category should be used when an individual has had an episode of illness that met the criteria for Schizophrenia but whose clinical picture now does not contain any prominent psychotic symptoms, yet signs of the illness persist. Emotional blunting, social withdrawal, eccentric behavior, and mild formal thought disorder are common. Delusions or hallucinations may be present but may have lost their affective coloring. It is almost invariably associated with a chronic or subchronic course.

Conceptually, this category is equivalent to the category of In Partial Remission specified under the severity subtypes of some of the Affective Disorders.

Operational Criteria for Residual

A. Once had an episode of Schizophrenia with one or more psychotic symptoms (delusions, hallucinations, marked formal thought disorder, grossly bizarre behavior).

B. Current clinical picture does not contain any prominent psychotic symptoms.

C. Still shows signs of the illness, such as blunted or inappropriate affect, social withdrawal, eccentric behavior, or some evidence of mild formal thought disorder.

Classification of Course

The most appropriate category for characterizing the course of the illness to date is noted in the fifth digit.

1. Acute
   a. Sudden onset. Less than 3 months from first signs of increasing psychopathology to any of the psychotic schizophrenic symptoms, i.e., delusions, hallucinations, or formal thought disorder.
   b. Short course. Continuously ill with significant signs of Schizophrenia (delusions, hallucinations, formal thought disorder, catatonic symptoms, extreme social withdrawal, eccentric behavior, or unusual thoughts or perceptual experiences) for less than 3 months.
   c. Full recovery from any previous episode.
2. Subacute. Course is closer to that of acute than that of chronic. Example: First episode with fairly rapid onset and duration of 5 months. Example: Second episode with onset for this episode over a period of 6 months and full recovery from first episode.
3. Subchronic. Course is closer to that of chronic than that of acute.
4. Chronic. Significant signs of Schizophrenia [see (b) above] more or less continuously present for at least the last 2 years.
5. In remission. This should be used when in the past the patient met the full criteria and now is free of any clinical signs of the illness. The differentiation of Schizophrenia in Remission from No Mental Disorder requires consideration of the period of time since the last episode, number of episodes, and need for continued evaluation or prophylactic treatment. No precise guidelines can be offered at the present time.

When the course is noted as In Remission, the phenomenologic subtype should describe the phenomenology of the last episode of schizophrenic illness.

Chapter 59
Some Observations on British and American Concepts of Schizophrenia

Barry Gurland, M.R.C.P., M.R.C.Psych
Judith Kuriansky, M.Ed.

The Cross-National Project for the Study of the Diagnosis of the Mental Disorders in the United States and the United Kingdom began a series of studies in 1965, which are still continuing and being carried out by multidisciplinary teams based in New York and London (5,10). The central interest of this project is in methods and uses of classifying psychiatric practice and psychiatric patients in the United States and the United Kingdom.

The Cross-National Project has demonstrated that there are dramatic differences between British and American psychiatrists in their concepts of schizophrenia (2,6,7,11). In general, American psychiatrists have a wider concept of schizophrenia than their British colleagues. In this brief presentation we will make a few observations, based on our work, on the relative usefulness and on the stability of the two concepts of

The studies reported here have been funded by grants from the National Institute of Mental Health (Clinical Research Branch) and supplemented by funds from the New York State Department of Mental Hygiene and the British Department of Health and Social Services. In New York, the project is based in the Department of Geriatrics Research at the New York Psychiatric Institute and Department of Psychiatry, Columbia University, and in London, at the Institute of Psychiatry, Royal Bethlem and Maudsley Hospitals.

Project staff for the studies reported have included: (US) B. Gurland, L. Sharpe, R. Simon, J. Kuriansky, P. Stiller, and T. Farkas. (UK) J. Copeland, J. Gourlay, J. Cooper, R. Kendell, and N. Sartorius. W. E. Deming and J. Fleiss, were the main consultants for the United States, and B. Everitt, M. Shepherd, and J. Wing were the main consultants for the United Kingdom. J. Zubin was the International Advisor.

schizophrenia—the "British" concept which tends to be *narrow* or exclusive and the "American" concept which tends to be *broad* or inclusive.

DIAGNOSTIC DIFFERENCES RELATED TO PROGNOSIS

The first observation concerns the duration of hospitalization over the 2 years after index admission of 235 consecutive admissions aged 20–59 to state hospitals in New York. British-trained project psychiatrists, using a relatively narrow concept of schizophrenia, diagnosed the admissions independently of the American hospital psychiatrists who were using a relatively broad concept of schizophrenia (2). Duration of hospitalization (including only those days a patient was physically present on the ward) was measured by documentary information obtained from the New York State Department of Mental Hygiene in Albany, based on reports submitted by the individual New York State hospitals.

The amount of time spent in hospital by patients during the 2 years after the index admissions is expressed as a percentage of the duration of hospitalization to be expected on the basis of the sex, race, age, and marital composition of the given group of patients (i.e., the duration expected regardless of the diagnosis). Thus, where the duration of hospitalization of a given diagnostic group is 100%, it may be taken to mean that the diagnosis conveys nothing about the prognosis: percentages higher than 100% imply that the diagnosis indicates a poor prognosis and, conversely, lower than 100% indicates a good prognosis.[1]

The duration of hospitalization for the narrow-concept schizophrenics (N = 73) was 112%, and for the broad-concept schizophrenics (N = 150) it was 109%. Although the hospital psychiatrists, using a broad concept of schizophrenia, diagnosed twice as many schizophrenics as did the project psychiatrists, who were using a narrow concept of schizophrenia, the duration of hospitalization was much the same for both narrow- and broad-concept schizophrenics.

The group of broad-concept schizophrenics included the vast majority (69 out of 73) of the narrow-concept cases ("agreed schizophrenics") and also a substantial number of the cases called affective disorder by the project psychiatrists (disagreement cases). The disagreement cases had about the same prognosis (104%) as the "agreed" schizophrenics (113%), again reflecting similarity of prognosis for patients diagnosed with broad and narrow criteria. However, those cases agreed to have an affective disorder by both project and hospital psychiatrists showed a distinctly better prognosis than both the disagreement cases and the agreed schizophrenics. In other words, the 25 narrow-concept affectives had a better prognosis (54%) than did the 89 broad-concept affectives (88%). Thus the cross-national differences in diagnostic practice were less relevant to prognosis for patients diagnosed schizophrenics than for patients diagnosed as having an affective disorder.

DIAGNOSTIC DIFFERENCES RELATED TO PSYCHOPHYSIOLOGY

The second observation concerns the relationship between the two concepts of schizophrenia and psychophysiologic test performance. These data were derived in a

---

[1] Further details of this study can be obtained in mimeograph form from the authors.

collaborative study with Drs. Samuel Sutton and Gerald Bruder of Biometrics Research (1). Eighteen new admissions to a state hospital in New York were diagnosed by a project psychiatrist as having a schizophrenic or affective disorder in about equal numbers; but all 18 were called schizophrenic by the hospital psychiatrist. All these patients were tested by techniques measuring auditory threshold and reaction time facilitation. The test results were significantly correlated with the project diagnoses, but not with any subclassification (e.g., Chronic, Undifferentiated and Paranoid subtypes) provided by the hospital diagnoses on these patients. Thus the narrow concept of schizophrenia delineated a subgroup of the broad-concept schizophrenics, and this subgroup was distinguished from the remainder by its psychophysiologic test performance.

These observations suggest that both narrow and broad concepts of schizophrenia may be useful but for different purposes. Other evidence (4,5) suggests that yet other concepts may be useful for certain purposes.

CHANGES OVER TIME IN DIAGNOSTIC PRACTICE

The third observation is that in the absence of definitive evidence in favor of one or the other concept of schizophrenia, proponents of a given concept are liable to shift ground over time. We have used two methods to study the concepts of schizophrenia held by psychiatrists at the New York Psychiatric Institute over the period of time since 1930. One method involved blind rediagnosis of case records by a group of contemporary American academic psychiatrists (8). The other method, in collaboration with Drs. Robert Spitzer and Jean Endicott, applied the Research Diagnostic Criteria (13) to the case records (9). Both methods showed that in the 1930s the psychiatrists in New York held a relatively narrow concept of schizophrenia similar to that currently held by the British, but that this concept ballooned over the years to reach an apogee in the 1950s.

A further analysis of these data was used to compare the diagnostic concepts of a British psychiatrist, a group of contemporary American academic psychiatrists, the New York Psychiatric Institute psychiatrists of the 1950s, and the Research Diagnostic Criteria. The interest of this final observation is that the Research Diagnostic Criteria for schizophrenia roughly foreshadow the concepts of the draft proposal for DSM-III (12). Sixty-four case records were randomly drawn from admissions to the New York Psychiatric Institute over the period 1947–1956. The original hospital diagnoses were of schizophrenia in 77% of these cases. The British psychiatrist diagnosed 19% of the 64 case records as schizophrenic, and the group of contemporary American psychiatrists so diagnosed 47%. Specially trained raters independently classified these cases using the RDC criteria and found 33% to be schizophrenic. Thus, the breadth of the RDC diagnosis of schizophrenia fell between the relatively narrow concept of the British psychiatrist and the moderately broad concept of the contemporary American academic psychiatrists, but is in no way comparable to the very broad concept that prevailed in the 1950s.

We conclude that it is premature to select one or the other diagnostic concept of schizophrenia as the most useful one; at present it is clearly important that research reports on schizophrenia should specify the criteria employed for the concept of schizophrenia. DSM-III provides specific criteria for diagnosis and may offer an acceptable compromise between the concepts of schizophrenia held by contemporary British and American academic psychiatrists.

REFERENCES

1. Bruder GE, Sutton S, Babkoff H, et al: Auditory signal detectability and facilitation of simple reaction time in psychiatric patients and nonpatients. *Psychological Medicine* 5:260–272, 1975.
2. Cooper JE, Kendell RE, Gurland BJ, et al: *Psychiatric Diagnosis in New York and London: A Comparative Study of Mental Hospital Admissions*. (Maudsley Monograph no 20). London, Oxford University Press, 1972.
3. Gottesman I, Shields J: *Schizophrenia and Genetics: A Twin Study Vantage Point*. New York, Academic Press, 1972.
4. Gottesman I, Shields J: Genetic theorizing and schizophrenia. *British Journal of Psychiatry* 122:15–30, 1973.
5. Gurland BJ: Aims and organization and initial studies of the Cross-National Project. *International Journal of Aging & Human Development* 7:283–293, 1976.
6. Gurland BJ, Fleiss JL, Cooper JE, et al: Cross-national study of the diagnosis of mental disorders: Hospital diagnoses and hospital patients in New York and London. *Comprehensive Psychiatry* 11:18–25, 1970.
7. Kendell RE, Cooper JE, Gourlay AJ, et al: Diagnostic criteria of American and British psychiatrists. *Archives of General Psychiatry* 25:123–130, 1971.
8. Kuriansky JB, Deming WE, Gurland BJ: On trends in the diagnosis of schizophrenia. *American Journal of Psychiatry* 131:402–408, 1974.
9. Kuriansky JB, Gurland BJ, Spitzer RL, et al: Trends in the frequency of schizophrenia by different diagnostic approaches. *American Journal of Psychiatry*, accepted for publication.
10. Professional Staff of the Cross-National Project. The US-UK Cross-National Project, in *International Collaboration in Mental Health*. Rockville, Md, NIMH, 1973.
11. Sharpe L, Gurland BJ, Fleiss JL, et al: Some comparisons of American, Canadian and British psychiatrists in their diagnostic concepts. *Canadian Psychiatric Association Journal* 19:235–245, 1974.
12. Spitzer RL: Personal communication, 1976.
13. Spitzer RL, Endicott J, Robins E: *Research Diagnostic Criteria (RDC) for a Selected Group of Functional Disorders*. Unpublished manuscript, ed 2. 11/23/75. (Available from Dr. Spitzer, Biometrics Research, 722 West 168th St., New York, N.Y. 10032.)

Chapter 60
Can Diagnosis be Nonpejorative?

Loren R. Mosher, M.D.

Can diagnosis be nonpejorative? Yes, of course, it *can* be nonpejorative. Diagnosis serves many purposes: administrative, so a clinic head can know how many of which kinds of patients are being treated; research, so investigators can include certain types of patients in their study and exclude others; clinical, so a proper treatment may be assigned, and so forth. In none of these examples is diagnosis per se *necessarily* pejorative. Yet, it is possible to use "objective" diagnostic terms in a subjective manner that may have unintended, deleterious consequences.

The single most damaging connotation of the term schizophrenia is its association with progressive deterioration, an inevitable downhill course. Although there is ample evidence that such a negative outcome is in fact characteristic of only a minority of patients, the view of schizophrenic patients as capable of only a very limited recovery, at best, still exerts a strong influence over many mental health workers and creates an unnecessarily negative "set" which, in turn, colors their outlook on what can be "reasonably expected" from individuals given this diagnosis. For example, when confronted by troubling and troublesome behavior, ward staff are apt to *explain* the individual's behavior by his diagnostic label, e.g., he's acting in such and such a way *because* he's schizophrenic. This "explanation" serves many functions for staff: it may provide a means of distancing themselves from the patient, and it may give them a pseudounderstanding and a sense of certainty in an otherwise inexplicable situation.

From the patient's perspective, such use of this diagnostic label is pejorative because it invalidates him as a person and because it asks too little of him. That is, the diagnosis is being used to allow staff to avoid relating to the patient as a human being who is behaving in a way which may be objectionable, anxiety-provoking, or hostility-engendering; rather, the staff may relate to him in terms of their conceptions of the term schizophrenia. In this context a patient may, in effect, become his *diagnosis* and is related to as a label and as a nonperson. It is this person—the labeled patient—in this type of situation, with whom I wish to concern myself in this brief discussion.

The opinions expressed in this paper are those of the author and do not necessarily represent any official position of the National Institute of Mental Health.

Most of you have, at one time or another, been in a situation in which *you* were being related to on the basis of another's preconceived notion of you rather than on the basis of your current, actual behavior in the particular context. When caught in such a situation, I feel I must respond to these preconceptions in a manner that will correct them. If I am unsuccessful in this attempt, I am apt to become more and more annoyed that I can't have a "real" transaction with the other person. At such moments, my experience is one of being treated like an object by the other person because either I am not allowed to respond or, if I do, my responses are not heard or not responded to, as evidenced by a change in the other person's behavior toward me. When I am convinced that my efforts to be heard are fruitless, I characteristically respond in one of several ways. I may quietly retire to a position of hopelessness; I may leave the situation as rapidly as possible; or I may get angry and aggressive, usually by speaking loudly until the other person stops and pays some attention to what I have to say.

This description of my own experience in such relationships is, I believe, similar to what patients feel when they are related to on the basis of a preconceived set, i.e., as a diagnosis rather than as a person. If status and power differences are minimal (e.g., a patient with an aide or a Ph.D. chemist patient with a psychiatrist) or if the patient is not a veteran of several hospitalizations, or if he is particularly personable, he may be able to assert sufficient counterpower to overcome the set. However, if a patient becomes convinced his position is hopeless and responds in one of the three ways *I* might, he may well receive yet another label to explain his new behavior. My quiet withdrawal would be labeled "schizophrenic autism"; my active withdrawal, "schizophrenic's need for interpersonal distance"; and my aggressiveness, "unpredictable schizophrenic rage" or, these days, "too little Thorazine." It does not take many such interactions with the social environment for a patient to learn how he is expected to act and to come to feel that his views are not taken seriously, that he is powerless to change things, and that he cannot be understood.

Unfortunately, options available to patients are limited once they enter the hospital system. They usually are not free to leave and to find more hospitable (i.e., responsive) surroundings. Luckily for me, in contrast to a patient's experience, when I find everyone relating to me on the basis of preconceptions, I can feign illness or an emergency and leave. If only hospitalized, labeled schizophrenic persons had such opportunities!

It should be remembered that a disorganized person arrives at the first point of psychiatric intake with a poorly formed notion of "what's wrong." He and his family have come (or been brought) to the hospital to obtain an answer to the "problem" from the presumably powerful, doctor. Most often, the answer will be that the person who is hospitalized and diagnosed "schizophrenic" is the victim of an inherited disease (i.e., he and his family are not responsible for the affliction and therefore can do little about it); that the disease is believed to have a predictable, deteriorating course (in practice, if recovery is excellent, the diagnosis tends to be called into question); that it does, however, respond to medication which only the doctor can prescribe. Because he is seen as manifesting a disease (i.e., an endogenous process) the effects of interactional and contextual factors in determining his behavior usually are given little credence. As a consequence of these attitudes and interactions, the patient may begin to question his own experience of himself as a person and to view himself as other wiser and more powerful people do, i.e., as a powerless victim of a disease process over which he has little control and for which he has no responsibility. This is obviously also a view that is easier for his family to accept, especially since it is proffered to them at a time of crisis when they are assailed by questions and perhaps by guilt. Thus, a diagnosis may serve as a ticket of admission into a medically based treatment system which, because of its focus on disease, dysfunction, and disability, can lead to a cycle of spiraling negative expectations that may induct the patient into a career as a mental patient or schizophrenic. His new mental-patient identity and its attendant erosion of self-confidence and self-esteem do not prepare him to confront the competitive social and work world of society. However compassionately motivated, his family's view of him as "sick," "dependent," and nonresponsive will only hinder any attempts he may make at reassuming a mature adult status.

Let us assume the patient is a 20-year-old man, comes from a blue collar family, and has worked in the auto industry since high school graduation. He arrives home from a 20-day hospitalization very slowed down from high doses of antipsychotic drugs. He is rather unresponsive compared to his old self. He is unsure of his own capacities and abilities. His family was seen by a social worker several times while he was hospitalized; in addition, they attended a parents' group. In preparation for his return home, the family has been encouraged to learn the early signs of their son's decompensation so they can check to see if he is taking his medicine or bring him back to the hospital for more treatment before the disease gets out of control again.

Several months later, the ex-patient begins to feel he ought to be doing more than he is. Despite feeling rather lethargic, he returns to the automobile factory and asks for his job. His sick leave has run out but has been extended. The boss, quite legitimately, wants to know what happened and whether or not he is back to his "old self" and ready to work again. The 20-year-old assembler tells the boss where he's been, his diagnosis, and how he now feels. He asks to have his job back. The boss, while ambivalent about this "schizophrenic," feels obliged to take him back. Within 3 days, it is quite clear that the former patient's manual dexterity is impaired too much to be able to keep up on the assembly line and that his lethargy makes it difficult for him to stay alert for 8 hours. The employer decides, understandably, that his employee cannot "make it" as an assembler because he is a schizophrenic. Having asked his friends about the disease, he is now convinced that this young man is a hopeless case—not unlike his best friend's brother who spent most of his life in state mental hospitals.

The boss sits down with our hypothetical patient to discuss what he feels he must do, i.e., let him go. The assembler gets angry, believing he was not given a fair chance to prove his ability. The boss remembers the description of his friend's brother as one who got angry with little provocation because he *always* felt he was being treated unfairly. "Ah ha!" thinks the boss, "so this one's a paranoid schizophrenic too."

The assembler returns home angry and dejected. A fight ensues between himself and his father. That evening, he is readmitted to the hospital suffering from another episode of schizophrenia.

I wish this composite story was a fabrication. Oversimplified? Yes. Basically untrue? *No.*

Santayana (1) remarked that those who do not know history are destined to repeat its mistakes. With regard to psychiatric diagnosis, we still seem to be caught up in the late nineteenth century view of all diseases as qualitative departures from normal functioning, with single agents causing single diseases. The possibility that psychiatric disorders might be quantitative deviations from normality, like strength or IQ, which are capable of being present in varying quantities seems to exert little influence on today's classifiers who appear to be overwhelmed by the importance of the history of the spirochete in our field.

What are the characteristics of a good diagnostic system? There are four: (a) it should be objective; (b) it should be reliable; (c) it should be valid; and (d) it should be comprehensive and have minimal overlap between its categories. Is the present system lacking in objectivity and, hence, susceptible to nonpsychopathology-based influences? I believe it is. At least nine nonillness-related factors influence the assessment of psychopathology, some of which are race, sex, socioeconomic status, type of interview, and religious and political beliefs of the patient (2–15).

Is it a reliable system? Spitzer and Fleiss (16) in reviewing studies of interrater reliability found a mean kappa of 0.57 for schizophrenia. Cronbach et al. (17) recommend an acceptable risk level for individual decisions of 1 in 10 chances of error. One might raise serious questions about the use of a diagnosis with the consequences which schizophrenia has for the individual unless it can show an interrater reliability of at least 0.80, if not 0.90. But questions notwithstanding, we continue to use our present system despite a nearly 25% error rate.

Is our current diagnostic scheme valid? Unfortunately, in terms of construct validity, this most critical question cannot be answered. A construct can be validated by independently derived data from other sources. For example, for a complaint of gnawing epigastric pain, we have the stool guaiac and upper G.I. series as possible validators of a presumptive diagnosis of ulcer. At the present time there are no independent measures to help us validate the diagnosis of schizophrenia.

Does it allow us to predict outcome, i.e., does it have predictive validity? Recent data from the US team of the IPSS (18,19), findings from cross-cultural studies (20,21), and long-term European studies (22) indicate that diagnosis and prognosis are relatively independent. Although the diagnosis of schizophrenia is a poor specific predictor, it may have some limited predictive validity because it contains within it a group of persons with relative psychosocial incompetence. But there is considerable overlap in outcome between schizophrenics (even "process" schizophrenics) and patients with other psychiatric diagnoses. Thus, I believe we could make more accurate predictions of "adjustment" with a psychosocial competence measure independent of psychiatric diagnostic categories.

Does it allow us to give proper treatment? Yes, but in practice, the use of a diagnostic label for this purpose means we have disregarded a great deal of potentially important information. In addition, there is significant treatment assignment crossover between diagnostic groups (e.g., phenothiazines are effective in acute mania). Thus, I believe that a cross-sectional phenomenologic system would probably lead to fewer treatment assignment errors than is now the case.

Is it comprehensive and nonoverlapping? No. Blashfield (23) and others have pointed out that as coverage becomes wider, reliability falls and patients can be fitted into any one of several categories. On the other hand, Taylor and Abrams (24) recently illustrated that for the diagnosis of schizophrenia, a reliable, nonoverlapping system is not able to categorize between 30 and 50% of patients.

Why then, do we persist in the use of our present diagnostic system? Is the diagnostic habit the flywheel of psychiatric society? I think it is more than just habit: it allows us to remain attached to the rest of medicine; it gives us an aura of scientific respectability; it allows us to collect insurance payments; and motivationally most important, it allows us to preserve sameness in the face of ambiguity and uncertainty.

I believe it would be wise if psychiatry as a whole and its classifiers in particular would heed Sir Aubrey Lewis's (7) advice:

To set up a sharp distinction "in the interests of academic accuracy," when the distinction is not found in nature, is no help to thought or action.

I have discussed the diagnostic label *"schizophrenia"* with a number of patients. Interestingly, they often say that they do not mind the label itself, but it is the inaccurate attributions made to them because of it that they find objectionable. They know quite well when they are manifestly schizophrenic. They know it from their personal phenomenology at a point in time. They object to being *seen* as schizophrenic when they are not; they object to being treated as dependent children when it is not necessary; they object to having to lie to obtain work for which they are qualified; and they object to their not being listened to and taken seriously because they are, after all, "schizophrenic." Those who believe labeling and its consequence, stigmatization, either do not exist or are not important factors in the lives of individual patients have not talked to labeled persons. Rabkin's review (25) of research on attitudes toward the mentally ill details quite well the research evidence bearing on this question. She concludes that the bulk of the evidence indicates that being mentally ill is seen pejoratively. Although perhaps less *openly* expressed in the late 1960s, as compared with the 1950s, the prevailing view is nonetheless negative.

In closing, I would like to second the views of my patients. I do not object to the term schizophrenia per se. Rather, I decry the meanings, significances, and explanatory powers attributed to the term by many mental health workers and the public. My concern is whether or not this term *can* ever be purged of inaccurate and distorted attributions so as *not* to have the unintended, but unfortunate, consequences it currently has for many patients. If progress is to be made with regard to schizophrenia—whether it be etiologic progress or making the diagnosis nonpejorative—we need to expand, rather than restrict, our conceptual horizons. Unfortunately, instead we seem to be fitting ourselves more and more into the "conceptual straitjacket" Laing (26) described in his presentation at the last Rochester meeting on schizophrenia.

REFERENCES

1. Santayana G: *The Life of Reason,* vol 1. 1905–06.

2. Braginsky BM, Braginsky DD: *Mainstream Psychology.* New York, Holt, Rinehart & Winston, 1974.

3. Cooper JE, Kendell RE, Gurland BJ, et al: *Psychiatric Diagnosis in New York and London: A Comparative Study of Mental Hospital Admissions.* (Maudsley Monograph no 20). London, Oxford University Press, 1972.

4. Efron C: Psychiatric bias: An experimental study of the effects of social class membership on diagnostic outcome. Unpublished master's thesis, Wesleyan University, 1970.

5. Grinker RR, Miller J, Sabshin M, et al: *The Phenomena of Depressions.* New York, Hoeber Publishing Co, 1961.

6. Katz MM, Cole JO, Lowery HA: Studies of the diagnostic process: The influence of symptom perception, past experience, and ethnic background on diagnostic decisions. *Am J Psychiat* 125:937–947, 1969.

7. Kendell RE: *The Classification of Depressive Illnesses.* London, Oxford University Press, 1968.

8. Kuriansky JB, Deming WE, Gurland BJ: On trends in the diagnosis of schizophrenia. *Am J Psychiat* 131:402–407, 1974.

9. Langer EJ, Abelson RP: A patient by any other name . . . : Clinician group difference in labeling bias. *J Con & Clin Psy* 42:4–9, 1974.

10. Lee SD, Temerlin MK: Social class, diagnosis, and prognosis for psychotherapy. *Psychotherapy: Theory, Research and Practice* 7:181–185, 1970.

11. Rosenhan DL: The contextual nature of psychiatric diagnoses. *J Abnorm Psychol* 84:462–474, 1975.

12. Simon RJ, Fleiss JL, Gurland BJ, et al: Depression and schizophrenia in hospitalized black and white mental patients. *Arch Gen Psy* 28:509–512, 1972.

13. Strupp JJ: Psychoanalysis, "focal psychotherapy" and the nature of the therapeutic influence. *Arch Gen Psy* 32:127–135, 1975.

14. Temerlin MK: Suggestion effects in psychiatric diagnosis. *J Ner Ment Dis* 147:349, 1968.

15. Wenger DL, Fletcher CR: The effect of legal counsel on admission to a state hospital: A confrontation of professions. *J Health Soc Behav* 10:66–72, 1969.

16. Spitzer, RL, Fleiss JL: A reanalysis of the reliability of psychiatric diagnoses. *Brit J Psych* 125:341–347, 1976.

17. Cronbach LJ, Gleser GC, Harinder N, et al: *The Dependability of Behavioral Measurements: Theory of Generalizability for Scores and Profiles.* New York, John Wiley & Sons, 1972.

18. Strauss JS, Carpenter WT Jr: Characteristic symptoms and outcome in schizophrenia. *Arch Gen Psy* 30:429–434, 1974.

19. Hawk AB, Carpenter WJ Jr, Strauss JS: Diagnostic criteria and five year outcome in schizophrenia: A report from the International Pilot Study of Schizophrenia. *Arch Gen Psy* 32:343–347, 1975.

20. World Health Organization: *Report of the International Pilot Study of Schizophrenia,* vol 2. Geneva, WHO, in preparation. Also, see Chap 57, this volume.

21. Murphy HBM, Raman AC: The chronicity of schizophrenia in indigenous tropical peoples: Results of a twelve-year survey in Mauritius. *Brit J Psych* 118:489–497, 1971.

22. Bleuler M: A 23-year longitudinal study of 208 schizophrenics and impressions in regard to the nature of schizophrenia, in Rosenthal D, Kety S (eds): *The Transmission of Schizophrenia.* London, Pergamon Press, 1968.

23. Blashfield R: An evaluation of the DSM II classification of schizophrenia as a nomenclature. *J Abnorm Psychol* 82:382–389, 1973.

24. Taylor MA, Abrams R: A critique of the St. Louis psychiatric research criteria for schizophrenia. *Am J Psychiat* 132:1276–1280, 1975.

25. Rabkin J: Public attitudes toward mental illness: A review of the literature. *Schizophrenia Bulletin* 10:9–33, 1974.

26. Laing RD: The study of family and social contexts in relation to the origin of schizophrenia, in Romano J (ed): *The Origins of Schizophrenia.* New York, Excerpta Medica, 1967.

CONCLUDING COMMENTS
Roy R. Grinker, Sr., M.D.

At the First Rochester International Conference on Schizophrenia in 1967, giant steps forward were taken to clarify diagnostic concepts; yet much remains non-understandable, if not confused. Hidden agendas still indicate that reductionistic versus existential concepts continue to dichotomize a syndrome that should by now be viewed as a system composed of many components poorly controlled by the function of an organizing principle. Romano optimistically stated in 1967 that petulant adherence to polar positions had diminished (1). At this Second Conference it seems that all positions from the biogenetic to the social have become more complicated and difficult to pursue without increased sophistication and awareness of patterns of relationships. Biochemical information is in flux, family data and interpretations are softer, schizophrenic spectrums are sinks of confusion, and some diagnostic rubrics applied to subtypes of schizophrenics are more like linguistic inventions than empirical data.

At the First Conference Garmezy said it well: "Our great need is for integrative studies in schizophrenia that are contained within a longitudinal-developmental context" (2). I would add that such longitudinal studies must indeed be long-term, including as Garmezy states: "studies of high-risk groups," especially their "cognitive styles."

At this Second Conference an auspicious shift in the classification of schizophrenia for DSM-III by Spitzer and his committee indicates great progress by the elimination of terms such as latent schizophrenia or borderline schizophrenia (see Chapter 58). Both "latent" and "borderline" refer to proximity to psychosis, not to schizophrenia which either is present or is not.

Mosher's destructive suggestion that we abolish the term schizophrenia as pejorative bespeaks an antiscientific or at least an antipsychiatric viewpoint (see Chapter 60). We tried this approach in World War I using shell shock for all psychiatric diagnoses even though the victim may never have even heard a shell. Likewise, we used the terms combat-fatigue or operational-fatigue for everyone in World War II. Not only did these euphemisms not protect their bearers, but they were harmful in that they delayed appropriate therapy for neurotics and psychotics.

At one time we did not use terms such as syphilis or cancer, then considered as shameful diseases. Thus they remained untreated until public education taught otherwise; morbidity and mortality were thereby decreased. We should recognize that hiding behind such false faces as "problems of living," which are universal problems, will prevent proper and early treatment of any kind from being instituted early enough to save many schizophrenics from disaster. We need to recognize that our responsibility is to describe to the public a syndrome for which there is now hope for its amelioration, neither assuming that its psychotic extreme is therapeutic nor that its presence connotes inevitable social ostracism.

Sartorius, Jablensky, and Strömgren have summarized a valuable cross-cultural study which definitively indicates that schizophrenic patients can be discriminated in all cultures, and that the concept and classification is based on consistent symptom patterns even after a 2-year follow-up period (see Chapter 57). Differences, however, do exist in the course and outcome of schizophrenia across cultures. Here we have an empirical and explicit statement of both biogenetic and sociocultural factors involving the presence and course of schizophrenia.

REFERENCES

1. Romano J, in Romano J (ed): *The Origins of Schizophrenia*. New York, Excerpta Medica, 1967, pp 279–281.
2. Garmezy N, in Romano J (ed): *The Origins of Schizophrenia*. New York, Excerpta Medica, 1967, pp 201–213.

Chapter 61
From Symptoms to Vulnerability and Beyond: An Overview

Lyman C. Wynne, M.D., Ph.D.

My intended task was to integrate diverse contributions of this volume on the nature of schizophrenia. As I was drawn into the tangled skein of these chapters, I sensed a risk that the very richness of the concepts and data presented here had the potential, paradoxically, to impoverish my own hard-won (but tenuously unified) point of view. In 25 years as therapist and researcher with schizophrenics and their families, I have found that experience in this realm ever heightens my awareness of paradox and complexity—and of the magnitude of that which remains painful and obscure.

Hence, I proceed hesitantly, but am heartened by recall of William Blake, poet, artist, and visionary, who probed deeply into similar dark mysteries from a different perspective. In 1790 he wrote "The Marriage of Heaven and Hell," using images familiar to schizophrenics and perhaps to some of their therapists and researchers: "As a new heaven is begun, . . . the Eternal Hell revives . . . Without Contraries is no progression" (1).

In this volume on schizophrenia, Contraries abound. Following principles of Hegelian dialectic, should we seek and expect reconciliation to emerge from these contraries? Or, rather, will long-held and beloved beliefs remain entrenched and opposed? Or will these beliefs become transformed in meaning and substance, as with Blake's Angel "now become a Devil" with whom he "often read the Bible together in its infernal or diabolical sense"? Blake, assuming that angelic interpretations were already well known, promised that the world also should be given contrary diabolical interpretations "if they behave well" (1). Let us consider if we have behaved here in such a way that one day we shall read together of the infernal as well as the holy Contraries of schizophrenia.

During the past decade, four components of the concept of schizophrenia have emerged as increasingly distinct, with each component now examined with more sophisticated methods, and with the esteem accorded to each partially transformed. These components, which will be differentiated throughout this discussion, are:

1. the *symptom picture* at a given point in time
2. the *onset and course* of the symptoms through time

698

3. the relatively enduring *vulnerability* (diathesis, predisposition) to develop clinical symptoms ("etiologic" factors are those aspects of vulnerability which are specific or necessary, although not sufficient, in the "causative" chains leading to the symptoms)

4. *stressors* (the nonspecific internal or external factors that can convert vulnerability into symptomatology) *and supports* (the counteractive factors which can reduce or mask vulnerability).

SYMPTOM PICTURE AND DIAGNOSIS

Looking back to 1967, to the First Rochester Conference (2) and the Puerto Rico Conference on transmission of schizophrenia (3), I am startled to realize how great a transformation is now underway in professional attitudes about the diagnosis of "schizophrenia" and the kind of criteria and methods needed for the making of a diagnosis. In 1967, American and European views of psychiatric diagnosis in general, and of schizophrenia in particular, were dominated by one or another of the following divergent points of view: (a) diagnosis was a boring, unimportant distraction from the clinical work of understanding and treating patients, useful only to satisfy the bureaucratic needs of hospital administrators and record librarians; (b) the diagnosis and concept of schizophrenia was a "conceptual straitjacket that severely restricted the possibilities both of psychiatrists and patients" (4) and was likely to have pejorative consequences against which Dr. Mosher (see Chapter 60) has warned in the present Conference; (c) the diagnosis of schizophrenia could be valuable but was so loose and unreliable that it left patients and clinicians adrift without guidelines for rational treatment and did not permit researchers to carry out replicable or interpretable studies; or, in contrast, (d) some experienced European clinicians believed their diagnoses to be so solidly based that demands by researchers for "blind" diagnoses and reliability studies were regarded as unnecessary or insulting.

All these viewpoints have now receded in prominence. Although a new consensus has not yet been achieved, I perceive that the following changes are taking place in beliefs and practices about the diagnosis of schizophrenia: (a) the variety of symptomatic conditions diagnosed as schizophrenic is sharply narrowing; (b) biologic and contextual features *other* than symptoms are given more detailed and careful attention; (c) although the determinants of outcome are of great interest, long-term outcome is specifically not a *diagnostic* criterion; (d) there is a growing willingness to use operational, explicitly defined criteria for diagnosis; and (e) there is a rapidly crystallizing norm that standardized diagnostic interview schedules should be used in research as part of a recognized need for reliability and comparison studies.

"Schizophrenia" is now regarded as a disorder or syndrome of "characteristic," quite easily recognized psychotic symptoms, and less often either as a myth or as a circumscribed disease entity. An increasingly representative point of view is that of Gottesman and Shields: Schizophrenia is "a relatively specific syndrome and neither a disease entity nor an arbitrary figment nor an epithet" (5, p 208).

A Historical Note

Probably the most significant of these trends is the more explicit distinction between the overt symptomatology of the schizophrenic psychosis and diverse "underlying" phenomena. Thus, there is a growing interest in reserving the terms "schizophrenic syndrome" and "schizophrenic disorder" for the more or less episodic psychotic symptom picture, and to use distinct terms such as "schizotypy" and "schizotypal personality disorder" for the more enduring, "underlying," but nonpsychotic diathesis, predisposition, or vulnerability. In contrast, most past investigators, following Bleuler, have melded a selection of symptoms with their various hypotheses about underlying principles that could, hopefully, unify the kaleidoscopic symptomatology.

Emil Kraepelin initiated this effort at conceptual unification, based on assumed uniformity in course of illness and age of onset. In 1896, he concluded that a "distinct disease must exist" because of his "overpowering impression of the states of dementia quite similar to each other which developed" in the course and outcome despite "the most varied initial clinical symptoms" (6, p 3). Kraepelin later recognized the limitations of outcome as a diagnostic criterion, but he had nevertheless stimulated others to join the search for a unifying principle.

Most notably, Eugen Bleuler wished to bring psychiatry into the medical mainstream by formulating a disease concept that would replace the "chaos" and "incomprehensibility" produced by the earlier tendency to give numerous disease names to miscellaneous disconnected symptoms. In 1911, Bleuler wrote enthusiastically: "The Kraepelinian dementia praecox is an actual disease concept" (7, p 278). Bleuler wished to go beyond Kraepelin's clinical descriptions. Drawing upon analogues to medical diseases, he sought the "fundamental disturbance," the "anatomical findings," (p 273) and "the predisposition, on the basis of which psychic processes develop the symptoms" (p 349). Recognizing that an organic substrate could not yet be specified, he identified "primary" manifestations of the underlying predisposition, especially the disturbance of association "stemming directly from the disease process itself" (p 348).

Thus, Bleuler asserted that this unifying disease concept was "superior to any symptomatic one because we are dealing with absolute, not relative criteria—absolute in the sense that once the criteria are demonstrated, the diagnosis is under all circumstances assured" (p 283). Athough his emphasis on an hypothesized underlying disturbance helped Bleuler to create a consistent disease theory, application of this concept has not been easy for clinicians and empirical researchers. Bleuler himself recognized the problem: "It only remains to ask whether an only slightly marked affective disturbance is not already a schizophrenic one. These are difficulties which are inherent, not in the disease concept, but in our diagnostic shortcomings, and which apply to any disease. Whether a certain irregularity of breathing can already be considered as pneumonic bronchial breathing is a technical question, not one involving the disease concept" (p 283). Indeed, "the disease may remain symptomless for a long time" (p 349). "Proof that the various clinical conditions included in this concept constitute an entity is the . . . fact [that] these clinical states can pass over into one another" (p 279). Furthermore, "if symptoms are present at all, it is a matter of indifference as far as the disease-concept is concerned, whether they are barely noticeable or markedly severe: in every case they remain within the framework of schizophrenic symptoms" (p 284). In accord with this formulation, Bleuler introduced the "simple" subtype in which nonflorid symptomatic manifestations become evident only slowly over many years, and he suggested that "latent schizophrenia" is the "most frequent form, although admittedly these people hardly ever come for treatment" (p 239).

Over the years, many alternative hypotheses have been proposed about underlying and unifying principles, such as genetic concepts of "schizoidia" and psychodynamic formulations of loss of ego boundaries to replace or to embroider Bleuler's theory of "primary symptoms." Thus, Bleuler's approach enduringly stimulated theory builders and provided a resilient framework for the diagnosis of schizophrenia retained in most present-day texts. An expanded version of Bleuler's viewpoint was made official in the American Psychiatric Association criteria of DSM-II (1968) in which simple, latent, acute, schizoaffective and undifferentiated subtypes were all recognized. Since the florid symptoms were defined as secondary, diagnosis in the Bleulerian tradition often has been based on subtle evidence of the inferred underlying processes. However, this has meant that the criteria have been fluid, and that reliable methods have not emerged for assessing the underlying "primary" features. Nor did Eugen Bleuler assign himself the task of developing such methods. Rather, he sought and achieved his explicit goal of formulating a comprehensive disease theory based on hypotheses about the underlying processes. Bleuler made the diagnosis of schizophrenia when he believed there were evidences of latent tendencies or, in today's terminology, evidences of vulnerabilities.

Bleuler carefully acknowledged that his theory would require buttressing and clarification in future studies. However, contrary to current common belief, he did not regard schizophrenia as basically heterogeneous; he did not expect that two or more distinct disease entities would be identified. Confusion appears to have arisen when later readers have noted his subtitle, *The Group of Schizophrenias* (7), but have neglected to study his text: He insisted that he had defined a disease concept "with concrete delimitations," "a genus" although not a "species of disease" (p 279). He stated that "subdivision of the group of schizophrenias is a task for the future," but of greater importance to him was his conclusion that "thorough study of the psychopathology revealed everywhere the same fundamental phenomena" and "a complete absence of any distinguishable boundaries (at least with our present methods of investigation)" within the clinical picture of schizophrenia (p 280).

Over the years others have, of course, tried out many ways of dividing, narrowing, or broadening the boundaries in Bleuler's 1911 formulation. These later approaches have taken three major forms: (a) changes in the selection of overt symptoms regarded as diagnostic (see Section XIII); (b) the addition of a temporal dimension—premorbid development and/or onset and course (see Sections IX and XII); and (c) new hypotheses, methods, and data that fill in gaps and modify Bleuler's concept of the underlying processes (see the rest of this volume).

Langfeldt and other Scandinavians subdivided and narrowed the symptoms that they believed to be diagnostic of "true" schizophrenia and at the same time linked this subset of symptoms to a revived emphasis on poor outcome as a defining criterion (8). Although the Second Rochester Conference has demonstrated that the course of illness deservedly continues to be a problem of great practical relevance in planning treatment services, we now can see that the criteria of outcome need to be multidimensional (see Chapter 54), that the initial symptom picture is not a good predictor of several aspects of outcome, and that course can be affected significantly both by the modality of treatment and by the stressors and supports, especially in the family (9,10). Thus, there appears to be general support, although not unanimity, for conceptualizing symptom picture and course as separate axes or dimensions in the assessment of schizophrenia (see Chapters 54 and 58).

Kurt Schneider declared his agreement with Bleuler that "psychiatric diagnosis must be based upon the presenting situation, not on the course taken by the illness" (11, p 92). However, in other respects Schneider made a radical departure from Bleuler. He aimed to make a nontheoretical, purely descriptive approach to the florid symptoms in their own right. He contended that his symptoms of "first-rank" should have "decisive weight beyond all others in establishing a differential typology between schizophrenia and cyclothymia. . . . The value of these symptoms is, therefore, only related to diagnosis; they have no particular contribution to make to the theory of schizophrenia, as Bleuler's basic and accessory symptoms have" (11, pp 135,133).

Although Schneider took a strongly organic view ("Our concept of psychiatric illness is based entirely on morbid bodily change" [p 7]), his *symptom* criteria for diagnosis did not derive from his etiologic views. Nor did he follow Bleuler in basing diagnosis partly on subtle indications of vulnerability. Thus, Schneider's approach, beyond that of others, describes the symptom picture in isolation from the other three components of the concept of schizophrenia—the course, the underlying vulnerability (including hypothesized etiology), and the context of stressors and supports. Recent evidence suggests that Schneider's first-rank symptoms are not so distinctive for schizophrenia as he had believed, and they have not been validated by recent studies of the course of illness (12). Nevertheless, within the past decade, Schneider's influence has become far more pervasive than most American psychiatrists realize. The London-Maudsley psychiatrists, led by Wing and Cooper, have introduced a diagnostic framework heavily weighted by Schneider's first-rank symptoms. These criteria were incorporated into Wing's Present-State Examination (PSE), only slightly modified for use in the WHO study of schizophrenia (see Chapter 57), and now are prominent in the "characteristic" symptoms of the proposed DSM-III criteria for schizophrenia (see Chapter 58).

Despite widespread dissatisfaction with the vagueness of DSM-II criteria for schizophrenia, many American psychiatrists appear uneasy about what are perceived as premature constrictions of the proposed DSM-III. As a dynamically oriented psychiatrist who nevertheless has participated actively in WHO programs on schizophrenia since the initiation of that research in 1965, and now in the Task Force for DSM-III, I believe that reassurance and optimism is appropriate if the purposes and limitations of these diagnostic criteria are understood.

First, I feel confident that narrowed use of the diagnostic term "schizophrenic disorder" will be welcomed by those who legitimately have been concerned that at times both the public and the mental health professions indeed have used the label loosely and carelessly. The possibility of pejorative implications (see Chapter 60) that may add to the secondary handicaps of the patient (see Chapter 53) can be acknowledged as an unfortunate reality of unknown magnitude without entering unnecessarily into the quicksands of debate about whether "labeling" is a "primary" cause of psychiatric disability.

Second, researchers and the public alike are insisting that psychiatry evaluate and document its successes and failures in treatment far more fully, both with drugs and psychotherapy. For most schizophrenics, neuroleptic treatment clearly is powerful both in its antipsychotic actions and in its potential side effects, while lithium appears more effective for the affective psychoses and perhaps the schizoaffective disorders. Insofar as schizophrenia has been overdiagnosed, neuroleptics probably have been given inappropriately to patients who incorrectly were diagnosed as schizophrenic. Because of the effectiveness of lithium for manic-depressive disorders, the need for careful, reliable, and valid diagnosis becomes more pragmatic and urgent an issue than in the past.

Third, a multifaceted or multiaxial model of diagnosis for which DSM-III provides a beginning, will facilitate attention not only to the details of current episodic symptomatic distress and impairment but also to such dimensions as enduring personality patterns (Axis II in DSM-III), the psychosocial stressors (Axis IV), and highest level of recent functioning (Axis V). Guidelines for the assessment of the family context are a badly needed gap in DSM-III, but are currently being considered and developed for future use. Thus, "diagnosis" is becoming viewed as more than a label for presenting symptoms. This comprehensive approach to assessment is needed to demonstrate that psychiatric diagnosis can become a meaningful distillation of knowledge relevant to all aspects of treatment planning.

Fourth, the interaction of medication and psychosocial treatments is becoming understandable and amenable to rational and more comprehensive treatment planning (see Chapters 53–55), especially to cope with the vexing problem of frequent relapses. During the next decade, I expect that we shall witness a substantial resurgence of psychosocial treatments with schizophrenics—more selective, effective, and focused in relation to the kind of symptoms, the phase of symptom resolution, and the family context. Such programs will also draw far more heavily on family therapy and education and on social skill building, especially with those patients who have a poor premorbid history and who have few competencies to counteract their vulnerability to relapse (9).

Fifth, if patient samples are selected with the more operational DSM-III criteria for symptoms and course, we will narrow the basis for explaining away discrepancies between studies on the grounds, usually not documented, that the samples may have been diagnostically different. At present, we cannot readily group or regroup patients, in ways that could be replicated by others, to test hypotheses about either homogeneous subgroups or about larger clusters of patients and families. Although DSM-III certainly will not be the definitive answer to this problem, consistent application of these criteria will facilitate improved comparisons of findings between different studies and, in turn, the usefulness of the diagnostic criteria can be validated.

Undoubtedly both the field trials of DSM-III and the future use of this and other approaches will lead to fundamental changes in the dimensions, categories, and criteria of diagnosis. A key to success in these explorations is that the diagnostic criteria be regarded as working hypotheses, not as final conclusions, and be used to facilitate genuine dialogue between clinicians and researchers about definable issues. We have labored far too many years weighted down by diagnostic baggage, never unpacked and examined, and commonly regarded as a diabolical burden which has hampered our journey toward the presumed heavens of etiology and recovery.

THE CONCEPT OF VULNERABILITY

My viewpoint of schizophrenia is quite similar to that expressed by Joseph Zubin, namely, that vulnerability is the most crucial and least understood aspect of schizophrenia. I strongly endorse Zubin's suggestion that vulnerability be regarded as an integrating principle linking symptomatology with diverse variables relevant to etiology, pathogenesis, onset, course, and prevention.

Vulnerability (predisposition, diathesis) to schizophrenia can be defined as the individual's characteristic threshold beyond which stressful events produce decompensation manifest in the clinically diagnosable symptom picture. As Garmezy put it, predisposition is "indexed by those components of a genetic and/or cultural heritage which either singly or in combination determine the threshold of adaptive responsiveness to specific life experiences" (13).

Vulnerability as Enduring, Trait-Like Features

Zubin regards vulnerability as a stable trait that characterizes the individual independently of the presence or absence of psychopathologic episodes, which are nonenduring
"states" (see Concluding Comments, Section XII). The distinction between states and
traits suggests a strategy for identifying indicators of vulnerability: to attempt to discern
persisting features, optimally those that a) can be identified before first onset and help to
predict the later symptoms; b) continue concomitantly with the symptoms; and c) remain
during symptom remission and help to predict relapse. This strategy is followed with a
great diversity of methods in the high-risk research field described in this volume (see
Chapters 34–41, 43–45). Most of these programs begin the study of hypothesized vulnerability indicators in children or adolescents prior to the initial episode of schizophrenic
illness. However, Spring and Zubin (see Chapter 36) begin at a later stage, studying
attentional indices in adults who are at high risk for future schizophrenic episodes because
of a history of a past episode. Some will relapse, some not. Hence, their varying degrees of
vulnerability to future episodes fruitfully can be studied during remissions.

Vulnerability as a Developmental and Epigenetic Process

Compared with symptomatic episodes, vulnerability is relatively enduring but should not
be regarded as developmentally static or fixed. Although the genetic endowment remains
unchanged throughout life, its manifestations unfold only slowly in the course of development. Maturational lags and precocities may be controlled genetically and have been
implicated in childhood schizophrenia. It is possible, even likely, that adult schizophrenics
also have vulnerabilities that follow a maturational course building up in adolescence and
young adulthood and later subsiding. Conceivably, some recoveries in later life, described
by Dr. Manfred Bleuler (see Chapter 55), partially could occur on this basis.

The genetic components of vulnerability are inevitably shaped from conception onward
throughout development as the result of transactions of the individual with the psychosocial and physical environment. Furthermore, the transactional point of view implies
feedback loops in which the individual modifies the same environment that continues to be
formative of his personal qualities over time. Transactions seen in a developmental
context imply the concept of *epigenesis* that has been central in my thinking for many
years. This means that "interchanges or transactions at each developmental phase build
upon the outcome of earlier transactions. . . . Constitutional and experiential influences
recombine in each developmental phase to create new biologic and behavioral
potentialities which then help determine the next phase" (14). An important implication
of an epigenetic formulation is that prevention and treatment effectively can take place at
many points in what Gottesman and Shields call the "chain of consequences," without
modifying or even identifying the earlier "root" causes (5).

Diathesis-Stressor Models

It should be recognized that I have described only one version of a broader concept of
gene-environment relationships that go under the umbrella of the diathesis-stressor
models of etiology. Rosenthal has written an overview of this model as well as two

alternatives, monogenic-biochemical theories that deny significant experiential influences, and life-experience theories that deny any importance to specific genes (15,16). Of the three major kinds of models, diathesis-stressor theories are most in favor at present, perhaps more on philosophic grounds than on the basis of clear-cut evidence.

Rosenthal has described six versions of the diathesis-stressor model (16), one of which is the epigenetic view that I favor. Rosenthal calls this model "reciprocal escalation," meaning that the inborn diathesis (vulnerability) and stressors heighten each other in an intensifying process until the schizophrenic break occurs.

The looseness with which the diathesis-stressor models have been formulated thus far is apparent when one perceives that Rosenthal's six versions would be difficult to differentiate from one another. "Augmentation" is a version in which diathesis and stress somehow compound in the same phenotype, producing an overload leading to clinical schizophrenia. This appears to me to be a nondevelopmental description of reciprocal escalation.

"Variance analysis" is a version in which the diathesis is inferred but not specifically identified. By comparing genetic and environmental loadings in broad terms, the variance in the phenotype can be accounted for. This approach is not incompatible with the other versions and provides a statistical way of summarizing broad sources of the clinical phenotype without getting into sequences or details of development, or into the question of specific (necessary) etiologic factors versus nonspecific factors.

Other versions of the diathesis-stressor model are vague about the nature of the diathesis and how this may or may not change as the result of the impact of stressors. In the "activation" model, the diathesis is triggered toward schizophrenia by stressors, but the theory is unclear about whether or not diathesis may change during the course of development or as the result of a psychotic episode. However, if the clinical observation is correct that relapses are precipitated by less severe stressors than those that trigger onset of the initial episode, then vulnerability must have increased during or after the first episode.

It is my impression that a decade ago a general model of diathesis-stress (more accurately, stressor) was generally accepted. As research has proceeded, both on aspects of diathesis or vulnerability and on aspects of stressors, the complexities and the limitations of the models have become more apparent. First, the concept needs to incorporate a developmental perspective more fully. Second, the distinction between inborn and acquired components of diathesis or vulnerability was seldom made in earlier years. Third, the concept of stressor has been somewhat ambiguous. This term probably should be reserved for the immediate stressors that nonspecifically trigger or precipitate an episode. However, the concept of stressor also has been applied to any environmental factor, including repetitious patterns of life experience. In my view these factors more properly should be regarded as formative contributions to "underlying" vulnerability or predisposition, not as precipitating factors in acute symptomatic decompensation. For example, a lifelong social learning experience in which few interpersonal skills are acquired, with an absence of opportunities for learning adaptive skills relevant to the environment that the adult later will have to face, should be regarded as heightening vulnerability but not as constituting a triggering stressor. Future study of details surrounding circumstances for both acute onsets of schizophrenic psychoses and, even more neglected, for the study of insidious onsets, is badly needed to clarify the nature of these interaction effects in what once was incorporated loosely into the diathesis-stress model.

Acquired and Innate Components of Vulnerability

Although most discussions of vulnerability begin with a generalized comment about nongenetic aspects of a diathesis for schizophrenia, usually the possibility of acquired vulnerability receives little further comment. In this volume, the genetic aspects of vulnerability are most extensively explored; but, turning to environmental contributions, the most commonly accepted form of acquired vulnerability is biologic, based on evidence of changes produced by intrauterine or birth complications and possibly postnatal cerebral disorders. The reports by McNeil and Kaij (see Chapter 39), Sameroff and Zax (see Chapter 40), and by Kinney and Jacobsen (see Chapter 3) are especially significant in assessing this source of acquired vulnerability. The current conclusion seems to be that there is a nonspecific, nongenetic biologic contribution to vulnerability for psychopathology in general, and possibly more distinctly for process schizophrenia. Needing further study is the intriguing possibility that the interaction effects of genetic factors and obstetric complications produce a degree of vulnerability that leads to psychosis when both occur, but not with one in the absence of the other.

An important implication of an epigenetic-developmental frame of reference is that "predisposition" itself can be altered both through maturation and through experiential, learned components of vulnerability that interact with the biologic components. A prevailing viewpoint about family communication and other such variables is that if they contribute to schizophrenic illness, they presumably do so as triggering stressors. Brown, Birley, and Wing (9) and Vaughn and Leff (10) have shown that critical, hostile comments from emotionally overinvolved key relatives contribute to relapse of schizophrenic illness. On the one hand, these authors observe that the critical attitudes are more about long-standing attributes of the patient than about recent psychotic behavior. Hence, these family interaction patterns may well be enduring, although no studies using their methods have been carried out in high-risk subjects prior to onset of the initial episode. Goldstein et al (see Chapter 45) have found significantly more negative remarks in families of adolescents who become ill with schizophrenia spectrum disorders 5 years later. Such data suggest that family communication patterns may be formative to vulnerability rather than triggering or precipitating acute episodes.

My long-term research collaboration with Singer (see Chapter 46) has been oriented toward those familial patterns that may modify vulnerability. At the 1967 Puerto Rico Conference, I described our framework for study of the familial-environmental contributions to predisposition (17):

> We have assumed that in the long-term relationships which occur in family life there will be certain transactional patterns that will have occurred with high frequency. Such patterns are likely to have differing influences upon different individual family members because their susceptibility to formative change inevitably varies both constitutionally and experientially, depending upon such factors as stage of individual maturation and development and role within the family. We have been especially interested in those aspects of family life which appear to be patterned and recurrent, that is, "structural" or "stylistic."
>
> Similarly, with respect to those persons who are diagnosed as schizophrenic, we have felt that it was especially crucial to deal with structural or core features of the schizophrenic disorder, those aspects of the illness which seem to recur under a variety of circumstances, even in periods of remission from florid symptoms. For example, the so-called "formal" aspects of schizophrenic thinking disorders appear to be based upon relatively enduring response dispositions of the individual. Therefore, we have attempted to define and delineate the diverse

varieties of thought disorders but have found it necessary to go beyond conventional clinical formulations of thought disorder in order to make this concept operationally useful for research purposes (18,19).

This effort has led us into another pair of concepts: focal attention and shared focal attention. We have described these concepts in detail elsewhere (19,20). . . .

[In summary] we have been interested in those factors which are likely to have been predisposing rather than precipitating, enduring rather than only immediate. We have assumed that a variety of factors, both familial and nonfamilial, precipitate acute episodes of psychiatric disorder. We have, in short, been interested in those structural or stylistic features which might lead to an increased vulnerability to a number of possible precipitating circumstances.

Distorted life experiences over many years are less dramatic but probably more contributory to acquired vulnerability than exceptional, traumatic life events. Therefore, repetitious and enduring formative influences need to be assessed with especial care in developmental psychopathology and in prospective high-risk research (see Sections IX and X).

Specific and General Components of Vulnerability

There is perhaps no aspect of the concept of schizophrenia that has generated more heat and less light than the problem of etiologic specificity. Perhaps the most noteworthy exception to this rule is the illuminating dialogue between Gottesman and Shields, on the one hand, and Paul Meehl on the other, in the concluding chapters of the book *Schizophrenia and Genetics* (5) in which Meehl gives a penetrating critique of the clear exposition by Gottesman and Shields. My comments here will build upon and suggest certain modifications of their remarks. Gottesman and Shields begin with the working hypothesis that "a genetic contribution is necessary but not sufficient for schizophrenia to occur. Furthermore, the genes are conceived of as specific to schizophrenia, i.e., whatever else they may do, they increase the liability to schizophrenia rather than to high blood pressure, affective disorder, and so forth. The genetic contribution may or may not be the largest contributor to the variance of liability; in analysis of variance terms, it means an interaction effect preventing other variables from causing schizophrenia when the specific genetic etiology is missing. Since our model imposes the requirement of necessity on the genetic component of schizophrenia, it follows that the component is *important* regardless of any quantification that may subsequently emerge" (5, p 10).

Gottesman and Shields elaborate a schematic representation of combined sources of liability, both genetic and environmental. Here they include ingredients that commonly are neglected, especially assets that counteract or interact with the liabilities. Also, "general genetic contributors which serve as modifiers or potentiators together with general environmental contributors which serve as modifiers or potentiators, each define dimensions of liability which combine with the specific genetic liability to determine the net liability and the position of the individual vis a vis the threshold [for symptomatic decompensation] at a particular time" (p 332). Meehl points out that the meaning of the term "specific etiology" is much more ambiguous if one hypothesizes that the specific genetic factor is polygenetically transmitted than if one uses a monogenic model or even a major gene model with modifiers (5).

The problem of genetic interpretation is further complicated by recognition of the importance for vulnerability theory of what have been called "response dispositions" (21), a dimensionalized approach to temperament. These dispositions are partly hereditary. Through additive or interactive genetic processes, with later developmental modifications, the response dispositions could combine nonspecifically to produce much of, or even the total, genetic contribution to predisposition or vulnerability for schizophrenia. The temperamental dispositions that may be relevant to schizophrenia include the modulation of attention and the susceptibility to stimulus overload, strongly emphasized in this volume, as well as related patterns of cognitive and affective controls such as field dependence-independence, scanning control, rage readiness, stimulus sensitivity, social introversion, anxiety-proneness, impulsivity, and so forth. Of this staggeringly complex array of dimensions, none are usually thought to be specific for schizophrenia, but all may potentiate, inhibit, or mask the clinical manifestations. For example, a high readiness for rage, perhaps inborn, could make schizophrenic breakdown more likely, whereas controls of rage learned in the family environment could forestall decompensation. Meehl has lucidly discussed such possibilities (5), but there can be no detailed consensus about how to conceptualize *non*specific dispositional factors and stressors until agreement is reached about what, if anything, is indeed focal, specific, or intrinsic to *schizophrenic* vulnerability. As I see it, the geneticists have such a wealth of viable candidates as contributors to schizophrenia on a nonspecific, genetic basis, that the hypothesized *specific* genetic factor may well exist but be submerged from view for purposes of genetic analysis. On the other hand, the data on platelet MAO (see Chapter 38) suggest that genetic factors could be significant for psychiatric disorders with broader symptomatology than schizophrenia and, thus, technically could be nonspecific. My conjecture is that the environmental factors may turn out to be the *specific* contributions to schizophrenia, interacting with *nonspecific* genetic factors. However, traditional research starting with a genetic orientation has not incorporated methods or concepts that tap distinctive aspects of the family environment (see Section X) and that appear to differ from "stressors" leading to other disorders such as depression and psychosomatic illness.

An obvious difficulty with the specificity concept at this time is that the clinical diagnosis of schizophrenia, used as a phenotype for genetic analysis, has some value for getting genetic studies underway; but, as Meehl points out, "what we call the 'pathology' of the clinical disease is learned social pathology, related only derivatively to the . . . dispositions that are, strictly speaking, 'heritable'" (5, p 412). Because even the narrowly defined first-rank symptoms of Schneider fail to rule out many "false positives," judged from other clinical and laboratory criteria, further progress in genetic studies is likely to be limited until an endophenotype is discovered that appears closer to the hypothesized genes than is clinical diagnosis. In addition to the platelet MAO levels and the pendulum eye-tracking measures (see Chapter 37), the continuous performance task measure of Kornetsky and Mirsky (see Chapter 17), the reaction time "cross-over effect" measure described by Steffy (see Chapter 20), thought disorder as measured with the Delta Index in the Rorschach (22), and certain MMPI patterns (5), are under investigation currently.

Perhaps combinations of such indices will be helpful. Hanson, Gottesman, and Heston (23) have suggested the use of multiple childhood indicators of vulnerability to later schizophrenia—poor motor skills, large intra-individual inconsistencies in performance on cognitive tasks, and observations of "schizoidlike behaviors, including apathy, withdrawal, and emotional flatness, mixed somewhat paradoxically with emotional instability, irritability, and negativism."

A complication in the search for better phenotypal indicators of vulnerability is that expectable developmental changes in these indicators mean that the same features that are useful at one age may not be at another age. Therefore, studies of family pedigrees at a given point in time may call for different indicators for family members at different points in the life cycle. Despite these and other stumbling blocks, I predict that the next decade will show useful if not definitive breakthroughs in the identification of laboratory or test measures, biologic or psychologic, that will facilitate genetic studies of schizophrenia and that will help clarify whether or not there are specific genetic contributors as well as the more widely accepted nonspecific genetic contributors to liability.

Gottesman and Shields concede that "there may well turn out to be specific environmental liabilities of schizophrenia in addition to the general one we have provided for" (5, p 333). On the other hand, they interpret the recent adoption and fostering studies as providing negative evidence on this point. They state: "No evidence was found for the operation of the one particular environmental influence that had generally been assumed to be highly important—the presence of schizophrenia or related disorders in the rearing family. Focus must thus be shifted to individual vulnerability reacting with nonspecific and culturally common if not ubiquitous factors" (5, p 49). Similarly, Rosenthal (24) and Wender et al (25) have viewed parental psychopathology as a nonspecific "rearing variable."

I would suggest that this point of view is premature and probably misleading. First, the presence of schizophrenia in the rearing family is an inconsistent indicator of environmental contributions. For example, Anthony's clinical observations (26) suggest that parents with prognostically more severe "process" schizophrenia are apt to be symptomatically withdrawn and have longer hospitalizations that spare the offspring, compared to a more disturbing impact from either borderline or brief, florid episodes.

Second, studies oriented to genetic hypotheses have not examined family relationships in terms of hypothetically more specific variables but, rather, typically have ignored these factors or obtained global reports about such features as family conflict or broken homes. For example, Rosenthal, Wender, Kety, et al (27) have described a study of *general* qualities of parent-child relationships, not only, as the authors acknowledge, subject to the well-known shortcomings of retrospective recall, but also necessarily lacking any data on those features of family communication that have been most productive with methods using direct observation of interaction (see Chapters 44–46).

Third, the variables generated with these direct methods vary modestly and "logically" across situations (28) and predict consistently to independently collected data, for example, in peer and teacher ratings of school children (29). Variables such as the "balance" of interaction directed to and from family members are highly patterned statistically significant measures (30).

Fourth, in contrast to earlier procedures such as the Object Sorting Test, which quite easily was distorted by factors such as situational anxiety and educational background, techniques of studying family interaction have moved far in the past decade, can now be measured reliably and do not need to rest with global retrospective ratings. Seriously and consistently deviant communication patterns cannot be assumed to be "perhaps universal" (Gottesman's term when describing environmental factors in Chapter 5). To be sure, large population surveys need to be conducted with these standardized methods, as well as parametric studies of demographic and other factors that modify performance. However, small samples suggest that about 10% of randomly selected parents show frequent communication deviances of the special kinds we have found in families of schizophrenics (21). In families with normal and neurotic offspring, these "deviant" parents have spouses who clearly have positive corrective qualities. Hence, my current speculation is that family *systems* with seriously deviant communication patterns are found in only 5–10% of the population. If this hypothesis (conjecture!) is even roughly correct, then the *combination* of genetic vulnerability and acquired vulnerability from family communication sources would be rare indeed—possibly 1% or less of the population.

Because a great diversity of potent, nonspecific, or general liabilities and assets could contribute to the characteristic threshold level of vulnerability in an individual, we need to ask the question of how essential is a positive answer to the question of whether there is a *specific* etiologic factor for schizophrenia, or for any subgroup of schizophrenics. Perhaps we should take seriously the hypothesis of no specific etiologic factors, and try to identify the most potent constellations of general factors. Gottesman and Shields are worried that "the observation that schizophrenia may well be etiologically heterogeneous, with many biological and environmental causes, could lead to research nihilism and obscurantism" (5, p 1). They take the extreme case of a possible 100 causes, each accounting for 1% of the cases. However, it is quite reasonable to consider that the so-called general factors, whether they are genetic or environmental, are far from ubiquitous. After all, as Dr. Murphy has shown (see Chapter 52), combinations of cultural factors that may be relevant to schizophrenia are quite restricted to certain groups, occurring within a given locale with specific backgrounds and value systems, and thus applicable only to defined segments of the general population. Such cultural factors are not specific in the sense of being necessary for every case of schizophrenia, but would be similar to a few "big" nonspecific genes. Identification of a limited cluster of major though nonspecific environmental and genetic factors would move research, treatment, or prevention forward and be far from nihilistic. Another possibility that is quite conceivable is that the *combinations* of factors interacting with one another is what is *necessary*. In that sense, interaction effects may become "specific" and more important and interesting than the major effect of any single specific factor.

Because "communication deviance" and related factors emerge and have their possible impact within a developmental context, I have preferred to speak of these variables as "intermediate" between genetic endowment and clinical symptomatology (21). The sources of communication deviance must be formulated in terms of gene-environment interaction at multiple developmental stages. Such is a task of current high-risk research that incorporates both genetic and family communication variables. Similarly, the attentional and psychophysiologic response dispositions, described at length in this volume, are also "intermediate (21). The evidence in this volume suggests, on the one hand, the likelihood that measures of these dispositions soon will be useful as indicators of genetic vulnerability and, on the other hand, that these same attentional problems clearly are crucial components of schizophrenic disorders of language and communication familiar to the clinician (14,18,20, and Section VII of this volume).

EPILOGUE

During the Second Rochester International Conference on Schizophrenia, I was keenly aware of my designated role to provide a concluding overview. As the papers were presented, I felt bombarded by the fascinating, diversely technical discussions derived from many contrasting points of view and differing types of data. This complex experience evoked in me conflicting goals, either to attempt genuine assimilation and integration of these presentations or, constricting myself to just one or two issues, to set aside the alternative and opposing ideas. I became keenly and painfully aware as the Conference progressed that I was caught up in a straining effort to make sense of the proceedings as a whole. At the same time, I was jarringly reminded at the conclusion of the first day that the Conference was in my home setting, and that my clinical responsibilities to patients continued. I received an indirect but urgent message that a schizophrenic patient, who had progressed after a long inpatient stay to the Day Treatment Program, had begun that day to hallucinate again and had disappeared abruptly from a group meeting. I sought assistance through that expediter of modern communication, our telephone system; after seemingly interminable transfers and "holds," I made contact with the social worker who last had seen my patient, and we arranged to meet and to discuss what might be going on. I found myself wrenched from my efforts to understand the nature and meaning of neurotransmitters. Instead, I worked out a revised clinical plan through which treatment could continue with others while I was unavailable. This plan seemed sensible enough as written down in the hospital record. At the same time, my subjective experience was one of unease and increasing irritation over my failure to integrate this particularistic human relationship and the abstract principles of the Conference.

The next day of the proceedings was marked by recognition of our distinguished honorary degree recipients, and then, by a rapid change of content, to significant but mind-mazing data on the growing numbers of schizophrenics in this country, moving onward to the sociocultural factors that may influence the onset and course of these disorders, onward once again to intricate and controversial family and clinical studies, and finally to presentations on laboratory measures of reaction time, eye movement, neurophysiologic, and psychopharmacologic problems.

Prior to the Conference, I had sketched out preliminary comments for my overview; this preparation now seemed inadequate if not irrelevant. And so at the close of the day, irritable and drained, I returned alone to my hospital office, deliberately removing myself from meeting with colleagues, ostensibly to review my notes of the day's proceedings and to look over the draft of my paper, but also to try to cope with my dismay and perplexity about what was going on with the patient who no doubt knew (from posters in the hospital) that I was chairing a meeting on the nature of schizophrenia.

As I approached my office, I glanced down the corridor which stretched toward the other end of the Medical Center. From a seemingly enormous distance my patient was slowly walking toward me for a completely unscheduled meeting that now became an intrinsic ingredient in the schema of this day in my life. We entered the office and I put on a shelf the bulky conference papers, my manuscript and my notes. I turned from schizophrenia to a schizophrenic. We made contact with a handshake and a gesture; I then sat down to hear what this young man had been doing that day and what was absorbing him at this time.

What I did not hear and what I did not learn was more about his incredibly complicated background. I did not learn more about his two schizophrenic uncles with whom he presumably shares a genetic endowment. I did not learn more about the interrupted developmental flow, the warpings of his childhood, and the confused communication patterns that he had learned during the long years in which his extremely well-meaning but disharmonious parents fought for his loyalty. I did not learn more about his loneliness and lack of a "chum" during preadolescence, nor of his efforts at age 15 to make contact with a person of the opposite sex, a contact which had started in a blaze of fantasies and ended in ashes of confusion. I did not learn more about his experience of what Kurt Schneider would have called first-rank symptoms, a half-dozen of those catalogued in *Clinical Psychopathology* (11).

Instead, I learned of a sequence of events that had taken place with him while I was at the Conference. After two days of hallucinatory and paranoid withdrawal, he nevertheless had returned on the day of our meeting to the Treatment Program and had become absorbed in completing a project in ceramics. What I did hear from him concerned matters in which he, not I, was expert, matters in which the assets were his, not mine. I asked and learned about the technical skills he had used that day. I learned about the process of transforming clay by adding the proper amount of water so that the initial sculpting would hold together. I became engrossed in his description of the intricacies of glazing and the chemicals that he used to create a myriad of colors; I could only admire and envy his inventiveness and craftsmanship. As we talked, his angry hallucinatory experience receded, and the reality of his assets came into view; I became absorbed and animated, and I experienced him as sharing a similar experience. On the shelf lay my notes, unstudied, unreviewed, and unintegrated—I was able to set aside, to hold in abeyance that special form of madness. I rediscovered that a core of sanity, a sense of connectedness could co-exist alongside our continuing perplexities. We both regained, at least momentarily, the capacity for empathy and relatedness, and a shared focus for our attention; we gained and were grateful.

The event put together for me a different kind of integration than I had anticipated. Its unexpectedness brought to mind an aphorism of F. Scott Fitzgerald: "To record, one must be unwary." I also was reminded of another comment of Fitzgerald on the test of intelligence: "the ability to hold opposed ideas in the mind at the same time and still retain the ability to function." Thus I was brought full circle to Blake's cryptic insight: "Without Contraries is no progression." In a broader sense, the problem of schizophrenia and of schizophrenics, like our life as a whole, is filled with uncertainties, perplexities, mysteries, and paradoxes that continue to swirl turbulently even as we search for, and even may find "answers." We cannot grasp nor contain these tidal currents. With good fortune, perhaps we can understand more fully where we are in this flux, if we can find the conditions under which to become and remain more receptive.

In 1817, John Keats wrote a letter to his brothers, George and Tom, in which he arrived at a similar conclusion and coined the term "Negative Capability" to describe these qualities that I recommend to myself and to others:

> At once it struck me, what quality went to form a man of Achievement, especially in Literature and which Shakespeare possessed so enormously—I mean Negative Capability, that is, when man is capable of being in uncertainties, Mysteries, doubts, without any irritable reaching after fact and reason (31).

REFERENCES

1. Blake W: *The Marriage of Heaven and Hell*, in Perkins D (ed): *English Romantic Writers*. New York, Harcourt, Brace & World, Inc, 1967, pp 68–75.

2. See Romano J (ed): *The Origins of Schizophrenia, Proceedings of the First Rochester International Conference on Schizophrenia,* Int. Congress Series No 151. Amsterdam, Excerpta Medica Foundation, 1967.

3. See Rosenthal D, Kety S (eds): *The Transmission of Schizophrenia, Proceedings of the Second Research Conference of the Foundations' Fund for Research in Psychiatry.* Oxford, Pergamon Press, 1968.

4. Laing RD: The Study of family and social contexts in relation to the origin of schizophrenia, in Romano J, *op cit,* pp 139–146.

5. Gottesman II, Shields J: *Schizophrenia and Genetics: A Twin Study Vantage Point.* New York, Academic Press, 1972.

6. Kraepelin E: *Dementia Praecox and Paraphrenia.* Edinburgh, E & S Livingstone, 1919.

7. Bleuler E: *Dementia Praecox or the Group of Schizophrenias.* New York, International Universities Press, 1950.

8. Langfeldt G: *The Schizophreniform States.* Copenhagen, Munksgaard, 1939.

9. Brown GW, Birley JLT, Wing JK: Influence of family life on the course of schizophrenic disorders: a replication. *Brit J Psychiat* 121:241–250, 1972.

10. Vaughn CE, Leff JP: The influence of family and social factors on the course of psychiatric illness: A comparison of schizophrenia and depressed neurotic patients. *Brit J Psychiat* 129:125–137, 1976.

11. Schneider K: *Clinical Psychopathology.* New York, Grune & Stratton, 1959.

12. Carpenter WT, Strauss JS: Cross-cultural evaluation of Schneider's first-rank symptoms of schizophrenia: A report from the International Pilot Study of Schizophrenia. *Am J Psychiat* 131:682–687, 1974.

13. Garmezy N: The experimental study of children vulnerable to psychopathology, in Davids A (ed): *Child Personality & Psychopathology: Current Topics,* Vol 2. New York, John Wiley & Sons, 1975, p 172.

14. Singer MT, Wynne LC: Thought disorder and family relations of schizophrenics: IV. Results and implications. *Arch Gen Psychiat* 12:201–212, 1965.

15. Rosenthal D (ed): *The Genain Quadruplets.* New York, Basic Books, Inc, Publishers, 1963.

16. Rosenthal D: *Genetic Theory and Abnormal Behavior.* New York, McGraw-Hill Book Co, 1970.

17. Wynne LC: Methodologic and conceptual issues in the study of schizophrenics and their families. *J Psychiat Res* 6:185–199, 1968.

18. Wynne LC, Singer MT: Thought disorder and family relations of schizophrenics: II. A classification of forms of thinking. *Arch Gen Psychiat* 9:199–206, 1963.

19. Wynne LC, Singer MT: Schizophrenic impairments in sharing foci of attention: a conceptual basis for viewing schizophrenics and their families in research and therapy. Presented as the Bertram H Roberts' Memorial Lecture, Yale University, New Haven, Conn, April 26, 1966.

20. Wynne LC: Family transactions and schizophrenia: II. Conceptual considerations for a research strategy, in Romano J (ed): *The Origins of Schizophrenia.* Amsterdam, Excerpta Medica, 1967, pp 165–178.

21. Wynne LC, Singer MT, Bartko JJ, et al: Schizophrenics and their families: research on parental communication, in Tanner JM (ed): *Developments in Psychiatric Research.* London, Hodder & Stoughton, 1977, pp 254–286.

22. Goldfried MR, Strecker G, Weiner IB: *Rorschach Handbook of Clinical and Research Applications.* Englewood Cliffs, NJ, Prentice-Hall, 1971, pp 288–305.

23. Hanson DR, Gottesman II, Heston LL: Some possible indicators of adult schizophrenia inferred from children of schizophrenics. *Brit J Psychiat* 129:142–154, 1976.

24. Rosenthal D: A program of research on heredity in schizophrenia. *Behav Sci* 16:191–201, 1971.

25. Wender PH, Rosenthal D, Kety SS: A psychiatric assessment of the adoptive parents of schizophrenics, in Rosenthal D, Kety SS (eds), *op cit,* pp 235–250, 1968.

26. Anthony EJ: A clinical evaluation of children with psychotic parents. *Amer J Psychiat* 126:177–184, 1969.

27. Rosenthal D, Wender PH, Kety SS, et al: Parent-child relationships and psychopathological disorder in the child. *Arch Gen Psychiat* 32:466–476, 1975.

28. Doane JA: Parental communication deviance as a predictor of child competence in families with a

schizophrenic and nonschizophrenic parent. Doctoral thesis, Department of Psychology, University of Rochester, 1977.

29. Ritzler BA, Singer MT, Cole RE, et al: Parental communication deviance and competence of children at risk for schizophrenia. Presented at the Eastern Psychological Association meeting, Boston, April, 1977.

30. Cole RE, Kokes RF, Harder DW, et al: Relationship of family interaction to parent psychopathology. Presented at the 85th Annual American Psychological Association Convention, San Francisco, August, 1977.

31. Keats J, in Perkins D, *op cit* p 1029.

Author Index

Subject Index